MW00992500

OTHER MAGE TITLES BY WILLEM FLOOR

A Political and Economic History of 5 Port Cities, 1500–1750

The Rise of the Gulf Arabs, The Politics of Trade on the Persian Littoral, 1747–1792

The Rise and Fall of Bandar-e Lengeh, The Distribution Center for the Arabian Coast, 1750–1930

Bandar Abbas: The Natural Trade Gateway of Southeast Iran

Links with the Hinterland: Bushehr, Borazjan, Kazerun, Banu Ka'b & Bandar Abbas

The Hula Arabs of the Shibkuh Coast of Iran

Muscat – City, Society and Trade

Bushehr: City, Society & Trade, 1797–1947

Khark: The Island's Untold Story

Agriculture in Qajar Iran

Public Health in Qajar Iran

The History of Theater in Iran

A Social History of Sexual Relations in Iran

Guilds, Merchants & Ulama in Nineteenth-Century Iran

Labor & Industry in Iran 1850 -1941

The Rise and Fall of Nader Shah: Dutch East India Company Reports 1730-1747

Games Persians Play: A History of Games and Pastimes in Iran from Hide-and-Seek to Hunting

Salar Al-Dowleh: A Delusional Prince & Wannabe Shah

Studies in the History of Medicine in Iran

A Man of Two Worlds: Pedros Bedik in Iran, 1670–1675
Pedros Bedik
translated with Colette Ouahes from the Latin

Astrakhan Anno 1770
Samuel Gottlieb Gmelin

Travels Through Northern Persia 1770–1774
Samuel Gottlieb Gmelin

Titles and Emoluments in Safavid Iran: A Third Manual of Safavid Administration
Mirza Naqi Nasiri

Exotic Attractions in Persia, 1684–1688
Engelbert Kaempfer
translated with Colette Ouahes from the Latin

TRANSLATED WITH HASAN JAVADI

The Heavenly Rose-Garden: A History of Shirvan & Daghestan
Abbas Qoli Aqa Bakikhanov

Travels in Iran & the Caucasus, 1652 and 1655
Evliya Chelebi

Awake: A Moslem Woman's Rare Memoir of Her Life & Partnership with the Editor of Molla Nasreddin
Hamideh Khanum Javanshir

KERMANSHAH

City & Province 1800-1945

WILLEM FLOOR

MAGE PUBLISHERS

Library of Congress Cataloging-in-Publication Data
Available in detail at the Library of Congress

ISBN: 978-1-949445-00-8

Printed and Manufactured in the United States

MAGE PUBLISHERS
Washington, DC
as@mage.com
Visit Mage Publishers online at
www.mage.com

CONTENTS

ILLUSTRATIONS

TABLES

INTRODUCTION

Kermanshah is a city that usually is ignored by historians (apart from Mohammad 'Ali Soltani's 10 volume magnum opus), despite the fact that it was an important transit station on the trade route between Iraq and Iran as well as a gathering point for pilgrims going to and returning from Kerbela and Najaf. Also, it was the city that was more dominated by tribal politics than any other city in Iran. Kermanshah was also important because of its strategic position on the border with Iraq, whenever war broke out with the Ottomans. But two events in particular stand out in the history of Kermanshah. One which is rather well-known, viz. in 1916-17 Kermanshah was the capital of the short-lived *Mohajerin* movement and the battlefield between the combined Ottoman and German force and the Russians. This last event has been studied to a certain extent, although here, on this subject, much new information and nuance is made available. Also, the political events from 1906-1945 are discussed in great detail and this provides much new information on how provincial politics had a life of its own. In fact, it shows that indeed 'all politics are local,' for all so-called political differences may have been clad in a national and/or constitutionalist guise, but these differences were more determined by local cleavages than national ones. Also, Kermanshah remained a very conservative city, which elected reactionary tribal chiefs and landowners to parliament. The second event, although very important, is ignored by, if not entirely unknown to, historians, viz. that Kermanshah was one of the most important commercial gateways to Iran and, from 1920 to 1925, the government's most important non-oil revenue earner. The rise of the city as an important *bandar*, or entrepot is discussed in detail in this study.

It is a strange coincidence that it appears that on the Reza Shah period neither Persian nor British sources are available. Mohammad 'Ali Soltani, for whom no detail is too small or insignificant, devotes only six pages on this period, of which two are full page-sized photographs, and he is unable to tell us much about how the city fared during this period. Although he refers the reader to his volume on the Tribes of Kermanshah, the events discussed there don't concern the city itself, which is the main focus of this study. Indeed it would seem that relevant documents on this period in Persian archives are lacking. A search made in the archives of the municipality of Kermanshah yielded no additional information whatsoever. Also, copies of local newspapers from that period are not available in Persian archives and libraries. Likewise, there is a similar lacuna in the British national archives, for there are no Consular reports available about Kermanshah from May 1921 until January 1942, with the exception of one report for the year 1936. During that entire period there were British consuls in the city, be it there was a very high turnover of staff, but their reports either have been misfiled or have been lost.[1]

1. The very helpful staff of the National Archives in Kew Gardens were unable to locate them for me. The monthly Consular reports for the year 1943 are also missing.

These events as well as the broader historical context of the city and province of Kermanshah between 1800-1945 is told in seven chapters. The cut-off point of this study, the end of WW II, is artificial to some extent, be it that after 1945, political life in the city and the country took a totally different turn than in the previous period. This is a development that deserves its own book, because it would have made this one even more voluminous than it is already. The first chapter offers a history of the city until 1800. In chapter two the morphology and the main characteristics of the city and its inhabitants are discussed. Chapter three highlights the city's administrative institutions. Chapter four provides an overview of the administrative structure of the province and of its tribal population and their economic activities. Chapter five discusses the agricultural products and activities of Kermanshah province. Chapter six analyzes the trade of Kermanshah during the nineteenth and the first four decades of the twentieth century. The last and seventh chapter offers an overview of the development of the historical, in particular political, events that took place in Kermanshah during the 1800-1945 period. This study is concluded by a number of appendices, of which the largest one (appendix I) concerns the Jewish population of Kermanshah, which appendix is co-authored by Parisa Mohammadi, who also did the research in the Persian archives.

CHAPTER ONE

KERMANSHAH BEFORE 1800

Kermanshah or Kermanshahan is the name of the city that is first mentioned in the 10th century CE. Arab geographers usually called it Qarmesen (قرمسن), which is the oldest and most frequent form of the name, but also found are Qarmasin (قرماسين), Qarmashin (قرمشين), Qarmisin (قرميسين) and Qermisin (قرميسين). al-Istakhri, al-Muqaddasi and the anonymous author of the *Hudud al-Alam* wrote Kermanshahan, which was the Persian name for the city. The Jewish historian Nathan Ha-Bavli reports that the late 9th-early 10th century exilarch Mar ʿUqba was banished from 909 to 916 to a locality, not far from Baghdad, called Kermanshah.[1] Qazvini (13th century) writes that Qarmesen was situated close to Kermanshahan, as though they were twin cities; Yaqut gives both names, but says little about the town.[2] In the nineteenth century, the official name of the city was Dar al-Dowleh Kermanshahan, while the province was called Kermanshah.[3] Herzfeld submitted that Qarmesen was "the Kurdish pronunciation of Kermanshahan," but it is also possible that it was an older name of the settlement that grew into Kermanshah, or, as Qazvini, suggest that Qarmesen and Kermanshahan were twin-cities. Rabino mentions a local tradition, according to which Qarmesen was the name (perhaps non-Iranian) of an earlier or nearby settlement at a place called Kermanshah-e Kohneh (Old Kermanshah) in the district of Balada.[4] In the mid-17th century, two European travelers also reported that there were two settlements (city and town; town and village) at the location referred to as Kermanshah (see below).

Nothing is known about the origins of the city of Kermanshah. There have been no archeological excavations in the town of Kermanshah itself, but from the excavations at sites close to the city (Kangavar, Bisotun, Harsin, Nehavand, etc.) it is clear that its surrounding region was inhabited since pre-historic times as far back as 35,000 BCE.[5] Although allegedly built in Sasanian times, and situated in the Sasanian province of Eran-Asan-Kard-Kawad, Kermanshah is not listed among the cities mentioned in the *Shahrestaniha i Eranshahr*.[6] There exist two traditions about the city's foundation. According to Hamdallah Mustawfi, it was built by king

1. Neubauer 1895, II, pp. 77-88; Levi 1984, vol. 2, pp. 382-83.
2. Schwarz 1993, vol.4, p. 480; Le Strange1966, pp. 21, 186.
3. Floyer 1882, pp. 436, note.
4. Herzfeld 1968, p. 16; DCR 590 (1903), p. 7; de Morgan 1894, vol. 2, p. 100.
5. Matheson 1976, pp. 26, 120.
6. Daryaee 2002; Gyselen 1989, pp. 82-84. The identification with Kambadene, one of the so-called 'Parthian stations' is doubtful. Calmeyer 1996, pp. 13-14.

Bahram (r. 388-99 CE), who became known as Kermanshah, when he was governor of Kerman. However, the town that he founded probably was Kermanshah, a small town situated between Kerman and Yazd.[7] According to the other tradition, Kawadh, son of Firuz (488-541 CE) was the city's founder. Ibn Faqih relates that Qubadh (Kawadh) considered it the most pleasant place on the road between Ctesiphon (Mada'en) and Balkh, because of its tasty water and pleasant air, so that he founded Qarmesen and built himself a palace with 1,000 vine stocks used as pillars.[8] This tradition is reflected in Mustawfi's account, who mentions that King Qubad (Kawadh) restored the city, building there for his own use a mighty palace. His son, Anushirvan the Just, allegedly erected a platform, measuring one hundred ell square, and here at a great banquet the Emperor of China, the Khaqan of the Turks, the Raja of India, and the Caesar of Rome, all (in obeisance) kissed his hand.[9] This tradition of the rebuilding of the city may be true, because in 951 CE, Abu Dulaf implies that under the city was another one, for when one of the chiefs of Kermanshah wanted to build a court with annexes they found, when digging, another building, just like the one he wanted to build.[10] That the area was one that received much attention from the Persian emperors is clear from the many Achaemenid and Sasanian monuments that are found near the city (Bisotun, Kangavar/Godin Tepeh, Nehavand/Tepeh Giyan, etc).[11] Ibn Faqih even states that king Abarwiz (590-628 CE) made Kermanshah his residence, because in particular the breeze at sunset was a welcome cooler after the hot day.[12] It has been suggested that the original city was situated "north of the present site, on the opposite side of the Qara-Su in the vicinity of Taq-e Bostan."[13]

After the fall of Hulwan (640 CE), the conquering Arabs under Jarir b. 'Abdollah Bajali took Kermanshah peaceably.[14] Kermanshah was the center of the western quarter of the province of Jibal or Mah al-Kufa, which province later was known as Iraq-e 'Ajam. The western quarter around Kermanshah was called Kurdistan since Seljuq times.[15] It may have been at that time that the city moved to a hill north-west of the current city,[16] which may explain why European travelers mention two settlements, a village and a town (see below), when mentioning Kermanshah.[17] All Arab geographers agree with al-Muqaddasi that Kermanshah one of the most pleasant towns of the Persian kingdom.[18] According to Abu Dulaf, Qarmesen "is a fine and splendid town, though there are no remains inside it, except a house which is said to have been

7. Mustawfi 1919, p. 106; Daryaee 2002; Shirvani 1315, p. 294.

8. Schwarz 1993, vol. 4, pp. 481-82.

9. Mustawfi 1919, p. 106; Shirvani 1315, p. 294. Jami, in the second chapter of his *Baharestan*, reports the result of this alleged banquet of the four emperors.

10. Ibn Muhalhil 1955, p. 45.

11. Golriz 1357; Matheson 1976, pp. 26, 120.

12. Schwarz 1993, vol. 4, p. 482. On Abarwiz, see al-Tabari 1999, vol. 5, pp. 303-17.

13. Clarke and Clark 1969, p.18.

14. Schwarz 1993, vol. 4, p. 482.

15. Le Strange 1966, p. 186; Fragner 1972, p. 51; Schwarz 1993, vol. 3, pp. 479, 482 (al-Muqaddasi stated that Qarmasin (قرماسين) was part of Hamadan). Mah is the Arabic rendering of the Pahlavi appellation Mad (Media).

16. Clarke and Clark 1969, p.18.

17. DCR 590, p. 7; de Morgan 1894, vol. 2, p. 100.

18. Schwarz 1993, vol. 4, p. 481.

wonderful."[19] According to the *Hudud al-'Alam*, the first known source to mention the city's Persian name, Kermanshahan was a borough "on the road of the pilgrims, densely populated, prosperous and pleasant.[20] Ibn Wadih reported: Qarmesen "is one of the most important cities with many inhabitants, mostly non-Arabs, Persians and Kurds." Ibn Hawqal repeats Istakhri and added that, "it was a very pleasant town with streams, trees and fruit; the life necessities are cheap, there is pasturage and many cattle, also springs; the city offers agricultural products and merchandise." al-Muqaddasi, wrote that it was one of the prides of the Jibal. "It is pleasant, surrounded by gardens, the chief mosque is situated in the bazaar and is graceful. Azud al-Dowleh had a palace built there. The town is situated on the main road, its barley beer is highly praised." Bekri called the city an important place, while Muhallabi (2nd half 12th century) writes: "The city of Qarmasin is the largest and most important city of Jibal; it is thriving and has many inhabitants; from there also comes much saffron." Yaqut refers to it as "the well-known place, situated in a large plain and may be reckoned as one of the most beautiful cities of Iraq-e 'Ajam; there is much fruit and saffron, and also much merchandise; the inhabitants number 30,000."[21]

Kermanshah was militarily and economically important because of its location at the intersection of the great highway linking Baghdad to Khorasan with a trade route to Tabriz and Ardabil. Although a commercial town, Kermanshah was less important than Dinavar and Hamadan. Later it was one of the four major cities of Iraq-e 'Ajam, but it was still less important than Ray, Isfahan and Dinavar. However, because of its strategic location it was a staging area for troops.[22] Because of that it was also a target of military operations such as around 931, when the Ziyard ruler Mardavij pillaged and destroyed the area as far as Kermanshah and enslaved its people.[23] The city itself may have remained unscathed, because the Buyid ruler Azud al-Dowleh built a palace in Kermanshah's main street. Also, both the Buyids and the Kakuyids struck coins in the city.[24] Moreover, as noted above, Kermanshah was a pleasant and thriving city in the tenth century.

Under the Buyids, and probably earlier under the Abbasids as well, it seems that Kurdish governors ruled the city. The Kurdish Hasanvayhids (959-1047) who held sway at Sarmaj (near Bisotun) ruled over an area stretching from Dinavar to Shahrezur.[25] They were overthrown by the Annazids (990-1117), who held an area from Holvan to Dinavar. The Seljuqs, whose incursions into the area began in 1045, ousted the Annazids. The almost continuous century-long strife between Buyids, Hasanvays, Annazids, and Seljuqs had a negative impact on the economic development of the region.[26] The takeover of Kermanshah by the Seljuqs did not bring the

19. Ibn Muhalhil 1955, p. 45.
20. Minorsky 1937, p. 132.
21. Schwarz 1993, vol. 4, pp. 481-82; Le Strange 1966, p. 186.
22. Minorsky 1937, p. 132 (one of the "boroughs on the road of the pilgrims, densely populated, prosperous, ... and pleasant."); Fragner 1972, pp. 182-83; Le Strange 1966, p. 185.
23. Mas`udi 1965, vol. 5, p. 269.
24. Miles 1975, pp. 369-75.
25. One of the Hasanvayh rulers bore the title of *Saheb*. Spuler 1952, p. 102 (Saheb b. `Abbad, vizier of Mo'ayyed al-Dowleh); Bürgel 1965, p. 141 (Bakhtiyar b. Hasanawaih); Fragner 1972, p. 71. According to Ardalan 2004, pp. 27-28 the Hasanvayhs ruled until 1019.
26. Ardalan 2004, p. 28, n. 56.

necessary period of peace to recover. Because of Kermanshah's strategic location it was a much coveted city resulting in regional conflicts. In 1197/98, Kermanshah was sacked by the Khvarezmi Amir Mighajuk,[27] while some 50 years later, in December 1257, the city was destroyed and its inhabitants were killed by the Mongols.[28] One century later Mustawfi wrote that its name was still also written as Qirmisin. He described it as a village. "Kirmanshah was formerly a medium-sized town, but is now merely a village."[29] Thereafter, administratively, the Jibal province was divided into two parts. The western part was Kurdistan with Kermanshah as its main center, the other part became Iraq-e ʿAjam.

In the following centuries the city is occasionally mentioned in passing.[30] According to the early thirteenth century text *ʿAjayeb al-Donya*, there was a well in Kermanshahan where a stone statute of a man stood, which they called *kariz*. When they threw it into the well the water ceased to flow and when they put it back the water in the well started flowing again.[31] It seems that Kermanshah remained a small, insignificant place, which was only a stage on the pilgrimage road.[32] The town is not mentioned in historical accounts of the fifteenth century. Kurdish chiefs probably held the town as in previous centuries. With the establishment of the Safavid state it seems that this state of affairs somewhat changed. Under Esmaʿil I and Tahmasp I, Qezelbash governors were appointed to Dinavar, but none are mentioned for Kermanshah,[33] nor is the city mentioned in early Safavid sources. It was only after the fall of Baghdad in 1534 that Kermanshah became a frontier town and like the rest of the border area it was often in an unsettled condition. The Safavids, who used local tribes to protect the border, did the same with the Kermanshah area, where Kurds were used. Depending on the political and military situation these Kurds changed sides between Ottomans and Safavids whenever it was to their advantage. The Safavids used, among others, the Ardalans to defend the Kermanshah area. This tribe had first sided with the Ottomans, but later supported the Safavids, and at times, it tried to be independent from either side.[34]

In 1590, ʿAbbas I ceded Kermanshah and other Western provinces to the Ottomans. It was only in 1603 that Kermanshah was retaken as part of ʿAbbas I's major multi-year military campaign to recover his lost territory. In 1631, Khan Ahmad Khan I, the Kurdish ruler of Ardalan broke with the Safavids and had himself crowned at Harunabad as Shah Ahmad Khan. He struck money and had the *khutbah* read in his name; he made his capital in Kirkuk and ruled over a territory that included Kermanshah, Hamadan, Sonqor, Nehavand, Lorestan, Garrus and Ormiyeh, where he appointed his own governors. In 1636, at the battle of Marivan, Safi I

27. al-Ravandi 1921, p. 398.
28. Boyle 1975, p. 347.
29. Mustawfi 1919, p. 106; Le Strange 1966, p. 186.
30. Shabankareh 1376, p. 115.
31. Anonymous 1993, p. 451.
32. Mustawfi 1919, p. 162.
33. Nasiri 2008, p. 179.
34. Ardalan 2004, pp. 34 ff.

defeated him and put an end to the upstart Kurdish regime.[35] In November 1638, the Safavid army used Taq-e Vasetan, near Kermanshah as a staging area to march to Baghdad.[36]

The treaty of Zohab of 1639 between the Safavids and Ottomans established that Kermanshah remained part of Persia. Because of the peace Kermanshah remained a back water. It does not seem to have constituted a separate administrative jurisdiction prior to the reign of Safi I (r. 1629-1642), at least I have not been able to find any mention of such a fact.[37] Even thereafter the mentioning of a governor of Kermanshah is rare and then it seems that it was a kind of dependency of Dinavar, for the same governor who held Dinavar and Kermanshahan in another text is not mentioned as also being in charge of Kermanshahan, but only of Dinavar.[38] Sonqor, situated at 90 km from Kermanshah and consisting of two valleys, that of Gavehrud and Shajurud, together with Kolhar was often held at the same time by the governor of Sonqor and/or Dinavar. After 1636, this post became hereditary in the Zanganeh family.[39] It is only towards the end of Safavid rule that its name is regularly mentioned[40] and that there even was a *begler-begi* of Kermanshah (see Table 1.1).[41] In a Safavid geography written around 1670, its author only repeats what the *Nozhat al-Qolub* and the *Ajayeb al-Donya* report. In addition he writes that "it produces fruit from the cold and hot zone, while some pastures were set aside to raise animals."[42]

It is of interest to note that Kurdish governors of Dinavar only appear as of the late 1620s, despite the fact that in other border areas Kurdish governors already prevailed at an earlier date. Despite the increased importance and power of the Zanganeh family both at the provincial and national level this importance did not rub off on Kermanshah. Sheikh Ali Khan Zanganeh, Shah Soleyman's powerful grand vizier established *vaqf*s in Hamadan, and a caravanserai at Bisutun, but apparently not in Kermanshah.

---

35. Ardalan 2004, p. 39.
36. Esfahani 1368, p. 261.
37. The town of Kermanshah existed, of course, prior to that period. See, e.g., Bidlisi 1868, vol. 1, pp. 218-19, who mentions Kermanshahan as a halting place.
38. Vahid Qazvini 1383, p. 331 (governor of the *il-e* Kalhor-Zanganeh and of Dinavar).
39. Yusof 1317, pp. 227, 292.
40. Nasiri 2008, pp. 124, 129, 132-34, 163 (the governor of Kermanshahan used spies to monitor the movements of the Ottomans in 1695-96).
41. But in a document dated 1108/1697 only the governor (*hakem*) of Kermanshahan is referred to. Qarakhani 1353, doc. 6.
42. Mostofwfi-ye Yazdi 1989, p. 364.

Table 1.1: Governors of Kermanshah during the Safavid reign

Name	Year	Observations	Source
`Ali Beg Zanganeh a.k.a. Ali Baba	1038-1043/1629-1633	*Hakem* of Dinavar + Kermanshahan, Kolhar+ Sonqor	Yusof 1317, p. 273
Shahrokh Soltan Zanganeh	1043-1050/1633-1640	*Hakem* of Dinavar + Kermanshahan; *Hakem* of the *il-e* Kolhar-Zanganeh + Dinavar- succeeded by his brother	Yusof 1317, p. 246; Vahid 1383, pp. 294, 301, 317. 331
Sheikh Ali Khan Zanganeh	1049-1067/1639-1657	*Hakem* of Dinavar + Kermanshahan; Hakem *il-e* Kolhar-Zanganeh + Dinavar- succeeded by his brother	Vahid 1383, pp. 301, 317, 331, 569, 577, 626
Shahqoli Khan Zanganeh b. Sheikh Ali Khan	?-1686	*Hakem* of Kermanshah	Hedges 1887, vol. 1, 216
Shahverdi Khan Zanganeh b. Sheikh Ali Khan	1097-1103/1686-1692	*Beglerbegi* of Kermanshahan	Khatunabadi 1352, p. 547; Sanson1695, p. 80; Hedges 1887, vol. 1, 216
Mortezaqoli Beg; later Mehr `Ali Beg	1107/1696	deputy *hakem* of Kolhar, Sonqor + Kermanshahan	Nasiri 2008, pp. 124, 129, 133
N.N.	1108/1697	*Hakem* of Kermanshahan	Qarakhani 1353, doc. 6

The Ottoman traveler Evliya Chelebi left a short description of the town, which he visited in 1655. He described it as follows:

> Description of the castle of Kermanshah. It was built in 915 [1509-10] by Shah Esma'il and therefore it was called Kermanshah.[43] It is situated in the district of Hamadan in a vast plain. It is a beautiful brick building. It is pentagonal, has two gates, one thousand soldiers and it is a separate sultanate. At present it is under the shah's vizier, Sheikh 'Ali Khan Luri,[44] whose representative is its Sultan. Originally this city is on the border of Lurestan; it is a big city. All its buildings, gardens and orchards are well-made.[45]

The quasi-absence of the city in Safavid chronicles is also found in European travelogues.[46] The Sherleys' party passed the city around 1590, but did not mention it. Likewise, in 1618 Pietro

43. Chelebi arrived at this etymology as follows: *kerman* means 'fort, castle,' hence kermanshah meaning 'the king's castle.'

44. Meaning Sheikh Ali Khan Zanganeh, a Kurd, not a Lor. This means that Chelebi must have written or emended this part of his *Travels* after 1669, because Sheikh Ali Khan was grandvizier from 1669 until 1691.

45. Evliya Chelebi 2010, p. 208.

46. Tavernier 1713, vol. 1, p. 390 describes a route between Isfahan and Baghdad that passes through Nehavand-Kangavar and from there to Senneh, Pol-e shah, Mahidast and Harunabad and onwards to Baghdad, but he does not mention Kermanshah at all (see also Idem, vol. 1, pp. 194, 252). It possibly may be the small town that he mentions, situated near a relief in a mountain (more likely Bisotun), without stating its name. According to Tavernier, this town had many streams that watered it, good fruit, and excellent wine. The Persians believed that Alexander died there on his return from India. From there to Baghdad there was much date cultivation and people lived in huts made of date fronds. Tavernier 1713, vol. 1, p. 391.

della Valle passed through the plain of Kermanshah, from Mahidasht to Pol-e Qarasu, but he does not even mention Kermanshah, although he must have seen the small town. Raphael du Mans only mentions Kermanshah as the capital of the Kurds. There are only three European travelers who actually provide some information on the city, of whom Thevenot is the most descriptive. He writes the following:

> The Town where the *Chan* resides is about two miles distant from the Village; it is called *Kerman Shahon*, (that's to say the Kings Barns) because the countrey about bears plenty of Rice, which *Schah Abbas* gave for the *Zaret* or Pilgrimage of Devotion that was made to the Mosque of *Imam Hussein*. But the *Turk* being Master of it at present, the rice is sent to *Ispahan*. This is but an inconsiderable Town, nevertheless, it hath a covered *Bazar* well stored with Goods and Provisions for the Belly. There is a *Seraglio* in it for the *Chan* or Governour: The Truth is, though it make some better shew than the rest of the houses, it is indeed of no great worth, at least on the outside for I entered not the Gate, but saw some *Divans* for taking the air on.[47]

Whereas Thevenot writes that Kermanshah was a small town, in 1674 Bembo writes, "That city is large and near the border and about three miles from the town." Like Thevenot he makes a difference between the city and the nearby village, which he calls a town.[48] Hedges, who was in Kermanshah in January 1686, reported that Shahqoli Khan, the governor of the city and a son of Sheikh 'Ali Khan, forced the caravan to open various bales looking for gold and silver. Hedges was forced to pay him and his servants a sum of 15 *tuman*s in cash and goods to prevent further scrutiny.[49] Bembo, described a similar, be it less invasive and less costly scrutiny. The Khan's scribe took down everybody's name and the amount of merchandise in the caravan; this account was then signed by the governor of Kermanshah. "The signed account is then taken to an official who resides at the border, and he checks everything again, particularly the number of weapons, so that no one brings armaments to Baghdad under the pretext of using them, and he checks the number of men who go out of the country."[50]

Kermanshah disappears from the scene until the fall of the Safavids after the Afghan invasion of 1722. In early 1723, under Hasan Pasha, the governor of Baghdad, the Ottomans invaded Western Persia. Well before that time, Hasan Pasha had been in contact with Hoseyn 'Ali Beg, the deputy-governor of Kermanshah, who surrendered the city without any opposition in October 1723. This resulted in gentle treatment of the population. Shortly thereafter Hasan Pasha died in Kermanshah; he was succeeded by his son Ahmad Pasha, who in September 1724 also occupied Hamadan. The treaty of July 1724 between Russia and Turkey, assigned both provinces

---

47. Thevenot 1971, part 2, pp. 69-70.
48. Bembo 2007, p. 384. This reflects Yaqut's observation that there was a Kermanshah city and a Qarmesen town (see above). Only archaeological excavations may resolve this issue.
49. Hedges 1887, vol. 1, p. 216
50. Bembo 2007, pp. 384, 389 (check at the border).

to the Ottomans.[51] In 1726, the Ottoman position in W. Persia was challenged by Ashraf Khan, the Afghan leader. He defeated the Ottoman forces, which retreated and abandoned Kermanshah, returning to Baghdad.[52] In 1727, Ahmad Pasha returned with a large army to wipe out the disgrace of defeat and retake the lost provinces. However, Ashraf Khan preferred peace to war, as a result of which, both sides concluded a peace agreement in October 1727, by which Western Persia, including Kermanshah was ceded in perpetuity to the Ottomans.[53] Due to these military operations many villages in Kermanshah province were abandoned, according to Ottoman registers (*mühimme defterleri*).[54]

According to Otter, at the end of the Safavid period it was still a major city. However, when the Sunnis from Dargazin fled into Ottoman Turkey at an unstated date (presumably in 1730) they destroyed it.[55] In June-July 1730, Tahmasp Qoli Khan (the later Nader Shah) easily retook Hamadan and Kermanshah, because the Turkish troops fled to Baghdad after having been defeated at Nehavand.[56] In about March 1731, Ahmad Pasha retook Kermanshah and thereafter defeated Tahmasp II and retook much of W. Persia. However, the Ottomans offered the return of most of this territory, including Kermanshah, if they were allowed to keep Georgia, Armenia and other lands above the Aras. Tahmasp II agreed to this by treaty of January 1732. Although the Ottomans withdrew from most of the newly won territory such as Hamadan, they held on to Kermanshah. The treaty was not acceptable to Tahmasp Qoli Khan (the later Nader Shah) who deposed Tahmasp at the end of August 1732. He marched to Kermanshah which he retook in November 1732. The next month he left the city and marched to Baghdad.[57]

As of then Kermanshah became the staging area for Nader Shah's wars with the Ottomans, where he gathered much siege artillery. To that end he built a fort at about 6 km from Kermanshah, which was well garrisoned and equipped with arms, ammunition as well as with cannons and a cannon foundry. Because of its location, it controlled the routes to Baghdad as well as those inside the provinces of Kermanshah, Lorestan and Kurdistan.[58] In May 1736, Nader Shah again marched to Kermanshah with a huge and heavily armed force to decisively defeat the Ottomans in Iraq.[59] 'Abdol-Baqi Khan was sent to the Ottoman court to ratify the agreed upon peace agreement after Ahmad Pasha's defeat. He returned in November 1736 to Persia accompanied by an Ottoman ambassador. 'Abdol-Baqi Khan, who was governor of Kermanshah, wanted to embarrass the Ottoman ambassador because he felt that the Ottomans had not treated him appropriately. Therefore, he had the most beautiful tents erected outside the city and all the

51. Lockhart 1956, pp. 225, 234n, 258, 268-71; Idem 1938, pp. 12, 47; Axworthy 2006, p. 63; Longrigg 2002, pp. 130-31 (the governor of Kermanshah was Abu'l-Baqi Khan).

52. Lockhart 1956, pp. 290-91; Longrigg 2002, p. 134; Hanway 1753, vol. 3/1, p. 249.

53. Lockhart 1956, pp. 291-92; Longrigg 2002, p. 134

54. Calmard 2015.

55. Otter 1748, vol. 1, pp. 181-82.

56. Lockhart 1938, pp. 49-50; Axworthy 2006, p. 108.

57. Axworthy 2006, pp. 116-17, 128; Lockhart 1938, p. 97 (Abdol-Baqi Khan Zanganeh was governor of Kermanshah); Longrigg 2002, pp. 135, 137. CHI 1991, vol. 7, p. 302 gives 30 July 1731 as the date of the Ottoman retaking Kermanshah.

58. Perry 1979, pp. 5, 15; Ardalan 2004, p. 74; Axworthy 2006, p. 108; Tucker 2006, p. 100.

59. Lockhart 1938, pp. 237, 246,249-50; Ardalan 2004, p. 60 (in 1741 the *vali* of Ardalan collected 10,000 *kharvar* of wheat from Kermanshah for the Baghdad campaign).

town's inhabitants gathered to welcome the Ottoman ambassador, whom they greeted with several salvos from their muskets until he dismounted at his tent. There he was regaled to a magnificent banquet. The ambassador then entered the city and was lodged in the governor's residence. 'Abdol-Baqi Khan told his son Mostafa, who was governing the city during his absence, to take good care of the ambassador. To further embarrass the ambassador 'Abdol-Baqi Khan told him to take it easy and enjoy his stay and not hasten at all.[60] The province was rich in produce and cattle and herds, and supplied Isfahan with provisions.[61] Nader Shah was again in Kermanshah in January 1744, marching from Iraq via the city to quell uprisings in Persia.[62]

After Nader Shah's death in 1747, his murderer and nephew 'Adel Shah succeeded him. In the province of Kermanshah there were two strategic positions of great importance, viz. the city itself and the fort-arsenal, which held the key to W. Persia. Nader Shah had built and equipped the fort, which was situated on the Qara Su, at one *farsakh* from the city, as a forward base for his campaigns against Baghdad. Moreover, its strategic position, made Kermanshah a location of great strategic importance, because it was ideal as a military staging area as noted above. 'Adel Shah appointed Mortezaqoli Khan Zanganeh as governor of Kermanshah and Mirza Mohammad Taqi Golestaneh jointly with the *tupchi-bashi* as commander of the fort. However, Hoseyn Khan Zanganeh, *chavosh-bashi*, who had been blinded by Nader Shah on suspicion of treason, seized the city. He plundered its merchants, took its artillery and made a failed attempt to take Hamadan. Returning to Kermanshah he faced opposition. Mirza Mohammad Taqi Golestaneh was in Ardalan collecting taxes, when he learnt of Nader Shah's death. He left his 5,000 Afghan troops and hurried to Kermanshah where Hoseyn Khan Zanganeh made room for him. When 'Adel Shah appointed Amir Khan 'Arab Mishmast *tupchi-bashi* as commander of the fort Mirza Mohammad Taqi Golestaneh welcomed him. Hoseyn Khan fearing their combined force fled and joined Ebrahim Mirza, who one year after Nader Shah's murder, rebelled against his brother 'Adel Shah, who was killed. Ebrahim Shah, as he then called himself, sent a strong force to Kermanshah which was plundered, but his troops failed to take the nearby fort, which held Nader Shah's arsenal, the lynchpin to control over W. Persia. Hoseyn Khan had a kinsman appointed governor of Kermanshah and with 5,000 men marched to the city. Amir Khan forced them to hold out in a fort, but Ebrahim Shah sent additional troops that defeated Amir Khan. He withdrew after a three-week siege; however, the defenders realized that their future might be bleak if they did not make a deal with Ebrahim Shah. The latter welcomed their overture as he stood in need of the *tupchi-bashi*'s skills. Hoseyn Khan took possession of Kermanshah, which inconvenienced Mirza Mohammad Taqi Golestaneh. He left and went to Isfahan and using his contacts at the new court he was able to get Ebrahim Shah's authorization to oust Hoseyn Khan from Kermanshah together with Salim Khan. The latter evaded Hoseyn Khan's army and took the undefended city. He then induced Hoseyn Khan to trust him, killed him and installed Mirza Mohammad Taqi Golestaneh as governor of Kermanshah.[63]

---

60. Otter 1748, vol. 1, pp. 33, 37, 183-84.
61. Otter 1748, vol. 1, p. 181.
62. Axworthy 2006, p. 258.
63. Perry 1979, pp. 15-17; Ardalan 2004, p. 74-75.

Ebrahim Mirza failed to defeat the other pretender, Nader Shah's grandson Shahrokh Mirza. As a result, some of his troops returned home, among which were Kurds under Emamqoli Khan Zanganeh. He defeated Morteza Qoli Khan and Najaf Qoli Khan Kalhor, who opposed him and took Kermanshah, where he installed himself as governor. His rule only lasted a few months. Emamqoli Khan Zanganeh mobilized a large army and also tried to take the fort held by Mirza Mohammad Taqi Golestaneh and 'Abdol-'Ali Khan Mishmast. These were forced to ask Hasan Ali Khan Ardalan, the *vali* of Ardalan for help. The latter marched with a substantial force, which Emamqoli Khan rashly attacked with a much smaller force. As a result he barely escaped with his life, but later he was blinded by his enemies. The *Vali*, who then controlled Kermanshah, Hamadan, Malayer, Borujerd, Farahan and Kazzaz, appointed new governors, including Mehr 'Ali Khan Tekkelu at Kermanshah.[64] In 1750, Soleyman Pasha II Baban fled to Persia and with the help of troops from the Kermanshah area (*Vali* of Ardalan) he regained his governorship.[65]

Meanwhile a succession was had broken out in Persia between a number of contenders. In 1750, 'Ali Mardan Khan Bakhtiyari and Karim Khan Zand took Isfahan. While 'Ali Mardan Bakhtiyari moved south, Karim Khan moved west, because he wanted to secure his back by neutralizing the *Vali* of Ardalan and other chiefs in W. Persia. Mehr 'Ali Khan Tekkelu, governor of Hamadan opposed him but was defeated. Karim Khan then marched onwards and took Kermanshah, but not the fort. However, it remained under siege for 6 months and food was running low. But at that time, a group of the fort's foragers ran into a group of Kalhor besiegers. The two sides fought and the foragers, assisted by a sortie from the fort, defeated the Kalhors, pursued them to Kermanshah and expelled them for there. The besieged started celebrating and laying in new stores. The Zands could not, of course, accept this setback and Sadeq Khan Zand sent a force of 1,000 men to lay siege again. The besiegers proposed battle and defeated the Zands and made much booty. Now Mohammad Khan Zand, who had been appointed governor of Kermanshah, came and he changed tactics weakening the defenders. The siege lasted for another 6 months, so in total one year, while the defenders were waiting for relief from 'Ali Mardan Khan Bakhtiyari, whom they had contacted. The latter had fallen out with Karim Khan and saw assisting the besieged as a way to make his comeback. To improve his chances he went to Baghdad to ask for Soleyman Pasha, the governor of Baghdad's support, which he received. However, 'Ali Mardan Khan Bakhtiyari was slow in getting his act together. Meanwhile, discontent grew among the defenders, one of whom, hoping to gain reward from the Zands, blew up a gunpowder store. Despite the resulting breaches, the defenders repaired them and continued to hold off the attackers. What did not help the besieged was that support for the procrastinating 'Ali Mardan Khan Bakhtiyari was diminishing, while Karim Khan Zand decided to take a hand himself in taking the fort, just before 'Ali Mardan Khan Bakhtiyari's arrival before the city. In May 1753, after two years of siege, having been promised quarter by Karim Khan the defenders surrendered. 'Ali Mardan Khan Zand was appointed governor of the city and the fort. 'Abdol-'Ali Khan Mishmast and Mohammad Taqi Golestaneh, the former commanders of the fort became hostages and were attached to Karim Khan's army. After his success at Kermanshah,

64. Perry 1979, pp. 19-20, 56; Ardalan 2004, pp. 74-77, 80, 94-95.

65. Longrigg 2002, p. 179; Ardalan 2004, p. 77.

Karim Khan marched westward to dash any hopes 'Ali Mardan Bakthiyari may have held and decisively defeated him in June 1753.[66]

Initially, Karim Khan Zand was less fortunate in his efforts to eliminate the other major pretender, Azad Khan, an Afghan general. When in 1753 Azad Khan defeated Karim Khan Zand, some of his troops under Mohammad Khan Zand fled westward towards Zohab. The hostages 'Abdol-'Ali and Mohammad Taqi Golestaneh were captured by Azad Khan. The former had to accompany Azad Khan on his further campaign, while Mohammad Taqi Golestaneh was sent to Kermanshah to hold that for the Afghans. Heydar Khan Zanganeh, who had laid low for about a year, but hearing that Mohammad Khan Zand was recruiting, came down from the mountains and took Kermanshah. Mirza Mohammad Taqi Golestaneh, whose Afghan troops had made themselves very unpopular, decided to go over to the Zand cause and joined Heydar Khan Zand, be it with some apprehension. The city was abandoned, many buildings and its defenses were destroyed, most inhabitants were sent into the hills, and the roads were blocked, all these measures had as objective to deny Azad Khan a base of operations. As soon as Heydar Khan joined with Mohammad Khan he shot Mirza Mohammad Taqi Golestaneh in vengeance of the blinding of his uncle Emamqoli Khan Zanganeh in 1748. The Zand army now marched from Zohab to Kermanshah, where Mohammad Khan completed the destruction of the town started by Heydar Khan Zand. He expelled the last remaining inhabitants, demolished the remaining towers of the fort, dumped the fort's cannons into the Qara Su, and finally blew up the entire fort.[67] In 1774 there was a severe pest epidemic in Kermanshah.[68]

In 1776, Nazar 'Ali Khan Zand, who had been campaigning in Iraq in 1775 and was now facing a large Ottoman force led by the governors of Baghdad and Mosul, withdrew his forces from Kermanshah and went to Shiraz. However, there were still Zand troops in the area under 'Ali Morad Khan Zand. In 1777, the Zand troops, mostly Kurds and Lors, were defeated. However, the arrival of new Zand troops from Shiraz, who pushed the Ottomans onto their own territory as well as the conclusion of a peace treaty between the two states put an end to hostilities.[69] When in March 1779 news arrived of Karim Khan's death Nazar 'Ali Khan left Kermanshah and hurried to Shiraz. 'Ali Morad Khan succeeded his brother and was supported by Allahqoli Khan Zanganeh.[70] After the death of 'Ali Morad Khan, Allahqoli Khan Zanganeh made a bid for the throne, however, in 1785 he was killed in battle by troops led by Khosrow II of Ardalan. The *Vali* marched to Kermanshah intending to lay siege, but, on his arrival, Allahqoli Khan Zanganeh's uncle, Hajj 'Ali Khan Zanganeh, who was his deputy governor, surrendered the city. The latter was then appointed *beglerbegi* of Kermanshah, who, during his rule, seized the districts of Sonqor and Dinavar, which he added to his jurisdiction.[71] Thereafter, Khosrow Khan Ardalan the *Vali* defeated Ja'far Khan Zand, 'Ali Morad Khan's successor and wanted to make a bid for the throne himself. However, he had second thoughts about it and

66. Perry 1979, pp. 24-25, 38-41, 43-44; Ardalan 2004, pp. 85, 92, 95-96.
67. Perry 1979, pp. 55-57.
68. Sticker 1908-10, p. 269.
69. Perry 1979, pp. 190-81; Ardalan 2004, pp. 134, 138-39, 141-43.
70. Ardalan 2004, pp. 147, 150-51, 154.
71. Ardalan 2004, pp. 162-63, 166-67. Sepehr 1337, vol. 1, p. 49.

joined the cause of Aqa Mohammad Khan Qajar. Nevertheless, the *Vali* allowed Esma'il Khan Zand, who claimed to have become a dervish, to depart to Kerbela. However, the so-called dervish immediately raised an army and laid siege to Kermanshah's citadel. Hajj 'Ali Khan Zanganeh asked the *Vali* for assistance, who reacted quickly and defeated Esma'il Khan's troops.[72] Hajj 'Ali Khan Zanganeh's rule (1784-97) was allegedly much appreciated by his subjects. He was the last Zand governor and was succeeded by a Qajar appointed governor.[73]

72. Ardalan 2004, pp. 178-84. Sepehr 1, 60
73. Soltani 1381, vol. 1, pp. 286-87.

CHAPTER TWO

THE CITY OF KERMANSHAH

LOCATION

The city of Kermanshah is situated at "the southern extremity of a fine plain, through the center of which runs the Qarasu" at about 1,500 m above sea level.[1] The plain is 10 km wide (north-south) and 50 km (east-west), covered with small villages (30-50 houses) and is watered by three considerable streams, which, when joined, are called Qara Su. To the north the plain ends with the Parau mountain range that stops at Bisotun village.[2] The town itself stands on three or four gentle hills (Fath 'Ali Khan, Chiasorkh, and Kamarzand) at the foot of a range. By 1900, Chiasorkh hill, which was covered with small huts inhabited by Kurds, was the end of the town to the south. It was here that the gardens, orchards (with many walnut trees and poplars) and vineyards began, which were the first view of Kermanshah coming from the south-west. These gardens, with numerous small kiosks or pleasure-houses, were "laid out in walks, canals, and reservoirs of water, all of which" produced a pleasant and picturesque view.[3] Because it was situated on rising ground, within Kermanshah's walls there were some slight and other steep ascents, with eminences of different heights, and their corresponding valleys. One hill stood out and was known as Tepeh Alaf Khan or Sartepeh.[4] The intermingled area of gardens, orchards and vineyards, covered an uninterrupted area of some 7 km and were fenced off from each other by straight poplars that were used as timber and wind screen. The gardens offered an abundance of apricots, nectarines, peaches, morellos, cherries, mulberries, and so on.[5] In 1816, Buckingham described it as a "beautiful and extensive plain." Some twenty years later, Fraser described "the situation of Kermanshah [as] the most picturesque, and finest, in point of fact, of any city I remember seeing in Persia." In 1841, Teule observed that contrary to the past the city was no longer surrounded by large beautiful gardens. At that time the land was lying fallow and abandoned. Only towards the west of the city there still were some orchards.[6]

1. Kinneir 1813, p. 132.
2. Adamec 1976, vol. 1, p. 368; Mounsey 1872, p. 294; Gerard 1883, p. 40. Benjamin 1859, p. 206 wrote that the town was surrounded by large morasses, referring to the many streams, no doubt.
3. Olivier 1807, vol. 5, p. 14; Kinneir 1813, p. 132; Rousseau 1813, p. 85; Buckingham 1971, p. 99; Keppel 1827, vol. 2, p. 15; Fraser 1840, vol. 2, p. 185; Lycklama 1873, vol. 3, p. 455; Binder 1887, p. 346; Harris 1896, p. 251; Curzon 1892, vol. 1, p. 559; Rabino 1903, p. 3; Layard 1887, p. 224; Mitford 1884, vol. 1, p. 342; Bigham 1897, p. 185.
4. Buckingham 1971, p. 99; Layard 1887, pp. 224-25; DCR 590 (Kermanshah 1901-02), p. 3.
5. Candler 1919, p. 242; Mitford 1884, vol. 1, p. 342.
6. Teule 1842, vol. 2, p. 486.

Fig. 2.1: Kermanshah seen from the south. In the background Kuh-e Paraw (1907).

Almost 30 years later, Bellew wrote that coming from Hamadan, Kermanshah had a clean and neat appearance "and is decidedly the most flourishing place we have yet seen in Persia."[7] Wills wrote that the grassy plain that surrounded the city, was "a very unusual sight in Persia."[8] In 1920, Dr. Mary Griscom, described her first view of the city as follows: "As we wound up the slopes and looked back on Kermanshah, it seemed scarcely a town, but rather clusters of trees and irregularities in the mud. Little mud houses, a mud citadel, a colorless bazar – that was Kermanshah."[9] Major Greenhouse, the British consul wrote that from Sarab about 5 km of gardens extended to the city, which were enclosed by high mud walls and filled with all kinds of fruit trees common to the province.[10] In 1930, Reitlinger wrote:

> The acropolis of Kermanshah is seen suddenly and dramatically, ridge upon ridge of flat yellow houses broken by the tufts of orchards and the white splashes of modern buildings. Its situation is what one would expect of Kurdestan, but it has nothing to do with Persia, where they build on the open plain, with endless room

7. Buckingham 1971, p. 99; Fraser 1840, vol. 2, p. 185; Layard 1887, p. 225; Bellew 1999, p. 473. These sentiments were very much like those expressed by travelers 1,000 earlier, see chapter one.
8. Wills 1893, p. 109.
9. Griscom 1921, pp. 233-240.
10. AIR 20/663, Maj. Greenhouse, Notes on Kermanshah Affairs, May 1921, p. 17.

> to straggle outwards as the houses fall into decay. Even in mountain country the Persian instinct is not to make defensible cities clustering around rock forts, but to seek out the flattest valleys of the gentlest slopes.[11]

The approach from the east was entirely different. In 1797, Olivier noted that the south-western approach of the town stood in stark contrast to the ruined and/or abandoned villages and sparsely cultivated areas that he traveled through after he left Hamadan. Rabino was not less appreciative and stated that Kermanshah from the east offered a "mean appearance," one that was quite devoid of anything noteworthy. The only thing to relieve the tedium was that one saw "a few tin-covered minarets, the Neghareh Khaneh and the whitewashed walls" of the governor's palace, the only indication that you were approaching a town, not a village.[12] However, to Bellew, coming from Hamadan, Kermanshah appeared "clean, neat, and agreeable, and decidedly the most flourishing place we have yet seen in Persia."[13]

WALLS & GATES

In 1760s, the town had a castle; the buildings, both public and private were badly constructed and most of them were in ruins, due to the constant warfare that it experienced.[14] Later the fortifications were rebuilt and reinforced. In 1797, Kermanshah had strong fortifications with thick walls and a deep moat all around. The citadel likewise was very strong and had been built at Nader Shah's orders, who also had the town walls repaired with a view to provide a solid defense against the Ottomans.[15] Nevertheless, in 1807, Rousseau, the French consul-general in Aleppo opined that one or two decades prior to his visit it was but a miserable town. At the time of his visit the town was surrounded by a simple earthen wall with an old castle within, in which the governor lived.[16] In 1816, Kermanshah's three miles-circumference had an irregular shape, almost circular. In 1900, its circumference was 8,150 paces or 6.7 km, a walk of some one and a half hour. In the first decades of the nineteenth century, the thick walls were flanked with circular bastions, at stated distances, turreted, and pierced with loopholes and ports for cannon, but without a moat. The walls were not really a defense against modern artillery as they were mainly built of sun-dried bricks[17] and in 1816 there was yet no ordnance mounted on any part

---

11. Reitlinger 1932, p. 30. Coming from the west one had a lovely view of the city "half hidden in mists of blue wood-smoke- the mountains across the valley behind rugged and snow-powdered." McCallum 1930, p. 223, see also Hale 1920, pp. 220-21; Powell 1923, p. 231.
12. Olivier 1807, vol. 5, pp. 14, 24-25, 62-64, 159, 165, also vol. 6, pp. 271-273; DCR 590 (Kermanshah 1901-02), p. 3.
13. Bellew 1999, p. 437.
14. La Porte 1771, vol. 2, p. 256.
15. Olivier 1807, vol. 5, p. 23. According to Lambton, "Kirmanshah," *Encyclopedia of Islam*[2], the walls had been destroyed by Nader Shah, which clearly was not the case (see chapter one).
16. Rousseau 1813, p. 85.
17. Dupré 1819, vol. 1, p. 236; Buckingham 1971, p. 99; Fraser 1840, vol. 2, p. 194; de Sercey 1928, p. 296; Mounsey 1872, p. 294; Bellew 1999, p. 437. According to Beth Hillel 1832, p. 88, the city had "a high wall built of hewn stone."

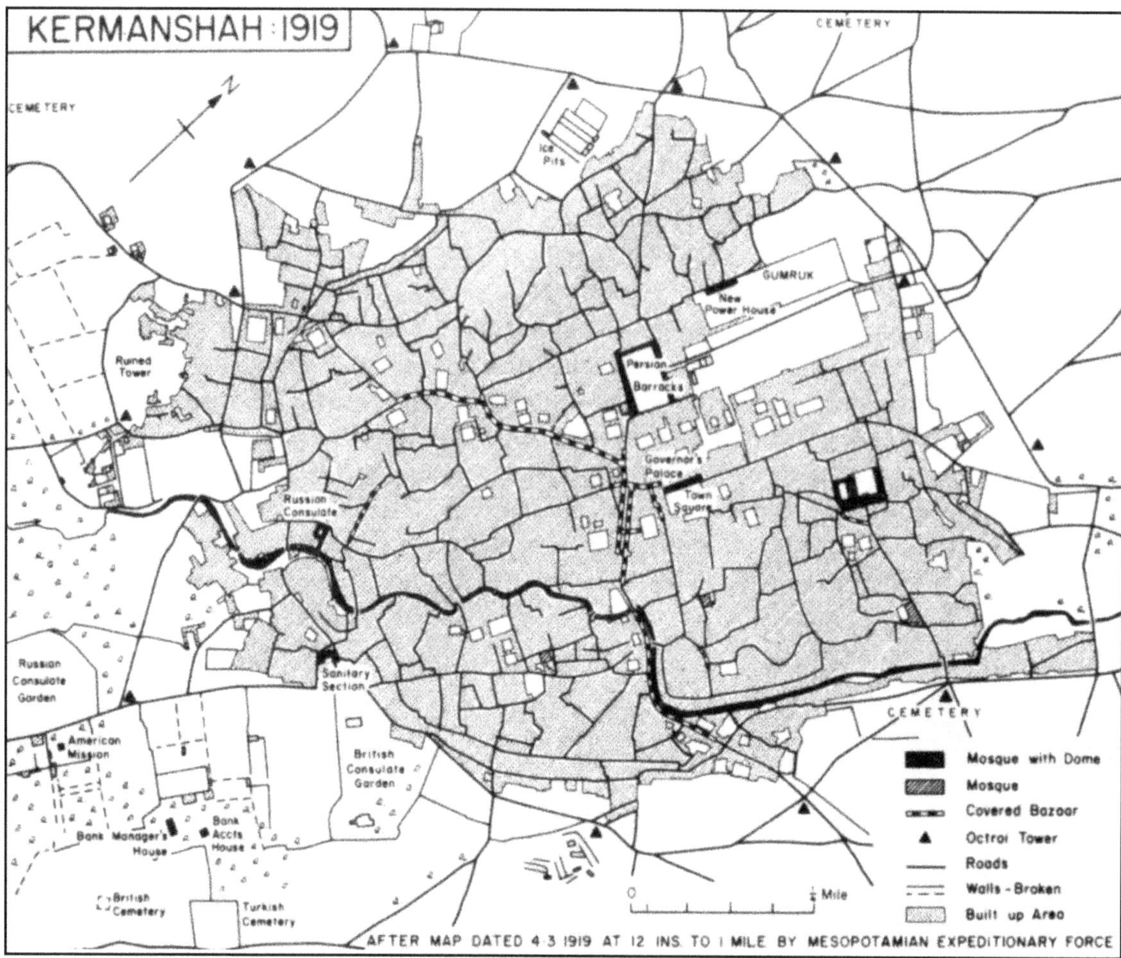

Fig. 2.2: Map of Kermanshah (1919). Source: Clark and Clarke 1969, p. 21.

of it.[18] In the 1820s, Armstrong described the city as "old and ruinous." The streets were filled with peasants and merchants, indicating its important commercial function.[19] In 1840 and around 1850, Kermanshah was still a fortified city, with towers at intervals along the wall.[20] By the 1880s, "the fortifications are in a state of miserable repair, as in fact is the whole place, the entire town presenting the appearance of fast falling into decay."[21] In fact, according to Mrs. Bishop, the ruinous city wall was "much too large for the shrunken city it encloses, parts of it lying in the moat, some ruinous loopholed towers."[22] In 1890, Curzon held the same view describing the ruinous walls and the moat filled with rubbish.[23] By 1900 no trace of the walls was left, "unless it be one or two towers now forming part of the houses of the poorer inhabitants."[24] This

18. Buckingham 1971, p. 99.
19. Armstrong 1831, p. 149.
20. Teule 1842, vol. 2, p. 481; Benjamin 1863, p. 206.
21. Harris 1896, p. 251.
22. Bishop 1891, vol. 1, p. 98.
23. Curzon 1892, vol. 1, p. 559.
24. According to Rabino, and he is the only one to mention this, Dowlatshah built a moat around the town, of which by 1900 no trace was left. DCR 590 (Kermanshah 1901-02), p. 4; Jackson 1910, p. 231 ("traces of the moat are visible where it has not been completely filled up.").

process of dilapidation of the walls may have already started in the 1830s, because Fraser in 1836 wrote: "The gate of the town has fallen in; there was hardly room for the horses to pass, and we rose almost entirely through ruins to reached the caravanserai."[25] By 1920, the town was still encircled by 14 loop-holed two-storied towers used as local Customs post for controlling commercial traffic.[26]

In 1807, Dupré noted four gates: the Baghdad kapou to the south, the Ispahan kapou to the east, the Feyz-Abad kapou to the west, and the Hadji-Nakhi kapou to the north.[27] Although around 1830, Beth Hillel reported that there were three gates, there were actually five gates, which in 1816, Buckingham listed.[28] By 1900 the five gates did not exist anymore, but their names were still used to identify the main entrances to the town. The one to the west or the Baghdad road was still called Darvaseh Kubber Aga, from a pretty little tomb there with a flower garden. It was later also known as Darvazeh-ye Chiasorkh. To the north-west was the gate called Darvazeh-ye Najaf Ashraf, which led to the Emad al-Dowleh mosque. There also was a gate called Darvazeh-ye Sarab that led to Mahidasht. The third gate was Darvazeh-ye Sharifabad, called after the person who built it, later called Darvazeh-ye Kaleskeh; the fourth gate to the north-east was the Darvazeh-ye Taq-e Bostan, later called Darvazeh-ye Qassab-khaneh, and the fifth gate to the south-east was Darvazeh-ye Isfahan, later called Darvazeh-ye Yahudiha.[29] Although ostensibly there were only five gates, the city was allegedly also known as "the City of the Seven Gates."[30]

CITY QUARTERS

Kermanshah was divided into three city quarters (*mahallehs*), which each were under a chief (*kadkhoda*), a function that was practically hereditary. The quarters (originally villages) were named: (i) Barzadamagh to the south and east to which the quarter of Sar-Tepeh was attached; in 1903 its chief was Mahmud Khan, Amin al-Ra'aya. Its sub-divisions were Barzadamagh, Gozar Chal Hasan Khan, Gozar Rajab 'Ali Khan, Kucheh-ye Sheikhavanda, and Kucheh-ye Bahramvandha; (ii) Feyzabad, which was the oldest part of town and was situated to the north, with Fath 'Ali Khan as *kadkhoda* in 1903, and in 1908, Naqi Khan- its subdivisions were: Zarrabiha, Gozar Sayyed Mohammad Rahim, Gozar-e Aqayan, Mahalleh-ye Yahudiha; and (iii)

25. Fraser 1840, vol. 2, p. 194.
26. AIR 20/663, p. 17.
27. Dupré 1819, vol. 1, p. 236.
28. Beth Hillel 1832, p. 88.
29. Buckingham 1971, pp. 99-100 (the Najaf Ashraf gate was named after a saint of that name, of which he gives the story); Rabino opines that it was either formerly was the gate for pilgrims going to Najaf and Kerbela, or that it "got its name from the fact that Mohammed Ali Mirza had new gates made for Nejef, and had the old ones brought to Kermanshah and put up at this spot." DCR 590 (Kermanshah 1901-02). Since Buckingham was in Kermanshah a few years after the gate had been built his explanation seems to be the more likely one. Soltani 1381, vol. 3, p. 481; Cherikof 1358, p. 93 (darvazeh-ye Sarab). Soltani also mentions the Darvazeh-ye Chal-e Hasan Khan in the east and Darvazeh-ye Gari-khaneh (Gomrok) in the N.W. of the city as well as Darvazeh-e Chenani, Soltani 1381, vol. 4, pp. 640, 642; Jackson 1910, p. 231 (5 gates).
30. Forbes-Leith 1925, p. 172.

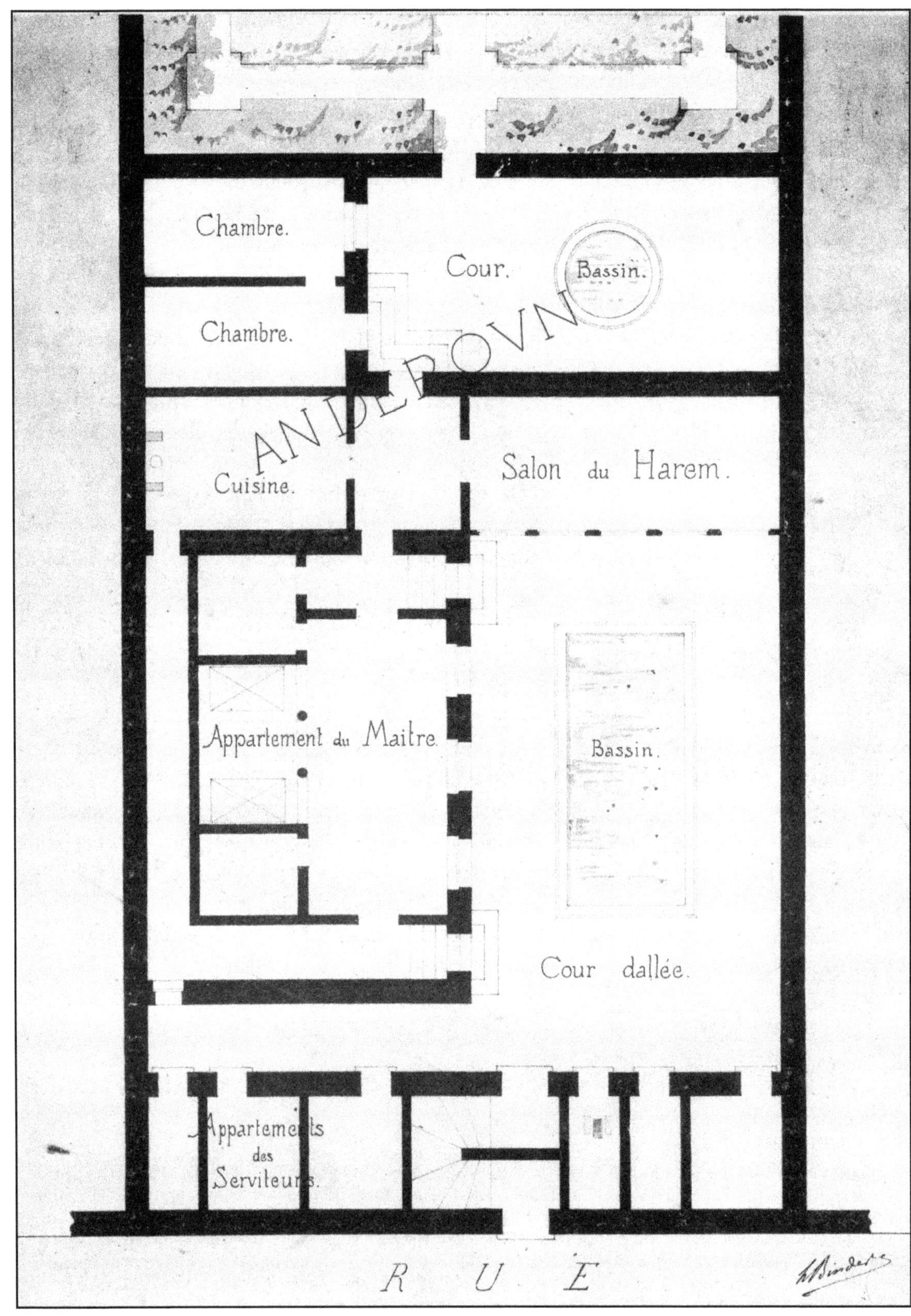

Fig. 2.3: Plan of Dr. Vaume's house (1886).

Meydan Mullah 'Abbas 'Ali to the west, with Akbar Khan as *kadkhoda* and as subdivisions: Meydan-e Mullah 'Abbas 'Ali, Gozar-e Qarabaghi, Sar Tepeh Mohammed 'Ali Beg, Kucheh-ye Saiavandeh, and Mahalleh-ye Chenani. In 1903, Sharif al-Molk was *kadkhoda-bashi* and was responsible for the other three *kadkhoda*s, but in 1908 he is mentioned as the chief of the Barzadimagh quarter. Feyzabad was the district where most notables lived, because the streets were wider and it was not close to the bazaars.[31]

HOUSES & BUILDINGS

In the 1940s, Kermanshah was described as a huge Kurdish village of huts and narrow alleys,[32] because most houses or hovels in Kermanshah were small, single-storied built in sun-dried brick around a courtyard. Therefore, after heavy rainfall some houses and buildings would be damaged.[33] The houses were all separated from the street by a clay wall. According to Wills, in the 1870s, each house "having an arched entrance closed by a heavy, unpainted door, with many big nails in it." In most of these dwellings there was little furniture apart from some floor cover and cushions. There was no separate bedroom or dining room, but at night bedding was placed in the living room, where people slept. Whereas one usually assumes that five or six persons lived in one small mud house, according to Rabino, in 1900 the Kurds huddled together. "Ten Kurds put up in a mud house consisting of three small rooms, and it is said that in no town in Persia are there so many inmates to a house."[34] According to his contemporary, Dr. Scott, houses in Kermanshah were overcrowded and unhygienic, usually 7-8 persons living in a one-room dwelling.[35] Only the notables and merchants had comfortable and even fine houses, which in 1797 mostly were two and some three story-buildings. On top was a terrace on which people slept during the summer months. However, from the outside this was not obvious as one could only observed high walls. This changed when tall buildings were constructed in the twentieth century. For example, from the balcony of Hotel Bristol the beds, many with mosquito nets, could be seen on the city's houses. The larger houses, such as owned by Vakil al-Dowleh, had a doorway giving access to a dark passageway, at the end of which there was a door opening to a square courtyard with rooms on both sides. From the courtyard a staircase led to a gallery. It further had above this a glass-room offering a view of the city and the plain. Also, there was a second courtyard, on one side of which were large rooms for guests, wile the rooms opposite from it were the owner's. The walls were decorated with colored tiles and the floor was paved.[36]

31. DCR 590 (Kermanshah 1901-02), pp. 4-5; Administration Report 1908, p. 39; AIR 20/663, Maj. Greenhouse, Notes on Kermanshah Affairs, May 1921, p. 18.

32. Government of Great Britain 1945, p. 525.

33. This happened, for example, in March 1920 when many houses and the outer wall of the barracks crumbled. FO 248/1293, Report Kermanshah 31/03/1920.

34. DCR 590 (Kermanshah 1901-02), p. 13; Dupré 1819, vol. 1, p. 237; Binder 1887, p. 351; Wills 1893, pp. 109-110; Whigham 1903, p. 271; Blücher 1949, p. 74.

35. Scott 1905, p. 622.

36. Olivier 1807, vol. 5, p. 24; Dupré 1819, vol. 1, p. 237; Floyer 1979, p. 435; Harris 1896, pp. 255-56 (with drawing); DCR 590 (Kermanshah 1901-02), p. 5; Powell 1923, p. 231; Blücher 1949, pp. 74-75.

Fig. 2.4: Courtyard of Vakil al-Dowleh's house (1895)

Other large houses had a slightly different arrangement, but all had a public (*biruni*) and a private part (*anderuni*) as may be seen from fig. 2.3, which shows the plan of an upper-class house typical for the country.[37] As winters were cold and the houses without much effective insulation people kept warm with a brazier (*manghal*) or sat around the *korsi* in dark rooms with closed windows. Only in the houses of the great it was comfortable living, because they "can afford plenty of firewood, and have glazed windows in their *khelwuts* [private] and principal rooms, and even in their mansions all beyond the apartments of the master himself is as bad as in other places."[38]

In 1807, Dupré found that there was nothing noteworthy to the city.[39] Because Kermanshah's increased role as an urban center was due to the Qajars, the main public buildings all date from that period and most were built by two of its most prominent governors. The first, who is sometimes described as the 'founder' or 'builder' of Kermanshah, was Mohammad 'Ali Mirza Dowlatshah and the other was his son, Emamqoli Mirza, Emad al-Dowleh. Dowlatshah was the builder of the palace or ark, which was the largest, a quarter of a mile in circuit, and therefore, "by far the most conspicuous building in the city."[40] According to Fraser, the palace had "an imposing exterior, its gate is built on a height, which adds to the effect of its own altitude and gave access to an arcaded passage [*talar*], from which by several traverses one reached a large court in which was the divan-khaneh or hall of public audience."[41] However, Layard disagreed. He noted that the palace's exterior was like all public and private buildings in Persia of plain mud-built walls, while, in 1840, the entire building was in a ruinous state.[42] In 1867, Wills observed that the *talar* in which he was received, which had a fountain, was decorated with mirrors and florid mural paintings; "these in this case were life-size full-length portraits of posture dancers and dancing girls, and were in ancient costumes, having been painted fifty years ago." Furthermore he noted that the *taqcheh*s or niches were filled with "chromo-lithographs in very dubious taste." There also were chandeliers at various heights and some 20 of old carriage-lamps stuck into staples in the walls. Finally, many cages with one nightingale in each of them were standing around.[43] Long vaulted passageways, with raised seats of brickwork on either side where guards and servants were sitting talking and smoking, connected some 12 courtyards that were surrounded by rooms and apartments, just like the houses of the notables. The various courtyards, usually with a fountain and a parterre of roses and/or other flowers in the middle, were the center of several other buildings that were attached to the palace or the *divan-khaneh*, as Naser al-Din Shah called it. These extensions were the Emarat-e Kashkul

---

37. Binder 1887, p. 345; Hinz 1938, pp. 18-19.

38. Fraser 1840, vol. 2, pp. 196-97. Lors supplied Kermanshah with charcoal. DCR 590 (Kermanshah, 1902), p. 25.

39. Dupré 1819, vol. 1, p. 237. His compatriot de Pagès, 1797, vol. 1, p. 326 held the same view as did many others such as A Correspondent, 1835, p. 404.

40. Southgate 1840, vol. 1, p. 137; Buckingham 1971, p. 104. Teule 1842, vol. 2, p. 483 considered the palace not noteworthy, although its gardens were attractive.

41. Fraser 1840, vol. 2, p. 190-91. In the *divan-khaneh* there were two "monolith of Sang Sumakh (porphyry) from the Bisutun Hills, considered a great rarity by the Persians." DCR 590 (Kermanshah 1901-02), p. 7. The governor's palace and arsenal probably were built on the site of the village of Kermanshah-e kohneh. Adamec 1976, vol. 1, p. 366.

42. Layard 1887, p. 231.

43. Wills 1893, pp. 113-14.

Fig. 2.5: Lambert Molitor's house in Kermanshah in 1910. © *Collection Molitor, Ed. Elytis* no. 107

(oblong building), the Anderun (women's quarters), the Emarat-e Bidistan, the Emarat-e Kakh (towers) between the Andarun and the Emarat-e Archain or Howz-khaneh (tank room), which was behind the *divan-khaneh* and noteworthy, although in decay by the turn of the century. The palace complex further included the stables, the Khalvat and other private apartments.[44] Visitors were usually received in the *divan-khaneh*, where, in 1840, the governor sat "surrounded by vases filled with sweet-scented flowers."[45]

There were also some buildings of interests in the city's suburbs. Dowlatshah was the builder of the *Bagh-e shahzadeh*, in which the *Kalleh-ye Hajji Karim* was situated, called after its builder, but it was also known as *Delgosha*. It was later renovated and repaired by his son. It was situated on the east of the Sarab, overlooking the city's gardens. *Delgosha* was used as the summer palace of the governor. It had its own small garden and terrace. From 1918-21 it was used as the British military hospital with a capacity of 200 beds. Other buildings of some interest were the *Pol-e Qarasu* and the *Jist* at Vakiliyeh.[46] *Afghan House*, which belonged to Khadduri,

---

44. Naser al-Din Shah, pp. 70-72. Already in 1840, much of the palace was in a ruined condition. The open halls around the Howz had "once been gorgeously and elaborately painted" while smaller side rooms were closed by beautiful lattice-work." Layard 1887, p. 231.

45. Layard 1887, p. 232.

46. DCR 590 (Kermanshah 1901-02), p. 7, note; AIR 20/663, p. 19. Perhaps the *Delgosha* is the same building in which the governor of Kermanshah received Olivier, who described the place of reception as "a very vast room" that was situated on ground level in a not too large garden, watered by a spring. In the room were some inferior [presumably wall] paintings, "two of which appeared to be of two Europeans." Olivier 1807, vol. 5, pp. 20-21.

Fig. 2.6: The Divan-khaneh with the courtyard of the barracks and the rooms of the soldiers (1911).
© *Collection Molitor, Ed. Elytis* no. 210.

a merchant. It was east of the road to Sarab, two-storied, well-built with 10 rooms, servant accommodations, large gardens and stables. From 1918-21 it served as a lodging for officers and as officers club. *Ejlaliyeh*, the property of Amir Koll, was a large house situated south of the city on the western bank of a stream. It consisted of two buildings with a garden in between. In 1920-21, the lower building was used as billet, and the higher building as hotel for families of officers. Across from the *Ejlaliyeh* were two good detached houses with gardens that were used as British military billets during their presence in the city.[47]

The palace's 300 m long front and main entrance was to the south-east on artillery square, which was flanked by the main bazaar that also was built by Dowlatshah. Therefore, it was initially known as *Meydan-e Now* and a place for the exercise of horses; later it was called *Meydan-e Tupkhaneh*, because guns were placed there and the military marched there.[48] The square was 32 m wide and 80 m long. In 1884, Hosam al-Molk built European-type gardens in the square that were planted with flowers and maintained by a number of gardeners.[49] In the following years the space and recesses around the square as well as the square itself was occupied by all kinds of craftsmen and traders and the square had become a market place and filthy. In 1900, Ala al-Dowleh banned all commercial activity in the square and evicted that craftsmen

47. AIR 20/663, p. 19.
48. Binder 1887, p. 347; Buckingham 1971, p. 104.
49. *Ruznameh-ye Iran* 1375, vol. 4, p. 2592 (no. 643; 04/12/1887).

around the square, who had sat up shop in small rooms (*hojrehs*). He cleaned, repaired, and repainted the square and embellished it with small fenced gardens in which plane trees were planted and had public lights installed that were lit each night. He further placed two rusty guns on either side of the square and a water tank in its middle. Other guns and mortars were place in the recesses around the square. "Every evening there is military parade, and at sunset, after the bugles and drums of the Neghareh Khaneh, to the south of the square, have ceased their deafening noise, the military band plays and the crowd settles in the coffee houses till two hours later when everything is quiet again."[50] Around 1920, apart from numerous coffee-houses there also were all the government offices, i.e. the palace of the governor, the offices of the police, the main Post Office and the office of the Eastern Telegraph Company. In the N.W. corner of the *Meydan* there was the *Masjed-e Jom'eh* and the gendarmerie barracks. To the west of the *Meydan* was another spacious square with the barracks .[51]

The large square or *Meydan* was surrounded by the main bazaar. In 1807, Dupré wrote that the *besesteins* [sic; *bazzazestans*] or markets were neither extensive nor elegant. Also, they were of a very common architecture.[52] Shortly thereafter new bazaars were constructed, which consisted of arcades occupying three sides of the square, the governor's palace occupying the fourth place, all of which was built by Dowlatshah.[53] In 1816, those bazaars that were finished were "lofty, wide and well lighted and aired, built of brick, with vaulted domes, rising in succession from the roof, and having a range of shops, about twelve feet wide in front, divided by a central perpendicular bar, and closed by double shutters. The benches before them are built of stone, conveniently low for sitting, and the shops are sufficiently spacious to contain a large variety of merchandise, and leave room for the keeper, visitor and assistant."[54] This bazaar comprised a series of "shops and stalls in recesses like those of a large khan; and having lanes linking them to the main bazaars in the different quarters of the town, and generally crowded with people.'[55] However, the straight wide vaulted lanes, built step fashion in the steepest part of the town, were extended thereafter with tortuous alleys.[56] During winter time the bazaar was uncomfortably cold, the apertures in the bricked domes letting in not only light and air, but also rain, snow and slush. In the 1930s, the bazaars were very clean and the shops neat and orderly.[57] In 1835, Fraser observed that "The bazaars half open, the owners of the shops cowering at the doors of their cells, and shivering over a pot of charcoal in their sheep-skin clothes, you are literally drowned in discomforts."[58] The main bazaar was the one that began at the *Meydan-e Tupkhaneh* (artillery square) and continued until *Darvazeh-ye Sar-e Qabr Aqa*. The extreme end of this bazaar was

50. *Ruznameh-ye Iran* 1375, vol. 5, p. 4087 (no. 1106; 03/07/1902); DCR 590 (Kermanshah 1901-02), p. 7; Grothe 1910, p. 93.

51. Powell 1923, p. 231; AIR 20/663, pp. 17-18.

52. Dupré 1819, vol. 1, p. 237.

53. *The Saturday Magazine*, no. 500, 18 April 1840, p. 145; Southgate 1840, vol. 1, p. 137.

54. Buckingham 1971, p. 109. According to A Correspondent 1835 b, p. 438, the shops were more spacious than in Turkey.

55. Buckingham 1971, p. 104. Teule 1842, vol. 2, p. 482 submitted that the bazaars are as unremarkable as the products they had to offer.

56. Binder 1887, p. 345; Reitlinger 1932, p. 31.

57. Alexander 1931, p. 24; Reitlinger 1932, p. 31.

58. Fraser 1840, vol. 2, p. 196.

called *bazar-e 'alaf-khaneh*; others bazaars included the *Rasteh-ye Rajab 'Ali Khan, Rasteh-ye Chal Hasan Khan, Bazzazkhaneh-ye Emadiyeh*, and *Bazzazkhaneh-ye Shahi*.[59]

Although, subsequent governors neglected city development and improvements, already in 1822, one-fifth of the buildings was in ruins.[60] It is unknown what the cause of this was (earthquake; rains), but some 20 years later Layard noted that "a great part of the town was in ruins."[61] The ruinous state of many buildings in the rest of the city and the dilapidated condition of the bazaars were getting worse during the second half of the nineteenth century.[62] The arrival of Ala al-Dowleh as governor in 1900 changed all that. He not only renovated the government buildings, but forced the owners of the bazaars to repair their property under threat of severe punishment. As a result, the bazaars were whitewashed and the caravanserais repaired. The governor also initiated a novelty to Persia by having the streets cleaned and street lights in the streets and bazaars all night long, a phenomenon that did not even exist in Tehran.[63]

Those that existed prior to 1835 all were built by Hajji Hashem Khan.[64] In 1850, there 16 caravanserais, "in 3 of which traders reside."[65] There were two kinds of caravanserais; one used for pilgrims, and the other for merchants and caravans. Of the latter kind, the most important one was the *Vakil al-Dowleh* caravanserai, which held the offices of the main merchants.[66] In 1900, the most important caravanserais were the *Vakil al-Dowleh, Postkhaneh, Gomruk, Emad al-Dowleh, Qeysariyeh, Bazzazkhaneh, Hajji Mo'in, Navvab*, and *Chaharsuq*.[67]

Emad al-Dowleh built the arsenal on an elevation in the middle of town. In 1890, it had two Austrian Uchatius 12-pounders, two brass smooth-bore six-pounders, and 500 Werndl rifles with a garrison of 500 men.[68] In 1902, the Arsenal was completely hemmed in by buildings and shops. It was basically a military warehouse. In 1902, it was said that it contained 700 Werndl rifles and 20 old muzzle loader guns of various sizes. The other guns that previously were kept in the arsenal had all been placed on the Artillery Square. These were: two Austrian 9 cm breechloaders; four Austrian 7 cm breech loading mule guns; four Austrian muzzle-loading 6-pounders (made in Tehran); 10 old mounted muzzle loaders of varying sizes and two mortars mounted on a gun carriage.[69]

The barracks were situated near the governor's palace and in the words of Rabino were untenanted hovels. It basically was a large square (146 m x 76 m) bordered on three sides by 128 small rooms, which each could accommodate 5-6 soldiers. The entire arrangement very

---

59. DCR 590 (Kermanshah 1901-02), pp. 4-5, 12.
60. Shirvani 1215, p. 492
61. Layard 1887, p. 225. Teule 1842, vol. 2, p. 482 (the city is in a very miserable condition. I am struck by the poverty wherever I look, even after having seen all the misery of the [other] Persian cities).
62. Bishop 1891, vol. 1, p. 101; Curzon 1892, vol. 1, p. 559.
63. DCR 590 (Kermanshah 1901-02), pp. 4-5, 12; *Ruznameh-ye Iran* 1375, vol. 45, p. 4087 (no. 1106; 03/07/1902).
64. Fraser 1840, vol. 2, p. 185. Some predated the Qajar era, see Olivier 1807, vol. 5, p. 15. Layard 1887, p. 225 stayed in one called *Aqa*.
65. Amanat 1983, p. 94.
66. DCR 590 (Kermanshah, 1902), p. 5.
67. DCR 590 (Kermanshah, 1902), pp. 72-75.
68. Curzon 1892, vol. 1, p. 559.
69. DCR 590 (Kermanshah 1901-02), pp. 8, 64.

much looked like the inner court of the *Shah 'Abbasi* caravanserai. The fourth side was a three-story building with rooms; they were dominated by the towers of the palace's *anderun* or women's quarters. Before the renovations of 1902 the place was a total ruin. Thereafter the square was used for drill practice and the adjacent rooms housed the soldiers. The top two stories of the building on the fourth side and the *andarun* towers had not yet been repaired in 1903.[70] From 1918 to 1921 the British military called these barracks 'the Persian barracks' and during the British military presence in Kermanshah during that period, the mechanical transport company, ordnance and supply depots were located there. There were rooms and stables facing the yard on all sides and on the east side three storeys, surmounted by a four-storied tower. North of the Persian barracks was a big walled enclosure in which the Customs was situated. Part of it was also used by the British as a depot.[71] In March 1920, heavy rains caused some houses to crumble as well as the outer wall of the barracks (*sarbaz-khaneh*). [72]

Despite all these buildings, Wills characterized the town as "straggling, with many open spaces."[73] Also, European visitors were not impressed with what the city had to offer in terms of places of interests. The general view summed by Whigham was that "The town is remarkable for no conspicuous building nor outward signs of wealth." Furthermore, that "the best that can be said is that it contains fewer ruined and unoccupied houses than most other towns in Persia."[74] According to Rabino, only the *Divankhaneh* plus the *Talar* and the *Howzkhaneh* were noteworthy.[75]

DEVELOPMENT PATTERN OF KERMANSHAH DURING THE QAJAR PERIOD

As mentioned above, Dowlatshah commissioned the main elements of the city such as the governor's palace (*Arg-e Hokmran*) and bazaar next to the central mosque, which remained from the Zand period. These were located in the heart of the town, around the central *Meydan*, or in other words they formed the central part of the three villages Chanani, Feyzabad and Barzadimak. The oldest Qajar endowment in Kermanshah belongs to Dowlatshah (1820). He donated a mosque, a madraseh, a cistern, a public bath, a caravanserai or *timcheh*, and thirty-two shops.[76] This endowment was located to the west of governor's palace and north of the bazaar. A second endowment belonged to someone named Farrash-Bashi (1866), who donated a *timcheh* located to the east of the governor palace and bazaar.[77] These building activities represent the

70. DCR 590 (Kermanshah 1901-02), p. 8.
71. AIR 20/663, pp. 17-18.
72. FO 248/1293, Report Kermanshah 31/03/1920.
73. Wills 1893, p. 110.
74. Whigham 1903, pp. 271-72; Mounsey 1872, p. 294 (no buildings or mosques worthy of note); Harris 1896, p. 256 (There is nothing to see); Lycklama 1873, vol. 3, p. 455 (only the gardens were worthwhile visiting).
75. DCR 590 (Kermanshah, 1902), p. 7.
76. Keshavarz 1382, p. 261.
77. Keshavarz 1382, p. 489

Fig. 2.7: The lower part of Kermanshah (*ca.* 1911). © *Collection Molitor, Ed. Elytis* no. 203.

beginning of the development of the city from its center to the west and east, although the town did not develop much outwardly, because it was build up very compactly.

Thereafter, accelerated development of the town took place to the west and south. En route to Kerbela, Naser al-Din Shah described Kermanshah and wrote the following: "I went on Fath-Ali Khan hill, the whole town was visible from there. There was another hill among the gardens known as *Chagha-Sorkh*. Much of the city is located on a hill."[78] The extension of the thriving bazaar toward the western gate or *Darvazeh-ye Sar-e-Qabr-e Agha* (*Chagha-Sorkh*), which was used by pilgrims, may be one of the reasons of the development pattern to the west of the city. Naser-al-Din Shah's comments about the bazaar also suggests this: "the most important street (*rasteh*) of the bazaar begins from *Tup-Khaneh* square and ends at the western gate (*Darvazeh-ye Sar-e-Qabr-e Agha*). [79]

After the 1870s, it seems that the eastern parts of the town began to grow, because other important endowments such as by Emad al-Dowleh (1890), Zahir al-Molk (1891) and Vakil-bashi are mostly located in the eastern part of the town. Hasan Khan Mo'aven al-Molk endowed the construction and embellishment of a large *takiyeh* that bears his name. Construction began in the 1880s and lasted till 1920. It is an outstanding example of tiled Qajar work with Persian and European patterns, a splendid example of the new iconography that came into being toward the end of the nineteenth century.[80] Many of these endowments were related to structures within

78. Naser al-Din Shah 1372, p. 60.
79. Idem, p. 60.
80. Peterson 1979, pp. 618-28; Salari 1371.

the Kermanshah bazaar. Therefore, the development of the town to some extent may be considered as subordinate of development of the bazaar as the main structural element in the town.

According to a 1919 British map, the administrative block (governor's palace, barracks) together with 1.2 km long bazaar was in the center of the city. The bazaar with its caravanserais was the commercial center and therefore, the focus of caravan traffic, which went into east-west direction across the city. Toward to the end of the Qajar period the development process to the south of the town gradually increased, and much of this process was because of the foreigners who lived in Kermanshah. The construction of offices and residences such as the Russian Consulate, the Ottoman Consulate, the American mission hospital and houses of the staff of the Imperial Bank of Persia made this a new residential area, despite the fact that this was an area with mainly gardens. Thus, the small European population was mainly concentrated in the S.E. outskirts of the city, east of Qal'eh-ye Kohan. In 1920, the British consul Greenhouse reported that "The latter is a walled enclosure, situated S. of the town, measuring 450 x 500 yards in which the huts of the British Military post were erected." The Indian battalion was camped 1.5 km east of Qal'eh-ye Kohan among gardens. Most mosques were situated in the north-eastern part of the city. As a result, the built up area was compact, more or less egg-shaped, 6 km in circumference. It extended 2.5 km from north-east to south-west and 1.6 km from north-west to the south-east and most of the city lay west of the Abshuran river.[81] In the 1930s, the Khiyaban-e Melli, a broad avenue with roundabouts was cut though the city from north to south, while also new modern buildings were erected, the most imposing were the new barracks.[82] Moreover, garages were built in the northern part of the city on the roads to Hamadan and Tehran, a grain-silo north-east of the city, while there was urban residential development, houses with spacious gardens, to the south-west.[83]

HOTELS

Travelers usually slept in a caravanserai. Around 1830, Beth Hillel reported that there were "capital houses built of hewn stone, of two stories for travelers, and keeping Merchants goods: these are called caravanserai; every kind of trade is exercised there."[84] Pilgrim caravans were spread out all over town and therefore, the number of caravanserais used as lodgings is not known; also many private homes were used as lodgings if there was a larger than usual number of pilgrims in town.[85] European travelers often lodged with Europeans working in Kermanshah, were put up in a house by the governor, or slept in a caravanserai or some other kind of lodging such as in private homes. After 1850, British officials usually stayed in the British agent's house.[86]

81. Clarke & Clark 1969, pp. 21-22; AIR 20/663, p. 25.
82. Government of Great Britain 1945, p. 525
83. Clarke & Clark 1969, p. 23.
84. Beth Hillel 1832, p. 88; Wills 1892, p. 110; La Porte 1771, vol. 2, p. 255.
85. DCR 590 (Kermanshah, 1902), p. 5; Sayyah 1346, p. 232.
86. Rousseau 1813, p. 86; A Correspondent 1835 a, p. 404; Harris 1896, p. 254; Floyer 1979, p. 437; Bigham 1897, p. 185; Cresson 1908, pp. 159-60.

Fig. 2.8: Street behind the Divan-khaneh (top) and a *charvadar* (1907).

Layard and Mitford rented a room in the *karavansara-ye Aqa*, "which was not over clean or free from vermin." Here they were assailed by hawkers who rented out water pipes as well as by barbers, who offered their services.[87]

It was only as of the 1920s that European-style hotels were established in Kermanshah.[88] The first of its kind probably was an unnamed hotel built at the end of 1919 near Bisotun, a stretch of the road where usually many robberies occurred. However, in the beginning of 1920 the area was quiet. The hotel was one "where many better class pilgrims and townspeople stay. It is not guarded and not molested."[89] In 1930, the American travel Reitlinger observed that "On the edge of the town, among Armenian garages and shops, stands the Hotel Bristol." ...It far exceeded my expectations. A pane or two might be broken in the bedroom window, but were made up for by the heat of a stove, lit at once by a venerable Georgian housemaid, a relic of feudal Russia. In the saloon, a carpeted place of luxury decorated with steamship posters and coloured Swiss views, was a dignified coterie [of Greeks] listening to a gramophone."[90] A few years later, Miss Alexander stayed at the same hotel which she called Kermanshah's principal hotel. She was less positive of the amenities offered than Reitlinger.

> The rooms themselves were clean and the beds comfortable, but my advice to newcomers is to make a thorough survey of one's room on arrival, and to see that all the necessities are there which we, as Europeans, may require. For it is annoying to return later to find that there is no towel, or only the damp leavings of the last occupant, that the jug is empty or the basin dirty. The tooth-glass is often absent, as is the key of the door, while it is easier to make the servant wrestle with the stubborn whims of the window, which refuses either to open, or lets in cold blasts of air, than to do it oneself. ... The public room of the hotel consisted of a large dining-room-lounge (this arrangement is usual in Persia). At one end it is equipped with small tables and chairs, the manager's desk, and a few shelves which formed the bar; while at the other was a large table on which papers were strewn, some more chairs and a gramophone as well as a wireless installation which gave forth at intervals, music and unintelligible talks from Moscow and Baku. Habitués strolled in for meals, dinner being seldom served before half-past eight, they remained late, however, often till midnight, chatting with the manager, or listening to the gramophone or radio.[91]

Balfour and his party, who stayed in the same hotel and in the same year as Ms Alexander found the hotel pleasant and comfortable enough, "though the ladies found it hard to resign themselves to its complete lack of sanitation." The amenities offered was also to their liking and Balfour found his stay sufficiently pleasant to include a description of his experience in Hotel Bristol.

---

87. Layard 1887, p. 225; Mitford 1884, vol. 1, p. 343.
88. Blücher 1949, p. 80.
89. FO 248/1293, tel. Consul to Legation, 22/04/1920.
90. Reitlinger 1932, pp. 30-31; Lingeman 1930, p. 10; Gray 1938, p. ix (daily, about 50 riyals).
91. Alexander 1934, p. 23.

> There was a cozy dining room with garish pictures of Swiss peasant scenes on the walls. Two naked, painted Atlases held on their shoulders golden globes with the faces of clocks, and a table was stacked, not with cheap magazines and handbooks, but with copies of the *National Geographic Magazine*. We had an excellent dinner of soup, meat and spinach, rice as light as only Persian rice can be, with a sharp sauce, chicken, fresh fruit cup, amber Persian wine to drink and a fizzy Russian mineral water.

When one of his companions told the owner that his hotel was superior to many they had stayed in on their journey from Great Britain, he said, as a matter of course: "Yes, you are now in a civilized country."[92] In 1935, Hotel *Bristol* was no more, but it was then styled as: 'Grand Hotel ex Bristol' or just *Grand Hotel* with rooms at about 50 riyals per day. In 1937, in addition, there was the *Hotel Hallal Bala*, with a daily rate of about 50 rials.[93] Finally, four other hotels are mentioned at that time, viz. Hotel *Bisestun*,[94] *Bozorg*, *Jahan* and *Continental*. There also were some inns (*mosafer-khanehs*) and restaurants, in particular along the Khiyaban-e Garazh.[95]

STREETS

The streets of Kermanshah were dirty, unpaved, narrow and winding. Those to the bazaar were often exceedingly crowded, so that Persian notables and their party went on horseback around town preceded by footmen and hangers-on, who had to make their way with sticks or heavy maces. In 1902, Ala al-Dowleh banned secular and religious notables to be accompanied by such large escorts, but, if the rule was respected, it did not last after his departure. Movement was so slow in the streets not so much due to people crowding the streets, but rather due to the long lines of animals of the caravans that moved in and out of the city carrying firewood and merchandise. However, throngs of beggars also often were an obstacle. Hardly any street was wide enough to allow wheeled traffic. By 1900, the Zarrabiha street and the one from the *Darvazeh-ye Sarab* to the *Chal-e Hasan Khan* were the only ones that were fit for carts.[96] Near the latter were situated the two largest caravanserais, *Amin Khan* and *Vakil al-Dowleh*.[97] Although the streets were dirty not much activity was undertaken to do something about it. In 1888, Hosam

92. Balfour 1935, p. 88.
93. Simmonds 1935, p. ix; Gray 1938, p. ix; Hinz 1938, p. 18 (he admired the prints showing scenes in German *Jugendstil* as well as adds recommending Junker's gas-fired bath-oven and visiting Germany).
94. [http://iranshahrpedia.ir/fa/indexer#limit:50|page:1|infix:هتل |]
95. Soltani 1381, vol. 1, p. 552.
96. Olivier 1807, vol. 5, p. 24; Keppel 1827, vol. 2, p. 50; Beth Hillel 1832, p. 88; A Correspondent 1835 a, p. 404; Teule 1842, vol. 2, p. 482; Layard 1887, p. 238; Sayyah 1346, p. 233; Binder 1887, p. 345; Wills 1893, p. 109; Floyer 1979, p. 433; Harris 1896, p. 257; DCR 590 (Kermanshah 1901-02), p. 5; Whigham 1903, p. 271; Cresson 1908, pp. 159-60; Grothe 1910, p. 90; *Ruznameh-ye Iran* 1375, vol. 5, p. 4091 (no. 1017; 26/07/1902). Blücher 1949, pp. 65, 74; AIR 20/663, Maj. Greenhouse, Notes on Kermanshah Affairs, May 1921, p. 17.
97. Grothe 1910, p. 90.

al-Molk considered improving the situation. He prohibited the throwing of refuse and the like into the streets and also intended to keep them clean, but this plan, as well as the ban, seems to have remained a good intention, given the unchanged condition of the streets thereafter.[98] In early 1892, Ziya al-Dowleh ordered the cleaning of the streets (*tanzifat-e baladiyeh*) to which end he employed workers from the *ehtesabiyyeh* (public cleaning service).[99] This order clearly had no lasting effect, because in 1902, Ala al-Dowleh ordered the streets to be cleaned and engaged workers from the *ehtesabiyyeh* to sweep them every day; also to lit lamps in those streets where lamps had been placed.[100] In 1913, "A carriage road round the town is being made, a great improvement, as only a few of the streets are wide enough for vehicular traffic."[101] In July 1913, more than half of a carriage road around the town was completed, which was indeed an improvement.[102]

Moreover, none of the streets were paved so that when it rained or thawed after snow fall and freezing temperatures streets became almost impossible to use. In 1835, Fraser had to endure such a situation. He could walk from the palace to the caravanserai almost entirely through the covered bazaars to stay dry.[103] However, Fraser wrote that when he wanted to leave Kermanshah he was not so lucky, for due to rain and snow he "went knee-deep in mud, torrents pouring down from every house; heaps of snow, six to ten feet in height, over which, both horse and foot-passengers must climb at the risk of slipping down into the gulf of mud at their feet, or toppling over the wall of some dwelling, overlooked by the snowy mountain on which they tread."[104] And even when he finally had left Kermanshah, he found that also outside the walls "we continued to trudge in mud, sometimes to the horse's knees."[105] The situation could become even worse than just streets turning into mud lanes. Because the Qarasu runs through the center of the city, it sometimes happened that it overflowed, which "is attended with very serious injury." This happened in 1821, when in the lower part of the town a considerable part of the population were swept away.[106] In 1867, Wills described the streets as follows: "The causeway was generally some three feet wide, and raised a yard wide and often two feet deep in mud or water, looking like a ditch, but it was really the road (save the mark!) for horses, mules, and camels."[107]

In the 1930s, the Khiyaban-e Melli, a broad avenue was cut though the city from north to south.[108] In 1934, with a budget on one million rials the Khiyaban-e Pahlavi and the Khiyaban-e Raf'atiyeh were made. For people's use some 100 droshkies were stationed in these streets.[109]

98. *Ruznameh-ye Iran* 1375, vol. 4, p. 2607 (no. 647; 21/01/1888).
99. *Ruznameh-ye Iran* 1375, vol. 4, p. 3088 (no. 767; 26/02/1892).
100. *Ruznameh-ye Iran* 1375, vol. 5, p. 4087 (no. 1106; 03/07/1902).
101. DCR 5204 (Kermanshah,1912-13), p. 5
102. Political Diaries vol. 5, p. 201.
103. Fraser 1840, vol. 2, p. 193.
104. Fraser 1840, vol. 2, p. 196.
105. Fraser 1840, vol. 2, p. 198
106. Keppel 1827, vol. 2, p. 15; Beth Hillel 1832, p. 88. There continued to be inundations. In April 1934, an entire city quarter was inundated; more than 200 houses were destroyed and 26 people died. *The Palestine Post*, Thursday 02/03/1934, p. 1; Idem, Monday 11/06/1934, p. 1 (with slightly different numbers)
107. Wills 1893, p. 110; Floyer 1979, pp. 433, 339.
108. Government of Great Britain 1945, p. 525
109. Soltani 1381, vol. 1, p. 554.

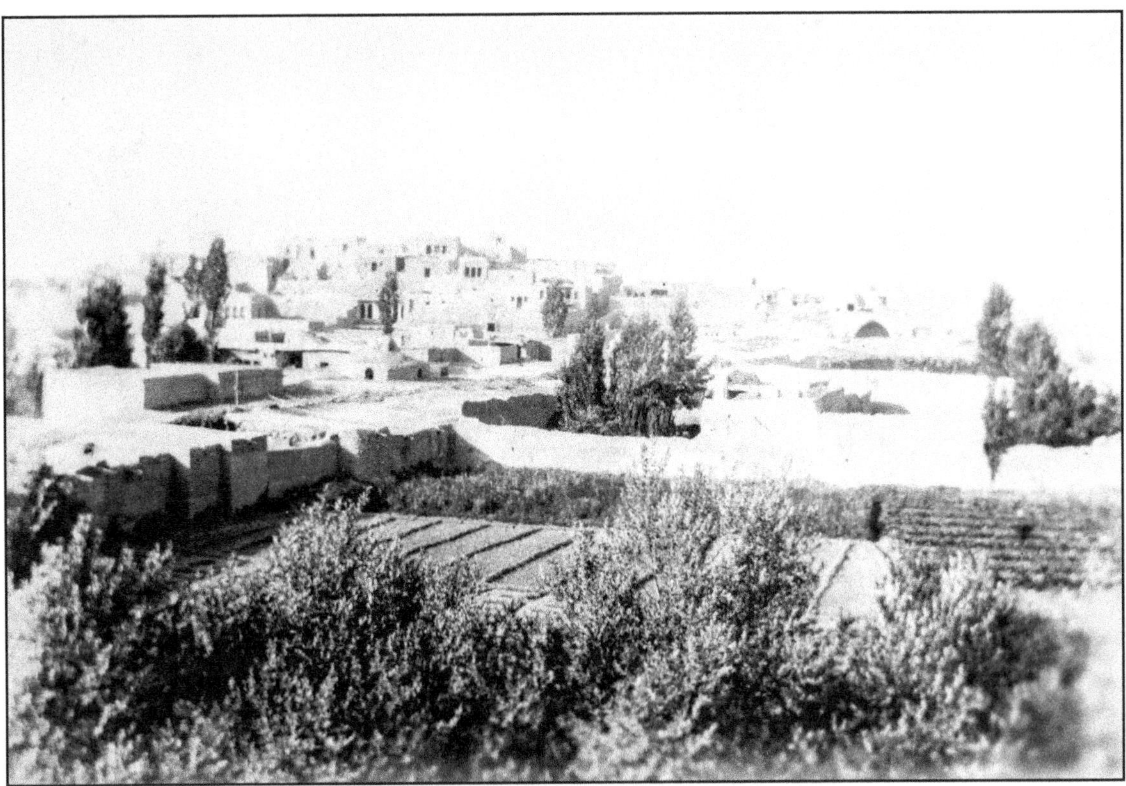

Fig. 2.9: Kermanshah 1912. © *Collection Molitor, Ed. Elytis* no. 116.

Of course, the purpose of making these broad streets was questioned by people, including the British consul who commented: "In demolishing old streets and in building in their place wide avenues flanked by the flimsiest of buildings-often mere facades erected to give an imposing impression- the local authorities cannot said to have benefited the population- in this district, at any rate- during the past few years."[110] In 1930, the main streets of the city were well swept.[111] The streets were kept wet by a number of men, who took water from the *jub* or water course along the road and threw its contents onto the street. If you were so unfortunate to just pass by you ran the risk to be soaked. Each sprinkler had the responsibility to wet a specific section of the road.[112]

By mid-1942 the main street of the city was in bad repair, made worse because of much military traffic passed through it. Therefore, the Mayor asked Kampsax or the British road making authorities to asphalt it, but it had no priority.[113] The asphalting off the main avenue finally begun in mid-March 1944 with the help of two large steam rollers.[114] In July 1945, the

110. FO 371/21900, f. 113.
111. Alexander 1931, p. 24.
112. Hinz 1938, p. 19.
113. FO 371/31402, Kermanshah Diary September 1942.
114. FO 371/40177, Kermanshah Diary March 1944. However, two months later the consul reported: "Leveling of the main street in Kermanshah is progressing. Asphalting has not yet begun." FO 371/40177, Kermanshah Diary May 1944.

Fig. 2.10, top: Kermanshah in 1911 as seen from the roof of Molitor's house. © *Collection Molitor, Ed. Elytis* no. 117.

Fig. 2.11, above: Kermanshah. © *Collection Molitor, Ed. Elytis* no. 193.

Fig. 2.12, opposite: Kermanshah and its gardens (*ca.* 1911). © Collection Molitor, Ed. Elytis no. 197.

British consul observed that the only main road of Kermanshah had been asphalted free of charge by Great Britain, but due to lack of maintenance and repair had become a series of pot-holes. The metalling of the road had to be paid by the Municipality, but its leaders, Mohammadi and Mo'ali disagreed, which paralyzed all municipal activities.[115] Until 1952, only 1.5 half of the avenues were asphalted, but by 1955 even the smaller alleys were being asphalted and several new avenues had been added.[116]

POPULATION

Although there is no census or other quantitative sources that would allow a reliable approximation of Kermanshah's population, it is clear that in the mid-eighteenth century it was a small market-town, whose people mostly lived from agriculture and animal husbandry. In 1735, Kermanshah had 10,000 inhabitants, according to Leandro di Santa Cecilia.[117] With the establishment of the Qajar dynasty and security in the country as well as the appointment of Mohammad 'Ali Mirza Dowlatshah, Fath 'Ali Shah oldest son as governor of Kermanshah, the town started thriving and growing in size. In 1802, Kinneir opined that Kermanshah was a flourishing town with about 12,000 houses or 60,000 people, which is unlikely as this is at odds

115. FO 371/45400, Kermanshah Diary July 1945.
116. RG 91-19-28, Frances Zoeckler to Board of Foreign Missions, 08/02/1956.
117. Buckingham 1971, p. 101; Santa Cecilia 1757, p. 19.

with population estimates from other contemporary sources.[118] For example, in 1790, Abbé Beauchamp estimated the population at 5,000-6,000, while the French consul in Baghdad, Rousseau, in 1807 estimated its population at had 16,000-18,000 inhabitants and in that same year his compatriot Dupré estimated that the city did not have more than 10,000 inhabitants.[119] Writing in 1816, Buckingham argued that the town had increased in size, in population, in affluence, and it was still growing. It then had about 30,000 inhabitants, but from "the space covered by houses, and the manner in which they were occupied, I thought the number of people here at least equal to half of those at Baghdad," which would make the estimate still higher.[120] In 1830, Kermanshah was ravaged by the plague, which reduced its population to 12,000 people. It was before the outbreak of the plague that Beth Hillel visited the town and estimated its population at more than 80,000 families or 300,000 people. As in the case of all other cities that Beth Hillel visited he invariably greatly overestimated the number of its inhabitants, unfortunately.[121] In 1835, an anonymous British traveler wrote that Kermanshah was "comparatively new as a town, having, not many years ago, been merely a village."[122] In 1837, the American missionary Southgate estimated its population at about 35,000.[123] In 1840, the French ambassador de Sercey opined that Kermanshah was one of the most important cities of Persia, with a population of 12,000, while his compatriot Teule estimated it at 20,000 to 25,000 people.[124] This very low number, according to the French officer Ferrier, was due to the misrule by governor Mohebb 'Ali Khan, as a result of which the population of Kermanshah had dropped by as much as 75%; the townsmen had gone to Azerbaijan, the nomads to Turkey.[125] In 1850, Keith Abbott reported that Kermanshah was a small town with about 5,000 houses or some 25,000 inhabitants.[126] In 1856, a British traveler estimated that the town had 20-25,000 inhabitants,[127] while Naser al-Din Shah en route to Kerbela in 1870 wrote that the town had 7,000 houses and 70,000 inhabitants, which seems to be much too high a population figure. In 1876, Floyer estimated the population at 40,000 people.[128] In the mid-1880s, Kermanshah allegedly had 30,000 inhabitants, according to Binder, a French traveler and Dickson, a British Tehran-based diplomat,[129] while Herbert, the latter's colleague in 1888 reported a decreasing population of 40,000 inhabitants or 6,000 houses, while in 1887 Mrs. Bishop put the number at 25,000 people only.[130] Normally a house is taken to represent five inmates. Kermanshah had the same number of 30,000

118. Kinneir 1973, p. 132.

119. Rousseau 1813, p. 85; Grothe 1910, p. 88; Dupré 1819, vol. 1, p. 238. Kinneir 1973, p. 132 wrote that the flourishing city had 12,000 houses, suggesting 60,000 inhabitants, which cannot be true as this is at too great odds with other contemporary sources.

120. Buckingham 1971, pp. 100-01.

121. *DCR* no. 3189, p. 39; Shirvani 1315, p. 492; Beth Hillel 1832, p. 89.

122. A Correspondent 1835 a, p. 404.

123. Southgate 1840, vol. 1, p. 137.

124. de Sercey 1928, p. 298; Teule 1842, vol. 2, p. 482.

125. Ferrier 1857, pp. 25-26.

126. Amanat 1993, pp. 93, 97.

127. Mounsey 1872, p. 294.

128. Naser al-Din Shah, p. 71; Floyer 1979, p. 435.

129. Binder 1887, p. 347; AP 76 (Report 31/10/1884), p. 7. Gerard 1883, p. 44 mentions 4,600 houses, or about 25,000 inhabitants.

130. DCR 113, p. 8.

inhabitants a decade later, despite the fact that the author wrote, "although allegedly it had much larger number 10 years ago. Bad government drove people elsewhere."[131] In 1890, Curzon estimated the population at 40,000.[132] By 1900, the fixed population was estimated at 50,000 to 60,000 with a floating population of 10% representing pilgrims.[133] In 1911, Mrs. Stead estimated Kermanshah's population at 45,000.[134] It appears that the population was still at the 60,000 level in the 1920s, although Forbes-Leith, who had lived in the area for some time, in 1924 estimated that the city only had 30,000 inhabitants.[135] In 1932 the population was estimated to be about 70,000 and a decade later 88,000 inhabitants.[136] In 1944, the American missionaries estimated that the population was over 100,000, higher than the 90,000 mentioned by the British consul.[137] In 1947, the British consul noted that "There is movement of people from rural to Kermanshah and from Kermanshah to Tehran, mostly the well-to-do to enjoy the luxuries of town such as electricity for a few hours day. [138] This migration explains why the city's population grew in size in the following decades.

Table 2.1: Estimated population (1735-1944)

Year	No of inhabitants	Source
1735	10,000	Leandro di Santa Cecilia
1795	5-6,000	Abbé Beauchamp
1807	10,000 and 16-18,000	Dupré; Rousseau
1810	60,000 ?	Kinneir -12,000 houses
1816	>30,000	Buckingham
1830	300,000 ?	Beth Hillel
1832	12,000	Shirvani
1837	35,000	Southgate
1840	12,000	de Sercey
1840	20-25,000	Teule
1850	25,000	Abbott - 5,000 houses
1856	20-25,000	Mounsey
1870	70,000 ?	Naser al-Din Shah - 7,000 houses
1876	40,000	Floyer
1882	25,000?	Gerard 4,600 houses

131. Harris 1896, 251; Bishop 1891, vol. 1, p. 101 held the same opinion.

132. Curzon 1892, vol. 1, p. 558, however, later he gives a figure of 60,000 inhabitants. Idem, vol. 1, p. 575. Bigham 1897, p. 186 gives a figure of 100,000 for 1895, which seems too high.

133. DCR 590 (Kermanshah, 1902), p. 13; Whigham 1903, p. 271; see however, *RMM* 2 (1907), p. 197, which gives the population as 30,000. In 1903, the Turkish consul estimated the population at 100,000, Rabino 60,000 and Baron Weydel, the Belgian customs chief put it at 40-50,000. Rolandshay 1904, p. 116.

134. Stead 1911, p. 128.

135. Wilson 1932, p. 19; Hale n.d., p. 206; Forbes-Leith 1925, p. 172.

136. Ebtehaj 1932, p. 148; Government of Great Britain 1945, p. 524.

137. RG 91-19-28, Annual Report Westminster Hospital Kermanshah 1943-44; FO 371/40177, Kermanshah Diary May 1944.

138. FO 371/45488 Kermanshah Diary March 1947.

Year	No of inhabitants	Source
1885	30,000	Binder; Dickson
1887	25,000	Bishop
1888	40,000	Herbert - 6,000 houses
1890	40,000	Curzon
1895	30,000	Harris
1900	40-60,000	Rabino, Ronaldshay
1911	45,000	Stead
1924	30,000 - 60,000	Forbes-Leith; Wilson
1932	70,000	Ebtehaj
1944	99,000 -100,000	Government of Great Britain; US missionaries

Note: Estimates that are at odds with the trend are marked by an ?

Most of the population were Kurds, but there also were Lors, and even some families of Afghan descent. The official language was Persian, which was understood in all towns and large villages in the province. The Kurds spoke a version of Kermanji, with variations in districts and tribes, and the Lors spoke a similar language. Turkic speaking villagers and tribesmen spoke a dialect not unlike Osmanli Turkish. The lower classes in Kermanshah spoke a local dialect, which was a mixture of Kermanji and Persian, according to Consul Greenhouse, a dialect being close to Sanjabi and Kalhori Kurdish. The various minority ethnic/religious groups, in addition to Kurdish and/or Persian, spoke their own language.[139]

EMPLOYMENT

Kermanshah had the usual tradesmen and craftsmen that most Persian cities had, being employed in metal working, wood working, building, ceramic, textile, leather, and food as well as agriculture related crafts and trades.[140] Apparently, they were organized as guilds. For in 1824, the mourning procession of Mohammad 'Ali Mirza was led "by the artisans: each craft had with it a black banner, and a horse equipped in the same mournful manner.[141] The fact that each craft was clearly represented separately from each other suggests a guild organization.[142] This conclusion is supported by the fact that around 1920, 20 guilds in Kermanshah had created a united organization to better defend their interests.[143]

139. Wilson 1932, p. 33; Ebtehaj 1932, p. 148; DCR 590 (Kermanshah, 1902), p. 15; Hale n.d., p. 206; Mann 1909, pp. 1123-24. According to Beth Hillel 1832, p. 89, Persian and Kurdish was spoken. Soltani 1381, vol. 1, pp. 265-78; AIR 20/663, p. 23.

140. de Sercey 1928, p. 298.

141. Keppel 1827, vol. 2, p. 55.

142. On guilds in Qajar Iran, see Floor 2010.

143. Ossetrov 1922, p. 571; partly translated by Ravasani n.d., pp. 227-28.

The gold- and silversmiths of Kermanshah were very good, in particular their *qalyan*-heads, teapots, milk pots, and silver cutlery (knives, forks, spoons), as well as a myriad of copper items.[144] In 1930, the tiny shops of gold workers, copper and brass smiths with all kinds of items such as jugs, bowls, urns, mule bells offered the only evidence of native products displayed in the bazaars.[145] Europeans were rightly amazed at the skills and ability of Persian metal workers to copy almost any imported product while using scraps of metal to do so. Buckingham reported that in Kermanshah muskets and pistols were made "of a good quality, and in sufficient request to be sent to different parts of Persia."[146] Bleibtreu, like Harris, reported that Kermanshah was known for good rifles and pistols. They were sold throughout Persia.[147] However, the best workmen in W. Persia were in Kangavar, who made excellent Martini rifles at 20 *tumans* (Rs 45)/piece and were able to copy anything. In Kangavar there were four gunsmiths, whose average production was 100 rifles/year.[148] It may well be that some of the skills the Persian gunsmiths displayed had been acquired through the introduction of European technology into Persia.[149] Mohammad 'Ali Mirza in Kermanshah like his younger brother and rival 'Abbas Mirza aimed to modernize his armed forces, to which end he had established "a foundry for brass cannon, under the superintendance of the Russian Yusef Khan, his Topjee Bashi, at which he intends casting all the ordnance for the city; and some coarse gunpowder is also made by the same man."[150] By the 1880s, this production of guns may have greatly reduced. At least, Harris reported that "The long tunneled bazaars are picturesque enough," but after finding some old arms there was nothing worth purchasing.[151] In 1920, there were only three gun makers.[152]

The construction of many public and private buildings implies the presence of carpenters, masons, builders and brick makers, the more because the tiles used in the various houses were made locally. For example, the interior of the Emad al-Dowleh mosque was covered with tiles made in Kermanshah. However, by the 1880s the tile makers craft did not exist anymore. In 1900, Rabino called "this manufacture, so far as Kermanshah is concerned, an art of the past."[153] The tile work of the Mo'aven al-Molk *takiyeh* was executed by the master tile maker Hasan Tahirani, who was induced to come to Kermanshah from Tehran.[154] There also was some pottery made.[155]

In the early Qajar period, printed cotton cloths and handkerchiefs were still made in great quantity in Kermanshah. However, later, like in most of Persia this industry was mostly replaced

---

144. Lycklama 1873, vol. 3, p. 473; also Brugsch 1863, vol. 2, p. 86; Binder 1887, p. 347; Soltani 1381, vol. 1, pp. 160-162; Blücher 1949, p. 79.
145. Alexander 1931, p. 24; AIR 20/663, p. 59.
146. Buckingham 1971, p. 110.
147. Bleibtreu 1894, p. 185; Buckingham 1971, p. 110 ("and in sufficient request to be sent to different parts of Persia").
148. Political Diaries 1, p. 352.
149. See Floor 2003 b, p. 257
150. Buckingham 1971, pp. 110, 101
151. Harris 1896, p. 256; Binder 1887, pp. 346-47.
152. AIR 20/663, p. 18.
153. DCR 590 (Kermanshah 1901-02), p. 8.
154. Peterson 1979, pp. 624-25.
155. AIR 20/663, p. 59.

by imports. By 1920, there still was some silk weaving, be it mainly in Hamadan.[156] Saddle cloths and felt coats (*yapanchis*) that were much used by the tribes in mountains were also made in Kermanshah.[157]

Carpet weaving added much to the province's wealth. Ferrier, referring to the situation in the 1840s, stated that "None can be more rich, soft, and beautiful; the patterns are in perfect taste, and the colours most brilliant," ... and, moreover, they were cheap and very durable, including its colors. Also "each side is presentable."[158] These were the product of cottage industries, because there were no large manufactories, which, when completed, were brought to the bazaar for sale.[159] The carpets of Kermanshah, if not celebrated, were as good as anywhere else made in Persia, at least until the 1860s. By 1870, the carpet industry was nearly extinct. By 1880, due to the rapacity of governors, plague and cholera not much of its once colorful production was left. The only positive point that could be said about them was that aniline dyes were not as much used in Kermanshah town as by the Kurds, according to Preece.[160] According to Mrs. Bishop, writing in 1887, Kermanshah was still famous for its carpets and she noted that "There are from 25 to 30 kinds, with their specific names." However, as Rabino rightly pointed out she must have been mistaken or referred to a previous period, because at the time of her visit the carpet industry was already extinct in the province.[161] Whigham agreed with Rabino and reported that "there are no carpets of any value made in Kermanshah, nor is there any manufacturing industry of any sort."[162] By 1900, two basic carpet designs were still produced, the Herati and the shawl design, both of low quality. Gelims were more appreciated, especially those woven in Harsin, Kerend and a few other places, because they were easily sold and rarely confiscated by governors or tribal chiefs.[163] These carpets and gelims were woven by the nomads. The carpets were coarse and not long lasting, but the gelims had an excellent reputation and thus enjoyed good sales. By 1910, carpet production had improved due to the growing use of natural dyes instead of anilines.[164] This was due to effective marketing by German firms and the easiness of the use of their product. In July 1906, Messrs. Burgher and Behrens, two German nationals taught the chief dyers of the town the use of synthetic indigo.[165]

Despite the disappearance of the carpet industry from Kermanshah, some carpet dealers in the USA and Europe maintained that carpets were still woven at Kermanshah and they were not

---

156. Buckingham 1971, p. 110; AIR 20/663, p. 59. On the demise of the Iranian textile industry, see Floor 1998 and Idem 2009.

157. AIR 20/663, p. 59; de Sercey 1928, p. 298.

158. Ferrier 1856, p. 26; Blau 1858, p. 45; Mounsey 1872, p. 293.

159. Buckingham 1971, p. 110; Dupré 1819, vol. 1, pp. 230, 238; A Correspondent 1835 a, p. 404; de Sercey 1928, p. 298; Southgate 1840, vol. 1, p. 137; Fraser 1826, p. 357; Layard 1887, p. 239; Amanat 1983, p. 94; Benjamin 1859, p. 206; DCR 590, p. 20.

160. Adamec 1976, vol. 1, p. 358; DCR 590 (Kermanshah, 1902), p. 20; DCR 2260 (Ispahan 1879-99), p. 17.

161. Bishop 1891, vol. 1, p. 109; DCR 590 (Kermanshah, 1902), p. 20.

162. Whigham 1903, p. 274.

163. DCR 590 (Kermanshah, 1902), p. 19.

164. Küss 1911, part III, p. 27. "The carpet industry, for which Kermanshah was formerly so famous, is now almost instinct [sic; extinct], at least as regards to Kermanshah town and the centre of the province." AIR 20/663, p. 58

165. Political Diaries, vol. 1, p. 428.

made in Kerman as others suggested.[166] Or, they maintained that the Kermanshah rugs didn't come from the city, but from the surrounding mountains.[167] However, knowledgeable people such as D. H. Dwight, a long time resident of Hamadan, wrote that the name 'Kermanshah carpet' "grew out of ignorance or perverted ingenuity of dealers, who knew nothing about so remote a town as Kerman, who were confused by its similarity to the name of Kermanshah, and whose romantic eyes were attracted by the termination of the latter. A Kermanshah is just a better example of a modern Kerman carpet." However, he was mistaken when he also wrote that it was "hardly an exaggeration to affirm that no rugs are or were ever made there."[168]

Gloves were a difficult article to buy in the bazaar. Like in Turkey only gloves for the right hand were sold, which, moreover, were not often used, except when it was cold. There were both worsted and leather gloves. A British visitor reported that "The latter sometimes reaching to the middle of the fore-arm, not unlike the gloves of our dragoons. They often had fingers, in which they differ from those of Turkey, where I do not think I ever saw fingered gloves."[169] It is not clear whether these gloves were made locally or imported. The same anonymous British traveler, on arrival in Kermanshah wore red pumps with peaked toes, which he had worn since Baghdad. These were not comfortable and therefore, he bought shoes in Kermanshah. "The shoes had high iron-bound heels, were without peaked toes, made with black leather, and were the only shoes I had seen in the East made with welts, on the same principle as our own. They were clumsily done to be sure, and the leather badly dressed; but they were things in which one might walk firmly, and I was therefore well satisfied with them."[170]

To feed the population there were grocers, bakers and other food related crafts and trades. In Kermanshah, there was even a special kind of thick wheat bread, called *tap-tapi*, which was baked on the *saj* (a concave metal plate) to take as provisions when traveling or during the time of field work. Another kind was *kulbereh*, a round, very thick bread, made with wheat, barley and millet flour, which was mostly used in religious convents (*khanqah*) for the consumption by guests, pilgrims and devotees.[171] "In the confectioners' shops are sweet cakes of different sorts, small loaves, and sugar refined in the town, almonds and other comfits arranged in glass jars, and sweet drinks prepared in large copper and brazen vessels, covered with engraved devices and inscriptions."[172] Also, various kinds of sweetbreads were baked such as *kolucheh-ye shekari*, *kak*, *khanegi*, much of which were bought by pilgrims on their way to Kerbela.[173] Mostly mutton was consumed; goat meat was eaten by the very poorest only, while beef was rarely seen. The sheep were large and fat. "The butchers are clean in the manner of serving and dressing

166. Pushman 1911, p. 25.
167. Mumford 1915, p. 188.
168. Dwight 1917, p. 621; see also Lewis 1913, p. 347 (the so-called Kermanshah rugs come from Tabriz).
169. A Correspondent 1835 b, pp. 438-39.
170. A Correspondent 1835 b, p. 439.
171. Soltani 1381, vol. 1, p. 246 (*tap-tapi* was also baked in a *tanur-e zamini* or *tabun*); Basir al-Molk 1374, p. 134; Al-e Ahmad, 1333, p. 3.
172. Buckingham 1971, p. 111; Alexander 1931 pp. 24-25.
173. Soltani 1381, vol. 1, p. 248; Jackson 1909, p. 232 (sugar cakes). *Komaj* is a turmeric and cumin bread that's filled with chopped dates.

Fig. 2.13: Peddlers in the bazaar (1886).

them, though, from the very different modes of preparing dishes here and in Europe."[174]

There were, as yet, no coffee-houses in 1816, but "cook-shops, fruit-stalls, and confectioners' benches are very numerous." All kinds of food were to be had there. The cook-shops were very clean, "they offer kebabs, bread, rice, and sometimes steamed dishes. Most people in the bazaar send for food there, as it is not customary to go home to eat."[175] The food was brought to their location on a large circular pewter tray.[176] By the end of the 19th century there were many coffee-houses, in particular in the *Meydan-e Tupkhaneh*.

All kinds of good fruit and provisions were available in the bazaars. Fruit, which constituted a major part of people's diet during three months of the year, was available in abundance, in particular melons, grapes, peaches, and apples. There were also pears and plums, but more rarely, and every kind of vegetable common to the country, were good, and kept and served with cleanliness and care.[177]

Wine making and selling was exclusively done by Christians and Jews, "although the gain arising from it comes chiefly from the Mussulmans, whose private habits support what their

174. Buckingham 1971, p. 111.

175. Buckingham 1971, pp. 109-110; Mitford 1884, vol. 1, p. 343. Kebabs brought from a cook shop and a cup of green tea. Fraser 1840, vol. 2, p. 185; Grothe 1910, p. 91.

176. Layard 1887, p. 225.

177. Dupré 1819, vol. 1, p. 238; Buckingham 1971, pp. 109-10; Grothe 1910, p. 91.

religion forbids them openly to countenance. The business is carried on in private, but the great jars and other vessels arranged for the reception of the liquor, showed that the article was in good demand."[178]

Around 1850, Kermanshah was well-known for its tanneries and its trade in hides and pelts as well as the large number of pack animals and the production of all kinds necessaries needed for transportation.[179] The range of products included leather boots and shoes, canvass shoes, saddlery and various other leather goods.[180] On the *Meydan* was also the horse market, as well as outside the walls, on the north of the town, where many were seeking a horse. All the horses there were Persian. These were stronger than the Arabian horse, but exceedingly inferior in beauty, and also said to be so in speed and in sustaining privations of food and water.[181] In 1904, the cost of shoeing was 4 *qrans*; inferior shoes were 2.5 *qrans*. The horseshoes were different from those in use in Europe. "The shoe in universal use consists of a thin plate of iron of about 1¼ to 1½ inches wide, hammered to the shape of the hoof, which it nearly covers, and is fastened on by four or six large-headed nails. They last about 10 weeks."[182]

A significant share of the urban population was still engaged in agricultural activities such as market gardening, which in major towns still held first place in the 1850s.[183] In addition, there was the group of servants and retainers of all descriptions that served the government and leisure class. Finally, this sector included all those who had no regular employment and tried by hook and crook to make a living, or in other words, the poor. The services sector, the informal sector and that of the casual day laborers represented the bulk of the urban labor force. The majority of them were employed as unskilled laborers, mostly in menial jobs such as porters, charcoal makers, cobblers, sweepers, refuse gatherers (*kannas*), brick-makers and construction workers, in short, all low-paying jobs.[184] However, the demand for unskilled work was not enough to supply everybody with gainful employment. Consequently, streets and bazaars were overcrowded with poor and unemployed persons, ready to sell their labor for a piece of bread after 1870.[185] This may also partly explain the presence of sex workers. In Kermanshah, the prostitutes lived in the house of the public executioner. "The monopoly of whom [i.e. the prostitutes] was the largest source of this man's revenue."[186] In 1840, there also was a seller of slaves.[187] Although, at the Sultan's orders of December 1846, the governor of Baghdad prohibited the slave trade in the Ottoman ports of the Persian Gulf, the transport of slaves from Baghdad via Kermanshah to Persia continued for quite a number of years.[188]

---

178. Southgate 1840, vol. 1, p. 131; Rabino 1903, p. 15.
179. Blau 1858, p. 45.
180. AIR 20/663, p. 59.
181. Buckingham 1971, pp. 112-13.
182. DCR 3189 (Kermanshah 1903-04), p. 35; Adamec 1976, vol. 1, p. 359.
183. Issawi 1971, p. 286; Floor 2003 a.
184. Floor 2009, pp. 7-12.
185. Issawi 1971, pp. 48-50; Qazvini 1370, pp. 71-74.
186. Wills 1893, p. 110.
187. Teule 1842, vol. 2, p. 484. It still happened that occasionally persons were offered for sale. In 1898, a man offered Zahir al-Molk a young girl for 24 *tumans*. *Ruznameh-ye Iran* 1375, vol. 5, p. 3768 (no. 936; 05/06/1898).
188. Toledano 1982, pp. 101, 105-06; for the slave trade in Persia, see Floor 2012.

In May 1906, the cashier/bookkeeper of the *Imperial Bank of Persia* in Kermanshah, Mirza Esma'il Baqer Khan, opened *The English Stores*, a shop dealing in provisions and general stores. The fact that at that time there were 45-50 British subjects in the British consular district may have had something to do with this, although the British consul reported that its clientele were Persian.[189] Later that year, Mirza Esma'il Baqer Khan was arrested for fraud and an arrangement was worked out for him to pay back the stolen money. Two years later, *The English Stores* was practically closed, "which is as well, for its condition shed no lustre on the name it held," the British consul commented.[190] Another sign that modern products were in use and could be repaired in Kermanshah is the presence of a watch-maker (*sa'atsaz*).[191] For the arrival of modern factories and the like in Kerman, see Chapter Seven.

RELIGION

At the beginning of the Qajar period, most inhabitants of Kermanshah town were not any longer Ali-ilahis like most people in the province. Nevertheless in 1807, Rousseau observed that the town did not suffer much from intra-religious fanaticism.[192] This conversion to Shiism had apparently started in the eighteenth century. This trend was allegedly reinforced by Hajji 'Ali Khan, a former governor, who built the *Masjed-e Jom'eh* and allegedly had forced the inhabitants to pray there and this gradually converted the Ali-ilahis to Shiism. However, Mitford opined that in 1840 the majority of the population was still Ali-ilahi,[193] who, according to Keppel in 1824, were "held in greater abhorrence than Christians and Jews" by Shiites,[194] although there still were many of them in the city.[195] In 1920, according to the British consul, "in the city 50% are Ali-ilahis, about 25% are Bahais, but in secret. The rest are Shiites."[196] According to the British consul, the Ali-ilahis "are a sect that believes in successive reincarnations of the Deity. They hold that 'Ali was a divine reincarnation while Muhammad was his lawgiver. There are two groups (a) the *Atish Begi* who a re mainly in Damavand, Tehran, Kazvin and Azarbaijan, and (b) the *Haft Tawanan* of Kermanshah, Luristan and Mosul. A considerable proportion of the dervishes in Persian are Ali Ilahis."[197]

---

189. DCR 3683 (Kermanshah,1905-06), p. 5; Political Diaries, vol. 1, p. 352. This number decreased to 10 European and 8 Indian British subjects in 1910. DCR 4766 (Kermanshah,1910-11), p. 7. In 1905, Mirza Esma`il was also involved in a bread-ring. FO 248/879, Crossle to Grant-Duff, Tehran, 11/08/1906.

190. Administration Report 1908, p. 46; Administration Report 1906-07, p. 42. In August 1906, the British consul had already induced the governor to close the shop. FO 248/879, Weekly Diary ending 28 August1906.

191. IOR/L/MIL/17/15/11/3, Who's Who in Persia, vol. 2, p. 164 (Ja`far *Sa`atsaz*, who had a leading role in German and Democrat activities in 1915, and who was employed by the Municipality).

192. Rousseau 1813, p. 88. According to Teule 1842, vol. 2, p. 483 the population was entirely Shiite.

193. Buckingham 1971, p. 101; DCR 590 (Kermanshah, 1901-02), pp. 6, 14; Shirvani 1315, p. 294; Mitford 1884, vol. 1, p. 335.

194. Keppel 1827, vol. 2, p. 61

195. Shirvani 1315, p. 294.

196. AIR 20/663, pp. 23, 78.

197. IOR/L/MIL/17/15/11/3, Who's Who in Persia, vol. 2, p. 31; Napier 1919, p. 8.

By 1900, there still were conversions to Shiite Islam, because Rabino explicitly mentioned the *jadid al-islam* as a group.[198] Given the religious composition of the population these converts most likely were Ali-ilahis and Jews. In fact, in 1917 the governor of Kermanshah was a converted Jew, the son of Hakim Nasiri, the genitor of the Nasir al-Attiba family.[199] As far as the Jews were concerned, a convert could claim the property of his infidel family members, which injustice, needless to say, caused much misery, bitterness and resentment (see Appendix I concerning the Jewish population).

In 1816, there were allegedly only 20 Sunni families-settlers from Turkey in Kermanshah as well as some Arabs, but these were only sojourners. A century later there still were only a few Sunnis in the city.[200] However, by 1917, there some 1,000 Sunnis in the city.[201]

There were even fewer Christians in 1816 in Kermanshah. In that year, Buckingham found only one, viz. Yusef Khan, a Russian and the governor's *tupchi-bashi* and no Armenians at all. He did not count the few, mostly female, Georgian slaves that lived in the town among the Christians. In 1837, there were four Armenian families in the city. By 1900, there were a few Chaldean Christians, 30 persons, who had settled in Kermanshah; one made his living in trade, the others made arak and inferior wine.[202] As of the 1890s, American missionaries began their activities in Kermanshah.[203] In 1917, the were half a dozen of Chaldean families and one or two Armenians and Mr. and Mrs. Stead, the two American missionaries.[204] In 1921, there were some 50 Armenians and over 100 Assyrians. There was an Armenian church as there was in the smaller towns, while there was a Chaldean bishop at Senneh.[205]

There were no Zoroastrians, though Rousseau counted three in 1807, while by 1900 there was also an unknown number of Babis living in Kermanshah.[206]

RELIGIOUS SITUATION

To guide believers onto the right path there were many religious leaders, who did not always set a good example to their flock. The main religious official in Kermanshah in 1824, was the *mullah-bashi*, "who was the prince's associate in every species of debauchery." He was drunk every evening and during Ramazan he held a party with friends and three boys.[207] This kind of

---

198. DCR 590 (Kermanshah, 1901-02), p. 14.
199. Hale n.d., p. 206; Soltani 1381, vol. 4, p. 379.
200. Buckingham 1971, p. 101; DCR 590 (Kermanshah, 1901-02), p. 14.
201. Hale n.d., p. 206.
202. Buckingham 1971, p. 101; Beth Hillel 1832, p. 89 (a few Armenians); Southgate 1840, vol. 1, p. 137; Teule 1842, vol. 2, p. 483; DCR 590 (Kermanshah, 1902), p. 15.
203. Presbyterian Church 1919-20, p. 265; Harris 1896, p. 252 ("a missionary and his wife were there attending to the medical mission and the schools").
204. Hale 1920, p. 206, 208.
205. AIR 20/663, pp. 23, 78. In 1908, Haworth found that the 60 family Christian community in Senneh was better treated by their Moslem neighbors than elsewhere in Persia and in good economic circumstances, and there was more wealth in Senneh in general than he had seen elsewhere in Persia. Political Diaries vol. 3, p. 311.
206. Buckingham 1971, p. 101.
207. Keppel 1827, vol. 2, pp. 59-60, 70.

Fig. 2.14: Kermanshah and the Red Hill (*ca.* 1911). © *Collection Molitor, Ed. Elytis* no. 199.

immoral behavior by many members of the Moslem clergy not only gave rise to Babism, but also to the conflict about the Constitution in 1907 between the conservative notables, to which most leading olama belonged, and the trades people (see Chapter Seven). Around 1900, the leading Shiite clerics were Mirza Asadollah Imam Jom'eh, Mohammad Saleh Mojtahed, son of Hajji Aqa, Aqa Hadi Mojtahed and his son Aqa Rahim Mojtahed, Aqa 'Abdol-Qasem Mojtahed, and Aqa Hadi, son of Sheikh 'Abdol-Rahim Mojtahed. They had enormous influence in the last decade of the nineteenth century, but they lost much of their influence after the arrival of the forceful governor Ala al-Dowleh.[208]

However, what was not tolerated was the rise of religious people who claimed quasi-divine status. In 1901, a dervish named Fathollah in the village of Guran claimed to see dreams of the divine. As a result, many people joined him and the government concluded that he was becoming more than a public nuisance. Therefore, a military force was sent to seize him and his followers. The latter fled immediately when the troops arrived, so that they only found the dervish's grandson, who was sent to Tehran.[209]

The fact that Kermanshah for a long time had been but a small market town was reflected in the fact that in 1816, it had only four mosques, three of which were "smaller than those seen in the poorest villages of Egypt." The largest, close to the palace, was funded by prince Dowlatshah.[210] Although in the mid-1830s, this Friday mosque was the only considerable one in Kermanshah to be seen, some 20 years later Mounsey wrote that there were "no mosques

208. DCR 590 (Kermanshah, 1901-02), p. 13. On Shiism and Sufism in Kermanshah, see Soltani 1381, vols. 6-10.
209. Heravi 1372, p. 745.
210. Buckingham 1971, p. 105; Kinneir 1973, p. 132; Olivier 1807, vol. 2, p. 24.

Fig. 2.16: The Divan-khaneh seen during a religious festival (*ca.* 1911). © *Collection Molitor, Ed. Elytis* no. 56.

worthy of note" in Kermanshah.[211] In 1840, Mitford noted the total absence of minarets. He was told that "they had been pulled down and forbidden as they commanded a view of the interior of their houses; it strikingly illustrated a remark I have read, of a town without a spire being like a face without a nose."[212] By 1900, the oldest mosque was the Friday one, built by the grandfather of the current Zahir al-Molk. "There are none of great antiquity, and those existing now are more for the benefit of the settlers from other parts of the country than for the native population"[213] At that time there were eleven mosques.[214] In 1920, there were 12 mosques and nine *takiyehs*, which were only used at Moharram and Ramazan.[215] One of these mosques, at least its dome, stood out in the 1930s, because of its silvery cover, which was because it was covered "with flattened kerosene tins."[216]

Reza Shah abolished the Moharram ceremonies, which did not seem to have met with much opposition, although, the abolition meant a loss of income for the lower class religious. The Shah also in other ways reduced the role of the religious class, such as in education, the judiciary and in the registration of deeds and contracts. In the past the religious class had a quasi-monopoly on education and the judiciary, which Reza Shah greatly marginalized by secularizing the education and the judicial system. Its members also earned much money as public registrars.

211. Southgate 1840, vol. 1, p. 137. Mounsey 1872, p. 294.
212. Mitford 1884, vol. 1, p. 342.
213. DCR 590 (Kermanshah, 1901-02), p. 6. see also the Naser al-Din Shah's journey to Kerbela.
214. Soltani 1381, vol. 1, p. 561.
215. AIR 20/663, p. 18.
216. Hay 1937, p. 21.

However, the creation of the Registration Department made their services obsolete.[217] After Reza Shah's abdication the ban on Moharram processions remained in force, but in January 1944 (Moharram 1363 *qamari*), some enthusiasts, 2-3 dozen in all, went to Bisotun to engage in traditional head-cutting. However, in general, the people of Kermanshah seemed to have become adverse to this display. *Rowzeh-khvani* was allowed and reports indicated that their number had increased.[218] Indeed, it seemed that religious fervor was on the rise. In December 1944 (Moharram 1364), although all processions and demonstrations were banned during Moharram, some processions gathered in mosques, but the police did not allow them to go into the streets.[219]

The lassitude in strictly following Shiite rules as noted in the use of mosques is also evident in that of the *hammam*s or public baths. In 1810, Kermanshah had 14 *hammams*.[220] These baths were of a superior kind, according to Buckingham. "There are said to be equal to the one we visited and four or five frequented only by the poorer classes." One of the first kind was close to palace.[221] The palace's women's quarters had its own bath-house.[222] These bath-houses had no access to running water and, therefore, used a well to supply their needs.[223] As in other towns, men blew long horns on the roofs of the baths to let the public know that they were open for business.[224] By 1900, there were about 30 public baths, of which five or six were of higher quality. According to Rabino, "They are not made great use of by the working classes, who, not being of the Shiah persuasion, do not attach so great an importance to bathing."[225] However, people did not go to the public baths for hygienic reasons, to clean themselves, but rather for religious reasons, viz. to cleanse themselves ritually. Even if people had wanted to clean themselves for health reasons then they should not have gone to the public baths, because their water was "only changed once or twice a year."[226] The situation was very much like that in Hamadan, where in March 1907, the governor:

> Ordered that the water in the baths was to be changed once a week and that all shop-keepers were to place lights outside their shops outside to light the streets. These abominable ideas, however, smacked too much of European influence and the good Mullahs of the town protested against the evil, saying that a change of water once a year was good enough for any one, more than that was unholy,

---

217. FO 371/20048, f. 134b. In general, see Amir Mohammad, *Tarikh-e Sejell va Thabt-e Ahval dar Iran*. Tehran: Negarestan-e Andisheh, 1395
218. FO 371/40177, Kermanshah Diary January 1944.
219. FO 371/45400 Monthly Diary Dec. 1944.
220. Kinneir 1973, p. 132.
221. Buckingham 1971, pp. 105-09 (with a detailed description).
222. Naser al-Din Shah 1363, p. 71.
223. Soltani 1381, vol. 1, p. 556 (the stokers were also responsible the water pump, once modern pumps were installed)
224. Mitford 1884, vol. 1, p. 343; Soltani 1381, vol. 1, p. 560.
225. DCR 590 (Kermanshah, 1901-02), p. 6.
226. DCR 3189 (Kermanshah 1903-04), p. 39.

Fig 2.17: "Cleansing one's body in the *hammam*" (from the satirical weekly *Molla Nasral-Din*)

> while lighting the streets was an invention of the devil. Thus Hamadan continues in religious darkness and the baths in the odour of sanctity.[227]

This situation evokes the condition of the bathhouses in Persia as depicted in the satirical Azeri language journal *Molla Nasral-Din* (see fig. 2.17) and as described by Maraghe'i in his *Safarnameh-ye Ebrahim Beg*, concerning his visit to the bathhouse of the Imam Reza shrine in Mashhad:

> When we got to the bathhouse, the odor of the stinking water, virtually, started to choke me; a pit filled with stinking water or *kor* water! The greasy water was the color of a peacock feather, its odor was nauseating. Without a doubt, this filthy water was the source of all kinds of contagious diseases. All the blind and bald people in the whole city with all their rankles, men and women, day and night, immersed themselves in the three-months old filthy water. In fact, I was shocked to learn that neither the city authorities nor the olama cared about contagious diseases and contaminations of which this stinking water was the source. By naming it *kor*, they thought they could eliminate all those diseases. I think, attributing any kind of cleansing quality to such water would be a desecration

227. Political Diaries, vol. 2, p. 101.

Malaria was prevalent throughout the year, excepting the winter months. The types of anopheles found were *M. culicifacies*, *M. funesta* and *M. rossii*.

Tuberculosis in most of its forms was frequently encountered. Amongst children the type was mostly adenitis and bone disease, while the women owing to the *pardahnashin* system, are frequent sufferers from lung affections. Men, in spite of the open air life they lead, often catch the disease owing to their insufficient dietary, venereal excess and habits of opium smoking.

Leprosy is not commonly seen, and when met is mostly of the tubercular type. No attempts at segregation are made and lepers for the most part make their living by begging.

Syphilis in all its forms is common. So far no case of primary syphilis has been treated in the dispensary, as the disease in that stage is either treated by a native doctor or, more commonly, neglected.

Gonorrhoea is infrequent, it is treated by the local talent. Most of the cases so treated suffer from gleet which however is disregarded.

Ascarides is very frequently encountered. Most of the patients who come to the dispensary ask for santonin and now it is almost a routine practice to administer santonin in obscure stomach complaints. During the year 336 cases were seen.

Rheumatic affections are common and are largely due to insufficient clothing and the exposed life the people lead.

Diseases of the nervous system are fairly numerous, consisting for the most part, of sciatica, facial neuralgia, epilepsy and locomotor ataxy.

897 cases of eye complaints were treated during the year, the large majority consisting of granular ophthalmia and its sequelae.

Respiratory diseases, laryngitis chiefly of syphilitic origin, chronic bronchitis, bronchial asthma and emphysema.

Digestive complaints. Gastritis and enteritis accounted for 496 cases, due to the unsuitable food of the poorer classes.

Skin affection were frequently seen, mostly tinea favosa and syphilitic affections.

Only 2 cases of opium poisoning were treated during the year, which is surprising in face of the fact that opium smoking is practically universal. This may be due to the low percentage of morphine in Persian opium.

Fifty-five operations were performed during the year. The more important operations were:-

Removal of sequestrum of palatal process of the upper jaw.

Two excisions of rodent ulcers, in both cases at the inner angle of the eye.

Fistula in *ano*.

Lateral lithotomy, child 6 years old: 1 calculus uric acid 10 grain, 1 phosphatic 12 grams.

Case of extensive phospahatic deposit on tubercular ulcer of the bladder was operated on by a Persian doctor under the impression that it was vesical calculus, unsuccessfully. Later 220 grains were removed piecemeal.

Strangulated hernia, right side. Herniotomy. Contents, caecum with long mesentery and ileo-caecalintus susception. Manual reduction failing, the caecum was opened and reduction effected,

Three senile cataracts.

One iridectomy for glaucoma.

Numerous operations for entropion, ectropion, etc.

Result: Cure in all cases except the herniotomy which died to days later.

H. Crossle, M.D. Captain, I.M.S.
Consular Surgeon, Kermanshah

Source: Administration Report 1908, pp. 50-51.

> to our holy religion, which observes sanity as one of its principal tenets. How could such water, which is a blend of so many people's filth and excretions, be cleansing?... I decided that I would never go to a bathhouse in Persia again.[228]

By 1912, there were 36 all privately-owned bath-houses. These bath-houses were rarely covered with tiles and it was only in 1937 that Hasan 'Ali Ashrafi, the chief of the municipality, for hygienic reasons, issued a notice detailing what changes needed to be made, which included tiling walls as well as the installation of showers.[229]

There were no cemeteries inside the city Kermanshah, which was exceptional for Persia. Outside the city there were two big ones: *Qabr-e Aqa* and *Qabr-e Feyzabad* or *Tepeh-ye Ghazi Beg*. There were no *imamzadeh*s in or near the city. There was only a small arch, the remains of the cupola of a tomb, the burial place of Sayyedah Fatimah, the female attendant of *al-Ma'-sumeh*. "At 3.5 farsakh from Kermanshah there is near Kinisht, a village called Pir Gheyb or Pir Kabir, but if there ever was an Imamzadeh is not known."[230] In 1934, Foruhar, president of the Municipal council proposed to purchase a hearse to transport bodies to the cemetery. He also proposed to open a new cemetery 3 km outside the city and to close the existing cemeteries of *Mosalla, Sayyed Saleh, Bala Jub* at the east and west of the city. From 1935, corpses were transported by carriage and not on a wooden bier (*tabut*) any longer. In 1939, the Municipality bought a second hearse carriage.[231] There was no cemetery for Christians. Thus, when Ms Anderton, a Roman Catholic English governess in Farmanfarma's family died on 1 May 1905, her body was taken to the British Consulate. Lacking a cemetery she was buried next to the Consulate grounds.[232] In March 1911, the Russian consul and the Customs administration raised the possibility of the establishment of a European cemetery. At that time, two Belgians were interred outside the city on a hill, and the Customs administration had authorized the investment in a cemetery there. However, the British consul did not think that hill to be the right place for a cemetery and he suggested they might be re-interred in the possible new place. In a corner of wasteland of the British Consulate four European had been buried: Ms Anderson, Mr. Meier (Swiss), Mr. Wagner (Belgian) and Mr. Sonet, near that plot of land there was a temporary tomb where Mrs. Haworth's remains perhaps would be sent to.[233] In 1941, the British proposed to establish a British military cemetery as part of the Consulate's grounds.[234] It would seem that none of these proposals ever were realized.

---

228. Maraghe'i 1364, p. 27. A *kor* is still water that fills a container, whose length, breadth and depth are three and a half spans each, i.e. the volume of water will be 42,875 cubic span, although 36 cubic span is enough.

229. Soltani 1381, vol. 1, pp. 560-61. By 1966, there were 63 bathhouses. Clarke & Clark 1969, p. 109.

230. DCR 590 (Kermanshah, 1902), p. 6; A Correspondent 1835 a, p. 404; see Clarke & Clark 1969, p. 21 (1919 map) for locations; he also indicates a separate Turkish cemetery.

231. Soltani 1381, vol. 1, p. 555.

232. Political Diaries, vol. 1, p. 97.

233. FO 248/1031, McDouall to Tehran, 16/03/1911; FO 248/1073, McDouall to Townley, 12/03/1913.

234. FO 369/2706, Code 234, file 11526. Clarke & Clark 1969, p. 21 (1919 map) shows a British cemetery, which is not mentioned in British correspondence of that time.

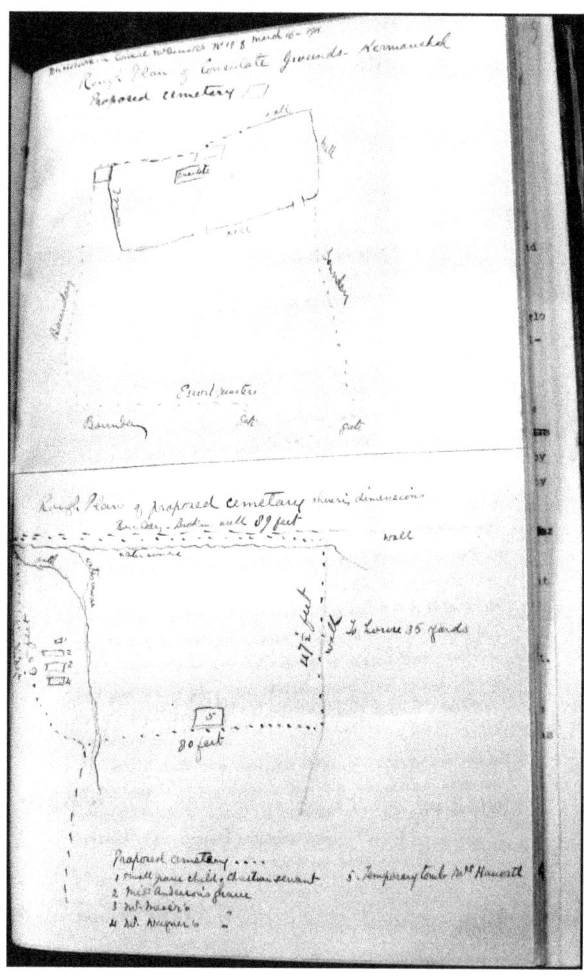

Fig. 2.18: Proposed location of the European cemetery (1911).

CHRISTIANS

In 1895, an unnamed Christian missionary couple was engaged in medical and educational activities.[235] This may have been a Christian from Urmiyeh called Kasha Mooshi.[236] He accompanied Mr. Stead, an American missionary and his wife, when they arrived in Kermanshah in April 1905. He complained that a certain Agha Mehdi had written a paper against them and was trying to get signatures in the bazaar. This action was caused by their exceeding zeal, which was resented by some. The British consul warned Mr. Stead to be aware of Moslem susceptibilities.[237] Prior to the arrival of American missionaries the few Christians had no religious leader. Because conversion of Moslems was not allowed, the missionaries needed another target group in the city to justify their presence. One American missionary commented that the presence of a large Jewish community served "as an excuse for our being permitted to work among so large a Moslem population."[238] And indeed, apart from educational, medical and social activities aimed at all religious groups, they focused their religious activities on Jews and Ali-ilahis.[239] Baron Weydel, the Belgian chief of the Customs Department, urged his employees, all nominal Christian or liberal Moslems, to attend church.[240] The American missionaries had a chapel in Feyzabad and a mission residence in the S.E. suburb.[241] Use was made of a converted Persian boy, trained at the Tehran High school to preach. Collections were also made, which were used for evangelistic activities and furnishing the chapel in the dispensary.[242] The British and Foreign Bible Society employed a certain Mirza Ephraim as bible colporteur, who was always in conflict with the

235. Harris 1896, p. 252.

236. It was later reported that it was Kashe Mooshe Dooman, a native of Urmiyeh who had started an outstation in Kermanshah. *The Continent*, Volume 53 (6 July, 1922), p. 877.

237. Political Diaries, vol. 1, p. 97.

238. Whipple 1900, p. 814.

239. Presbyterian Church 1919-20, p. 265.

240. Presbyterian Church 1904, p. 242.

241. Presbyterian Church 1904, p. .

242. Presbyterian Church 1915, p. 313.

Steads.[243] In 1922, Kasha Mooshi Dooman's home served as the church.[244]

During the 1918 famine the Steads saved thousands of lives. They also cared for many of the orphans among the refugees. Mr. Stead established a small orphanage and adopted 63 Armenian and Syrian orphaned girls, who were clothed, fed, and educated with the help of the American Near East Relief.[245] But when Mrs. Stead left on a furlough, Mr. Stead was left alone with his sixty-three little Kurds, Armenians and Syrians and with the responsibility of their physical and spiritual welfare. The orphans continued to be coal-oiled every Friday, and bathed and given a clean dress, dingy gray from the frequent boilings, on Saturday. The four older girls alternated, two and two about, in cooking for Mr. Stead and the orphans and teaching a little school started for the children. In the morning they were given a mixture of coarse cereal and bread, at noon, stewed pumpkin and soup, at night, more bread.[246] The orphanage lasted at least until 1928, for in that year it was decided that funds might be used for establishing a school for the Assyrian children.[247] In 1932,

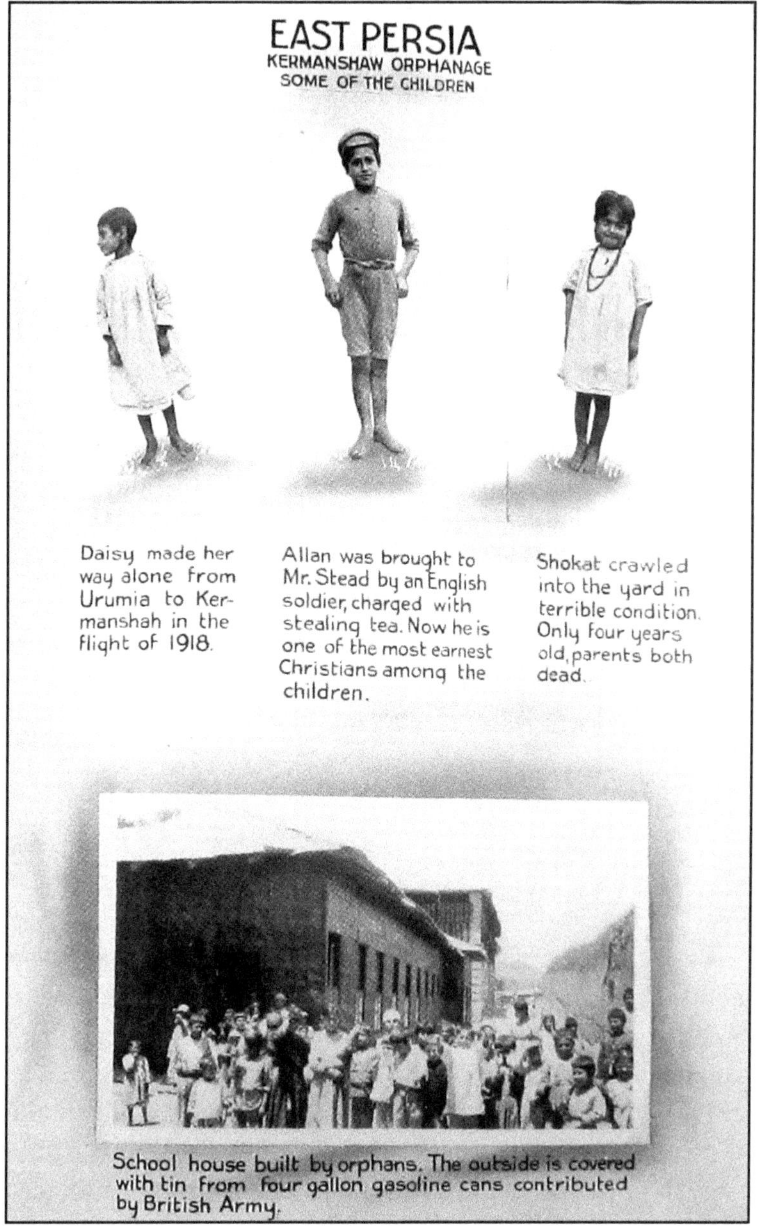

EAST PERSIA
KERMANSHAW ORPHANAGE
SOME OF THE CHILDREN
Daisy made her way alone from Urumia to Kermanshah in the flight of 1918.
Allan was brought to Mr. Stead by an English soldier, charged with stealing tea. Now he is one of the most earnest Christians among the children.
Shokat crawled into the yard in terrible condition. Only four years old, parents both dead.
School house built by orphans. The outside is covered with tin from four gallon gasoline cans contributed by British Army.

Fig. 2.19: Mrs Stead's orphanage (1918)

243. Administration Report 1908, p. 46.
244. *The Continent*, Volume 53 (6 July, 1922), p. 877.
245. Griscom 1921, pp. 233-40; Barton 1930, p. 101.
246. Griscom 1921, pp. 233-240 (with a photo of people waiting for food).
247. Presbyterian Church 1928, p. 5.

it was reported that many of these orphans did well in the mission schools and that some were working as teachers and nurses in the mision schools and hospital.[248]

BABIS

A few Babis, including the famous poetess Tahereh (Qorrat al-Eyn) passed through Kermanshah in 1840s and tried to draw adherents to their cause and faith. However, they were attacked by a mob, in a not so spontaneous demonstration, and expelled from the city.[249] In 1869, the Babi leaders passed through Kermanshah en route to Tehran.[250] Despite this lack of success, compounded by their suppression after 1852, the Babi/Bahai doctrine apparently found fertile soil in Kermanshah. During Ramazan (June-July) 1918, some fiery speeches were given against the Bahais in the city's square.[251] In 1920, according to the British consul, about 25% of the population were Bahais, but in secret. Nevertheless, Bahai enthusiasts were beaten on occasion. On 17 June 1920, at the end of Ramadan there was an attempt to excite religious zeal against Bahais. The governor expelled the leading Bahai merchant from the city and had a Bahai preacher mildly beaten. This appeased the mullahs. Sometimes, such as in January 1921, matters took a turn for the worse, when a Bahai leader was killed in the streets.[252]

DRESS

"People's dress is plain; the men all wear a high cap of black curly fur, generally of sheep and lamb's-skin. The tightness of their dress about the body and arms, and its looseness below, for sitting cross-legged and kneeling, do not harmonize together. The long slender locks of hair, hanging behind their necks, give an air of boyishness to some, and the thick bushy masses of a stiffer kind an aspect of ferocity to others." Dress is either dull green or blue, with the absence of rich shawls, bright shalloons, gilded and silver arms, &c.. Kurdish peasants have "conical caps, short jackets of thick white woolen." Arabs like in Baghdad with a fez and small turban; the Shushtaris "turbans of brown cotton shawl, crossed with white, and amply folded round the head, while one end is suffered to hang loosely behind."[253] In 1917, Hale described the dress of the Kurdish populace as being dark colored loose garments and baggy trousers. The head dress was "flat and circular on top, concave on all side, and very, very large."[254] "Women veiled with

248. RG 91-19-28, Westminster Hospital Report no. 2, 1932.
249. Jasion 2004, p. 189.
250. Soltan 1381, p. 344.
251. FO 248/1204, Kermanshah report no. 6, 02/08/1918 by Lt. Col. Kennion.
252. AIR 20/663, pp. 23-24, 78; FO 248/1293, Report Kermanshah, no. 6, 30 June 1920.
253. Buckingham 1971, pp. 111-12; Keppel 1827, vol. 2, p. 34, note (Persians wear sheepskin hats); Wills 1893, p. 110.
254. Hale 1920, p. 206.

white cloth tied over the forehead and hanging low on the breast, with a grating work of hollow thread before the eyes, and the great outer cloth or scarf, of checked blue cotton."[255] Merchants wore a *labadeh*, a long coat, over a white collarless shirt and around their head a silken (*shir-shakari*) sash. Over it they wore a small white fez around which they wrapped a wide band. Sayyeds wore a red fez around which they wrapped a green or black sash. The fez headwear was imported from Baghdad. Jews and Christians, who worked in offices and the banks or who were merchants wore European clothes. Their headwear was either a round cardboard hat or a small felt hat. Jewish merchants from Baghdad wore a red fez. However, Jewish herbalists wore the same clothes and headwear as Moslem herbalists and there was no difference between their shops either, so that you did not know whether you saw a Moslem or Jewish herbalist.[256] In short, people's dress in Kermanshah was quite varied.[257]

As of 1930, it was compulsory for men to wear European clothes and to wear the so-called Pahlavi hat, "a small round military cap with a peak. This is made in all colours, the smart young men usually having it to tone with their suits, or in the same material."[258] They came in all colors, but the smart set wore them usually in the same color as their costume. Also, the Shah's portrait was stamped on the lining. People had one year to change to European clothes, i.e. coat, trousers and hat. This also held for anybody who wanted to enter Persia.[259] In 1935 European hats had to be worn, which were not immediately procurable, either at the price or style wanted. Therefore, "The Governor of Kermanshah asked the British Consul to lend him a Homburg."[260] The change in male dress code was not at all appreciated, but people were resigned to what was felt to be the inevitable, given the strong enforcement by officials, police and military in both towns and villages. When Reza Shah visited Shahabad (ex-Harunabad) in 1935, he almost sacked Asadollah Mirza Shehab al-Dowleh, the governor of Kermanshah on the spot, because he had seen some villagers without the required kepi hat. The governor kept his job by pointing out that the men were in Kurdistan, not in his governorate.[261]

More problematic was the enforced unveiling of women, which was decreed in 1936, against which there was much opposition. The population expressed their support for Sheikh Bahlul in Mashhad, who had spoken out against the enforced adoption of European headwear as well as the unveiling of women. Out of protest, many merchants in Kermanshah took down Reza Shah's portrait from their walls.[262] However, the effect of the unveiling decree was also immediately noticeable in the opposite sense. In particular female teachers were among the first women to adopt European clothes and a beret as headdress. "These girls affected thick cotton stockings of a crude shade of soap pink, and seemed unable to keep them pulled taut."[263] The change in

---

255. Buckingham 1971, p. 112; Keppel 1827, vol. 2, p. 34.
256. *Rahavard* 23, p. 275.
257. For more and detailed information, see Soltani 1381, vol. 1, pp. 249-64.
258. Alexander 1934, p. 24.
259. Alexander 1934, p. 24; Stark 2001, pp. 3, 10, 50.
260. Hay 1937, p. 296.
261. FO 371/20048 (15/04/1936), f. 135.
262. FO 60/416 (1936, p. 18).
263. Hay 1937, pp. 20-21.

dress also had a financial cost, because it was an additional household expenditure, which, generally speaking, most households, being poor, could ill afford.[264]

WATER & CLIMATE

The water supply of Kermanshah was abundant, although its water was "heavy and indigestible." In 1807, good drinking water came from a single spring at the city's entrance. This was probably water that was hauled from a spring near the village of Sarab Said south of the city, a spring that irrigated the large gardens to the south of the cty, as well as from *Cheshmeh-ye Ebrahim Zaher* and *Cheshmeh-ye Sineh-Goleh-ye Zard*. Water for the tanks in the houses of the notables was obtained from the *Qanat-e aghani*, *Ab-e jabbeh-khaneh*, *Ab-e dowlat-khaneh*, and *Nahr-e Mehdi Khani*, which were located south-west of the city.[265] However, the water of the Sarab spring ran in an open channel and was liable to pollution from the villages on the banks of the stream. The Sarab split into various smaller streams, which supplied water to the various city quarters, such as *Nahr-e Do Dang* and *Nahr-e Mir Sayyed 'Ali* that supplied Feyzabad, while *Nahr-e Mehdi Khani* and *Shorot Gelow* supplied Chenani and part of Feyzabad. The Sarab also powered watermills that grinded grains to produce flour for the city's bakeries.[266]

In July 1913, Farmanfarma, the governor at that time, sent two engineers to assess the feasibility of a canal from the Qarasu to supply the northern part of town with water,[267] but there was no follow-up. In May 1916, Dr. Feistmantel, the Austrian Legation physician, proposed to make a *qanat* to supply the city with good water to be financed out of the corpse tax revenues, which always had been used for the maintenance of a quarantine station on the pilgrimage route.[268] Water supply became more problematic over the years and in 1944, during a drought, there was an increasing shortage of water, which contributed to public health problems. During the summer and fall of 1944, British army tankers came every day to the main square to distribute water to people. Many people had to buy clean water and others fetched water from open water-channels. The latter were a source of dispute between rival users: market gardeners, who had no right to it and unscrupulous householders who stole their neighbors' water. To put an end to this problem, in June 1944, the governor created a committee to oversee fair water distribution. Although by year's end the water issue was less pressing *Majles* elections were approaching. Therefore, in December 1944 Mr. Zanganeh, a *Majles* deputy, for the first time showed an interest in the welfare of his constituents. He met with local notables about town improvements such as covering a water course used as the city's drain, building two or three more *qanat*s to increase the water supply to Kermanshah and laying a water pipe where last summer and autumn

---

264. FO 371/21900. f. 112.

265. Dupré 1819, vol. 1, p. 237; DCR 590 (Kermanshah, 1902), p. 10; Shirvani, 294 (most houses have running water). In 1966, this spring supplied "100 to 140 litres per second in spring but only 100 to 190 litres per second during the dry season." Clarke & Clark 1969, p. 97.

266. Scott 1905, p. 621; Soltani 1381, vol. 1, p. 555-56.

267. Political Diaries vol. 5, p. 201; FO 248/1073, Kermanshah Diary no. 27, ending 03/07/1913.

268. IOR/L/PS/10/284, File 2612/1912 Pt 2 'Persia. Tehran Sanitary Council', Neligan to Townley, 08/04/1914.

Fig. 2.20: The Qara-Su at Kermanshah (*ca.* 1911). © *Collection Molitor, Ed. Elytis* no. 201.

British army tankers came every day to distribute water to people during drought.[269] These three *qanat*s were apparenly later built, for in 1966, they provided "50 to 100 litres per second when they converge at Cheshme Rozan in the south-west of the city."[270]

Not to be outdone by a rival, in April 1945 Mr. Sasan, another *Majles* deputy wanted to interest APOC to give a piped water scheme to Kermanshah. The British consul thought this would be great, because the existing unsanitary system caused much sickness. However, he mused, it probably was a re-election maneuver as Mr. Sasan had not shown any interest in his constituents before that time.[271] Mr. Sasan actually went to Abadan, from where, in June 1945, he returned empty handed, because APOC did not want to pay for the piped water scheme.[272] Perhaps in reaction to this development, one month later, the Shah contributed 2.5 million Rls to the proposed piped water scheme of Kermanshah. Prof. Winsor of the American Irrigation Institute came to study the possibility of bringing water from the Sarab and Qara Su river. If possible, it was intended to form a limited liability company to provide additional funds.[273] Nothing came of these plans, because in March 1947 the water scheme was discussed by the Consulting Company, but like in 1945 problems were raised as to water rights, lack of confidence

269. FO 371/40177, Kermanshah Diary June 1944; FO 371/45400 Monthly Diary December 1944.
270. Clarke & Clark 1969, p. 97.
271. FO 371/45400, Kermanshah Diary April 1945.
272. FO 371/45400, Kermanshah Diary June 1945.
273. FO 371/45400, Kermanshah Diary July 1945.

Fig. 2.21: Kermanshah under snow as seen from the roof of Molitor's house (*ca.* 1911).
© *Collection Molitor, Ed. Elytis* no. 375.

in shareholding company, and the race for personal gain.[274] As a result, it was only in 1954 that piped water was introduced to the city.[275]

In 1903, Rabino opined that despite the total absence of sewers Kermanshah was a healthy place.[276] However, Kermanshah was unique, because part of the city had sewers. The reason why Rabino wrote there were no sewers is, because he had a European notion of sewers, not what passed as such in Kermanshah. For this sewer was in fact the Abshuran stream (formed by several Sarab springs) that bisected the city and in which people threw their waste and sewage. During the rainy season the stream overflowed its banks and easily evacuated the sewage from the city. However, in the lower part of the city the stream was uncovered and thus, was like an open sewer and a public nuisance. This in particular was the case in summer, when water was scarce and the Abshuran was reduced to a trickle, so that much of the sewage was not moved, remained lying and thus, constituted a public health risk. Part of sewage was used to manure the vegetable fields, but most flowed into the Qara Su. The occurrence of endemic stomach and intestinal diseases (in particular, diarrhea and dysentery) among the population was mainly blamed on the irrigation of vegetables with this polluted water.[277]

---

274. FO 371/45488, Kermanshah Diary March 1947.
275. Soltani 1381, vol. 1, pp. 555-56.
276. DCR 3189 (Kermanshah 1903-04), p. 39
277. Dupré 1819, vol. 1, p. 237; Scott 1905, p. 621; Adamec 1976, vol. 1, p. 372; Clarke & Clark 1969, p. 100; DCR 3189 (Kermanshah 1903-04), p. 39.

Apart from household refuse and night soil, industrial activities such as that of the butchers (*sallakh*) polluted the Abshuran. This was because the slaughter-house was situated east of the city in a hollow, a.k.a. *chal-e qassab-khaneh*, right next to the Abshuran. Because of the pollution of the Abshuran public health suffered.[278] Therefore, in 1887, Hosam al-Molk I prohibited people living along the river to throw filth and refuse in it.[279] In January 1890, Hosam al-Molk II announced his intention to regulate refuse and water disposal after an outbreak of cholera.[280] In 1902, Ala al-Dowleh banned the washing of corpses in springs and streams in the city that were used by people as drinking water, citing the potential of causing diseases. Therefore, he built a corpse washing-house (*ghossal-khaneh*) outside the city. At the same time, he also banned the washing of clothes and old rags (*kohneh-shu'i*) in these same springs.[281] However, the ban was not very well implemented, although it was a beginning. To ensure unhindered supply, and later less polluted water supply, the city employed water managers or *mir-ab*s. Wells were uncommon, expect in the Meydan-e Mollah 'Abbas 'Ali district. The tanks of the houses were mostly interconnected, water flowing from house to house and waterborne diseases like cholera were thus easily spread, the more so since the water in the tanks was used for all household chores.[282] In 1919-20, Amir Nezam, the governor tried to improve the city's sanitation, but with little success.[283] It was only in 1966 that a beginning was made with construction of a sewerage network. Until its completion the Abshuran and its tributaries continued to function as an open sewerage system.[284]

Because Kermanshah is one of the cities at the highest altitude in Persia, summers are markedly cooler than temperatures in the lowlands, such as towards Baghdad, once its most important trading partner. The reverse side is that its winters are colder with significant snowfall. In 1912, the maximum temperature was 106 degrees Fahrenheit in July, while the minimum temperature was 3 degrees Fahrenheit in February.[285] The rainy season is from November to March, while the summers are dry thus, negatively impacting the water supply situation in the city. In 1920, total annual rainfall was 15.55 inches or 39.49 cm (see Table 2.2).

Table 2.2: Maximum and minimum temperature and rainfall September 1919-March 1921

Month	Average maximum shade temperature	Average minimum temperature	Maximum	Minimum	Rainfall in inches
September 1919	91.6	56.7	99.0	51.8	Nil
October	83.4	46.7	90.8	36.8	Nil
November	70.5	37.4	82.1	26.1	0.08

278. Soltani 1381, vol. 1, p. 549; AIR 20/663, p. 18.
279. *Ruznameh-ye Iran* 1375, vol. 4, p. 2607 (no. 647; 21/01/1888).
280. *Ruznameh-ye Iran* 1376, no. 707 (25/01/1890), p. 2827.
281. *Ruznameh-ye Iran* 1375, vol. 5, p. 4091 (no. 1017; 26/07/1902).
282. Scott 1905, p. 621; AIR 20/663, p. 18.
283. AIR 20/663, p. 19.
284. Clarke & Clark 1969, p. 100.
285. DCR 5204 (Kermanshah 1912-13), p. 5.

Month	Average maximum shade temperature	Average minimum temperature	Maximum	Minimum	Rainfall in inches
December	49.0	30.6	61.4	11.0	2.92
January 1920	44.8	27.6	54.0	12.0	1.52
February	39.5	22.9	51.4	8.5	2.33
March	60.4	36.8	70.0	28.1	4.61
April	67.8	43.7	81.0	30.0	1.22
May	80.7	49.0	89.0	39.6	0.62
June	93.7	58.1	103.0	47.7	Nil
July	99.1	62.3	106.8	59.0	Nil
August	97.4	62.5	107.0	53.2	Nil
September	90.7	54.5	105.8	46.0	0.66
October	78.4	50.0	97.1	40.1	0.67
November	57.1	36.0	74.2	19.8	2.47
December	39.4	22.6	47.9	10.6	1.45
January 1921	39.3	22.5	52.5	6.5	2.85
February	42.2	22.3	57.0	7.8	3.715
March	56.7	32.7	71.0	23.5	2.275

Source: AIR 20/663, May 1921, pp. 44-45.

Some travelers held the climate to be generally unhealthy.[286] However, Whigham was rather positive and so was the British consul Greenhouse. "The climate is exceedingly cold in winter, not unlike that of England in spring, and unpleasantly hot for only two months in the summer, when the inhabitants retire as much as possible to the pretty gardens and orchards which lie a little further up the slope to the south of the town."[287]

286. Harris 1896, p. 251.

287. Whigham 1903, p. 272; AIR 20/663, pp. 47-48.

MEDICAL CARE

As in other cities in Persia malaria was a main problem, tuberculosis was also frequently encountered, while syphilis, eye diseases, rheumatic affections, diseases of the nervous system, respiratory diseases, digestive complaints and skin affections were very common." The usual illnesses are fever, small-pox and diphtheria."[1] Typhus fever and relapsing fever were endemic in towns and villages in early summer and cholera and dysentery later, while pneumonia and influenza prevailed in winter. There were no local authorities who were able to give reliable statistics on the number of sick and of mortality.[2] Trachoma was very prevalent among the Persians. What was not very hygienic was that "They have a custom of dyeing the nails, hair, beard, eyebrows, and eyelashes a bright red, with a substance called henna. A beauty doctor, a woman, goes from one family to another to do this, always using the same filthy brush."[3] Despite all this Kermanshah was a healthy place in 1900, according to Rabino.[4]

The prevalence of malaria was due to people's unsanitary habits and the universal custom of having a water tank in the courtyard of the house. Moreover, the water ran from the tank of one house to that of the next, and as in these tanks the cooking utensils and house linen were washed, the water generally used for drinking purposes was polluted and contaminated; this also caused many stomach and bowel complaints.[5] Meat was transported by animals to shops, which were unhygienic due to flies attracted by the meat. This situation lasted till the end of spring, but in summer, butchers called it *gusht-e gondan* or 'putrid meat.' They either reduced slaughter to a minimum, or closed their shops and did something else. It was not only the butchers that caused public health problems, for other shops selling foodstuffs also were quite unhygienic premises.[6]

Although typhoid fever and malaria were endemic, the population was immunized and consequently, people rarely died of these diseases. Also, venereal disease was rampant and inherited syphilis was said to effect a large number of people. Despite this and the fact that a large percentage of the male population were opium smokers, public health was rather good in the 1930s. This held in particular for the rural population whose health was rather robust. Also, in the 1940s, there were no outbreak of serious epidemics in the city and province.[7] Although in general, public health was good in the city, it was bad in the districts due to lack of medical

---

1. Administration Report 1908, pp. 49-54; DCR 3189 (Kermanshah 1903-04), p. 39. Teule noted that the so-called Aleppo boils did not reach as far as Kermanshah. Teule 1842, vol. 2, p. 483. On the public health situation in Persia in general, see Floor 2004.
2. FO 248/1313, Weir, consul Kermanshah to FO, London 10/7/1919.
3. McClintic 1917, p. 103.
4. DCR 3189 (Kermanshah 1903-04), p. 39
5. Administration Report, p. 50; DCR no. 3189, "Trade of Kermanshah and District for the year 1903-04," (London, 1904), p. 39. In July 1945, there was less malaria than normal due to drinking water supplies more abundant than usual. FO 371/45400, Kermanshah Diary July 1945
6. Soltani 1381, vol. 1, p. 549. This reminds one of the situation in the 1670s, when, according to Chardin: "The Persians who are pretty well to pass, seldom eat the Entrails, Feet, or the Heads of Beasts, it goes against their Stomachs. The poorest sort of People only eat them, buying 'em in the Shops that dress nothing else. They call the Cooks that dress them, *guende-paikaun*, as who should say, Cooks for the rotten Pieces." Chardin 1811, p. 59. *Guende-paikaun* or, properly, *gandeh pak-kon*, meaning, remover of rotten [parts].
7. FO 371/21900, f. 116.

attention and supplies. A case in point was Rovanshir, where in May 1944, out of a population of 400 some 80 died of malaria. Appeals to Tehran did not result in any medical assistance.[8]

Unfortunately, during the Qajar period the city suffered many times from epidemics such as the plague and cholera, or suffered the debilitating effects of famine on people's health. For example, until October 1834, Kermanshah had been uninterruptedly ravaged by the plague for three years and consequently its population was much reduced.[9] Therefore, the first thing Fraser saw approaching Kermanshah was an "extent of the acres, absolutely, of fresh graves all within the last two years. ... [Inside the town followed] "the roofless walls of the houses whose inhabitants now tenanted these graves."[10] In 1872, Bellew likewise when approaching the walls saw many new graves, "filled during the last two years with the bodies of fifteen thousand people who have died here." Most had come from the countryside in search of food, but found stone instead of bread.[11] In January 1861 plague broke out at Kermanshah. Unfortunately, this coincided with a year of drought and scarcity of foodstuffs.[12] In 1868, cholera broke out again at Kermanshah and onwards to Iraq.[13] On 25 September 1889, there was a cholera outbreak in Kermanshah, which followed the pilgrim route from Kerbala and stopped at Qom. At that time half of the city's population fled to its environs, while the other half was making arrangements to do the same. By 5 October the city was empty of its people. On 3 October, 30 people and the next day ten died of the ailment, but the death rate started to drop as of 7 October and the outbreak continued till the end of November 1889.[14] In 1904, there was a serious outbreak of cholera only in the town and province. There were no cholera in 1905, but many died due to due to a variety of other diseases, made worse by the effect of the 3-year semi-famine conditions.[15] In December 1905, it was believed that cholera had broken out at Qasr-e Shirin. However, it soon became clear that it was not cholera, but another sickness, which caused many deaths at Qasr-e Shirin.[16]

There also was something like a "sickly season," as the British consul Captain Haworth called it, that began at the end of August. In September 1907, Hayworth reported that "one person, at least, is ill with fever in every house in the city. This would give a total of some 10,000 people suffering."[17] Perhaps this was the flue locally known as *misheh*.[18] There was not a single day in the year that some member of the Russian community was not down with the fever, according to Russian doctor in that same year.[19]

---

8. FO 371/40177, Kermanshah Diary April 1944; Idem, Kermanshah Diary May 1944.
9. Shirvani 1315, p. 294. According to Teule 1842, vol. 2, pp. 483-84 the plague raged four times in a century in Kermanshah, which four years earlier had almost depopulated the entire city.
10. Fraser 1840, vol. 2, pp. 193-94.
11. Bellew 1999, p. 437.
12. Soltan 1381, vol. 4, p. 343.
13. MacNamara 1876, pp. 353; Bryden 1869, p. 149.
14. Abbasi and Badi`i 1372, pp. 73-74; Mullen 1889-90, p. 18; Scott 1905, p. 620.
15. DCR 3683 (Kermanshah 1905-06), p. 5; Administration Report 1905-06, p. 46; Scott 1905, p. 621.
16. Political Diaries, vol. 1, pp. 237, 255.
17. Political Diaries, vol. 2, pp. 348, 358.
18. FO 248/1204, Kermanshah report no. 8, 05/10/1918 by Lt. Col. Kennion. On influenza in Persia, see Floor 2018 b.
19. Political Diaries vol. 1, p. 569.

Given the state of medical knowledge and hygienic conditions in Kermanshah there was not much that the people and the authorities could have done. Although in the first half of the nineteenth century some of the doctors in Kermanshah allegedly were so renowned that people from other parts of Persia sought their treatment and healing, their number and effectiveness did not make a difference to the majority of people in Kermanshah[20] As a result, most of the inhabitants of Kermanshah relied on folk medicine.[21] Despite this there were early attempts at preventive medicine. In 1812, Dr. James Campbell won the gratitude of 'Abbas Mirza, whom he cured of a venereal complaint, while he also vaccinated his entire family.[22] This success led to the employment of Dr. John Cormick by 'Abbas Mirza as his personal physician, whom he instructed to start a vaccination campaign against smallpox. Although children in some villages were vaccinated the campaign was stopped, due to popular opposition.[23] His older brother and rival, Mohammad 'Ali Mirza, governor of Kermanshah also had a smallpox vaccination campaign carried out in the border area with Iraq. Jean de Murat, a French trader, carried out the vaccination campaign in Kermanshah. According to his own account, he introduced smallpox vaccination in Baghdad in 1809. Only through the intervention of Grand Mufti, Ahmad Effendi, had he been able to actually perform the vaccinations. He then trained natives of Mosul and Erevan so that they might do the same in their towns. His wife trained a few Christian women in the vaccination technique, one of whom continued vaccinations in Basra after de Murat and his wife had left Iraq. De Murat declared that he had vaccinated more than 4,500 children up to 1819. In that year, the governor of Kermanshah invited him to become his chief interpreter. In that town he vaccinated more than 500 people, amongst which 25 Qajar princes and princesses. When the prince-governor died in 1822, de Murat wandered from Kermanshah to Hamadan, Tehran, Kashan, on to Isfahan and finally Jolfa, where he still resided in 1828. "He vaccinated at all those towns and kept up vaccination at Julfa," about which he sent regular reports to Dr. McNeil, the surgeon of the British Legation. It would seem that de Murat "got his lymph from Dr. Milne at Busreh."[24] The manner in which vaccination took place "was to prick the skin with a sharp piece of silver and afterwards to introduce the lymph with a quill." Later unarmed bone points were used.[25] However, the vaccination effort was but a single event and there was no systematic national sustained and comprehensive follow-up, which only happened in the twentieth century.

Another attempt at preventive public health measures was taken in 1852, when cholera broke out. The then grand vizier, Amir Kabir, imposed a quarantine at the border with Iraq.[26]

---

20. Soltani 1381, vol. 1, pp. 531-33; Fasa'i 1378, vol. 2, p. 995.
21. On the state of public health and medical knowledge and care available in Qajar Iran, see Floor 2005 and Idem 2018 b.
22. Wright 2001, p. 123.
23. Ebrahimnejad 2002, pp. 99-100.
24. Colvill 1872, pp. 68-69; Adamiyat 1348, p. 324. In 1234/1818, Hovannes Moradiyan, i.e. Jean de Murat, carried out vaccinations in Kermanshah province. Soltani 1381, vol. 1, p. 531; Eqbal 1326, pp. 69-71. Teule 1842, vol. 1, p. 474 observes that in Sonqor inoculation was widely practiced, but vaccination was still unknown.
25. Colvill 1872, p. 70.
26. Adamiyyat 1348, p. 326; for the ongoing international discussion on the need for quarantines as reported in the Persian press see Government of Iran, *Vaqaye`-ye Ettefaqiyeh*, vol. 1, pp. 500, 579; vol. 2, pp. 913, 2778 (*kerakhtin, qeranteyn, qerantineh*).

This action most likely was in response to measures taken by the Ottoman authorities. Following the 1851 Paris International Sanitary Conference, the Ottomans initiated a system of quarantine control in the Persian Gulf and at the Persian border, because they believed the plague entered their lands via Persia such as in 1831.[27] This effort led to a spasmodic follow-up by the Persian authorities, probably induced by stringent measures taken on the Ottoman side of the border. In November 1856, the Persian government tried to stop pilgrims going from Kermanshah, where cholera had broken out, to Iraq, where the Turkish authorities since 1854 had imposed quarantine rules. The pilgrims were kept 10 days at the border and then the Persian authorities wanted to keep them there for another 10 to 20 days. Food was running out, however, and given the lack of order and organization the estimated 15,000 pilgrims forced their way into Iraq and several people, including soldiers, were killed.[28] After 1851, Ottomans had quarantine control in Basra. However, only 3,300 average/year entered via Basra, but most people came via Persia.[29] Outbreaks in the 1860s and 1870s of cholera and plague led to blame-naming by both sides. On 13 June 1853 there was cholera at Hamadan and Kermanshah.[30] In September 1856, it reached Hamadan and Kermanshah. Pilgrims at Khaneqin broke the quarantine and further spread the disease. It ravaged Kermanshah.[31] On 19 December 1860 the disease was very severe at Kermanshah. In mid-December 1860 the disease broke out in Tehran with many deaths also in January 1861, with an a total of about 1,000; on 31 July 1861, in Hamadan 80 cases daily were reported; on 28 August 1861 it appeared at Kermanshah where allegedly 300 deaths/day out of population of 25,000 occurred.[32] The Ottoman authorities accused Persia from neglect, while Dr. Tholozan, who represented Persia, argued that the plague had its origin in both Persian and Iraqi mountainous Kurdistan.[33] In 1889-90, at Khaneqin, there was another imposition of quarantine on arrivals from Persia. By that time Persia also had a quarantine structure in place as is clear from steps taken to stop the spread of cholera in September 1889, when not only travelers, but also fruit, meat, and charcoal were not allowed to cross the border.[34] In November 1892, Mirza Ebrahim, the *hafez al-sehhat*, the medical sanitary officer, gave orders that certain foodstuffs and drinks should not be allowed to be brought into the city or be sold. This order was given because there had been a number of deaths and he wanted to contain the outbreak of the disease.[35]

When in November 1903 cholera broke out in Kerbela the Ottoman authorities banned the movement of pilgrims and the transport of corpses to be buried in the Shiite holy places. They also informed the Persian authorities to inform pilgrims and families wishing to transport corpses to Iraq that this was banned for the time being. Although the Persian authorities had this message

---

27. Bulmus 2012, p. 155.
28. De Gobineau 1959, p. 34.
29. Bulmus 2012, p. 155.
30. Amanat 1983, p. 213; Petermann 1865, p. 225.
31. MacNamara 1876, p. 238; Amanat 1983, p. 213.
32. MacNamara 1876, p. 240.
33. Bulmus 2012, pp. 155-56.
34. Bishop 1891, vol. 1, p. 70; Abbasi and Badi`i 1372, pp. 69-71. The *Ruznameh-ye Iran* 1375, vol. 4, p. 2847 (no. 707; 25/01/1890) reports that there had been no cholera in the city since 50 days.
35. *Ruznameh-ye Iran* 1375, vol. 4, p. 3166 (no. 787; 27/11/1892). In mid-January 1893 the *Ruznameh-ye Iran* 1375, vol. 4, p. 3183 (no. 791; 31/01/1893) states that that since 40 days the disease had gone.

publicly announced in the bazaars there were still pilgrims leaving or were already on the move. Therefore, also strict quarantine measures were imposed and the director of Customs, Molitor, was given full powers to apply the rules. From Tehran, 50 (or 150) Cossacks were sent to help impose the quarantine as well as tents and medicines. Dr. Cesari and Dr. Mirza Heydar Khan were the physicians in charge. There were quarantine stations at Qasr-e Shirin, Mahidasht and Bisotun, which were operated by the Customs department.

On 30 January 1904, the Ottoman authorities announced that the cholera epidemic in Iraq was over and that pilgrims and corpses were free to move again. However, on 16 March 1904, the ban on the movement of pilgrims and corpses was re-imposed, because cholera had broken out again in Iraq, notably in Baghdad. At the border with Persia quarantine measures were enforced and the same measures were taken in Persia. The governor of Kermanshah ordered the *kargozar* to issue travel permits to Iraq no longer. On 5 April 1904, in the Jewish quarter, the first case of cholera was identified. Nevertheless, pilgrims were allowed to depart, provided quarantine rules were observed during their journey. The governor of Kermanshah was ordered to see to it that the epidemic would not spread to other parts of Persia and to that end he had to establish a committee, which had to liaise with Dr. Ra'uf Bey Wam.

In Kermanshah itself there were several additional cases of cholera had been identified several steps were taken to prevent the disease from spreading. An old caravanserai was set aside as cholera hospital, mostly for poor people, but it was of little use. The sale, of fruit in the bazaar was forbidden for some time. Preventive measures so that other provinces would not become infected, such as cleaning the town, disinfecting houses and clothes of patients, notification of cases, free distribution of medicines and disinfectants etc. was started but the weak governor stopped it after being pressured by a few bigoted and discontented people against European innovations. On 21-22 April 1904, there was a demonstration against the European physicians who were carrying out the protective measures. It was said that there was no cholera outbreak, but the doctors had poisoned the water supply. Thereafter, all sanitary measures were discontinued.[36]

On 10 April 1904, four Persian physicians issued a report that they had seen no cholera in the city. However, the quarantine measures were still in place. In fact, at Qasr-e Shirin, instead of 2 days 9 days of quarantine had to be observed. This made sense, because in Kangavar cholera was widespread and had killed a number of people. Here and elsewhere the viability of the quarantine system was severely tested and found wanting, when one of the well-known olama of Najaf, Aqa Fazel Mameqani, traveled with a large number of his disciples (*tollab*) on pilgrimage to Mashhad. The cleric had refused to obey the rules at Kangavar, which had resulted in an attack by his disciples and local supporters of the quarantine staff, notably of Dr. Ra'uf Bey, an Ottoman physician. Although Mameqani had promised that he would not go to Kermanshah after having left the mess he had created in Kangavar he went straight to Kermanshah. Here, the quarantine staff refused the group entry into the city and insisted that it took up lodgings in the quarantine station to determine that they had not been infected with cholera that was raging at that time in Najaf. The disciples told the health officials that, "the footsteps of His Eminence (*hezrat-e aqa*) are sacred and merciful and wherever he sets foot the

36. Scott 1905, pp. 621-22. On cholera epidemics in Persia, see Floor 2018 b, chapter one.

calamity will be lifted. There is no need for quarantine." When the health officials pointed out that His Eminence and the likes of him had been present in Najaf and Kerbela and that it had not prevented the epidemic to strike there, the disciples reacted by giving them a severe trouncing with their sticks. After all, one does not question the word of a leading religious personality in Persia. Then they moved quickly into Kermanshah. The next day a few of them fell ill and that same day 23 of them died. The remainder of the group spread out and traveled to Borujerd, Isfahan, Hamadan and other places and nobody dared to stop them and thus the cholera spread. Finally, via Qom, they arrived at Tehran and spread the disease there. The rich and mighty took to the hills, the weak and the poor remained behind and many of them fell victim to the disease, "as is usually the case," Hajj Sayyah, who reported this event, wrote.[37] Because of the ignorance of Aqa Fazel and his companions, compounded by their arrogance and intransigence, cholera first swept through the city and then throughout the entire country. When on 8 May 1904, the son of one of the leading mullahs of Kermanshah died of cholera, people panicked and one-third of the population left the city camping under trees and in villages. As a result, the disease spread throughout the entire province. Mortality was varying; in Hajjiabad there were 40-50 dead on a population of 250, but in other villages it remained in the single digits. Seeing that it was outside the city as bad as inside the people returned on 30 May. Because the quarantine stations could be easily bypassed the system was not effective. The result was 5,000 dead in Kermanshah on a total of 68,000 in the country as a whole, figures that were generally believed to underestimate the real level of mortality.[38] On 27 August 1904, P. Raucq was sent to Kermanshah to organize a sanitary service. He died of cholera at the end of 1904.[39]

In February 1908, M. Cesari of the Customs Department told Captain Hayworth, the British consul that quarantine in Persia was but a political measure and that the existence or not of plague was irrelevant.[40] In April 1908, Dr. Bongrad came from Tehran and went to Qasr-e Shirin to initiate quarantine against plague, assisted by M. Cesari. They returned in June.[41] Cholera re-appeared in Kermanshah early in October 1910 and its virulence increased toward October 15, when there were 45 deaths. It decreased after October 18, and there were no cases after 8 November. It also prevailed in the villages, but there are no data available of the havoc wrought there. There was an outbreak of small-pox among children in July 1910, which reached its height in October, when adults also were attacked. There were no cases after December.[42] In

37. Sayyah 1346, pp. 535-36; DCR 3189 (Kermanshah 1903-04), p. 39; Scott 1905, p. 622.

38. Scott 1905, p. 621. When it was thought that the epidemic was over the governor reduced expenditures for health activities. After insistence that it was not over more funds were made available. Thereafter, it seems that there was more government interest in improving the quarantine system and public hygiene in general. Rusta'i 1382, vol. 1, pp. 339-42, 394-99; Soltani 1386, p. 148.

39. Destrée 1976, pp. 117, 346.

40. Political Diaries, vol. 3, p. 134. François Cesari was a Corsican, who, after having failed to enter the *Ecole polytechnique* in Paris, tried his luck in Russia where he worked as a correspondent for a few months for the *Journal français de St. Pétersbourg*. He then went to Mashhad where he had been engaged as French teacher for Eyn al-Molk, the governor's children. However, he was greatly disappointed both in the study interest of his pupils as well as in the promised salary. Therefore, he went to Ashqabad, where he stayed with the Reveille family for a few months. Later he accompanied d'Allemagne to Mashhad. In 1902, he was so fortunate as to be hired by the Persian government. d'Allemagne 1911, vol. 1, pp. iii, iv.

41. Administration Report 1908, p. 48.

42. DCR 4766 (Kermanshah 1910-11), p. 7.

1911, there was no outbreak of an epidemic, although typhoid prevailed in last few months of that year.[43] There were no epidemics in 1911.[44] However, as of 18 December 1911 there was an outbreak of cholera on the road to Bisotun and beyond; about 37 died in nine days, according to Dr. ʻAbdollah Khan, the government sanitary physician.[45] On 13 February 1913, Dr. ʻAbdollah left to the Guran district on receiving news that a plague-like disease had broken out there. However, he concluded that it was anthrax and that there was no danger for epidemic.[46] At the end of May 1913 pest had broken out in various villages near Kermanshah - 8 villages, between Mahidasht and Harunabad; later also in the Kalhor district. Dr. ʻAbdollah Khan was sent to takes steps, while quarantine was imposed. Tehran sent Dr. Heydar Mirza, who had much experience in this field; he was accompanied by some troops, including Cossacks with *Na'eb* Reza Khan. On 23 August 1913, Dr. Heydar Mirza reported to Farmanfarma that there was a case of plague, who then decided to impose a quarantine until the end of August. Orders were given to send 50 *kharvar* of lime to disinfect the houses. On 28 August, Dr. Heydar Mirza reported that all houses had been disinfected and there were not any new cases and thus, the governor decided to lift the quarantine. On 9 September 1913, Dr. Heydar Mirza declared the village of Jameh-Shuran safe and that disinfection work in other villages had begun. On 22 September Dr. Heydar Mirza reported that in fact the plague had raged for 11 months in a number of villages and that some 500 people had died. By the end of August 1913, villages such as Zebiry, Badrey, and Harunabad had been disinfected, i.e. the walls were lime-washed and all huts made of wood and branches were burnt. On 10 September 1913, the whole province was declared to be plague free. In early November 1913 small-pox was very prevalent in Kermanshah.[47] By 1918, typhus had been rife throughout the country for two years and Mrs. Stead helped combat the epidemic both among the British military and Persian citizens. Lack of supplies made it impossible for the American missionaries to open the dispensary when in June 1918 they stopped famine relief.[48] Also, in later years a system of health inspection was maintained. In the 1930s, travelers arriving from Iraq at Qasr-e Shirin were sent to the local dispensary-hospital where they had to show their certificate of recent vaccinations and inoculations to be allowed entry into the country.[49]

A related sanitary problem was that of the transport of corpses, which in and by itself constituted a potential public health threat. Initially, there was no quarantine station at Qasr-e Shirin, although there was one on the Iraqi-Turkish side of the border. The dangerous transport of corpses was controlled from Kermanshah where a medical officer gave a permit for the corpse when it was totally desiccated or if it had a certificate proving it had been interned for at least

43. DCR 5204 (Kermanshah 1912-13), p. 5.
44. DCR 4994 (Kermanshah 1911-12), p. 7.
45. IOR/L/PS/10/283, File 2612/1912 Pt 1 'Tehran Sanitary Council', PV 5 February 1912, p. 79.
46. Political Diaries vol. 5, pp. 69, 168.
47. IOR/L/PS/10/283, File 2612/1912 Pt 1 'Tehran Sanitary Council', PV 3 JUne 1913, pp. 160-61; PV 5 June 1913, p. 166-67; PV 5 August 1913, p. 176-77; PV 2 September 1913, p. 181; PV 7 October 1913, pp. 185-86, 189-92 (report Heydar Mirza about the pest in the villages that he visited). McDouall to FO, 25/09/1913; Soltani 1386, p. 198; FO 248/1073, Kermanshah Diary no. 45, ending 06/11/1913.
48. Annual Report by the Presbyterian Church in the U.S.A. Board of Foreign Missions, Volumes 82-83, p. 266.
49. Alexander 1934, p. 19.

three years. Only when an epidemic broke out a sanitary post was established at Qasr-e Shirin.[50] Therefore, in Kermanshah the medical public health officer from the National Sanitary Council examined how well the corpse was packed and whether it could be transported to Khaneqin. If positive, the coffin was sealed, which was opened in Khaneqin for a second inspection, and, if not acceptable, it would be immediately buried locally. The medical inspection fee due in Kermanshah was 2 *tuman*s per corpse plus 1 *qran* for sealing wax, and in Khaneqin 0.5 Turkish pound.[51] In 1907, the tax on corpses was raised to 7 *qran*s and was not kept any longer by the local authorities in Kermanshah, but by the National Sanitary Council. The money was spent to build a quarantine station between Kermanshah and Kerbela. The Council also persuaded the government to allot it 10% of the taxes on horses and carriages to be used for free public vaccination. Given the outbreak of cholera in Kermanshah, among others, the government made funds available to finance, doctors, drugs and lazarets.[52]

LOCAL MEDICAL CAPACITY

At the turn of the twentieth century, Kermanshah had a population of some 50,000 inhabitants, but no mention is made of any medical institution.[53] There were some traditional Persian doctors trained in Galenic medicine, who early in the nineteenth century were widely know across Persia, in particular its occulists (*kahhalan*). For example, Hakim Kermanshahi gave Vesal Shirazi his sight back[54] During the rule of 'Emad al-Dowleh, Kermanshah also famous physicians such as Hajji Mirza Hoseyn Hakim-bashi and Mirza Zeynal-'Abedin Hakim-bashi.[55] There was even one physician who had been trained, or at least had personal knowledge of Western medicine. In 1872, Bellew met in Kermanshah Mirza Sadeq Khan, *hakim-bashi* who had walked the London hospitals and spoke good English.[56] During Hosam al-Saltaneh's government Shams al-Atteba' was the physician of the governor's establishment. By the turn of the twentieth century well-known physicians included 'Abdollah, son of doctor Mohammad Khan Kermanshahi and Mirza Mahmud Khan *doktor-e eyalat*.[57]

There were also traditionally trained Jewish physicians who treated Moslem and other patients in Kermanshah and environs. The most well-known among them were Hakim Nasir or Nasir al-Atteba' and *Hafez al-Sehhat*, who converted to Islam in 1893. In addition, there were herbalists and sellers of protective amulets, who were the ones who 'treated' most people.[58] In

---

50. Government of Great Britain 1945, pp. 412-13. For a more detailed description of the transportation of corpses, see Appendix VI.
51. DCR 590 (Kermanshah, 1902), pp. 12-13. In 1904, 35 *qran*s per corpse had to be paid to the Turkish authorities in Kermanshah and 0.5 Turkish pound at Khaneqin, where there was a permanent Turkish quarantine station. Pilgrims had to pay 10 piasters, gold quarantine tax at Khaneqin. Scott 1905, p. 622.
52. Elgood 1951, p. 531
53. DCR 590 (Kermanshah 1902), p. 13.
54. Rusta'i 1382, vol. 2, p. 406.
55. Soltani 1381, vol. 1, p. 532.
56. Bellew 1999, p. 438.
57. Soltani 1381, vol. 1, pp. 533-34.
58. Yerushalmi 2010, p. 98; Soltani 1381, vol. 1, p. 538.

addition to Jewish and Moslem herbalists (*attar*), there were other traditional practitioners such as barbers (*salmani*), who were found in the *Meydan-e 'Allaf-khaneh* as well as 'dentists' who drew teeth.[59] There also was a government appointed public health official (*hafez al-sehhat*) in Kermanshah, the result of the establishment of the Public Health Committee in 1877 in Tehran. In 1885, the French physician Dr. Vaume was sanitary medical officer for the Persian government.[60] However, he, like his colleagues, had no funds at his disposal to take public health measures, such as proposed by Dr. Schlimmer.[61] In 1861, Zeyn al-'Abedin Khan Tabib was appointed as *hakim-bashi* of Kermanshah.[62]

In 1926, there were some 20 Persian physicians working in Kermanshah and 19 apothecary shops. [63] In the 1920-30s, there were more Persian physicians in the city, who had received modern medical training. For example, in 1925, 'Abdol-Hoseyn Khan Elhami was the city's public health official (*tabib-e sehhiyeh-ye baladi-ye Kermanshah*).[64] In 1934, Dr. Habibollah Khan Rafi' al-Mamalek practiced medicine; he had studied in Europe,[65] while Dr. 'Abdol-'Ali Khan Kalimi had studied medicine in Syria at the American College.[66] Dr. Ahmad Khan, born in 1878, studied in Turkey; in 1909 was appointed chief physician of the Western army and Kermanshah (*ra'is-e sehhiyeh-ye tip-e savar-e lashkar-e gharbi va Kermanshah*).[67] In 1912, Mirza Hoseyn Khan Doktor was chief of physicians of Kermanshah and Kurdistan and chief of the Kermanshah hospital and the brigade.[68] Dr. Mirza 'Abdollah Khan was the public health chief of the West (*ra'is-e sehhiyeh-ye gharb*) and resided at Kermanshah.[69] In 1931 the municipality created a public-health (*behdari*) section for the medical treatment of poor people by physicians such as Fakhr Pezeshkan and Ebrahim Khan Tizabi, who received 690 and 300 rials/month. In that same year, the municipality also established a mental institution in the *Bagh-e Hajj Aqa Mohammad Mehdi Feyz Mahdavi*. It employed some staff, and the institution was served in turns by doctors Allah Khan Mo'ed, 'Abdal'Ali Khan Aresta, Ahmad Khan and others. Furthermore, a house for invalids was created in the *Shabestan* of the Amir-e Nezam Garrusi Mosque, south of the Friday Mosque, which for years had been abandoned. It daily housed 82 men, 69 women and 11 children.[70] However, this arrangement did not work so well, in fact, not at all. In 1934, the municipality had asked the Westminster Hospital to care for indigent patients, for which service it paid less than one-third of the cost of patients it sent. However, by mid-1935 the Municipality was many months in arrears. Dr. Packhard complained that if this situation of

---

59. Soltani 1381, vol. 1, p. 534; in general, see Floor 2005.
60. Abbasiyan and Badi`i 1372, p. 74; (in 1889) Binder, p. 354.
61. Schlimmer 1970, pp. 215, 454.
62. Rusta'i 1382, vol. 2, pp. 538-40. In 1908, there was a Persian doctor who must have received training in modern medicine, because he operated on a patient. Administration Report 1908, p. 50; see also the Textbox above.
63. Soltani 1381, vol. 1, pp. 535-36.
64. Rusta'i 1382, vol. 2, pp. 118-21.
65. Rusta'i 1382, vol. 2, pp. 280-81.
66. Rusta'i 1382, vol. 2, pp. 414-15,
67. Rusta'i 1382, vol. 2, pp. 486-87.
68. Rusta'i 1382, vol. 2, pp. 563-65.
69. Rusta'i 1382, vol. 1, pp. 101-03, vol. 2, 702.
70. Soltani 1381, vol. 1, pp. 553-54.

non-payment continued he and his staff might reach the point where they only would accept charity cases for which they had funds available.[71]

Since 1919, physicians had to be licensed to be able to practice and Kermanshah was one of the cities where examinations took place to establish whether a doctor could get a license.[72] However, in 1936 the British consul concluded that "nor are the local doctors and dentists any better now than 20 years ago. The same filthy 'hammams' which were patronized twenty years ago are still used and germ-laden kanat-water is boiled over and over again for successive batches of bathers now, just as it was a century ago. Sanitation and public hygiene are as little understood now as they were before the present era of progress was ushered in."[73] In April 1944, there were only six reputable pharmacists, according to the local committee for the Imperial Pharmaceutical Institute.[74]

DISPENSARY & HOSPITAL SITUATION

In early 1882, Ziya al-Dowleh had announced his intention to establish a hospital (*bimarestan*) for the poor and pilgrims outside Kermanshah, but he does not seem to have done so. Also, given the description it it more than likely that it was the intention to establish a traditional hospice, or *dar al- ziyafat* or *dar al-shafa* rather than a modern hospital.[75] On 27 December 1904, 'Abdol-Hoseyn Mirza Farmanfarma, when governor of Kermanshah, opened a newly built hospital in the town for sick pilgrims. However, when Farmanfarma was dismissed one year later the hospital was neglected and became dilapidated. When Farid al-Molk visited it in 1905 it had no patients, although its doctor, 'Abdollah Tabib and its director 'Ali Reza were present. The physician told the new governor that Farmanfarma had given 70 *tuman*s per month, which was insufficient for the operating expenses of the hospital, excluding the salary of the doctor and the cost of charcoal that amounted to 100 *tuman*s per month. Farmanfarma had wanted to secure funding for the hospital by allocating a certain percentage from the tax paid for the transport of the corpses going to Kerbela to be paid by the chief of the Customs Department, who wrote that this was a decision to be taken by Tehran.[76] According to the British, Farmanfarma's real objective in establishing the hospital "was to obtain a free gift of land for personal gains." He tried to mount the same scheme two years later in Kerman.[77]

This medical gap was filled by the British consulate and American missionaries. The British opened a charitable dispensary and Civil Hospital, at an unknown date, probably starting in 1904

71. RG 91-19-28, The Westminster Hospital Annual Report 1934-35.

72. Rusta'i 1382, vol. 1, pp. 32; See Soltani 1381, vol. 1, p. 535. If the health authorities believed that somebody was practicing without a license a notice was sent. Rusta'i 1382, vol. 1, pp. 94-95.

73. FO 371/21900, f. 113.

74. FO 371/40177, Kermanshah Diary April 1944.

75. *Ruznameh-ye Iran* 1367, vol. 4, p. 3084 (21/02/1882).

76. Soltani 1381, vol. 1, pp. 533-534, quoted from Farid al-Molk Hamadani 1345, pp. 64-65, 228, 238, 223; Rusta'i 1382, vol. 1, pp. 333; Presbyterian Church 1904, p. 242.

77. Political Diaries, vol. 1, p. 379.

when their Consulate was opened, because it had an IMS physician on its staff.[78] The Russian consulate-general offered similar services, as a physician was attached to it. Dr. Ost left in early December 1905, but it seems that there always a physician was attached to the Russian consulate. In early 1912 Dr. Valensky arrived. Dr. Stead had hoped that the Russian Consulate would maintain a dispensary as it had done before, but since the British had closed theirs (see below), the Russians had no political reason for having one.[79] Therefore, thereafter the Russian physicians were merely Consulate doctor, except in special cases, such as in March 1913, when there was a suspected outbreak of cholera in the Kalhor district, where the Russian consular physician was sent to investigate.[80] In 1917, the wife of the Russian assistant-consul happened to be a dentist, who had a flourishing practice during her short stay in Kermanshah.[81] On 24 March 1908, the Turkish physician died of typhus. On 25 July 1908, he was replaced by Dr. Paraskevopolous.[82] It is not known whether the Ottoman consulate-general offered similar services, although a physician was attached to it.

The staff of the Customs administration had their own physician, who, in 1906, was the same one in charge of Farmanfarma's hospital, which was located inside the Customs compound and was financed by the Customs employees. In mid-1906, the Russian physician visited the hospital and offered to take it over and begin a dispensary there. He estimated that an investment of 6,000 *tumans* would be necessary to bring the hospital up to standards, which meant the end of this plan. Consul Crossle, a physician himself, believed that the hospital might be more efficiently run and would not require more than 4,000 *tumans*/year in operating cost. Mr. Waffelaert was amenable to this idea, and Crossle therefore, argued that this medical opportunity "should be exploited by us and not allowed to get into the hands of the Russians."[83] However, nothing came of it.

In 1905, the British Consulate dispensary had a daily average attendance of 60-80 out-patients, who received medical advice and medicine free of charge.[84] In 1906-07, the dispensary saw an average of 100 patients per day. Most were Kurds, but the number of non-Kurdish patients was increasing.[85] In 1908, the British dispensary was transferred from the Consulate to more commodious quarters in town, consisting of: a surgeon's office, a hospital assistant's office, a dispensing room, two dressing rooms, two small waiting rooms, one for male and one for female patients; an operating room, one small ward for emergency cases and a hospital assistant's quarters. It was open for 174 days in that year, because for the remainder of the time, the medical staff accompanied the consul on tour. In 1908 it treated 20,981 patients of which 8,000 were males, 10,762 females and 5,942 children. At the Civil Hospital a total of 308 in-house patients were

78. Administration Report 1905-06, p. 45; Administration Report 1908, p. 49; Wilson 1941, p. 114.
79. RG 91-1-12, Medical Report- Kermanshah Station, Year ending June 30th 1912 (Blanche Wilson-Stead).
80. Political Diaries, vol. 1, p. 237; Administration Report 1908, p. 45; January 1907 Russian physician Velonsky. Political Diaries, vol. 2, p. 29; Further Correspondence Persia no. 1 (1914), p. 60.
81. Hale n.d., p. 226.
82. Administraton Report 1907-08, p. 64.
83. FO 248/789, Crossle to Grant-Duff, 10/09/1906.
84. DCR 3683 (Kermanshah 1905-06), p. 5.
85. Administration Report 1906-07, p. 43.

treated, of which 284 were men and 24 women. The dispensary performed also simple operations.[86] In January 1910, the British hospital and dispensary was closed, although, for some time, a hospital auxiliary remained attached to the Consulate.[87] Later a sub-assistant surgeon, Mir Mushtaq Ali, served at the Consulate, but on 4 May 1912 he returned to India and was not replaced.[88] Dr. Stead regretted the closure of the two Consular dispensaries observing: "With both the British and Russian medical work shut off Kermanshah is very badly in need of a good physician and surgeon."[89]

Despite the British and Russian medical services offered to the population of Kermanshah, there was still room for more of the same. In 1907, after their arrival, the 25-year old American missionaries, Mr. B. W. Stead and Mrs. Stead, the latter, who was a physician, also known by her maiden name as Dr. Blanche Wilson, offered medical services in Kermanshah. That same year, she opened a small dispensary and for two years carried on an active medical practice. She saw 20-35 patients/day in the forenoon. Very few left without hearing the gospel. Mrs. Stead also made medical house calls to bind wounds etc. as well as did some minor operations, such as a compound fracture wound. She also turned her house in a temporary hospital for a poor Jewess who was living in a dirty dark room.[90] In 1907, Mrs. Stead enlarged her dispensary with a few rooms and henceforth also received in-patients. After a year furlough in the USA, the Steads returned to Kermanshah in 1911. The wounded of the street fights between royalists and constitutionalists (see Chapter Seven) in 1912-13, were the first in-patients in a hastily constructed first medical building by the Steads. This general clinic was usually attended by 50-70 Moslem women/day.[91]

In 1915, there was a Belgian physician, Dr. Bruneel, who was attached to the Customs administration. It is not known whether he provided medical care to other people. In January 1915, Dr. Bruneel offered to buy all medicines still stored in the British consulate. The British consul asked the Legation for permission to do so, as there was no physician any longer there and it this way the medicines would be put to good use. However, when the German occupation force came looking for Dr. Bruneel on 24 January 1916, he decided to flee to Basra, where he, be it seriously wounded due to treachery of his Kurdish guide, arrived in mid-February 1916.[92]

WW I brought other problems as well. Between 1915 and 1921 Kermanshah was held by three different foreign armies (see chapter seven). All three occupation forces, i.e. the Turks, the Russians and the British had their own military hospital. The local Persian administration

86. The more serious operations included "removal of sequestrum of palatal process of upper jaw; excision of rodent ulcers in the inner angle of the eye, fistula *in ano*, lateral lithomy, cataract, iridectomy." Administration Report 1908, pp. 49-54.

87. FO 248/999, McDouall to Tehran 08/01/1910. On 14 May 1914, Mr. Stead told Farid al-Molk that he had repaired a house in the city which he wanted to use as a residence and as a hospital. Hamadani 1354, p. 401.

88. FO 248/1073, McDouall to Townley, 09/01/1913.

89. RG 91-1-12, Medical Report- Kermanshah Station, Year ending June 30th 1912 (Blanche Wilson-Stead). There was indeed no European physician any longer in the city and Lambert Molitor asked one to come from Hamadan for the birth of his son in 1911. Molitor 2018 a.

90. Stead 1907, p. 234; RG 91-19-28, Westminster Hospital Report no. 2, 1932.

91. RG 91-19-28, Westminster Hospital Report no. 2, 1932; `Eyn al-Salṭaneh 1376, vol. 1, pp. 377, 865; Elgood 1951, pp. 511-512, 534; Waterfield 1973, pp. 139-140; Presbyterian Church 1915, p. 313.

92. Laureys 1996, pp. 320-23; FO 248/1112, McDouall to Legation, 26/01/1915; Soltani 1381, vol. 4, p. 794.

and its Turkish allies in 1915 used a building in the heart of the city as a hospital. However, this hospital seems to have had limited capacity, for when wounded from the fight at Bidsorkh were brought to Kermanshah in January 1915 there was no hospital where they might be treated.[93] In February 1915, Turks withdrew from Kermanshah leaving Dr. Stead in charge of a (make-shift?) hospital full with Turkish sick and wounded.[94] With the Russian troops that took Kermanshah came a medical unit that was supported by an American Red Cross team. It decided not to use that hospital, because typhus had raged there. Moreover, it had not been fumigated. Because many wounded were expected the US-Russian medical team moved to Del-gosha, a deserted Kurdish village some 1.5 km outside town. In a Persian Khan's palace with nice gardens the surgical hospital was set up. Because the capacity of the village was too small to put up the wounded, raised beds were built of boards, with an awning over them, along the walls of the gardens. Straw mattreses and pillows were made and all gauze available in the bazaar was bought. Each soldier was given such a covering as protection against mosquitos. Most of the work was done by American doctors, one Russian doctor and nurse, and two *feldscher*s and two *sanitar*s.[95] Hundreds of wounded came in each day. Medical staff from other places, the American missionary and the IBP banker all helped. The operating room, though well-lighted had a mud floor. There was neither a sterilizer nor rubber gloves. Sterile supplies came in sterile paper packages; cotton was dipped in biochloride before it was sterilized. When carbolic acid and alcohol were finished they used arak, denatured alcohol and bichloride in mercury tablets. Potassium permanganate was used for all dressings. The American-Russian medical staff used granite plates and basins that were sterilized with alcohol. Clean water came from a spring at 3 km distance. Soiled dressings were burnt, but when wet they smoldered all day. Therefore, the staff tried burying them, but at night they were dug up and taken by enterprising Persians, who washed them in a stream nearby, dried them and then sold them in the bazaar. The Russian nurse handed everything with sterile forceps and handed all that was needed to the staff. The sanitars removed the bandages. Operating was done in the morning; light wounded were sent back when they had recovered; more serious cases remained in the hospital and then were sent in carts to Russia. The soldiers came in all kinds of conveyances from the front usually after 3-6 days travel. On 28 June 1916, the medical unit was told to leave Kermanshah. The caravan with sick and wounded arrived on 5 July in Hamadan, where there were three Russian hospitals (Red Cross, Military and *Zemsky Zayust*).[96]

> The patients were to be sent first, then household and hospital supplies, and lastly the sisters were to go; the doctors were to remain with the retreating army. All went to their various duties, some into the operating room, dressing the newly wounded, while others packed the supplies or prepared the sick and wounded for the trip back. We had an amputation case that evening, a patient who came to us with a tourniquet on his leg, which had been there, presumably, for two days.

---

93. Ezz al-Mamalek 1332, p. 84.

94. RG 91-19-28, Westminster Hospital Report no. 2, 1932.

95. In the Russian health system a *feldscher* was a health care professional who provided various medical services limited to emergency treatment and ambulance practice. A *sanitar* was a medical orderly.

96. McClintic 1917, pp. 102-06.

> The most important things were moved, although some had to be left behind and were loot for the Persians. The covered vans were piled high with articles and upon these the convalescent soldiers, who were too weak to walk, sat holding on. All sorts of conveyances were used to carry us back: two-wheeled carts; lineakas [large wagonettes], carriages with low side seats; horses, donkeys, and camels. Each person was armed with a rifle, bayonet or revolver and all the cartridges he could carry.
>
> As we rode slowly out of Kermanshah, the roofs were filled with townspeople to see us leave. Some were sad, others gay, due to the excitement which prevailed. Now for a long journey again, without food or water, in the scorching sun; but as I look back, we were kept so busy with the dreadfully sick, delirious, and heavily wounded, that little thought was given to our own personal needs. Each evening when the tents were pitched, the dinners were cooked, medicines given out, and each soldier, lying on the ground or in the wagon, was made as comfortable as could be, in his heavy uniform and boots.
>
> The "Zemsky Zayust," [Land Association] one of the foremost organizations in Russia, had wayside stations. What a treat to the half-sick, distressed soldiers who had to walk! With their boots off, they would struggle along, nothing to eat or drink all day, to these places, which would provide for them. About one o'clock in the morning, the second night out on the road, our mounted patients, who were in the front of this long march were attacked by a tribe of the fierce, wild Kurds. They removed all the dressings and bandages, thinking money was concealed under them. One sanitar was seriously injured, all the soldiers were in a state of collapse, and the march was delayed until the next afternoon. The sisters acted very bravely, working hard to quiet the soldiers, and because of this had the St. George's medal conferred upon them. A Russian soldier receives for bravery the St. George's Cross, with a black and orange striped ribbon.[97]

The Turks returned on 29 June 1916 to Kermanshah, allegedly establishing no less than 11 hospitals in Kermanshah. The Turkish commander asked Dr. Stead to help in these military hospitals, which likely were residential buildings that were used as such. For a long time she had charge of the Russian wounded and sick.[98] The Turks also commandeered a house that they turned into a a convalescent hospital. The Turkish troops cut down its big walnut trees, which were used as firewood.[99] When the Turks left on 27 February 1917, the Russians set up their own hospital structure. However, by October 1917, "the Russian Red Cross has closed its local hospital, but the Russian Land Association has two hospitals manned by women doctors and nurses, male orderlies, and one or two surgeons." There were no wounded, but many sick suffering from typhus

97. McClintic 1917, pp. 105-06.
98. RG 91-19-28, Westminster Hospital Report no. 2, 1932.
99. Hale n.d., p. 225.

and malaria and the wards were congested. The hospital was not optimally managed, but the women in charge, although worrying about the fate of their families back home, persevered and coped better than the Russian officers and soldiers. Among the last Russians to leave were the nurses at the one remaining hospital.[100] That hospital was discontinued before February 1918 when the last Russian soldiers had left. In June 1918, Dr. Stead wrote that "for more than two years typhus has been rife throughout the whole country." When typhus struck the British troops in Kermanshah they were unprepared. There was "a young doctor, inexperienced as far as typhus was concerned, no hospital, no beds or bed clothing or hospital appliances. It also happened that I was buying tents for relief work and had enough on hand to supply the extras needed for both islolation and hospital camps."[101] Therefore, the British built a hospital complex outside Kermanshah, which they used until April 1921, when they withdrew all their troops from Persia.[102]

In July 1918, typhus and cholera were prevalent. Amir Koll, the acting governor, took sanitary measures; although the city became cleaner, much needed still to be done.[103] In September 1918, following the famine, Kermanshah was struck by the worldwide influenza pandemic, which caused many deaths, especially in the villages. By the end of October all villages in Mahidasht and Kermanshah valleys had 8-10 graves. Due to last year's famine people had no resistance.[104] Hall, the Bank manager wrote: "Pneunomia and malaria on top of it have caused many deaths, particularly among the Indians, and the hospitals here and in Hamadan are full of sick. ... Half the population seems to have suffered more or less."[105] In December 1918, Hall reported that "the hospitals are no longer congested, and the work of the doctors (and padres) is less onerous than it was."[106] Not only the local population suffered from the pandemic, but so did the British troops. Forbes-Leith wrote when he returned to Persia after WWI: "I lost many friends and my men from all kinds of foul disease, and under such conditions it is little wonder that many of my brother officers, especially those who until the war had never been out of England, regarded Persia as a veritable Hell on earth."[107] During the famine and the pandemic Dr. Stead worked tirelessly, providing famine relief, setting up an orphanage and caring the sick, both Persian and British. Dr. Stead's work was much appreciated by everybody, including the British Parliament.[108]

Her dispensary had suffered during the Great War. In fact, during 1917-18 the dispensary had to be closed due to the hostilities and the lack of medical supplies.[109] In 1919, Mrs. Stead was able to re-open the dispensary, but she provided only medical care to out-patients. Meanwhile,

---

100. Hale n.d., pp. 212, 216; McClintic 1917, p. 40.
101. Presbyterian Church 1919 a, p. 266 ("Lack of medical supplies made it impossible to open the Dispensary when we closed down the famine relief at the first of June.").
102. Hale n.d., p. 226.
103. FO 248/1204 Kermanshah report no. 6, 02/08/1918 by Lt. Col. Kennion.
104. FO 248/1204 Kermanshah report no. 9, 01/11/1918 by Lt. Col. Kennion. On the influenze pandemic, see Floor 2018 b.
105. Hale 1920, p. 237.
106. Hale 1920, p. 240.
107. Forbes-Leith 1927, p. 21.
108. RG 91-19-28, Westminster Hospital Report no. 2, 1932.
109. Presbyterian Church 1919 b, p. 266. In 1921 the dispensary was closed due to the absence of Mrs. Stead. Presbyterian Church 1921, p. 335.

some of her work was seen to by the British Medical Corps, although as of March of that year the latter received orders to no longer treat civilians.[110] On Dr. Stead's return in March 1920 she opened the dispensary in her sewing room, where she received 30 patients every day. In 1921 the dispensary was closed due to her absence. When the British army left Kermanshah in April 1921, it offered the huts that had served as their military hospital for sale to the American missionaries. The 21 huts, 12 of which 80 feet long, were nicely located on a hill outside the city. Moreover, they were located at a distance from one another such that this made the establishment of a cottage-hospital possible. The Americans bought them for 3,350 *tuman*s, much below market value, but they had to break down the 'ideal hospital' as they had neither the staff to guard them nor a doctor to work there, while looting of building materials had already occurred.[111]

THE WESTMINSTER OR AMERICAN CHRISTIAN HOSPITAL

It happened that when Dr. Harry Packhard was returning to Persia (Urmiyeh) he found Dr. Stead very ill at Qasr-e Shirin, where she had been visiting friends. He took her to Kermanshah where she died on 21 February 1922 in Kermanshah, aged 52 years. The Eastern Mission asked that Dr. Packhard stay in Kermanshah and finish the hospital building and remain there until the arrival of Dr. Bussdicker, the new physician. Dr. Packhard not only built the hospital, but also a physician's residence and a chapel in memory of Dr. Stead, funds having been made available by her husband's supporting church in Kansas City. When Dr. and Mrs. Bussdicker arrived in Kermanshah at the end of October 1922, the hospital had been finished and the first patient had been admitted. Because Dr. Bussdicker did not speak Persian the Eastern Mission asked Dr. Packhard to stay for the winter. He left in the spring of 1923, and Dr. Bussdicker and his wife, who was a trained nurse, continued the medical work helped by some half-trained girls and ignorant boys. Their work was facilitated by the arrival of a nurse, Miss Mary Edna Burgess, who joined the medical team in 1922.[112]

In 1926, Dr. Packhard returned to Kermanshah, while Dr. and Mrs. Bushdicker R.N. went to Rasht for 18 months. When the Bushdickers returned to Kermanshah in 1928, Dr. Packhard was also permanently assigned to Kermanshah. Because the work load increased, they were able to convince a meeting of the American missionaries in 1928, of the need for a permanent second physician. The meeting also decided to ask the missionaries of the Kermanshah station to draw up plans for the adequate housing of their medical work, while it went on record that a second physician was needed in Kermanshah.[113] Dr. Packhard who returned to the US in 1930 was able to convince the Westminster Church in Bufalo, N.Y. to build a new hospital in Kermanshah rather than in Urmiyeh as had been the original plan.

110. Presbyterian Church 1920, p. 318.

111. Presbyterian Church 1922 a, pp. 68, 368-369.

112. Presbyterian Church 1922 b, no. 48, p. 27.

113. Elgood 1951, pp. 511-512, 534; Waterfield 1973, pp. 139-140; Presbyterian Church 1919 b, p. 266; Presbyterian Church 1921, p. 335; Presbyterian Church 1928, pp. 12, 17.

Meanwhile, the Bushdickers with one graduate nurse continued their medical work in Kermanshah, later, in 1931, joined by Dr. Packhard.[114]

In 1932, the Presbyterian church in Buffalo made $30,000 available to build the Westminster Hospital in Kermanshah. Ground was broken in March 1932 and on 17 October 1932 the first patients were admitted to the 75 bed, 4-storey hospital, although painting and carpenter work was still going on. One of the outstanding features of the new hospital was that there was running water everywhere it was needed, which made it almost unique in Persia.[115] The men's ward was on 2nd and 3rd floor. The 2nd floor ward had 10 beds and two small private rooms. This floor was almost reserved for patients sent by the city health department and were all the poorest and hopeless patients. Many had chronic diseases and were mostly there to ease their last days and have them die in comfort. The third floor had two wards with 21 beds, an enclosed porch with four beds for TB patients and five private rooms. Most patients there were able to pay all or part of their expenses. Some were still full charity patients. The women's ward was on the top floor; here were also the operating rooms. There were three wards with resp. four and six beds, two general and one obstretical with four beds. There were six private rooms of which two obstretical. There also was a porch that was partly enclosed with glass windows with four beds; the open part had 4-6 beds, but it was only used in summer.[116]

The women's ward and clinic was very important as it provided targeted and much needed quality care to women. Ceasarians were performed and general obstretics care was given. These obstetrics services were a boon for the women of Kermanshah because there was no other venue, apart from some midwives who dabbled in medicine. When Dr. Jenny Stead, who intermittently was available, between 1932-37, and in 1938 Dr. Mary Zoekcler, and, as of 1944, Dr. Frances Zoeckler, more special attention could be given and these female physicians were in charge of the women's ward and the women's clinic.[117] As of 1940, Mrs. Packard conducted a baby clinic (feeding problems, weight loss, slow development, digestive troubles), which was continued after she and her husband retired in 1943. Here women of all layers of society intermingled, rich and poor, European and Persian.[118] Because of their contribution, starting with Dr. Stead, the Westminster Hospital or *Bimarestan-e Masihi* (the Christian Hospital) was known among the people of Kermanshah as *Bagh-e Hakim Khanom* or *Bimarestan-e Amrika'i* (The Female Doctor's Garden or the American Hospital).[119]

---

114. RG 61.3.46, Bushdicker/Kermanshah to Huntwork/New York, 29/09/1957.
115. RG 91-19-28, Packard to Butzer 03/06/1933; RG 91-19-28, Westminster Hospital 1933.
116. RG 91-19-28, Annual Report Westminster Hospital Kermanshah 1938-39.
117. RG 91-19-28, Westminster Hospital 1933; RG 91-19-28, Report of Westminster Hospital July 1, 1933 to June 30, 1934; RG 91-19-28, Kermanshah Medical Report 1937; RG 91-19-28, Annual Report Westminster Hospital Kermanshah June 30, 1938; RG 91-19-28, Annual Report Westminster Hospital Kermanshah 1938-39; RG 91-19-28, The Westminster Hospital Bulletin. vol. 2/1. October 1939; RG 91-19-28, Annual Report Westminster Hospital Kermanshah 1944-45; Government of Great Britain 1945, p. 410.
118. RG 91-19-28, Report Westminster Hospital Kermanshah 1940.
119. RG 61-3-46, Muradian to Bussdicker, 06/08/1959.

Fig. 2.22: The Westminster Hospital or *Bimarestan-e Masihi* (2017).

In 1932, Ms Fulton R.N. opened a Nurses Training School.[120] Over a three-year period, the student-nurses received lessons in ethics, practical nursing, personal hygiene, dietetics, bacteriology, materia medica, anatomy, physiology and English; all subjects were taught by the American medical staff. After a six-month probation period, the student-nurses learned nursing skills, both on the job and in theory, and after three years received their diploma, nurse's cap and a pin.[121] In 1936, the Ministry of Education decided to start nurse training schools in Tehran, Tabriz and Mashhad and at its request the Mission allowed American nurses to teach there half of their time with a contract for 3 years. Because Kermanshah had no government nurse training school the government allowed the Westminster Hospital to continue to operate its school, adhering to the government program. The only inconvenience was that the government required two-year training, whereas the Westminster Hospital had a 3-year program, which it preferred. However, by adhering to the government rules, it ensured government recognition of the diploma of their graduates.[122] The recognition of the Westminster Hospital nurse training school by the government also meant that it only could admit girls who had graduated from the 9th grade. This posed a probem, because in 1939, there were only about 20 graduates in Kermanshah, of which the hospital was only able to induce one to come. But the hospital badly need nurses. Therefore, it allowed 3 sixth class graduates to join the nurse training school on the condition

120. RG 91-19-28, Westminster Hospital News vol. 1/3 -15/09/1932.

121. RG 91-19-28, Westminster Hospital Report 07/03/1933; Arasteh 1967, p. 124.

122. RG 91-19-28, Kermanshah Medical Report 1937.

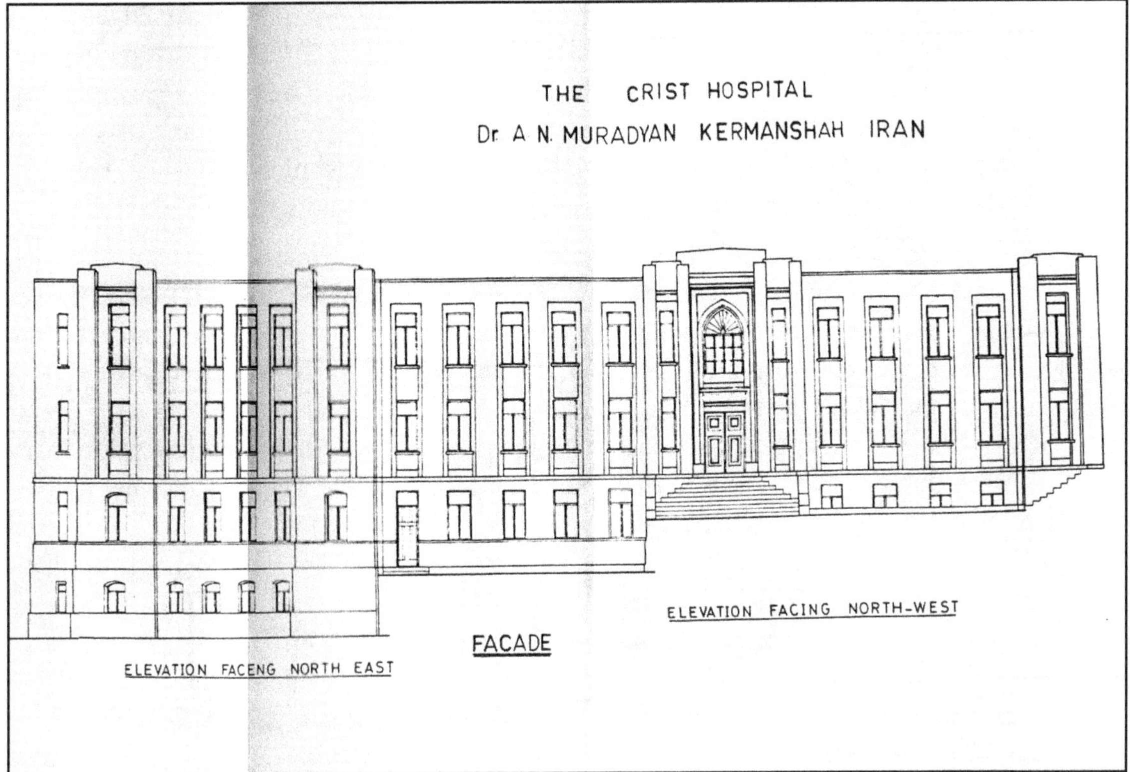

Fig. 2.23: Drawing/Facade of the The Westminster Hospital or *Bimarestan-e Masihi* (1952).

that they would continue to study and get their 9th grade graduation and only then they would get their American diploma. Unfortunately, there was a high attrition rate of both student and graduate nurses. The head of the training school opined that the nurses didn't come because they had the idea of service, but rather came to get away from home and when trained, knowing English and the typewriter they received attractive offers with easier work and better pay. Marriage was another reason why nurses left their service.[123]

Until 1940, the Westminster Hospital was the only civil hospital in Ostan V, although there was a great need for it in several of its towns. There were some health officers working in Kermanshah, but they were unable to satisfy the needs of the population, while the existing military hospitals were not even able to care for major surgery of the troops in the region.[124] In fact, before the Westminster Hospital was even completed the military authorities asked its physicians to perform 270 hernia operations on new conscripts as soon as possible.[125] In 1940, later than was expected, a *Red Lion and Sun* state hospital was established in Kermanshah, which was able to care for the most distressing cases that before were all sent to the Westminster Hospital. Because the Department of Health required that the state hospital took care of all charity cases in the region this lightened the burden somewhat for the Westminster Hospital. This meant that it was able to focus on more highly specialized work for which its staff was

123. RG 91-19-28, Annual Report Westminster Hospital Kermanshah 1938-39.

124. RG 91-19-28, Westminster Hospital Report no. 2, 1932.

125. RG 91-19-28, Westminster Hospital Report no. 4, 1932.

qualified. During a visit by Dr. Packhard to the *Red Lion and Sun* hospital he observed that three doctors, one druggist, one midwife and several helpers were caring for 27 patients quite satisfactorily and that a new grant enabled them to install another five beds. The Westminsiter Hospital collaborated with the staff of the state hospital in the area of X-ray and its superior facilities in obstretics and surgery.[126] In 1943, when the 75-bed Westminster Hospital had only one physician, the *Red Lion and Sun* state hospital employed 5 doctors for 35 beds.[127]

In January-February 1943 the public health situation in Kermanshah was disastrous. According to Dr. Mohammad Daftari, the Director of Public Health, there were 1,230 deaths due to typhus alone.[128] The only institution that was able to provide effective help, and even that was not adequate, was the Westminster Hospital. In 1941, Dr. Packhard had been transferred to Hamadan, but fortunately he was back in 1943 to help battle the typhus outbreak. Shortly thereafter, he and Mrs. Packard retired after having served for thirty-seven years as a missionary physician. The common people as well as the local authorities paid exceptional tributes to him. To deal with eventual further outbreaks of typhus in Kermanshah the government opened a Typhus Hospital in that city.[129] At Dr. Daftari's request, the British Army made a sample disinfector, which was handed to him in January 1944. At his follow-up request, the British Army emptied 12 bitumen drums to be turned into disinfectors. Dr. Daftari also became the chairman of the local committee of the Imperial Iranian Pharmaceutical Institute for the control of the sale of drugs by reputable pharmacists, which was formed in January 1944. Members of the committee included the Director of Finance and Dr. Bussdicker of the Westminster Hospital.[130] In June 1945, some cases of cholera were reported. The Public Health Department said there were none and posted a notice in the local press saying that those who spread false information would be punished in accordance with the law. [131] In the first quarter of 1945, the public health situation of the entire province was much better.[132]

After Dr. Packhard's departure, Dr. Bussdicker was working alone until 1944 when Dr. Mohammad A'zam Zanganeh, a graduate of Tehran and Bern Universities, joined him, attracted by a special financial arrangement. He remained for a number of years until the early 1950s and thereafter went in private practice, but he also served as otolargynologist consultant for the hospital. Dr. Zanganeh also referred his patients to the hospital. In 1946, Dr. Frances Zoeckler joined the medical staff and took over the women's ward and clinic. She left in 1953 on furlough and was replaced by Dr. Burton Dyson, who in 1955 returned to the USA. Dr. Zoeckler returned

---

126. RG 91-19-28, Report Westminster Hospital Kermanshah 1940. The arrival of this civil state hospital was already expected in 1932. RG 91-19-28, Packhard to Speer, 30/07/1932. Soltani 1381, vol. 3, p. 897 although not giving a date, implies that the first stone of the Red Lion & Sun hospital was laid around 1930.

127. RG 91-19-28, Annual Report Westminster Hospital Kermanshah 1943-44.

128. FO 371/40177, Kermanshah Diary February 1944; Idem, Kermanshah Diary March 1944.

129. RG 61.3.46, Bushdicker/Kermanshah to Huntwork/New York, 29/09/1957.

130. FO 371/40177, Kermanshah Diary January 1944 (there was also a hospital at Shahabad); FO 371/40177, Kermanshah Diary December 1943. There were also people who misused their position. There were articles in the press about doctor Abedin, who was accused of charging 200 rials for a vaccination certificate, whereas the people concerned had been vaccinated in Tehran; doctor Abedin denied it. FO 371/45400, Kermanshah Diary February 1945.

131. FO 371/45400, Kermanshah Diary June 1945.

132. FO 371/45400, Kermanshah Diary February 1945; Idem, Kermanshah Diary March 1945.

in September 1955, who wrote enthusiastically: "In 1952 a water piped system was a dream, now we have it with a purification system."[133] Dr. Zanganeh was replaced by Dr. Art Moradian, who had been trained in the USA. Ms Estelle Chambers was still the head of nursing.[134] The hospital closed in 1958, coinciding with the retirement of Dr. Bussdicker, because the mission was unable to recruit and send doctors and nurses.[135] The gap in the resulting supply of medical care was assumed by the government hospital.

EDUCATION

There were a number of traditional *maktab-khaneh*s where children were taught the principles of reading and writing as well as memorized parts of the Koran and Persian poetry. The monthly fee was 0.5 to 2 *qran*s per month per pupil. Girls were seldom taught by a *molla-baji*. Only sons of the elite had access to books, such as the *Shahnameh* and Nezami's *Divan* and received an education in literature.[136] In 1902, the first modern school was established by Mirza Hoseyn 'Ali Khan Mohandes in his own house, which was named *Mohtashamiyeh*, so named because it was established with the financial help of Mohtasham al-Dowleh; it had some 40 pupils, who were taught Persian, French, arithmetic and marching. 'Ala al-Dowleh endowed the school with 200 *tumans*/annually, Ehtesham al-Dowleh paid the rest. This school was closed around 1912. The second school was the *madraseh-ye nezami* (military school). It enjoyed great support from governor Ala al-Dowleh. He had the more than 50 pupils dressed in infantry dress and made their principal, Sayyed Javad Khan Sartip-e Tupkhaneh, train the children to march with small Werndl rifles, in accordance with Austrian military regulations. Sometimes, they performed this exercise on the *Meydan-e Tupkhaneh*, sometimes outside the city. The pupils were taught the military arts, music, artillery, and drill. Exams were taken at government house in the governor's presence. 'Ala al-Dowleh also supported a third school, the *madraseh-ye eslamiyeh* founded and led by a former Jew, Sheikh Mohammad Sa'id Jadid al-Eslam, also in his own house. Later, with the help Mirza Esma'il Khan and others he was able to establish the school in other premises. At the school Persian, Arabic, French, and arithmetic were taught, while its pupils likewise engaged in drill practice. Some of his students, of the 'Emad al-Dowleh family, most of whom had learnt French quite well, according to Eugene Aubin, were employed at the Telegraph office. Sheikh Mohammad Sa'id closed his school in 1907, because he wanted to open one in Hamadan. When Farmanfarma became governor Sheikh Mohammad Sa'id got into a dispute with Sheikh Mohammad Taqi, as a result of which the former resigned from the school. With the help of the new governor he established the *madraseh-ye 'elmiyeh-ye eslamiyeh*. This led to the closure of the two other schools, whose pupils gradually all moved to the new school. In 1915-16, the *mohajerin* insisted that the school drop the appellation *elmiyeh*. The *madraseh-ye*

133. RG 91-19-28, Frances Zoeckler to Board of For. Missions 08/02/1956.
134. RG 61-3-46, Bushdicker/Kermanshah to Huntwork/New York, 29/09/1957.
135. Miller 1989, p. 328.
136. Soltani 1381, vol. 1, p. 279.

'elmiyeh-ye eslamiyeh itself was closed in 1919. In February 1912, Mlle Porpier [?] and Ebrahim Musavi wanted to establish a boys and girls school, for which the then governor granted permission. However, it seems nothing came of it, presumably because of the changing political climate.[137]

In 1902, in addition to the *Ehteshamiyeh* school of Hoseyn 'Ali Khan, the *Nezami* school, and the *madraseh-ye eslamiyeh* of Sheikh Mohammad Sa'id there was another modern school, where Persian, some French, English, geography and arithmetic was taught. Kasha Mooshi, a Christian convert trained in Tehran, started a school with 20 Moslem, 8 Chaldean, and 5 Jewish pupils. Later this number grew. According to Whipple, among the daily attendants of the school run by Kosha Moshee were three princes, several noblemen and two sayyeds and others, because of "the higher branches taught and its high moral character." At these modern schools, pupils paid 10 *qran*s per month except for Kashe Mushi's school, which was financed by the American missionaries. None of these schools made a real dent in the almost general state of illiteracy among the population, which was estimated to be at 97 percent.[138] This American support for a local Persian school may have come about by the refusal of the Persian government in January 1894 to permit the American missionaries to open a school in Kermanshah to teach Christian and Jewish children. The American request to open school was in response to a letter, dated 1 March 1904, from a Mr. Hoax (no pun intended), asking to send a teacher to Kermanshah because their children were not allowed to enter Moslem *maktab*s. This letter was signed by people with Jewish and Christian names.[139] Later, the American missionaries started a school in their home. However, the number of pupils was very limited and this school received less attention in 1918 due to the desperate state of affairs in the town. During the first half of the year the school had seven children that were staying in the home of the missionaries and two from an enlightened Persian family. The three oldest children taught in turns the others and were taught themselves when any of the missionaries were in town.[140] By 1922, there was a new school building, which was built by the orphans that Mrs. Stead had taken into her care in 1918. The outside of the building was covered with 4-gallon gasoline tins donated by the British Army. The school had 72 students at that time.[141]

There were also a number of other schools in Kermanshah, although they were mostly short-lived. In 1903, Mirza Taqi Shirazi, a clergyman, founded a high school that by 1907 had 50 students. The subjects taught were: Persian, Arabic, arithmetic, Islam, rhetoric, calligraphy and the basics of French.[142] In 1906, the *Roshdiyeh* school was established, but it lasted only five months. In 1908, the *Hoquq* school was started by a number of prominent persons. The school lasted until Salar al-Dowleh's rebellion in 1909. After the suppression of the rebellion in 1911, Mo'azed al-Dowleh, using this school's furniture, started a government school named *madraseh-ye motavasseteh-ye Ahmadiyeh-e dowlati*. Hajj Mohammad Taqi Esfahani deeded a piece of land and building to start a school named *Nosrat* in March 1910. He also gave funds

137. Soltani 1381, vol. 1, pp. 280, 282-85; vol. 3, pp. 475-76; Hamadani 1354, p. 398; Aubin 1907, pp. 337-38. The *Ruznameh-ye Iran* 1375, vol. 5, p. 4092 (no. 1017; 26/07/1902) mentions all three schools.

138. DCR 590 (Kermanshah1902), p. 6; Whipple 1900, p. 814; Presbyterian Church 1904, p. 242.

139. US Government 1895, pp. 486ff.

140. Presbyterian Church 1919-20, p. 265-266.

141. For a photo see, Presbyterian Church 1922 a, pp. 368-369 (in between), 372.

142. *Revue du Monde Musulmane* 1907/3, p. 59.

so that 30 orphans could attend this school. However, he got into conflict Mohammad Mehdi Mo'in al-Tojjar, the principal and the school was closed. Later he deeded the land, building and its furniture to Mo'azed al-Dowleh to open a state school named *Nosrat*. In 1913, Lambert Molitor, who was in charge of the Customs and Taxes of Kermanshah, suggested to local merchants to finance two schools for girls and boys by levying a small fee on imports. Mo'azed al-Dowleh pursued this idea and, as a result, the merchants agreed to pay 1 *shahi* per imported package. The Customs Administration started levying the 1 *shahi* on 7 February 1913. Also, in October 1913, a meeting was held at Government House to discuss access to education, which should be free for the poor. It was suggested that expenses should be paid out of the income of *vaqf* lands, "of which little now reaches the objects for which it was devised." On 29 November 1919, the *Madraseh-ye Mohamadiyeh* was opened by its principal Mirza Nasrollah.[143] In 1913, the Ministry of Education decided that one-third of revenues of rural *vaqf*s would be paid to the *madrash-ye 'elmiyeh-ye eslamiyeh*. Mo'azed al-Dowleh proposed to allot 25 *tuman*s of the monthly *haqq al-towliyeh* of the Emad al-Dowleh mosque and 25 *tuman*s/month of the *owqaf* to the state schools. During WW I revenues for the schools dropped precipitously, because customs revenues had plummeted. To make up the shortfall the schools put on theatrical performances. Some notables also paid a monthly amount for the schools, such as Amin al-Mamalek, who gave 10 *tuman*s/month. The *Nosrat* school had to close temporarily due to lack of revenues.[144]

In 1911, Mirza Esma'il Khan Mo'azed al-Dowleh was charged with the supervision of educational affairs. On 7 January 1916, Sayyed Abu'l-Qasem Behbahani was put in charge of the educational affairs. This was a difficult period, with the warring parties occupying the city and trade blocked, and, as a result, schools were closed temporarily. In October 1916, the provisional government allotted instead of 25 *tuman*s of taxes 100 *tuman*s/month to the state schools. Some of the *mohajerin*, such as Eskander Mirza, also taught at the schools for a while. The provisional government also started a training school for officers. After its flight, the furniture was used for the *Ahmadiyeh* state school. On 6 June 1916, Hoseyn Aqa Soltanzadeh was appointed inspector of the schools. When on 28 March 1917, Sayyed Abu'l-Qasem had to go to Tehran for a short while, Mirza Hoseyn Amin-e Homayun Kermanshahi was put in charge of educational affairs, and he appointed Mehdi Khan as inspector. In 1917, a theatrical performance was organized for the benefit of the school which yielded almost 1,200 *tuman*s. On 8 October 1917, when Sayyed Abu'l-Qasem returned, he found a school system in disorder, although the *Nosrat* school had opened again. Every teacher did what he liked and the quality of teaching was inadequate. The revenues from the customs were non-existent and from the treasury the schools only received 25 *tuman*s/month. The famine, the severe cold and the pandemic were not conducive to a good functioning school system either. Sayyed Abu'l-Qasem called a meeting with the responsible department heads. As a result, new inspectors were appointed and a temporary budget was agreed upon. As of 1918, the one-third of the 1 *shahi* fee from the Customs was again paid to the *Mohammadiyeh* school. In that year a new school

143. Soltani 1381, vol. 1, pp. 286-89 (Soltani gives 1305 *shamsi* as the year, which is incorrect); FO 248/1073, Kermanshah Diary no. 44, ending 30/10/1913. In November 1913, Ali Qolij, a strong man gave a performance for the benefit of the schools. FO 248/1073, Kermanshah Diary no. 47, ending 20/11/1913.

144. Soltani 1381, vol. 1, pp. 290-91.

Sharaf was opened. On 28 August 1918, Sayyed Abu'l-Qasem went to Tehran and was replaced by Sheikh 'Ali Asghar who remained in office until 31 October 1918, when he resigned. He was replaced by the acting chief Mirza Mahmud Fakhr al-Eslam on 30 December 1918.[145]

It would require a separate book to discuss the further development of both government and private schools in Kermanshah, moreover, that book has already been written by Mohammad 'Ali Alavi-Kiya and Mohsen Rostami-Guran, who offer a detailed study about the development of the school system in Kermanshah.[146] Here it suffices to state that it was only in the mid-1930s that much progress was made in providing education to the people of Kermanshah. In 1926, Sayyed 'Abdol-Hoseyn Soltan was appointed chief of education (*ra'is-e ma'aref*) for Kermanshah. He introduced the Ministry of Education's programs to the schools in Kermanshah. Before that time, Mirza Ahmad Javaheri had provided educational guidance on a voluntary basis. Although many new government school were established in Kermanshah and the small towns of the province, nevertheless, the standard and level of education remained low. The government tried to improve the quality of education both by attracting better teachers and by paying more. In secondary schools much emphasis was given to physical exercise and students were encouraged to join the scout movement. Sports also formed part of the curriculum, in particular football and volley-ball, which games drew more players as their popularity increased. In 1937, free-of-charge night classes were started, which after initial hesitation to attend soon were hardly able to meet demand. The British consul noted that religious instruction (note: not education) was limited to two hours per week, although he opined "that Iranian children of the present day would benefit by having religious instruction in the schools." The consul thought so, because moral teaching would instill a sense of honesty, a virtue that was sorely lacking in Persians, in his opinion.[147] On March 20 1945, the Education Department held a ceremony in the *Shahpur* school for graduating students. Mr. Shokra'i stated that at that time there were 3,733 students in the province and the education budget amounted to Rls. 4,211,360/year.[148]

NEWSPAPERS

In 1906, 'Abdol-Karim Gheyrat Kermanshahi published the *Shehab-e Thaqib* periodical, the first newspaper published in Kermanshah. In 1907, Abu'l-Qasem Lahuti published the newspaper *Bisotun*. In 1909, the *Kermanshah* newspaper appeared, which was founded by Mirza Ahmad Khan Vaziri Mo'tazed al-Dowleh and its editor was Sayyed Hedayatollah Fasih al-Motakallemin. It was published until 1911. A newspaper with the same name was again published as of April 1927 with Farajollah Kaviyani as editor. At that time it was published 3 times weekly and its politics were conservative. The third newspaper was *Rastakhiz*, which was published in 1915

145. Soltani 1381, vol. 1, pp. 280, 287-88, 291-93.
146. Alavi-Kiya and Rostami-Guran 1384; see also Soltani 1381, vol. 1, pp. 279-331.
147. FO 371/21900, f. 116.
148. FO 371/45400, Kermanshah Diary March 1945. In October 1945, Mr. Shokrai, director of the education department was replaced by Hoseyn Ali Ahsani. FO 371/45400, Kermanshah Diary October 1945.

and edited by Taqi Yazi writing as Pur Davud. It was printed in Baghdad. It ceased publication when the Russians occupied the city. *Akhbar* was published during the provisional government by Mirza Nasrollah Khan Shirazi Jami Jam and it was published until February 1917. Because of the editor's name it was also known as the *Jam-e Jam* and it published war news. *Harfha-ye Hesami* was published when the *Mohajedin* government was in place in 1915. Mirza Kazem Malekzadeh was the editor of Democrat newspaper *Gharb-e Iran* , which was published since August 1916. Its editor was hit by a bullet and later died; he was replaced by Mehdi Khan Forupur, whose last issue was no. 20. For in June 1918, Majd al-Molk banned its publication. *Afsaneh* and *Bakhtar* were newspapers of which we only know that it was under Mirza 'Ali Asghar Khan Ehtesham al-Maleh in December 1917 and soon thereafter both newspapers as well as a third were closed down, because they were violently anti-British. *Bisotun* was published by Abu'l-Qasem Lahuti and Farajollah Kaviyani. It only issued 12 numbers, when due to internal conflict it ceased publication and Lahuti had to leave Kermanshah on 2 January 1918. It resumed publication under Ahmad 'Ali Khan Sheybani and as of May 1918 by Mahdi Farahpur, who in July received a license for its publication. This was the first license to publish a newspaper issued to Kermanshah. In mid-1918, *Bisotun* had an English speaking editor, Shabani, who was to translate and publish articles from the British press, but he left to Tehran at that time.[149] It stopped publication in the early 1920s, but appeared again in 1925 and reappeared in 1943 as the local daily organ of *Tudeh* with Sa'adat as editor. It then regularly appeared until 2 February 1949, when it was banned. The British believed that this Kermanshah newspaper received paper via the Soviet Consulate. In February 1921, *Sabah* was published by Mirza Mehdi Khan Mo'tamed al-Tojjar, which had scientific and literary articles. It continued publishing until about February 1928. The *Kawkab-e Darakhsan*, with Sheikh Ahmad Javaheri as editor, received its license in November 1923. It started publishing in 1925 until 1928, and it resumed publishing in March 1949 as a monthly. Only three issues were published, because when its editor died it stopped publishing. In 1925, *Makhzan-e Danesh* was published by Sayyed Kazem Khan. In that same year *Ruznameh-ye Rahbar* was published. First, under Mirza Naqi Khan Rahbar, then by Hoseyn Shakiba and as of the beginning of 1927 till April 1927 by Farajollah Kavyani. As of 1951 it was republished by Rahbar. *Fesahat* was a literary journal published by Mohammad Javad Shebab Jalili and as of 1932 under Farajollah Kavyani. It ceased publication in 1935, when the publisher died. Other newspapers included *Siyasat-e Sharq* by Mohammad Vazir-zadeh, which appeared in 1927 and ceased publication after a few months. *Parav* was published by Heydar Mazhar as of 20 February 1928, however the publisher was unable to get a license. *Majalleh-ye Da'vat-e Eslami* under Sayyed Mohammad Taqi Vahedi was published from 1927 until 1934. *Majalleh-e Okhuvvat* appeared in 1928, but after 12 issues it stopped publication. *Kawkab-e Gharb* (Star of the West) was published by Hajji 'Abdollah Mostashar 'Ali Ne'mati as of 1929. Its editor was Sayyed 'Abdol-Karim Gheyrat. It appeared for the second time from 1932 to 1937, edited by Feyzollah Sa'adat. It reappeared in the fall of 1942, twice per week. It was a conservative and religious publication. On 29 November 1934, *Taq-e Bustan* was published

149. FO 248/1204 Kermanshah report no. 3, 11/06/1918 by Lt. Col. Kennion.

by 'Abdol-Rasul Pashmi. Only four issues appeared and on 18 December 1934 the paper ceased publication.[150]

COMMUNICATIONS

A modern Postal service was organized since 1873, which fell under the Ministry of Posts and Telegraphs. In Kermanshah there was a regional director who was responsible to the Ministry in Tehran. The postal service was limited to town and villages having a post office. When there were good roads the mail was sent in fourgons, which changed at post houses, on average 120 km per day. Off the main roads and in winter the mail was carried by pack animals or by courier, who traveled on average 45 km per day.[151] In the 1880s, a weekly and satisfactory postal service existed between Tehran and Kermanshah.[152] In 1890, there was only one post station between Kermanshah and Khaneqin, which was at Sarpol, where the mail changed horses. From Kermanshah to Tehran there were many *chaparkhaneh*s and a *chapar* service.[153] In March 1906, the governor asked the Posts to be taken away from the Customs Department and placed in the hands of a Persian as the pensions were paid very irregularly. True, the existing situation was bad, but after the change it became worse.[154] Therefore, the post office was located in the customs house caravanserai on the northern edge of the town. The mail for Hamadan and Tehran left on Mondays and Thursdays and from there on Wednesdays and Satudays; for Baghdad on Wednesday and in return on Sunday. There also was a mail route to Harsin that left on Wednesday and mail from there was received on Thursday. The mail took seven days to Tehran and to Baghdad four days, using respectively 6 and 2 post horses; although in winter both destinations took two additional days. To Harsin the mail was taken by foot messenger or *qased*.[155]

In 1911, many horses were stolen by rebels or brigands so that the carriage company, which carried the mail, was unable to carry the mails to the Turkish border as of October and later, due to death of the manager, it ceased operations.[156] In 1912, there was an attempt to start a cart postal service, which failed, partly due to high fodder prices. As a result, postal service was highly irregular until February when the local government provided horsemen to carry the mail, but for parcels great delays remained.[157] At the end of 1912 the mail was much delayed; there was a new contractor Mr. Aghaniantz, who was not as yet fully operational as he had not sent

150. Haddad 'Adel, Elmi, and Taromi-Rad 2012, p. 79; Soltani 1381, vol. 1, p. 333-38; FO 248/1204, Kermanshah report no. 3, 11/06/1918 by Lt. Col. Kennion; Idem, tel. Greenhouse/Kermanshah to Legation, 02/03/1918; FO 371/45400, Monthly Diary December 1944.

151. AIR 20/663, p. 141 c.

152. *AP* 76 (Report 31/10/1884), p. 7; Adamec 1976, vol. 1, p. 373.

153. Curzon 1892, vol. 1, p. 51; Adamec 1976, vol. 1, p. 373.

154. Administration Report 1906-07, p. 41. The postmaster prince Isa Mirza was dismissed and replaced by Akram al-Dowleh. Political Diaries, vol. 3, p. 317.

155. Adamec 1976, vol. 1, p. 373-74.

156. DCR 4994 (Kermanshah 1911-12), p. 7.

157. DCR 5204 (Kermanshah 1912-13), p. 5.

any animals, which caused a great delay in the delivery of the mail.[158] In 1917, there was no post service of horses, due to the war. Therefore, the British consul occasionally arranged for a foot or mule messenger to take the mailbag to Basra through Posht-e Kuh.[159]

In 1930, the Post office was on the main square.[160] There are no data available how well or not the post office functioned in the post-war years. However, it would seem that in 1944 the quality of the service had gone down. In January 1944, 'Abdol 'Ali Misdaqi became the new director of P&T. However, in May the British consul complained that there was a need for improvement, because a letter from the governor to Major Oakshott in Sanandaj took 13 days, over a distance that normally was but a 4-hour drive.[161]

As of 1867, there was a telegraph station in Kermanshah, connecting it with Europe.[162] Messages in Latin script could be sent to Tehran, Khaneqin and Baghdad, to the other stations Persian had to be used. The charge was 2.75 *qran*s per 10 words for the interior, and 4.5 *qran*s per word for Baghdad. The *farrash* delivering the telegram asked for a fee of 10 *shahi*s. Messages to Europe were best sent via Tehran, because via Turkey the message became incomprehensible due to mutilation during transmission.[163] The station was located in one of the courtyards of the palace, opening on the *meydan*.[164] In 1911, "after the occupation of Kermanshah by rebels the telegraph was interrupted, and the post irregular and unreliable."[165] In September 1911, the telegraph connection between Hamadan and Tehran was restored, but the line to Baghdad had not yet re-laid. During the troubles all poles were taken away, so that since October the telegraph was interrupted.[166] During WW I telegraph service, of course, became unreliable, only to be restored after 1918, when the British military built new telegraph lines between Khaneqin and Kerend (3 lines), Kerend to Hamadan (2 lines), and Hamadan to Qazvin (1 line). The lines were maintained and operated by British staff under the director of P&T in Iraq pending an agreement with the Indo-European Telegraph Department (IETD). The Persian Telegraph Department was "permitted to use one of these lines during a certain period of the day." It also operated its own lines between Hamadan and Bijar, Senneh, Tehran and Soltanabad (via Dowlatabad) as well as between Borujerd and Khorramabad. These Persian-owned lines were not part of the IETD's trunkline. Each provincial governor had a director of Telegraph in his administration, because during the winter months the telegraph was the only means to maintain contact with the outlying districts, "and throughout the year are one of the principal means whereby the Government maintains its authority." Although breakages were frequent these were "usually repaired within

158. FO 248/1073, Kermanshah Diary no. 1, ending 2 January 1913; FO 248/1073, Kermanshah Diary no. 3, ending 16 January 1913; Political Diaries vol. 5, p. 39.
159. Hale n.d., pp. 199, 205.
160. Alexander 1934, p. 25.
161. FO 371/40177, Kermanshah Diary May 1944.
162. Binder 1887, p. 345.
163. Adamec 1976, vol. 1, p. 373.
164. DCR 4994 (Kermanshah 1911-12), p. 7.
165. DCR 4994 (Kermanshah 1911-12), p. 5
166. DCR 5204 (Kermanshah 1912-13), pp. 5, 7.

a remarkably short time, and, considering the difficulties which [are] here to be found, the working of the Department may be considered most creditable."[167]

> Delays (which are often considerable) occur when messages are transferred from one line to another, and where messages here to be sent over a line not operated by the Department. The officials in charge of Telegraph offices receive very small pay, but are able to supplement this until their income become [sic] considerable by the indiscriminate setting of the contents of messages.
>
> Telegrams from the United Kingdom to Persia cost 2/8 per word, but from Persia to the United Kingdom 8.50 krans per word. Non official telegrams are subject to much delay and take as much as six days in transit. For inland telegrams the rate is 4 krans for the first 10 words and 8 shahis for each additional word.
>
> The excess of receipts over expenditure is considerable and the Telegraph Department forms a satisfactory source of revenues for the Persian Government.
>
> Source: AIR 20/663, pp. 141 b-c.

After the departure of the British in April 1921, there were no major problems any longer with the telegraph service.

In 1911, a telephone service was installed in Kermanshah city.[168] In 1921 there was a telephone line between Kermanshah and Hamadan, while the former also had a telephone exchange. In 1924, there were 121 telephone subscribers, who paid 20-25 *qrans*/month for their telephone connection; this number had increased to 502 in 1948.[169] As of 1935, there also was a line connecting Kermanshah with Naft-e Shah, "of one pair of 150 lbs. cadmium copper wire connected to trunk switchboards at Karmenshah and Naft-i-Shah. Also carries five intermediate telephones bridged across the lines."[170] A major problem was the theft of the copper wire in the 1940s (see Chapter Seven).

In January 1918, a rough landing-ground for aeroplanes was made, where on 16 January 1918, a couple of RE 8's landed, which caused much sensation in the city.[171] The small field was located at 18 km N.E. from the city north of the Kermanshah-Hamadan road and measured

167. AIR 20/663, pp. 141 a-b.

168. DCR 4994 (Kermanshah 1911-12), p. 7.

169. AIR 20/663; Hadow 1925, p. 32; Roberts 1948, p. 26. During the presence of British troops in Kermanshah the telephone office was in the British camp and the British controlled both directions; there was apparently no opposition against this. FO 248/1204 Kermanshah report no. 3, 11/06/1918 by Lt. Col. Kennion.

170. IOR/L/MIL/17/15/24, 'Military Report on The Anglo-Iranian Oil Company's (South Iranian) Oilfield Area', p. 33.

171. Hale n.d., p. 219. The RE-8 was a British two-seat bi-plane reconnaissance and bomber aircraft.

385 x 425 meters. As the soil was heavy it was not possible to land there after it had rained. By 1921 the landing strip was overgrown and required about four days of work to be fit again for landing.[172] Later the landing strip was hardened and extended, for on 21 April 1928, Junkers Weekly Airmail Service started its regular air service in Persia. The company also landed in Kermanshah on its flight from Tehran, Hamadan and Baghdad. However, Junkers discontinued its service, when the government did not renew its concession that expired at the end of February 1932.[173] In 1935, the Persian government began irregular flights to Kermanshah. There is no mention of a flight connection between Baghdad and Kermanshah. In fact, Gray, the British commercial counselor at that time, suggested only a car from Baghdad to Tehran. He further noted that there was no civil aviation at that time in Persia and that a service between Tehran and Baghdad was contemplated.[174] In March 1938, a regular air service between Baghdad and Tehran was opened, sponsored by the Persian government, operated by an airline called *Iranian State Airlines*. It carried, mail, passengers and freight once per week and called on Kermanshah on the outward and return flight.[175] A weekly mail and passenger air service Tehran and Kermanshah began on 6 April 1942. The runway was extended from 880 to 1500 m.[176] In 1948, there were only occasional diversions of flights to Kermanshah by a private Persian company, while the *Iranian State Airline* executed irregular service between the main cities.[177]

ELECTRICITY

In 1929, Harun Qasri (Harun Ilyahov and Co.) became the first producer of electricity in Kermanshah with an engine of 25 kW direct current, which he erected in the Chahar Bagh, on the northern side of the Friday Mosque. A short time thereafter Hajj Da'i erected a 30 kW alternate current plant at the Chahar Rah-e Ojaq. For the time being these two producers satisfied the small demand of the town. The Municipality told Harun Ilyahov to cover the northern part of town and Hajj Da'i's Lighting Company the southern part of the city. When Harun Qasri ceased operations, Hajj Da'i established a Lighting Company. In 1943, this Company operated two MAN engines of 375 H.P. that supplied the city's needs, but at a new location, viz. south of the city at Seh Rah Rafi'atiyeh.[178] Until 1954, electricity service was of poor quality and only available for a few hours in the evenings. In many parts of the city, the lights were on only

172. AIR 20/663, p. 22.

173. Mahrad 1997, p. 151; Ebtehaj 1932, p. 148; Lingeman 1930, pp. 36, 49. For Junker's flight schedule, see Appendix II.

174. Ellwell-Sutton 1941, p. 100; Gray 1938, pp. viii, 27.

175. *The Palestine Post*, Monday 28/03/1938, p. 5.

176. FO 371/31402, Kermanshah Diary April 1942.

177. Roberts 1948, p. 25.

178. Hamed and Habibi 1376, p. 96. According to Soltani 1381, vol. 1, p. 550, the first power company was named Harun Ilyahov and Co., which had a 1,800 kW engine to power a grain mill to make *ard-e qannadi*. It was erected in the Feyzabad quarter. In 1933 the Lighting Comp. was created by Abbas Hajj Da'i to provide light to the quarters, thus before Harun Qasri went out of business.

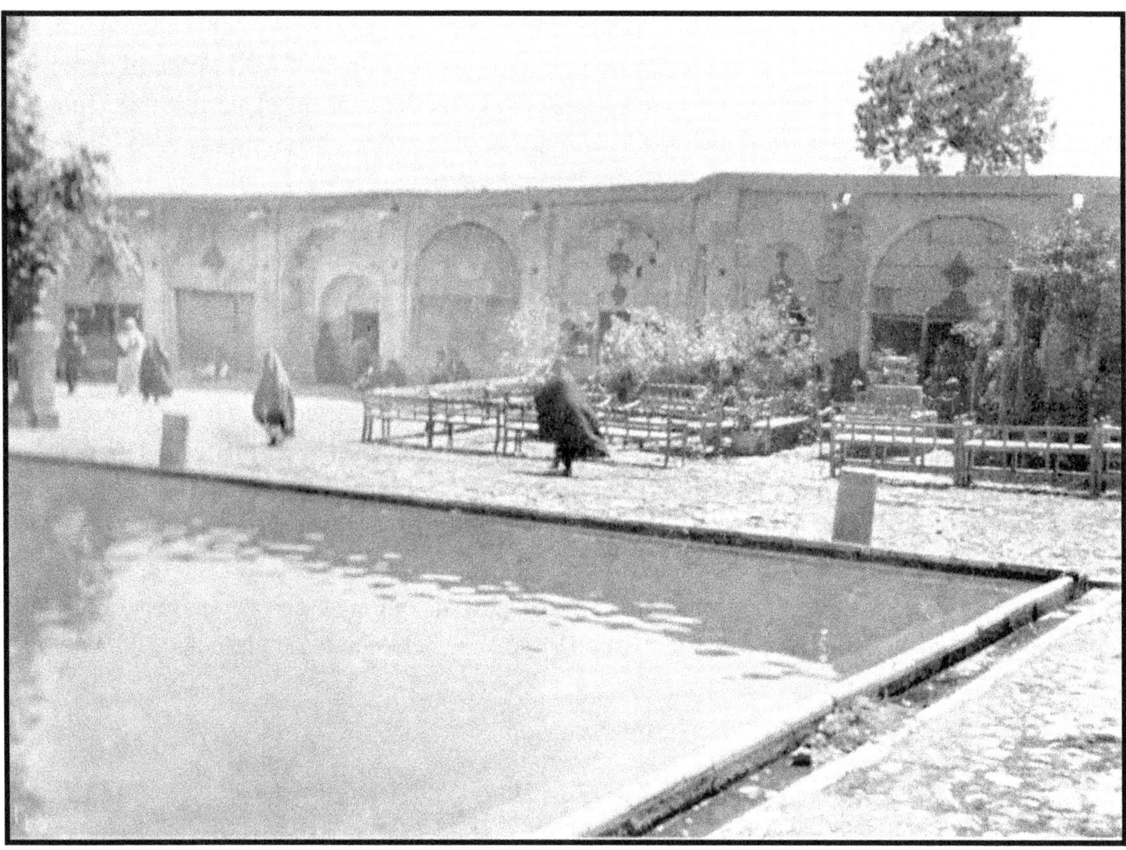

Fig. 2.24: Tea-house on the Meydan (1907).

certain nights of the week and off the rest of the time. But as of 1955, the electricity consumer had 24-hour service.[179]

AMUSEMENTS

There were no parks or other places to play. Children either played in the streets, in courtyards and, if they went to school, in the school yard.[180] People went to Bisotun or other parts for picnics etc. There was only one option for indoor sports, viz. the *zurkhaneh* such as that of Mortezaqoli Mirza.[181] In 1937, the city acquired its first sport playing field, a piece of land that the Municipality set aside for physical exercise, opposite the *Dabirestan-e Nezam*. It also levied a 3% impost to expand the field's facilities.[182]

179. RG 91-19-28, Frances Zoeckler to Board of Foreign Missions 08/02/1956.

180. For the kind of games played, see Floor 2012 and Soltani 1381, vol. 1, pp. 208-15, 220-22.

181. Lycklama 1873, vol. 3, p. 476; Blücher 1949, p. 75, 80. For sport and in particular wrestling activities, see Soltani 1381, vol. 1, pp. 216-19, 223-27, 228-38.

182. Soltani 1381, vol. 1, p. 556. For other amusements such as libraries, hunting and music, see Soltani 1381, vol. 1, pp. 208-15, 239042, 357-408

PHOTOGRAPHY

Three years after the invention of photography in 1839 this new technology was also used in Persia. It reached Kermanshah probably in the early 1860s. For in 1865, the Dutch traveler Lycklama à Nijeholt reported that prince Mortezaqoli Mirza Saram al-Dowleh had a photography laboratorium in that city.[183] In 1867, he made very good photos of Wills and Pierson, the IETD agent in Kermanshah.[184] Saram al-Dowleh did not remain the only photographer, for Mirza Mobin Khoshdel Kermanshahi, who died in 1906, as well as Sayyed Shams al-Din Dowlatabadi Badi' al-Sanaye' also made photographs. Other photographers, who worked in the second decade of the twentieth century, were Sani' al-Sadat 'Akkas and Asadollah Kermanshahi. Later they were joined by Yunanan 'Akkas.[185]

CINEMA

In December 1920, two unnamed enterprising Persians began operating a small cinema.[186] In 1931, Mosavver al-Dowleh received permission to start a cinema, called *Foruhar* at Kh. Shah Bakhti North; it had its own electric engin. In 1936, it closed because Mosavver al-Dowleh left to Europe and he had no manager to replace him. In 1933, Hedayatollah Palizi (Vakil al-Dowleh III) opened a cinema with a summer and winter salon in one of his own buildings adjacent to the new Kh. Shahpur, which also had its own power source. At first, it only showed silent movies, thereafter talking ones until 1955. In 1941, Hasan 'Ali Khan A'zam Sanjabi opened the cinema *Homa*, which later was renamed *Iran*.[187] As of 1942, a British cinema van showed newsreels and films, both in Kermanshah and smaller rural towns. In 1944, the British showed 'Mrs. Miniver.' People did not consider the connection between successive power outages in January 1945 and the fact that one of the two cinemas had a generator, owned by the owner of the power supply company, unlike its unfortunate competitor, who depended on the city's power supply, a strange coincidence.[188]

---

183. Lycklama 1873, vol. 3, p. 479.
184. Wills 1893, p. 116.
185. Soltani 1381, vol. 1. p. 530.
186. FO 248/1293, Report Kermanshah, no. 11, up to 10 December 1920.
187. Soltani 1381, vol. 1, pp. 551-52 (with a list of cinemas established after 1941).
188. FO 371/45400, Monthly Diary January 1945.

RADIO

In 1917, the British had an Anzac wireless station at Kermanshah, which allowed them "to get Reuter's daily news hot from Basra." However, the unit left on 1 January 1918, thus Kermanshah returned to radio silence until 11 January, when an Australian wireless party came, replacing the Russian wireless, which they had dismantled on 8 January.[189] However, it was only in 1958 that the first public radio station was established in Kermanshah.[190]

STORY TELLING (*NAQQALI*)

In Kermanshah there was a kind of performers who were engaged in entertaining acts that were called *shamurti*. Usually, such an entertainer performed on the outskirts of town and spread his carpet there.[191] Among the Kurds there were so-called *goranibech*s, reciters of songs, who moved from house to house chanting their poems; during the day they did their normal job and in the evening they became artists.[192] Jewish storytellers were much in demand in Kurdistan.[193] According to Sabar, "The general theme of the tale may well be familiar to the audience, but a skillful teller can still captivate his listeners with it again and again. The tales vary in length from an hour's telling to installments filling several long winter nights."[194] It is of interest to note here that *shahnameh-khvani* and knowledge of the epic was very popular and strong among the Kermanshah Kurds, who played an important military role in guarding the border and being engaged in other warlike exploits. Each tribal unit had their own *shahnameh-khvan*s, who were much respected in tribal assemblies. Many verses were therefore adapted for popular consumption and translated into Kurdish.[195]

THEATER

Various forms of theater existed in Persia that also were performed in Kermanshah. Apart from slap-stick theater such as *baqqal-bazi* and *ru-howzi* as well as open-air festivals such as *mirmiran* and *koseh-geldi*, there was religious theater (*ta'ziyeh*).[196] From the beginning of the twentieth

---

189. Hale 1920, pp. 210, 216, 219; The Anzac operated a Russian wireless station. Dunsterville 1932, p. 22. The Germans in Kermanshah had no radio station in 1916. Blücher 1949, p. 80.

190. Soltani 1381, vol. 1, p. 546.

191. Soltani 1381, vol. 1, p. 352.

192. Aubin 1907, pp. 87, 91-92.

193. Sabar 1982, p. xxxvii

194. Sabar 1982, pp. xxxvii-xxxviii.

195. Soltani 1381, vol. 1, p. 349. For an overview and discussion of the various forms expression of popular theatrical and story-telling, see Rashidirostami 2018.

196. Abbasi and Badi`i 1372, p. 73; Rashidirostami 2018.

century these traditional forms of theatrical performance received competition from modern European-type theater.

In Kermanshah, the first modern play was performed through the good offices of 'Ali Khan Zahir al-Dowleh when he was its governor in 1907. The proceeds were about 2,000 *tumans*, which were given to the Scientific Islamic School (*madraseh-ye 'elmiyyeh-ye eslamiyeh*).[197] There is no news about theater in Kermanshah for another decade until October/November 1917, when the British bank official Hale, who had just been transferred from Berjand to Kermanshah attended a theatrical performance in his new posting. He wrote:

> Also, I have been to a Persian play-a product of modernity brought out by the democrats in aid of some educational scheme. One or two of the actors had come from Teheran, but the rest were locally-produced amateurs, including a couple of Chaldeans. The play commenced about nine o'clock and went on till after midnight. It was a representation of life in a provincial town some years back, centring round a pleasure-loving, stupid, ignorant, idle and thoughtlessly tyrannical governor and his rapacious and hypocritical satellites, with a sidelight on the superstitious credulity of a family of oppressed villagers, the greed of the tax-collector, and the ruthlessness of an unfeeling village headman. The whole thing was a satire on the old types and manners and the old system, which persists largely in the present day: it was exaggerated and overdone, perhaps, but it contained many telling points, and was remarkably well acted.[198]

In 1930, Mir Seyf al-Din Kermanshahi founded the Kermanshahi Drama Studio (*Estudiyu-ye Deram-e Kermanshahi*). He had learned the theater trade, in particular that of making decors, in Moscow, Tiflis and Baku. After the death of his wife Boyuk Khan Nakhjevani invited him to Tabriz where he worked for the "Sun and Lion Theater." Then he was hired by *Jame'eh-ye Barbod* and after some time he worked for *Nakisa* and other theater groups in Tehran. Finally, he began to work as an independent. Kermanshahi introduced the use of the term "studio" in Persia and also the making of attractive professional decors. The "Studio" worked among others with Mohammad 'Ali Soltani, Rahim Namvar, 'Ali Adhari, and the actresses Iran Daftari, Helen and Maryam Nuri and Niktaj Sabri. The group went out of business due to a variety of other reasons such as financial, artistic, organizational, location and not to forget the competition. For example, when "Studio" staged its play *Leyla and Majnun* in secret its competitors were rehearsing the same play at the same time. Although probably unrelated to this event, Kermanshahi committed suicide in 1932.[199]

Another name connected with the beginning of theater performances in Kermanshah is that of Mir Seyf al-Din. He returned to Tabriz from Tiflis in 1930. He then moved to Tehran where

---

197. Soltani 1381, vol. 1, p. 353.

198. Hale 1920, p. 210 (the Russians also organized theatrical performances at their hospital to entertain the soldiers). However, Blücher 1949, p. 80 states that in 1916 there was no theater at all, most likely referring to the period when the city was under Turkish-German control. There were some theatrical performances by schools to raise money, see above.

199. Osku'i 1992, pp. 146-52; Floor 1396, p. 288.

he came into contact with the first attempts of theater. There he learnt the trade and then put on a performance of "Leyla and Majnun" and later one of "Khosrow and Shirin" with Daryabegi and Ms. Moluk Zarrabi. Mir Seyf al-Din then decided to work on his own and opened his own theater. He did various plays such as "Yusef and Zoleykha," "Mashhadi 'Abbas," and "'Aziz and 'Azizeh" which had professional decors. On July 26, 1933 he performed "*Arshin Mallalal*" that had been translated at his request. He died two days later; he had just been told by the government either to abandon theater or to leave Persia.

However, Mir Seyf al-Din was not the first to organize a theater in Kermanshah, but a group known as *Hey'at-e Te'atral-e Aramaneh* led by Mirza Taqi Khan. They performed at the opening of the first teachers training school in Kermanshah. The school's hall also served for later performances. They also wrote pieces and taught acting to those interested. The group became serious when GholamReza Parsa took over its management. One of the plays that he put on was "Napoleon." The group continued to perform until 1941. In 1944 they started to rehearse for "The doctor in spite of himself" and later also staged plays such as "The Merchant of Venice." Parsa also used Armenian women for female roles for the first time in Kermanshah. There also were other groups that put on performances in the 1940s.[200]

In 1943, Col. Shahrokhshahi, the commander of the Kermanshah Brigade periodically put on variety shows (music, comical sketches, etc) in the officers club. On one occasion in January 1944, "a crude, but amusing burlesque of a grain hoarder, seeing making up black market books of account was staged. He looked like Haji Lubiya whose activities to corner the beans market were reported in the past." People loved it and even the British consul was amused.[201] Not only the military, but also schools staged theatrical performances such as in February 1944. This was on the occasion of the celebration of the foundation of Tehran University at the *Shahpur* school, when the guests were presented with a theatrical performance from a *Shahnameh* episode.[202] In February 1947, there was a theater show to celebrate the return of some troops from Kurdistan.[203]

STANDARD OF LIVING

There was little change in the diet of Persians until recent times. At least one type of flat bread was always part of every meal. For bread was the major staple, accompanied by vegetables, potherbs, fruit, yoghurt, nuts with, sometimes, small amounts of rice and cheese plus sweetmeats as an occasional special treat. Meat was a luxury few could afford. The variety in the diet was further limited by the seasonal availability of certain products due to limited methods of preservation. There were also differences between rich and poor consumers, and to a lesser degree

200. Soltani 1381, vol. 1, pp. 353-54. See further Khalaj, Mansur. *Tarikhcheh-ye Namayesh dar Kermanshah* (Tehran, 1364/1985), which I was unable to obtain and read.
201. FO 371/40177, Kermanshah Diary January 1944.
202. FO 371/40177, Kermanshah Diary February 1944.
203. FO 371/45488 Keimanshah Diary February 1947.

between urban and rural consumers. Caloric intake was less during winter, and was at its lowest level by early summer, i.e. just prior to the harvest.[204]

When the harvest was good, landowners usually did not form a bread ring to create an artificial grain shortage in urban areas, and when the governor was not too oppressive, generally speaking food was cheap.[205] In the early 1830s, a British traveler observed that in the bazaar goods were weighed using rough stones on the scales. The kebab shop was constantly busy and employed three persons. According to him, two or three kebabs with bread was quite a sufficient meal for a moderate person; he bought four skewers of *kebab-e kubideh*, which cost 3.5 pence plus half a penny for the bread in which they were wrapped. At a bakery he bought more bread for 1 penny. Thus, for less than 6 pennies two persons had a very pleasant and sufficient meal, with plenty of bread and much fruit, a fact that compared favorably with the situation in Great Britain.[206] In 1840, Teule was struck by the general aspect of poverty of the town's population more so than in other Persian cities. Although life necessities were cheap, anything imported was expensive.[207] However, when a bad governor ruled the province life could become very bad indeed. This was the situation under Emir Mohebb 'Ali Khan (1844-48), who so oppressed the inhabitants of the province that General Ferrier, who stayed for some time in Kermanshah, was totally taken aback. Ferrier had seen other examples of oppression and thus, he remarked that if Mohebb 'Ali Khan only would have taken 2 or 3 times more than was normal from the inhabitants they would have been able to cope. However, "he has completely stripped them. [...] the peasantry have hardly bread to eat, and when they complain of their grievances to Court and endeavour to obtain justice, they are treated as rebels, condemned to be bastinadoed, and Mohib remains governor." The translator of Ferrier's book, who himself had been in 1846 in Kermanshah, had seen that the governor "had coolly seized what every man possessed, and had driven away their flocks and herds to his own estates at Makoo near Ararat. The people were picking grass in the fields to eat, and the children were naked and emaciated, except the stomach which was unnaturally swollen. In one street I passed through in the town [of Kermanshah], the people were lying on each side at the last gasp of death from starvation. I shall never forget one whole family, father, mother, and several children, lying together in a heap, unable to move from inanition."[208]

The situation reverted to normal during Naser al-Din Shah's reign when Eskandar Khan Sardar Devallu (1849-52) and Emamqoli Mirza Emad-al-Dowleh (1852-75) were governor. Referring to the situation around 1870, the British physician Wills wrote that "the people were well fed and well clothed." Also, that Kermanshah was the cheapest place in Persia; bread cost 2 p./7 lbs; mutton 14 p./7 lbs or 2.p./lb.[209] In 1880, Hajj Sayyah noted that bread was cheap in Kermanshah.[210] However, these prices and that situation of plenty only existed in good years. In early April 1890, people began worrying when spring rains seemed insufficient. As a result,

---

204. For more information, see Floor 2015, chapter 8.
205. On the bread supply situation in Persia in general and on bread rings in particular, see Floor 2015 chapter 9.
206. A Correspondent 1835 b, p. 439.
207. Teule 1842, vol. 2, p. 482.
208. Ferrier 1856, pp. 25-26.
209. Wills 1893, p. 109, 112.
210. Sayyah 1346, p. 233.

the price of wheat rose to over 3 *tumans* 3,000 dinars/*kharvar* and was unobtainable. Everybody was waiting for better rains, which fortunately happened on 29 April. Wheat was then sold at 2 *tumans* 6,000/*kharvar* and barley at 17,000 *tumans*/*kharvar* and its price continued to drop. Despite the good harvest, bakers sold inedible bad bread, a practice used all over Persia to drive up the price of good bread. In reaction, the governor took their chief to task.[211] In October 1896, when food prices were still high the price of charcoal rose significantly, due to the existence of a charcoal ring that artificially drove up its price. The governor had those involved arrested and the price immediately dropped to a normal level.[212] In 1898, food prices rose quickly and in March long lines were seen in front of the bakeries and the threat of public disturbances was real. During the year the situation did not improve, so that in November 1898 Eqbal al-Dowleh, to regulate the bread situation, convened a meeting of olama, notables, and trades people. It was decided that for a period of 10 months every day 70 *kharvar*s of wheat would be supplied to the bakers (*khabbaz-khaneh*). Landlords would receive 8 *tuman*s per *kharvar*, while wheat from state lands would be sold at 6 *tumans*. Bakers had to sell bread at 750 dinars per *man* of 3 kg; the entire affair was operated under the supervision of Mohtasham al-Dowleh.[213] To show that the government cared about people's welfare the deputy-governor in May 1902 ordered the price of bread to be brought down from 4 *man* per 1 *qran* to 5 *man* per 1 *qran*. Of course, no information is given how the bakers reacted to this 20% loss of income, who, usually reduced the quality and/or weight of bread.[214]

Table 2.3: Prices of life necessities in 1890-1902

Wheat	Barley	Rice	Bread	Rowghan	Meat	Year
2 T	1 T 6000 d	-	250 d	8500 d	2000 d 5 *shahis*	08/1902
1 T 3000 d	11000 d	-	1 *qran 4 man*	16000 d	-	06/1902
2 T	1 T 5000 d	2000 d	250 d	6000 d	1600 d	10/1901
2 T	14000 d	2000 d 5 *shahis*	1 *qran 4 man*	5500 d	1650 d	07/1901
3 T	18000 d	-	1 *shahi*	8000 d	-	05/1901
4 T	3 T 2000 d	2400 d	400 d	6000 d	2500 d	01/1901
4 T 5000 d	3 T 4000 d	2250 d	450 d	7000 d	2000 d	11/1900
4 T 6000 d	3 T 6000 d	2000 d	650 d	5000 d	2000 d	10/1900
7 T 5000 d	5 T	-	-	-	-	12/1899
8 T	4 T 5000 d	1500 d	800 d	5000 d	1800 d	07/1898
7 T	-	-	700 d	-	-	03/1898
9 T	8 T	-	-	-	-	01/1899

211. Abbasi and Badi`i 1372, pp. 71-73. In early 1892, Ziya al-Dowleh intervened when he believed that bakers were selling bread at too high prices (*geran-forushi*). *Ruznameh-ye Iran* 1375, vol. 4, p. 3088 (no. 767; 26/02/1892). Prices were also high because of the loss in value of the Persian currency, which hit the lower classes in particular, see Matthee, Floor, and Clawson 2013, pp. 194-99.

212. *Ruznameh-ye Iran* 1375, vol. 5, p. 3623 (no. 900; 05/12/1896).

213. *Ruznameh-ye Iran* 1375, vol. 5, pp. 3844 (no. 955; 23/01/1898), 3811 (no. 947; 15/11/1898).

214. *Ruznameh-ye Iran* 1375, vol. 5, pp. 4084 (no. 1105; 28/06/1902). On bakers' behavior to government intervention in general, see Floor 2015.

-	-	-	600 d	-	1600 d	08/1898
-	-	1500 d	400 d	8000 d	3000 d	03/1898
3 T	2 T	-	-	-	-	11/1897
5 T	4 T 5000 d	-	500 d	9000 d	4000 d	04/1897
-	-	-	500 d	-	2000 d	01/1897
1 T 8000 d	-	-	1 shahi	-	2000 d	12/1896
4 T 8,000 d	4 T	1750 d	450 d	9000 d	1500 d	09/1896
2 T	1 T 2500 d	-	-	5000 d	1250 d	01/1894
2 T	-	30 *shahis*	-	14000 d	-	11/1890

T = *tuman*; d = dinar; 1 *qran* = 1,000 dinar; 1 *shahi* = 200 dinars.

Wheat and barley prices are per *kharvar* of 300 kg; all other items are per *man-e Tabriz* or 3 kg.

Source: *Ruznameh-ye Iran* 1375, vol. 4, pp. 2948, 3283; vol. 5, pp. 3598, 3623, 3640, 3664, 3724, 3747, 3783, 3787, 3844, 3868, 3895, 3950, 3955, 3971, 3999,4016, 4036, 4084, 4095.

Although the harvest of 1903 and 1904 had been bad, the one of 1905 also was a poor one; the third year in a row. Almost all landowners were withholding stocks hoping for higher prices. The barley harvest was a failure, while the wheat harvest yielded less than average. In April 1905, many poor people from outside the city flocked to the town in search of food. The poor were so desperate that they drank the blood of sheep that were slaughtered. Therefore, on 3 May a meeting was held at the home of the Imam Jom'eh, one of the largest landowners, to organize a collection of food supplies for the poor. It was decided that each month 60 *kharvar* (18,000 kg) of wheat would be given by the notables and one bakery would be opened, where the poor could get bread. In July 1905, the gardens near Kermanshah were attacked by locusts and the damage was terrible. "All fruit trees are bare and ground crops all destroyed," on which people lived for 3 months per year. The price of food rose gradually, and led to an increase of prices of all commodities, which had downward effect on trade.[215] According to Mo'tamadi, Farmanfarma imported wheat from outlying districts to resolve the bread situation. Wheat was at that time 4 *qrans*/*man* and was sold by him to the bakers. As a result, the wheat price did not exceed 1 *qran* for 2 *man* and 10 *shahis*/*man*. At that time many Kurds came to town, many of whom were fed in a few mosques. As they were able-bodied men, Farmanfarma began a food-for-work program to make a road from the Feyzabad gate to the Qarasu; he also used them to plant trees along that road, which was henceforth called the Khiyaban-e Farmanfarma.[216] Mo'tamadi not only exaggerated the role of Farmanfarma, but he omitted to mention that the food scarcity was aggravated, if not caused, by a bread ring run by Farmanfarma.[217] Mirza Esma'il (Baqer), an employee of the IBP (*Bank-e Englis*), was involved with Farfarmanfarma's bread corner in 1905 together with the notorious Mo'aven al-Ra'aya, who all made large profits from people's misery. There were small riots in town and murders outside were frequent. Because Mirza Esma'il acted under the guise of being an employee of the IBP, when people rioted they, on one occasion, demonstrated against the Bank and threw not very seriously stones at Mr. Rabino, the Bank's

215. Administration Report 1905-06, p. 46; Political Diaries 1, pp. 107, 139, 157.
216. Soltani 1386, p. 147.
217. Political Diaries vol. 1, p. 157.

local manager, and the matter was easily settled by the deputy-governor.[218] One of those riots was caused by an altercation between a servant of Mo'in al-Ra'aya and one of Aqa Rahim on 31 May 1905. As the two men were bitter rivals, both rallied their supporters to have a "spontaneous" demonstration turned into a riot complete with shooting and closed bazaars. The deputy-governor urged the Imam Jom'eh and other olama to put an end to it, but the gentlemen could not agree on a common action.[219] Mo'tamadi also is too optimistic about the relief measure agreed upon in May, which clearly was inadequate, if it worked at all, because around 20 August 1905, the Imam Jom'eh of Kermanshah, when walking through streets, was threatened with death if the price of wheat was not soon reduced. Therefore, he discussed the death threat with the deputy-governor and proposed to force landowners to send supplies to the city so that the price of bread would come down to 10 *shahi*s per 3 kg, or 5 *tuman*s/*kharvar*. At that time, wheat was sold at 6 *tuman*s and rising. Barley was also expensive at 6-7 *tuman*s/*kharvar* and was expected to rise to 10 *tuman*s, due to hoarding.[220]

On 30 August 1905, the deputy-governor called a meeting of notables, who decided to operate 60 bakeries, each one would receive 150 *man* of wheat (2,700 *kharvar*/month). After mid-September wheat was sold at 5 *tuman*s/*kharvar* and bread at 10 *shahi*s/*man*. It was also decided that the official fiscal conversion rate (*tas'ir*) of taxes paid in kind would remain fixed at that rate for one year.[221] However, the British consul reported a different course of events. In early September 1905, the Imam Jom'eh held a meeting to urge landlords to sell part of their stock in the bazaar at a fixed rate of 50 *qran*s/*kharvar*. The grain owners refused to do so as long as Farmanfarma, the governor, a major and very wealthy and greedy landowner, continued hoarding his stocks in the hope of higher prices in winter. After mid-September 1905, the landowners met again and decided that wheat owners should sell stock to bakers at 65 *qran*s/*kharvar* and that bakers be forced to sell bread at 6 *qran*s/*man* of 2.9 kg. The British consul observed: "If they do it will be good, else there will be famine."[222]

Although there was no famine, the plan was not well executed. When Farmanfarma was sent to Kerman as governor at the end of December 1905 again some small troubles broke out in Kermanshah, about which he did nothing. Bread in town was so bad that the foreign consuls complained to the governor, who ordered to cut off the ears of two bakers and give them the bastinado. This had little effect and bread remained bitter so that the men of the consular escort refused to eat it. The continued high cost of bread in December coincided with a severe cold of 22 degrees in town, when people needed more sustenance. It even happened that two pilgrims froze to death in their *kavajehs*.[223] Farmanfarma left richer than when he had arrived, because he not only benefited from the bread situation, but he also bought many properties in Kangarvar, Sonqor and Dinavar during his governorship from the province's revenues.[224]

---

218. Administration Report 1905-06, p. 46; FO 248/879, Crossle to Grant-Duff, Tehran, 11/08/1906.
219. Soltani 1381, vol. 3, p. 479.
220. Political Diaries vol. 1, p. 157.
221. Hamadani 1354, pp. 230, 233.
222. Political Diaries vol. 1, p. 179.
223. Political Diaries vol. 1, p. 269.
224. Soltani 1386, p. 148.

In January 1906, the price of bread rose and was 1.5 *qrans/man* of 2.9 kg.[225] Although there was much rain in May 1906 and a bumper harvest was expected, the harvest was a disappointing one and the grain of poor quality. As a result, the bread price remained high. This caused turmoil in the city and one mullah preached against the IBP and the Customs as the cause of the trouble. The governor pacified the populace and had grain brought in from the villages. However, whereas in 1905 the price of wheat had been 9-10 *tumans/kharvar*, in August 1906 it was 12 *tumans* and it was expected to further rise in winter. Also, the price of all other foodstuffs had risen proportionally. The *beglarbegi*, the chief of bakers, had been instructed by the governor to deal with the problem. He issued an order that henceforth bread should be sold at 1 *qran* 3-4 *shahis/man*, while the bakers bought their wheat at 1 *qran* 4 *shahis/man*. Consequently, "bread is made of wheat mixed with bran, straw and even dirt."[226] In 1907, there was great scarcity in town and grain and bread prices rose very high.[227] Dr. Stead observed that in 1907, despite a good harvest and the best water supply since years, people were living from hand to mouth. "Everywhere people are depressed and discouraged."[228] According to Mo'tamadi, in March 1907, the daily expense of a family of four did not exceed 2 *qrans*/day. Because bread was 1 *qran* for 4 *man*; meat was 1 *qran* and 1 *'abbasi* per *man* and *rowghan* was 4 *qrans/man*; other articles also were cheap.[229] However, the year 1907/08 had been exceptionally dry, only 18 inches of rains fell, while the usually rushing streams till the end of June were now dry. Fortunately, the prospects for 1908 were good, because of ample rains. The crops were very good and the price of wheat of 8 *tumans* before the harvest dropped to 35 *qrans* per *kharvar* thereafter. In the Guran district wheat even cost 20 *qrans* per *kharvar*, but it was too expensive to bring it to Kermanshah. The price of barley also fell, viz. to 14 *qrans/kharvar*.[230] There was little snow in the winter of 1907/08. As a result, many springs ran dry, but despite this the crops did well. The price of barley fell to 15 *qrans* per 650 lbs and wheat to 30 *qrans*; chopped straw was sold at 10 *qrans*. Although the quantity of ice stored was lower than normal, the proximity of permanent show in the mountains compensated for this loss, so that the price of ice only rose a little.[231] The German traveler Grothe recorded in 1910 that 12 flat breads cost for 1 *qran*, while roasted yellow beets cost 1 *shahi*.[232]

Table 2.4 suggests that there was a slight increase in the price of wheat during the first decade of the twentieth century. At the lower end, at harvest time, the price tended to be around 30 *qrans* when the harvest was good, but later in the year it rose to 50 *qrans*. In the years 1912-13 the price of wheat normally was 5-10 *tumans* or 50-100 *qrans* per 650 lbs, but in 1913 it rose to 37 *tumans* or 370 *qrans/kharvar*, and even higher in Hamadan. Although there was a good

225. Political Diaries 1, p. 279.

226. Political Diaries vol. 1, p. 370; FO 248/879, Crossle to Grant-Duff, Tehran, 11/08/1906; Idem, Crossle to Tehran 23/08/1906; Idem, Crossle to Tehran 05/09/1906.

227. Political Diaries 1, p. 97.

228. Stead 1908, p. 18.

229. Soltani 1386, p. 151.

230. Administration Report 1907-08, pp. 62-63.

231. Administration Report 1908, p. 46.

232. Grothe 1910, p. 91.

crop in that year, the price of wheat sky-rocketed because much of the crop was destroyed by raiders and passing troops (see below chapter seven).

Table 2.4: Prices of life necessities in select years (*qrans/kharvar*)

Product	April 1890	1909	1911	1913
Wheat	30.3	35-50	30-50	50-100
Barley	20.6	14-25	-	
Straw	-	10-20	-	

Source: `Abbasi and Badi`i 1372, p. 71-73; DCR 4365 (1908-09), p. 6; DCR 4766, p. 8 (1910-11); DCR 5204 (1912-13), p. 6.

Despite the slight rise of the price of food and the very high prices in times of scarcity, natural or artificial, the level of wages for unskilled labor, i.e. for the majority of the urban labor pool in Kermanshah did not rise at all, as shown in Table 2.5.

Table 2.5: Daily wages for unskilled labor (1909-12), according to season (in *qrans*)

1909-10	1910-11	1911-12	1912-13
1-1.5	1-1.5	1-1.5	1-1.5

Source: DCR 4559, p. 7; DCR 4766, p. 7; DCR 4994, p. 7; DCR 5204, p. 5.

In this respect the situation of Kermanshah was not atypical for the situation in other cities and towns in Persia, be it that the province of Kermanshah usually had a significant grain surplus (see Chapter 5). In January 1913, the price of wheat rose from 20 to 23 *tumans*/*kharvar*; barley to 20 *tumans*. Bread cost 2 *qrans* per *man* for full weight; 1.75 *qrans* for short weight. Kurdish rice cost 5 *qrans*/*man* and Sadri (Rasht) rice 10 *qrans*/*man*.[233] A committee of *mojtaheds* and notables was formed to spend the collected money among the poor. They reported having sent home 350 strangers and having fed some 800 daily. Some were employed in roadwork, those unable to work were kept in a rented caravanserai and were fed twice per day. The committee asked for more subscriptions.[234] In the third week of January 1913, there was only two months of grain in store. There was grain in the villages to the north at Mian Darband, but this could not be transported for fear of robbery by the Pairawands. Farmanfarma, the governor, appointed the son of Hajji Hasan Kalantar to see to it that no grain was stored in the city. Therefore, he checked shopkeepers and others who had grain for their own use, and they paid him a fine if they had some. However, although the bread situation was worsening, it was no use complaining, because Farmanfarma took no action.[235]

233. FO 248/1073, Kermanshah Diary no. 1, ending 2 January 1913.
234. FO 248/1073, Kermanshah Diary no. 15, ending 10 January 1913.
235. FO 248/1073, Kermanshah Diary no. 4, ending 23 January 1913; Political Diaries vol. 5, p. 38.

Export of grain from Turkey was banned in March 1913 and there was almost a famine on the Persian border.[236] In March-April 1913, scarcity in Kermanshah continued; the absence of rains was worrisome. Straw at 1 *qran/man* was almost unobtainable. Wheat cost 32 *tumans/ kharvar*. The government supplied some of the bakers with a small amount of grain daily, while other bakers had to buy their grain in the market. The official price of bread was 2 *qrans/man*, but the bakers sold bread at short weight. Also, bread was bad as it was made of uncleaned wheat. "It was reported from Kurdistan that grain had fallen from heaven and the same substance has been found in waste stony ground at Kermanshah. It is probably of the nature of a truffle but very dry. It is ground and mixed with flour to make bread. The Governor, with subscriptions collected, is sending away those of the destitute who do not belong to the town. They receive some cash and an order on the Governor of Kangawar or Sungur for a further grant and are forwarded to these places. Of the local destitute, a number is kept and fed in a caravanserai."[237] People were very encouraged when it started to rain on 1-2 April 1913. Not only people were suffering so were their animals, because there was no straw in the villages, and animals were fed on roots of herbs. [238]

As a result, a large number of rural people came to Kermanshah in search of food. In reaction, a Poor Fund Committe (*Hey'at-e e'anat-e foqara-ye Kermanshah*) was formed in March 1913 under the presidency of Farfamanfarma. The Imperial Bank of Persia subscribed 100 *tumans*, the Russian consul 50 *tumans*, but the British consul did not contribute as his Minister saw no reason to do so. However, if McDouall considered it necessary to do so, he would give 50 *tumans*, on condition that the gift would be in McDouall's name.[239]

The governor used the monies collected by the Poor Fund to send those poor who were not city inhabitants away with some money and an order on the governors of Sonqor or Kangavar for a further grant. A number of the local poor were kept and housed in a caravanserai.[240] The governor banned the export of grain from the city, while the villagers who had no grain ate acorns.[241] The price of wheat fell from 32 to 26 *tumans* and barley to 33 *tumans* per *kharvar* of 650 lbs. By the end of April barley was sold at 15 *tumans*, but the price of wheat had not further dropped, although wheat had been brought into the city either by the governor or the Customs to prevent famine. Except for wheat, the downward trend of prices continued, because of the good rains. By end May 1913, the price of wheat was still at 32 *tumans* and barley at 25 *tumans*, despite the fact that in the plains the price of wheat had fallen. It was said that Farmanfarma prevented grain from coming from Qasr-e Shirin, because he had still much grain in storage. Fortunately, in the first week on June 1913 the price of grain was falling.[242] This may have been

---

236. Political Diaries vol. 5, p. 69.
237. Political Diaries vol. 5, p. 103.
238. FO 248/1073, Kermanshah Diary no. 14, ending 3 April 1913.
239. FO 248/1073, enclosure in McDouall to Tehran, 24/06/1913.
240. FO 248/1073, Kermanshah Diary no. 13, ending 27/03/1913. See also next page. The grain fallen from heaven probably was taranjabin (Lecanora esculenta), see Floor 2015, p. 27.
241. FO 248/1073, Kermanshah Diary no. 15, ending 10/04/1913.
242. FO 248/1073, Kermanshah Diary no. 17, ending 24/04/1913; Idem, Kermanshah Diary no. 18, ending 01/05/1913; Idem, Kermanshah Diary no. 19, ending 08/05/1913; Idem, Kermanshah Diary no. 22, ending 29/05/1913; Idem, Kermanshah Diary no. 23, ending 05/06/1913.

due to the following event. At the end of May 1913, grain of a white substance that tasted like maize (*Leconora Esculante* or manna) profusely fell from the skies in the city's environs. People believed that this was a gift of God given the high prices of food.[243] At the beginning of July 1913, the price of wheat was 10 *tumans* and barley 8 *tumans*, as a result of grain coming into the city. The price of bread was 1.5 *qran/man*.[244] Shortly thereafter, Farmanfarma banned the sale of grain to others than bakers and bread was then at 1.20 *qrans/man*.[245] In early August 1913, Farmanfarma gave orders that all wheat brought into the city had to be taken to the wheat market for sale to the bakers and not to homes of the owners. As a result, less wheat was arriving and it was said that this order had as objective to keep the price of grain high, which at that time was 8 *tumans/kharvar*.[246] The price of wheat gradually rose to 15 *tumans* and no wheat was coming in. The authorities wanted to compel each landowner to send part of his crop for the bakers, but as the sale of wheat was not free they were afraid of bringing it for sale. It was also said that Farmanfarma was secretly buying wheat and storing it in the villages, expecting the price to rise to famine levels, although the harvest was very good.[247] In mid-October 1913, the price of wheat remained at 15 *tumans*, but supplies were plentiful and therefore, there was no anxiety.[248] By month's end bread was plentiful, wheat was at 14 *tumans*, at which price there were no buyers. The fall in price was attributed to Farmanfarma's absence in Harsin.[249]

In October 1914 there was a drought in the province and therefore, bread was expensive. However, Farmanfarma sent men to the outlying districts to get wheat. Thus scarcity of bread was prevented. As a result, wheat, although rationed, was abundant and half of the bakeries baked all night.[250] In February 1915, the price of grain was falling. Wheat was 25-30 *tumans/kharvar* and barley 18-22 *tumans*. Bakers were forced to buy part of the grain requirements from the Revenue Administration at 4 *tumans/kharvar*.[251] Thereafter, the situation did not improve, because of the fighting that took place between Ottoman and Russian forces from December 1915 to March 1917 as well the destruction that the fighting had caused to the people, their land and animals.

The troubled condition in and around Kermanshah at the end of 1917 was not solely due to the despoliation of the province by Turks and Russians, a weak government and internal political dissent, but mostly because of famine conditions that were experienced in much of Persia and, in fact, in the entire Middle East. The worst conditions prevailed in western Persia, in particular in Tabriz, Ormiyeh, Salmas, Khoy, Hamadan and Kermanshah, due to the fact that in addition to famine conditions the people of that area also suffered from what is nowadays euphemistically

243. *The Sentinel*, Friday 18/07/1913, p. 12. In Kurdistan some kind of grain fell from heaven and the same occurred in Kermanshah. "It is probably of the nature of a truffle, but very dry. It is ground and mixed with flour to make bread." FO 248/1073, Kermanshah Diary no. 13, ending 27/03/1913. The grain fallen from heaven probably was *taranjabin* (Lecanora esculenta), see Floor 2015, p. 27.

244. FO 248/1073, Kermanshah Diary no. 27, ending 03/07/1913.

245. FO 248/1073, Kermanshah Diary no. 28, ending 10/07/1913.

246. FO 248/1073, Kermanshah Diary no. 32, ending 07/08/1913.

247. FO 248/1073, Kermanshah Diary no. 38, ending 18/09/1913.

248. FO 248/1073, Kermanshah Diary no. 42, ending 16/10/1913.

249. FO 248/1073, Kermanshah Diary no. 44, ending 30/10/1913.

250. Soltani 1986, pp. 197-98.

251. FO 248/1112, Kermanshah Diary 11/02/1915.

Fig. 2.25: People waiting for food during the famine of 1918.

called 'collateral damage' from the warfare between Ottoman and Russian troops.[252] For at least three years (1915-18), agriculture in the fertile and productive Mahidasht and Kerend plains had been in abeyance, due to the war, and the seed grain had been consumed in most cases.[253] The situation was made worse by the influenza pandemic, typhus, cholera and the undernourished conditions of the majority of the population.[254]

In January 1918, "In spite of the departure of the Russian troops the price of bread stands at seven times its normal figure. Famine relief has started in all the large towns, where deaths of starvation are increasing in number."[255] For that reason Col. Kennion advised the British government not to send troops beyond Qasr-e Shirin, because "the only supplies that he can guarantee are firewood and some fresh meat but that the purchase of the latter owing to the state of the approaching famine to that that part of their country has been reduced would be very unpopular."[256] In February 1918 food prices dropped; bread was 4.5 *qrans/man*; wheat 600 *qrans/kharvar*; barley and maize 460 *qrans/kharvar*. A famine food-for-work road making project over the Kerend plain was started led by Mr. Stead. In that month 1,400 men, women and children were at work, many of whom would have died without this.[257] Such a project was

252. See, e.g. the description of the situation in the Kermanshah area by Kuhestani-nezhad 1381, p. 43. For the situation elsewhere in Persia, such as in central Persia, Semnan, Isfahan, and Ardabil, see Idem. and Floor 1915.
253. Napier 1919, p.12.
254. Forbes-Leith 1927, p. 21. In general, see Floor 1915, chapters 8-9.
255. Hale n.d. p. 217.
256. IOR, L/P&S/12/84-87, From GOC Baghdad to CIGS, 14/01/1918 (secret).
257. FO 248/1204, Kermanshah report 17/02/1918 by Lt. Col. Kennion.

really needed, because "The price of bread, which had dropped somewhat, is going up again, and the famine continues to develop."[258]

Although people went hungry and/or died from hunger this was not because there was no grain. The Democrats in Kermanshah accused Col. Kennion of exporting grain to Baghdad, while it was in fact, e.g., the Kurds who were selling grain to the Turks at fantastic prices. It was Kennion who asked the British Legation to intervene with the Persian government to take action at Senneh, the capital of Kurdistan, where people were starving. He himself contacted landowning tribal chiefs such Sardar Rashid to likewise take action.[259] In early February 1918, Kennion was also looking ahead to the next harvest season. He noted that villages between Qasr-e Shirin and Harunabad were depopulated and ruined and it would take long before they regained prosperity. Also, that the inhabitants along the Kermanshah-Kerend road had no seed grain, while sowing had to start in 45 days. Therefore, he suggested to the British authorities that they would advance 200 tons of grain, which was available in Mesopotamia. His suggestion was adopted and in early March he made arrangements for seed distribution to all. The biggest difficulty was getting adequate security for these advance seed deliveries. He commented: "Persians are notoriously selfish in such matters, the well-to-do feel no obligation to help the poor." As an example, he cited the case of Kermanshah where people made difficulties to transport grain to famine-stricken Kerend.[260] Despite these actions, prices were rising although an imposed grain embargo maintained prices at lower level than in the districts where famine conditions prevailed.[261] In April 1918, the weather was ideal for crops, but only one-third of the possible area had been sown, mainly due to the damage done by Turkish and Russian troops. As a result,

> The peasants are largely destitute, and the villages on the line of march from the Turkish frontier are mostly in a state of ruin and desertion. Wheat has risen to eight times its normal price, and the British have been carrying out extensive road construction here and down the line and in Hamadan to relieve the poor, who are dying by scores daily. Thousands of them, mostly women and children, are mere half-demented skeletons, incapable of labour till they have been fed for some time. The American missionaries are taking a most active part in the work of relief and maintenance. The situation is worse in Hamadan, where cannibalism has occurred.[262]

However, the scenes in Kermanshah were also shocking as is clear from the writings of Candler, the representative of American Committee for Near East Relief. In that city Candler expressed his feeling as follows:

---

258. Hale 1920, p. 223.

259. FO 248/1204, Legation to Kennion 01/02/18 ("Can you get 'spontaneous' telegram from Kermanshahis thanking us for our famine work?"); Idem, Legation to Kennion 01/02/18; in general, see Sharifi Kazemi 1395, pp. 70-75.

260. FO 248/1204, tel. Lt. Col. Kennion/ Qasr-e Shirin 11/01/1918; Idem, Kermanshah report no. 2, 13/03/1918 by Lt. Col. Kennion; Napier 1919. p. 12..

261. FO 248/1204, Kennion to Legation, 14/03/1918.

262. Hale 1920, pp. 228-29.

> I was shocked to see a boy dead in the bazar. He was lying by the side of the road, his hands clutched, and some horse grain sticking to his lips as if he had been unable to swallow his last meal. The bazars were crowded, but no one seemed to take any notice of him. A little father on I passed another body of a young man, mere blotched skin and bone in loose rags. The crowd stepped to one side indifferently. There were children lying on skins in the mud crying piteously. [These children may have been professional beggars whose number had swollen significantly.] Twenty or thirty died in the streets every day uncared for by their own people, and many dead lay dead in the houses. There was a public scavenger who collected the bodies in the evening and threw them into a pit outside the city. The law of the jungle held in Kermanshah. When hunger gripped a family the husband would sometimes turn his wives and children into the street or abandon his home himself. The weakest went to the wall. I was changing some rupee notes at a money-changer's and gave a keran to a starved woman who was standing by. Four other women were on her like vultures, tearing at her hands and dress, howling and sobbing in a frightful way. I saw another woman, not strong enough to protect herself, buy a fold of bread at a stall; it was dragged from her and torn to strips like meat thrown to animals.[263]

The number of dead was so high that the *ghossal-khaneh*s of Mosalla, Balajub and Feyzabad could not handle the washing and burial of the corpses. The price of wheat rose from 3 to over 200 *tumans/kharvar*. The governor supported by the notables brought grain from Hamadan and made Fathollah Khabbaz responsible for the bread situation in the city. He, with the cooperation of his fellow guild members Sayyed Hoseyn Mostafa'i and Sayyed Morteza Musavi and others, was able to deal with this temporary problem. Because the crop situation in the Thalatheh district (Malayer, Nehavand and Tuyserkan) was relatively good Amir Koll helped to supply Hamadan and Kermanshah.[264]

The British force suffered no shortage, but had to pay high prices, but had mutton always and also various kinds of fish from the river such as carp, which Persians rarely ate.[265] They were not the only ones, for "There was food in Kermanshah for those who could afford it, and many of the well-to-do; but they seemed incapable of pity or any disinterested act."[266] As a result, they suspected those who helped of political motives, because there was plenty of food, but the Shah, officials and merchants organized bread rings for their own benefit, thus creating an artificial shortage in the market.[267] Candler was appalled by this attitude, because whereas

263. Candler 1919, pp. 243-44.

264. Soltani 1381, vol. 1, p. 548; vol. 4, p. 840.

265. Hale 1920, p. 229; Edmonds 2010, p. 227. About the lack of interest in eating fish, see Floor 2003, pp. 586-87.

266. Candler 1919, p. 245. According to Consul Cook, who also served in Persia in 1917-18, "The rascally merchants who in the last war saw women and children die in the streets here of hunger while their ambars were full have not changed this war." FO 248/1414, Cook to Hankey/Tehran12/07/1942.

267. Post 1920, p. 71; Candler 1919, p. 245. On the problem of hoarding and bread rings, see Floor 2015.

> The carnage of a battlefield has a touch of sublimity in it; but in famine there is no idealism, only a degradation, enforced and pitiless, a nakedness of despair which seems the negation of a watchful and interested God. Here one saw in humanity a physical and moral hideousness, as if the Almighty had relegated man to the false gods he had established by choice.[268]

Nevertheless, the American Near East Relief saved thousands by organizing and financing relief work on roads, because when the American missionaries first gave away food the mob rushed them and the strong (men) pushed aside the weak (women and children). The missionaries had to throw it over their heads to reach the weak, but then the strong ran back, and so the only way was to beat them off.[269] To circumvent this problem relief tickets were distributed so that the least capable of work would be the first to receive aid, but these were pushed aside and trampled upon by the surging crowd. Sticks did not help. "One was robbed and looted."[270] Mrs. Stead, who was engaged in relief work for destitute people, added a women's gallery to the chapel, so that women were separated from the men. She gave employment or other relief to the famine-stricken.[271] She also employed people in road work enabled to do so by British financing. In June 1918, the British Consulate financed the work of 9,600 famine workers on road work and neighborhood improvements in Kermanshah.[272] Despite prospects of a good harvest the price of bread was driven up by a bread ring. To break the ring a large volume of barley destined for the road workers was made available to the bakers. This had the desired effect.[273]

On 9 July 1918, after three months, the Famine relief was stopped as the famine was over. When the famine was most severe and prices highest aid was given to 3,480 people, mostly women and children. Although the harvest was excellent, the crop was average, because the seed sown was below normal. Prices remained higher than usual, because all available donkeys had been commandeered for road-making, little wheat was brought to the city. However, a more serious cause was hoarding by the landowners. Also, many villagers held grain reserve in case of a recurring famine. The maize crop was also good, except at Kerend.[274] There was no improvement in this situation, because in September 1918, some 60,000 Christian refugees from the Urmiyeh region descended on Kermanshah, who were forwarded to Baghdad.[275] However, this took time and consequently, Armenian refugees were living "on a dole of bread and a bowl of soup every day" from the Americans.[276]

Therefore, the price of grain remained high, while it was feared that buying grain for the British troops would drive up price. To avoid an artificial famine the British military authorities

---

268. Candler 1919, pp. 246-47.
269. Candler 1919, p. 245.
270. Candler 1919, p. 246.
271. Presbyterian Church 1919-20, p. 265.
272. Edmonds 2010, p. 228; FO 248/1204 Kermanshah report no. 3, 11/06/1918 by Lt. Col. Kennion.
273. FO 248/1204 Kermanshah report no. 3, 11/06/1918 by Lt. Col. Kennion.
274. FO 248/1204, Kermanshah report no. 6, 02/08/1918 by Lt. Col. Kennion; Hale n.d., p. 234.
275. Hale 1920, pp. 235-36.
276. Post 1920, p. 71.

proposed to establish a grain control scheme in Kermanshah province, just like they had done in Hamadan. As sowings were below normal, but the harvest was good, there was no shortage of food grains. However, stocks were below normal. Owners always kept large stores of grain, which had been depleted during the famine. As a result, available grain was only that year's harvest which was sufficient for both civilians and a moderate number of troops. However, owners did not sell enough in the market, so that the price of wheat was 38-40 *tumans*/*kharvar* in August 1918, somewhat rising towards the end of September. These prices compared favorably with those prevailing in the surrounding areas. Owners clearly want to hoard their stock to obtain even higher prices in the future. As this would create an artificial famine, drive up prices of other goods and labor, which would drive up the price of British occupation, "of which the sole beneficiaries would be a comparatively small class of landowners." In the past the governor was able to deal with such a situation by forced sales of grain. However, now the government had very little authority and power, unless backed up by the British. The tribes were so well-armed that the government was unable to face them. They not only had refused to pay any taxes during the last few years, but also had encroached on other people's lands, so that the owners were unable to pay taxes. With little revenues the government was unable to pay its troops and other employees. The British were willing to support the government in collecting taxes and enforcing the grain control scheme. However, at that time there as yet no governor. The daily needs of the city of Kermanshah were estimated at 90 *kharvar* or 33,000 *kharvar*/year. Based on past experience, the availability of 30 *kharvar*/day (10,000 *kharvar*/year), partly coming from revenue grain, was sufficient to supply the poor with bread and regulate the bread price. The remainder of the daily needs were assumed to be consumed by the landowning clas and their dependents and those who had access to grain. This meant that the grain control scheme should cover the 60 *kharvar*/day, which should be sold at not less than 30 *tumans*/*kharvar* for wheat and 20 *tumans*/*kharvar* for barley, given market conditions. Grain should be retailed at a slightly higher price to cover cost and this would function as the target price for the province. This daily amount should be divided among the landowners (excluding districts west of Kerend), and if need be enforced. The British would advance the money for the purchase of grain, and the grain should be sold for cash to the bakers and others by a city committee, which would then reimburse the British authorities. The maximum requirements of the British troops in the province and of Persian labor employed by it were estimated as follows:

Table 2.6: Wheat availability and needs, 1918

A. East of the Pay-Taq Pass B. West of the Pass

Place	Wheat required	Barley and maize required
Kerind to Mahidasht (troops)	300	1,900
Kerind (labor)	600	-
Khosrowabad	600	-
Harunabad	600	-
Kermanshah	1,000	3,500
Bisotun	1,200	900
Sahneh	650	-

Kangavar	850	1,900
Total	5,800	9,200

B. West of the Pass

Qasr-e Shirin to Pay Taq	1,700	2,500
Pay Taq to Taq-e Gharreh	900	2,500
Total	2,600	5,000

It was expected that wheat requirements for Zone A would pose no problems, but that part of the maize and barley required would have to be imported from Lorestan and Nehavand, provinces that were outside the grain control scheme. However, it was expected that prices there would reflect those in Kermanshah province, as it was proposed to publish the maximum price that would be offered, which would be 5 *tumans* above the Kermanshah target price. The price of the control scheme would be impacted by the sale of grain from the crownlands (*khaleseh*), where the government's share was one-third of the gross output. The revenues in kind were as follows:

Table 2.7: Revenues in kind, 1918

District	Nominal demand	Estimated actual recovery
Sonqor	1,300	600
Kangavar	800	500
Sahneh	1,000	500
Dinavar	1,000	600
Crown land- Beglerbegi's	1,000	200
Ditto - Imam Jom`eh's	1,300	400
Ditto (kariz, kerakoneh, ect.)	900	600
Mahidasht	300	100
Daru Faraman	500	300
Baladeh	300	300
Chamchemal	?	400
Total approx.	8,200	4,700

Source: FO 248/1204, Kennion to Civil Commissioner, Baghdad, 24/08/1918.

Of the total revenues in kind 2,700 *kharvar* were reserved for the Persian troops and administration, leaving 2,000 *kharvar* available for the British. The *khaleseh* official told Kennion that with British help he might be able to collect an additional 2,000 *kharvar*, but not more due to the depopulation of many villages. The above figures excluded the revenues from Zone B, which were mostly crown lands in hands of the tribes. This meant, until Zone B was brought under government control, that the control scheme only took into consideration the crown lands of Zohab and Bishewa. For the moment, grain from Zone B could be obtained by offering to pay in cash, because all grain had already been stored. In this way another 1,000 *kharvar* might be obtained. In a meeting in September with the newly arrived governor, Salar-e Lashkar this grain control scheme was discussed. He agreed grudgingly, saying that first stocks had to be built up, as there were none at the moment. To that end it was decided to first establish a stock for the troops 500 tons and the city 1,000 tons after which the scheme might be initiated. [277]

The Revenue Department sent an agent to the crown lands of Zohab and Bishewa in the Qasr-e Shirin district to asses government's demand for revenue. It was proposed to buy this grain for military needs.[278] On 13 Moharram or 19 October 1918, the governor met with the major landowners. He told them that they had to provide 12,000 *kharvar* for the city which would cover the needs till the next harvest. This amount was divided among the landowners, according to their landholding size, and they were responsible to supply bakers allotted to them with sufficient grain to keep the bakeries open till afternoon. Prices were fixed for wheat at Rls 40/*kharvar* and bread 3 *qrans* 2 *shahis*/*man*. To enable grain to be brought in the British military authorities released 1,000 local animals under their control, 400 more than they originally had intended to do.[279] Excellent rains in November 1918 as well as in 1920 led to brisk sowing. Some damage was done to the tobacco and rice crops in 1920 and prices were higher; wheat sold for 20 *tumans*/*kharvar*. However, bread was cheap, although wood was sold at 40-80 *qrans*/*kharvar*.[280]

I have not been able to find any information on the food situation in Kermanshah between 1919-30. Undoubtedly, in years of a bad harvest the same problems as mentioned above occurred in the province as they did thereafter. However, it seems that no major food problem occurred in Kermanshah during this period. In 1936, the British consul compared the bad food situation of 1936 with that of some 15 years ago and thus implied that the intervening years were better than either of these two bad years.[281] In 1930, the central government established a national grain monopoly with itself as the sole buyer. It did so with a view of keeping crop prices artificially low. In that same year, under the mayor of Kermanshah, Mohammad Hasan Khan Madani (Dabir-e A'zam), for the first time a pricing committee was formed with guild members, representatives of the governor and the municipality to set maximum prices of bread and food stuffs that were published. Because prices in the market were lower the committee was forced to collect prices every day from the market. This situation continued until 1935 when Nasrollah Mostashari and Yavar Foruhar were chairmen of the municipality.[282]

The perhaps unintended consequence of the grain monopoly was that it had a negative impact on the rural population. For the peasants were forced to subsidize the urban consumers,

---

277. FO 248/1204, Kennion to Civil Commissier/Baghdad, 24/08/1918; Idem, Kennion to Civil Commissier/Baghdad, 09/09/1918; Idem, Kermanshah report no. 8, 05/10/1918 by Lt. Col. Kennion.

278. FO 248/1204 Kermanshah report no. 7, 12/09/1918 by Lt. Col. Kennion.

279. FO 248/1204 Kermanshah report no. 9, 01/11/1918 by Lt. Col. Kennion; Idem, Kermanshah report no. 8, 05/10/1918 by Lt. Col. Kennion.

280. FO 248/1204, Kermanshah report no. 10, 03/12/1918 by Lt. Col. Kennion; FO 248/1293, Kermanshah report no. 9, up to 10 October 1920; Idem, Report Kermanshah no. 11, up to 10 December 1920.

281. FO 371/21900, f. 112. There was drought and hunger in Kerend in 1921, but it is not known whether that situation was local or province-wide. Malekzadeh et al. 1392, p.100 (doc. 43).

282. Soltani 1381, vol. 1, pp. 554-56.

and in particular the urban elite, by sacrificing their own desire for better and increased consumption. Peasants were penalized by (i) the difference in the government price of wheat, barley and other grains and those prevailing in the free market and (ii) the disregard for the local needs that were considered secondary to that of the big cities.[283] Moreover, (iii) the manner in which this policy was implemented made its impact even more negative. Furthermore, (iv) landlords and those in the supply chain were upset by the (a) oppressive behavior of the government's collection agents; and (b) the late or non-payment for the delivered grains.[284]

In 1936, the British consul in Kermanshah stated that "the same poverty and misery is to be found both in the country and in the town now, just as it existed fifteen years ago" and he only noted a slight improvement in living conditions for government officials. This group only constituted some 5% of the urban population of Kermanshah, but they were generally better off than the rest of the population. They were able to afford new clothes, furniture, other household goods, including items of European origin, as well as social expenses such as visits to the cinema. The remaining 95% was not better off, in fact worse off than a decade earlier, because most consumer goods had become more expensive and therefore, they suffered a fall in living standards.[285] Although it appeared as if the standard of living of the villagers had improved somewhat due to government favoring farming activities, but the higher income was offset by higher prices for most goods that they had to buy in the market. Therefore, 90% of the rural population still lived in the same conditions and with the same standard of living as in previous years and over all only about 10% of the population experienced a somewhat better living.[286]

In the mid-1930s prices had risen, while wages did not keep pace. Increased taxation and customs duties as well as foreign exchange control and high cost of import licenses drove prices up. New octroi taxes in 1937 further caused consumer goods to rise in price while there was no corresponding increase in purchasing power. These developments "caused great hardship and bitter discontent, especially among the poorer and middle classes."[287] The price the grain monopoly paid for wheat intended to give landowners and peasants a profit, which the government expected them to invest to gradually rebuild and modernize the villages and to increase output by better use of water. Some landowners started by building small bathhouses in a few villages; some placed brick-faced fronts on houses that were built along a tree lined street. However, these few and limited changes made no real impact, for otherwise village life remained entirely unchanged.[288] The result of this policy of monopolies and exactions was that even people in fertile lands such as around Kermanshah were reduced to a state of semi-starvation. This was due to the above mentioned four points, but in particular, because peasants were discouraged from planting grains given the too low a price the government was willing to pay. This trend coincided with a drought in 1939 and as a result there was not enough grain in the state granaries, as landlords were unwilling to sell and hoarded their grain.[289]

---

283. Katouzian 1981, p. 133.
284. Tayarani 1372, pp. 20-21 (with examples).
285. FO 371/21900, f. 112-13, see annexes B and C.
286. FO 371/21900, f. 112.
287. FO 371/21900, f.115.
288. FO 371/31402, Kermanshah Diary December 1941.
289. Azari 1371, p. 4.

Consequently, the cost of living continued to rise during 1939-40. In April-June 1940, grain stocks almost ran out, and bread price rose from 1.60 rials to 3.50/*man* of 3 kg. Bread during that period was inedible as it was adulterated with dirt and impurities. Moreover, the Sugar Monopoly had mismanaged sugar stocks in Kermanshah, which were almost exhausted and in April/May 1940 sugar was sold at 60-80% above the normal price. The price of building materials dropped (see Table 2.8) because there was less building activity since the war had broken out in Europe. However, it was expected that prices of building materials would rise again because hundreds of houses were demolished by the Municipality for making new avenues through Eastern Kermanshah. Moreover, direct taxation did not change. In fact, the Finance Department tried via all means to collect more revenues. The arbitrary way in which this was done to all sections of society made the government and the regime unpopular. One new tax was 50% tax on electricity, which all electricity consumers had to pay. Some 40 people decided to disconnect from the grid, including the *Bisotun* and *Bozorg* Hotels.[290]

Table 2.8: Comparative statement in Rials of building materials, Essential Foodstuffs and Fuels 1937-40

		18 September 1940	September 1938	September 1937
Commodity	**Unit**	**Rials**	**Rials**	**Rials**
Lime	Per kharvar	50	60	50
Mortar	”	75	70	50
Bricks (kiln baked)	1,000			
White	”	200	240	140
Green	”	200	230	140
Red	”	150	170	100
Beams 2 meters	100	620	640	450
3 meters	100	900	1,000	700
4 meters	30 cm each	13	14	10
5 meters	60 cm	21	22	17
Wages of labourer	Day	5-5.50	6	5
mason	”	20-28	20-28	15-22
carpenter	”	20	20	14
carpenter asst. (*shagerd*)	”	10	10	5
Bread (*lavash*)*	3 kilos	1.60*	1.60	1.50
Flour (white)	3 kilos	10.0	5.50	7.0
Mutton	3 kilos	9.60	8.0	8.80
Beef	3 kilos	6.50	5.0	6.40
Eggs	100	20.0	14.0	12.50
Sugar #	3 kilos	17.40 #	13.25	13.0
Tea	Packet of 500 gr.	28.0	23.0	20.0

290. FO 248/1414, Economic Report Kermanshah. March-Sept 1940, 18/09/1940.

		18 September 1940	September 1938	September 1937
Commodity	**Unit**	**Rials**	**Rials**	**Rials**
Raughan	3 kilos	36.0	31.0	34.0
Rice	3 kilos	10.0	8.50	8.50
Cheese	3 kilos	16.0	16.0	16.0
Charcoal	300 kilos	140.0	140.0	160.0
Firewood (logs)	300 kilos	42.0	40.0	40.0
Kerosene oil	18 liters	21.50 (not. incl. tin)	21.15	22 (incl. tin)
Candles	Half dozen	3.0	2.25	3.0

* Official price of bread: in practice bread costs 1.50 to 2.20 Rials per *batman* of 3 kilogrammes.

Offical price of sugar sold by the Sugar Monopoly Company's shops; in practice most people find it necessary to buy from other shops where sugar is sold at 19.50 to 20.50 Rials per *batman* of 3 kilos.

Source: FO 248/1414, Economic Report Kirmanshah. March-September 1940 (18/09/1940).

The occupation of Persia by the Allies in August 1941 did not improve the situation in Kermanshah or in other provinces, because the harvest had been bad in that year in most of the country. Moreover, the devaluation of the rial on 1 October 1941 made the fixed price of wheat and barley less attractive for landowners. The central government did not want to raise this price fearing popular discontent in the major cities. What made matters worse was that the abdication of Reza Shah was seen by the landowning class as an opportunity to make a killing by artificially making the price of grain rise.[291] They were quite successful in doing so, although they and the Persian public in general blamed the Allies for these problems. However, the truth was different. The *Times* correspondent reported from Kermanshah at the end of August 1941 that "large stocks of grain had been found by the advancing troops and that local scarcities were "evidently due to faulty distribution," as he put it euphemistically.[292] Throughout the war years the landowners and bureaucrats would continue their profiteering habit by hoarding and price speculation of life necessities.

The security situation had much improved by December 1941. Peasants could plow and sow, which had been unsafe in October and November. Fortunately, wheat supplies were sufficient until the next crop. However, there was already a sugar shortage and many products were becoming scarce.[293] The shortages became more pronounced in January 1942 and prices rose sharply. Sugar stocks were low and were expected to run out by March 10, if no additional supplies would become available. Matches had almost disappeared and cigarettes were getting scarce leading to price speculation above the official fixed price. Imported cotton piece-goods were almost unobtainable and locally made piece-goods were also scarce. The Persian authorities were trying to manage this by limiting the quantity one could buy. Although the wheat situation was satisfactory and local stocks were expected to last till July, the 1942 crop was expected to

291. Lloyd 1956, p. 159.
292. Skrine 1962, pp. 79, 94; for the situation in Persia in general, see Floor 2015 and Sharifi Kazemi 1395.
293. FO 371/31402, Kermanshah Diary December 1941.

be 30% below the average volume. Therefore, the British military authorities and consul, who were worried about popular disturbances, urged the governor (*ostandar*), the head of the municipality and the chief of police to take steps against hoarders and profiteering before the situation became really bad. The local authorities were encouraging peasants to plant maize, rice, and peas during the late winter and early spring, which would be a welcome addition if wheat would be in short supply.[294]

In February 1942, the economic situation improved somewhat due to the fall of prices of some goods. However, stocks of imported goods were almost gone and their prices rose due to speculation. Sugar stocks were also very low and if they would run out the British would be blamed. Fortunately, the situation with wheat and bread was different, as supplies were adequate. Also, the price of bread controlled by government at 3 rials/*man* compared favorably with rest of Persia. This fact made a difference in containing popular discontent which threatened to become serious in October 1941, before the arrival of *Sepahbod* Shahbakhti. He defied the authorities of Tehran who said that bread had to be priced at 4.5 rials/*man*. Qiyami, the governor (*farmandar*) of Kermanshah district was energetically trying to combat hoarding and profiteering to bring down the cost of living. Imported hardware, glass ware, woolen goods, drugs etc. were offered at record prices, the result of holding and speculative buying. Trying to control prices meant that the local authorities would have to face vested interests. Spare parts and tires for cars were already scare and it was expected that in a few months many cars would not be able to run. Therefore, the British authorities suggested local authorities to switch to animal transport in the coming summer and fall months. Heavy rains promise good harvest, but mild weather exposes plants to late frost.[295]

As the authorities were unable or unwilling to do something about the shortages this situation led to continued hoarding and profiteering and caused prices to rise and resentment, despite the passing of an anti-hoarding act by the *Majles* in March 1942. As expected the British were blamed for the inability of Persian authorities to control prices and stop abuses by rapacious officials and merchants.[296] Fortunately, grain stocks were sufficient to meet local demand till the next harvest. In fact, there was even surplus grain. From December 1941 till April 1942, some 8,647 tons of wheat and 2,015 tons of barley were sent to Tehran, Yazd, Kerman and Isfahan. Less beets were grown despite government encouragement to grow more. Cotton was also less grown than in the late 1930s.[297] Crop prospects that had looked positive in April looked poor in May 1942, because the expected rains had not come. In fact, it was expected that *Ostan V* would produce 25% less, because in some parts crops had dried up and in others yields looked to be disappointing.[298] Therefore, at the suggestion of the British Legation, the Persian government accepted the appointment of British officers in the main wheat-producing areas, whose

---

294. FO 371/31402, Kermanshah Diary January 1942.
295. FO 371/31402, Kermanshah Diary February 1942.
296. FO 371/31402, Consul to FO, 28 March 1942.
297. FO 371/31402, Kermanshah Diary April 1942.
298. FO 371/31402, Kermanshah Diary May 1942.

task it was to induce unwilling farmers and landowners to sell their grain to the government and to see to it that government officials really paid for grain delivered.[299]

During most of June 1942 there was almost nobody in charge of Kermanshah as Amir Koll was a mere figurehead, while Qiyami had gone for three weeks to Tehran and did not want to return. His energy and honesty had brought him into trouble with other officials in Kermanshah, supported by powerful merchants and landowners, who were engaged in profiteering and hoarding and by the intrigues of Majidzadeh, the Director of the Finance Department. He received no support from Amir Koll, which made his position untenable. But without a capable governor of the Kermanshah district (*farmandar*) the grain and *rowghan* collection would be in trouble and might go from bad to worse, or so the British feared, and the same held for the distribution of consumer goods in Kermanshah and its districts. Because of these intrigues the bread quality deteriorated. The Municipality and the Economic Department blamed each other, while the uncontrolled bakers and millers made large profits. Although there were big hoards of *rowghan* in town, the price rose to Rls 115/*man*, which was unaffordable to most at that price. At the urging of the British consul a meeting was held between the Persian authorities and the merchants. It was decided that 15% of the *rowghan* stock would be sold in Kermanshah at the price of Rls 80/*man*. The main hoarders, however, said the 15% share only applied to what would be sent to Tehran and other towns. Therefore, for some time they did not use local stocks for export, but what came from surrounding districts. Meanwhile, the Finance Department made no effort to apply the rules of the anti-hoarding laws that intended to keep prices and complaints down, and build up stocks. Finally, the Ministry of Finance in Tehran sanctioned the 15% rule, but Majidzadeh also received a telegram saying that *rowghan* could be exported from Kermanshah to Tehran without any hindrance provided the merchant could show a permit issued in Tehran.

The rest of country was also in need of grain and therefore, the Finance Department received orders to send 2,000 tons of wheat to Tehran from the Kermanshah district and 2,500 tons to Isfahan from the outlying districts. Majidzadeh said there was no wheat and he sent 500 tons of barley instead, then he left to Bijar (Kurdistan) where he said 4,000 tons were available if there was transport. The harvest was expected to be 80% of the normal output. The figure was somewhat suspect, because losses reported due to weather and agricultural pests (*senn*) were exaggerated to provide cover for hoarding and smuggling to Iraq. In June 1942, a British Cereals Collection officer came whose task it was to ensure that grain collection from growers would be without problems, especially in the tribal areas, and to protect the peasants from cheating and ill-treatment by officials. The British consul did not expect that the local officials of the Ministry of Finance would help the British officer as this would cut into their peculations and allow them to blame the British rather than the Persian government for the results of grain collection. On the other hand Persian officials refused to go into certain tribal areas, such as that of the Kalhors, who openly said that they would give little to Persian officials.

Meanwhile, nobody seemed to be in charge of the bread situation and the various responsible local authorities wasted time blaming each other rather than attacking the problem. The Economic Department blamed the Municipality for the bad quality of bread, which did not

299. Lloyd 1956, p. 159.

control the bakers, who filched the good flour supplied to them. The Municipality countered that the flour was already much adulterated when it arrived. The Justice Department said it could not do anything, because neither the Economic Department nor the Municipality presented it with good cases of hoarding and profiteering that it might prosecute. Moreover, until the end of June 1942 it maintained that the local courts had not yet received the text of the anti-hoarding laws passed in March or the regulations published on 4 June 1942 in the Ministry of Justice Gazette. In short, it looked as if all government departments wanted to obstruct any improvement and wanted things to remain as they were under the easy-going governor. This resulted in a rather ironic situation, for when the latter brought a case against a lorry owner who had damaged his car the police reported that the file had been 'lost'.[300]

To get a better understanding of the food supply situation the central government introduced a new scheme of assessing and collecting the wheat harvest. The landlords opposed the new scheme. One said the new scheme meant: "be honest and lose, or bribe us and we agree to your figures." The Finance Department argued that this was a poor excuse, because the crop estimation commission consisted mostly of landlords and that it was unable to cope with those who underestimated crops. On 19 July 1942, Majidzadeh, the director of the Finance Department told the British consul that there was only for 12 days wheat in Kermanshah. Despite this nothing was done against hoarders. Meanwhile the entire administration had almost come to a standstill because the popular district governor Qiyami had left, while Majidzadeh continued his intriguing against the governor.[301]

It was expected that after the harvest the pillaging would start including of the grain stored for government use. General Shahbakhti only made one officer and 30 men available to provide protection in the main wheat growing area. Although the assessment commission left in early July 1942 there was still no harvest estimate at the end of the month. According to the British consul, "they are mostly lazy and slipshod and have no data from last year to go on. As the former system of brutality, bribery, cheating and extortion cannot be used so widely this year, the officials seem to be at a loss." The officials used the presence of two uniformed British officers to browbeat growers insinuating that this year the British wanted to have the grain for themselves, resenting the presence of the officers as a check on their normal peculations. They didn't like it at all when the officers went out on their own to speak in Persian to the peasants. The British consul with some bitterness commented that "The rascally merchants who in the last war saw women and children die in the streets here of hunger while their *ambar* were full have not changed in this war, and in the provinces exercise even more influence on the officials than they do in Tehran."

In the second half of July 1942, the bread supply and the quality of bread remained bad, although the director of the Finance Department said that stocks were adequate. However, the bakers and millers were in league to adulterate the flour in the absence of municipal control. They sold part of the pilfered flour in the black market and sold the normal customer lighter bread (*kam-forushi*), who had to wait for hours in line and being told there were shortages. Therefore, the poor consumers just took the bread and did not even complain about its bad

300. FO 371/31402, Kermanshah Diary June 1942.
301. FO 371/31402, Fletcher to Legation, 20/07/1942.

quality. At a meeting on 25 June the mayor blamed the court, which only imposed small fines, while the president of the courts said after that three fines the mayor had the authority to suspend the baker and over 20 bakers had been fined over 8 times and were still allowed to continue. As a result of the meeting, the bread quality improved and the director of the Finance Department hastened to get new surplus in that already had been earmarked by the Ministry of Finance, which only focused on stockpiling grain at Tehran, which curiously remained as short of stocks as the provinces where it came from.

As to *rowghan* the proposal agreed upon in June remained a dead letter. Merchants were allowed to export it without handing over the stipulated 15% at a fixed price. They only signed undertakings that when called upon they would deliver, knowing full well that the corrupt officials would not do so. It was an eyewash for the consulate just as the anti-hoarding laws were an eyewash to the British authorities in Tehran, because no Persian officials had the intention to implement them.

The new government price of wheat was Rls 1,400/ton or Rls 420/*kharvar*. Influential landlords and peasants were generally unwilling to sell preferring to wait for a higher price later. Peasants also were angry at the government for not supplying them with tea, sugar and cloth, which were distributed at the official price in the towns, but they only could get them at very high 'free' prices, in which government officials had a remunerative interest. Many people were hoarding, officials and middle class families included. Armenian buyers, who bought grain for British army road workers, could not get wheat even at Rls 1,700/*kharvar*.[302] By the end of July 1942, the town bread supply had become easier; coming in small quantities by stop-gap methods; meanwhile, hoarding and smuggling continued.[303] The price of wheat in the free market was 500-650 rials/*kharvar* and at Qasr-e Shirin 750 and more and at Khaneqin they paid 1,250. This was only £32/ton, whereas in Iraq it was £40/ton. The Persian rate was £10 and, therefore, smuggling was impossible to stop, which would require honest border guards, "which is even more impossible." Even from east of Kermanshah caravans were going to Iraq. The governor himself stopped one of 150 donkeys that was coming from Dinavar. Supplies of tea and sugar from India reached the market here; piece goods from Tehran for sale to villagers when they have sold their ghee, wool and grain. The price of wool was lower this year, because there were no German buyers.[304]

According to Col. Fletcher, the political adviser of the consulate, in August 1942, the cost of living was twice what it was one year before, while incomes had not risen. Hoarding was partly to blame, because middle-class families stored wheat, rice and ghee, and for their current needs bought in the market. Although British troops brought many provisions with them, the consul surmised that their presence had to have an upward effect on prices of fruit, vegetables and meat. Moreover, the price of firewood trebled in July 1942 due to lack of transport and peasants working on military roads and works.[305] Also, the misguided (or perhaps deliberate) policy by the government in Tehran contributed to a further deterioration of the food situation. When in July 1942, there was only one week of supply in Kermanshah, there was plenty in the

302. FO 371/31402, Kermanshah Diary July 1942; FO 248/1414, Consul to Hankey/Tehran, 12/07/1942.

303. FO 371/31402, no. 41, Consul to FO, 02/08/1942. For the various distinct groups of smugglers, see Sharifi Kazemi 1395, pp. 155-59.

304. FO 371/31402, Kermanshah Diary July 1942; see also Sharifi Kazemi 1395, pp. 154, 175.

305. FO 371/31402, Kermanshah Diary August 1942.

government store in Kangavar and Sahneh. However, the Ministry of Finance in Tehran gave orders not to send any of it to Kermanshah. Col. Fletcher argued that such interference should stop, because the Ministry deliberately wanted people be discontent. Therefore, he pleaded for action by the British Legation to stop the rise of bread prices, otherwise he feared there would be riots.[306]

Although bread prices came down, the food situation was still unresolved. Middle and large landowners refused to supply or even sign an undertaking to hand over their surplus and the authorities did not threaten them. Small landowners only gave an undertaking for the smallest quantities which also would take a long time to collect, "because of slow commissions which first have to examine their case." The Director of the Finance and the Economic Department admitted that his estimate officials had given totally useless and unreliable reports and that he had to recalculate everything. Even those who signed undertakings complained that the Economic Department showed little interest in collecting it. Meanwhile the grain remained in the open ready to be stolen by marauding Kurds. The prevailing dishonesty and corruption totally stifled the food issue even when grain was available. As a result, in August 1942 there were bread riots in Kerend, Nehavand, Malayer, and Asadabad all small centers of wheat producing areas. In Kermanshah there also would have been riots were it not for the presence of British troops, which people believed would have intervened. Also, because the British political adviser had almost forced Amir Koll, the governor to go in person to the bakeries and had the worst bakers dealt with and their shops closed.

Until that time, bakers adulterated flour, half baked bread and sold short weight bread, but until this mild British intervention no Persian official had done anything. Because they noticed that this action gave rise to pro-British feelings they reacted by saying that they also would take firm steps to maintain the improved situation. The bakers complained about the government prices with which they claimed they could not make a profit. However, the bakeries that were closed offered to pay almost £200 in bribes to an official in one day to be allowed to reopen. The British consul opined that "The authorities know what needs to be done, but they don't know whether Tehran or they need to take action and so nothing gets done." According to the regulations, 26 August 1942 was the last day that merchants and those holding stocks of food-stuffs and other goods had to hand in their inventory lists. In Kermanshah no steps were taken, allegedly because the printed forms had not arrived from Tehran and thus, no official felt a need to do anything. The prime-minister sent Amir Koll, the governor a strongly worded message that hoarders must be dealt with. Mostashari, the city's governor, said that he would post it. The Director of the Finance and Economic Department, who was partly to blame for the problems, "though he is more honest and conscientious than others," was replaced on 30 August 1942 by Naha'i to the great satisfaction of Majidzadeh, the director of the Finance Department.[307]

In August 1942, to better deal with the worsening food situation, Tehran established a Food Department within the Ministry of Finance and in September 1942, this Department was upgraded to a separate Ministry of Foodstuffs. Mr. Sheridan, an American business man, was

306. FO 248/1414, Col. Fletcher to Gen. Maine 01/08/1942.
307. FO 371/31402, Kermanshah Diary August 1942.

appointed its advisor in October 1942, about the same time that Arthur Millspaugh was invited to once again become Administrator General of Finances.[308]

Landlords screamed when, in October 1942, 52 of them were arrested by the governor, among whom two of his uncles, much against his will and after pressure from the British consul and the British political adviser. After a few days he let 40 of them go. The prime-minister sent a telegram thanking him for being so firm, while he almost with tears in his eyes told the 40 that he was sorry for what he had done to them. The bakers took their cue from this and two days later bread was worse than ever before by filching wheat for sale in the black market. There were long lines of customers at the bakeries, who paid heavily for their immunity. A few days later 1,500 workers of Kermanshah Petroleum Company (KPC) struck saying they could not get bread in the morning before going to work. The British consul arranged for this important plant to continue the release of 7.5 tons of wheat (a week's supply) for distribution by KPC management. The governor started to talk about a ration scheme to prevent peasants from coming to Kermanshah to get cheap bread, but he needed £1,000 to print the ration cards, but he did not get the approval from Tehran. The British Consulate then arranged to transfer the matter into hands of the mayor. It was then proposed to mix wheat flour with 20% barley to force middle class hoarders to use their own stock of wheat flour rather than eat coarse bread from the bakeries. Of course, the bakers mixed 40% barley plus husks, making bread almost inedible and reducing the lines at the bakeries. According to the British consul, "The scenes around the bread shops are heart rending" and this in the middle of a major grain producing area.

Because of the arrests of the 52 landlords more wheat was collected. The increase of the government price of wheat of 1,400 to 3,500 rials brought in more wheat from smaller growers. But it remained doubtful whether big landowners would also sell their surplus. The director of the Finance Department believed he only would be able to collect 10,000 tons of the 15,000 that he needed for Kermanshah and its district. In Kurdistan there was just enough for Senneh and little else for export. As both Amir Koll and the chief Finance officials were landowners there was little chance that pressure would be brought on them. According to the British consul, "Persia in 1942 is something like England prior to 1832, with the land-owning classes in control of all local administration and virtually in control of Parliament and of the Cabinet, with two classes in the country - one bloated with wealth and the other abjectly poverty-stricken and hungry, with no one to care what happens to it."

Local merchants made huge profits from sales to the British army and by local speculators from rising prices on all goods. Much money was sent to Tehran, Tabriz and Isfahan to buy tea, textiles and other goods. "The cost of living is rising daily, hoarding and profiteering is rampant; the culprits are known to everyone, but nobody does anything under the new laws only passed in March. Tehran made things worse by buying up stocks of peas, beans, and potatoes." Local prices rose 400%, so clumsily the buying was done. The *Bank-e Melli* manager and two of the biggest merchant hoarders colluded and cleared 1 million rials. at the expense of the Bank and the hungry people. Smaller hoarders followed suit and the situation of the ordinary consumer was becoming desperate. Shopkeepers continued to raise prices and the vicious circle continued. Only the very poor who only ate bread escaped this. People were afraid that next February there

308. Lloyd 1956, p. 161. Millspaugh 1946, p. 40, for an analysis of the country's situation on his arrival.

would be famine and "this is only due to incompetence and maladministration at the higher levels." The British consul argued that only American and British intervention could prevent further deterioration.[309]

In November 1942, the first representative of the new Ministry of Foodstuffs (*Khvarbar*), a Mr. Rokni, arrived taking over from the director of the Finance and the Economic Department, i.e. all matters concerning sugar, wheat, barley, and rice. However, he did not make much headway with his easy-going work-shy staff. The jealousy of the Finance Department kept him short financially, while his task of collecting grain was suddenly taken away from him after a few days of his arrival by the free-lance unofficial buying agent Mr. Naamani [No'mani?], who had an astonishing contract from the American adviser, which would make him £10,000 in a few weeks, if he would do all that he promised to. The terms of his contract stated that he would receive a commission of 100 rials on what he bought up to 9,000 tons and 125 rials on the next 2,000 tons. These 11,000 tons were officially supposed to be reserved for Kermanshah and district. Any wheat beyond that he would get 200 rials and was to be sent to Tehran. Similar arrangements were made with a buyer at Sanandaj and Hamadan. Unless these buyers have more backing than the local officials they will get as far. Landowners opposed him and the biggest ones had already covered themselves in Tehran.

During the first half of November 1942 the scenes of long lines at the bakeries continued, while the bakers stole part of the flour with the connivance of the municipal authorities. Wheat stopped coming into town when the new Ministry of Foodstuffs ordered its officials not to pay the new agreed higher price to landlords who had not carried out their delivery undertaking, and this for the past two years. If landlords had been eager to deliver wheat at the new price the rule would have made sense, but this was not the case, supplies came in slowly and landlords were not willing to sign any undertaking. As a result, there was no supply of grain and no willingness to sign undertakings. The landlords thought that the Minister, Mr. Farrokh, was only trying to trick them out of the higher price after they would have revealed their hidden stocks. In fact, the situation became worse, because he also ordered that the price should not be paid to those who had only leased land last year, the price only to be paid to landowners. The latter were annoyed that renters who had paid rent in accordance with the lower prices for wheat should benefit on a level with themselves. "Until this class is removed from Persia there is little hope for it," the British consul commented. It took an entire month to have these two rules canceled, but the damage had been done. Little confidence in the government remained.

Despite promises from Tehran that it would only take the surplus above local needs it took more, whenever the capital needed more. Hoarding and cheating had reached such an extent that even if landlords would sign undertakings only 7,000 tons would be available. When four lorries from Tehran came to forcibly take wheat and barley the inhabitants prevented any grain from leaving. The gendarmes did not intervene, sympathizing with the villagers. If the government could show that there was five months in stock peasants would not oppose export of grain, but due to inefficiency and corruption and failure to press large landlords this was not the case.

309. FO 371/31402, Kermanshah Diary October 1942.

At the advice of Mr. Sheridan, the American food policy adviser, the government doubled the price of bread at the beginning of November 1942. This caused serious hardship as wages had not risen and the poor only ate bread. Also, the bread was heavy adulterated with barley, more than the official 30% rate. The rise in price had its intended effect, for the middle class started to use their own stocks of pure flour and some of the peasants who had come into Kermanshah for cheap bread returned. The British consul was very much upset about this measure and commented: "The poor, of course, had to cut their consumption in half, while the unfeeling officials talked about the improved bread situation. Mr. Sheridan may congratulate himself on this achievement, but no humane person in touch with realities can."

At the end of the November 1942 good rains fell and sowing began. Also, the war news was better and people didn't expect that there would be fighting in this part of the world and hoarders were more willing to eat their own stock or sell it. Large landowners still held out for famine conditions, but if the Anglo-American plan to bring in 25,000 tons of grain would work they might change their mind. Although through their friends in the Ministries they would try to get hold of his grain and thus still achieve their objectives. An inspector came from Tehran to investigate the 400% price rise of beans and peas due to the director of the *Bank-e Melli* and two hoarders. He made a damning report, but the British consul believed it was doubtful there would be any reaction; "after all in Tehran there are worst cases." Ironically, in the same month of November, Tehran ordered the *Bank-e Melli* to buy potatoes. Its director did so immediately and the price rose from Rls. 1,000 to 2,200/*kharvar*. He then started buying potatoes in Hamadan, probably in competition with the local bank there, and brought hundreds of tons to Kermanshah, although it was thought they were for Tehran. Over 2,000 tons were dumped in a damp store and started rotting. Tehran ordered to sell them at 6% above cost price, or 2,120 rials. However, the speculators had made their killing (over 10 million rials) and the price had gone down to 900 rials, so that the potatoes had to be sold at half price or left to rot. "Nothing will be done to bring the guilty to justice."

A rise in the price of bread meant a rise in price of every other commodity. Speculators increased the price of tea, sugar and rice. The Central Bank and *Bank-e Melli* said they would restrict the money supply to prevent speculation, but given the inefficiency and dishonesty of *Bank-e Melli* this was expected to have little effect. In November 1941 the cost of living was 400% higher than in August 1941. At the end of November prices dropped a little, probably because of better war news and Mr. Rokni's announcement that he was going to control the books of merchants and investigate recent transactions.

To resolve the bread situation, the central government decided to initiate a program of food rationing, but nobody knew how it would work and when it would start. Mostashari, the mayor, told the British political advisor that rationing would start in one week and on the same day he told the consul that it would happen in one month. Meanwhile, he took no action at all against hoarders and profiteers. Also, endless difficulties and intrigues prevented its implementation. Several thousand of useless sheets were printed locally, and others were expected to arrive from Tehran, but they were not to be used until the rationing had been tried in Tehran itself.[310] The presence of the Allied troops and the building of new roads and other projects, although

310. FO 371/31402, Kermanshah Diary November 1942; Idem, Fletcher to Tehran, 09/11/1942.

employing some 67,000 Persian workers, also had negative effects on the economy. The infusion of additional funds increased the money in circulation and had an upward effect on the already existing inflation. Also, all these construction activities limited the availability of transport capacity to the civilian economy and dislocated distribution of civilian goods. Finally, the overall effect was an increased demand for food and other goods, which encouraged hoarding and speculation.[311]

The central government also tried to manage the hoarding and profiteering by issuing new regulations, viz. that traders had to keep records of their stocks and transactions. The Economic Department officials had a field day with these rules by focusing on the small shop-keepers, who were illiterate and collected bribes for exemption. The situation became so bad that the shop-keepers were threatening a strike in protest.[312] Although the harvest of 1943 was very good the bread situation grew more troublesome. There were bread demonstrations in 1943 at various cities, including Kermanshah.[313] In December 1943, the wholesale price of food remained steady, with a slight drop in the sugar price. The Municipality's 2-weekly retail price list showed little or no change. Merchants ignored the list as inspectors could be induced to overlook overcharging. Smuggling of goods to Iraq remained brisk and customs officials on both sides were corrupt.[314] On 8 December 1943, the Shahabad sugar mill started working until 24 December. Some 5,000 instead of 10,000 tons of beets were collected and that only because the lorries partly worked clandestinely. Sugar content was 12% so that 600 tons of sugar was produced. In Kermanshah the sugar, tea, cloth situation remained unsatisfactory. The price of tea rose by 20%, due to new price regulations, which led to increased smuggling. Cloth supplies to the districts were almost nil, and the underclad situation of tribesmen, women, and children was serious. The resentment about this was heightened by the correct conviction that townspeople received preferential treatment.[315]

In January 1944, grain collection was almost complete. Ilam and Qasr-e Shirin were deficitary areas and were supplied from Gilan with 15 lorries. The *Amlak* produced little grain, which was disappointing, although part of the year's profits were high on this property. Enough grain was collected to supply the deficit areas. Stocks at Kermanshah were 6,000 tons, with 3,000 in the outstations. Total grain collected was 22,500 tons. On the black market the price of wheat dropped a little to 1,500 rials. Some 8,200 tons were shipped from the surplus to Tehran. Another 1,200 tons would follow transported by the British army. The bread situation in Kermanshah remained satisfactory and therefore, people were not upset that the surplus was leaving. The Justice Department received orders to flog offenders against the Food Laws. The governor called the heads of the departments to follow up with a view to get some culprits as a salutary example. However, bribery and corruption in the Supply Department was "as flagrant as ever." Rains were late but plentiful and widespread accompanied by mild weather, promise of good crop.

---

311. Lloyd 1956, p. 162.
312. FO 371/31402, Consul to Legation, 20/12/42
313. Tayarani 1372, p. 24 (with details).
314. FO 371/40177, Kermanshah Diary December 1943.
315. FO 371/40177, Kermanshah Diary January 1944.

Ebtehaj Sami'i, the director of the Department of Supply (*Khvarbar*) was attacked in the newspapers, the writer probably hoping to get a pay-off. Sami'i admitted that there was corruption by the underpaid employees, but he said they were punished when found out. This may have been true, but the alleged punishments had no impact whatsoever on the Department's behavior. Collection of grain continued mainly from peasant-owners with the sugar-barter scheme. Some 1,500 tons were collected. In February the barter scheme was to be extended to landowners who already had supplied as per their undertaking and it was expected that another 3,000 tons would be collected. The black market price of wheat steadily declined and was at 900-1,150 rials/*kharvar*, according to quality; barley at 500 rials/*kharvar*. The bread situation in Kermanshah was satisfactory, although there was some drop in quality for a few days, when wheat was not properly cleaned due to a wage dispute with the cleaners. After resolving this there were no more problems. It looks as next crop will be good.

In February 1944, Ebtehaj Sami'i was again attacked in the press. The campaign was waged by the recently formed *jami'at-e mahalli-ye Kermanshah*, or a local watch committee. Its members were young and progressive and "their aim is the encouragement of works of improvement and public utility, the exposure of scandal and corruption, and the promotion of the citizens in general." The bread situation remained satisfactory in Kermanshah. The number of 'government' bakeries was reduced from 60 to 30. Those bakeries that were not 'government' any longer were 'free', subject to certain conditions and could become 'government' again, if required. The daily issue of flour to bakeries fell from 30 to 20 tons. There was increased smuggling of tea and cotton piece-goods to Iraq for Nowruz requirements. The black market price of wheat rose to Rls 1,300/*kharvar* probably helped by the radio announcement about the 15% sugar barter scheme. This was embarrassing because in Kermanshah not 15 but 10% sugar was given.[316]

In March 1944, the bread situation continued to be satisfactory. The 'government' bakeries sold bread at the official price of 9 rials/*man*, made from flour that was 2/3 wheat and 1/3 barley. The 'free' bakeries sold 100% wheat bread at 12 rials/*man*. There was a growing demand for 'free' bread and government bakeries complained about the lack of demand for their bread. The Department of Supplies delivered only 10 tons/day of flour to the 'government' bakeries, which had been 30 tons/day previously, a drop partly due to the halving of the number of 'government' bakeries in February and partly to preference for good wheat bread. The situation in Qasr-e Shirin was also good, where only 100% wheat bread was sold.

In that same month, the governor (*ostandar*) held a meeting with the Supply and Finance Departments to discuss the distribution of tea, sugar and cloth. He emphasized the need for equal treatment of townsmen and tribesmen. The distribution of sugar, tea, and cloth was transferred from the Supply Department to the Finance Department per 21 March 1944. In stock was 100,000 m of cloth, but 300,000 m more had been demanded from Tehran. A small quantity of cloth was given to Col. Mokri to distribute among 60,000 people in Posht-e Kuh. What people needed there was also more rain to get a good crop. Also, pasturage was lacking and the tribes felt the pinch; also of water as not enough snow had fallen. Qa'em-maqami, the manager of the Shahabad sugar mill said that Tehran proposed to close the mill and two others, because they were uneconomic. This would be unfortunate for this modern plant, despite the fact that it was

316. FO 371/40177, Kermanshah Diary February 1944 (Money was in demand and rates were 21-28%).

far away from beet growing land. However, 1,200 ha were already under cultivation. Also, 500 families would be without income.

The markets were very active, especially in good such as. *rowghan*, piece-goods and tea, because of *Nowruz*. The upsurge in trade was reflected in the rise of interest rates from 15-21% to 21-28% and there was good demand for money. Purchase of wheat via the sugar barter scheme ended at the end of Esfand (February/March). The black market price of wheat rose to 1,450 rials/*kharvar* , but fell in second half month to 1,150-1,200 rials. In short, prices for food items were reasonable, but that of tea rose 50% and thus, smuggling of tea to Iraq continued.[317]

In February 1944, Javad Shirvani, head of the *Amlak* at Shahabad had gone to Tehran, although he was needed to arrange for leasing the crown lands, and soon as possible, else it was feared that this would negatively impact the production of these lands. However, his return in April did not improve the situation. He continued to be obstructive in leasing lands, so that there was the risk that they would not be cultivated at all. In fact, it was worse, because he and six so-called 'inspectors', who accompanied him from Tehran, told the tribal chiefs and their tribesmen that with the departure of Col. Fletcher, the Political Advisor, henceforth they would have to listen to them, who had no intention to return back any arable lands or pasturage. The British consul was much upset about the bad handling of this issue both in Kermanshah and in Tehran. He suggested that perhaps the Finance Department should be given powers to resolve this issue speedily. The British Legation put pressure on Tehran, so that in May 1944 Shirvani received orders to lease the crown lands immediately.[318]

In April 1944, the black market price remained steady at 1,250 rials/*kharvar* for wheat and such large quantities were coming into the market that the last 5 days of the month supply to 'government' bakeries was only 0.9 tons. Practically the whole town ate 'free' bread at 4 rials/kg while 'government' bread was sold at 3 rials/kg. People preferred it, because they were able to eat it, if need be without cheese or condiments, which they could not with 'government' bread, which had a 1/3 barley mixture. Bakers bought grain at 4 rials/kg and gained 30% in baking in weight of bread and were more than happy to sell it at 4 rials. The abundance of black market grain, signaling withdrawal of government from market, was a reflection of a good next harvest.

Supplies of sugar and piece-goods for Posht-e Kuh arrived, but the Finance Department had no money to pay for their transport, which delayed the highly needed distribution. The market was active; prices rose in tea, *rowghan* and piece-goods. Much *rowghan* was sent to Tehran. It seemed that smuggling to Iraq had ceased, but tin ingots, spices, electric wire and other goods were still illegally imported. Large quantities of hides also arrived. Interest rates rose to 24-36% and there remained a good demand for money. Local food prices rose somewhat.[319]

In May 1944, there was extensive damage to the grain crop in Sanjabi, Mahidasht and Miandarband, due to a combination of frost, very mild weather, and rains and crops withered

---

317. FO 371/40177, Kermanshah Diary March 1944.

318. FO 371/40177, Kermanshah Diary February 1944; Idem, Kermanshah Diary April 1944; Idem, Kermanshah Diary May 1944. The consul advised that "the Ra'is-e Khvarbar needs to be kept an eye on, but dealing in cloth, tea and sugar have just been handed over to Finance, which is run by a competent Kurd." FO 248/1433, Calvert, Kermanshah to Bullard/Tehran, 30/03/1944.

319. FO 371/40177, Kermanshah Diary April 1944.

by heat. In 1943, these areas had supplied 15,000 tons or almost half the surplus of Kermanshah. The damage was less to wheat, which ripens later, than to barley. The government only paid 2,600 rials instead of previously 3,000/ton which made collection more difficult. As no pressure was put on landowners, let alone punishment, there were still 75 landowners who had failed to satisfy last year's undertaking. The black market reacted immediately. The price of wheat rose from 1,250 to 1,900 and settled at 1,650 rials. Free bread became scarce and rose to 6 rials/kg so that 2/3 of the town was eating 'government' bread again. Since 8 May the government supply of flour rose to 15-17 tons and upwards to 20 tons/day. People didn't like 'government' bread, while millers and bakers didn't like working for the government; they liked the free market, where they made higher profits. Millers and bakers adulterated the bread and threatened to strike, with the objective to have the government issue them wheat and barley flour separately, so that they could sell wheat bread in the free market at a large profit. The millers complained that the water supply was not enough for their mills and that the government rates were too low. They rather worked for private buyers who paid 2 to 3 times more. Fortunately, the government had much grain in store, so it had leverage *vis a vis* the bakers and millers. Also, during the last two months some shopkeepers were flogged for profiteering. A grocer, three wine sellers and a baker received 50 lashes each. Another grocer and wine seller were each fined 901 rials. High retail prices remained, however, because no hoarding landowners were punished. The market was quieter than in April except for *rowghan*, but prices remained mainly stable. Nevertheless, demand for money was good, even at 28-36% interest rates. Also disappointing was that only five *kharvar* of sugar was sent to the tribesmen in Posht-e Kuh and no piece-goods at all. Piece-goods were distributed only in Kermanshah; booths were set up in the principal mosque, where 74,000 persons were said to have been supplied with 3 meters each; leaving 14,000 people unserved.

There were two developments in May 1944 that held out the hope that the management of the bread issue would improve. (i) Hutchinson the US advisor to the Finance Department arrived; he was responsible for all Finance Department work, price stabilization, grain collection and distribution, as well as distribution of monopoly goods. The opium and tobacco monopolies and the *Amlak* were also under his control and all employees were under his orders. Although the Transport Department was outside his jurisdiction, he could demand transport priorities. He had a meeting with Shirvani about the *Amlak*, but he gave distribution of monopoly goods first attention. (ii) The second development was that the Ministry of Finance appointed a commission to investigate alleged "misappropriation of official money in the sugar and the piece-good warehouses." The main target was Ebtehaj Sami'i, the director of the Cereals and Bread Department, formerly the *Khvarbar*. He was accused by Qubadian in the *Majles* on 9 May 1944 and was the target of newspaper articles in the past. Ne'matollah Varta headed the commission, whose members sent for their families to spent a nice summer in Kermanshah so the investigation was going slow.[320]

In June 1944, the free market wheat price was 1,700-1,800 rials; therefore, more government flour had to be baked. This meant that between 23-24 tons/day were delivered to the bakers, while it was close to 30 tons during the winter of 1943. The millers were very unhelpful, blaming

---

320. FO 371/40177, Kermanshah Diary May 1944.

water supply. They milled only 16-17 tons/day, the rest had to come from mills at Sahneh and Kangavar, or taken from the small reserve stock. On 17 June the bakers struck for one day. The government's ability to provide sufficient bread to consumers was not to the liking of millers and bakers, who longingly thought back of the situation of the summer of 1943, when 'government' bread became scarcer and worse in quality. 'Government' bread was plenty in supply at 3 rials/kg, while free bread was in short supply, at 6 rials/kg.

The Cereals and Bread Department was reinforced by the arrival of 'Ali Akbar Nasih, nominally inspector of grain collection. The estimating commissions were at work in the field doing crop estimations, which made the investigation of the *Khvarbar* by Varta's commission very difficult. The preliminary estimate was a total of 19,000 tons or 15,000 less than last year. This meant that only 5,000 tons were available for Tehran rather than 20,000 in the past year. The crop area near Kermanshah that produced 17,000 tons last year had only produced 3,000 tons this year. Therefore, it was hoped that the *Amlak* would produce a small surplus. Last year the *Amlak* and parts of the Garmsir lying outside it only were able to supply Shahabad, Kerend, Ilam, Gilan, Sar-e Pol-e Zohab, and Qasr-e Shirin. Attempt also were made to get grain from Kurdistan that did not supply any last year. Lt. Col. Ataollah of the Cereals and Bread Department in Tehran tried to convince the heads of the Justice Department to take punitive actions against landowners who didn't honor their last year's undertakings (*ta'ahhod*); however, they did not believe it was legal. There also were rumors alleging that the *bakhshdar* north-west of Kermanshah kept the sugar sent for the tribes or sold it to them at high prices. Javad Shirvani belatedly showed signs of cooperation. After months of delay finally two important lands were leased. There was very little trade in June, prices fell a little. As a result, money became cheaper and interest rates fell from 28-40% at beginning of month to 18-27% at the end.[321] Millspaugh reported that in the first three months of 1323 [March-May 1944] "substantial progress has been made in the distribution of sugar, tea and cotton piece-goods ... Reports from Meshed, Shirraz, Isfahan, Ahwaz and Kermanshah indicate that the distribution of monopoly goods is proceeding more extensively, not only in the towns, but also in the villages and among the tribesmen. Complaints of non-distribution have remarkedly decreased; and, instead we are receiving from all sections reports of actual distribution to the people."[322]

In December 1944, grain prices rose 20% from110 to 120 rials/*kharvar*. There was no change in the price of 'free' bread and average daily issues of government flour to 'government' bakers fell from 15.5 tons in November to 14 tons in December. Some 1,500 tons of additional grain was bought in the Kermanshah collection area and at the end of December total purchases were 10,749 tons of wheat 4,800 tons of barley. Some 1,300 tons were sent to Tehran, so 12,000 tons were in stock for Kermanshah and its branches. E.C. Hutchinson, the American Director-General of Finance decided to revert to the old system of keeping his own trucks rather than having to obtain them from EBR (the Road Transport Administration or *Edareh-ye Barbari-ye Rah*) which did not work well. Some 100 tons of sugar, and some tea and piece-goods were distributed in tribal areas. Hutchinson did not allow tribal leaders to pick these up in Kermanshah, fearing

---

321. FO 371/40177, Kermanshah Diary June 1944.

322. IOR/L/PS/12/3396, Report of the Administrator General of the Finances of Iran for the months of Ordibehest and Khordad 1323 (April 21-June 21 1944), p. 5.

resale to the black market; he brought them into tribal areas, but that was as far as he was able to go. Tea stores were in excess of need, but sugar stocks were almost finished. The Shahabad sugar mill began operating on 6 December. Nasratollah Azadi, director of customs at Qasr-e Shirin stopped trans-border trade of piece-goods, sugar from Persia and grain from Iraq, but his superiors did not like this; although it was illegal they knew about, and therefore, the matter was referred to Tehran. In the bazaar prices rose by 10%. According to the *Bank-e Melli* manager, the lower prices in the fall were engineered by some merchants who realized that the war was not yet over. They started panic selling of some of their goods, only to buy them back at lower prices, to be resold later at higher prices. [323]

In January 1945, crop prospects looked good as snow and rain fell. The ban of cross-border trade drove up prices in Qasr-e Shirin to 20 rials per 3 kg. Since then the import of grain was allowed for local use and the price fell to 13 rials. Prices of grain in the free market rose in Kermanshah due to transport difficulties. Bread rose slightly from 12 rials for *sangak* bread and 13 rials for *lavash* bread in November-December 1944 to respectively 14 and 16 rials in January 1945. The government issue of flour had to be increased from 14 tons/day in December to 19.5 tons/day in January 1945. About half of this was milled in a mill driven by a diesel motor rented by the Finance Department in the city last summer. Some 1,900 tons of purchased grain entered the city in January, so by the end of the month 17,472 tons were in stock of which over 12,000 tons was wheat. 886 tons of barley and 61 tons were sent to Tehran. The bazaar was quiet, while prices tend to drop on news of advances in Europe by Russia, so that prices of piece-goods and sugar dropped by 5-20%. Merchants tended to only do cash business. *Rowghan* also rose in price as had grain.[324]

The Prime Minister wrote to Hutchinson that his authority concerning cereals and bread, the distribution of monopoly goods, rent control and the *Edareh-e Barbari-ye Rah* (which he never had anything to do with) were at an end. The press were denouncing the Finance Department for its inability to issue new food coupons; these were only available on considerable payment. The Cereals and Bread Department ordered bread to be mixed with 25% barley. Hutchinson preferred a few weeks delay, because those who did not want to eat the adulterated bread "trust the bakers to make it inedible" would have difficulty buying 'free' wheat, adequate supplies of which were not available, until winter transport problems were over and next year's harvest was in. The result would be expensive 'free wheat' which reduced their scope to buy wheat at the official price. Official purchasing was at an end, but it was still happening. Due to the war news, the market was dull and there was little business, except for potatoes, which rose considerably in price.[325]

In March 1945, Salehi, chief of the Supply Department advised to change the 25% barley ratio to 15% barley in bread, which was done. If flour would be properly cleaned the bread would be as palatable and white as 100% wheat bread, he believed, but it did not keep so well. The government wanted to get out of the bread business, and if people did not like this bread

323. FO 371/45400 Monthly Diary December 1944. Mahmud Salehi was the head of the Kermanshah Cereals and Bread Department.

324. FO 371/45400 , Monthly Diary January 1945.

325. FO 371/45400, Kermanshah Diary February 1945.

and bought bread in the open market then this objective was achieved. If the price of 'free' bread went up it did not matter as the government was out of the business of buying grain. Moreover, good harvest prospects and better transport after the winter kept price of bread stable. The situation was less rosy concerning sugar. Only brown sugar was available and people had hoped for white sugar for *Nowruz*, so there was much criticism. This was bad PR for the Persians, Salehi said, because when the Americans were in charge they supplied all-wheat bread and white sugar, but the moment Persians took over there was barley-wheat bread and brown sugar only. Moreover, there were complaints that people had not received their sugar ration for three months. Trade was dull; there was hardly any business. Favorable war news made merchants hesitant to enter into new commitments. In spite of *Nowruz,* prices remained stationary, except for *rowghan* that rose from 30 rials to 400 rials per 3 kg.[326] Jahanshahi wanted the Ministry of the Interior to fire Mr. Moqaddam, the *bakhshdar* of Kermanshah, who was involved in sugar, tea, cloth corruption in distributing these to out-districts, which was none of his business. He asked the British consul to back him up.[327]

In April 1945, the bazaar was quiet; the impending end of the war was a deterrent for buying and selling. Prices were static except for *rowghan*, which fell considerably, although large deals were done at the end of the month.[328] There was some alarm about the arrival of locusts in Posht-e Kuh. Action was undertaken, but this was done half-heartedly and was very ineffectively executed, but as it was a sparsely cultivated region and there was no further spread there was no cause for alarm. Otherwise, crop prospects looked positive thanks to good May rains. Landowners and peasants were worried as the government price of grain went down and the government did not buy grain any longer. As a result, trade in the bazaar was stagnant, while some prices dropped after V day, but later rose again. However, prices of *rowghan* rose considerably and people started to complain. The *Tudeh* party asked the municipal council (*anjoman-e shahrdari*) to intervene. It decided to ban the export of *rowghan* to other parts of Persia. This caused a crisis between the council and the mayor (*shahrdar*) Mohammadi, who took the position that the decision was illegal and unenforceable. Therefore, the *Tudeh* took action by having their 'police' stop trucks loaded with *rowghan* from leaving Kermanshah and took an undertaking from merchants and transporters not to transport *rowghan* outside the province. Jahanshahi considered the whole affair illegal and the council withdrew its decision.[329]

When in June 1945, the government stopped buying barley the price dropped from 800 to 400 rials/*kharvar*. Sugar distribution in the province was a source of much discontent. E'temadi, the director of distribution stated that at the end of July he needed 800 tons to supply what was needed for 1323/1944 and 1,000 tons for 1324/1945, or a total of 1,800 tons, while the government had only authorized 600 tons to be supplied by the Shahabad mill. Even this amount could not be transported because of problems with the Road Transport Department (*edareh-ye barbari-ye rah*). As a result, some tribes had not received sugar during four and some even for 7-8

326. FO 371/45400, Kermanshah Diary March 1945
327. FO 248/1451, Consul Davis/Kermanshah to Moneypenny/Tehran, 05/03/1945
328. FO 371/45400, Kermanshah Diary April 1945.
329. FO 371/45400, Kermanshah Diary May 1945.

months. Moreover stocks were low (see Table 2.9). Nevertheless, the market remained quiet and prices were somewhat higher.[330]

Table 2.9: Tea and sugar stocks, June 1945

Sugar, brown	90 tons (gross)
Sugar, white	60 tons (gross) of which 32 tons were required for Kermanshah town, leaving only 28 for the tribes.
Tea, foreign	40 tons
Tea, Iranian	53 tons
Tea, mixed	10 tons

Source: FO 371/45400, Kermanshah Diary June 1945.

In July 1945, the Economic Department distributed 300 tons of sugar to the tribes; estimates of money pocketed by officials ranged from 600,000 to 900,000 rials. Ashtiyaneh, the inspector of the Economic Department in place of Mr. Salehi, its director was away on sick leave, had trouble with the bakers about the sale of government flour. With good crop prospects prices of wheat dropped from 1,500 to 800 rials/*kharvar* so that the difference between 'free' and government flour was smaller. Bakers making 'government' bread had difficulties selling it. Therefore, Ashtiyani decided to end the 20% barley mix and also to make sure that flour was better sieved and grinded than before. He had to get rid of 600 tons government flour that would not keep. Therefore, he wanted to close the 'free' bakeries for some time or force them to accept government flour. This caused opposition. A commission was formed and finally it was decided that bakers had to buy government flour or pay a fine of 4,000 rials. 'Free' bread sold at 10 rials per *man* and government bread at 9 rials, but its quality was not so good. Government bread bakers claimed that at this price they could not sell their bread and therefore, its price had to come down. Ashtiyani told them that this was impossible. The government had bought grain at high prices and subsidized the sale of bread, suffering significant losses. Meanwhile, grain prices continued to fall. Fortuitously, at the end of July there was a thunderstorm. Because people believe that when ripe grain is rained upon it does not keep, and therefore, landlords and peasants were selling their surplus. The government bought very little. The bazaar was active, but prices did not rise much. Interest rates were at 12-18%. There was a strong demand for tea and cotton piece-goods.[331]

Table 2.10: Wholesale prices in Kermanshah, March, May 1945 (in rials)

	Weight	03/45	05/45
Tea, Indian	300 g	*Rls* 200	190
Tea, Iranian	Idem	30	45
Rice	3 kg	33	32

330. FO 371/45400, Kermanshah Diary June 1945.
331. FO 371/45400, Kermanshah Diary July 1945.

Cheese		70	45
Salt	”	6	-
Onions	”	14	-
Charcoal	”	3	5
Firewood	”	2.30	-
Washing soap	”	200	-
Straw	”	3	-
Oranges	Each	3	-
Mutton	-	-	80
Goat's meat	-	-	48
Barley	-	-	8

Source: FO 371/45400, Kirmanshah Diary March 1945; Idem , Kirmanshah Diary May 1945.

In August 1945, wheat was aplenty and prices fell. There was no distribution of government sugar and tea; distribution of government cloth had not taken place for many months. The market overall was dull, and prices slightly dropped.[332] In September 1945, the Supply Department received 900 tons of sugar from Tehran. It proposed to distribute it to villagers who had received nothing for over one year. This caused an outcry from urbanites and tribesmen who were better organized than villagers. In Kermanshah no cloth had been distributed for 15 months; in the outstations much longer and elsewhere never at all. The Supply Department was short of cloth. It only had 204 bales in stock and it needed 1,000 bales to distribute 3 meters/p.p.

Wheat was abundant; its price was 850 rials per *kharvar*. The estimated surplus was 50,000 tons, but the government did not intend to buy and landlords and peasants had to sell it with great difficulty. The government target for this area was to buy 20,000 tons and so far it had received commitments for 15,000 tons. It had no intention to buy the remaining 5,000 tons. 'Free' bread was available aplenty at 8 rials/*man*; this was cheaper than 'government' bread which was not for sale and no government flour was supplied to bakers.[333] Consequently, there was worry about the sale of the 1945 surplus. There was even some grain left from 1944. There were hardly any buyers locally and no demand from the rest of Persia, while prospects for export were dim. The situation with sugar and piece-goods was still as bad as before. The Director of the Supply Department complained about the disorganization in the Tehran Depot. He finally went there in person and received 900 tons of sugar at Soltanabad and 1,000 bales of cloth at Khorramshahr with the promise that these would be transported to Kermanshah as soon as possible, but he received nothing, also no reply to his telegrams.[334]

332. FO 371/45400, Kermanshah Diary August 1945.

333. FO 371/45400, Kermanshah Diary September 1945.

334. FO 371/45400, Kermanshah Diary October 1945.

Table 2.11: Comparison of food prices, December 1943-September 1945 (in *rials*)

Product	End Dec1943	End Jan 1944	End Feb	End March	End April	End May	End June	30 Nov	31 Dec -44	31 Jan 1945	28 Feb	30 April	30 June	July 31	August 31	September 30
Wheat kharvar	1,500	1,000 (av)	1,300	1,150-1,200	1,250	1,650	1,700	950-1,000	1,100-1,200	1,500	1,500 -1,600	360	265	255	245	255
Barley kharvar	800	500	500	550	600	750	600	470	500	800	800	2,000	15	16	16	14
Peas 3kg	2,250	2,200	2,000	2,000	2,100	2,100	-	2,000	1,800	2,400	2,500	2,500	24	22	21	24
Beans 3kg	1,500	1,350	1,100	900	1,250	1,500	1,250	850	800	1,100	1,100 -1,150	1,300	13.5	14	15	20
Potatoes 3kg	750	800	600/700	550	900	900	1,200 (new)	800	1,400	1,500 - 1,700	2,000 - 2,200	1,500	1,000	800-900	785	835
Rowghan 3kg	240 per 3kg	240	222	230	255	243	226	200	290	370	360	900	300	300	400	350
Mutton-retail 3kg								64-72	90	88	100	112	64	81	80	75

Source: FO 371/40177, Monthly Diary December 1943-June 1944; FO 371/45400, Monthly Diary November-December 1944, January-September 1945.

By the end of 1945, the food situation in Kermanshah had returned to normal. The government had totally withdrawn from direct involvement in the purchase and distribution of food grains and other basic necessities and let the market function. Everybody had learnt from this experience and the food supply situation never again reverted to that of the many hunger years that had been typical for a great number of years prior to 1945.

CHAPTER THREE

ADMINISTRATIVE STRUCTURES

CITY GOVERNMENT

The governor (*hakem, hokmran, vali*) of Kermanshah, who was appointed by the Shah, resided in the governor's palace that had been built by Dowlatshah. He carried out his daily business in the official part of the palace, the so-called *divan-khaneh* or Government House. In carrying out his tasks the governor was assisted by the following officials, just like in any other large town in Qajar Persia. The first assistant was the deputy-governor (*na'eb al-hokumeh*), followed by (2) the provincial accountant and his staff (*ra'is daftar* or *vazir-e maliyat*), (3) the secretary and his staff (*monshi-bashi*), (4) the army accountant and his staff (*lashkar-nevis*), (5) the chief judicial officer (*ra'is-e otaq-e tahqiqat*), (6) the commercial agent (*ra'is-e tejarat*), (7) the chief attendant and his staff (*farrash-bashi*), (8) the chief orderly (*ardel-bashi*), (9) the chief of guards and his staff (*keshikchi-bashi*), (10) the chief of the riflemen and his staff (*tofangdar-bashi*), (11) the chief retainer and his staff (*qollar-aghasi bashi*), (12) the treasurer (*sanduqdar*), (13) the chief out-runner and his staff (*shater-bashi*), (14) the mayor of the city (*kalantar*), and (15) the chiefs of the city quarters (*kadkhoda*s) and the market overseer (*darugheh-ye bazar*).[1]

The functions of the first four officials are clear from their title. The deputy governor assisted the governor in whatever task the latter assigned to him, while he also officiated for the governor during his absence. The *vazir-e maliyat* was in charge of the collection, recording and management of the provincial revenues; he was also referred to as *pishkar*. The *monshi-bashi* was in charge of the governor's secretariat, drafted all outgoing correspondence and handled all incoming messages. The *lashkar-nevis* had the responsibility to see to it that the provincial army was maintained at strength and paid and to monitor any changes in its financial, administrative and other arrangements.[2] Apart from the provincial army (see chapter four), there always was a regiment from outside the province, which served as the city's garrison. Around the turn of the twentieth century, it was usually not more than 500 men strong, armed with Werndl rifles,

1. DCR 590 (Kermanshah, 1902), pp. 11-12; Lycklama 1873, vol. 3, p. 472; Soltani 1381, vol. 1, p. 547; *Ruznameh-ye Iran* 1375, vol. 4, p. 3396 (no. 860; 26/12/1894); vol. 5, pp. 4007 (no. 1006; 01/08/1901).
2. Adamec 1976, vol. 1, p. 372.

Fig. 3.1: The governor's palace in 1839.

which they had to return when disbanded.[3] The *ra'is-bashi-ye tahqiqat* was in charge of the administration of justice, dealing with requests, complaints and crimes; the chief-executioner (*mir-ghazab*) carried out executions, while the chief goaler (*dustaqban*) was in charge of the prison and its inmates, who were incarcerated in *divan-khaneh*'s complex. At the end of 1896, the *majles-e tahqiq* was renamed *otaq-e divan-khaneh* or *otaq-e divan-khaneh-ye 'adliyeh*.[4]

In 1881, there was a *ra'is-e tojjar* in Kermanshah and Kurdistan as in many other cities.[5] This official dealt with matters concerning trade and seems to have sent most cases for judgment to the town's *mojtaheds*. These would judge the case and have their decision executed by the *ra'is-e tojjar*.[6] In case of bankruptcy, especially when Europeans were involved, these would apply for help to the *ra'is-e tojjar*. This usually resulted in the convening of a *majles* or meeting of the parties concerned to try and find a solution to the conflict. After about 1880 such cases were referred to the *kargozar* or agent for foreign affairs.[7]

The *farrash-bashi* was the chamberlain, who was in charge of all of the governor's servants. The *ardel-bashi* was the governor's chief orderly; each day he provided relevant people with

3. DCR 590 (Kermanshah 1901-02), pp. 63-64.
4. *Ruznameh-ye Iran* 1375, vol. 5, pp. 3523 (no. 876; 23/02/1896), 3683 (no. 915; 10/01/1897)
5. E`temad al-Saltaneh 1294-96, vol. 3, appendix, 7; Adamec 1976, vol. 1, p. 372.
6. Aubin 1908, p. 36. At least since 1896, there was a *majles-e tejarat* in Kermanshah, which was under the rotating chairmanship of a government official. *Ruznameh-ye Iran* 1375, vol. 5, pp. 3523 (23/02/96), 4007 (01/08/1901), 4087 (03/07/1902).
7. Floor 1977, pp. 61-76. For a case study, see Idem 1983.

the password for the palace, so that they might enter and be about the palace after curfew (see below). The *keshikchi-bashi* was the chief of the governor's bodyguards. He watched over his tent at night and rode by his side when he went outside the palace. The *tofangdar-bashi* was the governor's arms carrier when he went hunting as well as chief of the hunting staff. The *qollar-aghasi bashi* introduced the governor to the people of the city when he was newly appointed and to the villagers, when he made a tour in the province. The *sanduqdar* was the treasury cashier. The *shater-bashi* was the chief of the runners.

The *kalantar*, who in Kermanshah also was referred to as *kadkhoda-bashi*, was the chief of the *kadkhoda*s. The *kalantar* was in charge of the local crown lands and the guilds (*mobasher-e khaleseh va asnaf-e bazar*), the management and policing of the city as well as of organizing firefighting and of price control. In these tasks, he was assisted by the *kadkhoda*s (for the quarters) and the *darugheh* (for the bazaar).[8] The role of the *kadkhoda* was to maintain law and order in his quarter and see to it that the taxes were collected. This task also involved policing the quarter as well as judging and sentencing light offences. The *kadkhoda*s also had to keep track of births and deaths (assisted by the *ghossalan* or body washers); their executive arm were known as *'asas*, or watchmen.[9]

In the early twentieth century, and presumably also prior to that time, robberies were very common in and outside town, although the thieves were seldom caught.[10] Moreover, if caught, when offenders had perpetrated their crime in another quarter there was little chance that punishment would follow. For example, in July 1906, thieves robbed the British Consulate. The consul commented that "There is no police and all misdemeanours are referred to the Kadkhuda" of the quarter. If the ruffian is from another part of town he will not be questioned, and it is a wonder that not more robberies are committed.[11] The *darugheh-ye bazar* and his *'asas* or night watchmen were responsible for the safety of the bazaars at night.[12]

People were supposed to be in their homes after "the signal drum is beat three times after sunset, at the last sound of which the streets must be cleared of every individual on pain of

8. Until mid-1892 the office of *kalantar* had been in the family of Hasan Khan, but he was dismissed for unjust behavior and replaced by Abdollah Khan. *Ruznameh-ye Iran* 1375, vol. 4, pp. 3104 (no. 771; 22/04/1892), 3315 (no. 824; 12/04/1894), 3379 (no. 840; 29/10/1894); vol. 5, pp. 3582 (no. 890; 01/08/1896) 3899 (no. 969; 30/12/1899); Adamec 1976, vol. 1, pp. 372-73. Originally, the title *beglerbegi* was given to a governor of a big province (see Floor 2001, p. 96), but in the late Qajar period instances are found where the *kalantar* of a big city was referred to as *beglerbegi* (see e.g. Floor 1971 a). When in February 1913 a shop in the *bazzaz-khaneh* was broken into, the *darugheh* was flogged and dismissed. FO 248/1073, Kermanshah Diary no. 7 ending 13/02/1913.

9. Political Diaries, vol. 3, p. 161; Soltani 1381, vol. 1, p. 457; *Ruznameh-ye Iran* 1375, vol. 4, p. 2824 (701; 19/11/1889). On the function of the *kadkhoda*, see Floor, "Kadkhoda," [iranica.com].

10. Political Diaries, vol. 1, pp. 411, 428. However, from reading the reports from Kermanshah in the *Ruznameh-ye Iran* (too many to list) one gets the impression that the roads were safe and that the occasional robberies were efficiently resolved by the capture of the culprits and the return of the stolen goods. Only once is there a report that the *qarasuran* had not been doing a very good job and, therefore, Ziya al-Molk changed all the road guards from Tang-e Bidsorkh to Qasr-e Shirin. *Ruznameh-ye Iran* 1375, vol. 4, p. 3131 (no. 778; 10/08/1892). For European newcomers the nights in the city seemed disturbing, because it "was customary that the Kurds were continually firing their guns outside town for the fun of it, which Waffelaert [the Belgian Customs official] mistook for being fired upon." Political Diaries 1, p. 103.

11. Administration Report 1906-07, p. 39.

12. Adamec 1976, vol. 1, p. 373. On the function of the *darugheh*, see Floor 1971.

death."[13] This ban lasted till dawn. People could only be outside their homes, if they had a password (*esm-e shab*). In Kermanshah there were two passwords that one could get from the *ardel-bashi*, the governor's chief orderly. One was for the town and the other for the artillery square. A third password was for the governor's palace and only meant for the inmates of the palace. In 1872, Bellew was able to leave the town after curfew at 10 p.m. through the good offices of Vakil al-Dowleh.[14]

It was not just a signal drum that was beaten, but an entire music band or *naqqareh-khaneh* gave the signal. To the south of the palace was a small building that dominated the terraces and was embellished with, what Binder considered to be artless paintings. Each evening, at sunset 5-6 musicians went there to play. The music started with a solo by the tambourine, then the big drum joined, after which followed calmer music, then a clarinet was played, and finally all of them played together, including the long trumpets that made an infernal noise. When the music stopped, the trumpets gave three last blows, after which followed a cannon shot.[15] In 1889 the *naqqareh-khaneh* was located southern part of *Sabzeh-Meydan* over the entrance gate of the Customs House, facing north. It was a small room with only one opening, the other three sides were walls. The musicians played for 20 minutes.[16]

The security officials (*kalantar*, *kadkhoda*, *darugheh* and *'asas*) brought transgressors of the law to justice. There was a dual judicial system of ad-hoc religious or *shari'ah* courts presided over by *qadi*s and ad-hoc secular or *'orf* courts administered by secular government officials. In the rural areas, where some 90% of the population lived, village and tribal leadership as well as landowners applied mostly customary law. Islamic law was applied in case of marriage and divorce, but often inheritance rules still followed customary rules in rural areas. In the city of Kermanshah, the practice was that (i) misdemeanors were taken care of by local institutions such as the chiefs of the extended families, chiefs of the city quarters and of the guilds applying customary law; (ii) felony cases were in general dealt with by the secular authorities such as the police chief (*darugheh*) and the governor applying customary law. The latter usually issued sentences by executive order without basing himself on any law. The bastinado and public executions usually were carried out in the *Meydan-e Tupkhaneh*; (iii) torts were either dealt with by the secular or the religious judiciary, the latter in particular if it concerned matters of family law; (iv) civil disputes were mostly dealt with by the religious judiciary applying Islamic law or by the mercantile community in case of trade related disputes, and (v) after the 1880s, cases involving both Persian and foreign subjects were referred to the *kargozar*. Although there were exceptions to this categorization, in general it held true.[17]

Cases of felony were the governor's jurisdiction, who could meet out any kind of sentence that he considered to meet the crime or that he considered to be politically expedient. Apart

13. Buckingham 1971, p. 103.
14. Rabino 1903, p. 5; Bellew 1999, p. 440.
15. Binder 1887, p. 347; Teule 1842, vol. 2, p. 483.
16. Soltani 1381, vol. 1, p. 553.
17. On the issue of the judiciary in general, see Floor 1983 a, pp. 113-147; Administration Report 1880-81, pp. 24-25. On the *kargozar*'s court, see above.

from the bastinado, criminals might be punished with mutilation or death.[18] These punishments were carried out in a variety of ways. Dr. Wills described a case of the punishment of two women.

> One day in Kermanshah I was surprised to meet a procession in the streets. First came all the lutis or buffoons, the public musicians singing and dancing, then a crowd of drunken roughs, then a few soldiers with fixed bayonets, then the "farrash-bashi," or "principal tent-pitcher" - in reality the Imad-u-dowlet's head-man - on horseback; the executioner, clad in red, and his aides; then two wretched women, their heads shaved and rubbed with curds, their faces bare and blackened, *dressed in men's clothes*, and both seated on one donkey, led by a negro, with their faces to the tail (their feet had been beaten to a pulp); then a crowd of some two thousand men ,women, and children. On inquiry I learnt that these women were attendants at a public baths, and had betrayed the wife of a tradesman into the hands of an admirer, who had secreted himself in the bath with their connivance. The woman complained, the man fled, and justice (Persian justice) was being done in the two unfortunate women. The Imad-u-dowlet had severely bastinadoed them and then gave them over to the executioner to be paraded through the town and then banished-after they had been handed over to the tender mercies of all the ruffians of the city. The first part of the sentence had been carried out, and they had been led thus through the bazaars from dawn till afternoon; the executioner taking, as is customary, a small tax from each trader according to his degree. I learnt afterwards that the mob defiled these women, and one died of her injuries; the other wretch either took poison or was given it by her offended relatives the next morning. Such is Persian justice.[19]

But there were many variations on the theme of justice. When entering the citadel of Kermanshah in 1867, Wills noted a man "nailed by the ear to a wooden telegraph post." It was a villager who had cut the telegraph wire and he was put here as a warning for others for 36 hours, after which he was thrown in prison.[20] In April 1890, the governor had two bandits beheaded in the presence of the heir of the man they had killed.[21] In 1901, a man had stolen a bale of cotton and was immured alive. The onlookers made remarks while the bound man struggled vehemently and vainly to prevent his fateful lot. One was so violent that it was difficult for the executioners to immure him and orders were given to still the man with a knife. At that time, two poplars in front of the IBP building, served as a scaffold. If condemned to die on the scaffold, the criminal had one leg tied to each tree and then was slowly cut open with a pair of scissors at orders of Ala al-Dowleh.[22] In 1911, Farmanfarma had some men, who had broken their pledge to him, killed by *tukhmaq* or rammer (i.e. their head was crushed like wax) just as

18. For an interesting case involving the killing of a soldier, see *Ruznameh-ye Iran* 1375, vol. 4, p. 2675 (no. 664; 30/09/1888).
19. Wills 1893, p.122 (italics in the original).
20. Wills 1893, pp.112-13.
21. Abbasi and Badi`i 1372, p. 71.
22. Rolandshay 1904, pp. 112, 116.

he had promised in the amnesty.[23] In the 1920s, the square was still used for public executions such as hangings, to which end a scaffold would be erected there. "Directly below it was a tank, or pool, in which the women of the town were doing their washing."[24]

The co-existence of two different judicial courts and sets of rules could be a cause of frustration and confusion. For example, when the half-share of a garden next to Consulate came into possession of the IBP, as the land was security for a loan, which was not paid despite having been granted an extension, the IBP wanted to build a house on it for its manager. This caused local opposition; the *mojtahed* of course backed the debtor, while the *kargozar* refused to act. In late April 1907 the debtor even claimed that he had paid the money to the *mojtahed* within the required time. This method had been indeed agreed upon, although no money was paid, but it made settlement more difficult. Capt. Haworth suggested that if opposition was really serious to refer the matter to IBP's head office in Tehran. However, in early May the IBP gave up its claim due to a flaw in the deed.[25]

After 1909 or so, many administrative changes took place in the manner in which the provincial administration was organized. Whereas before that time the governor was responsible for all aspects the province's administration (taxes, customs, judiciary, law and order) after that year the governor was assisted by an array of new departments and officials such as the deputy governor, *kargozar*, chiefs of treasury, Customs, army, police, gendarmerie, Telegraph and Post, *'adliyeh*, of which only the deputy-governor was directly responsible to the governor. The other officials were all responsible to their respective Ministries in Tehran.[26] Around 20 January 1909, Sa'd-e Homayun arrived from Tehran with orders to established a modern court of justice (*'adliyeh*) in Kermanshah.[27] There are not many data on the organization of the judiciary of Kermanshah after WW I. There was a court of appeals (*estinaf*) in 1945, which implies that there also should have been the court of first instance (*ebteda'i*), the criminal court (*jaza'i*) and the petty court (*solhiyeh*). This seems likely since there was a public prosecutor in Kermanshah and a head of the Justice department.[28]

MUNICIPALITY

In 1913, in accordance with the Municipality Law of 20 June 1907 (*qanun-e baladiyeh*), Farmanfarma, the governor, appointed Sa'd Homayun to organize the establishment of the municipality or *baladiyeh* and arrange for the cleaning and lighting of the streets. In the

23. Soltani, Nahzat, p. 179.
24. Powell 1923, p. 231.
25. Political Diaries, vol. 2, pp. 162, 183, 189.
26. AIR 20/663, p. 24.
27. Political Diaries, vol. 3, p. 46; FO 248/1073, Kermanshah Diary no. 11, ending 13/03/1913 (the `*adliyeh* under Mo`tazed al-Dowleh "appears to be doing good work and is praised by everyone").
28. FO 371/45400, Kermanshah Diary April 1945 (Mohammad Shahverdi public prosecutor); FO 371/45400, Kermanshah Diary October 1945 (Mr. Ma'qul, director of the Justice Department and President of the Court of Appeal, who was very popular locally).

Fig. 3.2: Meydan Kermanshah (1907).

beginning its work was mostly ceremonial, basically charged with the same tasks as the *farrash-khaneh* prior to that time. However, once the tasks for the municipality were formulated, the new institution basically took over the duties that previously had been the responsibility of the *beglerbegi*, *farrash-bashi*, *kadkhodas* and *darugheh-ye bazar*. As such, the municipality was charged with the supervision of the trades and crafts and collecting taxes from them, the quality of bread as well as activities such as cleaning the streets and the lighting of the oil lamps of government-house as well as of the lanes and streets in the evening. These latter two tasks were carried out by the municipal staff. In 1914, governor 'Abdol-Hoseyn Mirza dismissed Abu'l-Fath Mirza and replaced him with *beglerbegi* Asad Khan. This change coincided with the time of the famine, the influenza pandemic and the bitter cold.[29]

In early 1920, the latent bad feelings between Moderates and Democrats became overt. The *ra'is-e baladiyeh*, Amir Mojallal was removed from his post due to ill-health and Beglerbegi was put in his place by the governor. The former was a Democrat the latter a Moderate. The Democrats insisted that there should be elections, but the governor refused, because of strong party feelings. A compromise had to be reached for the selection of the four members of each of the three city quarters. Half to the Democrats and half to the Moderates, while Beglerbegi remained in function. Neither party really cared about the *baladiyeh*, but it was just for the Democrats an opportunity to test their strength. It was expected that when *Majles* met an attempt

29. Soltani 1381, vol. 1, pp. 547-48 (gives the name of the first mayor as Abu'l-Fath Mirza); FO 248/1073, Kermanshah Diary no. 19, ending 08/05/1913. "Taxes on the means of transport to cover municipal expenses were put in force on 24th October." FO 248/1073, Kermanshah Diary no. 44, ending 30/10/1913. Apparently, an earlier attempt to collect this tax at the bridge in January 1913 had not worked well. FO 248/1073, Kermanshah Diary no. 15, ending 10 January 1913.

would be made to annul the election of the four Moderates from Kermanshah. The party feelings subsided somewhat when news came of the demise of Sayyed Sadr at Kerbela.[30] In May 1920, there was still no municipality (*baladiyeh*) in running order and the city's cleanliness needed much improvement.[31]

At the end of September 1920, Mirza Hasan Khan Mohandes al-Molk resigned from his post as deputy-governor and he became *ra'is-e baladiyeh*. However, the prospects for a well-functioning municipality were not very bright. In October 1920, once again the governor announced that municipal elections would be held and that a new *ra'is* has already been appointed.[32] Apparently the situation improved somewhat thereafter, because the British consul reported in December 1920 that "municipal affairs begin to improve; thefts are few."[33] The execution of the various municipal tasks was rather sloughenly, because not all staff were given a specific task, so that many of these tasks were not carried out. In 1926, the only municipal workers were those who had to sweep and sprinkle the streets as of sunrise; in the evening they also lit and later extinguished the lamps and the lanterns in the streets and passageways. Initially, the municipality employed 12 street sweepers (*roftgar*), 3 *na'eb*s, 5 *mir-ab*s, and some workers and clerks. The chief of the municipality earned 157 rials; the lowest paid was the *garichi* who received 9 rials/month. During 1925-29, the Municipality employed 24 workers (*karmand*), 30 street sweepers, *na'eb*s, *mir-ab*s, and lantern lighters.

In mid-September 1929, Ebrahim Khan Mo'tamed Darakhshan was appointed head of the municipality. He made changes by hiring educated people, so that the municipality had a secretariat, accounting, hygiene (*tanzifat*), food supply, workers affairs, buildings, execution and inspection, health and assistance sections. Furthermore, he summoned the heads of the guilds and gave them hygienic rules to follow, such as that their work place had to be tiled, their workers had to wear clean white aprons and especially butchers had to cover their produce. Sellers of foodstuff (*khvarbar)* had to use white copper kettles to offer their wares. Henceforth transport of meat was to be done with hooks on the animals and be covered with white covers. The slaughter-house had to be relocated to a better place. In that same year rules for the collection of imposts of the guilds were issued. For the first time, houses, shops and real estate were inventoried and a database was created, also of the guilds. The municipality collected imposts on real estate (8%), weigh-bridge, *seyfi* permit, cinema and theater, garages and hotels, and restaurants, cafes, factories, slaughter-house, and various others, in addition to fines. In 1932, the municipality had revenues of 224,738 rials.[34]

As late as 1930, the music of the *naqqareh-khaneh* was heard at sunset, when "five or six respectable citizens climbed the top of a ruined tower and banged drums, beat cymbals, whistled on flutes, and tooted upon horns for about half an hour."[35] In 1934 this custom was discontinued,

30. FO 248/1293, Kermanshah Report no. 2, 29/02/1920.
31. FO 248/1293, Weir to Civil Commissioner, Baghdad 04/06/1920. "Notes on Kermanshah notables and officials." May 1920.
32. FO 248/1293, Kermanshah Report no. 9, up to 10 October 1920.
33. FO 248/1293, Kermanshah Report no. 11, up to 10 December 1920.
34. Soltani 1381, vol. 1, pp. 548-49, 552.
35. Reitlinger 1932, p. 31.

the musicians were sacked and even at Ramazan the gun was not fired anymore to announce the beginning and end of the month of fasting. On 15 November 1934, merchants petitioned the municipality to reinstate the *naqqareh-khaneh*, because most people had no idea of the right time and had no watch. However, the decision was not revoked.[36] In 1934, Foruhar, with a bank loan, was able to buy a fire truck, while in 1938, the *baladiyeh* was renamed *shahrdari*.[37]

Table 3.1: Mayors and their terms in office (1941-45)

Name	Years
Hosam al-Din Arefi	?-5 April 1942
Feyzollah A`zam Zanganeh	05/04-25/07/1942
Morteza Abu Dhar	1322?/1943
Sahebqerani	1323?/1944
Sa`id Fozuni*	?- 15 April 1945
Ali Asghar Mohammadi	15 April-September 1945
Kazem Sharifi	September 1945-?

Source: Soltani 1381, vol. 1, p. 557 (for those with *Shamsi* dates) and sources in the text (with CE dates).

* Soltani has Mansur Fozuni.

From 1921-25, part of the *divan-khaneh* was used to house the Municipality. During 1925-29 it was housed in the former telephone building, in the southern part of the Amir-e Nezam Garrusi Mosque. During 1930-37, the Municipality was housed in the Tavakkoli building in Kh. Sepah. From 1938-41, it was housed in the Nabash Sharqi building, employing 50 workers and 150 cadres.[38]

The inefficiency of the Municipality was made worse by the uncertainty about its available budget, both as to its level and the time of its approval. Although there was a willingness to establish open-air municipal markets (at the urging of the British consul), the governor did not obtain the required approval from Tehran. Finally, after much correspondence, the municipal budget, which included the financing for these markets, was approved. The delay in approval of the municipal budget also meant that the Municipality was unable to benefit from two steam rollers that were in Kermanshah to extended the runway. They surfaced the new road in front of the Consulate, but the municipal budget not yet having been approved, local authorities were unable to have them also roll the main street properly and so, they left it.[39] There continued to be problems with the municipal budget, even though the Municipality collected 3% octroi (‘*avarez*) on local produce brought into the city to finance part of its budget.[40]

---

36. Soltani 1381, vol. 1, p. 553.
37. Soltani 1381, vol. 1, p. 560.
38. Soltani 1381, vol. 1, p. 560.
39. FO 371/31402, Kermanshah Diary May 1942.
40. FO 371/40177, Kermanshah Diary March 1944.

On 5 April 1942, Arefi, the mayor was replaced by Feyzollah Zanganeh (Zahir al-Molk), an uncle of Amir Koll. Arefi was ineffective, lacked energy and was unable to control prices.[41] The British consul described the situation as follows:

> The Municipality has no budget whatever so for this year even for its most crying needs, including the salaries of its employees. It appears that Qiami would not let the useless figure-head of a Mayor and his equally useless council frame their own budget in March, and took it up with him to Tehran sometime later for arrangement at the Ministry of Interior.[42]

Zahir al-Molk, according to the British consul, was an unintelligent, inexperienced old man who had held no government post for over 20 years. It was difficult to accuse him of venality, but he certainly took advantage of the situation for his own and his relatives' interests and was allowing flagrant mismanagement to go on. The former governor had fired a score of the worst municipal employees a few months earlier, but they all had been able to get hired again filling their pockets with contributions from "bakers, millers and market gardeners now that bread and water are artificially made scarce under a frightened, muddled and inefficient administration which takes its cue partly from Tehran." On 25 July 1942, Zahir al-Molk resigned as mayor after a meeting requested by the British consul who pointed out that "the chief cause of the dangerously worsening local situation was the idleness, inefficiency and blatant corruption of the whole Municipality of the town and its officials." [43] The dismissal of the mayor did not improve the bread situation, which was characterized by the worsening quality of bread and rising prices.[44]

In mid-January 1944 an election committee was formed for the municipal elections in Kermanshah in February. Governor Fahim al-Dowleh asked Tehran whether the Jews (10,000 in number) would be allowed to vote, which they had requested. The Ministry of Interior informed him that Jews were allowed to vote; they had in the past, but not the last eight years.[45] In the mid-1930s, Reza Shah had taken some steps to disenfranchise Jews, including by dismissing them from government service.[46] On 13 February the elections were held for the 14 member municipal council. Some 600 men, mostly those not entitled to vote, gathered in front of the Municipal building and later at the *ostandari* to demonstrate in favor of Allameh, the former chairman. Allameh, who was described as a "well-known, if rather seedy demagogue" and unsuccessful candidate for the *Majles*, was debarred by the governor from standing for the municipal election. There was no disturbance but Fahim al-Dowleh fearing some postponed the election to a later date. [47] In mid-May 1944, Morteza Abuzeyr was appointed head of the

---

41. FO 371/31402, Kermanshah Diary April 1942; FO 248/1414 ,Cook to Legation, 23/07/1942.
42. FO 248/1414, Consul to Hankey/Tehran, 12/07/1942.
43. FO 371/31402, Kermanshah Diary July 1942. In a letter consul Cook wrote: "the useless figure-head of a Mayor and his equally useless council." FO 248/1414, Cook to Hankey/Tehran12/07/1942.
44. FO 371/31402, Kermanshah Diary August 1942
45. FO 371/40177, Kermanshah Diary January 1944; Idem, Kermanshah Diary February 1944.
46. Political Diaries vol. 7, p. 165; Political Diaries, vol. 12, pp. 43, 161.
47. FO 371/40177, Kermanshah Diary February 1944.

Municipality and assistant *ostandar*, according to the radio and Tehran newspapers. Because of his youth this came as a shock to older officials. In fact, Jahanshahi refused to move until Fahim al-Dowleh was back. Shortly thereafter, Morteza Abuzeyr's appointment was cancelled, because Fahim al-Dowleh had not approved it. He believed that Dr. Mo'aven, the *Majles* deputy was behind the appointment.[48] Although in July 1944 elections were held for the municipal council there was still no council as the decision had to be taken by the Ministry of the Interior.[49]

After a long wait, finally in March 1945, Kermanshah had a municipal council again. Its composition was as follows: (i) president, Hajji Mojtaba Abu'l-Ma'ali, a lawyer; (ii) vice-president, Bagher Maniani, a chemist. (iii) Others included: Heshmat Dowlatshahi, a large landowner as secretary; Hajji Mohammad Hariri and Ahmad Arjomand, merchants, and three landowners. Of these nine five had *Tudeh* leanings (the president, vice-president, and secretary). This caused discontent in town, because it was believed that Mo'aven and Zanganeh, both *Majles* deputies, had arranged in Tehran to get this *Tudeh* majority. Many regretted that Tavaquili [sic; Tavakolli?], a large and influential landowner was not included. Despite misgivings people hoped that the council would at least repair the main street.[50] Mohandes Sa'id Fozuni, the rather popular mayor went to Tehran to try and be reappointed; he hoped for the support of the municipal council. However, he had gone in vain, for on 15 April, Mr. 'Ali Asghar Mohammadi, the new *ra'is-e shardari* arrived.[51]

Mohammadi, the new *shahrdar* complained that the president of the council (*anjoman*), Mr. Abu'l-Ma'ali frustrated all efforts to improve the town, repair the streets, and remove refuse. Ma'ali has a bad reputation in town and had *Tudeh* sympathies. Mohammadi wanted to go to Tehran to have him removed, if not he would resign as he could not get any work out of him. Jahanshahi took no position but tried to make peace between the two.[52] Aslan Farhang returned from Tehran, and became assistant to *shahrdar*; he had been sent away to Tehran on suspicion of malpractice with the distribution of the bread rations.[53] In September 1945, after three months, Mohammadi was relieved as mayor by the governor. He was a young man, but his inability to work with Ma'ali decided Kalantari get rid off him, although he was appreciated by people who gave him a good send-off. His replacement was Kazem Sharifi, whose brother had been mayor of Kermanshah five years earlier. People wondered whether he would fare better with Ma'ali, who had *Tudeh* leanings, and felt strong in opposing the mayor seeing that governor did not like this.[54]

---

48. FO 371/40177, Kermanshah Diary May 1944.
49. FO 371/45400, Kermanshah Diary February 1945.
50. FO 371/45400, Kermanshah Diary March 1945.
51. FO 371/45400, Kermanshah Diary March 1945; Idem, Kermanshah Diary April 1945. Sa'id Fozuni, mayor of Kermanshah until April 1945, returned as Inspector of the Economic Department. FO 248/1451, Consul Kermanshah to Moneypenny/Tehran, 08/09/45.
52. FO 371/45400, Kermanshah Diary June 1945.
53. FO 371/45400, Kermanshah Diary July 1945.
54. FO 248/1451, Consul Kermanshah to Moneypenny/Tehran, 08/09/45.

POLICE

Around 1922, a modern police force replaced the old system of the *kadkhoda*s and *darugheh-ye bazar* and their men, although as of September 1909 a chief of police had immediately started hiring men and took steps for policing the town. In April 1913, there still was a police chief (*ra'is-e nazmiyeh*) in the city, who was ineffective.[55] Also during WW I Kermanshah continued to have a police chief separate from the traditional *kadkhoda* system. The new police force was also named *nazmiyeh* and was under a police chief.[56] Mohammad Khan Amir Showkat (born about 1883), was chief of police of Kermanshah for five years in total. He resigned in 1922, the CO of the Western Division found him too influential.[57]

After 1921, the police (*nazmiyeh*) was reorganized and centralized under the Minister of the Interior, who was locally represented by the governor. The police chief or *ra'is shahrbani*, as he was later called, was in charge of daily operations. Recruitment was done locally and men with a good military record and education were selected. However, they were poorly and irregularly paid and bribes were taken. In 1930, "The town police wear a brown woollen tunic-during the colder weather- and huge cap, the *kalpak*, and it is a serviceable and well-made uniform."[58] By the end of the 1940s, the police wore a light blue uniform with a small French type helmet of the same color. The police were in charge of keeping law and order, while a special department was in charge of checking the travel permit (*javaz*) of all travelers and police important roads. Outside Kermanshah, as in every Persian city, there was a police post, where travelers were held up for at least 30 minutes. Balfour, to entertain his readers, ridiculed the entire police control procedure as follows: "He would note the numbers of our cars, the numbers of our passports, the numbers of our various licenses and permits and any odd number he could find, add them up, take away the number he first thought of, and stand in puzzled contemplation for some minutes" before the car.[59] Ms Alexander was not condescending and more to the point and practical. She noted that the particulars of each traveler's passport were recorded in Persian, which made it impossible to verify whether the date had been correctly recorded. She further noted that the traveler's father's full name, which was and is not mentioned in Western passports. The traveler was invited to take a seat after which the *javaz* or travel permit was made out, "explaining our route, the wherefore of our journey and any information necessary. This one was made out like an itinerary, so that the formality had not to be gone through at every town we stopped at."[60] There also was a police station on leaving the town where the *javaz* was inspected and signed. Thereafter, the *javaz* had to be shown on leaving and entering every town in Persia.[61]

---

55. Political Diaries, vol. 3, p. 734; FO 248/1073, Kermanshah Diary no. 14, ending 3 April 1913.
56. AIR 20/663, p. 9.
57. He claimed descent from the Zand tribe. As gendarmerie officer he fought against Mohammad `Ali Shah in 1911 and was in Kermanshah during the early part of the war. IOR/L/PS/20/224, 'Biographies of the notables of Fars and certain Persian officials who have served at Shiraz. Delhi: Government of India, 1925', p. 53.
58. Alexander 1934, p. 26.
59. Balfour 1935, p. 87.
60. Alexander 1934, p. 20.
61. Alexander 1934, pp. 22, 30; McCallum 1930, p. 223.

There also was a traffic police, which wore a band of green, red and white. In Kermanshah, they stood on small circular platforms of at least 60 cm high to keep the police man "out of the mud and from being splashed. The shelter crowning it was exactly the same as an umbrella, fastened to a 10 foot pole and *made from old kerosene oil tins*, neatly cut to shape, joined and edged with a waved border of the same material, as an ornamentation, like a fancy frill to a parasol."[62] Foot police were armed with a revolver and a baton during the day, and at night they also had a carbine. Mounted police wore revolvers, rifles and sabers, both day and night. Plain clothes police and detectives (*qaragah*) worked for the criminal investigation department. They also served as the government's security service and investigated political activities, including those by foreigners.[63]

Table 3.2: List of police chiefs (1940-45)

Name	Date	Source
Col. Jahangiri	?- November 1941	FO 371/31402, Kermanshah Diary January 1942
Col. Artta	January-May 1942	FO 371/31402, Kermanshah Diary January 1942
Col. Javad Assefi*	June 1942-8 October 1945; since Jan. 45 assisted by Maj. Esma`il Rafi`i (Zell al-Soltan's family, former SPR)	FO 371/31402, Kermanshah Diary June 1942; FO 248/1451, Consul to Bullard, 06/10/45; FO 371/40177, Kermanshah Diary January 1944
Lt. Col. Esfandiary*	8 October 1945- ?	FO 248/1451, Consul to Bullard, 06/10/45
Major Mashallah Shakiba	8 October 1945-? appointed as inspector, a new function	FO 248/1451, Consul to Bullard, 06/10/45

* Col. Asefi, the police chief had Tudeh leanings. FO 248/1451, Consul Davis/Kermanshah to Moneypenny/Tehran, 08/09/1945. Lt. Col. Esfandiary was asst. police chief in 1943, and had reputation of being dishonest. FO 248/1451, Consul Kermanshah to Bullard/Tehran, 06/10/1945

GENDARMERIE

To keep the major trade arteries safe so-called road guards (*rahdaran* or *qarasuran*), who were drawn from the population (sedentary and/or tribal) living along these roads, were employed to prevent robberies and catch robbers. They were paid from the revenues of the road-tax (*rahdari*) that they collected. However, this system broke down after 1907, due to a weak central government that was unable to pay the road guards. As a result, road guards either became robbers themselves or levied higher taxes and fees from trade caravans and travelers. To avoid the creation of a British-officered force of road guards, which an irate Great British government wanted to impose, the Persian government proposed an alternative that was acceptable to London. Therefore, in 1911, the Gendarmerie force was created, officered by supposedly neutral

62. Alexander 1931, p. 26.
63. IOR/L/MIL/17/15/39, Notes on the Iranian Army. General Staff, India, 1940, p. 33.

Fig. 3.3: Farmanfarma with Lambert Molitor and General Hjalmarson, commander of the gendarmerie (*ca.* 1911). © *Collection Molitor, Ed. Elytis* no. 213.

Swedish officers, to police the roads and rural areas and protect the lives and property of travelers and the population. They wore white or grey Astrakhan hats with the royal badge and a rough grey and khaki uniform. In 1914, the infantry force numbered some 13,000 and was badly trained, badly paid and badly dressed. They were spread out over the country, but their number was still too small to be everywhere and, therefore, in many regions, such as Kermanshah, road guards were still operating, be it that they were a burden on travelers (see Chapter six). The mounted part of the gendarmerie force, like the road guards, was organized along tribal lines, i.e. under their own chiefs, bringing their own horse and arms. They only served in their own district and when called upon. On paper the force amounted to 38,000 men, while there also was an artillery force with some 5,000 men with some 100 breach and 150 muzzle loading and mountain guns. During WW I, some fought with the Democrats, Germans and Turks against the British and Russians, some of whom, as well as others, in 1916 joined the South Persia Rifles drawn by well-paying employment.

After WW I an effort was made to use the old gendarmerie force to police the major roads. This was not very successful, because the gendarmes were still badly paid and trained and also often badly led. The chief of the gendarmerie (*ra'is-e zhandarmeri*) was based in Kermanshah, where they had large barracks. The gendarmerie served as guards at the governor's palace, the consulates, and at the city's perimeter. Small detachments were stationed in small towns, at bridges and road posts along the trade route. In early 1919, there were about 600 men with British and Turkish rifles, with 100,000 British and 60,000 Turkish rounds. Their pay was always in arrears, they had bad discipline and their officers had little control. They were of poor physique and as fighters they were held in contempt by the tribesmen. They seldom distinguished themselves when operating in the rural areas.[64]

In short, they were an almost useless force. The governor, for example, wanted A'zam al-Saltaneh gone, who had strong tribe behind him, while he only had an unreliable gendarme force. Therefore, he wanted to wait till the spring when hostile tribes might come available to expel him.[65] In March 1920, at last the gendarmes received rifles without which they were useless. Major 'Abdol-Reza Khan, their commanding officer, was energetic and tried to make a force out of them, but their pay, of course, was in arrears.[66] Despite, or because of, good intentions the gendarmes remained a public nuisance and were even expected to become a danger. According to the British consul, the CO was a good officer. He had learnt that apparently 6,000 *tumans* pay was available in the Bank for Major 'Abdol-Reza in Tehran and he asked whether this might be made available as soon as possible.[67] By October 1920, the attitude of the gendarmes had not improved, partly due to the greed of the governor Sarem al-Dowleh, with whom the gendarmerie officers got into conflict about the division of the spoils after the killing of the chief of Harsin.[68]

After 1921, the gendarmerie was reorganized and instead of under the Ministry of Interior it was placed under the Ministry of War. The old gendarmerie force was 'replaced' by the mounted gendarmerie (*amniyeh*), who wore a light blue uniform, with leather accouterments and a blue helmet. They kept guard in block-houses that usually were built on heights overlooking major through roads.[69] In 1939, they were absorbed into the army at which time they numbered about 10,600. The *Amniyeh* was organized in regiments, who policed roads and rural districts. An independent battalion was in charge of guarding the border. They wore a blue cotton uniform, khaki puttees and *givehs*. Each regiment or independent battalion had a bureau for police work, such as investigations. A regiment was divided into 6-9 companies, each under a company commander, 3 platoon commander and 150 n.c.o.'s and armed policemen. An independent battalion had 4-6 companies. They were armed with a variety of old rifles and they didn't have automatic weapons. For discipline they were under the GOC of the division in the area in which they were stationed. In 1940, there was a total of 10 regiments and 15 independent battalions.[70]

During the WW II, the gendarmerie was organized in districts (*nahiyeh*), and each *nahiyeh* consisted of 3 *guruhan* or 250 men. Under the *ra'is-e nahiyeh* was a *ra'is-e hang*.[71] However, "The gendarmerie continued to be a byword for impotence and corruption." Senior posts were not filled for a few months and a capable officer was needed to establish a semblance of

64. IOR/L/MIL/17/15/39, Notes on the Iranian Army. General Staff, India, 1940, pp. 2, 33-34; AIR 20/663, pp. 8-9 (2nd part)
65. FO 248/1293, Kermanshah Report no. 2, 29/02/1920.
66. FO 248/1293, Report Kermanshah 31/03/1920.
67. FO 248/1293, tel. Consul to Legation, 23/07/1920.
68. FO 248/1293, Report Kermanshah, no. 9, up to 10 October 1920; Soltani 1381, vol. 4, p. 852.
69. Alexander 1934, p. 26; Hinz 1938, pp. 17-18.
70. IOR/L/MIL/17/15/39, Notes on the Iranian Army. General Staff, India, 1940, pp. 2, 33-34.
71. FO 371/45400, Kermanshah Diary April 1945.

efficiency. Major Ala'i, who arrived as inspector at first was interested to do just that, but soon he talked about leaving.[72] He clearly could not handle it. He suggested to the horrified governor (*ostandar*) to let certain prisoners escape and then shoot them while fleeing. According to Ala'i, to get an appointment, Ministry officials claimed as pay for an appointment to Kermanshah 2,000 rials/month.[73] Despite these employment circumstances, Col. Schwarzkopf, the American officer engaged to reform and put the gendarmerie on a good footing had a policy of removing an officer if there were complaints about him. He would then be placed somewhere else, and then he would be fired if there would again be complaints.[74] In mid-January 1944, Col. Yamini (*ra'is-e nahiyeh*) and as his assistant, Major Mohammad 'Ali Tatar Dorudian, the new *ra'is-e hang* and a former SPR arrived. Col. Hoseyn Yamini said that he needed 6 months to re-establish efficiency and 3 *guruhan* (about 250 men) to get to strength. Col. Yamini returned from Tehran to ask for men and machines. Although he was promised motor cycles and perhaps jeeps, he was considering to ask for a transfer. He had three *guruhan* or 250 men short of the official strength. Dorudian was dismissed, accused by his colleague Yamini of corruption, according to the British consul, due to friction and jealousy. Yamini was disheartened by the lack of men and size of task because improving this situation is and uphill battle and therefore he wanted a transfer.[75] The British wanted Yamini to return, because his interim was no good and the gendarmerie officers were corrupt.[76]

When officers were from Azerbaijan or had family there they would be circumspect in taking action, making sure not to upset Russian interests. For example, the acting commander of the gendarmerie Col. Mowlavi had relatives in the Russian zone.[77] In March 1945, Col. Mowlavi, was judged to be incompetent and was sent to Tehran for alleged corruption concerning silver smuggling and pilgrim traffic.[78] In April 1945, when Col. Kamal, formerly from Urmiyeh, took over, his command (*nahiyeh*) was split into two. One for Kermanshah and Posht-e Kuh, the other for Hamadan and Kurdistan. Both district commanders were directly responsible to Tehran.[79]

Table 3.3: Commanders of the Gendarmerie (1942-47)

Name	Date	Source
Col. Na'ini Nejad	September 1942-? deputy-commander	FO 371/31402, Kermanshah Diary September 1942
Major Ala'i	?-December 1943; inspector	FO 371/40177, Kermanshah Diary December 1943

72. FO 371/4017, Kermanshah Diary December 1943.
73. FO 248/1433, Calvert to Bullard, 19/01/1944.
74. FO 248/1414, Col. Fletcher to Tehran, 09/11/1942.
75. FO 371/40177, Kermanshah Diary May 1944.
76. FO 371/45400 Monthly Diary Dec. 1944.
77. FO 371/45400, Kermanshah Diary February 1945.
78. FO 371/45400, Kermanshah Diary March 1945.
79. FO 371/45400, Kermanshah Diary April 1945.

Name	Date	Source
Col. Hoseyn Yamini	17 January 1944-end? 1944 Maj. Mohamad `Ali Dorudian Tatar (former SPR) was his assistant	FO 248/1433, Calvert to Bullard 18/01/1944
Col. Mowlavi	February 1945-April 1945 acting	FO 371/45400 , Kermanshah Diary April 1945
Col. Kamal	April 1945-?	FO 371/45400 , Kermanshah Diary April 1945
Col. Abu'l-Hasan Ahanin	January 1947	FO 371/45488 Kermanshah Diary January 1947

The two forces, police and gendarmerie did not cooperate very well. For example, in June 1945, 14,000 feet of telephone copper wire was stolen from the Kermanshah Petroleum Company (KPC); the police said since the theft occurred outside the town limits it was a problem for the gendarmerie, who said that it occurred inside those limits and that the police should take care of the case. The temporary governor was unable to force them to work together, which they finally did.[80] The theft of telephone lines continued, because it was very lucrative. In August 1945, 3,000 yards of copper wire were stolen between Kermanshah and Bisotun,[81] and the same happened in September, although this time a part of it was recovered.[82] Finally, the Persian authorities adopted the British scheme, applied during the war, to make the tribal chiefs or village chiefs (*kadkhoda*s), who were responsible for the telephone line, pay, when robberies occurred.[83]

CUSTOMS

In 1797, Agha Reza, the Customs official came to inquire at the caravanserai, what goods Olivier and party had brought with them to calculate the customs due. He seems to have been in the employ of the governor, because the latter appointed him to look after the party of Frenchman.[84] It seems that until the transfer of customs to the Belgians, the customs office was located in a caravanserai in the bazaar.[85] The collection of the province's customs duties was farmed out to the highest bidder by the governor. In 1807, the Customs farm yielded 14,000 *tuman*s to the governor. The Customs duties were 2.5% for imports and exports; those in transit only paid one '*abbasi* per load. Butchers paid one *shahi* per head of animal, half a piaster was due on the sale of a horse, and the sealing duty on textiles was four *qarapul*s per single dyed or printed fabric. Also, at Sar-e pol toll was levied at a rate of 8 *para*s per riding horse and double that amount

80. FO 371/45400, Kermanshah Diary June 1945.
81. FO 371/45400, Kermanshah Diary August 1945.
82. FO 371/45400, Kermanshah Diary September 1945.
83. FO 371/45400, Monthly Diary January 1945; Idem, Kermanshah Diary April 1945.
84. Olivier 1807, vol. 5, p. 15f.
85. A Correspondent 1835 a, p. 404.

Fig. 3.4: Courtyard of the Customs building (*ca.* 1911). © *Collection Molitor, Ed. Elytis* no. 50.

per pack-animal.[86] Around 1845, customs revenues were 13,000 *tumans*.[87] The manner in which the imposts were levied was often arbitrary and irregular.[88]

The price of farming the Kermanshah province's customs increased gradually, another indication of the increase of trade. In the 1870s, the customs were farmed for 150,000 *qrans*, in 1881, for 200,000 *qrans*, for the year 1896-97 Vakil al-Dowleh paid 480,000 *qrans* and for 1897-98 the *kargozar* 'Abdol-Khaleh Khan paid 600,000 *qrans*. In 1898-99, prince Nosrat al-Divan paid 670,000 *qrans*.[89] According to Destrée, in 1899, Persian merchants paid 0.5%, Europeans 5% and Ottomans 12% customs duty.[90] However, Rabino reported that the customs duty was 2% for Persians and 5-6% for foreigners, while lamb-skins paid 5%.[91] In 1897, customs control was slack and evasions were enormous, so that the farmer lost on his investment. A syndicate of merchants formed to take over the collection of customs duties, but other events intervened.[92]

86. Dupré 1819, vol. 1, pp. 226, 238-39.
87. Ferrier 1971, p. 27.
88. Teule 1842, vol. 2, pp. 481, 493-94.
89. Adamec 1976, vol. 1, p. 351f; according to DCR 2260 (Isfahan, 1897-99), p. 15 and Whigham 1903, p. 280, in 1897, the customs were farmed for 86,000 *tumans*.
90. Destrée 1976, p. 50.
91. DCR 590 (Kermanshah, 1902), p. 24.
92. DCR 2260 (Ispahan, 1879-99), p. 15.

Fig. 3.4: In front of the Customs building 1910. © *Collection Molitor, Ed. Elytis* no. 74.

On 17 May 1897, Amin al-Dowleh, the Prime Minister (1896-98) signed a contract with the Imperial Bank of Persia (IBP) to receive 850,000 *qran*s monthly to pay government expenditures in exchange for receiving the customs revenues of Bushehr and Kermanshah. The IBP took over control of these Customs departments, but withdrew in August of the year after the government of Iran repaid its loan.[93] Because Mozaffar al-Din Shah (r. 1896-1907) needed more money again, Amin al-Soltan, the new Prime-Minister was able to secure a loan from Russia in the fall of 1898, with the Customs revenues of Northern Persia and the income of the fishing concession of the Caspian Sea as security. In March 1899, Amin al-Soltan placed the Customs of Kermanshah and Azerbaijan under the management of Belgian officials to increase government revenues. In 1900, Amin al-Soltan was able to obtain a new Russian loan on security of all customs revenues, except those of Fars and the Gulf Ports. Because under Belgian management the customs revenues of Kermanshah and Azerbaijan had increased substantially, Amin al-Soltan decided to place the entire national customs system under Belgian officials, which led to a 600% increase of total customs revenues in one year.[94] As a result, as of 21 March 1900, the customs department of Bushehr came under the direct management of the central government.[95]

93. Saldanha 1986, vol. 7/2, p. 177.
94. Jones 1986, vol. 1, pp. 82-86.
95. Adamec 1976, vol. 1, p. 374.

Although the Kermanshah Customs were officially placed under European supervision since March 1899 it was only as of October that a Belgian official was in place.[96] In late 1899, lacking staff, J. Naus the chief of the Belgian customs officials hired by the government of Iran, placed Pollaco, an employee of a maritime company to regularize the customs at Kermanshah. Instead of lowering the official customs duties to attract more trade and thus boost revenues as the customs farmers did he applied the official tariff to each category of merchant and product. Because up to that time Persian merchants paid 0.5%, Europeans 5% and Ottomans 12% all goods were imported as being Persian. Pollaco put a near end to this practice and in September 1900 he had collected 100,000 *tumans* in revenues including road taxes (*rahdari*), where before his time never more than 75,000 *tuman*s were collected.[97] In 1900, Baron Weydel took over the direction of the Customs department of Kermanshah, who, for the year 1900-01 collected 1,098,383 *qran*s (inland customs had been abolished). For 1901-02 he collected 3,041,851 *qran*s, of which he sent 2,960,000 *qran*s to Tehran. Also that year, as of 14 February, a new uniform duty of 5% was applied to everybody, including Persians, expect Ottoman subjects, who paid 6% for imports and 12% for exports. The new tariff was accepted without opposition. These last two years (1900-02) included *rahdari* of 1.10 *qran*s (22 *shahi*s) on goods entering and leaving. *Hava'i*, a tax on good entering and leaving the city, was also collected.[98] In that last year, Bushehr's customs revenues were 1 million pounds so that Kermanshah's revenue were 20% lower.[99]

The change in customs duties was not the only change that took place. Prior to the Belgian administration, the customs-house was government property. Goods deposited there had to pay a fee, the government being responsible for goods stolen. However, the government sold the warehouse to a private operator, so that the customs-house was no longer responsible. However, the governor still charged the relevant fee and special collectors were appointed to watch the caravans and collect the tax of 1 *qran* per every 12 loads. The Customs administration constructed a new compound as well as warehouses in the Bagh-e Shahzadeh.[100]

The organization of the Customs department of Kermanshah province was as follows. The central office was at Kermanshah, while Qasr-e Shirin was the main collecting and control station. In 1900, on the Persian side the *charvadar* bill was checked at the Customs frontier post and then the goods were sent to the Customs office at Kermanshah.[101] Qal'eh Sazbi was the first Persian border station, across from Khaneqin and was held by Hosam Nezam of the Sanjabis.[102] In addition, there were minor offices at Dubrulleh near Mandali, which was also a collecting station; Sarab Gilan was a control station, while there were minor offices at Eywan, Tanab, and

---

96. DCR 3189 (Kermanshah, 1903-04), p. 18; Whigham 1903, p. 270.

97. Destrée 1976, p. 50, who gave different rates as well. According to MacLean, prior to 1899 the customs rate was 2% but in reality 1-1.5% *ad valorem*. MacLean 1904, pp. 59-60. According to DCR 590 (Kermanshah, 1902), p. 24, which also has different customs duties, 90,000 *tumans* were collected.

98. DCR 590 (Kermanshah, 1902), p. 24; Whigham 1903, p. 280; DCR 3043 (Kermanshah, 1902-03), p. 7. Around 1830, *rahdari* was levied from non-Moslems at half a day's journey from Kermanshah coming from Nehavand. Beth Hillel 1832, p. 88.

99. Whigham 1903, p. 281; Adamec 1976, vol. 1, p. 374.

100. DCR 590 (Kermanshah, 1902), p. 24; Adamec 1976, vol. 1, p. 374.

101. MacLean 1904, pp. 59-60.

102. Political Diaries, vol. 3, p. 117.

Qal'eh Sabzi. The post at Ushkuri/Khushkuri situated 3 *farsakh* from Qasr-e Shirin and 0.5 *farsakh* from the border was established to prevent the use of caravans on the direct road leading to Zohab. To prevent smuggling armed horsemen controlled the border. In Kurdistan province, the Customs department had a dependent depot with minor offices at Senneh, Sakkis, Baneh, Paveh and Merivan. In 1909, already for two years, Ban was occupied by Turkish troops, Marivan was in revolt, and the Saqqez office was non-existent due to disturbed state of Persia. There also was a control station at Hamadan.[103] Despite the disturbed state of the country, there was not much smuggling of arms on this border.[104] However, smuggling increased significantly during unsettled times, in particular during the two World Wars, and whenever there were shortages in Qasr-e Shirin or in Iraq. The Customs department was invariably complaining that there were not enough border guards to effectively control the border so as to prevent smuggling, while regulations were not always optimal. For example, border officials asked Tehran that tribal chiefs be made responsible for the fines of tribal members when caught smuggling.[105]

Table 3.4: Branch offices of the Customs department, 1905

Location	Observations	*Tumans*
Qasr-e Shirin	-	4,500
Gilan	-	3,200
Eyvan and Sawmur	-	1,700
Senneh	Kurdistan	}
Sakkis	Kurdistan	}
Baneh	Kurdistan	}7,200
Merivan	Kurdistan	}
Javanrud Pareh	-	100
Hamadan	-	300
Hush Kuri	-	150
Kerend	*Bureau de surveillance*	...
Mahidasht	*Bureau de surveillance*	...
	Total	17,150

Source: Administration Report 1905-06, p. 49.

Since the new tariff, which on 14 February 1903 came into force, goods were only weighed, the value declared by merchants was just recorded without verification, as duty was levied per weight.[106] Under the new tariff instead of a uniform 5% *ad valorem* duty on imports and exports, a schedule of specific duties by category of goods was imposed. Especially injurious to British interests was the imposition of a weight tariff on piece goods, because Indian cottons were

103. DCR 3043 (Kermanshah, 1902-03), p. 7; DCR 4365 (Kermanshah,1908-09), p. 8; Adamec 1976, vol. 1, p. 374.
104. Administration Report 1905-06, p. 47
105. Sharifi Kazemi 1395, pp. 142-49, 154-59, 170-71, 180-84.
106. DCR 3189 (Kermanshah,1903-04), p. 18; Whigham 1903, p. 270; Entner 1965, pp. 53-55. The Kermanshah Customs revenues were security for the repayment of a recently contracted loan.

Fig. 3.5: Lambert Molitor with from left to right Lotfollah Mirza and Mirza Eshaq Khan (*ca.* 1911).
© *Collection Molitor, Ed. Elytis* no. 80.

heavier than those imported from Russia. As to British exports, grain, depending on the category, henceforth paid a tariff ranging from 3.5 to 20% and opium 8.5%, whereas export of dried fruit, almonds, and raw cotton, which were all exported to Russia, were exempted from export duties. The merchants protested against the new tariffs and wanted 3-month delay, but the government refused.[107] As of *Nowruz* 1913, the Customs and Finance Department began collecting an animal tax at the bridge and all animals entering the city were included.[108] As of 1910, a manifest had to be shown at the customs-house at Qasr-e Shirin whence goods come in bond under seal.[109]

In 1904, A. Molitor was in charge of Customs assisted by M. Fabri. As director, Molitor was also in charge of the Hamadan, Malayer and Kurdistan customs. As a result, he had no time to supervise his subordinates, with resulted in lower collections. In 1905, it was Waffelaert, assisted by Baron Fallon, who only served one year. Both men had excellent relations with Capt. Gough, which was a major change compared to Waffelaert's behavior in Bushehr towards the

107. Entner 1965, op. 68ff; Saldanha 1986, vol. 7/2, p.180-81; Administration Report 1902-1903, p. 2.
108. Political Diaries vol. 5, p. 103.
109. DCR 4766 (Kermanshah, 1910-11), p. 5.

Fig. 3.6: Customs agents before Lambert Molitor's departure in 1913. © *Collection Molitor, Ed. Elytis* no. 208.

British consulate.[110] In December 1905, Waffelaert was replaced by Mornard.[111] Most of the locally hired staff were Bahais.[112]

In mid-August 1906 there was an expression of strong feeling in Kermanshah against the Belgian-managed Customs administrations. While passing through the city Mr. Waffelaert was insulted by "some raggamuffins," while a mullah who had earlier preached the death of Europeans apparently had done so with the Customs officials in mind. A planned demonstration was called off, apparently at instructions from Qom. The reason for the hostile attitude towards the Customs officials was "due to the heavy tariff and the successful way in which smuggling is prevented with the consequence of heavy fines." People also felt that the Customs administrations should be run by Persians not by foreigners.[113]

The Customs revenues were partly used for local expenses; the rest was sent via the Russian Bank to Tehran, except for 10,000 *qrans*/week paid to IBP.[114] As of 1906, all customs revenues were remitted via the IBP and 3,000 *tumans* via the Russian Bank to Hamadan. In that year, E.

110. Political Diaries 1, p. 167.
111. Political Diaries, vol. 1, p. 255.
112. Political Diaries, vol. 3, p. 318.
113. FO 248/879, Crossle to Tehran, 23/08/1906.
114. Administration Report 1905-06, p. 47.

Waffelaert was again in charge of the Kermanshah office. Haworth, the British consul, who had good personal relations with him, considered him pigheaded, because he accused Shawal Levi, a British subject of smuggling. The Jewish merchant in question had taken goods to Posht-e Kuh, where there was no Customs office. Therefore, Waffelaert accused him of taken these goods illegally across the border! Haworth was convinced that Waffelaert was misled by his assistant Baron Viktor Staudach, a Persian subject of Austrian origin and a Moslem, about whom he commented: "His habits are entirely Persian and he is more unscrupulous than most Persians. I am glad to see him dismissed later."[115] The matter was referred to Tehran, which ordered to return the goods and mules to Shawal Levi. Waffelaert was replaced on 27 January 1907 by J. B. Heynssens. Deville was inspector as of March 1907, but left in May to return in the fall to take over from Heynssens. However, the latter did not leave after all and Deville was then appointed Inspector-General of the Posts and left in February 1908. He was replaced by Cattersell, who in March 1908 was replaced by Cesari. The latter, who was said to be a Russophile, was a Frenchman. In February 1908, Cesari told Hayworth, the British consul, that quarantine in Persia was a political measure and that the existence or not of plague was irrelevant. As a Frenchman he wanted to hurt German trade and he used the quarantine rules to delay or damage goods such as in case of cloth goods, which, if well fumigated, lost their color. Therefore, Hayworth considered him a scoundrel.[116] In early August 1908, Cesari was fired due to quarreling with the Belgians.[117] As of March 1908, A. Cattersel was acting director of Customs until the arrival of Lambert Molitor on 24 July 1908. Cattersel then went to Qasr-e Shirin, but left on 8 January 1909.[118] L. Molitor, who was assisted by Z. Vilain in Qasr-e Shirin since August 1910, remained in function until mid-1913.[119] On 26 May 1913, E. De Kerkheer succeeded Molitor; he was assisted by K. L. Collette, while E. Authelet assumed the function of inspector of taxes.[120] In 1914, Deweerdt, who spoke Persian, became director of the Customs department, while P. Guillaume as of 5 May 1914, was inspector of taxes. In January 1916, Deweerdt was arrested by the Germans. He was allowed to leave to Baghdad to return to Brussels, which was also in German hands. On his return to Belgium he died in the hospital on 19 February 1916, due to the terrible conditions he had suffered in Turkey.[121] The Ottoman consul also arrested Thomas and his son Towfiq, who were Christians and Ottoman subjects. They were being accused of heading a British-Russian network of spies and therefore, were sent to Baghdad.

---

115. Administration Report 1906-07, pp. 41, 43; Political Diaries, vol. 1, p. 167; Political Diaries, vol. 2, pp. 27-28 (with more details), 45. On Staudach, see Slaby 1985, p. 190.

116. Political Diaries, vol. 3, p. 134.

117. Administration Report 1906-07, p. 44; Administration Report 1907-08, p. 64; Destrée 338; Political Diaries 2, p. 55; vol. 3, pp. 35, 134, 265, 419 (earlier he had been fired twice by M. Naus, "but each time received definite orders from the Shah to re-employ him," because the Russians had more clout than Naus. Nevertheless, Cesari had been very useful to Naus "in picking up curios.")

118. Administration Report 1908, p. 49; Destrée 1976, pp. 332, 341. The employees of the Customs Department were allegedly all Bahais. Political Diaries, vol. 3, p. 318.

119. Destrée 1976, pp. 342, 348. R. Sonet died in Kermanshah of typhus in 1913. Destrée 1976, p. 347.

120. Political Diaries vol. 5, p. 167. Authelet was in charge of Qasr-e Shirin as of June 1913. Political Diaries vol. 5, p. 200; Destrée 1976, pp. 327, 329-31, 334.

121. Destrée 1976, pp. 335 337; Laureys 1996, pp. 319-24; Soltani 1381, vol. 4, p. 794-95 (he had been hiding in the house of Mr. Stead, the American missionary. Despite protests by the *kargozar*, because this deed constituted a violation of Iran's neutrality, Deweerdt was arrested).

Thomas's wife appealed to the Committee of National Defense that asked the consul to relent. He said he could not, but suggested that Eqbal al-Saltaneh, the governor of Kermanshah wire Enver Pasha. This had the desired success, although their return was subject to the demand that Eqbal al-Saltaneh endow a building he owned to the Islamic school in the city. This he did before his departure; the gift was to be effective only on the return of the father and son.[122] In 1917 and thereafter, Mr. Hunin was the Belgian customs director.[123] In 1932, the hiring of Belgian administrators was discontinued and the Customs Department henceforth was entirely in Persian hands. In 1935 a new Customs House was built.[124]

BANKS

Prior to the creation of a national Mint in 1877, in each major town, copper coins were first computed as *shahi*s, then via ghost dinars converted into the local ghost *tuman*. This means that copper coins had a value in dinars, although neither the government nor the bazaar needed to respect this value. This, however, made it easy for the authorities, usually the local mint-master, to tax copper by reducing the accountancy value of coins made of that metal. Consequently, many European travelers commented on the variation of local moneys. In 1809, Fraser wrote, "The number of abbassees in a real differ in different provinces, but are in general from five to six, and there are about as many pool-e-siahs in each abbassee; the former, when found, for it is not current every where, is of silver; the latter are lumps of copper, heavy and shapeless, with a few letters stamped on one side."[125] Part of the reason for the existence of these variations, at least until the establishment of the national mint in 1877, was that the local mints simply did not stick to the official standards for weight and fineness.[126]

Before 1877, the Mint of Kermanshah turned out fairly good coins. Pechan, the Austrian mint master in Tehran, made assays in 1866, resulting in 4.97 grains, fineness 880, value in francs 0.9719. The Kermanshah *qran*s were better than the average of other Iranian mints, and consequently, "have nearly all re-minted." Most coins were holed by Kurds to make ornaments for their womenfolk. Much specie was collected in Kermanshah and weekly large amounts were sent to Tehran. "Despite this, large amounts of coins accumulate here, brought by pilgrims and passed from hand to hand from village to village until it finally is used in town to buy clothes etc."[127] On 2 May 1896, Eyn al-Saltaneh reported that, following the shah's assassination, the IBP refused to accept copper money. The price of silver skyrocketed. In Kashan one *tuman* of

122. Soltani 1381, vol. 4, pp. 797-98.

123. Edmonds 2010, p. 219. However, it is also reported that Mr. Vercheval was appointed director of Customs at Kermanshah. IOR/L/PS/10/211, Meshed Diary no. 22 for the week ending 2nd June 1917.

124. Soltani 1381, vol. 1, p. 541 (see here also for Qasr-e Shirin and other border posts). In 1945, Mr. Pezeshkpur was the Director of Customs. IMG 8027- FO 371/45400 , Kermanshah Diary February 1945.

125. Fraser 1984, p. 74, note; see also Dupré 1819, vol. 2, pp. 477-80.

126. On the monetary situation in Iran at that time, see Matthee, Floor and Clawson 2013, chapters 6 and 7.

127. DCR 590, p. 25. On the monetary system of Iran and the new national Mint, see Matthee, Floor, Clawson 2013.

silver cost 2.5 *tuman* in copper money. Each *qran* had risen to 45 *shahi*s and nobody accepted these coins. "In Hamadan, Malayer and Kermanshah two *tumans* is one *tuman*."[128]

By 1900, the currency used in Kermanshah were the new coins, especially the *do hazari*, 1 *qran* coins, when they had no holes got 3% premium, old coins were at a discount of 1-1.5%. Copper coin were still in circulation at a rate of 61 *puls* = 1 *qran*, of which allegedly 10,000 *tuman*s of copper coin were still circulating. Nickel coins, of which 3,000 *tuman*s were put into circulation in Kermanshah in 1901 were readily accepted and in the villages were preferred to copper. In 1902, "there are now some 10,000 tomans of copper coin still in circulation. Of nickel coin in 1900, 3,000 tomans were put in circulation and readily accepted and in the villages preferred to copper."[129]

Prior to the arrival of modern banks in Kermanshah financial transactions were arranged by wealthy merchants and *sarraf*s. However, the *sarraf*s were merely money-changers with no influence over the market whatsoever. Their guild paid 60 *qran*s in guild taxes (*asnafiyeh*). Since 1901, the Persian bank *Sharekat-e Amte 'eh-ye Omumi*, had a branch office in Kermanshah.[130] It was closed when in 1902, the Imperial Bank of Persia (IBP) opened a branch office at Kermanshah and facilitated trade transactions. The IBP had its share of problems, especially after the 1907 discovery that the Kermanshah branch managed by Hyacinth Rabino had extensive bad debts. His father, Joseph Rabino the general manager of the IBP in Iran, reported to the Board that the heart of the problem was that Hyacinth, before leaving the branch in 1905, had "neglect[ed] all proper precautions so that his action is the primary cause of the disaster."[131] In August 1906, Consuls Gough and Crossle alerted Tehran about the dealings of Esma'il Baqer, an employee of the Bank, who already under Hyacinth Rabino had been engaged in private trading, and under his successor, Mr. Milligan, continued to do so, under the guise that he did so on behalf of the IBP. He also was engaged in a bread ring in 1905 and was about to start a new one in 1906 and all these activities reflected badly on the Bank and the British. Gough advised Tehran to move Esma'il Baqer from Kermanshah and replace Mr. Milligan.[132] The extent and the seriousness of Esma'il Baqer's dealings became known when, on 11 October 1906, Capt. Haworth arrived as the new consul. One day later Shawal Levi told him that Esma'il Baqer, the IBP cashier/bookkeeper was about to abscond. Haworth had him arrested by the governor. This was a shock as he was one of the most influential men in Kermanshah and owner of the *English Stores*. Until the age of 15 he had been educated in Great Britain and later he was educated at the American school in Beirut.[133]

The fraud of bookkeeper Mirza Esma'il Khan Baqer created many problems. He had been left unsupervised and gave loans to himself and all and sundry, against property, which was against IBP rules. Shawal Levi, "who was in some matters a partner of Baker deserves well of

128. Eyn al-Saltaneh 1376, vol. 1, 952.
129. DCR 590, p. 25.
130. DCR 590, p. 14.
131. J. Rabino to G. Newell, 17 July 1907, quoted in Jones 1968, vol. 1, p. 105.
132. FO 48/879, Gough to Grant Duff, 11/08/1906; Idem, Crossle to Grant Duff 20/08/1906.
133. Administration Report 1906-07, p.42; Political Diaries, vol. 1, p. 517; FO 248/879, Weekly Diary ending the 17th of October 1906.

Fig. 3.7: Building of the Imperial Bank of Persia (2017) © Marc Molitor

the Bank." The affair was a 9-days wonder in town. Mr. Arkless, the IBP accountant stated that Esma'il gave merchants ante-dated receipts purporting to be from the bank, because he was not on speaking terms with the Manager. Worse was that all, private and Bank, transactions were made out in the name of Esma'il Khan Baqer Modir-e Bank. While the Bank books showed a Bank loan a creditor could claim that he did not owe money to the Bank, or "brings up receipts which concerned private matters and attempts to set them off against Bank claims." This combined with the unsettled situation in the city made it almost impossible to recover money from a recalcitrant debtor.[134]

Mr. Messeroy of the IBP Tehran came to investigate the matter and inquired into the quarrel between the two bank employees. He concluded Esma'il Baqer had more authority than should be given to a *mirza*; his signature was sufficient for receipts.[135] In November 1906, Messeroy decided not to take legal steps against Esmail as (1) he could settle all claims from his guarantors, and (2) had enough money to torpedo the way to justice, and with his help there was a better chance to recuperate funds. Also, he regretted his deeds.[136] When he was released from his arrest in December 1906, Esma'il Khan Baqer took up his old life. He dined and played

134. Administration Report 1907-08, pp. 62, 64 (staff); Political Diaries, vol. 1, p. 517; FO 48/879, Crossle to Grant Duff, 20/08/1906.

135. Political Diaries, vol. 1, p. 525; FO 248/879, Weekly Diary ending the 31st October 1906.

136. Political Diaries, vol. 1, p. 534.

bridge with officials of the IBP, who did so to keep him in a friendly state of mind to get the Bank's money back, which they did not expect to be able to without his cooperation. Milligan, the IBP manager hoped to get the money from Esma'il' estate. The latter was "one of the most influential and respected men in the town. He also was received by the governor, with whom he gambled and who treated him as a honored guest." Likewise, government officials and the Ottoman Consul General received him, although the latter once protested that the man's reputation was being whitewashed. Only the British consul did not receive him. This situation as well as the fact that he was one of the leading merchants, who wanted to import only British goods as much as possible, put the British consul in a bind. He also wanted to import goods from Mohammerah via Posht-e Kuh, a route promoted by the consul. Finally, the Russian Consul General had offered Esma'il Khan Baqer two years' credit for importing Russian piece-goods. Baqer had not yet accepted the offer and the IBP asked Ziegler in Tehran and Isfahan whether they might offer Baqer a competitive deal.[137] Nothing came of all these plans and Mirza Esma'il Baqer left Kermanshah. In September 1911, he was in Bushehr under the name of Mirza Esma'il Khan. He tried to get a job with the APOC and the governor Movaqqar al-Dowleh made him director of the revenue administration (*amin-e maliyeh*). His father was a *monshi* in the British Residency and some mullahs called him a *kafir* or infidel.[138]

The IBP continued to have problems. 'Abdol-Ahd, a Turkish subject and IBP cashier resigned mid-January 1907. By weight of the money bags it was found that some 600 *tuman*s were missing. In the presence of the British and Ottoman consuls the 36 bags were opened and counted. To resolve the problem it was referred to the IBP head office in Tehran. This event as well as the private quarrels of IBP staff complicated matters for Mr. Messeroy the IBP inspector. The IBP manager was a friend of Esma'il Khan Baqer, while the accountant, Mr. Arkless championed 'Abdol-Ahd. The consul blamed many of the local issues he had to deal with, including the Shawal Levi affair, to the IBP office quarrels. Although Mr. Arkless finally admitted 'Abdol-Ahd's guilt it was too late to patch up the frayed relations. The consul, therefore, preferred that all of them be transferred as these quarrels and scandals hurt British prestige.[139]

On 9 September 1907, Messrs. Soane and Forbes Manson arrived to replace respectively the IBP manager and accountant.[140] In August 1908, Mr. Schindler, son of General Houtum-Schindler became manager of IBP Kermanshah replacing Soane.[141] As a result, of these staff changes the IBP was doing better; in 1908 many debts were paid and some partly, although bad debts remained. In the same year, the Bank was once again struck by a scandal. In this case the cause was Mr. Soane, the Bank manager since September 1907. He was sent to Great Britain on sick leave and took a Roman Catholic woman, formerly a servant at the British Consulate, with him. The woman's husband complained, and although Soane denied the whole affair he

---

137. Political Diaries, vol. 1, p. 517; Political Diaries, vol. 2, p. 28;
138. Political Diaries vol. 4, p. 450.
139. Political Diaries vol. 2, p. 56; FO 248/907, Haworth to Ahmad Bey, Turkish Consul-General, 31/01/1907; plus reply and enclosures.
140. Political Diaries, vol. 2, p. 357.
141. Political Diaries, vol. 3, p. 265.

was forced to resign from the Bank.[142] During WW I Capt. Dewar-Durie was the manager of the IBP, who served as a uniformed British officer at that time.[143]

Mr. Pine of the Russian Bank came on 29 August 1908 to open a branch at Kermanshah. He stayed for two months and then put Mr. Aghans in charge, an Armenian, who previously had worked in the Customs department and then for the IBP. This Bank, which did not do much business in Kermanshah, was closed in 1917 and was not reopened.[144] In May 1920, the Ottoman Bank opened a branch in Kermanshah. It had to discontinue operations because of IBP's exclusive banking concession. For the same reason the British government persuaded the British Eastern Bank not to open a branch there either.[145] Thus, the IBP remained the only bank in the city until 1931, when the *Bank-e Melli*, which was established by the *Majles* in 1927, opened a branch office in Kermanshah, shortly thereafter followed by the *Pahlavi* Bank and the *Ottoman* Bank.[146] In 1930, when you wanted to change money in Kermanshah you either went to the IBP or, which was illegal, you went to the bazaar, where you obtained a better rate. But this was not as easy as one might think, because that service was not available every day or beset with some risk. If it was a fasting day (*wafad*)[147] then the entire bazaar was closed.

> Or it is the Friday of the Moslems, the Saturday of the Jews, or the Sunday of the Christians. In the first case, the two greatest sheepskin buyers of the two, alleged millionaires, will be absent, and without their lead there can be no bidding for foreign money. In the second case the two rich men, it is true, will be in their offices, but without a secret lead from the Jews they will not be buying, and the whole bazaar knows it. In the third case the English-managed bank will be closed, and some tremendous fall in sterling will be rumoured.[148]

On any other day, over many glasses of tea and after much talk, the traveler finally and wearied made a transaction gaining some extra *tuman*s in the process.[149]

The Ottoman Bank House had made a deal for a take over when governor asked the British consul to intervene and break off the deal for a better offer. The building was supposed to be converted into a hospital, a plan already several years old, and meant to make money for some individuals, among which the governor. As a result, the sale of the Bank was postponed until later.[150]

---

142. Administration Report 1908, p. 46 ("This official had always given trouble and his departure will be a relief to everyone. Nevertheless, his conduct and disgrace are unfortunate, for he is an oriental scholar of a very high order."); FO 248/938, Haworth to Tehran 05/05/1908; Idem, FO 248/938, Diary no.19 ending November 3rd 1908. For Sir Arnold T. Wilson's laudatory biography of E.B. Soane (which does not mention the above affair), who converted to Islam in 1905, see Soane1926, pp. ix-xvii.
143. Edmonds 2010, p. 219.
144. Administration Report 1908, p. 46; Political Diaries, vol. 3, p. 318.
145. Wilson 1932, p. 268; Jones 1986, vol. 1, p. 194; IOR/L/PS/10/531/3 (1919-1920).
146. Ebtehaj 1932, p. 148; Government of Great Britain 1945, p. 524.
147. Reitlinger wrongly assumed that it was a fasting day, but it was a day of mourning on account of a decease or a *vafat* (وفات), presumably of an important person.
148. Reitlinger 1932, p. 36.
149. Reitlinger 1932, p. 36.
150. FO 371/45488 Kermanshah Diary May 1947

Fig. 3.8: Photo showing Mrs. Durie, Mrs. Nikolsky, Mr. Dekerckheer, Farmanfarma, Mr. McDouall, Mr. Authelet, Dr. Volansky, Mr. Dewar Durie, governess, Mr. Mac Gregor, Mr. Nikolsky (Kermanshah 1913). © *Collection Molitor, Ed. Elytis* no. 218.

FOREIGN CONSULATES

OTTOMAN EMPIRE

Ottoman Turkey had a Consul-General in Kermanshah since at least the 1860s. Traditionally the title of his function was *bash-shahbandar* or Consul-General[151] In the 1890s, the Ottoman Consul-general felt like he was in an outlandish and far-away place, but he was happy to make much money of the passports pilgrims needed. He spoke Turkish, French, a little Arabic, but no Persian.[152] This probably was Majid Bey who died in May 1901 in Kermanshah.[153] In 1906, Kerim Bey was Consul General; Ahmad Bey was consul (*shahbandar*). In the first half of September 1906, a group of Turkish subjects took refuge or *bast* at the Telegraph office to protest against their Consul-General and sent telegrams to Baghdad, Istanbul, and Tehran. They accused him of hindering their affairs. Tehran asked the governor to resolve the matter but he was unable to do so. In reaction to the protest, Kerim Bey asked to be replaced, because he had been five years in town. In October 1906, the protesting Turks came out of *bast* and came to British consul

151. Lycklama 1873, vol. 3, p. 472.
152. Harris 1896, pp. 256-57.
153. *Ruznameh-ye Iran* 1375, vol. 5, p. 4004 (no. 995; 02/06/1901).

to complain about their Kerim Bey; they had left *bast* because the governor and Kerim Bey had given assurances as to their safety, but when leaving the Telegraph office Kerim Bey seized a number of them and intended to deport them to Turkish territory. Haworth said he was unable to help. The Turkish subjects were still in *bast* toward the end of September.[154] Kerim Bey, the Ottoman Consul-General was transferred on 10 February 1907. However, there was a delay in the implementation of this decision. It was only on 28 September 1908, after seven years, that Kerim Bey left. Consul Ahmad Bey officiated, but he was shortly thereafter transferred to Bushehr.[155] On 5 December 1911, 'Abdol-Karim Bey was replaced as consul-general by Sa'ad Bey.[156] In January 1918, Mahmud Bey the Turkish consul went to Senneh.[157] After the withdrawal of the Ottoman troops on 27 February 1917, for some time no new Ottoman consul was appointed. In the early 1920s, Raqib Bey was Turkish consul, who left in February 1926. He was replaced by Jalal al-Din Bey, who spoke Italian and French fluently.[158]

The Ottoman consul had a consular guard, just like his Western colleagues.[159] In May 1913, the Turkish consular guard of 15 men, was refused permission to enter Persia. Samsam al-Mamalek disarmed them at Qal'eh Sabzi, but Farmanfama told him to restore their arms and take them to Turkish territory. From there they made a detour and illegally crossed the border and came to Kermanshah.[160]

GREAT BRITAIN

There was no British Consulate in Kermanshah, although since 1850 at the urging of the British consul in Baghdad and supported by the charge d'affaires in Tehran, there was a native agent to promote British trade and affairs. The first such agent was Agha Khalil, a Shiite Arab from Baghdad. The latter was Henry Rawlinson's trusted muleteer, whom he made British agent in Kermanshah. He was succeeded around 1870 by his son Aqa Hasan, Vakil al-Dowleh. The latter was the man to see, for he was not only the wealthiest man of Kermanshah, but also the local big man of the governor. Aqa Hasan Vakil al Dowleh died on 26 February 1893. He was replaced by his son 'Abdol-Karim.[161] In January 1907, the IBP inspector asked the British consul to sit on a commission to look into the affairs of the late Vakil a-Dowleh, a Turkish subject. The IBP wanted to protect its interests, but the consul also wanted to protect the rights of the heirs, who in the past lost heavily due to the executors of the will, particularly, Farmanfarma and the Imam

154. Political Diaries, vol. 1, pp. 482, 489, 498, 517.

155. Political Diaries, vol. 2, p. 101; Idem, vol. 3, p. 311; Administration Report 1906-07, p.42; Administration Report 1908, p. 49; Political Diaries, vol. 3, p. 311.

156. Hamadani 1354, p. 387.

157. FO 248/1204 tel. Lt. Col. Kennion 10/01/18.

158. FO 416/78, Intel. Summary No. 3, ending February 6, 1926; Idem, Intel. Summary No. 5 ending March 6, 1926.

159. The Turkish Consulate's escort left to Baghdad on 2 December 1912. Political Diaries vol. 5, pp. 12, 103.

160. Political Diaries vol. 5, p. 132; Further Correspondence, Persia no. 1 (1914), p. 108.

161. IOR/Z/E/4/20/K60 (1849-1850); IOR/Z/E/4/20/B8 (1849-1850); IOR/Z/E/4/20/T55 (1849-1850); *Ruznameh-ye Iran* 1375, vol. 4, p. 3195 (no. 794; 09/03/1893); Lycklama 1873, vol. 3, p. 472 (Hadji-Ghalil); Wills 1893, p. 109; Sayyah 1346, p. 232; Binder 347; Soltani 1373, 3, p. 379; Administration Report 1905-06, p. 45; Bird 1891, vol. 1, pp. 99-100; Gerard 1883, p. 44. On Vakil al-Dowleh, see FO 881/7228.

Jom'eh. He opined, because the Vakil al-Dowleh family had represented British interests from 1848 until 1903 it deserved British support.[162]

Although the British agents were seen as consul, by locals and foreigners alike, they were not and therefore, Curzon proposed to replace the native agent with a British vice-consul to promote trade along the Baghdad-Kermanshah road. In 1901, the British government offered the IBP to take charge of the Consulate although it had no agency in Kermanshah. When, one year later, the bank opened a branch office in Kermanshah, the government withdrew its offer.[163] Nevertheless, in 1903, Rabino, the IBP manager was acting-consul. In 1904, the British Consulate was established by Capt. Cough, who relieved Rabino and bought a house for use as the Consulate near the Delgosha. He was assisted by Capt. Williams, the consular surgeon.[164]

Table 3.5: List of British consuls, 1903-1947

Name	Date	Source
L.H. Rabino	23/02/1903 - 23/03/1904	
Capt. Cough	23/03/1904-10/10/1906; assisted by Capt. Williams I.M.S., the consular surgeon	Administration Report 1905-06, p. 45; Hale 1920, p. 205
Capt. Haworth I.M.S.	11/10/1906-23/07/1909	Political Diaries, vol. 1, p. 517
Capt. Crossle I.M.S.	23/07/- 21/08/1909	Political Diaries, vol. 3, p. 674
McDouall, William	21/08/1909-?/12/1916	Political Diaries, vol. 3, p. 698
Knox, Geoffrey George	06/-?/1910	FO 248/999, Acting consul G.G. Knox to Tehran, 11/07/1910
Lt. Col. R. L. Kennion	?/12/1917-?/09/1918	FO 248/1293, Kermanshah Report, no. 6, 30 June 1920
Major L. Weir	26/09/1918-17/06/1920	FO 248/1293, Kermanshah Report, no. 6, 30 June 1920; Diaries, vol. 3, p. 698
Major F.S. Greenhouse	17/06/1920-?/05/1921	Idem
Patrick Cowan	27/01/1921- 12/1930	FO 416/79, Intel. Summary No. 19 ending September 18, 1926
V. Newton	10/1922-09/05/1923	Soltani 1378, vol. 1, p. 17
Finch, Jon Philip Gordon	22/05/1922-17/06/1927	Idem
H.A.D. Haviland	28/11/1930-17/04/1931	Idem
Ch. A. Gault	Acting 06/04/-07/11/1933	Idem
Summerhouse?, Chr. Henry	Acting 01/-?/1934	Idem
Ch. A. Gault	Acting 1935	Idem
J. F. R. Vaughan-Russell	01/1936- ?	Idem
A. J. Gardner	20/08/-25/09/1937	Idem
Sarel?, Rudig Francis Gisbert	1938	Idem; vice-consul

162. Political Diaries, vol. 2, p. 29.

163. Whigham 1903, p. 283.

164. Administration Report 1905-06, p. 45; Hale n.d., p. 205.

Name	Date	Source
K. J. Simpson	Acting 1939	Idem
E. Wiltshire	Acting 1939	Idem
W. H. Young	10/01/-14/09/1939	Idem
F. H. Gamble (Cambell?)	1942	Idem; vice-consul
J. F. R. Vaughan-Russell	1940-28 May 1942	FO 371/31402, Kermanshah Diary December 1941
F.A.G. Cook	28 May 1942- ?1944	FO 371/31402, Kermanshah Diary May 1942
F. H. Gamble (Campbell?)	1943	Soltani 1378, vol. 1, p. 17
A.J. Edden; interim/ vice-consul	01/01/1944-10/02/1945	Soltani 1378, vol. 1, p. 17; FO 371/45400, Kermanshah Diary February 1945; Vice-consul W.H.B. Houghton. FO 371/45400 , Monthly Diary January 1945
A.W. Davis	11/02/1945-?/12/1946	FO 371/45400, Kermanshah Diary February 1945
R.N. Pullar	December 1946-?	FO 371/45488 Kermanshah Diary December 1946

In 1907, the Consulate buildings were built on a high ridge east of town, where it suffered much from excessive snow and winter frost.[165] The buildings withstood the onslaught from that first winter and continued to serve as the Consulate until 1917, when the departing Ottoman troops burnt them down. The British consulate was only rebuilt in 1923.[166] Therefore, when Col. Kennion and his wife returned to Kermanshah in 1917, they first stayed in one of the staff houses of the IBP.[167] Later the consulate was established in a large house on the southern outskirts of the city, above and east of a stream, normally the residence of the Belgian head of Customs.[168]

Until 1926, the British consul had an escort of Indian sowars. However, in that year the government of India withdrew the sowars. Cowan, the British consul in Kermanshah then wanted to arm Persian *gholams*. Tehran hearing about withdrawal of the sowars at Kermanshah, wrote that all Indian sowars should be withdrawn from Persia and consuls should not employ any armed personnel.[169]

---

165. Political Diaries 1, p. 97; AIR 20/663, p. 19.
166. IOR/L/PS/11/123, P 2560/1917 (22 May 1917-27 Jul 1917); IOR/L/PS/10/634/3 (1923-1924); NA, WORK 10/338; Hay 1937, p. 21; Edmonds 2010, p. 219.
167. Edmonds 2010, p. 219.
168. AIR 20/663, p. 19.
169. FO 416/79, Intel. Summary No. 19 ending September 18, 1926. The British Legation became an embassy in February 1944. FO 371/40177, Kermanshah Diary February 1944.

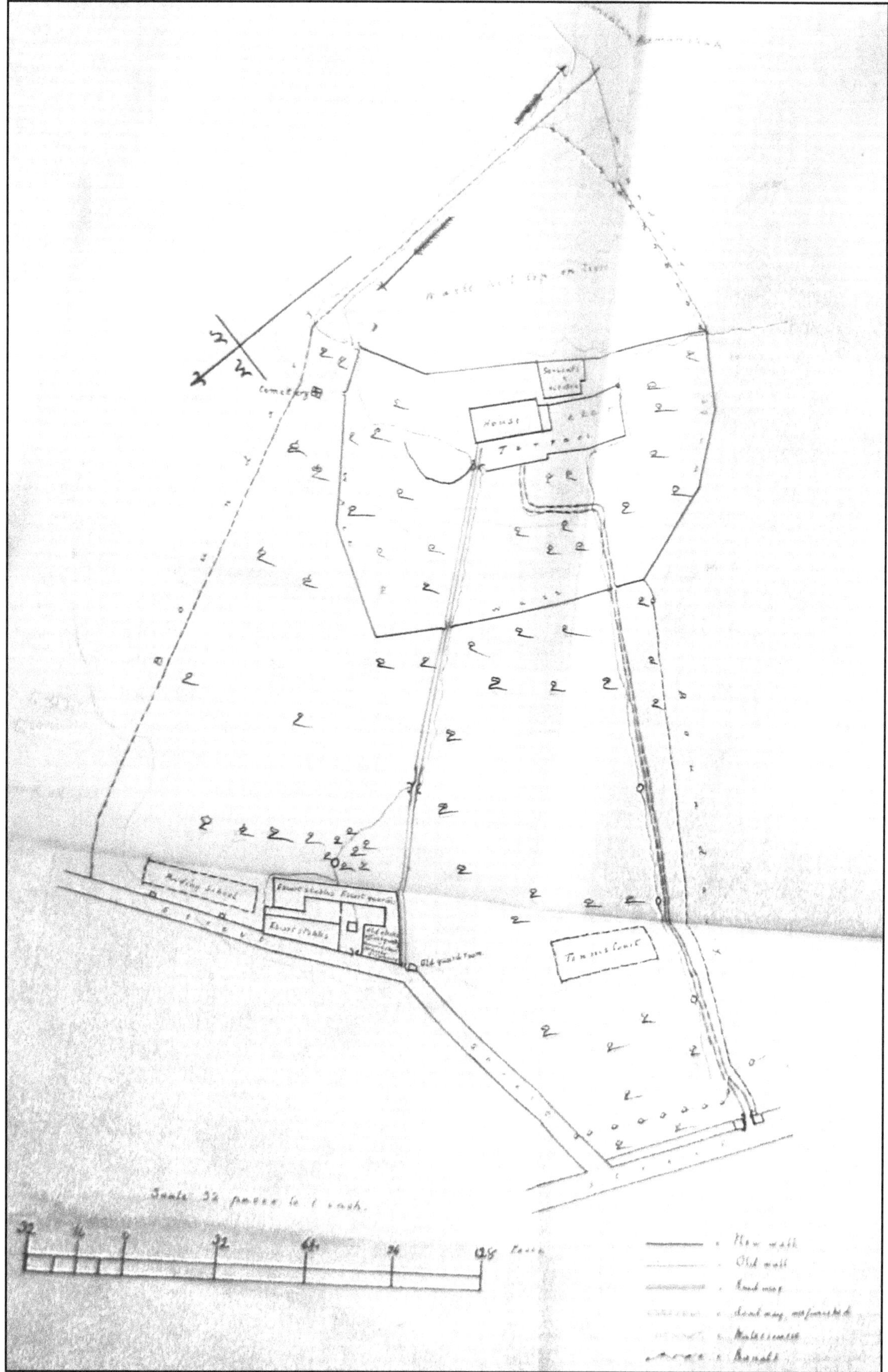
House
Cemetery
Riding School
Old guard room
Tennis Court
32
16
0
32
64
96
128
New wall
Old wall

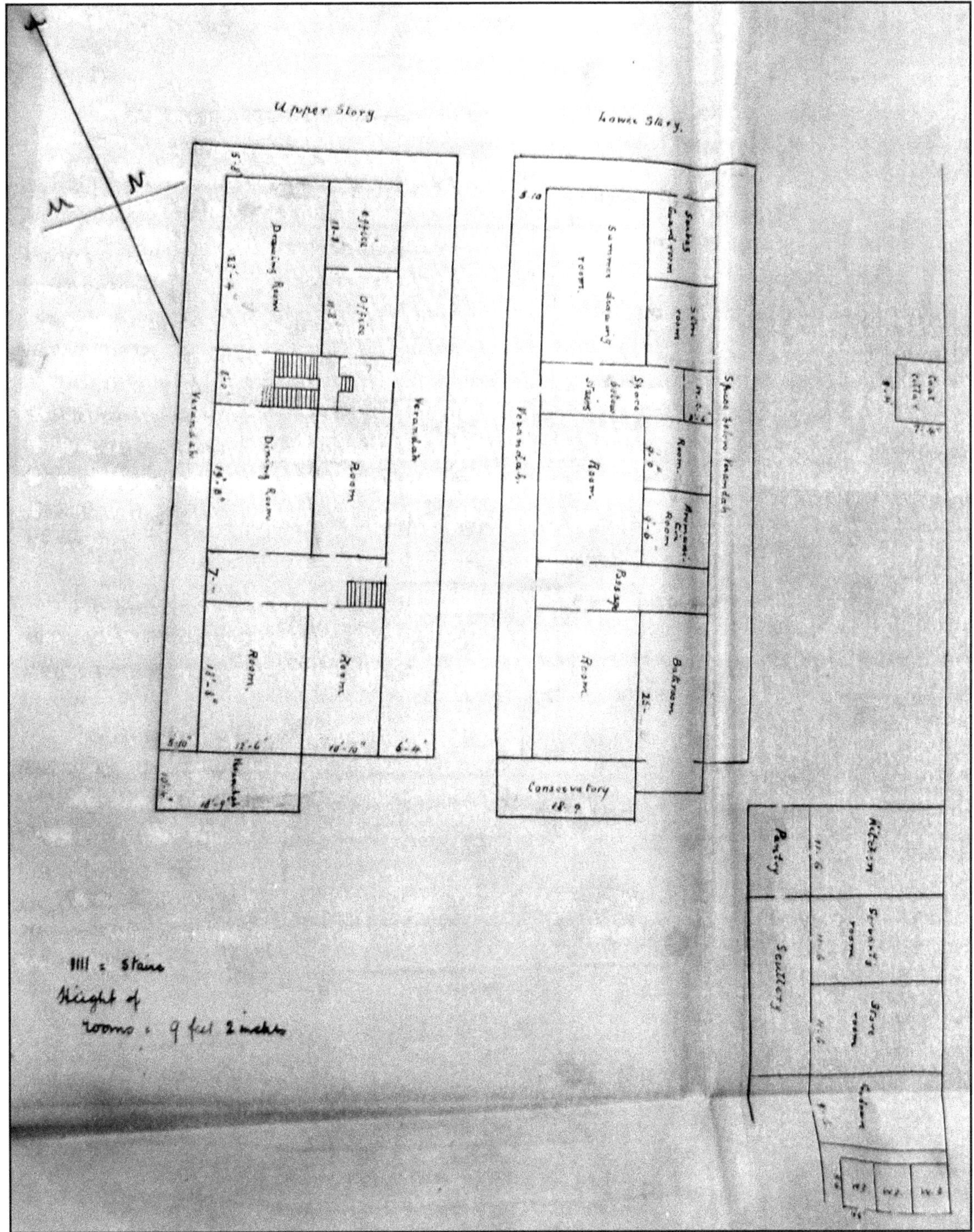

Fig. 3.9 and 3.10: *Opposite and above,* Plans of the British Consulate 1909.

RUSSIA

Russia established a Consulate-general in Kermanshah since 1903 to promote its political interests, because there were neither Russian citizens nor any Russian trade in Kermanshah. The consulate was headed by Mr. Nikolski and as of April 1906 he was assisted by Mr. Petrov. In December 1904, Dr. Ost, a Russian physician, arrived to serve at the Consulate. Dr. Ost left one year later on 17 December 1905, although there was as yet no news of a successor. At that time, the Russian consul traveled to Senneh, the first time in three years that he had left town.[170] Nikolski left on 11 October 1906 for 6-months leave to Europe; Petrov was acting consul during that period. To promote Russian trade, Nikolski sent agents (*vakil*) to Qasr-e Shirin and Khorramabad to reside there permanently. In November 1906, he appointed an important local merchant Vakil al-Tojjar as Russian agent in Senneh. The British were not able to learn what his duties or object of function were. Petrov left in July 1907. Dr. Volansky, the Consulate's physician, left at the end November 1908, but Nikolski remained as consul.[171]

During WWI the Consulate was closed for some time, when both the British and Russian consuls were forced to leave to Hamadan in August 1915 and only returned in June 1917. There was still a Russian consul (Cherkassov) and an assistant consul in March 1918.[172] Per 31 December 1920, the Russian consulate was closed. The Russians wanted to sell the Consular garden of 71,700 sq. meters (over 12 acres) for 1.5 *qran*/sq. m which compared favorably with the then current land price of about 3 *qran*s. The British government made an offer to buy the garden.[173]

---

170. Political Diaries 1, p. 428; Grothe 1910, p. 84.

171. Administration Report 1905-06, p. 45; Administration Report 1906-07, p. 42; Administration Report 1907-08, p. 64; Administration Report 1908, pp. 47, 49; Political Diaries, vol. 1, pp. 9, 255, 505, 539; Political Diaries, vol. 3, p. 389. When Lambert Molitor arrived in Kermanshah in 1908, the European colony consisted of the Russian consul, his wife and their two children, the secretary of the consul, and the Polish physician. Also, the British consul and his wife, the director of the IBP and his wife, and one IBP staff member. Molitor 2018 a.

172. Hale n.d.,pp. 216, 226; Edmonds 2010, p. 219.

173. FO 248/1293 tel. Consul to Legation, 31/12/1920; Idem, Kermanshah Report no. 1, 31/01/1920.

Table 3.6: List of Russian consuls (1903-45)

Name	Date	Source
Nikolski	1903-11 October 1906; April 1907- ?	Political Diaries vol. 1, p. 428
Petrov	Vice-consul; acting 10/06-04/07	Administration Report 1905-06, p. 45; Administration Report 1906-07, p. 42
Dolgopolov, acting	?- June 1915	FO 248/1112, Kermanshah Diary ending 14/01/1915
Baron Cherkasov	23 June 1915-March 1918	FO 248/1112, McDouall/Hamdan to Legation, 23/06/1915
	1918-1919 uncertain status	
Berlin	1922	See text
Lidin	1923?-December 1925	See text
Lovodsky	December 1925-?	See text
	1937-1941 closed	
Viatcheslav Chvetsov	21 January-October 1942	See text
Vladimir Troukhanovsky	October 1942-April 1943	See text
Elie Oserov, acting consul	April 1943-January 1944	See text
Nikolai Klimov	January 1944-26 March 1945	See text
Pankatrov, acting consul	26 March-1 August 1945	See text
Mirochine	1 August 1945-?	FO 371/45400, Kermanshah Diary August 1945

It was only in 1921 or early 1922 that a Soviet Russian consul was appointed to Kermanshah. The first Soviet consul was Mr. Berlin, who, in May 1922 appointed 'Ali Akbarov as his consular interpreter.[174] A certain Belaev, a Bolshevik agent in Kermanshah, without success, was trying to organize the labor class on Bolshevik lines. He was dismissed from the Consulate in July 1922 and returned to Moscow.[175] This did not stop Mr. Berlin from being engaged in political activities, for on 28 October 1923, the High Commissioner in Iraq received news that Mr. Berlin tried to collect all Iraqi extremists then in Persia and was trying to make Kermanshah the center for anti-British and anti-Iraq government activities. This activity was supported from Tehran, for M. Shumayetski wired M. Berlin as to various related anti-British activities and developments.[176]

It is not clear when Berlin was replaced by Lidin, the second Soviet Russian consul, who in December 1925 in his turn was replaced by Lovodsky as consul in Kermanshah.[177] In 1932,

174. IOR/L/MIL/17/15/11/3, Who's Who in Persia, vol. 2, p. 25. However, the British also reported that a certain Lebedev was appointed Russian consul in Kermanshah in April 1922, which apparently did not happen. IOR/L/MIL/17/15/11/3, Who's Who in Persia, vol. II, p. 187.

175. IOR/L/MIL/17/15/11/3, Who's Who in Persia, vol. 2, p. 84.

176. IOR/L/PS/18/C210, 'Bolshevik Intrigue in Persia since October 1922', p. 28.

177. FO 416/78, Intel. Summary No. 30 ending December 12, 1925; Russians opened a commercial agency at Qasr-e Shirin; a cloak for making propaganda into Iraq and Posht-e Kuh. FO 416/80, Intel. Summary No. 5 ending March 5, 1927.

the British, Turkish and Soviet Russian consulates are mentioned.[178] In 1937, the Russians closed their consulate which they reopened after the invasion of Iran. On 21 January 1942, Viatcheslav Chvetsov arrived as consul. He was assisted by 2 vice-consuls and one secretary who spoke English.[179] In May 1942, vice-consul Soldatoff left, but two other Russians arrived, including the gate keeper. This meant there were six Russians, who did not employ any Persians.[180] In October 1942, Troukhanovsky, the new consul arrived, who was young and spoke English.[181] Vladimir Troukhanovsky left in April 1943. Acting consul was Elie Oserov, who was assisted by vice-consul Pankratov. M. Maisky was the next consul, who's contacts with the British consul were in Persian.[182] Nikolai Klimov was his successor, an English speaker, taking over from Elie Oserov, the vice-consul who had been acting since Vladimir Troukhanovsky had left in April 1943.[183] He was succeeded by Nikolai Klimov, who was assisted by senior vice-consul Arkady Avakov and vice-consul Pavel Pankratov. Klimov left on 26 March 1944 with his family; Pankatrov was acting consul.[184] Mirochine, the new Soviet consul arrived on 01/08/1945, assisted by Pankatriv and vice-consul Kochelev.[185] In May 1944, the following persons were living in the Soviet Consulate: one consul, two vice-consuls plus six other Russians. With wives they numbered in total 15 persons, not counting children.[186] Although Allies, the British and Russian consulates monitored each others activities, nevertheless, the Russian Consulate used the British Army signals for their telegrams.[187]

IRAQ

In May 1942, Iraq opened a consulate in Kermanshah with ‘Abdol-Rahman al-Fellahi as its consul.[188] Naser al-Din Bey Gilani was Iraqi consul until July 1943, when he was appointed consul-general in Tehran.[189] In February 1945, M. Zeki was the Iraqi consul. In that month he issued 200 visas to pilgrims, which probably was one of his main tasks.[190] As of July 1945, the Iraqi consulate also represented Syrian interests, of which there appeared to be none in Kermanshah.[191]

178. Ebtehaj 1932, p. 148.
179. FO 371/31402, Kermanshah Diary January 1942; Idem, Kermanshah Diary February 1942.
180. FO 371/31402, Kermanshah Diary May 1942.
181. FO 371/31402, Kermanshah Diary October 1942.
182. FO 371/40177, Kermanshah Diary December 1943.
183. FO 371/40177, Kermanshah Diary January 1944.
184. FO 371/45400 Monthly Diary Dec. 1944; Idem, Kermanshah Diary June 1945; Kermanshah Diary February 1945; Kermanshah Diary March 1945 (Avakov, Soviet vice-consul); FO 371/45400, Kermanshah Diary June 1945.
185. FO 371/45400, Kermanshah Diary July 1945; Idem, Kermanshah Diary August 1945; Idem, Kermanshah Diary April 1945.
186. FO 371/40177, Kermanshah Diary May 1944.
187. FO 371/40177, Kermanshah Diary May 1944.
188. FO 371/31402, Kermanshah Diary May 1942. In April 1932, King Faysal had visited Kermanshah, where he was received by Reza Shah. *The Palestine Bulletin*, Thursday 28/04/1934, p. 1.
189. *The Palestine Bulletin*, Thursday 19/07/1934, p. 5
190. FO 371/45400, Kermanshah Diary February 1945.
191. FO 371/45400, Kermanshah Diary July 1945.

KARGOZARI

Because there was an Ottoman consul in Kermanshah, the Persian Ministry of Foreign Affairs had to be represented by a *kargozar*. The creation of the office of *kargozar* was the result of the implementation of the Treaty of Turkomanchay (1828), when a special office (*divan-e mohakemat-e kharejeh*) was created to deal with cases that arose between Persians and foreigners. The office of *kargozar*, which came into being in the late 1830s, was the successor of the secretary (*dabir*) of that office, although a fully developed *kargozari* was only established around 1880, according to Martin and Nouraei. It is not known when the first *kargozar* was appointed to Kermanshah.[192]

All matters between Persians and foreign subjects had to be taken up with the *kargozar*. These cases varied from simple theft to bankruptcy. In dealing with the cases before him, the *kargozar* had to take into account local opinion, because he was pressured from all sides to decide this or that way. Also, often the governor interfered, in particular in cases of theft, where compensation had to be paid. In such cases, "when the thieves are not discovered the victims are entitled to only half the amount stolen." Exceptionally, in June 1906, to please the British consul the governor paid in full 150 *tumans* the sum stolen from a British subject. However, to a Turkish Jew had been robbed, he paid only half. Similarly, when in the night of 29 June 1906 thieves entered the British Consulate's grounds and stole 20 *tumans* and some clothes the governor promised to pay in full when the thieves were not found.[193] However, when at the end of 2 June 1906, some soldiers tried to steal fruit from the British Consulate's garden the governor did not get involved. When the gardener discovered them they dragged him to the governor, but were caught by the Consulate's Clerk and Mirza. The latter insisted that the soldiers be bastinadoed in the Consulate instead of at the barracks. It was finally agreed that the punishment would take place at the *kargozar*'s residence. Led by trumpeters the soldiers were marched there and trussed up, but then the Clerk and Mirza forgave the beating, hoping that this public display would send a strong message.[194]

In Kermanshah one of his major activities was that of the passport office. In 1902, those traveling to Baghdad or Kerbela had to pay one *qran* for a passport. The fee for a visa was 12.6 *qrans* for every six months. Passport for other countries cost more, the fee varying from 1.20 to 30 *qrans* depending on the traveler's rank.[195] In March 1907, Farid al-Molk Qaraguzlu Hamadani, *kargozar* since 1903, was dismissed and replaced by Sharif al-Molk.[196] The latter was a pleasant man for whom no bribe was too small. In April 1908, the three foreign consuls approached their Legations to have the *kargozar* removed because of his corruption. The British consul had approached the Russian consul already in September 1907, but it was only 8 months later that the latter believed that it needed to be done.[197] Mohammad Reza Khan Asaf al-Molk

192. Martin and Nouraei 2005.
193. Political Diaries, vol. 1, pp. 403, 411.
194. Political Diaries, vol. 1, p. 428.
195. DCR 590 (Kermanshah 1901-02), p. 12.
196. Administration Report 1906-07, p. 43; Political Diaries, vol. 1, p. 482; Soltani 1381, vol. 3, pp. 481-82.
197. Administration Report 1907-08, p. 64; Political Diaries, vol. 2, p. 199 (according to Petrov, the Russian vice-consul, the *kargozar* "would accept a bribe of three Krans (one Shilling)"; Political Diaries, vol. 3, p. 143.

was *kargozar* in 1921 and 1922. The British considered him "a poisonous individual and one whose word cannot be relied on."[198] There continued to be *kargozars* in the city until 1927, when Reza Shah did away with the function as part of his abolishment of the Capitulations.

Fig. 3.10: *Above,* Betsy and Lambert Molitor in the courtyard of their house. © *Collection Molitor, Ed. Elytis* no. 0110
Fig. 3.11: *Facing page (top),* Reception at the Molitors in the spring of 1913, present are: McDouall, Lambert Molitor, Dr. Volansky, Mr. Dekerckheer, Mr. Authelet, Mrs. Molitor, Mrs. Durie, Mr. Nikolsky. © *Collection Molitor, Ed. Elytis* no. 219.
Fig. 3.12: *Facing page (bottom),* Betsy and Lambert Molitor in front of their house.
© *Collection Molitor, Ed. Elytis* no. 0390.

198. IOR/L/MIL/17/15/11/3, Who's Who in Persia, vol. 2, p. 71.

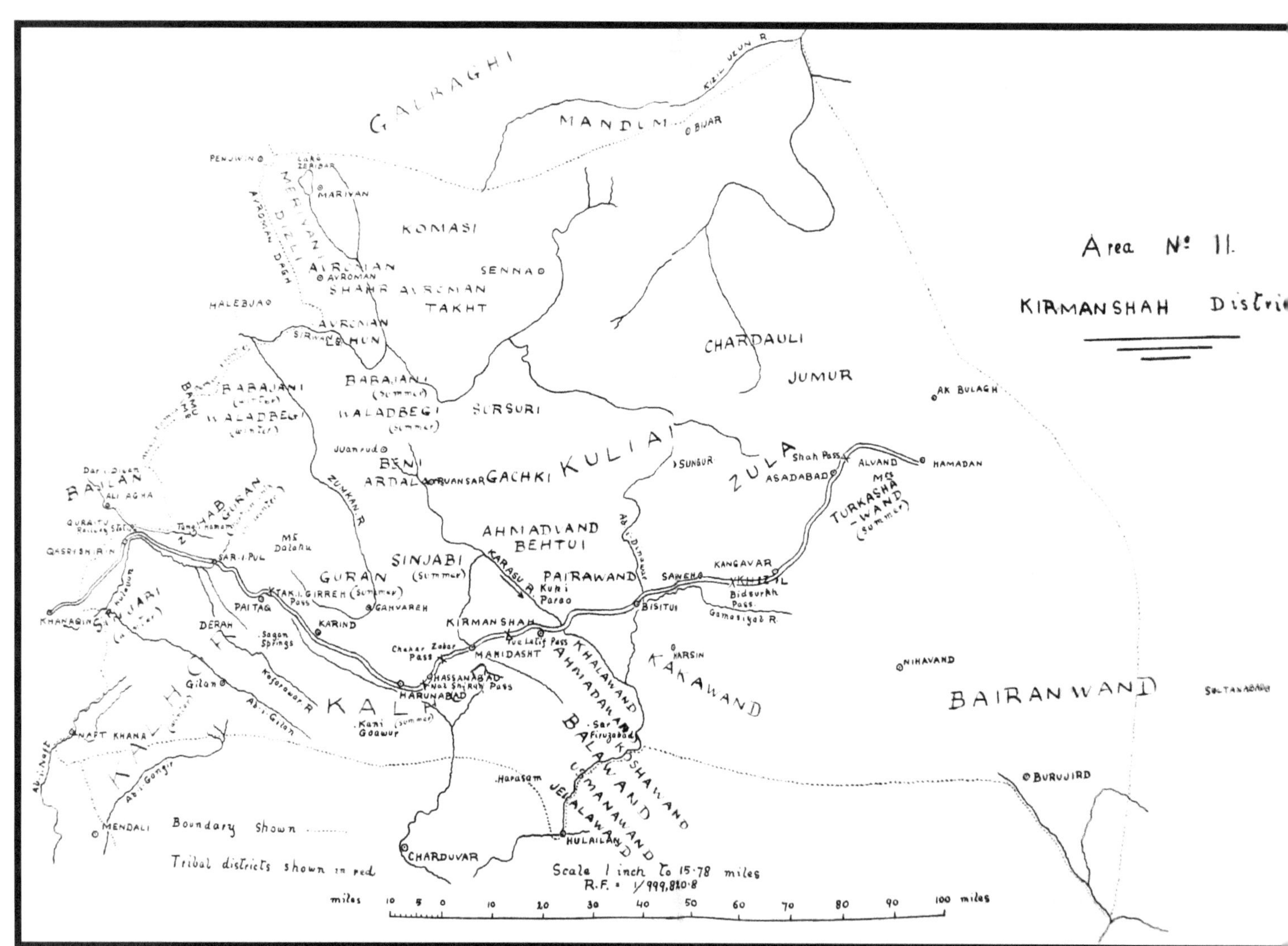

Fig. 4.1: Tribal map of the Kermanshah Consular district (1920).

CHAPTER FOUR

THE PROVINCE OF KERMANSHAH

SITUATION OF THE PROVINCE

The province bordered on the Baghdad *vilayat* (Qal'eh Sabzi) to the west, on Lorestan Kuchek (Posht-e Kuh) to the south, Kurdistan to the North and East. It was characterized by broad parallel plains, where the sedentary population lived, and mountains, populated by the pastoralists, mostly following a north-east and south-east direction. Mt. Dalahu is the highest mountain and is always snow-capped. Other high mountains include Kuh-e Parraw, Kuh-e Hulaneh and Kuh-e Delakhani. The mountains offer pasturage to the herds and were covered with trees such as oak, elm, sycamore, and some small conifers. The trees of the Kermanshah plains were the willow, poplar, Oriental plane and walnut, and fruit trees of N. Europe; palm trees were found in the gardens of Sar-e pol-e Zohab and Qasr-e Shrin. There was also much game such as bear, wolf, wild goat, gazelle, partridge, sand grouse, geese, duck and other migratory birds (bustard, snipe, quail).[1]

CLIMATE

The climate of the province was mild in summer but cold in winter, except in the Zohab district and the plains near the frontier and in the lower parts of the Kalhor country (in the region of Mandali) where it tended to be hot in summer. Snow on the mountains was heavy in winter and spring rains were normally plentiful. The maximum July temperature of the town of Kermanshah was 37.2° C. and the minimum January temperature 3.5° C. Annual rainfall was 372.7 mm.[2] The year 1907 was exceptionally dry with only 45.8 cm of rain. "On one day only did snow worth mentioning fall with the result that what are usually rushing streams until the month of June are now dry beds, while many springs which generally last till the heat of summer are also

1. DCR 3189 (Kermanshah 1903-04), pp. 32-34; Adamec 1976, vol. 1, p. 355-58.
2. CHI 1968, vol. 1, p. 247.

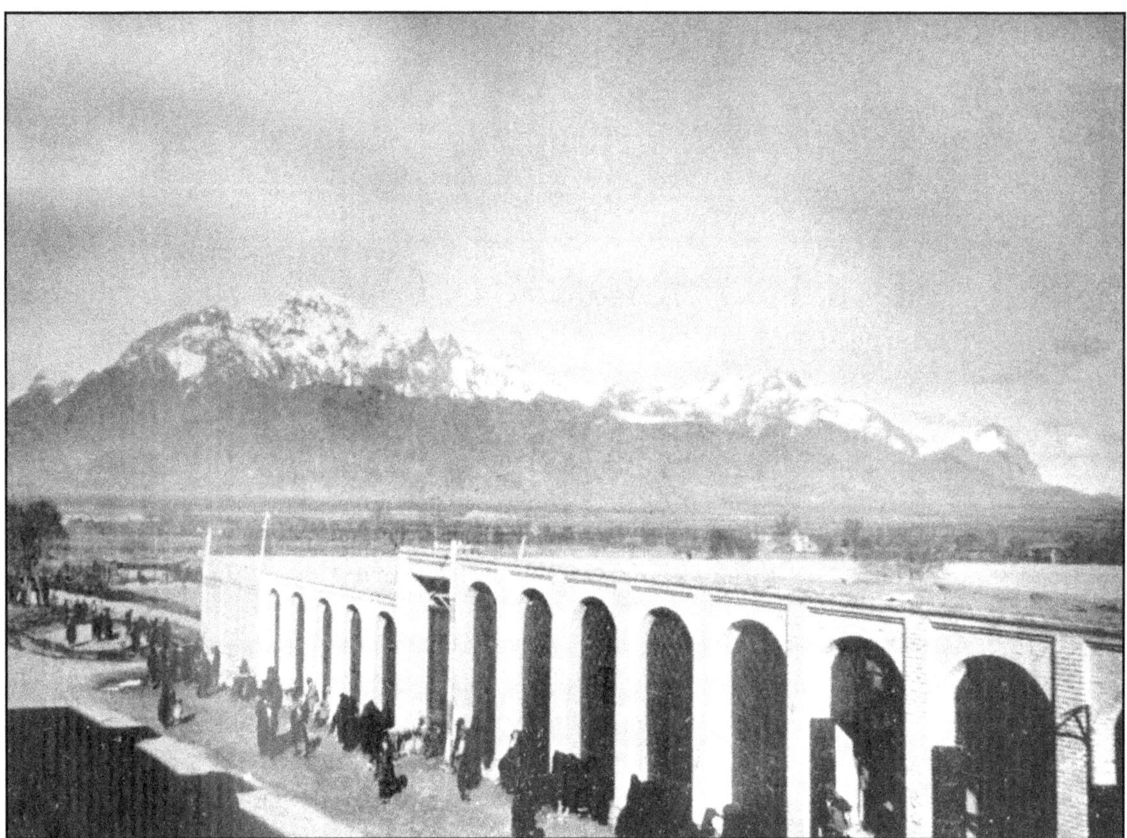

Fig. 4.2: Kermanshah plus Mt Bisotun (1930)

dry or at best have but a small trickle. Fortunately rain fell at the proper seasons for the crops of 1908 and thus no great harm has been done beyond that, owing to the warm winter, there is hardly any ice stored for next summer."[3] Indeed, due to the mild winter and very hot summer, ice ran out. Fortunately, the permanent snow in the hills offered a good alternative at a slightly higher price. February (12.9) is normally the coldest and 15/7 to 15/8 the hottest (103.2) month of the year. Rainfall was only 15.39 inches.[4]

ADMINISTRATION

The governor (*hakem*) of Kermanshah, who was appointed by the Shah, was assisted by a number of officials, some of which also dealt with provincial affairs such as (i) the provincial accountant and his staff (*ra'is daftar* or *vazir-e maliyat*), (ii) the secretary and his staff (*monshi-bashi*), (iii) the army accountant and his staff (*lashkar-nevis*), (iv) the chief attendant and his

3. Administration Report 1907/08, pp. 62-63.
4. Administration Report 1908, p. 46.

staff (*farrash-bashi*), and (v) the chief of the riflemen and his staff (*tofangdar-bashi*).[5] Often the governor of Kermanshah also held the governorship of Kurdistan as well as that of Lorestan and Borojerd, in which case he was also referred to as *Vali-ye Gharb* (governor fo the West). In a few cases Khuzestan was also added to his jurisdiction.

As of 1936, Persia was divided into five so-called *ostans* or regions. Kermanshah was part of *Ostan* V, which consisted of Kermanshah, Kurdistan and Lorestan. The provincial governor was henceforth called *ostandar* and the governors, including of Kermanshah city, of the towns and districts were called *farmandar*. The sub-district chiefs were called *bakhshdar*. At Qasr-e Shirin there was both a *hakem* and *sarhaddar* until 1936. The one responsible for civil matters and the other for border security. Thereafter, although the functions did not change, the titles did and henceforth were called respectively, *bakhshdar* and *kalantar-e marz*.[6] In 1944, the Soheyli Cabinet, one day before its demise, separated the Kurdistan *farmandari* from *Ostan* V and made it directly responsible to Tehran. The *ostandar*, Fahim al-Dowleh held this for illegal as Persia was divided into *ostans* and this could only changed by law not by a cabinet decision; also he felt that it was dangerous because it might fuel the independence movement in Kurdistan, the more so since the Cabinet decision used the word *esteqlal*. He wired Tehran to reverse it, since Soheyli made the decision hours before his resignation.[7]

The province was divided into districts (*boluks*) and market-towns (*qasabehs*), which each was under a deputy-governor, who were all, but one, appointed by the government. In the 1840s, the province had only five districts,[8] but in 1902, it was divided into 19 *boluks*.[9] There were two types of districts. Those which included "a town or villages of a non-tribal nature and tribal districts. The Governors of the former are selected from the town notables, or the leading land-owners of the area concerned and in the case of the latter the chief of the tribe concerned is usually appointed Governor although a town notable is sometimes appointed if a tribal chief is found to be unsatisfactory."[10] In 1902, this division with the appointees was as follows:

Qasr-e Shirin	Vacant
Zohab	Mansur al-Molk of the Gurans
Kerind	Ehtesham al-Mamalek of Kerind
Guran	Mansur al-Molk
Kalhor	Da'ud Khan, Sardar-e Mozaffar of the Kalhors
Mahidasht	Appointed from city. Hajji Agha Khan
Huleilan and Zardalal	Vali of Posht-e Kuh
Harasan & Dizgaran	Sheikh Hadi, *mojtahed*

5. DCR 590 (Kermanshah 1902), pp. 11-12; Lycklama 1873, vol. 3, p. 472.
6. FO 371/40177, Kermanshah Diary March 1944. The *sarhaddar* or *kalantar-e marz* was an official of the Ministry of Foreign Affairs.
7. FO 371/40177, Kermanshah Diary March 1944.
8. Ferrier 1971, p. 26.
9. DCR 590 (Kermanshah 1902), p. 33.
10. AIR 20/663, non-paginated (2 pages before p. 43).

Minaderbend & Zardarbend	Appointed from city
Duru Faruman	Ditto
Chamchamal	Fakhim al-Saltaneh
Dinavar	Appointed from city
Kulia'i & Sanghur	Mansur al-Dowleh
Khodabandelu	Appointed from city
Harsin	Ditto
Sehneh	Appointed by owner Vazir al-Daftar from Tehran

Source: DCR 590, pp. 38-39.

The deputy-governors, who were 'appointed from city' were usually called *na'eb*; the other were referred to as *hakem neshin*, and the governor always as *hakem*. Kangavar was often under Kermanshah, but its governor was almost always Sar Aslan, whose family had held this post for five generations by 1900. In 1902, it was an independent governorship. Asadabad was usually under Kermanshah, but sometimes under Hamadan as in 1902, when the post was vacant.[11] In what follows a short description of offered of each district or *boluk* as described in 1902 by Rabino, with additional notes by Major Greenhouse, British consul in 1920-21.[12]

Boluk of Kermanshah. This is the district with Kermanshah as its center. At some 10 km from the city is Baladeh, which in 1902 was under Mahmud Khan, the chief of the government grain stores. The inhabitants of this district have no pasture land and therefore, give their cattle to the Chapankarehs or shepherd families of other tribes to graze in Huleylan, for which grazing rights are paid.

Boluk of Vastam. This small district north of Kermanshah Kowbandeh Saleh to Hajjiabad and extends from the Qarasu to Kinisht and the Parow mountains. The district is practically entirely owned by Hajji 'Abdol-Rahim Vakil al-Dowleh. It is inhabited by the Peyravand, a small tribe of 500, who in summer reside in the Parow Mountains and in winter rent *qeshlaqs* near Qasr-e Shirin.

Boluk of Miyan Derbend. This district, also called Bilavar, borders on Kurdistan and the Kermanshah, Kuliya and Posht Derbend districts. Its inhabitants are mostly Ahmadavand Behtu'i. Zir Darband had some 20-30 hamlets, each with 10-120 people.

Boluk of Posht Derbend. This district, also called Bala Derbend, is north of Kermanshah. Its inhabitants are Koliya'is and Ahmadavand Behtu'is and other Kurds. The Ahmandavand are Shiites. In winter they reside in quarters near Qasr-e Shirin and in summer at some 30 km from Kermanshah, where they live in hamlets and till their fields. They supply horsemen (sowars) to the government.

Boluk of Dinavar. This district forms a large plain and is situated on the road from Kermanshah to Tabriz. The inhabitants, who live in some 50 hamlets are poor and a mixture of Koliya'is,

---

11. DCR 590, pp. 38-39 The list only shows 16 *boluks* (plus Asadabad and Kangavar). In addition, Sar-e Pol is also mentioned as a district. Administration Report 1905-06, p. 45. Although Huleylan (45 km from the city) was bought by the Vali of Posht-e Kuh it was part of Kermanshah. Administration Report 1907-08, p. 51.
12. DCR 590, pp. 33-61; AIR 20/663, pp. 25-40, 90; see also Rabino 1905, pp. 6-17.

Jelilavand, Maki and Nanekali. There also are many Jews, but no trace of the former Armenian population. The district has large rice fields, but in 1902 these were greatly reduced in size due to the 3-year drought.

Boluk of Koliya'i. This district is north and east of Kermanshah and is bordered by Kurdistan, Asadabad, Dinavar and Posht-e Derbend. It has some 150 mostly wheat producing villages and its inhabitants are mostly Koliya'is. The town of Sonqur is well watered and surrounded by villages and gardens; its governor is responsible for collecting the revenues. Forage and fuel are aplenty, while the pastoral population raises horses and mules.

Boluk of Sahneh. The district's chief place is Sahneh a small town some 60 km east of Kermanshah, situated on the main road between Bisotun and Kangavar. In 1920 it had 1,000 inhabitants and was surrounded by fruit gardens, in particular groves of walnut trees. In the past the district was *khaleseh* or crown property, but towards the end of the nineteenth century it was given as a hereditary *toyul* to Vazir Daftar of Tehran. Its chief produce is wheat and opium. Its inhabitants include the Khodabandlu tribe.[13]

Boluk of Kangavar. This district is very fertile with Kangavar as its chief place. Its population of mainly Khezels and Afshars live in some 35 villages and are Shiites. The district is adjacent to Asadabad, Koliya'i, Nehavand and Khezel and only in 1902 was added to Kermanshah. The post of governor is usually held by the chief of the local Afshar tribe, who is the largest landowner in the district and owned a nice house in Kermanshah.

Boluk of Asadabad. This district with chief place Asadabad (or Sa'adabad) was only added to Kermanshah in 1902, and is located 40 km from Kermanshah on the road to Hamadan. At a later date, before 1920, it fell again under Hamadan. In 1920, it was a town of 500 houses and 3,000 inhabitants and situated on the trade route. It had a small bazaar and only a small stream for its water supply. Extensive gardens were to the S.E. of the town. Since the beginning of the twentieth century the town was under the influence of the Farmanfarama family that practically owned the entire valley. It had a large house at Janatabad, 5 km S.W. of the town.

Boluk of Hersin. Its center is a small tribal market town, with 800 houses and a population of 1,500 in 1920, situated 50 km east of Kermanshah on one of the main roads to Lorestan. There are many good buildings in the town that could house 500 men, but one of its suburbs, called Lak, was in ruins in 1920. The town, surrounded by a level plain of 8 km circumference, was built in a well-watered valley. The inhabitants were Laks, of which the pastoral part summered in Khaveh and Alishter, two Lorestan districts. Although the sedentary inhabitants were mostly Laks, the town had a strong relationship with the Kakawand (Delfan) tribe, who used the Harsin valley as summer quarters, often even taking possession of the town itself. This fertile district included many villages and gardens and a few pastoral settlements. In Hersin good gelims were woven. Many young people from Hersin took government service (Cossacks, gendarmes, *farrash*es) in Tehran and therefore, they were less oppressed by local governors, because they had easy access to high officials in Tehran. In 1920, the valley paid 2,000 *tuman*s in taxes and the immediate surrounding 1,500 *tuman*s. The town had a *kalantar*, a *kadkhoda*, and the leading

13. Napier 1919, p. 7.

clergy were two brothers, the Qadi and Ra'is al-Olama. By 1920, a gendarmerie unit was stationed in the town.

Boluk of Chamchamal. Its chief place was Bisotun and it was composed of some 250 hamlets. Its owners were notables from Kermanshah, notably Vakil al-Dowleh. The inhabitants were a mixture of tribes, but mostly Zuleh and Zanganeh.

Boluk of Duru-Faraman. This district, east of Kermanshah, encompassed some 50 villages and hamlets. Its inhabitants were Laks who were Ali-ilahis. There also was a small Ahmandavand tribe.

Boluk of Mahidasht. Its chief place was Mahidasht, a halting stage 22 km on the road to Kermanshah. In 1876, Floyer described it as "a small village with a caravanserai. The people here seemed poor and wretched. They had no flocks, and consequently the almost universal employment of spinning was wanting, and they sat listlessly about the muddy streets, doing nothing and waiting for the spring."[14] In 1920 it had a population of 500 and 100 houses, a small bazaar and one caravanserai. The Ab-e Marik flowed N.W. of the town under a high brick bridge. Its large plain, dotted with some 400 villages and hamlets, was well watered and was one of the most productive in Persia. "It is said to furnish two-thirds of the grain supply for the town of Kermanshah, and its grain fetches 4 krans more per kharvar than that from other parts of the province." Most inhabitants were Kalhors and had a reputation for thieving. Other inhabitants were Sanjabis and Zanganehs; the latter were Shiites. Small Lori tribes were also to be found there (Osmanavand, Shaharzuli, Khormavoi). The rural population and their cattle moved with their pastoral kin in summer to their summer quarters on the Iraqi border.

Boluk of Harunabad. The village, situated on the trade route, was one of the chief places of the Kalhors and in 1920 had a population of 1,000, living in 200 houses and one caravanserai. The Kalhor chiefs collected an 'entertainment tax' from all those passing through the village. The rates were 140 *qran*s per 100 camels or mules vice-versa, and for a single journey 1 *qran*/ head. The district was some 58 km south-east of Kermanshah, with Harunabad or Haruniyeh as its chief place. The entire population were Kalhors, the most powerful tribe in the province. Their *yeylaq* or summer quarters were some 50 km from Kermanshah; their *qeshlaq* from Mandali to Qasr-e Shirin; both areas were very fertile and mostly *abi* land.

Boluk of Guran. This district was populated by the Guran tribe about half of which were sedentary (*deh-neshin* or *yeylaqi*), the other half being pastoral (*garmsiri*). It extended from Mahidasht to Harun Nishin Khan (near Baneh). Their winter quarters were in the plain of Zohab. The people produced wheat, tobacco and gelims for their own use.

Boluk of Kerend. This district with Kerend as its chief place, also included many large villages such as Harir and Khosrowabad. The town was situated on the Qasr-e Shirin-Kermanshah road. It was built at the mouth of a gorge in a high rocky ridge through which runs a stream watering the town and gardens (which extend about 1.5 km to the south across the road) down to the Ab-e Kerind. In 1876, it had about 1,000 houses, according to Floyer and its people were mostly employed in agriculture. They are Ali-ilahis and are divided into four clans, viz. "the Zarday, Shuar, Nou Darwan, and Nou Chem." In 1920 the town had about 800 inhabitants. The town's

---

14. Floyer 1882, pp. 440-41.

mostly sedentary inhabitants, as well as of the surrounding villages, were mostly Kerindi Kurds. Part of them migrate to Zohab in winter. Some Guran and Kalhor tribesmen also usually lived in the town. In the district there were also Laks, such as the Jalilawands. The plain of Kerend was famous for its seedless *asghari* grapes as well as other kinds of fruit. The women of the town of Kerend wove gelims, while many men were engaged in cutlery, metal work and gun making. They did not make cartridges; these were imported from Baghdad, recapped by hand and repeatedly used until worn out.[15]

Boluk of Zohab. This was the largest district in the province, but contained few villages. In fact, during the summer the plain of Zohab, though well watered, was mostly deserted. The greater part of the plain up to Sarpol was transformed into rice fields. At Hurin and Sheykhan wheat and rice were cultivated. Qasr-e Shirin was the largest settlement and was well provisioned to serve trade and pilgrim caravans. Its inhabitants were Bajlans, Jafs, Sanjabis, and Sharafbeynis. This district has been Ottoman territory until 1816, when Dowlatshah annexed it. According to the 1823 Treaty between Persia and Ottoman, it should have been returned. However, "neither has the Persian the will to render this act of justice nor had the Pasha of Baghdad the power to enforce it."[16]

Boluk of Eyvan. A large district bordering on Lorestan and Mendali. Its inhabitants were mainly Eyvanis, who were cultivators and had some cattle.

Boluk of Huleylan. This district bordered on Lorestan and was owned by the Vali of Posht-e Kuh. It was inhabited by Lor tribes. The Chupankeras of various tribes who grazed the cattle of the Kermanshah villagers leased pasturage there from the Huleylans.

TAXATION

How much revenues were collected and on the basis of what kind of tax schedules in the province in Kermanshah is not known, because for most years no published data are available and for the years that such data exist these only indicate the minimum amount collected, as governors always collected more than was their due. As elsewhere in Persia, the land or agricultural tax was the most important source of revenue. Around 1810, the province's nominal revenue was 15,000 *tumans*/year.[17] In the mid-1840s, the revenues of Kermanshah province (of only five districts) amounted to 60,000 in taxes and 13,000 *tumans* in customs, or a total of 73,000 *tumans* equal to £35,000 at that time.[18] In 1901, the land tax was fixed at 72,000 *tumans*. Additional sources of revenue (customs, guild tax, etc). yielded some 30,000 *tumans*, or a total of about 100,000 *tumans*. This last amount was the so-called fixed revenue or *asl*, which is what the governor of the province had to collect according to his revenue register or *ketabcheh*, which

---

15. DCR 590, pp. 53-57. In 1876, Floyer 1882, pp. 442-44 noticed small villages in this district, "all showing signs of activity in the manufacture of woollen carpets of a zigzag pattern not very handsome." Floyer was also pestered in Kerend by "journeyman tinkers, ironmongers, etc., who manufacture all sorts of handy travelling implements for sale to the pilgrims." See also Gerard 1883, p. 45; Napier 1919, p. 10. In 1906, consul Gough "saw some of the rifles manufactured in the town. These rifles are not at all badly turned out, and cost from 20 to 30 Tomans apiece (roughly from Rs. 50 to Rs. 75)." Administration Report 1905-06, p. 50.
16. DCR 590 (Kermanshah 1901-02), pp. 57-61; Administration Report 1907-08, p. 62.
17. Kinneir 1973, p. 132
18. Ferrier 1971, p. 27.

Fig. 4.3: Prince Mohammad Vali accompanied by Kurdish horsemen in 1911. © *Collection Molitor, Ed. Elytis* no. 128.

was issued by the government in Tehran. In addition, flexible irregular revenues or *farq* were collected, because the fiscal assessment was 30 years old by then. However, how much additional revenue this represented each year is unknown. Rabino was told that for a number of years, prior to his arrival in March 1902, the acting governor had asked the government in Tehran for 30,000 *tumans* to balance his accounts.[19]

After the Customs administration had been taken over by the Belgians, they also became involved with the financial management of the province. In 1905, the system worked as follows. The taxes, based on registers issued by Tehran, were collected by the deputy-governors, who, after deducting for military forces and administrative expenses, remitted the balance to the Treasury, which was administered by the Customs administration. After payment of the pensions the net balance was sent to Tehran. In 1904-05, the revenues for Kermanshah amounted to 451,900 *tumans*. This was quite an increase compared to 1901-02, despite the fact that the fiscal assessment was still not up-to-date, which led to fraud.[20] For the year 1907-08, more detailed data are available on the revenue schedule of Kermanshah province, as follows:

19. DCR 590 (Kermanshah 1901-02), pp. 33, 65; DCR 113, p. 8. For an analysis of the functioning of the fiscal system, see Floor 1998.

20. Administration Report 1905-06, p. 49.

		Cash	*Tomans*
Kermanshah and Sanghur			108,084 ½
Sehna and Kangavar			4,580
Asadabad			4,600
	Total		117,264 ½
		Grains	Kharwars.
Kermanshah and Sanghur			9,180
Sehna and Kangavar			537
Asadabad			1,600
Total			11,317
		Straw	Kharwars.
Kermanshah and Sanghur only			2,513

However, due to the disturbed conditions in the province, the government only collected a little of that. These revenues were mainly used to pay the pensions and stipends to princes, the mullahs of Kerbela and Najaf and the four regiments and contingents of horsemen (*savar*s). Other expenditures included the expenses to receive important pilgrims and expenses of the tribal chiefs. In 1901, the latter expenditure was said to amount from 12,000 to 20,000 *tuman*s/year.[21] Some of the tribes met their fiscal obligations by providing men to perform military service. Others, who did not, had to pay taxes, usually in kind. We don't know how much the tribes in Kermanshah paid, but if the level of taxation of the tribes in neighboring Kurdistan is an indication then it was not much. The per capita tax burden ranged from 18 *shahi*s (1 *qran* = 20 *shahi*s) for the Ketkis to 6 *qran*s 2 *shahi*s for the Durajis, with an average of 3 *qran*s.[22]

POPULATION

Although there was no census, it seems that there is general agreement that the population of Kermanshah province was some 300,000 to 350,000. In 1902, Rabino counted some 60,000 families in all, which at five persons per family is some 300,000 people (see Table 4.1). However, he also noted that the tribes always gave low numbers as to their number to cheat the tax man.[23] The people were divided into sedentary (*dehneshin* or *yeylaqi*) or pastoral (*sahraneshin* or *garmsiri*). In the mid-1830s, the population was composed of Turks, Lors and further away Kurds.[24] Towards the end of the nineteenth century, most villagers were Lors or Kurds. There

21. Administration Report 1907-08, p. 63; DCR 590, p. 65.
22. DCR 590, p. 62.
23. DCR 113, p. 8; Curzon 1892, vol. 2, p. 557; DCR 590, p. 63. Administration Report 1908, p. 40 gives a list of only the largest tribes, whose numbers are in general agreement with those of Table 4.2. The only major difference are the Bajlans, which allegedly numbered 1,000 families in 1908.
24. Southgate 1840, vol. 1, p. 323.

Fig. 4.4: Visit of two chiefs of the Bajlan tribe to Kermanshah in 1909. © *Collection Molitor, Ed. Elytis* no. 51.

also was some Turkish population in Sonqor and in Tavalabi village, who were Sunnis. Most of the Kurds of Kermanshah province were Ali-ilahis; there also were Christians who enclosed their wives, unlike the Kurds. There also were many Shiites, and a few Sunnis near the border.[25] The Kurdish women went around unveiled, some of them wore hoopskirts made of wattles, a red skirt and a shirt. "The men wear a bell-shaped flat-topped felt kullah or cap, sometimes like a brimless silk hat, and generally with a silk scarf twisted round it. In their girdles a formidable knife, the handle ornamented with brass, horne, and bone."[26]

Table 4.1: Estimated population of the province of Kermanshah (1900)

Name	Number of families	Summer quarters	Winter quarters
Aivan	2,000	Lurestan	Mandali
Harasam	200	Lurestan	Mandali
Huleilan	700	Lurestan	Mandali
Samareh	100	Lurestan	Mandali
Zengeneh	2,500	Sedentary in	Mahidasht

25. Binder 1887, p. 348; DCR 590, p. 14; Curzon 1892, vol. 1, p. 554 (350,000 Kurds; for a breakdown by tribe, see Idem, p. 556).

26. Napier 1919, p. 13; Binder 1887, p. 348.

Name	Number of families	Summer quarters	Winter quarters
Osmanavand	400	Sedentary in	Mahidasht
Ahmadavand Behtui	400	Sedentary in	Mahidasht
Jelilavand	300	Sedentary in	Mahidasht
Mafi	200	Sedentary in	Mahidasht
Nanekali	300	Sedentary in	Mahidasht
Kuliai	4,000	Mostly sedentary in	Sunqur
Sahna and dependencies	700	Mostly sedentary in	Sunqur
Khodabendlu	500	Mostly sedentary in	Sunqur
Zouleh	1,000	Mostly sedentary in	Sunqur
Gurans	5,000	Mahidasht	South of Kerend
Kalhurs	12,000	Harunabad	South-west of Kermanshah
Sharafbaini	1,000	Kerend	
Sanjabi	4,000	North of Kermanshah	Mahidasht
Kerindi	4,000	North of Kerend	Kerend
Bajlan	200	North of Kerend	Zohab
Jelalavand	500	North of Kerend	Zohab
Chamchamal and Dinavar	3,000	North of Kerend	Zohab
Hersin and Duru-Faraman	3,000	North of Kerend	Zohab
Petty tribes of Mahidasht	500	North of Kerend	Zohab
Kermanshah	12,000	North of Kerend	Zohab
Sarab	500	North of Kerend	Zohab
Baladeh and Pairavands	3,000	North of Kerend	Zohab

Source: DCR 590, p. 62.

In 1920, consul Greenhouse estimated that 75% of province's population were Moslems. The Kurdistan tribes were mostly Sunnis, while the Kalhors, Koliya'is, Ahmadawands and part of the Gurans were Shiites; the Sanjabis were Ali-ilahis as were the Othmanavands, Jalalavands, and part of the Gurans. Baba Yadgar, the religious center of the Ali-ilahis was some 15 km NNW of Paytaq.[27]

Table 4.2: List of the main tribes, their chiefs and number of tents 1902, 1905

Chief	Tribe	No. families 1902	No. tents or houses 1905
Da'ud Khan, Sardar-e Mozaffar or Saham al-Molk	Kalhor	10,000	12,000
Hoseyn Khan Mansur al-Molk	Guran	6,000	8,000
Habibollah Khan; Shir Mohammad Khan, Samsam al-Mamalek deposed	Sanjabi	2,000	3,000

27. AIR 20/663, p. 78; see also Napier 1919, p. 8, according to whom the Kalhors were Shiites and the other tribes were all Ali-ilahis.

Chief	Tribe	No. families 1902	No. tents or houses 1905
Mohammad Reza Khan, Zahir al-Molk, governor of Kermanshah	Zanganeh	4,000	4,000
No special chief, a broken class	Kuliai	4,000	6,000
Frontier tribe; Karim Khan, Shoja` al-Mamalek	Bajelan	1,000	600
Frontier tribe: Soleyman Khan, Shahab al-Mamalek	Sharafbayani	700	300
Ali Morad Khan, Ehtesham al-Mamalek	Kerindi	4,000	4,000
Mohammad Khan, Fath al-Mamalek	Ahmadwand	-	700
Mohammad Reza Khan, Zaher al-Molk	Nana Kalli	-	1,000
Governor appointed by governor	Pairwand	-	300

Source: DCR 590, p. 33f; Administration Report 1905-06, p. 48.

It would require a separate book to write about the various tribes in Kermanshah province. Therefore, I provide a brief description of the major tribes, not only because of their size, but also because they played a more important role in local politics than the others. Also, detailed information is only available about a few major tribes and that for a limited period only. As to the smaller tribes, information is mostly absent and what is there is incidental. Moreover, they were usually attached to a larger tribe such as in the case of the "Ahmadevand, Jellewend, Biwanji, Usmanawend," who were attached the Zanganeh tribe.[28] Although the leaders of the Zanganeh tribe, as prior to the 19th century, continued to play a dominant role in Kermanshah, little is known about this tribe during the 19th and 20th century, apart from the fact that its leaders continued to play an influential role in local politics (tribal or otherwise). The prestige and influence that its leaders enjoyed was not in proportion to the economic or military importance of this sedentarized tribe.[29] In the first two decades of the twentieth century, the Sanjabis also had great influence among the other tribes, for the following reasons:

> i. through small numerically, they were the most efficient tribe and the best fighters.
> ii. they maintained more cohesion than other tribes.
> iii. the personality of 'Ali Akbar Khan and his brothers.[30]

The Kalhors, who, because of their numerical superiority, should have dominated all other tribes, suffered from lack of cohesion, and therefore, were less of a power than they might have been. Nevertheless, they were a major rival of the Sanjabis and the two were usually hostile to each other. Each tribe, ruled by a paramount chief, was a combination of sub-groups under

---

28. Administration Report 1908, p. 40; DCR 590, p. 42. For information on the smaller tribes, see, e.g., Rabino 1905, pp. 17-23, 32-37, 39-40.

29. Napier 1919, p. 8. For more details on the Zanganeh, see Rabino 1905, pp. 39-40.

30. AIR 20/663, Maj. Greenhouse, Notes on Kermanshah Affairs, May 1921, p. 81. "The two small Sunni Muhammadan tribes, the Taishi and the Kara Mir Waisi, are affiliated to the Guran." Napier 1919, p. 8.

Fig. 4.5: Sardar Mokri and his Kurdish horsemen (*ca.* 1911). © *Collection Molitor, Ed. Elytis* no. 241

*kadkhoda*s or headmen, who tried to be as independent as possible from the tribal chief. Their loyalty to the paramount chief was ensured through coercion, marriage, cajoling, financial and other benefits. In February 1914, for example, Sardar Moqtader (Ali Akbar Khan Sanjabi) arrested two *kadkhoda*s of the Sufi section of the Sanjabis and refused to release them. The Sufis then moved to the border and Samsam al-Mamalek tried to reconcile them.[31] On 17 June 1906, consul Gough visited Da'ud Khan Kalhor's camp; there was a party in honor of Javan Mir Khan, his son, who married that day. Both father and son were much married (respectively 12 and 5 wives) to strengthen their position as tribal chief.[32] The tribal chief was responsible for payment of the annual taxes that were paid in kind and military service. The tribes were always late or disinclined in paying their taxes, and therefore, the governor of Kermanshah and his officials periodically went among the tribes in their summer quarters to collect those arrears.

As elsewhere in Persia, the tribes migrated twice per year between their summer and winter quarters, spending their summer in the uplands and the winter in the foothills from Mandali northwards around Gilan and Zohab. In the spring, the tribal groups migrated to the mountains and built huts from branches. After sowing their grain they moved their huts to the fields when the grain started growing. In September they went to their villages; the huts were set up in the

31. Political Diaries vol. 5, p. 421.
32. Political Diaries vol. 1, pp. 103, 427.

court yards, in which they lived while they repaired their homes; in winter the huts were used as fuel.[33] Table 4.3 shows where these quarters were for the various tribes, while it also indicates that some were mostly or entirely sedentary in large villages around which the rest of the tribe circulated. What the table does not show is that there also were sedentary Sanjabis, who therefore, were known as Yeylaqi Sanjabis. Given scarce resources and rivalry tribes might fight over access to land. In 1913, for example, there was fighting between the Sanjabis and Arabs in Iraq where the former had grazing lands.[34] In the summer of 1920, the Sanjabis wanted to get more grazing grounds at the expense of the Bajlans, but the governor decided that there was no justification for the claim and denied the request.[35] The actual boundaries of a tribal district were known to each tribe by way of certain physical features and land marks, although the demarcation of the districts was elastic and had to be secured by the threat of force. Although there was much inter-tribal as well as intra-tribal rivalry, and even enmity, if need be they appealed to their rivals to survive. For example in January 1920, because the grazing grounds of the Sanjabis were burnt they asked the Kalhors for permission to use theirs.[36] Such an occurrence seems to have occurred regularly, for in December 1920, the Turkashavand and the Jomur paid the Kalhors 2,000 *tumans* to be allowed to use their grazing land.[37]

Table 4.3: Approximate estimate of tribes in the Kermanshah and Kurdistan districts (1920)

Tribe	No. of houses	Name of chief	Summer quarters	Winter quarters
1.Kalhor	5,000 (8,000 rifles)	Soleyman Khan Amir-e A`zam	Guawar to Mahidasht	Gilan and near Mandali
2.Sanjabi	1,500 (3,000 rifles)	Qasem Khan Sardar-e Naser	North end of Mahidasht plain	Jebel Baghchah near Khaneqin and Aqdagh
3.Qalkhani	1,000	Qaser Soltan Rashid al-Saltaneh	Kuh-e Delahu	Zohab plain
4.Qalkhani	1,200	Asadollah Khan, Sardar Masnur and Qambar Soltan	-ditto-	-ditto-
5.Gahwarah	900	Gholam `Ali Khan	Gahwarah	Gahwarah
6.Bibiyani	200	Feyzollah Beg	Kuh-e Delahu	Zohab
7.Jaf	1,000	Ali Beg Soltan	Kuh-e Delahu	Quretu
8.Neyrizhi	500	Akbar Khan (d)	Near Gahwareh	Near Gahwareh
9.Tofangchi	1,000	Jahanbakhsh Zargham al-Saltaneh	Takht-e Gah near Mahidasht	Zohab
10.Ahmadwand	400 (400 rifles)	Farrokh Khan	Miyan Darband and Post-e Darband	Sedentary as in previous column

33. IOR/L/PS/10/283, File 2612/1912 Pt 1 'Tehran Sanitary Council', PV 7 October 1913, p. 189.
34. Political Diaries vol. 5, p. 103.
35. FO 248/1293 , Report Kermanshah, no. 7, up to 12 August 1920.
36. FO 248/1293, Kermanshah Report no. 1, 31/01/1920.
37. FO 248/1293, Report Kermanshah, no. 11, up to 10 December 1920.

Tribe	No. of houses	Name of chief	Summer quarters	Winter quarters
11.Kuliai	4,000 (200 rifles)	Hoseyb Qoli Khan Sardar-e Amjad (d)	Sedentary near Sanghor	Dinavar and Bilavar
12.Peyrawand	200	Hashem Khan, headman	In Mt. Parao	near Kermanshah
13.Bani Ardalan	2,000	Abbas Khan, Sardar Rashid	Ruvansir	Ruvansir
14.Jaf	500	Mohammad Rashid Beg Vali of Juvanrud	Juvanrud	Juvanrud
15.Babajani	500	Mohammad Saleh Beg	Near Juvanrud	East of Bamu
16.Waladbegi	200	Ya`qub Beg	Near Juvanrud	North of Zohab
17.Avroman Luhun	2,000	Ja`far Soltan Sardar-e Mo`atazed	S.E. of Avroman Dagh	
18.Avroman Takht	1,000	Majid Khan, Hoseyn Khan	East of Avroman Dagh	
19.Dizli	1,000	Mahmud Khan (prisoner of British)	Practically part of Avroman Takht	
20.Meriwan Khanisanan	600	Mahmud Khan (prisoner of British)	S.W. of Zeriwar Lake	Idem
21.Meriwan	800	Kay Khosrow Khan	S. and S.E. of Zeriwar lake	Idem
22.Mandumi	700	Lately badly defeated by force from Senneh and leading men all killed	Idem North of Senneh. West of Senneh road	Idem
23.Galbaghi	800		Between Senneh and Saqqez	Idem
24.Chardauli	900	Baqer Khan (d. ?)	S. of Hamadan-Senneh road	Idem
25.Garrusi ?	2,000	?	In neighborhood	of Bijar (Garrus district)

Of above (3) to (9) are generally known as Gurans. (13) to (16) are generally in close alliance under Sardar Rashid. (17) to (21) have very few sowars in comparison to others.

Source: FO 248/1293, Notes on Tribal Situation Kermanshah, May 1920, attached to Consul Kennion to Civil Commissioner/Baghdad, 04/06/1920.

Almost the entire population of the province was tribal or affiliated with a tribe, which made that local politics were tribal. The tribes wanted to be left alone, to their own way of life, which included trade, agriculture, husbandry and plundering each other, and, if they could get away with it, plundering trade caravans. According to the British consul Greenhouse, the tribes were not interested in either Persian or Kurdish nationalism or Pan-Islamism.[38] Also, they were often feuding with one another and contemporary reports are filled with accounts of tribal raids and

38. AIR 20/663, non-paginated (section Political Attitude, before p. 82).

fights. For example, in 1906, Shir Mohammad Khan Samsam al-Mamalek, chief of the Sanjabis, who was in charge of the road at Qasr-e Shirin, crossed the border with 200 men and stole more than 1,000 sheep, cows and horses and killed 2-3 Turks. The governor ordered Samsam al-Mamalek to return the property, but received no reply.[39] In October 1906, two nomad chiefs in Asadabad were fighting, endangering the 2,000 families living in that district, and therefore, the governor sent his son with troops to quell the disturbance.[40] In October 1920, Sardar Naser Sanjabi and his 280 men returned very satisfied; they had been able to punish their hereditary enemies, the Lodi tribes of Khaneqin and returned with 50 *tumans* each of loot plus some extras.[41]

Some tribal chiefs also held governorships of small towns, and sometimes even were appointed as governor of the province, creating a potential conflict of interests. Also, the provincial army, which was used for both internal and external provincial duties, consisted of local tribal units, which complicated the use of force against rebellious tribes. For example, pilgrims returning from Kerbela were robbed near Harunabad, i.e. in Kalhor country, and the governor ordered Da'ud Khan Kalhor to recover the stolen property.[42] In April 1908, the Koliya'is refused to pay any taxes and the governor sent Da'ud Khan with his Kalhors to bring them to heel.[43] Therefore, each tribal chief had an agent in the city to ensure that his interests were properly represented at the provincial administrative level. The importance of the tribes, in particular the big ones, increased during times of political unrest, when the central government was incapable of exercising its authority, as is clear from the situation after 1907.

Given the tribal nature of both urban and rural society, and the pivotal role that the city of Kermanshah played, both as the main population center in the province and as the seat of the representative of the central government, "it may be taken as an axiom that as tranquility in the town and district of Kermanshah depends on the state of affairs in Tehran so does the tranquility of the tribes of Kermanshah depend on the state of affairs in the town of Kermanshah and that of the Gurans or the Kalhor: it is therefore obvious that a quiet town and a united and friendly Kalhor will produce that peace and order which it is our object to obtain, more particularly along the military road- the line of communication for northern Persia."[44] To ensure that peace and quiet reigned in the province and that the tribes paid their taxes, all governors customarily dealt with the tribes in winter, when they were all at Zohab in the plains and not in their mountain lairs. In this way, with adequate military force and diplomatic skills, the central government representative, i.e. the governor was able to get his dues and ensure tribal allegiance.[45] "A strong and astute governor general is required in Kirmanshah to keep the tribes in order, as inter-tribal-intrigue is constantly in progress, and liable to result in hostilities at any time. Persian

39. Political Diaries vol. 1, p. 482.
40. Political Diaries vol. 1, p. 505.
41. FO 248/1293, Report Kermanshah, no. 9, up to 10 October 1920.
42. Political Diaries vol. 1, p. 482.
43. Political Diaries, vol. 3, p. 143; *Ruznameh-ye Iran* 1375, vol. 4, p. 3104 (no. 771; 22/04/1892).
44. FO 248/1293, Consul to Civil Commissioner/Baghdad, 04/016/1920.
45. FO 248/1112, McDouall to Legation, 02/02/1915; *Ruznameh-ye Iran* 1375, vol. 5, pp. 3984 (no. 990; 02/03/1901).

governors are adepts at fostering petty intrigues in a tribe, and thereby keeping malcontents up their sleeve to use as occasion may demand."[46]

KALHORS

The Kalhors were the most important tribe of the province and the strongest numerically. Since about 1700, the leading lineages were the Shahbazis or Hajjizadehs, the Mohammad 'Ali Khanis and the Kazem Khanis. Until 1902, the chiefs were always chosen from the first two of these three families. The Shahbazi lineage allegedly migrated from Isfahan in the remote past. Around 1840, Mohammad 'Ali Khan Shahbazi, chief of the Kalhors died. He had three sons, Mohammad Hoseyn, Mohammad Hasan and Zeyn al-'Abedin. The oldest son succeeded his father, but after a few years he resigned, and Mohammad Hasan became tribal chief. However, the youngest brother, Zeyn al-'Abedin bribed the authorities in Kermanshah and arranged for his brother to be imprisoned for two years in Kermanshah, after which he was exiled to Tehran. Zeyn al-'Abedin was chief for two and a half years and was a tyrannical chief, who even evicted his young son Reza Qoli Khan and forced him to fend for himself. Zeyn al-'Abedin was killed in the Esma'il Beg pass (near Harunabad) in revenge for the murder of Asad Beg, a leading member of the tribe. At that time, Emad al-Dowleh was governor of Kermanshah (1868-75) and he sent for Mohammad Hasan Khan from Tehran, whom he appointed chief or *hakem* of the Kalhors. After some years, probably around 1876, Mohammad Hasan Khan was deposed by his nephew Reza Qoli Khan, during a change of governors in Kermanshah. Reza Qoli Khan was able to remain *hakem* of the Kalhors until the spring of 1881, when he was replaced by his uncle Mohammad Hasan Khan, after having failed to deal effectively with the problems caused by the Ahmadavands. Reza Qoli Khan replaced his uncle again, but, when Hosam al-Molk was deputy-governor of Kermanshah (1884-88), he was sent to Isfahan. Zell al-Soltan sent him to Tehran where he was imprisoned and died. His brother, Mohammad 'Ali Khan, who was also imprisoned in Tehran, escaped and many tribesmen stated that they only would acknowledge him as tribal chief. At that time, Farrokh Khan, another Hajjizadeh family member, was *hakem* of the Kalhors, but he was expelled and Mohammad 'Ali Khan de facto assumed the function of *hakem* of the tribe and henceforth was known as Mohammad 'Ali Khan Ilkhani. Soon thereafter he was confirmed in his position by Tehran, but his position was challenged, when, in the beginning of 1900, the governor of Kermanshah took the position of *Ilkhani* away from him and re-appointed Farrokh Khan *Panjah-bashi* in his place. However, after many complaints about Farrokh Khan, Mohammad 'Ali Khan was able to regain his position by mid-1900.[47]

---

46. AIR 20/663, p. 82.

47. DCR 590, pp. 46-47. Mohammad 'Ali Khan was appointed *Ilkhani* of the Kalhors in April 1893. However, before and after his appointment there continued to be challenges to his position. *Ruznameh-ye Iran* 1375, vol. 4, pp. 3166 (no. 787; 27/11/1892), 3214 (no. 799; 11/05/1893), 3335 (no. 829; 13/06/1894); vol. 5, pp. 3950 (no. 982; 15/10/1900), 4019 (no. 999; 22/08/1901). For a story about the origin of the Hajjizadeh name of the lineage, see DCR 590, p. 48; see also Rabino 1905, pp. 25-32.

Thus, until the end of the nineteenth century, the Hajjizadeh lineage held the chieftainship (*Ilkhani*). However, in August 1902, Mohammad 'Ali Khan Amir Tuman was unseated by Da'ud Khan, Saham al-Mamalek, the head of the Khaledi section, who, already for some time, had been playing an influential role in Kalhor affairs and was often mentioned in the same breath as the *Ilkhani*. The Khaledi, one of the leading sub-divisions of the tribe, allegedly originated in the Nejd in Central Arabia.[48] In his turn, Da'ud Khan's eldest son, Javan Mir Khan Zargham Lashkar, challenged his father's position, became his rival and fought against his father. In May 1905, Da'ud Khan and his son came to Kermanshah to settle their dispute, which ended in an uneasy truce.[49] In early May 1908, the behavior of Da'ud Khan and his son Zargham al-Dowleh had so much upset many section chiefs that at the end of September 1908 they invited *Sartip* Mohammad 'Ali, the previous chief to join them and accept the leadership of the tribe. Mohammad 'Ali, who was pretender to the leadership and therefore, was still called *Ilkhani*, left Kermanshah with 60 men. Da'ud Khan, however, collected his *savar*s and 'convinced' the tribe to accept him. Da'ud Khan sent 700 men after Mohammad 'Ali Khan to prevent him from making his claim. As a result, he had to flee to Kermanshah via Posht-e Kuh with the help of the Vali. By that time Zargham al-Dowleh, the youthful son of Da'ud Khan had returned from Tehran, where, on his departure, he was given title of Salar Eqbal and 300 *savar*s funded by the Kermanshah's revenues. Finding Mohammad 'Ali Khan at Kermanshah he decided to kidnap him. Unfortunately for him it was 19 Ramazan (15 October 1908), a day of mourning of the Shiites,[50] and Mohammad 'Ali Khan's wife and relatives went to the mosque asking for justice. The mullahs and townspeople agreed and asked A'zam al-Dowleh, the deputy-governor, - his father was out of town- to take action; he was only too glad to do so as neither he nor his father had the means to make Da'ud Khan pay his taxes. The governor told Salar Eqbal to release Mohammad 'Ali Khan, to which he replied impertinently. The deputy-governor then sent him a message that he was serious and again a rude reply was given. A'zam al-Dowleh then ordered Salar Eqbal to be arrested. He was in the house of Amin al-Mamalek, the Kalhor agent and started firing at the men who had come to arrest him. However, people wanted justice and, therefore, the house was besieged on 18 October. During that day Khan Baba Khan Shiani died, possibly killed by the Salar Eqbal, because he was getting too powerful endangering his fathe's position. Because the Kalhors had no provisions they agreed the next day to surrender if the *mojtahed*s swore on the Koran that no injury would be done to them. Salar Eqbal further agreed to pay all arrears and to release Mohammad 'Ali Khan. This was agreed to. The next day there was a fight between the Kalhors and the Sanjabis, but the Kalhors were beaten off with some loss on their side. Da'ud Khan was furious with his son and marched to Mahidasht, but paid the taxes due and left his younger son as hostage in place of Salar Eqbal. Da'ud Khan was also furious because the governor, Zahir al-Molk Zanganeh, refused to allow him to send a telegram to the Shah, and tried in vein to have Molitor send a telegram on his behalf. The younger son was released when Zahir al-Molk returned to Kermanshah, thinking it would be better to have good relations with the tribes. "A governor taken from a local tribe naturally thinks of himself

---

48. *Ruznameh-ye Iran* 1375, vol. 5, pp. 3868 (no. 961; 29/07/1899), 3984 (no. 990; 02/03/1901); DCR 590, p. 47.
49. Political Diaries vol. 1, pp. 103, 427.
50. On the eve of 19 Ramazan 40 h.q. (15 October 661) Imam `Ali was attacked with a poisoned sword in the mosque of Kufa, hence known as *shab-e zarbat* or the night of the slaying.

and not of the people of the town," who had wasted time and effort and some lives to put 25,000 *tumans* in the governor's pocket.[51] In March 1909, Salar Eqbal, Da'ud Khan's eldest son, died after a fall from his horse while hunting. "This is locally regarded as the direct intervention of providence and is certainly a good thing for the district, for he gave promise of being worse than his father and indeed was gradually weaning a number of the Kalhur tribe from Daood khan, who, it was generally expected, he would kill in time, as Daood Khan himself had killed his own father by degrees in prison."[52]

After Da'ud Khan's death in 1912, the chieftainship was shared between Soleyman Khan Amir A'zam, son of Da'ud Khan and by 'Abbas Khan Amir Mo'azzam, grandson of Da'ud Khan, who both were teenagers at that time. Although it is also reported that in 1918 Soleyman Khan was 28, and so, if correct, in 1912 he must have been 22 years old. Because of 'Abbas Khan's support for the Ottomans and the Germans in WW I, Amir Koll, at that time governor of Kermanshah, appointed Soleyman Khan chief of the Kalhors in April 1917. However, Soleyman Khan had much difficulty in retaining his position owing to the hostility and intrigues by his nephew and rival 'Abbas Khan. According to the British, Soleyman Khan, although pro-British, "unfortunately lacks both brains and personality and is inclined to be lazy and self-indulgent," whereas "Abbas Khan, who, although pro-German during the war, is by far the better man."

The British began dealing with the Kalhors in February 1917, when Soleyman Khan joined a force of local levies under the British consul Kennion, who were cooperating with Russian forces from Soltanabad toward Qasr-e Shirin.[53] The Kalhor *savars* pushed back the Turks and engaged them in Mandali, but soon thereafter, Soleyman Khan heard that 'Abbas Khan had raided his district from Posht-e Kuh and withdrew to look after his own affairs. The reason was that in June 1917 Amir Koll had made Eyvan over to Soleyman Khan. In return for his services during the Salar al-Dowleh rebellion, the valley of Eyvan, near Mandali, and the water of Saunar, both an integral part of Kermanshah province, were leased to the Vali. This was a major obstacle, because formerly, these were leased to Da'ud Khan, the father of Soleyman Khan. The Kalhors lost the lease because of Da'ud Khan's support for Salar al-Dowleh's rebellion in 1912, and his son wanted to have it back.

Therefore, the Vali of Posht-e Kuh countered this change of the lease by sending 'Abbas Khan to attack Soleyman Khan. Although the latter retired and gave up the project for the time being, he never renounced his claim to Eyvan. At a big meeting of tribes, at Bindar in July 1917, which was attended by the British and Russian consuls, a reconciliation was effected between the two rival chiefs, but it proved to be superficial. The ostensible cause of the rivalry and quarrel between the two chiefs was landed property, most of which really belonged to the Vakil al-Dowleh or Palizi family of Kermanshah and to which neither chief had any real claim, but the enmity

51. Administration Report 1908, pp. 43-44; Political Diaries, vol. 3, pp. 176, 331, 343; Soltani 1386, pp. 154-57; FO 248/938, Diary no.19 [sic, must be 18] ending October 20th, 1908; Idem, FO 248/938, Diary no.19 ending November 3rd 1908.

52. Political Diaries, vol. 3, p. 527 (during the funeral, the son of a leading Kalhor chief, whom Salar Eqbal had killed, laughed out loud; in reaction the deceased's brother drew his revolver, but bloodshed was prevented).

53. For earlier contacts, see Political Diaries, vol. 3, pp. 353-54.

was really the result of intrigues of the Vali of Posht-e Kuh, whose policy it was to maintain a disunited Kalhor tribe.

In 1918 the tribe took part in the operations conducted by the British against the Sanjabis and after the defeat of the latter they became the paramount tribe in the province. The change of governor in 1919 led to tribal unrest. Until August 1919 the Kalhors still had two chiefs, Soleyman Khan Amir A'zam and 'Abbas Khan Amir Mo'azzam. As they were rivals the section chiefs changed their allegiance to one or the other, according to whim. The tribe was disorganized and no responsibility for robberies could be assigned to either chief. In August 1919, Soleyman Khan got practically the entire tribe to his side. 'Abbas Khan came to Kermanshah where he received 450 *tumans*/month and a grain allowance to stay away from the tribal area. The Persian government recognized Soleyman Khan as sole chief and he received robe of honor.[54]

However, the presence of 'Abbas Khan in the city was a source of disquiet for Amir Nezam, the governor, as he was intriguing to get his position as tribal chief back. This was facilitated by two facts: (i) the Kalhor section chiefs didn't like having one chief; formerly they played them off against each other; and (ii) Soleyman Khan's rule had become less popular as he became more tyrannical. Salar Heshmat, maternal uncle of 'Abbas Khan, wanted to stoke the fire and joined his nephew in Kermanshah. The British consul Greenhouse told him that if he did not return Amir Nezam was entitled to seize all his possessions and so he left.[55] With the change of governor and of the British consul 'Abbas Khan saw an excellent opportunity to return to Kalhor country and make his claim. He fled from Kermanshah and tried to oust Soleyman Khan Amir A'zam. 'Abbas Khan had the support of at least two factions, but Soleyman Khan had the majority of tribe with him. The British consul sent a telegram to Qasr-e Shirin asking that the Gurans join the latter. The Persian government sent 200 gendarmes, accompanied by a few British consular mounted guards, to Soleyman Khan as a sign that he was recognized as the sole chief of the Kalhors by the Persian government. Before their arrival the forces of Soleyman Khan and 'Abbas Khan clashed; the latter, who had not more than 300 men, was defeated. Most Guran chiefs sided with Soleyman Khan and joined him at Gilan. The Tofangchi section was absent. Akbar Khan, chief of the Neyrizhis, was killed by 'Abbas Khan's men. However, otherwise there were few casualties on either side. 'Abbas Khan allegedly fled to Eyvan and then to Asmanabad in the Vali of Posht-e Kuh's territory, who, allegedly, was not happy with him. The government asked him to be handed over, but such a gesture was contrary to tribal custom.[56] 'Abbas Khan was under the influence of his maternal uncle Salar Heshmat, who induced him not to return to Kermanshah. Despite his victory, Soleyman Khan had to change his ways, according to the British consul, if he wanted to keep his rule, because he spent his days and nights sleeping and gambling. Among the Kalhors, 'Abdollah Khan *farrash-bashi* Zarghameh al-Saltaneh was influential. He was of the Kauchai subsection of the Khaledi section. He spoke French and helped the British in building the road to Qasr-e Shirin. Soleyman Khan's confidents were Sayyed Ya'qub of Siyahchigeh village in Mahidasht and Salar-e Arfa' of the Kazemkhan section.

54. FO 248/1293, Tel. 32, Consul to Legation, 13/04/1920.

55. FO 248/1293, Report Kermanshah, 31/03/1920.

56. FO 248/1293, Tels. 32 and 34 , Consul to Legation, 13/04/1920 and 22/04/1920.

The relations of the Kalhors with other tribes was generally good except with the Vali of Posht-e Kuh, their neighbor, and attempts made for the two leaders to make up were unsuccessful. The chiefs of the Kalhors was always at enmity with the Vali of Posht-e Kuh, whom they disliked and feared. The chief of the tribe also had a permanent feud with the Sanjabis since 1900 or thereabouts, when Da'ud Khan Kalhor killed three Sanjabi chiefs and 30 *savar*s at Harunabad and the Sanjabis were prepared to help 'Abbas Khan, Soleyman Khan's rival, who had intermarried with the Sanjabis.[57]

Table 4.4: Approximate estimate of the Kalhor tribe, showing sections (1920)

Name	No. of houses	Names of headmen	Summer quarters	Winter quarters	Remarks
Khaledi subsections			Guawar	Gilan	
Shirakah	150	Azim Khan	Do	Do	
Alirezawand	150	Ahmad Agha, Javan Mir	Do	Do	With Amir-e Mo`azzam
Piragah	200	Safar Khan	Do	Do	With Amir-e Mo`azzam
Kauchai	200	Abdollah Khan, Kahkhoda Hajji	Do	Do	
Reutawand	150	Arfat/Olfat Khan	Do	Do	
Khulaga	100	Naser Khan	Do	Do	
Abdul Mamdi	50	--	Do	Do	Chief is of this family
End of Khaledi subsections					
Siahsiah	700	Seyf-e Lashkar	Rawani	Posht-e Gilan	
Shian	500	Samsam Lashkar	Shian	1/2 Shian; 1/2 Posht-e Gilan	
Kazem Khan and Darabegi	700	Salar Arfa	Gulin; Barfabad	Direh	Originally from Eyvan
Kulapa	200	Hoseyn Qoli Khan	Momini near Harisam	Near Mandali	
Kuchmi	300	Abbas Khan	Do	Do	
Shuan	100	Nosrat Lashkar	Shuan	Shuan	Sedentary
Shahini	50	Fateh Beg	Shuan	Shuan	Sedentary
Kamara	50	Eqbal Soltan	Kamara	Kamara	Sedentary
Harunabad	70	Mahmud Khan Kalantar	Harunabad	Harunabad	Sedentary
Kulajub	100	Qoli Khan, `Ali Mardan Khan	Kulajub	Kulajub	Sedentary
Mineshi	250	Farajollah Khan	Kifraur	Kifraur	Aliolahi

57. FO 248/1293, Consul Kennion to Civil Commissioner/Baghdad, 04/06/1920.

Name	No. of houses	Names of headmen	Summer quarters	Winter quarters	Remarks
Khaman	250	Mahmud Khan	Zabiri	Gilan	Originally from Shahrgol near Halabjeh
Kargah	200	Farrokh Khan, Habib Jowhar Khan, Nassur	Mahidasht	Near Mandali	Noted thieves
Aliwandi	50	Dawairij Khan	Mahidasht	Direh	
Beydak Begi	60	Esma`il Khan	Mahidasht	Rikhak	
Bazkalai	60	Ahmad Beg	Guawar	Gilan	
Mansuri	300	Mehdi Qoli Khan	Tang-e Mansuri	Tang-e Mansuri	
Gurgeh	50	Mahi Khan	Mahidasht	Gilan	
Zeykalkani	70	Namdar Khan	Gulin	Direh	
Lareni	50	Adjudan	West of Harunabad	Gilan	
Shahrek	30	-	Do	Do	
Goleni	50	-	Do	Do	

Major Greenhouse one year later listed slightly different Khaledi subsections: Shiraka, Piraka, Reutawand, Ghulam Ali, Said Muhammad, Chiraghali, Barga, Kuchay, Salih, Said Murad, Waraka, Mumay, Saiyed Razzee, Kurkee, Jaonza, Burik, Rejab, Said Khan Kasan, Ali Dost Bapir, Salika, Farhad Beg, Khir Wais, Jadir, Rashid, Abdul Mohammadi, Baz Kala. AIR 20/663, pp. 92-95.

Source: FO 248/1293, Notes on Tribal Situation Kermanshah, May 1920, attached to Consul Kennion to Civil Commissioner/Baghdad, 04/06/1920.

As to the Kalhors, in 1920, governor Sarem al-Dowleh stated that he had orders from the Ministry of Interior not to take any action concerning ‘Abbas Khan whatever happened. As a former ally of the *Mohajerin*, ‘Abbas Khan had a strong claim on the Democrats and had to be conciliated. All deportees from Kermanshah, except for Sardar Rashid, were of course befriended by Democrats. He had received instructions to befriend ‘Abbas Khan in every way possible.[58] ‘Abbas Khan remained in Eyvan with the Vali and did not want to return.[59] In August 1920, Amir A‘zam came to town and usurped ‘Abbas Khan's position and prevented his return. Certain Kalhor chiefs then stated that they wanted neither as their chief, but they changed their minds again, when they were told that this was accepted, after which they split up into factions. Summoned to town both chiefs settled their differences, but they quarreled again one week later. Greenhouse then observed that the headmen again fully supported Amir A‘zam. As a result, Soleyman Khan was 9,000 *tumans* lighter, but he became supreme chief of the Kalhors, while ‘Abbas Khan lost the chieftainship by quibbling over an extra 3,000 *tumans*.

The first 10 days of Moharram (end of September 1920) coincided with the arrival of 1,000 men of Vali Posht-e Kuh with ‘Abbas Khan into Kermanshah provincial territory against Amir A‘zam. They refused to withdraw professing friendship towards Great Britain. The Kalhors

58. FO 248/1293, Conversation Consul Greenhouse with Sarem al-Dowleh, 24/08/1920.
59. FO 248/1293, Report Kermanshah, no. 5, 31 May 1920; FO 248/1293, Tel. Consul to Legation, 30/07/1920.

scattered into the Mahidasht and Kerend valleys. The deputy governor and Greenhouse went to Kerend, because neither the Vali's agent nor 'Abbas Khan had any faith in the Persian government's promises. The two met with Mir Sa'id Mohammad Khan Ashraf al-Ashayer of Saidmarreh, the Vali's agent there. An agreement was reached. The Vali's troops would be withdrawn and 'Abbas Khan would come to Kermanshah with the promise of receiving the same treatment as Amir A'zam; fighting was to cease. The promise was immediately broken by the Vali's agent and Amir Mo'azzam did not agree to his part either. In reaction, the Kalhor sections started hostilities, including an action against the Char Zabar Pass. 'Abbas Khan was then invited by the deputy governor, Col. Gaskell (Perscom) and consul Greenhouse at Harunabad under safe conduct. After much toing and froing he came provided that the deputy governor promised he would be well treated by Sarem al-Dowleh; that no difference would made in treating Soleyman Khan and himself; and that no third party would be appointed chief of the Kalhors, if they reconciled. Greenhouse made no promises. 'Abbas Khan returned with the negotiators; en route Greenhouse persuaded him to join them unconditionally. The two chiefs failed to agree and were sent in the same car to Tehran to get some fresh air. This had a good effect on the Kalhor chiefs and the Gurans who had become restless. The Vali withdrew his men. Thereafter the tribal situation was good and was expected to remain so as long as the chiefs remained in Tehran. The candidates for the chieftainship of the Kalhors were influential and wealthy. The bidding reached 12,000 *tumans* in four days, but the Prime Minister spoiled the game by appointing *Ra'is-e Qoshun* E'temad Homayun as chief. According to consul Greenhouse, he "is better than most and if supported will suffice." The bone of contention remained the land of which 7/8 belonged to Raf'at al-Saltaneh and Vakil al-Dowleh's heirs, who finally obtained possession of their property after years of hopeless trying.[60] Indeed, it looked as if E'temad Homayun had the Kalhors under control. He had a nice income of which the governor received 60%. The value of the Kalhor chieftainship was put up above 50,000 *tumans*.[61]

GURAN CONFEDERACY

The Guran confederacy was next in importance. The Gurans after the Kalhors were the most numerous tribe. The tribes which formed the Guran confederacy originated from different areas and continued to have conflicting ideas and interests. Little is known of the early history of the Gurans, or whether it was even a confederacy more than in name. According to Rawlinson, who raised a regiment of Gurans, this tribe came into being as follows:

> Shortly after the time of Sultan Murad [r. 1623-1640], the Kalhur tribe, which had been driven out of Dartung and Darnah, assumed to themselves the peculiar

60. FO 248/1293, Report Kermanshah, no. 9, up to 10 October 1920. The probably cause of the land conflict is that the leading Mohammad `Ali Khani clan had sold all its property to Hajji Aqa Hasan, the late British agent, and therefore, the new tribal chief felt that he had title to that former Kalhor land. The other leading clan, the Hajjizadeh had converted all their property into *vaqf* to the benefit of their descendants. DCR 590, p. 46.

61. FO 248/1293 , Report Kermanshah, no. 11, up to 10 December 1920

> designation of Gurans, which had been previously applied to the Kurdish peasantry as distinguished from the clans; and these Gurans, at the same time, broke into three distinct tribes of Kalleh Zanjiri, Kerindi and Biwaniji, the names being derived from their several place of residence. They are said, with the connivance of the Government of Kermanshah, to have driven the Bajlans out of Darnah in about the year 1700, and to have obliged the latter to confine themselves to the plains, in which, shortly afterwards, the Bajlan Pasha founded the town of Zohab.[62]

Dr. Mann concluded from his studies among them that "this district was in olden times inhabited by a sedentary population who spoke the so-called tajik dialect of the interior of Persia. The population has been overpowered by the Kalhurs and Zengennehs and thus formed a new tribe, under the name of Gurans. The sedentary families of the Gurans have preserved their old language, whilst the nomad families speak the Kalhur and Zengeneh Kurdi."[63] Whatever the truth about the tribe's origins, it is evident that in recent times, it was merely an administrative division of Kermanshah province, as the various tribes were completely divided against themselves and the paramount chief was not able to exercise his authority over them.[64]

The Gurans were half nomadic (*garmsiri*) and half sedentary (*deh-neshin* or *yeylaqi*); the tribe had few horses. They were mostly Shiites and some were Ali-ilahis. Their military ability was great and they were assiduous raiders. However, the confederacy was not united, and in particular the two Qalkhani sections were mutually hostile. Certain sections had good relations with the Sanjabis. In 1917, the 60-year old Hoseyn Khan, Mansur al-Molk was chief of the Gurans. He was a drunkard and opium addict and too weak to rule his tribe, so that its eight sections were always in revolt. As a result, Mansur Khan was little respected. He was friendly to Europeans and pleasant, but not in a prosperous conditions. From time immemorial his family had been in charge of the Gurans. His daughter married Da'ud Khan Kalhor, which alliance helped him to remain in power.[65]

Table 4.5: Approximate estimate of Guran confederacy, showing sections (1920)

Name	No of houses	Names of chiefs	Summer quarters	Winter quarters	Observations
Guran confederacy	4-5,000	i. Sardar Eqbal of the Gahvareh; ii.Salar Mansur			Sardar Eqbal is now leading chief but ii. is ex-chief and his rival
1.Qalkhani	1,000	Qader Soltan, Rashid al-Saltaneh	Kuh-e Delahu	Binah and Pirah	700 rifles; 1,200 *tumans*/y taxes

62. DCR 590, p. 52.
63. DCR 590, p. 52; see also Rabino 1905, pp. 23-25.
64. See e.g., FO 248/938, f. 29 (undated February 1908 Diary from Capt. Haworth); Idem, Kermanshah Diary ending 4th March 1908.
65. IOR/L/MIL/17/15/11/3, Who's Who in Persia, vol. II, p. 198; see also DCR 590, p. 51.

Name	No of houses	Names of chiefs	Summer quarters	Winter quarters	Observations
2. Qalkhani	1,200	Abdollah Beg; Sardar Mansur & Qanbar Soltan	Do	Do	600 rifles; Abdollah Beg is 70 and seldom leaves his house. His brother Qanbar Soltan is the disturbing factor in the tribe, good fighting man; taxes: 1,200 *tumans*/year
3. Gahvareh	900	i. Sardar Eqbal; ii. Gholam Ali Khan, Salar Mansur	Gahvareh	Gahvareh	400 rifles. Taxes 1,200 *tumans*/yr. The chiefs are rivals; each command approx. 200 rifles
4. Bibiani	200	i.Feyzollah Beg; ii. Ali Beg Soltan ot Taishay is chief of a small section	Kuh-e Delahu	Zohab	100 rifles. Taxes: 1,000 *tumans*/yr
5. Jaf of Guran Taishay	5 and 6:	Ali Beg Soltan	Kuh-e Delahu	Quraytu	5 and 6 have 300 rifles and pay
6. Jaf: Qader Mir Waisa	1,000	Kadkhoda Mostafa I and II	Do	Do	750 *tumans*/yr in taxes
7. Tofangchi	1,000	Jahanbakhsh Zargham al-Saltaneh and his brother Sohrab	Takht-e Gah	Zohab	200 rifles
8.Bowanij	400	Hoseyn Khan is very old; his only son Ali Jan is 30	Bowanij a.k.a. Kanahar	Bishewa	100 rifles; very peaceful; they are really under Kerend, but enter in Guran politics.
Neyrizi	500	Mohammad Beg, a youth	Gahvareh	Zohab	200 rifles; 550 *tumans*/yr taxes. Reza Khan, the eldest of the chiefs family and Shahbaz Khan killed the late chief.
Neyrizi subsections					
Kwaik	150	Abdollah Beg, Moh. Hatem, Moh. Mir Ali, Seyfak Latif	Siahana	Zarinjab, Zohab	
Chighabur	50	Mahi Khan	Chighabur	Zarinjab	
Neliki	100	Ali Morad Khan	Gahvareh	Zarinjab	
Aliakhai	150	Soleyman Beg	Halel	Zarinjab	
Neyrizi	200	Aziz	Near Gahvareh; Chigha Chubin	and Biamush Kolkul	

Source: AIR 20/663, pp. 108-09; FO 248/1293, Notes on Tribal Situation Kermanshah, May 1920, attached to Consul Weir to Civil Commissioner/Baghdad, 04/06/1920. For a slightly different division of the tribe in only six branches, see DCR 590, p. 51.

The Qalkhani sections were notorious as raiders. In the early days of WW I, they intrigued with the Turks against the Russians, and, led by Qanbar Soltan Sardar Mansur and Rashid al-Saltaneh caused much annoyance to the latter. Mansur al-Molk was captured by the Russians in 1917 and taken to Hamadan; he fell ill and died in Kermanshah. A peaceful agreement was subsequently arranged in July 1917, when a Russian representative visited the Gurans and assured them of the goodwill of the Russian people. The Gurans were well represented at the big tribal meeting at Bindar in July 1917.[66]

Thereafter, Salar Mansur (Gholam 'Ali Khan of the Gahvareh), governor of Sonqor, was the paramount chief of the Gurans. He was married to a daughter of 'Abdol-Baqer Mirza of Kermanshah. He was not a strong leader and personal enmities biased his actions. The rivalry between the two Qalkhani sections determined Guran politics. The one was under Qader Soltan; Rashid al-Saltaneh was allied with the Sanjabis, which kept Qanbar Soltan from raiding the former. The other section was under Qanbar Soltan and Asadollah Beg, and made Jahanbakhsh Tofangchi- who was a waverer to either party- side with Qanbar Soltan. The Baziyanis formed the escort of the tribal chief and therefore, were also named *Tofangchiha*.

In 1917, Bahram Soltan, Rashid al-Saltaneh Qalkhani was the leading Guran personality, although Gholam 'Ali Shah Salar Mansur was nominally chief. Rashid al-Saltaneh professed friendship to the British, but in spite of this he gave sanctuary to the outlawed Sanjabi chiefs ('Ali Akbar Khan and Sardar Zafar) in June 1918. This was probably due to a desire for Sanjabi support against Jahanbakhsh Khan Zargham al-Saltaneh of the Tofangchi section of the tribe, who was rapidly becoming his rival as a leading spirit among the Gurans. The British consul with a British force moved to Bovanij (Kanahar) and frightened Rashid al-Saltaneh and imposed terms on him. (for details, see Chapter Seven). This undertaking was signed by Rashid al-Saltaneh, Sardar Mansur and other chiefs. Subsequently, he was also made responsible for security on the road to Qasr-e Shirin. This aroused the jealousy of the Qalkhani and Kalhor chiefs, and in September 1918, Sardar Mansur assisted by the Javanrud Jaf chiefs attacked him. After a fight which lasted three days Rashid al-Saltaneh was said to have died. He was succeeded by his eldest surviving brother Qader Soltan, who took his brother's title.

At the end of January 1918, Kennion visited Rashid al-Saltaneh Qalkahni, now chief of the Gurans at Piran, who was then on bad terms with the Sanjabis. He was ready to render any service to Great Britain, but his tribe was then very disunited. Sardar Khan Neyrizhi, ostensibly friendly to Rashid al-Saltaneh was friends with the Sanjabis. Asadollah Beg and Qanbar Soltan supported Rashid al-Saltaneh. Gholam 'Ali Khan, the nominal head of the Gurans had little power.[67] In January 1919, a British force surrounded the camps of the Neyrizhi section who had delayed in handing over stolen property. The chief, Shahbaz Khan, was deposed and Akbar Khan appointed in his place, but in the summer of 1920, Akbar Khan was murdered by Reza Khan and Shahbaz Khan. Mohammad Beg, the murdered man's brother, was made chief of the Neyrizhis and Qanbar Soltan was fined 5,000 *tumans* for sheltering Shahbaz Khan, although he

66. IOR/L/MIL/17/15/11/3, Who's Who in Persia, vol. II, p. 198.
67. FO 248/1204, Kermanshah report, 17/02/1918 by Lt. Col. Kennion.

denied it, the other by Soleyman Khan Kalhor. The governor promised capital punishment for them when caught..

After WW I, unlike the pre-war situation, the Gurans refrained mostly from raiding. Regular subsidies were paid to Qanbar Soltan, Salar Mansur and Rashid al-Saltaneh to keep the trade route safe and as an earnest of British goodwill and as an inducement to work with them. The road guards were paid by the British until the end February 1920. After that Tehran had to control the road with the gendarmes or to pay the *qarasuran*. Neither happened. Lack of money in the revenue office of Kermanshah was the reason. Capt. Reedy wanted to double the gendarmerie from 600 to 1,200 men to have a strike force and to have enough men to police the road. This had been proposed to Tehran. According to consul Greenhouse, if this did not happen, "we may pay road guards monthly drawn from Customs receipts." As a result of the intrigues of the governor of Kermanshah and Rashid al-Saltaneh, Salar Mansur was forced to give up his position as chief of the Gurans in the summer of 1920. He was succeeded by Sardar Eqbal, his half-brother, who was said to be the puppet of Rasid al-Saltaneh. Sardar Eqbal was a success as governor, according to the British, because he was on much better terms with Rashid al-Saltaneh and Qanbar Soltan. Meanwhile, Amir Koll supported intrigues to reinstate Salar Mansur, but Salar Eqbal and Salar A'zam were relatives and hostile to Salar Mansur. It was expected that a change of governor at Kerend would be the first step to return Salar Mansur and upset the tranquility of the Gurans.[68]

Greenhouse visited Sardar Eqbal in Gawareh and found it to be quiet. He also noted that Sardar Eqbal had little military authority. After his departure the Qalkhanis started to quarrel. Rashid al-Saltaneh's brother was trapped and held prisoner until the British Kerend agent and the governor of Kerend settled the quarrel. Jahanbakhsh, Zargham al-Saltaneh as usual was blamed by both sides and his removal was requested. There were, of course, intrigues to restore Salar Mansur, who was still in Kermanshah and full of grievances, complaining that he was bankrupt and hoped to become chief again. These intrigues were supported by Amir Koll of the Zanganeh, but these were not immediately successful. Meanwhile, Reza Khan Neyrizhi of the Gurans has been released. Rashid al-Saltaneh was in contact with Amir Naser Sanjabi and Amir Mo'azzam Kalhor which upsets the other tribes.[69] In 1921, after the fall of Sarem al-Dowleh, the governor of Kermanshah, Salar Mansur was able to regain the chieftainship of the confederation. During the Arab insurrection of 1920, 100 Qalkhani *savar*s were sent to cooperate with the British, but they proved unsatisfactory and were dismissed immediately. Jahanbakhsh Tofangchi Zargham al-Saltaneh continued to be responsible for a lot of unrest in the tribe.[70]

---

68. FO 248/1293, Report Kermanshah, no. 11, up to 10 December 1920
69. FO 248/1293, Report Kermanshah, no. 7, up to 12 August 1920.
70. FO 248/1293, Report Kermanshah, no. 11, up to 10 December 1920

Fig. 4.6: Samsam al-Mamalek Sanjabi and his retinue (1912). © *Collection Molitor, Ed. Elytis* no. 0265

SANJABIS

The Sanjabis originally were part of the Guran tribe, but they split off in the nineteenth century and formed a separate tribe. The tribe had five branches: Chelevi or Chelebi, Golgol, Daliyan, Darkhur, and Sufi. The real Sanjabis numbered only some 500 in 1900, but other nomadic groups had joined them and together with the sedentary population of their villages they numbered some 4,000 families. The traditional hereditary chiefs of the tribe were drawn from the Chelevi or Chelebi family. However, in 1898, Shir Khan, Samsam al-Mamalek, was appointed chief of the tribe by governor Mirza Mohammad Khan Eqbal al-Dowleh Kashani. By inheritance the real chief would have been Asadollah Khan, Salar Mokarram Chelevi. The Sanjabis led a pastoral life and were considered the best military fighting tribe in the province. They were internally divided into two groups, but a strong chief usually held the tribe well in hand. Their summer habitat was near Mahidasht and their winter quarters were near Khaneqin and Aq Dagh.[71]

In 1900, a brother and two uncles of Samsam al-Mamalek as well as 30 Sanjabi *savar*s were killed by Da'ud Khan Kalhor at Harunabad. Since then there always was strife between the Sanjabi and Kalhor chiefs. Although the Kalhors and Sanjabis had become friendly early in 1908, in November 1908 they had fallen out again. The reason was that when the tribal contingents that had gone to Tehran had lined up for the Shah's inspection the Sanjabis had taken the place of honor. Therefore, Da'ud Khan Kalhor supported the claim of Habibollah Khan, the heir

71. AIR 20/663, p. 102 (table); DCR 590, p. 58; *Ruznameh-ye Iran* 1375, vol. 5, pp. 4004 (no. 995; 02/06/1901); Soltani 1381, vol. 3, p. 480; Rabino 1905, pp. 37-38.

of the Chelevi lineage to the chieftainship of the Sanjabis. Although Samsam al-Mamalek had been an efficient chief, some sections of the Sanjabis were unhappy with Samsam al-Mamalek and especially with his second son Shoja' Lashkar. In mid-November 1908, the Kalhors and Gurans gathered at Sar-e Pol to attack Samsam al-Mamalek at Qasr-e Shirin, and therefore, people were leaving the town. The objective of the attack was to reinstate Habibollah Khan and seeing the superior force facing them the Sanjabis went over to the attacking side. Da'ud Khan and Habibollah Khan told Samsam al-Mamalek that unless he vacated Qasr-e Shirin they would attack. Samsam al-Mamalek had no choice but to flee with his family, taking asylum, of all people, with Da'ud Khan Kalhor, thus depriving himself from any outside support. Habibollah Khan took over the leadership of the tribe and the governorship of Qasr-e Shirin. Samsam al-Mamalek's son, who had been with a Sanjabi force in Tabriz in royal service, with the support of the town's people was able to convince the authorities in Tehran that his father had to be reinstated. Orders were given to that effect and Zahir al-Molk was ordered to take action against Da'ud Khan. However, this was like ordering a grasshopper to attack an elephant, unless other tribes would be called in, for the only force that Da'ud Khan feared was that of the Vali of Posht-e Kuh. In mid-December 1908, Da'ud Khan released Samsam al-Mamalek who went to Mahidasht. Going through the motions, Zahir al-Molk even gathered an army (part of his own regiment, some Koliya'is, and city *savars*) to move against Da'ud Khan and held a review and artillery practice on 25 December 1908, but then his 'army' was disbanded. Habibollah Khan paid Zahir al-Molk a bribe, who confirmed him in his new position and Da'ud Khan arranged matters in the same way. Apart from the villages plundered around the city nobody suffered. The Kalhors remained rebellious for some time, even infesting the trade route for sometime, although in January 1909 Da'ud Khan asked governor Zahir al-Molk to meet with him at Mahidasht to settle their problems. In doing so he wanted to show that he was more important than the governor by coming to him, but Zahir al-Molk told him that he would send his grandson. At the end of January 1909, Samsam al-Mamalek came to Kermanshah and took asylum in the telegraph office.[72] In May 1909, Da'ud Khan said that the prime mover against Samsam al-Mamalek had been his late son Salar Eqbal (d. March 1909) and that he was ready to reinstall him as chief of the Sanjabis. The two made up and became friendly. This not only meant that Habibollah Khan had to give up the governorship of Qasr-e Shirin, but also rather than the central government that it was the Kalhor chief who dismissed and appointed governors and, in addition, who would be the chief of the Sanjabis![73]

After Shir Khan Samsam al-Mamalek's death (in 1916?), his three sons formed the ruling family. The oldest son, Qasem Khan, Sardar Naser was the tribal chief; his two brothers were 'Ali Akbar Khan, Sardar Moqtader and Hoseyn Khan, Sardar Zafar. The Shirkhan family married into the Kermanshahi princely family of 'Abdol-Baqer Mirza. There was a long and bitter feud between the Shirkhani and Chelevi families, because of the latter's displacement as chiefs and the refusal of 'Ali Akbar Khan to divorce or properly maintain his Sanjabi wife, the daughter

---

72. Administration Report 1908, p. 45-46; Political Diaries, vol. 3, pp. 365, 379, 389-90, 411, 429, 437 (*yaghi*), 445. Samsam al-Mamalek was in debt to he IBP, but tried to bilk the Bank claiming that his debt was to Esma`il Baqer. FO 248/907, Haworth to Tehran,12/09/1907.

73. Political Diaries, vol. 3, p. 606.

of Asadollah Khan Chelevi. The Shirkhanis were Shiites, while practically all the Sanjabis were Ali-ilahis, and for this reason they were not altogether popular with the tribe.

In 1914, ‘Ali Akbar Khan was the dominant person in the tribe and one of the strongest men in the province. He was very ambitious and aspired to gain complete supremacy and the governorship of Kermanshah. He fought against the Germans in 1915, but in 1916 was induced to change sides by German gold. Soleyman Mirza, an ultra-Democrat acted as German agent among the tribe; bribery and the spread of German propaganda resulted in influencing the tribe to favor the German and Turkish cause. In 1917, ‘Ali Akbar Khan fought against the Russians and was outlawed by them. He remained allied with the Germans and Ottomans until the end of WW I. In January 1918, Soleyman Mirza was arrested at their camp at Qal‘eh Sabzi, on account of his continued intrigue with the German agent von Dreuffel. This upset the tribe, but brought about no change in their anti-Allied feelings. Their continued hostility during the advance into Persia of the ‘Dunsterforce” in the spring of 1918 resulted in the British organizing a tribal force to reduce them to submission.

This combined force of all the tribes in the province was assisted by British mountain guns, machine guns and airplanes. With some difficulty the combined force of Kalhors and Gurans was kept united and maneuvered into position. Eventually they caught the Sanjabis at the Zimkan river at a time when it was in flood and heavy punishment followed, the Sanjabis losing 300 men killed; many of them were drowned in the swollen river and 80,000 head of sheep were taken. This defeat completely crippled the tribe for the time being. ‘Ali Akbar Khan was wounded in the arm and he and Sardar Zafar wandered around as mere outlaws and eventually fled to Tehran. Sardar Naser was deported to Kerbela and Amanollah Khan Chelevi was appointed the chief of the tribe. The Sanjabis remained quiet after their punishment in 1918. Amanollah Khan was not a success as chief, because he exercised power not always as he should, and, as a result, became very unpopular. The British described Amanollah Khan “as the leader of the Chelevis; a useless and morose man.” In August 1919, Amanollah Khan was replaced by Sardar Naser, who was permitted to return from Kerbela and, according to the British, was the best of the three brothers. He was a sensible man and a good tribal leader and kept good control. Under Sardar Naser the tribe recovered rapidly, soon regained its position as the most efficient and the most united tribe of the province.

Salar Zafar was allowed to return from Tehran where he had fled with ‘Ali Akbar Khan. However, he was a born intriguer and a Democrat and he created disorder so that the three sons of Samsam al-Mamalek (Sardar Naser, ‘Ali Akbar Khan, and Salar Zafar) might regain their dominant position held before April 1918. He was allowed to go to Qasr-e Shirin and was arrested, because he was implicated in the flight of Amir Mo‘azzam from Kermanshah. With Salar Zafar’s arrest, the Sanjabis remained of secondary importance. Although Sardar Naser was still their chief, he kept his own views and knew that not everybody accepted him. ‘Ali Akbar Khan was still popular among the tribe, who admired and, at the same time, were terrified of him. He was still in Tehran from where he intrigued. The British consul realized that the two brothers could not be exiled permanently, and he suggested that perhaps after 6 months they might be allowed to return, provided the tribes gave reasonable sureties.

The tribal situation showed that there was an increase of intrigues from the town and a revival of Sanjabi interests. This caused counter agitation and was quieted by Salar Zafar’s deportation. According to the British consul, Salar Zafar, was "erratic and altogether unsound in mind," who openly avowed Bolshevik principles to the governor and carried a cipher that let no doubt of his seditious activities in Kurdistan and Lorestan.[74] In August and September 1920, when the Arab insurrection in Iraq had spread to Khaneqin and Kuretu, a force of 280 Sanjabi *savars* under Sardar Naser co-operated with the British in the Khaneqin area for some six weeks. They were opposed there to their hereditary enemies, the Dilos, and rendered most useful service.

There was enmity between the tribe and Sardar Rashid of Ravansir, as they encroached on land belonging to the latter and because 'Ali Akbar Khan had been too intimate with Hamideh Khanom, Sardar Rashid's wife. In March 1921, Sardar Naser, acting under orders of the governor, led his *savars* to attack the Neyrizhi Gurans, who were with Qanbar Soltan in Posht-e Tang-e Zohab. They were unsuccessful in rounding up the people wanted and acquired some loot. In April 1921, information was received that 'Ali Akbar Khan and Sardar Zafar had been released from Tehran.[75]

KOLIYA'IS AND HARSIN

The Koliya'is are a Shiite Kurdish tribe. Around 1900, they numbered about 4,000 families, who lived in an area between Asadabad and Kurdistan and were under the governor of Sonqur. They had been wealthy, but in the 1860s their wealth was plundered by 'Ali Qoli Mirza, the governor appointed by his father Emad al-Dowleh. They were engaged in husbandry and had vast pasture lands, where they raised horses and mules.[76]

The situation in the Koliya'i district was unsettled during the second decade of the twentieth century. Harsin was controlled by the Kakawands from Lorestan, whose chief, A'zam al-Saltaneh, Baqer Khan, often known as Khan Darra, had usurped the governorship of Harsin, which belonged to Kermanshah province. Intermittently he paid taxes; he oppressed the peasants and took taxes (*baj*) whenever he could. Qavam al-Dowleh, the governor of Lorestan pressed him to pay Lorestan taxes, which he was reluctant to do.[77] In January 1920, the followers of A'zam al-Saltaneh Kakawand and the Qazi of Harsin clashed, two men of the former were killed and some were wounded on both sides. A'zam al-Saltaneh was afraid of losing his position and sent for 2,000 tribesmen.[78] In February 1920, the conflict was temporarily settled by Mo'tazed al-Dowleh, who had been sent by Amir Nezam, the governor of Kermanshah, to resolve the quarrel. Blood money was paid for the two killed men and property robbed from the Qazi would be returned. The governor wanted A'zam al-Saltaneh gone, but he had a strong tribe behind him

74. FO 248/1293, Report Kermanshah, no. 7, up to 12 August 1920.
75. AIR 20/663, pp. 100-01.
76. Rabino 1905, p. 35.
77. FO 248/1293, Note on the Town and District of Kermanshah May 1920. "He [A`zam al-Saltaneh] fought against the Russians, but was now more friendly. Together with Sardar Amjad Hasanawand he headed a Lor confederacy opposed to Nazar Ali Khan Amra'i." IOR/L/MIL/17/15/11/3, Who's Who in Persia, vol. 2, p. 83.
78. FO 248/1293, Kermanshah Report no. 1, 31/01/1920.

and the governor's only armed force consisted of unreliable gendarmes. Therefore, he decided to until spring when hostile tribes might come available to expel him.[79] The situation in Harsin remained problematic[80] and therefore, the unsatisfactory condition of this district continued. To improve matters A'zam al-Saltaneh had to be removed. He made matters worse when he sent an official (*ma'mur*) from Qavam al-Dowleh, governor of Lorestan, packing when he came to demand payment of taxes, on account of him being the chief of the Kakawands.[81] As expected Qavam al-Dowleh replaced A'zam al-Saltaneh by his brother Ebrahim Khan as chief of the Kakawands. It was expected that both governors of Lorestan and Kermanshah jointly would take action to remove him.[82] In June 1920 still no action was taken. Threats and diplomacy having failed, it seemed as if the governor bided his time. The son of Sardar Fateh lived in Harsin watching developments and playing off one town party against the other. Khan Saheb Heydar Qoli Kabuli and Ja'far Qoli Kabuli, both British subjects, were the greatest sufferers of the impasse. The Imam Jom'eh supported A'zam al-Saltaneh, his son-in-law, and Agha Rahim *mojtahed* was deeply financially interested in the Kabuli brothers.[83] Despite his formal dismissal as chief, Baqer Khan A'zam al-Saltaneh felt strong enough to refuse to pay any taxes any longer. In early August 1920, Sarem al-Dowleh, the governor of Kermanshah, therefore, sent a force of gendarmes under Major Salar Nezam to attack and remove him. No fight took place, because Baqer Khan was murdered. His considerable property was not found having disappeared a few days before, which the governor was very busy looking for. As a result, his brother Ebrahim Khan was then able to assume the chieftainship of the Kakawand and Harsin and matters settled down. [84]

Harsin and Baqer Khan were not the only problems that arose in the Koliya'i district. There were increasing also complaints against Amir Amjad, the chief of the Koliya'is and, therefore, it was decided that he had to be replaced.[85] Koliya'i affairs would be simplified by the death of Amir Amjad. Although he kept absolute order in the district, this happened at the expense of the inhabitants, whom he squeezed much. His enmity with his relatives, Fateh Khan and Khvaneyn of Bilavar, prevented him from cultivating and, therefore, much of Koliya'i was unproductive. The Farmanfarma family who owned most of Asadabad wanted to get more land in neighboring Koliya'i district, where they had some villages, which might complicate matters.[86] Amir Amjad's death in May 1920 eased the situation; his son was temporarily put in charge pending the appointment of a new chief of the Gurans. Mohammad Khan, the brother of the murdered chief was made chief of the Neyrizhi section.[87] Because the son of Amir Amjad, 'Ali Akbar Khan (rich and depressed) and Nosrat Khan were quarreling, they were both summoned

79. FO 248/1293, Kermanshah Report no. 2, 29/02/1920; Soltani 1373, vol. 1, p. 850.
80. FO 248/1293 tel. 32 Consul to Legation, 13/04/1920.
81. FO 248/1293, Kermanshah Report no. 4, 30/04/1920.
82. FO 248/1293, Report Kermanshah no. 5, 31/05/1920.
83. FO 248/1293, Report Kermanshah no. 6, 30/06/1920.
84. FO 248/1293, Report Kermanshah, no. 7, up to 12 August 1920. The result was a conflict between Sarem al-Dowleh and Major Salam Nezam about the loot taken. Soltani 1381, vol. 1, p. 581.
85. FO 248/1293 tel. 32 Consul to Legation, 13/04/1920.
86. FO 248/1293 tel. Consul to Legation, 30/07/1920.
87. FO 248/1293, Report Kermanshah, no. 5, 31 May 1920.

to Kermanshah, but 'Ali Akbar only wanted to come with a guarantee from the British consulate that he would not be bled too heavily.[88]

ECONOMIC ACTIVITY

Agriculture, husbandry (about which later) and weaving, were the main economic activities in the province. Carpets were not made anymore, only at Hamadan and Soltanabad. The Guran made saddlebags or *gorjin* and rugs of coarse texture. *Gilim*s were made allover the province in large numbers. Kurdish carpets, mostly from Senneh, were sold at Senneh, Tabriz and Kermanshah.[89] In addition, the rural population produced much *rowghan* or clarified butter and tallow of goats, cotton in small quantity, packing bags, black hair tents and wooden combs and clay chaplets, which were greatly appreciated. They also made many felt rugs or *namad*s and there were many *giveh* shoemakers.[90]

The British traveler Rich observed that wood was becoming more and more scarce around Senneh in the 1820s. A man from Kermanshah, who had a foundry, contributed greatly to the destruction of the plane forests, because he only wanted plane tree (*chenar*) charcoal. This was worse than even timber cutting. "The agents for cutting wood never venture to carry money with them into the forests. The workmen are all paid at Halabjeh (south-east of Solimaniyeh) which is the nearest town in the district."[91] Export of charcoal from Kurdistan to Iraq continued throughout the nineteenth century, and only came to a halt when the government interfered in one way or the other. For example, "the imposition of quarantine on arrivals from Persia has all but stopped the supply of charcoal" in Kaneqin, and most of the inhabitants were going without a fire.[92] Others were less positive. Mrs. Stead wrote that "Many of the tribes live by blackmail and robbery and by sheep and goat herding."[93] Because of poverty and weakening of central government control many were engaged in highway robbery.

There also was trade, because the various products made and produced by villagers and pastoralists had to be sold. Also, both groups needed a variety of products that they did not make themselves, in particular cotton and sugar. In Kermanshah Province trade was mainly in the hands of Chaldean Christians.[94] There also were peddlers, who operated in other commercial branches such as in the wool trade. In Kermanshah, these peddlers were called locally *charchi* or *sahra-row*, they bought the wool in small quantities, either for cash, or against goods supplied.[95]

---

88. FO 248/1293, Report Kermanshah, no. 7, up to 12 August 1920.
89. AIR 20/66358; Gouvernement de France 1914, p. 95; Curzon 1892, vol. 1, 558 (brought to Kermanshah and sold in Istanbul).
90. DCR 590 (Kermanshah 1901-02), pp. 18-19; Amanat 1983, p. 94.
91. Rich 1836, vol. 1, p. 106.
92. Bishop 1891, vol. 1, p. 70.
93. Stead 1911, p. 128.
94. DCR 4365, p. 9.
95. DCR 3189, p. 26.

In 1685, grand vizier Sheykh 'Ali Khan Zanganeh, who, in the face of a monetary crisis caused by silver shortage, commissioned the exploitation of silver mines in the province of Kermanshah. Sheykh 'Ali Khan had issued an order to start working the silver mines in mountains of the province of Kermanshah and to procure a few camel loads of silver. From this silver a number of '*abbasi*s were struck at minimal cost, but due to the high cost of production the mining operation was discontinued.[96]

Kurdistan is also part of the geological zone, which contains petroleum resources and roughly stretches from Kirkuk to the Persian Gulf. Known oil fields were located at Chia-Sorkh, Shah-Morad, Karim Khan, Bazargar, Hurin, Gahvarreh and Shiyan in addition to other localities. There was also evidence (ancient cemeteries and fire temples) that many of these had been used since antiquity. The way in which the Kurds mined these naphtha wells at the beginning of the twentieth century was as follows:

> There is usually a well some 24 feet deep in the shape of a funnel, the top being 15 to 30 feet wide and the bottom 10 feet. At the bottom is a wooden platform giving access to two smaller wells some 30 feet deep. In these wells salt water and naphtha collect. The wells are emptied every five or six days by means of a bucket. The salt water is turned into tanks for evaporation, and the salt is sold in Kasr-i-Shirin at 1 kran a batman. The crude oil, which fetches at the well 4 krans per 4 Imperial gallons or tin (32 lbs. British), is taken to the still, which is now in Kerim Khan's village on the Kurretu River. The capacity of the still is only 70 Imperial gallons. Out of one charge of 35 gallons lamp oil are produced. The oil is sold at the still to the Kasr-i-Shirin Jews at 7½ to 8 krans per tin of 4 Imperial gallons, and is resold at Kasr-i-Shirin at 10 krans a tin.[97]

The first exploration for oil in Kermanshah province was made in 1901, after de Morgan's earlier observations on the region's prospects for oil. Preparatory work and drilling began in 1903 under Mr. Rosenplaenter, despite all kinds of technical difficulties. On 14 January 1904, he struck oil in the second well that he drilled. In 1906, consul Gough visited the d'Arcy wells, which "were guarded by tribesmen and everything in good order. The wells were both spouting, though not a very large amount of il was coming out." Thereafter, work was discontinued by May 1914. The drilling site received quite a number of important visitors in that year, amongst whom were Farmanfarma, the governor of Kermanshah, the Imam Jom'eh, government officials and religious leaders all of "seemed very keen on receiving a substantial present from us, especially in the shape of some shares of our Company." The number of these visitors increased to such numbers that Rosenplaenter had to start a separate Moslem. i.e. a *halal* kitchen, for them.[98]

---

96. Matthee, Floor and Clawson 2013, p. 128. On mining, see Floor 2000 and Idem 2003.

97. *DCR* 3189 (Kermanshah 1903-04), p. 38. "The oil wells belong to the Bajilan [Kurds], but the Chiahsurkh camp is on Guran territory." Adamec 1976, vol. 1, p. 83. See also De Morgan 1894, vol. 2, pp. 81-87, 182 (sites, production method, end-uses). There was also export of white naphtha or bitumen to Baghdad, though it is not clear whether this came form the Kurdistan or the Shustar wells. Olivier 1807, vol. 5, p. 321.

98. Ferrier 1982, pp. 55, 65-66; Administration Report 1905-06, p. 50. For Farmanfama's correspondence concerning the oil drilling at Chia Sorkh during this period, see Ettehadiyeh et al. 1395.

In 1934, drilling was resumed as a result of the negotiations in 1933 leading to the revision of the oil concession APOC (see Chapter Seven).

In 1904-05, some 12 tons of salt at £25 were exported from Kermanshah.[99] It was also consumed in Kermanshah province, where bread in 1885 was made with "wheat, maize, and ballotas [*balut*], a kind of acorn. The dough is placed on sheet-iron or *saj* and baked, but the dough is badly kneaded, badly fermented and therefore heavy and indigestible."[100]

PROVINCIAL ARMY

The Kalhors, Gurans, Kerendis and Zanganehs each provided a regiment for service in and outside the province.[101] The chief being the colonel (*sarhang*), while the sub-chiefs, in charge of a company, had the rank of *soltan* or captain.[102] The nominal strength of the provincial army was four regiments of 800 men each, 150 artillerists and 400-500 irregular cavalry. Only the Kerendi regiment had a military band. The Zanganeh regiment was formed as follows: Kendouleh 2 companies; Namivand 2 companies; Osmanavad 1; Kerkuki 1; Shamshir Chubi 1, and Chehri 1. The cavalry was formed by Nanekali 50; Ahmadavand Behtui 100 horsemen. The Gurans provided one regiment with 8 companies, each nominally 100 men, under a *soltan*. In 1902, the infantry came from the following localities: Takht-e Gah, Gahvareh, Baziani tribe, Nirijli tribe, Kalleh Zanjir, Biyabani tribe and Jafs of Palan. The Bazianis were the life guard of the Guran chief and were referred to as *tofangchiha*. They also occasionally supplied 100 horsemen to the government. The Kerendi regiment was composed as follows: Kerend 2 companies, Biwanji 2, Jelalavand 2, Rashidali 2, and Rijab was the military band. The Kalhor regiment was formed by: Khaleddi 1 company; Shiani 1; Kazem Khani 1; Harunabadi, Shahini and Shuan 1; Kuchimi and Kalojubi 1; Kuleppah 1; Charzebari 1; and Bedaghbeghi and Alavandi 1. It had no band.[103] Military service meant that all or part of the district's the land revenue was earmarked to pay for the upkeep of the regiment. Part of the revenue was earmarked for the regiment.[104] The regiments were nominally 1,000 men, but rarely mustered "300 of "ragged, ill-armed men."[105] Each year one regiment would relieve another of its task of guarding the city (*qaravoli-ye shahr*).[106]

The artillery was under a separate commander. In addition, there was an irregular cavalry (*savars*) paid by the government. In 1900, this cavalry was composed as follows: Sanjabis (400), Ahmadavands (150), Nanekulis (50) Sharafbeynis (100) and Bajlans (150). How many and from

---

99. Government of Great Britain 1906, p. 437.
100. Binder 1887, p. 352.
101. Administration Report 1905-06, p. 49. In general, see Motallebi 1384.
102. Napier 1919, p. 8.
103. DCR 590 (Kermanshah 1901-02), pp. 43, 46, 51-52, 55; see also Napier 1919, pp. 8, 10.
104. DCR 590 (Kermanshah 1901-02), pp. 46, 52.
105. Administration Report 1905-06, p. 49.
106. *Ruznameh-ye Iran* 1375, vol. 5, pp. 3483 (no. 866; 12/10/1895).

which tribes these *savars* had to be supplied was the governor's prerogative and therefore, was subject to change. For example, the Sharafbeynis and Bajlans had only been recently singled out for this service.[107] In addition, the government could draw on the tribal levies in case of need, which could supply another 5,600 men:

Table 4.6: List of tribal levies, 1901

Name tribe	Number
Zengeneh	200
Kalhur	4,000
Kerindi	50
Sanjabi	200
Ahmadavand Behtui	50
Bajlan	150
Sharafbaini	200
Nanekali	50
Kuliai	700
Total	5,600

Source: DCR 590 (Kermanshah 1901-02), p. 64

The tribal chiefs who supplied the soldiers gave statements of how many men were serving. As the amount did not reflect actual cost, both the governor and the tribal chief benefited from this, because all regiments were under strength. The cut both parties received was called perquisite or *madakhel*. In this way the tribal chief 'bought' his position. The soldiers received less than the official statements reported, because their officers also needed their cut. Officially soldiers received 1.5 *sir* of bread per day and 7 *qrans* per month, and if they worked every day their official pay was 10 *qrans*. However, in reality, if they were paid at all, payment was always in arrears and less than the official rate. Therefore, soldiers eked out a living in all kinds of jobs such as carpenters, bakers, butchers, etc. The horsemen (*savar*) officially received 15 *tumans* per year when on duty and 3 *tumans* when off-duty.[108]

The territorial army (*qoshun* or *nezam*) of long standing had much declined since 1907 and thereafter remained at a very low strength and was badly equipped. It was not called up for training or duties regularly. "Consequently their discipline is bad and their officers have little control over them. The men are of poor class, and poor physique. They are despised as fighters by the tribesmen, and seldom distinguish themselves when out to operate in the district." There was a commander or *ra'is-e qoshun* in Kermanshah. The term *nezam* was replaced by *qoshun* in 1922 by order of Reza Khan, who began an army reform, establishing a new modern army.[109]

107. DCR 590 (Kermanshah 1901-02), pp. 63-64.

108. Adamec 1976, vol. 1, p. 363.

109. AIR 20/663, pp. 9, 81-83; Napier 1919, p. 10. On the establishment of the new army, see S. Cronin, *The Army and the Creation of the Pahlavi State in Iran, 1910-1926*. London: IB Tauris, 1997.

CHAPTER FIVE

AGRICULTURE

INTRODUCTION

Kermanshah province had a fertile soil and an abundant water supply throughout the year. With more efficient methods peasants might produce 300% more, while they only produced for their own use and large tracts of land lay unused. Therefore, together with the provinces of Azerbaijan, Khorasan, Khamseh, and Hamadan, Kermanshah was in particular known as one of the cereal producing zones. Moreover, it was a major area where cattle was raised; hence much of the province's land was either under cultivation or used as pasture. Both agriculture and animal husbandry were negatively affected by i. attacks of tribesmen of the settled population; ii. internal tribal disunity and fighting; and iii. uncertainty about political developments and instability of the government. Also, near Kermanshah and on the borders of Kurdistan there was a shortage of peasants. As a result, peasants produced mainly for their own consumption and much excellent arable land was not cultivated.[1]

Because Kermanshah is mountainous much rain water was retained, either naturally or artificially, in the mountain valleys, where river water was used to irrigate the crops. Therefore agriculture was either *deymi*, i.e. does not need to be irrigated, or *abi*, i.e. it needs irrigation. To irrigate the land use was made of water wheels,[2] not much investment was required, because hardly any *qanat*s existed in this part of Iran. Dry farming was practiced in most parts of the province. Rain fed or *deymi* land was sown with grains and allowed to fallow the next year; irrigated or *abi* land was sown with grain in one year and with *seyfi* (summer garden crops such as water melons, melons, cucumbers, etc.) the following year.[3] A belt of forest 10-15 miles wide in western border of the mountain with oak, oak scrub, ash and hawthorn. However, the trees were stunted rarely reaching a height of 6 m. In the rest of province there was no forest, except here and there some oak scrub stands, all stunted the more so towards the east. The villagers cultivated the poplar everywhere for commercial purposes; the main item for roofing.[4]

1. Polak 1862, p. 130; Ibid. 1865, vol. 2, p. 136; Olivier 1807, vol. 5, p. 24; AIR 20/663, p. 51; Lambton 1953, p. 304.
2. Adamec 1976, vol. 1, pp. 126, 147, 236, 291.
3. Rich 1836, vol. 1, p. 134; Dupré 1819,vol. 1, p. 238; DCR 590 (Kermanshah 1902), p. 15.
4. AIR 20/663. According to Mr. Edwards of the Oriental Carpet Company at Hamadan told Napier 1919, p. 6, that the purchase of "a plot of land with sufficient water rights, planted with poplars, would return 10 per cent. per annum on cost of purchase within five years and 100 per cent. from ten years onwards."

In Kermanshah province, as in the rest of Persia, land was either crown land (*khaleseh*), revenue assignment (*teyul*, either for life or as pension), private property (*milk*, for large landowners or *khordeh malek* for small village landowners) and endowments (*vaqf*).[5] In the Kermanshah area there were many small landowners and peasant-proprietors around the towns, but farther away from the town land was in the hands of large landowners, some of whom owned large tracts, including over 50 villages. In short, most proprietors were large landowners and there were very few peasant proprietors.[6] Gardens, which allegedly were not common near Kermanshah, often were owned by landowners and were managed by a *bostanchi*.[7]

In the province, landowners only supplied the land and water, cattle and labor was supplied by the villagers. The predominant division of the harvest was that two-thirds went to the peasant. The various irregular imposts collected by landlords from their peasants as well as the division of the agricultural produce between landowners and peasants usually was as follows:

> (i) on *abi* land one-third, sometimes one-fourth of the harvest, which happened when the landowner also supplied seed and oxen the villagers only get one-fourth of harvest;
>
> (ii) on *deymi* land, one-fifth of the harvest;
>
> (ii) landowners also get a further 6% on the harvest share of villagers.
>
> (iv) further varying small perquisites, depending on agreement between villagers and landowners. Some of the usual charges are on one pair of oxen or *sar juft*:
>
> 1 *tuman* and 2 or 3 loads of fuel or straw, or 1 *man* ghi (*rowghan*) and 5 *qran*s, or
>
> 1 lamb and 5 *qran*s. Sometimes the perquisite is as small as 2 *qran*s and 1 fowl or 1/4 *man* ghi (*rowghan*). Villagers also have to supply labor free of charge when their masters are building. For gardens owners get one-third of produce.[8]

There were various other ways in which the crop was divided between the landowners and the peasants. Near Bisotun (Kermanshah) a farmer was working on a principle called 'sakko kali.' "He received the seed (wheat), and the land was of course free. He paid yearly one fowl, six eggs, seven donkey-loads of cut-straw, five krans for each pair of bullocks he used, and one load of wood. After that he kept for himself two-thirds of the crop he raised."[9] In Baladeh, a district of Kermanshah, the villagers, who had no pastureland, gave their cattle to the Chupankaras, or the shepherd families of some of the tribes, to be taken to the pastures of the Huleylanis and other groups, for which rent was paid.[10] However, the general rule seems to have been *nesf-e*

5. On land ownership see Lambton 1953 and Floor 2000.
6. FO 371/40222 (26/11/1943); Lambton 1953, p. 269.
7. Lambton 1953, p. 324. However, in 1920, Major Greenhouse observed that "nearly every village has its fruit garden." AIR 20/663, p. 57; Napier 1919, p. 12 (at Kerend, surrounded by rich gardens, the Turks before withdrawing cut large numbers of fruit trees); see also the description of the *boluk*s or districts in chapter four.
8. DCR 590, p. 33; Lambton 1953, p. 309. For an overview of the many unofficial imposts that could be levied from both male and female villagers, see Soltani 1381, vol. 2-3, pp. 1028-41.
9. Floyer 1882, p. 431.
10. Adamec 1976, vol. 1, p. 85.

kari (equal parts), i.e. the peasant providing labor and seed and the landlord paying for the harvesting. If the landlord only provided the land, the peasant received five-sixths (*dah-o-do*).[11] In certain parts peasants had to pay rent in cash.[12]

AGRICULTURAL CROPS.

The province of Kermanshah produced a large variety of agricultural commodities such as grain, and gall nuts, but the cultivation of opium, gums, castor oil, tobacco and saffron only became important after the 1870s. Other items that the province produced included indigo, maize, clover, alfalfa, as well as fruits and vegetables such as melons, water melons, grapes, cucumbers, egg plants and tomatoes for local consumption. Fruit was abundant in some districts.[13] Because it had excellent pastures, Kermanshah produced many sheep, horses, mules and their by-products such as guts, hides and wool.[14] In what follows I discuss the most important crops produced in the province.

Castor oil

The cultivation of the castor oil plant was found in many places.[15]

Chopped Lucerne was known as *tarit* or *tarid*, a term that was also used to refer bread crumbled into milk or soup. It was grown mainly as fodder for the winter and it was locally known as *onza*[16] At Kermanshah, Bellew saw hundreds of mules and asses transport loads of lucerne into the town [17]

Collyrium for the eyes (eye-powder or *qotur*) also known as *tutiya-ye elvend* was made in Kermanshah from a plant, which was said only to be found on the Elvend mountains. It was in great demand all over Iran.[18] Eyeshade (*tutiya*) was also made from soot of the burnt skin of the *gavan* plant, which was called *cheraghu*. The bushes were roasted over a fire and the soot was collected on an earthenware saucer or on an iron grate.[19]

---

11. Government of Great Britain 1945, pp. 435-36.
12. Lambton 1953, p. 272.
13. Fraser 1826, p. 357; Olivier 1807, vol. 5, p. 24; Amanat 1983, pp. 93-94; Binder 1887, p. 346; DCR 3189, p. 22; Olivier 1807, vol. 5, p. 24.
14. Fraser 1826 , p. 357; Olivier 1807, vol. 5, p. 24; Binder 1887, p. 346; Curzon 1892, vol. 1, p. 558.
15. DCR 3189, p. 34.
16. Eyn al-Saltaneh 1376, vol. 2, p. 1540; DCR 3189, p. 34 (clover).
17. Bellew 1999, p. 415.
18. DCR 3189, p. 46; Schlimmer 1970, p. 146.
19. Floor 2003, p. 510.

Cotton

Kermanshah produced much cotton, which therefore was sold at a low price in town.[20] Its price in 1849 was 1.75 *qran* per *man* of 6.5 lbs, although usually it sold at 2 *qrans*.[21] In 1865, Polak noted that until recently all cotton had been processed locally.[22] This remained so for many parts of Iran such as Kermanshah where around the turn of the twentieth century cotton was still only grown for local consumption.[23]

Dates

Dates were mostly produced around Mandali.[24]

Fruit

Every village had an orchard with apricots, quinces, peaches, apples, pears, mulberries, grapes, raisins, melons, nectarines, figs, cherries, walnuts and almonds. Fruit was of an exceptional quality, expect in the east, but little effort was spent on their cultivation such as pruning, prevention of insects, etc.[25] *Kharbuz* or *kharbuzeh*, the sugar melon (*Cucumis melo*), was one of the many varieties of melons cultivated in Iran. Melons were grown everywhere and may be considered as one of the chief food crops of the country. "I am told that in this part of Persia [Golpeygan], and in Kermanshah, melon-fields are to be seen three of four miles in length, and a mile and a half in breadth. I really believe there is no exaggeration in the statement."[26] In Kermanshah province, the fruits of Kenduleh, Harsin and Sahneh were also famous and were brought to town for sale. "Kerend has excellent grapes; dried figs from Rijab are well known, and Gahwarreh at one time had fine apples. Oranges and lemons are received from Mendali (Turkey)."[27] This trade had grown considerably in the second half of the century. There was, for example, large export of dried fruit from Kermanshah. This town, however, was also supplied from Hamadan, Malayer, and Iraq-e 'Ajam. The fruit was packed in boxes or bales and sent to Baghdad and Bombay.[28] *Gojeh-ferangi* or tomatoes (*Lycopersicon esculentum*) were grown in Kermanshah and in central Iran for local consumption at the turn of the twentieth century. The seeds had been imported from Europe.[29] There also was cultivation of other garden crops such as cucumbers and egg plants.[30]

---

20. Dupré 1819,vol. 1, p. 238; Teule 1842, vol. 2, pp. 485-86.
21. Amanat 1983, p. 93.
22. Polak 1865, vol. 2, pp. 166-167.
23. DCR 3189, p. 34.
24. DCR 590, p. 22.
25. AIR 20/663, pp. 57-58.
26. Sheil 1973, p. 223; DCR 3189 (Kermanshah 1903-04), p. 34 (melons, water melons).
27. DCR 3189, p. 34; "Grapes of a very fine quality and of 14 varieties, are abundantly produced and there are many other fruits." Amanat 1983, p. 94. The region was already well-known for its fruit, such as the *shah-anjir* or the king of figs, in the tenth century, Abu-Dulaf, p. 45
28. DCR 2260, p. 17; Dupré 1819, vol. 1, p. 238.
29. DCR 3189, p. 34. The fruit initially was also known as *badenjan-e ferengi* or European egg-plant, see Floor 2003, p. 344.
30. DCR 3189, p. 34.

Gall Nuts were brought for sale by the Goran and Jaf tribes, in 1849, at prices from 200 to 300 *qrans* per *kharvar* for mixed kinds, white, blue and green.[31]

Gaz or Manna

The oak-manna was often also classed as a *gaz-angabin*, e.g., by Polak, probably because it was considered as just an inferior type of *gaz*. The fact that it was not the only inferior kind of manna may have something to do with it. Kermanshah produced, for example, an inferior kind of manna, "called Geze Alafi. The Gez i guti found here is all from Isfahan. A few boxes of Gezengebin are prepared here. Gez Alafi costs about 3½ krans per mann and is used for medicinal purposes."[32] The French traveler Ferrier also just classed the Kermanshah *gaz* in the same category as that of Isfahan. "Manna, guzengebine, abounds in the province of Kermanshah; the Persians mix it with flour and sugar, and make it into little cakes; these they consider great dainties, and export them to all parts of Asia."[33]

Grain Production

The industry of Kermanshah and its environs was agriculture, and, as a result, it was one of the major wheat-growing provinces and it was "well known for the quantity and excellence of its wheat, and the great number and superior qualities of its mules."[34] Wheat and barley were normally found there in great abundance and very cheap; and even when it was expensive it was cheaper than anywhere elsewhere in Iran.[35] The total output of the province of Kermanshah in a normal year was about 180,000 *kharvar*s (80,000 tons) after supplying the needs of the population of about 350,000 persons.[36] Capt. Napier's estimate in 1875 of a harvest of 380,000 *kharvar* (139,000 tons) seems to be a year of high production, while in 1902 the harvest, minus local consumption, resulted in the unprecedented surplus output of 250,000 *kharvar*.[37]

---

31. Amanat 1983, p. 93.
32. DCR 590, pp. 19-20.
33. Ferrier 1857, pp. 26-27; Amanat 1983, p. 94 ("ghezenghebeen in Kermanshah").
34. Southgate 1840, vol. 1, p. 137; DCR 2260, p. 16.
35. In 1849, wheat was very cheap, "5 Kerans (4s/6d) for 650 lbs or 1072 bushels, was the price of wheat, but it is usually 10 to 12 Kerans for the same weight. Barley was at 2 1/2 Kerans, though generally 8 to 10 Kerans." Amanat 1983, p. 93.
36. DCR 2260, p. 16; DCR 113, Herbert, Report on the Industries, p. 8 (More grain cultivated than before, "and not more than one-third of the land formerly cultivated is under the plough."); DCR 590, p. 16 ("The great industry of Kermanshah and its neighbourhood is agriculture. The people are chiefly employed in tilling the fields"). Polak observed, "the cheapest cereals are always in Kermanshah, where wheat straw costs per *kharvar* 0.2 – 0.8 Ducat." Polak 1862, p. 130.
37. DCR 590, pp. 15-17.

Table 5.1: The usual output of Kermanshah was estimated to be 200,000 *kharvar* (1903)

Name location	Quantity/*Kharvar*
Kalhor	20,000
Mahidasht	25,000
Sanjabi	12,000
Guran	20,000
Kerind	15,000
Mian-Darband	6,000
Bilavar	6,000
Chamchamal	5,000
Sungor and Kuliai	20,000
Sahna	8,000
Dinavar	8,000
Khadabendelu	4,000
Hersin	5,000
Huleilan	5,000
Kasr-i Shirin	20,000
Assadabad and Kangavar	21,000
Total	200,000

Source: *DCR* 3189, p. 33.

Gums

The various contemporary sources give different locations for the production of tragacanth (*katira*), but agree that Kermanshah was one of the most important production centers.[38] The best gum reportedly came from Kermanshah; the next best from Rafsanjan and Fars. The first quality of tragacanth gum of Fars was said to be equal to the second quality of Kermanshah. Bushehr, which also exported tragacanth, received its best qualities from Borujerd by way of Isfahan, from the hills in the district of Kadirabad in Fars and from Bajigah near Shiraz.[39] In the trade with Kerman and Yazd various kinds of *katira* were mentioned, including *katira-ye tighi*, *jalabi*, *safid*, *safid-qalam*, *qalam*, and *Kerman*.[40]

Foreign observers feared that the indiscriminate tapping of the plant giving *katira* would soon cause the supply of gums to diminish. Already by 1900 the fields in the vicinity of Kermanshah were said to be almost completely exhausted. Rabino, at that time consul in Kermanshah therefore wrote:

---

38. Schlimmer 1970, p. 203; Stolze & Andreas 1885, p. 14; Polak 1865, vol. 2, p. 287; MacLean 1904, p. 22; Dupré 1819, vol. 2, p. 373 (Kurdistan and N. Persia). Gum tragacanth and mastic in Kermanshah normally cost respectively 60 and 80 *qrans*. Amanat 1983, p, 93.

39. Gleadowe-Newcomen 1906, p. 87; DCR 3189, pp. 27-29; DCR 3951, pp. 16-17.

40. Mahdavi and Afshar 1389, pp. 391, 470, 474-76.

> Speaking of the gum industry in the province of Fars, Lieut. Colonel C.A. Kemball, in his report on the trade of the Persian Gulf for the year 1900 (No. 2631 Annual Series), says: "It appears that the peasantry employed in the collection of the tragacanth work in a reckless manner, causing much damage to the plants, which are burnt down, after (before) incision, to such an extent as to render the same field unproductive for some years to come. Though the tragacanth fields are numerous and extensive, they will not be able to withstand the wholesale depredations which are now being perpetrated on them, unless the Persian Government undertakes their supervision with a view to maintaining and improving the industry." What Lieut. Colonel C.A. Kemball says about Fars applies equally well to Kermanshah, Luristan and Kurdistan.[41]

However, other observers were less alarmed by the increased cutting down of *astralagus* bushes. "Though the process by which white gum is produced proves destructive to the older shrubs which are burnt down to get it, so extensive are the regions still untouched, and owing to the fact that it is an indigenous and self-propagating plant, there is no probability of Persia being unable to continue to export in the future quantities as large as, if not longer than, she has exported in the past."[42]

However, Rabino's fears as to the situation around Kermanshah seemed to have been realized. Already in 1903, the fields around Kermanshah were almost completely exhausted.[43] During 1909-10, only 60 tons of *katira* was collected within 20 miles of Kermanshah and 290 tons from beyond. One of his successors commented in 1910, "a greater quantity was formerly collected at Kermanshah many plants have been destroyed by the process of burning which is employed to drive the sap into the roots and so obtain more."[44] It would seem that peddlers collected *katira* in small quantities. These in turn sold it to intermediaries (*dallal-e dowrehgerdha*). This made it a somewhat difficult branch of trade for major operators, for one of Iran's capitalists, Amin al-Zarb, complained that you just could not get large quantities of *katira*, because these intermediaries were not well-known and had no fixed abode and prices. In addition to these intermediaries and peddlers (*pilehvar*), block-printers (*chitsaz*) also bought small quantities of one to two *man* from the villagers for their own needs.[45]

In particular in western Iran, after the grain harvest, many inhabitants of Kermanshah and its surrounding villages spread out of the countryside after to collect gum tragacanth, which, when collected, they sent into town, where it was sorted, packed and exported.[46] In Hamadan, in 1907, for example, a Russian Armenian employed 50 young Armenian girls to sort the gum tragacanth that he had collected.[47]

---

41. DCR 3189, pp. 27-29.
42. Gleadowe-Newcomen 1906, pp. 87-88.
43. DCR 3189, p. 29.
44. DCR 4559, p. 6.
45. Mahdavi and Afshar 1389, p. 469-72 (there was no pre-harvest (*salaf*) sale of tragacanth).
46. *AP* 1899, 101, pp. 16, 18; see also DCR 590, p. 19; DCR 2260, p.16.
47. Grothe 1910, p. 193.

There are four principal qualities of gum tragacanth offered for sale in the Kermanshah market: -The first quality is received from Burujird, Nehavend and Kermanshah, and fetches unsorted from 28 to 32 krans per maund tabrizi. It is sorted into three classes, which fetch about 35 to 36, 30 to 31 and 28 to 29 respectively. The second quality is received from Kurdistan, Kermanshah, Nehavend and Burujird, and fetches unsorted from 11 to 18 krans per maund. It is sorted into five classes, fetching about 22, 18, 14, 12 and 8 krans per maund respectively. The third quality ("Zardeh" in Arabic) is known in Persia under the name of "Arrehbor" (cut with a saw), as the gum exudes from the branches which have been cut with a saw. Arrehbor costs 8 to 11 krans per maund. When sorted the different classes fetch 12, 9, 8 and 6 krans per maund respectively. It is obtained from Mount-Dalahu, Pusht-i-Kuh, Khoremabad and Burujird. The fourth quality, or stone gum, which is known under the name of Kurreh (Kora), is obtained from Mount-Dalahu, Pusht-i-Kuh, Khoremabad and Burujird. It is [27] quoted now at from 7 to 7½krans per maund. The prices were much lower in former years, 4 to 5 krans being asked for 1 maund. When sorted the different classes fetch 10, 6 and 4 krans per maund respectively.

The first quality katyra is obtained from the plant known as "Gavan-sefid" or white gavan, by incisions, from which the gum exudes. Second quality is obtained from the yellow gavan which is a larger plant than the gavan-sefid. The top of the plant is burnt, and when the leaves are all consumed the fire is put out and incisions are made. The following morning the gum which has oozed out of the incisions is gathered. This operation is repeated three or four times, the quality improving each time. The Arrebor gum exudes from the branch of a small tree, the top of which has been burnt and the branches then cut with a saw. The branches are cut three to four times. The plant yielding Kora is treated in the same way as that yielding Arrehbor gum. The operation is repeated three times, and the quality of the gum deteriorates each time. After seven years' constant tapping the gavan plant dries up.[48]

Indigo

In Kermanshah some indigo was grown for local consumption.[49]

Maize

In addition to wheat and barley, some maize was also cultivated in Kermanshah, where it was grown for local consumption.[50] It may have been the same variety cultivated in Kurdistan. It was

48. DCR 3189, pp. 27-29. According to Bader 1915, p. 1054, there were five qualities of tragacanth (*kevin*)
49. Southgate 1840. vol. 1, p. 324; Amanat 1983, pp. 93; DCR 3189, p. 34.
50. DCR 3189, p. 34.

"a kind of corn called '*bahara*', which is sown in spring, and requires artificial irrigation, which probably referred to maize."[51]

Opium

Opium production in the first half of the nineteenth century was mainly for the domestic market. In Kermanshah, peasants produced "an inconsiderable quantity for local consumption only – of fine quality."[52] According to Teule, in 1840 its production was of no import.[53] In the 1860s the production of opium was begun and continued to grow in Isfahan, Yazd, Fars, Kerman, Khorasan, Khuzistan and Kermanshah to such an extent that in the 1870s it had become one of the major crops.[54]

Opium cultivation for export had only begun in the late 1860s at Behbahan, and in Borujerd and Kermanshah only in 1875. In 1883, Polak wrote that the best quality opium was produced in Isfahan, followed by that of Yazd and Shiraz, and finally by that of the western provinces Borujerd, Malayer, and Kermanshah. The opium from the colder provinces was firmer and less moist than from other provinces such as Isfahan, Fars and Yazd. It also differed in color, the one being brown-red and contained less morphia, the other being yellow colored.[55]

In Kermanshah, the granary of Iran, opium cultivation was not considered as being more profitable than of cereals, "the expenses attending the former being so much greater." However, because opium was easily sold for cash immediately farmers preferred it to cereals and not for the superior profit compared with other crops.[56] This consideration seems to have been the major factor in the southern provinces as well. The British Commercial Commission in 1904 concluded that, "the drug and crop are easily disposed of for cash by the grower, and opium, unlike cereals, does not form a medium in which the Governors of districts may demand the payment of taxation. This is the chief reason why the Persian cultivator grows it so extensively."[57]

Opium was only cultivated in the immediate neighborhood of the town Kermanshah, and the output remained small: 300 boxes. In 1885, the output was only 180 boxes. Other opium came to Kermanshah from Borujerd, Nehavend and Hamadan. A box weighed from 20 to 22 *man* (130 to 143 lbs.) and cost about 2,800 to 3,200 *qran*s around 1900. Opium was also cultivated at Sahneh and some other villages in small quantities. After local consumption needs had been satisfied 100 to 150 boxes were exported via Baghdad. The rest was from Nehavend, Malayer, Borujerd, Dowlatabad, Lorestan, Hamadan, where the cultivation was being increased, and even from Isfahan. "Great progress could be made here in the cultivation of opium, but the villagers are too poor to supply the necessary capital for the expenses of gathering the opium and the

51. Rich 1836, vol.1, p. 134.
52. Amanat 1983, p. 93.
53. Teule 1842, vol. 2, p. 486.
54. Stack 1882, vol. 2, p. 37 and vol. 1, p. 38; for more details, see Floor 2003, pp. 435-38.
55. Floor 2003, p. 451.
56. Floor 2003, p. 439.
57. Gleadowe 1906, p. 89; MacLean 1904, p. 26 drew the same conclusion.

merchants do not trust them enough to make advances."[58] The system of opium cultivation was not much different in Kermanshah.

> The land intended for the cultivation of opium is cleared and ploughed in autumn and the seed is thickly sown in the month of Mizan (September 23 to October 24). The young plants show above the ground soon after the fields have been watered; and after the end of the cold season, during the months of Hamal and Saur (March 21 to May 22), the ground is manured. The plants are then thinned out, and at the end of the month of Jawz (May 22 to June 23), when the seed vessels mature, the lancing of the poppy heads begins. The lancing is done with a three or seven-bladed knife, and the following morning the juice which has juiced out of the wound is scraped off with a knife. The operation is repeated three times, the plant being allowed a day or two's rest. The quality and quantity of the juice constantly deteriorate. Fine weather is necessary to mature the plants, but if at the time of harvest it is very hot and dry the juice will not run so plentifully from the poppy heads, whilst through heavy showers of rain the opium may be lost. The opium is gathered in copper vessels, usually cooking utensils.[59]

A very detailed cost calculation provided by Rabino for the preparation of raw opium in Kermanshah shows the following:

The following are the expenses for producing 30 maunds tabrizi of raw opium:

	Expenses/Krans
In autumn	
10 maunds* of seeds	5
Ploughing, four days	6
Making the 'kards,' five days, six laborers, per day	30
Sowing the seed, three days, three laborers, per day	6
Irrigation, four times	12
In spring	
1,000 loads of manure	100
Spreading the manure	5
Thinning the poppies	20
In summer	
Collecting the opium	150
Total	334

58. DCR 590, p. 19; DCR 2260 (Isfahan 1897-99), p. 17; DCR 3189, p. 46; DCR 3189, p. 21. "The Luristan opium being daimi (i.e., not watered) was said to be of better quality than the opium cultivated in the usual way. It is sown by the Kakavand and other Lekk tribes, whose territory borders on that of Kermanshah." DCR 3189, p. 23.

59. DCR 3189, pp. 21-25.

> 10 maunds of seeds are sown in 1,000 '*kards*' or rectangles measuring 3 by 2 *zars*.
>
> 30 maunds of raw opium fetch from 180 to 300 tomans, 6 to 10 tomans per maunds. The necessary funds for the cultivation of opium are generally supplied by the proprietor or lessee of the village, who receives two-thirds of the crop and pays the villager, apart from al expenses, 10 *krans* per maunds of opium per maund produced.
>
> The white variety of the poppy is the one that is grown. Seed is obtained from the previous crop and the ground is allowed no rest. Severe cold may damage or destroy the crop. The usual yield of 1,000 *kards* of land is 30 maunds, but the amount produced may reach 60 maunds.[60]

The labor after the harvest was hard as well. Peasants also extracted oil from the seeds, which was used for making soap and as cooking fat for the poor. The poppy plant's stalks were dried and used as a cooking fuel. The peasant also boiled the heads to make a soothing drink.[61]

Rice

There were also extensive rice fields in Kermanshah province, in particular at Zohab, Gilan (Kalhor), Dinavar and Hamadan valleys. Rice production was for local consumption only. One rice variety cultivated was known as *berenj-e rasmi*, and was of inferior quality. The effort to introduce *ambarbu* rice from Mazandaran by the governor of Kermanshah in 1853 apparently had come to nought. By 1900, rice was still nearly all consumed locally, but some of it was exported to Khanekin and Mendali.[62] In neighboring Kurdistan, rice was chiefly gown chiefly in Shahrezur. "The district of Sherour is one of the most fertile in Persia, and is particularly abundant in rice-grounds."[63]

Total crops was estimated at 16,000 *kharvar* from:

Khaleseh villages	4,000
Razian and Bilavar	2,000
Dinavar	2,000
Chamchama	12,000
Zohab and Kalhor	6,000
Total	16,000 *kharvar*

60. DCR 3189, pp. 21-22. See also the estimate by MacLean: "The cost of preparing 12½ Shah mans is about krs. 60, and the price of prepared opium in September 1903 was krs. 120 to 125 per Tabriz man." MacLean 1904, p. 26, and earlier by Rabino, the cost of preparing one case of opium of 140 lbs. f.o.b. including transport and duty is about 630 *qrans* per 10¾ *man-e shah* of 13 lbs. each = 139¾ lbs." DCR 3305, pp. 6-7.

61. Merritt-Hawkes 1935, pp. 151, 167.

62. Amanat 1983, p. 93 ("in the husk 13 to 14 Kerans- ordinary value, 20 to 23 Kerans per 100 mens = 650 lbs clean, rice 50 Kerans.); E`temad al-Saltaneh 1368, vol. 2, p. 1149; DCR 3043, p. 7 (the rate is 56-85 *qrans* per *kharvar*); DCR 3189, p. 33.

63. Morier 1818, p. 314; Rich 1836, vol. 1, pp. 114, 134; for other locations see Cherikof 1358, pp. 101, 135, 158-60.

In 1902, rice sold from 20 March to October at 5.5 to 7.5 *tumans* per *kharvar*; rice in 1903 was sold immediately after the harvest at 6.5 *tumans*. In winter the price rose to 7 *tumans* and in March it fell to 5 *tumans*. Cleaned rice cost 17.5 *tumans* per *kharvar*.[64]

Other Cereals

Lentils, millet, and Indian corn were cultivated in trifling quantities.[65]

Rubia Tinctorum or the madder plant (*runas*; its roots, *rodan*, *rodang*). This valuable dyestuff for the textile industry was very common in Iran. Olivier found it growing wild in Kermanshah, Hamadan and Tehran, and other travelers noted its wild state in Kerman, Khuzistan, and Khorasan. Around 1810, wild madder was brought to town by the nomads, whence, as was done later in the century, Hindu traders exported it to India.[66] In 1910, the British consul at Isfahan reported: "the average amount of madder handled in Isfahan during the last 5 years is about 47,000 shahmans, all consumed in Persia. Since 1906 no more export. About this 20% is used in Isfahan for dyeing; the remainder goes to Soltanabad, Hamadan, Kermanshah, Fars, Ardistan, etc. The average crop is 60,000 shahmans."[67]

Saffron

Already in the tenth century it was reported that Kermanshah produced much saffron.[68] In the 1740s, Otter reported that it was still cultivated in the province.[69] Although it is not known how much was produced its cultivation is still mentioned.

Sugar Beets

The cultivation of sugar beets was unknown in Kermanshah until it was decided to build a sugar mill at Shahabad that started operating in 1935. Each year the area under cultivation with beets was extended. The 1939 crops was below the average of the three preceding years because of agricultural pests. The 1940 harvest was expected to amount to 25,000 tons, yielding some 3,000 tons of sugar.[70]

Tobacco

In Kermanshah, "tobacco is cultivated in the Guran district, which is said to number 50 villages or settlements. Gahwareh is the chief village of the Guran district and the centre of the tobacco

---

64. DCR 3189, p. 34.
65. Amanat 1983, p. 93.
66. Amanat 1983, p. 106, 133; Polak 1862, p. 139; Olivier 1807, vol. 5, pp. 335-336; Morier 1818, p. 230; Gleadowe 1906, p. 86; Dupré 1819, vol. 1, p. 265.
67. DCR 4838, p. 23; DCR 5048, p. 23.
68. Schwarz 1993, vol. 4, pp. 481-82; Le Strange 1905, p. 186.
69. Otter 1748, vol. 1, p. 181.
70. FO 248/1414, Report on the Commercial and Economic Situation ... in the year 1319.

growing district. It is 11 *farsakh*s distant from the town of Kermanshah. The tobacco is brought to town in sacks by the villagers."[71] A large quantity of tobacco was also exported from Kermanshah to Tehran and the districts. "It is certain that a large quantity of tobacco is exported to Turkey, evading Persian and Turkish customs alike. This is done by the Jaffs and other tribes when migrating from their summer to their winter quarters. The customs authorities are well aware of the fact, but apart from the seizure of a few loads of tobacco they are unable to prevent this abuse."[72]

Tutun or *tutun-e chepoq* was the second and common variety of tobacco (*Nicotiana rustica*). It was used exclusively in the common pipe (*chepoq*), and later also as cigarette tobacco. It was also known as Turkish or Turkoman tobacco, and resembled Indian tobacco. It was in particular cultivated in Kurdistan and Kermanshah. A large quantity was also grown in Azerbaijan, around the lake of Urumiyeh, which, according to E'temad al-Saltaneh, produced the best *tutun* of Persia, and indeed, in the 1890s, obtained a price that was six times higher than that produced elsewhere in Iran.[73] In Kermanshah province a small quantity of tobacco of some 2,000 to 5,000 *kharvar*s of tobacco per year continued to be grown and sold, at prices ranging from 0.75 to 10 *qran*s per *man*, according to quality. Much of it was exported to Tehran and the districts.Packing cost 13.5 *qran*s per case of 25-30 man. An unknown quantity was smuggled into Ottoman lands by the Jafs and other tribes during their migration. The customs authorities on both sides of the border were aware of this but they were unable to do something about it.[74]

Therefore, Azerbaijan imported large quantities of *tutun*, locally known as *nokta*, from Turkey. The local produce was exported to Russia's Asian provinces. "The tobacco smoked is usually Samsoon, a common kind of coarse Turkish; or Koordi, a mild tobacco, nearly white in colour, but with a pungent flavour; there are many other varieties. This Koordi looks like coarse sawdust, and is quite dry, and is simply the leaf-stalk and stem of the plant coarsely pounded; to look at it, no one would suppose on a first inspection that was tobacco at all: the best comes from Kermanshah."[75]

Vegetables

Various vegetables were produced such as: potatoes, cabbage, beans, lettuce and peas.[76] Around 1850, about 1,000 *kharvar* of peas were produced every year in Kermanshah province; some 2,000 were exported to interior of Persia; prices were 12-15 *qrans* per *kharvar*. Pulses of several kinds and horse beans were produced all in trifling quantities.[77]

---

71. DCR 3189, p. 32; DCR 3043, pp. 3, 32.
72. DCR 3189, p. 32 (Kermanshah merchants are Dai-Golam, Hajji Ali Bazaz, Hajji Mirza Hussein, Seyyed Nasrullah and the Sharekat Amteeh Omoomi).
73. Perkins 1843, p. 429; Polak 1862, p. 143 (it was straw-yellow in color); *AP* 65 (1871), p. 240; Stolze & Andreas 1885, p. 13; Schlimmer 1970, p. 402 (*tutun-e Eslambuli*); Issawi 1971, p. 250; E`temad al-Saltaneh 1368, vol. 1, p. 50; Gleadowe-Newcomen 1906, p. 90.
74. MacLean 1904, p. 48; DCR 3189, p. 32.
75. Wills 1893, p. 33.
76. AIR 20/663, p. 26
77. Amanat 1983, p. 93.

Animal Husbandry

Because land, fodder and water were abundantly available horses, mules and donkeys and other animals were produced in large numbers. Each village had its own flock of sheep, while the tribes has large flocks, their main source of income. Mules and horses were bred in considerable quantities in the nineteenth century. Nomads kept a small number of horses, mainly to produce mules. Those who needed to buy horses had to go to the tribes, such as in Hamadan and Kermanshah province, as few were brought to the city and few were exported to Baghdad, due to the high Ottoman import duty.[78] The shah and the various prince-governors all kept large horse herds. In the days of Mohammad ʻAli Mirza, governor of Kermanshah, 500 brood mares were kept in Deira valley and the Kermanshah horses were renowned. In the late 1830s, scarcely a hundred remained and all were inferior animals.[79] The horses, which had much Arab blood in them and were well adapted for both draught and saddle, were highly esteemed.[80]

In the second half of the nineteenth century the quality of horse breeding fell. Horses were bred by the Sanjabis, Kalhors and Koliya'is, as well as in Kurdistan and in a few villages. The Kalhors did not have many for sale, because they had many horsemen; they sold a few to pilgrims. Sanjabi horses had much Arab blood, and though rather small were better than the other horses. They were said to have 1,000 horses and mares, producing 200 foals/year; they were good for draught and beast of burden. The Koliya'is had 500-600 horses, producing some 100 colts/year; their horses were said not to be very strong; occasionally they bought mares from the Jafs and Khezels for breeding. Some 50-100 Arab horses were brought by pilgrims every year from Baghdad. They obtained prices of 30 to 100 Turkish pounds and were seldom offered for sale.[81]

Trade in horses was only local and supply-demand was in equilibrium.[82] Colts with good blood fetched 20-30 *tumans*, when 1-2 years old; the Jaf ones were sold at 40-50 *tumans*. One or 2-year old *yabus* were sold at 15-16 *tumans*. An ordinary horse, 4-5 years old, sold at 30-40 *tumans* among the tribes. The best time to purchase was about one months after *Nowruz*; in winter horses and mules were expensive, because of the great demand for transport. Young horses for caravans were trained when 3-4 years old to carry loads; 500 *man* (150 kg) was the usual load for a developed horse, sometimes 70 *man* (210 kg) was carried. A horse lived 15 to 20 years.[83]

Kermanshah was well known for the great number and superior qualities of its mules."[84] Mules were in particular used as a pack animal throughout the southwestern and western parts of Iran, in particular in Fars, Behbahan, Isfahan, Khuzistan, Lorestan, Kurdistan, Kermanshah, Hamadan, Tehran, and Azerbaijan. In these parts of the country the mule and donkey prevailed, and in some areas the mule monopolized the transportation sector. Mules were bred by Sanjabis,

78. Polak 1865, vol. 2, p. 100; Amanat 1983, p. 94; Adamec 1976, vol. 1, p. 359; de Bode 1845, vol. 2, p. 91-92; see also vol. 1, pp. 337, 368, 394; DCR 3189, p. 35 (with details of the Sanjabi, Kalhor, and Koliya'i horses). DCR 590, p. 18.

79. Rawlinson 1839, p. 40.

80. Ferrier 1856, p. 26; Adamec 1976, vol. 1, p. 341.

81. DCR 3189 p. 34.

82. DCR 4365, p. 8.

83. DCR 3189 p. 35; Adamec 1976, vol. 1, p. 359.

84. Southgate 1840, vol. 1, p. 137; Amanat 1983, p. 94.

Koliya'is and Kalhors in Kurdistan and in Harasan and near Kermanshah; especially famous were those by the Kalhors and Sanjabis. The best, however, were from Posht-e Kuh. Some 2-3,000 mules were produced per year in the province; all mules were produced by mares. A 1-year old mule cost 30-50 *tumans*; a good 3-year old mule cost 70-80 *tumans*, but might also might be had at 55 *tumans*, but they were less developed. When 3-4 years old the mule was accustomed to carry loads of 35-40 *man*, and when 5 some 50-60 *man*. The usual load was 320-390 lbs. and this was carried for 20-30 miles day after day. The lifetime of mules was 20-30 years; shoeing was 3 *qrans*. A complete packsaddle for a mule was 14 *tumans*.[85]

As many as 400 baggage mules could formerly be hired at places like Kermanshah, Senneh, Bijar, Hamadan, Saqqez, Khorramabad, Borujerd, Kangavar, Dowlatabad, Soltanabad, Khvonsar, Isfahan and Shiraz. In Kermanshah also 500 *yabus* and mules could be easily purchased for transportation purposes.[86] The muleteers (*charvadars*) preferred to buy the hardy mules over 4-years old from Kermanshah at prices ranging from 50 to 100 *tumans*. Below that age mules could be bought in the villages.[87]

Likewise many donkeys were bred in the province.[88] Riding donkeys used by mullahs and merchants came from Helleh, Baghdad, Shiraz, Yazd, and Kerman were bought at 25-50 *tumans*. The ordinary small black or grey donkey was used by the villagers and tribesmen. It was the means of transport locally; they were bred in the province and cost 10-25 *tumans*. Each village had some 10-50 donkeys; shoeing was 1.5 *qrans*. The usual load was 216 lbs for a donkey.[89]

No camels were bred in Kermanshah province. Some 2,000 to 3,000 camels came each year from Isfahan, Qom, Yazd and Kashan and carried loads from Kermanshah to Tehran or Isfahan or returned without loads. Arab camel men from Baghdad took loads to Hamadan, and sometimes to Tehran. Usually they took no loads for the return journey except during the wool season; they also took grain to Turkey, but very rarely a few cases of gum.[90]

Table 5.2: Estimated transport availability at selected centers (1920)

Location	Mules	Camels	Donkeys	Horse carts
Qasr-e Shirin	100	-	100	-
Kerind	300	-	300	-
Kermanshah	2,000	-	10,000	-
Kangavar	N	I	L	-
Hamadan	4,000	2,000	1,000	1,000

Source: AIR 20/663, p. 75.

85. DCR 3189, p. 35; DCR 4365, p. 8; Administration Report 1908, p. 49 (Lt. Williams of the Indian Army bought 500 mules and went via Baghdad).
86. Adamec 1976, vol. 1, p. 248 (also prices, payload, and daily distance).
87. DCR 590, p. 18.
88. DCR 590, p. 18.
89. DCR 3189, pp. 35-36.
90. DCR 3189, pp. 35-36.

Some cows and oxen were bred in the province, but there were no surplus cows.[91] The peasantry of Kermanshah had to import them from Lorestan. The nomads also used cows and oxen to plow their fields and carry their tents and belongings, and seldom parted with them. Beef in Kermanshah was good; oxen that refused to carry the yoke were sold to slaughterhouse.[92]

Sheep were plentiful in the province and formed part of the nomads' wealth. Around 1840, Lorestan furnished the bazaars of Borujerd, Nehavand, Hamadan, and Kermanshah with mutton, cheese, and butter and with charcoal prepared in woody Lorestan and transported by their oxen and donkeys.[93] The remainder of the year mutton came from Kermanshah, Malayer, and Kurdistan (Ardalan). The latter animals were very lean and therefore need fattening, but they were preferred to those of the Bakhtiyaris and Qashqa'is because they were hardier. Even the Tehran bazaars were stocked with Kurdistan mutton, for these sheep were larger than the ordinary species and fetched a higher price.[94] In the 1840s, the Kurds took 70,000 sheep/year to Tehran; many also were exported to Turkey. In fact, in the mid-1840s it was expected that they would send all their herds to Turkey in future, because of the governor's oppression.[95] The tribal and rural population of Kermanshah continued to supply sheep and goats to cities as far as Tehran and Baghdad, where entire flocks were driven, about 25,000 per year. By 1902, there was a preference to sell all their sheep to Ottoman lands.[96]

Herds of goats were kept in the mountainous districts; goat hair was used to make tents. Goat skins were either dried for export to Baghdad and Marseilles, made into coverings for ghi or *rowghan*, or turned into water skins or *mashq*s, of which every nomad family had two or three of them.[97]

91. DCR 590, p. 18.
92. DCR 3189 p. 36.
93. De Bode 1845, vol. 2, pp. 292-293.
94. De Bode 1845, vol. 2, pp. 90-91.
95. Ferrier 1856, p. 26.
96. DCR 590, p. 18 (guts).
97. DCR 3189 p. 36.

CHAPTER SIX

TRADE

THE DEVELOPMENT OF TRADE OF KERMANSHAH

INTRODUCTION

The annual turnover of trade in Kermanshah was influenced by a number of factors. The most important factor that affected trade was the weather. As 80% of Kermanshah province's population earned their livelihood in agriculture, their incomes rose and fell in harmony with the harvest. This was the case in 1905, when trade with Baghdad fell due to the increase of the cost of living caused by three years of partial famine in Kermanshah as well as scarcity and higher cost of animals.[1] After such a stretch of bad harvests, peasants used their hard cash to repair water channels and replace oxen rather than buy foreign manufactured goods.[2] When in 1906 there were good spring rains, the British consul reported that these were indicators of "prospects for a good harvest, which would increase imports."[3] This not only held for the province itself, but also for the markets that it served. Because poverty in its hinterland, for whatever reason, was not good for trade either as people would not be able to buy imported goods.

But it was not only the weather that determined a peasant's income, but also protection from oppression by governors, officials, landlords and brigands. For example, the population of Kermanshah at various period fell significantly due to tyrannical behavior of governors. Less population meant less production, meant less purchasing power, meant less demand for and production of goods, which resulted in less trade. In 1912, the occupation of town and province by rebels was bad for trade, because they forced merchants and people to make 'loans,' which impoverished them, which depressed trade.[4] Similarly, security on the roads and a positive

1. DCR 3683 (Kermanshah 1905-06), p. 3.
2. Lingeman 1928, p. 17.
3. DCR 3683 (Kermanshah 1905-06), p. 5.
4. DCR 5204 (Kermanshah 1912-13), p. 3; DCR 4994 (Kermanshah 1911-12), p. 5.

business climate, when it existed, had an upward effect on trade, or a downward one if it did not. In 1902, the roads were safe during the rule of governor Ala al-Dowleh, whose firm rule was good for trade.[5] In 1903/04, trade was negatively impacted when there was some panic due to the abnormal number of bankruptcies in August-September; but thereafter the market recovered.[6] Trade usually also decreased when conditions in the country were unsettled and disturbed, as was the case after 1907.[7] Further, the cost and availability of labor and transport affected the cost and the rapidity by which the market might be served. In 1905, transport more expensive, especially from Baghdad as Ottomans commandeered all pack animals for military operations.[8] In 1908, trade increased, despite the disturbed state of the country, but this was partly due to safety on the road and because there were no delays in river boat transport between Basra and Baghdad, whence Kermanshah received and sent much of it trade.[9] Trade was also trade affected by the fall of the value of the *qran*.[10] The consul in Kermanshah reported that in 1902-03 trade was prosperous, despite the fall of the *qran*, which nevertheless reduced the profit margin of importers.[11] Sometimes, some of the above factors coincided negatively impacting trade. For example, in 1911, the interruption of the telegraph was a drawback for importers, because the price of imports depended on value of the British pound in local currency. Moreover, at that time the road was unsafe and therefore, goods accumulated at Kermanshah. As a result, during the first three months of 1912 there was almost a stoppage of imports. Goods after leaving Baghdad were left at caravanserais, especially at Khaneqin at the Ottoman border.[12] During WW I, obviously there was no trade with Baghdad. However, as of 1918 there were no restriction on trade, which quickly rose to such a level that by 1921 Kermanshah was Persia's most important customs revenue earner. However, by 1925 the commercial position of Kermanshah was under serious pressure due to government policy favoring southern ports and discouraging transit trade via Iraq. The drop in commercial activity was partly cushioned by increased smuggling, but this could not restore Kermanshah's role as one of Persia's major import markets. Finally, market behavior and developments such as competing products and prices as well competing routes, about which more later, all influenced the volume of trade. What did not change was that the province exported more than it in imported.[13]

5. DCR 3043 (Kermanshah 1902-03), p. 8.
6. DCR 3189 (Kermanshah 1903-04), p. 18.
7. DCR 4100 (Kermanshah 1907-08), p. 3; DCR 4559 (Kermanshah 1909-10), p. 5
8. Administration Report 1905-06, p. 47; DCR 3683 (Kermanshah 1905-06), p. 3.
9. DCR 4365 (Kermanshah 1908-09), p. 6.
10. Administration Report 1905-06, p. 47
11. DCR 3043 (Kermanshah 1902-03), p. 2.
12. DCR 4994 (Kermanshah 1911-12), p. 5
13. Küss 1911, part III, p. 27.

ROUTES AND TRANSPORTATION COST

The commercial importance of Kermanshah gradually increased after the opening of the Suez Canal and this was related to the fact that it was the frontier town on the trade route between Baghdad and Persia. Therefore, to understand the commercial role of Kermanshah it is necessary to realize that in the nineteenth and early twentieth century trade could reach the Persian consumer via various routes, some of which were competing to supply the same markets. The most important routes were:

1. Via Trabson to Tabriz;
2. Via the Caucasus from Poti to Tabriz;
3. From the Volga across the Caspian to Resht or Astarabad;
4. From Karachi via Qandahar to Farrah, Herat and Mashhad or Qa'en-Nishapur;
5. From Bandar Abbas via Kerman and Yazd;
6. From Bushehr via Shiraz to Yazd and Isfahan;
7. From some other Persian Gulf port other than Bushehr and Bandar Abbas;
8. From Basra at the head of the Persian Gulf to Baghdad and then to Persia via Kermanshah or Shustar.

All these routes were actually used and there were ups and downs in the volume of trade transported via each of these routes during the period mentioned. Some of these routes were in competition with each other, such as nos. 1 and 2 as well as nos. 5 and 6 both with no. 8 (see below), and between most of them with the new ports and new roads that were developed in the 1920s (see below). Some routes were as yet only routes of local importance. Using route no. 7 would require developing new infrastructure, along a more arduous, less safe and not shorter road. The same held for the Shustar route. Sometimes, these various routes were not in strong competition with each other, as each had a comparative advantage as to their hinterland. Route no. 8 required sailing to Basra, then clearing Turkish customs and changing to river craft, then breaking up bulk and then to cross an unsafe animal tract between Baghdad and Kermanshah, where Persian duties would have to be paid. Therefore, for most of the nineteenth century, this route was only used for consumption along the Tigris, in Kermanshah and Hamadan.[14] As a consequence, until 1920, Kermanshah hardly was in competition with the Persian Gulf ports as a port of entry, because it supplied a totally different hinterland. It was only in Tehran that the Baghdad route clashed with the Bushehr and Shiraz track, "and there Bushire has matters practically its own way as far as ordinary goods are concerned. When it comes to pianos or other heavy articles, then the shorter land journey from Baghdad is preferred."[15] What made Kermanshah attractive as a point of transshipment was its strategic position, situated as it is between 400 km-500 km equidistant from Baghdad, Tehran Isfahan, Rasht and Tabriz to which direct routes existed.[16]

---

14. Pelly 1865, p. 59.
15. Whigham 1903, p. 275.
16. Curzon 1892, vol. 1, p. 558; DCR 590, p. 23; Adamec 1976, vol. 1, p. 365.

In the first half of the nineteenth century, Kermanshah was partly supplied from Dezful with indigo, cottons and dates, requiring to travel for six days over a bad road, passing over mountains and having to cross two unfordable rivers, while there were no towns or villages en route during 6 days of travel.[17] However, towards the end of the nineteenth century, goods from Dezful had to go via Baghdad and Kermanshah, such as in 1908, due to tribal feuds, "while 60 years ago it went regularly to Hamadan and C. Persia."[18] Kermanshah also was supplied from Tabriz for a few decades, but this changed after 1870 (see below). This was not known to many, including Whigham, who wrote: "South of Hamadan, Tabriz has no influence whatsoever, though in the 'Gazetteer of Persia,' published several years ago by the Indian Government, and not brought up to date, the amazing statement is made that Kermanshah is supplied with foreign goods from Tabriz."[19]

The commercial route from Baghdad to Tehran went via Kermanshah. Goods were transport by boat from Mohammerah to Baghdad, and from there by caravan to Tehran. In 1907, the length of the journey and its cost were estimated by the US consul in Tabriz as follows: Mohammareh-Basra 2-6 hours; Basra-Baghdad 5 days going, 3.5 days returning; due to traffic congestion 14 days/average; Baghdad- Qasr-e Shirin 6 days; Qasr-e Shirin-Kermanshah 7 days; Kermanshah-Tehran 20-25 days. The cost of the river journey were $6 per 1,000 lbs or 40 cubic feet and by land $7-13 per 520 lbs to Kermanshah. From Kermanshah to Tehran $10-13 per 520 lbs were charged. Total travel time came to two months and the total charges $40-50 per 640 lbs.[20] This, of course, was an average of travel time and cost, if there were no problems. In reality, each leg of the route had its problems.

BASRA-BAGHDAD LEG OF THE ROUTE

Most of Kermanshah's trade came via the Persian Gulf, where a variety of steamship companies called on Basra. Here goods for Persia were transshipped. Prior to 1841 river sailing boats (*serafina*) were used on both the Tigris and Euphrates. As of the 1860s, river steamers were mainly used, which made the journey shorter in time, to wit: 52-60 hours by steamer compared to 40-60 days. By 1900, all cargo for Persia was transshipped in Basra to Baghdad without Customs inspection. There were two Companies that provided steamer service. In 1895, six steamers were used. Two (*Mejdiyeh* and *Khalifa*) were operated by Stephen Lynch & Co., a British company established in 1861. The other four steamers belonged to the Ottoman government, which had appointed an official based in Basra to manage the Company. In 1879, the Lynch. Comp. had been transformed into the Euphrates and Tigris Steam Navigation Company (ETSNC), which employed one additional steamer, which was kept in reserve. The *Mejdiyeh* was 216 feet long 36 wide and drew 5 feet of water and carried 400 tons weight with 120 hp

---

17. Kinneir 1973, p. 459; Southgate 1840, vol. 1, p. 137; Blau 1858, p. 45.
18. Wilson 1941, p. 72.
19. Whigham 1903, p. 276.
20. Doty 1908, p. 630.

Fig. 6.1: River steamboat between Basra and Baghdad (1894).

engine. The *Khalifa* was like the *Mejdiyeh* only four feet less wide and carried 50 passengers less. The Turkish steamers were smaller and in poorer condition, so that seldom more than two steamers out of four were at work. Freight from Basra to Baghdad was higher than the cost of transportation from Basra to London. Until August 1899, only Turkish steamers were allowed to use tow barges, but the British ones made more profit, because they sailed regularly; the Turkish service was slow. In 1907, the Turkish steamers left three times per week, while the ETSNC left six times per week. The distance between Basra and Baghdad was 800 km, which the steamers did in three days. From Baghdad to Basra it took them four days. During low water (September-November) travel time doubled. The ETSNC through rates in 1900 from Basra to Baghdad were: 35*s.* per 1,000 kg for loaf sugar and 37*s.* per ton for all other cargo. Bombay cargo was ton weight, others according to tonnage scale; local cargo was by weight. According to MacLean, the Turkish steamers were less careful in handling goods, less speedy in handling claims, but charged 4*s.* to 6*s.* less. The freight for the return journey from Baghdad to Basra varied from 7*s.* 6*d.* to 22*s.* per ton weight. December-April was the off-peak season and consequently rates were lower. If steamers didn't suffice, merchants still used small sailing vessels, (rates: 15*s*. to 20*s*. per ton), but no insurance was available for this kind of transportation and therefore, usually only for cereals and merchandise of little value, and in emergency, goods were shipped in that manner. Another draw back was that sail ships took an indefinite time to arrive.[21]

There was general complaint about lack of steamer capacity; goods were often blocked at Basra for 4-6 months.[22] However, carrying capacity on the river was limited. There were frequent delays between Basra and Baghdad towards the end of the summer, because of the shallowness of the river. For example, in 1901, the river was much lower than usual at this season and vessels drawing more than 3.5 feet of water could not pass. This resulted in an accumulation of goods, which added to the already congested situation at Basra. This congestion was great and sometimes added 6 months in waiting time, which was further increased by the complicated quarantine rules at Basra.[23] Rabino had a different take on the delays in 1901, admitting that the delay at Basra was annoying, but he submitted that it was not a great drawback, because even if the goods would come on time the merchants "would delay before ordering goods so as not to overflow the market of Kermanshah."[24] Once the goods reached Baghdad there were further delays because wharfage at Baghdad was cramped. At Baghdad, goods for Persia paid 8% *ad valorem* import duty, but were entitled to a refund of 7% on presentation of a countersigned transit pass within 6 months. "Those who have lodged security only had to pay 1% with a guarantee of 10 *para*s per packages for the 7%." Transit goods were warehoused at Baghdad free for 30 days. Importers sold their goods to native merchants trading with Persia, but many also traded directly with Manchester (see below).[25]

BAGHDAD-KERMANSHAH LEG OF THE ROUTE

In the tenth century CE, the Baghdad-Kermanshah-Hamadan road was known as the Khorasan road and in Achaemenid times as the Royal road, which attests to its importance for trade and traffic since ancient times.[26] From Baghdad to Kermanshah and beyond all transport was by pack animals. Mules carried goods throughout the year, while from May to November camels were also used. However, on the road between Baghdad and Qasr-e Shirin camels were used the whole year.[27] The reason why camels could only transport good beyond Qasr-e Shirin for six months was because "camels from Arabia cannot travel in winter on account of the mud and

21. Hurner 1896, pp. 643-45; MacLean 1904, p. 60; Issawi 1967, pp.146-53, 181; Doty 1908, p. 630 (in 1907 the cost of transportation by river was $6 per 1,000 lbs or 40 cubit feet, depending on the Company's preference, which took on average 5 days upriver and 3.5 days for the return trip).

22. MacLean 1904, p. 60.

23. Whigham 1903, pp. 307-08. In 1907, the British Company had 3,000 tons waiting, this stifling the development of trade. In March 1907, Messrs. Lynch received permission to use their third steamer. DCR 3865, pp. 8-9. According to Doty 1908, p. 630 due to congestion the average duration of the river trip between Basra and Baghdad was 14 days.

24. DCR 590, p. 21 note.

25. MacLean 1904, pp. 59-60 (with a listing of the rates).

26. Le Strange 1905, p. 228; Mustawfi 1919, pp. 161-62; Fragner 1972, pp. 11-14.

27. DCR 4365, p. 5; Hurner 1896, p. 645.

slippery ground."[28] Mules covered the distance between Baghdad and Kermanshah in 12-14 days, whereas camels needed 18-22 days.[29] The average mule load was 3-3.5 cwts., 325-390 lbs, 50-60 batman, or 120 okes. Roughly, seven mule loads equaled one ton. A camel carried 400 lbs. Goods had to be well packed in two strong well-insulated oblong boxes of not more than 120-150 lbs. each and measuring 30x24x24 inches in case of light goods and smaller in case of heavier goods. Two bales was also possible, in which case the weight could be 10% more.[30] By 1910 about one-third of all trade in Baghdad was with Persia.[31] Bigham related that his party had to stop frequently to shoot horses that had broken legs and had been left by their owners to die.[32]

From Baghdad to Kermanshah one either went via Khaneqin or via Mandali. By 1900, the latter route was not used, because it was unsafe. [33] On the Khaneqin route there was a wagon service for passengers until Shahrabad (58 miles). [34] The road from Baghdad to the Persian border, some 8 km past Khaneqin, was mostly over level desert. The road only started climbing after crossing the border, which was indicated by a small tower. The Ottoman customs administration and the Tobacco Regie built from Hurin to Sheikhan to Baghcheh, eight towers (*kishleh*) from which they controlled the border. Although the sites of the towers were arbitrarily chosen they were accepted as border markers.[35] "The bad part of the road, near the Tak-i-Girra Pass, cannot be much better than the Bushire-Kotals, especially in winter and spring, when snow and rain add to the horrible state of the stony portion of the track. Only the extent of the road is not so great."[36] In 1870, this road "had been made practicable for carriages," because Naser al-Din Shah and his suite traveled in carriages to Kerbela.[37]

Table 6.1: The halting stations and distances on the Baghdad-Tehran route

Name of station	Distance in *farsakh*	Approximate distance in miles
Baghdad (T)	-	-
Beni Saad/Orta Khan	-	15
Yakubieh or Bakuba (T)	-	14
Shahrabad	-	26
Kizil Robat (T)	-	18
Khanikin * (1,000 feet) (T)	-	17

28. DCR 590, p. 21 note.
29. Hurner 1896, p. 645; Doty 1908, p. 630 (Baghdad- Qasr-e Shirin 6 days and then another 7 days to Kermanshah at a cost of $7 to 13 per 520 lbs..
30. Hurner 1896, p. 645; DCR 4365, p. 6; DCR 4559, p. 6; DCR 4766, p. 7; DCR 5204, p. 5
31. Sauer 1914, p. 1107.
32. Bigham 1897, p. 185. The abandoning of wounded riding and pack animals by their owners was a common occurrence on the Persian roads.
33. MacLean 1904, pp. 59-60.
34. MacLean 1904, pp. 59-60; Issawi 1967, p. 181.
35. Adamec 1976, vol. 1, p. 356
36. Whigham 1903, p. 307; Curzon 1892, vol. 1, p. 51; Rolandshay 1904, p.110.
37. Floyer 1882, p. 440.

Name of station	Distance in *farsakh*	Approximate distance in miles
Kasr-i-Shirin (1,700 feet) (T)	5	18
Sar-e pul-e Zohab (T)	5	18
Kerind * (5,250 feet) (T)	8	29
Harunabad	6	20
Mahidasht	6	22
Kermanshah * (5,000 feet) (T)	4	14
Bisitun	6	21
Sahneh	4	16
Kangavar * (T)	5	18
Asadabad (T)	6	23
Hamadan * (T)	6	25
Milagird (T)	7	25
Zerreh	4	16
Nubaran * (T)	9	32
Shamiran	4	14
Khushkek	5	19
Khanabad * (T)	6	22
Robat Kerim	8	32
Tehran (3,800 feet) (T)	7	28
Total	112	412

Source: Curzon 1892, vol. 1, p. 51; see also DCR 590, p. 69; Issawi 1967, p. 181. Telegraph stations are marked (T).

In winter, caravans leaving Kermanshah took the road to Qom instead of going to Tehran, leaving the normal route at Kangavar and passing through Parispah (19 miles), Nanej (30 miles), Dizabad (25 miles), Saruk (19 miles), Siahwashan (27), Jairud (21), Salian (16) to Qom (21).[38] In 1932, the halting stations on the road from the border to Kermanshah were as follows:

Table 6.2: Halting stations between the border and Kermanshah, 1930

Halting station	Distance in kms	Observations
Khosrovi	0	
Qasr-e Shirin	24	Quarantine; garages; tea shops
Sarpol	53	Bas reliefs; summer retreat
Paytagh	68	Elevation 5,300 feet
Sorkheh Dizeh	80	Tea shops;
Kerend	104	PTT; tea shops; elevation 5,380 feet
Shahabad	139	PTT; tea shops; garages; rest houses; large village
Hasanabad	157	Tea shops
Mahidashti	177	Tea shops; garage; large village
Kermanshah	204	Elevation 4,860

38. Curzon 1892, vol. 1, p. 51.

Source: Ebtehaj 1932, pp. 146-47.

The road was in good shape throughout the year, but during winter it might be closed for a few days due to snow, such as at Pay Taq.[39]

TRANSPORTATION COST

Transportation rates varied per season and the price of grain; they were highest in winter and spring and lowest in the fall and summer, when camels competed.[40] Also, during periods of increased demand such as a heavy pilgrim season prices rose; in 1894, to 80-90 and even to 130 *qrans*. In that same year, if transport cost were paid in *qrans*, the calculation was 10 *paras* less than the official *qran* rate, i.e. 1.75 instead of 2 piasters.[41] Rates also varied per product; the rates for cotton goods were lower than for other products, the most expensive rate was for cassia (£9/0/9 per mule and £6/6/6 per camel).[42] In 1894, rates for mules were higher (3 to 4 *qrans*) than for camels, because they were faster. However, although camels were slower, on average they also carried at least 10% more load. This may explain why the rates for mules were usually always higher than for camels. In 1912, for example, the rate from Baghdad to Kermanshah per camel was 76.5-96 *qrans* per 487.5 lbs and per mule 93.5-119 *qrans*. Although rates were unusually high in that year, the higher rate for mules than for camels was not.[43] Transport rates were also affected by insecurity on the road, robberies, demand of illegal road taxes (*rahdari*) and military operations. In 1905, rates rose significantly, especially from Baghdad, when the Ottoman army commandeered all pack animals for military operations.[44] In 1911, rates between Kermanshah and Hamadan were abnormally high due to scarcity of animals (see Table 6.3).[45] Mules were available throughout the year and between 200 to 400 were always immediately available; with forewarning 500 to 1,000 could be obtained.[46] The fourgon (4-horse cart) was preferred by the British authorities, and increasingly also by many merchants. However, carts were useless for petrol and oil, for which camels and donkeys were the best means of transportation.[47]

Most goods to Kermanshah were for Hamadan and therefore, transport usually was contracted for Baghdad-Kermanshah or to Hamadan or even to Tehran. This gave the Baghdad-Kermanshah route an advantage over the Bushehr-Shiraz-Isfahan route, where animals

39. Ebtehaj 1932, p. 147.
40. MacLean 1904, pp. 59-60; DCR 4766, p. 6.
41. Hurner 1896, pp. 645; DCR 590, p. 24.
42. Issawi 1967, p. 182 (with other examples of different rates per product).
43. Hurner 1896, p. 645; Issawi 1967, p. 181 (in 1910, the rate for cottons per camel was £5/16/9 and for mules £7/5/10); DCR 5204, p. 4; DCR 5419, p. 5 (126-180 *qrans* per camel and 135-198 *qrans* per mule for a load of 487.5 lbs).
44. Administration Report 1905-06, p. 47; DCR 3683, p. 4; Wilson 1941, pp. 151, 259; DCR 4766, p. 7. In 1907, according to Doty 1908, p. 630 total time from Basra to Tehran required 2 months travel, with a total cost of $40 to $50 per 640 lbs.
45. DCR 4994, p. 6.
46. Adamec 1976, vol. 1, p. 365.
47. AIR 20/663, pp. 74, 140.

only could be hired for the stretches between the cities, thus causing delays at Shiraz and Isfahan.[48] However, in spring there also were delays of a few days on the Baghdad-Kermanshah route, when muleteers stopped to graze their animals by the road. Muleteers refused to stop this practice and even fines for delays that normally were effective were useless at that time of the year. During winter when the passes were snowed under there also would be delays.[49]

Table 6.3: Transportation cost from Kermanshah per mule/in *qrans* (1901-27)

To/Year	1901-02	1904-05	1908-09	1909-10	1911-12	1913-14	1926-27
Baghdad	27-28	15-40	25-35	20-40	25-40	100-140	120
Borujerd	-	-	20-50	-	-	-	
Hamadan	40	40-60	60-90	25-50	75-200	80-140	90
Isfahan	-	-	60-90	-	-	-	220
Khorasan	-	-	120-40	-	-	-	
Resht	120	-	60-70	-	-	-	
Senneh	18	-	20-30	15-30	-	-	120
Soltanabad	-	-	20-50	-	-	-	
Tabriz	-	-	90-140	-	-	-	260
Tehran	125	80-100	80-120	-	-	-	220

Source: DCR 590, p. 24; DCR 3043, p. 9, 18; DCR 3420, p. 6; DCR 3683, p. 4; DCR 3953, p. 3; DCR 4365, p. 6; DCR 4559, p. 7; DCR 4994, p. 6; DCR 5419, p. 5; Lingeman 1928, pp. 45-46

What is clear is that, in normal years, the rates from Kermanshah to the interior of Persia were higher than those of the returning mules. Also, the rate from Baghdad to Kermanshah was higher than for the return trip. This was due to the fact that imports into Kermanshah from Baghdad were many times higher than its exports. What is further striking is that rates from Baghdad to Kermanshah grew markedly from 1910 onwards, mainly due to the unsettled situation of the province. Moreover, rates from Kermanshah to Baghdad increased even faster after 1912 (see Table 6.3). In 1913, mules, carrying 320 lbs, took 12 days and camels, carrying 450 lbs, 20 to 25 days from Baghdad to Kermanshah. In July 1913, freight rates were 0.5 *mejdiyeh* per *man* of 6 *oke*s for mules, a somewhat higher for camels. This was considered to be unusually high.[50]

Table 6.4: Transportation cost to Kermanshah in *qrans*/per mule/per *kharvar* (1904-14)

From/Year	1904-05	1905/06	1906-07	1908-09	1909-10	1911-12	1913-14
Baghdad	60-120	80-85	72-99	80-90	60-100	70-120	100-140
Borujerd	-	-	-	15-30	-	-	-

48. MacLean 1904, pp. 59-60; DCR 4365, p. 6.
49. DCR 4994, p. 5; AIR 20/663, p. 75.
50. Sauer 1914, p. 1107.

From/Year	1904-05	1905/06	1906-07	1908-09	1909-10	1911-12	1913-14
Hamadan	20-30	-	-	15-20	8-15	14-20	40-60
Resht	-	-	-	70-80	-	-	-
Senneh	-	-	-	6-12	10-28	-	-
Soltanabad	-	-	-	20-40	-	-	-
Tehran	50-60	-	-	50-60	-	-	-

Source: DCR 3043, p. 9, 18; DCR 3420, p. 6; DCR 3683, p. 4; DCR 3953, p. 3; DCR 4365, p. 6; DCR 4559, p. 7; DCR 4994, p. 6; DCR 5419, p. 5

Curzon reported that in 1890, 20,000 to 25,000 laden mules annually left and entered Baghdad. In 1904, 17,000 camels, 59,000 mules and 15,000 donkeys came from Baghdad to Kermanshah.[51] The cost of transportation on this leg of the route was very high. In 1895, the American consul in Baghdad, Rudolph Hurner calculated that taking 60 *qrans* for transport on imports and 30 *qrans* for export that 100,000 Turkish *liras* or £90,000 or $444,000 were paid for transport to and from Kermanshah.[52]

In 1900, roughly transport from Baghdad-Teheran was £14/ton and £20 from Bushehr to Tehran, while the land journey was 320 km shorter. Despite this more European goods still came via Bushehr than via Kermanshah. There were two reasons for this: total transportation cost and transportation time. First, it cost as much to send goods from Basra to Baghdad (510 miles) as to send them from London to Basra. Rates from Basra to London in 1900 were £1/12/6 per ton, including transshipment charges at Basra (breaking of bulk plus 1% transit duty), but the river freight from Basra to Baghdad varied from 10/8 to £11/19/1 per ton. The rate from Basra to London was steadily £31/10 to £4 per ton, including freight from Basra to Baghdad.[53] Moreover, there was the higher duty at Kermanshah, because of extra transport cost, "which is taxed by the customs in addition to the cost value of the goods. So that actual charges per ton come to nearly, if not quite, as much as the freight from Bushire to Tehran."[54] Second, due to the delays on the Basra-Baghdad river route (see above) total time of transportation from London to Tehran via Baghdad was twice that of transportation via Bushehr. From Bushehr to Tehran transport of goods usually took 6 months, but Whigham saw two stoves in Tehran that took one year to come from Basra.[55] Therefore, he argued that efforts should be made to improve the Baghdad route to enable British businessmen to better compete with the fast penetration of Russian goods in N. and W. Persia. However, he noted that there was little interest to pressure the Ottoman government "to improve the Tigris river service which at present is a quite unnecessary obstacle in

51. Curzon 1892, vol. 2, p. 577; Administration Report 1905-06, p. 47
52. Hurner 1896, pp. 645; Curzon 1892, vol. 1, p. 578. (The Turkish *lira*—from *libra* or pound—was introduced in 1844. 1 Turkish lira = 34 *qrans* = 13.6 rupees or 18 *s*). The abbreviation *s*. (from *solidus*) denotes the shilling, a unit of currency, formerly used in the United Kingdom. Twenty shillings equal one pound, and 12 pennies (*d*.) equal one shilling. The abbreviation *d*. (from *denarius*) denotes the penny, a unit of currency, formerly used in the United Kingdom. Twelve pennies equal one shilling.
53. DCR 2712, p. 4; DCR 590, p. 23. According to Doty 1908, p. 630, under normal conditions the trip from Kermanshah to Tehran took 20 to 25 days at an average cost of $ 10 to $13 per 520 lbs.
54. Whigham 1903, pp. 307-08.
55. Whigham 1903, pp. 307-08.

Fig. 6.2: Tea-house at Pay Taq (1935)

the way of the development of the Bagdad route." Such a policy would also see to investment in the improvement of the Baghdad-Hamadan road rather than the one from Ahvaz to Isahan. This neglect he blamed on Curzon, who dismissed the importance of the Baghdad road and underestimated the volume of trade passing through it.[56] Given this situation of high cost and time of transportation it is clear that trade would benefit enormously if there would be a railway between the Persian Gulf and Khaneqin, a subject that became a much contested project within that of the Baghdad Railway project.[57]

SECURITY ON THE ROAD

An important factor that influenced the cost and flow of trade was security. In Persia, security on the road was farmed out, for certain identified distinct stretches of the road in each tribal area to local chiefs, who were allowed to collect a road tax (*rahdari*). In return these chiefs were supposed to guarantee the safety or travelers and trade caravans. In case a robbery happened, the local governor had to compensate the victims. When there was a strong government the system worked reasonably well, but when there was a weak governor, or when the central government in general was weak and even powerless, as was the case after 1907, it did not.

56. Whigham 1903, pp. 277-78.
57. DCR 2712, p. 4; DCR 590, p. 23; Issawi 1971, pp. 191-93.

Throughout the nineteenth century, there were no major road security issues in Kermanshah province. This did not mean that there were no cases of attacks and robberies, but these were no major or chronic problem. This would change after 1907, and even more so, during and after the two rebellions by Salar al-Dowleh (1907 and 1911-12), which affected Kermanshah province. Moreover, because of the Customs agreement of 1903, all inland imposts on trade, including *rahdari*, had been abolished. This posed a dilemma, either the government paid the road guards or *qarasuran* or they were going to continue to levy *rahdari*, or would even start extorting payments, and worse, started robbing passenger and commercial traffic. For example, in April 1909, Fath 'Ali Khan, the Afshar chief of the road guards at 'Abbasabad said that his men only received grain for their horses and some flour for themselves and 4 *qran*s monthly, therefore, it was only natural that they asked some extra toll to add to their income. Even some robber chiefs themselves complained about the lack of safety and the government. The road between Hamadan and Kermanshah was held up by Lors between Bisotun and Kangavar.[58] In September 1909, Fath al-Eyalah, chief of the *qarasuran* exacted money from the muleteers on all transport; despite orders from the governor to pay back the money he refused as he claimed the right to charge a fee on all wool.[59] In November 1912, after the Ilkhani's *qarasuran* exacted heavy sums on the Bisotun road, the director of Customs refused to pay his and their wages. The *Ilkhani* countered by saying he would not allow government grain to enter Kermanshah until he was paid.[60]

In November 1912, some 800 pilgrims returning from Kerbela were attacked by the Qalkhani Guran under Qambar Soltan at the Pay Taq pass and stripped of everything. Five of them were killed and 20 wounded. Farmanfarma asked the inhabitants of Kermanshah for a contribution to enable the pilgrims to return home. The Qalkhani band also robbed several caravans. Because of this some 1,000 pilgrims going to Kerbela asked Farmanfarma what they should do. He advised them to go the Kerend, engage guards there to escort them to the border. He ordered 50 Cossacks and 50 tribal levies to accompany the pilgrims to Kerend and arranged with Ehtesham al-Mamalek Kerendi, the governor of Kerend, to send 300 of his men to Qasr-e Shirin every week to enable pilgrims to pass unmolested. The roads to and near Hamadan were also unsafe in November 1912.[61] Despite these steps, in late November 1912, the road to Qasr-e Shirin was still unsafe; and there were raids near the gates of Khaneqin.[62] Nevertheless, Farmanfarma gave assurances to the merchants that the road to the border was safe.[63] On 30 November 1912 a large pilgrim caravan was attacked by the Qalkhani at Khosrowabad, in the Kerend district. On 3 December 1912, small groups of pilgrims were robbed at the Pay Taq pass and another on 9 December again at Khosrowabad.[64] According to consul McDouall,

58. Political Diaries, vol. 3, p. 651.
59. Political Diaries, vol. 3, p. 734.
60. Political Diaries vol. 4, p. 629.
61. Political Diaries vol. 4, p. 630
62. Political Diaries vol. 4, p. 646.
63. Political Diaries vol. 4, p. 646.
64. Political Diaries vol. 5, p. 13

> Exactions on the road from the frontier to Kermanshah, and from the latter place to Hamadan, are very heavy, and there is no safety on the road. I have reason to believe that the transporters would gladly pay a smaller fee and for all if no further exactions were made. During the last year it is estimated that the road guards have collected between 150,000 tomans (30,000£) and 200,000 tomans (40,000£) between the frontier and Kermanshah alone. One British subject, owning ninety-one camels on each trip, paid 15 krans (7*s.*) on all on each camel, divided between twenty different posts.
> Rahdari is abolished, but it seems impossible to prevent the collection of fees called karasurani or "salamat-rao" from the muleteers. and this may not be covered by the abolition of rahdari.[65]

McDouall estimated that an amount of 80,000 *tuman*s would be sufficient to establish an effective road guard system, which could be financed by charging 7 *qran*s from the border to Hamadan and 3 *qran*s from Hamadan to the border. He based his calculation on the most recent commercial data, which suggested that annually some 100,000 pack animals were involved in the trade to and from border-Kermanshah-Hamadan and vice-versa.[66]

In December 1912, some *mojtahed*s and *rowzehkhvan*s denounced the cruelties of the roads guards as being worse than the massacre at Kerbela. Farmanfarma begged them to stop exciting people against him, as it was Moharram, and to give him time to take care of the problem. The roads were indeed very unsafe and little merchandise was transported. For the last 6 months there had been no parcel post, although the normal post still came twice per week. On 19 December a caravan arrived form Hamadan, but since the road was not safe it remained at Kermanshah. Goods were also accumulating at Qasr-e Shirin. A pilgrim caravan was escorted to Kerend but after that town, when the guards had left, they were robbed. The mail from Baghdad did not come, because the Turkish postmaster at Khaneqin refused to hand them over. On 22 December 1912 news arrived that at Walashgerd, beyond Kangavar 40 loads had been robbed. Farmanfarma ordered Ehtesham al-Dowleh, governor of Nehavand to control that road and Agha Rabi'eh to assist him.[67] To address the road safety crisis, Farmanfarma told the road commission (composed of himself, the director of customs and revenues and his assistant, the *kargozar*, and several others) that only the appointment of the Kakawands as road guards would make the road to Kangavar safe, because they were the most notorious robbers on that road. Their contract stipulated that they would receive a fixed sum of money, no illegal fees to be collected, and if they did it would be deducted. The commission signed the contract and sent it to the chief of Kakawands for his approval, in which case the Hajjizadehs would be replaced.[68]

---

65. IOR/L/PS/20/261/7, Persia. No 1 (1913). Further correspondence respecting the affairs of Persia, p. 283, no. 521, McDouall to Townley 05/12/1912.
66. IOR/L/PS/20/261/7, Persia. No 1 (1913). Further correspondence respecting the affairs of Persia, p. 283, no. 521, McDouall to Townley 05/12/1912.
67. Political Diaries vol. 5, p. 13.
68. Political Diaries vol. 5, p. 13. The functioning of the Commission of Roads, Telegraphs and Postal Service had been a problem from the beginning. It was only since January 1913 that the Director of Customs regularly attended its meetings. In that month he received orders to pay out of his receipts the military and administrative expenses and check the number of men paid. Political Diaries vol. 5, p. 38.

As a result, the Kangavar road was safe as the Kakawands only asked an official fee of one *qran* per animal at the bridge at 1.5 km from Kermanshah. The road to Baghdad was safe, but merchants had to pay heavily for that.[69] In early January 1913, Ebrahim Khan, brother of Baqer Khan, the chief of the Kakawands, came to see Farmanfarma and offered women and children as hostages for the tribe's good behavior on condition that the tribe be placed under Kermanshah. Farmanfarma replied that Sardar Akram had arranged for them to police that road and given his relationship with the Sardar he could not remove them from his jurisdiction. The safety on the road to Baghdad remained problematic. The road-guards exacted up to 35 *qran*s/mule and stole small packages. Therefore, merchants were afraid to use that road, because given these high cost importers hardly could make a profit.[70]

In March 1913, the leading camel owners asked the director of Customs at Qasr-e Shirin what the arrangements were for the safety of the road for the coming season, as they had been asked to send their camels to Mohammerah, and before deciding they wanted to know the state of the road. He was unable to give them reassurances as he had to wait for a reply from Kermanshah. The Customs department was trying to arrange for the use of the Gilan road, via a detour, passing three Sanjabi posts, and thereafter through Kalhor country to Kermanshah. In that case muleteers only had to pay 6 *qran*s between Qasr-e Shirin and Kermanshah as compared to 25 *qran*s on the normal road. However, the problem was that in summer the Gilan road lacked water and supplies, because the Kalhors had left for their summer quarters. The Customs department was also looking into another route via Badkuba, two stages from Baghdad to Mandali and Saomar and then via the Eyvan valley to Mahidasht through Kalhor country. This was once a main road but had fallen into disuse. It was used by Nader Shah to invade Iraq and he made it passable for cannons. On the Gilan road the Sanjabis collected one *qran* at five places in the 12 km of their territory and the Kalhor one *qran* at five places in 130 km, "or ten Krans per animal in all against twenty-five on usual route." Pilgrims stated that the Kalhors treated them well although they had to sleep in the open air for two nights.[71]

In that same month, Farmanfarma did nothing about the claim of robberies on the Baghdad road and it was unlikely that he would do so. In the commission he said that it was difficult to pay the road-guards as this would cost at least 1,000 *tuman*s/month. It was better to pay the consulate 100 *tuman*s taken from the Russian pilgrims; he did not mention the British claims. Heavy exactions by road-guards continued to be levied, while freight from Baghdad cost 32 *tumans* per 75 *man*.[72] Although the regular roads were safe in April 1913, few caravans passed. From Qasr-e Shirin there were great delays in transporting goods, because freight from there

---

69. Political Diaries vol. 5, pp. 13-14. FO 248/1073, Kermanshah Diary no. 1, ending 2 January 1913; Idem, Kermanshah Diary no. 3, ending 16 January 1913 and no. 4 ending 23 January 1913.

70. Political Diaries vol. 5, p. 38. As other tribes guilty of robbery had been pardoned, in March 1913 the Balawands offered 50 sowars and hostages if they also were pardoned. However, Farmanfarma replied that they had to pay. Political Diaries vol. 5, p. 69. Farmanfarma's insistence on payment may have been due to the fact that, on 22 November 1912, the Balawands had raided villages at 6 km from the city and had killed two men. Political Diaries vol. 4, p. 646. For Farmanfarma's justification not taking action against the tribes and put a stop to the exactions, see FO 248, 371, McDouall to Townley, 22/02/1913.

71. Political Diaries vol. 5, pp. 69-70; FO 248/1073, Kermanshah Diary no. 9, ending 27 February 1913.

72. Political Diaries vol. 5, p. 70.

was 18 *tumans* per load. In March 1913, due to short supplies shopkeepers bought cotton and Russian sugar from Hamadan and Tabriz, which had never been seen before in Kermanshah.[73]

In April 1913, the roads were safe, although the Kalhors began levying fees like the other tribes.[74] The Baghdad road was reasonably safe, although there were some robberies. Soleyman Khan, the Kalhor chief, sold the guarding of the road at Zaweym between Mahidasht and Harunabad to two of his subordinate chiefs for 1,500 *tumans*/year. 'Ali Khan *qarasuran-bashi* had the road to east of the Mahidasht bridge and 'Abdollah Khan *farrash-bashi* to the east, but they operated as partners. One muleteer claimed that he had to pay 60 *tumans* in all; Farmanfarma sent for 'Ali Khan and cursed him; he reimbursed 30 *tumans*, but the muleteer did not get anything. At the end of May 1913, caravans from Baghdad paid 25-30 *qrans* per animal, which was collected by force. The cameleers told the Turkish consul that if this practice continued they would not go beyond Qasr-e Shirin in the future. On 20 May the commission gave the road-guard a fixed rate of pay and banned the levying of fees. However, since the chiefs had farmed out the collection of fees it had only some effect.[75] In June 1913, the roads were safe, and although exactions were much less, the cameleers complained about them to the Turkish consul.[76] In July 1913, the roads continued to be safe, but almost all caravans from Baghdad took the Kalhor route. Fees were still levied at many places. One merchant said the charge was three *tumans* per camel from the border to Kermanshah and the same on the return, when most animals had no load. The normal freight was 75 *qrans* per 75 *man*, but to cover road fees it had risen to 125 *qrans*. About 1,000 camels without a load were stopped because Soleyman Khan demanded 12 *qrans* per camel. The Qalkhani Guran chief offered to let them pass for less at the Pay Taq pas. The British consul suggested that it was likely that Farmanfarma and the Turkish consul received a percentage from that fee.[77]

Although the Baghdad road remained safe and the post was regular in August-November 1913, freight on the Baghdad-Kermanshah route rose to 18 *tumans* per 75 *man*. Cameleers complained about heavy exactions, especially by Kalhors and said they would not return. There were also some robberies. In October 1913, from the border to Kermanshah, the Kalhors and Sanjabis collected four *tumans* per camel and the same fee for unloaded camels on return. The camel men charged this fee this on top of their freight rate.[78] Farmanfarma told McDouall only a military expedition could stop the exactions to which end he intended to march with a force of 1,5000 Gurans to the border area. However, he wanted to have 200 Cossacks with cannons from Hamadan and further suggested the McDouall arrange for additional support of 100 gendarmes. According to Mr. Authelet, the Belgian Customs officer at Qasr-e Shirin the tribes were afraid of Farmanfarma, who, if he wished, could put an immediate stop to the exactions.

---

73. Political Diaries vol. 5, pp. 70, 103.

74. Political Diaries vol. 5, p. 132.

75. Political Diaries vol. 5, p. 168.

76. Political Diaries vol. 5, p. 201.

77. Political Diaries vol. 5, p. 232. In July 1913, 70 donkeys belonging to a caravan were grazing 3 km outside the city and were stolen by Lors, some of whom were refugees, some were robbers. The *ra'is-e nazmiyeh* and his police went in pursuit, but failed to get them. Farmanfarma sent Mashhadi Hasan to Khalawand to try to recover them. Political Diaries vol. 5, p. 231.

78. Political Diaries vol. 5, pp. 269, 301, 329, 365.

Therefore, McDouall believed that Farmanfarma's proposed expedition only served to line his pockets and punish the Sanjabis, whom he hated, because they were friends of the Bakhtiyaris. However, if Farmanfarma would be recalled then only with the help of the Sanjabis his successor would be able to deal with the tribes. For that reason Tehran gave no permission for the expedition.[79] In December 1913, Khabir al-Sanaya, the Telegraph Superintendent, who was remaking the line to Qasr-e Shirin told Farmanfama that the road-guards made him pay 16 *tumans* and the Qalkhanis demanded five *qrans* per pole for permission to erect them in their district. From Kermanshah, the work had reached Kerend, although some new poles had already been stolen. At the end of December 1913 the roads were safe, but exactions on the Baghdad road were worse than ever, due to an increase of freight as a result of Russian goods penetrating to Qasr-e Shirin. In January 1914, less or no fees were collected from pilgrims, except by the Qalkhanis.[80] In February 1914, the roads were safe and no fees were extracted. Samsam al-Mamalek Sanjabi wrote from Qasr-e Shirin that at Farmanfarma's order the collection of road fees was stopped, but that his guards did not receive any pay from the government as others did. As usual this caused problems. At two places muleteers were forced to buy barley at exorbitant prices, while the telegraph was only working as far as Sar-e Pol Zohab. On 14 February 1914 some pilgrims complained that Qalkhanis robbed them at the Pay Taq pass. In April 1914, the roads were safe and Tehran sent orders to pay the road-guards. Farmanfarma issued a circular note praising the Revenue administration and asked all to support it.[81]

Of course, during the war years the roads to Iraq were closed to normal traffic. In 1917 tribal guards, the so-called *qarasuran*, at instigation of the British consul were used to guard the trade road in their tribal area to support the Russians in maintaining security and communications. However, this objective lasted only until October 1917, when the Russians withdrew their troops. But as soon as trade between Kermanshah and Baghdad picked up the need for road protection was felt again.[82] The governor ordered Mo'tazed al-Molk to reestablish the system of road guards between Kermanshah and Qasr-e Shirin on the scale fixed by Farmanfarma. He was not totally successful as chiefs of the Kalhors, Gurans, Kerends and Bajlans did not agree to the rates, which were fixed when grain was cheap. The matter was referred to Tehran.[83] To add insult to injury Mo'tazed al-Molk's caravan was attacked, an attack instigated by Gholam 'Ali Khan, Salar Mansur, the nominal chief of the Gurans. Mo'tazed al-Molk contacted Rashid al-Saltaneh who was more powerful. He returned everything and promised to keep Gholam 'Ali Khan in check. The governor then sent Sheikh Hoseyn, another agent, to arrange for the road guards. He paid some little money, but the pay was not enough given the famine rates, and therefore, Kennion concluded that given the importance of the road to the British military, the consulate had to provide additional payment. He commented that "On one hand it is undesirable that we take road guards in hand. The Russians tried it and failed because of Democratic agitation against the *Polis-e Gharb*, which was portrayed as another SPR under foreign control in this area." He

79. FO 248/1073, McDouall to Townley, 30/12/1913.
80. Political Diaries vol. 5, p. 398.
81. Political Diaries vol. 5, pp. 421, 449, 482, 493.
82. AIR 20/663, p. 9.
83. FO 248/1204 Kermanshah report 17/02/1918 by Lt. Col. Kennion.

also realized that British involvement required the support from the Persian government otherwise the nationalists would agitate against it. "On the other hands the pay does not reach the guards. Either the chiefs' agent in Kermanshah or the chiefs themselves misappropriate the money and the guards revert to age-old practice by blackmailing caravans or brigandage." The governor had no control over the tribes, because he had no armed force.[84]

Apart from financial problems there also was the problem that the tribal chiefs often were unable to control certain sections of their tribe, such as in June 1918, when the Kalhor chiefs were unable to exercise authority, in particular over the Kargah section.[85] Between Qasr-e Shirin and Kermanshah there were no major problems on the road, at that time, although there were several thefts of animals. At the urgent request of the Kalhor chiefs Kennion initiated a paid road guard system on a trial basis. In return they promised in writing to pay the guards and recompense any loss due to robbery, security of telegraph, etc. The reason was that as in the pre-war years the road guards between Kermanshah and Kangavar had not been paid for a few months by the Revenue Department. Therefore, Kennion went ahead with the trial payment in view of the importance of a safe road, because due to the non-payment of the road guards thefts on the road were on the increase.[86]

In the months thereafter the situation improved, because the road guards demanded less blackmail than usual, as many tribesmen were used in the British-paid roadwork from the Kulbanan pass to Mahidasht, in which activity the Kalhor tribesmen were making much money.[87] Likewise, the Gurans refrained mostly from raiding, which had been their favorite activity before 1914. The British paid subsidies to Qanbar Soltan, Salar Mansur and Rashid al-Saltaneh. These subsidies lasted until the end of February 1920. After that date the Persian government was supposed to control road with gendarmes or pay the road guards. Neither happened due to lack of money in the revenue office of Kermanshah. The British proposed Tehran to double the size of the gendarmerie from 600 to 1,200 men to have both a strike force and have enough men to police the road. The British consul suggested that if Tehran did not accept this proposal that the consulate might have to pay road guards on a monthly basis, the money being drawn from the Customs receipts.[88] Despite the additional British pay, the road guards (*qarasuran*) were never paid with regularity and in early 1920 they were owed five months in arrears. The money promised was invariably misappropriated and therefore, they had to blackmail and demand illegal fees from caravans. As a result, they gradually ceased to function, while the gendarmes were never an effective force to replace them.[89]

---

84. FO 248/1204 Kermanshah report 17/02/1918 by Lt. Col. Kennion; Idem, Kermanshah report no. 2, 13/03/1918 by Lt. Col. Kennion. At the Bindar conference on 19 July 1917, the Russian Colonel (later General) Zakharchenko had been able to induce the Sanjabis, the Bajlan and other tribal groups to form the so-called *Polis-e Gharb*, after the model of the SPR to provide security on the roads. However, due to opposition by the Nationalists, the force was never established. IOR/L/MIL/17/15/11/3, 'Who's Who in Persia (Volume II)', pp. 81, 187, 398; IOR/L/MIL/17/15/11/5, 'Who's Who in Persia (Volume III) Arabistan, Luristan, Isfahan & Bakhtiari', p. 3.

85. FO 248/1204 Kermanshah report no. 4, 18/06/1918 by Lt. Col. Kennion.

86. FO 248/1204 Kermanshah report no. 3, 11/06/1918 by Lt. Col. Kennion; Idem, Kermanshah report no. 4, 18/06/1918 by Lt. Col. Kennion; Idem, Kermanshah report no. 6, 02/08/1918 by Lt. Col. Kennion.

87. FO 248/1204 Kermanshah report no. 8, 05/10/1918 by Lt. Col. Kennion.

88. FO 248/1293, Consul to Civil Commissioner/Baghdad, 04/016/1920.

89. AIR 20/663, p. 9.

In July 1920, the road guards threatened to strike, because their arrears had not been paid. The necessary money had been allocated, but then the revenue authorities refused to pay arguing that the guards had been dismissed.[90] Finally, in early October 1920, the road guards were paid part of their 5-months arrears, but at the same time the Revenue Department announced it had no more money. Consequently, practically all road guards resigned and no satisfactory steps were taken to replace them. The British consul commented that if Tehran wanted to discontinue the system of road guards it should publicly say so and assume the responsibility for the robberies and the collection of illegal fees, which responsibility was now borne by the road guards. Moreover, the gendarmes were a most unsatisfactory and unpopular force and, until the time that gendarmes would become an efficient organization, they were no viable substitute to serve in the tribal districts. Because the pilgrim season was beginning and traffic was increasing, while large sections of the road were not policed, Greenhouse advised the payment of the arrears and announcement who in future would be responsible for robberies and the like, the more so, since half of the road guards officially stated they bore no responsibility for guarding the roads.[91] Tehran realizing that it had to do something to avoid creating an unacceptable situation in early December 1920 announced that it intended to pay road guards for past and current months, not in cash but in revenue notes. Also, taxes on traffic would henceforth only be collected at two locations. In practice they were collected at every halt by gendarmes and road guards, in addition to illegal taxes by tax collectors. Another illegal tax was taken at Khaneqin, but the British agent was ordered to help Arab muleteers to refuse this. There was some improvement in the behavior of the gendarmes, but complaints about illegal imposts continued.[92]

With the increase of trade, road protection also increased, in particular after the coup d'etat of February 1921, when, in addition to the gendarmerie (whose performance improved over time), there also was an increased presence of the army in connection with the pacification of Kurdistan and Lorestan. Nevertheless, it still happened that there were attacks on road traffic such as on 21 and 24 January, 1926 when there were two attacks on motorcars on the Qasr-e Shirin-Kermanshah road. One person was murdered. Reza Shah went to the War Office on 26 January and ordered the Minister of War to go to Kermanshah immediately and relieve the commanding officer of the Western Division of his command.[93] Thereafter, it seems that incidents of that nature were rare, also because trade with Iraq had fallen off significantly.

ROAD IMPROVEMENTS

As noted above, it was also necessary to improve the roads in Persia itself leading to Kermanshah. The indifferent state of roads and bad handling of goods by muleteers caused much interruption

90. FO 248/1293, Kermanshah Report no. 7, up to 12 August 1920; Idem, Tel. Consul to Legation, 30/07/1920.
91. FO 248/1293, Kermanshah Report no. 9, up to 10 October 1920; Idem, Tel. Consul to Legation, 02/10/1920; Idem, Tel. Consul to Legation, 05/10/1920; Idem, Tel. Consul to Legation, 01/10/1920.
92. FO 248/1293, Kermanshah Report no. 11, up to 10 December 1920.
93. FO 416/78, Intel. Summary No. 3, ending February 6, 1926.

and loss of business on the Khaneqin-Kermanshah leg of the route. "Merchants' resources are severely tried by all this."[94] Under Farmanfarma, the governor in 1902-03, the Shah was requested to grant a concession for the road from Kermanshah to Khaneqin. It was proposed to make a 30 m wide road with ditches on both sides and six halting stages. It was further planned to establish a transport service with 40 fourgons, 20 phaetons and 400 mules and tolls to be levied like on the Enzeli-Tehran road. The investment would be financed by merchants and notables of Kermanshah. However, the following year the road project fell through.[95]

The Russians neither waited for the British nor the Persians and with Russian financing, supervision and management the Qazvin-Hamadan road was completed in 1905 and, as a result, (Russian) trade increased via that road. In early November 1905, the 174 km long Qazvin-Hamadan road was not yet ready for wheeled traffic, but work was progressing as was the construction of the eight *mehmankhaneh*s or rest-houses. The latter were completed by February 1906 and all, except for two, were connected by telephone with Hamadan and Qazvin. The drawback of the rest-houses was that there were not built near villages and therefore, supplies were difficult to obtain at them. As a result, caravans went to the villages for shelter. Although in May 1906 the road was still not ready for wheeled traffic, 9-10 Russian officials supervised the use of the road to which end three toll bars had been erected; one in the middle and one at each end of the road.[96] Normally, including halts, a car traveled this road in 8-10 hours, but in winter, if there was snow in the pass, it took two days. After 1915 no more posting-horses were available. However, until the end of 1917, "the Russian road-personnel kept the surface in fair repair, and also kept the Sultan Bulagh pass free from snow in winter."[97]

This Russian project led to the discussion of the need to establish a Persian Company (directors included the Prime Minister, the Foreign Minister and Amir Afkham, the then governor Kermanshah) with a capital of £100,000 to build a carriageable road from Qasr-e Shirin to Hamadan.[98] Although initially it remained but talk, partly because of the political upheaval of the country during 1906-09, but finally in 1909, the Company built a road between Kermanshah and Qasr-e Shiran that was passable for carriages, while it also started a post and passenger service. Already in January-February 1910, the new road felt the impact of inclement weather when due to heavy snow passage was interrupted.[99] In 1911, a Russian subject operated a twice-weekly carriage service between Kermanshah and Khaneqin.[100] In 1918, the pioneers of the Mesopotamia Expeditionary Force improved the surface and realigned the worst zigzags of this road at the Taq-e Gireh pass. However, the 20 km stretch of the road in Mahidasht plan and 29 km stretch of the road in the Kerend plain became quagmires after heavy rain. The latter road was made into a metalled road in 1918 as part of the famine relief food-for-work program.[101]

94. DCR 5204, p. 5.
95. DCR 3043, p. 8; DCR 3189, p. 39.
96. Political Diaries, vol. 1, pp. 218, 306, 397 (the road had many culverts and 3 stone-bridges); DCR 3683, p. 4.
97. Napier 1919, p. 5.
98. DCR 3683, p. 4; Political Diaries, vol. 1, p. 370.
99. DCR 4766, p. 8.
100. Adamec 1976, vol. 1, p. 365.
101. Napier 1919, p. 11.

By 1914, the cost and time of transportation for both commercial and passenger traffic between Basra-Baghdad (820 km) and Kermanshah-Tehran (800 km) was as shown in Table 6.5. The French embassy, recommended the following firms, which were specialized in arranging both forms of transportation, to wit: Lynch Bros & Co.; Toumaniantz in Tehran; Berk Puttmanna in Baghdad; Mohammad Reza, Seyfollah or Nasrollah in Kermanshah.[102]

Table 6.5: Basra-Baghdad-Kermanshah-Tehran trade route - travel time and cost per segment (1914)

Route	Duration	Cost
Basra-Baghdad	3-5 days	25-28 *tumans* per 100 batman
Baghdad-Qasr-e Shrin	5-6 days	25-28 *tumans* per 100 batman
Qasr-e Shirin - Kermanshah	8-10 days	25-28 *tumans* per 100 batman
Kermanshah-Tehran	23-38 days	30 *tumans* per 100 batman
Total for goods	45-50 days	562-592 *qrans* per 100 batman
For travelers:		
Baghdad -Qasr-e Shirin	3-4 days	60 *tumans* per passenger/carriage
Qasr-e Shirin to Kermanshah	6-7 days	45 *qrans* per mule/passenger
Kermanshah -Tehran	5-6 days	150 *tumans*/wagon

Source: Gouvernement de France 1914, pp. 121-22.

Various British observers had suggested to develop a road from Mohammerah to Khorramabad. In 1913, the Persian Railway Syndicate (PRS) obtained a concession to develop a railway along that route and surveys of the track had started in April of that year. This was in reaction to the Russian railway concession obtained for the Jolfa-Tabriz route. The PRS realized that their railway would mean a loss to Baghdad, but they believed that the planned Baghdad railway would more than compensate for this. For only a railway connection between Baghdad and Kermanshah would mean the loss of trade with Persia, which amounted to about one third of total Baghdad trade. The PRS believed that their railway would ultimately continue towards Hamadan, Tabriz and Jolfa, while the Baghdad railway (the concession was only to Khaneqin) would continue to Kermanshah and Hamadan and then connect to Tehran. Such a development would above all benefit Baghdad, which would be the main distribution center for the Persian trade.[103] However, WW I intervened and the post-war situation had dampened British interest in the railway scheme, but not in trade between Baghdad and Kermanshah.

Because traders in Basra had heavily invested in cottons and other goods even before the fall of Baghdad in March 1917 there was there was an accumulation of goods in that port, because transport to Baghdad was still difficult and to Kermanshah trade was still restricted and sometimes stopped altogether. The opening in June 1918 of the road to Khaneqin and Kermanshah

102. Gouvernement de France 1914, p. 122.

103. Sauer 1914, pp. 1105, 1107; Administration Report 1913, p. 88; Wilson 1941, pp. 222, 225-28. These railways were but a part of the Indo-European Highway earlier dreamed about by some military planners and politicians, see e.g., Capenny 1900, pp. 523-34.

was a major event, because it had been closed to commercial traffic for three years during WWI.[104] However, it was only on 2 November 1918 that the British military commander announced "complete freedom of trade and the relaxation of blockade restrictions." Even so transportation rates were very high. Before the war the rate for a camel load was $8.80 but now it was $73![105] Fortunately, there was pent up demand in Persia, in particular for cotton piece goods, sugar and tea. Although transportation rates were very high, due to demand for transport by the military, merchants were willing to pay the high rates given the strong demand for these goods.[106] The transport situation improved after 1920. In 1916, the British army built a railway connecting Basra with Nasriyah, while the connection with Baghdad was completed in January 1920. A link from Baghdad to Khaneqin was built as well. As of that time, cargo could not only be forwarded by boat, but also by the Basra-Baghdad Railway, thus avoiding Customs inspection at Basra. Freight was £8.10s to £10 per ton. From Baghdad to Tiruk goods went by rail. Transport cost for merchandise per load of 10 tons was Rs305 per package, Rs1 13 *anna*s per 50 kg. "Nearly all imported merchandise destined to Kermanshah and beyond is dispatched by forwarding agents at Baghdad who advance the transport charges by rail to Tiruk and by animal or wagon thence onward." Goods were transported at the risk of the consignor, who had to make his own arrangement against theft and damage by weather. Transport cost was 216 *qran*s per 300 kg, which took about 20 days. From Tiruk to Kermanshah transport was by pack animal, wagons and lorries. The cost per animal or wagon was 180 *qran*s per *kharvar* of 300 kg. This trip lasted 6-8 days. By postal wagon the charge was the same but the journey lasted three days. Transport by truck from Tiruk to Kermanshah was mostly in the hands of the Mesopotamia Persia Corporation. Transportation cost were Rs80 to Rs100 per 300 kg, duration 5-8 days (glassware, earthenware and furniture excepted). It was also possible to insure the goods when transported by truck. There were also additional packing instructions, which were somewhat more stringent than in the nineteenth century. "For caravan transport on the Baghdad route into Persia (Kuretu-Tehran) packages should not exceed in weight 80 kilograms each, and boxes should weigh even less. Boxes should be strongly planked and carefully joined, and, in addition, should be wrapped in gunny and tied round with strong rope. If the contents be injurable by damp, boxes should further have a zinc lining. Bales should be ironbound. Sacks, if used, should be double."[107] The road from Iraq to Kermanshah also had improved. In October 1918, the IBP manager Hall traveled in two days from Kermanshah to Baghdad, the only good road with a length of 640 miles. He wrote: "The road on this side of the frontier has been metalled to a great extent, and sappers and steam rollers are still busy on it, and will be for some time to come. The villages that formed the old caravan stages are still in utter ruin."[108] By the end of December, most British troops were leaving Kermanshah, "but the sappers and pioneers remain, and the road-making goes on. Will they complete the work, I wonder, or will they leave the road in parts

104. Heizer 1920, p. 524.

105. Heizer 1919, p. 793. According to Hale 1920, p. 233, the Baghdad road was open to trade already in June 1918 and "caravans of merchandise are streaming along it."

106. Heizer 1920, p. 524.

107. Temple 1922, pp. 20-21.

108. Hale n.d., pp. 238-39.

a rough unfinished monument, to draw, for a decade, the smiles and imprecations of muleteers and camelmen and motorists, instead of their blessings for a generation?"[109]

To maintain the road between Kuretu and Hamadan the Persian government levied a road tax as of 1921. However, the manner of its collection as well the lack of the publication of the tax schedule led to arbitrary demands for payment against which the British government protested. For example, cars coming from Hamadan had to pay different amounts than those coming from Kuretu. It also did so, because there had been no formal announcement of the imposition of the new tax. In July 1921, a touring car traveling from Kermanshah to Tehran paid the following taxes:

Table 6.6: Road taxes paid between Kermanshah and Tehran (1921)

Leaving Kermanshah	**20** *qrans*
Entering Kangavar	20
Do. Asadabad	20
Do. Hamadan	20
Do. Qazvin	20
Leaving Qazvin	10
Entering Tehran	20
Total taxes	150 *qrans*
In addition road tolls had to be paid:	
Kermanshah - Hamadan	115.15
Hamadan - Qazvin	141.00
Qazvin - Tehran	92.00
Total tolls	348.15 *qrans*
Total of taxes and tolls	498.15 *qrans*

Moreover, usually no receipts were given and if they were these were incomplete, lacking the name of the place. Also, in this particular case the receipt for Qazvin given was for 10 *qrans*, while 10 more were taken on leaving Qazvin, which was illegal as this charge was included in the payment of 20 *qrans*. The British government therefore requested that (i) the tax schedule be published and that (ii) receipts were obligatory, stating the amount paid and the road section it covered, had to be numbered and counterfoiled.[110] It is unclear whether this request was positively implemented, but it seems unlikely. However, in 1924, the road was kept in good condition by the Persians.[111]

Transportation rates remained high in the 1920s. How high these rates must have been is indicated by those of 1926-27, which had fallen by 40-50% compared with the year before the transport crisis of 1925-26. What is further of interest that there was a significant increase in

109. Hale n.d., pp. 241-42; Griscom 1921, p. 236.
110. FO 371/7829, f. 26-27 (23/08/1921).
111. Forbes-Leith 1925, p. 170; Kirsch 1927, pp. 218, 220.

the use of trucks in Persia from 103 in 1924 to 967 in 1926. The rates per lorry from Baghdad to Kermanshah in 1926-27 was 200-225 *qrans* per *kharvar* and 220-250 *qrans* per *kharvar* for Kermanshah to Tehran.[112] In the following years the number of trucks grew and increasingly replaced animal transportation.[113] Between 1920 and 1940, the Iraqi leg of the route to Kermanshah had not much changed. Basra continued to offer the advantage of a port where goods including heavy packages, could be unloaded direct from the steamer on to quay. Further that goods could be forwarded by river steamers or by rail to Baghdad, then by rail to the railhead at Khaneqin or by lorry through Khaneqin to Kermanshah and Tehran. Iraqi Railways took charge of the collection of the goods at Basra and their delivery in Kermanshah, Hamadan and Tehran. "Goods can in any case be sent as far as Khaneqin on a through B/L and it frequently saves time and expense to ship goods destined to Persia to Basrah instead of Baghdad. There is a transit duty of 1/2 per cent." Despite these various advantages, the Basra-Baghdad-Kermanshah route was generally regarded as more expensive than the Bushehr route but it offered a saving of time in the winter months, because the Kermanshah road was very rarely closed. From 1930, onwards, there was in addition increased competition from the Mohammarah-Khorramabad-Tehran route.[114] Also, trucks were prevented from using the roads leading to Kermanshah, because after heavy rain storms washed away much of the road's upper surface or even obliterated parts of a road. And traffic on these roads "consisted chiefly of motor lorries and passenger omnibuses, both usually overloaded." These omnibuses had no windows and instead had wire netting along the sides, which looked like cages. These prevented that both passengers and their luggage were ejected onto the road while the bus lurched along. Moreover, passengers used the netting to attach their water bottles, lamps and *qalyans*. There also were "big covered waggons drawn by four horses abreast, which are peculiar to this part of the country, Kermanshah being specially noted for them. They are clumsy looking vehicles, the horses being harnessed only by traces, the swingle-tree extending a couple of feet beyond and on either side of the waggon, so as to allow enough space for the two outside horses."[115] In addition to a regular bus service in the 1930s, there was also a fast passenger service between Tehran-Baghdad v.v. offered by Overland Line, which used strong six-seater cars to drive in four days between the two capital cities. The drivers were experienced French and British drivers. The cost was 500 German marks per person and each person was allowed 3 kg of luggage. If passengers wanted to continue to Damascus an additional 100 marks had to be paid. The drivers ran a tight schedule which they made passengers adhere to.[116]

---

112. Lingeman 1928, pp. 6, 26. In December 1920, there were 60 private cars in Kermanshah. Most high officials and notables had cars. AIR 20/663, p. 140.
113. Lingeman 1930, pp. 34-35, 48 (rates).
114. Lingeman 1930, p. 7.
115. Alexander 1931, pp. 20-22, 29.
116. Kirsch 1927, pp. 222-23.

KERMANSHAH'S HINTERLAND

Apart from its strategic location, Kermanshah was one of the most populated provinces with many towns, which was good for trade as it ensured an attractive market. In fact, by 1900 Kermanshah through Hamadan also supplied Khorasan, Kurdistan, Tabriz, Garrus, Tehran, Ardabil, Qom, Kashan, Zanjan, and Isfahan.[1] This is what Whigham argued and stressed in his effort to convince his readers in the British government to develop the Iraqi transit route. He wrote that Kermanshah province had a large "agricultural and pastoral population living in countless villages, with a congeries of smaller towns like Burujird, Khoremabad, Sultanabad, Daolatabad, Kangawar, Nahawand, Sena, and many others all within a circle, whose centre lies between Kermanshah and Hamadan, and whose radius is about a hundred miles. This a country well worth developing."[2] British cottons and French sugar were supplied to "a great number of agricultural villages and small towns with Khoremabad, Burujird, Sultanabad, Daolatabad and Hamadan as chief clients."[3] Nevertheless, Kermanshah town was not the most important trading center in Western Persia.[4] Even though the Baghdad-Kermanshah trade route acquired increasing importance after the mid-1880s, it was Hamadan that was the main distribution center supplying Central Persia.[5] In 1907, it was estimated that 20% of imports for the British consular district remained at Kermanshah, while the rest went to Hamadan (and then to Senneh, Soltanabad, Borujerd, etc. For 1910, it was estimated that 25-30% were consumed in the province itself.[6] Also, Kermanshah did not even have one-fifth of Hamadan trade.[7] Kermanshah through Hamadan also supplied Khorasan, Kurdistan, Tabriz, Garrus, Tehran, Ardabil, Qom, Kashan, Zenjan, and Isfahan.[8] Kermanshah's function as an important transshipment center not only held for imports, but also for exports. For example, dried fruit for Baghdad, came from Hamadan, Malayer and Iraq.[9]

Nevertheless, according to the US consul in Baghdad, "Kermanshah is the emporium from whence all is sent to different destinations."[10]According to the British consul in Kermanshah, in 1903, the city's trade relations with other towns in Persia was as follows, which gives a very good insight in the forwarding nature of the trade of Kermanshah.

Table 6.6b: Kermanshah inland trade

Exports to:	
Tehran	Goods from Baghdad: ghee, tutun, peas, wheat, sheep

1. DCR 3189, p. 40.
2. Whigham 1903, p. 309.
3. Whigham 1903, p. 276.
4. DCR 4365, p. 6.
5. MacLean 1904, p. 46; FO 60/463 Report (1884), not foliated.
6. DCR 4100, p. 3; Küss 1911, part III, p. 27.
7. Administration Report 1907-08, p. 64.
8. DCR 3189, p. 40; DCR 4559, p. 5; DCR 590, p. 22.
9. DCR 3189 p. 36.
10. Hurner 1896, p. 645.

Hamadan	Goods from Baghdad: tutun, peas, dates, gall-nuts from Luristan, grease, ghee, raw hides
Isfahan	Manchester prints, iron, tea, cow-hides, wool, gilims and gaz-alafi
Resht	Bitter gums, gum tragacanth, Mexicans, white and grey shirtings, dates from Mendali
Soltanabad	Tea, sugar, Manchester goods
Kurdistan	Tea, sugar, tombaku (water pipe tobacco) of Kashan
Qom	Tutum, dates, white and grey shirtings, Mexicans, wheat
Kashan	Thread, white and grey shirtings, Mexicans
Borujerd	Tea, sugar, prints.
Imports from:	
Tehran	Russian prints, cloth, hardware and glassware
Hamadan	Naphtha, superior quality from Resht, Russian prints, cloth and velvet, and Russian glassware and hardware
Isfahan	Native cotton and woolen goods (such as qalamkars, prints, lahafs, abbas), gaz, givehs
Soltanabad	Carpets and tragacanth
Kurdistan	Carpets and tragacanth and gum known as sa`lab.
Qom	Copperware from Kashan, tumbaku, henna, cotton
Kashan	Copperware, tumbaku, henna, cotton, Kashan and Yazd silk goods
Borujerd	Carpets, opium, and tragacanth
Saveh	Pomegranates
Tabriz	Kerchiefs for the Kurds.

Source: DCR 3189, pp. 31-32.

Kermanshah lost much of this forwarding function after 1930, when the central government preferred trade to use all-Persian routes. The instrument to achieve this was the Foreign Exchange Control act, which regulated how much foreign exchange would be made available to importers. Kermanshah received very low allocations, as a result of which its importance as trading town waned (see above).

PILGRIMS

Because Kermanshah was situated on the major route to Baghdad and the holy places of Kerbela and Najaf, it greatly benefited from all through traffic, in particular from the passage of travelers (dead and alive) and pilgrims, which afforded it some measure of affluence.[11] It was already a halting stage for hajj pilgrims in the tenth century.[12] In April 1882, Capt. Gerard had to pay at Khaneqin, after having left Sabyi, the Persian border post, 2 *qran*s per head as quarantine dues, without medical examination.[13]

11. de Sercey 1928, p. 298.
12. Minorsky 1937, 132; Thevenot 1971, part 2, p. 67 (1660s).
13. Gerard 1883, p. 45.

According to a German physician in Ottoman service, who was in charge of the quarantine service in Khaneqin at the end of the nineteenth century, pilgrims usually started coming in April; the frequency of caravans was highest in spring and autumn, in particular during August-November period. Thereafter until April it was quiet. A pilgrimage lasted several months. The pilgrimages could be divided into four groups, each one related to a special Moslem festival: i. *Eyd-e Qorban* in the month of *Dhu 'l-Hijjah*; ii. *Ashura* in the month of *Moharram*; iii. *Arba 'in*, i.e. the transport of Imam Hoseyn's head from Damascus to Medina 40 days after the beheading; and iv. *Eyd-e ziyarat*, the normal pilgrimage that happened 20 days after Moharram. The Shiite pilgrims went to Kerbela, Najaf and many also to Samarra. Only a few continued to Mecca. Most Persian pilgrims came from Isfahan, Khorasan, Tabriz, Tehran, Rasht, Yazd, Qom, Shiraz, Mazanderan Qazvin, Borujerd, Baku, Urmiyeh, Kuba, Ardabil and Kermanshah. Mazanderani pilgrims usually came riding on a camel and wore a filthy dress, while Khorasanis often rode a horse or camel. Arab pilgrims coming from Iraq went to Imam Reza's shrine in Mashhad.[14]

In the late nineteenth and early twentieth centuries the British consuls in Kermanshah estimated that each year some 50,000 to 100,000 pilgrims passed through the town. In the first decade of the twentieth century, some 25,000 pilgrims hired mules or horses en route to Kerbela. Those pilgrims riding a quadruped needed a passport; pilgrims on foot, women and children did not require a passport. Wealthy Persians went by *takht-ravan* or litter and women usually in *kajaveh*. Therefore, it was not possible to estimate the number of pilgrims on foot as they were not supplied with passports. The pilgrims caravans usually had a *chavush* or guide who sang religious songs. The caravan was lead by a *pish-ahang*, an ornamented mule or horse with many bells. Large sums of money were exported by these pilgrims. Before leaving Persia, the pilgrims paid 20 gold piasters per passport at the Turkish Consulate-General in Kermanshah. Each year, this yielded about 5,000 Turkish pounds; in 1903/04, this amounted to 8,200 Turkish pounds. On entering Khaneqin the pilgrims had to pay a quarantine or sanitary tax of 10 gold piasters. Between 1903-13, there was an annual average of 42,000 travelers traveling via Khaneqin. It was estimated that each pilgrim spent some 200 *qran*s during a 60-day stay in Iraq. In addition to pilgrims, each year a large number corpses passed through Kermanshah en route to Kerbela. According to Bulmus, between 1909-14 annually an average of 3,900 bodies passed through Khaneqin, peaking in 1912-13 when 7,558 corpses passed. Only dry bodies were permitted pass, unless the corpse was less than 12 hours old when crossing. For corpses the Ottomans in Kermanshah charged 35 *qran*s of which 27.5 *qran*s or 5 piaster gold were remitted to the government account, the rest was for expenses. A further tax of 0.5 pound at Khaneqin; the cost of taking a body to Kerbela was 35-60 *tuman*s and higher. It also happened that muleteers threw the corpses into the Diyala river at Khaneqin to keep the rest of the money, but measures were taken to prevent this. Thus, pilgrims were a significant part of the local economy, because they spent the night in the city, bought food and other necessaries, brought money to change and they paid part of their way by selling all kinds of goods.[15] Therefore, during winter,

14. Saad 1913, pp. 96-97, 110.

15. DCR 3043, p. 8; DCR 3189 pp. 36-38. Adamec 1976, vol. 1, p. 344; Bulmus 2012, pp. 155-56; Saad 1913, pp. 100, 106, 114-15; see also IOR/L/PS/10/231, File 842/1912 'Sanitary Mission to Turco-Persian Frontier', p. 36. The Gazetteer and Whigham, 1903, p. 275 state that annually 100,000 to 125,000 pilgrims passed through Kermanshah en route to Kerbela, clearly having read DCR 2260 (Isfahan, 1879-99), p. 16, which provides these

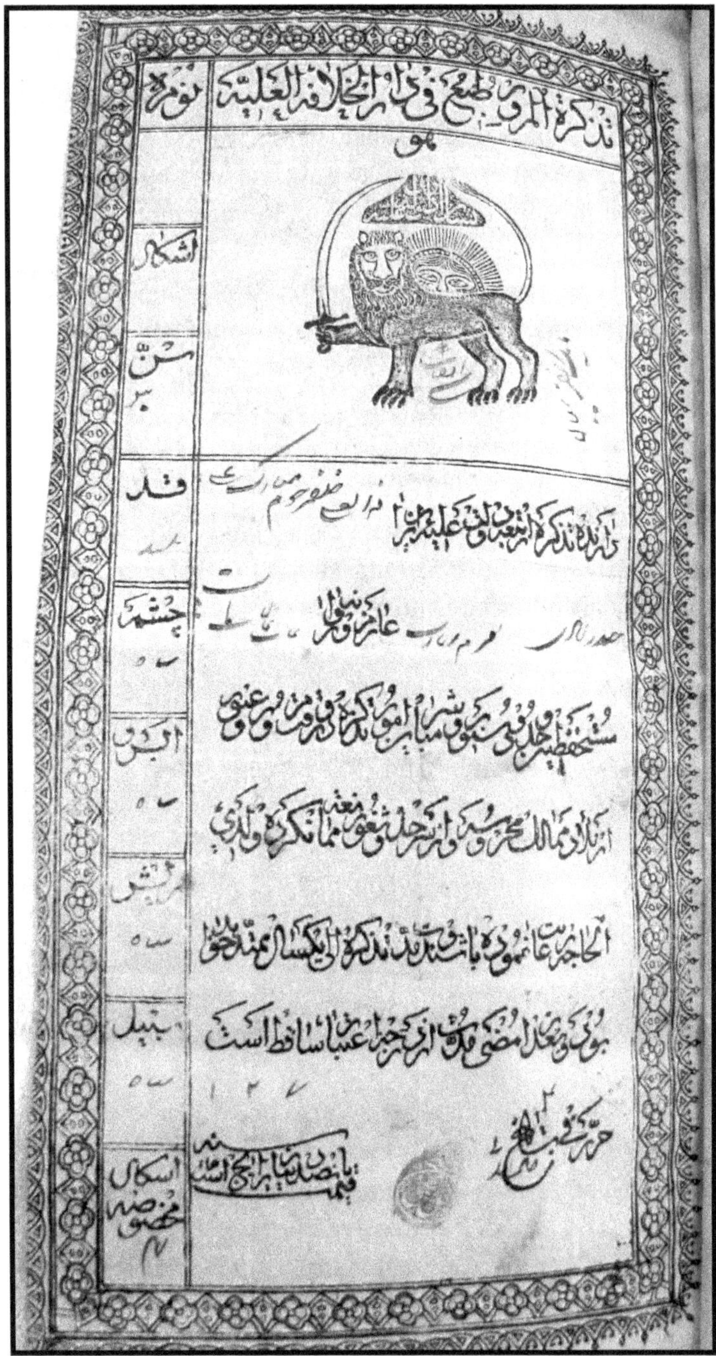
تذکرة المرور طبع فی دار الخلافة العلیة

Fig. 6.3: Persian printed passport for a visit to Karbala/Baghdad (1850)

some governors (Hosam al-Molk I and II) gave 200 to 500 sets of clothing to the poor and pilgrims against the severe cold and Hosam al-Molk II even built a caravanserai for the comfort of the pilgrim in 1891. Some took steps to facilitate pilgrim travel and help them when in need. In early 1892, Ziya al-Dowleh paid for the housing, cost and food for the poor and pilgrims coming into town, but thereafter they were sent on their way. This governor also took steps, for the first time, to regulate prices of foodstuffs sold to pilgrims and travelers at the caravanserais. To ensure that his order would be obeyed he had the price list affixed at the entrance of each caravanserai.[16] In 1907, much money, some 500,000 *qrans*, arrived from Baghdad (from the pilgrims) and Basra.[17] Those pilgrims who were not wealthy tried to pay their way to and from the places of pilgrimage by taking all kinds of merchandise with them. Consequently there is a proverb referring to this practice: *ham ziyarat, ham tejarat* (both pilgrimage and trade). Pilgrims also brought many articles for sale from their

figures. However, the British consuls in Kermanshah gave the lower figures as did Curzon 1892, vol. 1, p. 558. An estimate from the late 1880s, gives the number of 120 to 130,000 pilgrims, about 3,000/year came from Baku via Resht. DCR 113, p. 8. In 1894, Hurner 1896, p. 642, even estimated the number of pilgrims at 200,000 and about 2,000 corpses.

16. *Ruznameh-ye Iran* 1375, vol. 4, pp. 2715 (no. 674; 07/07/1889), 2853 (no. 708; 04/02/1890), 3023 (no. 751; 26/07/1891), 3084 (no. 766; 21/02/1892).

17. DCR 4100, p. 4.

places of pilgrimage such as soap from Mecca, rosaries from holy cities, circular pieces of earth from Kerbela, used by devout Shiites to put their head when praying, ands many similar items that could be sold in Persia at considerable profits.[18].

Consequently, pilgrim caravans were very large. Bellew met one of about 2,000 mules, camels and donkeys, and as many men and women. Such a caravan made so much noise that the sounds of its approach were heard a few minutes before it arrived.[19] Joining a pilgrim caravan was sometimes a mixed blessing for those travelers, who were not Shiites. On the one hand a sizable caravan provided some measure of security en route, but on the other hand, non-Shiites were continuously exposed to all kinds of troubles and difficulties. The pilgrims, often led by the example of the mullah who was the leader of their group, would heap abuse on the 'unclean' travel companion[s] and started quarrels and altercations, which sometimes led to the use of violence. Even the closeness of a sleeping carpet of a non-Shiite could become the source of anger. A Persian, employed by Layard 1887, to teach him Persian while traveling from Baghdad stopped drinking and eating of the of the same vessel with him, after having been threatened by the mullah of the pilgrims. Even sitting with him was embarrassing for the 'teacher'.[20] However, this was not everywhere or with everyone the case. One British travelers opined:

> From all I could learn by information or personal experience, their feeling is not as nearly offensive to us as we understand it to be. They have certain formalities connected with the preparation of their food, the omission of which renders the food and those who eat it impure. Hence they do not generally allow a Christian to partake with them of their own food, but they cannot bear that he should prepare his own food in their vessels, and still less do they like to partake of food that he has prepared, I am persuaded that the objection to eat of his fare is not so much an objection to him personally as to the food itself, or rather to its mode of preparation.[21]

Although, border and health control rules were well-known it still happened that there were problems for pilgrims. In February 1942, there were vehement articles accusing a certain doctor Abedin of charging 200 rials for a vaccination certificate, whereas the persons concerned already had been vaccinated in Tehran. Also, in the same month, 18 Indian pilgrims who had exit visa and no funds were stranded at the border, but through the intervention of a British field sergeant they got their visa.[22]

---

18. Saad 1913, p. 111; Layard 1887, p. 235.
19. Floyer 1882, pp. 441-42.
20. Layard 1887, pp. 228-29; Mitford 1884, pp. 327-28.
21. A Correspondent 1835 b, p. 438. However, see Southgate 1840, vol. 1, p. 80, who makes it crystal clear that being a non-Moslem was what made you unclean.
22. FO 371/45400, Kermanshah Diary February 1945.

THE GROWTH OF TRADE

Although the presence of a strong and trade-promoting ruler in the person of Dowlatshah in Kermanshah during the first two decades of the nineteenth century must have had a positive impact on the economy, but, as to trade, we have no quantative data to confirm this supposition. However, that this was indeed the case, is suggested by reports from later observers, who blamed the downturn in trade and prosperity of the city on the misrule of his successors. However, there were other forces at work that had not much to do with the internal conditions of Kermanshah. In the early 1820s, the Tabriz trade gained importance. Before that time most imports entered Persia via Bushehr and Baghdad. Because these routes were long, expensive and not always safe, trade looked for other cheaper routes. The change at Tabriz was related to the transfer of the staple from Izmir to Istanbul around 1820. Persian merchants were able to buy European goods cheaper thereafter at Istanbul, which they at first shipped via Scutari and Erzerum to Tabriz. This route was quite an improvement to channel European goods via Turkey. Moreover, by 1832, trade from Istanbul via Baghdad and onward via Kermanshah, or via the desert through Khuzestan, had become impractical by that time, due to internal troubles in the Baghdad pashaliq, and the caravans therefore traveled via Erzerum and Tabriz.[23] The sharp reduction in trade via the Tiflis-Tabriz route coincided with the growing insecurity on the Bushehr-Shiraz and the Baghdad-Kermanshah routes. This resulted in a considerable drop in Southern imports, which partly moved to the Trabzon-Tabriz route, and thus established the dominance of this northern route for the next 40 years. This not only held for textiles, but also for sugar. A further factor was the introduction of steam navigation between Istanbul and Trabson in 1826, which was expanded thereafter and reduced transportation cost significantly.[24]

As a result of these developments, Kermanshah became a much reduced town, the more so as it suffered the vagaries of the plague from 1830-34. In 1835, the American missionary opined that "the city seems less thriving than Hamadan, though the trade from Baghdad passes through it. It has only half as many caravans, nor is there to be seen the same throng in its bazaars. The people speak of it as having greatly declined since the days of Mohammad 'Ali Mirza."[25] In that same year, Fraser, when leaving Kermanshah observed that "we went through a ruined bazaar and many lanes of ruined houses,"[26] indicating the town was not prospering. In 1840, Teule observed that Kermanshah did more business with Isfahan than with Baghdad.[27] In 1844, Jones remarked that the city had 'a mean appearance' and that "decay presents itself whichever way the eye of the spectator turns."[28] The French officer in Persian service, Ferrier, wrote that Mohammad 'Ali Mirza enriched the town with his charities and the people lived in the enjoyment of plenty. However, they were driven out by the tyranny of his successors who only pursued their private interests. The splendid bazaars of Kermanshah were deserted, and if somebody exposed his goods for sale, "his venture rapidly disappears under the hands of an undisciplined

23. Abrahamian 1983, p. 286; Longrigg 2002, p. 248-49, 262-74.
24. Issawi 1971 a, pp. 92-103; Idem 1971 b, p. 19f; Longrigg 2002, p. 262ff; Floor 2003 b, pp. 334-35.
25. Southgate 1840, vol. 1, p. 136.
26. Fraser 1840, vol. 2, p. 196.
27. Teule 1842, vol. 2, p. 482.
28. Jones 1849, p. 289.

soldiery, who give themselves up to every description of excess, certain that they do so with impunity.[29] Likewise, Keith Abbott remarked that "The town and Bazars are in every respect mean, and proclaim the decay of all that could once have rendered the place of consequence ... with reference to commerce."[30] In the 1850s, Kermanshah was still known to be a commercial town of some local importance, but it clearly was not one of the major trading centers.[31] In fact, Keith Abbott wrote: "Like many other towns in Persia, it has in former days been of some importance, which it does not now posses." [32]

Up to 1870, the Trabzon-Tabriz trade route was the main channel for imported goods to Persia. Tabriz supplied most of northern and western Persia throughout the entire period. The decline in trade at Tabriz after 1866 was caused by a number of disasters. The first one was the failure of the silk crop due to the spread of the disease of the silk worm as of 1866, which reduced purchasing power significantly. This disaster was followed by the general famine of 1871-73 in Persia, which caused the death of tens of thousands, both human and animal life, resulting in reduced demand for imports and higher transportation cost due to lack of transport animals and high cost of fodder. These problems had barely run their course when the Russian-Turkish war on 1877 made transportation of goods via Poti or Trabson impossible as both armies commandeered pack animals to ensure a steady supply of goods. This route became even less attractive by the exemption on European goods transiting via the Caucasus. Major importers therefore were forced to import goods via the Bushehr-Isfahan and the Baghdad-Kermanshah-Hamadan trade routes,[33] a development further reinforced and helped by the opening of the Suez Canal in 1869, cheaper transportation cost in the Persian Gulf due to the use of steamers and the establishment of a steamer service on the Tigris.[34] As a result, Kermanshah became the port of entry for all goods entering Persia from Baghdad and coming from Great Britain and India via the Persian Gulf and the Tigris. "The rates of transport on the Bushire route are also considerably cheaper than those of Trebizond-Erzeroom, where for the last year [1892-93] they have ruled at 3 ½ l., per kantar (500 lbs. weight) as against half the amount merchants were accustomed to pay."[35]

Various Routes and Distances, in Day's Marching, by which Merchandise arrives in Persia

From Trebizond to Tabreez	from 32 days in winter to 70 days in summer, when the beasts of burden are permitted to pasture along the route.

29. Ferrier 1856, pp. 24-25.
30. Amanat 1983, p. 93.
31. Blau 1854, p. 54.
32. Amanat 1983, p. 93.
33. *AP* 68 Tabreez (1867), p. 500; *AP* 66 Tabreez (1870), p. 961; *AP* 58 Tabreez (1872), p. 1190; *AP* 65 Azerbaijan (1872), p. 968; *AP* 75 Tabreez (1873), p. 205; *AP* 75 Tabreez (1877-78), p. 1696; MacLean 1904, p. 46; *AP* 68, Ghilan 1867-68, p. 297; Küss 1911, p. 91; Issawi 1971 a, p. 84; Idem 1971 b, pp. 22-27; FO 60/463, Report on the Trade (1884), not foliated.
34. Küss 1911, p. 91; Issawi 1971 a, p. 84; Idem 1971 b, pp. 22-27; FO 60/463, Report on the Trade (1884), not foliated; *AP* 75 Tabreez (1878), p. 1696.
35. DCR 1440, p. 4; see also Issawi 1971 b, pp. 23-27; Adamec 1976, vol. 1, pp. 343-4. For the transport rates and duration of the trip via the various supply routes in 1907, see Doty 1908, p. 630.

Tabreez to Teheran	14 days to 18 days.
Baghdad to Teheran	via Khanakhin, Kermanshah, and Hamadan, about 28 days, according to the season.
Bushire to Teheran	about 46 days, including stoppages.
Bushire to Shiraz	10 days.
Shiraz to Ispahan	14 days.
Ispahan to Teheran	14 days.
Teheran to Tabreez	18 days.

Source: DCR 1440, p. 6.

Indeed trade via Kermanshah continued to increase. This was all the more remarkable because the import of local Iraqi goods had dropped significantly by that time. Whereas around 1860, normally two-thirds of total exports from Baghdad went to Persia, representing a value of about 34,000 dinars, in 1877-1879 exports of local Iraqi goods only represented 13,000 dinars, or 5.5% of total exports of local goods from Baghdad. However, transit trade to Persia (sugar, cottons, tea, metals) was 125,000 dinars that year. And although Baghdad exports of local products continued to drop, so that by 1900 it was of no importance, Baghdad's transit trade to Persia continued to grow.[36] In 1884, the secretary of the British Legation in Tehran reported that "I learn that a marked increase has taken place in the importations from Europe by the Baghdad and Hermanshah [sic] route, especially of sugar, grey and white shirting, and T-cloths."[37] The Baghdad-Kermanshah trade route had acquired some importance after the mid-1880s with Hamadan as the main distribution center supplying Central Persia.[38] Table 6.7 shows that there was a drop in trade in 1889. If this is correct, then it must have been a temporary event as trade thereafter shows significant growth. Even though the 1889 figure also indicates that total Persian transit trade of £540,000 represented 25% of total Baghdad trade.[39] However, it would seem that Curzon underestimated the trade of Kermanshah. When in 1898, a syndicate of merchants formed to take over the customs of Kermanshah, to determine how much to pay they assessed the average of trade over the three previous years they found that there was a 50% difference with 1897. They estimated imports after 1894 at £530,000, or the average of trade for 1894, 1895 and 1896 was at a level of £812,304 imports and £138,600 for exports [40]

Table 6.7: Total imports from Baghdad 1885-1897 in loads of 356 lbs.

Goods/Year	1885	1889	1894	1897
UK piece goods	8,000	7-8,000	-	22,000
Indian cottons	-	1,000	-	-

36. Issawi 1971 a, pp. 120-21.
37. AP 1884-85, 76, Report by Mr. Dickson on the Trade of Persia, Tehran 31/10/1884, p. 5 (also in FO 60/463).
38. MacLean 1904, p. 46; FO 60/463, Report (1884), not foliated.
39. Curzon 1892, vol. 2, p. 577-78. (The 1889 customs house figures for Kermanshah (viz. imports at £232,530 and exports at £95,266) only bears out the Baghdad figure for imports as the exports were much lower).
40. DCR 2260, p. 18.

Goods/Year	1885	1889	1894	1897
Drugs, metals	-	7,000	-	-
Sugar	-	6,000	20,000	-
Total	33,700	23,000	80,000	73,950
Total in £	-	-	-	822,000

Source: Curzon 1892, vol. 2, 578; Hurner 1896, pp. 645; DCR 2260, p. 15

Therefore, it was no wonder that consul Preece observed that "There are but few towns in Persia which show to-day so flourishing a condition from a trade point of view as Kermanshah and this in spite of oppression by the local governors and the badness and the unsafety of the roads radiating from it." ... "It is practically the only route available for Western Persia, now that the Luristan road can no longer be relied upon, supplying such districts as Kurdistan, Hamadan, Irak, and even competing seriously with the trade of the European merchants in Ispahan. At one time a certain portion of the trade filtered down from Tabriz, but now very little comes through that town; such Russian goods as naphtha, glassware, and hardware as have a sale in the bazaars come via Hamadan from Resht."[41] By the end of the century the province equaled, if it did not excel, any other province in its general state.[42]

By 1900, as port of entry of British and Indian goods, Kermanshah was hardly behind Bushehr, only 10% less annual turnover. According to Whigham, Kermanshah imports could be increased, because the Persian Manufacturing Company sent its carpets via Baghdad, while Messrs. Ziegler, as of 1903, sent its £60,000 worth of carpets via Resht and the Caucasus, because of the "irritating delays of the Tigris river service," although that route was at least 20% more expensive than via Baghdad.[43] Whigham further submitted that Curzon pushed the Karun scheme, which money, in his view, would be better spent on improving the Baghdad route. He also argued against the proposed Dezful-Borujerd road that Curzon favored, because it would not bring British piece goods closer to Hamadan and Kermanshah, as it the itinerary was longer than via Baghdad and the route went through an area without settlements.[44]

In 1906, there were good spring rains, which signaled that prospects for the harvest were good, which would increase imports. And indeed, trade with India increased, due to larger imports of sugar and spices. The increase of French trade at that time was due to larger sugar imports.[45]

Table 6.8: Total imports into Kermanshah via Turkey 1904-1914 in £

Year	Imports	Exports
1895-97 (average)	822,000	140,700

41. DCR 2260, p. 15.
42. Adamec 1976, vol. 1, pp. 336-37.
43. Whigham 1903, p. 281.
44. Whigham 1903, p. 282.
45. DCR 3683, p. p. 4.

Year	Imports	Exports
1901-02	866,000	182,731
1902-03	?	?
1903-04	894,812	193,918
1904-05	836,949	217,564
1905-06	745,674	165,032
1906-07	1,014,366	294,903
1907-8	1,240,445	230,679
1908-09	1,397,114	300,420
1909-10	1,259,138	321,662
1910-11	1,433,201	280,188
1911-12	1,124,261	287,908
1912-13	875,302	274,264
1913-14	1,301,123	252,405

Source: DCR 590; Whigham 1903, p. 280; Administration Report 1905-06, p. 46; Administration Report 1907/08, p. 63; DCR 4559, p. 8; DCR 4766, p. 8; DCR 5419, p. 6. Adamec 1976, vol. 1, pp. 361-62 (has slightly differing figures).

In 1906-07, trade further improved.[46] However, due to disturbances during the of summer 1907 trade almost stopped and recovered slowly, although total imports grew. Thereafter practically all the money arriving from the districts was needed for the customs. Trade during 1907-08 continued to grow, because merchants considered the Basra-Baghdad-Kermanshah route the safest route in Persia from the south.[47] Despite the disturbed state of the country trade increased in 1908-09, partly due to safety on the road, but dependent on boat transport between Basra and Baghdad.[48] Although trade was impacted by political unrest and lack of safety on the trade road, the upward trend in imports continued. The Kermanshah level of imports was higher than that of Bushehr and was slowly reaching the level as that of all Southern Persian ports, and finally exceeding them.[49]

The years 1911-13 were bad for trade due to occupation and plunder by rebels of town (February 1912) and province, who, moreover, forced merchants to make loans. This impoverished both the population and merchants. At the end of May 1912 government forces retook the city and province, but the roads remained unsafe for months afterwards. Also, food and fodder was scarce and prices were abnormal. During July-October 1912 there was an increase in trade, when goods that had accumulated at the border were brought in. In November there were robberies again on the road, the season that camels came into the hills; also exactions for safe road passage by road guards and tribesmen caused drop in trade as importers could not make a profit. In January 1913 the roads were safe again, but transport rates remained high. Camels brought

46. Administration Report 1906-07, p. 42.
47. Administration Report 1907-08, pp. 63-64; DCR 4100, p. 4.
48. DCR 4365, p. 6.
49. FO 248/938, Haworth to Resident, Bushire 06/08/1908.

goods from Baghdad to Qasr-e Shirin where they remained in bond, merchants sending donkeys to being in small quantities occasionally.[50]

Because the city and province of Kermanshah were the scene of battle, occupation, famine, and the influenza pandemic during 1915-18 there was little trade, because the route to Baghdad was closed to trade. Anyway, no data are available, even about local trade, which must have continued to ensure that the population was fed and clothed. According to a British official writing in 1918:

> The trade of this town has sunk to a low level as the Baghdad route has been closed since November 1914, and the Shiraz route is closed also, and some of the other routes are infested with robbers. A way, however, has been open for some months from Basra through the hitherto closed territory of the Vali of Pusht-i kuh, and caravans of tea and sugar are coming up by slow degrees. These commodities fetch a hundred per cent. profit, and are sold at prices far beyond the reach of the poor.[51]

After the British capture of Baghdad in March 1917, trade with Baghdad slowly restarted and in 1918 continued to flourish. Trade's major problem was the lack of pack animals, which were mainly used for military uses and roadwork. In September 1918, merchants were paying 10-12 *qran*s/donkey/day to get their goods to Hamadan.[52] Trade was also constrained by the lack of a functioning postal and telegraph system. Civilian mail was delayed due to military necessities and, therefore, letters from Baghdad often took three weeks to reach Kermanshah. However, civilian telegrams from Baghdad to Kermanshah posed no problem and were sent via military lines. Contrariwise, telegrams from Kermanshah to Baghdad had to be sent via Karachi. Moreover, the Persian telegraph often broke down, causing further delay.[53] After the war's end in November 1918, all trade restrictions with Iraq were lifted. However, the above mentioned problems, in particular that of transport remained an obstacle. The transport system came even more under pressure, because pilgrim traffic also resumed and was increasing. In November 1918, 514 passes were issued, in December, 1367. However, restrictions on carrying corpses to Mesopotamia were not lifted, which gave rise to the smuggling of corpses by Arabs via Posht-e Kuh on riding camels by Arabs, which was a very lucrative business.[54]

Whereas in April 1920 there were no problems on the roads this was different in July. Arriving caravans constantly complained about exactions. The reason was that all revenue taxes were farmed lowly, and all farmers took more than their due, and they all fleeced the muleteers. Moreover, the road guards had not been paid for 3-5 months, and the gendarmes not for two months. Also, the responsibility and duties were divided between them, with unsatisfactory

---

50. DCR 4994, p. 5; DCR 5204, p. 3.
51. Hale n.d. pp. 217-18 (06/01/1918).
52. FO 248/1204, Kermanshah report no. 8, 05/10/1918 by Lt. Col. Kennion; Idem, Kermanshah report no. 9, 01/11/1918 by Lt. Col. Kennion.
53. FO 248/1204, Kermanshah report no. 9, 01/11/1918 by Lt. Col. Kennion.
54. FO 248/1204, Kermanshah report no. 10, 03/12/1918 by Lt. Col. Kennion; Idem, Kermanshah report no. 11, 31/12/1918 by Lt. Col. Kennion.

results.[55] Trade remained dull, though merchants made good money due to high prices and the fall in exchange rates following the events in Baghdad (Arab rebellion) and Resht (Bolshevik incursion). The Mesopotamia Trading Corporation opened a big garage in Kermanshah, which was managed by a Brit; the company had several lorries and cars on the road. In addition, there were some 60 cars, public and private, in town. Petrol was sold at prohibitive rates. The road was safe, although there had been some robberies, despite the fact that road guards had still not paid for 5-7 months.[56] Even though the railway was not yet open to civil traffic, some goods reached Baghdad, but unofficially and with difficulty.[57]

Because of the aftermath of WW I, in particular the Russian revolution and the troubles in the northern province of Gilan, the commercial role of Kermanshah increased significantly. In fact, by 1920-21, not including petroleum exports, Kermanshah was Persia's most important customs revenue earner, underlining the importance of the Basra-Bagdad-Kermanshah trade route.[58] This route was already growing in importance before the war, while the construction of a railway between Basra-Baghdad and Baghdad-Khaneqin made this route in particular attractive for the transportation of fragile and perishable goods. Also, the closure of the northern trade routes was another and major factor that boosted the importance of this route. "From the figures in Table 6.9 it will be seen that imports via Kermanshah which amounted to kran 190 million in 1921-1922 exceeded in volume those of any other customs post in Persia, in spite of the 1 per cent. transit tax to which all goods passing through Iraq are subjected. In winter caravans leave the metalled road near Hamadan and make their way to Tehran via Sultanabad and Qum or direct via Nobaran in order to avoid the Aveh Pass north of Hamadan and the intense cold of the Kazvin plain." As is clear from is stated earlier in this chapter, Kermanshah was already the major port of Persia in the first decade of the nineteenth century. Manchester goods still were imported in large quantities, although there was a fall in their imports due to fierce competition from other European countries with depreciated coinage.[59]

Table 6.9: Import and Export by Major Customhouses (1920/21 - 1923/24) in *qrans*

Customs house	Imports 1920/21	Exports 1920/21	Imports 1923/24	Exports 1923/24
Kermanshah	145,625,040	33,201,315	194,338,059	61,483,413
Bushehr	98,043,706	32,314,481	277,660,769	505,193,516
Sistan	29,411,393	3,088,563	58,355,674	26,056,956
Tabriz	3,345,248	11,247,355	46,691,768	39,372,960
Caspian ports	6,582,180*	1,186,578*	57,574,989	58,588,879
Parcel post	2,301,188	2,717,149	5,091,725	5,411,253
Total	482,000,000	138,000,000	672,164,675	739,758,253

Source: Temple 1922, p. 10; Hadow 1925, p. 47.

55. FO 248/1293, Tel. Consul to Legation, 30/07/1920.
56. FO 248/1293, Kermanshah Report no. 7, up to 15 September 1920.
57. FO 248/1293, Kermanshah Report no. 9, up to 10 October 1920.
58. Temple 1922, p. 10.
59. Hadow 1923, pp. 10-11.

*no data from Resht due to revolutionary activities

As of 1924, the position of Kermanshah was being challenged, due to the increased use of the northern trade routes, which reduced traffic on the Basra road. However, Kermanshah, excluding oil, remained by far the most important import town of Persia. An additional development was that due to better maintenance the Baghdad route saw a significant development of car traffic between Persia and Beirut.

> A regular motor service connecting Tehran with Beirut is now run weekly by the Eastern Transport Company, 13, Pall Mall, London, which is also contemplating the development of freight traffic by motor lorries along the same route, giving European exporters the choice of consigning goods to Basra or Beirut, according to the nature of their goods. Between Basra and the Persian frontier the Iraq railways have developed a fast service of through goods wagons, which recently delivered a consignment of machinery at the Persian frontier within seven days of arrival at Basra. By shipping this consignment to Tehran by motor-truck it was possible to deliver 10 tons of machinery at the Persian capital within 40 days of its leaving London.[60]
>
> The fall in transit duties in Iraq also provided an incentive to increase the use of this route.[61] In 1925, the rates of animal transport on the Khaneqin-Tehran route fell by 40-50% compared with the year before the transport crisis of 1925-26. This crisis was partly offset was a significant increase in the use of lorries in Persia from 103 in 1924 to 967 in 1926.[62] The trade of Kermanshah came under greater pressure from developments both in the north and south. In the north Russian competition had become so fierce that by 1920 Hamadan had lost most of its entrepot function. Likewise, the major investments made in harbor improvements of Mohammerah as well as the new roads built in the south the Mohammarah-Khorramabad-Tehran route constituted a major competitor for the Iraq transit route to Kermanshah. Merchants considered it to be more expensive than the Bushehr route, but it had the advantage of saving time, because in winter the Kermanshah road was seldom closed. On both roads there also was an increased use of lorries.[63]

In October 1930, business, which was already suffering from a drop in trade, was at a standstill due to "an epidemic of bankruptcies."[64] Trade did not recover from this, because of the

---

60. Hadow 1925, pp. 30-31.
61. Hadow 1925, pp. 30-31, 47.
62. Lingeman 1928, p. 26. On the importance and growth of car transport, see Clawson 1993.
63. Lingeman 1930, pp. 7, 29, 34-35.
64. Lingeman 1930, pp. 27, 29. In September 1930, there was a large number of bankruptcies in Kermanshah. Baghdad merchants claimed that they lost 1 lakh of rupees. The Persian merchants estimated their loss at 2.5 million *qrans*. However, the Baghdad merchants were bilked out of their money, because of the slow and non-transparent legal system in Persia that favored bankrupt merchants. In fact, the Persian merchants continued trading as if nothing untoward had happened. Only big Baghdadi merchants were able to get some payment

imposition of the Foreign Exchange Control killed the import and forwarding trade which had enriched this city.[65] Consequently, in 1935, the Basra-Baghdad-Khaneqin to Kermanshah route was "not so much used now as previously, the import quotas for goods arriving through the Kermanshah Customs having recently been considerable reduced. Traffic is being diverted to the all-Iranian routes through Mohammarah and Bandar Shahpur." As for the Beirut-Baghdad route and on to Kermanshah, "This route is not cheaper and rarely quicker than the Mohammareh route. Transit duty through Iraq is one-half percent."[66] Because of the state monopoly of trade and high duties good money could be made by smugglers. This happened in all border regions and thus, also in Kermanshah. In 1936, Tehran appointed a new police chief to suppress smuggling activities. He arrested one of the largest smugglers plus 50 traders whom he did business with. The subsequent investigation suggested that the governor was paid-off and therefore he was recalled. The garrison commander was also suspected of involvement, but he remained.[67]

In the following years there was no change in this situation. The government continued to discourage trade via Baghdad, resulting in less commercial activity in Kermanshah. In fact, export data were not an good indicator for the health and level of local trade, as most export goods came from outside the province and were just in transit. Local importers did not receive a bigger import quota, and merchants just accepted the hard reality that if they want imported goods they had to get them from Tehran. As a result, instead of import trade merchants shifted to inter-bazaar trade, i.e. the selling local agricultural surpluses.[68]

Because of WW II, trade with Baghdad was restricted, which led to smuggling; from Persia mainly grain and tea, and from Iraq semi-luxury goods. In some cases these goods were actually declared, duty was paid, but no questions were asked. Legal trade was constrained by Iraqi customs regulations, which restricted the export to Persia of much needed goods (tires, sugar, piece-goods, and some less essential goods) at a time when the Persian government made foreign exchange available for such imports. Kermanshahi traders had only connections in Baghdad, not in India, from which they might have been able to import them. Therefore, they clamored for the easing of the Iraqi regulations, which did not happen, providing another incentive for smuggling. A good indication of this illegal trade was the increased business of the local bank, which had to handle a lot of Iraqi notes to pay for smuggled goods from Khaneqin. The *Bank-e Melli* had stopped doing commercial business, basically limiting itself to exchange dealings. Smuggling continued to increase, such that in October 1942, wealthy people in Sanandaj

---

from 'honest' Persian merchants to the value of 15-20% of the sum due; of the less 'honest' ones a few gave a small part of their debt. *The Palestine Bulletin*, Thursday 30/01/1930, p. 3

65. FO 248/1414, Vaughan-Russell Economic Report Kermanshah. March-Sept 1940.
66. Simmonds 1935, vii; Gray 1937, p. vii. In 1933, merchants in Baghdad were still optimistic about the prospects of trade with Kermanshah. Although Mohammarah was increasingly taking over from Basra, Baghdad was still able to supply a considerable share of Kermanshah's requirements. Also, there was then still hope about the advantage of the desert route from Beirut via Syria to Kermanshah. *The Palestine Post*, Thursday 02/03/1933, p. 2.
67. FO 60/416 (1936, p. 18); on smuggling in Lorestan, see Stark 2001, p. 50.
68. FO 248/1414, Vaughan-Russell Economic Report Kermanshah. March-Sept 1940.

complained that they could not get firewood or charcoal from Marivan as the Kurds and their donkeys were too busy smuggling.[69]

MERCHANTS

The growth in trade was also evident in the growth in the number and importance of the merchants in Kermanshah. In the late 1840s, according to Keith Abbott, its "mercantile community is composed of some 50 small traders, who carry on a limited traffic with places and Countries around, principally with Baghdad, Isfahan, Tabreez, Cashan, and Hamadan."[70] Around 1900, there were about 200 merchants dealing mostly in Manchester goods obtained direct from Manchester or through Baghdad, in sugar from Marseilles, and in opium, gums, goat-skins, carpets and wool, which they exported to Baghdad and England. There are six first-class merchants dealing with London, Bombay and Baghdad with a bazaar credit over £100,000 and they are said to have property of the same value. Another ten whose credit is £25,000 deal only with Baghdad and Persia. Also, many second-class merchants dealing with Baghdad and Persia, but in a small way, who have a credit of £1,000 to £2,000.[71] One of the most prominent of these was 'Abdol-Rahim Khan Vakil al-Dowleh, who combined trade with banking and landownership. His father, Hajj Agha Mohammad Hasan, Vakil al-Dowleh, came from Baghdad with Henry Rawlinson and became a British subject. He entered trade on a large scale and amassed a considerable fortune. After his death, his son 'Abdol-Rahim inherited most of his lands and possessions.[72] According to Curzon, Vakil al-Dowleh, the British native agent, had amassed great wealth being from official rapacity because of British protection. In 1890, he owned or built six caravanserais in the city, owned 100 of the 250 villages of Kermanshah and purchased the Delgosha garden. On Queen Victoria's Jubilee he feted the city of Kermanshah with an illumination (*cheraghani*). The British government awarded him for his services a CMG.[73]

Nevertheless, the merchants and bankers (*sarrafs*) of Kermanshah were really, with rare exceptions, but agents for the Baghdad or the Hamadan wholesale importers.[74] There were about twenty Ottoman Jews, who controlled the greatest part of the foreign and export trade through their family and friendship contacts with their co-religionists of Hamadan and Baghdad. Kashani merchants imported from Kashan tobacco, native silk goods, copper-ware, to a total amount of some 100,000 *tumans*, which they covered by exports to Kashan of prints and foreign goods received from Baghdad. Yazdi merchants imported henna and Yazdi silk from Yazd to the amount

69. FO 371/31402, Kermanshah Diary July 1942; Idem, Kermanshah Diary September 1942; Idem, Kermanshah Diary October 1942; FO 248/1414, Confidential note, Business in Iraqi Dinars, Kermanshah 07/09/1942.

70. Amanat 1983, p. 93.

71. DCR 2260, p. 16.

72. Harris 1896, p. 254; Bellew 1999, p. 473 (In 1872, Agha Hasan, 18 year old son of the British agent Vakil al-Dowleh.)

73. Curzon 1892, vol. 1, p. 559. A CMG means a Companion of the Most Distinguished Order of St. Michael and St. George awarded to men and women who render extraordinary or important non-military service in a foreign country.

74. Administration Report 1907-08, p. 64.

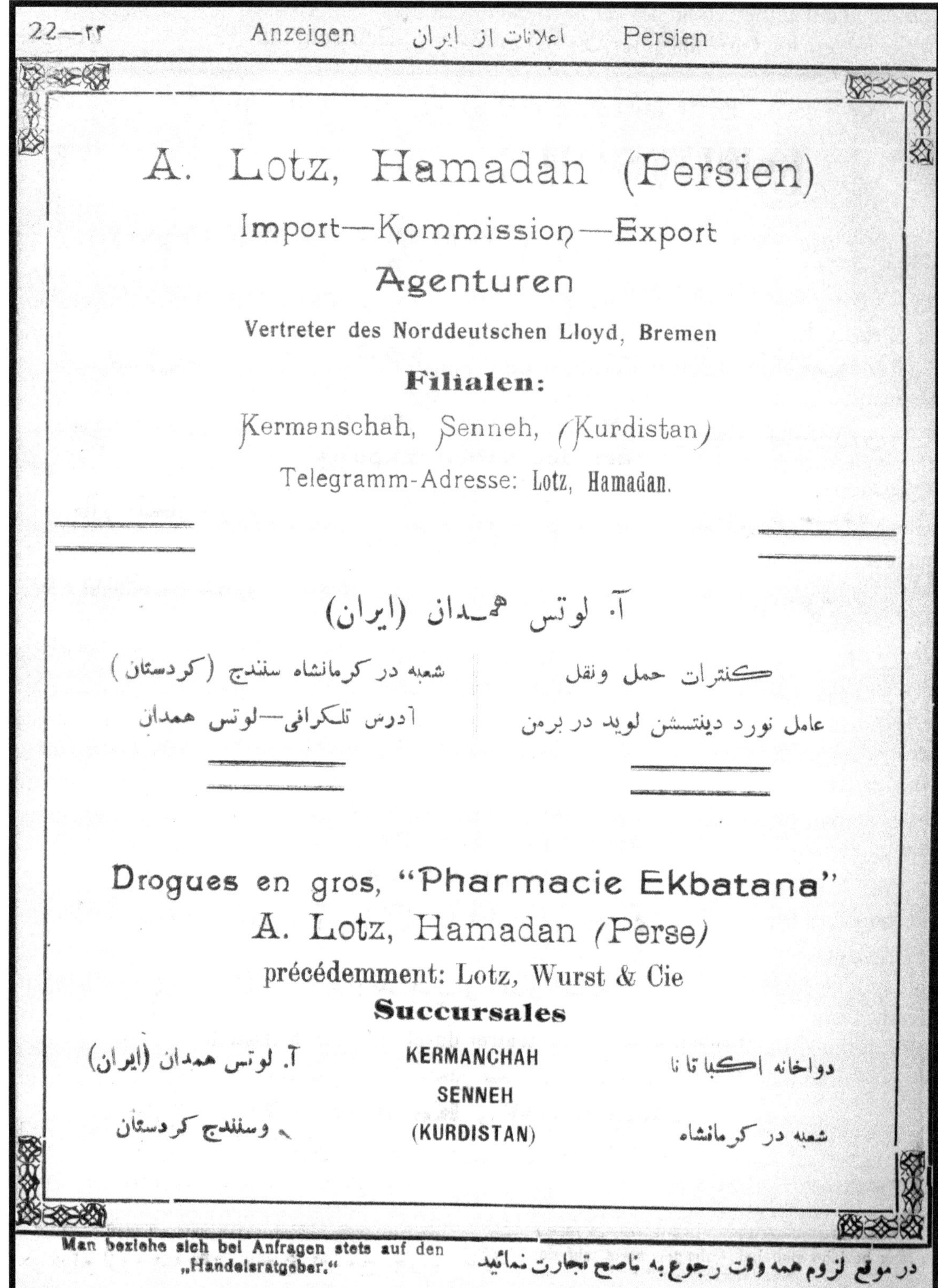

Fig. 6.4 Commercial advertisement of the Lotz pharmacy (1910).

of 20,000 *tumans*, and exported an equal amount of foreign goods to Yazd. Isfahani merchants imported native prints and cotton goods, such as *qalamkars*, prints, *lahafs*, *abas*, etc., and *gaz* and *givehs* from Isfahan, and exported to Isfahan Manchester prints, iron, tea, cowhides, wool and gelims. Their imports came to 100,000 *tumans*, but were exceeded by their exports. Hamadan merchants imported naphtha, rice, Russian prints, glassware and hardware (coming from Rasht), and exported to Hamadan dates from Mandali, gall-nuts, grease, ghee, raw hides, tea, spices, iron, lead, Manchester goods and window glass. The exports exceeded the imports. Some Hamadan merchants worked exclusively as commission agents for releasing goods from the customhouse and forwarding them to Hamadan.[75]

In 1910, the following merchants are listed as being among the most important. (i) the Russian Banque d'Escompte as sub-agent; (ii) A. Lotz, Pharmacy Hamadan (import-export); (iii) David Sasoon & Co, London; (iv) Singer & Co.; (v) Sykes, Manchester & Haji Ahmad Hamadani, (vi) Haji 'Ali Akbar Isfahani, (vii) Hajji Yusef, (viii) Hajji Mohammad Hoseyn Arab, (ix) Haji Mohammad Taqi Esfahani, (x) Haji Sayyed Ali, (xi) Haji Sayyed Asadollah, (xii) Haji Sayyed Habib, (xiii) Haji Sayyed Hasan, (xiv) Yusef Dallal, (xv) Mirza Fathollah Ra'is al-Tojjar, (xvi) Mirza Manuchehr (tragacanth), (xvii) Salman Messelun and (xviii) Thomas Rassam (export of tragacanth and raw cotton).[76]

Credit was usually allowed for three months, and for a few for six months, without any guarantee.[77] During June-August, money usually was scarce due to demand to buy wool. In 1911, although there was less wool, merchants did not want to show they had cash due to the uncertain political situation. Also, unlike normally no cash arrived from Baghdad during the winter. Therefore, it was expected that credit would come under pressure due to arbitrary demands on merchants by the various warring parties.[78]

STRUCTURE OF TRADE

It is difficult, if not impossible, to determine which countries were Kermanshah's main trading partners, because prior to 1900 we have no trade statistics for this town and province. Around 1800, part of the textiles imported from India was re-exported to the Ottoman Empire and the Arabian Coast. Olivier noted a caravan leaving Kermanshah for Baghdad loaded with, amongst other things, muslins, Indian textiles and Cashmere shawls.[79] There also was considerable and growing importation from the Ottoman Empire, amongst other things, chintzes (*indiennes*), prints, light cloth, silks, velvet, moirés, brocades, gallons, and spangles.[80] Trade moved mainly via the Baghdad-Kermanshah route until the 1820s, when the Turkish route via Erzerum-Khoy

75. DCR 590, p. 14; Adamec vol. 1, pp. 355-56; Küss 1911, part III, p. 27.
76. Küss 1911, part III, p. 28.
77. DCR 4559, p. 5; DCR 4766, p. 6.
78. DCR 4994, p. 7. credit was good, few failures; DCR 5204, p. 5.
79. Olivier 1807, vol. 5, p. 323; vol. 6, pp. 269, 321; Milburn 1813, vol. 1, p. 120. This was not a new development, but already existed for centuries.
80. Bélanger 1838, vol. 2, p. 431; Stocqueler 1832, vol. 2, p. 14.

offered a more cost-effective alternative to the Tiflis-Tabriz route, which was being promoted by the Russian government after its conquest of that part of the Caucasus. Also, the Baghdad-Kermanshah route suffered from border raids by the Persian governor of Kermanshah and the general unruliness in the Baghdad pashaliq.[81] One thing is clear, throughout the Qajar period, all exports went to Baghdad and from there these were forwarded to Europe, mainly Great Britain, and the Ottoman market. In 1912, all exports still were sent to Baghdad for further dealing, except for some to USA.[82]

It would appear that Kermanshah's imports were mainly from Europe, which were forwarded from the Levant via Baghdad or via Tabriz.[83] In 1849, Abbott noted that a considerable quantity of British cottons were sold in the Kermanshah bazaar, while in 1885, Binder noted British prints and Marseille sugar in the bazaar.[84] A British heavy-striped print (*tampush*) sold well in Kermanshah.[85] In 1902, in Hamadan, 75% of foreign goods were from W. Europe and came via Baghdad.[86] Towards the end of the nineteenth century, it would seem that Great Britain was the major trading partner. In 1911, half of British imports into Persia passed through the Kermanshah customs house.[87] So dominant were British products that "The name 'British' is accepted among the Kurds as the words 'Hall marked' are in the UK." This was in particular due to British guns and knives, of the latter especially the name Rodgers was considered the true test. "It happens that village Kurds are sold goods as inglis, which are not."[88]

Table 6.10: Total imports into Kermanshah via Turkey 1904-1914 in £

Country	1901-02	1903-04	1904-05	1905-06	1906-07	1907-08	1908-09	1909-10	1910-11	1911-12	1912-13	1913-14
UK		-	642,302	507,335	725,321	933,075	1,076,036	921,530	1,014,635	732,018	552,650	834,655
India		-	64,988	74,855	86,262	159,781	140,702	154,466	147,011	131,073	144,564	171,085
Turkey		-	62,008	52,462	53,273	40,249	69,733	83,382	106,351	122,835	92,337	129,199
Belgium		-	1,387	673	1,566	23,762	66,971	61,855	137,833	119,302	65,888	130,000
France		-	68,901	109,918	147,641	82,768	22,091	30,695	9,346	1,558	4,629	8,353
Germany		-	2,594	200	115	75	1,031	3,214	5,254	7,257	6.022	16,041
Austria		-	1,085	-	120	739	945	1,742	7,207	6,494	2,400	3,211
Sweden		-	240	-		-	304	1,714	3,450	959	2,578	4,118
Oman		-	-	-		-	1,249	1,325	1,469	1,700	2,648	4,186
Other		-	168	-		-	52	215	645	1,065	1,586	275
Russia		-	962	148	38	-	-	-	-	-	-	-
Total	865,749	894,812	844,635	745,674	1,014,366	1,240,449	1,397,114	1,259,138	1,433,201	1,124,261	875,302	1,301,123

Source: DCR 590, p. 22; Administration Report 1905-06, p. 46; DCR 4559, p. 8; DCR 4766, p. 8; DCR 5419, p. 6

81. Bélanger 1838, vol. 2, pp. 434-35; Longrigg 2002, pp. 240-49. Fraser 1826, pp. 380-83.
82. Fraser 1826, p. 363; DCR 4994, p. 6.
83. Fraser 1826, p. 365; Blau 1858, p. 45; Amanat 1983, pp. 93, 97.
84. Amanat 1983, p. 97; Binder 1887, p. 347.
85. MacLean 1904, p. 40
86. Whigham 1903, pp. 275-76.
87. DCR 4994, p. 5.
88. DCR 4100, p. 3.

Other countries played a minor role, but often dominated the market of a single commodity such as sugar (France; Belgium) and woolens (Austria-Hungary). Mercery and hardware, incl. purses, padlocks, locks, knives, penknives and razors were mainly of Russian or German manufacture or cheap local imitation. Lamps, lamp chimneys, boots and shoes were mainly French or Russian and came from the North.[89] The ranking of countries also changed over time. For example, in 1894, Great Britain, which sent cotton clothes, spun cotton, prints, copper and iron was the largest importer. France came second Franc with sugar, silk goods, and cognac. Third was a combination of Germany, Austria, and Switzerland, which sent hardware, red thread, tiles, clothes, *yazmah*, embroidered muslin, household goods, stationary and sundries. Finally came India that sent spices, coffee and tea and other drugs, while from Java came wood for construction.[90]

Not only did the ranking between countries change, but new ones also joined the competition for the W. Persian market. Belgian sugar and Swedish matches were absent from the list of imports in 1894, but both were prominent after 1900, in particular Belgian sugar that to a great extent replaced French sugar. Russian goods were totally absent in 1894 and in 1901, Russian trade was insignificant in the Kermanshah market, despite the fact that Russian trade in other parts of Persia was increasing. However, Russian goods were prevented from invading the Kermanshah market "by the cost of transport from Hamadan to Kermanshah, say 40 krans per kharvar."[91] For Russian goods exclusively came via Hamadan. In 1904, the British consul reported that "No Russian goods have yet reached Kermanshah by the subsidies Russian steamers from Odessa to Basra."[92] Transport cost was indeed the great stumbling block for Russian goods to compete in Kermanshah province, though these were quite common in Kurdistan, as is clear from the following.

> In the matter of transport the Russian goods, after a railway and sea journey to Enzeli, costing 1½ r. per pood, or after a railway and caravan journey to Tabriz, costing about 2 r. per pood, take 17 days from Tabriz and 12 days from Resht to Hamadan, the cost of transport in either case being 56 krans per 56 maunds tabrizi (1 kran per 6½ lbs.). Goods take about 25 to 30 days from Moscow to Hamadan. Manchester goods after a sea journey of say, 35, days from the United Kingdom to Busreh, and a river journey, of four to six days from Busreh to Baghdad, at an average freight of 3*s*. to 3*s*. 6d. per cwt., say, 18*s*. to 1*l*. 1*s*. per kharvar tabrizi (and very often after a delay in Busreh of from a few weeks to three or four months, according to the quantity of cargo and state of river, the months of July, August and September being the worst for the river journey), take 20 days by mule and 32 to 35 days by camel from Baghdad to Hamadan. The loss of interest on Manchester goods may roughly be given as follows: three

89. DCR 4559, p. 5.
90. Hurner 1896, pp. 644
91. DCR 590, p. 21.
92. DCR 3189, p. 31.

> to five months' interest on one-tenth of the price paid on arrival of the goods in Baghdad.[93]

Both Great Britain and Russia tried to bolster their market position by establishing a Consulate and a bank agency (see chapter three).[94] In 1905, more goods than before were brought from Russia. However, it was impossible to gauge the exact increase of Russian trade in Kermanshah, because these were not shown in customs lists. That is, the goods were recorded, but at Enzeli not at the Kermanshah customs. This also held for goods coming from Baghdad as customs did not record where they were going. However, a Russian agency to sell Singer machines opened in Hamadan. Two Russian agents came to Hamadan and Kermanshah with samples and taking orders for Russian cloth. Despite all that effort and the fact that the Russian Banque d'Escompte had an agent in Hamadan it did but little business.[95] Kurdistan, Bijar, Malayer, and Kermanshah were supplied by Hamadan with Russian prints. However, only certain designs of Russian cottons found a ready market, otherwise British cottons (gray shirtings, Mexicans, T cloth) all but monopolized the market. Russian cottons were offered at very attractive terms such as 23 months credit to the purchaser, while the exporter received a subsidy of 4 r. 65c. to 5 r. 40c. per *pud* (36 lbs.). In the case of Manchester goods "the importer has to pay one-tenth of the price in advance and nine-tenths on arrival of the goods in Baghdad."[96] In 1903, Russia exported about 750,000 *qran*s per year to Kermanshah, mainly prints, cloth, velvet, petroleum, hardware, tea and cigarettes. In 1904, a few Kermanshah merchants formed a syndicate and ordered as an experiment £2,000 worth of Russian cottons, mostly raised back prints. Exports to Russia were mostly lambskins (the most important article), walnuts; fox skins from the Guran and Zohab districts; otter skins; weasel ermine and wolf skins, a total of 20,000 skins. Old carpets were also sometimes exported to Russia, but by 1903 the supply was almost exhausted.[97] Ten years later petroleum was the only important commodity coming from Russia.[98]

By 1910, according to a German estimate, the Russian market share in Kermanshah was estimated to be about 20%, which is not borne out by British data. Russian fabrics were unable to compete with Manchester cottons, but had a strong market presence with tea glasses, glassware, samovars, lamps, and porcelain. The Firma Lotz in Hamadan tried to improve the German position in Kermanshah.[99] In 1913, the sale of Russian textiles had increased. Most of them were prints that were said to be of a faster dye than the Manchester tissues, of a greater variety of patterns and of medium quality. The Manchester goods were either of top quality and expensive or cheap but of inferior quality. However, the import trade in cottons was almost entirely carried on by Baghdad agents of Manchester firms who forwarded goods for sale.[100] A reflection of the much reduced, but still strong British market position, was the view of the shops in the

93. DCR 3189, pp. 41-42.
94. Küss 1911, part III, p. 27.
95. DCR 3683, pp. 3, 5.
96. DCR 3189, pp. 41-42.
97. DCR 3189, p. 30.
98. DCR 5204, p. 4 (with prices).
99. Küss 1911, part III, p. 27.
100. DCR 5419, p. 4; DCR 5204, p. 3 (sales of Russian prints dropped and German prints tried to take their place).

bazaar in 1930, which "were flooded with the cheap rubbish of Russia, Germany and Czecho-Slovakia."[101]

IMPORTS

In the 1820s, Kermanshah's import trade was with Baghdad, from where merchants brought specie, gold and silver as well as European manufactures brought from the Levant.[102] In the 1830s, the main trade relations were with Baghdad and Shushtar, "whence come cloths, from Isfahan by way of Kenghevar, from Hamadan, Sinneh, and Sulimanieh."[103] It had trade relations with Baghdad, and with Isfahan, Tabriz; it also imported and forwarded indigo, rice and dates from Khuzestan.[104] In the 1880s and 1890s, imports were Manchester and Indian piece goods, continental woolens and cottons, drugs, (pepper, coffee, tea, sugar, indigo, cochineal, spelter), metals and sugar (iron, steel, copper) and sugar.[105] In the decades thereafter piece goods and sugar continued to dominate imports. In 1920, the main imports were: sugar (Indian, Egyptian), Indian tea, Swedish matches, cloth and cotton goods, petrol, and motor cars.[106] Although data are lacking for most years, in 1933-34 the major imports products were cars, steel, cottons and machinery, in addition to the usual items.[107]

COTTONS

In 1850, "The manufactures of England are retailed in about 40 shops in the Bazar; the yearly importations of these goods being estimated to amount to 500 Horse Loads worth about £25,000" or about 5% of total European cottons, woolens and silks.[108] In 1901, a British heavy-striped print (*tampush*) sold well in Kermanshah.[109] Textiles were, if not the first then the second most important group of imported goods. For example, in Kermanshah, in 1885, textiles formed 22% of imports.[110] One of the reasons why mainly or increasingly, depending on the regional market, Persian traders were involved in the textile trade was the customs tariff. Foreign importers were subject to a different regime than Persian ones. While European had to pay 5% import duty, "Persians have imported T-red twills and prints from Baghdad, via Kermanshah, paying a total duty equal to 2 1/8 per cent; of course in some articles the difference is not so marked."[111] In

---

101. Alexander 1934, p. 24.
102. Fraser 1826, p. 365, see also p. 364! Beth Hillel 1832, p. 88 ("grain, wool, cotton, fat ghee, and honey, which are conveyed to Baghdad, and to other places.")
103. Southgate 1840, vol. 1, p. 137.
104. Blau 1858, p. 45.
105. Curzon 1892, vol. 2, p. 577; Hurner 1896, pp. 645.
106. AIR 20/663, p. 53.
107. FO 371/21900.
108. Amanat 1983, pp. 94, 97 (via Tabriz).
109. MacLean 1904, p. 40
110. DCR 113, p. 7.
111. DCR 2260, p. 12.

1910, cottons were the most important import commodity, and Manchester has practically the monopoly in Kermanshah and Hamadan. India supplied a small quantity of cheaper Mexicans.[112] "There is practically no competition with Manchester-made cottons in Kermanshah and Hamadan."[113] Even Russian red ground cotton goods, a popular fabric, were ousted by British cottons, which were of inferior quality. This was because a few Hamadan Jews had migrated to Manchester where they ordered inferior cloth made to sample. These goods were then exported to their friends in Kermanshah and Hamadan, who sold the cottons on commission. The firms were: Isaacs Bros. & Co - M.J. Somekh & Co.; Joseph Sassoon, Sykes & Co.; Yehouda Heskel & Co.; Shamash Bros. & Co.; J.J. Ini Bros. & Co.; E.S. David & Co. ; M.S.S. David & Co.[114] In practice this meant that the importation of cottons was almost entirely in the hands of Baghdad agents of these Manchester firms who forward most of them for sale to Hamadan, while Kermanshah supplied the neighboring villages. Dealers from Senneh and Kurdistan bought from Kerman importers. Due to bad trade conditions in 1913 there were few orders, therefore, Baghdad firms sent more of the cheaper kinds, thus making it appear that they were not as good as usual anymore.[115]

Russian prints only played a limited role. Kurdistan, Bijar, Malayer, and Kermanshah were supplied by Hamadan with Russian prints. Only certain designs of Russian cottons found a ready market, otherwise British cottons (gray shirtings, Mexicans, T cloth) all but monopolized the market. In 1913, the sale of Russian textiles had increased. Most of them were prints that were said to be of a faster dye than the Manchester tissues, of a greater variety of patterns and of medium quality. The Manchester goods were either of top quality and expensive or cheap but of inferior quality. However, the import trade in cottons was almost entirely carried on by Baghdad agents of Manchester firms who forwarded goods for sale.[116] In 1918, imports into Basra were $37 million, of which $17 million were cotton piece goods, 75% of which were for the Persian market. Exports from Persia that year were $10.4 million.[117]

HIDES

In the mid-nineteenth century Kermanshah still exported goat-skins, dressed or raw.[118] However, the city lost this function entirely to Hamadan where raw hides and lambskins from Baghdad were tanned in Hamadan and sold in Persia or sent to Russia via Tabriz and Rasht.[119]

---

112. DCR 4766, p. 5; DCR 4994, p. 5.
113. DCR 4559, p. 5.
114. Administration Report 1908, p. 47.
115. DCR 5204, p. 4; DCR 4994, p. 5.
116. DCR 5419, p. 4; DCR 5204, p. 3 (sales of Russian prints dropped and German prints tried to take their place).
117. Heizer 1920, p. 524.
118. Amanat 1983.
119. DCR 590, p. 22.

INDIGO

In Kermanshah some indigo was grown for local consumption,[120] however there also was import of indigo from Khuzestan.[121] In the mid-1890s, in Kermanshah aniline dyes were much less used, as well as in Lorestan and Malayer, who sent their carpets to Kermanshah, whence they were exported to Egypt, Syria, Baghdad and Bombay, where they had a ready sale.[122] However, that did not mean that no aniline dyes were imported from Baghdad, for they were until 1900, when the customs authorities took severe steps so that smuggling became costly to the smugglers, who were mainly Persian Jews.[123] The 1903 Customs Tariff imposed much higher duties on goods such as indigo. The British consul in Kermanshah calculated that the old tariff on indigo and *qermez* (crimson dye; cochineal) would have been 3,689.65 and 9,092.70 and, under the new tariff regime, amounted to 125,000 *qran*s for both items jointly.[124] It did not make much difference, for aniline dyes continued to be smuggled through Kurdistan and were for sale in the Kermanshah bazaar. As a result, not one carpet in 10 was free from this artificial dye; its brightness appealed to Persians.[125] In fact, imports and the use of artificial German indigo increased, because it was cheaper and easier to work with than the natural one. By 1910, German synthetic indigo threatened the dominant role of natural indigo at Kermanshah and Hamadan.[126] The year 1911 was the year that synthetic indigo overtook natural indigo. Despite some increase in natural indigo, synthetic indigo nearly equaled it in weight, and if it had not been for the First World War synthetic indigo would have marginalized natural indigo.[127] The price of German synthetic indigo had dropped significantly due to the competition of two German firms for the market. In 1913, the price of Indian indigo was 50 *qran*s and German indigo 30 *qran*s per *batman*.[128]

Table 6.11: Indigo import into Kermanshah during 1885-1913

Year	Chemical lbs.	£	Natural lb.	£
1885	-	-	150 loads	8,570
1897	-	-	150 loads	4,400
1901-02	5,694 *man*	1,024	2,253 *man*	2,289
1902-03	-	-	1,343 *batmans*	1,263
1903-04	-	-	5,768 *batmans*	4,896
1904-05	-	-	5,768 *batmans*	5,153

120. Amanat 1983, pp. 93; DCR 3189, p. 34.
121. Blau 1858, p. 45.
122. DCR 2260, p. 16-17.
123. DCR 590, p. 23.
124. DCR 3043, p. 16.
125. DCR 4100, pp. 3-4.
126. DCR 4766, p. 6; DCR 4994, p. 6.
127. DCR 5204, p. 6.
128. DCR 5419, p. 4.

Year	Chemical lbs.	£	Natural lb.	£
1905-06	-	-	38,216 lbs	5,046
1906-07	-	-	53,619 lbs.	9,092
1906-07	-	-	72,448 lbs.	27,884
1908-09	14	260	353	6,708
1909-10	127	2,435	926	19,469
1910-11	191	2,833	649	13,156
1911-12	405	6,702	240	4,564
1912-13	375	5,827	427	7,377
1913-14	-	-	3,783 lbs	16,284

Source: The imports of indigo via Kermanshah 150 loads at 200 tomans, or 30,000 tomans (£8,570) in 1885. DCR 113, p. 7; DCR 590, p. 26, 28; DCR 3043, p. 11, 16 (10,442 batman at £3,224 of *kermez* from France); DCR 3189, pp. 9, 19; *DCR* 3420, pp. 4, 13; DCR 3683, p. 12; DCR 4365, p. 15; DCR 4559, p. 11; DCR 4766, p. 10; DCR 5204, p. 9 (chemical = Germany; natural = India). DCR 5419, p. 7. The data for 1903-1907 also include the importation of *qermez* (cochineal); these have not been deducted because they represent less than one percent of the total imports for each year.

In nearby Soltanabad large quantities of Indian indigo and German synthetic indigo were imported from Kermanshah for its manufacturing industry.[129] Consequently, being a major consumer, here also the use of natural indigo had fallen off considerably, for by 1913 mostly synthetic indigo was in use.[130] Likewise, the same phenomenon was repeated in Azerbaijan. Indigo imports in Tabriz had a value of £2,030 in 1904-05 and £3,216 in 1903-04. Six years later, in 1910-11, indigo imports were at £3,579, or a level similar to that of 1904, but imports dropped in 1911-12 to £2,293. The decrease was due to the introduction of synthetic German indigo, "which will probably in time monopolise the market."[131]

PETROLEUM

Petroleum was the only article of daily use imported from Russia. In 1910, some 5,000 iron casks arrived at Kermanshah, containing 10, 12 and a few 16 gallons each; it sold at 2-2.5 *qran*s per *man* of 6.5 lbs.[132] When there was interruption of supply of Russian petroleum American petroleum was imported from Baghdad, which was inferior.[133] The import of this and other oil products from Abadan, via Baghdad, came to an end after the construction of the oil refinery in Kermanshah in 1935 (see above).

129. DCR 5048, p. 53; DCR 5254, p. 72.
130. DCR 5521, p. 50.
131. DCR 5088, p. 5; DCR 3507, p. 5.
132. DCR 4766, p. 5.
133. DCR 4994, p. 6 (with prices).

SUGAR

During the first decade of the twentieth century, sugar imports from France decreased, while those from Belgium increased. The reason was because French sugar was packed in cumbersome boxes. Contrariwise, Belgian sugar was packed in gunny bags, which were more easily handled and lighter and preferred despite higher breakage. Packing in bags cost 8% per gross weight; in case of boxes was double this percentage.[134] Loaf sugar was packed in sacks with 32 loaves each, "cases being unsuitable for mule transport." Each sack weighed 115 lbs.[135] Sugar was "only imported in small quantities in winter, the risk of moisture being very great."[136]

By 1913, Russian loaves, which had to compete with Belgian sugar in Hamadan, was strongly marketed in Kermanshah and sold ¼ *qran* per *man* cheaper than the Belgian sugar. It was also marketed in small loaves like the Belgian sugar, because consumers did not like large loaves either. Russian sugar could not really compete with the Belgian sugar in Kermanshah, provided that the transport rates from Baghdad were normal. Therefore, Russian sugar was sold in Soltanabad.[137] The British did not worry too much about whether sugar came from Belgium, France and/or Russia, as they were not competing in that market. However, if Belgian sugar was replaced by Russian sugar it would mean a decrease in trade from Baghdad, which meant a loss for British shipping interests.[138] In 1927, there was a decline of imports of sugar via Kermanshah, a decline that continued thereafter, as a result of the general decline of international trade in Kermanshah (see above).[139]

WOOLENS

Although woolens were all declared as coming from Great Britain, but in reality came most from Austria, with only some coming from Great Britain and Germany. The woolens were mostly for local consumption.[140] The market for woolen goods in Kermanshah amounted to £30,000, which was almost entirely in foreign hands.[141]

---

134. DCR 4365, p. 7; DCR 4994, p. 6 (prices); DCR 5204, p. 4 (prices).
135. DCR 4559, p. 5.
136. DCR 590, p. 21 note.
137. DCR 5419 p. 4; DCR 4766, p. 5; DCR 590, p. 22.
138. DCR 590, p. 21.
139. IOR/L/PS/11/276, P 689/1927 : 13 Jan 1927-10 Feb 1927.
140. DCR 4994, p. 6; DCR 590, p. 22; DCR 4766, p. 5; DCR 5204, p. 4.
141. Administration Report 1908, p. 48.

MISCELLANEOUS IMPORTS AND EXPORTS

In 1910, about 5% of total imports was tea from Russia. Most glass also came from Russia.[142] In the 1820s, the export trade with Baghdad consisted of grain, cotton, silk, tobacco and pipes, drugs, dyes, cotton goods, silk goods, Kerman and Kashmir shawls and woolen goods.[143] In the 1880s and 1890s, exports via Baghdad for the transit trade consisted of: wool, cotton, carpets, raw silk, opium, gum tragacanth, and dried fruit, while exports for local consumption was composed of: wheat, tobacco, *rowghan*, dried and fresh fruits.[144] In the twentieth century there was no major change in the composition of export products. In 1910, Kermanshah's exports were mainly: wheat, opium, raisins, apricots, walnuts, gum tragacanth, wool, skins, while guts were a recent newcomer.[145] A decade later the main exports were: carpets, skins, guts, tobacco, opium, and gum tragacanth.[146] Although data are lacking for all other years in the 1930s it would appear that in 1933-34 the major export products were: carpets, casings, gum tragacanth, dried fruit, vegetables, potatoes and hides.[147]

DATES

Dates from Kermanshah (mostly from Mandali) were distributed all over N. Persia including Isfahan.[148]

DRIED FRUIT

There was some export of dried fruit, mostly raisins in small boxes from Hamadan, Malayer and Persian Iraq, "but no great care is taken in the packing."[149]

GHEE (CLARIFIED BUTTER)

There was much production of ghee (*rowghan*), which usually governors banned to be exported to the interior. In 1904, an export permit cost 50 *qran*s per *kharvar*. Ghee was sold at 4-6 *qran*s at the beginning of spring, and 10-12 *qran*s in winter; it was usually bought in the summer by the rich people to be sold in winter at famine prices.[150]

---

142. DCR 4766, p. 5.
143. Fraser 1826, p. 363. In 1807, butter was exported to Baghdad. Dupré 1819, vol. 1, p. 238.
144. Curzon 1892, vol. 2, p. 577; Hurner 1896, pp. 645.
145. Küss 1911, part III, p. 27.
146. AIR 20/663, p. 53.
147. FO 371/21900.
148. DCR 590, p. 22.
149. Amanat 1983, p. 94; Dupré 1819, vol. 1, p. 238; DCR 4994, p. 6; DCR 3189, p. 36.
150. DCR 3189 p. 36.

GRAINS

Baghdad usually imported grains from Kermanshah.[151] In those areas where conditions to produce cereals were propitious and where communications to the nearest market were good, a grain market quickly developed. Part of the export was stimulated by the fact that caravans returned without freight, as was the case in Kermanshah, despite the fact that the freight rates to Tehran were almost twice higher than those from Tehran! In 1903, Rabino reported that, "much wheat is exported to the interior of Persian by camelmen, who, having no goods to transport for the return journey, buy wheat and barley for their own account and sell it wherever profitable, thus paying for the keep of their camels and making a small profit."[152] This made perfect sense in view of the much higher cost of outbound transportation as compared with inbound traffic. Therefore, "owing to the cost of transport it only pays to export it when there is a scarcity with high prices in Mesopotamia."[153]

Table 6.12: Rate per camel load on routes to and from Kermanshah (1904-05)

Route	From – in*qrans*	To – in *qrans*
Kermanshah to Baghdad	15	40
Tehran to Kermanshah	50	60
Hamadan to Kermanshah	20	30
Baghdad to Kermanshah	60	120
Kermanshah to Tehran	80	100
Kermanshah to Hamadan	40	60

Source: DCR 3420, p. 6.

> Another incentive was the often very low price of grains in Kermanshah. Peasants had to sell their grain immediately after the harvest to get cash to buy their various needs for the next winter. In 1875, after a bumper crop grain prices were a slow as 8 *qrans* per *kharvar* (about 7 *s*/ton). Despite this grain was unsaleable until November, because landowners still had full granaries from last's years harvest. To make room for the new grain, they had to feed wheat to their cattle and even burn it. Similar prices prevailed in 1902, when wheat was sold at 8 *qrans* (7 d. per cwt) and barley at 10 *qrans* per *kharvar* (9 d. per cwt). Usually, sales of barley in particular picked up during winter, because then large caravans of pilgrims passed through Kermanshah en route to Karbala.[154]

151. Dupré 1819, vol. 1, p. 238.
152. DCR 3189, p. 33.
153. DCR 4559, p. 7.
154. DCR 590, pp. 16-17; Curzon 1892, vol. 1, 558 (110,000 tons surplus); Whigham, p. 272. "There are two ways of storing grain in the province of Kermanshah. The usual way is to dig a large hole and lay straw in it; the grain is then poured in the middle and the hole covered over and Kahgelled. Each hole contains from 6 to 7 kharvars, and grain thus stored can be kept for many years, unless it be eaten by insects. The other way is to put the grain in store rooms, where it occasionally gets damaged when the rain-water leaks through the roof. As soon as insects

Even in a wheat surplus province such as Kermanshah, a bad harvest might have serious consequences for the population. This was the case in 1885, when the harvest was not good, wheat rose from 17 *qrans /kharvar* to 25 *qrans*. In 1886, the harvest was better, but the wheat price was still at 20 *qrans* and, as a result, there was no export of grain to Baghdad.[155] In 1897, when wheat prices were 25 *qrans* (1*l*,2*s*., 6*d*.) per ton, although still cheaper than elsewhere in Persia. However, because of a dry winter, prices in 1897-98 rose to 125 *qrans* per *kharvar*.[156] The same happened in 1903, when 25% less wheat was produced than normal. Consequently, prices, which, in 1902, had been 11-12 *qrans* rose to 25-33 *qrans* per *kharvar* (about 300 kg), thus at least doubling and even trebling in certain cases.[157] The British consul reported, "of late years, however, this surplus has been disposed of by export, either to the interior or to Baghdad, with the result that there is no grain reserve. Consequently, the crops having failed for the last two years, great scarcity prevails. Villagers not being allowed to buy grain in town, have to live on peas, lentils and maize. The nomads have suffered very severely. Wheat started at about 40 krans per kharvar, and rose to 100 krans in town and to 250 krans in the province. Barley started at 36 krans per kharvar, and rose to 90 krans in town and 200 krans in the province."[158]

In 1903, this mishap occurred in Kermanshah, the granary of Persia par excellence. One can imagine what impact similar events might have on less well-endowed areas. It did not matter whether the area normally was a surplus area, for even the granary of Persia, Kermanshah, suffered sometimes seriously due to crop failure. In 1904 the British consul reported, "The grain crop this year was bad, and showed a deficit of 25 per cent. on the usual output. Three causes are mentioned: locusts and insects, which this year caused great destruction; insufficient rainfall; ravages and depredations of the Kakawands and Tirhan Amrais, and of the Kalhor and Sanjabi sowars or horsemen sent in pursuit."[159] In 1903 the deficit was 25% of normal output. In October the new grain was sold immediately after the harvest at 15 *qrans* per *kharvar*; last year's barley fetched 15 *qrans*. This year's barley was sold at 26 to 28 *qrans* immediately after the harvest. Last year the stores had been emptied as owners sold it at whatever price they could get; this together with crop failure caused rise in prices. From October to March wheat fetched 25-33 *qrans* per *kharvar* depending on quality.[160] The best wheat came from Mahidasht, Duru-Faraman and Do-Kushkan. In winter barley was sold at 25-388 *qrans* per *kharvar*; in March price fell to 33 *qrans*. The grain crop (*galleh*) usually is one-third barley and the rest wheat, but this year in some parts the barley crop failed.[161]

are found in a store, or when the grain has been damaged by water, it is either given to the cattle or destroyed as it has no chance of sale. By the first system proprietors are not obliged to empty their granaries to make room for new crops." DCR 590, p. 16, note *.

155. DCR 113 (1887), p. 8.
156. DCR 2260, p. 16.
157. DCR 3189, p. 32.
158. DCR 3420, p. 6 (table with rates of transport).
159. DCR 3189, p. 32.
160. DCR 3189, p. 32.
161. DCR 3189, p. 33.

The local deficit situation was partly due to natural causes, partly to disincentives created by the government of Persia. The government was in the habit to ban the export of grain when in one or more parts of the country there was a bad harvest, or worse, a famine. Such a policy had a negative impact on agricultural output of Kermanshah province. When in 1902, the government of Persia imposed a heavy export tax on grain, because of deficits in other parts of the country this had a downward impact on grain production and made things worse rather than better. The same held true for the temporary bans on export of grain during periods of scarcity and high prices. In 1902, according to the British consul, "the heavy duty imposed on grain, heavy as far as this province is concerned, is a great drawback to the welfare of the inhabitants of Kermanshah. Large amounts of grain are left rotting in the villages, and it is not unusual to see proprietors of hundreds and even thousands of kharvars of grain unable to pay for their daily expenses."[162] Although wheat continued to be exported from Kermanshah to Iraq, Isfahan, Tehran and Soltanabad, taxes levied by the governor five *qran*s per *kharvar* (300 kg) for interior, and three *qran*s per camel-load and two *qran*s per mule-load for Iraq, were no incentive.[163]

Although it was understandable that the government of Persia wanted to ban grain export when part of its population was suffering from a lack of food this policy did not resolve this issue. However, to get an idea of how difficult it was to help another part of the country one has to realize that "though Teheran is but 300 miles from Kermanshah, it cost at least twelve times what the grain is worth on the spot to transport it over that distance,"[164] and these rates applied to a normal year![165]

Heavy duty on grain export was not to the advantage of Kermanshah population. Large quantities of grain were left rotting in the villages, "and it is not unusual to see proprietors of hundreds and even thousands of kharvars of grain unable to pay their daily expenses." It was not possible to export to the interior of Persia due to high transportation cost, it would be best to allow export grain to Baghdad at a rate of 15-20% ad valorem, instead of the current rate of 100 to 140%. Officially only 8,125 *kharvar* were exported, but more wheat and flour is smuggled over the border. At the end of the year, transport rates being favorable, some wheat was exported to Soltanabad. Total output was 200,000 *kharvar*, which was sold at 10-18 *qran*s per *kharvar*. Barley sold at 18 *qrans*.[166]

When in 1924, the price of wheat was so low that the landowners near Bisotun could not make a profit by transporting it to the market, they spread the rumor of a miracle having happened at the rock relief, in which either a lame man walked or a blind man saw, nobody knew precisely what. As a result, "the lame and the blind peasants flocked here in the thousands, with the result that the local price of grain trebled itself, and the landowners waxed fat on their blasphemy."[167]

---

162. DCR 3043, p. 6.
163. DCR 3189, p. 33.
164. DCR 590, p. 17; Whigham 1903, p. 273.
165. For a detailed discussion of this problem, see Floor 2015.
166. DCR 3043, pp. 2-3.
167. Forbes-Leith 1925, pp. 173-74.

GUMS

Two kinds of gum were exported from Kermanshah. Gum tragacanth (*katira*) and gum mastic (*saqqez*), both were marketed in three qualities. The former was more expensive and was all exported via Baghdad, the latter to Russia. Gum tragacanth (*katira*) came from Borujerd and Nehavand, with inferior quality from Kurdistan and Borujerd. It was collected in the mountains from wild bushes; the roots were exposed, an incision was made from which the exuding gum was collected in the late summer.[168] Gum mastic (*saqqez*) came from the Huleylan Posht-e Kuh forests in three qualities: white, yellow and black gum, which cost respectively 5, 4, and 3 *qrans* per Tabiz *man*. Unsorted *saqqez* gum was bought at 4-5.5 *qrans* per man this year; all *saqqez* gum was exported to Russia. Although it was a considerable trade, there are no data available, because these were either recorded in the Tabriz or the Resht customs-house.[169]

From 1895 to 1897, an average of some 2,7 million *qrans* of tragacanth was exported per year to Baghdad. In 1899, some £55,000 pounds were exported to Baghdad.[170] The total exports to Baghdad in 1903 amounted to 136,072 *man*, representing a value of say 40,000 pounds. First quality *katira* stood during the year at 18 to 22 *qrans*, whilst the second quality only fetched 8 to 12 *qrans* per *man*.[171]

Table 6.13: The cost of exporting *katira* from Kermanshah to Baghdad in 1903

Packing &c., per *man*	0.50 *qrans*
Freight to Baghdad, per *man*	0.50 *qrans*
Customs duty and sundry expenses at Turkish Custom-house	4 per cent.
Commission if the gum be sold in Baghdad	1½ per cent.
Cleaning and sorting the gum in Baghdad	2 per cent.
Commission paid in Baghdad if the gum be sent to London to be realized there for account of the Kermanshah merchant, per load of 50 *man*	1 *qran*

Expenses on gum sent to London amount to 1*l*.T. per case of 1¾ cwts. The commission charged in London is 2½ per cent.

Source: DCR 3189 p. 27.

Because of disturbances in Lorestan in 1904 there was a very limited supply of gum tragacanth. The total amount put on the Kermanshah market was only one-third of the amount disposed of every year, which led to a 10 percent rise in the price of the gum. Exports to Baghdad amounted to 1,496 *kharvars* in 1904, against 1,410 *kharvars* in 1903. About a quarter of that volume was exported to Russia via Resht to Tabriz. Of the gum exported from

168. DCR 4365, p. 7; DCR 4994, p. 6 (prices 34-40 *qrans* for 1st quality; 17-25 *qrans* for 2nd quality and 12-15 *qrans* for third quality); DCR 5204, p. 4 (prices 28-39 *qrans* for 1st quality; 17-23 *qrans* for 2nd quality and 10-16 *qrans* for third quality).

169. DCR 3189, p. 29. 3,000 loads of 50 *man*; *katira* 500 *kharvar*, Armenian firms and Persians send agents to by gums for Russia. Idem, p. 30.

170. *AP* 1899, 101, p. 16, 18; DCR 590, p. 27, table II.

171. DCR 590, p. 19, 68 (The customs house tariff in December 1902 was: Gum tragacanth no. 1 = 30 *qrans*; No. 2 =18 *qrans*; no. 3 = 13 *qrans*; arrebor = 8 *qrans*; gooreh = 5 *qrans*).

Kermanshah to Baghdad, about seven-eighths went to London, one sixth to France and one sixteenth to Germany.[172] In 1905, some 414,917 *man* were exported, whereas the year before it was only 159,140 *man*. The gum not only came from the area around Kermanshah (only some 20%), but in particular from the hills around Borujerd and Nehavand, Malayer and beyond, while an inferior quality came from Kurdistan and Borujerd. In 1910, there was still export of some 290 tons, but quantities were going down due to the disturbances in the border areas, and would dry up altogether, after 1915 due to World War I.[173] However, as of 1919 export of gums was resumed.[174]

GUTS

A lot of guts were exported from Kermanshah to Tiflis and Istanbul via Hamadan and Resht; they were used as wrappers. "About 40 sheep and goats are killed daily in Kermanshah and during the pilgrim season the number may reach 140. In summer, when the nomad flocks are near the city, for every tree goats one sheep is killed, whilst in winter it is the reverse. Guts from goats are about 17-18 *zar-e Tabrizi* long and sheep guts 24-30 *zar*. The guts have to be cleaned and made into length of 28 meters. 1,000 guts, uncleaned, cost 9-20 *tumans*, yielded about 700 cleaned and prepared guts getting 40 *qrans*. Until quite recently guts were simply thrown away."

Number of guts

	From	To
Kermanshah	18,000	20,000
Sonqor	500	700
Kangavar	700	800
Asadabad	800	900

In 1903, in total some 20,000 to 22,400 guts were exported with a value about 1,000 to 1,300 *tumans*.[175]

OPIUM

In Kermanshah, raw opium was either brought to Kermanshah and sold to the export merchants or sold on the spot to peddlers (*jambaz*), who disposed of it in town. The export merchant very often bought opium in small quantities. When he had a sufficient quantity of opium, he stored

172. DCR 3189, pp. 27-29.

173. DCR 3420, p. 6; DCR 4365, p. 7; DCR 4559, p. 6; DCR 5204, p. 4; Bader 1915, p. 1054 (with list of countries to which it was exported).

174. FO 371/21900.

175. DCR 3189, pp. 30-31.

it in large copper pans, until it was prepared for export.[176] It was indeed not unusual that other production centers supplied a regional staple, which in turn might supply another larger regional staple, as the case of Kermanshah demonstrates. In Kermanshah province opium cultivation had been of marginal importance, and only for local consumption, until the cultivation for export began. Opium cultivation on a larger scale and for export only started in 1875 in Kermanshah and Borujerd. Since 1876 the production in Kermanshah had been as follows:

1876 250 *man* of Tabriz
1877 350 *man* of Tabriz
1878 1,000 *man* of Tabriz
1879 1,500 *man* of Tabriz
1880 2,000 *man* of Tabriz
1881 2,000 *man* of Tabriz

Within a period of five years the production of opium had increased by 800%. The local authorities considered this new export crop a windfall, and contrary to the practice in the south, they imposed a duty at a rate of one *man* in six in 1878. No impost was levied if opium was taken into town. An export duty of five *tumans* was levied on a load of 50 *man*. This fiscal policy was understandable, when one realizes that much of the Kermanshah opium was brought from Nehavand, Kangavar and Kerend. About 150 *man* of opium was prepared each year in Kermanshah for local consumption, the rest was taken to Isfahan.[177] By 1890, the production was as follows:

Table 6.14: Opium production in Persia by region, in cases (1890)

Yazd	4,000
Khorasan	3,000
Isfahan	2,300
Shiraz	1,200
Kerman	500
Borujerd	500
Kermanshah	300
Other locations	1,200
Total	13,000

Source: Floor 2003, p. 452.

There was no major change in the export from Kermanshah. In both 1903 and 1904 the total amount exported was 21,840 *batmans* (1903) and 20,422 *batmans* (1904).[178] As a result, Persian

176. DCR 3189, p. 21.

177. FO 60/449, p. 9.

178. DCR 3189, pp. 24-25 (Average price this year was 3,400 *qrans* per chest. 90% goes to Hong-Kong; 10% to London and Egypt.).

exporters became more careful and adulteration decreased. Rabino reported in 1904, "Kermanshah opium usually contains 8½ per cent. of morphia, and has at the present time a very good name on the Hong-Kong market, the adulteration which was practised some years ago, having ceased."[179]

The export of opium via Kermanshah remained steady. As in the nineteenth century, most of the opium exported from Kermanshah, in fact, 70 percent was collected from Kurdistan, Malayer, Nehavand, Borujerd, Lorestan and locally, the remainder was in transit from Hamadan.[180] In Kermanshah, one chest contained 140 loaves or cakes (*chuneh*) of 100 *methqal*s each. The chest contained consequently about 22 *man-e Tabriz* or 79 lbs. of prepared opium. To produce this amount from 27 to 33 *mans*, according to quality, of raw opium were required. The following table gives the yield of opium from various places.

Table 6.15: Opium yields, cost and efficiency of opium processing by four regions, 1903

Origin	Quantity		Cost of raw opium	Opium per *man*	Prepared opium
	From	To	From	To	
	Man	*Man*	*Tomans*	*tomans*	*man*
Lorestan	27	29	7 ½	11	22
Kermanshah	..	30	7 ½	12	22
Nehavend	32	33	6 ½	11	22
Borujerd	32	33	5 ½	9	22

Source: DCR 3189, p. 22

Kermanshah exported some opium to Baghdad, but the bulk went to Isfahan.[181] For export to Europe opium was sent in boxes of 200 lbs. containing 266 cakes each. For export to China, opium was packed in tin-lined cases, containing 140¼ lbs. net.[182] In Kermanshah, "a box of opium, that it is to say half a load, contains two small zinc cases each containing 70 loaves of opium, weighing 100 miscals each."[183] Because the export tax on each chest was heavy, and as the duty was levied per chest and not per pound, a small profit could be made by having light cases and making them hold, by careful packing, a little more. The cases were marked, "sewn up in hides, or, still better, dammered, i.e. packed in tarpaulin."[184] The expenses for preparing a chest of opium (22 *man-e Tabriz*) were as follows in Kermanshah:

179. DCR 3189 p. 23.

180. DCR 3189, p. 21; DCR 4365, p. 7; also DCR 4559, p. 6 (the best opium came from east Kermanshah, but the largest quantity from Lorestan, the rest from Hamadan, Nehavand and Posht-e Kuh). About 800 boxes during the year of 21 ½ man (139 ¾ lbs.) costing 300 to 450 *tumans*. DCR 4766, p 6.

181. FO 60/449, pp. 1-2; Administration Report 1874-75, p. 28; Administration Report 1878-79, p. 32.

182. Gleadowe-Newcomen 1906, p. 89; Floor 2003, p. 448.

183. DCR 590, p. 19; DCR 2260, p.17; DCR 3189, p. 46; DCR 3189, p. 21.

184. Wills 1893, p. 181.

Table 6.16: Cost of opium preparation in Kermanshah, 1903

	Expenses/*qrans*
Preparing the opium	40
Paper covers	4
Wrappers	1
Gunny	2
Case	6
Tin lining for case	7
Nails, oil, cloth, rope, &c.	1.25
Total	61.25

Source: DCR 3189 p. 23.

Another method was practiced in Isfahan and other places, where "adulteration takes place by scraping away part of the skin of the poppy head together with the juice (opium thus adulterated is named 'pourreh'), but I am assured that this does not take place in Kermanshah."[185]

In particular Yazd, Isfahan and Kermanshah produced opium sticks of lower morphia content for domestic use. In addition they also exported *shireh*, in particular Yazd, where "smokers collect the burnt opium off their pipes, and this blackened refuse [*shireh*] finds a ready sale in Khorasan, where it obtains as much as 25 tomans a man … and smoked by those who have fallen to the very lowest depths of its indulgence."[186] In Kermanshah too, a large amount was consumed locally, "there hardly being a family without its quota of opium smokers, and the habit is increasing year by year."[187] The Kermanshah opium was said to be very strong and was mostly used for local consumption. Pure opium was called *shireh*. For local consumption, opium was prepared in sticks and was sold at about 17 *tuman*s per *man-e Tabriz*. "About 20 kharvars of opium (raw) is consumed locally by the 'waffur' smokers."[188]

RAW SILK

About 18,000 *man-e shahi* or ca. 270,000 lbs of raw Gilani silk were exported to Baghdad and from there two-thirds was forwarded to Istanbul.[189] By 1880, the main silk districts apart from Gilan were Mazandaran, Astarabad, Kermanshah, Sabzevar, Torbat-e Heydari, Qa'en, Berjand, Kashan and Yazd.[190] When the silkworm disease hit Gilan, the main silk exporting province, the affected province imported eggs from Khorasan, particularly from Sabzavar (in addition to eggs from Japan and Kermanshah). These imports started in 1868 and lasted until 1878, when they

185. DCR 3189, p. 21.
186. DCR 1662, pp. 20-21 ("this was almost as high as the price of a *man* of opium (5.89 kgs.) in Yazd before being exported to China.")
187. DCR 4365, p. 7.
188. DCR 3189, p. 23.
189. Fraser 1826, p. 358.
190. Stolze & Andreas 1885, p. 20.

proved to be a total failure due to the fact that Khorasan and other parts of Persia had also become infected by the silkworm disease.[191] Two-thirds of the crop of 1869 had been the produce of Japanese seed imported by the Ralli Bros. and the remainder of seed from Khorasan and other parts of Persia (Kermanshah).[192] The Kermanshah eggs actually came from the vicinity of Baghdad. The resulting so-called Kermanshah cocoon had a light salmon color, and was large, almond shaped, and very clean.[193] After 1874, output had dropped despite the fact that every season new silkworm eggs from Sabzavar and Kermanshah had been imported.[194] In 1908, silk with a value of £34,000 in transit from Resht was exported and in 1918 silk with a value $221,236.[195]

TEXTILES

In the beginning of the nineteenth century carpets were exported to Baghdad, which, after the decline of the Kermanshah carpet industry, only was resumed around the turn of the twentieth century. Many carpets were exported to Europe and the USA. Part of these carpets were from Soltanabad produced under supervision of the Persian Carpet Manufacturing Company, Ltd and old ones or carpets from Sarukh. Also many carpets came from Lorestan, Malayer and their hinterland. The ordinary ones were exported to Egypt, Syria, Baghdad and Bombay.[196] Although Tabriz was Persia's carpet distribution center, by 1909, many were exported via Kermanshah, due to disturbances in Tabriz.[197]

Fabrics imported from India were partly re-exported to the Ottoman Empire. Olivier noted a caravan leaving Kermanshah for Baghdad loaded with, amongst other things, muslins, Indian textiles and Cashmere shawls.[198] But not only imported fabrics were exported. Isfahani and Borujerdi cotton and woolen goods such as *qalamkar*s, *aba*s, etc. as well as Yazd and Kashan silks were exported to Baghdad for sale there as well as in Egypt, Syria and Bombay; some high quality ones even were sent to Europe, but didn't sell well there.[199]

---

191. *AP* 65 (1871), pp. 234-35; *AP* 57 (1872), p. 169; *AP* 70 (1878-79), p. 471.
192. *AP* 65 (1871), pp. 234-35.
193. FO 248/906, f. 58.
194. *AP* 82 (1877), p. 748.
195. DCR 4365, p. 7; Heizer 1920, p. 524.
196. DCR 590, pp. 22-23.
197. DCR 4365, p. 8.
198. Olivier 1807, vol. 5, p. 323; vol. 6, pp. 269, 321; Milburn 1813, vol. 1, p. 120.
199. DCR 2260, p. 17; DCR 590, p. 23.

TOBACCO

Formerly much tobacco was exported to Baghdad, but since the introduction of the Ottoman Régie in 1883 export in 1887 fell to 3,000 loads.[200]

WOOL

The main production areas for sheep wool in the 1850s were Iraq-e 'Ajam, Golpeygan, Khorasan, Kermanshah, Nehavand, Lorestan and in particular Kurdistan and Kerman. In addition to the wool from the normal two clips, there was also the wool from killed and dead sheep, though it concerned smaller quantities.[201] In Kurdistan the annual output was estimated at 2 to 2.5 tons, of which 35% was fine and middle fine white; 40% ordinary white; and 25% black and gray. The staple markets for wool were Kermanshah and Tabriz, and for export from Kurdistan, Mosul and Erzerum. The quantities, according to Blau, were substantial, but the quality left to be desired due to bad handling.[202] Camel wool was known for its length, softness, and purity, and was produced in particular in the southern and eastern provinces. The main staples were Tabriz, Kermanshah and Kerman. There was export both to Europe (via Turkey) Russia and India.[203] Around 1890, there were two main wool exporting provinces: Khorasan and Kermanshah. Wool in the other provinces, such as Kerman, was mostly used in the local shawl and carpet industries, or, elsewhere wool production was not that important.

By the 1890s, after wheat, wool had become one of the most important products of Kermanshah, because of the vast flocks of the Lors and Kurds. As in the case of other parts of Persia exporters believed that its quality might be improved by breeding. Rural women used much of the wool for carpet weaving, tent covers, saddlebags, ropes, and other articles, including, yarns, for their own use, although the yarns were also exported to Iraq and Lorestan. After deduction of the wool used for the domestic market, some 1,000,000 lbs. were left for export via Baghdad. Little care was taken to clean the wool, there were no presses, either hand or hydraulic, so that the bales were bulky. All export was by camel.[204]

The Kermanshah wool, known as *pashm-e Kurdi* or Kurdish wool, came from Lorestan, the district of the Kalhors, Gurans, Sanjabis and Koliya'is, and from the vicinity of the town of Kermanshah. The Kermanshah wool was all *bahari* or spring wool, the *pa'izi* or autumn wool did not amount to much, and being of inferior quality, was used for the manufacture of *namad*s or felts, which formed the winter overcoats of most of the Kurds. In 1904, the total output was estimated at about 2,000 *kharvar*s of half-washed wool (*nim shosteh*), of which up to recent

200. DCR 113, p. 8.
201. Blau 1858, p. 71.
202. Blau 1858, p. 71 (also for prices in 1857). The direct export from Kurdistan to Turkey was also confirmed in 1859 by Dickson. *AP* 63 (1861), p. 59.For data on the export of wool to Russia and Turkey in 1845 see Nateq 1989, pp. 227-228.
203. Stolze & Andreas 1885, pp. 22-23; Dupré 1819, vol. 1, p. 443.
204. DCR 2260, p. 16.

years 1,500 *kharvars* went to Baghdad *en route* to the United Kingdom, Marseilles and the United States, and the balance was either exported to the interior of Persia or consumed in the province. However, since about 1901, it would appear that only 500 to 1,000 *kharvars* of wool was exported to Baghdad, whilst 200 *kharvars* were consumed in the province and the balance went to Soltanabad for the manufacturing of carpets.[205] The total output in 1902 was estimated at 2,000 *kharvars* of unwashed wool, which was reduced to half that quantity when washed. Only a small portion of this was spun in Kermanshah. Because of lack of demand in Europe exports were down, although some of the wool was sent to Russia via Resht and to the carpet industry in Soltanabad and Farakhan.[206] In 1903, the wool available for sale amounted to some 1 million lbs, which was exported to Baghdad.[207]

As in other parts of Persia, urban-based agents went around the nomadic camps to buy wool. A rather varied commercial system was in place to suit the needs either of the agents and/or of the non-sedentary population.

> The wool is bought from the tribesmen in four different ways, by (a) pedlars called locally 'charchi' or 'sahra-row,' who buy the wool maund by maund either for cash, or against goods supplied; (b) middlemen who buy the wool during the winter at 2 to 3 krans per sheep and take delivery in spring. A sheep bears about ½ maund tabrizi of unwashed wool; (c) middlemen, who at the clipping season visit all the villages or encampments in the wool districts and purchase from the villagers and nomads. These middlemen usually borrow money at 20 per cent. per annum from the wool merchants in Kermanshah, and repay them in wool at the rate of the day; (d) merchants, who advance money to the chiefs of the tribes, half the sum lent bearing no interest, but being against wool to be delivered in spring at a price fixed beforehand, sometimes as low as 20 to 25 tomans per kharvar, and the other half bearing interest at 24 per cent. and repayable in wool at the rate of the day or in cash.[208]

Because of this system of commercial sales of wool, and the consequent demand for hard cash for the purchase of wool and other agricultural products, money was usually very scarce in Kermanshah during the months of June, July and August. Late arrival of funds from Baghdad, local political unrest, and insecurity in the roads only reinforced this.[209]

> There is usually 10 per cent. of black of colored hair in the wool, this is sorted and sent apart to Baghdad for sale. The following are the expenses of 100 maunds or 1 kharvar of unwashed wool brought to town before being ready for export:

Category	Expenses in krans
Cost of 100 maunds in unwashed wool, say	500*

205. DCR 3189, p. 25.
206. DCR 3043 pp. 2, 6.
207. Adamec 1976, vol. 1, p. 358.
208. DCR 3189, pp. 25-26.
209. DCR 4994, p. 7.

Weighing and porterage	4
Loss on gunny bags, sewing	10
Storing	2
Porterage to the Kasaru River for washing	3
Washing (Nim Shusteh, half-washed) and guards	15
Total	534

The rate during the season varied from 40 to 60 tomans.

The 100 maunds, after being washed in this way, produce 60 maunds of wool costing consequently 534 krans. Before being put on the market in Baghdad the exporter has still the following expenses to meet on every 60 maunds:

Category	Expenses in krans
Cost of transport to Baghdad†	50
Permit expenses, Kermanshah Custom-house	1
Quarantine permit, Khanekin	2
Porterage from town gates to custom-house, Baghdad	3
Customs duty (1 per cent.) and expenses, Turkish custom-house	12
Brokerage, ½ per cent.	3
Commission, 2 per cent.	12
Total	83

† The loads vary from 50 to 70 maunds according to the strength of the camels.

The 60 maunds of half-washed wool have consequently cost in Baghdad 617 krans, to which must be added from three to five months loss of interest (12 per cent.) on capital employed.

In reply to an inquiry as to why more care was not taken in washing and sorting the wool, the Kermanshah wool merchants declared that no skin, cotton rags or pieces of string were contained in the wool exported by them. They did not wash the wool so well for export as for spinning in the country, as well as washed wool scarcely fetched a better price in Baghdad than the usual wool exported there.

As regards the pressing the bales, the process would only leave them loss, as (as far as they were concerned) the wool was only intended for the Baghdad market, and as bulky bales presented no more difficulty for transport by camel than pressed bales.

For spinning purposes the wool is washed with better care, the process costing 10 krans more than for washing for export. The 100 maunds only produce 50 maunds, which when spun are reduced to 47 or 48 maunds. The spinning, which costs 2 ½ krans per maund, is done by the Kurdish women at odd moments, a family taking 8 to 12 days to spin 1 maund. 40 to 50 kharvars of spun wool are

> now exported to Sultanabad for the carpet industry, and 30 to 40 kharvars are used locally in the province of Kermanshah for the manufacture of carpets, rugs, gilims and woollen cloths.
>
> The season for purchasing and exporting wool in Kermanshah is June, July and August. In January, Mendali merchants bought wool in advance from the Kalhor tribe at 3 krans per sheep, i.e., about ½ maund tabrizi. These merchants can afford to offer better prices than the Kermanshah merchants, as they get the Kalhors to deliver them the wool near the frontier and are thus saved freight from Kermanshah to the frontier, a journey of seven days by caravan. Pastures being poor this year the prospects are not very good.[210]

The level of exports was determined by local and international demand for wool, by the weather, and by the political situation. In 1904, the pastures were longer than usual covered with snow, due to a severe winter, and as a result thousands of sheep died. This led to both a lower quantity and quality of the wool clip in that year.[211] Contrariwise, in 1903, the wool clip was large and excellent quality due to the heavy rains during the winter. Export of wool had generally been increasing, but there were years when demand in Europe was weak, such as in 1902, when there was a drop in wool export by 600% in volume and in value from 265,170 *qrans* to only 40,755 *qrans*. To compensate for this loss exporters sent a certain quantity of wool to Russia via Resht, and the carpet industry of Soltanabad and Farakhan was also partly supplied with wool.[212] Although this was a temporary setback there were two trends, which changed the export situation. The first was one of decreasing production due to natural conditions as well as the worsening of the political situation. Whereas the former was temporary, the latter appeared to be structural, at least in the medium-term, because of local rebellions and banditries. The second trend was that of increased local consumption at the expense of export. Whereas this local share was still not significant around 1900 by 1910, the wool clip was estimated at 870 tons. "Of this about one-third was cleaned and spun at Kermanshah for carpet weavers at Sultanabad and Dowletabad and the remainder was forwarded to Baghdad."[213] In the next years there was a further decrease in the export of wool due to the increase in local demand. This was for wool to be spun and transported to the carpet manufactories at Hamadan and Soltanabad.[214]

Table 6.17: Export of wool from Kermanshah (1900-14)

Year	In lbs.
1900-01	636,879
1901-02	459,082
1902-03	74,964

210. DCR 3189, pp. 25-27.
211. DCR 3420, p. 6.
212. DCR 3043, p. 6.
213. DCR 4559, p. 6.
214. DCR 5419, p. 4. See also DCR 5204, p. 4.

1903-04	299,409
1904-05	387,926
1905-06	916,766
1906-07	1,030,913
1907-08	674,750
1908-09	290,920
1909-10	991,872
1910-11	887,936
1911-12	467,096
1912-13	156,617
1913-14	110,441

Source: DCR 3189 p. 6; DCR 3043, p. 6; DCR 3420, p. 6; DCR 3683, p. 6; DCR 4365, p. 21 (table 4); DCR 4559, p. 6; DCR 5419, p. 10 (table 4).

By 1909, wool export was decreasing due to increased domestic demand, mostly in Soltanabad.[215] Of the available 870 tons of wool in 1909, about 33% was spun at Kermanshah and by the carpet weavers of Soltanabad and Dowlatabad; the rest was exported to Baghdad.[216] To get as much wool as possible, Baghdadi merchants came to border districts to buy wool. A British firm with a carpet manufactory at Hamadan established a branch at Kermanshah to purchase wool and carpets.[217]

Table 6.18: Comparison of total value and quantity of wool imported and exported during 1904-1913

Year	Export	Import	Net Export	Export	Import	Net Export
	Qrans	*Qrans*	*Qrans*	*Mann*	*Mann*	*Mann*
1904-05	10,884,590	3,540,655	7,343,935	1,627,513	517,945	1,109,568
1905-06	13,212,568	4,577,631	8,634,937	1,855,071	628,940	1,226,131
1906-07	14,927,571	5,060,612	9,866,959	1,856,744	641,532	1,215,212
1907-08	12,078,311	3,105,657	8,972,654	1,592,026	424,168	1,167,858
1908-09	10,386,815	1,201,652	9,185,263	2,060,303	209,560	1,850,743
1911-12	209,517	68,384	141,133	1,541,825	556,952	984,873
1912-13	205,458	59,158	146,300	1,441,435	430,740	1,010,695
1913-14	225,608	70,749	144,859	1,517,124	462,078	1,055,046

Source: DCR 4487, p. 22; DCR 5515, p 16.

Wool exports did not reach the level of 1910 anymore before World War I. Before that period the province was the scene of the Salar al-Dowleh rebellion as well as the weakening of control

215. DCR 4365, p. 8.
216. DCR 4559, p. 6; DCR 5204, p. 4.
217. DCR 5204, p. 4.

of the central government, which resulted in insecurity in the roads. After 1914, the province became part of the battlefront between Turkish and Russian troops. The famine of 1917-18 and the unsettled nature of the area thereafter prevented the wool trade to attain its previous position. The decrease in the wool trade was more pronounced in Kermanshah than in Khorasan, where Russian troops after 1912 controlled much of the province. Nevertheless, it would seem that the market was stabilizing itself at a certain level rather than growing. Total trade in wool and woolen fabrics amounted to almost 34 million *qran*s in 1913 or 6,25% of total trade. Export were 14,8 million *qran*s or 2,25% of total exports.[218]

Fig. 6.5: The plain of Kermanshah at the foot of Mount Bisotun (1907).

218. Government of France 1914, pp. 78, 80.

CHAPTER SEVEN

Political and Administrative Developments in Kermanshah

EARLY QAJAR PERIOD

Kermanshah did not recover quickly from the destruction and other collateral damage due to the almost constant acts of violence that it suffered during the second part of the eighteenth century. It received further blows during the period leading to the fall of the Zands[1] and its prospects of becoming a center of some regional importance looked dim. This was the situation, when the Qajars defeated the Zands and appointed their own governor to Kermanshah in 1797. The first Qajar governor was the 25-30 year old Mostafa Qoli Khan Zanganeh (1794-97), the son of Allah Qoli Khan, who was appointed by Agha Mohammad Khan at the suggestion of the local *mojtahed* Aqa Mohammad 'Ali, whose support the first Qajar shah had sought in 1790.[2] Shortly thereafter Shah Ne'matollah, who had been banned, was executed by the governor at *mojtahed'* Aqa Mohammad 'Ali's order. Because people complained about his rule Fath 'Ali Shah dismissed Mostafa Qoli Khan Zanganeh and summoned him to Tehran, where he remained for the rest of his life. The shah then appointed Mohammad 'Ali Khan Shambayati Qajar (1797), who clashed with *mojtahed* Aqa Mohammad Ali, who asked the shah to dismiss the new governor.[3]

He was succeeded by Fath 'Ali Khan Qajar (r. 1798-1806).[4] In 1806, Fath 'Ali Shah appointed his oldest son Mohammad 'Ali Mirza Dowlatshah (1789-21) in his place. Until then he had been nominal governor of Fars, Qazvin, Khamseh and Gilan. Dowlatshah was a very driven and competitive person, either innately or to overcome his handicap that he was the son of a Tatar slave woman, or both. Whatever the reason he wanted to outperform his younger half-brother and rival for the throne, 'Abbas Mirza, whose mother was a high-born Qajar lady and, therefore, heir to the throne. Agha Mohammad Khan liked his grand-nephew and once asked him what he

---

1. Perry 1979. p. 225.
2. Soltani 1381, vol. 1, p. 287; Sepehr 1337, vol. 1, p. 60; Hedayat 1339, vol. 9, p. 241; Olivier 1807, vol. 5, p. 15, 21. The governor and all notables of the city paid homage to the corpse of Agha Mohammad Khan when his body was transported via Kermanshah to Najaf.
3. Soltani 1381, vol. 1, pp. 289-90.
4. Soltani 1381, vol. 1, p. 290.

would do if he was king. The 6-year old prince allegedly replied: "I'll kill you." Agha Mohammad Khan was furious and ordered the boy to be strangled, but his mother's intervention saved his life.[5] Already at the age of six Mohammad 'Ali Mirza rode a horse and handled a spear and when he became 14 he had his first weapons. Fath 'Ali Shah sent him with Sardar Hoseyn Khan to fight rebels in Khorasan. His behavior there was of such ferocity, also towards his own troops, that the shah recalled him and gave him women, hoping to soften him through the female touch. At that time, he was governor of Qazvin.[6] Initially he was advised by Ebrahim Khan Sardar Qajar Devellu as well as by Mohammad 'Ali Khan Shambayati Qajar. In 1808, DuPré wrote that his vizier was the governor of Hamadan, Mohammad Hoseyn Khan Qaraguzlu, to whom he delegated everything. He was further assisted by Mirza 'Abdol-Vahhab and Mirza Zaman Tabrizi as viziers.[7]

To show his father that he was more qualified than his brother 'Abbas Mirza to be the heir, he not only was daring on the battlefield, as shown in Khorasan, but also through his building activities in Qazvin, Shushtar, and Dezful. However, the stage where he made his biggest play was Kermanshah, which he transformed from a sleepy small provincial market town into a cultural and commercial center. The number of his buildings in Kermanshah were said to surpass most of those built in other towns in early Qajar Iran. In 1832, Shirvani writes that there were 10,000 houses in Kermanshah.[8] Almost as an aside, Dowlatshah made his place of residence a prosperous and growing town. In a way, he was the founder of the city and its affluence, which was inconsiderable before his time, and he took pride in embellishing it. A large palace in the center; a country house surrounded by gardens for his harem; a spacious mosque near his residence all paid by him. "The whole range of streets, bazars, caravanserais, baths, &c. which are now erecting are, however, building from advances of their future occupiers, in loans to the Prince, on the faith of his promise, that the sums shall be accounted for in their annual rents." Thus, the prince as owner of much land and buildings, "can be regarded only as a monied speculator in possession of an unrestrained monopoly."[9] Even 30 years later those days were remembered as fortunate and prosperous ones, when people lived in the enjoyment of plenty.[10]

In 1809, Dowlatshah's jurisdiction was enlarged and included Kermanshah, Zohab, Sonqor, Hamadan, Lorestan, Bakhtiyari, and Khuzestan. As an administrator Dowlatshah showed he had great ability. He was on top of all public affairs. Although his rule was mild, it was also firm. He did not eschew from taking harsh measures, such as when he had two men blown from a canon for a minor offense. In fact, allegedly the common punishment at Kermanshah was "burying a man alive, with his head downwards and his legs in the air." Dowlatshah also took a hands-on approach to his rule and, according to Buckingham, who observed this in 1816, "the prince sits for an hour or two early in the day to transact public business and receive visits; but

5. Chardin 1811, vol. 10, p. 238.
6. Jaubert 1821, pp. 212-13.
7. Dupré 1819, vol. 1, p. 240; Rousseau 1813, pp. 85-86. Aqa Jani Khan was his *ishik aghasi* or master of ceremonies. Rousseau 1813, p. 90.
8. Shirvani 1315, p. 492
9. Buckingham 1971, p. 102.
10. Ferrier 1856, p. 24.

it is covered with an awning against the sun, with fanciful designs.[11] As a result, he also kept the tribes of his jurisdiction under control, undoubtedly enabled by his reputation of "being the most able and warlike of all the princes of Persia," but also by channeling the warlike tendencies of the tribesmen and their lust and need for plunder into his various military campaigns. He was not a modernizer as his half-brother 'Abbas Mirza, but rather of a reactionary bent. Nevertheless, Brydges opined that Dowlatshah's mounted irregular levies were more impressive than 'Abbas Mirza's troops trained by British officers to fight according to European methods.[12] As such, Buckingham in 1816, reported that Dowlatshah was "thought by many to be most powerful of all the governors on the empire, not excepting the Shah himself."[13]

Dowlatshah also was "a great trader and encourages trade in others as long as it does not hurt his personal interests," and, according to Kinneir, it was a flourishing town.[14] He was also a well-read man, who, like other Persians at that time, was greatly interested in astronomy, occult sciences and history. Sir Gore Ouseley who met him in 1809 was impressed by his knowledge of European history and current events.[15] The prince was also a poet in his own right with his own *Divan*. He wrote a biographical dictionary of his own contemporaries, *Ma'ather-e Dowlatshah*, and invited a crowd of poets and musicians to his court. Dowlatshah's interest in the occult made him invite the Arab theologian and philosopher Sheikh 'Ali Ahmad Ahsa'i, the founder of Sheikhism to Kermanshah. He was financially supported by the prince and taught in Kermanshah until Dowlatshah's death in 1821. Many scholars came from all parts of the Shiite world to study under Shaykh Ahmad and his teachings enjoyed widespread support. At Mohammad 'Ali Mirza's request he wrote a number of treatises on theological subjects, including *al-'Esma va'l-raja'a* on corporeal resurrection. Despite, or because of, his endeavors, Dowlatshah asked Ahsa'i to provide him with a testimony of good conduct to ease his entry into the next world. The testimony was placed on his coffin to be sure that the message was not overlooked and delivered at the right place.[16]

But it was above all on the battlefield where Dowlatshah wanted to show his prowess. In August 1805 a quarrel between 'Ali Pasha, the newly appointed governor of Baghdad and 'Abdol-Rahman Khan Baban of Shahrazur, led to armed conflict. The Kurdish chief fled into Persia and asked for asylum, which was granted. 'Ali Pasha refused to vacate Soleymaniyeh as Fath 'Ali Shah had several times ordered him to do. The Pasha replied that he would forgive the chief and even allow him to return, but his fate was in the hands of the Ottoman Soltan, not the Shah. This was short of *lèse-majesté* and in May 1806 an army under Dowlatshah set out for Iraq. In November he defeated 'Ali Pasha and took Soleymaniyeh. Therefore, the new *vali* of Baghdad, who had killed 'Ali Pasha, sent the Arab Shiite jurist Sheikh Ja'far Najafi, the author of *Kashf al-Ghita*, to negotiate with the prince, whom he convinced to induce his father to cease hostilities and release the captured prisoners in exchange for 'Abdol-Rahman's reinstatement

11. Keppel 1827, vol. 2, p. 21; Buckingham 1971, pp. 101-02, 104.
12. Kinneir 1973, p. 130; Brydges 1976, pp. 253-56.
13. Buckingham, p. 178.
14. Buckingham 1971, p. 102; Kinneir 1973 , p. 132.
15. Ouseley 1819, vol. 3, pp. 347-49.
16. Algar 1969, pp. 68, 70; Momen 2003, p. 323.

in Shahrazur. Although the proposal was accepted, the new agreement did not resolve the structural problem of border disputes with the Pasha of Baghdad leading to new raids, partly brought about by dissident Pashas who sought refuge in Kermanshah.[17]

In 1807, the 18-year old Dowlatshah had an army of 20,000-25,000 men and a revenue of more than 3 million francs.[18] In competition with 'Abbas Mirza, he likewise tried to modernize his army along European lines, first by employing French officers from the mission of General Alfred de Gardanne to Persia in 1808 and soon thereafter by commissioning British instructors.[19] After 1814, at one moment, some eight European officers were employed in Kermanshah.[20] Although Dowlatshah attached great importance to military matters, in 1816 there was not one cannon on the walls of Kermanshah. "Seven fine long brass pieces, of Persian foundry, and apparently very old, were lying on the ground before the Prince's palace, and in another public square." But he had a chief of cannoneers. At that time, his army was estimated at 500 horse and 1,000 foot; "they are required to arm and clothe themselves out of their pay; no uniform, and undisciplined."[21]

In 1812, 'Abd ol-Rahman Baban governor of Shahrazur was defeated in skirmishes with Ottoman troops of a new *Vali* in Iraq, 'Abdollah Pasha, and again took refuge with Mohammad 'Ali Mirza, who then invaded Ottoman territory at the head of a large force, advancing to the vicinity of Baghdad. Mediation by Sheikh Ja'far Najafi put an end to Persian looting and destruction in exchange for 'Abd ol-Rahman Baban's reinstatement as governor of Shahrazur. Despite the appointment of Da'ud Pasha in 1816, a more forceful *Vali* of Baghdad, the Persians retained their military advantage for nearly a decade.[22] Dowlatshah wanted that advantage even reinforced, so that when in 1816, four French officers en route to Lahore arrived in Bagdad, Dowlatshah's vizier learning of their arrival invited them to come to Kermanshah and train his master's army. The next two years the four officers trained seven battalions, in accordance with European military rules. In 1818, Dowlatshah, declared war on Baghdad, without his father's consent. He appointed Devaux, one of the French officers, as commander of his army of 14,000 irregulars. Da'ud Pasha had some 22,00 men. Not awaiting the order to attack, Devaux ordered his troops to attack the Ottomans and planted his standard right among the enemy force. The Ottomans were routed and 6,000 were taken prisoner, all cannon and the pasha's tent were seized as well. Dowlatshah, who had not wanted to attack, given the enemy's superior strength, was overwhelmed by this success and in front of his troops embraced Devaux and bestowed on him the order of the Lion and the Sun and an expensive robe of honor.

In 1821, hostilities broke out again between Persia and Turkey about border issues. 'Abbas Mirza claimed that two tribes that were Persian subjects, had been given refuge by the *Saraskar* of Erzerum. Although the *Saraskar* was recalled after Persian protests, his successor was even

17. Longrigg 1925, pp. 253-36, 242-49.
18. Rousseau 1813, p. 85.
19. Fraser 1984, p. 225; Buckingham 1971, pp. 177, 180, 193; Rich 1836, vol. 1, p. 106; Kerr Porter 1821, vol. 2, p. 181; Jaubert 1821, p. 280; Keppel 1827, vol. 1, p. 320, vol. 2, pp. 14-21.
20. Keppel 1827, vol. 2, p. 19.
21. Buckingham 1971, pp. 102-03.
22. Hedayat 1339, vol. 9, pp. 481-82; E`temad al-Saltaneh 1361, vol. 3, pp. 1504-05; Soltani 1381, vol. 4, pp. 294-97.

less forthcoming and threw 'Abbas Mirza's representative, who had come to lodge a complaint, in prison. This was interpreted as Turkey's disinterest in amiable settlement and the Shah ordered his son to take military action. 'Abbas Mirza occupied a large swath of the border lands, including Bitlis. The Pasha of Baghdad pushed back by invading Shahrazur. Dowlatshah counter-attacked on the pretext of protecting 'Abd ol-Rahman's son and successor, Mahmud Pasha Baban, whom the Ottomans accused of disloyalty. Dowlatshah's operation was coordinated with 'Abbas Mirza's campaign. To support the military operation of his two eldest sons, Fath 'Ali Shah led an army towards the Iraqi border. However, before he had reached Hamadan, cholera broke out and the army was dispersed. In July 1822, cholera struck Kermanshah. Meanwhile, Dowlatshah had defeated the Ottoman force and pushed as far as the gates of Baghdad. He was dissuaded from taking the city by the intervention of Sheikh Musa Najafi, son of Sheikh Ja'far. Because of an outbreak of cholera this decision was an easy one to take. According to Devaux, Mohammad 'Ali Mirza was already ill at that time, and also had received orders to withdraw. During his withdrawal Dowlatshah succumbed to the disease at Taq-e Garra and his army lost 2,000 men; falling back to Hamadan the Persian army lost 30-40 men/day. Some of the disputed issues were partially settled in the treaty of Erzurum in 1823 after 'Abbas Mirza had further bloodied an Ottoman attempt to expel him. However, the treaty only led to a temporary lull in the troubled relations between Persia and the Ottoman empire, while the border areas remained in flux.[23] It would seem that not only 'Abbaz Mirza was happy that his most serious rival for the throne had died, but also Fath 'Ali Shah may have felt the same, because to Fraser's surprise his father did not show any grief on hearing the news of his oldest son's death.[24] This was different in Kermanshah where the new governor mourned his father in a public display, which, according to Rich, was peculiar to that city, where " they accompany the body to the grave with music and singing."[25]

Under Dowlatshah's rule, Kermanshah enjoyed a period of prosperity and social calm, due to increased trade and pilgrim traffic. This prosperity was needed, because the build up and maintenance of the big army and its use was a heavy burden for the province. At least one man benefited much from the increased military expenditures, viz. Mirza Hadi, the prince's Minister of War, who made a fortune in that function. After the prince's death he fled to Kerbela.[26] Despite all his achievements, the supporters of 'Abbas Mirza called Dowlatshah derisively by the less honorable name of Mir 'Ali Khan.[27] European observers judged Dowlatshah differently. Some admired his robustness, articulacy, and assertiveness, whereas his critics judged him to be volatile, imperious and willful. For example, in 1811 he allegedly threatened to stab himself if

23. For his attack toward Baghdad and a description of subsequent events, see Belge 1829, pp. 349-54; Hedayat 1339, vol. 9, pp. 597-604; US Government 1875, p. 54; Anonymous 1877, p. 514; E'tezad al-Saltaneh 1370, p. 145; Soltani 1381, vol. 4, pp. 299-300; Rich 1836, vol. 2, p. 298 (the Pasha had just sent his youngest son as hostage to Kermanshah).

24. Fraser 1840, vol. 1, pp. 145-46, 148-49.

25. Keppel 1827, vol. 2, p. 2; Rich 1836, vol. 2, p. 301. On this Kurdish custom to accompany religious and mourning ceremonies with chants and music, see Rashidirostami 2018, pp. 278-79.

26. Fontanier 1844, vol. 1/2, p. 13.

27. Jaubert 1821, p. 211.

his father denied him permission to attack Baghdad.[28] His strong ambition to be the successor to the throne is clear from an anecdote from his childhood (see above).[29]

Dowlatshah was survived by twenty-four children, including seven sons, of whom the eldest, Mohammad Hoseyn Mirza Heshmat al-Dowleh (r. 1821-26), succeeded him as governor of Kermanshah. His father had been governor of Kermanshah, Lorestan, Arabistan, but now his province became part of 'Abbas Mirza, the crown prince's jurisdiction.[30] During the Persian army's withdrawal, the Ottomans attacked and seized the fort of Mandali, which had a garrison of 300 Persian soldiers. Although the Ottomans had granted them quarter, if they surrendered, they killed the Persian soldiers. Devaux who had trained the garrison commander was furious and asked permission to retake Mandali. In 1821, Mohammad Hoseyn Mirza led part of a Persian military operation against the Ottomans. Devaux arrived at night, dividing his troops into three sections, attacked the fort from three sides. Devaux was able to enter, killing many and saving many Persian subjects from the Ottoman furor, and occupied the fort Mandali. Fath 'Ali Shah rewarded Devaux with the rank of Khan and one of the court painters was instructed to make a painting of one of Devaux's battles. The scene depicted the moment that Devaux planted the flag among his enemies, and the painting allegedly was hung in the royal palace.[31] In 1824, Da'ud Pasha retook the fort. Fath 'Ali Shah gave orders to send troops, but without waiting Mohammad Hoseyn Mirza with 5,000 men and five guns hurried to Mandali, which he retook in May 1824. As a result, he received the title Heshmat al-Dowleh. He was described in Persian sources as being as courageous and energetic as his father, but in 1826, Devaux left Kermanshah in disgust, because he characterized Heshmat al-Dowleh as pusillanimous, weak and untrustworthy, who spent most of his time in his harem. Devaux went to Baghdad where the Pasha appointed him governor of Hilla with the rank of general.[32] Keppel confirms this character assessment, writing that the French officers had always access to the prince, who was a drunk and debauchee.[33] The prince also put men in chain, to the great astonishment of his people, and killed some just to make the point that he could.[34] For that reason perhaps, a certain Hasan Khan was the governor, acting on part of the prince.[35]

Heshmat al-Dowleh still employed European military instructors. In 1824, there were two French, two Italian and one Spanish officer in Kermanshah.[36] The officers all had the Order of the Lion and Sun and another one, which was instituted by Mohammad 'Ali Mirza. After the war with Baghdad the French officers had suggested to the prince to establish a 'knighthood' as a reward for their services, one of which showed two lions fighting for the crown. This design was sanctioned by Fath 'Ali Shah.[37] The prince's Kurdish lifeguards wore European jackets,

---

28. Atkin 1980, p. 115.
29. Azod al-Dowleh 2014, pp. 107-08. For a slightly different version, see Chardin 1811, vol. 10, p. 238.
30. Keppel 1827, vol. 2, p. 23.
31. Belge 1829, pp. 352-53.
32. Belge 1829, pp. 349-54.
33. Keppel 1827, vol. 2, p. 68.
34. Fraser 1840, vol. 2, p. 192.
35. Keppel 1827, vol. 2, p. 20.
36. Keppel 1827, vol. 2, p. 14-15.
37. Keppel 1827, vol. 2, pp. 16-18.

otherwise they all wore different clothes.[38] When Keppel and some other British officers passed through Kermanshah en route to Europe, Heshmat al-Dowleh insisted that they come and visit him. Through a number of passage ways and turns one reached the *khalvat*, a small apartment where the prince sat on a chair. He said that he wanted to have a capital army himself drilled by British officers, as well as some of the muskets that were underway from Baghdad to the king's army. "He was a great drill himself, he said; delighted in military matters, and admired the English *Nizam* beyond everything." The prince asked that the British Envoy request the Shah to allow him this.[39]

Because of court intrigues 'Abbas Mirza had Heshmat al-Dowleh dismissed as governor of Kermanshah. He was replaced by Mohammad Taqi Mirza Hosam al-Saltaneh, a son of Fath 'Ali Shah, who ruled from 1826-29. His capital was Borujerd and he also governed Lorestan and Arabistan. Due to misbehavior, also by his officials, he was recalled and Heshmat al-Dowleh became governor for a second time. Allegedly, the people of Kermanshah had petitioned Fath 'Ali Shah to reappoint him. However, Hosam al-Saltaneh refused to accept his dismissal and gathered a force of Bakhtiyaris with which he tried to seize Kermanshah, but he was defeated and fled to Borujerd. The two sides met again and the conflict ended with Hosam al-Saltaneh fleeing to Tehran. Heshmat al-Dowleh was unable to keep law and order during the time when the province was ravaged by a severe outbreak of the plague that lasted uninterruptedly from 1832 until October 1834 and consequently Kermanshah's population was much reduced. This situation led to incursions by Lors and Bakhtiyaris. But what really led to his dismissal was his weather vane attitude towards the succession to the throne after Fath 'Ali Shah's death in 1834. He did not choose sides, but kept his options open toward all three contenders. Therefore, when Mohammad Shah acceded to the throne Heshmat al-Dowleh was dismissed and summoned to Tehran. He tried to flee but was captured and imprisoned in Ardabil for the rest of his life.[40]

In January 1835, Bahram Mirza Mo'ezz al-Dowleh, Mohammad Shah's younger brother became governor of Kermanshah, Lorestan and Khuzestan. Not much is known of what happened during his rule, apart from his request for British military advisers to modernize his army and a not so successful campaign against the Bakhtiyaris of Mohammad Taqi Khan in Khuzestan. In April 1835, Lt. Henry C. Rawlinson arrived in Kermanshah where he stayed for three years drilling a Persian regiment and getting acquainted with the Bisotun inscription that he later deciphered.[41] In early 1836, Bahram Mirza marched to Shushtar to subdue the Bakhtiyaris, which in reality became the prince's acceptance of the status quo. However, it was not this lack of military success, but his behavior, or rather that of his representatives, that led to his dismissal. This behavior must have been rather obnoxious because in March 1836 there were disturbances in the city denouncing Bahman Mirza. As a result, one month later he was dismissed. He was replaced by Manucher Khan Gorji Mo'tamed al-Dowleh (1836-38), who was welcomed by the same tribal leaders, who had opposed Bahman Mirza's rule. When Mohammad Shah needed

38. Keppel 1827, vol. 2, p. 56.
39. Fraser 1840, vol. 2, pp. 191-92.
40. Shirvani 1315, p. 294; Teule 1842, vol. 2, pp. 483-84; Fraser 1840, vol. 2, pp. 350; relations with the Gurans, p. 187; Keppel 1827, vol. 2, pp. 57-58; Shirvani 1315, p. 492; Bamdad 1347, vol. 1, pp. 193, 377; vol. 3, p. 376; Hambly, 1991 a, pp. 166-69.
41. Fraser 1840, vol. 2, pp. 190-91; CHI vol. 6, p. 173.

him to suppress the rebellious situation in Isfahan, Mo'tamed al-Dowleh was transferred and Isfahan was added to his jurisdiction of Kermanshah, Lorestan and Khuzestan. Mo'tamed al-Dowleh appointed a number of successive deputy-governors to administer Kermanshah, viz. Nur-Moḥammad Khan Qajar, Hajji Khan Saheb Ekhtiyar, 'Abdol-Hoseyn Khan Javanshir, and Mohebb 'Ali Khan Shoja' al-Dowleh Maku'i.[42]

In 1840, Sardar Nur Mohammad Khan Qajar was governor of Kermanshah. He was a man of middle age, handsome, with a deep black dyed beard. He wore a coat of the rarest Kashmir shawl and high cap of the finest lamb skin and a jewel-studded dagger in a shawl folded around his waist.[43] To de Sercey, the French envoy, he complained about problems caused by Kurds.[44] He was expelled from the town by a popular revolt around 20 May 1840. Teule who arrived one week after this event was surprised that the town was quiet and that there was no sign of past revolutionary activity. In fact, things seemed to looked better than before.[45] Sardar Nur Mohammad Khan was replaced by Hajji Khan Shakki, Saheb-Ekhtiyar (1841-42). Even before his arrival he seems to have had a bad reputation in Kermanshah, perhaps mainly because he was a fanatic Sunni in a governorate with fanatic Shiites. When he got into a dispute with the governor of Kerend, he wanted the entire population to be punished. They rose up and killed him instead.[46]

'Abdol-Hoseyn Khan Javanshir (1843-44) was the next governor. He was faced with a population that was still hot in the face about the events concerning Saheb-Ekhtiyar. Apparently, he did not dare to impose himself, because it was reported to Tehran that he was rather weak. Therefore, Tehran gave Mo'tamed al-Dowleh orders to involve himself more with the affairs of Kermanshah. At that time, he was leading operations against Mohammad Taqi Bakhtiyari in Khuzestan. One of his commanders was Mohebb 'Ali Khan Maku'i, who, after the successful completion of that campaign went to Kermanshah. 'Abdol-Hoseyn Khan Javanshir was afraid that Maku'i wanted his position and pressed the tribal leaders to declare for him. On his return to Kermanshah there was a letter from Mohebb 'Ali Khan stating that he had come to Kermanshah to put things in order. Javanshir replied that the people here did not want him and if he had learnt nothing from Saheb-Ekhtiyar's fate then that might be his fate as well. At that time, Mohebb 'Ali Khan received orders from Tehran to seize those who had killed Saheb Ekhtiyar; in case of opposition he had permission to kill them. Javanshir received this letter and again went to Qal'eh-ye Zanjir to discuss matters with the tribal chiefs. It was decided to send Mohebb 'Ali Khan a letter telling him to return to Tehran. On receipt Mohebb 'Ali Khan put his troops in battle order. Javanshir wrote the chiefs to prepare troops to oppose him and lure him into an ambush. Mohebb 'Ali Khan got hold of this letter and sent it by speed messenger to Tehran.

---

42. Soltani 1381, vol. 4, pp. 327-28; Fraser 1840, vol. 2, p. 186; Bamdad 1347, vol. 4, pp. 159-63; Hambly 1991 a, p. 155.
43. Layard 1971, p. 232.
44. de Sercey 1928, p. 297.
45. Teule 1842, vol. 2, p. 481.
46. Soltani 1381, vol. 4, pp. 330-32; FO 248/108, Mirza Mohammad Reza, news writer to Robertson/Bushire, 29 June 1842 ("It is reported that Hajji Khan Qaradaghlu received khilat from shah and was appointed governor of Kermanshah").

The reply was that Javanshir was dismissed and summoned to Tehran and Mohebb 'Ali Khan was appointed governor.[47]

One of the first things Mohebb 'Ali Khan Maku'i (1844-48) did was to break the unity of the tribal chiefs by killing some of them, while sending others to Tehran, where they were imprisoned. According to Ferrier, Emir Mohebb 'Ali Khan, governor of Kermanshah was the general who caused the failure at Herat through his cowardice. He also described him as an ignorant and cruel man.[48] Because of his misrule and oppression the splendid bazaars of Kermanshah were deserted, and if somebody offered his goods for sale, "his venture rapidly disappears under the hands of an undisciplined soldiery, who give themselves up to every description of excess, certain that they do so with impunity.... When the inhabitants quarrel they dare not apply to the normal tribunals, but are forced by the soldiers to make them the arbiters of their differences." Although there was a drop in revenues, Mohebb 'Ali Khan collected the same amount from those that remained. People complained in vain, because, being from Maku, he was patronized by his fellow compatriot Mirza Aghasi, the prime minister. In the eyes of the shah Mohebb 'Ali Khan's vices were transformed into virtues.

> The misery is frightful wherever his jurisdiction extends: the peasantry have hardly bread to eat, And when they complain of their grievances at Court and endeavour to obtain justice, they are treated as rebels, condemned to be bastinadoed, and Mohib Ali Khan remains their governor. This bad policy had produced its fruits: three-fourths of the population has emigrated; the townspeople to Azerbaijan, and the nomads to Turkey."[49]

In the mid-1840s he was confronted with an uprising of the Kalhor tribe. The governor had sent soldiers to collect taxes, when he himself was bedridden due to an old wound. The Kalhors and the people of Kermanshah considered this the right time to take action and besieged the castle. But the garrison was alert and dispersed the rebellious force. Tehran sent fresh troops to put the rebellion down. Hedayat said of him "he did what he did and said what he wanted." When Mohammad Shah died, his patron and compatriot, prime minister Mirza Aghasi was dismissed. This was a sign for the people of Kermanshah to rise up and they again besieged the citadel, took it and plundered it. Mohebb 'Ali Khan fled and reached the new shah's army camp, who was very angry with his unannounced and unauthorized appearance. He was seized, punished and had his wealth extorted.[50] In short, during Mohammad Shah's reign, the people of Kermanshah were impoverished and driven out by the tyranny of Dowlatshah's successors, who only pursued their private interests.[51]

47. Soltani 1381, vol. 4, pp. 332-33.

48. Ferrier 1856, p. 25.

49. Ferrier 1856, pp. 25-26. An editorial footnote to this book confirms this from the editor's own observations in 1846.

50. Hambly 1991 b, pp. 561-62; Soltani 1381, vol. 4, pp. 333-36.

51. Ferrier 1856, pp. 24-25.

NASERI PERIOD

Emir Mohebb 'Ali Khan's successor was Eskander Khan Qajar Devellu Sardar (1849-52). To ensure peace in the province Amir Kabir discussed the situation with the imprisoned Kurdish tribal chiefs, whom he sent with the new governor to Kermanshah. Thus, the new governor was surrounded by Zanganeh chiefs who managed the administration of the province for him.[52] In 1849, the Kakawands made Kermanshah insecure and plundered caravans and travelers, against which the new governor took swift and effective action. In 1851 Naser al-Din Shah visited Western Persia and Sardar went to Borujerd to meet the shah. Given the news about the bad economic situation the shah granted 12,000 *tumans* reduction in taxes. After the fall of Amir Kabir (1852), Sardar was transferred to Khoy and in March 1853 he was replaced by Emamqoli Mirza Qajar 'Emad al-Dowleh (1853-75), the sixth son of Dowlatshah. His first activity was to bring the tribes under control, raise troops and bring order to the border areas. He quelled Timur Khan Guran's rebellion and took strong measures against brigandage. The various tribes also contributed to the army that Naser al-Din Shah marched to Herat in 1854. When this attack on Herat led to a conflict with Great Britain, the olama of Kermanshah joined the call for jihad by the olama of Tehran.[53] In 1863, Lorestan was added to 'Emad al-Dowleh's jurisdiction. In 1868, the 'Emad al-Dowleh mosque plus rooms for the theology students in the goldsmiths' bazaar was completed. The 100 or so shops in the bazaar and the 'Emad al-Dowleh caravanserai were part of the foundation he established and their income had to be used for the mosque's upkeep.[54]

'Emad al-Dowleh had the reputation of being a wise and just governor. He made the town's trade and industry prosper and reduced the onerous taxes in the province.[55] Wills wrote that he was very wealthy and that he was "liked as a Governor, being stern, but generally just." His wealth was clear from his coffee-cup holders, which were of gold enameled, and decorated with rows of diamonds; his water pipes all of gold, and his personal one was so thickly encrusted with emeralds that it looked like green glass.[56] 'Emad al-Dowleh's youngest son and his favorite was a scoundrel and guilty of every crime possible. He even tried to kill his father, but only wounded him. His father ordered him chained, but two days later released him and he seemingly was received back in favor. However, this was a ploy to mute the population's minds. For shortly thereafter he was found dead, allegedly by his own hand.[57] The famine of 1870-71 also left its impact on the city, where some 15,000 people died. Many rural people flocked to the city, "but found instead a stone in place of bread." When Bellew entered the city in 1872, he saw a large number of "new graves, filled during the last two years." At that time, the Vakil al-Dowleh, who was very ill, said that the famine was over, the harvest had been good and prices had come down to normal levels.[58]

---

52. Soltani 1381, vol. 4, p. 338.
53. Motallebi 1395, p. 208; Soltan 1381, vol. 4, p. 343.
54. Soltani 1381, vol. 4, p. 343.
55. Binder 1887, pp. 346-47.
56. Wills 1893, pp. 112-13,
57. Wills 1893, pp.124-25.
58. Bellew 1999, p. 438.

On 17 October 1870, Naser al-Din Shah arrived in Kermanshah on pilgrimage to Kerbela.[59] During his visit to Kermanshah and onwards to Kerbela Naser al-Din Shah made use of carriages, which were left behind in broken down condition. In 1876, there were still seven or eight of them, three of which were owned by Aqa Hasan, Vakil al-Dowleh, who made outings with them. The drive itself was short, "for a road practicable for carriages led but a short distance from the town."[60] On the Shah's return from Kerbela ʻEmad al-Dowleh was dismissed; he was replaced by the second son of Dowlatshah, Tahmasp Mirza Moʻayyad al-Dowleh in 1871, while Lorestan was added to the jurisdiction. ʻEmad al-Dowleh accompanied the Shah to Europe in 1873 and on their return he, in March 1875, was once again appointed as governor of Kermanshah. He died in October of that same year and was succeeded by his oldest son, Badiʻ al-Molk Mirza Heshmat al-Saltaneh in 1875, who at that time was governor of Kurdistan. He only remained in office for the remainder of the official year (i.e. until March 1876), due to infighting among his siblings.[61]

The next governor of Kermanshah and Kurdistan was Soltan Morad Mirza Hosam al-Saltaneh (end 1876-80), 13th son of ʻAbbas Mirza. Locally he was known as "the conqueror of Herat". When Floyer visited him in 1876 he observed that the governor's army camp:

> Was well arranged, so far as details were concerned. Each subdivision of troops was well defined, and its head-quarters marked by a pole bearing a square bright tin, which blazed in the sun most brilliantly, and was decidedly better than a flag, which would during the rains have drooped miserably.
>
> But the conqueror of Herat was not happy in his choice of situation. He had pitched his camp on the banks of the river (the Kara Su or black water) which had overflowed its banks and inundated the surrounding country. The result was that the mud was knee deep, and that the soldiers had all taken off their trowsers and presented a most unmilitary aspect.
>
> We sent an ambassador to the commander-in-chief, and, while waiting, left our horses in the charge of grooms, and took the coffee in the tent of the 'sartip' or general.[62] The water was here as everywhere, but the sartip had spread a quantity of chopped straw on the ground and put his carpets over that. The result was that though we were sitting on mud and water we were quite dry, and I thought t myself that this might be the origin of the saying, 'like water under the grass'; the chopped straw being fry, hard, and springy, absorbed no moisture, and though water was running under us, we sat as if we were on the roof of a house. Or credentials having been presented, we ploughed through the mud from the

59. Soltani 1381, vol. 4, p. 344.

60. Floyer 1979, p. 439; Sayyah 1346, p. 232.

61. Bamdad 1347, vol. 1, p. 162; Soltani 1381, vol. 3, p. 359.

62. This *sartip* may have been "Bolair, a French general in Persian service for 35 years, formerly an engineer officer; had served in Algeria, and was at the siege of Herat; was now returning to Ispahan after reporting on frontier." Gerard 1883, p. 44.

> sartip's tent to that of the commander-in-chief, which was gorgeous and well guarded, no others being allowed within forty yards of it.
>
> The commander-in-chief was very courteous, and we had coffee in cups of silver studded with turquoises. He did not omit to remind me that he had been to England, and been presented to Her Majesty. He was dressed as a European, possibly in honour of my visit, and we conversed freely. Observing a prismatic compass sticking out of my pocket he asked various questions as to its use, and sent for a 'kibl-nama' of his own. This on arrival turned out to be an old French prismatic, with a clinometer included for the use of which he begged me to write him out a paper of instructions, which I readily promised to do.[63]

At the end of 1880 the people of Kermanshah rose up against Hosam al-Saltaneh, because of the heavy taxes he imposed. Also, due to complaints he was dismissed. Because the people expressed a preference for the re-appointment of Badi' al-Molk Mirza Heshmat al-Saltaneh, the latter, in April 1881, became the new governor.[64] He was a known quantity as former governor and because he and his family had chosen Kermanshah as their permanent residence. However, due to local conflicts and the insecure conditions of the province he was dismissed one year later. Gholam Reza Khan Shehab al-Molk was his successor, in both Kermanshah and Kurdistan, but his term of office was short.[65] He was replaced by 'Abdollah Mirza Heshmat al-Dowleh, who served as governor until early May 1882.[66]

Because of these frequent changes in governorships, which consequently were of short duration and characterized by turmoil, the situation in Kermanshah deteriorated. In addition, this gave rise to tribal revolts, which made Tehran decide to try something new and make Kermanshah province part of a new administrative structure, to wit: the new jurisdiction administrated by the Shah's oldest son Mas'ud Mirza Zell al-Soltan. On 5 May 1882, the latter became governor of Kermanshah, which became part of a new and very large jurisdiction that encompassed most of the central and southern provinces of the country, including Kurdistan. Therefore, in that same year, Zell al-Soltan appointed Mahmud Khan Naser al-Molk as deputy governor of Kermanshah and Kurdistan.[67] Because in 1884 Naser al-Molk was appointed Minister of Foreign Affairs, Hoseyn Khan Qaragozlu Hosam al-Molk became deputy governor and he held that function from 1884 until 1890.[68] One of his main activities was the killing of Javanmir and his Hamavands, who had been a headache in the past, but because of problems with the larger tribes he was appointed *sarhaddar-e gharbi* and governor of Qasr-e Shirin. However, once a thief always a thief; he and his followers continued with their brigandage despite warnings to

63. Floyer 1882, pp. 437-38.
64. Bamdad 1347, vol. 1, p. 189.
65. Soltani 1381, vol. 4, p. 364; Bamdad 1347, vol. 1, p. 189.
66. Soltani 1381, vol. 4, p. 364. According to Gerard 1883, p. 44, on 6 April 1882 the governor of Kermanshah was "Abdollah Mirza Hushnat-ud-Doulah, who was to be relieved shortly."
67. Bamdad 1347, vol. 4, p. 56.
68. Jaberi-Ansari 1321, p. 290.

stop. In 1888, the governor killed the brigand governor and his band.[69] When in 1888, Zell al-Soltan wanted to visit Kermanshah the population unanimously protested and asked the Shah to forbid the visit. The reason was that the prince traveled with a retinue of some 1,400 men, which would plunder the city, because they "take everything, but pay nothing."[70] This was also the year that Zell al-Soltan's jurisdiction was significantly reduced, and, among others, he was dismissed as governor of Kermanshah and Kurdistan. His deputy, Hosam al-Molk, thereafter continued as independent governor of Kermanshah and Kurdistan, while his son, Zeyn al-'Abedin Khan Qaragozlu Hosam al-Molk II was his deputy in Kermanshah. His father remained in office until his death on 25 October 1889, when the son took over. He also became governor of Lorestan and Borujerd. He resigned in 1892, after his son had married Mozaffar al-Din Mirza's daughter.[71]

Hasan 'Ali Khan Garrusi Amir Nezam became governor of a new so-called central province, consisting of Kermanshah, Kurdistan and Hamadan (1892-96). He deputized Anushirvan Mirza Ziya al-Dowleh, who arrived on 26 December 1891 in the city. During his time as governor he tried to improve the efficiency of the road guards, dealt with the internal Kalhor strife, and tried to prevent price-fixing by sellers of life necessities.[72] Because of heavy fiscal demands he was faced with riots in May 1893. The demonstrators surrounded the citadel, barricaded its entrance and cut the trees of his garden and destroyed the doors of the gate. 'Ali Mardan Khan Mir Panjeh-ye Kerendi was about the leave with his troops and asked the deputy-governor whether he should suppress the riot. He then was hit by a rock and thus his soldiers attacked the rioters. Their leader used this as an opportunity to loot 'Ali Mardan Khan's house and set fire to it, hoping that the Kerendi force would come to his house and leave the citadel. However, he did not leave the citadel. The entire disturbance lasted 9 hours. Then the Imam Jom'eh and Aqa Vali, two leading olama intervened. Once things quieted down Amir Nezam was alerted, who said that there should be no more disturbances until his arrival; if there would be, they should be suppressed by force. A similar message came from Tehran. People then dispersed and many took to the mountains, while some wanted to continue rioting. They once again attacked with arms and Ziya al-Dowleh sought refuge with 'Emad al-Dowleh. The rioters then dispersed. Nozhat Efendi, the Ottoman consul (*shahbandar*) also wired Amir Nezam to come. He then came, while sending a threatening letter to the rioters ahead of his arrival. Out of fear many fled, even across the border, although a few days later, after the public audience, a general amnesty was declared.[73] The Sanjabis had crossed the border, because of these events, which meant a weakening of the protection of the border, of which this tribe usually took charge.[74] Amir Nezam then appointed his own son Salar al-Molk as his deputy, who was but a boy. His behavior once

69. Soltani 1381, vol. 4, p. 369.

70. Saad 1913, p. 95.

71. E`temad al-Saltaneh 1345, pp. 765, 1014; Soltani 1381, vol. 4, pp. 372-76; *Ruznameh-ye Iran* 1375, vol. 4, pp. 2816 (no. 699; 05/11/1889), 2820 (no. 700; 29/11/1889); vol. 5, pp. 2599 (no. 645; 24/12/187), 2607 (no. 647; 21/01/1888).

72. *Ruznameh-ye Iran* 1375, vol. 4, p. 3023 (no. 763; 14/01/1892); 3088 (no. 767; 26/02/1892), 3131 (no. 778; 10/08/1892).

73. E`temad al-Saltaneh 1345, p. 1041; Soltani 1381, vol. 4, pp. 377-83; *Ruznameh-ye Iran* 1375, vol. 4, p. 3072 (no. 763; 14/01/1892).

74. Ehtesham al-Dowleh 1366, p. 257; Soltani 1381, vol. 4, p. 385.

again led to riots in 1896, occasioned by Naser al-Din Shah's assassination. He then appointed Zahir al-Molk Zanganeh Amir Tuman as his deputy in March 1897, who resigned a month later.[75]

MOZAFFARI PERIOD

In April 1897, Zeyn al-'Abedin Khan Qaragozlu 'Asheqlu Hosam al-Molk Amir Afkham was appointed governor of Kermanshah. One month after his arrival (in May), Mozaffar al-Din Shah appointed his 18-year old son Abu'l-Fath Mirza Salar al-Dowleh governor of Kermanshah, while Amir Afkham remained as his financial manager and chief executive officer (*pishkar*). The prince-governor arrived in the city on June 1897. In January 1898, Hosam al-Molk resigned. He was replaced by Zahir al-Molk Zanganeh Amir Tuman. The official newspaper *Iran* drew a positive picture of Salar al-Dowleh as governor by reporting that every day at least one or two hours he in person was in the *divan-khaneh* to deal with government affairs.[76] However, the reality was somewhat different. In a short period, through his exactions and oppression, Salar al-Dowleh was able to become a generally hated man. "His exactions were so heavy that he was removed in response to the appeals made by the victims." There were many meetings of those who had him removed, prominent among them was the Imam Jom'eh.[77]

In April 1898, Mirza Mohammad Khan Eqbal al-Dowleh Kashani (1315-19/1879-1902) was appointed governor. His deputy was Mirza Aqa Khan Ghaffari Kashi. To keep the tribes calm, the new governor confirmed Mohammad 'Ali Khan Ilkhani as chief of the Kalhors and he gave the chieftainship of the Gurans and border control to Hoseyn Khan Amir Tuman, that of the Sanjabis to Shir Mohammad Khan Samsam al-Mamalek, and made Hoseyn Khan A'zam al-Dowleh Zanganeh, chief of the Koliya'i tribe and governor of Sonqor. It was also the year that the Customs of Kermanshah were henceforth managed by the Belgians.[78] In 1901, Mehdiqoli Khan Majd al-Dowleh replaced Eqbal al-Dowleh.[79] Not much can be said about his one-year administration, but that the harvest was good, prices were low and he did not oppress the people to enrich himself.[80] On 15 September 1902, Ahmad Khan 'Ala' al-Dowleh was appointed

75. Soltani 1381, vol. 4, pp. 385-86; *Ruznameh-ye Iran* 1375, vol. 5, p. 3664 (no. 910; 24/04/1897).

76. *Ruznameh-ye Iran* 1375, vol. 5, p. 3702 (no. 920; 03/10/1897). The personal daily presence of the governor in the *divan-khaneh* or in the *talar-e hokumat* (from morning till evening) dealing with government affairs as well as that of his deputy and administrative staff, in particular the *mostowfis*, thereafter became a refrain in the reports from Kermanshah in *Ruznameh-ye Iran* 1375, vol. 5, pp. 3787 (no. 942; 31/08/1898), 3955 (no. 983; 14/11/1900), 3988 (no. 991; 20/03/1901), 3999 (no. 994; 20/05/1901), 4036 (no. 1003; 24/10/1901), 4047 (no. 1006; 17/12/1901), 4084 (no. 1105; 28/06/1902),4108 (no. 1021; 11/10/1902). It also occurred a few times in the newspaper before that time, e.g., *Ruznameh-ye Iran* 1375, vol. 4, p. 2852 (no. 708; 04/02/1890)

77. Administration Report 1905-06, p. 46; E`temad al-Saltaneh 1345, p. 1113 (appointment of Hosam al-Molk in 1312/1894-95).

78. Soltani 1381, vol. 4, pp. 470-71.

79. Majd al-Dowleh was a son of Isa Khan Vali Ehtesham al-Dowleh. He was born around 1850, accompanied the Shah three times to Europe, was the chief of the royal household, master-of-the horse, etc. In 1903, he was appointed Ilkhani of the Qajar tribe. Was illiterate and a reactionary and in July 1907 was arrested and forced to pay a considerable sum to obtain his release. IOR/L/PS/20/223, 'Who's who in Persia. Calcutta: General Staff, India, 1916', p. 204.

80. Soltani 1381, vol. 4, pp. 472-73.

governor of Kermanshah. In March 1903, people rose up against him, because of his oppressive measures. During his administration he renovated part of the city, the first modern school was established, and oil exploration began.[81]

In 1903, 'Abdol-Hoseyn Mirza Farmanfarma (1903-06) was appointed governor of Kermanshah. That same year both Russia and Great Britain opened Consulates in Kermanshah. Nothing much is known about the first years of his administration, apart from his establishment of a hospital in the city (see Chapter Two). More is known about his activities in the year 1905, which began as a rather quiet year, but ended with some serious food problems for the people of Kermanshah, which situation Farmanfarma made worse by the bread ring he led. For most of the year Farmanfarma was absent from the city. The reason was that in November/December 1904 a group of Lors had attacked Col. Douglas and Lt. Lorimer. The British government demanded the culprits to be punished and therefore, on 21 December 1904, Tehran ordered Farmanfarma to so. This required that he march into Lorestan, which he did not like to do. Therefore, he claimed that his wife (the Shah's daughter) was ill, but Lt. Dr. Williams IMS in Kermanshah refused to give him a supportive medical certificate as there were no grounds for it.[82] Finally, Farmanfarma moved in January 1905 to punish the tribe, an action monitored by Lt. Williams,[83] who reported from Kangavar at the end of January 1905 that the cold was severe. "Eggs, oranges, &c. were frozen as hard as stones. Four of Farmanfarma's soldiers succumbed to the cold and several others had their hands and feet frost-bitten. He considers that his sowars' uniform is too thin for this climate."[84] He arrived on 5 February 1905 at Borujerd; it was so cold that due "to the freezing of the lubricating oil the rifles of the escort would have been useless anywhere between Sulimanieh and Burujird." Farmanfarma believed that Mehr 'Ali Khan was behind the attack on British oficers. The number of troops at Borujerd was less than Tehran believed; instead of 10,000 with all stores there were only 1,500 soldiers with eight cartridges per man and no food. Farmanfarma told the now Capt. Williams he could neither guarantee protection nor food; even when he offered to pay for food and animals the governor said he was unable to do so.[85] In mid-February 1905 Tehran agreed with Farmanfarma's proposal to wait with action until the crops were collected, i.e. in 6 months' time.[86] Williams reported after his return on 5 May 1905 that Farmanfarma could do nothing against the Dirakwand Lors, unless by treachery.[87] In mid-July 1905 Farmanfarma wrote to Gough from Khorramabad that he had arrested 13 Dirakwands, 6 of whom had been directly involved in he attack, whom he had placed in prison in Borujerd.[88] On 21 August 1905, Firuz Mirza brought the Dirakwands captured by his father Farmanfarma. On 27 October 1905, after 10 month's absence, Farmanfarma returned from Lorestan. He informed the British consul that he had been unable to get more Dirakwands

---

81. Soltani 1381, vol. 4, p. 474-76.
82. Political Diaries vol. 1, p. 9. IMS means Indian Medical Service.
83. Political Diaries vol. 1, p. 18.
84. Political Diaries vol. 1, p. 45.
85. Political Diaries vol. 1, p. 56. While en route, Lt. Williams had been promoted to Captain.
86. Political Diaries vol. 1, p. 62.
87. Political Diaries vol. 1, p. 97.
88. Political Diaries vol. 1, p. 139.

and that he considered the matter taken care of.[89] During Farmanfarma's absence, his deputy Salar Mansur was acting governor.[90]

Shortly after his return, Farmanfarma resigned as governor of Kermanshah and Lorestan and left on 8 January 1906.[91] Farmanfarma was replaced by the governor of Hamadan, Zeyn al-'Abedin Khan Hosam ol-Molk as governor of Kermanshah and *Sarhaddar-e Iraqeyn*. His 20-year old son, who was most unintelligent, who had just received title of Hosam al-Molk, arrived on 16 January as deputy-governor. Henceforth, his father was called Amir Afkham, who entered Kermanshah on 9 March 1906.[92] Farmanfarma had kept the Lor prisoners separate from the ordinary felons and treated them moderately well. In the last week of January 1906, they were transferred by the new deputy to the common prison, where they received a simple ration of bread and no fire or light at night. Gough sent a verbal message to the deputy expressing hope that the Lors would be better treated as in a sense they were British prisoners. The message had no effect, so in early February consul Gough reminded him again. The deputy apologized and said he was inexperienced and but a boy, but he would heed the advice. While Gough was gone during the first week of February 1906, the governor of Kermanshah sent the Lor prisoners to Borujerd.[93] The tribes were quiet except that the second son of Da'ud Khan, the chief of the Kalhors was killed.[94] However, in mid-1906, the district was constantly disturbed and robberies were common; in July 1906 thieves even robbed the British Consulate. In early August 1906 there was much fighting among some tribes at Asadabad. To put a stop to the fighting, the elder son of Amir Afkham invited them under guise of friendship and then arrested them.[95]

CONSTITUTIONAL TURMOIL

This was the time that political tempers and tensions started to run high in Persia, because of the demand for political reform, in particular for a people's assembly or *Majles* and a Constitution. The political turmoil in the major cities of the country also affected Kermanshah, where the call for political change was heard and heeded. On behalf of the people of Kermanshah, the Imam Jom'eh's son went to Qom and later to Tehran to join and support the leaders of the Constitutional movement.[96] As in other cities the divisions among the people of Kermanshah, or rather among

---

89. Political Diaries vol. 1, pp. 147, 211.
90. Administration Report 1905-06, p. 46; Political Diaries vol. 1, p. 157.
91. Political Diaries vol. 1, p. 279, 285; Soltani 1381, vol. 4, p. 481.
92. Political Diaries vol. 1, p. 279, 285; Soltani 1381, vol. 4, p. 481. Zeyn al-Abedin Afkham al-Molk Hamadani Qaragozlu. Soltani 1386, p. 148. "Zeyn al-`Abedin Khan Amir Afkham (later Amir Nuyan). Has two regiments commanded by his sons Ehtesham al-Dowleh and Hesam al-Molk. Large landed proprietor in Hamadan, but is deeply in debt to the Russian Bank, Farmanfarma, etc. for 100,000 *tumans*. Is liberal though not highly educated, but has common sense. Head of the Qaragozlu Turks and locally known as 'the fox' on account of his cunning." IOR/L/MIL/17/15/11/3, Who's Who in Persia, vol. 2, p. 49-50.
93. Political Diaries vol. 1, pp. 289, 295, 352.
94. Administration Report 1905-06, p. 46.
95. Administration Report 1906-07, pp. 39-40.
96. Nazem al-Eslam Kermani 1346, pt. 1, p. 299, note 1.

the local elite, represented traditional local cleavages, rather than a coherent set of political objectives, let alone of one or more political programs. The local differences were not so much about a Constitution and all what that entailed, but rather about a shift in power relations. This led, among other events, on 8 July 1906, to a fight with swords in the city between two rival parties, during which some people were wounded. The governor cut off ears of three men and sent two influential men in chains to Hamadan and imprisoned another in the town. Mo'in al-Ra'aya, a local leader and head of one of the quarreling factions took refuge with the Turkish consul-general, who, however, handed him over to governor.[97] On 30 July 1906, the dismissal of anti-reform prime minister 'Eyn al-Dowleh was received with great demonstrations of joy; the whole town was illuminated in the evening.[98] In early August 1906, this early political success induced a well-known fanatic mullah to preach the death of all Europeans; the governor took steps and it remained quiet in town. This mullah was not Aqa Mohammad Mehdi, for in May 1907, the acting Russian consul Petrov suggested to his British colleague Haworth to jointly ask action to be taken, because one of the mullah's servants had beaten one of Petrov's servants. During their discussion Petrov opined that there was an anti-European feeling in Kermanshah and therefore, it should be made clear that "it would not be wise to do anything against Europeans." Haworth disagreed, because Aqa Mohammad Mehdi "was accused inciting the people against Christians and took care to see to it that the report was contradicted to him."[99]

In early September 1906, the text of the telegram sent by the British king to the asylum seekers in the British Legation in Tehran was distributed in Kermanshah and made a good impression on the people. To prevent popular turmoil, the governor charged 'Abdollah Khan, the *beglerbegi*, with the supervision of the price of wheat; he adopted strict measures and the quality of bread improved and the town remained quiet.[100] However, under the surface sentiments of some people ran high and hot. In early November 1906, Hoseyn, son of Hajji Shavan, a merchant, blew himself up while making a bomb. In his house 18 other bombs were found, 12 were filled. Friends and associates were arrested, who denied any knowledge. The bombs were made of gun metal made by a local blacksmith who was arrested. This apparently was the first case of a bomb being made in Persia for political purposes.[101] At that time, like in other cities, in response to the newly found political freedom, many associations (*anjomans*) were created such as *edelat* (justice), *asnaf* (guilds), *tojjar* (merchants), *khavanin va malekin* (Khans and landowners), *shahzadegan* (princes) etc. and they all asked the Shah, in writing and by telegram via the religious leaders of the reform movement in Tehran, Behbahani and Tabataba'i, to grant a Constitution and the establishment of a *Majles*. Also, the leaders in Najaf issued a fatwa supporting the Constitutional movement. Although the variety of these *anjomans* reflected the socio-economic classes that later would be represented in the first *Majles*, there is little information available on their actual political significance and activities, and even on their membership. It would seem that they rather were created as a vehicle for representing a claim

---

97. Political Diaries vol. 1, p. 421. Mo'in al-Ra`aya was released with a robe of honor (*khel`at*). Although the town was quiet thefts were frequent. Political Diaries vol. 1, p. 428.

98. Political Diaries vol. 1, p. 435; Administration Report 1906-07, p. 39.

99. Political Diaries, vol. 1, p. 441; vol. 2, p. 199.

100. Political Diaries vol. 1, pp. 467, 489.

101. Political Diaries vol. 1, p. 533.

for representation in the *Majles* rather than that of a political program or point of view. That did not mean that its members did not have political views, but these were still rather vague and parochial.[102]

When on 7 October 1906 the Constitution was granted, almost immediately, i.e. at the end of November 1906, elections began in Kermanshah for the *Majles* under the supervision of Asadollah Al-e Aqa, the Imam Jom'eh. The party of the clergy opposed electing a member to the *Majles*. "They maintain that if the Assembly becomes a settled fact, civil law will gradually oust the Shera or religious law." The Imam Jom'eh, the most influential *mojtahed* in Kermanshah, was in favor of the *Majles* so the others were expected to give up their opposition, the more so since the olama of Kerbela officially supported the establishment of a *Majles* by telegram.[103] On 13 December 1906, 20,000 cartridges arrived from Tehran plus tents and uniforms for three regiments allegedly for soldiers to be sent to the border, but in reality as a precautionary measure to quell disturbances in case of the Shah's imminent death. Tents for the troops were pitched in the *meydan* and recruits were drilled. When the Imam Jom'eh died on 4 January 1907,[104] there were no disturbances and neither when on 3 January 1907 the old Shah died and the new one acceded to the throne.[105]

In early February 1907, two 'parties' were formed for the election of the deputies for the *Majles* and the local assembly. One 'party' was powerful, because it had the backing of all the high government officials and of the leading clergy except for Aqa Mohammad Mehdi and the newly arrived Imam Jom'eh. The other 'party' comprised the town's people and bazaaris. "The people say that they are tired of the dishonesty of the Mujtaheds and Mullahs," and wanted to elect Agha Mohammad Mehdi and the Imam Jom'eh as their representatives.[106] There was indeed general discontent with the ruling class, whether political or religious. "They are disgusted with political, social and religious conditions and are clamoring for change." It was not only people in cities and towns, but also those in the villages were asking the US missionaries, "when will a foreign government assume control of Persian affairs, that we may have liberty and peace."[107] The main event was the failed attempt to establish a provincial assembly at Kermanshah, due to the enmity between the two contending groups, which were formed along the lines of the traditional cleavages pre-dating the constitutional revolution. "The natural formation of parties which followed the commencement of the elections proved a convenient peg upon which to hang the enmity which had previously existed between certain sections of the local community."[108]

---

102. Soltani 1386, pp. 148-49. The Persian translator of Grothe 1910, p. 84 (see Soltani 1381, vol. 1, p. 104), incorrectly translated *Handwerkerausstände* as *anjomanha-ye asnaf*, because it means 'strikes by artisans.'

103. Political Diaries vol. 1, p. 569; vol. 2, p. 28; Nazem al-Eslam Kermani 1346, pt. 2, pp. 71-72 (text telegram); Soltani 1381, vol. 4, p. 486.

104. Political Diaries vol. 2, pp. 9, 28-29.

105. Administration Report 1906-07, p. 40.

106. Political Diaries vol. 2, p. 73; Administration Report 1906-07, p. 40. For the remarks by the president of the *Majles* on the problems of the elections in Kermanshah, see Nazem al-Eslam Kermani 1346, pt. 2, p. 112 and Soltani 1986, pp. 148-49.

107. Presbyterian Church 1908, p. 346.

108. Administration Report 1906-07, p. 39.

The two parties represented the same people and interests as before the election, but they were stronger, because the stakes and potential gains were much higher than before. In February 1907 this became clear. The so-called aristocratic party, composed of landowners and most mullahs with their followers, were opposed to any change. The other party was composed of the common people, notably the tradesmen and one or two mullahs; their leader was *mojtahed* Aqa Mohammad Mehdi, whom the people followed. Before 1907, all power was in the hands of the official and religious class; the one had all physical might, the other all moral power. But people had enough of the tyranny of the officials and the corruption of the mullahs and wanted to grab power to freedom offered by the new system. Especially, the leading merchants would like to repay some of the oppressive behavior they had suffered.[109] The following persons were chosen as deputies: Hajj Mohammad Saleh Khan from the aristocrats, the Hajjizadehs on behalf of the landowners, Abu'l-Qasem Mirza for the princes, Hajj Malek Mohammad Tajer for the merchants and artisans.[110]

On 12 February 1907, some 3,000-5,000 people were gathered in Aqa Mohammad Mehdi's mosque. Thereafter it was made known that allegedly he had said that non-Moslems could not go through the bazaar when it rained as the water dropping from their clothes would drop in the cobbled gutter in the middle of the streets in which Moslems washed their potatoes and vegetables. On 20 February 1907, a deputation of the leaders of various groups called on Capt. Haworth, the British consul informing him that the report was false and was circulated by the mullah's enemies to make Europeans become hostile towards the people's party. They had elected their representatives and had informed Amir Afkham, who had not informed Tehran, and they were afraid that due to the opposition's intrigues that matters would result in bloodshed. The opposition informed Haworth that the representatives had not been properly elected and therefore, were not acceptable. Haworth discussed the matter with Amir Afkham, who told him that Tehran had ordered him to refer the matter of the elections to the Imam Jom'eh, who had died before definite steps could be taken. The aristocratic party wanted Aqa Sheikh Hadi as president of the *anjoman-e velayati*, but the people had elected Aqa Mohammad Mehdi. Both had refused the appointment, but as Moharram approached Amir Afkham urged Aqa Mohammad Mehdi to temporarily accept the function to avoid disturbances. This enraged the aristocratic party. Therefore, Amir Afkham asked Tehran to send a Special Commissioner (*ma'mur*) to supervise the elections. Amir Afkham told Haworth that he did not want to remain governor once the council had been installed, because he would no longer have any real authority any longer. "All that would be required would be a revenue officer and I am inclined to agree with him," Haworth reported.[111] An additional reason may have been that Amir Afkham had become governor with the help of Kurdish chiefs, who were not in favor of the liberal movement in the

109. Administration Report 1906-07, p. 40; Soltani 1386, p. 150 calls the two parties: liberals and conservatives.

110. Soltani 1386, p. 149. For Malek Mohammad's message to the *Majles*, see also Soltani 1381, vol. 4, pp 488-49.

111. Political Diaries vol. 2, pp. 73, 81; FO 248/907, Kermanshah Diary ending February 30th, 1907 (the deputation consisted of "Haji Sayed Habib, tajir; Haji Moin ul. [sic], tajir; Abdul Hassan Khan, a Khan; Haji Hussain Ali, sarraf bashi - the first named is one of the elected members, the others are heads of of their respective sections").

Majles and refused to send deputies to Tehran, which gave rise to opposition from the mullahs and merchants.[112]

Moharram, which started on 14 February 1907, was quiet, but, in the second half of February 1907, Tehran replied that no commissioner would be sent. Amir Afkham was reconfirmed in his function, so it was expected that he would try to have his own man appointed. Meanwhile, the governor acted as if a commissioner would still arrive and he did not interfere in the local conflict. In early March 1907, a larger deputation visited Haworth complaining that their telegrams did not reach Tehran, but he explained that he could not interfere in the elections.[113] On 14 March 1907, tired of waiting for the commissioner, all traders and employees of the town took *bast* in the Telegraph Office and those not able to enter were to be found on the roofs of the houses around the *meydan-e tupkhaneh* and closed the bazaar.[114] According to Grothe, the crowd of people on the *meydan* had been mobilized by a few mullahs with slogans such as "For the People" to curry favor with the populace and gain power. This slogan appealed to people's hope for "cheaper bread" and "lower taxes." Tents had been erected, while a red banner proclaimed "For the People." In addition to strikes by the artisans, there also were fights and the discharge of firearms, following spirited orations in some parts of the city. Some people were killed, and the subsequent burials gave rise to new orations and fights; the whole affair was enabled by mild, dry March weather. When a few days later it started raining hard for a few days and the streets turned into red mud baths, political activists changed into stay-at-homes.[115] The 3,000 people or so of Kermanshah sat in *bast* in the Telegraph Office for more than 30 days and the cost of food, apart from help from some notables and landowners, was borne by Sayyed Asadollah and Sayyed Habibollah, the Malek brothers. Each day, Sayyed 'Abbas Malek, the son of Habibollah and his son-in-law, Sayyed Habib Rastgar, and Hajj Mirza Abed Moshir al-Ra'aya, paid two *qrans*/p.p. based on the people in the number of tents. This was generous, because at that time the daily expense of a family of four did not exceed two *qrans*/day.[116]

On 17 March 1907, Tehran ordered that Mo'in al-Ra'aya and Ra'is al-Tojjar with Sheikh Mohammad Hasan, hardly aristocrats, but leading members of the aristocratic party, were to be seized and expelled from town. They had advance notice and left before this happened. The next day, Hajj Rostam Beg Sarabi, a member of the people's party passed the house of *mojtahed* Abu'l-Qasem Ra'is al-Olama, where the aristocratic party often met. Here Hajj Rostam Beg Sarabi was received with shouts and stones; he ran to the square shouting that they had been trying to kill him and incited his adherents to attack Ra'is al-Olama's house, which they did. The conservatives, in particular Mo'in al-Ra'aya and Mo'aven al-Molk, who were diehard

112. Aubin 1907, pp. 324-25.

113. Political Diaries vol. 2, pp. 90, 101.

114. Political Diaries vol. 2, p. 151; Soltani 1386, p. 149. According to Aubin 1907, p. 326, the reason for the *bast* and closure of the bazaar was the governor's partiality in a dispute between two Sayyed merchants and a member of the family of a Kurdish chief.

115. Grothe 1910, pp. 83-84.

116. Soltani 1386, p. 150.

fanatics, had many thugs and riflemen in their employ. Therefore, the attackers were met with gunfire, and four were killed and two wounded.[117]

As a result, Amir Afkham was sacked due to incompetence in dealing with the political situation of Kermanshah. Two days before his dismissal, he fled in the night for fear of reprisals by the population. He was joined by the Mo'tazed Daftar, his retinue of hangers-on, his servants and their luggage as well as his soldiers, all going to the *qahvehkhaneh* at Hajjiabad. Although the British consul was not impressed with him as governor, he nevertheless concluded that of all the governors, "he was the sole one who showed any power of meeting the difficulties or understanding the trend of affairs and had the Commission from Tehran been sent to decide on the legality of the elections at the time he demanded much of what happened subsequently might have been avoided."[118]

SEYF AL-DOWLEH

In his stead, Soltan Mohammad Mirza Seyf al-Dowleh, younger brother of 'Eyn al-Dowleh was appointed.[119] He was governor of Borujerd, and, according to the British consul, "a person far more incompetent to deal with the matter before him." People left the asylum, when he sent a telegram promising to take care of their grievances, and thus, disturbances halted temporarily. He arrived on 2 April 1907 and, without announcement, the day after his arrival he hung a man from prison in the *Meydan* to intimidate the populace. He lasted two months.[120] It was soon learnt that Seyf al-Dowleh was weak and avaricious, who cared for little else than raking in money. On 16 April he visited the local assembly and promised to send an official to attend future meetings. He had no intention to do so and his remark was just to lull his adversaries into security; he only meant to gain time. The assembly waited for the official, but received the reply *farda* (tomorrow). It then sent a strongly worded letter demanding a reply; he then wrote that the official would come in two days. Meanwhile the head of the *Majles* in Tehran wrote that

---

117. Administration Report 1906-07, pp. 40-41; Political Diaries vol. 2, p. 151; Soltani 1386, p.150; Aubin 1907, p. 326. "Together with his brother, Mo`in al-Ra`aya (both of obscure origin), Mo`aven al-Molk rose to prominence in the service of the governors of Kermanshah prior to the Constitutional movement. Although he later espoused Salar al-Dowleh's cause, he did not identify with any political party. Thereafter he was "asked to restore order in the city and since then enjoyed great unofficial authority. Also, he was in charge of food supply during the current famine [1918]. Is fairly honest, friendly to the British, and against the Sanjabis, who occupied some of his properties in Mahidasht." IOR/L/MIL/17/15/11/3, 'Who's Who in Persia (Volume II)', p. 227.

118. Administration Report 1906-07, p. 43; Administration Report 1907-08, p. 51; Political Diaries vol. 2, p. 162; Aubin 1907, pp. 326-28.

119. Soltan Mohammad Mirza, Seyf al-Dowleh (b. ca. 1852). "Was chamberlain of Naser al-Din Shah, governor of Tuyserkan, Nehavand and Malayer. Later governor of Qazvin (1901) and Astarabad (1903). Brother of Eyn al-Dowleh. Failure as governor of Kermanshah due to his ineptitude; he only half-heartedly apologized for the *bast* of 2,000 people on the Consulate grounds and the firing at them, and then only when pressed by Tehran. He was dismissed to make reparations to the British government, but reappointed in October 1907, but he did not assume the governorship due to objections made by the British Legation. In July 1908 he was appointed governor of Khuzestan and spent most of his time as the guest of Sheikh Khaz`al, who was married to his grand daughter. In 1911 he supported Salar al-Dowleh." IOR/L/MIL/17/15/11/3, Who's Who in Persia, vol. II, p. 335-36.

120. Political Diaries vol. 2, pp. 151, 162; Soltani 1381, vol. 3, p. 489; Idem 1386, p. 151; Stead 1908, p. 18.

rather than spill blood perhaps it would be better not to have a local assembly at all in Kermanshah. At that time a son of a *mojtahed* from Kerbela passed through and stayed, promising to try and reconcile the parties. After two days' grace, at the beginning of May 1907, Seyf al-Dowleh again tried to lull the local assembly in security by ordering Mo'in al-Ra'aya and Ra'is al-Tojjar with Sheikh Mohammad Hasan expelled from town. This was done and they went to Sarwinao, a village of Rais al-Tojjar at some 18 km from Kermanshah. Haworth, the British consul, did not trust Seyf al-Dowleh's good intentions towards the people. He was guided by Zahir al-Molk, who was strongly opposed to the new regime, although he was too old to do anything rash. He told Haworth that although he had high hopes of the new Prime Minister: "How can it be expected that those, who up to the present had power, even of life and death, should, without a word, become subservient to a Mejlis of trades people?" Zahir al-Molk induced the leaders of the people to ask Seyf al-Dowleh to remove the artillery camp from above the town, to which he agreed on the promise that they would cause no trouble.

In April 1907, Balawand Lors, friends of Mo'in al-Ra'aya, looted villages as close as 44 km from Kermanshah and carried off sheep. They had assisted Mo'in al-Ra'aya during the recent riots in Kermanshah. Seyf al-Dowleh sent a group of horsemen in pursuit, who were defeated. Meanwhile, in Lorestan Salar al-Dowleh had rebelled against his brother, Mohammad 'Ali Shah. At the beginning of May 1907, Salar al-Dowleh's troops, mainly consisting of Lors, were marching toward Nehavand. Because they were badly equiped and provisioned they plundered the area around Nehavand and Hamadan. Tehran gave orders to its regional governors to oppose the rebel-prince. Meanwhile, there were rumors that Salar al-Dowleh was approaching with an army from 20,000 to 60,000 men. However, the prince's military might was rather limited and therefore, uncertain about a military outcome of the rebellion, Salar al-Dowleh approached the British consul on 16 May asking him to mediate between him and his brother, Mohammad 'Ali Shah. Haworth wrote to Tehran and the Shah promised his brother's safety and a pardon. Because of his opposition to the government Salar al-Dowleh enjoyed some popularity among the 'popular party' in Kermanshah. According to Grothe, the rank-and-file of this party believed Salar al-Dowleh to be "the affable, generous royal prince, who would rap the rich and big thieves on their knuckles" and they cheered him on. However, it appears that most people were very worried about Salar al-Dowleh's eventual success. On 30 May 1907, the British consular Mirza came back with Salar al-Dowleh's reply; he wanted to continue as governor of Lorestan, Arabistan, Borujerd and Nehavand. He ignored the content of the consul's letter and said unless his demands were met he was not responsible for the consequences. He would not attack Kermanshah because it had consuls and a Bank, but he would sack Nehavand and Dowlatabad.[121]

Seyf al-Dowleh was an extremely weak man and unable to reconcile the bickering factions in town. In particular, the bazaaris were refractory; every other day they would close the bazaar and refuse to sell their goods.[122] On 1 June 1907, a mullah belonging to the popular party,

---

121. Administration Report 1907-08, p. 52; Political Diaries vol. 2, pp. 183, 189, 199, 209; IOR/L/PS/20/260/2, Persia no.1 (1909) Correspondence respecting the affairs of Persia, December 1906 to November 1908,' Spring-Rice to Grey 18/06/1907, p. 30 (no. 27); Grothe 1910, pp. 85-86.

122. Stead 1908, p. 18.

accompanied by a few hundred partisans rode through the bazaar. When Vothuq al-Mamalek, *lashkar-nevis* (accountant-general of the army), one of the moving spirits of the aristocratic party, did not get out of the way fast enough, the mullah's escort cursed and then attacked him. When he was wounded and bleeding, his escort fired their revolvers and a riot broke out which lasted all day. The next day, the Kerend regiment and Sanjabi *savar*s (Vothuq al-Mamalek was a relative of the commander of the Sanjabi *savar*s) joined by a mob of the worst ruffians looted the town; the bazaar was hastily closed, but the soldiers broke open the shops and the entire bazaar was sacked. They looted the 1,500-2,000 shops in the bazaar, from the *Dahaneh-ye Meydan* till the end of *Mahalleh-ye Tavileh-ye Tupkhaneh* also known as the *Chaharrah-e Akharat*. Ra'is al-Olama issued a fatva that the looting was lawful as the Constitution-wishers were acting against the Imam of the Age. The insecurity in the city lasted two weeks and the financial loss was enormous; one Russian subject lost 20,000 *tuman*s or £4,000. "Many merchants who were worth thousands in the morning had nothing in the evening." The looting was the sign for general lawlessness and fighting broke out all over the city. Men were stopped and in broad day light stripped of their clothes. Foreigners went only outside when accompanied by 6-12 soldiers. People said Seyf al-Dowleh had given the order to loot the town intending to favor the aristocratic party, which true or not, happened and much of the loot ended up in the house of A'zam al-Dowleh, who later became the acting governor. As a result of the fighting 13 people were killed and the people's party, all 2,000 of them, took refuge in the British Consulate. On 1 June 1907, the British Consulate's staff, learning that people wanted to take refuge in the Consulate, had closed the gate; however the garden had no walls and thus, on 3 June people came pouring in. On 4 June, Haworth arrived at the Consulate coming from Kangavar and found it very crowded.[123]

Some 2,000 people camped at the British Consulate. Life and property in the city were not safe.[124] Among the campers was Aqa Mohammad Mehdi, the leader of the popular party, his brother, and four of the six elected members of the local assembly, and the chiefs of all trades. Haworth insisted that they handed in their arms and he received orders from the Legation to get rid of the *basti*s or asylum seekers peacably. Both the Shah and Amin al-Soltan, the Prime Minister, wrote and blamed the British consul for protecting the looters; thus, ironically the victims of the plunder were blamed for the turmoil.[125] Haworth together with his Russian colleague were at Kangavar when the riot occurred. The two consuls had gone there to try and meet with Salar al-Dowleh, but en route learnt that he had moved towards Kermanshah and so they had decided to return. On arrival in the city, Haworth found "part of the bazaar looted to the last pin, many merchants being penniless and the chiefs of the people's party in refuge at the Consulate. They refused to leave unless things were righted for them. The chief priest was very offhand and said that if I did nothing he would telegraph to London." After Aqa Mohammad Mehdi had apologized for this outburst Haworth went to see the governor, whom he considered to be responsible for the riot. He showed Haworth telegrams from Amin al-Soltan, the Prime Minister, stating that Aqa Mohammad Mehdi, the *mojtahed*, had incited the riot and the consul,

---

123. Administration Report 1907-08, pp. 53-54; Stead 1908, p. 18; Soltani 1386, p.150; Grothe 1910, p. 85; FO 248/907, Diary for the month of June 1907.

124. Stead 1908, p. 18.

125. Administration Report 1907-08, p. 54; FO 248/907, Diary ending 16th July 1907.

therefore, could not keep him. Haworth told him that he would not use force to expel anyone from the Consulate. "At that period I was informed that the Shah was at telegraph office and had sent a message asking if I proposed to help rioters to riot. I replied I was helping nobody, that I would telegraph the British Minister and act according to your orders, that the people had come to the Consulate without my permission and all I wanted was if they have wrongs they should be righted that they could leave Consulate. I consider Governor has played with people and that on the whole they are in the right." The governor favored the aristocratic party and, therefore, he was unable to bring peace and quiet to the city, because the people did not trust him. If the governor would expel Aqa Mohammad Mehdi there would be more fighting, unless the leaders of the other party were also expelled. The Russian consul did not agree with Haworth on this last point. Haworth also feared that fighting would break out in the Consulate' grounds if the governor would try to expel the *mojtahed*. The British consul made it clear to the governor that he refused to get involved "in the matter at all, as I am a stranger." However, because he had asked the governor many questions to learn how matters had come about the latter, concluded that Haworth sympathized with the people, the more so, because he refused to expel them from the Consulate. The situation was not only bad in the city, but also in its environs where all villages were deserted and the Kalhors and other tribesmen were plundering along the road.[126]

Haworth had orders not to chose sides, but the people believed that the British were the reason that they had a Constitution, that Edward VII had sent a genuine telegram congratulating the *Majles* (the Russian consul had planted that idea) and the British having a constitutional government themselves would therefore help them. This perception was reinforced by the sympathetic tenor of articles in the British press. Despite his neutrality, and not being able to expel the *basti*s, the aristocratic party believed Haworth to be a most cunning and wily diplomat, as he wrote with some self-deprecating glee.[127] Those who had been plundered went to Tehran and sat *bast* in the *Majles*. There was almost agreement on an adequate compensation by the government when Amin al-Soltan was assassinated on 31 August 1907 and the poor victims had to return empty-handed to Kermanshah.[128]

SALAR AL-DOWLEH

On 6 June 1907, the British consul received messages from Salar al-Dowleh, announcing that Kermanshah would be the capital of his kingdom. One letter was an enclosure to Aqa Mohammad Mehdi asking him to raise the religious banner, for without force the people would not be able to obtain their rights. Every able man should get a sword and don the white kaftan of the jihad. If the Mullah did not do this then he was worse than a Christian, a Jew, and an idolater. Another

126. FO 248/907, Haworth to Legation, 26/06/1907.
127. Administration Report 1907-08, p. 54; FO 248/907, Diary ending 16th July 1907.
128. Soltani 1386, p.150.

Fig. 7.1: Salar al-Dowleh in Kurdish dress (*ca.* 1911). © *Collection Molitor, Ed. Elytis* no. 132.

letter stated that if by 22 June the British government had done nothing he would start hostilities.[129] As per his instructions the British consul let Salar al-Dowleh know that the Shah assured his pardon and life, if he submitted. On 12 June 1907, Haworth received, via his Minister, a letter from Amin al-Soltan and the *Majles* to Aqa Mohammad Mehdi promising him safety and a full enquiry in Tehran or Hamadan. He had to tell Aqa Mohammad Mehdi to accept this offer and leave the Consulate. The latter asked for two days to think about this; he wanted the inquiry in Kermanshah and he hoped that his messengers would reach Tehran in that time to get this tabled. Indeed it worked, for Zahir al-Dowleh, governor Hamadan was told to go to Kermanshah and investigate the matter. On 9 June there was a battle between Salar al-Dowleh's and Amir Afkham's men at Nehavand. His artillery chief did not hit anything, having been told if he did he would be beheaded later. Salar al-Dowleh, who was caught unaware by the skirmish, ran to the fight, shot the artillery chief and aimed himself two shots that hit Nehavand's walls. When Da'ud Khan Kalhor arrived with 1,500 men Salar al-Dowleh and his Lors withdrew to Khorramabad. Because of his sudden movement the British consul's letter did not reach Salar al-Dowleh and was returned to him. Therefore, on 13 June a copy of that letter was sent offering him a pardon, as before. Because of the rebellion, the province was unsettled and robberies were taking place, including in the city. In fact, five robberies took place at the Consulate; even one gun was stolen from the bed of a sleeping guard. On 14 June on the high ground on either side of the Consulate groups of men started firing at each other in the Consulate grounds below, among the refugees. Seyf al-Dowleh said that this was the work of the refugees themselves, but Haworth did not

129. Stead 1908, p. 18; Administration Report 1907-08, pp. 54-56; Political Diaries vol. 2, pp. 253-54. Similar letters had been sent all over the country. IOR/L/PS/20/260/2, 'Persia. No 1 (1909). Correspondence respecting the affairs of Persia, from December 1906 to November 1908', Spring-Rice to Grey, 18/06/1907, p. 31 (no. 27)

believe this. He was authorized to leave to the IBP building for his own safety, but since he believed the action was aimed at the refugees and not at him he stayed. The refugees reacted: "if we are not safe under the British flag, what will happen if we leave the Consulate?" On 18 June, Haworth received a letter from Nazar ʻAli Khan, Fath Lashkar, Salar al-Dowleh's father-in-law and commander of his troops.[130] In this letter he wrote that he accepted a new governor for Lorestan, but not Mojur al-Saltaneh; als,o no Bakhtiyaris were to be sent, because these were his hereditary enemies, and if so, he would take to the hills and become a brigand. Tehran refused the offer and therefore, he resumed his old life. A punitive expedition sent against him had no result, because at the end of 1907 he took Khorramabad and the governor, Mojur al-Saltaneh, sought refuge in the house of the Imam Jomʻeh. However, the Vali of Posht-e Kuh attacked Nazar ʻAli Khan's positions from the West, while the Bakhtiyaris attacked from Khorramabad to the south. After his defeat Salar al-Dowleh accompanied by one servant fled to Kermanshah and on 19 June totally unexpected took refuge in the British Consulate, to the great surprise of Haworth. According to Grothe, Salar al-Dowleh had waited too long and had not taken advantage of his popularity among the have-nots. If he had gone to Kermanshah in May 1907 he would have been received with open arms and he would have an excellent and strong defensive base for his future operations. Haworth thought that the prince had accepted the pardon, but soon it was clear that Salar al-Dowleh had not received either of the two letters sent to him. He made new demands (being allowed to leave the country to a British possession), which Haworth forwarded to Tehran. The *Majles* had decided that Salar al-Dowleh should be handed over to the Persian government and on 22 June at night (to save his face) Haworth transferred him to Zahir al-Dowleh.[131]

ZAHIR AL-DOWLEH

Although the governor of Hamadan was sent to put things in order in Kermanshah the semblance of government in the province had changed into anarchy. Trade was down, because many traders were bankrupt after the plundering of the bazaar and despite a good harvest and the best water

130. "Nazar Ali Khan Sardar Akram II (b. ca. 1860). Chief of the Amra'i (sub-section of the Tarhan tribe) and one of the principal figures in W Lurestan. He has his headquarters at Tarkhan and is usually at variance with the Persian government. The Tarhan and Delfan tribe were more or less united under him, whose title of Vali-ye Pish-e Kuh gave a him a legal claim to exercise authority over them. However, under no circumstance would any large portion of the tribe support any one cause of individual. In 1903, Nazar Ali Khan was pursued by Salar al-Dowleh assisted by the Vali of Posht-i Kuh, but they could not get him. In 1907 Salar al-Dowleh made peace with him, when the prince rebelled against his brother Mohammad Ali Shah. He married Nazar Ali Khan's daughter and when pressed sought refuge with him. Early 1909, Nazar Ali Khan refused to hand over the taxes that he had collected from the Baranwand to Amir Afkham. He and the Vali of Poht-e Kuh are old enemies, but if politically beneficial they relax their enmity. Is addicted to alcohol and opium." IOR/L/PS/20/223, 'Who's who in Persia. Calcutta: General Staff, India, 1916', p. 395.

131. Administration Report 1907-08, pp. 55-56; FO 248/907, Diary ending 16th July 1907; Grothe 1910, pp. 86-87; Stead 1908, p. 18. The shooting incident at the British Consulate was discussed in the British House of Lords, where it was reported that "the fire was directed not against Englishmen but against Persian Party opponents, who had taken refuge in the Consulate. The Persian Government have expressed profound regret, and sent very strong orders to the Governor to punish the guilty persons and prevent a repetition of the outrage." *The Hansard*, HC Deb. 20 June 1907, vol. 176 cc609-10.

supply since years people were living from hand to mouth. "Everywhere people are depressed and discouraged. Many are disappointed and are openly murmuring their government and are discontended with their religion."[132] It was not so much their religion as the behavior of a large number of the religious class that people were discontent with. A glaring and not exceptional example was the management of a religious foundation (*vaqf*) outside Kermanshah by some mullahs. They were embezzling its revenues and, therefore, the heirs seized the property and fort. "The charge is naturally quite correct," the British consul commented. However, when in early May 1908, Dr. Bongrand went there the occupiers mistook the Consul's white sun hat for the white turban of a mullah and started shooting. They apologized, but it was an indication of the people's strong feelings and the state of the country without a governor.[133]

Such was the situation when on 1 July 1907, Salar al-Dowleh left Kermanshah accompanied by Seyf al-Dowleh, the ex-governor, because Zahir al-Dowleh was appointed governor of Kermanshah.[134] As enquiry commissioner he had come to Kermanshah on 20 June and went to see the asylum seekers and tried to convince Aqa Mohammad Mehdi to leave. He then went to the telegraph office where some of the aristocratic party had taken refuge to persuade them to go home. Although the commissioner telegraphed Tehran that the asylum sit-in was over, 75% still remained as the chiefs of trades wanted some pledge through the British consul and only left two days later. Zahir al-Dowleh now tried to settle the local conflict. The two parties did not cause further disturbances, but robberies and murder also happened frequently and it was not safe to go out at night. Outside the town, Dowlatmand, a petty Lor chief, was plundering the country side. On 11 August a large crowd went to Zahir al-Dowleh and asked him what he intended to do as he had done nothing so far. They vilified him and accused him of inducing them to leave their asylum under false pretense. He was unable to pacify them. On 12 August 1907 he held a meeting, but none of the leaders of the popular party showed up, only some members of the aristocratic party. Meanwhile, Aqa Mohammad Mehdi was summoned to Tehran in connection with its inquiry into the cause of the riot. This was because many believed that Zahir al-Dowleh would not be impartial and, therefore, he gave out that he went to Tehran for this separate inquiry.[135]

Aqa Mohammad Mehdi and Zahir al-Dowleh had agreed that he would leave alone and unescorted, to avoid the appearance of being under arrest. He received 500 *tuman*s for expenses, which money was borrowed from the Imperial Bank of Persia (IBP). A few days later it became known that Aqa Mohammad Mehdi had not gone to Tehran, but to Iraq, because he was stopped at the border, as he had no passport; he wired Zahir al-Dowleh that he had confidence in him and had decided to go to Kerbela to devote himself to religious matters; he asked for a passport, to which Tehran agreed. Later it became clear that Zahir al-Dowleh had arranged for the 'flight'

132. Stead 1908, p. 18.

133. Political Diaries, vol. 3, p. 167.

134. Both the Russian and the British consul had complained to their Legations about Seyf al-Dowleh and the *kargozar*, because the latter was almost openly obstructive and the former was not to be trusted "and I should consider him to be the last man to bring back Kermanshah to peace and quiet." FO 248/906, Haworth to Tehran,10/06/1907.

135. Administration Report 1908, p. 57; Political Diaries vol. 2, pp. 299, 315-16; FO 248/907, Diary ending 16th July 1907.

and the money, having played on the fear of Aqa Mohammad Mehdi of what might happen in Tehran; moreover, his major stumbling block to reach a settlement was gone. The next month Zahir al-Dowleh made further inquiries; both parties remained calm, but became increasingly discontent. Finally, Zahir al-Dowleh informed Tehran that Salar al-Dowleh was the cause of the looting as his inflammatory letters had triggered the riots; Seyf al-Dowleh also shared the blame and responsibility, as did some others. However, Tehran did not accept this explanation. In the beginning of October 1907, a handbill (*shabnameh*) was posted in the main street stating that unless Zahir al-Dowleh found a solution for those who had been looted he would be killed by a group of 10 men, who had agreed to do so. Meanwhile, the city environs became more unsettled, but Zahir al-Dowleh did not take any tough measures as he did not think them proper. Shortly thereafter, prince Zafar al-Saltaneh was appointed commander of the forces of W. Persia. He made A'zam al-Dowleh, Zahir al-Molk's son, head of the Zanganeh tribe, commander of the forces in Kermanshah, but before taking up this post he first had to pay 2,000 *tumans*.[136] According to Sheikh Farajollah Mo'tamedi, 'Ali Khan Zahir al-Dowleh helped those who had been looted, which clearly was not the case. However, he only helped some students of Sheikh Mohamad Taqi Shirazi, the principal of the *madraseh-ye Eslamiyeh*, who received all they had lost.[137]

On 9 October 1907, Zahir al-Dowleh was again appointed governor of Hamadan, he refused until he had been paid for his time as governor of Kermanshah. Then Seyf al-Dowleh who, to a great extent, had been responsible for all the disturbances, was reappointed governor of Kermanshah. He was ordered "to pay the value of the goods [80,000 *tumans*] lost in the looting and was to recover the amount from those who were to blame." The notables of Kermanshah, who had benefited and now would have to pay, did not like this. Nor did the British Legation that opposed his appointment and thus, Seyf al-Dowleh did not assume his governorship. On 2 October much firing happened at 200 m from the British Consulate; the Consular guard turned out and troops also came from the *kadkhoda*; but the assailants had moved on to firing at the Turkish Consulate and the Telegraph Office. Haworth believed that its purpose was that he would report that the situation was unsettled since the appointment of Seyf al-Dowleh. On 15 November, Zahir al-Dowleh was reappointed governor of Kermanshah; on hearing this people took asylum in the Telegraph Office, for Seyf al-Dowleh had been sent as the guilty party for the looting and had to compensate them. On 22 November 1907, two commissioners arrived from Tehran; originally sent to supervise Seyf al-Dowleh executing his orders, now they would do the same with Zahir al-Dowleh. The people's party had grown in power and its militia started drill exercises.[138]

Soleyman Mirza, a young eloquent prince and one of the leaders of the popular party, began to deliver speeches against the Anglo-Russian Convention of 31 August 1907. This Convention aimed to secure British and Russian interests in Persia and to be a vehicle to bring about political stability to the country. To that end the two powers divided Persia in two spheres of influence

---

136. Administration Report 1908, p. 58; Political Diaries vol. 2, pp. 315; 347-48, 397-98; FO 248/907, Diary ending 14th August 1907.

137. Soltani 1386, p. 152.

138. Administration Report 1908, p. 59; Political Diaries, vol. 2, pp. 405-06,424-25,453; IOR/L/MIL/17/15/11/3, Who's Who in Persia, vol. II, p. 336. "The British Indian detachment at Kermanshah consisted of one duffadar and seven sowars." *The Hansard*, HC Debate, 20 June 1907, vol. 176 cc609-10; Grothe 1910, p. 85.

and one neutral zone in between these two. To assuage Persian nationalist feelings the two powers stated that they were committed to respect the integrity and independence of Persia.[139] The publication of the news about the Convention caused much resentment among nationalist circles in Persia, however, not in Kermanshah, where Soleyman Mirza failed to rouse support for his cause and he gave it up. Zahir al-Dowleh, whose daughter had married the grandson of Zahir al-Molk, became less supportive of the popular party and complaints grew about him. It was publicly said that if he did not take bribes his agents did; also "his apathy was worse than the rapacity of an ordinary Hakim." The two commissioners, who had arrived on 22 November 1907, reminded him that he was appointed to recover the looted money and if he did not want to do that he'd better resign. He then 'imprisoned' the chiefs of the local regiments, including his new in-laws (A'zam al-Dowleh, chief of Zanganeh regiment; Ehtesham al-Mamalek, chief of the Kerend regiment; Moqtader al-Molk, chief of the artillery, Vothuq al-Mamalek *lashkarnevis-bashi*). They were 'imprisoned' by day and returned home at night. He also imprisoned the three *kadkhoda*s of the city quarters concerned. He then promised that the money should be paid in 10 days and opened a public subscription, to which those arrested had to contribute substantially! On the 7th day (12 December), seeing the futility of it all and not being able to keep his promise to recover the money due to the people before 15 December, he left the city at night; his wife and family had left two days earlier, allegedly to visit her sick daughter in Tehran, to avoid raising suspicion.[140]

ZAHIR AL-MOLK

Meanwhile, the political problems remained unresolved, and caused problems throughout the year and this was reflected in the frequent change of governors. Because there was no governor, the 85-year old Reza Khan Zanganeh Zahir al-Molk, the influential Zanganeh chief took over in December 1907 and was later confirmed as deputy-governor; the 9th governor in that year. He was an old-style governor, who could not accept involvement of the lower classes and tradesmen in government. His idea of justice was cutting of limbs and the like, instilling fear, and as a result, the town became and remained silent.[141] Zahir al-Molk also told the militia to stop drilling and the local assemblies to stop meeting "as he did not understand new ways." The militia had been formed at the end of November and was composed of two groups. One had 25 men consisting of princes and Khans etc. and the other consisted of some 40 followers of Mo'in al-Ra'aya. The militia, which was well-armed, was supposed to get its own uniform, but, for the time being, drilled in uniforms of Persian soldiers. After a while the *anjoman*s of Tabriz, later followed by Isfahan, withdrew their recognition of Mohammad 'Ali Shah because of his disrespect for the Constitution. This also had an impact on Kermanshah, which learnt about this from Tabriz. Mo'in al-Ra'aya, a former aristocratic party leader, made a speech calling for the formation of a cavalry, the seizing of the guns in the arsenal, and to march to Tehran to support

139. F. Kazemzadeh, "Anglo-Russian Convention," iranicaonline. org.

140. Political Diaries vol. 3, p. 13

141. Political Diaries vol. 3, p. 13.

the *Majles*. When Mohammad 'Ali Shah gave in, people said it was all due to misunderstandings and evil advisers. Because of the telegraph, communications were quick, and, as a result, the popular party found cohesion. The militia began its drill again and the governor did not object. On 28 December 1907 telegrams arrived from Sheikh Fazlolllah Nuri saying that the Constitution was against the *shari'ah* and another telegram from the *Majles* warning people against the Sheikh.[142]

Mojtahed Kamal al-Din read the two telegrams at a meeting he had called as well as a telegram from Kerbela that stated that the *Majles* was in accordance with the *shari'ah* and opposition to it made you an unbeliever. The Imam Jom'eh rose and said only Kerbela's voice was valid in this matter. As a result, a telegram was sent to the *Majles* offering full support and one to Fazlollah Nuri disassociating themselves from him. The Shah promised Russia and Great Britain that he would obey the Constitution, and calm reigned in Kermanshah. On 2 January 1908, despite orders from Tehran to prevent him from returning, Aqa Mohammad Mehdi returned with the blessings of the olama of Kerbela. He was jubilated, a dozen caparisoned led horses (*yadak*) were sent to greet him, one from governor and one from *kargozar*. "The people went in thousands and kissed Mehdi's hands and feet and even the feet of his horse. Mehdi now pretends to great absorption from the world and abstention from temporal affairs. He is, however, the religious chief of the local assembly." Even those opposing him and his enemies, such as Mo'in al-Ra'aya, went to greet him.[143] Although the 'popular' party seemed to be in a strong position, the *kargozar* told the consuls that in his view there was a strong party in favor of the old regime and that it would not give up power without bloodshed. At that time, a minor mullah who spoke against the Shah was beaten up by his fellow mullahs, while Soleyman Mirza, the leader of the progressives, was nearly killed by a group of sayyeds, who called him a 'Babi'. The 120-man strong militia showed up on 6 January 1908; to make them look bigger as a group, soldiers and others temporarily filled their ranks and made it look as if there were 400. The 30-40 princes and Khans also drilled but the whole activity did not make further progress.[144]

On 11 January 1908, Zahir al-Molk, who was appointed C-in-C of the border forces left to Qasr-e Shirin; his son A'zam al-Dowleh took over as deputy governor. He immediately acted with great harshness and brute force, but did not care whether he punished the guilty or the innocent. Until the end of the year, he made much money, especially from the muleteers. Tehran had forbidden muleteers crossing the border, which he allowed, if they paid him. There were no further fights; the people's party being too strong; also the border problems demanded the full attention of the officials. However, despite its strength, how was the people's party going to deal with the loss of income and employment for the official class and their hangers-on under a constitutional government? The tribes had all the power and were not pro-Constitution. So, if opposition to the Constitution were to grow in strength there would be much armed support in

142. Administration Report 1908, p. 60, Political Diaries, vol. 2, p.461, 473-74; vol. 3, p. 2, 35.

143. Political Diaries, vol. 3, p. 47; Administration Report 1908, p. 61; FO 248/938, Diary ending January 7, 1907[sic, must 1908].

144. Political Diaries, vol. 3, p. 48; FO 248/938, Diary ending January 7, 1907 [sic, must 1908]. Sayyed Akbar Shah was a supporter of Mohammad Ali Shah and the conservatives. Soltani 1381, vol. 4, p. 499. The most respected prince in town, Mohtasham al-Dowleh trained an artillery militia in mid-December 1907. Political Diaries, vol. 3, p. 14.

Kermanshah. In October 1907, the Turks reinforced their troops along the border. Baneh was so far the only place occupied by them. There were some 1,500 infantry, 250 cavalry and three cannons. They laid claim to the districts of Zohab and Samur.[145]

In February 1908, neither pilgrims nor caravans were allowed to go to Baghdad. In mid-February 1908 A'zam al-Dowleh beheaded several men in the city's square for highway robbery, after which the corpses were dragged through the streets as a warning to others. He later beheaded another six men. In mid-March a man called Karim cut the throat of Aqa Rahim, "one of the leading reactionary mullahs and the most corrupt of them all." One of his students attacked Karim, so that the mullah's throat was not totally slit. He was still alive and was treated by Dr. Loqman al-Soltan, but most people hoped that he would die. His killer was blown from a gun. As a result, the royalist party gained strength.[146] At the end of February 1908 there was almost a major riot. A certain Sayyed Akbar, a partisan of Sheikh Fazlollah Nuri, had come from Tehran and was received with open arms by the royalist party, whose members paid him many visits. In reaction, Soleyman Mirza, one of the leaders of the popular party and Inspector of Education, went with some men of the Nationalist militia to the house in which Sayyed Akbar was staying. He drew a line around the entrance and said: "as Sayed Akbar was preaching against the Constitution it was not desirable that he should be allowed to receive visits." The royalist party turned out in force and Soleyman Mirza had to flee pursued by a crowd that called him a 'Babi' and wanted him expelled from the city. Shopkeepers closed the bazaar fearing fights. Tehran was induced to issue orders to expel Sayyed Akbar to Kerbela and he left on 3 March 1908. The event showed how strong the royalist party was as it could count on support from all big landowners and high government officials. They favored the old regime because under it "their power was unlimited and their incomes large." Also, the tribes would support the royalists if a civil war would break out, although they gladly would plunder both sides.[147]

In mid-April 1908, A'zam al-Dowleh Zanganeh was dismissed. The Prime Minister, probably at the suggestion of Soleyman Mirza, who had gone to Tehran, asked A'zam al-Dowleh to explain the legality of his executions. Toward the end of April 1908, Vazir Akram was appointed governor of Kermanshah. However, the chiefs of the local tribes met and wired Tehran that they were satisfied with Zahir al-Molk as governor. As one of the tasks of the governors was to keep the tribes in order, they, of course, preferred to have one of their own as governor. A'zam al-Dowleh was severely criticized by the newspaper *Majles*. One of the persons executed by him was a boy of 16 accused of "moral offences." There was no proof, but the accusation sufficed.[148]

---

145. Administration Report 1907-08, pp. 61-62. "Hoseyn Khan Zanganeh, A`zam al-Dowleh II, eldest son of Zahir al-Molk Zanganeh. Whenever his father is governor of Kermanshah he is his deputy and to all intents and purposes governor. Is rather bloodthirsty and fond of money, "but has not the power to rule so large a province." Relies on intrigue and is a most unsatisfactory ruler. Like most of his family deeply indebted to the IBP." IOR/L/PS/20/223, 'Who's who in Persia. Calcutta: General Staff, India, 1916', p. 55.

146. Political Diaries, vol. 3, pp. 81, 117; Soltani 1381, vol. 4, p. 501; Idem 1386, pp. 162-63.

147. FO 248/938, Diary ending 4th March 1908.

148. Political Diaries, vol. 3, p. 149 (The Kalhors, who paid no taxes either, ironically had been sent to make the Koliya'is pay taxes, but returned on hearing that a new governor was appointed).

However, at the end of April 1908, Vazir Akram resigned and was appointed governor of Tehran, which he had not even left. As a result, Kermanshah was without anyone in charge of the government. The *kadkhoda* of the quarter in which the British Consulate was located came to see the consul saying that robberies were frequent in the quarter and that he was worried, being responsible, because the Consulate had no walls. He suggested that Haworth ask for more guards from A'zam al-Dowleh. The *kadkhoda* clearly hoped that the consul would report about the dismal state of affairs in the city to Tehran.[149] In early May 1908, the two parties were waiting for the new govenor. The *anjoman* took the case of the 16-year old executed boy seriously; it was said that all A'zam al-Dowleh's ranks and titles were taken away. The local *anjoman* demanded him to be sent to Tehran and the new governor had received orders to such effect. It was expected if it came to that he would escape to Kerbela. There was no defense for his behavior and, according to the British consul, he "is a most objectionable person at all times."[150] Zahir al-Molk refused to send his son to Tehran and was furious with the authorities there. On 9 May 1908, there was a rumor that there would be rioting and shopkeepers began to remove their goods to their homes. The town was rife with rumor and there was constant firing at night. Two murders were committed between 9-12 May. It was said that Zahir al-Molk was behind the rumors and unrest to frighten candidates for the post of governor, so that the only one willing to take the job would be he. Matters got worse, when the Koliya'is and Kurdistan tribes started fighting each other. The city was surrounded by fighting and plundering tribes. A'zam al-Dowleh, who held the command of the garrison regiment, gave out that as he had been dismissed he did not want to do anything and thus, it was dangerous to go out at night. The town had "never been in such a bad situation before," according to the British consul.[151] After Vazir Akram's resignation Qa'emmaqam was appointed governor of Kermanshah, but nobody expected him to come and fill the job. Meanwhile, there was no governor or deputy and the situation in the province became worse. The local situation remained bad until 19 May 1908, because there was no nobody in charge and criminals were not punished. However, on that day Zahir al-Molk took over again as deputy governor and the incessant firing during the night stopped and the town became somewhat safer. The Prime Minister ordered that A'zam al-Dowleh be sent to Tehran for punishment, but as his father was the deputy governor this did not happen. [152]

The Kakawands, joined by other Lors, continued to hold the road to Hamadan and were raiding villages. The Kakawand Lors crossed the provincial border, the villagers fled, the robbers occupied the villages along the Tehran road, looting much between Chachamal and Bisotun, 40 km from Kermanshah. Mr. and Mrs. Stead at 50 km from Kermanshah were robbed of everything in May 1908. Mr. Stead only kept his pants; his servant was totally stripped. From Mrs. Stead they only took her jacket and outside skirt, she would not have been touched, but too late the Lors realized she was a woman. According to the British consul, "Lors will not rob or molest women; as sign of good faith between two tribes that want to make peace, women are often sent as flags of truce to complete the first arrangement." The Kakawands occupied the Tehran road

149. Political Diaries, vol. 3, p. 161.
150. Political Diaries, vol. 3, p. 167.
151. Political Diaries, vol. 3, p. 176.
152. Political Diaries, vol. 3, p.188; Administration Report 1908, p. 40.

and the tribes around Kermanshah were fighting each other and all roads were unsafe. For three weeks there was no authority in the town, and life went on without "an uproar." Only two murders were committed, and although the culprits were known they walked out of town. The Kakawands continued their robbing spree and were joined by other tribes and they divided the country into spheres of influence, "just like the English-Russian convention as the local wags remarked." At the end of three weeks many pilgrims from Kerbela had amassed because they could not continue their journey; they asked the local *mojtahed*s to intervene, who informed A'zam al-Dowleh that since his brother Fakhim al-Saltaneh was governor of Chamchamal he received an allowance for the upkeep of *savar*s, thus he had to protect the pilgrims in his district. Fakhim al-Saltaneh collected a few *savar*s and promised to escort the pilgrims as well as some muleteers. The post wagon also was ordered to join, but allowed the pilgrims to go first. The Kakawands attacked, the escort fled, and the pilgrims were stripped; the muleteers could save most of their loads. Fakhim al-Saltaneh then had the nerve to demand 10% for the protection he had given them! Meanwhile, as expected, Qaemmaqam resigned, and prince 'Azizollah Mirza Zafar al-Saltaneh was appointed and was expected to arrive with troops in Kermanshah in June.[153]

The attacks by the Kakawands had an interesting conclusion. Habibollah, chief of one the raiding bands of the Kakawands suddenly died. The superstitious Lors blamed this on them having robbed pilgrims. His rival, Khani then claimed the chieftainship of the Kakawands and wired from Kangavar that he regretted the action taken of which he had no knowledge and that if claimants came to Kangavar he would give them their goods. In the last week of May 1908, a group of pilgrims was looted by followers of Hasan Khan, the *kalantar*, who himself had been looted by the Kakawands, who seemed to have left the road by that time altogether. Meanwhile the Balawands looted the Zanganehs, the Koliya'is were fighting the Kandula'is and the Kalhors had an internal succession fight. At the end of May 1908, Zahir al-Molk was ordered to restore security in the governorate. Zafar al-Saltaneh, who had been appointed governor, had left Tehran with a small force. The workers of the Customs Department went on strike after Asghar Selim, a ruffian and follower of Mo'in al-Ra'aya had beaten one of their colleagues. Tehran ordered Zahir al-Molk to punish him and decreed that he himself was responsible for any losses incurred, but he refused as the man was in his son's party. As a result, all Customs employees left handing the key to Zahir al-Molk and telling him that he was responsible for whatever happened.[154] In early June 1908, the Customs were open for business again; Asghar Salim was taken to Customs-house accompanied by the *farrash-bashi* with the sticks, there he apologized and was forgiven.[155]

The town was quiet, while the Kakawands had returned home. There were even signs of progress, because some of the leading men began construction projects; the vizier of the province, Mohtasham al-Dowleh improved his house "and many rooms would not disgrace Europe." Mo'in al-Ra'aya, "the chief stormy petrel of the district," built a fine *rowzeh-khaneh*, "if the exterior were worthy of the interior, the result would be worthy of note as an addition to

153. Political Diaries, vol. 3, pp. 176, 207 ("At the beginning of June 1908, Dowlatmand, chief of section of Belawend tribe and a successful brigand was murdered, which was a godsend to the villages south-east of Kermanshah on which he levied a tribute"); Administration Report 1908, p. 40.

154. Political Diaries, vol. 3, p. 188-89, 195; Soltani 1381, vol. 4, p. 503.

155. Political Diaries, vol. 3, p. 195.

the town."[156] On 6 June 1908, Mohammad 'Ali Shah sent a telegram saying that the people were his sons and that he had arrested various people, who were making trouble. On 9 June telegrams from Resht and Mazandaran were received saying that Mohammad 'Ali Shah was opposed to the Constitution and that they had renounced their allegiance to him. Hundreds of copies of this telegram were distributed throughout Kermanshah. Then a reply was sent from Kermanshah to the Shah stating that people were glad that he was doing everything to support the Constitution. On June 14, a telegram from Isfahan arrived that 14 cities that formerly had the right to mint money had deposed the Shah and appointed his son under a regent. Kermanshah replied that it would follow the lead of Tabriz, a promise it could not carry out because "the tribes would swamp it in ten days once the Shah's authority had been determined in Tehran." The new governor, 'Azizollah Mirza Zafar al-Saltaneh, according to Mo'tamedi, a stupid and arrogant man, arrived on 14 June without a single soldier and hardly with a servant. Fortunately, the town was sick of fighting and the two opposing parties were ready to be friends for the moment.[157]

On 23 June 1908, news arrived of Mohammad 'Ali Shah's coup d'etat. People in the city of Kermanshah did nothing, although if the telegraph office had not been occupied they might have risen up. The villagers did not care who was in charge as long as they were left alone and could do their work.[158] When news arrived that Mohammad 'Ali Shah had won, people accepted the fait accompli. The British consul believed that the occupation of the Telegraph Office was planned by the Shah's party. Before the coup, Zahir al-Molk had telegraphed the Shah that he could count on the Kurdish tribes and offered his services; the other chiefs also offered to send 2,000 men. Zahir al-Molk's offer was refused, but the others were accepted, but only for 200 horsemen. However, the chiefs had difficulty mobilizing 200 men as all the small chiefs refused to supply men, saying it was too costly for them. Finally, 200 Kalhors and 200 Sanjabis left under respectively Zargham al-Dowleh, son of Da'ud Khan and Shoja' al-Lashkar, son of Samsam al-Mamalek. They kept their men under control and no looting was allowed.[159]

Fights between the tribes were constant; outside city it was still not safe. In mid-August 1908, the Kakawands again infested the Tehran road; Fakhim al-Saltaneh with 200 *savar*s, 400 soldiers and some artillery was sent to punish them and recover stolen property. This operation had to be done together with the governor of Lorestan who was at Borujerd. However, only Fath al-Soltan, better known as Nazar 'Ali Khan Amra'i, showed up. Some goods, notably, mules were recovered and a portion was sold back at profitable rates, the rest was divided between the two chiefs.

On 18 July 1908, Zafar al-Saltaneh left for Kurdistan to install Hajji Mohammad Khan, his deputy there. To complicate matters, Amanollah Khan Eqtedar Nezam arrived on 27 July 1908 to replace Hajji Mohammad Khan as deputy governor, be it that this was irrelevant by that time. Because in early August 1908, during his absence, Zafar al-Saltaneh was dismissed as governor of Kermanshah and appointed governor of Kurdistan, a favorite move to exile an undesirable person. Apparently, Zafar al-Saltaneh was too pro-Constitutional for the Shah's liking. In July

156. Administration Report 1908, p. 39; Political Diaries, vol. 3, p. 201.
157. Administration Report 1908, pp. 41-42; Political Diaries, vol. 3, p. 207; Soltani 1386, p. 154.
158. Political Diaries, vol. 3, p. 217.
159. Political Diaries, vol. 3, p. 225.

1908, Haworth had left Kermanshah to visit Kurdistan and when he returned on 28 September he found that Mohammad Reza Khan Zahir al-Molk was governor again, who had paid 25,000 *tumans* and later another 5,000 *tumans* to get the post. He had agreed to collect the current year's and last year's arrears, which was impossible, but fate intervened on his side. He was an old man and in practice his oldest son Mohammad Hoseyn Khan A'zam al-Dowleh was governor.[160] Nobody believed the good intentions of Mohammad 'Ali Shah, although the Shah's coup d'etat raised little reaction in Kermanshah; people were sick of fighting and the peasants only cared about their work and whether the roads were safe. People told each other that Russia had promised massive military aid to the Shah, while Zahir al-Molk wired the Shah that all Kurdish tribes were at his disposal. The Shah had sent an agent to the olama asking them to sign a document that stated that a Constitution was not required. However, before they had to do some real soul-searching about what to reply, on 4 October 1908 a telegram arrived in which the Shah stated that he would convene a new *Majles* in November, but that Tabriz would be disenfranchised.[161] Everybody, even officials, in private agreed that a Constitution would be the best way to resolve the country's problems.[162] Zahir al-Molk remained governor, but he was powerless, "though Governor to-day he may be only the chief of a small tribe tomorrow, a position he has always to consider." He only wanted to get as much money as he safely could get and wanted to have nothing to do with the past. Zahir al-Molk, who was a disaster as governor, according to Haworth, had not yet collected all the revenue and was likely to lose money.[163] In late January 1909, Zaher al-Molk disclaimed any responsibility for losses that foreigners incurred in the past, even during his administration, although the *kargozar* had received orders that he was responsible. However, the governor refused to carry out any orders from Tehran that had financial implications.[164]

In the first half of March 1909, the *mojtaheds* of Kerbela sent a letter to the olama of Kermanshah that those who did not support the Constitution were unbelievers and thus, they had to choose. Also, that the governor had to release Sayyed 'Abdollah, a member of the *Majles*, who had been imprisoned in the fort after the Shah's coup d'etat. Zahir al-Molk replied he had his orders and they should address their request to the Shah. "He also added that it seemed quite unnecessary to do anything as if the country was to receive a Constitution, it would be given to Kermanshah also; if not, what was the good of compromising themselves. This advice agreed so absolutely with the private opinions of the priests that they followed it completely. The people also had replied to them that as the priests had not assisted them in 1907, so now they refused to close their shops to help the priests."[165] Haworth observed that "so little information of the

---

160. Political Diaries, vol. 3, pp. 241, 265, 317; Soltani 1386, pp. 154, 164; FO 248/938, Dairy no. 17 ending October 4th, 1908; Administration Report 1908, pp. 42-43.

161. Administration Report 1908, pp. 42-43; Political Diaries vol. 3, pp. 217, 317.

162. Administration Report 1908, p. 45-46.

163. Administration Report 1908, pp. 45-47.

164. Political Diaries, vol. 3, pp. 461-62.

165. Political Diaries, vol. 3, p. 527; for more about the banning of Sayyed `Abdollah, Sayyed Behbahani's brother, see Soltani 1386, p. 164. Sayyed `Abdollah, according to the British, a notorious *Majles mojtahed*, had arrived in Kermanshah supposedly en route to Kerbela. However, he stayed in a village near Kermanshah. Soltani 1381, vol. 4, p. 503.

state of affairs in the north reaches Kermanshah." Rumors were rife and the announcement of the Constitution was expected any moment.[166]

On 1 April 1909, a Jewish man was executed by blowing him from a gun, for killing an artillerist or *tupchi*, although it was said that his brother had done it. After the gun was fired the man was uninjured. Some of Imam Jom'eh's followers immediately freed him. He had called on Hazrat-e 'Abbas and had been saved; the whole town was illuminated that night in honor of this saint's miracle. The executioner or *mir-ghazab* had remorse, renounced his sons, left his job and joined the Imam Jom'eh's staff. A relative of the "executed" Jew, who was employed by the German chemist Lotz, was also overcome, and converted to Islam. However, the ungodly said that the Imam Jom'eh had bribed the executioner. People were not happy with Zahir al-Molk in April 1909. The Imam Jom'eh was suspected of being a Constitutionalist and Zahir al-Molk complained to the Shah about him. Zahir al-Molk and his son A'zam al-Dowleh were quarreling about the methods of government and distribution of the spoils as a result of which the *divankhaneh* was empty and judgments were no longer heard.[167] On the occasion of the news of the granting of a Constitution on 4 May 1909 orders were given for one night of illumination or *cheraghani*, but the people of Hamadan insisted on doing it for three days.[168]

ZAHIR AL-DOWLEH, AGAIN

On 1 June 1909, Zahir al-Molk handed in his resignation, which was not accepted, because there was no one else who wanted the job.[169] In early June 1909 there was an attempt to form new local assembly, but it was decided to wait for the new governor. On 13 June 1909, Zahir al-Dowleh arrived, who had been reappointed governor. The town was quiet, although there was some firing at night which the governor ordered to cease.[170] There was a split among the population. On one side, there were Sayyed Kamal al-Din (a *mojtahed* from Tehran and brother of Sayyed 'Abdollah who had arrived two years ago en route to Kerbela), Mohtasham al-Dowleh, Qavam-e Ra'aya (better known as Kelbi) and his sons, most princes and notables as a well as Zahir al-Molk. On the other side were Hoseyn Khan Mo'in al-Ra'aya and the local *mojtahed*s, although they did not openly give their support. Only recently the two parties had sworn friendship and unity on the Koran together. However, the intrigues of the sons of Kelbi, who were the instigators of all local trouble, led to their falling out. Mo'in al-Ra'aya's party put up notices saying that Kamal al-Din was an undesirable and should be expelled from town. Kamal al-Din's party was stronger and prepared to resist, so trouble was brewing. On 13 July 1909 the bazaars

166. Political Diaries, vol. 3, p. 568.

167. Political Diaries, vol. 3, p. 606.

168. Political Diaries, vol. 3, p. 635. Lotz had a pharmacy in Hamadan and apparently a branch in Kermanshah as well. Küss 1911, part V, p. 22.

169. Political Diaries, vol. 3, p. 651; Soltani 1381, vol. 4, p. 509.

170. Diaries, vol. 3, pp. 659, 667.

were closed. In the night of 18 June 1909, the house of the Mir Ghazab was attacked and everything looted; he was wounded and died the next morning.[171]

The main event was the unexpected arrival at the British Consulate of Mo'in al-Ra'aya, Ra'is al-Tojjar and Uzuk al-Mamalek, the leading men of the popular party early on 15 July 1909. Kamal-Din's party had proposed a subscription to be raised to pay for the expense of those send to defend the Constitution. Mo'in al- Ra'aya disagreed with the proposal, because the money would be misappropriated. He favored that those who could afford it should pay and send men; this led to ill-feeling between the two parties. Later Mo'in al-Ra'aya's party posted notices that Kamal al-Din should be deported as an undesirable. The same day there was a scuffle between Hasan Khan, brother of Mo'in al- Ra'aya and a man of Kamal al-Din's party; he complained to Kamal al-Din, who complained to Zahir al-Molk, who controlled the only regiment in town and was only too willing to settle old scores. He demanded that Mo'in al-Ra'aya, Ra'is al-Tojjar and two others (incl. Zahir al-Molk's son) should leave town, else he would fight. They refused and in the night of 13-14 July a fight broke out that lasted well into the next day. Zahir al-Molk who had control over the regiment, arsenal and artillery used all three, which were government property, to settle a private quarrel! In the afternoon of 14 July, Zahir al-Molk placed the government cannons where they overlooked the houses belonging to his main opponents and fired. The firing continued till the evening and two persons on either side were killed. According to Lambert Molitor, more than 5,000 shots were fired. The governor was too weak and could not do anything and remained in his house and nobody blamed him as Tehran did not give him the means to do anything. On the night of 14 July, Zaher al-Molk was reconciled with his son and Mo'in al-Ra'aya thus lost his main supporter and gave up. Mo'in al-Ra'aya, Ra'is al-Tojjar and Uzuk al-Mamalek left town that night, but they were waylaid by Mirza 'Ali Khan, chief of the *qarasuran*. They fled to the Turkish Consulate, but were refused entry, and then they had taken refuge in the British Consulate's grounds, which was easy as these were eight acres in extent and were not walled. Capt. Crossle told them to leave, but they refused, because they would be killed if they would do so. Of the Consulate's escort of eight men the consul sent four to protect them. The consul reported the matter to the governor, who was not willing to interfere himself. The British consul lodged a formal complaint and asked the governor for guards to protect the Consulate, but the governor replied that he was unable to. Zahir al-Molk had handed out the rifles in the arsenal to his men and refused to supply guards from his regiment. Meanwhile, Zahir al-Molk looted and burnt down Mo'in al- Ra'aya's house, and later he burnt down the town house of the Ra'is-e Tojjar and his new house outside the city. Zahir al-Molk demanded that Crossle hand over the refugees so that they might be tried. His messengers were accompanied by a large group of people, who threatened to take the *bast*is by force, if need be. During two nights attempts were made to get at the asylum seekers, but the intruders were beaten off. On 16 July 1908, Zahir al-Dowleh informed the British consul that he had resigned and that he would not act as governor for as long as Zahir al-Molk used government property for a private quarrel. In the morning of 17 July Da'ud Khan Kalhor arrived with 200 *savar*s and demanded that unless Mo'in al-Ra'aya was handed over to him he would plunder the city. Later that day news arrived that Mohammad 'Ali Shah had abdicated, which refocused

171. Political Diaries, vol. 3, p. 673.

people's attention on other than local events. On 18 July Da'ud Khan left after talks with the Consulate's Mirza and Zahir al-Molk, but before doing so, he sent a telegram to Tehran demanding that Mo'in al-Ra'aya be handed over to Zahir al-Molk. After discussions one of them left on 27 July and the others on 3 August 1909. Sepahdar A'zam wired that Great Britain and Russia had greatly helped in obtaining the Constitution and therefore, there should be no ill-will toward them. Kamal al-Din sent a message to the British and Russian consuls to thank their government for their support, and called on the consuls on 29 July.[172]

Meanwhile, life around Kermanshah assumed its usual pattern. This time, the Koliya'is and Kandulehs rebelled and attacked the villages of Zahir al-Molk and his family. On 5 August 1909, the governor received a telegram with orders that Zahir al-Molk had to march against the Kakawands and the Koliya'is to put down the disturbances. He left the next day with one regiment and two guns and returned on 12 August without having had any success. The Koliya'is had joined with Da'ud Khan Kalhor and considered attacking Zahir al-Molk. They wrote to the governor that they were Constitutionalists and intended to take revenge on Zahir al-Molk who attacked them out of a personal grudge not because of political reasons. The local situation became even more tense, when Sepahdar, the Prime Minister, wired the governor that because the Constitution had been granted the *feda'i* soldiers were to be abolished. However, they refused to be disbanded and annoyed people with petty extortion threatening violence if they were not paid.[173]

Tehran ordered the governor to send Sayyed Kamal al-Din to Tehran without delay to answer charges of having organized disturbances in Kermanshah. The Sayyed made excuses – he had local debts and no means to pay for the trip. The governor then paid 500 *tuman*s for them and told him to leave. Kamal al-Din then wired Kerbela saying he was summoned to Tehran without cause and whether he should go? He left anyway on 23 August 1909. At the end of August 1909, Mo'in al-Ra'aya was at Taq-e Bisotun and collected men to enter town, ostensibly to recover property looted from his brother's house. After discussion there was reconciliation between him and Zahir al-Molk who promised to recover the looted property. Sepahdar, the Prime Minister, wired the governor that Mokhtar al-Saltaneh was appointed commander of the military in Kermanshah and would arrive with his own regiment shortly. This was really needed and would clip the wings of Zahir al-Molk; Mokhtar al-Saltaneh arrived on 15 August alone, his regiment was following. On 6 September 1909, Tehran wired that Zahir al-Molk and his sons A'zam al-Dowleh and Amir al-Moqtader had to come to Tehran. Some of his partisans wired Tehran on behalf of the Kermanshah people that if he would leave the town would be in disorder and asked that he had not to leave. Tehran replied they had to come.[174]

On 5 September 1909, the *mojtahed*s of Kerbela sent a telegram enjoining the people to pay the taxes that the government levied; it was their duty also to follow the government's orders. Earlier, after Mohammad 'Ali Shah's coup d'etat, they had sent a similar text but declaring all

172. Political Diaries, vol. 3, pp. 697-98; FO 248/698, Crossle to Tehran, 18/07/1908; Destree 1976, pp. 194-95; Molitor 2018a.

173. Political Diaries, vol. 3, p. 698.

174. Political Diaries, vol. 3, p. 716.

taxes were illegal (*haram*).[175] On 24 September 1909, Mokhtar al-Soltan, the new army commander, received 100 Sanjabis; the soldiers from Tehran had not yet arrived. Because the *mojaheds* of the city were divided they could not be used. Zahir al-Molk was not going to Tehran but considered going to Kerbela. Because Da'ud Khan Kalhor had threatened to arrest him if he passed through Qasr-e Shirin he left the city on 24 September via Posht-e Kuh.[176]

The rebelling Kandulehs (a sub-division of the Zanganeh) submitted to Zahir al-Molk in October 1909. They had to surrender their rifles in exchange for a receipt. This was done in a public place and they asked for the return of the receipt that they had signed when the rifles were given to them the first time. Mo'in al-Ra'aya supported them, but A'zam al-Dowleh, Zahir al-Molk's son cursed him and asked why he interfered. Mo'in al-Ra'aya's brother then drew his revolver, and only intervention by the olama prevented a fight. Mo'in al-Ra'aya's opponents persuaded the local *anjoman* to ask Mo'in al-Ra'aya to leave the city. He went to Da'ud Khan Kalhor and his brother went to the Koliya'is. Then Da'ud Khan wrote to the local *anjoman* that since he officially was Ra'is al-Ashayer (chief of the tribes) he was coming to the city, because they were unable to keep order. He would not interfere with anybody, except that he wanted to recover the damage done to Mo'in al-Ra'aya's house from the perpetrators, which he estimated at one million *tuman*s. The notables were very much afraid, because Zahir al-Molk had gone to the Vali of Posht-e Kuh. The latter wrote that Da'ud Khan Kalhor had to make peace with A'zam al-Dowleh, and Zahir al-Molk wrote his son to go to Mahidasht and do so. The *mojaheds* in Zahir al-Molk's camp fearing to be left in the lurch, threatened to attack the house of Sayyed Hasan Owjaq, Da'ud Khan's agent where Mo'in al-Ra'aya's children were. The notables appealed to A'zam al-Dowleh who promised to take the *mojaheds* with him to Mahidasht and that they would be included in any reconciliation. On 11 October Da'ud Khan Kalhor came to Mahidasht and A'zam al-Dowleh, most notables and their friends and the leaders of the *mojaheds* went there on 12 October. Zahir al-Dowleh wrote to Tehran that as long as he had no force he could not accept any responsibility. Meanwhile, Mokhtar al-Saltaneh wanted to resign as commander since no reinforcements had arrived.[177]

About 8 November 1909, there was a fight between Da'ud Khan Kalhor, supported by most tribes, and the Sanjabis, supported by the Jafs of Kurdistan, the Ahmadawand Chelabis, and Turkish refugees. Zahir al-Dowleh was ordered to support Da'ud Khan, but as there was opposition by some groups against further fighting in Kermanshah, which might lead to a religious war, the Jafs being Sunnis, he delayed before sending troops. Then the Sanjabis withdrew, not wishing to fight government troops. Da'ud Khan used the occasion to plunder some villages and therefore, the roads were unsafe.[178] At the end of November 1909, Zahir al-Dowleh resigned and was replaced by Reza Qoli Khan Nezam al-Saltaneh, who did not arrive immediately. As a result, in December 1909, the city was unsafe, as there were many robberies. The Baghdad road was rather safe, but on all other roads there were robberies. The telegraph was several times

175. Political Diaries, vol. 3, p. 717.
176. Political Diaries, vol. 3, p. 734.
177. FO 248/968, Diary ending 13th October 1909.
178. IOR/L/PS/20/261/1, Persia no. 1 (1911), Further Correspondence Respecting the Affairs of Persia, p. 8.

interrupted by the Kakawands, who destroyed several kms of lines and took away the material.[179]

NEZAM AL-SALTANEH

In January 1910 the city was quiet, Zahir al-Dowleh having left on 2 January, awaiting the arrival of the new governor, who came on 5 January. Nezam al-Saltaneh arrived with 100 horse and 500 infantry; at the end of the month 200 Sanjabis and 50 Nanakali horsemen arrived, while an additional 200 men were raised and drilled locally. The new governor preserved order in the city, but did not take severe action against disturbers of the peace. His treasury was empty. Early February 1910, Nezam al-Saltaneh ordered Salar Mas'ud, the governor of Qasr-e Shirin and chief of the Gurans to come to Kermanshah to pay his taxes. He replied that he could not leave the border, but he was summoned again. Salar Mas'ud then consulted with Da'ud Khan Kalhor, who ordered the roadguards to stop levying illegal fees from the caravans.[180]

During March-May 1910, the city remained quiet and was effectively policed. Also, the province was quiet. Nezam al-Saltaneh moved with his troops through the province arresting various offenders; three of the more important ones in the city (Hajj Rostam Beg, Kelbi, Asghar Selim) were sent to Tehran. The local assembly wanted them tried in Kermanshah, but Nezam al-Saltaneh insisted that they had to go to Tehran. This had a good result, because some of the tribes submitted to him and sent forces to join him. He had by then 2,000 men. Also, Da'ud Khan Kalhor and other important chiefs seemed to be inclined to obey the government.[181] In May 1910 the roads were safe, while the province was quiet except at the Kurdistan border where tribes were fighting. Nezam al-Saltaneh was negotiating with Da'ud Khan Kalhor and waited for Bakhtiyari horsemen before moving from the city. Da'ud Khan seemed to be apprehensive of the force being gathered. There was some discontent with the governor's harsh methods to maintain order, but he immediately arrested two of the ringleaders that put a stop to the agitation.[182] Although he would change his opinion later, in May 1910, the new British consul McDouall had a positive view of Nezam al-Saltaneh, whom he described as a very capable governor of the old school. Although his rule was despotic, he committed no oppressive or barbarous acts, but, with the support of the *Majles*, ruled along constitutional lines, having the *nazmiyeh*, *adliyeh*, and *baladiyeh* carrying out their respective duties. However, the provincial assembly or *anjoman-e velayati* had no power.[183] The *anjoman-e velayati* of Kermanshah city was composed of Hajj Aqa Mohammad Mehdi Mojtahed, president; Mohammad Baqer Mirza

---

179. IOR/L/PS/20/261/1, Persia no. 1 (1911), Further Correspondence Respecting the Affairs of Persia, p. 15.

180. IOR/L/PS/20/261/1, Persia no. 1 (1911), Further Correspondence Respecting the Affairs of Persia, pp. 23, 31.

181. IOR/L/PS/20/261/1, Persia no. 1 (1911), Further Correspondence Respecting the Affairs of Persia, p. 38, 46, 52. According to Lambert Molitor, since his arrival, Nezam al-Saltaneh's authority was feared throughout the province and there was order and security. He put a stop to the road attacks by the Kakarendis and the illegal imposts collected by the Kerassourans. The local administrative offices the governor had established functioned more or less well. Molitor 2018 a (letter 02/04/1910).

182. IOR/L/PS/20/261/1, Persia no. 1 (1911), Further Correspondence Respecting the Affairs of Persia, p. 62.

183. FO 248/999, McDouall to Tehran, 25/05/1910.

Khosrovi, deputy-chief; Abu'l-Hasan Khan Sanjabi, Sayyed 'Abbas Malekzadeh, secretaries; Hajj Mirza 'Abed Moshir al-Ra'aya, Hajj Beg Mohammad Razzaz, Mirza Javan Khan Vazir, members. Sheikh Mahmud was the representative for Kangavar, while there also was one for Qasr-e Shirin, Sonqor and Koliya'i.[184]

Since July 1909, when Constitutional forces ousted Mohammad 'Ali Shah, the government in Tehran was dominated by the Bakhtiyari chiefs. This fact was not appreciated by many conservative groups in W. Persia, in particular by the Vali of Posht-e Kuh and other Lor tribal chiefs, who were the traditional enemies of the Bakhtiyaris. Therefore, anti-Bakhtiyari activities with anti-Constitutional overtones came into being. In July 1910, for example, there were signs of an anti-Constitutional movement in Kermanshah, including a document allegedly signed by eight *mojtaheds* from Kerbela, although there was no confirmation of its truthfulness from Baghdad. The document was religious and anti-foreign in nature and assailed the self-interestedness of the government and press in Tehran and the tyranny of the new local institutions in the provinces (see Appendix IX). Also, it informed the readers that a few days earlier a meeting had taken place in Borujerd of local chiefs and olama, who professed allegiance to Mohammad 'Ali Shah. The Russian agent there confirmed this, but acting British consul Knox was sceptical and ascribed this propaganda campaign merely as a justification for plunder and as well as an anti-Bakhtiyari activity. There also was a rumor of a Koran being circulated that had been sealed by various tribal chiefs by which means they aimed to rally those that wanted to reduce Bakhtiyari power. Peasants and small towns people indeed suffered from tyranny, but not so much from the government in Tehran, but rather from their local chiefs, and, more so than before. Nevertheless, there was a general conviction that the government in Tehran was incompetent and corrupt. However, that did not concern the tribesmen, who didn't care about religious or political intrigue, except when it was to their immediate advantage.[185]

Attention was temporarily diverted from the anti-constitutional agitation, when in the night of 23 July 1910, a soldier of the Kerendi regiment was shot in the garden of the Russian Consulate. Soldiers used to enter the garden at will at night to pluck fruit and two gardeners had been wounded by them. On the night in question the soldier had come close to consul's house and was warned and chased away, but he returned one hour later and was shot by a guard. As a result, on the night of 23 July there was an anti-Russian demonstration, some 100 soldiers called out at Mr. Lissowski and some stones were thrown. The Persian staff fled and Lissowski was alone with two Cossacks. Before they became threatening the soldiers were dispersed by Persian Cossacks sent by Nezam al-Saltaneh. A guard of 50 men was then posted and various officials came to apologize. On 25 July Nezam al-Saltaneh himself apologized to Mr. Lissowski and advised that Russian Cossacks better not be seen in the streets for the moment. However, the Kerendis were still angry and groups of them continued to pass by the Russian Consulate and rifles were directed at it, but Persian Cossacks intervened before shots could be fired. Lissowski intended to leave Kermanshah in case these incidents did not stop, but the British consul Knox (who temporarily held the function during McDouall's absence) told him he would try to pressure Nezam al-Saltaneh to disband the Kerendi regiment and get a fresh one. The governor after

184. Soltani 1386, pp. 173-74.
185. FO 248/999, Acting consul G.G. Knox to Tehran, 11/07/1910.

some frank talk agreed to disband the 100 Kerendis of the city's regiment and try to disband the rest of the regiment as well and get fresh troops. That same afternoon the Kerendis were paid and escorted out of the city. However, anti-foreign feelings were still strong in the city.[186]

On 7 July 1910, Da'ud Khan Kalhor had withdrawn to Harunabad, but returned on 15 July to Mahidasht with a large force, although intending to submit to the governor. The next morning, with a large body of men he rode to the governor's tent, where they had an unsatisfactory discussion. Da'ud Khan said he had not come earlier fearing treachery and was dismissed. The Russian and British consuls, seeing Da'ud Khan's high-handed behavior, told the governor that their Legations supported his endeavors. He thanked them and said he hoped that there would be peace now, now that Da'ud Khan had submitted. The two consuls also contacted Da'ud Khan by letter expressing the hope that all differences could be settled without bloodshed and advised him to accept the governor's terms. Da'ud Khan still made difficulties about paying his taxes. There was opposition in Kermanshah against local government institutions. This held in particular for the local police, who were very unpopular and at the end of July there was a disorderly demonstration against them. Hearing this the governor came to town and publicly abused the chief of police, who resigned but was immediately reinstated at orders from Tehran and the governor apologized. Otherwise the town was quiet with some occasional firing at night and some casualties and wounded.[187]

By mid-1910, the governor's former authority had considerably waned. He had been firm during the first months, which earned him many enemies. These were led by the Aqa Mohammad Mehdi, leading *mojtahed* and chief of the unpopular local government, which he tried to control, and the chief tax collector, whose perquisites were interfered with and both made complaints against him in Tehran. Although McDouall believed that Nezam al-Saltaneh allowed the new institutions do their work, a local source states that he disliked Constitutionalists and therefore, opposed the newly created court of justice (*adliyeh*) headed by Lesan al-Dowleh and that was further composed of Mohammad Javad Khan Samsam al-Dowleh, Abu'l-Hasan Khan Zanganeh and Amin al-Shari'eh. Nezam al-Saltaneh maintained that complaints should be dealt with by the governor. Lesan al-Dowleh resented the governor's interference so much so that the Democrats in Tehran urged the government to dismiss him. Most of the complaints were unjustified, but they weakened Nezam al-Saltaneh's position so that he relaxed his rule. Nezam al-Saltaneh was not a demanding rapacious governor. He did not look for bribes; although in the conflict with Da'ud Khan many were killed he was content with a payment of 1,000 *tuman*s. Also, when in early September 1910, four large caravans and many pilgrims were plundered near Kangavar, Nezam al-Saltaneh sent a force there, although it was outside his jurisdiction, showing more sense of responsibility than previous governors had. Apparently, the attacks were the work of the Khezel and Kakawand tribes, instigated by Sardar Akram, who was in Harsin.[188]

Cholera broke out in early October 1910 and spread over the city and province. The governor, officials, troops and 80% population left the city. There was panic and no business was done.

186. FO 248/999, Acting consul G.G. Knox to Tehran, 28/07/1910; Idem, Knox to Tehran, 30/07/1910.

187. IOR/L/PS/20/261/1, Persia no. 1 (1911), Further Correspondence Respecting the Affairs of Persia, pp. 72, 84, 96.

188. IOR/L/PS/20/261/1, Persia no. 1 (1911), Further Correspondence Respecting the Affairs of Persia, p. 100; Soltani 1381, vol. 4, p. 544; Idem 1386, p.173.

The only troops in town were the Persian Cossacks and the governor's escort. On 20 October 1910 there was a report about renewed fighting between the Sanjabis and the Kalhors near Qasr-e Shirin. Habibollah Khan with troops from Da'ud Khan Kalhor attacked Samsam al-Mamalek, the previous Sanjabi chief (see Chapter Four), but he was repulsed with heavy losses. He then tried to get more new troops. The governor of Kerend was ordered by Nezam al-Saltaneh to support Samsam al-Mamalek. By the end of October the cholera epidemic had run its course and many, who had fled the city, returned home. Nezam al-Saltaneh still remained outside the city, which did not put an end to the many robberies in the city's environs. During that time, Nezam al-Saltaneh offered his resignation, thus avoiding being dismissed. His resignation was not immediately accepted by the government until it had found his replacement. On 19 November 1910, Nezam al-Saltaneh was appointed governor of Fars and on 28 November he left Kermanshah. In the interim period two deputy-governors were appointed, while the leaders of the rival factions swore to work together. On 16 January 1911, 'Ali Taqi Mirza Rokn al-Dowleh, his successor, arrived in Kermanshah accompanied by 45 Persian Cossacks. The new governor tried to improve the police force under a new chief; there still were numerous petty robberies, although otherwise quiet prevailed in the city. Meanwhile D'aud Khan Kalhor refused to come and pay his respect to Rokn al-Dowleh, while the latter refused the offered services of 200 Kalhor *savar*s. Although Tehran appointed Samsam al-Mamalek Sanjabi governor of Qasr-e Shirin, but since Da'ud Khan Kalhor opposed this he could not take up his post.[189]

Partisan conflicts still marred the political scene of Kermanshah, which ostensibly concerned the return of property looted in 1909, but in reality was but the continued conflict between two old warring factions, the Democrats and the Moderates. Hajj Rostam Beg, one of the faction leaders had been detained in Tehran, but escaped and returned to Kermanshah. On 21 February 1911, to avoid an outbreak of renewed fights between the two rivals, Aqa Mohammad Mehdi held a *majles* and sent for Hajj Rostam Beg and Mo'in al-Ra'aya and told them to reconcile. Mo'in al-Ra'aya said that if Hajj Rostam Beg brought the goods looted from him and burnt them in the *Meydan* he would be satisfied. Aqa Mohammad Mehdi said to leave that to him and so ostensibly the two were reconciled. A telegram was sent to Tehran about this and Rostam Beg did not object and Aqa Mohammad Mehdi affixed the seal of the *anjoman* to the telegram.[190] The reconciliation did not improve the security situation in the city. Robberies were frequent at night. Police expenses were to be paid from the *edareh-ye thalatheh*, so far only 400 *tuman*s were paid, which was insufficient. An investigation by the *anjoman-e velayati* showed that the rest of the money was spent on expenditures of the *edareh*. The *anjoman* ordered the *edareh* to reduce its staff and move into the governor's palace. When a man wanted by the police fled into Aqa Mohammad Mehdi's house the servants repulsed the police. When the *mojtahed* heard of

189. IOR/L/PS/20/261/1, Persia no. 1 (1911), Further Correspondence Respecting the Affairs of Persia, pp. 100, 112, 118; Soltani 1381, vol. 4, p. 544; IOR/L/PS/20/261/4, 'Persia. No 3 (1912). Further correspondence respecting the affairs of Persia.', pp. 5, 29, 42.

190. FO 248/1031, Diary no. 8, week ending February 23rd 1911; IOR/L/PS/20/261/4, 'Persia. No 3 (1912). Further correspondence respecting the affairs of Persia.', p. 42.

this he sent the man and the servant to police headquarters. Meanwhile, Hajj Rostam Beg and Mo'in al-Ra'aya held secret meetings with their supporters.[191]

This was not the only local turmoil. On 25 and 26 March 1911, two attempts were made to break into the British Consulate at Kermanshah. On the first occasion two men were arrested, and on the second the *savar*s' quarters were entered, two uniforms and some goods were taken, and shots were exchanged with some thirty men, believed to be seeking revenge for the arrest of their two comrades the day before. The British Consul notified the Governor and took steps to defend the Consulate. A warning reached the Consulate that the band concerned threatened to kill the Indian sowars, and on 28 March stones were thrown at the British Consulate; but the men, finding it well garrisoned, made no further attempt, but then robbed the house of a notable in the town. The same night the brigands fired at the British Consulate, but, when the fire was returned, departed. The local authorities placed troops at the Consulate for its protection, and Sir George Barclay held the Persian government responsible for the safety of the Consulate and of British subjects, and urged the punishment of the culprits.[192]

YAR MOHAMMAD KHAN

On 30 April 1911, Rokn al-Dowleh resigned as governor and was succeeded by Mohtasham al-Dowleh as governor pro tem. He had not been a good governor, was very greedy and accepted bribes as low as 200 *tuman*s, according to Mo'tamadi.[193] At that time Yar Mohammad Khan came to Kermanshah, his place of birth where he was less well-known than in Tabriz or Tehran. He had made a name for himself while fighting in the defense of the Constitution in Tabriz and in 1909 had gone to Tehran. Here he joined fellow-Democrats such as Yeprem Khan, but after the Atabeg Park event on 7 August 1910 (forced disarmament of *mojahed* fighters by the Democrats and Bakhtiyaris) he was arrested on 21 March 1911, and was imprisoned for two weeks. He was sent under guard to exile to Iraq, but at Dizabad he fled and arrived on 12 April in Kermanshah. The next day he presented himself to the *anjoman-e velayati* and offered to obey that body or the national *Majles*. "He explained that he had left Tehran at the personal request of the Regent, but, finding that he was being sent under guard, he had escaped from it." In the meantime, Tehran had given orders to the authorities in Kermanshah to arrest him.[194] Yar Mohammad Khan, previously had been a member of the artillery (*tupkhaneh*) section of the Kermanshah garrison and was one of the partisans of Aqa Mohammad Mehdi Mojtahed. When he met with the *anjoman-e veyalati* he was accompanied by his guards. During that meeting the commander of the Cossacks came in and showed Aqa Mohammad Mehdi Mojtahed, the president of the *anjoman* an order from Sepahdar, the Prime Minister, for Yar Mohammad Khan's arrest. The president told the officer not to take any action as this would only result in trouble. Meanwhile, Rokn al-Dowleh, the governor had ordered Yar Mohammad Khan's arrest and to

191. FO 248/1031, Diary no. 9, week ending March 2nd 1911; IOR/L/PS/20/261/4, 'Persia. No 3 (1912). Further correspondence respecting the affairs of Persia,' p. 53.

192. *The Hansard*, House of Commons Debate 12 April 1911, vol. 24, pp. 457-58.

193. Soltani 1381, vol. 4, pp. 548-49.

194. Hamadani 1354, p. 367.

that end the chief of police Mirza Karim Khan surrounded the building in which the *anjoman* met, which was next to the *Bidestan-e Divankhaneh*. However, one of Yar Mohammad Khan's friends entered the meeting and told those assembled that the building had been surrounded. He had mobilized Yar Mohammad Khan's armed friends, who, when he left the *anjoman*'s premises, fired some shots as a signal for his friends to start firing at the police. The police and/or soldiers fled, but not before three *mojaheds* and four passersby were killed.[195]

Yar Mohammad Khan was quite popular in his hometown; his main enemy was Mo'in al-Ra'aya, one of the faction leaders who kept a guard of some 100 men. On 1 May 1911, Mo'in al-Ra'aya went to house of Aqa Mohammad Mehdi where he was to meet others to send a telegram asking for the retention of Rokn al-Dowleh as governor and the expulsion of Yar Mohammad Khan. However, the others did not come and when he left he was shot from the roof of the bazaar and died. Mo'in al-Ra'aya's brother, Akbar Khan, was with 50 men in Sonqor. It was feared that he would get support from the Koliya'is and therefore, the acting governor sent a force to stop him. The bazaar was immediately closed and shopkeepers removed all they could to their homes. Yar Mohammad Khan came with a force and told the people not to be afraid and that he would guarantee their safety, but was unsuccessful in doing so. The killer remained unknown, although some said that he was of the Kalbi faction, as two of Kalbi's sons had been killed by Mo'in al-Ra'aya's faction. Others said that the killer was sent from Tehran with connivance of Yar Mohammad Khan and that Aqa Mohammad Mehdi and Amin al-Mamalek were also doomed. However, according to Mo'tamadi, some of the thugs of the Mo'ini brothers had been with the police chief during the attempted arrest of Yar Mohammad Khan on 13 April. Therefore, later, incited by Yar Mohammad Khan, Kazem Kur ('the one-eyed,' but a good shot), a man close to Qavam al-Ra'aya, who hated the Mo'ini clan, shot the oldest of the Mo'ini brothers, Hoseyn Khan Mo'in al-Ra'aya, who was hit by 10 bullets died. Mohtasham al-Dowleh, the acting governor wanted to leave with his family and so did many others, but he was persuaded to stay. He telegraphed Tehran to send a governor immediately to prevent any further trouble. However, the opposite happened. For Kelbi and Asghar Selim, two trouble makers, who had been sent to Tehran by Nezam al-Saltaneh and had been released, were retuning to Kermanshah, which promised an outbreak of new troubles.[196]

The Democrats in Tehran telegraphed Yar Mohammad Khan that he and his supporters had to come to Tehran; they even sent him their back pay and travel money. The majority of the members of the provincial *anjoman* supported Yar Mohammad Khan as did many local notables and they urged the government in Tehran to pardon him, which had the desired result. One of his friends, Sharif Khan Kadkhoda threw Yar Mohammad Khan a big party to thank his supporters. As a result, to all intents and purposes Yar Mohammad Khan assumed the command of local military affairs, which put him in a very strong position.[197]

---

195. Soltani 1386, pp. 174-75; Idem 1381, vol. 4, pp. 546-48.

196. FO 248/1031, McDouall to Tehran, 02/05/1911; IOR/L/PS/20/261/4, 'Persia. No 3 (1912). Further correspondence respecting the affairs of Persia.', p. 65; Soltani 1386, pp. 158 ("A thug Asgar Salim, an enemy of Hoseyn Khan's faction"), 174-75.

197. Soltani 1386, pp. 174-75; Idem 1381, vol. 4, pp. 546-48; Hamadani 1354, p. 367.

THE SALAR AL-DOWLEH YEARS

After Rokn al-Dowleh's dismissal, first Samsam al-Saltaneh Bakhtiyari was appointed as his successor, and than Sardar Mo'tazed. In the meantime, Mohtasham al-Dowleh was acting governor and was able to keep order in the city. He was successful in convincing Yar Mohammad Khan to leave the city to avoid an armed fight between his men and those of Akbar Khan, Mo'in al-Ra'aya's brother. McDouall reported on 12 June 1911 that Akbar Khan had left the city to attack the village of Hajj Rostam Beg. Moreover, inside the city both sides had erected fortifications, and there had been some sniping between them. The bazaar was closed and people were afraid for the looming turmoil.[198]

Thus, the city had barely absorbed political murder and turmoil, when a new chapter in its history began, to wit: the occupation of the city by the rebel prince Abu'l-Fath Mirza Salar al-Dowleh, who had already made an unsuccessful bid to mount the throne in 1907. After his ouster from the throne and Persia in July 1908, the ex-Shah, Mohammad 'Ali Mirza made plans to regain it. In November 1910, with the Tsar's permission, the ex-Shah traveled from Odessa to Vienna, accompanied by Sho'a' al-Saltaneh, his second brother, to meet with his third brother Salar al-Dowleh to finalize the plan for his return to power. The ex-Shah, together with Sho'a' al-Saltaneh, would raise tribesmen around Astarabad, while from Ottoman territory, Salar al-Dowleh would raise Kurdish support and invade Iran. In Vienna, they discussed their plan with Hartwig, the former Russian minister in Tehran, who repeated the official Russian position that although Russia could not support them, it would do nothing against them.[199]

On 18 July 1911, news was received that Mohammad 'Ali with some followers and plenty of arms supplied by the government of Russia had landed at Gumush Tepeh and marched to Astarabad to retake the throne. Salar al-Dowleh came from Baghdad in disguise, went to Sanandaj, convinced some tribal Khans unhappy with Tehran policy to join him and made it his temporary base of operations. Bahador al-Saltaneh Kordestani reported the prince's arrival and activities and asked forces to be sent to oppose him.[200] There was also suspicion and some evidence that Salar al-Dowleh had received some support from the Ottoman government.[201]

In June 1911, Salar al-Dowleh was said to have some 4,000 men in Kurdistan, where he acted totally independently.[202] On 29 June he sent five letters to Moshir-e Divan, Asaf-e Divan, Hajj Mo'tamad, Vakil al-Molk and Habib Tajer informing them that with 6,000 Jafs and Mokris he was marching to Kurdistan to take vengeance on the Constitutionalists and renew respect for the olama. He gave orders that all partisans of the Constitution had to be arrested, who, after his arrival, would be punished. Also, to get the support of the Kurdish chiefs on whom he would bestow upon them the titles of al-Dowleh, al-Saltaneh and Sardar. The prince wrote that he supported the constitution and the rights of the olama and Islam. He also wrote letters to Tehran,

198. IOR/L/PS/20/261/4, 'Persia. No 3 (1912). Further correspondence respecting the affairs of Persia.', pp. 65, 80

199. Kazemzadeh 1968, pp. 598-600; Adhari 1378, p. 75; Malekzadeh 1328, vol. 6, pp. 267-73. Arshad al-Dowleh mistakenly mentioned that they met in Odessa. Moore 1914, p. 33.

200. Adhari 1378, docs. 13, 14, 20.

201. Adhari, p. 18, docs. 21-22, 25.

202. Mo`ayyer al- Mamalek 1361, pp. 25, 32, 37; Eyn al-Saltaneh 1377, vol. 5, p. 3433 (merchants telegraphed not to ship goods to Azerbaijan as they would be all seized).

Kermanshah, Hamadan, Borujerd, Qazvin, Zanjan, Garrus, Soltanabad etc. The olama of Kurdistan supported him in his bid for the throne.[203]

On 2 July 1911, the prince took Garrus and Kurdistan where in the name of the ex-Shah an illumination (*cheraghani*) was organized. The government in Tehran was paralyzed and it took one week before orders were given to take action against the rebel prince. Tehran appointed Sardar Jang and Sardar Zafar commanders of the Bakhtiyari troops with orders that they had to defeat Salar al-Dowleh, while they were also given the governorships of Kermanshah, Hamadan, Kurdistan, and Lurestan.[204] On 17 July 1911, Salar al-Dowleh took Senneh and environs and was expected to take Kermanshah thereafter. He proclaimed Mohammad ʻAli as Shah, himself the latter's crown prince (*vali- ʻahd*) and telegraphed orders to the *Majles* to invite Mohammad ʻAli to return. The Prime Minister, Sardar Asʻad immediately promised to make tribesmen available to oppose him.[205] In this connection it is interesting to note that ʻEyn al-Saltaneh wrote in his Diary that many, including the prince's followers, expected that after taking Tehran war would break out between the two brothers, because Salar al-Dowleh was hell-bent on becoming Shah.[206]

Salar al-Dowleh also wrote to sympathizers in Kermanshah, such as the Moʻinis, viz. Akbar Khan Moʻaven-e Lashkar, Sheikh ʻAli Asghar, Hasan Khan Moʻaven al-Molk as well as the Hajjizadeh clan headed by Farrokh Khan Ilkhani, Hajj Hasan Kalantar, Aqa Qoli Farrash-bashi his nephew, Moʻtazed al-Mamalek, Hajj Sharif Khan Moʻtamadi and his adherents and many others of the leading olama, such us Aqa Rahim Mojtahed and Aqa Mahmud, brother of Hajj Aqa Janbazi, who declared themselves for his cause. The prince also made it clear to his supporters in Kermanshah that the court of justice (*adliyeh*), the police office (*nazmiyeh*) and the telephone office had to be plundered. The prince's leading supporters met and arranged that on 11 July 1911 some (*luti*s and *owbash*) attacked and looted the three institutions. They also burnt documents concerning taxes on salt, opium label (*taryak banderol*) and gum tragacanth (*katira*). Two days before the attack governor Rokn al-Dowleh had gone to Tehran, ostensibly to prepare the defense against Salar al-Dowleh, thus leaving the field open and free to him. According to Farid al-Molk, because there were no longer any police the authorities sent the traditional executors of law and order (*gazmeh*, *aʻtas* and *qaravol*s) into the various city quarters.[207]

On 21 July 1911, McDouall reported that Salar al-Dowleh had wired Amir al-Mamalek that he placed Kermanshah under his control with orders to respect and protect the Consulates, keep order in the city, and convey the local authorities to Tehran, and to collect food and fodder for 7,000 horse and 10,000 foot, who left on 19 and 20 July. Several officials were threatened by

---

203. Mardukh, p. 286; Adhari 1370, doc. 25; Mostowfi 1324, vol. 2, p. 353.

204. Dowlatabadi 1362, pp. 122, 126.

205. Hamadani 1354, p. 374; IOR/L/PS/20/261/4, 'Persia. No 3 (1912). Further correspondence respecting the affairs of Persia', Barclay to Grey 17/07/1911, p. 94 (no. 186), (nos. 187, 189); Eyn al-Saltaneh 1377, vol. 5, p. 3495. Nobody opposed the prince's entry into Senneh; in fact, he was welcomed out of fear, while rich people had already fled to save their money. Adhari 1378, doc. 31.

206. Eyn al-Saltaneh 1377, vol. 5, pp. 3511-12; Idem, vol. 7, p. 5599.

207. Soltani 1386, pp. 175-77; Hamadani 1354, p. 373; Eyn al-Saltaneh 1377, vol. 5, p. 3458 (Nazar `Ali Khan was plundering near Mahidasht and said he would come shortly to the city; the `*adliyeh* was closed and the entire city was in uproar). On the *gazmeh* etc, see Floor 1973.

the crowd and fled to the British Consulate; McDouall arranged that Amir al-Mamalek took care of their safe departure.[208] Salar al-Dowleh left Kurdistan on 24 July 1911, but before he left he sent telegrams to the acting and deputy governors to continue their duties. Meanwhile, groups from each tribe were joining Da'ud Khan Kalhor, who since 23 July was camped at Qal'eh-ye Delgosha, 1.5 km outside Kermanshah, to support the prince.[209] On 30 July 1911, Salar al-Dowleh entered Kermanshah with 2,000 men, reinforced by 4,000 local levies, and the next day received representatives of all classes of the population. All Tehran appointed officials had already left town which made any resistance unlikely. Those who had taken asylum in the British Consulate had left on 29 July with a safe-conduct from Da'ud Khan Kalhor. One of his main supporters, Aqa Mahmud the *mojtahed* was often in the prince's presence, who stayed in the city until 24 August.[210] Salar al-Dowleh asked Molitor, the Belgian official in charge of the Kermanshah Customs administration, to hand him the Customs revenues (representing some 60,000 *tuman*s/month), who refused and referred the prince to Tehran. However, on 17 August he took more than 23,000 *tuman*s from the Customs office. At that time, the Kalhor and Sanjabi chiefs were in Kermanshah as well as the Vali of Posht-e Kuh. Salar al-Dowleh ordered the merchants not to pay customs duties anymore. He also ordered Da'ud Khan Kalhor to seal the state arsenal and granary.[211] Neither the Customs revenues nor the wealth of the city's population were beyond his grasping hands, in particular the wealth of those who supported the Constitution. The prince had them tortured and forcibly exacted much money from them and others, while some were even killed.[212] In an undated telegram (probably end July-early August 1911) to Mo'azed al-Saltaneh, the Minister of Post and Telegraph, Salar al-Dowleh boasted of his large force led by Sardar Mozaffar, chief of the Kalhors, Amir Jang Vali of Posht-e Kuh and Sardar Akram Nazar 'Ali Khan, the latter two from Lorestan, who were marching to defend the ex-Shah's rights. Further that the Qalavand, a section of the Dirakwand, had dislodged the rebellious Bakhtiyaris in Arabistan, and that Mohammad Khan Asanlu of Zanajan with 50 *savar*s had taken that town in his name.[213] Probably at the end of July 1911 Khalil Khan Azerbaijani and two Armenians arrived in Kermanshah. They had been selected by the Committee of Democrats in Tehran to kill Salar al-Dowleh. When a package arrived for them the director of the post office became suspicious. He alerted the prince, who ordered the package to be opened. It contained explosives to make bombs. The three men were arrested; Khalil Khan was killed

---

208. IOR/L/PS/20/261/4, 'Persia. No 3 (1912). Further correspondence respecting the affairs of Persia.', p. 99 (no. 207); Hamadani 1354, p. 374. Sayyed Akbar Shah, later Ashraf al-Va`ezin, incited the city's ruffians to carry out the looting. Molitor 2018 b, p. 1

209. IOR/L/PS/20/261/4, 'Persia. No 3 (1912). Further correspondence respecting the affairs of Persia', Barclay to Grey 17/07/1911, p. 94 (no. 186); Idem, Barclay to Grey, 26/07/1911, p. 106 (no. 220). Sharif Khan Amir al-Mamalek, ex-kadkhoda and reactionary, had convinced Da'ud Khan Kalhor to invite the prince to come to Kermanshah. The other tribes, intimidated by this move, promised their support. Mo`tazed al-Dowleh, pishkar of finances, Lesan al-Saltaneh, chief of the `adliyeh, and Mobasher Homayun, chief of police fled to Tehran. Molitor 2018 b, p. 1.

210. IOR/L/PS/20/261/4, 'Persia. No 3 (1912). Further correspondence respecting the affairs of Persia', p. 151 (no. 319); IOR/L/PS/20/261/4, 'Persia. No 3 (1912). Further correspondence respecting the affairs of Persia', Barclay to Grey 01/08/1911, p. 118 (no. 247); Hamadani 1354, p. 374 (ass. governor and police chief took refuge), 376 (Salar entered on 4 Sha`ban), 377, 379. Eyn al-Saltaneh 1377, vol. 5, p. 3488 (the prince burnt the *adliyeh* and *nazmiyeh* offices; he hung and imprisoned some people).

211. Destree 1976, pp. 210-11; Adhari 1378, pp. 21-22 (docs. 35-36); Hamadani 1354, p. 376; Adhari 1378, docs. 35-36, 48-49.

212. Soltani 1386, p. 183; Shuster 1968, p. 115; Mo`ayyer al- Mamalek 1361, p. 53, 73; Adhari 1378, p. 21; IOR/L/PS/20/261/4, 'Persia. No 3 (1912). Further correspondence respecting the affairs of Persia.' Barclayto Grey 12/08/1911, p.129 (no. 274). Molitor 2018 b, p. 1.

213. Afshar 1367, pp. 2005-06, doc. 1.

in prison. The two Armenians, who were Ottoman subjects, were taken to Qal`eh Sabzi at the border where the chief of the Sanjabis killed them.[214]

On 8 August 1911, Mohammad 'Ali Mirza, the ex-Shah sent Salar al-Dowleh a telegram asking him to hurry to Tehran, where there were only 3,000 Bakhtiyaris as defensive force; a delay might cause the ex-Shah a major problem.[215] After having filled his coffers with his ill-gotten gains, on 23 August 1911, Salar al-Dowleh accompanied by Da'ud Khan and a mix of Kalhor, Sanjabi and Jaf tribesmen (ca. 10,000 men) and 16 guns left Kermanshah into the direction of Malayer. He appointed his younger brother 'Abdol-Fazl Mirza 'Azad al-Soltan governor of Kermanshah, with Mohtasham al-Dowleh as his vice-governor and *pishkar*. Farid al-Molk was appointed *kargozar*. Before he left he sent a telegram to the *Majles*. Amir Mofakhkham Bakhtiyari, who had been governor of Lorestan for some months, was ordered to oppose Salar al-Dowleh. Amir Mofakhkham left Borujerd with 2,000 men. His cousin, Sardar Zafar, who, in the beginning of August 1911, had left Tehran to Soltanabad, was to join him. However, there were doubts about the loyalty to the central government of both Sardar Zafar and Amir Mofakhkam; the latter was near Malayer by that time.[216]

After Amir Mofakhkham's departure from Borujerd, the Lors declared for the prince and joined his force, who appointed his father-in-law, Nazar 'Ali Khan, governor of that town. Given that situation, and the uncertainty whether Amir Mofakhkham would oppose or join Salar al-Dowleh, the defensive position of the central government in Tehran looked weak. The more so, because if Amir Mofakhkham would join him, only Sardar Zafar with 500 men at Soltanabad would be between him and Tehran. From Kermanshah, Salar al-Dowleh first went to Dowlatabad and neared the position of Amir Mofakhkham. Hamadan was already in the hands of his adherents. On 12 August a group of notables had come to Kermanshah to discuss with the prince the mechanics of his taking over of the city, which his vanguard entered on 16 August. On 20 August 1911, according to Shuster, Salar al-Dowleh was said to be at Hamadan with 10,000 men and 16 cannons, which was erroneous. The ex-Shah was well informed, because indeed government forces in Tehran only numbered 3,000 men. As a result, panic broke out among the governing class in Tehran. The more so, because other sources reported even much higher numbers of the prince's troops. On 31 August 1911, Barclay reported that Salar al-Dowleh with 10,000 men intended to march to Qazvin after having taken Hamadan. 'Eyn al-Saltaneh remarked that the prince's soldiers "do not know any language, no Turkish, no Persian, not any other language (they are Sowjbulgahi Kurds)."[217] However, apparently Salar al-Dowleh skirted Hamadan and

---

214. Molitor 2018 b, p. 2.

215. Adhari 1378, p. 22. There were people, such as grain owners in Taleqan, who actually liked the idea that the prince would take Tehran, because they expected the price of wheat to go up, allowing them to make more profit. Eyn al-Saltaneh 1377, vol. 5, p. 3526.

216. IOR/L/PS/20/261/4, 'Persia. No 3 (1912). Further correspondence respecting the affairs of Persia,' p. 167 (no. 366), 168 (no. 367); IOR/L/PS/20/223, 'Who's who in Persia. Calcutta: General Staff, India, 1916', p. 55; Malekzadeh 1328, vol. 6, p. 292; Dowlatabadi 1362, p. 128; Eyn al-Saltaneh 1377, vol. 5, p. 3488. According to Molitor, the prince had assembled a force of 20,000 tribesmen. Molitor 2018 b, p. 2.

217. IOR/L/PS/20/261/4, 'Persia. No 3 (1912). Further correspondence respecting the affairs of Persia,' pp. 152 (no. 322, 325), 167 (no. 366), 168 (no. 367); Hamadani 1354, pp. 378-79; Shuster 1968, p. 121; Mo`ayyer al- Mamalek 1361, p. 86, 91 (threatening telegram), 98-99; Jurabchi 1363, pp. 66 (40,000 men), 76 (30,000; Kolhar were said to have joined him); Malekzadeh 1328, vol. 7, p. 292; Dowlatabadi 1362, p. 133; Eyn al-Saltaneh 1377, vol. 5, p. 3494 (the prince threw a baker into his oven and the bread price dropped to 2 *shahis/man*, which made him popular with the people of Hamadan. He also arrested several people in that city). Some of the plunder of Hamadan was later sold in Tehran, for some items, see Eyn al-Saltaneh 1377, vol. 5, pp. 3571, 3574.

went to Nehavand, where his troops ravaged the villages in the city's environs.[218] Earlier in August 1911/Sha'ban 1329, the *Majles* ordered Salar al-Dowleh to be arrested and promised to pay 25,000 *tumans* for him, dead or alive.[219] In reaction Salar al-Dowleh sent an angry telegram to the *Majles* and telling the delegates that the ex-Shah and he were coming to Tehran to teach them a lesson.[220]

Meanwhile, the Bakhtiyari government in Tehran was trying to raise a force to oppose the ex-Shah's forces. On 12 August 1911, Ja'far Qoli and Gholam Hoseyn, two Bakhtiyari chiefs telegraphed from Isfahan that they had raised 2,000 *savars*, who would hurry to the defense.[221] Only four days later the same chiefs complained that the *savars* still had not received their rations and fodder (*jireh va 'aliq*), to which end 30,000 *tumans* had been promised. They themselves had expended 50,000 *tumans* to buy horses for these *savars*. The cost for rations and fodder from Isfahan to Tehran was 20,000 *tumans*. In Isfahan, the daily expenditure was 1,500 *tumans* for 3,000 *savars*.[222] The lack of funds continued to bedevil the effectiveness of the government forces, which problem was only partly alleviated by a loan from Great Britain and Russia.

Salar al-Dowleh learnt about the ex-Shah's defeat on 3 Ramadan or 28 August 1911. This news did not discourage him, in fact he saw this as an opportunity to advance his own claim to the throne. When the ex-Shah was still in Iran, Salar al-Dowleh called him Shah and himself the latter's *vali- 'ahd* or heir-apparent.[223] However, after the ex-Shah's defeat on 12 August 1909, Salar al-Dowleh made a bid for the throne for himself. He allegedly struck money with the text: *Sekkeh bar zar mizanad salar-e din - yavarash bashad amir al-mo'menin*" On the reverse side stood: al-Soltan Abu'l-Fath Shah Qajar, however, numismatists, so far, have never seen such a coin.[224] He also was seen with a *jiqeh* on his hat and in his proclamations he also styled himself 'Shah' and in his telegrams addressed the cabinet as 'Our Ministers' and the Majles as 'Our Majles.' On 19 September 1911, Salar al-Dowleh in telegrams to the *Majles* refered to himself as 'Our Majesty' or as He referred to himself as Salar al-Dowleh *Shahehshah-e koll-e mamalek-e Khuzestan, Lorestan va Iraq-e Ajam*, and announced that he would be in three days in Qom.[225]

On 6 September 1911, Salar al-Dowleh defeated Amir Mofakhkham in Malayer district; many arms fell into his hands, and the town was plundered. He continued to advance towards Tehran unopposed, while Amir Mofakhkham withdrew to Soltanabad, where his cousin Sardar

---

218. Hamadani 1354, pp. 380, 383.

219. Bamdad 1347, vol. 1, p. 48; Ettehadiyeh and Sa`vandiyan 1366, p. 88; Dowlatabadi 1362, p. 130; for the text see Shuster 1968, p. 88.

220. Adhari 1378, p. 20.

221. Afshar 1367, p. 2007, doc. 3 (the hijri date 16 Shah`ban = 12 August; the solar 22 Asad = 19 August).

222. Afshar 1367, pp. 2007-08, doc. 4. The money was still not paid and the permission for a loan for 10,000 *tumans* was not given either. Afshar 1367, p. 2008, doc. 5.

223. Soltani 1386, p. 183.

224. Yaghma'i 1363, p. 140; Bamdad 1347, vol. 1, p. 49; Enayat 1340, p. 315. The text on the coin sates: "Salar al-Din struck [coins] on gold, may the Lord of the Believers [Ali] be his friend."

225. Enayat 1340, p. 315; Mostowfi 1324, vol. 2, pp. 594, 598; Bamdad 1347, vol. 1, p. 50; Shuster 1968, pp. 134-35; *The New Hazell Annual and Almanack*, vol. 28 (1913), p. 305; IOR/L/PS/20/261/4, 'Persia. No 3 (1912). Further correspondence respecting the affairs of Persia.', Barclay to Grey 19/09/1911, p. 159 (no. 352).

Zafar had 500 Bakhtiyari reinforcements.[226] However, the two Bakhtiyari chiefs did not face the prince again, for on 10 September 1911, Amir Mofakhkham marched via Golpeygan and Khonsar to Bakhtiyari country and Sardar Zafar and Sardar Jang left to Qom. They had 1,500 well-armed men with them and left a bad impression that they left without a fight. As a result, the people of Soltanabad wrote to Salar al-Dowleh asking for his protection. He replied the same day, writing that if the request had not arrived he would have come with 30,000 men and 22 guns to destroy their town completely. Two days later 400 of his men occupied the town led by the well-known robber 'Abbas Khan Chenari. During his stay the prince collected 50,000 *tuman*s in taxes. The poor people of the Soltanabad district were first fleeced by the Bakhtiyaris and then by Salar al-Dowleh, who appointed Seyf al-Dowleh, brother to 'Eyn al-Dowleh, as governor.[227]

Going around Soltanabad, Salar al-Dowleh went to Nobaran with 4,000 men intending to march to Tehran either via Saveh or Zarand. According to one source, whom Eyn al-Saltaneh believed to be lying, the prince had 20,000 men, whose column stretched for 24 km; he had a music band complete with drums (*balaban*), 16 guns, and the troops were divided into seven sections. These troops launched plunder raids as far as Saveh; many looters returned home after that, according to Mo'tamedi. When the prince chose the route via Saveh a combined force of 2,000 men consisting of Armenians under Yeprem Khan and Bakhtiyaris, under Sardar Mohtasham and Sardar Bahador, were sent to oppose him. The Bakhtiyaris of Sardar Zafar from Qom also joined them. The battle took place on 27 September at Bagh-e Shah, 13 km from Saveh (144 km from Tehran - between Nobaran and Qom) and Salar al-Dowleh's force of some 4,000 men consisting of Kalhors, Lors and other tribesmen was completely routed, suffering 300 deaths. The tribesmen fled and Salar al-Dowleh, who probably was at Nobaran, fled into the direction of Hamadan. Government forces did not pursue him, although these had suffered few losses. Because the defeated rebel prince had not been pursued it was feared that he might try and raise new troops, because the force that had defeated him was occupied with plundering, while there was complete disorder of which anyone might have taken advantage. In fact, at Salar al-Dowleh's request, Nazar 'Ali Khan Amra'i even aided some beleaguered supporters of the prince at Eshtrinan. It was also reported that Salar al-Dowleh had contacted Sowlat al-Dowleh Qashqa'i and Qavam al-Molk asking them to oppose the Bakhtiyaris.[228]

---

226. IOR/L/PS/20/261/4, 'Persia. No 3 (1912). Further correspondence respecting the affairs of Persia.', Barclay to Grey 11/09/1911, p. 154, (no. 334); IOR/L/PS/20/261/5, 'Persia. No 4 (1912) Further correspondence respecting the affairs of Persia', p. 23-24 (no. 53); Adhari 1378, doc. 40; Dowlatabadi 1362, p. 138; Hamadani 1354, p. 381; Eyn al-Saltaneh 1377, vol. 5, p. 3507 (500 Bakhtiyaris were killed). According to Malekzadeh 1328, vol. 6, pp. 292-93, the Bakhtiyaris fought very well when attacked, but Amir Afkham, who was watching from afar, ordered his troops to withdraw as he had already decided to go some place else. However, the result was a defeat and loss of arms, which Malekzadeh ascribes to Amir Afkham's support for the ex-Shah. This defeat caused panic in Tehran. Molitor 2018 b, p. 2.

227. IOR/L/PS/20/261/5, 'Persia. No 4 (1912). Further correspondence respecting the affairs of Persia', p. 21 (no. 51); Malekzadeh 1328, vol. 6, pp. 293-95 (in Malayer, he was joined by another 1,000 Kurds and Lors and his total force was estimated to be 30,000 strong); Mostowfi 1324, vol 2, pp. 594, 598; Eyn al-Saltaneh 1377, vol. 5, p. 3543 (people did not know who were worse, the Lors or the Bakhtiyaris); Bamdad 1347, vol. 1, p. 50; Shuster 1968, pp. 134-35; *The New Hazell Annual and Almanack*, vol. 28 (1913), p. 305. Salar al-Dowleh received men, arms and ammunition from Amir Afshar in Zanjan. Adhari 1327, docs. 37-38.

228. Dowlatabadi 1362, pp. 183-87; Eyn al-Saltaneh 1377, vol. 5, pp. 3552, 3570-71 (here it is reported that at Saveh the prince had 22,000 men, who were mostly armed with muzzle-loaders (*sar-por*), daggers, swords and cudgels

The total rout, first of the ex-Shah's forces, and then followed by that of his brother, meant that the only undefeated royalist force in Persia was that of Shoja' al-Dowleh in Tabriz, who, after these two defeats (Mohammad 'Ali and Salar al-Dowleh), became discouraged, also due to many desertions from his ranks.[229] The people of Tehran on learning Salar al-Dowleh's defeat breathed a sigh of relief, because everybody had been afraid and greatly worried.[230] After Mohammad 'Ali's forces were defeated and in reaction to the confiscation of the properties of Sho'a' al-Saltaneh and Salar al-Dowleh on 4 October 1911, the Russian Legation intervened to protect its financial interests (Salar was heavily indebted to the Russian Bank) stating he was a Russian subject, thus, preventing the confiscation of Salar al-Dowleh's property.[231]

On 8 October 1911, a telegram arrived from Sardar Zafar and Sardar Jang, who were in Hamadan, addressed to olama and merchants of Kermanshah announcing their impending arrival in Kermanshah and instructing them to arrest 'Azad al-Soltan until officials arrived to investigate his exactions. The prince learning this fled to the Turkish Consulate. In the evening Hajji Sayyed Habib, Malek al-Tojjar went there with others demanding the return of 1,600 *tumans* he had paid the prince, who, being helpless paid him. When the text of the telegram became known the population robbed any Kalhor they met in the streets. Sardar Mozaffar Da'ud Khan Kalhor left for Delgosha, the government house 1.6 km outside the city. The next morning he brought 'Azad al-Soltan there. Some notables went there and tried to induce him to come to the city and carry on the government swearing to support him. The prince refused saying he would accompany the son of the Vali to join his brother Salar al-Dowleh. Ahmad Mirza from the Khezel tribe came with 50 *savars* from Salar al-Dowleh and gave the prince a secret message from his brother. McDouall believed that the prince wanted to go to Najaf and appeal to Akhund Khorasani, as he had been forced by his brother to come to Kermanshah; he took more interest in agriculture than politics. Faced with his refusal the notables in consultation with tribal chiefs sent a telegram to the prime minister saying that in spite of their telegram the city was left without a governor

---

for looting. His mountain guns had been no match for the Schneider guns (3- and 5-shot) that the government forces had). Prior to the battle there had been a skirmish between the Kalhors and th Koliya'is, who had mistaken each other for being government troops. This resulted in many dead among whom Akbar Khan Kermanshahi, Mo`aven al-Molk's brother. Molitor 2018 b, p. 2.

229. IOR/L/PS/20/261/5, 'Persia. No 4 (1912). Further correspondence respecting the affairs of Persia', pp. 23-24 (no. 53); Adhari 1378, doc. 39, 46-47, 50, 52 (plunder); Malekzadeh 1328, vol. 7, pp. 65-67, 117; Dowlatabadi 1362, pp. 141-44, 172-79, 181-82; Hamadani 1354, p. 382; Eyn al-Saltaneh 1377, vol. 5, pp. 3534, 3543, 3560-63 (when in Hamadan the prince threw his two guns into a pond). For a short description of the battle and the carnage of dead and wounded afterwards, see Moore 1914, pp. 60-61; see also Malekzadeh 1328, vol. 7, pp. 53-64 and Saki 1343, p. 349; Soltani 1386, p. 182 reports that if the Bakhtiyaris had pursued the prince they would have been able to end the rebellion. People of Saveh and the various neighboring villages that had been plundered complained about the treatment they had received from both government officials and the rebels. Adhari 1378, p. 23 (docs. 43, 47-48). Hamadani 1354, p. 383 (After Salar al-Dowleh's defeat Amir Mofakhkham went on pilgrimage to Kerbela realizing that people knew that he was a partisan of the prince).

230. Dowlatabadi 1362, p. 183. However, shortly thereafter there was a lot of gunfire to be heard in Tehran during the night and people were sure that Salar al-Dowleh had come and they could not sleep all night. The next morning it became clear that a camel driver had fallen into the city's moat and the guards believed that the prince's army had come. The poor camel man was hit by some 2,000 bullets. Eyn al-Saltaneh 1377, vol. 5, p. 3544.

231. Mostowfi 1324, vol. 2, pp. 594, 598; Bamdad 1347, vol. 1, p. 50; Shuster 1968, pp. 134-35; Malekzadeh 1328, vol. 7, pp. 68-69; *The New Hazell Annual and Almanack*, vol. 28 (1913), p. 305; Mo`ayyer al- Mamalek 1361, pp. 102, 108, 111. At that time, it became known that Salar al-Dowleh had put some 300,000 *tumans* of extorted money in the Bank. Eyn al-Saltaneh 1377, vol. 5, p. 3546.

and in a state of anarchy. Then Salar al-Dowleh arrived with a great force and they had no choice but to submit and support him. Some were forced to accompany him, but fled when he engaged government forces. If there was an impartial governor they would follow him, otherwise they would resist. They signed a telegram, which was sent to others for their signature. Mohtasham al-Dowleh cut out "otherwise will resists," from the text, but he did not sign it. Ehtesham al-Dowleh, the Kerend chief refused to sign as well, because he had been forced to join by Salar al-Dowleh and had documents to prove it. Some merchants were forced to affix their seals. Late in the afternoon the Sardars sent another telegram from Hamadan instructing Mohtasham al-Dowleh to assume the duties of government and arrest the telegraph superintendent, who had suppressed telegrams but also circulated false ones. There was a crowd in the Telegraph office, which immediately wanted to beat up the superintendent, who was then arrested. McDouall commented that if soon no governor arrived with sufficient force the city would fall back into anarchy.[232]

The reactionaries in Kermanshah, notably Sharaf Khan Amin al-Mamalek, feared punishment by the Bakhtiyaris for their past deed. They did not want government troops in the city and, therefore, sent a delegation to Hamadan, consisting of Sardar Ejlal, Amir Moqtader and Salar Ashraf, promising to ensure law and order in Kermanshah if the government did not send any troops. When this was accepted on the delegation's return it was decided to find out Da'ud Khan Kalhor position toward Salar al-Dowleh. If he remained loyal to the prince their plan to keep order in the city was not feasible. Sardar Moqtader was sent to Da'ud Khan and if the latter remained loyal to the prince the Sardar should not return to the city but go to Iraq. When he did not return it was decided that Sardar Ejlal also had to go to Iraq. Before he left money was obtained from the Customs to pay for the local force to keep order in the city.[233]

Despite Salar al-Dowleh's defeat on 27 September 1911, Salar Homayun, one of his agents in Kermanshah, demanded Molitor to hand over the Customs revenues to him. Molitor delayed doing so, while asking the government for military assistance, because there were still many supporters of Salar al-Dowleh in the city, whose possible violent reaction he rightly feared. Moreover, the environs of Kermanshah were being plundered by Amanollah Khan, the rebel son of the Vali of Posht-e Kuh. The situation within the city remained precarious. In October 1911, one of the notables asked Molitor for the money to pay for the organization of a local militia, but he refused, as it would anger Salar al-Dowleh's party in the city. The Russian consul advised Molitor to close the Customs for a few days and remain at home.[234] The ex-Shah's and his brother's partisans were still quite active near Kermanshah in October 1911. Fearing an attack on the city, which was in a state of some disorder, many people, including the governor, Ehtesham al-Dowleh left for Baghdad and Kerbela at the end of October 1911. Salar al-Dowleh, who showed up again in the neighborhood, appointed Farrokh Khan Ilkhani to replace him, but the head of Hajjizadeh clan was unable to maintain order. In November 1911, the situation in

---

232. FO 248/1031, McDouall to Tehran, 10/10/1911; IOR/L/PS/20/261/5, 'Persia. No 4 (1912). Further correspondence respecting the affairs of Persia', p.139 (no. 53)

233. Molitor 2018 b, p. 2.

234. Soltani 1386, p. 211; Destree 1976, pp. 211-13; Hamadani 1354, pp. 384-85; Adhari 1378, p. 24 (doc. 54). After his brother's defeat `Azad al-Soltan fled to Kerbela. IOR/L/PS/20/223, 'Who's who in Persia. Calcutta: General Staff, India, 1916', p. 55.

Kermanshah became increasingly worse due to the rise in robberies such that McDouall had placed Britsh flags on warehouses containing British goods. On 27 November, McDouall wired Tehran that he feared the pillaging of the city.[235] On 21 November 1911, news was received that a force of Bakhtiyaris had defeated Salar al-Dowleh, who had fled with the chief of the Deyrawands to Khorramabad. This news made Amanollah Khan, the rebellious son of the Vali, decide to depart from Delgoshah and leave the Kermanshah area.[236]

Due to the unsettled and insecure situation in the city and province, people continued to flee to the holy places in Iraq. The British vice-consul at Kerbela reported on 30 November 1911 that the number of pilgrims was higher than usual due to the influx of refugees from Kermanshah, about 4,000 of them; princes, Khans, merchants, and others. Ehtesham al-Dowleh, the former governor of Kermanshah was one of them. Ehtesham al-Dowleh told the British vice-consul in Kerbela that Salar al-Dowleh wanted civil war. Therefore, he and others wanted to apply for Turkish citizenship; others would do so in the Consulates inside Iran. Akhund Kazem Khorasani had told Ehtesham al-Dowleh that he regretted the situation, but had not indicated that he would take a position.[237]

There were continued skirmishes between government forces and rebels in December 1911. Caravans were plundered and trade routes were closed and 'Abbas Khan, grandson of Sharif al-Molk killed villagers, plundered and burnt 27 villages belonging to Vakil al-Molk; the Customs was closed since the end of November, while the population of entire villages moved to Turkish territory.[238] Therefore, on 1 Dec 1911, Khosrow Bakhtiyari wired from Hamadan that there was a need to pursue Salar al-Dowleh who was gathering men and growing in strength. Also, his *savar*s were being discouraged by the long idleness, non-payment and sickness. He again asked for a reply to earlier telegrams.[239] However, Tehran had more problems than Salar al-Dowleh and was as yet unable to take forceful action. However, it sent A'zam al-Dowleh as acting-governor of Kermanshah, who arrived there in early December 1911. A`zam al-Dowleh, Sardar Ejlal's father, was a reactionary and supporter of the ex-Shah. He was detained in Tehran, but was released when he swore loyalty to the constitutional government. Accompanied by Saud Beg, the Ottoman consul, he arrived on 30 November in Kermanshah. After his arrival, Salar al-Dowleh's enemies urged him to fight the prince's supporters. A`zam al-Dowleh considered this useless for as long Da'ud Khan supported Salar al-Dowleh. Therefore, he excused himself saying that he had to put his affairs in order due to his long absence from the city. However, Farrokh Khan Hajjizadeh and other Salar supporters forced him to ;leave the city, before he had the chance to collect troops. Therefore, A`zam al-Dowleh had to decide whether to leave or stay and oppose the prince's supporters. He decided to oppose them and on 2 December 1911

---

235. IOR/L/PS/20/261/6, 'Persia. No 5 (1912). Further correspondence respecting the affairs of Persia', p. 35 (no. 89); IOR/L/PS/20/261/4, 'Persia. No 3 (1912). Further correspondence respecting the affairs of Persia.', p. 132 (no. 302); Hamadani 1354, pp. 386-87; Adhari 1378, docs. 53-56 (attack on government buildings such as police and telephone; also road robberies and general insecurity).

236. IOR/L/PS/10/212, File 211/1912, 'Turkish Arabia Summaries,' p. 5; Hamadani 1354, pp. 386-87.

237. IOR/L/PS/10/212, File 211/1912, 'Turkish Arabia Summaries,' p. 5.

238. Destree 1976, pp. 211-13; Adhari 1378, p. 25 (docs. 55-57, 59, 62). At that time Mojallal al-Soltan was trying to raise tribal support for the ex-Shah in Kurdistan. Dowlatabadi 1362, pp. 72-73.

239. Afshar 1367, pp. 2014-15, doc. 16.

hostilities broke out between the two sides, which lasted three days. A`zam al-Dowleh's main fighters were the Kandeluhis, who had occupied the main positions in the city. In secret, Farrokh Khan was able to induce their chiefs to join his side. He also alerted Salar al-Dowleh that the city was in his hands and that the prince could return. The prince wrote to the brother of one of the great mojtahed's of the city that if its people would abandon their enmity toward him they would have nothing to fear from him.[240] His arrival led to fights between his and Farrokh Khan's followers. However, on 15 December the city was quiet and the next day Salar al-Dowleh with a small force arrived. Initially there was still some fighting between government forces and the rebels. A'zam al-Dowleh, the acting governor, and some of his supporters fled to the British consulate and took asylum to avoid that the city would be plundered. At that time Salar al-Dowleh took the Customs revenues by force. Molitor had no choice as Salar al-Dowleh threatened him and his staff. [241] The prince appointed Farrokh Khan governor of Kangavar who, at the end of December 1911, threatened to sack that town, if it did not surrender to him.[242]

On 18 December 1911, the British and Russian consuls met with Salar al-Dowleh. He told them that he had news that some people at Saqqez had invited the Turks, and they replied that they would report it to their Legations. He then told them that he had given orders to repair the telegraph line and re-establish the postal service. As to A'zam al-Dowleh and others, who were in *bast* in the British Consulate, he said he would pardon them and gave his parole that their property would not be interfered with. However, the presence of A'zam al-Dowleh and four others leaders (his son Fakhim al-Dowleh, Abu'l-Hasan Khan deputy of the *anjoman*, Hajji Rostam Beg, Mehdi Pahlavan Reza and 'Emad al-Ra'aya) in Kermanshah was not advisable, it would be better if they were absent for two months. If he allowed them to stay, and even if they did nothing, their enemies might cause disorder and accuse them of it. He gave his word that they would be safely conducted to the border, or to a safe place on the road to Tehran, and each consul could send a man or two to observe. McDouall pointed out that in Shiraz Nezam al-Saltaneh had given his word, but that Qavam al-Dowleh still had been attacked and his brother had been killed. Salar al-Dowleh said "I am not Nezam al-Saltaneh,' to which McDouall said, 'yes, but your followers are like the wild Qashqa'is.' McDouall told him he would ask the *basti*s what they wanted. Apart from the five persons that he would pardon the rest might safely return to their homes, but if they again gave offence and took *bast* they would be tried and if found guilty punished, to the consuls' satisfaction. The consuls then said but two of our subjects had their properties seized; Salar al-Dowleh told them to give the details in writing and that he would look into it. Since he had no news from Mohammad 'Ali Mirza for two months; he intended to stay for Moharram and spend the winter in Lorestan and Kurdistan. In spring he would collect

---

240. Molitor 2018 b, pp. 3-4.

241. After his brother's defeat `Azad al-Soltan fled to Kerbela. IOR/L/PS/20/223, 'Who's who in Persia. Calcutta: General Staff, India, 1916', p. 55; IOR/L/PS/20/261/6, 'Persia. No 5 (1912). Further correspondence respecting the affairs of Persia,' Barclay to Grey 21/12/1911, p. 29 (no. 87); IOR/L/PS/20/261/6, 'Persia. No 5 (1912); Further correspondence respecting the affairs of Persia', p. 35 (no. 89). IOR/L/PS/20/261/5, 'Persia. No 4 (1912). Further correspondence respecting the affairs of Persia', Barclay to Grey 22/12/1911, p. 136 (no. 318); Malekzadeh 1328, vol. 7, p.159; Adhari 1378, p. 26 (doc. 62); Dowlatabadi 1362, p. 72; Hamadani 1354, pp. 387-90 (Farrokh Khan died on 22 December 1911).

242. Adhari 1378, doc. 61; Hamadani 1354, pp. 388-89. Shortly thereafter cholera broke out in the city and one of the first victims was Farrokh Khan Hajjizadeh. Molitor 2018 b, pp. 4-5.

his forces and march to Tehran. He had not wanted to come to Kermanshah but Farrokh Khan had begged him. He had dispatched governors to Hamadan, Malayer and Kolila'i. Some mullahs had shown him a telegram advocating boycotting Russian goods etc. On arrival he had only 200 *savar*s, which were joined by locals, about 700, but he said that Nazar 'Ali Khan and his son Sardar Mozaffar would be here in two days with their men.[243] The five *basti*s were ready to leave for Hamadan, provided they would have solid guarantees for their safety. McDouall suggested that guards and a guarantee from Sardar Mozaffar would be sufficient. Salar al-Dowleh said that this would take too long, and that they should leave before Moharram when feelings were high. Finally, he agreed that two agents from both consulates and from two leading *mojtahed*s could accompany the safe-conductees. Beyond Kangavar they would be safe. McDouall sent message to Salar al-Dowleh and added that it was not his function to send *savar*s, but if the Russians would, so would he.[244]

Meanwhile, Salar al-Dowleh tried to reinforce his position by raising fresh troops of which he allegedly had gathered some 3,000 men to oppose the government. On 2 January 1912, to the great consternation of the city's inhabitants, the prince and his Lors plundered the fodder and other provisions from the warehouse of Mirza 'Ali Khan Qarasuran-bashi. Ten days later it was found that the arsenal had been totally emptied of arms and gunpowder.[245] On 6 January 1912, Salar al-Dowleh demanded payment of 33,800 *tuman*s with credit receipts signed by the IBP manager Hamadan and 42,000 *tuman*s from bills on the 'Ali Akbar Brothers of Borujerd, which he claimed he had the right to encash. The IBP manager, who had orders not to pay Salar al-Dowleh, had no choice but to pay the prince, who was the only force in town and threatened to take the entire IBP branch treasury if he refused. At that time the IBP had 260,000 *tuman*s in cash and notes, of which 120,000 *tuman*s had been packed for transport. The rest was in the safe, which was above ground and could easily be demolished and, therefore, fearing greater loss, he paid. Salar al-Dowleh told the British consul that he did not want to fight the Persian government, if they left him alone. If not, he would attack Tehran in the spring. He would be content with an area from Azerbaijan to Khuzestan; he also was willing to pay taxes to Tehran.[246] The *basti*s finally decided that they did not want to leave, despite Salar al-Dowleh's assurance of safe-conduct. Salar al-Dowleh told the Consulate's *monshi* that he could not be responsible for the safety of foreigners if the *basti*s remained in the Consulate, because their presence aroused people's ire. He suggested informing the Russian consul as well.[247] Two weeks later, on the night of 15 January 1912, shots were fired from all sides at the Consulate. McDouall told the Consular guard only to fire if they saw any people in the grounds. The *basti*s and their servants, some 30 people, were all armed and ready to fight, but had orders from A'zam al-Dowleh not to fire unless attacked. In the morning of 16 January, Salar al-Dowleh sent for the British

243. FO 248/1031, McDouall to Tehran, 19/12/1911; Hamadani 1354, pp. 386-87 (on 21 December Nazar Ali Khan was in Kermanshah), 392 (he and the *Vali* left the city on 05/02/1912).

244. FO 248/1031, McDouall to Tehran, 21/12/1911; Hamadani 1354, pp. 389-91.

245. Adhari 1378, p. 26 (doc. 63); Hamadani 1354, pp. 391-92. Salar al-Dowleh's troops also, with violence and torture, exacted much money from the people of Kermanshah. Molitor 2018 b, p. 5.

246. FO 248/1053, McDouall to George Barclay, 06/01/1912; Idem, McDouall to Tehran, 06/01/1911; Adhari 1378, p. 26 (docs. 64, 70).

247. FO 248/1053, McDoulall to Tehran, 09/01/1912. In mid-February 1912, the government offered the prince a pension of 12,000 *tumans*, if he left to Europe. Dowlatabadi 1362, p. 74.

monshi and swore he had nothing to do with the shooting incident. He had investigated the matter and was sure that these had been partisans of the *basti*s to inculpate him. He wanted to see McDouall, who let him know that he first needed to punish the culprits, whom he thought were Salar Homayun's ruffians. Nazar 'Ali Khan sent a message to express his sorrow and informed McDouall that the previous night four of his men had been absent; he had arrested them and if guilty he would punish them.[248]

YAR MOHAMMAD KHAN TO THE RESCUE

In early January 1912, Farmanfarma was again appointed governor of Kermanshah with the task to defeat and oust Salar al-Dowleh. To that end he had two regiments of soldiers, 800 Bakhtiyari *savar*s and *mojahed*s at his disposal. However, he had not much faith in the soldiers and therefore, mainly relied on the *mojahed*s. The latter were a force of some 300 men under Yar Mohammad Khan Kermanshahi. Together with a few cannons and maxims this force left Qazvin for Hamadan, where it arrived at the end of January 1912. On 6 February the *mojahed*s took Sahneh, near Kermanshah, and Salar Mokram, who held the place for Salar al-Dowleh fled. Two days later, the *mojahed*s, who constituted the vanguard of a small government force under Yar Mohammad Khan, arrived at Bisotun, from where he wired Yeprem Khan asking for arms and ammunition. Salar al-Dowleh on learning of this threat sent a force against him, but Yar Mohammad, knowing the terrain better than the prince, instead of continuing via the road marched through the hills and entered the city during the night.[249] He only had a few men with him, who they took position in a few houses and started firing at daylight. As a result, Salar al-Dowleh, Da'ud Khan Kalhor, and the son of Farrokh Khan all fled, apparently believing that their partners had betrayed them. McDouall only allowed A'zam al-Dowleh to leave until the government forces had taken the town, as he had promised Salar al-Dowleh. After dark Yar Mohammad Khan entered the palace. In the evening all three rebel leaders gathered at Mahidasht and tried to retake the city but were repulsed. During the night a fight took place at the Qarasu bridge, where about 10 *mojahed*s were killed, and on both sides some 200 men participated. The rebels then withdrew to Manzileh, east of Kermanshah. A'zam al-Dowleh left the British Consulate where he had taken refuge since 15 December 1911, and took charge of the governorship again. After Salar al-Dowleh's departure from Kermanshah on 8 February, the

248. FO 248/1053, McDouall to Tehran, 16/01/1912.

249. According to Molitor, Yar Mohammad Khan had orders to remain in Hamadan waiting for reinforcements. However, he wanted to liberate his fellow Kermanshahis and marched to the city, arriving on 7 February 1912 at Bisotun. Salar al-Dowleh sent 700 Kalhors against him, but they were defeated at Sarpol-e Qarasu, The mojaheds lost 30 men, but that same night entered the city. The next day there was fighting throughout the entire day in the city, resulting in the withdrawal of Salar al-Dowleh and his troops. It would seem that Molitor, who wrote this after the events, commingled some of the various activities, because the fight at the Qarasu took place one day later. Molitor 2018 b, p. 5.

Fig. 7.2: Mojaheds who fought against Salar al-Dowleh (1912). © *Collection Molitor, Ed Elytis* no. 231.

Constitutional flag was raised. The next morning with a few gunshots the *mojaheds* forced the bazaaris to close the bazaar.[250]

Even though the fighting was over, still some people were killed. For example, Sharaf al-Molk Kurdistani, chief of the Jafs, was not killed during the fighting, because he was at the house of Aqa Mahmud, brother of Aqa Mohammad Mehdi. However, the morning after the fighting (9 February) he was shot with his nephew and two servants by the *mojaheds*. The Kurdistanis in town signed a testimony that it was the *mojaheds* who had killed him and that the townspeople were innocent and sent the document to their tribe to prevent them from killing Kermanshahis. Aqa Mahmud was arrested, also Aqa Rahim, Hajji Aqa Vali, Aqa Sayyed Reza Qomi and the Sheikh al-Eslam of Hersin, all *mojtaheds*. Salar al-Dowleh's whole correspondence was found in the palace as was Aqa Mahmud's dispatch case. The extraordinary government commission looked into the case against them. There was no doubt of Aqa Mahmud's guilt; the commission decided he had to pay 4,000 *tumans* and be sent to Tehran with the others. During the night Yar Mohammad Khan, who said he was acting on orders from Tehran, ordered his execution and Aqa Mahmud was hanged at daylight on 12 February. The others were sent

250. 'Persia. No 1 (1913). Further correspondence respecting the affairs of Persia', pp. 11-12; Political Diaries vol. 4, p. 518; IOR/L/PS/10/212, File 211/1912 'Turkish Arabia Summaries', p. 6; IOR/L/PS/20/261/6, 'Persia. No 5 (1912). Further correspondence respecting the affairs of Persia', p. 119 (no. 304); Political Diaries vol. 4, p. 518; Malekzadeh 1328, vol. 7, pp. 160-61; Adhari 1378, docs. 71, 73-77; Dowlatabadi 1362, p. 78; Eyn al-Saltaneh 1377, vol. 5, p. 3649; Hamadani 1354, p. 393; Ettehadiyeh and Sa`vandiyan 1366, vol. 1, pp. 136-37.

to Tehran; Aqa Rahim was also expected to be executed. On 9 February, two officers of the Zanganeh regiment, two executioners, and two others were shot (Salar Rashid Kurdistani, Hajj Rostam Khan, Soltan Safar Khan of the Zanganeh regiment, Shehab Nezam and his brother). The government force consisted of about 200 *mojaheds*, 100 Kolia'i horsemen and local soldiers and volunteers, perhaps 1,000 in total. They had plenty of ammunition and wired Farmanfarma, who had been recently appointed as governor of Kermanshah, for reinforcements. The city was quiet, but people were in terror.[251] The city was placed under martial law. Sayyed Mohammad Rowzeh-khvan and Na'eb-Sadr took refuge in the British Consulate on 11 February because the *mojaheds* were looking for them, who accused them of political offences, but they claimed they could prove their innocence. The former was accused of having taken messages from Salar al-Dowleh to A'zam al-Dowleh when in *bast* trying to persuade him to surrender and also of preaching against the Constitution, which on the latter point McDouall thought he had not. Na'eb-Sadr had always been the go-between for the clergy and the governor and had done the same under Salar al-Dowleh. On 15 February 1912, the local authorities gave assurances that if they did not leave their homes, they would not be arrested, out of consideration of the British consulate that had saved their lives.[252] Although the local population had aided Yar Mohammad Khan in taking the city, the *mojaheds* behaved as conquerors and rather badly towards their compatriots. This did not make the *mojaheds* very popular, the more so, while they had only suffered at most 15 men dead and wounded, the towns people had lost more than 500 among the non-combatants.[253]

Salar al-Dowleh went to Mahidasht after he left Kermanshah on 9 February 1912; he sent his wife to Kalhor country and with Sardar Mozaffer and the city Khans he moved to some 16 km from the city camping on crown-lands.[254] His troops plundered all environing villages and he sent messengers all around exhorting people to join his forces. The city was in good order and the defenders were busy fortifying the town. Via the Russian consul a letter arrived from Salar al-Dowleh on 17 February 1912 informing the consuls that he was going to take the town and that consuls and foreign subjects should withdraw to the villages "till he had punished the unruly." He made that point, because some of his followers ascribed their earlier defeat to the presence of Persian officials in the British consulate, and if they wanted to win they had to destroy it. He said he would allow them to plunder the consulate and the IBP. Meanwhile, the Kakawands let none pass into direction of Kangavar. Needless to say that this situation was not good for trade.

---

251. FO 248/1053, McDouall to Tehran, 13/02/1912; Malekzadeh 1328, vol. 7, p. 161; Adhari 1378, pp. 26-27 (docs. 73, 75); IOR/L/PS/20/261/6, 'Persia. No 5 (1912). Further correspondence respecting the affairs of Persia', Barclay to Grey 15/03/1912, p. 120 (no. 306); Adhari 1378, p. 27 (docs. 78, 80, 84); Hamadani 1354, pp. 393-94; Molitor 2018 b, p. 6. According to Dowlatabadi 1362, pp. 79-80 one of the reasons for the arrests and executions was to extort money from the town's people.

252. FO 248/1053, McDouall to Tehran, 15/02/1912. The government offered Salar al-Dowleh a pension of 12,000 *tumans* and restitution of his estates, as he is very poor, on condition that he would keep order in Kermanshah, hand over the city to the governor, and leave Persia. IOR/L/PS/20/261/6, 'Persia. No 5 (1912). Further correspondence respecting the affairs of Persia', Barclay to Grey 12/02/1912, p. 68 (no. 171).

253. Dowlatabadi 1362, p. 79.

254. IOR/L/PS/20/261/6, 'Persia. No 5 (1912). Further correspondence respecting the affairs of Persia', Barclay to Grey 15/03/1912, p. 120 (no. 306); Adhari 1378, p. 27; doc. 81 - at Yar Mohammad Khan's request Yefrim Khan had sent some cannons as the former believed that in that case he could defeat the prince's force, but they had not arrived yet - docs. 83, 85.

SALAR AL-DOWLEH, AGAIN

At that time, 'Ettela' al-Dowleh was president of the court-martial and army commander (*ra'is-e qoshun*), and president of a special commission. Gates were erected in several places and messengers sent to Farmanfarma, the appointed governor, asking to send reinforcements as soon as possible. Some chiefs, including Sardar Akram, wrote that they submitted to the government. Salar al-Dowleh's supporters were encouraged, because Farmanfarma did not come. The government had only a small force and part of that was willing to desert or help the rebels; the latter formed a large body of troops. On 18 February 1912 skirmishing started. On the night of 21 February there was firing west of Kermanshah where volunteers had made barricades supported by some *mojaheds*. At sunrise the volunteers joined the rebels, who then occupied Chiya Sorkh, a hill suburb of the city. Then they occupied one-third of the bazaar, but were driven back by the *mojaheds*, who suffered many casualties, but held out at a barricade until the next morning. On 22 February, the rebels (Kurdistanis, Sanjabis, town Khans) entered the city at several points and by 9 p.m. the town was theirs. The government officials and Yar Mohammad Khan fled, the latter without informing his *mojaheds*, toward Dinavar with much ammunition. On both sides some 40 men were killed. On 23 February 1912, Salar al-Dowleh and Sardar Mozaffar went to the palace. When the Kalhors arrived, who had done little fighting, they started plundering. They did not respect the houses of the Consular staff who flew the Russian or British flag. In the bazaar only the caravanserai of Vakil al-Dowleh, filled with British goods, and the *bazzaz-khaneh* escaped the looting. During this time many men, women and children were killed.[255]

The rebels searched everywhere for *mojaheds* and several were arrested, with the help of the towns people who had turned against them because of their oppressive behavior. In total, Salar al-Dowleh hung 102 Constitutionalists in one day, including 'Ettela al-Dowleh, the *kargozar*. His body was partly burnt and then thrown to the dogs. The others met a similar fate. Due to Yar Mohammad's defeat, Farmanfarma, the new governor, en route to Kermanshah returned to Tehran. Because Hamadan remained in government hands the government in Tehran ordered Farmanfarma to return to Hamadan and face Salar al-Dowleh. He was to leave again with a force of Cossacks. Salar al-Dowleh sent troops to take Kangavar and Sahneh, and intended to march on Hamadan.[256] The prince sent those troops there, because after their expulsion from Kermanshah, Yar Mohammad Khan had fled to Kangavar. Here Sari Aslan, the local governor, supported the government in Tehran. From there, they wired Yeprem Khan asking him for supplies as well as urging him to come in person as soon as possible. They further sent letters urging to send them arms and ammunition, because they had enough men, but not arms, to

---

255. IOR/L/PS/20/261/6, 'Persia. No 5 (1912). Further correspondence respecting the affairs of Persia', Barclay to Grey 12/03/1912 and 15/03/1912, pp. 117 (no. 297), 121 (no. 307); IOR/L/PS/20/261/7, 'Persia. No 1 (1913). Further correspondence respecting the affairs of Persia', p. 14-15 (no. 22); Dowlatabadi 1362, pp. 80-82 (with a list of plundered warehouses and houses); Adhari 1378, p. 28 (docs. 86, 101-102); Hamadani 1354, pp. 394-95; Malekzadeh 1328, vol. 7, pp. 161-62. Molitor 2018 b, p. 6.

256. IOR/L/PS/20/261/7, 'Persia. No 1 (1913). Further correspondence respecting the affairs of Persia', pp. 11, 14-15 (no. 22); Political Diaries vol. 4, p. 518; Adhari 1378, p. 28 (docs. 94, 99); Dowlatabadi 1362, pp. 82-83; Eyn al-Saltaneh 1377, vol. 5, p. 3649; Hamadani 1354, pp. 395-97. A`zam al-Dowleh and his son had fled to the village of Kanduleh, where they were arrested by one of their own men, Qanbar Khan, sergeant of the Zanganeh regiment. In the night of 25 February 1912, at the orders of Da'ud Khan Klahor, they were strangled. The next day their bodies were hung in the meydan and suffered all kinds of ignominy. Molitor 2018 b, p. 6.

enable them to destroy the rebel-prince. Salar al-Dowleh sent Sari Aslan a letter reprimanding him for not presenting himself and promising that he would destroy Kangavar. This caused panic among its inhabitants who asked Tehran to send troops to prevent this.[257] Tehran only sent nice replies thanking them for their fervor and to put Sari Aslan's mind at peace he was informed that the ex-Shah had left Iran and now Salar al-Dowleh had to be expelled as well.[258]

Salar al-Dowleh was always looking for ways of getting money and sometimes he did so not by using force, but by false claims with a hint of the use of force. On 14 March 1912, McDouall reported that at the request of the *kargozar* he opened a bag that Salar al-Dowleh had deposited at the IBP, from which the prince claimed 95,000 *tumans* were missing when he returned to Kermanshah. McDouall stated that the claim was false, but Salar al-Dowleh claimed compensation from IBP; he refused to apologize and thus the Bank was in danger.[259] The prince also imposed a forced contribution of the merchants of Kermanshah; each had to pay 3,000 to 5,000 *tumans* for his expenses, so that he could dismiss his troops, whom he told to be back by *Nowruz*, because then he would march to Hamadan. Some of his supporters, such as Baqer Khan of the Kakawands, Nazar 'Ali Khan Amra'i and Hasan Pasha Koliya'i were attacking and plundering villages, notables and anybody on the roads to and from Kermanshah, so that pilgrims remained in Khaneqin afraid to travel to Kermanshah. All these various activities caused economic and human distress and much physical destruction.[260]

On 1 March 1912, Barclay instructed McDouall, together with his Russian colleague, to suggest to Salar al-Dowleh to accept the Persian government's offer "of 6,000 *tumans* for himself and 6,000 *tumans* for his family, revocation of the confiscation of his estates, on condition that he keep order in Kermanshah and the places under his occupation, hands them over to a governor appointed by the Persian Government and then leaves Persia with an undertaking not to return to the country without the previous consent of the Persian Government."[261] A few days later, the British and Russian consuls informed Salar al-Dowleh about the offer made by the Persian government and strongly advised him to accept. However, he refused to do so, but in lieu, on 14 March, he made a counter-proposal in a very long letter, basically demanding the ceding of W. Iran under his rule as a quasi-independent ruler. The two consuls immediately advised him "to make a more reasonable proposal," but he refused, because Tehran would undoubtedly demand changes anyway.[262]

On 30 March 1912, McDouall was instructed to urge Salar al-Dowleh once again to accept Tehran's terms and hand over the occupied lands to Farmanfarma and to leave Iran. The two Powers fully supported the military action the Persian government was taking, to which end

257. Adhari 1378, pp. 28-29 (docs. 73-74, 81, 83, 87-88, 94-97, 99).

258. Adhari 1378, p. 29 (docs. 77, 98).

259. IOR/L/PS/20/261/6, 'Persia. No 5 (1912). Further correspondence respecting the affairs of Persia.', Barclay to Grey 15/03/1912, p. 121 (no. 307); Malekzadeh 1328, vol. 7, pp. 161-62.

260. Adhari 1378, p. 28 (docs. 89, 90-93, 103). Molitor 2018 b, p. 7. According to Hamadani 1354, pp. 398-99 the prince imposed a contribution of 5 to 50 *tumans* per household. The prince also appointed Ehtesham al-Dowleh as governor of the Thalatheh governorate.

261. IOR/L/PS/20/261/7, 'Persia. No 1 (1913). Further correspondence respecting the affairs of Persia', pp. 9-10 (no. 14).

262. IOR/L/PS/20/261/7, 'Persia. No 1 (1913). Further correspondence respecting the affairs of Persia', pp. 15-16 (no. 23) (at that time the prince had only 500 men in the city); Dowlatabadi 1362, p. 84.

they had made considerable funds available. If he refused, which was contrary to their interests, Russia and Great Britain would not help him get a pension and provide protection in the future. Both consuls met Salar al-Dowleh on 6 April to relate the message, but he refused, saying that, because the Legations were acting as mediators he felt vindicated and declared himself Shah. He had not come to get a pension, but to restore order and religion, to save the country from a corrupt and incompetent government and a child king. He said compare the state of this province with the rest of the country. McDouall said trade in Kermanshah was at a standstill, which the prince denied and said roads were safe. According to McDouall, "He is so filled with his idea of his own greatness that he cannot be convinced to see reality." The next day Salar al-Dowleh left Kermanshah going to Harunabad, Da'ud Khan Kalhor's headquarters, to speak with local chiefs and arrange their quarrels and collect more men. McDouall did not think the Vali would come. On the same day the two consuls also informed several tribal chiefs and city notables about their message to Salar al-Dowleh. McDouall told the Sanjabi chief the contents of the telegram, who promised to deal with the Kalhors, if Farmanfarma would come immediately with 300 men and guns. Otherwise the tribes would be forced to join Salar al-Dowleh. Farmanfarma who was then at Qazvin, was confident that with his forces he could take care of the problem; also by negotiating with the Sanjabis. Everybody now took the position that the resolution of the Salar al-Dowleh rebellion was in Farmanfarma's hands.[263]

Meanwhile, Salar al-Dowleh had created a commission of justice (*'adalat*) consisting of the *kargozar*, Aqa Rahim *mojtahed*, and Malek Mohammad, a bankrupt merchant. On 7 April 1912, Salar al-Dowleh left to Gilan, ostensibly to meet with the Vali. He had been in vain trying to have the Vali come to Kermanshah, who finally said that he would meet him in Gilan, provided he would hand over his rebel son Amanollah Khan in chains. Salar al-Dowleh left with 200 men and left the justice commission in charge of Kermanshah with the Ilkhani as executive. There were only 250 levies in the city the rest had gone home. It was said that the Gurans and Kalhors had fought. The Guran-Sanjabi combination was quiet, because they knew that Salar al-Dowleh would not support Da'ud Khan and they only joined the prince out of fear of Da'ud Khan in his present position.[264]

McDouall was instructed to make public the communication made to Salar al-Dowleh on behalf of the Legations; the Russian consul had no such instructions, which put the onus on the British. Malekzadeh implied in his comments on these events that the Russians did not want to do anything to hinder Salar al-Dowleh. On 7 April 1912, McDouall first informed Samsam al-Mamalek who told him that his son 'Ali Akbar had formed a combination against Da'ud Khan Kalhor, but was now quiet as Da'ud Khan was Salar al-Dowleh's most trusted supporter and he was not strong enough to oppose Salar al-Dowleh, if he supported Da'ud Khan. If a man of rank like Farmanfarma arrived with some 500 men and two guns his presence would be sufficient and then they could easily deal with Da'ud Khan. This had to be quickly, or else the

---

263. IOR/L/PS/20/261/7, 'Persia. No 1 (1913). Further correspondence respecting the affairs of Persia', pp. 18 (encl. 3 in no. 23 and no. 24), 53-54 (no.125); Malekzadeh 1328, vol. 7, p. 163 .

264. FO 248/1053, Diary no. 3 from March 31 to April 11th 1912. On 7 April 1912, a detachment of 100 Russian troops were sent to Hamadan to avoid that it would fall into the hands of adherents of Salar al-Dowleh. IOR/L/PS/20/261/7, 'Persia. No 1 (1913). Further correspondence respecting the affairs of Persia' Barcley to Grey, 07/04/1912, p. 8 (no. 12); Hamadani 1354, p. 399.

tribes would be obliged to join, or at least send some men to the prince. McDouall also informed Aqa Mohammad Mehdi who at once left for his village as of then there was no ranking *mojtahed* in town, apart from Aqa Rahim. On 3 April 1912, he sent a copy to the Vali and to Qasr-e Shirin to vice-consul Soane for publication and talks with tribal chiefs. McDouall also sent for the Ilkhani, the son of Farrokh Khan, head of the Hajjizadehs in town and *de jure* chief of the Kalhors and told him about the contents of the communication. He said that his position was different as he had properties inside and outside the city, which now were usurped by Da'ud Khan; his first object was to protect the town and he would not yet change his course. On 13 April some 100 of Salar al-Dowleh's adherents met at the house of Aqa Rahim. The principals being the Ilkhani, Salar Mozaffar, and Mashdi Hasan, brother of the late Mo'in al-Ra'aya. Aqa Rahim said the contents of the British message had made him afraid and he thought of leaving. The others said there was nothing from the Russian consul and the British were the enemy of Salar al-Dowleh. Aqa Rahim suggested writing to Tehran that they were poor inoffensive people and they would submit to anyone who came with a force and ask for amnesty. The others refused. They finally wrote a letter to Salar al-Dowleh stating that since he had left, the British consul had spread stories that Mohammad 'Ali had left and that Salar al-Dowleh must leave and that the government in Tehran was powerful. Therefore, it was imperative that he got the Vali to join and immediately return to Kermanshah with the Vali's forces or they would leave town. If the Vali did not come and he could not do anything they had to see to their own safety. McDouall commented that because the Russian consul said nothing and the Turkish consul was at the prince's service the people thought that only the British were the prince's enemy and when he returned he would make life difficult for British subjects. Salar al-Dowleh had no loyal friends, they only joined him out of fear, some for plunder, others because they had committed too much to him, and some even if they would get government pardon knew that they would be murdered because of their ill-treatment of the people. Only quick action by Tehran might put an end to this, and to prevent that the Vali and the Sheikh of Mohammareh join Salar al-Dowleh. There was no news from Gilan, only rumors, but it seemed that the Vali would not join Salar al-Dowleh, who "like Sardar Akram is known to be offended at the honour heaped on Daood Khan, a man of no birth."[265]

In April 1912, Salar al-Dowleh again threatened Molitor to pay him the Customs monies; the latter ordered Vilain at Qasr-e Shirin to stop all goods going towards Kermanshah. Salar al-Dowleh considered this an act of treason and told him to order Vilain to let the goods depart.[266] By mid-April Salar al-Dowleh had become very unpopular in Kermanshah due to his exactions. He was still in Kalhor country to raise more support.[267] Salar al-Dowleh left Gilan on 28 or 29 April 1912, where he had gone to obtain support of Vali, who only came there after having received a safe-conduct from the prince, because Da'ud Khan Kalhor was his enemy. While

265. FO 248/1053, McDouall to Tehran, 13/04/1912; IOR/L/PS/20/261/7, 'Persia. No 1 (1913). Further correspondence respecting the affairs of Persia', pp. 9 (no. 14), 52 (no. 125), 54-55 (no. 125); Malekzadeh 1328, vol. 7, p. 164.

266. Destree 1976. pp. 247-48.

267. IOR/L/PS/20/261/7, 'Persia. No 1 (1913). Further correspondence respecting the affairs of Persia', p. 38 (no. 84). At the end of March 1912, both the Russian and British consular agents were instructed to jointly inform Mojallal al-Soltan that taking Hamadan in the name of Mohammad Ali, the ex-Shah, was contrary to wishes of both Legations. Adhari 1378, doc. 104.

Fig. 7.3: Farmanfarma's army en route in 1911. © *Collection Molitor, Ed. Elytis* no. 131.

there, the Vali lived in his own tents and he and his men fed themselves refusing to be the guest of Da'ud Khan Kalhor, "who, he said, was a robber and could only entertain him from his unlawful spoils." The Vali told the prince he could only support the royalist troops under certain conditions: no looting, chiefs should support their men, no molesting of travelers and traders, and no extortion of merchants and others. The prince acceded to these conditions, but the Vali seemed not to have put much faith in this commitment, because he returned home. While in Gilan, Salar al-Dowleh married a daughter of Da'ud Khan, the Vali being present at the wedding. It was said to be the 10th matrimonial alliance of the prince during this campaign. From Gilan he hurried to Kermanshah to face Farmanfarma's advance. The townsmen of Kermanshah were wavering in their support and asked him to declare his intentions and in reply he said he would meet the enemy. He had already summoned 'Ali Akbar Sanjabi to join him at Gilan, where he did not come due to this feud with Da'ud Khan.[268]

Meanwhile, Salar al-Dowleh did not get his reinforcements, mostly because the various tribes did not trust each other. Samsam al-Mamalek replied to Salar al-Dowleh that given his quarrel with the Kalhors he would not come to Kermanshah as long as they had not left.

268. IOR/L/PS/10/212, File 211/1912 'Turkish Arabia Summaries', pp. 7-8. IOR/L/PS/10/212, File 211/1912 'Turkish Arabia Summaries', pp. 7-8; Dowlatabadi 1362, p. 85.

Fig. 7.4: Salar al-Dowleh and Da'ud Khan Kalhor and his sons (1912). © *Collection Molitor, Ed. Elytis* no. 386.

Moreover, there was trouble on the border caused by the Kalhors and therefore, he could not spare a man. Sardar Mozaffer, the Kalhor chief, in his turn told Salar al-Dowleh that he could not come until the Sanjabi contingent had left Kermanshah and furthermore that he would come when the Vali came. The latter wrote that he would come, but he had an excuse for a delay. This situation was troublesome for Salar al-Dowleh, because he could not do a thing without the Kermanshah tribes. Therefore, he wrote to his supporters that so-and-so had already come to encourage them to come as well.[269] On 1 May 1912, Salar al-Dowleh sent a telegram to Townley saying he had been joined by the Vali and that he was returning to Kermanshah and then would march to Hamadan. He had instructed Amir Mofakhkham to march to Soltanabad and Mojallal al-Soltan to Hamadan, where government forces were ready to march to Kermanshah.[270]

In early January 1912, 'Abdol-Hoseyn Mirza Farmanfarma had been appointed governor of Kermanshah with the task to counter Salar al-Dowleh's depredations. On 6 April 1912, Farmanfarma finally left Tehran for Hamadan with a considerable force. He stopped at Qazvin for a while and then proceeded to Hamadan. Farmanfarma's troops consisted of levies from his

269. IOR/L/PS/20/261/7, 'Persia. No 1 (1913). Further correspondence respecting the affairs of Persia', p. 74.
270. IOR/L/PS/20/261/7, 'Persia. No 1 (1913). Further correspondence respecting the affairs of Persia', p. 32 (no. 72).

estates in Asadabad, Maragheh and Miyanj, in addition to 400 Bakhtiyari *savar*s, 150 Cossacks, amongst whom was by Reza Khan Mir Panj Makzimi (the later Reza Shah), who commanded the artillery (Maxim guns). There also were levies from the villages of Amir Nezam Qaraqozlu and 300 *mojahed*s under Yar Mohammad Khan.[271] A force of 600 Bakhtiyaris under Shehab al-Saltaneh and Ziya al-Soltan followed somewhat later with orders to march to Zanjan and then to wait for further orders. Meanwhile, Amir Nezam, the governor of Hamadan fortified the town. On 3 May 1912, Salar al-Dowleh returned to Kermanshah with 600 men. The Sanjabis and other smaller tribes had not openly broken with Salar al-Dowleh, but had sent no representatives to him in Gilan. The prince told the British consul McDouall that he wanted to fight government troops some 12 miles outside Hamadan to avoid casualties among civilians and damage to foreign goods. He asked the consul to convey this to the government in Tehran. The British Minister considered this letter a joke, which had been written before the prince knew that his troops had been defeated at Hamadan. Salar al-Dowleh sent 15,000 men under Da'ud Khan Kalhor, now titled Amir A'zam, to Hamadan to defeat Farmanfarma. The latter took almost one month to march from Tehran to Hamadan, and on 3 May 1912 he advanced against Mojallal al-Soltan. The two armies met on 5 May; they fired at each other and then fled. "Mujallal winning because he looked round first, and discovered that he and the enemy were playing the same game." Farmanfarma lost three Schneider field guns and some mountain batteries with all their ammunition, and allegedly had only 150 men left. Officially it was said that their breechblocks had been removed before they were abandoned. Farmanfarma withdrew to Hamadan waiting for reinforcements. These were Armenian *fada'i*s under Kerri Khan, but there was disaffection in their ranks. The Bakhtiyari force at Zanjan was ordered to join Farmanfarma. Meanwhile, Yeprem Khan, with 200 Armenian *fada'i*s sent as reinforcement, left Tehran on 7 May and hastened by car to Hamadan to take command of the entire government force. After his arrival on 11 May, Yeprem Khan rallied the government troops, who were reinforced by the Bakhtiyaris.[272]

On hearing about the quarrel between the tribes, Kazem Khan Sanjabi and Salar Arshad Kurdistani, who had been with Mojallal al-Soltan when he defeated Farmanfarma, returned on 5 May 1912. Mojallal al-Soltan wrote to Salar al-Dowleh that he should send him reinforcements, instead of leaving some of his force in Kermanshah to deal with the tribal quarrels. Salar al-Dowleh sent some olama to Samsam al-Mamalek, who then visited the prince, who embraced him, called him father and gave him 3,000 *tuman*s. Samsam al-Mamalek said the tribes would not accept a government by the Kalhors; if they met there would be a fight; they could not serve in the same army. Salar al-Dowleh promised, 'serve me and you won't have to submit to Sardar-e

---

271. Farmanfarma'iyan 1382, vol. 1, p. 360; Afshar 1367, pp. 2016-17, docs. 18, 20-21 (on 21 November 1911, he complained that promised gunners and soldiers had not come and that Mr. Lecoffre, who was supposed to pay the force's expenditures, had left, the more so since all foodstuffs were expensive in Hamadan). On 4 Qus 1329/27 November 1911, he complained that the soldiers had not been paid and were hungry. He asked for wheat and barley to be made available immediately so that the soldiers would not die. Afshar 1367, p. 2018, doc. 22

272. IOR/L/PS/20/261/7, 'Persia. No 1 (1913). Further correspondence respecting the affairs of Persia', pp. 37-38 (no. 84); Farmanfarma'iyan 1382, vol. 1, pp. 356-58; Dowlatabadi 1362, p. 84; IOR/L/PS/20/261/7, 'Persia. No 1 (1913). Further correspondence respecting the affairs of Persia', pp. 41 (no. 87), 43 (no. 93), 44 (nos. 96, 98) 53-55 (no. 125), 57 (no. 126), 65-66 (no. 136-37, 140-41), 72; Malekzadeh 1328, vol. 7, pp. 164-65; Soltani 1386, pp. 187-89 (Salar al-Dowleh lost 500-600 men, the government 50). According to Molitor, Salar al-Dowleh's troops were commanded by Abdol-Baqi Khan Char Dowli and Qasem Khan Sardar Naser, son of Samsam al-Mamalek Sanjabi. Molitor 2018 b, p. 7.

Mozaffar.' He asked for 800 men to be sent to Mojallal al-Soltan. Samsam al-Mamalek appeared to have agreed, returned to his village to see his son 'Ali Akbar, who was the real head of the 'tribal 'combination.' It was expected that if Farmanfarma would defeat Mojallal al-Soltan then they would not join Salar al-Dowleh. Sardar Mozaffar wrote to Ehtesham al-Mamalek of Kerend that he was right to punish the Kalhors. Apparently, he was afraid of the strength of the 'combination' and only intended to fight when attacked. He was expected to join at Kangavar for the advance. The Ilkhani was at Sahneh with 300-400 men. Meanwhile, Salar al-Dowleh did not get his reinforcements, mostly because the various tribes did not trust each other. [273]

On 14 May 1912, Salar al-Dowleh met with McDouall to explain, one again, that he was a patriot who only wanted to restore order. He could do it better than the current government and, moreover, he would be more useful to the British than Sardar As'ad, who was beholden to the Russians. Although given their past behavior toward him he had no reason to love the British, but he was convinced only the British government would be able to guarantee Persia's integrity and independence. Therefore, he would do everything to support British interests and had given orders to respect British goods. McDouall asked him about the jihad that Kurdish olama had declared at the instigation of Mojallal al-Soltan, who had told them that the government in Tehran had sold out to Russia and Great Britian and that he had said that foreign goods would be first looted. The prince replied that this was a trick played by his enemies, because Mojallal al-Soltan could not tell such stories without his orders.[274]

On 19 May 1912, Yeprem Khan, after reconnoitering enemy positions, attacked Mojallal al-Soltan. The battle at Surcheh began at 9 a.m. and ended by 4.30 pm, when Yeprem Khan was killed by a sniper. Immediately, panic broke out, because Mojallal al-Soltan's reinforcements arrived at that time, but Kerri Khan kept order by ruthless shooting the first men who fled. Then another three hours of fight ensued and Mojallal al-Soltan was defeated; he suffered 300 casualtie. Government forces' losses were 30 killed, including Yeprem Khan. Salar al-Dowleh's lustre waned and he withdrew to Kermanshah with some 80 men.[275] Farmanfarma marched quickly toward Kermanshah to prevent Salar al-Dowleh from reinforcing himself, en route taking Sehneh. On 27 May, the Ilkhani reported that Salar al-Dowleh had defeated the advance guard of government reinforcements. Da'ud Khan Kalhor (Sardar Mozaffar) joined him on the evening of 28 May and camped at Sahneh to make a final stand. In the morning (29 May) government forces attacked with maxims and artillery. Da'ud Khan tried to capture the artillery under Reza Khan, but got shot in the leg and withdrew, but died en route. Because Da'ud Khan, his oldest son, as well as many other Kalhor leaders were killed the rest of the tribesmen fled to their own country. The Hajjizadehs of the Ilkhani section fled to the hills. When news arrived of his army's defeat and flight, Kazem Khan Sanjabi was with Salar al-Dowleh and left

273. IOR/L/PS/20/261/7, 'Persia. No 1 (1913). Further correspondence respecting the affairs of Persia', p. 74 (encl. 2-4 to no. 166).

274. IOR/L/PS/20/261/7, 'Persia. No 1 (1913). Further correspondence respecting the affairs of Persia', pp. 73 (no. 166).

275. IOR/L/PS/20/261/7, 'Persia. No 1 (1913). Further correspondence respecting the affairs of Persia', pp. 48 (no. 113), 52 (no. 122), 72-73 (no. 166), 86 (no. 173); Soltani 1386, p. 188 (Salar al-Dowleh lost 500 men, the government 50 men); Eyn al-Saltaneh 1377, vol. 5, pp. 3709-10; Hamadani 1354, p. 401; Adhari 1378, p. 29 (docs. 104, 107-08). Concerning Yefrim Khan's death and funeral, see Eyn al-Saltaneh 1377, vol. 5, pp. 3703-04.

immediately for his own district. Salar al-Dowleh, Mojallal al-Soltan and his men, with one gun, fled to Lorestan where he took refuge with the Vali. On 30 May 1912, Farmanfarma arrived in Kermanshah without firing a shot; the town remained quiet.[276] To keep it that way, Farmanfarma made it known that he understood that those who had fought with Salar al-Dowleh had done so to protect themselves, or were forced to do so, and he declared a general amnesty provided they did not extend any further support to Salar al-Dowleh.[277]

Since the arrival of Farmanfarma there were no disturbances in the city. However, the situation in the districts remained unsettled, and he took no steps against Salar al-Dowleh's followers, who, in July 1912, still held some villages near Kermanshah. On 7 June 1912, Salar al-Dowleh with 200 men was near Mian Do-Ab, allegedly to force the government to return his confiscated estates.[278] On 28 June 1912, Salar al-Dowleh wrote that he was in Kurdistan and that tribal chiefs needed to present themselves to him.[279] In July 1912, it was reported that Salar al-Dowleh was at Saqqez and was going to the Tabriz area in a Russian village where Mojallal al-Soltan had already arrived. It was also reported that he was collecting additional forces and that Nazar 'Ali Khan had joined him. As of 2 July, Mojallal al-Soltan had taken refuge in Ne'matabad, the summer-quarters of the Russian consul, who, in accordance with his Minister's instructions, gave orders to arrest him. He was then taken to Russia, after having signed a document that he would not return to Iran.[280]

On 12 July 1912, all Bakhtiyaris and *mojaheds* left for Bisotun and had gone one stage beyond it, because Farmanfarma had no money to pay his troops. He informed Tehran that unless it sent money he was forced to take it from Customs receipts, else the Bakhtiyaris and *mojaheds* would abandon him and depart altogether and Salar al-Dowleh could take over again.[281] The only troops remaining in Kermanshah were the Hamadani *feda'i* regiment and 500 of Farmanfarma' own *savars*, as well as some local troops, and more of the latter were expected. The military leaders were dissatisfied because they had nothing to do and were dispersed over town; also, because those who asked for pardon from Farmanfarma were told to come later, implying that he did not trust them, which they maintained he could. The British, Ottoman and

---

276. Soltani 1386, pp. 188-91; Malekzadeh 1328, vol. 7, pp. 165, 167-75; Hamadani 1354, pp. 402-03; Adhari 1378, p. 29 (docs. 109-111); Eyn al-Saltaneh 1377, vol. 5, pp. 3849-50 (details on this battle by Da'ud Khan); IOR/L/PS/20/261/7, 'Persia. No 1 (1913). Further correspondence respecting the affairs of Persia', pp. 65-67 (no. 136-37, 141, 146), 72-75 (no. 166). The battle took place in the plain of Samangan, between Sahneh and Bisetun. Salar al-Dowleh was waiting in the Delgosha, his getaway in case he lost, just outside Kermanshah. Molitor 2018 b, p. 7.

277. Soltani 1386, p. 189.

278. IOR/L/PS/20/261/4, 'Persia. No 3 (1912). Further correspondence respecting the affairs of Persia', p. 78 (no. 154), 112 (no. 225).

279. Ettehadiyeh and Sa`vandiyan 1366, p. 191.

280. IOR/L/PS/20/261/7, 'Persia. No 1 (1913). Further correspondence respecting the affairs of Persia', pp. 91 (no. 181), 99 (no.191), 111-12 (no. 227). This news contradicted earlier news, according to which Nazar `Ali Khan Amra'i and the Vali of Posht-e Kuh, Salar al-Dowleh's principal protectors, had submitted to Tehran, while Salar al-Dowleh was a fugitive en route to Tabriz, fearing that his former allies would arrest him. IOR/L/PS/20/261/7, 'Persia. No 1 (1913). Further correspondence respecting the affairs of Persia',Townley to Grey 24/07/1912, p. 106 (no. 217); Adhari 1378, doc. 112.

281. Political Diaries, vol. 4, p. 586; IOR/L/PS/20/261/7, 'Persia. No 1 (1913). Further correspondence respecting the affairs of Persia', pp. 60 (in April 1912, the government had promised the Armenians new elections, but did not do so), 102 (the Minister of Finance begged for an advance from Russia and Greta Britain to pay the troops at Kermanshah, else they would leave), 105, 131.

Russian Consuls met Farmanfarma on 14 July; he told them that the government troops had left without permission and that the presence of 300 *mojaheds* with a maxim and two guns was necessary, because many of the local troops had sided with the rebels in the past and were untrustworthy. Therefore, a loyal group would keep them honest. Salar al-Dowleh was then at Alishtar in Lorestan with Nazar 'Ali Khan Amra'i, Sardar Akram with about 700 men. Nazar 'Ali Khan was in regular contact with Farmanfarma and had informed him that Salar al-Dowleh would be willing to submit, if he was offered a governorship. Shortly thereafter he and the Vali made their submission to the government.[282] Salar al-Dowleh also wrote directly to Farmanfarma trying to shame him for what he had done to his family.[283] Farmanfarma asked the government in Tehran to send him money to pay his troops, else there was the possibility that Salar al-Dowleh would undo all the gains that had been made. At that time, he had been able to get the support of 400 Guran *savars*, but they left.[284]

YAR MOHAMMAD KHAN DEFECTS

In August 1912, Salar al-Dowleh was plundering parts of Kurdistan. On 15 August there was news that Salar al-Dowleh was 55 km from Kermanshah, and therefore, on 12 August, Farmanfarma left with his army to Senneh to restore order.[285] On 19 August 1912, Yar Mohammad Khan and Mosayeb Qoli Khan arrived at Kermanshah having deserted Farmanfarma one stage from Senneh; they had 300 *mojaheds* with them. They declared for Salar al-Dowleh, who had promised to restore the *Majles*. Yar Mohammad Khan published a notice that his action was not out of enmity to Farmanfarma, but out of desire of the opening of the *Majles* and a change of government. In Kermanshah, they were joined by Salar al-Dowleh's previous supporters.[286] According to Sheikh Mohammad Mehdi Kermanshahi, the reason for Yar Mohammad Khan's defection was that Farmanfarma, who did not like the lower class *sardars*, had told Yar Mohammad Khan that he was on his own. It is true that their relationship had been festering from the beginning of 1912. Farmanfarma was very unhappy with Yar Mohammad Khan during the preceding months, even writing that "I will not go with Yar Mohammad Khan to paradise."[287]

---

282. IOR/L/PS/20/261/7, 'Persia. No 1 (1913). Further correspondence respecting the affairs of Persia', pp. 105 (no. 213), 106 (no. 217), 139 (no. 283); Adhari 1378, p. 30 (docs. 110-111). Molitor also reports that the troops left because Farmanfarma did not want to take action against Salar al-Dowleh's followers. Molitor 2018 b, p. 7.

283. Adhari 1378, p. 30; Farmanfarma'iyan 1341, pp. 500-03.

284. Adhari 1378, p. 30 (doc. 113, 115); IOR/L/PS/20/261/7, 'Persia. No 1 (1913). Further correspondence respecting the affairs of Persia', p. 131 (no. 280).

285. IOR/L/PS/20/261/7, 'Persia. No 1 (1913). Further correspondence respecting the affairs of Persia', pp. 99 (no. 191), 165 (no. 328); Hamadani 1354, p. 407.

286. IOR/L/PS/20/261/7, 'Persia. No 1 (1913). Further correspondence respecting the affairs of Persia', pp. 129 (no. 279), 165 (no. 328); Hamadani 1354, pp. 407, 409.

287. Soltani 1386, p. 192; Farmanfarma'iyan 1382, vol. 1, pp. 358-59; Eyn al-Saltaneh 1377, vol. 5, p. 3654 calls Yar Mohammad Khan, a bush-cutting gum collector' (*gavan-kan katira begir*). Adhari 1378, pp. 31-32, citing Ali Naqipur, *Yar Mohammad Khan Sardar-e Mashruteh*. Tehran, 1369/1990, pp. 15, 166, 174, ascribes the split to the corrupt traditional elite politicians in charge of the Tehran government as well as to the bad relations between the two men, Yar Mohammad Khan blaming Farmanfarma for the unnecessary deaths of his friends.

However, it would seem that the real reason for Yar Mohammad Khan's defection was Tehran politics. The Democrats were hell bent on unseating the current government and were willing to use any means to do so with the objective to have elections for the *Majles*, which had been closed since late 1911. Therefore, the Democrats gave Yar Mohammad Khan, who was one of their supporters, the order to join forces with Salar al-Dowleh. The strange reasoning was that having an alternative government led by Salar al-Dowleh and Yar Mohammad Khan in charge of W. Persia would give the Democrats a strike force to oust the Bakhtiyaris and Naser al-Molk, the Regent, and take control of Tehran and the state. Yar Mohammad Khan knew that the local force that Farmanfarma had left behind did not exceed 500 men, who, moreover, were no threat to his battle-hardened *mojaheds*. He quickly took control of the city, helped by local Democrats, and arrested Seham al-Dowleh, Farmanfarma's deputy-governor and other partisans. That same afternoon, Yar Mohammad Khan published a proclamation in which he called Naser al-Molk a traitor and that he only wanted to re-establish freedom and the Constitution and therefore, would continue to fight until these two objective were in place and the *Majles* reopened. He also sent a telegram to Tehran demanding the dismissal of the Regent, a change of the composition of the Cabinet reflecting that of the *Majles* and the Constitution.[288] Farmanfarma regretted Yar Mohammad Khan's defection after all efforts and expenses made, which, he suggested, would give only new life to Salar al-Dowleh's rebellion.[289]

According to Mo'tamedi, prior to his defection, Yar Mohammad Khan in secret had written to Salar al-Dowleh that he was disappointed in doing the government's bidding and that he would support his cause, if he would appoint him commander of his troops, and later as Prime Minister, after he had put him on the throne. In reply Salar al-Dowleh sent 15,000 *tumans* in gold to Yar Mohammad Khan, which he had to collect near Sanandaj. On hearing this Yar Mohammad and 400 *mojaheds* left Kermanshah during the night, and rode to Sanandaj and then personally went around Kurdistan to recruit fighters. He allegedly collected 25,000 men and marched on Kermanshah to seize Farmanfarma and his arms. Farmanfarma knew about his defection and prepared a defense with a force of Sanjabis, some Bakhtiyaris and Armenians.[290]

On 3 September 1912, Salar al-Dowleh returned to Kermanshah with 500 men and some Kurdish chiefs, among whom 'Abbas Khan Javanrudi. Yar Mohammad received him warmly; he had 1,000 men, and perhaps more outside the city.[291] After his arrival, Salar al-Dowleh again threatened Molitor and told him that if he did not open the Customs he would retaliate against his staff, who were afraid and demanded that Molitor realize that he put their lives in danger by his refusal to obey Salar al-Dowleh. Molitor was between a rock and a hard place; his anguished staff and merchants urged him to keep the Customs open, which would give Salar al-Dowleh the opportunity to extort money from them. Molitor asked Tehran permission to close the Customs, which did not help much, because the prince took the Customs funds by force. Part

---

288. Malekzadeh 1328, vol. 7, pp. 240-43.
289. Adhari 1378, p. 33 (doc. 116).
290. Soltani 1386, pp. 192-93.
291. IOR/L/PS/20/261/7, 'Persia. No 1 (1913). Further correspondence respecting the affairs of Persia', p. 152 (no. 303). According to Hamadani 1354, p. 410, the prince returned on 1 September.

of the money seized, Salar al-Dowleh paid to 'Abbas Khan, who promised to dislodge Farmanfarma from Senneh. The tribes took a wait-and-see policy and did not join either side.[292]

At the end of August 1912, Townley reported that the situation in Kermanshah was confused. The government did not know that rebellious *mojaheds* had taken the town; it hoped to recover the town with the help of the Bakhtiyaris levies, 500 of whom were with Farmanfarma; 150 were en route from Soltanabad and 350 were to be sent from Tehran. Farmanfarma stated that all would be well if Tehran would send him 35,000 *tumans*. Yar Mohammad Khan, the rebel leader promised the same result for 40,000 *tumans*, both parties appeared to want to squeeze the government.[293]

The Bakhtiyari tribesmen and the *mojaheds* said they were willing to return if they were paid their arrear pay. There were also complaints that Farmanfarma took the spoils of war to enrich himself and that neither the government nor the troops who took them got any share. ... Before it was clear which side Yar Mohammad Khan and his men was on, the central government sent a young Armenian, Mirza Yanz [Yans], former *chef de cabinet* of Yeprem Khan, to resolve the differences between the Moslem *mojaheds* and the Armenians who had remained loyal to Kerri Khan. However, he arrived too late and failed in his mission. He not only was unable to convince the Moslem *mojaheds* to return, but he associated himself with the loyal *mojaheds* and the Bakhtiyaris and sent a petititon to the government saying that the forces had been fighting for months for the Constitution and the *Majles*, but that the former was ignored and elections for the latter were not even contemplated. After considerable hesitation Farmanfarma's troops were induced to return to retake the city.[294]

On 8 September 1912, Salar al-Dowleh and Yar Mohammad left Kermanshah and with 600 men marched to Kurdistan. They were threatening Senneh, where the governor took refuge in the Turkish consulate, while the inhabitants fled in terror. The government in Tehran did not know where Farmanfarma was, who one week earlier had taken Senneh. Tehran wanted him to leave Senneh and take Kermanshah back from Salar al-Dowleh.[295] When Salar al-Dowleh and Yar Mohammad Khan left the city both forces passed each other without firing a shot; apparently one force took the highway the other the rebels a less frequented mountain road. The other version is that the armies indeed passed in sight of one another without exchanging a blow, because the Bakhtiyaris and *mojaheds* refused to fire on Salar al-Dowleh and his men.[296] A third version given is that "the object of each of the Commanders appears to be plunder. The theory current here for some time a tacit understanding between Salar-ed-Dowleh and Firman Firmah is now regarded as probably correct. ... Salar-ed-Dowleh and Firman Firmah may

292. Destree 1976, pp. 248-49. While all this was going on the government in Tehran paid 200 *tumans* per month for the upkeep Salar al-Dowleh's wives and children in Tehran. Adhari 1378, doc. 117.

293. IOR/L/PS/20/261/7, 'Persia. No 1 (1913). Further correspondence respecting the affairs of Persia', p. 146 (no. 293).

294. IOR/L/PS/20/261/7, 'Persia. No 1 (1913). Further correspondence respecting the affairs of Persia', Townley to Grey 02/10/1912, pp. 187-89 (no. 370 plus enclosure); Malekzadeh 1328, vol. 7, p. 244. According to Hamadani 1354, p. 410 they left on 10 September/

295. IOR/L/PS/20/261/7, 'Persia. No 1 (1913). Further correspondence respecting the affairs of Persia', Townley to Grey19/09/1912, p. 156 (no. 318),174 (no. 338); Malekzadeh 1328, vol. 7, pp. 244-45.

296. IOR/L/PS/20/261/7, 'Persia. No 1 (1913). Further correspondence respecting the affairs of Persia', Townley to Grey 02/10/1912, pp. 187-88 (no. 370).

exchange towns."[297] Whatever the truth, a fact is that the two opponents changed cities without firing a shot.

FARMANFARMA

After having returned to Kermanshah on 14 September 1912, there was continued friction between Farmanfarma and the chiefs of the Bakhtiyaris and the *mojahed* troops. The *mojaheds* had insulted the Russian flag on the house of a Russian subject and Farmanfarma feared assassination if he did not take action. He informed McDouall that the Bakhtiyaris and *mojaheds* did not obey him when ordered to pursue Yar Mohammad Khan and they also refused to pursue Salar al-Dowleh. After they had looted some villages he was afraid to do anything. From the Bakhtiyari leaders, Shehab al-Saltaneh and Ziya al-Soltan, McDouall learnt that they were dissatisfied with Farmanfarma, who had taken no steps to punish the rebels and only wrote letters to them rather than using force. He gave appointments to men who were rebels and did not even force them to pay fines to get a government pardon. Also, they did not trust the *mojaheds* and feared that some might even join Yar Mohammad Khan. An additional problem was that the current *mojahed* commander did not have the influence that Yeprem Khan had; they had all been proud to serve under him, but after his death said why should they serve under an Armenian? They would no longer fight and had wired Tehran that they were no longer responsible for the security of the province and were leaving. In the afternoon of 19 September 1912, the Bakhtiyaris and Armenian *mojaheds*, some 800 men left the city, returning to Tehran. Farmanfarma immediately asked McDouall to recommend to Tehran that the Bakhtiyaris and *mojaheds* had to be recalled and money to be given to him to raise a local force. Previously (July 1912) he had said that he needed 300 *mojaheds*. McDouall felt that a local force could not be trusted as long as Salar al-Dowleh was in Iran. The same held for the tribes, with the possible exception of part of the Sanjabis, because the tribes were only loyal to themselves and no one else, government or pretender, and were ready to join either side for plunder. A local force in charge of the arsenal would immediately defect to Salar al-Dowleh if he promised it the looting of Hamadan, and probably the nucleus of the defectors would be Hasan, Mo'in al-Ra'aya's brother; in short a situation as bad or worse than tribesmen.[298] When at Kangavar the chiefs were able to convince the deserting force to stay there until Tehran had sent relief troops. They stated that they had been fighting for a constitution and the *Majles*, and refused to continue fighting when the former was ignored and no hope for the latter to be summoned. However, Tehran was only able to send 150 Bakhtiyaris and no more. Without them the government force in Kermanshah had no fighting value. The British and Russian Ministers told the Bakhtiyari Prime Minister and Minister of War that if they could not raise Bakhtiyari troops and stop them from meddlding in politics they would withdraw their support from the Bakhtiyaris. This resulted in part of the Bakhtiyaris at Kangavar returning to Kermanshah, while the rest went to Hamadan

297. IOR/L/PS/10/212, File 211/1912 'Turkish Arabia Summaries', p. 5.
298. FO 248/1053, McDouall to Tehran. 19/09/1912; Hamadani 1354, pp. 411-12.

Fig. 7.5: Consul Nikolsky and Farmanfarma (1913). © *Collection Molitor, Ed. Elytis* no. 220.

to reinforce the garrison there. Salar al-Dowleh was said to have gathered 7,000 men and appeared to no longer claim the throne but wanted an independent Iran under a constitutional government.[299]

SALAR AL-DOWLEH DEFEATED

Although Kermanshah was in government hands again this did not mean that the city was safe and secure. As stated above part of the troops were unwilling to fight given the political situation in the country that did not agree with the reasons why they had been fighting and had left. Moreover, Salar al-Dowleh threatened the city again, while most of the government troops had gone to 'Abbasabad. When alerted to the threatening situation its leaders wired the olama that they would be back in Kermanshah by 30 September. Meanwhile, Salar al-Dowleh had wired McDouall that he would leave 27 September for Kermanshah, and on 28 September it was reported that Yar Mohammad Khan was with a force at Kamarian at 35 miles from Kermanshah. Farmanfarma repeatedly had asked for funds, as he believed that local levies would fight for

299. IOR/L/PS/20/261/7, 'Persia. No 1 (1913). Further correspondence respecting the affairs of Persia', Townley to Grey19/09/1912, pp, 156 (no. 318),173; Idem, Townley to Grey 02/10/1912, pp. 187-88 (no. 370); Malekzadeh 1328, vol. 7, p. 246; Hamadani 1354, pp. 416-17.

him if paid. The tribes were not willing to fight for him, even when well paid, unless the Bakhtiyaris force would be there. The 250 Cossacks were not reliable, because it was due to their cowardice or worse that he had lost in May at Hamadan. On 26 September 1912 a large group of people came to the Russian and British Consulates with a petition, an action instigated by Farmanfarma, and the petition only was agreed upon after many meetings and all swearing together. The people really wanted security. Salar al-Dowleh had looted the city in February and the villages were plundered by both parties. Heavy sums were exacted by Salar al-Dowleh and smaller sums by Farmanfarma. The people would submit to anyone as long as they were left in peace. Farmanfarma had orders to hold the city, but he only had enough men to hold the citadel. The petitioners also asked the consuls to protect them, who replied that they only would protect the *basti*s, but not their families and property in the city.[300]

> We the undersigned people of Kermanshah each one representing one community and it is a long time that we are not masters of our lives, property, good name, and honor. Everyone from every side attacks this one handfull of earth. Except killing and plunder it has in the end no other result for the unfortunate people of Kermanshah and especially in these days we see that our honour (irz va namus), lives, and property, are really in danger. Therefore, we are compelled to take refuge in the Consulate. We beg you the representative of a Great Power neighbour to the unfortunates to obtain, in whatever way you know, safety of life, honour, and good name, for we can endure no more and until you give us security of life, property and good name we will not leave the Consulate, and request that the government troops for war and the troops of Salar ed-Dowleh do not enter the town but fight outside.
>
> Seals of mujtahids as follows:
> Sultan al-Ulema, Aga Muhammad Mahdi, Aga Sheikh Hadi, Aga Rahim, Imam Juma, Aga Abul Hassan, Aga Shams ed-Din, Haji Aga Wali, Shuja al-Ulema, Zahir al-Ulema, Aga Muhammad Sadiq, Naib Sadr.
> Following princes and Khans. Amin al-Mamalek, Sardar Iljal, Mutazid ed-Dowleh, Zafar Ashraf, Samsam as Sultan, Akram ed-Dowleh, Amir Muqtadir. Mutazid as Sultan, Naser ed-Diwan, Abul Hassan Khan, Mansur ed-Diwan, Shuku‘ as-Sultan, Haji Hassan Khan Kalantar, Quli Khan, As‘ad ed-Dowleh. Muhammad Jawad Mirza, Salar Muhtisham, Sarem as-Sultan, Mirza Ali Khan, Muhammad Taqi Khan, Chiragh Ali Khan, Seyeed i Nizam, Abu Seyeed Khan, Fathullah Khan, Ebrahim Khan, Muawen al-Mulk, Haji Ibrahim.
> Following merchants and traders. Rais et-Tujjar, Haji Seyid Habibullah, Haji Saeyd Baqir, Haji Mulla, Tahir Sarraf, Hussein Hasan, Muhammad Tahir, Muhammad Ali, Malek Muhammad, Haji Ali Akbar, Amanullah Khan. Maled

300. IOR/L/PS/20/261/7, 'Persia. No 1 (1913). Further correspondence respecting the affairs of Persia', pp. 175 (no. 434), 202-03 (no. 395); Hamadani 1354, p. 414; Adhari 1378, p. 33 (doc. 120; a day later they sought refuge with the Ottoman consul-general). Eyn al-Saltaneh 1377, vol. 5, p. 3684 refers to the total insecurity in the Hamadan area caused by all sides, whether rebel or government.

Mohammed, Aga Barar, Sayid Muhammad Ali, Seyid Mohammed, Seyid Mustafa, Shuja el-Nizam.[301]

On 3 October 1912, Salar al-Dowleh and Yar Mohammad Khan with 1,000 men arrived at Mian Darband, 35 miles from Kermanshah. The two consuls requested that they not fight in the city; they gave Farmanfarma two days to leave the city and face them in the field. Farmanfarma had given his troops orders to leave on 6 October. However, on 5 October 1912 at 2.30 a.m. Yar Mohammad Khan attacked the city. He entered the town through the *darvazeh-ye mahalleh-ye Barzeh Dagh* in the s.e. and the *darvazeh-ye mahalleh-ye Chenani* in the west and took control over a large part of it. Farmanfarma held the government buildings, the Bakhtiyaris and Sanjabis ChiaSorkh with two guns. At 9 a.m. Yar Mohammad was shot in the head. He had 50 Kalhors with him who fled immediately and came to the British Consulate asking for asylum, which was refused, apart from a few wounded men. The rebels withdrew fighting and there was shooting till afternoon. At that time, some 300 Kurds came to the British Consulate, while under heavy fire seeking asylum. Farmanfarma promised their life if they surrendered. McDouall disarmed them and found that their only arms were some clubs. They were escorted to their own district; the wounded were taken to the Farmanfarma hospital. McDouall estimated that only some 200 persons had died. This number differs significantly from that of Mo'tamadi, according to whom most of Yar Mohammad Khan's force, which was centered in the gardens south-east of the city awaiting news, was shelled by the Bakhtiyaris and Armenians. Even two weeks later they were still burying the about 3,000 dead Kurds. After this defeat the Kalhors tried to join the fight, but they were defeated by the Bakhtiyaris. It was generally believed that Yar Mohammad's death meant the end of Salar al-Dowleh's rebellion. Yar Mohammad's second-in-command, Hoseyn Qoli Khan was able to escape with his men.[302] Thus, finally peace returned to the city after four years of unrest, Molitor, the Belgian Customs officer wrote. Nevertheless, he wanted to leave, because he blamed the Russians for having fomented disorder in Kermanshah as it was one of the main routes through which British goods entered.[303]

---

301. FO 248/1053, Petition of *bastis*; IOR/L/PS/20/261/7, 'Persia. No 1 (1913). Further correspondence respecting the affairs of Persia', pp. 203-04 (no. 395)

302. IOR/L/PS/20/261/7, 'Persia. No 1 (1913). Further correspondence respecting the affairs of Persia', pp. 177 (no. 348), 204 (no. 395), 212 (no. 414); Soltani 1386, pp. 192-95; Malekzadeh 1328, vol. 7, pp. 247-48; Hamadani 1354, p. 415; Eyn al-Saltaneh 1377, vol. 5, pp. 3654, 3668. Yar Mohammad Khan had taken the city at night due to Mo`aven al-Molk and Ilkhani, who were supposed to guard the gates. These traitors, who led Yar Mohammad Khan to the Divankhaneh, were protected by Farmanfarma, because they were partners in another crime, in this case of the local bread ring. Molitor 2018 a (letter 22/10/1912 to Mornard); Idem 2018 b, p. 8 (600 Kurds and mojaheds died). For details about the battle in Kermanshah and an appreciation of Yar Mohammad Khan, see Soltani 1381, vol. 3, pp. 640-71; see also the contemptuous opinion of Eyn al-Saltaneh 1377, vol. 5, pp. 3665 (Yar Mohammad Khan, the bush cutting gum collector was appointed army commander, governor of Kermanshah and marcher lord (*sarhaddar*) of both Iraqs, while Mojallal al-Soltan became governor of Kurdistan and the prince's deputy). 3760.

303. Destree 1976, pp. 249-50.

FARMANFARMA, AGAIN

When the danger of Salar al-Dowleh was a ghost of the past, Farmanfarma all of a sudden received more assistance. Jahanbakhsh, a Guran chief, arrived with 200 *savar*s to join Farmanfarma. But there was still some local trouble. On the night of 11 November 1912, the sons of Hajj Mo'adel and Hajj Rostam Beg escaped from prison in the palace and were said to be in the Turkish Consulate, which the consul denied. On 14 November, the assistant-governor Saham al-Dowleh left to Asadabad and other villages with a gun and 200 men to secure the city's environs. Despite his more secure position Farmanfarma felt he needed to strengthen it. Therefore, his agents asked the notables to sign a testimony that praised his administration with the request to retain him, but many refused, because it contained some falsehoods. In early November 1912, 'Abbas Khan, grandson of the late Da'ud Khan Kalhor, sent back the 10 Cossacks sent to support him as chief of the Kalhors. It appeared that 'Abdollah Khan the *farrash-bashi* of the late Da'ud Khan, who escaped when Yar Mohammad was defeated, told 'Abbas Khan and Soleyman Khan, son of Da'ud Khan, who were collecting forces to attack each other, that Salar al-Dowleh was attacking Tehran and that the ex-Shah had returned and they should be ready to assist the former, and thus, they reconciled.[304] Despite the arrival of more assistance in November 1912, the government was losing control over the city, every night there were robberies in the outskirts of the city. Without an armed escort, officials were unable to leave the city. The roads to and near Hamadan were also unsafe.[305] On 23 November 1912, Farmanfarma received news that Hoseyn Qoli Khan Mojahed with the son of Hajj Rostam Beg and the Balawands intended to attack the city that night. He made preparations and the inhabitants hid their goods. However, the rumor was false; Hoseyn Qoli was pardoned and was expected to join the governor. Because Farmanfama reinforced his palace people became afraid; on 30 November 1912 he said because he did not get funds that he had resigned.[306]

What did not help in this situation was that in November 1912 the Persian Cossacks asked Tehran for permission to depart. On 6 December 1912, with the only maxim gun, the force of 150 Cossacks left to Tehran. Their presence had been a great support for the governor's authority, who now only had 300 infantry and about 300 levies, "armed with obsolete pattern rifles." The tribes had 4,000 repeating rifles plus ordinary ones.[307] Hoseyn Qoli Khan, the *mojahed*, who had refused to side with Yar Mohammad Khan and had joined Farmanfarma, negotiated with the rebels with the result that all but Salar Mozaffar returned. He had sought asylum in the Turkish Consulate. When Mo'aven al-Ra'aya arrived, all adherents of Salar al-Dowleh were in town; most of them robbers and ruffians who had plundered the city in February 1912.[308] One of them, 'Ali Aqa Kheshtmal had broken into the government grain store when Yar Mohammad Khan held sway in Kermanshah and sold its contents to him. But Farmanfarma had a use for

304. Political Diaries vol. 4, p. 629.

305. Political Diaries vol. 4, p. 630.

306. Political Diaries vol. 4, pp. 630, 646; vol. 5, p. 12; IOR/L/PS/20/261/7, 'Persia. No 1 (1913). Further correspondence respecting the affairs of Persia', p. 277 (no. 518).

307. Political Diaries vol. 4, pp. 630, 646; vol. 5, p. 12; IOR/L/PS/20/261/7, 'Persia. No 1 (1913). Further correspondence respecting the affairs of Persia', p. 277 (no. 518)\.

308. Political Diaries vol. 5, p. 12.

this as well as for other ruffians. This one he sent to 'Abdollah Khan, the *farrash-bashi* of the late Da'ud Khan Kalhor to induce him to come back into the government fold. 'Abdollah Khan was the man who had brought Salar al-Dawleh to Kermanshah and was with him till the end and he fled when Yar Mohammad Khan died. He was said to have looted goods to the value of £100,000. 'Abdollah Khan was at Mahidasht and willing to come in on condition of an amnesty and he promised to give presents. Meanwhile, the town was unsafe. The Ilkhani and his followers in town were no longer used as road guards and many of these ruffians were induced to leave. Prices were high which invited robbery. In the night of 23 December 1912, three persons were murdered in their house, which was plundered. Several merchants were robbed. The modus operandi of the thieves was that they pretended to bring a letter and when the door was opened a dozen men rushed in. The inhabitants were kept under guard while others plundered the house. On 2 January 1913, two robbers were caught and executed. Also the house of a notorious robber, Mohammad 'Ali Cenal, was plundered and burnt by the governors' Cossacks. The British consul wondered whether Farmanfarma finally would begin to govern, which he had not done so far. Merchants were rightly afraid and had hired guards.[309] According to Molitor, Farmanfarma opposed any reform at Kermanshah that ran counter to his personal interests.[310]

Farmanfarma's task was in principle made easier when in December 1912, Tehran and Moscow concluded an agreement by which Russia would make a monthly guaranteed sum of 30,000 *tuman*s (about £6,000) for the governor of Kermanshah for an indefinite period for administrative expenses and upkeep of the military force.[311] Thus, Farmanfarma's repeated complaints of lack of funds and blaming his inability to do his job thus, had lost its justification. Would he now finally begin to rule and bring order to the province? Unfortunately, his activities continued to be focused on enriching himself and enflaming the existing disorder rather than reducing it. Farmanfarma treated the Qalkhanis well as they paid him *pishkash*. As a result, even those robbed by them while on pilgrimage were not allowed to complain.[312] On 3 January 1913, 'Abdollah Khan *farrash-bashi* of the late Da'ud Khan arrived with 2,000 *tuman*s of the Kalhor revenue and 50 *savar*s; these were engaged for the government by the Customs department. 'Abdollah Khan was still in the city and his presence and that of the Ilkhani was a source of danger. On 8 January the two parties passed each other in the street; the Ilkhani men taunted the others, but 'Abdollah Khan restrained his men and reported the incident to Farmanfarma. Thereafter, the latter detached some of the Ilkhani's men to other parts of the city and he told everyone that he intended to arrest the Ilkhani if possible. This was to frighten him to flee with his men, because the Farmanfarma believed it would be dangerous to arrest him. However, McDouall blamed Farmanfarma's self-interest, pointing out that in 1910 Nezam al-Saltaneh had arrested several faction leaders who had more men and did nothing. Ilkhani's men tried to rob Molitor's house on 18 January; the result was two dead. The Ilkhani also exacted some money from Hajji Ahmad, a leading merchant. On 23 January 1913, the Ilkhani with all his men left town to a village 10 km away. On 25 January Farmanfarma left with 200 men and two

309. FO 248/1073, Kermanshah Diary no. 1, ending 2 January 1913.

310. Destree 1976, p. 305

311. IOR/L/PS/20/261/7, 'Persia. No 1 (1913). Further correspondence respecting the affairs of Persia', p. 266 (no. 501).

312. FO 248/1073, Kermanshah Diary no. 15, ending 10 January 1913.

mountain guns and surrounded the village. After some shots the Ilkhani, his brother and some followers escaped through the part where the Kalhors were. The village was then taken and the Ilkhani's son, ShahRokh, who had committed some murders in the last two years, was captured and shot by a *mojahed*. The Kalhors left the Ilkhanis' men among the villagers after disarming them. Farmanfarma did not pursue the Ilkhani who was said to have taken refuge with Sardar Akram. Later it was reported that none of the tribes wanted to help him. He wrote to Farmanfarma that he had always obeyed him and had fled to avoid fighting with him. According to McDouall, the province was in such a state that it would be difficult for the governor's successor to establish even some semblance of order.[313]

Tehran wanted to send a police chief (*ra'is-e nazmiyeh*), but Farmanfarma said this was not necessary, because he had appointed a good man, Mahmud Khan *mojahed* as such.[314] In the last week of December 1912 there had been a dispute between Kalhors and Sanjabis concerning the winter pasturage, which resulted in fighting. In January 1913, peace was arranged between the Kalhors and Sanjabis by the section chiefs.[315] On 29 January 1913, Farmanfarma received a letter from the Kalhor and Sanjabi chiefs that they offered to attack the Qalkhani Gurans, who were then in the Zohab plain; if not, the latter would return to their hills after the winter, where it was difficult to attack them. This was to punish them for their many robberies at the Pay Taq pass. Farmanfarma declined having been paid off by the Qalkhanis.[316]

According to McDouall, it was hopeless to expect anything from Farmanfarma. The latter officially informed him that he would sent Hoseyn Qoli Mojahed to recover stolen goods belonging to British subjects, but he did not go, because Farmanfarma asserted that he could not reduce his force in town. At the same time, Farmanfarma received money from the Kalhors and others, probably the money from these very same robberies. He claimed that he was unable to do anything without money, when money was given he then said that he wanted rifles, and finally he disclaimed any responsibility as he resigned. When Farmanfarma heard there was a new cabinet in Tehran he withdrew his resignation. He got all the bad characters into town, but refused to arrest them. His non-action after the failed robbery at Molitor's house upset the Europeans. The leader of the robbers was known, but Farmanfarma did not allow any action to be taken. Unless Farmanfarma was made personally responsible for goods stolen nothing would happen, McDouall wrote. But even against such an eventuality Farmanfarma had taken steps by placing all his property under Russian protection. According to McDouall, Kermanshah needed an active governor to keep trade going, and British trade was the only action in town. What he did not consider a good option was to let Farmanfarma go and leave Kermanshah without a governor.[317]

---

313. Political Diaries vol. 5, pp. 37-38; FO 248/1073, Kermanshah Diary no. 3, ending 16 January 1913; FO 248/1073, Kermanshah Diary no. 4, ending 23 January 1913; 'Persia. No 1 (1914). Further correspondence respecting the affairs of Persia', p. 25 (no. 51).

314. FO 248/1073, Kermanshah Diary no. 3, ending 16 January 1913. For the organization chart and pay of the police force established by Farmanfarma, see Soltani 1381, vol. 4, pp. 765-67. McDouall issued a notice that "in future any person guilty of offences against the central of provincial government if they take refuge at the consulate will be handed over to the authorities." FO 248/1073, McDouall to Townley 16/01/1913.

315. Political Diaries vol. 5, pp. 12, 37.

316. Political Diaries vol. 5, pp. 37-38.

317. FO 248/1073, Kermanshah Diary no. 6, ending 23 January 1913.

Samsam al-Mamalek, the Sanjabi chief, continued trying to make an alliance among all the tribes of Kermanshah through marriage and intrigue against the Kalhors. The alliance seemed to be strong enough to defeat the Kalhors. Samsam al-Mammalek had included several notorious bandits in the league, such as Mahmud Khan, governor of Bisotun. Farmanfarma remained in the city but did not take any responsibility as governor.[318] Meanwhile, he continued to repeat his old refrain that he could do nothing against tribesmen; to do that he needed money, rifles, cannons, ammunition and men. Also, money alone was useless, unless he could send it to Tabriz to have men come from his estates and have arms and ammunition come from Europe and India. McDouall urged him to take some action to open the road to Baghdad, but Farmanfarma said that he could not put pressure on the tribes, because if he did, they all would become defensive. He had only ammunition for a few hours of fighting. He had asked Tehran for all he needed and he was willing to leave for Europe if nothing was sent. Molitor confirmed the lack of ammunition and he said Farmanfarma would be more active if he received what he had asked. McDouall suggested to use the Sanjabis and the Kalhors against Qalkhani robbers, which Farmanfarma said would cause chaos and total insecurity. Farmanfarma's assurance that he would promote British interests was hollow as these all depended on the road being open. Although thereafter goods were arriving via the Kalhor road where exactions were less, their volume was only 10% of the monthly average.[319]

In March 1913, the Ilkhani was still in Gokal village with two notorious thieves, Sayyed Mahmud and Mohammad 'Ali Ginel, and some 10 men. He tried to get a pardon from Farmanfarma, "who knows that he has some money in the Bank through his cousin 'Ali Pasha Khan." The latter was paid by the government and with 30 *savar*s guarded the Dizabad road. In the same month, the Director of Finance and Customs received 30,000 *tuman*s from the Treasurer-General for provincial expenses, to be paid monthly. Farmanfarma was expecting 150 *savar*s from his estates in Azerbaijan and on their arrival, he intended to leave on a tour to Qasr-e Shirin to put the road in order. Preparations were being made. He was very bitter against the Sanjabis who helped him against Salar al-Dowleh in May 1912, because they were friends of the Bakhtiyaris. Also, they robbed some goods and exacted illegal fees, but so did the Kalhors and Qalkhanis, who had fought against him.[320]

Hoseyn Qoli Mojahed accused Mohammad Khan Mojahed, the chief of police, with whom he was on bad terms, to employ bad characters as policemen, which, according to McDouall was untrue. What was true was that Hoseyn Qoli Mojahed had hired some unsavory characters as *savar*s and taken them under his protection.[321] The security situation inside the city did not improve, the more so, because Hoseyn Qoli Mojahed paid his men only a small part of their wages, who, therefore, took goods without paying, harassed women and sometimes killed people. However, Farmanfarma considered him capable, as he arrested robbers, and therefore, refused to punish them. The only positive sign was that the trade roads were safe and the post

318. IOR/L/PS/20/261/7, 'Persia. No 1 (1913). Further correspondence respecting the affairs of Persia', p. 306 (no. 561).

319. FO 248/1073, McDouall to Barclay, 22/02/1913.

320. Political Diaries vol. 5, pp. 68-69.

321. FO 248/1073, Kermanshah Diary no. 8, ending 20 February 1913; Idem, McDouall to Townley, 17/04/1913 (the chief of police, Mohammad Khan, a very capable man, but in a difficult position).

Fig. 7.6: Cavalry crossing the Qara Su near Kermanshah (1912). © *Collection Molitor, Ed. Elytis* no. 232.

was more regular; it took 10 days from Tehran and Baghdad, and 6 days from Hamadan. The Qalkhani Guran chiefs, who were in the city, told Farmanfarma who the robbers were in Pay Taq. However, he dare not arrest them, but sent somebody to get the stolen goods.[322] To reward 'Abdollah Khan *farrash-bashi* for settling the differences between the Kalhors and Farmanfarma, he was given a widow of Da'ud Khan in marriage, who was the daughter of the late hereditary Ilkhani Mohammad 'Ali Khan, and famed for her beauty.[323] However, despite the patching up of relations, Soleyman Khan Sardar Firuz, son of Da'ud Khan, was still afraid to come to Kermanshah and asked for a safe-conduct. This was granted, except for the payment of revenues and the British claims.[324]

Farmanfarma was playing games, with himself as the game master, with the objective to significantly improve his financial position. From the very beginning he used the argument that he needed money to restore tranquility to the province, and when Tehran sent money, he said that he needed arms and ammunition. Another ploy of his was to regularly threaten or submit his resignation to get his way with the central government. In May 1913 Farmanfarma said he

322. FO 248/1073, Kermanshah Diary no. 14, ending 03/04/1913.
323. FO 248/1073, Kermanshah Diary no. 11, ending 13/03/1913.
324. FO 248/1073, Kermanshah Diary no. 12, ending 20/03/1913.

had telegraphed Tehran his resignation as he did not receive ammunition. Also, Kurdistan was taken from him, about which he was pleased, but it was also considered to separate Malayer from which the current Kermanshah garrison was drawn.[325] Towards the tribes of Kermanshah, Farmanfarma pursued a policy of playing them off against one another and using the possible threat of his support to one of the rival parties to influence their uncertainty. In early 1913, Farmanfarma had decided to isolate the Sanjabis, partly because of ʻAli Akbar Khan Sanjabi had refused to sell Farmanfarma a horse that he had set his heart on.[326] Farmanfarma'iyan intimates that this enmity was due to Sanjabi support for Salar al-Dowleh.[327] However, that support was rather weak, and finally the Sanjabis defected and helped Farmanfarma defeat Salar al-Dowleh. If it was the real reason, why did Farmanfarma not have the same enmity towards the Kalhors, who were Salar al-Dowleh's main supporters till the very end? The real reason was that the Sanjabis had good relations with the Bakhtiyaris, whom Farmanfarma hated. As a result, ʻAli Akbar Khan, who had been already more than one month at Mahidasht, did not come to Kermanshah and sought allies and went to make friends with Salar Rashid Kurdistani. Farmanfarma showed friendship to the Qalkhani Gurans to use them against the Sanjabis. When in May 1913, Ehtesham al-Mamalek Kerendi did not come to Kermanshah, because he was afraid that Sanjabis would trespass on his territory when returning from the plains, Farmanfarma sent some Cossacks to Kerend to make the Sanjabis stick to their usual route.[328] Although Farmanfarma for personal reasons targeted the Sanjabis, this did not mean that this tribe was always behaving well. This questionable behavior was not so much the fighting in April 1913 between Sanjabis and Arabs in Iraq, where the former had grazing lands, as this was a rather normal occurrence between all tribes. However, Samsam al-Mamalek Sanjabi, who was in charge of Qasr-e Shirin, tyrannized its inhabitants and exacted money from them.[329]

In May 1913, Farmanfarma pleased with his arrangement with the Gurans turned to the Kalhors, whose chieftainship was shared by ʻAbbas Khan, grandson and Soleyman Khan, son of the late Da'ud Khan, both boys were under 18.[330] The Sanjabis seeing through Farmanfarma's plans tried to form a united tribal front against the governor. Samsam al-Mamalek Sanjabi tried to unite the Kalhors, Sanjabis, Kerendis and Neyrizhis to oppose Farmanfarama and the Qalkhanis. The British consul doubted that the Kalhors would join such a tribal front, as they were counting that travelers would pass through their country, so fighting was not in their interest. However, Samsam al-Mamamlek made a speech to the Kalhor chiefs and said he had been their enemy, had joined Farmanfarma to fight against them, but as tribesmen: "why kill each other; let's be friends, maintain order in the province, but, while obeying Farmanfarma not to allow him to extract money from them." All kissed his hands and the two young chiefs said

---

325. Political Diaries vol. 5, p. 131 (The Peyravand, who depend on the sale of their produce to Kermanshah, were recently (May 1913) pardoned on condition of not robbing anymore but did so again); Soltani 1381, vol. 4, p. 768.

326. FO 248/1112, Kermanshah Diary 04/02/1915; FO 248/1073, Kermanshah Diary no. 29, ending 17/07/1913 (Samsam al-Mamalek bemoans that government service is not rewarded and that he better give the celebrated horse to Farmanfarma).

327. Farmanfarma'iyan 1382, vol. 2, pp. 265, 267.

328. Political Diaries vol. 5, p. 131; FO 248/1073, Kermanshah Diary no. 16, ending 17/04/1913.

329. Political Diaries vol. 5, p. 103.

330. Political Diaries vol. 5, p. 131; FO 248/1073, Kermanshah Diary no. 16, ending 17/04/1913.

he was their father and made an alliance and matrimonial contracts.[331] Another result of the bid for unity was that Ehtesham al-Mamalek Kerendi made peace with the Kalhor and Sanjabi chiefs, his former enemies. They now all agreed in their enmity towards the Qalkhani Gurans; the smaller tribes were also with them.[332] In June 1913, 'Ali Akbar Khan, son of Samsam al-Mamalek Sanjabi, told two gendarmes that he did not understand why Farmanfarma favored the Qalkhani Gurans who were robbers and murderers? The Sanjabis had and did not act against government and had asked the governor to treat them fairly and punish the Qalkhanis or allow them to do so and not to grant Qalkhanis land at Zohab. If Farmanfarma failed to do so, the Sanjabis would inform the town's notables and telegraph Tehran. If there was no result, they would be forced to oppose Farmanfarma, though remaining faithful to the central government in Tehran. The gendarmes reported this to the police chief, who told Farmanfarma. The latter continued to sow dissension among the tribes to prevent them from joining Samsam al-Mamalek. He reminded the Kalhor *kadkhoda*s of Samsam al-Mamalek's enmity towards them and that he had protected them against the Bakhtiyaris and Sanjabis. This intervention had some success, because some *kadkhoda*s wrote the governor that they would disobey their chiefs.[333] On 5 June 1913, prime minister Eyn al-Dowleh wired Farmanfarma that Lorestan and Borujerd were added to his province, which as of then consisted of Kermanshah, Thalatheh (Malayer), Borujerd and Lorestan. Hamadan apparently was not included. Farmanfarma was not expected to accept.[334]

SALAR AL-DOWLEH, INTERLUDE

Although Salar al-Dowleh had fled to Astarabad and in the first part of 1913 was killing and plundering in the Caspian provinces he still had supporters in Kurdistan and Kermanshah. In April 1913 he wrote to some of them that he would be returning and his supporters were looking forward to that. Also, news was circulating in the city that the prince would arrive shortly, which the British Consulate in Kermanshah quickly discredited by making it known that at that time the prince was in Bandar-e Gaz.[335] Nevertheless, the rumors that the prince had occupied Mazandaran and would come to Kurdistan, which then did not have a governor, caused much anxiety in Kermanshah.[336] It also resulted in activities by Salar al-Dowleh's local supporters.

> I am informed that Mahmed Khan, ex-mujahid, the chief of police [of Kermanshah] , one of those who deserted Yar Mohamed when that officer

331. Political Diaries vol. 5, pp. 131-32; FO 248/1073, Kermanshah Diary no. 18, ending 01/05/1913.

332. Political Diaries vol. 5, p. 167

333. Political Diaries vol. 5, p. 168; FO 248/1073, Kermanshah Diary no. 22, ending 29/05/1913. The Sanjabis were under a curse and therefore, could never fight against the central government. Likewise, the Vali of Posht-e Kuh who said: "we have a familial curse [*la`nat-nameh*] that we should not oppose the central government." Soltani 1384, p. 117.

334. Political Diaries vol. 5, p. 167. On 18 July 1913, Sardar Mo`tazed and forces arrived in Kermanshah. He acted for Farmanfama when he went on tour. Political Diaries vol. 5, p. 231.

335. FO 248/1073, Kermanshah Diary no. 18, ending 01/05/1913.

336. FO 248/1073, Kermanshah Diary no. 21, ending 22/05/1913.

> declared for Salar ed Dowleh, and who has caused general satisfaction by his organization of the town police, is very anxious about the future. I understand that he had reported to Farmanfarma that under pretence of gambling there are nightly meetings of adherents of Salar ed Dowleh at the house of Salar Mozaffur, and he fears that they are in consultation with Salar ed Dowleh. This Salar Mozaffur is a man of low character and responsible for many of the executions and plunderings when Salar ed Dowleh was here. He was for some time in "bast" at the Ottoman consulate but has now been pardoned and favoured by Farmanfarma, probably because he can tell where some of the loot left behind, when Salar ed Dowleh left, is concealed. This was the man who negotiated between the town people and Salar ed Dowleh to bring that prince here from Luristan in December 1911. Stories of renewed activity by Salar ed Dowleh are being circulated by his adherents.[337]

In May 1913, Salar al-Dowleh's supporters in Kermanshah continued to spread stories of his victories and his occupation of various towns. They were believed to be in secret contact with him via dervishes or pilgrims. The fact that Farmanfarma had started making new fortifications only reinforced the belief among the population that Salar al-Dowleh would be coming and increased their anxiety.[338] There was also an increase in plundering of villages, which was said to be due to the rumors of Salar al-Dowleh's successes and his expected return, and "to the absence of any punishment for such offences."[339] On 5 June 1913, there was finally an end to the rumors, because on that day Farmanfarma received news from Tehran that Salar al-Dowleh had fled into the direction of Kurdistan and was instructed to take steps to arrest him, if he came to Kermanshah.[340]

The Russians felt embarrassed by the prince's actions and sent Persian Cossacks under two Russian officers to arrest him. Salar al-Dowleh had fled to the Jaf Kurds. By mid-June 1913, he was at Divan Darreh, 10 *farsakh* from Senneh, where the Kalbegis had joined him. He wrote to many people and sent messengers to Senneh, saying that he had come to restore order, that these districts were especially his, and he appointed Vakil al-Molk as its governor. Meanwhile, 'Eyn al-Dowleh, the Prime Minister, telegraphed Asar al-Divan, the governor of Senneh, that troops were en route, that this time no pardon would be given to the rebels, and that he had to see to it that the prince was unable to raise a force. This news was said to have a positive effect on the people of Senneh, where the prince was said not to be welcome. Salar al-Dowleh sent a letter to Aqa Habibollah, the agent of the IBP in Senneh, writing him not to flee again, but to trust him and "to greet the traders his dear children from him." Salar al-Dowleh wrote to Soleyman Khan, the son of Da'ud Khan Kalhor, that he had come to revenge his father. He showed the letter to the Kalhor *kadkhoda*s who told him not to join the prince again, and therefore, he sent an evasive answer. The heads of the other tribes were also in correspondence with the rebel-prince, but it was believed that they used this as leverage to get Farmanfarma agree to their

337. FO 248/1073, McDouall to Legation, no. 49, 24/05/1913.
338. FO 248/1073, Kermanshah Diary no. 22, ending 29/05/1913.
339. FO 248/1073, Kermanshah Diary no. 23, ending 05/06/1913.
340. FO 248/1073, Kermanshah Diary no. 24, ending 12/06/1913.

demands and that it was very unlikely that they would join him. Nevertheless, people in Kermanshah were very worried, because they knew that the prince's supporters were in contact with him. Also, he would come to take control of the Customs, being in need of money. Farmanfarma intended to send Sayyed Akbar Shah and Ra'is al-Tojjar to advise Salar al-Dowleh to remain where he was, in which case he would intercede for him with the government. However, when pointed out that the two emissaries were not to be trusted, he abandoned this plan. Officials at Miyan-Band intercepted a bundle of letters from Salar al-Dowleh to Salar Mozaffar, Hasan Mo'aven al-Ra'aya, the Kalhor chiefs, and others, as well as their replies to him, which they handed over to Farmanfarma.[341]

Farmanfarma made preparations to oppose him, to which end he had recently received reinforcements. Nevertheless, the notables of Kermanshah criticized him for not being firm with Salar al-Dowleh and his followers. Farmanfarma had allowed former supporters of the prince to return to Kermanshah, including Salar Mozaffar, the prince's main supporter and responsible for most of the exactions and executions during his stay in the city. In May 1913, Farmanfarma even invited him to an official military review at the *Meydan*. "This caused much cursing by the native spectators and soldiers, including the Cossacks, who were cursing the Farmanfarma and the government for allowing it."[342] The governor told the British consul that he knew what people said and although Salar al-Dowleh as "his brother-in-law and cousin is dear to him," he would act against him if he rebelled. Townley, the British Minister in Tehran also had doubts about Farmanfarma, because "his loyalty is somewhat doubtful, and he is as arrant a coward as Salar." It was known that Salar Mozaffar had sent a messenger to Salar al-Dowleh, who was reported to have arrived in Qaratowreh district, 14 *farsakh* from Senneh, where there was no one to oppose him.[343] It may well be that Salar Mozaffar carried a proposal from the governor, because Prime Minister 'Eyn al-Dowleh replied to Farmanfarma's offer to negotiate with Salar al-Dowleh "that the prince had caused so much loss to life and property that negotiations would be impossible and measures were being taken to capture him." Farmanfarma sent official copies of the telegrams from the Telegraph Office to the tribal chiefs concerning the troops en route and measures taken against Salar al-Dowleh. The Sanjabi and Kalhor chiefs forwarded the letters sent by the prince to Farmanfarma. When letters from Salar al-Dowleh arrived for two Qalkhani chiefs, on duty with 200 men in Kermanshah, they fled. On 22 June, in Senneh, notables, olama and tradesmen held a meeting to decide whether or not to receive Salar al-Dowleh. It was

---

341. FO 248/1073, Kermanshah Diary no. 26, ending 26/06/1913; Shahedi 1381, pp. 654-55. Government of Great Britain 1914, p.149 (no.307); Idem, Townley to Grey, 18/07/1913, pp. 124 (no. 277), 125 (no.282); IOR/L/PS/18/C144, 'Extracts from Annual Persia Reports, 1906, 1909, 1910, 1911, 1912, 1913 regarding loans, and complete reports for 1908 & 1913', pp. 15; IOR/L/PS/10/212, File 211/1912, 'Turkish Arabia Summaries,' p. 12; Adhari 1378, doc. 1; Hamadani 1354, p. 426.

342. FO 248/1073, Kermanshah Diary no. 21, ending 22/05/1913. Farmanfarma had invited all unsavory bad characters, who fled after Salar al-Dowleh's defeat, back into town with the argument that it was safer as he could keep an eye on them. Therefore, people suspected that the governor himself was a supporter of the rebel-prince. FO 248/1073, McDouall to Legation, 24/05/1913. Even in November 1913, McDouall reported "the policy of Farmanfarma appears to be to support adherents of that prince [Salar al-Dowleh] against his opponents as he supports the Kalkhani against the Sinjabis." FO 248/1073, Kermanshah Diary no. 46, ending 13/11/1913.

343. Government of Great Britain 1914, p.126 (no. 285- Townley to Grey, 23/07/1913); see also pp. 126-27 no. 287, p.149 (no.307); IOR/L/PS/18/C144, 'Extracts from Annual Persia Reports, 1906, 1909, 1910, 1911, 1912, 1913 regarding loans, and complete reports for 1908 & 1913', pp. 15; FO 248/1073, Kermanshah Diary no. 25, ending 19/06/1913.

unanimously decided to refuse him entry and the notables were asked to mobilize men to take care of the town's defense. They wrote the prince that supplies were short and they feared the anger of the government, therefore, he was not welcome and if he would come they would oppose him. On 29 June the notables with some 1,000 men left to oppose Salar al-Dowleh, who only had some 100 Kalbegis and 50 Turkish Jafs with him at Kuleh, at some 8 *farsakh* from Senneh. Unable and unwilling to meet with this force, Salar al-Dowleh fled from that location.[344] However, he remained at about 10 *farsakh* from Senneh, but moved each day to a different village. He still had a small force of Kalbegis and Jafs with him, and tried to extort 5,000 *tumans* from a village headman by torture. On 4 July 1913, a force led by Russian officers with four guns and 50 loads of ammunition arrived and camped outside Kermanshah.[345]

Salar al-Dowleh, supported by some Jafs and Kalbegis, was near Sennah, moving from one village to the other and extorting money from the *kadkhodas*.[346] On 17 July 1913, Salar al-Dowleh surrendered to the Russian officer in charge of the Cossacks who had been sent to arrest him.[347] Shortly thereafter the prince asked for permission to visit a sick friend and gave his parole that he would not flee. However, he did not return and went among the Kurdish tribes to raise troops. When this failed Salar al-Dowleh surrendered to the Cossack force sent after him.[348] With the good offices of the Russians, Salar al-Dowleh negotiated the payment of a pension of 10,000 *tumans* or £1,800 per year and an outfit allowance of £600 from the Persian government on condition that he went to Switzerland. If he would return to Persia he would lose his pension and Russian goodwill. Salar al-Dowleh left Kermanshah on 5 October 1913 under escort of a Russian officer plus a detachment of Cossacks for Rasht and Europe. He arrived in Baku on 23 October 1913. A Russian officer escorted him all the way to the Swiss border, where his pension was monthly paid by the Russian Legation.[349]

FARMANFARMA, LAST TIME

With the Salar al-Dowleh threat out of the way, the main topic of discussion in the city in mid-September 1913 were the elections for the *Majles*. Farmanfarma had received strict orders

344. FO 248/1073, Kermanshah Diary no. 27, ending 03/07/1913.

345. FO 248/1073, Kermanshah Diary no. 28, ending 10/07/1913.

346. Political Diaries vol. 5, pp. 200-01.

347. Shahedi 1381, pp. 654-55. Government of Great Britain 1914, Townley to Grey, 07/07/1918 and 18/07/1913, pp. 124 (no. 277), 125 (no. 282), 149 (no.307); IOR/L/PS/18/C144, 'Extracts from Annual Persia Reports, 1906, 1909, 1910, 1911, 1912, 1913 regarding loans, and complete reports for 1908 & 1913', pp. 15; IOR/L/PS/10/212, File 211/1912, 'Turkish Arabia Summaries,' p. 12; 'Persia. No 1 (1914). Further correspondence respecting the affairs of Persia', Townley to Grey, 07/07/1913, p. 124 (no. 277); Adhari 1378, doc. 1; Hamadani 1354, p. 426.

348. IOR/L/PS/10/212, File 211/1912, 'Turkish Arabia Summaries,' p. 10; 'Persia. No 1 (1914). Further correspondence respecting the affairs of Persia', p. 160 (no. 324), p.151 (no.311); Adhari 1378, p. 39-40.

349. Government of Great Britain 1914, Townley to Grey, 17/09/1913, p. 152 (no. 319); Idem, Townley to Grey, 07/10/1913, p. 164 (no.339); Fortescue 1920, pp. 30, 33; Eyn al-Saltaneh 1377, vol. 5, p. 3947 (he left Tehran in a car); Kazembeyki 2003, pp.195-96; Colby and Churchill 1914, p. 534; Sharif Kashani 1362, vol. 3, p. 789; Political Diaries vol. 5, pp. 200-01; Ettehadiyeh and Sa`vandiyan 1366, vol. 1, pp. 211-14; IOR/L/PS/18/C144, 'Extracts from Annual Persia Reports, 1906, 1909, 1910, 1911, 1912, 1913 regarding loans, and complete reports for 1908 & 1913', pp. 15; Adhari 1378, p. 39 (docs. 156-57).

to organize the elections, although he opposed them. It was expected that he would recommend to appoint somebody from Tehran, if there were riots in the city. Names of candidates mentions included: Mo'tazed al-Dowleh, the president of the *'adliyeh*, Mohammad Baqer Mirza, chef de cabinet, Mo'azed al-Molk, the *kargozar* and Sheikh Morteza. They were all members of the *E'tedaliyun* party and the last two were favored by Farmanfarma, because he thought that they would support him in Tehran.[350] Private meetings were held by Democrats in opposition to Farmanfarma. Samsam al-Soltan Kalhor was mentioned as a potential candidate, while Sayyed Hoseyn Kazzazi, member of he last *Majles* and a Democrat arrived from Tehran, clearly also staking his claim. Dr. Heydar Mirza's name was also mentioned as a candidate. Farmanfarma was waiting for the elections to have taken place in Tehran, before holding them in Kermanshah.[351]

In early October 1913, a conflict broke out between Farmanfarma and his deputy who also was governor of the city of Kermanshah, Sardar Mo'tazed, when the latter wanted to collect certain fees that Farmanfarma wanted for himself. The Sardar was very much upset and allegedly told to the messenger said: "that he was ashamed of Farman Farma's conduct. He, being a wealthy man, drew pay for all his servants and grooms as government sowars and collected presents from brigands instead of punishing them. Such things were all very well under the ancient regime, but with Europeans in charge of the Treasury it did not do and he heard from Tehran that His Highness was the laughing stock of the capital. As he was afraid of sharing the disgrace he was writing to Tehran to try and obtain his own recall."[352]

The two men settled their conflict and shortly thereafter, Farmanfarma with 1,000 men and four guns was at Harsin with some levies from the Ahmandavand Gurans and Kangavar, but no Kalhors and Sanjabis. He promised the Kakawand chiefs that no harm would befall them, if they gave him satisfaction.[353] On 9 November 1913 there was a fight between the Sanjabis and Qalkhanis; of the latter some were killed; they complained to Farmanfarma, who said he would come and see to things, but he did not and thus, both parties made peace. Meanwhile, Farmanfarma continued his policy of sowing dissension among the tribes. On 30 November 1913 Farmanfarma returned with his force from Harsin. He had exacted much in cash and kind from Kakawands. The Turkish claims of 28,000 *tuman*s against the Kakawands was settled with 6 *tuman*s. Farmanfarma offered 60% payment for the British claims, which probably would be accepted.[354] In February 1914, 'Abbas Khan Kalhor went to Zohab with some chiefs and met with Shir Khan Qalkhani and other Guran chiefs; they conferred with Sardar Moqtader (Ali Akbar Khan Sanjabi) and swore an alliance with him.[355]

---

350. FO 248/1073, Kermanshah Diary no. 39, ending 25/09/1913.
351. FO 248/1073, Kermanshah Diary no. 40, ending 02/10/1913.
352. FO 248/1073, Kermanshah Diary no. 42, ending 16/10/1913.
353. Political Diaries vol. 5, p. 329.
354. Political Diaries vol. 5, pp. 364-65. See also FO 248/1073, the Kermanshah Diary nos. 43-47. In mid-December 1913, it was learnt that `Abdollah Khan Farrash-bashi had been seriously wounded in a fight and `Abbas Khan slightly. FO 248/1073, Kermanshah Diary no. 51, ending 18/12/1913.
355. Political Diaries vol. 5, p. 421.

WORLD WAR I PERIOD

THE EVE OF AXIS INTERFERENCE

On 2 August 1914, shortly after the outbreak of WW I, Turkey signed an alliance with Germany to join the war against the Allied Powers. As yet Persia was not impacted by this development. Business at the border was as usual, although in October 1914, the Turkish authorities were ill-treating pilgrims and Persian residents at Khaneqin; the road to Qasr-e Shirin was closed. As a result, there was great scarcity at Khaneqin, which depended for much of its daily necessities on Persian imports. Hearing about the maltreatment of pilgrims, Sardar Moqtader went to the border and sent a message to the Khaneqin authorities demanding an explanation, adding, if they wanted a fight he was as always ready, but they should not harass defenseless pilgrims. He threatened to take it out on any Turkish soldier found on his side of the border. The Turks sent a conciliatory reply, referred his complaint to headquarters and stopped harassing pilgrims.[356]

It was only in December 1914 that for the first time, signals were given that the Turks were interested in having Persia join the war with them. At that time, "Turkish subjects occasionally talk of 'Jahad' and are told that the only 'Jahad' for Persians was one against Turkey." In fact, in every mail the *Ettehad-e Eslam Society* of Baghdad sent pamphlets calling on Persians to join their brothers in Islam. One preacher in Kermanshah commented that only when they were in trouble the Turks said that Persians were fellow Moslems.[357] Given the tense situation caused by the various calls to arms the Turkish authorities exercised strict censorship on all postal articles entering the country. Letters had to be in French or Arabic only and in open covers.[358] Although in reaction to the British occupation of Basra in December 1914, a jihad proclamation was circulated in January 1915, the olama at Kermanshah suppressed it, arguing that the olama of Kerbela "only endorse defence if Islam is attacked and no result is probable here."[359] At that time the new *Majles* was dominated by members of the clergy and in particular by a clerical-political party, which wanted an alliance with Great Britain, which partly explains this neutral reaction. In November 1914, Townley, the British Minister in Tehran wrote to Sir Edward Grey, the British Foreign Secretary:

> The clerical section of this party, with whom I am on friendly terms, has sent me spontaneous assurances that during the first ten days of Moharrem no pro-Turkish sermons will be preached, and advantages of siding with us will be sedulously put before the people. Messages have also been sent to the Ulemas of Mesopotamia and of the Shiah faithfully telling them programme of Persian Government, and that priests do not favour a Turkish policy, and exhorting

356. Political Diaries vol. 5, p. 548.
357. Political Diaries vol. 5, p. 569.
358. Political Diaries vol. 5, p. 569; vol. 6, p. 2.
359. Political Diaries, vol. 6, p. 2.

> them not to preach holy war, of an intention to do there have been some signs at Mohammerah and Kermanshah.[360]

Meanwhile, local politics in Kermanshah continued as if there was not a looming problem at the border. On 22 July 1914, Farmanfarma had written to the Consuls that he would postpone his resignation until after Ahmad Shah's coronation and he asked that any future correspondence not be addressed to him. At the end of August 1914 the Russian consul tried to prevent Farmanfarma's resignation; he arranged for a telegram to be send by a number of notables to Tehran, but he failed to have the bazaar closed down.[361] In August 1914, after the election, the vote count showed a majority for each of the Democrat candidates, but there was no official result yet.[362] However, Farmanfarma did not want the Democrats to win, as he belonged to the *E'tedaliyun* or Moderates, and therefore, in September, he incited a certain Hasan to disband the election commission with the excuse that the elections had been carried out incorrectly. People protested, the bazaar was closed, the Koliya'is declared themselves to be Moderates and the Sanjabis and part of the Kalhors announced they were Democrats. Farmanfarma, who could not prevent that Kermanshah had become a Democrat stronghold, remained with his deputy Asadollah Khan Sardar Mo'tazed in Kermanshah until early October 1914. Even before he left the deputies were chosen, but he telegraphed Tehran that some people had complained about irregularities in the elections.[363]

When Farmanfarma left Kermanshah no successor had as yet been appointed. The absence of a governor from Kermanshah had a negative effect. Some bad characters were making trouble and the British consul feared that if they were not stopped, the situation might get out of hand. Sardar Ejlal, the acting governor and the *kargozar* were local men and thus, had to protect their private interests. Many *shabnameh*s were thrown into the British Consulate's doorway, many partly decipherable. Several targeted the *Alliance Israélite* calling to expel all Moslem pupils from their school or the Jewish quarter would be attacked. One said: "close the school for one month, or else." The chief of police increased patrols in that quarter. Another *shabnameh* called for a meeting in the main mosque on 1 January 1915, but the olama did not know anything of this. Other *shabnameh*s were directed against Europeans, especially the Russians. Sardar Ejlal only sent for some merchants belonging to the Democrat party and told them to stop this activity, as if it were the Democrats doing this, which was unlikely, as Qavam al-Olama, the local leader of the Democrats and other prominent Democrats had sons at the *Alliance* school. Everybody thought that the instigators were Mehdi 'Abdol-Rasul and Mirza Nasrollah, who both were interested in establishing a rival school. Previously, Mehdi 'Abdol-Rasul had often given trouble to the American missionaries for the same reason. Mirza Nasrollah had been refused Turkish protection and was a known bad character. He would have been expelled from Kermanshah, if

360. IOR/L/PS/10/463, File 3136/1914 Pt 2 'German War. Situation in Turkish Arabia & Persian Gulf' Townley to Grey 18/11/1914. He further reported that the Cabinet, though sympathetic towards Great Britain, wanted to maintain a complete and strict neutral attitude, because it feared that public opinion would disapprove of an open espousal of Great Britain and its allies.
361. Political Diaries vol. 5, p. 524-25.
362. Political Diaries vol. 5, p. 524.
363. Soltani 1378, vol. 1, p. 110.

he had not been hired as the Russian consulate's *monshi*.[364] Later Farmanfarma used him for his intrigues against the Democrats and he was given the title of E'temad al-Tojjar. At the beginning of 1915, he was said to be an intimate of the Turkish consul, which may have inspired the text of some of the letters. Yusef Elwindi, a Turkish Christian was also said to be involved. Some *shabnamehs* asked the olama to denounce the proclamation to assist the Turks or to take to the field themselves. These activities were in line with that of the Ottomans in general and in particular, of the Ottoman consul, who in the last week of December had put pressure on the preacher (*khateb*) of the Friday mosque to read the *khotbah* in the Ottoman Sultan's name. The preacher informed the governor and the consul received orders from his embassy to desist. On 4 January 1915, Sheikh 'Abdol-Hamid, who had become a Turkish subject, left with a group of ruffians to join Ottoman forces in Iraq; they were sent off by other ruffians; in short, there was great insecurity in town. The *kargazor* reported that the Turkish consul had given nationalization papers to some 200 persons in the Senneh area.[365]

AMIR MOFAKHKHAM

In early January 1915 the appointment of Lotf 'Ali Khan Amir Mofakhkham Bakhtiyari as the new governor of Kermanshah was announced. His imminent arrival immediately created a problem. Mr. Deweerdt, the finance director said that he was unable to pay the troops Amir Mofakhkham wanted to bring with him and Tehran informed him it was unable to send money. If the soldiers would remain unpaid it would reduce Amir Mofakhkham's prestige and it also might lead to disorder. Deweerdt suggested the new governor stop recruiting soldiers. The British consul felt that he could not tell Amir Mofakhkham that he did not need any soldiers, because to bring order to the province he needed those, unless he used the Sanjabis who could provide 1,000 men. On the other hand, if he did not want to leave the city of Kermanshah he only needed a personal guard. To put the province in order the Kalhors needed to be forced to pay revenue.

364. It was not the only time that the Russians hired unsavory characters. Dolgopolov, the acting consul, employed a *monshi*, who was a local prince and somewhat mad or 'divaneh.' His relatives made fun of him. "Baha al-Soltan and Mehdi Abdol-Rasul have convinced the acting consul to give in writing to the notorious Mehdi Hasan, Mo`aven al-Molk, a paper certifying his loyal services and usefulness in keeping order. He was part of Salar al-Dowleh's men, who plundered the city when he took it. Although Salar al-Dowleh's man he was employed by Farmanfarma, because he was one of the last old faction leaders and had a band of ruffians in his pay. He lately has been restraining his ruffians as his position is precarious awaiting arrival of the new governor. Kargozar is troubled that Russian and Turkish consulates are neighbors as Dolgopolow is very nervous and he's afraid something might happen when Cossacks and courts go out to meet the new governor. Dolgopolow does not care to meet others, even Russians." FO 248/1112, Kermanshah Diary ending 14/01/1915

365. FO 248/1112, McDouall to Tehran, 07/01/1915; Idem, Kermanshah diary ending 07/01/1915. In the week thereafter, some more *shabnamehs* were distributed. "The Nazmiyeh know who by, but as they are not the men accused by acting governor they cannot do anything." FO 248/1112, Kermanshah Diary ending 14/01/1915. Around 10 January 1915, Khalifeh Rasul with 200 ruffians left Kermanshah to fight with Turks.

Amir Mofakhkham or his representative then had to go with a force to Harunabad. Formally there should have been three local regiments, but none were in service at that time.[366]

Before the new governor left Tehran, Sepehr went to see him on 17 December 1914, promising German support and gave him a portrait of Wilhelm II.[367] Because of the weather Amir Mofakhkham wired ahead that people shouldn't come to officially welcome him (*esteqbal*). He arrived on 18 January 1915. The welcoming group consisted of several chiefs. Amir Mofakhkham had 200 men with him; his son followed with another 200, and another 600 were to follow later.[368] This account of the *esteqbal* contradicts that of Mo'tamedi, who writes that the new governor was so full of himself that those welcoming him had to take off their shoes and were not allowed to sit in his presence, thus upsetting the elite of Kermanshah. As a result, most notables refrained from further seeing the governor. Therefore, Amir Mofakhkham's stay in Kermanshah was bound not to last very long.[369] Sardar Moqtader had a famous horse, which he showed to Amir Mofakkham. The latter asked for a horse of the same stock. Farmanfarma had coveted that horse and when Sardar Moqtader did not give it to him it was one reason for his quarrel with the Sanjabis.[370]

Amir Mofakhkham did not make major changes in the provincial administration. Sardar Ejlal continued as assistant to the governor; Mohammad Baqer Mirza, the *shahzadeh-bashi*, continued as *chef de cabinet*. Also, some clerks were rehired. However, Mahmud Khan, the ex-chief police was arrested, because of some rifles and horses that had disappeared. To many people this seemed to be an injustice, because he had remained faithful to the central government, when other *mojahed*s had joined Salar al-Dowleh's rebellion. He and 24 men took refuge in the British Consulate. Of these, 17 had joined the police and their rifles and horses were accounted for, but now the administration claimed that he was responsible for the seven others.[371]

In February 1915, insecurity in the city increased. Amir Mofakhkham published a statement that Persia was neutral and he banned any support of the Turks, probably also in reaction to the increased activity by the Turkish consul. This sign was torn down by some of the town's ruffians, who were Turkish subjects, which led to a clash with the police. Amir Mofakhkham met with the Turkish consul and then dismissed the chief of police, the son of Bahador al-Soltan. Meanwhile, some people and mullahs were collecting subscriptions for the volunteers, some of whom, such as Khalifeh Rasul and his party returned. Meanwhile, 30 Persian Cossacks with a maxim gun arrived in Kermanshah and reinforced the local troops.[372] 'Ali Akbar Sanjabi advised Amir Mofakhkham to take no action against the Kalhors in Kermanshah, because if he did they

---

366. FO 248/1112, McDouall to Legation, 19/01/1915. Lotf `Ali Khan Amir Mofakhkham, "a man of no education and an intriguer." Begin 1915 appointed governor of Kermanshah and resigned summer 1915. "Old and stupid, very religious." Was at odds with the other Bakhtiyari Khans (he was a partisan of Mohammad Ali Shah) and was appointed Ilkhani in 1921-22. IOR/L/MIL/17/15/11/5, 'Who's Who in Persia (Volume III) Arabistan, Luristan, Isfahan & Bakhtiari', p. 23.

367. Sepehr 1337, p. 137; Soltani 1381, vol. 4, pp. 774-75

368. FO 248/1112, Kermanshah Diary ending 21/01/1915; Political Diaries, vol. 6, p. 26.

369. Soltani 1386, pp. 198-99.

370. FO 248/1112, Kermanshah Diary ending 04/02/1915.

371. FO 248/1112, Kermanshah to Legation, 26/01/1915.

372. FO 248/1112, Kermanshah Diary ending 21/01/1915. Political Diaries, vol. 6, p. 26.

would leave the city and no others would come. McDouall advised Amir Mofakhkham to go to see the Kalhors before spring, because in Kermanshah all governors customarily dealt with the tribes in winter, when they were all at Zohab. The governor wanted to go, but complained about the lack of money for his troops.[373] Therefore, Sardar Ejlal went to Gilan (Kalhor district) to collect the taxes and the *pishkesh*. Soleyman Khan Kalhor refused to pay and said that 'Abbas Khan Kalhor was a boy and they did not owe 17,500 *tuman*s. When 'Abbas Khan said that he was not a boy, Soleyman Khan reacted: "then you pay your share, I won't pay mine."[374]

THE GERMANS AND OTTOMANS ARRIVE

Surprisingly Kermanshah, which was in the Russian zone of influence, was not secured by Allied forces, despite its strategic location.[375] This 'negligence' to guard the backdoor to W. Persia was due to the fact that Great Britain did not want to wage war on Turkey, and did not expect any Turkish or German activity in a part of Persia, where none of the Allies had any immediate interest. Although Russia was at war with Turkey it did not take any preventive steps either, probably believing that the Axis powers had no designs on W. Persia. However, Axis activities could only be launched through there as Azerbaijan and Khuzestan were respectively under Russian and British control. Germany considered the universal Persian opposition against British and Russian presence in Persia and their violation of its neutrality a perfect vehicle to undermine the position of the Allies. Contrariwise, Turkey played the pan-Islam card to mobilize anti-Allied support in Persia. Although Turkey was a neighbor, it was the Germans who would take the lead in Persia to undermine the Allied position. Consequently, most of Germany's anti-Allied activities was channeled through Kermanshah. This, of course, resulted in a conflict between the European antagonists on Persian soil. The first time that they did so was in 1915. To start anti-Allied activities in W. Persia the German embassy wanted to have a consul in that area. The man chosen by default was Max Otto Schönemann, an old-Persia hand, who had managed a factory and a commercial firm in Tabriz and who knew that part of Persia well. Therefore, he had been appointed as consul in Tabriz, but as this was in Russian hands he could not go there, and thus, Soltanabad was selected as an alternative, because of the presence of a German-friendly community that managed the local carpet industry.[376]

The first sign that the Axis forces were going to undertake anti-Allied activities in Persia was the rather innocuous news that at the end of January 1915, a German consul for Soltanabad had arrived at Qasr-e Shirin with four attendants. The Turkish consul had rented rooms for him at Kermanshah. A second sign was the news that a Turkish force was sighted at Shahburan,

373. FO 248/1112, McDouall to Legation, 02/02/1915.

374. FO 248/1112, Kermanshah Diary 25/02/1915; Idem, Kermanshah Diary ending 29 January 1915. Both chiefs were boys, probably only 15 years old.

375. Already in 1888, Major-General Charles Metcalfe MacGregor, *The Defence of India: A Strategical Study*. Simla, 1884, p. 347, had pointed out that in case of war with Russia Baghdad could be reached quickly via Kermanshah and thus, vice-versa.

376. For the reasons of German involvement with Persia and its initial leading role as compared with that of Turkey, see Gehrke 1377, vol. 1, pp. 67-92; Bast 2002, pp. 112-16.

halfway from Baghdad. The Turks had already entered Persia in Azerbaijan (Maragheh; Urmiyeh) and Kurdistan, where at Chia Sorkh in Bajlan country they sealed the APOC rooms and put the Bajlans in charge of the oil wells, which were in the part of the Bajlan region allotted to Turkey by the frontier commission.[377] On 11 February 1915, the *kargozar* reported that Schönemann with two Afghans and two Caucasians had illegally and armed entered into Persia and was staying at Qasr-e Shirin for some time making propaganda among the tribes. He warned that if the government did not intervene the Russian consul would arrest him.[378] By the second week of February 1915, there were rumors that Turkish troops were at Qasr-e Shirin, which refers to the force led by Ra'uf Bey (see below). Amir Mofakhkham wired Samsam al-Mamalek Sanjabi, the governor of Qasr-e Shirin, who replied as long he was there, no Turk would cross the border. The German consul was still at Qasr-e Shirin, probably influencing the tribes, or so thought the British consul. Meanwhile, Turkish troops were making preparations at Qezel Robat some 35 km away. They asked Samsam al-Mamalek to let them pass en route to Kermanshah. He refused to do so, unless the Persian government told him differently.[379]

By mid-February 1915, Amir Mofakhkham received a report from Samsam al-Mamalek that a certain Sheikh Hasan had come to him on behalf of the olama with a document that called on Persians to join the Axis powers in their war against the Allies. Samsam al-Mamalek told him that Persia was neutral. Moreover, he should contact the governor at Kermanshah with such matters as he only executed the latter's orders. Meanwhile, some Turkish officers with 150 men came to Chia Sorkh ostensibly for the oil wells, but really to contact the tribes. Indeed, the Mandali Sayyeds asked the mother of Soleyman Khan Kalhor to induce the Kalhors to join the Turks. She promised to send some men, but she had to do so secretly, because Amir Mofakhkham was coming shortly to collect the taxes. Samsam al-Mamalek further reported that the German consul, who was joined by three other Germans and much baggage, send him a note advising him to ignore the Turks, but rather support Germany, which had no designs on Persia and acknowledged its neutrality. The Sanjabi chief further wrote that he could handle the Turkish force at Shahburan if it tried to cross the border. However, if regular Turkish army troops with guns would come he needed reinforcements from the government. The governor ordered Samsam al-Mamalek to maintain his position.[380]

According to Amir Mofakhkham, allegedly 300 cases of arms and ammunition had arrived at Qasr-e Shirin for the Germans. He opined that it would be better that Samsam al-Saltaneh went to Qasr-e Shirin to deal with this. The *sarhaddar* reported that Schönemann was preparing arms and proposed to intervene and have him escorted to Iraqi border. Samsam al-Mamalek contradicted the *sarhaddar* and was suspected to be on the Ottoman side by Tehran, possibly also because some olama had preached unity with the Ottomans, while his winter pasturage was partly on the Turkish side of the border. On 18 March 1915, the *sarhaddar* reported that consul Schönemann was very friendly with Samsam al-Mamalek, with whom he had daily contacts

377. FO 248/1112 Kermanshah Diary 04./02/1915; Political Diaries, vol. 6, p. 26; Ansari 1353, p. 127; Ducrocq 1923, p. 149 (the Turks at first prevented Schönemann from entering Persia); Soltani 1381, vol. 4, p. 774 (re Chia Sorkh).

378. Sepehr 1337, p. 145; for further developments, see Bayat 1381, pp. 35-37.

379. FO 248/1112 Kermanshah Diary 11/02/1915; Idem, Telegram Legation to McDouall, 11/02/1915.

380. FO 248/1112, McDouall to Legation, 16/02/1915; Bayat 1381, pp. 36; Soltani 1381, vol. 4, p. 776. There also were pro-Turkish activities at Malayer, see FO 248/1112, Kermanshah Diary 18/02/1915.

and went hunting. According to Schönemann's servants, Samsam al-Mamalek had said that if Schönemann brought him arms he would raise 4,000 men and join forces with the Ottomans. According to the Russians, Schönemann had distributed 40,000 cartridges among the Kurdish tribes.[381]

In addition to looming German trouble, there also was some other, be it minor, trouble coming from Iraq, this time religious-tinted trouble. After a cold reception at Qasr-e Shirin, Sheikh 'Ali, Sheikh al-Iraqeyn, son of the late Zeyn al-'Abedin, a leading Shia cleric came to Kermanshah where he arrived on 18 February 1915. He had sent a telegram from Qasr-e Shirin that he was coming and asked to prepare lodgings for him. The local olama were upset, because they did not want him to preach jihad, since after the troubled Salar al-Dowleh years they only wanted peace. Sheikh 'Ali had photos and letters from the olama in Kerbela, which did not get him a welcome reception, because the olama of Kermanshah basically ignored him. They told Sheikh al-Iraqayn to keep quiet and if he had anything to say to do so in Tehran as they would do nothing without orders from Tehran. Therefore, he stayed with the Turkish consul. Sheikh 'Ali was not the only one that tried to induce Persians to join the Axis cause. Those of Tavileh (near the Persian border) wrote to 'Ali Akbar Sanjabi that they had joined the Turks for jihad and invited him to join as well. He replied that he was in the service of the Persian government. Samsam al-Mamalek and the director of Customs at Qasr-e Shirin reported that Salar al-Dowleh and Amir-e Heshmat with 1,000 Turkish soldiers had come to Chia Sorkh, where the Bajlans, Fatah Beg Jaf and some Jaf tribesmen had joined them. Samsam al-Mamalek advised Amir Mofakhkham to take action against these tribes. With his son he could subdue them. Amir Mofakhkham promised to send 'Ali Akbar Sanjabi Sardar Moqtader to join his father at once with all available horsemen.[382] Sardar Moqtader said he would leave as soon as possible and that he had warned the governor about the Bajlans; he had arrangements with the Babajani tribe who would make the Jafs return. On 26 February 1915, Sardar Moqtader with 400 men arrived at Qasr-e Shirin (a distance of 170 km, which was quite a feat to do so in less than 48 hours). His father had 300 men, therefore, it was felt that there was no more danger.[383] At that time the Kalhors, Sanjabis and Gurans made much money by selling grain from Gilan and Zohab to German officers who supplied the Turkish force that was positioned near Qasr-e Shirin.[384]

On 26 February 1915, Schönemann with Capt. Wilhelm Paschen and another German, a physician (probably Dr. Niedermayer) and five Turks and several Persian servants arrived in Kermanshah. Schönemann wanted to rent a house for two months and hire 150 unemployed

---

381. Soltani 1381, vol. 4, pp. 776-80. Around 20 March 1915, with two Turkish officers, Schönemann had tried to get the Sanjabis to cooperate. IOR/R/15/2/1996, 'Who's Who in Mesopotamia, General Staff, India (Serial No. 372)', pp. 362 (on 8 April Germans with 70 boxes of rifles), 359. Schönemann himself reported that in February 1915, he and Samsam al-Mamalek had agreed to a covert collaboration, which resulted in the capture of Fathollah Khan, the *gholam-bashi* of the IBP en route to Baghdad, who allegedly had documents on the spy organization of the British in W. Persia. Ansari 1353, p. 128.

382. FO 248/1112, Kermanshah Diary 12/02/1915; Idem, Kermanshah Diary 25/02/1915 (Sheikh Ali was instead referred to as Sheikh Hasan); Idem, Kermanshah to Legation, 23/02/1915; Idem, Kermanshah Diary 18/03/1915; Gehrke 1377, vol. 1, pp. 137-38; Ducrocq 1923, p. 85. On the conflicting information about the presence, or not, of Salar al-Dowleh at the Persian-Iraqi border during WW I, see Floor 2018, pp. 105-113.

383. FO 248/1112, McDouall to Legation, 27/02/1915.

384. AIR 20/663, p. 79.

Fig. 7.7: Schönemann in his Tabriz factory (1910)

*savar*s, but when Amir Mofakhkham heard this he told them not to do so. Schönemann allegedly called himself a Moslem and made clear that he had come to cause trouble in Kermanshah and expel the British and Russian consuls. He dined with the Turkish consul every night. On 4 March 1915, Amir Mofakhkham left with his son and 300 soldiers to Zohab returning via Gilan (Kalhor district) to collect taxes. Before his departure, he appointed Montazam al-Daftar as governor of Kermanshah. He was a young man with no experience, whom he had taken as *monshi* from Tehran. Fateh Beg Jaf said that he was loyal to Persia, while Sardar Ejlal collected 10,000 *tuman*s from the Kalhors.[385]

Schönemann rented a house for 6 months and paid 300 *tuman*s in cash. He initially hired 20 men whom he armed with rifles and revolvers. He wanted to hire *savar*s from some local leaders, who refused. He also bought cartridges of all patterns. Schönemann's hired guns went around in streets armed, which was contrary to police regulations, and therefore, the British consul informed the *kargozar* about this. The *kargozar* told Schönemann's *monshi* that this was not allowed. Schönemann then wrote to the British consul that if he had a problem he should write officially to the *kargozar*, who then would write officially to him. Because the *kargozar* did not want to get involved writing to someone who had no official position, he sent a verbal reply saying it was no concern of consuls, but a police regulation. Schönemann then replied that

385. FO 248/1112, Kermanshah diary 04/03/1915. According to Gehrke 1377, vol. 1, p. 140, Schönemann felt threatened by the strong local influence of the British and Russian consuls, the more so, since had no protective force as the consuls did. They allegedly distributed money among their partisans to counter German influence.

his men would comply with the regulations, as long as they were not on duty. The *kargozar* wrote to the Ministry of Foreign Affairs, which asked the German Legation to send Schönemann as soon as possible to Soltanabad.[386]

Schönemann's house was visited by many people who wanted to be hired as guards. He gave out that he did not like to offend them by refusing to see them. It was also said that he had commitments from several Khans for *savar*s. However, there was no proof. Schönemann inspected all potential hires, but said he would hire them when needed. He was constantly changing the men who were in his service, probably to try them out. Meanwhile, two more Germans had arrived, who were going to Isfahan as consul and vice-consul with 14 mule loads, which looked like they contained ammunition and rifles. Another four Germans were still in the city. Two of them gave their names as Prof. Iritche and Dalkersone, but on the telegram the real name of one of them, Zugmayer, was to be seen. By that time Schönemann had mobilized enough local support, including among the gendarmerie that he felt to be in a strong position and that the influence of the British and Russian consuls had decreased.[387] In fact, according to Zugmayer, Schönemann had induced a number of employees of the Telegraph office to give him the original text of all his telegrams so that the British could not make use of them, if they ever would get hold of the German code. Also, he received all the drafts of the telegrams sent by the British consul, which the latter did not destroy but simply threw in the waste basket.[388]

Here, I want to say something about Schönemann's background. In 1907, Max Otto Schönemann came as a carpenter to Persia, first working in Khoy.[389] However, he clearly wanted to achieve more and in 1908 came to Tabriz to seek betterment. There he put himself under Russian protection, meeting with Vladimir Minorsky, who was consul in Tabriz at that time.[390] Schönemann then got involved with a certain Mr. Grumach of Berlin to continue Mr. Mossig's business of the Aslan Company, and, because of that in a legal dispute.

> When in the summer 1908 Mr. Mossig, local manager of the Aslan Company, a German firm, returned to Berlin, he left the management to Mr. Jacobs, a Nestorian of Persian nationality, without any exchange of documents. In the fall of 1908, Mr. Schuneman produced a power-of-attorney from the Aslan Company and took over the stocks from Mr. Jacobs against a signed receipt. Mr. Schunemann then declared that Mr. Jacobs had not transferred all the stock received from Mr. Mossig and claimed 4,000 *tuman*s. the value of the goods not delivered. The case was tried at the Russian Consulate-general under whose protection Mr. Schunemann then was. Mr. Schunemann was ordered to produce certain

386. FO 248/1112, Kermanshah Diary 12/02/1915; Idem, Kermanshah Diary 18/03/1915; Gehrke 1377, vol. 1, p. 137.

387. FO 248/1112 McDouall to Legation/Townley, 16/03/1915; Idem, Kermanshah Diary 18/03/1915; Gehrke 1377, vol. 1, p. 140. On 13 April 1915, the following Germans arrived in Kermanshah: Litten, Wustrow, Col. Heller, Friedrich, Jacob. Niedermayer, Oscar, Silder [sic; Seiler?], Tukef, Dr. Niedermayer, Wagner, Fasting. IOR/R/15/2/1996, 'Who's Who in Mesopotamia, General Staff, India (Serial No. 372)', p. 126.

388. Ducrocq 1923, p. 164.

389. Nasiri- Moghaddam 2016, p. 411, doc. 109. According to FO 248/1112, Kermanshah Diary 18/03/1915, "he was once a carpenter at Urmiyeh."

390. Ansari 1353, p. 126.

> documents in support of his claim within 12 days, failing which he would have to pay Mr. Jacobs 5 tomans per day until the conclusion of the case, the money to be returned in the event of Mr. Schunemann winning the case. He never produced the documents, but invoked the assistance of the Anjuman to settle his claim, whereupon the Russian Consul General washed his hands of the case.
> The unfortunate Mr. Jacobs, who wished to leave Tabriz, was detained by the local authorities, whom Mr. Schunemann held responsible for the 4,000 tomans claimed, in the event of Mr. Jacobs departure before the settlement of the case. Ijlal-ul-Mulk, therefore, referred the matter to arbitration -one of the arbiters being Mr. Hildebrand Stevens - and the result was a decision in the favour of Mr. Jacobs. Nevertheless, the Acting Governor, intimidated by Mr. Schunemann, was afraid to let Mr. Jacobs go. For several months the case dragged on before various local authorities, until at last it came before the Ministry of Justice, where both parties signed an engagement to refer the case to arbitration and abide by the decision of the arbiters. The arbiters appointed by Mr. Schunemann and Jacobs themselves, were Mr. Grunberg, local agent of the Austro-Orientalische Gesellschaft, and Mr. Stevens respectively. After several months of deliberation the arbiters gave their award in favour of Mr. Jacobs, and the Ministry of Justice issued the usual confirmatory decree. Mr. Schunemann, ignoring his signed engagement, made several attempts to bring the case before the Karguzari, but the Karguzar, in view of the arbitral proceedings at the Ministry of Justice, refused to take cognisance of the case. ... Mr. Schunemann who is an ignorant man, and equally untrustworthy, must have totally misrepresented the facts to his Legation.[391]

Unfortunately, I have not been able to establish whether Schönemann finally paid. At any rate, Schönemann believed that the Russian Consulate had not supported his side very much. Therefore, he referred the matter to the local *Anjoman*, which made Mr. Pokhitonov, the Russian consul so angry that he withdrew Schönemann's Russian protection. In reaction, Schönemann induced the German Ministry of Foreign Affairs to appoint him consul in Tabriz. This smudge on his career was no obstacle for this appointment, for in early April 1909 Schönemann informed the foreign consuls in that city that he had assumed function of German consul. Nicholas, the French consul wrote that Schönemann had raised the German flag in front of his house, but that he had not contacted any of the other consuls in Tabriz in person.[392] He was able to establish a small woodworking factory in Tabriz, was engaged in import of machinery as well as of drugs, and household articles,[393] while he also was the head of a carpet company at Tabriz.[394] He managed this company until he left in 1914 for Berlin to volunteer his services for anti-Allied activities in Persia. In Kermanshah, the British consul McDouall noted that whilst the other Germans who came to that city in 1915 were polite, Schönemann was not. Because of having

391. FO 248/974, no. 25, Smart to Sir George Barclay, Tabriz 21 August 1908 (fol. 426).
392. Nasiri- Moghaddam 2016, p. 411, doc. 109, p. 423, doc 114.
393. See the commercial ad in Küss 1911, part V, pp. 24-25.
394. FO 248/1112, Kermanshah Diary 18/03/1915.

spent some seven years in Azerbaijan, Schönemann spoke Azeri, but not Persian and therefore, he employed Naser al-Vezareh as his interpreter in Kermanshah.[395]

Amir Hozur, the police chief, who was appointed new chief of police on 24 March 1915, was helping the Germans and introducing people to them as *savar*s. He received money for himself and his *kadkhoda*s. Two *kadkhoda*s accepted; a third reported it to Amir Mofakhkham who reported it to Tehran. The chief of police also had hidden from the deputy-governor that the Schönemann's servants went armed into the bazaar contrary to police regulations. Schönemann told the *kargozar* to complain about him in Tehran. The *kargozar* told the British consul that he should not give the Germans a reason to riot, as his guards were all local ruffians, who told their friends that they would rob the two banks in the city. Although the local authorities did not acknowledge that the four Germans had any official standing, they had orders from Tehran to treat them well until they moved on. Dolgopolov, the Russian consul, suggested to McDouall that they should arrest the Germans to which end he had wired his Legation.[396] On 21 March 1915, the Germans hoisted their flag. The *kargozar* protested and they did not do so thereafter. When riding about town the Germans were accompanied by 30 men; they had engaged Mo'in Nezam and Bahador Nezam, two gendarmerie officers with 25 *savar*s each, who wore a uniform.[397] On 30 March 1915, Dr. Erich Zugmayer and Capt. Griesinger left for Isfahan via Borujerd, where they met with Nezam al-Saltaneh, the governor of Lorestan, who promised them his support; in Isfahan they were met by the Swiss citizen, Geo Weber of the Hamadan carpet company, who was German consular agent in Hamadan.[398]

On 13 March 1915, Khorshid Bey, a Turkish Kurd attacked a village near Qasr-e Shirin. The Sanjabis pursued him and killed a few of his men and returned with plunder. Among those killed was a Turkish officer, Esma'il Haqqi, the leader of Turkish propaganda for Persia, while another was taken prisoner and, moreover, important papers were taken.[399] The Turks who were massing troops at the Kuretu oil wells asked Amir Mofakhkham to remove Samsam al-Mamalek from Qasr-e Shirin. They were annoyed because the Sanjabis had recovered confidential papers from the body of the killed Turkish officer. The Amir wanted Samsam al-Mamalek to return the Turkish rifles, who refused, because they were proof that the raiders were Turkish soldiers. He was also miffed because the Persian government expected him to defend the border, while it

---

395. FO 248/1112, Kermanshah Diary 18/03/1915.

396. FO 248/1112 McDouall to Townley, 20/03/1915. In fact, in mid-March, Mo`aven al-Dowleh, the Minister of Foreign Affairs refused to acknowledge Schönemann as consul in Soltanabad and told the German Legation that he had to leave Persia. However, Kardoff, the German charge d'affaires, was able to have the Minister reverse his decision. However, when the Minister learnt that Schönemann was not leaving for his post he threatened to withdraw his approval. Kardoff's intervention again prevented this. Gehrke 1377, vol. 1, pp. 140-41.

397. FO 248/1112, Kermanshah Diary 25/03/1915; Soltani 1381, vol. 4, p. 782 (the *kargozar* wanted to put an end to the hiring of sowars, but the governor disagreed as they were for the protection of the Germans).

398. FO 248/1112, Kermanshah Diary 01/04/1915; Bast1997, p. 20. It would seem that in general the German agents working in or crossing Persia en route to Afghanistan were well received by the various governors they met, but none went so far as to state that they supported the German cause. Wilhelm Paschen declared after his capture: "I can only say that all governors between Isfahan and the Afghan border came out to meet us and declared themselves our friends: they would probably do as much for you if you were passing that way." IOR/L/PS/10/210, Protocol of the Interrogatory ... of Wilhelm Paschen, 31 July 1916, appendix to Meshed Diary no. 33 for week ending the 12th August 1916; see also Ducrocq 1923, pp. 153-55.

399. FO 248/1112, Kermanshah Diary 18/03/1915; Idem, McDouall/Hamadan to Tehran 29/05/1915.

neither paid his *savar*s nor provided ammunition, while each cartridge cost 1.5 *qran* for his magazine rifles.

On 27 March 1915, Soleyman Khan came with 500 Kalhors to the governor's camp. Two days later the governor arrested him. The reason for his arrest was that he brought 3,000 *tuman*s saying: "this is all I have." The governor sent him to his revenue official to make up the accounts. Soleyman Khan said he was not afraid of some donkey *savar*s and if they arrested him what would they do. On being told the governor had him arrested as well as his brother and 15 Kalhor tribesmen; the other Kalhors fled taking the governor's transport, some 200 mules, with them. His son, Sardar Mo'azzam went in pursuit of them. The governor wired Kermanshah to immediately send him Mahmud Khan Hajjizadeh Kalhor, called Ilkhani, the son of the late Farrokh Khan, and *de jure* Ilkhani of the Kalhor, with all their *savar*s. Other levies and ammunition followed. When Hajjizadeh Ilkhani arrived, the governor made him chief of the Kalhor tribe with the title of Sardar Mozaffar. The governor also arrested the Qalkhani chiefs, because they were responsible for robberies at the Pay Taq pass.

The Germans and Turks at Mandali allegedly had asked 'Abbas Khan Kalhor Sardar Eqbal to send them *savar*s. He told them that he had to go see the governor at Zohab, but Mahmud Khan and 'Abdollah Khan *farrash-bashi* would meet with them. These two allegedly promised 800 *savar*s who would receive pay and a German badge. When 'Abbas Khan Kalhor heard about Soleyman Khan's arrest he allegedly sent all women and children to Mandali and himself with 1,000 *savar*s remained at Gilan. He allegedly promised the Germans 1,000 *savar*s; he himself would be paid 500 *tuman*s/month; other chiefs 100 and the *savar*s 25 *tuman*s each. The *savar*s had to come with a horse, while the Germans would give them rifles. The Turks promised to destroy the Sanjabis and give Qasr-e Shirin to the Kalhors and Soleyman Khan. Amir Mofakhkham sent 1,200 men against him, consisting of Ilkhani Kalhors, Sanjabis and Bakhtiyaris. The Yeylaqi Sanjabis (i.e. those who don't go to the winter quarters) were also sent for. McDouall pointed out to the deputy-governor if they would leave then there would be no armed force near Kermanshah to call upon, if need be. He then wired the governor pointing out that he needed a force in the city, in case of disturbances. The chief of police had only 100 men who were not all reliable. Otherwise, there were only 100 soldiers and Capt. Mamunov with his 30 Cossacks to protect the city. At McDouall's insistence, the *kargozar* had orders given to enforce the rules about bearing arms in the city; the main offenders were Schönemann's people, whom he asked again to respect the rules. The Democrats told McDouall that they did not want to oppose Great Britain, although admitting that some members might have acted irresponsibly.[400]

At the end of March 1915, the German and Austrian ambassadors entered Persia via Qasr-e Shirin and went to Kermanshah, where they arrived on 11 April. Schönemann, with many of his hired *savar*s and the Ottoman consul Rafiq Bey went to greet them, as did Samsam al-Mamalek. Four more Germans arrived at Kermanshah. Schönemann was hiring more men, who allegedly were all ruffians and of the criminal class, former supporters of Salar al-Dowleh. For some there was an arrest warrant; they were said to number 300, but McDouall believed that

400. FO 248/1112, McDouall to Townley 06/04/1915; Idem, Kermanshah Diary 01/04/1915; Idem, Kermanshah Diary 08/04/1915.

this was an exaggeration. The olama did not want to hear talk about jihad, unity of Islam and war, they only wanted to keep the peace in the city.[401]

Meanwhile, a force of Turkish irregulars and Kurdish tribesmen, a few thousand strong, commanded by Hoseyn Ra'uf Bey crossed the border taking Qasr-e Shirin on 12 April 1915.[402] In mid-January 1915, he had arrived in the border area and began gathering Turkish forces in that area, apparently assisted by German financing. He aimed to spread the Panislamist message and propagate the jihad among the Persians and thus, have the people rise up against the Russians and British. However, he, and others, would find that there was little interest in his message among the mainly Kurdish tribes of Kermanshah.[403] Initial reports estimated the force at 10,000 men with guns. Later, it was estimated at 500 regulars, 1,500 irregulars. Its commander Hoseyn Ra'uf Bey sent an ultimatum to Amir Mofakhkham that if Soleyman Khan was not freed within 24 hours he would attack Qasr-e Shirin and Samsam al-Mamalek. Dabir Homayun, the Persian agent at Khaneqin, asked for a two day's delay and went to the governor's camp. He wired Tehran that said he was negotiating with the Turks, and that Tehran should not interfere. The German ambassador offered to mediate between Amir Mofakhkham and Hoseyn Ra'uf Bey, while, at the same time, he asked the Ottoman government to recall Ra'uf Bey immediately, as this incursion ran counter to German strategy for Persia. Qavam al-Olama told the *kargozar* that if the governor would release Soleyman Khan he would be ruined and the Kalhors would come to Kermanshah and plunder it. The *kargozar* said that the Turkish consul had ordered the Turkish troops not to move, because the entire matter would be resolved amiably. Qavam al-Olama told his fellow Democrats that Sardar Ejlal, the *kargozar* and other Moderates wanted to disgrace Amir Mofakhkham and make the way free for Farmanfarma. By early May 1915, some Turkish troops were at the foot of Pay Taq, i.e. the border formerly claimed by the Turks. The Sanjabis had all left, leaving nothing, even the green crops were gone. They had asked for permission to attack the Turks, but Tehran gave no definite reply; the Sanjabis asserted that they could have easily defeated them. The Turks asked the Qalkhanis to close the Pay Taq pass, but the Amir had already left the plains. The Turks had offered Soleyman Khan 60,000 *tuman*s if he would join them; when he was arrested they promised Amir Mofakhkham to pay his tax arrears and the proved claims for his release, if he would not support the Sanjabis. The Germans were against Ra'uf Bey's taking of Qasr-e Shirin. Also, at Kermanshah, there was differences of opinion between the two Axis members. The Germans were against Amir Mofakhkham and the Turks were for him. Meanwhile, the situation in Kermanshah was quiet; many *savar*s hired by

---

401. FO 248/1112, Kermanshah Diary 08/04/1915; Soltani 1381, vol. 4, pp. 780-84; Gehrke 1377, vol. 1, p. 177. For a photo of the German ambassador's entry into Kermanshah on 13 April 1915, see Litten 1925, p. 227.

402. On the Iraqi population's reaction to this force's exactions and forced conscription during its march to the Persian border, see Political Diaries, vol. 6, p. 26. Hoseyn Ra'uf Bey, a friend of Enver Pasha. Formerly, captain of the cruiser 'Hamidieh'. Arrived in February 1915 at Mandali. Returned to Bagdad November 1915; left to Istanbul; was appointed chief of the naval head quarters staff on 13 March 1916. However, under the entry 'Rifaat Bey,' *The Times* reported that this happened on 16 February 1916. Later, president of the Council of Ministers at Ankara. IOR/R/15/2/1997, 'Who's Who in Mesopotamia, General Staff, India (Serial No. 10)', pp. 100-01; Ducrocq 1923, p. 122; Soltani 1381, vol. 4, p. 780.

403. Gehrke 1377, vol. 1, pp. 136-37, 139; Ducrocq 1923, p. 122. (Berlin gave him £50,000, rifles, and machine-guns that were sent to Baghdad)

Schönemann were leaving him. Samsam al-Mamalek was reported to be at Kerend, where it was reported the Turks arrived during the first days of May.[404]

Amir Mofakhkham released the Guran and Kalhor chiefs at Kerend and left the same day for Kermanshah. Sardar Ejlal and other townspeople conspired against him and told him to leave town. He was prepared to do so, but the Turkish consul convinced him to stay. Amin Bey, president of the Turkish consular court supported the conspirators. Tehran ordered Amir Mofakhkham to stay and confirmed him as governor and asked the olama to maintain the peace. However, the pressure was mounting and now both Democrats and Moderates were asking Amir Mofakhkham to leave. The governor remained in the palace but was entirely powerless. Hoseyn Ra'uf Bey wired from Zohab, offering to help him restore order as the Turks were friends of the Bakhtiyaris. The governor gave a non-committal reply. Meanwhile, having been abandoned by the Persian government, Samsam al-Mamalek and Mohammad Baqer Mirza felt that they had no choice but to seek asylum in the German consulate as protection against the Turks. There was much friction between the German and Turkish consuls about this. Meanwhile, Fateh Beg Jaf with two guns was reported to be moving towards the Sanjabi tribe.[405] The opposition of the Democrats to the Turks and German support for the Sanjabis probably was because two of Samsam al-Mamalek's sons were married to daughters of Mohammad Baqer Mirza, who was believed to be a Democrat. Moreover, his son and relatives, including a *Majles* deputy, were all strong Democrats. Given this strong link between the Democrats and the Sanjabis and the fact that the Germans professed to be friends of the Democrats this 'alliance' is understandable.[406]

DEPARTURE OF THE RUSSIAN AND BRITISH CONSULS

According to Soltani, it would seem that with the threat of Hoseyn Ra'uf Bey's force at Kerend, the arrival of the German and Austrian ambassador, and the increasingly threatening behavior by Schönemann, who enjoyed strong support from the Democrats, led to the departure of the British and Russian consuls and their compatriots.[407] Gehrke writes that Schönemann had been able create such a threatening situation in Kermanshah that the British and Russian consuls had assumed a defensive position. By having turned the Indian guards at the British consulate and the 20 Persian Cossack guards at the Russian consulate he maneuvered them into a siege-like position when the German and Austrian ambassadors were about to arrive, which induced these two consuls and their compatriots, including the IBP, to leave Kermanshah.[408] However, the

404. FO 248/1112, Mc Douall/Hamadan to Legation 05/05/1915; Idem, Kermanshah Diary 08/04/1915; Bast 1997, p. 21; Gehrke 1377, vol. 1, pp. 137 (grew to 3,000), 177-79; Soltani 1381, vol. 4, p. 781. IOR/L/PS/20/223, 'Who's who in Persia. Calcutta: General Staff, India, 1916', p. 362 (2,000 men).

405. FO 248/1112, McDouall/Hamadan, Kermanshah news, 27/04/1915; Idem, McDouall/Hamadan to Legation, 05/05/1915; Idem, McDouall/Hamadan to Tehran, 29/05/1915; Soltani 1381, vol. 4, p. 785.

406. FO 248/1112, McDouall to Legation 08/05/1915.

407. Soltani 1381, vol. 4, pp. 781-83.

408. Gehrke 1377, vol. 1, p. 180. Abdu Rabb, the dragoman of the British Consulate General at Baghdad supported the Turks as interpreter and "seems to have seduced the Indian sowars." FO 248/1112, McDouall/Hamadan, Kermanshah news 27/04/1915; Idem, McDouall/Hamadan to Legation, 05/05/1915.

British consul had no intention to leave at all, for it was Dolgopolov, the acting Russian consul who proposed to withdraw the consulates. According to McDouall, there was no reason for the departure, but the Russian proposal implied that there were reasons unknown to the British. The real reason may have been "the nervousness" of the acting Russian consul, about which McDouall had been complaining earlier. In the second half of March 1915, this "nervousness," even had become dangerous in his opinion. Dolgopolov's *mirza* told the *kargozar* that the consul feared an attack on his life. When there was a dispute between a Persian servant of the Turkish Consulate with one of the Russian Consulate the *kargozar* had to intervene. Although the two servants patched up their quarrel, the Russian consul felt so threatened that he built a wall between his roof and that of the Turk, as they lived in adjoining houses. According to McDouall, "Everybody would like to see him him leave as he is seen as a danger." This would have been no problem, given the presence of his deputy, the level-headed Mr. Kirsanov.[409] On 13 April 1915, that is one day after Ra'uf Bey crossed the border and took Qasr-e Shirin, Dolgopolov left Kermanshah without informing McDouall, who was told that Dolgopolov had orders and that the Persian Cossacks would be withdrawn. These were the only troops in town and were to conduct the Europeans to a place of safety. McDouall still would not have left then, but that very night the Imperial Bank house was fired upon and therefore, he decided to leave. He justified his decision further by pointing out that, "The Russian consul with his Cossacks leaving indicates that it was a Russian decision and Kermanshah being in the Russian sphere me remaining there might be interpreted as being anti-Russian and locally would have been interpreted as our policy not being theirs." Moreover, the main Turkish force did not go beyond Kerend, but there were Turks with the Kalhors that could come without detection to Kermanshah. Therefore, the danger was not from the Turks but from the Kalhors, who, being in rebellion, might have attacked and looted Kermanshah. Also, as McDouall was not allowed to hire *savar*s, whilst Schönemann had more than 100 men and the position of the Persian government was doubtful, he, therefore, had no choice but to go. In fact, the governor with a large force had been unable to stop the Turks at the Pay Taq pass and McDouall had not received an answer as to his safety.[410] It is of interest to note that McDouall did not mention in his justification for withdrawal from Kermanshah that his Indian escort had defected to the Ottoman Consulate and the Persian Cossacks had gone to the German Consulate. When the two ambassadors left Kermanshah they were preceded by the Indian *savar*s in their parade dress and the Persian Cossacks followed them.[411]

On his departure, McDouall left several local reporters behind in Kermanshah including his *monshi*. The latter later reported that after the Europeans left panic prevailed in the city. Merchants and shopkeepers closed their shops and hid their goods. The Post and Telegraph stopped working. The villagers of Mahidasht all fled; everybody was afraid that the Kalhors and the Turks were coming and strong messages were sent to Schönemann and Hoseyn Ra'uf Bey not to come. The latter stayed at Pay Taq, but the tribesmen were urging their chiefs to march in the hope of looting Kermanshah. The force at Pay Taq consisted of: Turkish infantry

---

409. FO 248/1112, McDouall to Townley, 26/03/1915.
410. FO 248/1112, no. 31, McDouall/Hamadan to Legation, 14/07/1915.
411. Sepehr 1337 p. 166.

600, cavalry 200 commanded by Hoseyn Ra'uf Bey and Beha Bey; Turkish tribesmen 100; Kermanshahi tribesmen: 'Abdollah Beg *farrash-bashi* 30 *savar*s; Parviz Khan Bajlan 30 *savar*s; Safar Khan Guran 20 *savar*s; Fatah Beg Jaf 40 *savar*s; Soleyman Khan and 'Abbas Khan Kalhor 150 *savar*s. Guns four; ammunition eight loads. Ahmad Beg Jaf and Beha Bey had gone to punish the Sanjabis, but they had orders not to fight. The Germans were putting pressure on Ra'uf Bey, whose behavior created problems for them in mobilizing local support, in particular their effort to induce prime minister Eyn al-Dowleh to their side. A tentative agreement arranged by Capt. Sarre in May 1915 failed as did the attempt by the German ambassador in Istanbul to have Ra'uf Bey recalled. The latter was openly supported by Enver Pasha, the Minister of War, and therefore, the Germans had to live with this unwanted reality.[412]

Amir Mofakhkham told Mohammad Baqer Mirza that the Turkish consul had shown him a letter from Hoseyn Ra'uf Bey in which he wrote that if Samsam al-Mamalek would come to the Ottoman Consulate and apologize he would be forgiven. The Amir advised him to do so, and so, with permission of the German consul and with Mohammad Baqer Mirza, he went there. The Ottoman consul was very pleased about this and told Samsam al-Mamalek that he would write immediately to Hoseyn Ra'uf Bey about this. Two days later the consul said a reply had come, but instead of Samsam al-Mamamlek Mohammad Baqer Mirza went. The consul asked: "where is Samsam al-Mamalek, why has not he come to see me these last two days?" He then gave Mohammad Baqer Mirza Hoseyn Ra'uf Bey's reply: "As long as Shir Khan is in the Turkish consulate he is safe, and as long as his sons don't seek asylum their assurance of safety is not given." Samsam al-Mamalek was very angry and showed the letter to everybody and there was an outcry in the city against this. On 11 May he left the city to join his sons and his tribe in the hills of their summer quarters. The Sanjabis were ready to drive the Turks out of Persia, if Tehran would give permission. Ra'uf Bey with his 1,500 men asked Amir Mofakhkham to punish Samsam al-Mamalek and made some other conditions. The governor referred the matter to Tehran, which contacted Istanbul. The commander of the Persian Cossacks in Kermanshah asked the governor for a Schneider gun to fight Schönemann. Tehran wired that attacking a diplomatic representative was out of the question.

Meanwhile, the local opposition against Amir Mofakhkham continued; since his return from Zohab he daily wired Tehran asking for orders and money; he was owed 60,000 *tuman*s and his men had not been paid. Therefore, he informed Tehran that if in three days he would not get a positive reply he would resign and leave. He felt that he had no other choice considering the opposition he was facing and his lack of funds. Therefore, he sent his men to the Qara Su camp. On 3 May 1915 he left the Qara Su camp with his men and went straight via Borujerd to Kemereh and left the city in Schönemann's hands. The *kargozar* informed Tehran that not only the people, but also the tribes were opposed to the governor and sent letters to that effect, incited by Schönemann. He suggested to immediately appoint a new governor. The more, because without gendarmerie in the city (all had gone as escort for the two ambassadors) it was difficult

412. FO 248/1112, enclosure in McDouall's letter no. 10 of 12/05/1915; Bast 1997, p. 25; Gehrke 1377, vol. 1, pp. 202-05, 222; Ducrocq 1923, p. 88, 132-37, 149 (German-Turkish conflicting objectives).

to maintain order.[413] According to Sheikh Mohammad Mehdi Kermanshahi, at that time, it could be said that all matters in Kermanshah were decided by Schönemann.[414]

In the absence of anyone in authority, not even a deputy-governor, the notables cooperated to maintain order. Mokhtar al-Saltaneh, the army commander and Abu'l-Fath Mirza, the acting chief of police, were in charge of keeping order. People were angry about Samsam al-Mamalek's treatment by the Turks and about Ehtesham al-Mamalek, governor of Kerend's letter who wrote: the Turks are "pressing me to sign to support them, if I don't they'll destroy the town, what to do?" As a result, the whole city was united in not letting in the Turks. Copies of Ehtesham al-Mamalek's letter were sent to Amir Mofakhkham, the olama and the *kargozar*. Amir Mofakhkham said that he was no longer governor and the matter did not concern him. People got together and wrote a letter to the Kalhor and Guran chiefs, saying: "Persia is neutral, you are loyal to Iran; you have to separate from them, because if Turks advance our country will be destroyed. If you don't listen you may expect nothing from us and we will oppose and fight you." They also sent a copy of this letter to the Turkish consul.

Tehran sent a stream of telegrams, which showed support for Samsam al-Mamalek and praised the Sanjabis. The central government also sent telegrams to the Guran and Kalhor chiefs and the olama saying Persia is neutral, you must be too and not be guilty and ally you with one party or the other. The people and olama were pleased with these messages and replied in a positive sense and that they were neutral. However, they also asked Tehran: "why is a Turkish army within our borders trampling villages and crops and people." Meanwhile, Schönemann was slowly discharging the *savar*s he had hired.[415] Mo'tasem al-Molk officiated as acting governor, until a new governor was appointed, with 'Ali Khan Sardar Ejlal Zanganeh (Amir Koll) as his deputy.

In early May 1915, Soleyman Khan Kalhor wrote to the people of Kermanshah, if you don't hand over the Ilkhani, who had been appointed Kalhor chief, and other Hajjizadeh leaders, he would join the Turks and attack Kermanshah. They refused. Prime Minister 'Eyn al-Dowleh wired Soleyman Khan that if he didn't remain neutral Tehran would support the tribes against him. 'Abbas Khan told Soleyman Khan that he would never attack the Sanjabis, who were his relatives. Sardar Ejlal, the acting governor, told people that the Turks would not have a chance against Great Britain and Russia and if the Turkish troops would come to Kermanshah it would be occupied by Russia and their women would fall into the hands of Russian soldiers. Those opposing entry of the Turks were the olama, the Hajjizadehs, Mo'aven al-Molk, who held sway over most of the town's ruffians, Sayyed Hasan Owjaq, agent for the Guran chief, Amin al-Mamalek, agent for the Kalhor chief, and the *kadkhoda-bashi* of the town. All the Gurans, including the Qalkhanis swore an alliance with the Sanjabis.

---

413. FO 248/1112, Kermanshah news 04/05/1915; Idem, McDouall/Hamadan to Tehran, 29/05/1915; Soltani 1381, vol. 4, pp. 783-85, 788; Idem 1986, p. 202. According to another British source, Amir Mofakhkham resigned on 7 July 1915. IOR/R/15/2/1997, 'Who's Who in Mesopotamia, General Staff, India (Serial No. 10)', p. 22

414. Soltani 1986, p. 203.

415. FO 248/1112, Kermanshah news 04/05/1915.

ATTACK BY HOSEYN RA'UF BEY

In the night of 9-10 May 1915, some 60 Turks arrived led by five officers, some went to the Ottoman Consulate, others to a caravanserai. The townspeople wanted to attack the Ottoman Consulate but the olama said let's first inform Tehran. 'Eyn al-Dowleh replied, "Persia is neutral, so the Turks must not enter Kermanshah." The Turkish ambassador asked him to wait till 12 May before taking any action. The officers said they had not come to fight but to talk to the olama. As it was not safe for the Turks to go out into the streets the olama came to a house close to the Turkish Consulate. Through an interpreter, the officers said that they had come on a peaceful mission. The olama replied: "why not notify the authorities and ask permission from Tehran?" The senior officer was embarrassed and said that it was too late to do that now that they had arrived. Persia and Turkey were friends and had the same religon. Great Britain and Russia intended to seize them both. Therefore, he asked them to join Turkey to expel them both. Sayyed Reza Qomi, the agent of Sayyed Kazem of Najaf, said: "Persia is neutral and no Persian may help any of the parties. So far we have restrained the people, but it may get out of hand any moment and they will attack you." Samsam al-Mamalek left Kermanshah to go to Sanjabis and promised the town's people help. Leaders of the people went to the arsenal to get weapons. Its commander said that without orders from Tehran he could not give them. They said that then they would take them by force. Samsam al-Mamalek allegedly asked Tehran for permission to expel the Turks; he did not want any help, only permission. At that time, Schönemann had only 50 *savar*s, while there were 65 foot and 20 mounted gendarmes at Kermanshah under Capt. Sonesen. Another 120 gendarmes had left Hamadan to join them. They guarded the British Consulate and the Imperial Bank. The Turkish force at Pay Taq was estimated to consist of 400 regulars, 800 untrained irregulars in uniform and some tribesmen.[416] While things remained quiet in the city, its leaders were trying to make the Kalhors and Sanjabis work together and met their chiefs at Mahidasht. Tehran had given permission to the townspeople to defend Kermanshah if attacked by the Turks, but the Sanjabis did not receive permission to attack the Turks. Samsam al-Mamalek still wanted to attack them, if the olama of Kermanshah would guarantee that Tehran would not punish him. At that time, there were 250 gendarmes at Kermanshah, indicating that those coming from Hamadan had arrived.[417]

People in the city were constantly having meetings. Those of the Turkish party were: two sons of Sayyed 'Abbas of Mir 'Abdol Bagi & Sons, 'Abdu Rabb the dragoman of the British Consulate in Baghdad, and Mehdi 'Abdol-Rasul. They brought money from Hoseyn Ra'uf Bey. They deceived some people, amongst whom Mo'aven al-Ra'aya, who, after meeting the Turkish consul, said he would remain neutral and did not attend any meetings. Sayyed Hasan Owjaq, agent for the Gurans was also gotten to as was Amin al-Mamalek, agent for the Kalhors. Some preachers were bribed not to preach against the Turks. The division among the people was widening, but the olama prevented open quarreling. Ahmad Aqa Mir 'Abdol-Baqi wrote a letter that the town was pro-Turkish and added forged the seals on it and took it to the Turkish camp. This became known and people cried that he had betrayed them. Sayyed Hasan, the head of the

416. FO 248/1112, Mc Douall/Hamadan to Legation, 19/05/1915; Soltani 1381, vol. 4, p. 786.
417. FO 248/1112, McDouall/Hamadan to Legation, 22/05/1915.

firm, immediately wired Kerend to order him back, but he had already passed that town. Slowly the opposition against the Turks was decreasing. Some were seduced by money, others blamed Sardar Ejlal, the acting governor, of playing a double game. Others would oppose the Turks if it was made their worthwhile, but only the Turks were spending money. When Sardar Ejlal ordered Soleyman Khan Kalhor to come to Mahidasht, the Turkish consul asked why he had done so without consulting him, an indication of growing Turkish influence.

Ehtesham al-Mamalek, the governor of Kerend, who had asked for help, was ordered by 'Eyn al-Dowleh to remain neutral. He showed the telegram to Hoseyn Ra'uf Bey, who said that it was a British forgery and told him, he either joined him or he would destroy the town. To get help, the Kerendis went to the head of the Ali-ilahis, Sayyed Rostam, who arranged an alliance between the Sanjabis and the Gurans. They wrote to Soleyman Khan, who sent an agent to make peace with Samsam al-Mamalek. The latter agreed, but subject to consultation with his allies in town. Five men from the city would meet the two chiefs. The telegram from 'Eyn al-Dowleh had been sent by messenger with a letter from the townspeople. Ebrahim Adhem, a Turkish officer with a flag and escort, who always was with Soleyman Khan, drew his revolver to shoot him, but Soleyman Khan said 'no.' He told the messenger to ask Amin al-Mamalek to come with others to arrange the peace. Sardar Ejlal also wanted to be there and asked them to wait, because he had to ask permission. A few days passed during which the Ottoman consul told Hoseyn Ra'uf Bey not to attack. Those who went were: Sayyed Hasan Owjaq and Amin al-Mamalek (suspected to be pro-Turkish), Qavam al-Olama, prince Salar Nezam, and 'Abdol-Hasan Zanganeh (anti-Turkish). It was at this time that the British consular *monshi* left Kermanshah, when he learnt that the Turks wanted to capture him.

Schönemann told the people of Kermanshah that Germany only wanted Persia's independence and trade with it, not like Turkey to make it dependent on it. He said he would talk to Hoseyn Ra'uf Bey, whom he considered to be mad. Meanwhile, the Turks in small groups of 4-5 in civilian dress entered the city. Some of them hired volunteers. With the Turks were also some Indians ('Abdu Rabb, Khodayar Khan and the Consular *savars*). Khodayar Khan showed letters in Indian script purportedly saying that the British had been kicked out of India and the proof was that they were not advancing on Baghdad. Amir Heshmat Feda'i passing through Kermanshah wrote to friends not to trust the Turks, he had fought for them, but now he'd rather fight for the Russians against them. A servant of Salar al-Dowleh had written his family that Amir Heshmat had convinced the prince not to collaborate with the Turks and to return to Europe. 'Abdu Rabb hearing this said that Amir Heshmat was an infidel and only because the Turks had refused to make him governor of Azerbaijan he had abandoned them. Lahuti Khan, then in Schönemann's service, said that if he were not in German service he would have shot 'Abdu Rabb for slandering such an honorable man.[418]

The five representatives returned to Kermanshah after having made peace between the Sanjabis and the Kalhors. Ebrahim Adhem, the Turkish officer, was very rude to them and told them if they were not gone in two hours he would arrest them. Soleyman Khan negotiated with them in secret in another house. He said he was afraid but if the Shah, the Prime Minister, and

418. FO 248/1112, McDouall/Hamadan to Legation, 26/05/1915; Idem, McDouall/Hamadan to Legation 29/05/1915.

the Minister of the Interior would grant him a pardon and the townspeople would swear an alliance with him, he would get rid of the Turks from his district. Sardar Ejlal and the *kargozar* wired Tehran asking for this pardon. The British did not believe Soleyman Khan, taking the position that the Kalhors were inveterate liars, but if they or the Russians would give assurances they might do what they said. It was unlikely that the Turks would make peace with Sanjabis; Sardar Moqtader had made a night attack on their fort and killed a few of them and captured two Guran chiefs, who were his enemies. The Qalkhanis thieves also attacked them, so that some of the irregulars were deserting. The Turks moved from the top to the bottom of the Pay Taq pass. The Turks tried to incite the Kalhors to attack the Sanjabis saying that the captured Guran chief was under their protection. Schönemann was mediating and argued that the Turks and Samsam al-Mamalek had to come to terms. Together with Capt. Sonesen he went to Sarab Nilufer to meet Samsam al-Mamalek. They wanted to win over the people, bring the army and go to Hamadan to incite people against Great Britain and Russia.[419]

The Kalhors were still with the Turks; the other tribes were ready to attack them. After Schönemann had seen Hoseyn Ra'uf Bey he went to see Samsam al-Mamalek (with Sonesen and Mohammad Baqer Mirza) and arranged for Samsam al-Mamalek to see Hoseyn Ra'uf Bey with Sonesen to ask for pardon. On 1 June 1916, Sonesen and Schönemann went to Samsam al-Mamalek's house to take him to Ra'uf Bey. The Turks had moved from Sorkh-e Rizeh to Sar-e Mil, and from there had gone to Kerend; 100 of them were at Harunabad. Hoseyn Ra'uf Bey wrote to Hoseyn Khan, chief of the Gurans that if he did not come to him he would come to Gahvareh and destroy them.

McDouall feared that if Samsam al-Mamalek would received assurances from Hoseyn Ra'uf Bey that nothing would prevent the Turks from going to Kermanshah. In early June 1915, there were only two Germans in Kermanshah with a few local guards, including 16 Persian Cossack deserters. Samsam al-Mamalek had asked a written guarantee from the Turks, which was given by Mohiy al-Din, a Turkish officer in Kermanshah. People informed Tehran which wired Samsam al-Mamalek ordering him not to join the Turks. He was delighted with this; the telegram was not in code and also forbade Soleyman Khan to attack the Sanjabis saying that nobody could annex Persian territory, it belonged to the Persians. Schönemann was upset by this; the Turks moved closer (12 km) to Kerend. The Kerendis wired Tehran if the government would not help them they would oppose the Turks on their own. The Turks sent the Indians and some Kermanshahi volunteers to Kerend; they also hired some 100 men under Hajj Safer's son. The Turks took a suburb called Chiga Sorkh for their troops, which was located on a hill commanding the town.[420]

On 5 June 1915, Mohiy al-Din, the Turkish officer left Kermanshah for good with the Indian and other *savar*s. The Turkish consul returned the houses and furniture that he had rented for these troops. He himself was also secretly storing goods with friends and seemed to be preparing to leave. Hoseyn Ra'uf Bey was still at Kerend with detachments at Khosrowabad and Harunabad in Kalhor country. Through the mediation of Nazar 'Ali Khan, the Sanjabis, Kalhors, Gurans, Qalkhanis and Jafs made peace and signed an agreement to respect Persian neutrality and not

419. FO 248/1112, McDouall/Hamadan to Legation 02/06/1915; Soltani 1381, vol. 4, pp. 786-90.
420. FO 248/1112, McDouall/Hamadan to Legation, 09/06/1915.

to quarrel among themselves; they sent the text to townspeople who were asked to join them and henceforth act together, which they signed. All tribal chiefs concerned intended to come to Kermanshah. The Kalhors made the following demand: a written pardon for Nazar 'Ali Khan Amra'i and themselves; the title of Amir A'zam for Soleyman Khan and Sardar Mozaffar for 'Abbas Khan; that no governor would be appointed over the Kalhors; and that Eyvan (a district between Gilan and Post-e Kuh that Tehran had given to the Vali) would be granted to them. If granted they would abandon the Turks; Sardar Ejlal wired these demands to Tehran and urged the government to satisfy these demands.[421] In mid-June 1915, the gendarmes seized a load of ammunition for the Turkish consul. The people were pleased about this, but asked why did not that happen with Schönemann's shipments?[422]

The people of Kermanshah were not happy with the tribal chiefs and their big escorts coming as they damaged the crops near the town. Also, they wanted the new governor to come as soon as possible. After Hoseyn Ra'uf Bey took some flocks from Ehtesham al-Mamalek he took them back. Hoseyn Ra'uf Bey asked him to send his son Salar Ashraf to amiably settle their problem, but when he came he was arrested as well as Hasan Khan the *sarhaddar*, the *kargozar*'s agent. A group of sayyeds went to ask for their release and were fired upon and some were killed and wounded. The arrest of the son happened as follows: The son of Sayyed Rostam, the religious head of the Gurans, visited Ehtesham al-Mamalek with a small escort. Ra'uf Bey gave orders to send those Sanjabis to him. The governor sent his son to explain who the visitors were and his son was immediately arrested. A deputation was sent to the Turkish camp and was fired upon; among the fired upon dead were some Guran sayyeds. Sayyed Rostam asked Aqa Bakhsh, whom the Ali-ilahis consider the incarnation of a deity, for help. He sent his son and Kakawand Lors and called on his followers to begin a jihad against the Turks.[423]

On 13 June 1915, the Turks plundered some villages and then began bombarding and besieging Kerend. After some fighting the 80-year old Ehtesham al-Mamalek asked for quarter. He was put in chains as was his son. Then the soldiers began a massacre and killed over 1,000 persons, allegedly including babies and women having their beasts cut off. Then the whole village, including the caravanserai of pilgrims was plundered, "even the Jewish merchants living there. Some were killed, the rest fled and no one was left in Kerind. They did not leave a dinar or an old mat, all was pillaged."[424] When the tribes learnt about the sack of Kerend, the Sanjabi Sardars and the Qalkhanis met at Gahvareh at the house of Sayyed Rostam. The Gurans and the people from the city also came. 'Ali Akbar Khan Sanjabi met with the city's leaders at the house

421. FO 248/1112, McDouall/Hamadan to Legation, 15/06/1915 ("The wife of the president of the Turkish court has taken refuge with Mrs. Stead.").

422. FO 248/1112, McDouall/Hamdan to Legation, 19/06/1915.

423. FO 248/1112, McDouall/Hamdan to Legation, 30/06/1915.

424. FO 248/1112, Translation of a letter from Sardar Haidar Quli Khan Cabuli to McDouall dated Kermanshah June 27, 1915. Bast 1997, p. 25 mistakenly situated the attack on Kerend at the beginning of July 1915. The British Indian sowars of the Consulate, who in April had gone over to the Turks, also fought with Hoseyn Ra'uf Bey's force; a duffadar was in charge of the maxim gun. The Indian sowars let McDouall know that they regretted their desertion. FO 248/1112 no. 30, McDouall/Hamadan to Legation, 17/07/1915. In Kerend during the fight between Ra'uf and the Keredinis (17 September), the Jews were plundered and fled to Kermanshah. There the financial agent levied a heavy tax on grapes and raisins thus preventing Jews from making wine (January 21). Adler 1916, vol. 18, p. 149.

of prince As'ad al-Dowleh and they swore to act together. On 18 June 1915, some 300 volunteers left Kermanshah to so the same. The chiefs that were in town left in the afternoon with 700 *savar*s to help the Kerendis. On Tuesday morning (22 June), just after midnight, a joint Sanjabi-Guran force under 'Ali Akbar Sanjabi attacked the Turks at Kerend, who were in a caravanserai, from three sides and fought until sunset. Casualties, mostly wounded, were estimated to 150 on the Turkish side and 120 on the side of the tribes. After 'Ali Akbar Khan had taken the Turkish headquarters the Turks raised the white flag. The Kalhors had not joined the fight. Sardar Akram Pishkuhi, an Ali-ilahi sent some *savar*s and Salar Rashid (Ruansir Valizadeh) also joined the tribes.[425]

The Kalhors said Hoseyn Ra'uf Bey wanted to occupy the province, while 'Abdu Rabb, Khodayar Khan and Edham Beg came to Kermanshah and said that Hoseyn Ra'uf Bey wanted an excuse to be able withdraw honorably and, to that end, he needed a letter from the people of Kermanshah. A group of men were nominated to discuss this with him, but they did not leave because of the attack of Kerend. These men brought money to induce the people of the city to support the Turks. Amin Bey, the president of the Turkish consular court, tried to bribe the olama. Three of them Aqa Mohammad Mehdi, Aqa Rahim and Sheikh Hadi refused, but Qavam al-Olama, the leader of the Democrats, Aqa Vali and Ashraf al-Va'ezin and some others did. On 26 June 1915, Sardar Ejlal wanted to leave the city; he was angry because people were openly accusing him of having been bribed by the Turks. Apparently, 'Abbas Khan had given 2,000 gold liras to him, and also gold for the *kargozar*, and others. Sardar Ejlal pressed the notables to join Schönemann and Capt. Sonesen to make peace and they were obliged to do so. Mohammad Baqer Mirza wrote to 'Ali Akbar Khan that the city had decided that the fighting had to stop and peace be made. If this had not happened, Hoseyn Ra'uf Bey would have been finished. Aqa Rahim *mojtahed* had allegedly accused Sardar Ejlal of making a mess of the whole affair and destroying the city "and swore if he left and withdrew he himself would oppose him, 'whatever you have seen it is your own fault.' He returned in the afternoon to Government House, where 2 days earlier people had placed a dog saying this is his father "who takes bribes from and helps the Turks." On Friday night (25 June) Tehran wired the *kargozar* ordering him to go to Hoseyn Ra'uf Bey to ask him whether ornot he had come by orders of his government, which his embassy denied. If not, he had to leave, if on his own account, he had to say so. If he did not want to give an answer in writing the *kargozar* had to write a report so that Tehran could decide what steps to take with the Turkish government.[426]

On 26 June 1915, some Qalkhanis came into the city to sell some of the loot taken from the Turks. People laughed when they walked through the bazaar dressed in a Turkish soldier's coat

425. Moberley 1987, pp. 61-62; Ansari 1353, p. 128; FO 248/1112, Translation of a letter from Sardar Haidar Quli Khan Cabuli to McDouall dated Kermanshah June 27, 1915. FO 248/1112 McDouall/Hamadan to Legation, 30/06/1915; Soltani 1386, p. 203; Idem 1381, vol. 4, p. 787, 790 (the Kerendis were supported by the Sanjabi and Guran tribe in the defense of their town); Litten 1925, pp. 208-09 (who writes Schünemann). On the Iraqi population's reaction to this force's exactions and forced conscription during its march to the Persian border, see Political Diaries, vol. 6, p. 26; FO 248/1112 no. 25, McDouall/Hamadan to Legation, 23/06/1915.

426. FO 248/1112, Translation of a letter from Sardar Haidar Quli Khan Cabuli to McDouall dated Kermanshah June 27, 1915; FO 248/1112 no. 25, McDouall/Hamadan to Legation, 23/06/1915 (Around 9 June some Indians arrived with arms and ammo for Schönemann; they had joined the Germans in France. On 13/06 they left towards Soltanabad.); FO 248/1112, McDouall/Hamadan to Legation, 30/06/1915; Soltani 1381, vol. 4, p. 787.

with a fez on their head. At sunset Shevket Bey, the Turkish consul, returned with an escort and near the gate people hurled abuse at him and shots were fired. They fled and the chief of police arrested some of the men, while the Turkish Consulate was heavily guarded. The Turks in the Consulate were packing up, preparing to leave, if need be. On 25 June, some 150 gendarmes with one gun left for Kerend. If these notables had not taken Turkish gold the whole affair would be over and the Turkish troops expelled from Persia, according to a local Afghan resident. It was said that 200 tribesmen and 400 Turks killed.[427]

A group consisting of Roshani Bey, the German and Turkish consuls, representing Hoseyn Ra'uf Bey, and Zahir al-Olama, Qavam al-Olama and the *kargozar* for Persia, at the orders from Tehran, went to Kerend to arrange a truce. After the Turks had raised the white flag, Schönemann gave a written undertaking that the Turks would withdraw to Turkey or from the province as desired. Also, that they would release Ehtesham al-Mamalek's son, while 'Ali Akbar Khan would release the two officers who had surrendered. A 3-day truce was agreed to finalize matters. 'Ali Akbar Sanjabi talked with the city's leaders at Gahvareh who said Hoseyn Ra'uf Bey had to leave the province and cross the border. Hoseyn Ra'uf said he'd rather die. 'Ali Akbar was furious with Schönemann that the Turks did not carry out their promises and swore to kill the Turks if they did not withdraw. The town was united and the gendarmes were powerless. Finally, Schönemann's mediation (assisted by Capt. Sonesen and Count Kanitz) was able to settle the conflict, when Hoseyn Ra'uf Bey signed an agreement to withdraw on 29 June 1915. This, of course, solidified German influence in Kermanshah. According to the agreement, the Turks would leave to Sar-e Pol-e Zohab to wait for orders from Istanbul that would be transmitted via the Turkish embassy in Tehran. Furthermore, a commission was formed concerning the plundering of Kerend. It consisted of two representatives of the Persian government, the *kargozar*, and one each for the Sanjabis, Gurans, and Kalhors, and one from Hoseyn Ra'uf Bey, which would meet at Kerend. The tribes returned to their districts and the townspeople to the city. The attack on Kerend led to the fall of Prime Minister 'Eyn al-Dowleh. But for Schönemann, the Turks would have been pushed back to Khaneqin. The Kalhors played a double game; 'Abdollah Khan *farrash-bashi* and Karim Gordeh with 200 *savar*s had joined the Turks in the fight and the looting of Kerend. Sardar Ejlal and some others approved of this and did not report it to the government. Anti-Turkish feelings were still high in the city. When a Sanjabi sold a Turkish rifle in the bazaar, the Turkish consul had it seized; people were insensed and besieged the Consulate; he was forced to return the rifle.[428]

By mid-July 1915, the Turks were still at Sar-e Pol Zohab; en route they robbed and killed villagers and gave ammunition to Aqa Fateh Jaf, who had a quarrel with the Qalkhanis. The 200 Kalhors under 'Abdollah Khan and Karim Gordeh were still with Ra'uf Bey. The Turks asked 300 liras from the town of Qasr-e Shirin. The Captain of the Gendarmes wanted to drive out Turks, but Schönemann told him that it was none of his business. Kermanshah was quiet, but people were annoyed with their leaders, who were criticizing Farmanfarma, which people

---

427. FO 248/1112, Translation of a letter from Sardar Haidar Quli Khan Cabuli to McDouall dated Kermanshah June 27, 1915.

428. Moberley 1987, pp. 61-62; Ansari 1353, p. 128; FO 248/1112, McDouall/Hamadan to Legation, 30/06/1915; Idem, McDouall/Hamadan to Legation, 07/07/1915; Soltani 1386, p. 203; Idem 1381, vol. 4, p. 790; Litten 1925, pp. 208-09.

considered irrelevant as talk was cheap. The more so, because despite the agreement to withdraw, Hoseyn Ra'uf Bey felt thwarted and even told the *kargozar* that he had intended to massacre the people of Kermanshah. Emin Bey, president of the Turkish Consular Court told a *mojtahed* that the Ottoman government would punish Ra'uf Bey. The man who fired at Showket Bey on 26 June was still in prison; through intercession the Turkish embassy was willing to let him go as a sign of Islamic unity, provided that the leaders of Kermanshah signed a telegram that they were friendly now with the Turks; none would sign.[429]

The Turks remained at Sar-e Pol where they were intriguing with the tribes hoping to create confusion to be able to come back. There were no replies from Tehran and none were expected, while the *Majles* was closed. The Kalhors were still with Hoseyn Ra'uf Bey and perhaps 'Abbas Khan and Jahanbakhsh were expeected to also join them. Jahanbaksh had taken refuge with Sardar Eqbal and he sent him with his brother to the Gurans to arrange his affairs. The Sanjabis did nothing, even made up with Soleyman Khan, Sardar Nosrat, who intended to marry a daughter of Qasem Khan Sardar Naser Sanjabi. Sardar Eqbal was annoyed and opposed to Sanjabis. Mo'azzam al-Saltaneh, the deputy of the new governor, Eqbal al-Dowleh, came, saw and regretted that he had done so.[430]

BRITISH AND RUSSIAN CONSULS PREVENTED FROM RETURNING

To counter German influence, Great Britain and Russia decided at the beginning of August 1915 to send their consuls (McDouall and Cherkasov) back to Kermanshah. The British and Russian Ministers had asked Eqbal al-Dowleh, the governor of Kermanshah (at that time still in Tehran) to guarantee the safe entry of their consuls into Kermanshah. In reply the Persian government ordered Major Edwal, who commanded 200 gendarmes, as well as the Cossack brigade in Sanandaj to make that happen. However, the gendarmerie was unable to do so. The reason was that Captain de Maree had been defeated by Lor tribesmen and had lost 200 of his 800 gendarmes. Both he and Nezam al-Saltaneh, the governor of Lorestan, had barely escaped with their lives. This led to the British Minister's (Marling) comment that apart from their "pro-German attitude it shows that Swedish officers are incapable of safe-guarding the roads." Edwall admitted that he did not know where the 800 gendarmes were, but he hoped to find most of them, but he could not provide the requested escort. Marling was against letting McDouall return, but it was at the request of the Russians to accompany their consul that he gave in. "Kermanshah being in the Russian zone I deferred to my Russian colleague as to the reestablishment of the consulates there. I told de Etter that they should not leave without an escort, he agreed, but forgot to send message and they left." The Persian government ordered Lt. Sonesen to send an escort, but he refused claiming that his men had no horses. De Etter then threatened to send two squadrons of Russian Cossacks and this had desired effect.[431]

429. FO 248/1112, McDouall/Hamadan to Legation, 14/07/1915 (Schönemann and Count Kanitz were in Kermanshah).

430. FO 248/1112, McDouall/Hamadan to Legation, 21/07/1915.

431. FO 416/63, Marling to Grey, Tehran 30/08/1915.

The two consuls left Hamadan on 8 August 1915, accompanied by an escort of Persian and Russian Cossacks. Meanwhile, Schönemann prepared Kermanshah to oppose the return of the two consuls. The town's inhabitants were scared, fearing that fighting would take place as well as an occupation by the Turks. To allay their fears Schönemann promised that he would not ask Hoseyn Ra'uf Bey to come to his assistance. On 7 August 1915, Schönemann left Kermanshah with 500 Kalhors, Sanjabis and Nazar 'Ali Khan's tribesmen. On 13 August, Schönemann arrived at Sahneh and fortified the place. He did the same at Bisotun. The Ilkhani allowed him to pass on payment. He allegedly said, "just like Great Britain has occupied Bushehr I have occupied Kermanshah." In reply to the governor who asked by telegram what he had to do, Tehran replied that he had to maintain neutrality and peace in the district. On 15 August, a Kalhor messenger from Schönemann came to the governor saying that the two consuls were coming to expel him from Kermanshah and by their intrigues caused the killing of some of his men. He had no choice but to take action, however, he did not want hurt any Persian subjects who were neutral. He requested the governor of Kangavar to ask the two consuls to withdraw else he would attack. The governor forwarded Schönemann's letter to Tehran and asked for instructions. On 16 August 1915, the bazaars in Kangavar were closed. Sayyed 'Abbas Lari, the leading *mojtahed* discussed the situation with the British consular *monshi*. The Kangavar *mojtahed*s decided to write to Schönemann that the consuls were guests and would come to Kermanshah with the permission and authority of the Persian government. They asked Schönemann not to advance, otherwise they had to oppose him. To McDouall it was clear that Schönemann did want the two consuls on the postal road. At Sahneh he had gathered a force of about 100 men, half townsmen, half Gurans. They had joined him for the money, and therefore, it was doubtful whether they would fight.[432] Schönemann replied to Sayyed 'Abbas Lari that out of respect for him he would not come to Kangevar, but the consuls had to go and he should not be deceived by people whose deeds in Azerbaijan and Bushehr and elsewhere were well-known and spoke for themselves. The *mojtahed* replied that if Schönemann advanced he would call a jihad. Schönemann went to Kermanshah but his 100 men remained there.

In Kermanshah allegedly two-thirds of the people supported the British position. In meetings they pointed out that the consuls had every right to return to their Consulates. If the Germans were allowed to forcibly oppose their return this would probably result in the foreign occupation of Kermanshah. They finally wired the Minister of Interior in Tehran that Schönemann had collected a bunch of criminals and tribesmen to oppose the return of the consuls; they were not involved in this and were prepared to go with a sufficient force to conduct the consuls to Kermanshah. In the evening of 17 August 1915, the Prime Minister wired the governor that it was was his duty to protect the consuls and repel any attempts by Schönemann to attack them.[433]

Schönemann went to Kermanshah on 17 August 1915 and returned to Sahneh on 19 August. He then wired the olama and governor of Kangavar that he gave the consuls three days to depart, if they did not he would come to Kangavar. The governor sent him a copy of the Prime Minister's telegram. Schönemann replied he would not come, and in afternoon, Mirza Reza Khan, his *monshi* came with an oral message. He tried to induce the governor not to interfere, who replied

432. FO 248/1112, McDouall/Kangavar to Legation, 16/08/1915.

433. FO 248/1112, McDouall/Kangavar to Legation, 18/08/1915.

that he had his orders. On 18 August, Kirsanon, the Russian vice-consul in Baghdad arrived with 30 Russian horsemen. Therefore, McDouall doubted that Schönemann would fight.[434]

Schönemann remained at Sahneh with an outpost at the Bidsorkh pass. He had one maxim gun and was fortifying the pass to which end he had brought masons, picks etc. from Kermanshah. Nazar 'Ali Khan's men were reported to have left him after Schönemann refused to pay what they demanded. Nazar 'Ali Khan then offered his help to the British, if Great Britain would induce the Persian government to reinstate him at Pish-e Kuh. Schönemann told the people of Kermanshah he could not let the consuls return as the road via Kermanshah was the only one that enabled Germany to have communication with the interior of Persia and their return would close it. Schönemann's faction of the Democrats were supporting the Germans at the orders of the Democrats in the *Majles*. The Germans spent much money and induced a number of people to their side or made them neutral. The British consul believed that the majority wanted the consuls to return even with the support of British and Russian troops, because their only fear was an advance by Hoseyn Ra'uf Bey. The latter was still at Sar-e Pol, but the Kalhors had left with whatever they could steal from him. Allegedly 150 men deserted and with their arms fled to the Kalhors. Hoseyn Ra'uf Bey continued to misbehave; he burnt some people alive and burnt the Ali-ilahi shrine at Baba Yadgar. The tribes, including the Kalhors and Jafs sworn an alliance to attack the Turks angered by the attack on the shrine and the occupation of their winter quarters.

On 20 August 1915, four German officers with seven loads of specie arrived in Kermanshah, also Atif Bey with 12 soldiers. The Swedish commander of the gendarmes undertook nothing without Schönemann's endorsement. Meanwhile, Kirsanov without his escort returned to Hamadan.[435] In the evening of 25 August it was reported that Schönemann with some Lors and Gurans had left Sahneh toward Kangavar. The town was safe as long the surrounding hills were held. Early in the morning of 26 August Schönemann occupied some of the hills vacated by the townspeople and the governor, Mirza Farajollah Khan, son of Sari Aslan, because he could only rely on his household servants. Schönemann wrote to the governor stating that he gave the consuls 3 hours to leave else he would attack. One hill was held by Persian Cossacks, who complained they were fired upon from the town. On both sides two people were killed and Schönemann sent a Baghdadi tribesman, Sayad al-Soltan, claiming to represent the Persian government, to prevent bloodshed. The governor sent the olama to say that the consuls would leave if he would withdraw. Finally, the governor saw Schönemann himself and after his return, he took the responsibility to conduct the two consuls safely to Hamadan. Schönemann had 200 men and two maxims plus some of Nazar 'Ali Khan's men, other Lors, some Gurans with Jahanbaksh Khan or his brother, and the son of Hoseyn Khan Guran, also some Kakawands and Khezels. Schönemann's force also occupied the road to Hamadan. The Persian government's gendarmes were sent, but only arrived at Kangavar when Schönemann's attack was in progress and they then decided not to join the fight and continued to Hamadan; the two consuls decided to do the same given Schönemann's superior position and force. In the afternoon, they left

434. FO 248/1112, McDouall/Kangavar to Legation, 21/08/1915. Some German agents in Persia were not enthused about this action by Schönemann and wrote: "he justifies his enormous expenditure of money by saying that he could not otherwise have held the Kerman[sic; shah] line of communication. IOR/L/PS/10/651, File 464/1917 Pt 2 'Persia: Bushire hinterland situation', p. 21.

435. FO 248/1112, McDouall/Kangavar to Legation, 25/08/1915.

accompanied by the governor and reached Asadabad. The governor of that place had orders to assist Kangavar and he supposedly had sent 200 men, but the consuls did not see any. Here they received a telegram that Schönemann had withdrawn as soon as the consuls had left. The Persian government then ordered Capt. Mamonov at Senneh to go to Kangavar, but the consuls had already left. It was the British Minister's opinion that the consuls only might return to Kermanshah with the support of 800-900 men plus two maxims. McDouall commented that "if allowed we could raise 1,000 horsemen and go."[436] Schönemann stayed at Bidsorkh and when the consuls reached Asadabad he and his men returned to Kermanshah. The Persian government demanded that the German embassy dismiss Schönemann. In reply the German ambassador blamed the entire incident on the British and Russians; Schönemann had only defended himself, given the fact that the Allies arrested German consuls in the areas of Persia that they controlled, without permission from the Persian government.[437]

Jalil al-Dowleh, a Moderate, who was head of the municipality of Kermanshah and was doing his best for the British, soon after Mo'azzam al-Saltaneh's arrival was replaced by Asad Khan Beglerbegi through German and Democrat intrigues. Asad Khan was the chief friend of the Germans. "Most of the people were annoyed at the Democrats helping the Germans and several meetings have been held at Jilli-ed-Daulah's house which had resulted in over a thousand Democrats joining the Moderate party ... these say they will not assist foreigners but most of them are secretly ready to help us." Allegedly, the Sanjabis and Gurans raided Turkish territory in retaliation for the burning of shrine. An Indian correspondent wrote that many, at least 250 were willing to escort the two consuls to Kermanshah. McDouall suggested that if the Persian government would nominally hire them Britain could pay them.[438] McDouall clearly was engaged in a bout of wishful thinking, or believed what his local sources reported to him, as there were not that many Persians, who supported British interests, as popular support for those who attacked these interests bears out.[439]

The tribes were very angry about the burning of Baba Yadgar. Mohammad Baqer Mirza restrained them from outright attacking Ra'uf Bey's force, but they had a large force at Kerend. The Kalhors who had deserted Ra'uf Bey often robbed his camp. At Kangavar, the bankrupt merchant Mohammad Ja'far, Askar Khan, chief of the road guards and one Abu Taleb were hiring men for the Germans. They offered 30 *tuman*s/month per horseman, 15 for foot and 100 for a commander. The people at Kangavar were said to be divided into three groups: 1. those who didn't want to be bothered; 2. those who were pro-German; and 3. those who could be bought. On his return to Kermanshah, Schönemann told his men that he only could pay them 3 *qran*s/day or 9 *tuman*s/month. They said if he did not pay they would hoist the Russian and the British flag. He then promised to ask his government to pay them as before. On 4 September 1915, a gendarme came to Kangavar saying Schönemann would be coming. Lunch was prepared and finally two men arrived with 15 Kermanshahi *savar*s with German badges, and five mounted

436. FO 248/1112, McDouall/Hamadan to Legation, 28/08/1915; FO 416/63 Marling to Grey, Tehran 30/08/1915. "Kangavar is important transit point through which Germans can send arms into Persian; we need to control that." FO 248/1112, no. 47, McDouall/Hamadan to Legation, 28/08/1915.

437. Miroshnikov 1963, p. 45; Hale n.d., p. 207.

438. FO 248/1112 McDouall/Hamadan to Legation, 10/09/1915.

439. Soltani 1386, pp. 205-06.

Gendarmes. The two men were dressed in European khaki riding suits with top boots and Persian caps. They told the governor's *farrash-bashi* that they were Turkish officers, Mahmud Nadim and Jalal Bey, who were going to Tehran to arrange that the force at Sar-e Pol might be withdrawn without attacks by the tribes, who shortly would go to their winter quarters. They left to Malayer in the afternoon.[440]

In early October 1915, 30 loads of German munitions arrived in Kermanshah, including iron for fortifications and land mines. Some 300 Turkish troops were gradually smuggled into the city, who wore Persian caps and German badges, while also 70 Germans from Baghdad arrived. Schönemann was enlisting men and he wanted to raise 20,000 men to assist defend Baghdad.[441] Allegedly Schönemann gave tribes access to winter quarters in Iraq as their own were burnt, if they would not attack Hoseyn Ra'uf Bey. There were 30 Germans in Kermanshah, including mechanics. They hired Kerendi smiths to make, or rather assemble, magazines and automatic rifles. Moreover, each night ammunition was arriving from Baghdad. Schönemann was the de-facto governor of Kermanshah, who went around on a motorcycle. There were about 400 gendarmes; half local men; many of the original gendarmes had left. The Persian government had abandoned Kermanshah to the Germans and the notables were in communication with Germans.[442] By the end of September 1915, Hoseyn Ra'uf Bey left Sar-e Pol to Baghdad. Some 60 Persians under Ebrahim Beg, a Caucasian, who had joined him, returned to Kermanshah without arms and joined the Germans, who sent arms and pamphlets to Isfahan. Shahzadeh Hoseyn, a notorious ruffian in German employ, got into a fight with a man and people complained and were ready to attack him; he was then fired and 50 men threw down their badge and were fired as well.[443]

TRIBES AGREE TO SUPPORT GERMANS AND TURKS

At that time, the Allies were unable to take immediate action against the Germans in Kermanshah, because their forces were fully occupied elsewhere in Persia and Iraq. Because the Germans believed that the Russians would try to capture Baghdad via Kermanshah, Count Kanitz was sent to that city to prepare counter-measures to prevent this. Spending much money, he made alliances with various tribal groups, stocked arms and ammunition, and surveyed the terrain to prepare defensive measures. At that time, according to the British, there were at least 60 Germans, and 250 Austrians, mostly prisoners of war who had escaped from Russian prisons, with 80,000 rifles, seven or eight machine guns and bombs. There also were some 300 Turkish troops, who wore Persian caps with German badges, while more were being enlisted in Iraq.[444] To shore up Persian support the Germans hammered their message: 1. respect for Persia's

---

440. FO 248/1112, McDouall/Hamadan to Legation,18/09/1915 (Friends at Kermanshah said that if the Persian Government ordered Samsam al-Mamalek to escort consuls he would do so).

441. FO 248/1112, Telegram McDouall/Hamadan to Legation, 13/09/1915.

442. FO 248/1112, McDouall/Hamadan to Legation, 22/09/1915.

443. FO 248/1112, McDouall/Hamadan to Legation, 02/10/1915.

444. Moberley 1987, p. 112. Kanitz's activities, who had promised much and spent much money, ran totally counter to what the German Minister, Reuss, tried to achieve in Tehran. Bast 1997, p. 30.

sovereignty, integrity and neutrality and 2. support for Persia's desire to be rid of British and Russian domination. This tailor-made message had the desired result for many people and political groups were ready to collaborate with the Germans.[445]

On 26 September 1915, Hajji Mirza Mehdi Khan, secretary of the Persian Legation in Istanbul and Fawzi Bey, the new military attaché at Tehran, came to Kermanshah to assess the damage caused by Hoseyn Ra'uf Bey. Fawzi Bey was accompanied by 11 Persian students who had been trained at Turkish military schools. Fawzi Bey not only brought about a reconciliation between the tribal leaders and Hoseyn Ra'uf Bey, but was able to induce the tribes to support their cause. Mohammad Baqer Mirza, one of the leading Democrats, tried to induce the various tribal leaders to join forces. This was, of course, strongly supported by Schönemann, who already employed a large number of members of various tribes to which end he spent large sums of money. The British suspected that the Germans wanted to use their tribal support to reinforce Turkish troops at Baghdad.[446]

In early October 1915 the leaders of the Kalhors, Sanjabis and Gurans met at Mahidasht and agreed to jointly oppose the British and Russian occupation of Persia. Fawzi Bey brought some Koran manuscripts, some to be sent to others towns, and asked in name of this holy book to join them. At a meeting in the *kargozari* it was agreed that:

> As on the coming of the Turkish army certain regrettable incidents took place between the tribes and the army which are contrary to the good understanding between Persia and Turkey therefore at this time Mirza Mehdi Khan secretary to the Persian Embassy at Constantinople and Fauzi Bey military attache to Turkish Embassy at Tehran have come to enquire into these events. At the Karguzarate the Tribal chiefs undertake that from and after this date they will safeguard the passage of Turkish passengers and merchandise from Kaleh Sabzi to Kermanshah and their followers will carry this out and not allow any loss or damage provided that Turks assure the safe passage of Persian travellers, pilgrims, and merchandise and that Husain Raouf's forces should leave Khaniqin in that no such events should occur in future.
> Sealed by Karguzar; Samsam el-Mamalek Sanjabi; Suliman Sardar Nusret Kalhur; Ali Akbar Sanjabi Sardar Nasir; Salar Mansur son of Husan Khan Guran Sardar Muazzam.[447]

Hoseyn Khan Guran was paralyzed and was unable to attend. Ehtesham al-Mamalek and his Kerendis refused to sign and sent the government in Tehran a claim for one milion *tuman*s in damages. Fawzi Beg signed a paper that Persian merchants could safely pass and that Hoseyn Ra'uf Bey would leave Khaneqin to Baghdad. Mohammad Baqer Mirza and Qavam al-Olama had made peace between Schönemann and the Sanjabis and 'Ali Akbar Khan Sardar Moqtader had met Schönemann and allegedly received a large sum which pacified him. The Sanjabis also

---

445. Soltani 1396, pp. 205-06.

446. FO 248/1112. No. 56. Camp Hamadan, Oct. 9,1915. McDouall to Marling; FO 371/2435. Tel. No. 1940. Sept. 14,1915. Cox to Secretary to the Government of India.

447. FO 248/1112, no. 56 (09/10/1915).

signed because they wanted Qasr-e Shirin and Samsam al-Mamalek had been made governor there again. In exchange the tribes were to provide *savar*s, viz. the Sanjabis, Kalhors and Gurans 300 each, the Kerendis 50 and 20 foot, and the Ahmadavands 25. Ostensibly these *savar*s were to assist the gendarmes to protect the road, each in their own tribal district. Each *savar* received 9 *tumans*/month nominally from the Persian government, but in reality from Schönemann. In this way Schönemann had all the tribes under his thumbs and prevented the governor raising *savar*s making excuses such as migration to winter quarters and roads have to be guarded. In addition to Kermanshahi *savar*s and those of Nazar 'Ali Khan, he sent the son of Hajji Mo'adel to the Peyravands[448] and also send to the Koliya'is and Kurdistanis. They had to undertake to provide a number of *savar*s, who only would be called upon when needed, but would be paid while at home; in this way he raised 2,000 men.

Eqbal al-Dowleh in need of men, telegraphed Mo'azzam al-Saltaneh to send him 300 tribal levies as an escort for which he would pay. Schönemann believed that this was a scheme to escort the British and Russian consuls back. He had already engaged 300 *savar*s through Sardar Ejlal Zanganeh and 'Abbas Khan Kalhor; he paid one installment and gave them German badges. Sardar Nosrat hearing this also wanted to be hired. Not all tribes had jumped on the Turkish-German bandwagon. One Hasan Khan Koliya'i had entered German service and showed up with his men wearing German badges. Mansur al-Soltan arrested and ill-treated them saying: "you want to give Germans access to Kuliai lands?" Schönemann sent some *savar*s to free them as they were under German protection. Nevertheless, McDouall lamented: "The chief reason of the decay of British and Russian influence is that while we were in Hamadan at first, though some of the tribes and townspeople were with Schunemann the majority both of the tribes and town were our partisans and expected us to come with sufficient force, others, too, were afraid of thwe consequences if they joined Schunemann, but since the Kanhavar affair and our return to Hamadan and time has passed and they have no news of our coming people have become hopeless and no longer expect us to return and Schunemann's position had much improved na di increased by large sums he has paid and is paying. The situation is now like it was in the time of Salar-ed-Dowleh. Schunemann being in the prince's palace. The house of Rais-et-Tujar is the German Consulate and Ali Akbar [Khan Sanjabi] lives there whom Schunemann addresses as Amir Jang, he he himself lives in the house of Seyed Mohammed Guniferrush with the sowars." Sayyed Hasan Owjaq promised to bring *savar*s and the position of the Moderates, to whom Schönemann showed much friendship, had much improved. Meanwhile, there was dissension in the ranks of the Democrats, some were pro-German, others wanted to maintain neutrality. Eqbal al-Dowleh telegraphed that the Turkish embassy did not want Samsam al-Mamalek as governor of Qasr-e Shirin, which was his condition to make peace with the Germans and Turks. According to McDouall's sources, "All tribes and most townspeople have become paid servants of Germans except the Hajjizadehs due to Naser Divan." The city's defensive capacity was being strengthened. By night much ammunition was arriving as well as many 18-year old Germans. McDouall sent the *kargozar* a telegram announcing the British victory at Kut al-Amara, which was published in the city. Schönemann immediately countered with a print sheet of German victories in Europe sending copies to olama and notables. To extend his sphere of inflence, Schönemann placed *savar*s at the villages to Kangavar and even sent some to

448. The Peyravands were led by six *kadkhodas*, "but no chiefs, and various cousins are continually fighting for the chieftainship." Napier 1919, p. 10.

Hamadan. On 9 October 1915, he left to Bisotun, apparently to see the Kakawands. The German commanding the *savar*s went to see Jahanbakhsh to arrange the peace between Guran and Sanjabis as agreed at Mahidasht meeting.[449]

Meanwhile, the Germans extended their activities to Hamadan, where consular agent Weber and Lt. Erdmann raised men and enjoyed strong local support, with the objective to expel the British and Russian consuls. The local governor, Amir Afkham, was unable to impose himself and the situation became dire. Against the will of the Persian government, the Russian ambassador sent the 300 men of the Persian Cossack Brigade, which was officered by Russians, to Hamadan where they took up position at the strategic Mosalla Qal'eh. The local population was afraid that a fight might break out between the Cossacks and the pro-German local gendarmerie and other local pro-German forces. At that time, the Persian government decided to disband the national Gendarmerie, which was hailed by the British, but deplored by nationalist groups. However, the government had no money to pay the force, the arrears in pay were substantial. Moreover, the British decided to stop their subsidy for the Gendarmerie, because they believed that its Swedish officers had been important conduits for German propaganda and support.[450]

MIGRATION OF NATIONALISTS TO QOM

The Persian government was increasingly put under greater pressure by the opposing European powers to join their side. This sometimes was of a very direct and personal nature. Toward the end of November 1915, Major de Maree informed Farmanfarma if he did not join the nationalist party all his properties in W. Persia would be destroyed. Farmanfarma then asked the British and Russian Ministers whether he would be compensated by their governments if this happened.[451] Allied mistrust of the Persian government grew after it became known that there had been secret negotiations with Germany in early November 1915. This resulted in a draft mutual defense agreement, in case of an attack by Great Britain and Russia. Germany further promised to finance the cost of war, to supply large quantities of arms and ammunition, training and officers to Persia as well as to grant it a loan of 500,000 *tuman*s to be paid in monthly installments. The loan was to be secured by the Customs revenues. Persia promised not to join the Allies, to make 100,000 soldiers available, to allow a German bank to be established in Persia and to confiscate the assets of the IBP and, in case of war with Great Britain and Russia, was only to begin hostilities after 50,000 rifles had been supplied. The Allies warned the Persian government that if it signed such a treaty they would take appropriate steps to protect their citizens. The Persian government denied the existence of the agreement. However, from German sources it is clear that it existed, although it had not been signed. It would appear the Mostawfi al-Mamalek, the Prime Minister,

---

449. FO 248/1112, McDouall/Hamadan to Legation, 09/10/1915; Idem, McDouall/Hamadan to Legation, 16/10/1915.

450. FO 416/63. Tel. No. 296. Marling to Grey, 26/08/1915. According to Russian and German sources, Swedish officers received payments from the German Ministry of Foreign Affairs. Miroshnikov 1963, p. 46; Ducrocq 1923, pp. 83-45, 150-53; Blücher 1949, p. 16 (concerning Germanophile Swedish officers).

451. FO 416/63, Marling to Grey, 26/11/1915.

was waiting for the arms to be supplied and the loan payments to begin before he considered signing. Fear for the reaction of the Allies also played a role.[452]

German influence was at its highest at that time and even the Allies feared a German takeover and the establishment of a pro-German government in Persia. The Germans continued with their preparations to stop an expected Russian attack on Baghdad. When the alliance between Persia and the Allies became known, Germany reacted by warning Persia that it would suffer the fate of Belgium and Serbia when German forces would march to invade India.[453] To cooperate with the British against the Turks in Iraq and counter German activities in Kermanshah, Russia sent to Persia about 15,000 men, half of whom were mounted, with 46 guns, which advanced to Kermanshah, Tehran, Isfahan and Qazvin. However, due to bad roads their progress was slow. General Baratov entered Enzeli on 30 October 1915 and established his headquarters two days later in Qazvin.[454] Subsequent talks between the Persian government and the Allies did not improve the situation. Totally unexpected, on 15 November 1915, many *Majles* deputies and nationalist supporters, fearing Russian occupation of Tehran and demands by the Allies, fled the city and went to Qom. Ahmad Shah who also had considered leaving at the very last moment decided to stay, having been persuaded by the Allied ambassadors of the dire consequences for himself and the country if he would leave. The arrival of fresh Russian troops at Karaj, threatening Tehran, induced Ahmad Shah on 2 November 1915, whose carriage was ready for departure to Qom the entire day, to remain in the capital. In Qom, this group of nationalists, which was referred to as *mohajerin* or migrants, established a committee of national defense (*komiteh-ye defa'-e melli*), at the instigation of German ambassador Reuss and Schönemann who had gone to Qom as well.[455]

Meanwhile, the situation in Hamadan was serious. The city was in the hands of pro-German forces and the Persian Cossacks, although the Germans argued that the Russians controlled the city. The Persian Cossacks had been reinforced and numbered 550 men; they had taken up positions at Mosalla Qal'eh. Also, there was a Russian consular guard of 40 in Hamadan, while 200 additional Russian soldiers had come from Tehran. The British consul had a guard of 100 cavalry and 50 infantry of the Indian army, which made the consulates look like forts rather than diplomatic buildings.[456] The pro-German forces received support from Kermanshah. Tribesmen as well as gendarmes from elsewhere joined them, so that some 2,000 gendarmes were present in the city, who were commanded by Major Mohammad Taqi Khan Pesiyan and two Swedish officers. It was *Moharram* and the olama harangued the believers, stirring up

452. Gehrke 1377, vol. 1, pp. 300-04; vol. 2, pp. 890-97; Sepehr 1337, 264; Dowlatabadi 1330, vol. 3, 312; Miroshnikov 1963, p. 48; Slaby 1982, p. 300.

453. Miroshnikov 1963, p. 50.

454. IOR/L/MIL/17/15/72/1, 'Critical Study of the Campaign in Mesopotamia up to April 1917: Part I - Report', p. 119; Erdmann 1918, p. 120; Ducrocq 1923, pp. 183-84.

455. Vahid al-Molk 1378, pp. 21-22; Miroshnikov 1963, pp. 49-50; Blücher 1949, p. 26; Ezz al-Mamalek 1332, pp. 50-63; Adib al-Saltaneh 1332, pp. 17-20; Malekzadeh Hirbod 1328, p. 22; Divanbegi 1351, pp. 4-6; Soltani, Nahzat, pp. 207-08; Gehrke 1377, vol. 1, pp. 348-50; Ducrocq 1923, p. 184. On the events leading to the movement of the *mohajerin*, also see Salar-Behzadi, 1372, pp. 608-37.

456. Miroshnikov 1963, p. 45; Erdmann 1918, p. 114 (Russians had sent 200 horse and 50 foot as reinforcement; the British in addition to the Indian escort had hired a few hundred sowars; the German consular agent had only 60 sowars).

anti-Allied feelings by referring to Russian behavior in Tabriz and their shelling of the Imam Reza shrine in Mashhad in 1912. However, despite the tense atmosphere there were no disturbances. Finally, Pesiyan offered the Persian Cossacks unhindered departure and when this was refused he attacked and surrounded Mosalla Qal'eh on 22 November 1915. After a short fight the Cossacks, who had hardly resisted, surrendered and were disarmed. McDouall burnt ciphers and secret documents; he was in contact with the governor, but not with his Russian colleague as his house was in the zone of fighting. The governor could do nothing and the gendarmerie officers refused to see him or the consuls when he sent for them. The Russians did not take part in the fight. The Persian Cossacks held out in a caravanserai, shooting occasionally. The governor arranged that if the Cossacks surrendered their arms the Russian consul and escort would be allowed to leave immediately; the British were given till noon the next day and would not be molested. The Germans and the gendarmes refused to let the money of the IBP be moved. Some of the Persian Cossacks joined the gendarmes, the majority left to Qazvin. Pesiyan became military governor after he had arrested Salar Lashkar, the governor. The British colony and McDouall left at noon 22 November. On 25 November they met the Russians and Cossack 50 miles from Hamadan and then proceeded to Qazvin. This was a great victory for the Germans and the Persian nationalists, the more so, because similar events took place in Shiraz, Arak and later also in Isfahan, Yazd and Kerman. However, these developments were strongly denounced by the Persian government, who made it known that Persia maintained friendly relations with Great Britain and Russia.[457] On 24 November, the German consular agent wired from Hamadan: "thank God, the German and Persian mujahids have driven their enemy from Hamadan and British and Russian consuls left for Qazvin and property and cash of British bank detained and mujahids pursue the enemy."[458]

Meanwhile, on 21 November 1915, 'Ali Akbar Sanjabi with 200 *savar*s, 'Abdollah Khan *farrash-bashi* Kalhor with 100 *savar*s went to the German force at Berenjan[459] (16 km from Kermanshah on the Senneh road) to oppose the Persian Cossacks. The gendarmes with Sonesen returned as the Cossacks had withdrawn. Other chiefs came into town to help the townspeople and see 'Ali Akbar Khan Sanjabi. The *savar*s had suffered many casualties during previous fighting. 'Ali Mohammad Khan, a Kolia'i then at Kermanshah had undertaken to supply 50 *savar*s out of fear for Qavam al-Olama and Imam Jom'eh, but friends of the British prevented this, after which he did not want to support the Germans.

On 26 November 1915, a telegram from the Committee of National Defense at Qom arrived addressed to the olama, notables and people of Kermanshah, calling on them to unite as 'Persia, the Crown and Throne' were in danger. It was signed by four deputies. The Democrats wanted to send telegrams to Qom, Tehran and Hamadan; it was proposed to hold a meeting in the house of the Imam Jom'eh, because Aqa Rahim, the principal *mojtahed* refused to have it in his house or to attend it. The meeting was attended by 'Ali Akbar Sanjabi, Jalil al-Dowleh, 'Abdollah

---

457. FO 248/1112, McDouall/Qazvin to Legation, 30/11/1915; Miroshnikov 1963, p. 50. For an account how the German led force took Hamadan, see Erdmann 1918, pp. 141-54; for the Moharram processions, see Idem, p. 136f.

458. FO 248/1112, McDouall/Qazvin to Legation, 23/12/1915. According to Erdmann 1918, pp. 154-55 they obtained 300 modern rifles with much ammunition, two machine-guns, mountain equipment, 30,000 rounds of ammunition, mules, horses, and 135,000 *tumans* in cash.

459. Perhaps Babajan?

Khan *farrash-bashi* Kalhor, Mohammad Baqer Mirza, Qavam al-Olama, Amin al-Mamalek, Sayyed Hasan Owjaq, As'ad al-Dowleh, and others. But the leading olama and many notables did not attend. Mehdi Mo'tamed al-Tojjar produced a draft reply stating that they were ready to defend themselves against the British and Russians. A discussion took place and against it spoke: Hasan shoemaker, Sayyed 'Ali, head of the *bazzaz-khaneh*, Taqi shoemaker, A'sad goldmith, Hasan packsadler, and Meshdi Agha'i baker. They asked why should we listen to four fugitive deputies. Finally, a draft was produced in which it was said that the people were united and ready to obey the orders of the government (*owliya-ye omur*) and did not support any foreigners.

On 25 November 1915, the Turkish consul circulated a gelatin news sheet[460] stating that the British had been defeated at 'Azizeh; three steamers had been captured and one sunk in the Euphrates. Also, that Khalil Bey had reached Baghdad with reinforcements, airplanes and armed cars. The Italians had withdrawn from Tripoli due to the *mojaheds* there. In the bazaar Sayyed 'Ali, head of the *Bazzaz-khaneh* openly cursed those who took German gold, which caused damage and pillage to the town. Abu'l-Fath Mirza, chief of police, assisted the Germans. Mohammad Baqer Mirza and Qavam al-Olama wanted to send 200 *savars* to Hamadan to show their support. Sheikh 'Ali, brother of Mo'aven al-Molk opposed this saying that if the Russians had no intention to attack this would induce them to do so, and this would cause damage to the town. Also, a draft telegram circulated against the return of the consuls, but *mojtahed* Aqa Rahim prevented most of the olama from signing it. In general, the city's elite did not want to assist the Germans.[461]

Meanwhile, the Russians had sent 300 men to Hamadan to protect the foreign consuls, not knowing that these had already left for Qazvin. On 30 November the Russian force was confronted by armed Persian gendarmes at the Soltan Bolagh pass and were forced to withdraw. The nationalists cried victory. In reaction, the Russians sent a force of 3,000 men and after hard fighting at Saveh it was able to force the Persian force to withdraw to Hamadan. The defeat caused panic in the city and the pro-German elements fled. On 16 December 1915, the Russian force took Hamadan and hoisted the Russian flag over its Consulate.[462] The Russians had been successful in ousting the hostile force from Hamadan, despite the fact that they had a shortage of boots and ammunition.[463] Part of the Russian force defeated a Persian force and marched southward taking Qom in mid-December. By early January 1916, Kashan and Isfahan had fallen into Russian hands.

---

460. A photographic process in which gelatin is used as the dispersing vehicle for the light-sensitive silver salts. The process, introduced in about 1880, superseded the wet collodion process, in which a wet negative was produced from a nitrocellulose (collodion).

461. FO 248/1112, McDouall/Qazvin to Legation, 23/12/1915.

462. FO 371/2724, No. 90, Consul Kermanshah/Hamadan to Legation, 05/01/1916; "The Times", 11/12/1915; Miroshnikov 1963, p. 51; Blücher 1949, p. 28 (9 December); Ezz al-Mamalek 1332, pp. 63, 65, 77; Adib al-Saltaneh 1332, p. 21, 30.

463. FO 371/2724, Marling to FO, 24/03/1916.

'NATIONAL' GOVERNMENT IN KERMANSHAH

When the Germans failed to turn the Persian government they tried to influence the Committee in Qom. From Qom, Count Kanitz asked Major Edwall and the other Swedish officers in Tehran to disarm the Persian Cossacks, to kidnap the Shah and take him to Qom, and thereafter to oppose the Russian incursion. Failing that the Swedish officers had to defect to the German-Turkish side with their troops. If they refused they would be dismissed from the ranks of the German army, where they held ranks in the reserves. Most officers (Edwall, Frick, Sonneson, Kjellstrom, Erikson, Prawitz, Hellemark, Pousette, de Maree) had already chosen the German side, only a few remained in Tehran (Gleerup, Lundberg). The second gendarmerie regiment under Major Frick marched to Qom and put himself under the orders of Kanitz, who later would use the regiment to defend Saveh and Qom in November-December 1915. Taken aback by the development of events in Tehran, on 2 December 1915, the Committee of National Defense in Qom signed an agreement of cooperation with Germany. The Moderates undertook to assist and co-operate with the Germans for Perso-German interests in all cities of Persia. The Germans promised to assist the Committee and its allies in the various cities of Persia with money, arms, ammunition and officers.[464] However, Germany was only able to supply some small arms and a small number of officers. On the other hand, the disparate forces that formally proclaimed their support for the Committee's goals were so varied and disunited that the formation of a truly national force under one leadership that might withstand Allied forces was a practical impossibility. This became very clear after the Russian army, despite heavy opposition from Persian nationalist forces, began its unstoppable march towards Kermanshah. After successes at Saveh and Robat-e Karim, the Russians defeated the Persian force at Arak on 21 January 1916 and moved toward Borujerd, where they met with a friendly welcome from the Lors, who ensured that Lorestan remained peaceful.[465]

Meanwhile, the Moderates were trying to put together a national leadership that would appeal to broad segments of society. After Mokhber al-Saltaneh had refused, Mosavat, one of the leaders of the Moderates, accompanied by Count Kanitz and a few German officers went to Borujerd to ask Nezam al-Saltaneh, governor of Borujerd, Lorestan and Arabistan to accept the leadership role. Count Kanitz had discussed the issue already with Nezam al-Saltaneh in the summer of 1915 and on 26 December 1915 the two men signed an agreement. The Germans promised arms and technical assistance and would advance funds for the expense of the war, while Nezam al-Saltaneh, who (including his heirs in case of his death) would receive 20,000 *tumans* monthly and a guarantee of his property up to 2 million *tumans*, whatever the outcome of the war, promised: 1. To follow the orders of von Goltz, 2. Have at least 4,000 men ready by 14 January 1916 and then within two months an additional 6,000 men and, 3. Assume leadership of the movement and its armed force.[466] Schönemann was allegedly against this agreement with

464. Sepehr 1337, p. 258; Ansari 1353, pp. 129-30. For the text of the agreement with Schönemann, see Gehrke 1377, vol. 1, pp. 348-52; vol. 2, p. 905 (doc. 20).

465. Miroshnikov 1963, pp. 51, 69-70; Moberley 1987, p. 137-38; Malekzadeh Hirbod 1328, p. 23; Divanbegi 1351, p. 6; Bast 1997, p. 35.

466. Gehrke 1377, pp. 901-03 (doc. 18 with the correct date of month, but with the wrong year); Ducrocq 1923, pp. 98-99 (doc. 1), 187; Blücher 1949, pp. 28-29; Malekzadeh Hirbod 1328, p. 22; Divanbegi 1351, p. 7; Soltani 1386,

Nezam al-Saltaneh. He had been warned during his secret visit to Tehran in November 1915 by Mohtasham al-Saltaneh, the Minister of Foreign Affairs, who was a close relative of Nezam al-Saltaneh and sympathetic to the German side. He told Schönemann that his cousin was materialistic, unreliable, and ambitious, characteristics that Schönemann would experience for himself, as he wrote later.[467]

> Reza Qoli Khan. Mafi Nezam al-Saltaneh (Mojir al-Saltaneh and Salar-e Mo'azzam), born about 1863. Son of Heydar Qoli Khan Mafi and nephew of Hoseyn Qoli Khan Mafi, Nezam al-Saltaneh I. In 1894, Nezam al-Saltaneh and his family (Reza Qoli served as deputy-governor in 1893) were banned from the governorship of Bushehr for seven years, due to complaints about their misrule and British pressure. Governor of the Persian Gulf Ports (1902-04). When the Belgians took over the collection of the Customs he fraudulently presented himself to Tehran as one of the Qaids of Hayat Da'ud and received part of the subsidy given them in compensation. He inherited from his uncles the valuable Zireh district (Dashtestan) and the villages of Daliki and Bibira and the district of Khisht. He bought the Khaviz and Ahram districts in Tangestan. From 1905-08 he was governor of Khuzestan and established lasting good relations with Sheikh Khaz'al. In 1908 he returned to Tehran and succeeded his uncle as Nezam al-Saltaneh. In 1910, he was governor of Kermanshah and in January-September 1911 governor of Fars. "He had formed a compact of all Chiefs in the South, to witthe Wali of Pust-i-Kuh, Shaikh of Muhammerah and Soulat al-Doulah, the Ilkhani of the Qashqai, and shortly after his arrival in Shiraz picked a quarrel with Qawam-ul-Mulk IV and his brother, which ended in the brothers being sent to Europe under escort. On the way they were ambushed near Khaneh Zinian by the instigation of their enemy, Soulet al-Douleh (probably with the connivance of Nizam-us-Saltaneh). Nasr-ud-Douleh was killed, Qawam-ul-Mulk IV escaped to the British Consulate, Shiraz, where he remained in 'bast' for two months." His wife sent for the Khamseh tribesmen and this resulted in heavy fighting between Nizam-ul-Saltaneh and the Qawam quarter of Shiraz. "He also instigated a Persian regiment to force their way into the British Consulate." Abandoned by his Qashqa'i friends, he was dismissed by the Bakhtiyari cabinet which attached all his estates and ordered his arrest. He fled to Daleki where his friend Sheikh Khaz'al in October 1911 sent an Arab force to take him to Muhammarah. He went to Europe (mostly in Switzerland) where he remained until the beginning of 1914, when he was allowed to return. In June 1914, he became governor of Lurestan and Borujerd. When Mostawfi al-Mamalek in November 1915 sent a circular-telegram to all governors that Ahmad Shah would leave Tehran and was about to declare war on Great Britain and Russia he openly threw in his lot with the Turks and Germans, with whom he had earlier contacts. He promised to raise levies in Lurestan for which he pocketed money upfront, reportedly £80,000.

pp. 210-12; Idem 1381, vol. 4, pp. 792-93; Bast 1997, p. 35; Safa'i 1346, vol. 2, pp. 182-83.

467. Ansari 1353, pp. 129-30.

With a few hundred Lurs he marched to Hamadan but then turned to Kermanshah and joined the Mohajerin and the rest. He was routed at Asadabad by the Russians and fled to Kermanshah and fled with them when they withdrew. He was sentenced to 10 years of exile (he lived in Switzerland), but was allowed to return in the fall of 1921. He landed in Muhammarah, took control of his estates, which Sheikh Khaz'al had mortgaged in 1911 by a loan from the IBP to the latter. In 1922, he was governor of Khorasan. Was avaricious and played a baneful role in the South.

Source: IOR/L/PS/20/224, 'Biographies of the notables of Fars and certain Persian officials who have served at Shiraz. Delhi: Government of India, 1925', p. 60-61; IOR/L/MIL/17/15/11/7, 'Who's Who in Persia (Volume IV) Persian Baluchistan, Kerman, Bandar Abbas, Fars, Yezd and Laristan', p. 113.

When Nezam al-Saltaneh arrived from Lorestan in Kermanshah he had 4,000-5,000 men with him. According to Mirza Farajollah Khan Mo'tamadi, who acted as translator during these negotiations, Nezam al-Saltaneh demanded a payment of 500,000 gold liras in cash as compensation for his properties, which he feared would be confiscated. On 6 January 1916, after the first payment of 350,000 gold liras was delivered to Borujerd, Nezam al-Saltaneh only moved as far as Sahneh, at 10 km from Kermanshah. Here, he insisted on payment of the remaining 150,000 liras before moving to that city.[468]

Since early 1915, Kermanshah had become the center of German activities that increased in size and intensity during that year. The city had been without a governor for months so that neither government officials nor army personnel had been paid. When Eqbal al-Dowleh, the new governor, arrived in Kermanshah he tried to do something about this without much success. Despite the unsettled situation many inhabitants fully supported the Qom Committee, because they resented the Russian advance. However, there was also a strong reactionary group in the city, which opposed the Democrats. Moreover, there were differences between the Germans and the Turks.[469] Most of the neighboring tribes declared their support for the *mohajerin* movement.[470] The gendarmerie at Kermanshah, under Captain Sonesen, disarmed the Persian Cossacks garrisoned in town. On 10 December 1915, the gendarmes occupied all government offices and the PTT,[471] while tribal groups occupied all Customs stations in the province and arrested the Belgian head of the Customs Department. The gendarmes seized about 23,500 *tumans*, which were in the Customs office. Furthermore, the local Committee for National Defense appointed a number of persons to censor all publications and communications. As of that moment, Kermanshah was firmly in the hands of the nationalists and opposed to the Allies. This also became clear from the stream of German officials that came to the city. The German ambassador,

468. Blücher 1949, pp. 28-29; Malekzadeh Hirbod 1328, p. 22; Divanbegi 1351, p. 7; Soltani 1386, pp. 210-12; Idem 1381, vol. 4, pp. 792-93; Slaby 1982, p. 296 (Nezam al-Saltaneh received 80,000 *Reichs Mark* (RM) per month as personal income and 320,000 RM for his cavalry).

469. Vahid al-Molk 1378, p. 42.

470. Soltani 1381, vol. 4. pp. 793-95.

471. On behalf of the local *komiteh-ye defa`i-ye melli-ye Kermanshah*, which consisted of Mohammad Baqer Mirza Khosrovi, Qavam al-Olama, Sayyed Hasan Owjaq, Jalil al-Dowleh, and Sayyed Abbas, on 11 December 1915, for each office three persons were appointed to censor all mail and telegrams. Messages in code were banned. Soltani 1381, vol. 4, p. 794.

Prince Reuss, who had been recalled to Berlin, because of the failure of his policy to have Persia join the Axis powers, passed through Kermanshah on 13 December 1915 and assured the nationalists of German support. Dr. Vassel, who took over as German Minister in Persia and who had to renegotiate the agreement with Nezam al-Saltaneh, did the same on his arrival in Kermanshah on 6 January 1916. In fact, on the last day of January, in Sahneh, he gave Nezam al-Saltaneh a letter in which he committed the German government to defend the territory, political independence and economy of Persia, during peace negotiations after victory had been obtained. On 16 January 1916, Marshall von der Goltz Pasha together with Colonel Bopp, who was in charge of military operations in Persia, spent three days in Kermanshah and held talks with local leaders, German and Turkish representatives. Of the latter, Fawzi Bey, the military attaché as well as the Turkish consul were directing Turkish, mainly pan-Islamic, propaganda. Bopp had about 30 officers with him to train Persian troops. The arrival of the *mohajerin* in the city in early February 1916, fleeing before the Russian advance, made the situation in the city even tenser. A meeting of local religious, political and tribal leaders on 20 February 1916 decided to ask Nezam al-Saltaneh to form a national government.[472]

> Due to the importance of the present situation of the country and the necessity for maintaining the means of forces and effective policy for securing of the internal administration of the country, releasing His Majesty Ahmad Shah from danger and siege of foreign forces, and concluding political and military conventions and agreements, the committee of representatives believe that it is necessary to organise a council of executives which will be under your leadership to enact the duties according to opinions and programs which will be obtained by the committee of representatives.[473]

Nezam al-Saltaneh's relationship with the Germans became complicated because neither side seemed to be able to meet each other's demands. Kanitz *cum suis* were disavowed, because they had no authority to have made their various promises and commitments to the nationalists. Also, the Germans went out of their way not to create the impression that the institutions that the *mohajerin* had established were seen by them as governmental. On 31 January 1916, Dr. Vassel, who had taken over from Prince Reuss, made it clear to Nezam al-Saltaneh that if Persia did not enter the war German guarantees would be voided. Vassel also was at odds with Fawzi Bey. On the other hand, Nezam al-Saltaneh's position was strengthened by the acknowledgment of the Committee in Qom and the subsequent formation of a provisional government, which enabled him to conclude an agreement with Germany and Turkey. In addition of a government, there also was a consultative council in which both Democrats and Moderates were represented. Although, an 'alternative' to the government in Tehran, the new government's edicts were issued in the name of Ahmad Shah. In reaction, the Tehran government confiscated Nezam al-Saltaneh's property.[474]

---

472. Vahid al-Molk 1378, p. 42 (names); Soltani 1381, vol. 4, pp. 974-75 (the German military mission arrived on 2 January 1916), 798; Bast 1997, p. 34 (1 January). For the von der Goltz and Bopp mission, see Ducrocq 1923, pp. 100-10 (Instructions for von der Goltz), 124-25 and Gehrke 1377, vol. 1, pp. 203-95 and vol. 2, pp. 880-83, 898-900. For Vassel's letter, see Gehrke 1377, vol. 2, p. 908 (doc. 22).

473. Sepehr 1337, p. 309; Qudsi 1342, p. 33. According to Vahid al-Molk 1378, pp. 41, it was Dr. Vassel who had pressured Nezam al-Saltaneh to form a provisional government.

474. Soltani 1386, pp. 801-02; Idem 1381, vol. 4, pp. 799-800 (with composition and program); Gehrke 1377, vol. 1, pp. 359-64.

Fig. 7.8: Nezam al-Saltaneh Cabinet (1916). *From left to right:* Qasem Khan, Minister of Post; Mohammad `Ali Khan Mafi, Minister of Foreign Affairs; Sayyed Hasan Modarres, Minister of Justice; Nezam al-Saltaneh, Head of Government; Adib al-Saltaneh, Minister of Interior; Mohammad `Ali Khan Farzineh, Minister of Finance; Hajji `Ezz al-Mamalek, Minister of Public Works.

According to a report from Mashhad, in the second week of December 1915, Democrats met in the home of Mashhadi Taqi to form a cabinet that consisted of: Nezam al-Saltaneh, Prime Minister; Salar A'zam, Foreign Affairs; Adib al-Saltaneh, Posts; Hajji Esma'il Tabrizi, Education; and Hajji Seyid Mehdi, Interior. Soleyman Mirza was charged to make this known throughout Persia. Malik al-Sho'ara objected because not all Democratic societies in Persia had been consulted. He was told that in principle he was correct, but the Khorasan society had not contributed *mojaheds* to the common cause. All agreed that this was fair. Therefore, a circular letter was drafted to be sent to Sabzavar, Nishapur, Bojnord etc. instructing Democrats to make a list of all firearms in their possession, to buy more of them, especially from Russian soldiers, with a view to form *mojahed* levies.[475]

475. IOR/L/PS/10/210, File 52/1912 Pt. 2 'Persian Diaries,' Meshed Diary no, 51 for the week ending the 16th of December 1916, p. 2

Table 7.1: Composition of the first provisional government (February 1916)

Name 11/02/1916	Name 20/02/1916	Function
Nezam al-Saltaneh	Same	Chief
Sayyed Mohammad Sadeq Tabataba'i/ *Sayyed `Abdol-Mahdi	Sayyed `Abdol-Mahdi	Justice
Soleyman Mirza	Same	Interior
Mirza Mohammad `Ali Khan Kelup	Same	Finance
Mohammad `Ali Khan (Nezam al-Saltaneh's son)	Same	Foreign Affairs
Sayyed Hasan Modarres	Hajj Esma`il Rashti	Education
Mirza Qasem Khan	This is not in Soltani	Trade and Public Welfare
Vahid al-Molk with Adib al-Saltaneh	Same	* Post and Telegraph

Source: Gehrke 1377, vol. 1, p. 359 (does not mention the 11/02 Cabinet and Post & Telegraph); Soltani 1381, vol. 4, pp. 799, 801 (does not have Trade and Public Welfare and does not mention Tabataba'i). * = Soltani.

Nezam al-Saltaneh informed the German and Turkish governments of the new situation, asked for their assistance, and committed his government to fight the Allies, the enemies of Islam, in Persia. Both German and Turkish governments made encouraging noises of help without promising anything concrete. In fact, apart from 1,500 Turkish troops no other military help arrived. Dr. Vassel apart from congratulations with the formation of the new government only made encouraging noises. The Persian side, frustrated by lack of success on the battlefield, lack of money, lack of organization, real hardship and infighting blamed their problems on the Germans, who had promised much, but had under-delivered in their opinion. Therefore, Nezam al-Saltaneh approached Enver Pasha for support.[476]

Eqbal al-Saltaneh, the Tehran appointed governor, was asked to join the nationalists or leave, but when he opted to leave he was basically kept under house arrest, but later, on 1 February 1916, was allowed to depart under armed escort. Three days prior to his departure Nezam al-Saltaneh had placed the city under martial law. This did not stop two local ruffians (Hoseyn Kardi and Mahmud Khan) having a fight in the bazaar, in which the latter and seven of his men were killed. The killer fled and therefore, the gendarmes arrested Hajj Rostam Khan, one of the killer's lieutenants.[477] In February 1916, some small groups of fighters arrived to support the *mohajerin* movement, such as a force led by the former governor of Kermanshah, Amir Mofakhkham Bakhtiyari. He with his sons Hajji Ebrahim and 'Abdol-Qasem Khan joined the Germans.[478]

476. Sepehr 1337, pp. 309-10; Vahid al-Molk 1378, pp. 44. and 802. For letter to Kaiser Wilhelm II thanking him for his support and asking for more help as well as the congratulation letter from Berlin, see Soltani 1386, p. 802; Bast 1997, pp. 35-36; Ettehadiyyeh 2006, p. 22f.

477. Vahid al-Molk 1378, p. 42; Soltani 1381, vol. 4, p. 796.

478. IOR/R/15/2/1997, 'Who's Who in Mesopotamia, General Staff, India (Serial No. 10)', p. 22 (Amir Mofakhkham and Hasan Qoli Khan with 1,500 Bakhtiyaris were at Baghshahi on 15 April 1916, returning home, as the Germans had not paid him for two months. It was reported that Amir Mofakhkham was disheartened by the Russian successes); Soltani 1386, p. 803 (200 men); Idem 1381, vol. 4, p. 803 (400 Bakhtiyaris; 400 Kakawands).

RUSSIANS TAKE HAMADAN AND KERMANSHAH

After the fall of Hamadan on 16 December 1916, McDouall left Qazvin on 27 December to Hamadan where he arrived in a car lent by the Russian authorities. On arrival he found that his things that he had left there were practically untouched. The Manager of IBP also returned and the Bank was open for business by mid-January 1917. However, the postal service was not yet reestablished, but the mail was sent by Russian cars that commuted daily to Qazvin. The road to Kermanshah was still held by gendarmes and other nationalist forces. Nevertheless, the British consul was convinced that in Kermanshah there was a strong party that opposed the German presence.[479] The opposing Persian force consisted of a disparate group of defenders (gendarmes, nationalists, tribesmen and some 250 Turkish soldiers) that withdrew in two groups, one to Malayer and the other to Asadabad. Only the gendarmes were an effective fighting force, be it poorly armed and dressed; the tribesmen were not very useful and even unreliable, according to Blücher.[480] In fact, the German officers despised their Persian allies, calling them "caftan-types, Persian gang, and cowards," which were the mildest of epithets used. Dr. Vassel was very unhappy about this and wrote: "With that much indignation and so little humor anyone fails in the Orient."[481] The British military also considered tribal auxiliaries of limited use. Not only were they unreliable time-wise, but they were less effective away from their own district, where they knew the lay of the land intimately. Moreover, they lost heart once they suffered casualties.[482]

After heavy fighting, the Russian forces were able to defeat the opposing forces at both locations. The Persian forces, about 9,000 men strong, of which 1,000 gendarmes, regrouped at the Bid Sorkh pass, near Kangavar. Here they received support through the arrival of Nezam al-Saltaneh with some 3,000-4,000 men as well as the 1,500 man Turkish force. Nezam al-Saltaneh had his headquarters at Sahneh and he hoped to be able to protect Kermanshah awaiting the arrival of reinforcements from his foreign allies. However, the Turkish government needed all the help itself at Baghdad and therefore, did not send any additional troops. For the moment the Germans, led by Colonel Bopp, could only help by preparing an extensive system of trenches and other defensive measures, while clamoring to Berlin for immediate support. Count Kanitz was deeply disappointed in the performance of the Lor tribesmen on 15 January 1916, whom he had led into in battle by example, but afterwards they withdrew that same evening. Count Kanitz who had made grand gestures and promised much, realized that he had failed, became depressed and left. He was never found and probably committed suicide that same evening.[483]

---

479. FO 371/2724, Consul/Hamadan to Legation, 05/01/1917. For a personal account of the withdrawal of the Nationalist Persian force from Hamadan to Iraq, see Sayyah 1395, pp. 15-80.

480. Blücher 1949, pp. 29, 37, 38-51 (for his observations about the behavior of the Kalhors; contrariwise, the Sanjabis performed well in skirmishes); Moberley 1987, p. 144; Malekzadeh Hirbod 1328, pp. 26-27 (they only came for the German money); Erdmann 1918, p. 164 (the tribal forces such as the Lors, Kalhors, Ilkhanis, and Kakawands had failed at every occasion, except for the Sanjabis and the Bakhtiyaris).

481. Slaby 1982, p. 297; Ducrocq 1923, p. 189 (von der Goltz gave orders that such epithets should not be uttered about allies).

482. AIR/20/663, pp. 84-85.

483. Vahid al-Molk 1378, p. 39 (Dr. Vassel also was in Sahneh), 43; Qa`emmaqami, pp. 166-67; Blücher 1949, p. 29; Moberley 1987, p. 138; Ezz al-Mamalek 1332, pp. 80-81; Malekzadeh Hirbod 1328, p. 34; Divanbegi 1351, p. 17; Soltani 1381, vol. 4, pp. 795-96, 803, 811-12 (Bid Sorkh - the solar dates are wrong in stead of 1296 it should be 1294); Erdmann 1918, p.170.

The defensive strategy worked quite well, because for a few weeks the Russians were unable to push through to Kangavar. Therefore, they decided to go around the town and marched from Malayer to Nehavand, which they took on 13 February 1916. From there the much larger Russian force took Kangavar on 22 February inflicting heavy losses on their opponents. The Persian force retreated to Sahneh and then to Bisotun, which was taken by the Russians on 25 February. Then the Russians marched to Kermanshah warning that if there was any resistance they would destroy the city. This did not happen, because a delegation of olama and local leaders welcomed the Russians to the city on 27 February 1916, who imposed martial law. While promising law and order, including the order that Russian soldiers had to pay for goods at prices fixed weekly by the police as well as the appointment of an officer to hear complaints about misbehavior by Russian soldiers, the Russian commander warned that any hostile activity would result in the burning down of the house or village involved. Moreover, people had to surrender any enemy-combatant who was hiding with them as well as all arms, ammunition, lead and gunpowder belonging to enemy forces within three days after the imposition of martial law, on pain of punishment.[484] General Baratov arrived on 9 April 1916; there was an *estaqbal* 1.5 km from the city; on 10 April there was the hoisting of the flag followed by ceremonies.[485] Governor Eqbal al-Dowleh, who was still in the neighborhood, was set free from his escort, when, on his way to Kerend, he passed Kermanshah. The governor remained in a village, but wrote a letter to Baratov offering his services. He replied that he would not interfere with local administration and invited Eqbal al-Dowleh to the city, which he did on 1 March 1916. However, Tehran replaced him with Naser al-Saltaneh, who was assisted by Amir Koll as deputy. Mo'azed al-Molk continued to be *kargozar*, while all major offices were filled by members of the *E'tedaliyun* party. Major Sayyed Hoseyn Khan, who had been sacked by Col. Bopp for his collaboration with the Russians became head of the gendarmerie.[486] The road between Qazvin and Hamadan had become almost impassable. Motor wagons took seven days, while beyond Hamadan there was no road for cars. Pack animals took six days from Hamadan to Kermanshah. This made communications and intelligence gathering more difficult, the more so, because the Russian troops had neither aeroplanes nor wireless.[487]

The *mohajerin* and their supporters fled the city on 23 February 1916. It was a flight which they had not prepared for. It was each man for himself and many died of hunger and cold, because many people did not have winter clothes. Everybody had gone into the direction of Kerend, pursued by the Russians. The situation of the *mohajerin* and their supporters was desperate. Some tribal groups left as did the Swedish gendarmerie officers, while the German and Turkish representatives told Nezam al-Saltaneh that it might be best to withdraw to Baghdad. Baratov moved westward, but, the Turkish force commanded by Col. Bopp was able to stop the Russians at Pay Taq, even though it had to withdraw because they ran out of ammunition and desertion of the Kurdish tribesmen. When the Russians broke through on 4 May, the *mohajerin* left and the stampede of fleeing refugees reflected the panic that was felt in the town. Not being

---

484. Miroshnikov 1963, p. 51; Vahid al-Molk 1378, pp. 43; Gehrke 1377, vol. 1, pp. 370-74; Moberley 1987, p. 144; Ezz al-Mamalek 1332, p. 85; Erdmann 1918, pp. 164-71, 178 (blames the defeat at Kangavar to tribesmen from the Kurveh area, who were bought off by Russian gold and left the field); Soltani 1381, vol. 4, pp. 803, 807 (the gendarmerie restituted the 23,500 *tumans* to the Customs office prior to their flight from the city), 808, 810.

485. FO 371/2724, McDouall to Marling, 11/04/1916.

486. Soltani 1381, vol. 4, pp. 809 (text letter), 813.

487. FO 371/2724, Marling to FO, 24/03/1916.

able to defend Kerend they withdrew to Qasr-e Shirin, where they finally received some military support from the Turks, who considered the Russian advance a serious threat to themselves. Qasr-e Shirin was overwhelmed by the influx of refugees. At that time, it had some 4,000 inhabitants and all of sudden 7,000 refugees descended on the small town. As a result, food was in short supply. According to Mo'tamedi, who was in Qasr-e Shirin, the leaders of the *Komiteh-ye Defa'* only thought of themselves and how to get as fast as possible to Baghdad. Only the Germans and Turks did their best to help as much as possible those who had no transport. Likewise, in Baghdad, the Germans helped the émigrés with food and financial support, much more than the Persian notables. The Ottoman consul arranged that supplies could be brought from Khaneqin and environs. Also, some food was sent by Samsam al-Mamalek, the chief of the Sanjabis and by the Vali of Posht-e Kuh. The refugees were joined by *mohajerin* from Isfahan, amongst whom Soleyman Mirza, as well as one of the leaders of the Moderates, Modarres and other nationalist leaders. Due to their dire straits, conflicts arose among the nationalists and there was even an assassination attempt on Nezam al-Saltaneh. However, shortly thereafter the various factions made up and agreed to work together. They established an *Association of the Defenders of the Homeland*, which was led by Soleyman Mirza (*enqelabiyun*) and Modarres (*e'tedaliyun*). Its executive committee was set up at the end of March.[488]

On 19 March 1916, Nezam al-Saltaneh was with a Persian force and 4,000 Turks at Sar-e Pol. He allegedly was pursued from Kermanshah by Fath al-Eyalah and Sardar Ejlal, but got away to Huleylan and sought the protection of the Vali of Posht-e Kuh on 25 March. Dr. Vassel had ordered Schönemann to see to it that Nezam al-Saltaneh and the Committee would safely reach Iraq. Although they finally arrived their journey was arduous, not only due to the difficult mountainous terrain, but also by the hostile Lors, who considered the caravan of refugees only as an object of plunder. Even in Khorramabad they were not safe until the Vali arrived with a considerable force, which not only brought security, but also the means to safely reach Iraq. However, the *mohajerin*, including Nezam al-Saltaneh, were angry and embittered with Germany and Schönemann and by the end of April 1916, they deserted the waning power of the Germans.[489] Relations between the Germans and Turks changed after the death of von der Goltz Pasha on 19 April 1916. Enver Pasha took over command, he dissolved the German-Persian military mission, and made new arrangements with Nezam al-Saltaneh without giving the Germans much say in the talks. In fact, henceforth the German and Austrian officers only had an advisory role, which really meant that they were told what decisions had been taken. Most members of the German-Austrian military mission were withdrawn. At that time, the mission consisted of some 300 men, of which 100 Germans and the remainder mostly Austrians. This indicates that when

---

488. Blücher 1949, p. 36. See Dowlatabadi, vol. 3, pp. 366-67 for the mood and the anti-German and anti-*mohajerin* arguments made. Vahid al-Molk 1378, pp. 44-47; Ezz al-Mamalek 1332, pp. 86-87; Adib al-Saltaneh 1332, p. 30; Malekzadeh Hirbod 1328, p. 27; Soltani 1381, vol. 4, pp. 803-05, 813-14; Bast 1997, p. 36; Gehrke 1377, vol. 1, pp. 370-74.

489. IOR/L/MIL/17/15/51, 'Who's who in Mesopotamia, General Staff, India (Serial No.22)', p. 94; Ansari 1353, pp. 131-32; Gehrke 1377, vol. 1, pp. 365-70. For another report that relates a different account and route of Nezam al-Saltaneh's flight, see Soltani 1381, vol. 4, pp. 806-07.

the Germans were in command they had to rely mostly on Austrians to execute their plans.[490] In early July 1916, Schönemann was sent to Berlin accused of embezzlement.[491]

Whereas the Kalhors, Sanjabis and Gurans had been making much money in doing business with German officers, acting as supply officers for Turkish forces at Qasr-e Shirin (selling them grain from Gilan and Zohab), the reverse was the case when the Russians came. They did not treat the tribes well, did not pay at all or insufficiently for supplies, while there also was unbridled looting by Russian soldiers. According to Major Greenhouse, moreover, "Russian military officers interfered with a heavy hand in tribal affairs concerning the nature of which they were generally in complete ignorance." Due to their less than tactful handling of the tribes, the latter became mainly hostile towards the Russians. The anti-Russian faction consisted of Fateh Soltan (Koliya'i), Farrokh Khan (Ahmadawand), 'Ali Akbar Khan (Sanjabi), and Fateh Beg (Jaf). This group was not only pro-German and partisans of the Democrats but also wanted 'Ali Akbar Khan Sanjabi to be appointed governor of Kermanshah. Also anti-Russian were Sardar Rashid of Ravansar as well as the Qalkhani chiefs. Contrariwise, Sardar Amjad (Koliya'i), Soleyman Khan (Kalhor) and Majid Khan (Bajlan) remained pro-British and supported the *E'tedaliyun* or Moderates.[492]

TURKS COUNTER-ATTACK

Baratov's position became untenable when 13,000 British soldiers under General Townshend surrendered on 29 April 1916 at Kut al-Amara. The British defeat freed up Turkish forces, which now could be used against the Russians at Khaneqin. On 7 May 1916, the Russians had taken Qasr-e Shirin and inflicted much damage on the Turks at the Diyala river. However, on 2 June 1916, as a result of the changed tactical situation, Turkish reinforcements left Baghdad and marched towards Khaneqin. On 3 June 1916, the Russian attack on Khaneqin failed. Russian losses were 27 officers and 400 men. They took 80 prisoners and 200 loaded camels with provisions. Due to the heat and lack of water Baratov withdrew to Kerend; also, his troops were suffering from indigestion resulting in 20 deaths and 100 sick.[493] The situation was worrisome and a major cause of anxiety for the Allies. While the Russians were in Hamadan, the Turks induced Lors and Bakhtiyaris (including Amir Mofakhkham and his sons) to attack the Russians

490. Bast 1997, p. 38; Gehrke 1377, vol. 1, pp. 380-93; Slaby 1982, pp. 296-97 (The German officers treated their Austrian colleagues and soldiers as 'lesser assistants' and did not acknowledge their contribution). Schönemann left Posht-e Kuh for Baghdad on 03/03/1916. IOR/R/15/2/1997, 'Who's Who in Mesopotamia, General Staff, India (Serial No. 10)', p. 115.

491. IOR/R/15/2/1997, 'Who's Who in Mesopotamia, General Staff, India (Serial No. 10)', p. 115; IOR/L/PS/10/585, File 618/1916 'Persia: Swedish gendarmerie affairs' (Tel. no. 436, Marling to London 08/07/1916). However, it seems that Schönemann was back in Mosul in October 1917, charged to take gendarmes to Qasr-e Shirin. IOR/L/PS/10/612, File 3360/1916 Pt 1 'Persian correspondence (1916-17)', Tel. no. 78, Tehran Legation to Govt. of India, 29/10/1917, p. 9.

492. AIR 20/663, pp. 79-81.

493. Miroshnikov 1963, pp. 56-57; Gehrke 1377, vol. 1, pp. 394-95; Blücher 1949, pp. 36-37, 48-50, 52; Ezz al-Mamalek 1332, p. 87; Soltani 1386, pp. 213-19, 222; Idem 1381, vol. 4, pp. 813-14; FO 371/2724, tel. Marling to FO, 11/06/1916.

at Borujerd and Soltanabad.[494] The Germans were pleased, because the Russian defeat had been their tactical objective, which thus had been successfully achieved. The Turkish force under 'Ali Ehsan Bey of some 12,000 foot and 4,000 horse plus auxiliaries with 54 cannons outnumbered and outgunned Baratov's force of 4,000 foot and 6,000 horse with 20 cannons. On 1 July 1916 Baratov withdrew from Kermanshah and in mid-August from Hamadan, but he stopped the Turkish onslaught at the Soltan-Bulagh pass.[495] In the wake of the large Turkish force the *mohajerin* returned to Persia and took up positions at Kerend and later moved to Kermanshah.[496]

Gen. Beloselski expected the Turks (two divisions) to take Kermanshah. He opined that they should be encouraged to lengthen their lines of communications, which would allow the Russians to shorten and reinforce theirs.[497] This was a rather optimistic analysis of the situation, because the Russians were unable to send Baratov immediate reinforcements. On the Western Front the Germans were pressing hard and Russia could not spare any troops. Therefore, St. Petersburg asked whether an Indian Expeditionary Force might intervene.[498] On 30 June 1916, the Turks advanced from Mahidasht; they deployed 22-27 battalions; 1 regular cavalry brigade with numerous Kurds and 16 guns. After heavy fighting the Russians withdrew during the night to Bisotun covered by the Caucasus Cavalry Division, which held the bridgehead 8 km from Kermanshah.[499] Baratov had 9,000 men, but withdrew to Sahneh which had better defensive positions and its climate was better. From Tiflis, Grand Duke Nikolay Nikolayevich Romanov promised reinforcements, but not many.[500] Naser al-Saltaneh, the governor of Kermanshah left the city as did the IBP on 28 June 1916 having only returned on 6 March of that same year. [501] On the morning of 29 June, McDouall's Russian colleage told him that Kermanshah had to be evacuated. The next day he left Kermanshah with his entire establishment, all his baggage, and many refugees going to Kangavar. McDouall had to leave his books behind with a friend as well as government property such as carpets and furniture. Some papers and books had to be left in the safe, while he dismantled the telegraph so that it could not be used. On 2 July 1916, McDouall arrived at Kangavar where he received a message from Baratov to proceed to Hamadan. He waited until 4 July when his Russian colleague arrived. That night Baratov also arrived who gave him a seat in the car to Hamadan. Meanwhile, the Turks remained at Qara Su and reinforced positions there. On 5 July McDouall arrived at Hamadan with his entire staff. All the Persian officials and many others had also left and had come to Hamadan as well. Many people, especially Armenians, left Hamadan and went to Qazvin, although by that time the prevailing panic had somewhat decreased.[502]

---

494. AIR 20/663. For an assessment of the military situation at Soltanabad by Col. Kennion, see IOR/L/PS/10/612, File 3360/1916 Pt 1 'Persian correspondence (1916-17)' (07/12/1916).
495. Miroshnikov 1963, p. 60; Malekzadeh Hirbod 1328, p. 29; Divanbegi 1351, pp. 68-69; Soltani 1381, vol. 4, p. 814.
496. Dowlatabadi 1330, vol. 4, pp. 32-33; Divanbegi 1351, p. 70; Ezz al-Mamalek 1332, pp. 90-92; Adib al-Saltaneh 1332, p. 31; Soltani 1386, p. 222; Idem 1381, vol. 4, p. 814.
497. FO 371/2724, Tel. Marling to FO, 15/06/16; Soltani 1381, vol. 4, p. 814.
498. FO 371/2724, Tel. Buchanan/St. Petersburg to FO, 03/07/1916.
499. FO 371/2724, Col. March to DMI, 04/07/1916.
500. FO 371/2724, Marling to FO, 04/07/1916
501. Sepehr 1337, pp. 282-83.
502. FO 371/2724, Tel. Marling to FO, 05/07/16; Idem, McDouall/Hamadan to Marling 08/07/1916.

SECOND 'NATIONAL' GOVERNMENT IN KERMANSHAH

The Turkish troops entered Kermanshah on 1 July 1916. They were mostly Arabs under Mahmud Pasha, who made a speech in the main mosque saying that he had come at the request of the olama of Kerbela. The Turks had no coined money and paid in paper redeemable in one year after the war, which created mistrust among the population. On arrival, the Turks demanded bedding for 1,000 patients and 75,000 liras for expenses, which was paid by wealthy notables. Only a few Sanjabis and Gurans were in Kermanshah.[503] The Turks published a notice with the text *Askarmiz Kermashahder* or 'Our army is in Kermanshah; it cost 1 *qorush* but it was even sold at 1 gold lira or 100 times more. Shortly thereafter the *mohajerin* government arrived, which was given a great welcome by the people of the city. Nezam al-Saltaneh's newly formed government was heavily loaded with family members, such as his oldest son, Mohammad 'Ali Khan, who was appointed Minister for Foreign Affairs; the other son, Mohammad Taqi Khan, who became his father's secretary, and Salar Lashkar, his son-in-law and son of Farmanfarma, was in charge of the War Ministry. Nezam al-Saltaneh remained commander-in-chief of the armed forces, while Sardar Moqtader was president of the joint Perso-Turco-German military staff.[504] At that time, Dr. Vassel was replaced as ambassador by Nadolny, who came to Kermanshah accompanied by Blücher as his secretary. Nadolny repeated that Germany had no political designs on Persia, it only wanted to threaten the British position in India.[505]

503. FO 371/2724, Tel. Marling to FO, 04/08/1916

504. Blücher 1949, pp. 68-69; Qodsi 1342, p. 336; Safa'i, vol. 2, p. 160; Divanbegi 1351, p. 70; Hale 1920, p. 207; Ezz al-Mamalek 1332, pp. 97; Divanbegi 1351, p. 70; Soltani 1386, p. 221; Idem 1381, vol. 4, pp. 814-18; Gehrke 1377, vol. 1, p. 409.

505. Sepehr 1337, pp. 282-83; Blücher 1949, pp. 62-63; Divanbegi 1351, pp. 63, 68; Ettehadiyyeh 2006, pp. 22-26; Bast 1997, pp. 38-39; Soltani 1381, vol. 4, p. 821. Apart from Germany, Austria also had an official representative at Kermanshah, vice-consul Count Béldi. Slaby 1982, p. 300. However, at the time that Nezam al-Saltaneh returned to Kerman no German diplomats were present as they were on mission elsewhere. Gehrke 1377, vol. 1, p. 407.

Table 7.2: Composition of the second provisional government (July 1916)

	Gehrke		Soltani
Name	Function	Name	Function
Nezam al-Saltaneh	Chief	Nezam al-Saltaneh	Chief
Mohammad `Ali Khan Mafi	Foreign Affairs	Mohammad `Ali Khan Mafi	Foreign Affairs
Adib al-Saltaneh	Interior	Soleyman Mirza	Interior
Mohammad `Ali Khan Kelup	Finance	Mohammad `Ali Khan Kelup	Finance
Sayyed Hasan Modarres	Justice	Sayyed Hasan Modarres	Education and *Owqaf*
Sayyed Mohammad Tabataba'i	Justice	Sayyed Mohammad Tabataba'i	Justice
Mirza Qasem Khan	Post and Telegraph	Vahid al-Molk Sheynbani	Post and Telegraph
Hajji Ezz al-Mamalek	Public Welfare	Amanollah Ardalan	Public Works
Salar Lashkar	War	-.-	-.-

Source: Gehrke 1377, vol. 1, pp. 408-09; Soltani 1381, vol. 4, p. 806. -.- = not mentioned

Nezam al-Saltaneh had used his time in Baghdad to bolster his position among the *mohajerin* and increase his influence. He changed his government or rather the *Hey'at-e Hokumat-e Movaqat* (the provisional government council) and got rid of its Democrat members, while at the end of May 1916, in a secret meeting with Enver Pasha, a political and military agreement was concluded, which was ratified in June 1916. In the agreement Turkey gave assurances concerning the integrity of Persian territory, military support for the nationalists, and support for Nezam al-Saltaneh as head of the provisional government. Few people (whether Persian or German) were informed about this agreement, while Turkey henceforth had the upperhand in military affairs, a reality that was made official by a formal treaty among the three parties, much to the resentment of the Germans. On his return to Kermanshah, Nezam al-Saltaneh worked with his cabinet and a 20-member consultative body called *Hey'at Namayandegan* (council of representatives), with which he had a rather strained and arms-length's relationship.[506]

To create a semblance of a normal functioning government, Nezam al-Saltaneh took several steps such as collecting taxes, establishing a budget, appointing governors, fixing salaries of government employees, maintaining law and order, having a judiciary, the beginning of a health system, and other administrative structures as well as issuing regulations. He appointed Amir Naser Khalaj as governor of Kermanshah,[507] while he also appointed governors for Kerend, Sanandaj, Garrus, Nehavand, Borujerd, Malayer and Hamadan and assigned a gendarmerie force to each of them. Furthermore, the *Shir-e Khorshid-e Sorkh* organization was re-established and allegedly some hospitals were opened. One of these hospitals was opened and managed by

506. Ettehadiyyeh 2006, pp. 17-20; Bast 1997, p. 39. On German (Nadolny) efforts to renew German relations with Nezam al-Saltaneh and the latter's attempt to negotiate directly with Berlin, see Gehrke 1377, vol. 1, pp. 409-26.

507. Later he appointed Mohammad Baqer Mirza as governor. FO 248/1135, Consul Kennion in Qazvin to Tehran, 16/09/1916. Another source reports that on 12 June 1916, Shahnuzim [?], a relative of Farmanfarma, was appointed Vali of Kermanshah. IOR/L/MIL/17/15/51, 'Who's who in Mesopotamia, General Staff, India (Serial No.22)', p. 115.

Fig. 7.9: German banknote with Persian overprint (1916)

a German physician, who received medical supplies from Germany. Several schools were allegedly established. The provisional government was assisted by a German military mission under Captain von Loeben, which had to form and train the Persian gendarmerie, and a Turkish military mission that was to train a national Persian army. The daily training of these two groups was begun immediately and, by December 1916, 4,000 soldiers and 1,500 gendarmes were being trained. The soldiers wore a tan-colored uniform and caps. The *mohajerin* government wanted to mobilize in total some 12,000 men, based on the *bonicheh* system, i.e. the recruits were organized by place of origin or tribe. The Germans supplied the new recruits with Lebel rifles, captured in Belgium. The garrison of 3,000 men was housed in a number of caravanserais. The German mission also drafted a new penal code to be used by the provisional government in Kermanshah. The Turkish government was represented by the military attache Fawzi Bey, a Kurd and a former adjudant of Enver Pasha. The basis of the new Turkish-German cooperation in Persia was a military agreement (19 August 1916) and a political one (21 August), which manifested the secondary role of Germany. Law and order were partially restored, taxes were collected, the roads were repaired and traffic between the various towns was safe, and very importantly, the food markets of Kermanshah were better supplied. Apart from sugar there were no shortages in the city at only slightly higher prices than normal. The better food supply was enabled by German payments in silver, so that requisitions of food from the villagers was no longer required. The latter brought their grain to the city, while the pastoralists brought their animals. This also stimulated local crafts, thus partly compensating for the loss of the normal transit trade due to the war. To facilitate their financial support, the Germans opened a branch of the *Deutsche Bank* that issued banknotes, which were German imperial treasury notes (5 and 10 Mark notes of 1904/06) that were stamped with Persian nominations of 12 *tumans*, 10 *tumans* and 25 *tumans* respectively (see Fig. 7.9). These banknotes were backed by silver and provided

Fig. 7.10 Overprint Kermanshah postage stamps (1916)

financial assistance to Nezam al-Saltaneh's government to the tune of 360,000 *tuman*s monthly. The silver had been imported from the US, from which good *qran*s were minted in Berlin using Nadolny's cufflinks as model, which were made from Ahmad Shahi *qran*s, a keepsake of an earlier visit to Persia. The silver was transported from Berlin in three months' time by rail and on mules. In the beginning recipients of the banknotes presented them to the bank to be paid in silver on the same day, but after some time, when people had more faith in the notes, they often circulated for weeks in the bazaar, thus easing the cash flow problem for the German bank. Nevertheless, initially people checked whether the German struck *qrans* were of the correct weight and alloy.[508] Because of the war situation a shortage of postage stamps with the value of 12 and 24 *shahi*s occurred. Therefore, the post office of Kermanshah had three hand stamps made. One for the surcharge *Chahis* and the other for the surcharge 12 and 24. One *qran* stamps were thus twice surcharged, one time with *Chahi*s and the other times with either 12 or 24. These stamps were issued from January until the end of April 1917.[509]

> In late 1914, the gendarmerie Major Abu'-l-Qasem Lahuti had been sentenced to death for certain criminal acts and desertion from his gendarmerie unit in Qom. He escaped to the Kurds and was said to have acted as chief of staff of Akbar Khan Sanjabi, when he opposed Hoseyn Ra'uf Bey in 1915 at Kerend. When the tribes made peace with the Turks and Schönemann, he came to Kermanshah in early April 1915 in the company of Sayyed Esma'il Owjaq returning from Kerbela, whose house was an asylum. He then took refuge with Schönemann and the Turks in Kermanshah and trained local levies for them, as he was afraid of the gendarmerie officers, because he was still condemned to death. Privately he wrote the British consul that he was ready to help the British. When Nezam al-Saltaneh established his provisional government, he edited the *Bisetun*, an anti-allied publication. In March 1916, he went to Kermanshah and accompanied the British from there to Hamadan in July 1916. From there he went to Tehran with a letter from McDouall recommending him for employment. In August 1917, Durie [R.N. Dewar-Durie, IBP manager] recommended him for the SPR. As there was no vacancy he started an anti-British-Russian newspaper, writing that the British in the South had enlisted the fighting races on their side by employing them in the SPR and that the new road guards under the Zakharchenko agreement told

508. Divanbegi 1351, p. 64, 70; Blücher 1949, pp. 63, 70-72, 76, 98-99, 101, 104; Ezz al-Mamalek 1332, pp. 96; Soltani 1386, pp. 222-23; Idem 1381, vol. 4, pp. 818-21; Gehrke 1377, vol. 1, pp. 409-14, 426-28; Bast 1997, pp. 40-41; Mihanpur-Sayyah 1395, p. 118. The total amount spent by Germany to support the Persian nationalists in Kermanshah amounted to some 20 million *Reichsmark*, see Luft 2002, p. 53, n. 32.

509. Sadri, Mehdad 2002, *Persiphila. Standard Philatelic Catalogue. Iran-Qajar Dynasty*. n.p., p. 142.

the same story. After the February Revolution in Russia he became involved with revolutionary Russians among the occupying troops in Kermanshah, where in 1917 he helped to establish to *Ferqeh-ye Kargar*, the first workers organization in Persia. Later he went to Constantinople, where he became a journalist and a pro-Kemalist. Towards the end of 1921 he returned to Persia via Erzerum in the company of Amir Heshmat. He obtained an appointment in the Gendarmerie and used his position to engineer a mutiny among the Gendarmerie in and around Tabriz in February 1922. After his defeat he fled to Russia, where he remained.

Source: IOR/L/MIL/17/15/11/3, Who's Who in Persia, vol. II, p. 187; FO 248/1112, Kermanshah Diary 08/04/1915; see also Cronin 2004, pp. 121-23.

According to Blücher, several Persian newspapers were established in Kermanshah, which received their news from the German news organization *Wolf*, which transmitted them to the newly established the news organization *Iran*. Also published were the newspaper *Akhbar*, and *Bisotun*, an anti-allied publication, but the Turks did not allow the publication of *Rastakhiz* as it did not support their pan-Islamist message. Therefore, the Persian nationalists welcomed German support as a counter-weight against Turkish designs to dominate affairs in Persia, something of which the Germans were acutely aware. This rivalry combined with a serious lack of trust between the *mohajerin* and their German and Turkish advisors constituted a structural problem. Nadolny found it impossible to work with Fawzi Pasha, whose recall he demanded, while his relationship with Nezam al-Saltaneh was constrained. The latter wanted Nadolny to endorse the promises made by Kanitz, which he could not. Also, the Turks and Nezam al-Saltaneh had different objectives from the Germans.[510] The Turks emphasized their brotherhood in Islam: a message that was supported by the olama of Najaf and Kerbela. However, these sentiments were not shared, but rather opposed by many, including by the officers of the army trained by the Turks. The latter further stressed their defeat of the Russians in W. Persia and their victory over the British at Kut al-Amara and that they had no designs whatsoever on Persian territory.[511] However, despite their claim that they had no ulterior motives, the Turks levied a contribution on the people of Kermanshah; the latter in a few days had to contribute 3000 *lirah*s and 800 *kharvar* of grain.

The differences that had cropped up among the *mohajerin* at Qasr-e Shirin had not gone away. They had continued to fester in Baghdad, where Nezam al-Saltaneh had made a secret side deal with Enver Pasha, and they continued to do so in Kermanshah. This was the reason that Soleyman Mirza had not joined Nezam al-Saltaneh's government, although others claim it was jealousy and resentment of the latter.[512] The fact that many of the politicians, who were billeted in houses and caravanserais, had nothing else to do but discuss politics and their own difficulties, contributed to the problems. It did not help either that Nezam al-Saltaneh and his

510. Sepehr 1337, pp. 282-83; Gehrke 1377, vol. 1, pp. 435-48; Blücher 1949, pp. 62-63, 102-03; Cronin 2004, p. 122; Ezz al-Mamalek 1332, pp. 97; Malekzadeh Hirbod 1328, p. 31; Divanbegi 1351, p. 71, 73.

511. Sepehr 1337, pp. 379-81; Blücher 1949, pp. 72-73, 103-04; Soltani 1381, vol. 4, pp. 818-19. On the relationship between the provisional government and the German and Turks, see Ettehadiyyeh 2006, pp. 22-26; Bast 1997, pp. 41-42.

512. Qodsi 1342, p. 374; Blücher 1949, pp. 69, 103; Soltani 1381, vol. 4, p. 821; Ettehadiyyeh 2006, p. 19.

government were not very collaborative and mostly kept the 20-member consultative body in the dark about its affairs. To overcome their differences the various parties came to an agreement on 26 August 1916, stipulating that they would work together to achieve Persia's integrity and freedom in cooperation with the Axis powers. However, this did not stop a few radical Democrats being involved in a murder attempt on Nezam al-Saltaneh. To bolster Nezam al-Saltaneh's position he received an ancient sword from the Turks via the olama of Kerbela, which was given to him with much ceremony in Kermanshah by a representative of the Kerbela olama.[513] Meanwhile, the Turkish force attacked Baratov's positions at Asadabad, where he lost seven guns and then had to abandon Hamadan.[514]

During Ashura (Moharram: 28/10-26/11/1916), there were no disturbances in Hamadan as the people and the leading olama, except for Sayyed Mohammad Tabataba'i, opposed this. In fact, the displays of mourning were fewer than usual. In the night of Sunday 21 November 1916, Germans and gendarmes attacked the position of the Persian Cossacks on a hill overlooking the city, but they were repulsed. Then the gendarmes led by Major Pesiyan, Major Kaellstrom and Capt. Ericson attacked again capturing a maxim gun and all the Cossacks there. The remaining Cossacks withdrew to two caravanserais on the outskirts of the city and after 2-3 hours of firing (mostly into the air) all became quiet. In the early morning of 22 November, the consuls and their compatriots were told to leave the city. However, this departure was conditional on the handing over of all arms of the Persian Cossacks and the Russian Consular guards. Finally, the Russian guards were allowed to keep theirs, but the Europeans had to leave immediately. This meant the hurried evacuation of the Russian and British consuls and of their compatriots. The Russian community left at 3 p.m., but the British got permission to depart the next morning. They left at 7 p.m. on 23 November; their wagons were searched for arms and cash, because the Germans wanted to make sure that the IBP assets (138,000 *tumans*) would be theirs. En route, a group of mercenaries under a German officer went to the village of Latgah, where they broke open Amir Nezam's arsenal and took 3,000 rifles and much ammunition. At the Aq Bulaq road station, 200 gendarmes under Capt. Erdmann were the only enemy troops seen.[515]

After having taken Hamadan, the Turks marched toward Tehran, which caused much panic in the city and even the foreign embassies made preparations to flee. However, the Turks stopped at the Aveh or Avej pass and withdrew to Hamadan, where they reinforced their position. From Hamadan, Baratov moved to Aq Bulaq 21 km north of Hamadan on the Qazvin road. There was no news of Russian reinforcements that did not include artillery. The Soltan Bulagh pass (at 2.5 km elevation) was the only defense between Hamadan and Qazvin and Tehran ran the risk of being totally cut off from Qazvin. Marling, the British Minister saw three options:

---

513. Blücher 1949, pp. 64, 70, 76, 103-04; Moberley 1987, p. 194; Ezz al-Mamalek 1332, p. 91, 100-01 (with a photo of the sword reception ceremony); Malekzadeh Hirbod 1328, p. 31 (with photo of the ceremony); Divanbegi 1351, p. 72; Soltani 1381, vol. 4, p. 821; Ettehadiyyeh 2006, p. 20.

514. FO 371/2724, Tel. Marling to FO, 10/08/1916.

515. FO 371/2724, Cowan/Qazvin to Marling, 30/11/1916 (On 17 November 1916, Major Kaellstrom and Capt. Ericson had arrived from Qazvin.); Idem, Murray/Qazvin to Wood 02/12/1916. Total losses claimed by IBP due to war activities amounted to 883,824 *qrans* or about £180,000. Jones 1986, p. 171. Ali Ehsan Bey had his headquarters in the IBP manager's house, and he did not damage it when he left, unlike the Germans. Napier 1919, p. 6

1. Legations remain here in Tehran
2. Retirement to Mashhad allowing our colonies to reach Russia via e.g. Barforrush
3. Retirement to Resht; but if Sultan Bulagh position is forced this option is closed.[516]

On 15 August 1916, Marling reported that his Russian colleague received advice from the Russian general to partially evacuate Tehran and Isfahan. He had sufficient transport to evacuate all British citizens. Given Baratov's advice, the next day Marling moved women and children of the British colony to Resht; the men would remain till the last moment and, if need be, probably would go to Mashhadisar.[517] Consul Lt. Col. Kennion, who replaced McDouall, reported that Baratov was at Serdeta and his staff at Aveh. The Russian infantry was being withdrawn to the Soltan Bulagh pass; two cavalry regiments on the north side and guns near Kurujan were watching the enemy outposts at Aq Bulagh. The Russian troops at Senneh had been safely withdrawn. The total Russian infantry amounted to 11 battalions of 350 men each. The enemy's strength was three times that. Baratov decided to defend Soltan Bulagh, while the Russian troops at Isfahan were ordered to remain there. Baratov told Kennion that his troops needed 4-5 days rest to be able to stop Turks. Although Tiflis had promised reinforcements, Baratov said it would help if British troops in Iraq would advance.[518] Meanwhile, the enemy did not advance beyond Aq Bulagh. Although Kennion believed that the Russians would be able to hold their position, he nevertheless informed Marling that if Baratov had to withdraw the Allied community in Tehran would have only two days time to leave.[519] The Turks had one aeroplane that flew over the Russian positions, but Baratov's major problem was food supply; on 21 August 1916, Russian troops had received no bread for two days, but there was plenty of meat.[520] Fortunately, two weeks later Baratov received reinforcements: infantry 5,630; Cossacks 1,950; gunners 350. About 2,800 sick were evacuated. There were also some 1,000 sick at the hospital in Qazvin.[521] On 18 September 1916, Baratov informed the Legations in Tehran that the danger of a Turkish breakthrough was a thing of the past and that the ladies might return.[522]

Meanwhile, in October 1916, the Turks were collecting grain in Kermanshah and Hamadan, storing it at Hamadan and Asadabad, some going to Baghdad; as a result, there was scarcity in the bazaar and a famine was looming in Kermanshah. Aqa Na'eb al-Sadr had gone to

---

516. FO 371/2724, Tel. Marling to FO, 10/08/1916. According to IOR/L/PS/10/585, File 618/1916 'Persia: Swedish gendarmerie affairs' (Tel. no. 436, Marling to London 08/07/1916), only four Swedish officers were still at the Persian front (Sonessen, Kellrent, Hellemarck, Ericksen). The rest of the rebel Swedish officers had joined the German army; de Maree (under arrest) and the others had been dismissed for insubordination and had returned to Sweden.

517. FO 371/2724, Tel. Marling to FO, 15/08/1916; Idem, Tel. Marling to FO, 15/08/1916; Idem, Marling to FO, 20/09/1916 reports on steps taken for evacuation Tehran.

518. FO 371/2724, Tel. Marling to FO, 14/08/1916. Baratov had his corps headquarters at the village of Aveh, below the Soltan Bulagh pass, "once a prosperous village, it has suffered like all others in this war-swept area." Napier 1919, p. 6.

519. FO 371/2724, Tel. Marling to FO, 17/08/1916, reports in detail on the military situation at Sultan Bulagh.

520. FO 371/2724, Tel. Marling to FO, 21/08/1916.

521. FO 371/2724, Marling to FO, 05/09/1916

522. FO 371/2724, Tel. Marling to FO, 18/09/1916; Idem, report of the military adviser on the situation of the Russian troops on 14/08/1916.

Kermanshah, where orders for his arrest were given as being a British reporter. Although it was his brother Aqa Shah who was employed by the British, he thought it better to disappear. Nezam al-Saltaneh called up the Kerend and Guran regiments, and he sent 500 men to Hamadan. He also called up the Zanganeh and Kalhor regiments as well as the Hamadan regiments. The Turkish second-in-command gave a speech in mosque of Sheveren. He said that they had come to liberate Persia from the infidels and after and their money finished they would leave. Sayyed Mohammad Tabataba'i from Kermanshah with Sayyed 'Abdol Vahhab asked the Turks to remain, who agreed if funds would be made available. Therefore, the two sayyeds were collecting money and paying them. The total Turkish force was about 20,000; half in Hamadan; the rest in Kermanshah, Kurdistan and elsewhere.[523]

In November 1916, the Ottomans were still sending grain, tobacco, sugar, petroleum, etc. to Baghdad. In Kermanshah, the Turks exercised strict control over the city's security. A Turkish officer was based at the police station (*nazmiyeh*); every arrival was taken there and stayed for a day or two for examination. People leaving received a note and had to pay 5.25 *qran*s. One hundred Turks patrolled with local police in the streets to maintain law and order. Also, in other ways they were acting as an occupying power. The Turks were said to take conscripts; one from three families, who had to be maintained by these three families. At Hamadan there were complaints about exactions by the Turks and many of its notables left for Kermanshah. The Turks allegedly 'raised' another 20,000 *tuman*s from the Hamadan merchants. They also made money by charging pilgrims going to Kerbela as much as 40 *tuman*s for a pass.

There were no troops at Kangavar, but in the Asadabad pass there were many Turks. Soleyman Khan Kalhor and his sons were at Hamadan as were many other Kurdish chiefs and their followers. According to a pilgrim, who traveled from Baghdad to Qazvin, there were 700 Turkish troops and 3,000 Persians with two mountain guns at Kerend. At Kermanshah, there were 2,000 Turkish troops and 500 gendarmes. The Turks were recruiting men, both horse and foot, and had collected some 2,000 men in a variety of uniforms with badges inscribed: "Khalifeh of God, Liberty, Army of Nader, Unity of Islam, Defense of Islam, O Master of the Age (i.e. the 12th Imam)." Their main force allegedly was at Hamadan and in Kurdistan. Daily 15-16 wagons, in addition to mules, arrived with ammunition and provisions, some of it was for Hamadan and the rest was stored at Kangavar. An infantry soldier received 12 and a horseman 16 *tuman*s/month. Meanwhile, Germans arrived at Baghdad to assist at Kermanshah, while four heavy cannons had been sent from Baghdad. The Vali of Posht-e Kuh was said to support the Turks and his son was coming to Kermanshah. There were signs that the Turks moved in small parties at night to Bijar (Kurdistan), while at Zenjan, where they had laid mines, the Turks retreated to draw out the Russians. However, not all tribes supported the Ottomans and these attacked their supply lines. In November 1916, pilgrims from Iraq returned with a caravan with 25 animals with loads of cash for Kermanshah. It remained at Zohab, waiting for an escort, fearing an attack by the Gurans, who wanted the money. The Gurans had looted Kerend and had taken some rifles from the house of the governor appointed by Nezam al-Saltaneh.[524]

---

523. FO 248/1135, Consul Kermanshah/Qazvin to Tehran, 26/10/1916.

524. FO 248/1135, Consul Kermanshah/Qazvin to Marling, 25/11/1916; Idem, Consul Kermanshah/Qazvin to Marling, 04/12/1916; Idem, McDouall/Qazvin to Marling, 09/12/1916 (its annex has a very detailed overview of

Meanwhile, it was reported that the Turks were making fortifications near Kermanshah and had sent many reinforcements to Hamadan. Furthermore, a rumor was spread that the olama of Kerbela and Sayyed Kadhem had declared jihad obligatory on all Moslems; some then volunteered and put on a uniform, but the people of Kermanshah were disturbed and could not sleep. Nezam al-Saltaneh received a telegram from the Turkish and German Minister of War awarding him decorations. He replied that he was ready to shed his own blood and that of his family for Islam against its enemies as his ancestors had done. All property of Russians in Kermanshah was confiscated. The chief of police in Kermanshah was suspected and arrested, but he cleared the name and was reinstated. Nezam al-Saltaneh wrote to the Democrat Committee of Kermanshah that their support was a service to Islam and that they had to thank the Turks and the German emperor and pray for them. 'Ali Hasan Bey wrote to Nezam al-Saltaneh congratulating him with the decorations on behalf of the Turkish and Persian officers. War preparations were not without danger, because four German officers were killed in Hamadan when a room with explosives that they visited exploded. Six loads of money came for the Turks at Hamadan. They had the Koran read in front of troops while the Persians carried banner with the text 'O Hoseyn the martyr.'

But all was not well in Hamadan. In November 1916 it was reported that Turkish ammunition stocks were low and that, in preparation of the winter, the Turks were constructing grain warehouses. Also, there was severe cold weather in Hamadan and it was expected that many sick would be added to the 1,500 already laid up in hospitals in Kermanshah. The Turks cut down trees for fuel, while there was a shortage of food resulting in famine. These trees were from the dense groves of trees around Hamadan as well as the famous trees from the huge Sheverin garden, in which Baratov previously had his headquarters, and where the Turks cut some 2,000 trees, according to Napier. He also reported that the Hamadan tanneries produced large quantities of footwear for the Turkish troops. The differences and tension between Turks and Germans became evident when 'Ali Hasan Bey had a row with a German Major, who asked him why he did not attack and remained in garrison for 3 to 4 months in Hamadan exhausted the people of Hamadan? He replied, "the Russians have two men for one of ours and his government did not send any reinforcements. To which the German officer replied: "These are lies and you make delays" 'Ali Hasan Bey wanted to resign but his officers did not allow him. In Kermanshah merchants had a meeting about the Turkish notes; Nezam al-Saltaneh arrested the leader, fined him and let him go.[525]

---

the positions and Turkish and auxiliaries' troop strength). For a discussion of the fights between the Avroman and the Russians, see Advay 1392, pp. 182-206.

525. FO 248/1135, McDouall/Qazvin to Marling, 09/12/1916 (annex); Idem, Kennion/Qazvin to Tehran 04/12/1916; IOR/L/PS/10/612, File 3360/1916 Pt 1 'Persian correspondence (1916-17)', no, 13385, GOC to Chief General Staff, Simla, 18/11/1916. The Turkish government telegraphed Ali Hasan Bey ordering him to stay and that 30,000 men would come with supplies. Nezam al-Saltaneh also said he would send 30,000 men. FO 248/1135, Kennion/Qazvin to Tehran, 13/12/1916; Napier 1919, pp. 6-7.

Fig. 7.11: Russian soldier and locals in August 1917

RUSSIANS RETAKE HAMADAN AND KERMANSHAH

The defeat and withdrawal of the Russians and the fall of Hamadan had given rise to great optimism for the future among the *mohajerin* in Kermanshah. It was believed that once the Turkish force would have been supplied with enough ammunition and provisions it would continue its march to Tehran. The more so, since the Russians had so easily given in and only had assumed a defensive strategy. Likewise, in Iraq, Khalil Pasha believed that the British would not be able to rebound from their defeat at Kut al-Amara and make another attempt to take Baghdad. However, the Turkish command was mistaken. The weakening of their forces by sending the XIII Corps to Persia and the lowering of their guard in Iraq came at a heavy price for the Turks. In January 1917, a superior British force defeated Turkish forces in S. Iraq, took Kut al-Amara and marched to Baghdad. In need of troops the Turks ordered ʿAli Ehsan Pasha, the Turkish commander in Persia to withdraw his troops to join the defense of Baghdad, which he did immediately. The withdrawal was not only a complete surprise for the Russians, but also for the Persian force that had been trained at the end of 1916 in Kermanshah and had joined the Turkish force at Avej as well as for the Germans. The latter were ordered to withdraw to Kirkuk in a wire from General Gressmann in Baghdad, while, after some discussion, the provisional government decided to do the same and go to Kirkuk as well. The well-equipped Persian force dissolved during the retreat as many soldiers deserted and returned to their homes, taking their arms with them. To hide their participation they often hid and changed their clothes. On 2 March 1917, Baratov retook Hamadan and restored order. Russian troops also realigned the road over the Asadabad pass. In early February 1917, Russian troops had already taken control over Kurdistan, according to Mardukh. The news of the Turkish withdrawal from Kermanshah on 27 February 1917 led to public discussions among groups of people in the city's streets, who regretted this development and continued to express their support for the *mohajerin*. However, there was a run on the German bank to exchange notes for silver. Allegedly, the bank was able to meet all its obligations. People started leaving Kermanshah, but the various tribal groups did not attack or plunder the refugees. A substantial number of the *mohajerin* did not want to go to Baghdad, but instead sought refuge with the Sanjabis. Nezam al-Saltaneh, some members of his cabinet and the gendarmerie officers fled to Istanbul, where living conditions were harsh, while some others continued to Berlin. During their flight news arrived that the Tsar had abdicated on 15 March 1917, an event that had major consequences for the continuation of the war.[526]

On 11 March 1917, Baratov entered Kermanshah and with some delay, due to supply problems and a strong Turkish defense of the Pay Taq pass, he entered Qasr-e Shirin on 31 March. He pursued the Turks as far as the Diyala river. On 11 March 1917 the British took Baghdad, thus ending any possibility for the *mohajerin* to return.[527] During the Turkish occupation there had been a vast number of sick, mainly due to cholera, typhus and malaria. Mortality was 30 per day, mainly Anatolians. When the Turks departed, they left 2,500 dead in the cemetery.[528] By May 1917, Baratov had to withdraw most of his troops to Hamadan, because of Kurdish harassment of his supply lines, lack of supplies, sickness and decreasing morale among his men, due to political events in Russia. However, he left a substantial force at Kermanshah and other neighboring towns.[529] Despite the defeat of the Axis forces in Persia, the British feared the outbreak of either anarchy or a Democratic government in Persia hostile to British interests due to what the Viceroy of India called an "infinitely more genuine and widespread wave of democratic feeling." Therefore, he instructed the British Minister in Tehran to conciliate Democratic leaders with money, "and if this be possible money should not be spared." He was even prepared to "scrap the 1907 Convention" and give Persians a greater control in the SPR and financial matters. He concluded, "It is obvious that any attempt to continue old reactionary policy is doomed to failure in Persia and can only discredit deeply elsewhere." In short, Great Britain and Persia should form a joint front against an expected Turkish attack. However, if Persia would declare against the Allies, a political, commercial and military contingency plan was being formulated.[530]

---

526. Blücher 1949, pp. 107-112, 118; Mardukh 1351, vol. 2, p. 333; Ezz al-Mamalek 1332, pp. 102-05, 111-12; Adib al-Saltaneh 1332, p. 34; Malekzadeh Hirbod 1328, p. 33; Divanbegi 1351, p. 94f.; Soltani 1381, vol. 4, pp. 823-24; Napier 1919, p. 7; Ehtesham al-Saltaneh 1366, pp. 722-33; Qodsi 1342, vol. 1, p. 401. According to Sasani 1345, p. 30 the *mohajerin* consisted of four groups: i. those living on German money; ii. those living on Turkish money; iii. those who paid their own way, and iv. those who were spies. For those who came to Istanbul, see Idem, p. 35.

527. Blücher 1949, pp. 95-96, 106-09; Miroshnikov 1963, p. 62; Moberley 1987, p. 228; Ezz al-Mamalek 1332, pp. 102, 105; Malekzadeh Hirbod 1328, p. 32; Divanbegi 1351, p. 76; Edmonds 2010, p. 213; Soltani 1386, pp. 224-25. For an account of the withdrawal of the Nationalist force to Iraq, see Sayyah 1395, pp. 193-248.

528. AIR 20/663, p. 24 (1st part); Slaby 1982, p. 297 (typhus, dysentery and other illnesses, decimated the Austrian military detachment in Kermanshah by half in the space of three months).

529. Edmonds 2010, p. 213.

530. IOR/L/PS/11/127, P 4038/1917, Viceroy to India Office, 25/06/1917.

During the entire period of 1915-17, the American missionaries, Mr. and Mrs. Stead had remained in Kermanshah. They reported in early 1918 that:

> We have seen three military occupations and evacuations. The town was turned into a training camp for Kurdish cavalry and Persian infantry. Russian and Turks were fighting at our doors. There was a lot of havoc, many sick, wounded, and dying. Under the Turks it was easier to do evangelization work. In November 1916 the Persian autorities forbade Bible journeys outside the town, because the men might be in touch with the Russians. In spring 1917 the Russians took the town again.[531]

RUSSIANS DEPART

Until July 1917 the city remained without a governor, when Amir Koll, who had remained in Tehran and was governor of Arak/Soltanabad, was appointed governor of Kermanshah. A substantial Russian force of infantry and Cossacks still occupied Kermanshah, partly camping outside the city, but mostly lodging in houses from which the Persian owners or tenants had been ejected. Because the Russian soldiers molested the city's inhabitants Amir Koll arranged with Baratov to prevent this. The heads of the various departments also slowly came from Tehran, such as Mo'azed al-Molk, the *kargozar*, Major Lahuti Khan, commander of the gendarmerie and Salar-e Ashraf, the chief of police. Although the Russians had promised amnesty to all those who had left the city, on their return the Russian soldiers took their arms and horses. Amir Koll remained governor until the beginning October 1917, when he was appointed elsewhere. However, because of his good relations with the Russians, it was thought better that he remained. On 7 November 1917, Taqi Khan Majd al-Molk, nephew of Amin al-Dowleh, who had been several times minister, arrived in Kermanshah to replace Amir Koll, who became governor of Borujerd and Lorestan.[532]

The breakdown of discipline among the Russian troops after October 1917, followed by their withdrawal had consequences for Kermanshah. By the end of 1917, the Russian military was hardly a fighting force, because most of its members were heavily involved in revolutionary propaganda and discussions. Moreover, they were hungry and the Russian army was not very effective in feeding its soldiers. There was anti-Russian feeling in Kermanshah and the surrounding area because, among other things, the Russians commandeered wheat at derisory prices, which people suspected they sent to Russia, paying with devalued rubles for their purchases. Because the ruble had dropped much in value, the British bank ensured these food requirements by converting the ruble at a favorable rate into British pounds. Although the British had no troops in Kermanshah in 1917, it was mostly with the help of the British that the Russians

---

531. Anonymous 1918, p. 302; Hale 1920, p. 208.

532. IOR/L/MIL/17/15/11/3, Who's Who in Persia, vol. 2, p. 191; Soltani 1386, pp. 227, 230; Idem 1381, vol. 4, pp. 824, 837-38, 840-41."Even during the Russian occupation 'shulloks' [*sholugh*] or disturbances, marked by rifle firing, occurred almost nightly." Napier 1919, p. 8.

were able to buy grain from the Persians.[533] The result of the movements of undisciplined Turkish and Russian troops in 1917 and 1918 left the country in a state of famine. Russians were the worst offenders in oppressing and looting people. Often, they were very cruel, according to the British consul. The area west of Kermanshah had suffered much due to the various military operations. In May 1917, Kerend and Qasr-e Shirin were the only inhabited towns along the main road, with many impoverished villages.[534]

On 29 December 1917 a deputation of Kermanshah Democrats visited Col. Kennion to inform him that their objective was to maintain Persia's neutrality. If the British had the same objective they were willing to cooperate. Furthermore, they would stop German intrigues in the area. Kennion assured them that the British government had the same objective and that he did not think that British troops would be sent to Persia, even if the Russians left. He promised to report their view to headquarters.[535] The overture to the British was understandable, because at the end of 1917, due to the lack of control by the Russians, who had begun to leave, and the weak Persian administration, the town was "much disturbed by lawlessness-the work of ne'er-do-wells and political agitators." The tribes remained quiet at that time, while the British believed that German propaganda did not seem to work. However, according to Mardukh and other Persian authors the opposite was the case, although tribal opposition, with the exception of the Sanjabis, ceased almost completely. Also, after the departure of the Russian troops from Kermanshah the political agitation by the Democrats ceased, but a small section, called 'terrorists', remained active and were believed to be responsible for the murder of Mirza Esma'il Khan Mo'azed al-Molk, the *kargozar* or the Persian agent for foreign affairs. He was shot in the street, just when leaving the Russian consulate on 2 January 1918. He was a physician, who had helped the Democrats much. Apparently, he was killed at the instigation of Abu'l-Qasem Lahuti Khan, who fled immediately after the murder. Although Lahuti Khan's guilt was not proven, the *kargozar* was certainly killed by an extreme Democrat. Two days later an attempt was made on life of Mo'tazed al-Dowleh. Whether related to the earlier killing or not, Vothuq al-Mamalek, the *kadkhoda* of Feyzabad and a member of the *E'tedaliyun*, was also killed. The suspected killer, Major Abu'l-Hasan Khan fled the city. The city was very disturbed and each night guns were fired. The *E'tedaliyun* party then induced Mo'aven al-Molk to step in and maintain order and, using the split in the Democrats, the *E'tedaliyun* turned the tables on them. Mahmud, son of Hajji Safar and Na'eb Esmail, brother of Hajji Mirza Abid, two Democrat bandits were killed on 10 February 1918. These two political murders were blamed on the Moderates. Since then, the Democrat party was temporarily in eclipse. The new governor, Taqi Khan Majd al-Molk, a Democrat, who arrived on 4 November 1917, was, according to the local IBP manager Hale, "a man of straw." He was unable to stop the feuding that went on between the various political factions (Democrats and *E'tedaliyun*) in the city.[536]

---

533. Hale n.d., p. 209; Edmonds 2010, pp. 214-15, 219; Soltani 1386, p. 225; Moberley 1987, pp. 233-34; Soltani 1381, vol. 4, pp. 838-39.

534. AIR 20/663.

535. FO 248/1204, Kermanshah report 17/02/1918 by Lt. Col. Kennion.

536. FO 248/1204, Tel. Lt. Col. Kennion 10/01/18; Hale n.d., pp. 216-17; FO 248/1204, Kermanshah report 17/02/1918 by Lt. Col. Kennion; Soltani 1386, p. 230; Idem 1381, vol. 4, p. 841 ("he was a politician, a capable and learned man, but a bureaucrat"), 842 (Mo`azed al-Molk was the son of Naser al-Atebba' Jadid al-Eslam); FO

BRITISH TROOPS ARRIVE

Because of the collapse of the Russian state and its army, a vacuum threatened to come into being in W. and N. Persia, which might be filled by forces hostile to Britain. Therefore, the British government decided to fill this vacuum with its own troops. When Lt. Col. Matthews' advance group arrived in Kermanshah at the end of 1917 the remaining Russian troops looked with some hostility at them, because they believed German propaganda, which blamed the British for continuing the war.[537] Percy Cox, the British chief political officer in the Middle East, wanted to send a British force to Persia with the task of "getting in touch with and winning over the Nationalist element in Persian and organising levies for the purpose of repelling enemy parties endeavouring to penetrate between Resht and Kermanshah." In particular, he wanted experienced Persia-hands like Stokes, Noel and Soane to be involved in this mission. Because of logistics, Cox argued that only via Kermanshah could such a force be supplied with all its material needs.[538] Marling argued that there was a danger the extremist Democrats might form a new cabinet, which would endanger telegraphic communication with PErsia from London via Tiflis. Moreover, these same Democrats were in close touch with "Maximalist soldiers of Kasvin" and they hoped to get their support. Furthermore, Baratov's troops were an unreliable force and could not be counted upon and might even be withdrawn. Therefore, Marling strongly suggested that British troops, supported by armored cars, should take control over the Khaneqin-Hamadan road, which would have a stabilizing effect in Tehran.[539] Initially, London did not want to take such a decision given that "it would not be compatible with measures that were being taken to form a nucleus of Russian troops on voluntary basis."[540] Col. Kennion told Cox that the proposed force that was to support Bichakerov, was not really needed. But if Great Britian wanted to provide him with some overt support, the overflight of some aeroplanes would have a salutary effect. A landing field at Kermanshah could be arranged. Such a measure would also take the pressure of and give more time for the soil to dry, as in January the roads were still hardly passable. Also, Kennion urged the British government to formulate the mission objective of the proposed force before sending any troops to Persia. At that time, Kennion was having talks with moderate Democrats about a rapprochement with the British (see above), and they were adamantly opposed to the coming of British troops to Persia. If these talks would be successful, it was expected that the Kalhor tribe and Soleyman Mirza also would abandon their anti-British stance. However, if it was decided to send troops, Col. Kennion urged that prior to the arrival of British troops, the British government issued a proclamation informing the Persian public about the limited mission, in time and area, of these troops, which would reduce their

248/1204 tel. Lt. Col. Kennion/ Qasr-e Shirin 17/01/1918. Mardukh 1351, vol. 2, pp. 333-34; Dhowqi 1368, p. 14; Shamim 1347, p. 568

537. Bean 1942, p. 727. There was only an Armistice at that time, not yet an end to the war.
538. IOR/L/P&S/12/84-87, Cox, Baghdad to India Office, 20/12/1917.
539. IOR/L/P&S/12/84-87, Marling to FO, 17/12/1917
540. IOR/L/P&S/12/84-87, FO to Marling, Tehran, 07/01/1918.

opposition to such a measure.[541] It was decided that the proclamation would have the following content:

> 1. Step forced on us by German action in Persia which Persian government have not been and are not in a position to prevent.
> 2. As His Majesty's Government have no designs on Persian independence and integrity, troops will be withdrawn at the latest at end of the war. In the meantime hoped that the Persian people will realise that this step has been taken in their interest to prevent worse calamity.
> 3. Assurances given to respect religious sacred places.
> 4. Assurances given to respect persons property and institutions and no desire to interfere in administration. Supplies will be paid for at fair rates and inhabitants treated with consideration. On the other hand expect local authorities will preserve order wherever troops located.
> 5. As troops being sent in our and Persians joint interests it is expected that they will be met in a friendly spirit by Government, officials, tribes and people, which will be reciprocated. But acts of hostility will be punished.[542]

On 13 January 1918, due to floods and heavy rains, Cox considered it not feasible to send the British column beyond the Taq-e Gireh pass; moreover, food supplies would not be available. Therefore, he strongly argued to have the column not go beyond Khaneqin for the time being.[543] On 15 January 1918, the War Office instructed Cox to send the British column beyond Khaneqin, because its task was to support Bichkarov's attempts to close the Persian border, in particular to prevent any enemy representatives going to Tehran. The further movements of the column were left to Cox, based on the local supply and road situation. However, he had to contact Bichakarov, while he also might send aeroplanes.[544]

Meanwhile, in early January 1918, the Germans in the Sanjabi region wrote to the Democrats in Kermanshah that Russia, Turkey and Germany had signed an agreement not to enter Persia.[545] They urged them to make life difficult for the British, expel them from the city and that they would send funds. As a result, Mo'tazed al-Dowleh and Amir Koll were about to leave the city, but the *E'tedaliyun* convinced the latter to remain. The Democrats' agitation had calmed down with the continued withdrawal of Russian troops. However, "a small and not unsound section called 'terrorists' are active, however, and the assassination of Kargouzar on 2nd January is put down to them." As a result, the population was very apprehensive, but did not support the

541. IOR/L/P&S/12/84-87, Cox to India Office, Government of India, 11/01/1918; Idem, Telegram Marling to FO, 13/01/1918 (extreme Democrats only want total withdrawal; moderate Democrats are influenced by lies in the Tehran press. Marling had instructed Kennion to counter the "misunderstandings" and through personal contacts rectify the wrong impressions).

542. IOR/L/P&S/12/84-87, Telegram Civil Commissioner Baghdad to FO, 22/03/1918.

543. IOR/L/P&S/12/84-87, Telegram GOC Mesopotamia to CIGS, 13/01/1918.

544. IOR/L/P&S/12/84-87, Telegram CIGS War Office to GOC and GHQ Mesopotamia, 15/01/1918 (secret).

545. This probably refers to the armistice concluded between the Soviet Russia and the Axis Powers on 15 December 1917, after which peace negotiations began that resulted in the treaty of Brest-Litovsk of 3 March 1918.

inactive governor to get rid of pro-German agitators. On 8 January 1918, all Russian troops had left except 300 Khapyorski Cossacks, despite British supported efforts by Baratov to form a reliable Russian volunteer force. The Russian wireless left on 8 January 1918. On 11 January 1918, the Russian partisan force arrived at Kermanshah and General Mistouloff with the Khapyorski Regiment left a few days later.[546]

By the end of January, the only Russian fighting force still at Kermanshah was that of the anti-Bolshevik Col. Bichkarov and his Cossacks, who joined the so-called Dunsterforce. At that time, there were only a few Europeans in the city. In addition to Col. Kennion and his wife, there were the IBP manager and his wife, the Russian consul, and the American missionaries.[547] On 3 February 1918, Dunsterville reached Kermanshah where he stayed for rest of the year.

> On the north-east front a small column was sent at the beginning of January as far as Pai Tak, at the foot of the Tak-i-Girra Pass. It met with no opposition, and on its return occupied Kasr-i-Shirin. Towards the end of -the month the state of famine to which the Turks had reduced Northern Persia made it incumbent on me to endeavour to open the main trade route via Kirmanshah in order to get supplies to the poor inhabitants of the towns and villages, and to provide them with an outlet for their home manufactures. With this object in view I increased the garrison of Kasr-i-Shirin, and pushed small posts towards Kirmanshah. A large amount of tribal labour was also employed in improving the road, which was in a lamentable state of disrepair. The continuance of wet weather up to the present date, coupled with snow on the high ground east of the Tak-i-Girra pass, has rendered the maintenance of troops along the road a matter of extreme difficulty.[548]

Service in Kermanshah for the British troops was heavy and monotonous, which was partly relieved by the construction of hockey and football fields. Officers often went duck and snipe shooting.[549]

---

546. IOR/L/P&S/12/84-87, Telegram Cox to FO and India Office, 17/01/1918; FO 248/1204, Tel. Mr Hale, acting consul for Lt. Col. Kennion, 08/01/1918; IOR/L/P&S/12/84-87, Telegram CGS New Delhi to DM 1, 15/01/1918 (secret); FO 248/1204, Kermanshah report 17/02/1918 by Lt. Col. Kennion; FO 248/1204, Tel. Lt. Col. Kennion/ Qasr-e Shirin 17/01/1918. On 01/01/1918 "I left Kermanshah with ANZAC wireless station, so that there was no radio any longer at Kermanshah." FO 248/1204, Kermanshah report 17/02/1918 by Lt. Col. Kennion.

547. Dunsterville, p. 21; Hale n.d. 209; Moberley 1987, p. 273; Edmonds 2010, p. 227, 239 (for an overview of British forces in NW Iran); By mid-January all Russian troops had left Senneh. FO 248/1204, Tel. Lt. Col. Kennion/ Qasr-e Shirin 17/01/1918. Lazar Fedorovich Bicherakov (Bicherahov) (1882 -1952) - Colonel of the Terskoye Cossack Force (Tsar Army). After 1918 one of leaders and organizers of anti-Bolshevik activities in the Caucasus. From 1919 White émigré. Lived in Germany, during WWII he was head of the North-Caucasus Section of the Committee of Liberated Peoples of Russia (KONR) - anti-Soviet organizations that co-operated with the Nazis.

548. "Despatch of Lt. General W. R. Marshall, commander of the Mesopotamian Expeditionary Force." *Sixth Supplement to the London Gazette* 26 August 1918, p. 10152.

549. Lt. Col. P. S. Stony, *The History of the 26th Punjabis: 1857-1923*. Uckfield: Naval & Military Press, 2006, p. 75; for a description of the snipe hunting opportunities, see Wills 1893, pp.116-17.

SITUATION IN THE CITY IS VOLATILE

Despite the presence of British troops, the situation in the city remained volatile. In March 1918, two swashbuckling blackguards were having a pistol duel in front of the IBP, because of which the IBP guard was accidentally wounded. The IBP manager, Hale demanded that the governor arrest both men and have them pay 500 *tuman*s. One of them was protected by an influential person.[550] This refers to the troubles around Hajji Na'lband Sardar Sowlat (Sowlat Lashkar), a fighter for the constitutional movement (1906-09), a rowdy and *mojahed* of Sardar Yar Mohammad, who during Salar al-Dowleh's rebellion had engaged in looting and had become a local troublemaker with his band of freebooters and, therefore, was called 'the equal of the devil' (*thani athanyn iblis*). Before Amir Koll became governor, he had employed Hajji Na'lband and the city knew a period of security. However, later Hajji Na'lband resumed his criminal activities and usurped some of Vakil al-Dowleh's heirs' property. Because of Majd ol-Molk's weak administration, he had gathered a band of ruffians and expelled the Treasury guards from the gates of the city and collected taxes himself. Taqi Khan Majd al-Molk, the governor asked Amir Koll and other notables for advice to what he should do. As a result, Manuchehr Mirza 'Emad al-Dowleh III, the chief of treasury, with some other notables surrounded Sowlat's house, and fighting took place he and seven of his men were killed. Another event concerned Mirza Meshki, who was one of the *monshi*s of Da'ud Khan Kalhor. He was a ruffian and was killed at the governor's orders. After his death many carpets and other stolen goods were found in his house. Because the government was weak, anybody who could get 15 armed men around him in a quarter could rule over its people and play as if he were the governor. At that time, at the instigation of the conservative members of the *Bedayat* court, Sheikh 'Ali Mahallati was killed. In short, the situation in the city was unsafe and uncertain. For this reason Majd al-Molk ordered the newspaper *Gharb-e Iran*, the mouth piece of the Democrats, which was unrelentingly criticizing the *E'tedaliyun*, to bring some rest to the city.[551] The troubled condition in and around Kermanshah was not solely due to a weak government and political dissent, but mostly because of famine conditions that were experienced in much of the country (see Chapter Two).

By mid-March 1918, the most extreme Democrats had left Kermanshah, which may have been the reason why the town was quieter than usual, although there was firing of arms at night.[552] After the murder of fellow employees, the staff of the Revenue and Artillery departments went on strike around 12 March as a protest against the bad and ineffective administration. The olama and the merchants wired Tehran asking for a change of governor, stipulating that no Bakhtiyari would be welcome.[553] The people had reason to be dissatisfied as the province was in a bad shape. Tribesmen raided villages, the roads were unsafe, except in Kermanshah where British troops provided security. The Vakil al-Dowleh heirs were in dispute with the Hajjizadehs; the former had intermarried with Amir Koll, who arranged with the Kalhors to evict the Hajjizadehs from

550. Hale 1920, p. 227; FO 248/1204. Tel. Greenhouse to Legation 20/03/1918.
551. Soltani 1381, vol. 4, pp. 844-47, 487; Idem 1386, pp. 231-32.
552. FO 248/1204, Kennion to Legation, 14/03/1918.
553. FO 248/1204, Tel. Greenhouse to Legation, 14/03/1918.

the disputed land.[554] The governor was trying to get rid of the chief of police Abu'l-Fath Mirza, who was an undesirable element and an extreme Democrat.[555] Not only were the ragged Persian troops useless to the governor, but he himself was useless, being apathetic and incapable. Therefore, people flocked to the British Consulate as the only power, but in most cases the British could not do anything. What was needed was a capable governor to establish law and order, for it was impossible for the British consul to do so, even if this were desirable. The British consul made an exception for the food supply to avoid rising prices and grain not being collected, the British were prepared to come down hard on the tribes, if need be. The Jargah section of Kalhors and the Kalawands most needed this. The use of an aeroplane was believed to be ideal for this purpose, because no troops were needed and it was able to get where the terrain was difficult.[556] At the end of October 1918, Amir Koll was appointed governor of the Thalatheh (Malayer, Nehavand, Tuyserkhan), although his deputy Samsam al-Dowleh had already gone there, he considered the appointment to be beneath his dignity and made no haste to go there. In early December he still was in Kermanshah, waiting for *savar*s from Tehran to turn out Mehr 'Ali Khan from Nehavand; until that time, he did not move. At the end of December 1918, Amir Koll resigned as governor of the Thalatheh, although his deputy remained there.[557]

Heeding the dissatisfaction of the people and of the British, Tehran appointed a new governor, 'Abbas Mirza Salar Lashkar, son of Farmanfarma, who arrived on 27 August 1918. One of the first things he did was to re-establish the gendarmerie. He was hostile to the Democrats, and although Lahuti Khan wrote odes in his name from his place of refuge in Dowlatabad, these fell on deaf ears, because Salar Lashkar did not trust him.[558] People were satisfied with the appointment of Salar Lashkar as the new governor. But this satisfaction was tempered by his appointment of Amir Koll as acting governor, whom Kennion regarded "as useless as the late Governor Haji MajdulMulk and more of an intriguer and more avaricious."[559] Salar Lashkar made some changes. He ordered that without a police license, no arms could be borne in the city. Under Persian management this meant a tax on rifle owners, Kennion commented. The killing of political enemies and/or the settling of scores continued under his government, such as when a notorious criminal 'Abdol-Hoseyn Torkeh killed 'Ali Aqa Sadeq Tabrizi. Despite his links with powerful notables like Mo'aven al-Molk he was hanged. To establish order, the governor wanted to have an effective force of 300 *savar*s instead of Persian troops under Showkat al-Molk, who were useless. To pay for them he asked Tehran for 10,000 *tuman*s from the Customs revenues. In that case he also could collect the normal revenue, which would enable the Revenue Department to maintain its various establishments in Kermanshah, for which it had no money at that time.[560]

---

554. FO 248/1204, Kermanshah report no. 4, 27/06/1918 by Lt. Col. Kennion.
555. FO 248/1204, Tel. Kennion to Legation, 27/06/1918.
556. FO 248/1204, Kermanshah report no. 4, 27/06/1918 by Lt. Col. Kennion.
557. FO 248/1204, Kermanshah report no. 9, 01/11/1918 by Lt. Col. Kennion; Idem, Kermanshah report no. 10, 03/12/1918 by Lt. Col. Kennion; Idem, Kermanshah report no. 11, 31/12/1918 by Lt. Col. Kennion.
558. Soltani 1381, vol. 4, pp. 847-48; FO 248/1204, Kermanshah report no. 7, 12/09/1918 by Lt. Col. Kennion.
559. FO 248/1204, Kermanshah report no. 6, 02/08/1918 by Lt. Col. Kennion.
560. Soltani 1381, vol. 4, p. 849; FO 248/1204, Kermanshah report no. 7, 12/09/1918 by Lt. Col. Kennion.

Good war news gave hope to people that Turkey would soon withdraw from the war and Persia. Again, the Democrats put out feelers how they would be treated if they supported the British position in Persia. They were angry about recent Turkish behavior in Tabriz where some leading Democrats were executed and imprisoned; after talks with the British consul they promised to support Great Britain.[561] After the fall of Damascus, Aleppo and Beirut the armistice with Turkey on 30 October 1918 was not unexpected. There was widespread satisfaction that Turkey had to withdraw from NW Persia, although the sudden collapse of Germany and Austria was unexpected. To celebrate these events there were fireworks and a feast dinner.[562] And there was reason to celebrate as Kermanshah had rather escaped the vagaries of war. In February 1919, the American tourist Donald B. Watt arrived in Kermanshah, who wrote: "Kermanshah escaped the ravages of the Turks and the Russians so that it is a great relief to see a town which is not three-fourths ruined.[563]

THE SANJABI QUESTION

One of the issues that the British had to resolve was that of the tribes, who had collaborated with the Germans, in particular the Sanjabis, who, even after the fall of Kermanshah, continued to support the German/Turkish cause. The latter were still continuing to undertake hostile activities from Kurdistan and Sanjabi tribal land. In January 1918, Mahmud Bey the Turkish consul went to Senneh, where he incited the Marivans to go to Kermanshah and seize the British consul, who was at Qasr-e Shirin at that time. The Turks were not the only ones trying to make problems so were the Germans, who urged Democrats to make trouble in Kermanshah for Great Britain.[564]

At that time, Col. Kennion was at Qasr-e Shirin where he observed that the Sanjabis were at the Qal'eh Sabzi grazing ground, which indicated that they had peaceful intentions.[565] Therefore, as per his orders, to try and without the use of force to neutralize further anti-British Sanjabi activities, on 19 January 1918, Kennion visited the camp of Qasem Khan, the chief of the Sanjabis near Qal'eh Sabzi. There he met with 'Ali Akbar Khan, Hoseyn Khan and Soleyman Mirza. 'Ali Akbar Khan admitted that von Dreufel had visited him, but also the Qalkhanis. He only had come to buy supplies which they had not sold. They professed friendship for Great Britain and as long as it respected Persia's neutrality, no German would pass through, nor would they have any contact with them or sell anything to them. Soleyman Mirza, when he held a major position in Nezam al-Saltaneh's government in Kermanshah, was a well-known friend of the Germans and opposed to the Turks, justified his past position as being a patriot. He said that they had lost hope in the Germans and were ready to work with Great Britain if it proved

---

561. FO 248/1204, Kermanshah report no. 8, 05/10/1918 by Lt. Col. Kennion. For the situation in Tabriz, see Rais-Nia 2002.

562. FO 248/1204, Kermanshah report no. 10, 03/12/1918 by Lt. Col. Kennion.

563. Watt 1967, p. 45.

564. FO 248/1204, Tel. Lt. Col. Kennion 10/01/1918; Idem, Tel. Lt. Col. Kennion 12/01/18; Idem, Tel. Mr Hale, acting for Lt. Col. Kennion 8/01/1918.

565. FO 248/1204, Tel. Lt. Col. Kennion/ Qasr-e Shirin to Legation, 17/01/1918.

its friendship with deeds. As signs to the contrary he pointed to the SPR, British control over Customs, British action in Khuzestan, and its interference in the appointment of officials. Kennion told Soleyman Mirza that he was not competent to discuss such issues, but suggested that he leave the border area as that might raise suspicion; also, it would be better to reach his objectives in Tehran. Soleyman Mirza said that this would discredit him in the eyes of the Democrats, who would assume that Kennion had bribed him. If the British Legation, through the Persian government asked him to come to Tehran to discuss these questions he would come. Soleyman Mirza, according to Kennion, was fanatic about Persian freedom from foreign control and independence. However, he was willing to work with the British, if these ideals might be achieved, of course, with a prominent role for himself. Soleyman Mirza also wanted a man like Shuster to re-organize Persia's finances and a man like Stokes for the army. According to Kennion, he had great influence with Sanjabis.[566]

There was reason to believe that Soleyman Mirza continued intriguing with von Dreufel and therefore, the British decided to arrest him on 8 January 1918 in the camp of Qasem Khan, but he had already left in disguise. It meant that his ties with Sanjabis were broken off. Kennion opined that the Sanjabis might consider that he had broken his word. Sanjabi continued collaboration with the German was confirmed when on 16 February 1918 von Dreufel visited the Sanjabis at Hajilar. However, according to Sheikh Hoseyn, he was given a rude, cold reception. As there were no pro- and contra-Sanjabi factions information from there was not always reliable. On 17 February Kennion had a meeting with Rashid al-Saltaneh who wanted to attack the Sanjabis with other hostile tribes; these included the Kalhors under Soleyman Khan, and almost all the Gurans under Jahanbakhsh (Zargham al-Saltaneh), Qambar Khan and 'Abdollah Beg. He also hoped to draw Safar Khan Neyrizhi to his side. Rashid al-Saltaneh said because Bamu was then under snow, meaning there was no pasturage, it would be the best time to attack them. Kennion told him that it was not the desired objective at that time.[567]

However, that soon changed. In May 1918, the anti-Sanjabi tribes (Kalhors, Gurans), supported by the British attacked the Sanjabis. The British support consisted of light guns and aeroplanes. The Kalhors and Gurans seized some 100,000 sheep and much personal property, inflicting 50 casualties. Also, in the ensuing stampede, due to panic, 200 women and children drowned in the Zinkan river. Qasem Khan, who went to Kermanshah to complain, was arrested and sent to Baghdad. Sardar Naser came to the British consulate to complain and promised to bring in 'Ali Akbar, but he did not keep his promise. As a result of this attack, the power of the Sanjabis was broken. The Persian government severely reprimanded the Kalhor chiefs, and hinted that this was the more so, because they had acted at the behest of foreigners. The Kalhor chiefs were not greatly impressed and wanted Kennion to engineer that one of them was appointed governor of Kermanshah. When he refused, they suggested Amir Koll, which he nixed immediately. Kennion did not want any tribal chief as governor, although he agreed with them that Majd al-Molk needed to go as he was useless.[568] Majd ol-Molk had sent a telegram

566. FO 248/1204, Kermanshah report 17/02/1918 by Lt. Col. Kennion; Idem, Kermanshah report, 19/01/1918 by Lt. Col. Kennion.

567. FO 248/1204, Kermanshah report no. 2, 13/03/1918 by Lt. Col. Kennion.

568. FO 248/1204, FO to Consul (telegram ?275) 21/05/1918 (400 casualties). Idem, Consul to Balfour, Tel. no 441, 23/05/1918 (50 casualties). Majd ol-Molk received telegrams from the Persian government with an anti-British

to Tehran accusing Amir Koll to be in cahoots with the British and having incited people not to pay taxes. Therefore, nothing he said should be trusted, Kennion wrote.[569] The Kalhor and Guran chiefs behaved insolently to Majd ol-Molk, when he asked them to pay their taxes and give pledges of neutrality; he blamed Amir Koll for this attitude.[570]

'Ali Akbar Khan, who with followers had gone to Kuh-e Bamu, was driven out by Sardar Akram Valad Beg and was wounded in the arm. His brother Sardar Zafar was given refuge by Qambar Soltan Qalkhani.[571] Kennion arranged a meeting with Rashid al-Saltaneh and other Guran chiefs to settle the matter of 'Ali Akbar Khan's asylum and other outstanding issues; at the same time a column would threaten the Gurans from Bewanij. The Guran chiefs (but not Safar Khan) met Sardar Rashid and chiefs of the Kurdistani side, including Sardar Akram, Vakil of Javanrud, Shoja al-Mamalek and Zimlan at the end of June 1918. Rashid al-Saltaneh allegedly made overtures to have them befriend the Sanjabis. Sardar Rashid told Kennion that the Kurdistan chiefs induced the Gurans to make an agreement to expel 'Ali Akbar and his brother wherever they were. At that time, 'Ali Akbar was actually believed to be in Rashid al-Saltaneh's tent. The latter sent Kennion assurances of friendship including an agreement sealed by him, Qanbar Soltan, Asadollah Beg and 'Ali Beg, which said that they would not give asylum to the Sanjabi chiefs. 'Ali Akbar's arm was severely wounded. On 9 June 1918, the Kalhor chiefs left Kermanshah and went to Mahidasht where they tried to get a meeting with Sardar Rashid and other chiefs of the Kurdistan border area. Since the Sanjabi chiefs were defeated, the Kalhors tried to be acknowledged as the leading chiefs of Kermanshah and the successors of Sanjabis.[572] Rashid al-Saltaneh continued to give asylum to 'Ali Akbar even after having signed an agreement not to do so. With his influential relations in Kermanshah, 'Ali Akbar Khan was more than a tribal chief. On the one hand he was the face of the enemy party and on the other hand he was the link between the enemy outside and inside Persia. Kennion decided to see how Rashid al-Saltaneh's professed friendship would prove itself, before taking action against him.[573]

On 22 June 1918, Kennion met the Kalhor chiefs at Harunabad and took 'Abbas Khan to Kerend. Soleyman Khan with the chiefs followed to Gavareh. The Kurdistan chiefs had been asked to go to Qal'eh Zanjir. On 24 June Kennion marched with a column from Kerend to Bewanij and met Rashid al-Saltaneh and his two brothers. Rashid al-Saltaneh said hospitality was sacred like the Baba Yadgar, where 'Ali Akbar had been staying all the time. He did not like the fine of rifles, which was a new experience for Qalkhanis or the aeroplane that made a

---

content concerning the action taken against Sanjabis as well as the occupation by British troops of the Delgosha Government House. FO 248/1204, Kermanshah report no. 4, 18/06/1918 by Lt. Col. Kennion.

569. FO 248/1204, Copy transl. tel. no. 3619, Majd ol-Molk to Min. Interior, 07/07/1918. According to Kennion, Majd ol-Molk "is such a weak character that any unfavorable turn in Persia is reflected in his attitude." FO 248/1204, Kermanshah report no. 4, 18/06/1918 by Lt. Col. Kennion. He also wanted to make money, and therefore, wanted to appoint the Kalhor chief as deputy-governor of Qasr-e Shirin. Kennion vetoed this, "because now no tribal chief there is suitable." He then took 400 *tumans* from Majid Khan Bajlan and appointed him in that position. "I am taking steps to make him resign. He is unfit and it would cause trouble with the other tribes." FO 248/1204, Kermanshah report no. 4, 18/06/1918 by Lt. Col. Kennion

570. FO 248/1204, Kennion to FO, tel. no. 97, 13/06/1918.

571. FO 248/1204, Kennion to FO, Kermanshah summary no. 15, 02/06/1918.

572. FO 248/1204, Kermanshah report no. 3, 11/06/1918 by Lt. Col. Kennion.

573. FO 248/1204, Kermanshah report no. 4, 18/06/1918 by Lt. Col. Kennion.

reconnaissance flight while he and Kennion were talking. He finally gave in and the following day he signed with the other chiefs the following commitment: 1. payment of a finewithin seven days to the government of 200 rifles of which 25 must be British; 2. 800 sheep to be given via the British consul to friendly chiefs; 3. Sanjabi chiefs not allowed in Guran country, including at Baba Yadgar; 4. any British enemy to be seized and handed over; 5. a general promise of friendship and obedience; 6. a promise not to oppress the people of Kerend and Bewanij, whom they had been given trouble; 7. the Gurans to make peace with the neighboring chiefs, who were friendly to the British. The guns to be handed over had to be in serviceable condition. Bewanij, an open valley dotted with villages, was abandoned at that time, due to Qalkhani and Russian operations. In return, Kennion gave all chiefs a letter of forgiveness and amnesty and left an agent to collect the fine and left the next morning. The 'friendly' chiefs were disappointed because they had hoped for a chance to loot the Gurans. Kennion who knew that tribal chiefs were fickle, wondered how long their commitment would last. At any rate, 'Ali Akbar and his brother were believed to have left to the Babajani Jafs; his arm was suppurating, but other reports indicated that it was getting better.[574] Qasem Khan Sanjabi Sardar Naser returned; his brother 'Ali Akbar gave himself up to Nosrat al-Dowleh in Tehran where he stayed as political detainee. The Kalhors refrained from looting.[575]

SMUGGLING FOOD TO TURKEY

Short of food supplies, in early 1918, the Turks were either buying grain directly in Kurdistan or other consumer goods via Persian subjects living there. To that end Kurdistanis bought tea, sugar, and piece goods in the bazaar of Kermanshah, which Kennion believed likely were destined for Halabjeh. To pressure the local authorities to stop this trade he suspended passes for 'Ali Gharbi for a few days. On 10 Febrary 1918, the governor issued an order to ban passage of goods to Kurdistan except by the direct Senneh road. This and other measures Kennion took with the Avroman aimed to stop such traffic.[576] To prevent goods going to the enemy via Kurdistan he asked the governor to ban all traffic into that direction. Agreements and cash deposits were taken from traders asking for passes to import contraband goods from occupied territory. In this way they held themselves and some others jointly responsible to give notice of the intended departure of any caravan into the banned direction. Although the scheme seemed to work for the direct roads to Kurdistan, there continued to be much trade between Kermanshah and Hamadan and Sonqur and nothing prevented traders to go from there to Senneh. Therefore, on 11 June 1918, Kennion introduced a pass system for trade between Kermanshah and Hamadan. The governor and local officials opposed this system, because the former had placed an embargo on all trade to Hamadan due to high prices in Kermanshah, reserving for himself the right to give passes to traders who were allowed to go there. This he now was forced to

574. FO 248/1204, Kermanshah report no. 4, 27/06/1918 by Lt. Col. Kennion.

575. FO 248/1204, Kermanshah report no. 11, 31/12/1918 by Lt. Col. Kennion. This was brought about with the help of the Farmanfarma family, who also arranged a monthly pension of 300 *tumans* for `Ali Akbar. Ettehadiyeh-Sa`vandiyan 1366, vol. 2, pp. 680, 682, 692-93, 698-99, 737-38; Idem 1369, pp. 39-40.

576. FO 248/1204, Kermanshah report no. 2, 13/03/1918 by Lt. Col. Kennion.

withdraw.[577] Some Kurdistani chiefs liked the idea of border control and came to see Kennion. The most important one, Ja'far Soltan told him he had taken several villages on the Turkish side. He gave Kennion a written undertaking promising: 1. to defend the border against the Turks; 2. to arrest and hand over enemy agents; 3. stop trading with enemy via the Halabja road. He further arranged to have his men enlist in the Khaneqin Levy Corps.[578]

INFLUX OF REFUGEES

In September 1918, the passage of Armenian and Jelu refugees was proceeding without a problem. There were some robberies in the Jelu camp; therefore, some rifles were given to the refugees as protection. Their bread supply from Kermanshah was somewhat problematic, but the governor helped to resolve this matter.[579] Also, in October 1918, the stream of refugees from Urumiyeh continued, there was no sign of stopping it. They were utterly undisciplined and they didn't all go the the camps where food was available. In fact, they camped where they liked and, as a result, were at the mercy of Persians, who took the animals of these stragglers. Because of the addition of these hungry mouths, prices remained high.[580] In November 1918, some 600 Armenians, old men, (pregnant) women and children, preferred to temporarily stay in Kermanshah rather than go to Baquba. Although all downward transport was loaded with the sick and wounded it remained quite a challenge to get them there.[581] At the beginning of December 1918, the 600 Armenians were still in the caravanserai the British consul had hired in Kermanshah, Whenever possible, they were transported out. The conduct of the Armenian Irregular Regiments marching from Hamadan to Baquba was not good. Discipline was bad and they looted a village.[582] In June 1920, there were still a few refugees who received relief, which was only given in the form of cash. These were mainly families who did not want to go to Baquba and had found employment with the British military in various functions. Although all were receiving relief, they had good jobs and therefore, many reductions were made.[583] At the beginning of August 1920, the relief work was closed down. There were 50 refugees who were sent to Baquba, as they wanted to go there. [584] In December 1920, large numbers of Armenians passed through Kermanshah en route to the US; also, some Jews going to Palestine.[585]

577. FO 248/1204, Kermanshah report no. 3, 11/06/1918 by Lt. Col. Kennion.
578. FO 248/1204, Kermanshah report no. 4, 18/06/1918 by Lt. Col. Kennion.
579. FO 248/1204, Kermanshah report no. 7, 12/09/1918 by Lt. Col. Kennion.
580. FO 248/1204, Kermanshah report no. 8, 05/10/1918 by Lt. Col. Kennion.
581. FO 248/1204, Kermanshah report no. 9, 01/11/1918 by Lt. Col. Kennion.
582. FO 248/1204, Kermanshah report no. 10, 03/12/1918 by Lt. Col. Kennion.
583. FO 248/1293, Kermanshah Report no. 6, 30 June 1920.
584. FO 248/1293, Kermanshah Report no. 7, up to 12 August 1920.
585. FO 248/1293, Kermanshah Report no. 11, up to 10 December 1920

POST-WAR PERIOD

With the end of the war, trade with Baghdad was resumed, and there was a return to more normal conditions (see Chapter Six). However, the normal condition soon became abnormal when instead of typhoid fever Kermanshah in November 1918 was in the grip of election fever. The city was allowed to send four MPs to the *Majles*.[586] There were nightly speeches and conferences in the city to solicit votes. The Democrats were divided. Mer'at al-Soltan, the main Democrat, was a former member who sought re-election. He was the son-in-law of Mohammad Baqer Mirza. Other Democrats standing for election were 'Ali Akbar Khan and Qasem Khan Sanjabi. Because several Democrats had lost much due to the depredations by the Sanjabis, they refused to have anything to do with the latter two. Because of this split among the Democrats, the more united Moderate party stood the better chance. The expected winners were: Nosrat al-Dowleh, Mo'tazed al-Dowleh, Amir Koll and Naser Divan.[587]

Meanwhile, the town and district were quiet, due to the steps taken by governor Salar Lashkar who ruled with some firmness, and who was not afraid to apply capital punishment when needed. Local mounted police were posted along the main road from the city to Bidsorkh, while *qarasuran* or road guards guarded the roads elsewhere, including at Mahidasht and Harunabad.[588] Although Salar-e Lashkar was very wealthy he was greedy and corrupt. After complaints by some citizens, accompanied with a list of the sums of graft he had taken, he was replaced by Mohammad Rahim Khan Amir Nezam Qaraqozlu, who served for about one year and did not take one cent in graft![589] During Amir Nezam's administration the city and province were quiet, except at Harsin where followers of A'zam al-Saltaneh Kakawand and the Qazi of Harsin clashed; two of the former's followers killed and some were wounded on both sides. A'zam al-Saltaneh afraid of losing his position sent for 2,000 tribesmen. The presence of Amir Mo'azzam in the city was a source of disquiet for Amir Nezam as he was intriguing with his opponents.[590]There also were attempts by politicians in Tehran to get their clients posts in Kermanshah. Adibandi, for example, tried have to have Sowlat al-Molk replaced as chief of police. The British consul considered Sowlat al-Molk to be very good at his job and argued that there was no justification for his removal.[591] Likewise, E'temad Homayun, who had become CO of the Persian troops in October 1919, complained that Army HQ wanted to replace him, because he, like his predecessor, had refused to pay graft to Salar Lashkar. They wanted to replace him with Abu'l-Fath Mirza, who was inspector of Army finances at Tehran under Salar

---

586. FO 248/1204, Kermanshah report no. 10, 03/12/1918 by Lt. Col. Kennion (Both town and district are quiet); Idem, Kermanshah report no. 11, 31/12/1918 by Lt. Col. Kennion.

587. FO 248/1204, Kermanshah report no. 11, 31/12/1918 by Lt. Col. Kennion.

588. FO 248/1204, Kermanshah report no. 8, 05/10/1918 by Lt. Col. Kennion; Idem, Kermanshah report no. 11, 31/12/1918 by Lt. Col. Kennion.

589. Soltani 1381, vol. 4, pp. 849-50. Hajji `Abdollah Khan Amir-e Nezam, previously Sardar Akram. Had military training and experience and had served in several administrative functions, incl. as governor of Khuzestan (1897). He was very wealthy. His son, Hoseyn Qoli Khan Amir Nezam was the head of the influential Qaraguzlu family of Hamadan. "He is not a person of strong character, but he is very honest and sincere and universally respected." He was educated in England. IOR/L/PS/20/223, Who's Who in Persia, Calcutta: General Staff, India 1916, p. 41.

590. FO 248/1293, Kermanshah Report no. 1, 31/01/1920.

591. FO 248/1293, Tel. Consul to Legation, 13/01/1920.

Lashkar. The latter was on good terms with the Minister of War. When Salar Lashkar was governor Abu'l-Fath Mirza was chief of police and his tool and he had to leave as he was very much disliked. His appointment would be unpopular, moreover, he had no army training. Therefore, the consul hoped that when Sarem al-Dowleh, the new governor arrived that the chiefs of police, gendarmes, army and finance would not be changed. They all had strong letters of recommendation from the Legation and were doing their best with few funds and means at their disposal.[592]

In March 1920, the town was quiet, which tranquility was only disturbed by a policeman who shot another one in a personal quarrel. He was judged under martial law, was found guilty and was hung three days later. This was a stark difference with the dilatoriness of the *'adliyeh* in deciding cases and the dislike of the governor to hang criminals lest he become unpopular. There was also positive movement on the tribal front. Amir Nezam, accompanied by Naser Divan, his chief of the governor's office, and the *ra'is-e maliyeh* visited Qasr-e Shirin to settle revenues matters in Zohab, where the Gurans, unwillingly, paid taxes for the first time. Because the Gurans and Sanjabis were going to their summer quarters, British military transports were told to take the route of Darband-Istakhvan to keep the road open at Pay Taq for the tribes. Salar Zafar, a Democrat and an inveterate intriguer, went to Qasr-e Shirin. In early April 1920, the town still was quiet despite rumors of unrest in Tehran and the absence of Amir Nezam and the deputy-governor. After Amir Nezam returned from Qasr-e Shirin, he left for Tehran on 13 April 1920. He had pressed the Prime Minister for his resignation, because the government did not sufficiently support him, while the government departments that were controlled from Tehran acted too independently from him. Amir Nezam had earned a reputation of honesty and straightforwardness.[593]

THE LAST YEARS OF QAJAR RULE

The political situation in the city was good in the early 1920, although there were many rumors every day, most of which were false. They were spread as part of intrigues for positions, many of them from Democrats, who were few in numbers in Kermanshah. They had no influence and the party had no real head apart from Salar Zafar Sanjabi, who was under restraint in the gendarmerie barracks. The carrying of arms had been forbidden, except by persons with a license. Tribesmen who arrived at the city gate had to deposit their arms and pick them up on departure. Since this order had been issued there was less violence and thieving at night. Firing at night that had been common, became exceptional. There were some bad characters who might raise trouble when the police relaxed their vigilance, and there was a resurgence of thieving at times. People liked the quiet. Chief topic of interest was the expected arrival of the shah. After his passage Sarem al-Dowleh, the new governor intended to hold municipal elections. The town was waiting to see how the new governor would rule. It was expected that soon he would return

592. FO 248/1293, no. 31, Consul to Legation, 13/01/1920.
593. FO 248/1293, Tel. 32 Consul to Legation, 13/04/1920.

to Tehran politics after a few months and that again a son of Farmanfarma would hold the governorship. This would mean another period of corruption and uneasiness, of which the town was free under Amir Nezam.[594]

On 30 April 1920, the new deputy-governor Mofakhkham al-Molk arrived. The arrival of Sarem al-Dowleh was still uncertain as he might decide to have his capital at Hamadan.[595] Akbar Mirza Sarem al-Dowleh, the eighth son of Zell ol-Soltan, was born around 1885. Before coming to Kermanshah he was the governor of Isfahan, where he was dismissed due to intrigues by the Democrats. In 1906, on the orders of his father he had killed his mother, and for some time the British and Russian consuls did not receive him, "but he has managed to live that down." In 1918 he was Minister of Finance. He was said the have "a breadth of view, a constancy, a sense of justice, and a grasp of affairs which raise him above the crowd of living Persian politicians."[596]Ahmad Shah arrived on 28 and left 30 May 1920. The streets were decorated with carpets and people seemed to be genuinely enthusiastic and spontaneous about his visit. In the evening there were fireworks. On 14 May 1920, the very rich new governor Sarem al-Dowleh arrived. The bombardment of Enzeli by the Bolsheviks caused some excitement among the population, which was allayed by seeing British troops leaving Kerend in that direction.[597]

In August 1920, people were very dissatisfied with Sarem al-Dowleh and a change would be beneficial, according to the British consul. "His policy is weak and will lead to unrest; he is notoriously corrupt and unpopular." He demanded 5,000 *tuman*s per activity to be paid into the IBP; when the bank sent him the conformation and he found that because of changes in the rate of exchange the amount was 5 *tuman*s less he refused to sign. He even fought with his gendarmerie officers about the division of plunder. In one month, he changed five deputy governors often without good reason; he also opposed British policy with regard to the tribes. Trade was hampered by exactions, but he did nothing. "Can a good replacement be found?" Major Greenhouse asked Tehran.[598] Amir Koll might be temporary governor for a short time, Greenhouse suggested. He did not change his mind even though at the end of July 1920, Sarem al-Dowleh all of a sudden had decided to take energetic action. He sent Salar Zafar Sanjabi to Tehran as his political activities were dangerous. He also showed support for Amir A'zam Kalhor.[599]

However, the British Legation disagreed with its consul in Kermanshah, for it considered Sarem al-Dowleh's dismissal not desirable, because on return to Tehran, where he was influential, he would start intriguing against the government. The Legation informed Greenhouse that the PM would send him a reprimand and warning and a friend had written him privately about

---

594. FO 248/1293, Tel. Consul to Legation, 23/07/1920.

595. FO 248/1293, Tel. 32 Consul to Legation, 13/04/1920.

596. IOR/L/MIL/17/15/11/3, Who's Who in Persia, vol. 2, pp. 23-24; IOR/L/PS/20/224, Biographies of the notables of Fars and certain Persian officials who have served at Shiraz. Delhi: Government of India, 1925', p. 13 (In 1922 he was appointed governor of Fars, but he resigned after a conflict with the Military taking over his palace. He did not perform well in Fars due to "poor office work, indolence and seeking to win popular favour by ultra-democratic manner and by extreme parsimony.")

597. FO 248/1293, Report Kermanshah, no. 5, 31 May 1920.

598. FO 248/1293, Tel. Consul to Legation, 23/07/1920; Soltani 1381, vol. 4, p. 852.

599. FO 248/1293, Tel. Consul to Legation, 30/07/1920.

his mishandling of dealing with the tribes. "Let's wait what will be the result of this. If he fails to improve I'll ask for his dismissal."[600] The political uncertainty in Tehran had its impact on Kermanshah. From the governor downwards, everybody was waiting their cue from Tehran with the result that the administration was even more corrupt and slacker than usual. Only the presence of British troops kept the province quiet; Bolshevik agents made little inroads. In August 1920, the British consul observed that there had been no capital punishment in Kermanshah for many months and there were at least nine convicted murderers and robbers in prison. The alleged reason for not sentencing them was that there was no public prosecutor. This obstacle was waived by Tehran and the establishment of a martial court of law with chiefs of police and gendarmes and *ra'is-e qoshun* should see some hangings, Greenhouse opined hopefully.[601]

Sarem al-Dowleh tried to put the British consul at ease by educating him what it took to be a politician and/or governor in Persia. He told Greenhouse that he was well aware that the cabinet was against him and criticized him; he had done the same to them; Persian politics was like a water wheel. They were trying to blame him for revenue problems, which at the same time limiting his finances. He had fired prince 'Emad al-Dowleh for speculation, who had now been returned to him as chief inspector of revenues! He knew that British were not satisfied with him, he was sorry, but he had to make money and had to follow a policy of alliance with the *Mohajerin* and Democrats, who doubtless were contrary to British interests. He would try to be more careful and maintain his close connection with its interests. The *Mohajerin* now had great influence and power. He, Vothuq al-Dowleh and others like them, of course, were opposed to them in principle, but out of self-interest had to work with them. He admitted that like everybody else he was making money. But he and Vothuq al-Dowleh also had to spend it freely for political reasons. Even now Vothuq al-Dowleh from Bombay had to spend 1,000 *tuman*s to keep his political clique going or he would have to give up his political ambitions. This was because except in government there were no openings for an educated person. For 2,500 posts in say the Revenue Department there were 5,000 hungry applicants. Those unemployed had to be supported by those who wanted to make use of them later; his expenses equaled at least his bribes.[602]

With good news from Rasht, things promised to become normal; but then on 14 August 1920 the Arab uprising in Khaneqin stopped traffic and caused consternation and people realized the importance of events in Iraq. Prompt British action kept the border tribes quiet. Sarem al-Dowleh ordered 700 Kalhors, Gurans and Sanjabis to go to Qasr-e Shirin to defend the border, their payment was guaranteed by the British consulate. Some 100 Gurans came immediately, but were no good and were sent back. Sardar Naser arrived in full force; the Kalhors like their chiefs were fickle and unreliable and only 100 showed and were of little use; in all 400 came. They attacked Khaneqin and restored order. This action kept the border quiet. There were no

600. FO 248/1293, draft tel. Legation to Baghdad, 18/08/1920. Idem, draft letter Legation to Sarem 'warning' him about dissatisfaction with him because of his interference with the tribes and the frequent change of place holders hoping to benefit from this. Kennion, also asked Tehran to have Sarem al-Dowleh given orders to arrest Amir Mo`azzam, who refused to come in, which prevented the settlement of the tribe. FO 248/1293, Tel. Consul to Legation, 09/08/1920.

601. FO 248/1293, Report Kermanshah no. 7, up to 12 August 1920.

602. FO 248/1293, discussion Consul Greenhouse with Sarem al-Dowleh, 24/08/2920.

new elections in 1920; those elected in the preceding year were all Moderates and still had one year to serve. There was not much interest in Tehran politics in Kermanshah, there was already too much trouble locally. The city was quiet though as badly administrated as ever. The municipality existed in name only, but used up money, while city sanitation was deplorable. Sowlat al-Molk managed the police department very well and had the confidence of all classes and parties. Punishment for criminals caught could be harsh. A notorious thief was walled up and another hanged.[603]

In 1920-21, there were three main political parties in Kermanshah: the Democrats, the Moderates, and the Mullah or religious party. Democrats were few and their leader was Sardar Zafar of the Sanjabi tribe (in detention in 1921 in Tehran) and thus, they were without a leader. In Kermanshah the leading members were: Sayyed 'Abbas Khordeh, Tama Khan Qannad, Mohammad Chanain, and 'Ali Aqa Ehtesham. Apart from some extremists "their party principles entirely opposed Bolshevism." The Anglo-Persian Treaty of 1919 was at first well received by people in Kermanshah, except by extreme Democrats. They maintained that it would make Iran tied to and oppressed by Great Britain and if the Shah went to Europe the British would make him a prisoner. In Kermanshah political intrigue was less intense than in other cities. Likewise, the Jangali movement failed to interest people in Kermanshah. The same held for the Arab insurrection in Iraq; there was little sympathy for it. The Democrats were fairly friendly towards Great Britain. In 1920 there was a chance for the Persian Government to sign the treaty. In Kermanshah the impression was that Persians would be in a subordinate positions under British officials if the treaty was signed. Also, the official class feared for their peculations. The deputies did not want it to be known that they voted for the treaty and therefore, did not go to Tehran. The Kermanshah deputies friendly to Great Britain were: Amir Koll, Naser Divan, Mo'tazed al-Dowleh, and Firuz Mirza Nosrat al-Dowleh. Amir Koll never left Kermanshah claiming illness to avoid the responsibility. On 10 January 1921, Naser Divan and Mo'tazed al-Dowleh left to Tehran, and Firuz Mirza a few days later, he only had returned from Europe on 10 January 1921.[604] The British army left Kermanshah in April 1921.[605]

The February coup d'etat of 1921 was followed by a military governorship of Kermanshah; there were no disturbances. On 12 April 1921, Major Mahmud Khan Paludin, the recently arrived commander of the gendarmerie, with help of the Kalhor tribe, attacked the governor's palace and seized Sarem al-Dowleh, on orders from Tehran. He was assisted by Amir A'zam Kalhor, Mofakhkham al-Molk, deputy governor and his men, who were in large number in town at that time. Amir Koll and 'Abdol-Fateh Mirza Amir Qoshun took *bast* in the British consulate. There was some firing at the palace, some casualties, but disturbances were quickly over. Mahmud Khan declared himself military governor and imposed martial law. That same afternoon Sarem al-Dowleh and his deputy Mofattah al-Molk were sent in two carriages to Tehran under guard of 25 gendarmes and 25 Kalhors. Amir A'zam accompanied the party until Asadabad. He was

603. FO 248/1293, Kermanshah Report no. 7, up to 15 September 1920.

604. AIR 20/663, p. 5.

605. Presbyterian Church 1922 a, pp. 68, 368-369.

imprisoned but released when Ziya al-Din was ousted. The days thereafter, the town was quiet and outwardly, people were not disturbed.[606]

Major Mahmud Khan Puladin was confirmed as the military governor and head of the local gendarmerie. Mohammad Hoseyn Khan Thiqeh al-Molk was seconded to him as civil governor. On 25 July 1921, a dispute broke out between Democrats and the *E'tedaliyun* concerning the elections for the *Majles*; Thiqeh al-Molk stood for the Democrats.[607] On 7 June 1921 the notables protested against the new tax schedule imposed by Ebtehaj al-Soltan, *ra'is-e maliyeh*, the collection of arrears over 6 years of the destroyed properties for which a reduction had been granted. Also, they asked for the appointment of a competent governor. In early July 1921, the new tax measures were cancelled and Thiqeh al-Eslam was dismissed as governor awaiting the arrival of his replacement, Abu'l-Fazl Mirza'Azad al-Saltaneh, son of Mozaffar al-Din Shah, who was appointed in December 1921.[608] He did not care for the governorship very much given his past involvement (he had been governor in 1912 appointed by Salar al-Dowleh) and the location of the province. Also, the appointment of Ahmad Aqa Khan as commander of the Western Army by Reza Khan and of Mokhtari as chief police was not to his liking. While the Democrats favored the appointments made by the coup d'etatists, the *E'tedaliyun* and the tribal chiefs opposed them. Aqa Sayyed Hasan, Azad al-Saltaneh's son-in-law, was able to bring about that his father-in-lawwas set aside; he resigned and in July 1922 he returned to Tehran.[609]

He was succeeded by Mokarram al-Molk Qa'emmaqam-e Tabrizi, who was governor from October-November 1922 until the beginning of 1923. The military command remained with Ahmad Aqa Khan Amir Lashkar. The elections for the 5th *Majles* led to great tension between the Democrats and *E'tedaliyun*. The former sent from Tehran two killers Hoseyn Aqa Qafqazi and 'Ali Borujerdi to kill Hasan Khan Mo'aven al-Molk, in which they were successful. Later Aqa Sayyed Hasan Kazazi, a Democrat was killed. Given his services to the nation he was buried with military honors. Next came the influx of olama from Iraq after the disturbances in Kerbela.[610]

Mohammad Khan Sardar 'Azim was the next governor; he was a retired Cossack officer and father-in-law to Ahmad Aqa Khan, the commander of the Army of the West. In the fall of 1923 Ahmad Shah passed through Kermanshah en route to Europe, never to return to Iran. At that time the movement to establish a republic began.[611] In August-September 1923, Gholam 'Ali Mirza Dowlatshahi Mojallal al-Dowleh became governor. Reza Khan had married his daughter.[612] Millspaugh, the Administrator General of Finances, made changes in and established

606. AIR 20/663, Maj. Greenhouse, Notes on Kirmanshah Affairs, May 1921; Soltani 1381, vol. 4, p. 853; Idem 1386, pp. 235-36. Another British source, but not present in Kermanshah, states that Ahmad Khan Akhgar was the CO of the gendarmerie and arrested Sarem al-Dowleh, "but showed him great consideration." IOR/L/MIL/17/15/11/8, 'Additions and Corrections to Who's Who in Persia (Volume IV)', pp. 4-5.

607. Soltani 1381, vol. 4, p. 854.

608. Soltani 1381, vol. 4, p. 855-58.

609. Soltani 1381, vol. 4, p. 859.

610. Soltani 1381, vol. 4, pp. 861-66. Qa'em-Maqam Tabrizi, governor of Kermanshah in 1922, before that of Astarabad and Kurdistan, "friendly and intelligent." IOR/L/MIL/17/15/11/3, Who's Who in Persia, vol. 2, p. 311.

611. Soltani 1381, vol. 4, pp. 866-68.

612. Soltani 1381, vol. 4, p. 869.

inspections of the revenue departments. As a result, in 1923, 11 employees of the directorate of indirect taxes of Kermanshah were dismissed for disobeying orders and political activities.[613] In 1924, the procession of cars bringing the body of Major Imbrie, the US consul, to the railhead at Khaneqin passed through Kermanshah, accompanied by a number of senior Persian officers, while the whole garrison paid tribute.[614] Mojallal al-Dowleh was succeeded by Mohammad Khan Montazam al-Dowleh in January 1925. Around 11 November 1925 the Qajar crown prince left Kermanshah to depart from Iran.[615]

REZA SHAH PERIOD

Mohammad Khan Montazem was appointed governor of Kermanshah and took office on 26 February 1926.[616] He had the difficult task to represent the new regime and establish its authority in both city and the province. This was no easy task, because the province was in disarray, while "The state of the troops of the Western Division is deplorable. Unpaid and badly trained, they are in a state of discontent, and propaganda is making headway among them."[617] The dissatisfaction of the Kurdish tribes increased when Reza Shah continued his disarmament campaign. As a result, "Sardar Rashid, a notorious chieftain from the Ravansar region, who had already rebelled half a dozen times in the past and been pardoned, again raised the banner of rebellion, in connivance with Salar-ed-Dovleh, many local tribes joining in the revolt for the sake of plunder. This revolt very soon extended towards the north."[618] After this feeble and failed attempt in 1925, Salar al-Dowleh, the wannabe Shah of 1910-12, made another effort in July 1926 to attack Kermanshah by rallying dissatisfied Kurdish tribal elements. Reza Shah was very angry about Salar al-Dowleh's incursion, because he believed that the Qajar rebel had outside, i.e. British help. However, he was probably angrier about the unreliability of the troops of the Western Division. According to the British, "they are unfit to take to the field against the enemy. There are rumors of panicky retirements and of surrenders to the enemy without fighting. Reinforcements have reached Senneh and more are underway from Tehran."[619] An airplane returning from reconnaissance over the Salar al-Dowleh unsurrection area crashed near Kermanshah and was completely destroyed. The Russian pilot and the accompanying Persian officer were not seriously hurt.[620] The additional troop reinforcements made all the difference, Salar al-Dowleh was ousted and fled to Iraq and the Kurdish insurrection was suppressed.[621] Meanwhile, in Kermanshah there was very little interest in the insurrection in Kurdistan.

613. FO 461/73, f. 90b.
614. Forbes-Leith 1925, p. 172.
615. Soltani 1381, vol. 4, p. 874.
616. FO 416/78, Intel. Summary No. 5 ending March 6, 1926.
617. FO 416/79, Intel. Summary No. 15 ending July 24, 1926.
618. Arfa 1964, p. 203.
619. FO 416/79, Intel. Summary No. 17 ending August 21, 1926.
620. FO 416/79, Intel. Summary No. 18 ending September 4, 1926.
621. On Salar al-Dowleh's forays into Persia in 1925 and 1926, and its aftermath, see Floor 2018.

However, due to the absence of troops at the Kurdish front, a strong anti-dynastic feeling came to the fore in Kermanshah,[622] be it that this did not remain overt for long.

In April 1927, Reza Shah was still very dissatisfied with the condition of the troops of the Western Division and publicly said so to its commanding general.[623] In that year there was an administrative reorganization of the various provinces. As of then Kermanshah became the administrative center of the newly formed Ostan V, while henceforth the governors (*ostandar*) of the province (*ostan*) were named by the Minister of the Interior.[624] Reza Shah arrived on 18 April 1928 and was Amir Koll's guest. He arrived with Sarem al-Dowleh, Shokr al-Molk, Qa'emmaqam al-Molk, Aqa Mir, Amir A'zam and Amir Akram and an escort of 50-60 men in five lorries. During his previous visit to Kermanshah Reza Shah had used some violence, and this time also some local officials felt the "Pahlavi touch." The Chief of Staff was told he bungled the affair of Sayyed Ashraf who was pardoned. On 19 April there was an important meeting in the *Ejlaliyeh*, Amir Koll's residence; even the telephone was cut off. Amir Koll told the British consul that the meeting was only a gambling party to put the Shah in a good mood. He did not want to be governor of Posht-e Kuh and had paid a sum to be excused of this post; in his stead Ahmad Aqa Amir Lashkar, the commander of the Western Division was reappointed, also as governor of Posht-e Kuh. However, Reza Shah did not trust Amir Koll, according to the British consul, and wanted him to accept a governorship in Fars or Khorasan. On 20 April the Shah left for his property in Shahabad (Harunabad) returning the next day. On his return, the governor of Kurdistan, Ettela' al-Molk and a Kurdish chief came to see him. In the morning of 23 April 1928, Reza Shah left Kermanshah.[625] Although Kurdistan had been pacified, in 1932, there was still one independent army brigade in Kermanshah.[626]

Asadollah Mirza Shehab al-Molk was three times governor of Kermanshah during this period and seems to have left a rather good impression in that he tried to work for the well of the people. He was known to go out into the streets in the morning to ask people what needed to be done and gave instructions to take care of the problems raised by his interlocutors.[627] He was dismissed in 1933, when he was replaced by Mohsen Khan Aliabadi (Eqtedar al-Dowleh), who lasted not more than one year as he opposed Tehran's interference with the judiciary in Kermanshah and thus he was let go. His replacement was Ahmad Khan Mohseni 'Emad al-Molk who was appointed in November 1934, and of his accomplishments in Kermanshah, if any, nothing is known, but that he was dismissed in July 1935. Shehab al-Dowleh was reappointed, who remained in office until 1937, when he was dismissed.[628]

Although Kermanshah was the staging area for the disarmament and pacification campaigns in Kurdistan and Lorestan, the province itself was relatively quiet. The fact that in 1926 Reza

622. FO 416/79, Intel. Summary No. 19 ending September 18, 1926.

623. FO 416/80, Intel. Summary No. 7 ending April 2, 1927.

624. Soltani 1381, vol. 4, p. 895.

625. FO 371/13064, no. 21, Cowan/Kermanshah to Clive/Tehran, 23/04/1928. According to Soltani 1384, p. 118, Amir Koll was one of the close friends of Reza Shah and advised him on all matters concerning Kurdistan, Lorestan and Kermanshah.

626. Wilson 1932, p. 344.

627. Soltani 1381, vol. 4, p. 897.

628. Soltani 1381, vol. 4, p. 897.

Shah arrested most of the tribal chiefs and either put them in prison or banned them to other parts of Persia helped, of course. Control of public life was strict and dissent was suppressed. Economically the province suffered from its relative isolation after Tehran had decided that it preferred to supply the province via Persian ports rather than via the traditional Basra-Baghdad route (see Chapter Six).[629] Nevertheless, the province was not forgotten, because it also received its share of public investments and had its share of modernization projects like the rest of the country, even when the impact of this modernization was superficial.

MODERNIZATION OF THE CITY

The city also changed during this period. Modern wide avenues were constructed that were lined with buildings in a new style of architecture. Of course, not everybody was happy with these urban changes as many existing houses had to be destroyed, inconveniencing many people. But it gave the city a face lift, a slightly different appearance, one that indicated that things were changing. When Balfour and party entered the city in 1934 he observed that "Kermanshah was in the throes of modernization, and new bazaars of glazed brick were taking the place of the old. There were traffic lights, and even a traffic policeman mounted on an imposing dais at the junction of four streets. But there was no traffic."[630] These traffic daises were little round brick platforms. In Kerend there was even one, "placed in a tiny garden of minute bed and paths, marked out with bricks," with an umbrella-like shelter above his head. In Kermanshah there was only one of this type minus the garden right in front of Hotel Bristol. "The platform was at least two feet high, and kept the man out of the mud and from being splashed." The umbrella was fastened to a ten-foot pole and was made of kerosene cans, "neatly cut to shape, joined and edged with a waved border of the same material, as an ornamentation, like a little fancy frill to a parasol."[631]

Balfour must have been exaggerating to amuse his readers by ridiculing the situation in Kermanshah, when he wrote that there was no traffic in the city. True, in 1916 there were no cars in Kermanshah and in 1918 they still were a rare sight.[632] However, after 1920 there was a substantial increase in motorized traffic. This was due to the presence of the British army, which, when it departed in April 1921 sold its trucks (Fords). At that time Ebrahim Khan Guran and 10 young family members had been working with the British and had learned how to drive and repair cars. As nobody in Kermanshah had any knowledge of cars, Ebrahim Khan Guran bought the trucks and started a garage and a transportation company. Later he also acquired a car dealership.[633]

629. For a fictional account of the working and living conditions of urban and rural workers at that time, see Khodadad 1395, a Kermanshahi Communist, who wrote the first Persian workers novel that was published in 1936 in Kermanshah.

630. Balfour 1935, p. 88.

631. Alexander 1934, p. 26.

632. Blücher 1949, p. 79; Edmonds 2010, p. 221.

633. Soltani 1381, vol. 1, p. 545.

Fig. 7.12: The main street of Kermanshah in 1934.

By 1920, cars had become so numerous that the habit of keeping stocks of oil and gasoline in caravanserais had become dangerous. At that time, the British consul Greenhouse called a meeting of local merchants and Ra'is al-Tojjar and it was decided that all oil and petrol in bulk should be stored at one site far away from buildings. A committee was formed that choose a suitable site.[634] There was also an increase in car accidents; often due to ignorance of villagers about the rules of the road. Because all cars in 1920 were British, free medical and generous pecuniary compensation was given in each case. Because of the increase in the number of cars by December 1920 petrol was almost unobtainable even at 150 *qran*s and kerosene at 60 *qran*s per tin. At that time, the number of Persian owned cars in Kermanshah was 27, while all other cars in the city numbered 35. Although cars were a danger to pedestrians, they were not the only ones, because the ubiquitous 4-horsed fourgon was a danger to traffic. "It has no breaks and is seldom under control on a steep gradient."[635] The number of cars in the city kept increasing. In 1927, the Imperial Bank manager, McCallum, remarked that Kermanshah had masses of cars.[636] With this growth of car traffic there was a need for garages. In 1932, there were three: Reza'i, Hoseyni and Fuladi. In 1936, there were probably more, because Hinz submits that Kermanshah

634. FO 248/1293, Kermanshah Report no. 4, 30/04/1920.

635. FO 248/1293, Kermanshah Report no. 11, up to 10 December 1920.

636. McCallum 1930, p. 223.

had a remarkable large number of garages.[637] Among those garages were: Beyn al-Nahreyn, Milard, Guran, Sirafi, Afshar, Mahmudi, Isfahan and Tehran.[638]

Despite these signs of modernization, it was the general opinion of the few foreign visitors to Kermanshah that, apart from the bazaar, there was nothing much of interest to see, while the bazaar did not have much to offer.[639] The bazaars were very clean though; the narrow streets were swept, and the shops were neat and orderly. There were apertures in the bricked domes to let in light and air as well as rain and snow. "The shops were flooded with the cheap rubbish of Russia, Germany and Czecho-Slovakia." The only Persian products were the tiny shops of jewelers, gold workers, and copper and brass smiths. There were also food shops and bakeries with bread and sweetmeats.[640]

From the above the reader may get the impression that Kermanshah was hardly touched by modern technological progress and that the city remained stuck in the past. However, that was not the case. To supply the growing number of cars, electric machines and the like with the necessary oil products the city had an APOC depot, which was supplied by rail to Khaneqin and from there by truck.[641] However, Persia wanted that APOC rather than favoring Iraqi oil development began developing the oil field at Kermanshah. Therefore, during the negotiations in 1933 for the revision of the oil concession APOC agreed to develop the Naft-e Shah field in Kermanshah Province. In 1934, drilling was resumed by a separately established Kermanshah Oil Company. A small topping plant was built to reinject parts of the crude oil not wanted into the reservoir. Kermanshah was the end of the 158-mile pipeline that began at Naft-e Shah and had a capacity of 70,000 gallons/day to supply the small refinery of an annual 5 million ton throughput, situated 5 km from Kermanshah at the Qarasu river. The refinery was opened in 1935 in the presence of Prime Minister Forughi. The pipe had a pressure of 1,500 pounds/sq. feet and was insulated with asbestos and bituminous mastic. This refinery supplied N.W. and Central Persia with its fuel needs to various despots with a fleet of trucks in bulk and in tins. However, during winter when snow might make the roads impassable a storage tank in Qazvin fulfilled that function.[642]

The only other major modern industrial employer was the state-owned sugar mill at Shahabad that was built in 1935. Up to at least 1940, due to insufficient beet production, the sugar mill only worked 40-50 day per year, while the sugar refinery operated for another 30-35 days. To meet sugar demand Java sugar was imported that the mill converted into loaf sugar for the local market.[643] Therefore, employment was seasonal and varied from 700 people at peak time to 90-100 during the off-season, many of whom were technicians. The seasonal and mostly unskilled labor was mostly hired from among the surrounding rural district. In 1943 wages for unskilled labor were 15 rials/day and for skilled labor it varied from 500 to 1,600 rials/month

637. Ebtehaj 1932, p. 148; Reitlinger 1932, p. 30; Hinz 1938, p. 19.
638. Soltani 1381, vol. 1, p. 552.
639. Powell 1923, p. 232; Alexander 1934, p. 26.
640. Alexander 1934, p. 24.
641. McCallum 1930, p. 223.
642. Bamberg 2000, pp. 68, 70 (foto of the opening of the refinery); Hay 1937, p. 20.
643. FO 248/1414, Report on the Social and Economic Situation ... for the year 1319.

depending on the skills set. In rural areas payments differed per district. In Mahidasht a laborer received 1,000 rials cash for 9 months plus food, one suit of clothes and one pair of shoes. In other districts, notably Sanjabi, payments were in kind, 2-3 *man* of wheat/day.[644] In addition, employment was offered in other modern plants such as a cotton spinning factory built in 1930, while several knitting plants were operating in 1935. Furthermore, in 1935 a grain silo was erected.[645] Later mills for flour, rice and vegetable oils were added.[646] From the above it is clear that despite the establishment of these new modern industries the province of Kermanshah still remained very much agricultural, in which sector some 80% of the population was still gainfully employed. Likewise, the city still remained very much a traditional pre-industrial market and pilgrim town.[647]

WORLD WAR II PERIOD

On 25 August 1941, British troops moved into Persia, including Kermanshah, where the objective was to occupy the refinery and oil field and join up with Soviet forces, who invaded the country from the North.[648] The occupying powers divided the country into a British and a Russian zone; Kermanshah was situated in the British zone. Throughout the war years, apart from military security issues, which I will not discuss, the British were preoccupied with the following problems in Kermanshah: the food supply, the economic situation, the ineffective Persian administration and the lack of public support for the Allies. As the first two problems have been discussed above (chapters 2 and 4) I only discuss the latter two issues. All these problems were, of course, interlinked and the worsening of one of them impacted negatively on the others. The occupiers were not welcome and the attitude of the population in general was unfriendly towards the Allies and pro-German. Of course, such feelings were not unexpected, but the British clearly hoped that over time their presence would be seen as beneficial.

ALLIED PROPAGANDA

On 29 January 1942 the Tripartite Treaty was signed, which offered Persia protection, while creating a "Persian corridor" (*pol-e peyruzi*) for the Allies—a supply route from the Persian Gulf to Russia. Persia promised "not to adopt in its relations with foreign countries an attitude which is inconsistent with the alliance," while the Allies gave a guarantee that they would leave Persian soil within six months of the close of the war. If the Allies had hoped that the Tripartite Treaty signing would be welcomed by the population they were disappointed. People in Kermanshah remained unfriendly and the only thing that they appreciated in the Treaty was that

---

644. FO 371/40222 (26/11/1943).
645. Wilson 1932, p. 62; Floor 2009, p. 171.
646. Government of Great Britain 1945, pp. 459-60, 525.
647. Clarke & Clark 1969, p. Ael 1931, pp. 48-51.
648. Bamberg 2000, p. 237; Longrigg 1925, pp. 60-61.

it did not oblige Persians to serve in the Allied armies. The British consul put a good face on things by commenting that if only "Russian activities in N. and N.W. Persia were less hostile to the Persians the unfriendly attitude would improve." However, Persian officialdom, although now formally on the Allied side, could not be induced to organize a party to celebrate this event. Therefore, the British consul postponed the celebration until after the arrival of his Soviet colleague and even then he was not certain whether he would organize a celebration party. To counter German propaganda and to inform the local population about British positions, he was impatiently awaiting a cinema van, films with Persian text and battery-operated radio sets, and other PR materials.[649] On 28 February 1942, despite the lukewarm attitude of the Persian authorities to the Tripartite Treaty, a dinner party for 120 guests was given, which was a great success, at least according to the British consul. However, he also reported that local feelings remained cool towards the Allies.

The Persian military remained anti-British, but to improve this situation the Persian government as of April 1942, allowed them to meet with British officers.[650] This did not yield immediate success, of course. In fact, anti-British activities increased thereafter, in proportion to German successes around Rostov. Persian officers insulted people associated with Great Britain, threatening them with what would happen soon. The British consul was convinced that there was a kind of organized pro-Axis activity in the army, although General Shahbakhti, the commander of the Western Army, denied that such a thing even existed. However, General Razmara, who came for a visit to Kermanshah, admitted that it did. Because of Allied military reverses, in particular the fall of Rostov in July 1942, the anti-British sentiments gained momentum and not only among Army officers. As a result, those friendly to the British remained aloof, when the Germans were moving toward the Caucasus, while those who were anti-British were jubilant.[651]

Both Cook, the British consul and Col. Fletcher, the British Consulate's political adviser, believed that Kermanshah was a center of anti-British organizations, both civil and military. The anti-British feelings were more openly shown due to a failure to act against Persian fifth column activities, they argued. Therefore, Fletcher proposed to establish a temporary camp outside Kermanshah to intern pro-German sympathizers. However, if such sympathizers were officers of Shahbakhti's troops these should be sent straight to Ahvaz, else it would be a blow to the general's vanity. He even suggested that it might be a good idea to pay the tribes to stop being a nuisance to keep the lines of communication open should the war come to Persia. However, the British Legation disagreed and was of the opinion that both Cook and Fletcher exaggerated.[652]

---

649. FO 371/31402, Kermanshah Diary January 1942

650. FO 371/31402, Kermanshah Diary April 1942.

651. FO 371/31402, Kermanshah Diary July 1942. That is why in 1945, the British consul regretted that Col. Shahrokhshahi, the commander of the Kermanshah Brigade, who had done much to improve the morale of the troops and change the anti-Allies attitude of his officers, was replaced. FO 371/45400, Kermanshah Diary February 1945. On the attitude of Persia army officers in 1942, see Appendix IX.

652. FO 248/1414,Cook to Legation, 09/08/1942; FO 371/31402, no. 41, Consul to FO, 02/08/1942; FO 248/1414, Col. Fletcher to Gen. Maine, 01/08/1942.

Cook opined that Persian officials considered this issue of anti-British activity rather casually, which he did not. Any activity that he considered anti-British had his attention. Col. Ha'eri, the chief of the closed Cadet school, which was allegedly imbued with Nazi ideals, was told by Amir Koll, the governor, who also was his brother-in-law, that he had to leave to Tehran at British insistence, not because of these Nazi sympathies, but because he had talked too much to the Russians during a few parties! Because of these developments there were fewer visitors to the British Consulate, because Amir Koll told his officials not to visit or have anything to do with the British. When asked about this he admitted that the Soheyli cabinet had given him such instructions a few months earlier. Consul Cook commented: "If we have to return to the boycott and isolation of the Reza Shah period our work becomes difficult and unreal, especially in the British zone where numerous people are affected by the presence of our army. In the main street, one year after our entry, one does not find one British poster or calendar in a shop or cafe although thousands have been distributed by the consulate. Perhaps they deem it inadvisable to do so."[653]

Therefore, the British consul despaired, because he received insufficient PR material to counter pro-German propaganda. Moreover, the materials that he initially received were unsuitable and inadequate. In fact, the otherwise ineffective Amir Koll, the governor, did better than whatever British propaganda had done. In February 1942, he had three pro-German Persians arrested, showing his good-will towards the British. They were all friends of Dr. Fuchs, the head of the Municipal Hospital and they were sent to other parts of Persia. This arrest sent a strong message to other pro-Germans, who spread news of German and Japanese victories.[654] However, this was only one positive signal from an otherwise uncooperative administration. The British consul wanted to have Col. Artta [sic; ?] recalled, who had been appointed police chief in January 1942. As a policeman he had a very bad reputation and he was a close associate of General Rokn al-Din Mokhtari, the notorious police chief of Tehran under Reza Shah. In April 1942, he returned from Tehran with a promotion. The consul was very upset about this and suspected ulterior motives, for why else was this man sent to Kermanshah in the British zone and with a promotion? To the public at large it seemed to suggest that the British wanted to be associated with him. Therefore, the consul urged that he should be replaced as soon as possible. "We should try to get good people here; for whoever is employed here it reflects on us." In May 1942, Col. Artta was recalled after pressure from Great Britain, but also because people feared him.[655]

Also, the anti-British attitude was encountered in vital areas such as the supply route through which equipment was sent to Russia. While Great Britain was spending large amounts of money to improve the road to Hamadan for transporting goods to Russia, Persian Customs officials on purpose delayed these goods as much as possible. They insisted on making a list of everything the trucks carried, which, so the consul believed, was copied to the enemy. As a result, the trucks had to wait for 4-5 hours to complete Customs formalities. Cook insisted that better

---

653. FO 371/31402, Kermanshah Diary August 1942.
654. FO 371/31402, Kermanshah Diary February 1942.
655. FO 371/31402, Kermanshah Diary April 1942.

arrangements should have to be made with the Persian government that after all was officially allied with the Allies.[656]

British PR activities were hardly a good instrument as counter propaganda. In early 1942, the few films that were shown by the British in the cinemas were newsreels, most of them with Persian sound tracks, but unfit for PR purposes. Although British radio transmissions were improving, they were weaker than those of the Axis. Russian successes on the battlefield helped in this regard, but people still blamed Great Britain for Russia's behavior in N. Persia. The opening of the Russian Consulate in Kermanshah meant that many people feared that there would be more Soviet propaganda to encourage the poverty-stricken masses to rise up against the wealthy class and demand reforms. They asked: "why do they open a consulate in Kermanshah when there is no Russian interest here?"[657]

Although, as of April 1942, more Persian magazines were received, and public broadcasts were more listened to due to longer programs, no films were received.[658] In mid-1942, some 300 people came to listen to the nightly broadcast of the BBC and Radio Tehran news in Persian. Cook believed more people would come, if only he had a good loudspeaker, because then the program could be aired outside, which was better in the hot weather. The good news was that the cinema van finally arrived. The bad news was that the old and unsuitable news-reel films supplied by Cairo broke all the time. The inexperienced Persian operator could barely cope with this problem, so that if things would not improve Cook expected that "the experiment will not last long in his hands."[659] Although by July 1942, much material in Persian was available the films were still as unsuitable as before. Although there was a growing interest in the BBC radio news broadcast (142 in April and 168 in May), there was still much pro-Axis sentiment. In fact, German propaganda had a significant impact via privately-owned radio sets and a whisper campaign. To ensure that two hotels that had radio sets didn't air German programs plainclothes police were stationed there to prevent this.[660] Despite requests for better quality PR material and services, in July 1942 Cook concluded that these continued to be inadequate; the radio set did not have enough sound and people in the back of the hall could not hear it. The cinema van was a complete failure as it was handled by two unskilled youths; the projector was old and worn-out; the films from Cairo were brittle, ancient, patched and torn and had little PR value. He even reported that allegedly wholesale distributors of British magazines for sale in the provinces sold them as waste paper or as packing paper.[661] In August 1942, there was no change in this situation except that the cinema van had broken down and was returned to Tehran. Cook further drew attention to a potential intelligence issue. Many enemy aliens (Italians, Hungarians), who were working for Kampsax on road making projects, formed a potential danger, because even if they supported the Allies, the Nazis might pressure them through their family in Europe. Fortunately, for Cook the German onslaught in Russia stopped in the months after the German withdrawal

656. FO 371/31402, Kermanshah Diary July 1942.
657. FO 371/31402, Kermanshah Diary February 1942.
658. FO 371/31402, Kermanshah Diary April 1942.
659. FO 371/31402, Kermanshah Diary June 1942.
660. FO 371/31402, Kermanshah Diary July 1942.
661. FO 371/31402, Kermanshah Diary July 1942.

from Rostov in December 1941. As a result, people were more interested in the local food problem than in German propaganda.[662]

In September 1942, Cook tried to make his PR efforts more effective. He hired a shop to display British war posters, photos and created a place where people could read pamphlets. The visitors were mostly school boys and young men. About 200 people came every evening to listen to the BBC, but immediately thereafter they left without staying to listen to the Baku, Delhi and Tehran news bulletins. In that same month, the Russians also opened a small display near the British shop, but it was much less attractive, at least according to Cook.[663] Although by October 1942 British posters were to be seen all over town, people had no time for PR given the economic and the bread situation. According to consul Good, for 4/5th of the population, the best PR would be to put a few honest Brits in charge of the province with a group of honest Persians to get them out of this morass.[664] By November 1942, the British consul believed that the PR campaign was finally beginning to be more effective. Printed PR material was distributed and was seen everywhere. Whereas by then, the film van was a great success, the BBC radio program was listened to at 7.45 pm, but the transmission from Tehran was barely audible. Moreover, German broadcasts that were jammed in the past were very audible between 8.30-9 pm. But since they told so many untruths about the British occupied part of Persia, no longer had any impact, as people were able to verify those claims themselves.[665]

Perhaps more effective than films and posters was the good behavior of the British troops and that they paid for everything, because this left a good impression. The fact that British troops were overcharged when buying fruit, the result of Army supply officers buying at inflated prices from local contractors and who didn't bother to check with the British Consulate as to prices, also helped. Perhaps the best PR activity was the road work that was done in the province to which end the British paid large sums to rural workers; this much changed their attitude toward Great Britain. To further curry favor with public opinion the British put on the occasional military display such as the one with the fife and drum band given by the 1st Ghurka Rifles for 2,000 Persians in April 1942. The display did not quell the anti-British feelings, of course, the more so that, as yet, there were no Allied victories.[666] Allied successes at the end of 1942 (N. Africa, Pacific, and Stalingrad in February 1943) meant change. At least people no longer thought that war would come to Persia. Therefore, they began visiting the British Consulate again, which they had not done out of fear and at instructions from Tehran. Of course, bad-wishers continued to say that the British were responsible for the terrible bread situation, hoarding, and other problems.[667] Perhaps even more significant than battle field success was the Tehran Conference (28 November to 1 December 1943), which greatly impressed people, especially the statement concerning the independence of Persia. Merchants in particular, were pleased with the promise of material assistance after the war.[668] Using the background of the war events and

662. FO 371/31402, Kermanshah Diary August 1942.
663. FO 371/31402, Kermanshah Diary September 1942.
664. FO 371/31402, Kermanshah Diary October 1942.
665. FO 371/31402, Kermanshah Diary November 1942.
666. FO 371/31402, Kermanshah Diary April 1942; Idem, Kermanshah Diary June 1942.
667. FO 371/31402, Kermanshah Diary November 1942.
668. FO 371/40177, Kermanshah Diary December 1943.

of the local bread situation, as of 1943 the British followed a two-pronged approach to capture the hearts and minds of the population. One via the media of print, film and radio, and the other via the delivery of charitable assistance in the field of medical care and poverty alleviation.

I. In the first area, i.e. that of the media, as of mid-1943, Great Britain had a Radio Listening Hall in the *Meydan* with two large PR display boards. Not to be outdone the Russians placed one of their own next to it. The mobile cinema was a big success; at the Shahabad sugar mill the film 'Desert Victory' was shown, which previously and later was shown many times in Kermanshah city itself.[669] Also shown was the film 'Mrs. Miniver', the proceeds of which were for the RAF Benevolent Fund. The same film was shown for the whole week as an introduction to the Tehran Conference, a total of Rls 32,500 were collected. The day before, a film was shown in the *Shahpur* school for 600 school children, apart from the Tehran Conference, shorts were shown, which, as much as possible, had little to do with the war. The BBC Persian service from 2-2.15 p.m. was of little use in Kermanshah, because there was no electricity during the day time (apart from the KPC and the US mission with their own generator) and the number of radios with battery-sets was almost zero.[670] Due to warmer weather, the size of the audience grew, both in and outside the British radio hall. Allegedly, this counteracted German propaganda. Public opinion was now convinced of the Allied victory such that the Christian minorities and pro-British people were apprehensive of the day of departure of British troops.[671]

By May 1944, the British radio hall finally had a working amplifier and, as a result, instead of 300 there were 700 listeners in the main square in the evening. However, with more daylight electricity, it came too late available to also broadcast the Allied program from Tehran at 7 pm. The Anglo-Iranian Relief Fund (AIRF) traveled into the district to hand out cloth and newspapers, illustrated magazines and other PR material. The film van showed films to 400 children.[672] In June 1944, the news of the fall of Rome was greeted with applause in the Radio Hall; the overall reaction in town was surprisingly enthusiastic. There was also much public interested in the map room which showed the situation on the Eastern and Western front.[673] The film van had to be sent to Tehran for repairs and only returned on 25 December 1944. Its 16 mm projector was able operate off the electric grid, which gave it more flexibility than the 35 mm projector. Therefore, showings were resumed in private homes and the British Consulate.[674] In January 1945, the mobile film truck also showed films in other towns and in March around the province, where its service was well-received.[675]

II. The second line of propaganda was that of poverty alleviation. The organization engaged in that kind of work was the Anglo-Iranian Relief Fund (AIRF), which as of the first of January 1944 began providing food to a limited number of the poor. On that day, 1,000 free meals were

669. FO 371/40177, Kermanshah Diary December 1943.
670. FO 371/40177, Kermanshah Diary February 1944.
671. FO 371/40177, Kermanshah Diary April 1944.
672. FO 371/40177, Kermanshah Diary May 1944.
673. FO 371/40177, Kermanshah Diary June 1944.
674. FO 371/45400 Monthly Diary Dec. 1944.
675. FO 371/45400, Monthly Diary January 1945; Idem, Kermanshah Diary March 1945.

served at the local Poor House. The consul and other notables were present, which resulted in good publicity in the newspapers. In fact, the *Tudeh*-leaning newspaper *Bisotun* printed the AIRF report in serial form.[676] In February 1944, AIRF continued its program of free meals in the Poor House, viz. 1,500 meals consisting of bread and meat soup. In March another 1,500 meals were distributed. In April 1944, the AIRF meal program came to end; privately donated children's clothes were all given to the Poor House.[677] Its other activities, however, continued. In June, the British Consul distributed cloth and sugar to the poor in Ilam and Eywan on behalf of the AIRF. Further, one ton of sugar and 26 kg of tea were distributed to poor villagers. Also, free bread was distributed, which was paid for by wealthy landowners and others who contributed £1,500 to feed 1,650 poor persons daily.[678] On 20 December 1944, AFPPR gave gifts of sugar, tea, khaki drill and colored poplin to 100 people in the poor house.[679] On 19 March 1945, on behalf of AFPPR the British consul made *Nowruz* gifts to 100 poor school children (3 m of cloth each) and to 120 inmates of the Kermanshah poor house (300 gr sugar and 30 gr tea each). The poor house looked good and the poor well looked after, an improvement compared to the situation a few months ago, according to the consul.[680] Some presents from the AIRF were also made to poor rural inhabitants.[681] On 8 September 1945 or *Eyd al-Fetr*, the British consul distributed AFPPR goods to the Poor House which was in bad situation due to lack of funds.[682]

The British Consulate, and in particular the AIRF, were also active in providing medical assistance. Since July 1943, the AIRF operated a dispensary in Senneh, where, by April 1944, some 2,600 patients had been treated. In January 1944, it also gave 2,500 sulfanilamide tablets (an early anti-biotic medicine) to the same dispensary.[683] On 12 February 1944 extra hospital equipment was brought from Shahabad by the British military. AIFR gave 1,000 anti-diphtheria vaccines for school children, which were handed over to the governor. Medical supplies from AIRF also went to Senneh.[684] In June 1944, at Senneh, AIRF treated 874 patients at the free clinic.[685] The British army hospital treated the workers that built their barracks.[686] In January 1945, two mobile dispensaries arrived that were active in the Sanandaj and in Rowanshir areas.[687] In April 1945, the Anglo-Iran Relief Fund sent medicines, which were given to the mobile dispensary at Kermanshah and some to the hospital at Ilam.[688] By September 1945, the AIRF mobile dispensary at Sanandaj had treated 8,000 patients during the two years of its operation. Also, 10,000 Webrine anti-malaria tablets were distributed, which was an endemic disease there.[689]

---

676. FO 371/40177,Kermanshah Diary January 1944.
677. FO 371/40177, Kermanshah Diary February 1944; Idem, Kermanshah Diary April 1944.
678. FO 371/40177, Kermanshah Diary June 1944.
679. FO 371/45400 Monthly Diary December 1944.
680. FO 371/45400, Kermanshah Diary March 1945.
681. FO 371/45400, Kermanshah Diary April 1945.
682. FO 371/45400, Kermanshah Diary September 1945.
683. FO 371/40177, Kermanshah Diary January 1944; Idem, Kermanshah Diary April 1944.
684. FO 371/40177, Kermanshah Diary February 1944.
685. FO 371/40177, Kermanshah Diary June 1944.
686. FO 371/45400 Monthly Diary December 1944.
687. FO 371/45400, Monthly Diary January 1945.
688. FO 371/45400, Kermanshah Diary April 1945.
689. FO 371/45400, Kermanshah Diary September 1945.

In addition to these two standard PR approaches, there were the occasional more lighthearted and/or targeted public services offered. For example, in April 1944, the VIth Royal Mahratta regiment band played for an audience of 3,000 people. Some Persian officers asked whether it was possible to give a weekly concert, which showed how much the atmosphere towards the British had changed.[690] This is also clear from the fact that in January 1944 in the *Shahpur* school a certain Mr. Farahmandi formed an "English Culture Club" and advertised in English in the *Bisotun* newspaper with the request for help with lectures and magazines. The British Consulate provided assistance and it alerted the British Council for follow-up activities.[691] Also, the British cinema van went around the province, English lessons from Radio Tehran well received, for there was a great demand to learn English.[692] The other service was targeted towards public officials. The PRB lorry service apart from its normal work also gave the British the chance to offer rides to officials such as the head of the Municipality and department heads going to Tehran.[693]

The other Allied power represented in Kermanshah, the Soviet Union had its own PR program. Like the British the Russians showed propaganda films all around.[694] There were exhibitions, such as in April 1944, when in the *Shahpur* school an exhibition of photos of the battles of Leningrad and Stalingrad was held. The governor opened the exhibition, the Soviet and British consuls spoke, but, as the latter reported, attention was perfunctorily, because by that time people were inured to war news, which moreover was not fresh.[695] In January 1945, there was an exhibition of photos of Red Army medical services in the *Shahpur* School; but, according to the British consul, the speeches were too long and bored the audience, which left without looking at the pictures.[696] The Russian Consulate also offered Russian lessons by a local teacher.[697] Russian military officers visiting Kurdistan engaged in political activities such as inciting local nationalist feeling.[698] This aspect of Russian PR may explain why in March 1945 the Soviet Consulate refused to give a list of Russians in the Kermanshah area when the British consul requested that information in connection with a security scheme that was being drawn up.[699]

Both Consulates instead of offering services or goods, once in a while did the reverse and asked the local population for their help. In December 1943, 'the Fund for the relief of sufferers in the Soviet Union' opened at the end of November 1943 by the governor, collected Rls 200,000 as well as large gifts of clothes and other materials that were received by the Soviet consul, who expressed his thanks through the local press. Separately, Rls 120,460 was raised by a cinema

---

690. FO 371/40177, Kermanshah Diary May 1944.
691. FO 371/40177, Kermanshah Diary January 1944.
692. FO 371/40177, Kermanshah Diary April 1944.
693. FO 371/40177, Kermanshah Diary April 1944.
694. FO 371/40177, Kermanshah Diary April 1944; FO 371/45400, Kermanshah Diary April 1944.
695. FO 371/40177, Kermanshah Diary April 1944.
696. FO 371/45400, Monthly Diary January 1945.
697. FO 371/45400 Monthly Diary Dec. 1944; Idem, Kermanshah Diary April 1945.
698. FO 371/40177, Kermanshah Diary April 1944.
699. FO 371/45400, Kermanshah Diary March 1945.

show.[700] Likewise the British held, for example, 'A Prisoners of War Week' from 2-9 June 1944 organized by KPC, which included a football match and a fun fair, which yielded £350.[701] During the British Army Red Cross week (4-11 February 1945), £2,500 were collected, mostly from Kermanshahi citizens. Ulterior motives may have played a role in their generosity.[702] In October 1945, a check for Rls 10,000 was sent from AIRF for the Poor House which was in bad shape.[703] With the departure of the British troops and their liaison officer, the closure of AIRF and the dispensary at Sanandaj around October 1945, the British consul concluded that henceforth Great Britain would have less influence and information, but believed that things would not be like before the war, for the segregation policy of Reza Shah would not return to.[704] However, in 1946 the Prime Minister imposed limited contacts of Persians with foreign consulates.[705]

Although the PR program had its impact and more Persians became its consumers, there still were quite a few people who remained anti-British or anti-Allies. For example, in March 1944, brickbats were thrown at the British Consulate and at Col. Fletcher, during the *Majles* elections.[706] There also was the occasional negative PR such as when on 24 April 1944, two drunken US soldiers entered a house looking for women; an angry crowd threw stones at them. As a result, Kermanshah was declared out of bounds for US soldiers. Shortly thereafter, the city was in bound again, but for British soldiers only.[707] In April 1945, the main topic of conversation was the approaching end of the war; the British Radio Hall maintained by the PR Bureau was crowded during the evening broadcasts.[708] Public reaction to V-day was mixed; not everybody welcomed it. Merchants, landowners, and shopkeepers had enjoyed good war years and were not enthusiastic, fearing a drop in prices. The rest of the population was not very enthusiastic either, realizing that whatever benefit the end of the war might bring it would not help them. Political minded people wanted the Allies out, and nobody cared about the war with Japan.[709] In July 1945, the mood was quiet; the talk of the town was the election result in Great Britain and many believed that Great Britain had become Communist. On 25 July 1945, a celebration was held at the *Homay* Cinema of the second year of the Freedom Front with non-controversial speeches with a film at the end.[710] The month of August was quiet and the end of the Second World War passed by without any celebration, official or otherwise.[711]

---

700. FO 371/40177, Kermanshah Diary December 1943.
701. FO 371/40177, Kermanshah Diary June 1944.
702. FO 371/45400, Kermanshah Diary February 1945.
703. FO 371/4540, Kermanshah Diary October 1945.
704. FO 248/1451, Consul Kermanshah to Bullard, 06/10/1945.
705. FO 371/45488, Kermanshah Diary May 1947.
706. FO 248/1433, Calvert, Kermanshah to Bullard, 30/03/1944.
707. FO 371/40177, Kermanshah Diary April 1944.
708. FO 371/45400, Kermanshah Diary April 1945.
709. FO 371/45400, Kermanshah Diary May 1945.
710. FO 371/45400, Kermanshah Diary July 1945.
711. FO 371/45400, Kermanshah Diary August 1945.

The PR activities of both Great Britain and Russia had short-term objectives, viz. to counter-Nazi propaganda and the local negative view of the Allies. The methods chosen aimed to convince Persians that the British and Russians were the good guys, who only wanted the best for Persia and its people. The methods chosen (films, radio, reading material, health and food aid) only served to reinforce that message. Although Allies, both Great Britain and Russia tried to covertly undermine each other's position. The British did not seem to have a long-term PR objective in mind for the period after the war, whereas the Russians were engaged in political propaganda, in particular in Kurdistan and Azerbaijan, and by providing support for the local branch of the *Tudeh* party. The fact that with a population of 80,000 only, some 700 people showed up every night to listen to the BBC indicates that British propaganda had a very limited impact. This is understandable, because for the Persian public WW II was not their war, the Allies were occupiers, while their presence and their activities were not perceived as alleviating their daily struggle, in particular to be able to buy sufficient bread at an affordable price. Therefore, even if the propaganda materials had been more suitable and better delivered and targeted it is doubtful that these would have swayed the population of Kermanshah to look favorable on Allied presence in their country.[712]

LOCAL POLITICAL AND ADMINISTRATIVE DEVELOPMENTS

After the British invasion of Persia, and more in particular of Kermanshah, the security situation on the roads and in the rural areas immediately worsened, because, following the occupation, the entire Persian administration and its enforcement infrastructure (army, gendarmerie) was in total disarray. Trade was at a low ebb, brigandage increased and there was tribal unrest. To face these problems the British military insisted that the city's governor (*farmandar*), Azizollah Nikpay E'zaz al-Dowleh, although he was an effective administrator, be dismissed and a military governor appointed in his stead.[713] Likewise, the chief of police, Col. Jahangiri, was removed, because he was unhelpful to the British authorities.[714] To establish order, Gen. Shahbakhti decided that the best way to achieve that was to reverse government policy of strict control over the tribes. Instead, he "let the tribes pretty well run their own affairs by the device of appointing their own leaders to all the Government posts in their area, a device which has in fact worked well. The chiefs who had been exiled to Iraq by Reza Shah and had been living there more or less under our [i.e. British] protection and put this policy into execution, using

712. On the PR activities of the Allies in general, see Rowena Abdul-Razak, "But what would they think of us?" Propaganda and the Manipulation of the Anglo-Soviet Occupation of Iran, 1941-1946?" *Iranian Studies* 49/5 (2016), pp. 817-35.

713. FO 248/1414, Note 'Internal Situation Kermanshah" 02/05/1942; Malekzadeh et al. 1392, p. 275 (doc. 201).

714. FO 371/31402, Kermanshah Diary January 1942.

their influence to keep their tribesmen in order, in return for which we 'promised' or 'undertook' to give them our 'support.' "[715]

As a result of this change of policy as well as normal operations by the Persian military, the security situation in the province was much improved by the end of December 1941. There was less brigandage and goods and produce could move around the province without problem. Also, peasants could plow and sow, which had been unsafe in October and November. In Kurdistan the situation remained unchanged, however. The economic situation deteriorated, which made that the feelings against the Allies remained unfriendly, though these were somewhat alleviated by Russian success on the Eastern Front and the British victory in Libya. The entry of the USA in the war caused a brief sensation, but was overshadowed by the Japanese successes in the Pacific. Overall, people remained pro-German, but British propaganda had barely started due to lack of materials (see above).[716]

By the end of 1941, the Persian military had some success with their actions against minor tribes. As a result, government authority was established throughout Kermanshah province, except in some areas in Kurdistan. The winter of 1941-42 was bitterly cold and in January 1942 the roads were under a snow pack from more than 1 meter up to over 3 meters, which put a stop to all military activities. On 25 January 1942, Amir Koll Zanganeh came to take over as governor (o*standar*); on the same day Zeyn al-'Abedin Qiyami, an official of the Ministry of Interior, arrived as city governor (*farmandar*). At that time, the well-known Amir Koll was described as "an elderly man, with little administrative experience or ability and little energy." He was neither a strong character nor of an independent mind, but Qiyami was and the British hoped that Amir Koll would follow his advice. Amir Koll professed friendship for Great Britain, but he had little influence over Shahbakhti, the Persian general commanding the Western Army, who, although not unfriendly, was hardly pro-British. Also, Col. Artta [?], whom the British did not like, was appointed chief of police replacing Col. Jahangiri (see above).[717]

In February 1942, the economic situation improved somewhat due to the fall of prices of some goods. However, this was only a temporary phenomenon as shortages of all kinds of goods were in the offing, due to a lull in trading activities. Otherwise, the situation in town and province improved. Brigandage was down, so that public security was almost normal. However, Kurdistan was still unsettled, but elsewhere tribesmen were being unarmed.[718] The new governor went to visit the Kurds and asked them to air their grievances, which he communicated to Tehran. This was a considerable change from their contacts with General Shahbakhti, who showed no interest whatsoever in their grievances and only tried to show dissent among the tribes.[719] Hama Rashid,

715. FO 248/1451, Davis/Kermanshah to Moneypenny/Tehran, 12/05/1945 (he added that the government was in its right to change this policy, but since the chiefs "have been making a good thing out of Gendarmerie pay and sugar and tea distribution and such like perquisites which have come to them in their guise of Government officials they will not be very happy to have regular Persian Government officials in their mids again.")

716. FO 371/31402, Kermanshah Diary December 1941.

717. FO 371/31402, Kermanshah Diary January 1942.

718. FO 371/31402, Kermanshah Diary February 1942; Idem, Consul to FO, 22 March 1942 ("public attitude still unfriendly and military are still as anti-British as ever. Sugar shortage serious in province, except in Kermanshah town").

719. FO 371/31402, Kermanshah Diary April 1942; Idem, Kermanshah Diary December 1941.

the leader of the Kurdish rebellion, was defeated by General Arfa in April 1942, which for he time being meant that tribal opposition collapsed. Although Tehran had promised reforms it had done nothing to belay Kurdish suspicions.[720]

After a dispute with Majidzadeh, the director of the Finance Department, Qiyami threatened to leave, which would make Amir Koll unable to perform his duties, according to the British consul. Therefore, with much difficulty he was induced to stay.[721] However, after he went to Tehran for consultations Qiyami refused to return. As a result, administrative chaos and economic confusion prevailed in Kermanshah. Amir Koll offered his resignation after Qiyami left. Meanwhile, Sepahbod Shahbakhti interfered with everything. The local authorities did not know how to stop him and Amir Koll just gave in.[722] The administrative leadership was not only in a mess, so was almost the entire administration, both urban and rural. The *bakhshdar*s in Kurdistan had not received any pay for 6 months and threatened to resign. In Kermanshah, the minor municipal employees only had received 12% of their wages, which was all they had to live on during the last three months. The municipal budget was still not approved, when it should have been on March 21. At least 200 of the 500 staff of the Finance and Economic Department were redundant, while some only showed up once a month to pick up their pay.[723] Majidzadeh was openly intriguing to oust Amir Koll and perhaps also the mayor. Already, he had made the position of Qiyami untenable causing administrative chaos and economic confusion. The British consul commented, "Although arrangements for the retention of 15% of the ghee sent from Kermanshah has been sanctioned by Tehran, he is twisting other instructions in order to send out ghee without restrictions, knowing this will cause local popular excitement."[724]

Finally, in August 1942, a new city governor, Mr. Mostashari arrived, "a former mayor, of whose energy and ability nobody here thinks much, but he is well thought of by Tehran." He was handicapped by having a poor staff, no mayor and a bunch of corrupt municipal officials. He had no car and went around town in an old droshky. Col. Tabataba'i at Shahabad complained that he had no transport either and could not go around his jurisdiction. Col. Mokri, who kept Posht-e Kuh peaceful, was threatening to leave as Tehran gave him no car either. Apparently, nobody wanted to go back to the days of horses, mules and tents and camping, the British consul commented. There was not much, because even in Tehran there was a large fleet of cars, but without tires.[725] Because that was the real problem; tires were in very short supply and in July 1942, Consul Cook wrote that "if no new ones are coming transport will come to a halt including for the Governor and the governor. I have three-year old unsafe tires." What was really a problem was that the director-general of the Finance Department had no car to visit the wheat collection area at that important time.[726]

---

720. FO 371/31402, Kermanshah Diary April 1942; Idem, Kermanshah Diary May 1942.
721. FO 371/31402, Kermanshah Diary May 1942.
722. FO 248/1414, Telegram Consul to Tehran, 29/06/1942.
723. FO 371/31402, Kermanshah Diary June 1942.
724. FO 248/1414, Telegram Consul to Legation, 07/07/1942.
725. FO 371/31402, Kermanshah Diary August 1942; Idem, Kermanshah Diary July 1942.
726. FO 371/31402, Kermanshah Diary July 1942.

Meanwhile, there was growing insecurity in the tribal lands, where minor fights had broken out. As usual, whenever a problem arose, Amir Koll did nothing and the same held for the Kurdish *bakhshdar*s or sub-district chiefs. Gen. Shahbakhti, after pressure from the British Consulate, removed Jahan Bakhsh as *bakhshdar* of Mahidasht and replaced him with an officer as well as establishing five gendarmerie posts to stop excessive grain smuggling to Iraq. Jahan Bakhsh was almost openly not only the smuggling organizer, but also the leader of a gang of wheat robbers in the neighboring villages. He was brought to Kermanshah to give account of himself, but was immediately let go on bail. He acted on behalf of important members of the governor's family so he felt immune.[727] For most of September 1942 Amir Koll was ill, which was inconvenient at a time when the Prime Minister and the British consul harangued him to take action against his friends, profiteers and hoarders.[728] In September-October 1942, there continued to be some minor fighting and inter-tribal quarreling in Kurdistan, where there was no government control whatsoever and smuggling went on unhindered.[729]

According to consul Cook, "The local administration continues on its downhill path of indolence, fear, of responsibility, corruption, intrigue and general graft. All respect for it among the citizens, rich or poor, has definitely disappeared." The governor, Amir Koll, outdid his record for "incompetence, nepotism and jobbery" when after a few days, he let go a gang of recalcitrant landowners who had been arrested, in accordance with his own regulation for not delivering their surplus wheat. Col. Farrokh, "energetic and surpassingly fearless" was recalled to Tehran a few days after he had arrested the above-mentioned influential landlords. This made other officials even more leery to be proactive and do their duty. Mostashari, the city governor, "displays the lack of character, drive and initiative for which he was well-known here before he even arrived all he does is sent telegrams to Tehran." He did nothing about the bread situation and "to all intents and purposes is on the municipal payroll of the bakers and millers, while the people whom he is supposed fight for suffer hunger and bad bread." Mr. Nakha'i, the new director of the Finance Department tried to improve things, but he was handicapped by those around him. Asafi, the chief of police admitted that there were insufficient police in Kermanshah to keep order. Meanwhile, Sepahbod Shahbakhti remained above it all. He took the position that until Tehran gave one man here "full powers, clear instructions and proper responsibility" nothing could be done. He was the only person who enjoyed respect and popularity in the town and province.[730] However, the British did not want Shahbakhti as governor, because he had a very bad reputation, no administrative experience, and was believed to be one of the principal smugglers, while it was doubtful whether the Persian government would appoint him. Moreover, "even if we knew a good man we don't want to push a particular man."[731]

In October-November 1942, Shahbakhti and Amir Koll were in Tehran. It was rumored that Shahbakhti would not return, which, according to Col. Fletcher, the political advisor, meant that, "whatever his faults, the only capable official in Kermanshah will be gone." It was further

---

727. FO 371/31402, Kermanshah Diary August 1942.
728. FO 371/31402, Kermanshah Diary September 1942.
729. FO 371/31402, Kermanshah Diary September 1942; Idem, Kermanshah Diary October 1942.
730. FO 371/31402, Kermanshah Diary October 1942.
731. FO 248/1414, Note 'Internal Situation Kermanshah" 02/05/1942.

rumored that Amir Koll perhaps would not return, which, apart from his relatives, nobody would regret. During his tenure he only had feathered his own nest and despite his influence among tribes he was at the beck and call of any undesirable element rather than doing good for the province. True, the government did not pay him, gave him little backing, and he was surrounded by corrupt officials, but he did not even try to be a good governor. The only honest official who did his duty, Col. Farrokh, was removed from his post. However, he returned as chief of staff of General Shahbakhti, which was due to the latter and perhaps the British Legation. His replacement, Col. Mirfendereski had a bad reputation, although he presented himself very well as being competent and efficient.[732] Therefore, the British Legation considered whether Nikpay could not return as city governor (*farmandar*).[733] Because there were many robberies in the province and the presence of so many tribal chiefs in Kermanshah was considered too close for comfort to their tribal base, in December 1943 the British therefore, moved the leading ones to Hamadan.[734]

Unfortunately, sources dealing with the year 1943 are missing from the British archives and therefore, we don't know much of what happened that year, as there are no published sources, in Persian, English or any other language, dealing with that period. Probably in January 1943, Amir Koll was replaced as governor by Dr. Salehi, who remained in function until about August 1943.[735] His successor was Fahim al-Dowleh, who likely took office in October or November 1943. The British were quite happy with Fahim al-Dowleh. He worked closely with Col. Fletcher, the political advisor and he often went into the districts to solve problems. What he lacked, the consul opined, was a good assistant who could look after Kermanshah when he was outside the city. Also, Fahim al-Dowleh was good at running a team so that they harmoniously worked together, which was not the case with his predecessor.[736]

In December of that year he was busy organizing the election for the 14th *Majles*. There was some real competition, for there were several candidates standing for the four *Majles* seats. The ones who had the best chance to be elected were Messrs. Sasan, Montaser, Dr. Zanganeh, 'Abbas Qobadian, and Dr. Mo'aven. After the election Montaser resigned his place and offered it to Dr. Mo'aven, who was 5th in the running. Some disappointed candidates waged action to delay the election results. It was led by Hajji 'Abbas Hajji Da'i (President of the Chamber of Commerce, a wealthy merchant and a hoarder), who was backed by a local lawyer, Abu'l-Mo'ali and secretly supported by Hedayat Palizi (Raf'at al-Saltaneh). Hajji Da'i and Palizi were the 6th and 7th in the count. They mainly targeted Sasan, who headed the poll with over 15,000 votes, arguing that he had resigned from public function too late, and, therefore, his candidacy was invalid. The electoral college, under Hajji Da'i (a member and candidate for election!), made things difficult and at the end of December 1943 issued a certificate for the election for Dr. Mo'aven, Dr. Zanganeh, and Qobadian, but refused one for Sasan. Previously the electoral college had offered his seat, which was theirs to give, to Hajji Da'i, who wrote to the governor that he had accepted it. Copies of his telegram appeared in the local press. However, the electoral

732. FO 371/31402, Kermanshah Diary November 1942.

733. FO 248/1414, Secret Memo, Internal Situation - Kermanshah Administration, Tehran, 09/11/1942.

734. FO 371/40177, Kermanshah Diary December 1943.

735. FO 248/1433, Memo Tehran Legation, 17/02/1944 (he "was governor and acting-governor at Kermanshah when I was there last winter; ... he has remained without work for the last 6 months.")

736. FO 248/1433, Calvert, Kermanshah to Bullard, 30/03/1944; FO 371/40177, Kermanshah Diary December 1943.

college did not dare to give him a certificate of election. Finally, on 16 January 1944, Sasan's certificate of election was issued and all four *Majles* deputies left to Tehran in that month.[737]

After the postponed municipal elections in mid-January 1944, due to some trouble with a candidate, there was a real disturbance on 17 February, when there was a strike by the staff of the Telephone Company. The military telephone was not affected. The governor gave an ultimatum to the strikers to be back at work by 7 p.m. that same day, which had its desired effect. He promised to present their grievances to the government in Tehran. It was not the only extraordinary event in that month. Three army inspectors, Col. Farzami, Lt. Col. Mo'in Ansari and Major Pahlavan had written a negative report on the Kermanshah Brigade, but offered to write a positive one if its commander, Col. Shahrokhshahi paid them Rls. 40,000. The latter sent the negative report to Tehran with his comments about the bribery offer and asked what to do. He was told to pay the blackmailers in notes with consecutive numbers. On payday, Col. Dumont, US Army, arrived in Kermanshah and confronted the three inspectors. He took the money and they handed in their positive report. Because Col. Farzami was a relative of the Shah it was expected that this story would have a follow-up.[738]

In May 1944, the Soheyli cabinet made the Kurdistan governorate (*farmandari*) independent of *Ostan* V and placed it directly under Tehran. Fahim al-Dowleh held this to be illegal as Iran was divided into provinces (*ostans*) and this arrangement could only be changed by law not by a cabinet decision. Moreover, he considered it also to be dangerous, because it would fuel the Kurdish independence movement, the more so since the Cabinet decision had used the word *esteqlal* or 'independence.' He wired Tehran asking to reverse the decision, because Soheyli had made the decision hours before his resignation. However, the new Sa'id cabinet that was viewed as being the same as the previous Soheyli one declined to do so.[739] Therefore, Fahim al-Dowleh went to Tehran to discuss: 1. the separation of Kurdistan; 2. the difficulties of military control of that part of the *ostan* from Khorramabad, i.e. outside his jurisdiction; he proposed to make the Kermanshah brigade responsible; and 3. the mismanagement of the crown lands at Shahabad. However, he had little success, because a returning official said that the governor was 'still hunting for the Government.'"[740]

Jahanshahi, Fahim al-Dowleh's chef de cabinet, whom the British consul characterized as a minor official of little standing and significance, acted as interim-governor. In mid-May 1944, Morteza Abozeyr was appointed head of the municipality and assistant governor, according to the radio and Tehran newspapers. Because of his youth this came as a shock to older officials. In fact, Jahanshahi refused to move until Fahim al-Dowleh was back.[741] Shortly thereafter, Morteza Abozeyr's appointment was cancelled, because Fahim al-Dowleh had not approved it.

737. FO 371/40177, Kermanshah Diary December 1943; Idem, Kermanshah Diary January 1944.

738. FO 371/40177, Kermanshah Diary February 1944. I have not been able to find any further information on the handling of this case.

739. FO 371/40177, Kermanshah Diary May 1944.

740. FO 371/40177, Kermanshah Diary April 1944.

741. FO 371/40177, Kermanshah Diary May 1944.

He believed that Dr. Mo'aven, the *Majles* deputy was behind the appointment. Many department heads went into the districts and were asked for tea, sugar and piece-goods.[742]

On 11 August 1944, Fahim al-Dowleh had a stroke. The Persian government did not take any action, so that neither Jahanshah, his chef de cabinet nor Ma'qul, the head of the Justice Department took any action in the absence of authorization and instructions.[743] Tehran, finally gave instructions that the local affairs were to remain in the hands of Jahanshahi as acting governor. The British consul was none too happy about this, because despite having long served there he considered that Jahanshahi was unfit for the job. Therefore, he hoped for a speedy return of Fahim al-Dowleh or else a quick replacement. The consul opined that "one of the main pre-occupations of this Ostan is to see to the welfare of the tribes and secure their cooperation with the government, so a replacement better be an enlightened civilian." The British did not want a high-ranking military officer as governor, because this would constrain the Cdr of XIIth Brigade, Col. Shahrokhshahi, who took care of all military matters. In August 1944, there was a tribal conference in the city, with a follow-up on 16 December, when, at Sar-e Pol-e Zohab, Jahanshahi met with tribal leaders to discuss land rents, supplies, security of roads etc., all subjects of great interest to them. This was a clever political move, because it showed that Jahanshahi saw the tribes more than as brigands. However, a major point of friction was the demand of land rent on state lands along the Iraqi border north of Qasr-e Shirin, where the tribes (Guran and Jaf sections) had paid no rent for two years.

Fahim al-Dowleh remained in Tehran, because he was sick and therefore, nothing really happened. It helped that the tribes were in the Garmsir at a safe distance. Also, the old problems such as hunger, typhus, and unemployment largely had spared the town so far. Although in July 1944 elections were held for the municipal council there was still no council, because the results had to be validated and announced by the Ministry of the Interior. The talk of the town was when would the war in Europe end, although there was no interest in the war in Asia with Japan, However, not everybody liked to see the war ended, some 15,000-20,000 people belonging to or depending on the merchant class benefited from the high wartime prices and did not want these to come down.[744]

In February 1945, there still was no replacement of Fahim al-Dowleh and nobody was appointed at Shahabad, which was offered to Jahanshahi the acting governor. Despite local protests 'Abdollah Vahid was removed from Qasr-e Shirin, an honest man.[745] April 1945 was quiet, but still no new governor had been appointed, which was really needed, because the tribal migration to the Garmsir started in 4-5 weeks and once the tribes would be there a firm hand was needed. According to the British consul, Jahanshahi did not have that, while he also seemed to be raking in some money, while he still could. The main topic of conversation remained the approaching end of war, the Radio Hall maintained by the PR Bureau was crowded for the evening broadcasts.[746] In June 1945, Kermanshah was still without a governor. Mohsen 'Ali

742. FO 371/40177, Kermanshah Diary May 1944.
743. FO 248/1313, Consul to Legation, 18/08/1944.
744. FO 371/45400, Monthly Diary January 1945.
745. FO 371/45400, Kermanshah Diary February 1945.
746. FO 371/45400, Kermanshah Diary April 1945.

Qaragozlu (Sardar Akram) had been appointed as the successor, but later this was cancelled. Meanwhile, Jahanshahi's reputation suffered as more stories about corruption were heard. Also, "he temporizes everything and does not decide and does not take responsibility." The good harvest had a beneficial impact on people's mood; however, the sugar shortage caused discontent especially among the tribes.[747] Jahanshahi continued in office and his laisser-faire policy, which upset those officials who wanted to do something.[748]

Finally, on 19 August Fathollah Kalantari arrived as the new governor of *ostan* V. The month of August 1945 was quiet, and even the end of war passed by without celebration, official or otherwise. The only newsworthy event was that after a dispute with Mr. Ma'qul, the director of the Justice Department in Kermanshah Col. Mokri was relieved of his function as *farmandar* (governor) of Ilam. He had been there before the Allies came and had ruled the area with iron hand as in Reza Shah's days as a military dictatorship, but without troops. [749] Hoseyn Heshmat Sani'i was appointed *farmandar* of the city of Kermanshah and assistant governor of *Ostan* V. Jahanshahi left and the British consul who for months had been quite critical of him commented that "despite all Jahanshahi has done well; he was asst. farmandar when he became governor-general a.i. which put him at a disadvantage in dealing with senior officials in the province. Although lacking in authority and unwilling to take decisions, partly due to his lack of seniority, he kept the province quiet and orderly and had a good relationship with the Allies. Although rumors of corruption were heard this is not noticeable in his way of life. He declined the farmandari of Qasr-e Shirin as he suffers from malaria and climate is bad there."[750] At Qasr-e Shirin, the new governor, Kalantari showed that with his arrival things would change. He told the merchants that they were a band of thieves and smugglers. He was going to apply Customs rules very strictly and they should end trade with Iraq. The British had winked at cross-border trade, because legitimate trade was impossible, but grain, tea, sugar and cloth in small quantities made a difference. Of course, the governor had to apply the law, but this was not so easy as there was a deficit of grain at Qasr-e Shirin. Of course, people could buy grain at Kermanshah but transport cost were very high and, therefore, smuggling paid.[751]

POLITICAL DEVELOPMENTS

During the first years after Reza Shah's abdication there were no political activities in Kermanshah, at least none were reported. Although there had been elections for the *Majles* in December 1943, there had been no real political challenge, as all the candidates were local

747. FO 371/45400, Kermanshah Diary June 1945.

748. FO 371/45400, Kermanshah Diary July 1945 (Heydar Ali Sehhatpur became the new director of PT; he arrived on 19/07).

749. FO 371/45400, Kermanshah Diary August 1945 (Shokrai, the director of the Education Department was replaced by Hoseyn Ali Ahsani).

750. FO 371/45400, Kermanshah Diary September 1945.

751. FO 248/1451, Consul Kermanshah to Moneypenny/Tehran, 08/09/1945. On Persian policy and the reality of cross-border smuggling, see Kazemi 1395.

notables. However, more diverse political life started to heat up in the city in 1944; this time it was not the *Tudeh* party that was the source of the political heat, because that party suffered from internal problems. In September 1943, there had been a schism and since then the *Tudeh* party had led a lingering existence in Kermanshah. "The end came quietly at the end of February 1944," wrote the British consul, but that was hope rather than reality.[752] Nevertheless, the newspapers *Bisotun* continued to serve as the local daily organ of the *Tudeh* party with Sa'adat as editor. However, it was the '*Edalat* party, which in Kermanshah consisted of a dozen members, that suddenly developed an enormous activity in the beginning of March 1944. It was said to have 500-600 members, including some former *Tudeh'is*. According to the British, the sudden upsurge of the '*Edalat* party was engineered by 'Allameh, the failed candidate for the *Majles* elections, to give him a better shot at the next municipal elections. He saw, but later was denied visits with the British consul several times, because the latter rightly perceived these visits as a ploy for "acquiring credit." 'Allameh went around in the streets with a group of toughs, who were representatives of the '*Edalat* membership. Fahim al-Dowleh, the governor also had misgivings about 'Allameh, because he himself was a founding-member of the '*Edalat* party and he disliked 'Allameh's association with the party. He poured some cold water on 'Allameh's enthusiasm, who then returned to Tehran, while thereafter that party's activity died down.[753]

In May 1944, there was trouble at the Shahabad sugar mill among the some 100 resident technical staff there. At the beginning of April, a personnel manager from Tehran came. According to Qa'emmaqam, the manager of the mill, he was a *Tudeh'i*, and when he left there was a tendency of subordination, which was exploited by Sana'i, a line-kiln foreman. As warnings did not help Qa'emmaqam fired him. A few days later Sani'i showed up at the mill and was sent away. Qa'emmaqam contacted the British Consulate and the political advisor, but he was told it was his problem and that he had to show responsibility. He said that a visit from the Russian Consulate with the Leningrad exhibition did not help much to improve situation. However, according to the British, there was no evidence of any Russian covert activity. However, Hojabran of the Finance Ministry, a known communist sympathizer, started to interfere with the sugar factory, but this had as yet no discernable consequences. In fact, both the *Tudeh* and '*Edalat* party had gone into hibernation by that time. It was then that all of a sudden in May 1944, a branch of the *Peykar* party was formed in Kermanshah. On 22 May, the *Bisotun* paper announced the formation of a local committee with its headquarters and a bookshop there. Its leader supposedly was Giti-ara, a shopkeeper, but the local party only had a dozen members.[754]

The *Tudeh* party in Kermanshah was restarted by Mohammad Hasan Khosrovi and Sayyed Mohammad Kazazi probably in late 1944 with the help of Eng. Atiqehchi, who later came from Tehran. They founded the provincial committee of Kermanshah that was presided by Shehabpur. They set up an office on the outskirts of the city next to a garage and put up a sign over the door. They were able to attract the teachers of the *Shahpur* school by organizing a strike, when they

---

752. FO 371/40177, Kermanshah Diary February 1944.

753. FO 371/40177, Kermanshah Diary March 1944; FO 248/1413, A. S. Calvert to Trott/Tehran 09/06/1944. On the activities of the `*Edalat* party in Kermanshah, which was linked to conservative landowners, see Soltani 1378, vol. 2, pp. 425-34.

754. FO 371/40177, Kermanshah Diary May 1944. The *Peykar* party never amounted to much in Kermanshah, see Soltani 1378, vol. 2, pp. 440-42.

had a conflict with the head of the local education board (*ra'is-e farhang*). The teachers also frequented the club that *Tudeh* later opened. Also, a number of wrestlers joined the party, which was always useful in case there was a fight. The office was later moved near the *meydan-e shahrdari*. Shehabpur was succeeded by Mohsen 'Alavi as chief of the *Tudeh* party in the city, probably at the end of 1945.[755]

In December 1944, the local *Tudeh* party showed that it was alive again, when its members formed a trade union, a local branch of the *United Council of Workers and Toilers of Iran* (*Ettehadiyeh-ye Kargaran va Zahmatkashan*). Its aim was: to improve the lot of workers, through, among other things, a scheme of financial relief for sick and disabled workers. The *United Council of Workers* was part of the *Tudeh* 'Central United Council', which sent its congratulations. The British saw little difference between the Union and the *Tudeh*, because the members were the same and they shared the same office. The Union announced the opening of branches in various towns. Its local leader was Dr. Forutan, "an unqualified practitioner of unsavory reputation, who had been in prison for murder of his mistress." The Persian manager of APOC opined that his appointment could not be better for ruining the chances of the Union's popularity, as if it had been done by its enemies. Forutan staged two performances of a play in Hotel *Bisotun* on 13th and 14th December 1944 that was in such poor taste - a story about prostitution - that practically all "unprejudiced members of the audience" left jeering at the end of the first act, and a few days later an article in the Kermanshah newspaper appeared complaining about the play's bad taste. During the second night the audience consisted mostly of *Tudeh* members, many free, so the fiasco of first performance was not repeated. The Russian vice-consul also was in the audience.

Forutan sent a letter to the newspaper editor, Farajollah Kaviani, denouncing the police, the army, the education authorities, and the rich, "who wait in warm rooms and laugh at the poor." Kaviani did not publish Forutan's long epistle, but over three weeks in gruesome detail he published how Forutan and two friends had murdered a prostitute for her jewelry 20 years earlier. The serial ended with call on the Central United Council (CUC) to distance itself from a character like Forutan and to prevent him from having anything to do with labor matters. On 28 January 1945, Forutan replied in the *Bisotun* newspaper, "The Tudeh party and the Workers Union are not children and do not need a nurse." The workers and party had faith in Forutan. The open letter was copied to the CUC and published in the Tehran *Zafar* newspaper.

In the afternoon of 14 December 1944, Forutan held a political meeting in Hotel *Bisotun* where he denounced Sa'id, Sayyed Ziya al-Din and the Prime Minister. Col. 'Asefi, the chief of police berated him at the order of Jahanshahi. Fahim al-Dowleh had discouraged, if not banned all political activities in Kermanshah. Therefore, Jahanshahi did not tolerate any disturbances. On 21 December 1944, even troops had marched through the streets of the city, a hint to those who wanted to disturb the peace. Forutan then held a speech in his house on 21st. He did the same on the 22nd, for other *Tudeh'i*s, and followed members of the Dowlatshahi family, 2-3 of them were *Tudeh* members, to a mourning ceremony for a member of that family. In both meetings, Forutan boasted of his large following. However, the British consul was not worried, because in his opinion Kermanshah was not a fertile soil for labor action. Its economy was

755. Soltani 1378, vol. 2, pp. 230-31.

mainly agricultural, while the main industrial employer was the Oil Company, which was responsible for the welfare of some 9,000, workers and their families, or 10% of the city's population. Also, the construction of the British army camp at Bisotun provided good well-paid work.

On 7 January 1945, the *Bisotun* newspaper announced that Sayyed 'Abdol-Qasem Nadimi was the secretary of the '*Edalat* party and that henceforth every Friday meetings would be held in various parts of the town. Otherwise nothing was heard from or about '*Edalat*. To increase its market share, the '*Edalat* party supported the call of the mullahs for a religious revival, to counter *Tudeh* influence, which had an irreligious program. '*Edalat* had some support among shopkeepers but not among the city's notables. The latter, fearing the growing left-wing movement supported Sayyed Mahmud Tabataba'i, a mullah who had come in early December 1944 from Mashhad and Tehran preaching the principles of democracy, Islam and in particular the 10th commandment (thou shall not covet one's neighbor's house) in the mosques.[756]

In February 1945 there still was little political activity in town. The newspapers mainly focused on criticizing the authorities for delaying pilgrims going to Iraq, complaining about the proposed mixing of barley in the bread, sympathizing with the school teachers, who had not been paid their full salary, and softly moaning about the plight of workers, but hardly paying attention to the war, although people in town talked about it. *Tudeh* remained active but not in an obtrusive manner. On 3 February 1945, it celebrated the anniversary of the death of Dr. Arrani with speeches, in which speakers stressed that "we are all brothers irrespective of religion; we have nothing to do with the Russians or British; and that there would be no demonstrations." In short, it was a very quiet month, and even the *Tudeh* was quiet as it only grumbled about the quality of the sugar issued for *Nowruz*. As a counterpoint to *Tudeh* activities, the Department of Agriculture formed an Agricultural Committee composed of landowners and notables ostensibly to discuss ways to improve the prosperity of the province. However, one of its main objectives was to counter *Tudeh* propaganda to turn peasants against the land owners. Mr. Sobhani, the director of the Department of Agriculture was the president, while its members consisted of Mr. Jenahi, director of the Agricultural Bank, Mohandes Gharib, head of the Shahabad Sugar mill, and 15 large landowners. It was decided to make an inventory of irrigation possibilities. Sobhani proposed the introduction of silk worm eggs, while the introduction of new agricultural implements and improvement of peasant housing was also discussed.[757]

There was no major political activity. On 3 March 1945, there was large meeting of the labor union. In speeches labor rights were stressed and as well their importance of the labor class to the country. Red Army feats were referred to with admiration. The *Tudeh* speeches further harped on the social evils in Persia and the need to grant Russia an oil concession, which would be in Persia's interest. A *Tudeh* member claimed that the party and the trade union had 3,000 members, presumably including the branches. The speeches also referred to demonstrations at Sahneh, Kangavar, Bisotun, and Sonqur. Khalilpur, a student of the Agricultural School in Tehran, gave a fiery speech and promised a *Tudeh* revolution as soon as the 3,000 students would begin their training as officers. On both sides of the political spectrum sometimes feelings ran high. Several pilgrims were refused entrance into Iraq because they were alleged to be *Tudeh* members, while

756. FO 371/45400 Monthly Diary December 1944.
757. FO 371/45400, Kermanshah Diary February 1945.

on 30 March 1945, Major Rafiyeh, second-in-command of the Kermanshah Police was publicly insulted by Dowlatshahi, a prominent notable and *Tudeh* member, and forcibly ejected when he looked into a *Tudeh* meeting. The matter was referred to the Justice Department. Sayyed Ziya al-Din sent a certain Dr. Elahi to Kermanshah and Qasr-e Shirin to organize branches of his party. Dr. Elahi was told that it was better to wait until after the end of the war when the political situation in Persia would be clearer and he left. Mr. Sasan, one of the four *Majles* deputies was here to canvas for re-election;the last time he had the most votes.[758]

Tudeh activity was on the increase but not as yet aggressive. In fact, most of April 1945 was quiet, but more *Tudeh* political activity started with a strike on 30 March at the oil refinery. The strike did not last long, but the poor workers who followed *Tudeh* slogans were out of a job. It was more of a trial balloon than a real labor strike. If it had succeeded it might have had serious consequences for the oil works at Abadan. The British consul believed that the whole affair would not have happened if there had been a strong governor with efficient authority. According to him, Jahanshahi, who was well-meaning and hard-working, lacked initiative and exercised ineffectual authority. A more worrying looming source of unrest was the presence of about 300 unemployed UKCC drivers. They had been out of work for several months; some 70 workers came to the British Consulate in April 1945, attracting a large crowd, saying they would accept any work. Moreover, the British army would soon dismiss some 2,000 men when the construction of the Bisotun barracks was finished, while the Kermanshah oil industry also was downsizing. These workers could not be absorbed locally and the authorities had taken no steps to deal with this problem. The Trade Union was promising a weekly dole, while *Tudeh* was also promising pecuniary assistance. The source of those funds was unknown. The Workers Union attacked Mr. Montaser of the Kermanshah Oil Company with a typewritten tract accusing him of mistreating workers and kicking one to death. This was an indication of the rising discontent. The local *Tudeh* press also criticized the lack of education of the working class, which it portrayed as the cause of all evil. The British consul commented, “they themselves take no steps to correct this situation.”[759]

In May 1945, *Tudeh* was very active, also in smaller towns, villages and among the tribes. In the afternoon of 29 May 1945, the Workers Union, with agreement of *Tudeh*, called a meeting of the workers of the oil refinery in the Friday mosque. By 4.30 p.m. there were some 700 men who were harangued by several speakers saying the Oil Company belonged to Persians not the British, that its benefits belonged to the workers; they should get higher pay, better living conditions, more generous rations, etc. The next morning the Oil Company buses arrived as usual at the northern edge of the town to take workers to the refinery, but most refused to go, those who wanted to enter were prevented by intimidation by others. The clerical staff traveling by separate bus was not interfered with. Later in the day the strikers sent their demands, signed by 940 workers, to the Oil Company:

758. FO 371/45400, Kermanshah Diary March 1945; for the Tudeh party in Qasr-e Shirin, see Soltani 1378, vol. 2, p. 340.

759. FO 371/45400, Kermanshah Diary April 1945 (On 30/04, Col. Shahrokhshahi left, that he is a friend of Razmara will count against him with General Arfa, the present CoS, when his alleged crimes are examined. He is replaced by Col. Nosratollah Bayandor).

1. wages to be paid on Fridays;
2. ration to workers on the same scale as senior Company staff;
3. working hours reduced to 8;
4. men should not be forced to work overtime;
5. workers should not be threatened by reprisals;
6. insurance laws should be complied with.
7. health facilities to be made available to all workers.
8. delegates sent on behalf of strikers should not be victimized, and
9. workers should have the right to attend party meetings.

The demands were template and showed that neither the Union nor *Tudeh* had done their homework. Because actual workings hours were 7 3/4 hours/day; free medical care was provided to all workers; and workers' rights to attend political party meetings had never been called into question. Prior to the strike no complaints had been made to management and the entire affair had the hallmark of a non-spontaneous strike. It was the work of *Tudeh* party and Union leaders plus some disgruntled oil workers to show the strength of the party and union and test British reaction and resolve. If succeeded the same approach would have been tried in Abadan, the British consul believed. The Company pointed out that violence and stone throwing was the task of the police. However, the chief of police, Col. 'Asefi, an Azerbaijani, fearing to upset the Russians did not want to take any action, even when pressed by Jahanshahi. He said there was no sign of violence, although stones and bricks had been thrown. Col. Bayandor[760] acted immediately and placed soldiers at several points to maintain public safety. The Company rejected the demands and informed the workers that the regulations stated that if absent without leave for more than 6 days meant automatic dismissal. Therefore, more and more workers returned and staff members, who lived nearby and not in town, kept the refinery operating, though dispatch of refined products to the rest of Persia had to be stopped temporarily.

The Workers Union also held a May-Day demonstrations. Some 2,500 'members' marched from the lower end of the town to the center and back. It was a well-organized and orderly march, the police were absent, although Col. 'Asefi said that he had police with machine-guns station at various places, but nobody was able to spot any of those. The Union had its own 'police' who wore armbands and had been well schooled beforehand and kept perfect order. The wages of street sweepers were raised from 450 to 600 Rls/month, which may have been brought about by this demonstration. As a counteraction, the *'Edalat* Party held a meeting on May 8 in the afternoon, where its leader 'Allameh Vahidi held a speech praising democratic principles, the Allied war effort and some local officials. It was well attended. A Youth Movement was started by the Workers Union in Kermanshah, but as yet, developed little activity. A rival Athletic Club for Young People was also established.[761]

---

760. Col. Bayandor before coming to Kermanshah served in Saqqez, which was an isolated garrison, which was only supplied with the barest necessities "and he bare-facedly lined his pockets even when it meant starving his own officers and men. Such action is usually tolerated, but even Persian officials raised their eyebrows by his brazenness." FO 371/45400, Kermanshah Diary May 1945.

761. FO 371/45400, Kermanshah Diary May 1945; Soltani 1378, vol. 2, pp. 427-28; *Ruznameh-ye Zafar* 15 Khordad 1324, Year 1, no. 136 (which has a longer list of demands). img016??

There was a reduction in *Tudeh* and Union activity after the failed strike. The strike ended 6 June, when the six-day grace period expired and those workers who were absent were automatically fired. There was no problem in replacing workers; the first day 500 and the second day 1,000 men showed up. In all 363 men lost their job, of these over 100 who had a good record and were skilled were rehired after some time and some 120 new ones were hired. Thus, the Company downsized 140 men, which they had kept on out of humanitarian reasons, discharging 1 to 2 per week. The dismissed men appealed to Jahanshahi and the British Consulate, who referred them to the Oil Company.

A few days later, *Zafar*, the Tehran labor union newspaper, published a telegram from the Tehran Central Workers Union to the Kermanshah Workers Union stating that the strike had been without their knowledge or approval, that it should be ended as soon as possible, because there was still a war going on. This publication meant a loss of face of the leaders in Kermanshah. The failed strike and loss of work for 200 men was a disaster for the *Tudeh* and the Workers Union and a loss of prestige. For the entire month the leaders laid low, went out of town and their office was deserted. There were plans to organize demonstrations of laid-off workers with their famished families, but it did not take place. Neither Jahanshahi nor the chief of police was able to say what steps if any he would take if they had, only Col. Bayandor stated that he would take all measures necessary. On 27 June there was a *Tudeh* meeting at the house of Sayyed 'Abbas Tabataba'i. Mehdi Farahpur, editor of *Bisotun* was elected liaison between Kermanshah and Tehran and Sayyed Mohammad Kazazi was relieved of his post as secretary; no replacement was appointed. The *Bisotun*, the local *Tudeh* organ, accused the KPC manager Montaser and Labor Manager Mostowfi of foreign exploitation of Persian workers.

On 20 June 1945, *Tudeh* opened a branch at Qasr-e Shirin under Fraj Taheri. The first meeting took place on 22 June, and immediately thereafter an employee of the Finance Department was severely beaten because of non-supply of sugar for seven months. On 27 June there was another clash when *Tudeh* brought in ice to sell cheaply to the inhabitants. Those with vested interests attacked the lorry, the ice was looted and those selling ice were attacked and wounded. The police were unable to stop the riot, but made a few arrests. Unrelated to *Tudeh* activities was the strike on 23 June by employees of the Rationing Department of Kermanshah protesting the non-payment of wages during the last two months. When paid they went back to work. A possible other source of labor unrest arose when Ashtiyani, the inspector of the Economic Department, came from Tehran and fired 70 employees of the Cereal and Bread Department; allegedly he had orders to fire 200 in all. *Tudeh* asked him not to do so. Indeed, unemployment in Kermanshah was a major cause of worry. In addition to the 250 men fired by KPC and the 200 of the Cereals Department some 2,000 were to be laid off by the British Army. Although it was expected that some would return to their villages for the harvest season, nevertheless they would increase the ranks of the unemployed and would be welcomed by *Tudeh* with open arms.[762]

The *Tudeh* party was weakened by the failed KPC strike and a violent incident in Hamadan and further by the departure of Dr. Anvar Shaki, chief of the *Red Lion and Sun Hospital* at Kermanshah, who was one of their leading lights. Another leader, Mohsen 'Alavi, principal of

762. FO 371/45400, Kermanshah Diary June 1945; Soltani 1378, vol. 2, pp. 340-41.

the *Shahpur* school, was to be transferred shortly, while Eng. Atiqehchci had not much drive.[763] As a result, *Tudeh* was licking its wounds. Due to lack of funds it closed its office and moved in with the Workers Union in the garage sector. Mr. Shohab, from Tehran HQ came and took over the secretarial seals from Kazazi. In a meeting with members he said he had never seen such disorganization and incompetence and made accusations against local leaders, which was resented by them and their followers and led to a pandemonium. *Tudeh* activities in others areas were also low-key. In Hamadan the governor, Sardar Akram, warned 'Ali Akbar Nowrasi, the local *Tudeh* leader, not to hold public meetings or cause disturbances. In the villages, action against giving landlords their share in the crops died down. Attempts to open a branch office in Sanandaj completely failed due to action by government officials and landowners. The party was not even able to put up a signboard. At Kerend, where the British had Army and Airforce Leave camps, the main notable was Hayati, a local major landowner, of a family with ancient roots in the area. Two *Tudeh* members from Kermanshah tried to establish a branch of the party with the help of the commanding officers of the police and gendarmerie. However, their meeting, discussing how to recruit members, was attacked by members of the '*Edalat* party. Some damage was done. Two of the attackers were in the employ Abu'l-Hoseyn Hayati Kerendi, who were arrested and sent to Tehran. Although the authorities were pleased with the incident, Mr. Hayati got into some trouble. An inquiry was held in Kermanshah. The gendarmerie officer was summoned to Kermanshah, but the policeman was not, because Col. 'Asefi, who was believed to have *Tudeh* leanings, "displays a notable tenderness, where the Tudeh is concerned." Hayati and the two local officers made up, and the latter carried on as before. Kalantari, the governor, agreed with Hayati's objective, but not with his methods.[764]

In August 1945, there were no *Tudeh* activities due to internal recriminations that continued in exacerbated form indoors.[765] Sayyed 'Abdol-Qasem Kashani was released from internment after war's end; he stayed for a while in Kermanshah where his pro-German affinity was seen as martyrdom and increased his popularity. He made anti-Allied speeches and promised to return to politics.[766] In September Kashani left and was given great send-off.[767] *Tudeh* membership after the KPC fiasco had fallen by some 80%, but in October 1945 showed signs of revival, when its membership reached 300 and attendance at their meetings was increasing. The party focused its activities on canvassing laid off workers from KPC, British Army and the UKCC. They announced a demonstration to celebrate 28th anniversary of the Red Revolution.[768]

Events in Azerbaijan in 1946 hurt the *Tudeh* party and enlivened atmosphere in in Kermanshah. Crowds of tribal leaders came offering men, if they had been given rifles there would have 5,000 volunteers and a further 3,000 were promised by landowners. Expressions of loyalty and help were continuously sent to the central government and the governor. When Persian troops left in lorries for Kurdistan people cheered them wildly, when three months earlier

763. FO 371/45400, Kermanshah Diary July 1945.

764. FO 248/1451, Consul Davis to Moneypenny/Tehran, 08/09/1945; FO 371/45400, Kermanshah Diary August 1945.

765. FO 371/45400, Kermanshah Diary September 1945.

766. FO 371/45400, Kermanshah Diary August 1945.

767. FO 371/45400, Kermanshah Diary September 1945.

768. FO 371/45400, Kermanshah Diary October 1945.

they had been sheep like followers of *Tudeh* leaders. People avidly listened to the radio to learn about developments in Azerbaijan. When the Azerbaijani Democrat debacle became known people were happy, especially those with relatives at the front or going there. To celebrate the victory a march pass was held for the troops and those tribes that had promised to sent volunteers such as Sanjabis, Kalhors and Valadbegis. It had been a long time since that armed tribesmen on horse were welcomed as brothers by civilian and military authorities alike. This was followed by five hours of speeches and *tableaux-vivants* showing the valor of the Persian soldier and the craven heartedness of the Azerbaijani Democrats. The anti-Russian tone was not hidden. Only the Russian vice-consul attended. [769] As a result, the two main local *Tudeh* leaders, 'Alavi, director of Education and Dr. Shaki left Kermanshah on 10 October 1946, because they feared for their lives. *Tudeh* activities in the cities and the districts also fell significantly.[770] In March 1947, the Russian Consulate transformed the *Tudeh* headquarters office as the *VOKS* office.[771] In June 1947, attempts were being made to revive *Tudeh* under the banner of the *Bisotun* newspaper and one or two local notables. *Tudeh* opened a club and allegedly had a library.[772] The *Tudeh* revival was managed by the *VOKS* office. Cinema shows were given, *Bisotun* started articles in the old style, and some 40 members of the KPC joined the party. Given the prevailing corruption, the British consul found this success unsurprising. A fire that had destroyed the headquarters of the Democrat Party at Kermanshah was put out by the KPC. The fire was believed to have been instigated by the *Tudeh* party, the more because there were other similar fires in neighboring towns. [773]

Although *Tudeh* tried to mobilize the peasants and workers they were unable to create a significant basis for their political program. The conservative landlords and notables were more successful in doing so as they had the funds to distribute at the right moment, while they also had more social and economic control over the majority of the population that was still steeped in traditional values. The fact that Kermanshah had only a very small modern labor class, the natural basis for *Tudeh* was not very helpful either. As a result, Kermanshah remained a reliable politically conservative bastion known for its conservative traditional values.

INFIGHTING AMONG THE KALHORS

Another facet of political life in the Kermanshah was more traditional, i.e. old-fashioned infighting among the various tribal lineages. After Reza Shah's abdication and the return of exiled tribal chiefs these intrigues and fights started again. The most notable conflict was that which broke out among the Kalhor tribe. In 1924 Reza Shah had seized the properties of the

---

769. FO 371/45488 Kermanshah Diary December 1946.

770. IOR/L/PS/12/1156, Ext 5000/46(1) 'Persian Situation: Miscellaneous Reports', Tehran to FO (secret telegram) 13/10/1946. In this telegram it is also mentioned that the Landowners organization had sent a telegram to the prime minister thanking him for the appointment of the new governor-general, Shehab al-Dowleh.

771. FO 371/45488 Kermanshah Diary March 1947. VOKS was a Soviet agency created in 1925 to promote international cultural contacts between authors, artists, athletes, musicians and the like.

772. FO 371/45488 Kermanshah Diary June 1947.

773. FO 371/45488 Kermanshah Diary August 1947.

Kalhor (Bavandpur) chief, 'Abbas Khan Qobadian, Amir Makhsus at Harunabad, which was then renamed Shahabad (now Eslam-e Gharb) and he had installed a military governor there. Also, the lands belonging to Karim Khan Da'udian, the uncle of 'Abbas, were seized and forcibly exchanged for lands in Khorasan. In 1926, 'Abbas Khan was taken to Tehran, and spent 11 years in prison and two under surveillance. After 'Abbas Khan Amir Makhsus's arrest in 1930, Samsam al-Dowleh Yavari was installed a chief of the Kalhors, but, because he was totally uninterested in tribal affairs, he was dismissed after one year. Then Col. Esma'il Khan was charged with this task, who assisted by 'Ali Aqa A'zami, a servant of the old Kalhor chief Da'ud Khan (d. 1912), i.e. 'Abbas Khan's grandfather. Thereafter Col. Sharabi, followed by Col. Baqer Khan and then Col. Donboli was chief of the tribe until March 1941, who again were assisted by 'Ali Aqa A'zami. However, as of March 1941 'Ali Aqa A'zami alone was put in charge of the tribe as *bakhshdar* of Gilan and Eyvan, whose management was appreciated.[774] In 1941, 'Abbas Khan and many other interned chiefs were allowed to return. Members of the Qobadian lineage spent their time intriguing against the A'zamis and trying to get their lands back, in which they were partly successful. In June 1943, 'Ali Aqa was treacherously murdered in his house at Hasanabad by Hajji 'Ali Akbari (Hojabr), a relative of the Qobadian and Da'udian families, who escaped to Iraq. It was suspected, but never proven, that 'Abbas Khan and his relatives were behind this. After the murder of 'Ali Aqa, Col. Fletcher made the 21-year old son, Qasem Khan, *bakhshdar* of Gilan and head of Kalhor tribe and removed the Qobadian faction from the area in return for which the A'zamis kept good order. Col. Fletcher forced all the Qobadians to live in Kermanshah. However, Qasem Khan's appointment by the governorate of Kermanshah was not confirmed by Tehran. In early 1945, the Ministry of the Interior appointed Baluch Khosrovi, a regular official, but he was but a temporary buffer between the rivals. Because 'Abbas Khan continued to be difficult, interfering with tribal affairs, Col. Fletcher had him elected to the *Majles*. There he spent all his time not working for Persia but for his family, to restore its power and lands. Until the end of 1944 this was without success, but he managed to get the Ministry of Interior not recognize Qasem Khan's position at Gilan. In early September 1945, he struck even harder through Khosrow Khan, his brother, as governor at Shahabad, whose appointment the British considered unwise and provocative and indeed, it led to trouble. Moreover, Khosrow Khan's appointment was contrary to the promise by 'Abbas Qobadian and his family to abstain from all interference in tribal or political affairs, a promise given to the British and the Persian governments in November 1944. Also, there had been no consultation with the governor's office about this appointment, which was unusual. Khosrow Khan Qobadian began as governor of Shahabad by initiating a one-sided disarmament of the Kalhors with the assistance of soldiers put at his disposal. Also, for these government rifles permits had been given to those belonging to the A'zamis. Immediately after the disarmament one of the A'zami villages was attacked, one man was killed and a grain store was burnt. The British consul told the commanding officer of the troops that this situation was undesirable, who then put the disarmament activity on hold. Since it was unlikely that Khosrow Khan would cease his hostile actions against the A'zamis it was expected that the latter would resist further actions

774. Soltani 1384, pp. 118, 202, 204.

against them.[775] Indeed, the Qobadians encroached on A'zami lands from Mahidasht to Qasr-e Shirin. They also wanted to kill Qasem Khan and his half-brother Gholam Reza as they had killed their father 'Ali Aqa. On 20 August 1945, the A'zamis collected 200 armed men at Shahabad and the governor had to send gendarmerie Colonel Kamal with his gendarmes to becalm the heated spirits. On 22 August a representative of the A'zamis told the British consul that they could no longer stand it; either all 3,000 of them would take asylum in the British Consulate or go to Iraq, if Khosrow Khan remained governor (*farmandar*) of Shahabad. Pasha Khan, another brother, was reported to become *bakhshdar* of Shian, the center of the Hajjizadeh family property, where the Qobadians also had claims. His cousin, 'Ali Shah Da'udian, was said to be appointed *bakhshdar* of Gilan, another cousin, GholamReza Da'udian, as *bakhshdar* of Eyvan, and another, 'Abbas Keshtavand, as *bakhshdar* of Sar-e Pol and still another as deputy-director of the sugar mill at Shahabad. This familial arrangement served to re-elect 'Abbas Khan and to get rid of the A'zamis and regain all the properties they claimed from the royal domains department (*Amlak*), the A'zamis, the Hajjizadehs and from others. So far, the only firm appointment was that of Khosrow Khan, the other appointments were rumored to take place.[776]

In early September 1945, Fathollah Kalantari went on tour in the province, visited Khosrow Qobadian and took him to Qasem Khan A'zami in his village of Barfarad, 6.5 km from Shahabad. To the British consul's big surprise Khosrow Khan was not murdered! Kalantari hoped to settle the rivalry by inter-family marriage, also by making Qasem Khan *bakhshdar* of Gilan and Eyvan. However, it was still unknown whether the Prime Minister could stop 'Abbas Qobadian from pushing his brother Khosrow as governor.[777] 'Abbas Qobadian's position was very strong as leader of the Majority in the *Majles*. Therefore, Kalantari wanted British discrete support against 'Abbas Qobadian, Amir Makhsus. He wanted to give the *bakhshdari* of Sar-e Pol to Qasem Khan A'zami, which was under the governor of Qasr-e Shirin, so that the A'zami faction of the Kalhors would not be entirely left at the mercy of the Qobadians. The latter had their own candidate, someone who had risen from nothing to *bakhshdar* thanks to the A'zamis, whom he had abandoned.[778]

The settling of accounts between rival clans after Reza Shah's abdication and the return of exiled chiefs was, of course, not limited to the Kalhors. In the summer of 1943 Asghar Khan Bakhtiyar was banished with some other Sanjabi chiefs suspected of anti-British activities. In his place, Karim Khan Barkhodari was appointed *bakhshdar*. The latter was known for his avarice and oppression and had amassed a fortune at the expense of his tribesmen. At the end of 1944, Asghar Khan was allowed to return and started intriguing against Karim Khan, wanting his old function back. He accused him of having sold 20 government rifles, which he, Asghar Khan, allegedly had transferred to Karim Khan when he left. The army arrested Karim Khan for a few weeks, which was a blow to his influence and prestige. Jahanshahi, before his departure

775. FO 248/1451, Consul Kermanshah to Moneypenny/Tehran, 21/09/1945; Idem, Dacid to Moneypenny/Tehran 17/08/1945.

776. FO 248/1451, Consul Kermanshah to Legation, 23/08/45; FO 248/1451, Consul Kermanshah to Moneypenny/Tehran, 17/08/1945.

777. A.W. Davis. FO 248/1451, Consul Kermanshah to Moneypenny/Tehran, 08/09/1945.

778. FO 248/1451, Consul Kermanshah to Moneypenny, 13/10/1945.

in May 1944, agreed that Karim Khan should go, but there was no suitable replacement. Thus, for the time being he remained supervisor (*sarparast*) of the Sanjabis, while people complained about him, because they were no longer willing to stand his oppression, while Asghar Khan and the Persian army intrigued against him.[779]

779. FO 248/1451, Consul Kermanshah to Moneypenny, 08/09/1945.

Appendix I

The Jewish Community of Kermanshah

BY

WILLEM FLOOR & PARISA MOHAMMADI

HISTORY

Persian Jews are amongst the oldest inhabitants of the country. The origin of the Jewish Diaspora in Persia is closely connected with various events in Israel's ancient history. According to the earliest written reference to Jewish settlement in Persia, Shalmaneser king of Assyria, took Samaria and carried Israel away unto Assyria, and placed them in Halah and Habor. On the river Gozan and in the cities of the Medes. This exile took place in 722 BCE. There were some additional smaller banishments, beginning some thirty five years after the fall of Samaria. Most of the Jews were settled in the Northern Zagros Mountains, primarily in the region we know as Kurdistan.[1] Jews were one of the important religious minorities in Kermanshah, one of the important towns in the Kurdistan region. According to Moqaddasi, there were more Jews than Christians in the city.[2] The earliest mention of Kermanshah as a dwelling place of the Jews occurs in Nathan ha-Bavli's report from the 10th century.[3] Thereafter, sources are silent about the presence of Jews in this city until the early 18th century. The Armenian chronicler Arak'el of Tabriz listed the various Jewish communities in seventeenth century Persia, but no Jewish community in Kermanshah is mentioned. Surprisingly, they are not mentioned either in the other mid-seventeenth century chronicle of Babai ben Lutf, although Jews undoubtedly lived in the city during the Safavid period (1501–1736). If it were not for the fact that in the 1720s, the presence 53 Jewish households in Kermanshah is recorded in Ottoman survey registers, one would have believed that there were no Jews in this city.[4]

---

1. Loeb 1977, p. 274.
2. al-Moqaddasi 1362, p. 589.
3. Neubauer 1895, II, pp. 77-88; Levi 1984, vol. 2, pp. 382-83; Pirnazar 2010, p. 164.
4. Lewis 1984, p. 119; Moreen 1987, p. 40 (a rabbi from Kermanshah); Arak`el of Tabriz, *Book of History*. tr. George Bournoutian. Costa Mesa: Mazda, 2010.

POPULATION FIGURES

During the Qajar period travelers who visited the town and other foreign reporters provide us with data about the Jewish population in Kermanshah. In 1807 and in 1816, it was estimated that there were 20 Jewish families or some 100 persons in Kermanshah. They were the most miserable group among the population, according to Rousseau, the French consul in Baghdad.[5] Rabbi David de-Beth Hillel (around 1827) reports that there were 300 Jewish families with three synagogues, living among 80,000 Moslem families, which total population number is far too high (see Chapter Two). Most of the Jews were poor.[6] In 1837, the American missionary Southgate estimated the Jewish population at 60 families, while in 1840 the French traveler Teule estimated it at 150 houses.[7] Around 1850, Joseph Benjamin refers to the Jewish life, economy, and community of Kermanshah. He reports a small Jewish community of forty families. According to him, Kermanshah was a large, fortified city surrounded by a chain of mountains, and carried "a considerable trade," as well as a "costly carpets" industry.[8] Rabbi Castleman reported in 1860 that there were few Jews in Kermanshah, and that "they are not God fearing people."[9] According to Neumark, in 1884 there were 250 Jewish families. He describes a community with some highly esteemed members, such as Hakim Aqajan, who was a learned physician, a teacher well-versed in the Talmud, and a slaughterer of cattle and fowls, in accordance with Jewish ritual. The community had adopted many of the customs of their Jewish co-religionists in nearby Baghdad.[10] In fact, "in the streets, women cover their face with a thin black net- a Baghdad custom."[11] In a letter dated 4 January 1873, Isaac Luria, the head master of the *Alliance Israélite School* in Baghdad estimated that 600 Jewish souls lived in Kermanshah.[12] In 1888-89, it is reported that there were some 1,000 Jews, but in 1893, the Jewish population of Kermanshah numbered 2,000 people (120 houses, 450 families). In 1904, the French *Alliance Israélite Universelle* (AIU) bulletin, estimated the population of the Jews in Kermanshah city to be about 1,406 [13] and with it surroundings it had the fifth biggest Persian Jewish community with 3,800 persons.[14] By 1900, the Jewish population was about 150 houses or 750 people as well as 20 Jewish merchants, temporary residents from Baghdad.[15] The American missionary Whipple, passing through the city in 1900, reported that there were 1,500

5. Dupré 1819, vol. 1, p. 238; Buckingham 1971, p. 101; Rousseau 1813, p. 288.
6. Beth Hillel 1832, p. 89.
7. Southgate 1840 vol. 1, p. 137; Teule 1842, vol. 2, p. 483.
8. Benjamin 1859, pp. 205-206.
9. Castleman1942, p. 71.
10. Pirnazar 2014 quoting Neumark 1947.
11. Singer 1916, vol. 7, p. 468.
12. Yeroushalmi 2009, p. 67.
13. Yeroushalmi 2009, pp. 67, 83, 89, 111; DCR 590 (Kermanshah, 1902), pp. 14-15; Levi 1335, vol. 3, p. 813. According to Singer 1916, vol. 7, p. 468, in 1903 there were 1,406 Jews and their quarter had 135 houses.
14. Tsadik 2007, p. 9; Idem 2009, pp. 108-112; Levi 1335, vol. 3, p. 813; *Alliance Israélite BulletinAnnuel* 66, 1904, pp. 168-69.
15. Yeroushalmi 2009, pp. 67, 83, 89, 111; DCR 590 (Kermanshah, 1902), pp. 14-15.

Jews.[16] In 1917, some 1,500 Jews were said to live in the city, while in 1921, Maj. Greenhouse, the British consul, mentions several hundred.[17] In 1930, their number was reported to be 1,200,[18] while in 1944, the British consul estimated their number at some 10,000 souls.[19]

WHY DO THESE FIGURES VARY?

We know that it is difficult to provide an accurate number of the Jewish population during the nineteenth century Persia, due to the lack of a census, but there are some other reasons. According to Tsadik, Jews might have been afraid to report their real numbers for religious reasons. Tallying people was believed to inflict untimely death on those counted. Also, they might have been apprehensive about disclosing their true number out of fear that the Persian authorities would increase taxation.[20] But it seems that the *Alliance Israélite Universelle* numbers for 1904 were rather accurate, because it was in their interest to have precise figures, which, moreover, are borne out by other sources. It is not clear why the number of Jews given by the British consul for 1944 is nine times that of their number in 1930. This may be due to a typing error, for, according to Netzer, the Jewish population of Kermanshah in 1948 only numbered 2,864 persons.[21]

OCCUPATIONAL STATUS

Whereas Moslems were employed in any trade, craft or service in Persia, non-Moslems were subject to many restrictions for both religious and social reasons (see next section). This held in particular for Jews, the largest non-Moslem group in the city. As a result, Jews mostly belonged to the lower economical segment of society. Many Jews lived by small trade and hawking,[22] traveling between cities and villages, while the women stayed at home spinning wool and silk or weaving hand-knit footwear called *giveh*.[23] They probably were engaged in these activities, because small trade and hawking did not require having large sums of money or property. Furthermore, Moslems often did not allow Jews to open shops in the bazaars of their own cities.[24] It was only as of the early twentieth century that Jews were able to own shops and

16. Whipple 1900, p. 814.
17. Hale 1920, p. 205; AIR 20/663, p. 23.
18. *The Palestine Bulletin*, Monday 10/02/1930, p. 2.
19. FO 371/40177, Kermanshah Diary January 1944.
20. Tsadik 2007, p. 7.
21. Netzer 2001.
22. Buckingham 1971, p. 101; Southgate 1840, vol. 1, p. 137; Yeroushalmi 2009, pp. 67, 83, 89, 111; DCR 590 (Kermanshah, 1902), pp. 14-15. According to Rousseau 1813, p. 88 the small Jewish community was engaged as money changers and as physicians. In Khaneqin there were mostly small traders, merchants or money changers. Saad 1913, p. 72.
23. Kermanshahchi 2007, pp. 354-56; Singer 1916, vol. 7, p. 468 (The Jews were engaged in spinning; only some 30 were engaged in trade).
24. Tsadik 2005, pp. 275-282

businesses in the local markets of the city. However, Jews in Kermanshah had their shops in a part of the bazaar called the Jewish bazaar, where they mainly were engaged in selling herbs (*'attari*); some were making and selling wine,[25] and others were engaged in the carpet trade. Ebrahim Haim was one of the first people who opened his shop in this bazaar.[26] Table I.1 gives a breakdown of the employment of Jewish men in Kermanshah in 1903. Although there some differences between the two sources that provide these data, they basically agree on the type of employment, although the number of employed differ. Also, where one source (Levi) provides a number for each type of employment, the other (Cohen) does less so and only reports, for example, that 85 men were retailers, and that 68 men were gainfully employed as dyers, goldsmiths, carpet makers, barbers and teachers, seven worked as chimney cleaners and glaziers and one man was a porter.[27]

Table Appendix I.1: Occupation of Jewish men in Kermanshah in 1903

Occupation	Source/ Cohen	Source/Levi
Herbalist	129	-
Itinerant herbalist	-	70
Herb trader	-	22
Retailer	85	-
Merchant	-	55
Goldsmith	X	23
Itinerant fabric seller	-	44
Dyer	X	28
Porter	1	15
Hebrew teacher	X	2
Weaver	-	10
Distiller	-	2
Liquor seller	-	3
Barber	X	3
Synagogue servant	-	3
Well digger	-	3
Chimney cleaner and glazier	7	-

X = mentioned, but no number. - = not mentioned.

The large number of Jewish herbalists is not surprising, because Jews often worked as medical practitioners.[28] Jews were also represented in another medical professional branch, viz. as sellers of amulets and talismans. The mullah of the Jewish community made a living selling

25. DDSR, 1325-K12-P2-71.
26. DDSR,1325-K11-P9-233; Kermanshahchi 2007, p. 355.
27. Cohen 1992, p. 14; Levy 1335, vol. 3 pp. 813-14.
28. Yeroushalmi 2009, p. 98.

such items to superstitious Moslems.[29] Finally, there were Jewish physicians who treated Moslem patients both in Kermanshah and its environs.[30]

There were also a number of Jewish merchants, who were involved in the import- and export trade. Because of contacts with Jews in Baghdad and Great Britain, Persian Jewish merchants could import more cheaply than others directly from Manchester, and especially, because they took small profits.[31] Yusef Mir, Moshe Nissan, Moshe Lalehzar, Hakim Zadeha, Kerendian, Khvajeh Harun Ghasri, Ebrahim Laher (Kermanshahchi), Yusef Kashefi, Ya'qub and Davud Khalili were well-known Jewish merchants of this period.[32] Having business partners among the Jews of Baghdad resulted in the settlement of many Iraqi Jews in Kermanshah, and close family and socio-cultural ties existed between the two Jewish communities.[33] A 1904 report notes that Jews had a predominant role in the cotton textile import trade from Manchester via Baghdad into Iran;" at least 80 percent of the [Kermanshah and Hamadan] trade was in the hands of Jewish traders.[34]

MAHALLEH (JEWISH QUARTER)

Mahalleh means "quarter, district, neighborhood," a word widely used in Persian to refer to any given part of city or town that is distinguishable from the rest based on a particular demographic concentration.[35] To unobservant eyes Jews did not differ in their way of life or clothes from Moslems. In fact, in many respects their way of life reflected the behavior and culture of the Moslem population they were living among. Like Moslem men, they beat their wives and sometimes married two wives.[36] However, religious minorities such as Jews lived separately for both external and internal reasons. The external reasons had to do with their status as *zemmi*s, i.e., the people of the Book - Christians, Zoroastrians, and Jews. As *zemmi*s they were granted protection of their life and property as long as they recognized the Moslem authority and performed certain duties:[37] (1) to pay the *jezya* tax on an annual basis, (2) not contradict the protection articles, (3) not harm Moslems, (4) not display objects objectionable to Moslems, (5) not build houses of worship, not ring bells, and not construct buildings taller than those of Moslems, and (6) to accept the regulations imposed on them by the Moslems.[38]

---

29. Benjamin 1863, pp. 205-06 a; Floor 2005, p. 92.
30. Yeroushalmi 2009, p. 98; Singer 1916, vol. 7, p. 468.
31. Floor 1976, p. 122
32. Kermanshahchi 2007, p. 355.
33. Kermanshahchi 2007, pp. 354-56.
34. Tsadik 2005, p. 277
35. Sarshar 2002, p. 104.
36. Stead 1907, p. 234; Loeb 1977. According to Singer 1916, vol. 7, p. 468, "when a husband divorces his wife he has to pay her 12 tumans ($12)."
37. Tsadik 2003.
38. Tsadik 2003, pp. 401-403. However, according to Singer 1916, vol. 7, p. 468, "The community paid no special tax."

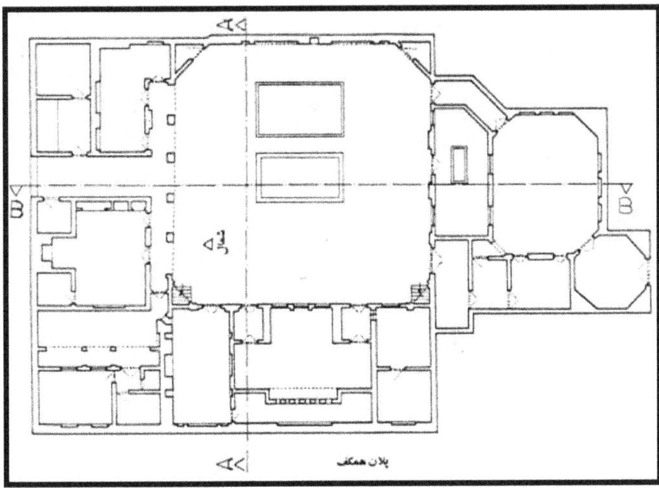

Fig Appendix I.1: Khvajeh Barukh house
(entrance to the *biruni*; walkway, and ground-plan, 2010)

An additional external reason was that under the Safavids, who converted the greater part of the population to Shiism, restrictions were imposed on minorities to encourage conversion to the Shiite creed of Islam.[39] These restrictions were the result of the Shiite Islamic concept of *taharat* or ritual cleanliness. Even touching an unbeliever, not necessarily a Jew, for its also held for other unbelievers, would require a Moslem to perform ritual cleansing (*vozu'*). Therefore, unbelievers lived apart with their own shops, because Moslems could not eat foodstuffs or wear fabrics that had been touched by the unclean hands or clothes of an unbeliever. Therefore, Jews were literally untouchable, unless of course you wanted to beat them up and plunder them or rape their womenfolk.

For internal reasons, Jews themselves preferred to reside in their own demarcated quarters as these would include central Jewish institutions such as synagogues as well as the public and/or ritual baths. Living with other Jews at the same place could guarantee the cohesiveness and identity of the Jewish community, and in times of anti-Jewish persecution it would be easier to close and protect the quarter. Also, because the Jews were very orthodox they, in their turn, considered non-Jews impure and refused to accept food or drinks from Moslems or Christians.[40] As for the government, the residence of Jews in

39. Tsadik 2003, p. 403.
40. Saad 1913, p. 72.

one locale allowed for a more efficient control over a specific group, thereby, for instance, expediting the collection of taxes. Thus, Moslem society sought to distinguish itself from non-Moslems so as to secure its own identity and difference. Moreover, in Shiite Persia, the alleged 'impurity' of the Jews was another impetus for their segregation to one area.[41]

The Jewish quarter or *mahalleh* in Kermanshah was located in Feyzabad, near the south-east gate, which therefore, was called the Jewish or Isfahan gate. The Abshuran stream, that carried off the city's sewage and two mosques, the Masjed-e Kuchek and the Masjed Sheikh Hadi indicated the limits of the quarter and marked it off from the city. Beyond the stream Jews were not allowed to own property.[42] Henry Stern who visited the city in 1845, wrote: 'The Jewish quarter is situated in an unhealthy part of the town. The Synagogue is an insignificant mud building and amidst a few wretched hovels, which are a striking proof of the misery of their occupants."[43] The Jewish quarter like other parts of the town had narrow streets, the one-room houses were shabby in which large families lived together. In winter, each family slept in this single room under the *korsi*[44] and in summer on big beds in the yard.[45] The houses of some rich Jewish families, such as that of Khvajeh Barukh, like that of the Moslem counterparts, had a public (male) and private (female) section. The Khvajeh Barukh house (Kakeh Barukh's house or Mal Kakeh Barukh in Kurdish) is the only remaining example of a Jewish Qajar house in Kermanshah, which is located in the former Jewish Feyzabad quarter in the Southern east part of the old city. The house belonged to a Jewish merchant and was built during the last decade of Naser al-Din Shah reign. It is one of the rare Qajar houses that has a private bathroom.

The centers of Jewish life in the *mahalleh* were three: the synagogue, the bath, and the cemetery.

SYNAGOGUE

The synagogue was the heart of a Jewish quarter and also, the main religious element of the Jewish community, which had various functions. In 1847, the *mahalleh* had three synagogues, which, in 1903, it still had as well as a Talmud Torah. The Jewish community did not have a charitable society.[46] In 1845, Stern only mentioned one, which he described as " an insignificant mud building."[47] "A crowd of Jews surrounded us and conducted to it. We had to wait several minutes while a messenger was dispatched for keys. On entering we descended to an extremely poor place of worship, affording the strongest evidence of poverty and oppression of the Jews

41. Tsadik 2009.
42. Kermanshahchi 2007, pp. 320, 353; Singer 1916, vol. 7, p. 468.
43. Stern 1854, p. 236.
44. A *korsi* s a type of low table with a heat source (usually a charcoal brazier) underneath it, and blankets thrown over it.
45. Kermanshahchi 2007, p. 354.
46. D'Beth Hillel 1832, p. 88; Singer 1916, vol. 7, p. 468. The poor were aided by a collection in the synagogue when they asked for help. During the month of Nissan, a temporary committee was established to raise funds for providing *matzoth* and other *Pesach* needs for the poor. *The Sentinel*, Friday 20/06/1924, p. 30.
47. Stern 1854, p. 236.

here. They told us that they repeatedly laid down expensive carpets, and ornamented the books of the law, but the soldiers had as often broken in at night and stolen every article of value."[48] The synagogue constituted the principal and often times the only center of Jewish communal life, which were struggling to survive and provide very basic services.[49]

THE BATHS

There were two baths in the Jewish quarter that were opened in early mornings to men and all day long were exclusive to women. Also there were a few *mikvah*s for religious matters.[50]

THE CEMETERY

The cemetery was a sacred place and the tombs of sainted Rabbis were pilgrimage sites. The cemetery was often referred to euphemistically as *bethayyim* (the house of the living) in Hebrew and in Judeo-Persian as *beheshtiyeh.* In Shiite Persia, Jews had their separate cemetery, since it is not permissible to bury infidels in Moslem graveyards. By the same token, it is forbidden to inter a Moslem in the burial places of infidels.[51] The British 1919 map of Kermanshah suggests that the Jewish cemetery of Kermanshah was located outside of the south-eastern gate of the town close to the Jewish quarter.[52] Allegedly, Ebrahim Kermanshahchi established the first Jewish cemetery in Kermanshah i.e. one where Jews could be buried in accordance with all religious requirements.[53]

SOCIAL STATUS

Jews and other unbelievers had a difficult life in Persia, because they never knew when a true believer would take advantage of their inferior status. This was also true for the Qajar period, when Jews in Kermanshah had to deal with difficulties concerning their status in the society. Jews were always the target of curses and vilifications, which was occasionally varied with the odd pogrom. The fact that they were under the protection and jurisdiction of the *kargozar* (the foreign affairs agent) since the 1860s, does not seem to have provided them with much protection.[54] A rabbi complained to Stern about the situation of the Jewish community in Kermanshah in 1845. He said: "why we are in the prison-bonds of the Ishmaelites [Moslems]? And treated

48. Stern 1854, p. 363.
49. Yeroushalmi 2009, 122. The *mikvah* is primarily used by the more Orthodox Jewish communities to symbolically purify the body. According to Jewish law, a *mikvah* must be connected to a naturally occurring water source and it must contain enough water to fully immerse a person of average stature.
50. Kermanshahchi 2007, p. 356.
51. Tsadik 2003, p. 396.
52. Clarke and Clark 1969, p. 21.
53. Cohanim 1993, p. 154.
54. DCR 590 (Kermanshah, 1902), p. 12.

us as dust under their feet ? why do the spoilers seize our property and kidnap our daughters under their defiled roofs?"[55] Persecutions of Jews would increase when a fanatical religious professional, who wanted to gain more spiritual brownie points (*thavab*s) by improving his political clout in this earthly paradise, raised his voice to attack the infidels. The easiest way for a cleric to prove his impeccable religious credentials was to provoke the anti-Jewish or anti-Christian sentiments of the people; unfortunately, a recurring practice that finds much credit until this very day. Of course, this left an imprint on the behavior of Jews and Christians outside their homes. A description of how Jews in Khaneqin coped with this structural intolerance quite likely also applied to those in Kermanshah:

> They put up with much. One day I asked our money changer (*sarraf*) why the Jews did endure so much so quietly. He replied: Before a Jew leaves his house, he remains standing at the door sill, takes of his tarbush (headdress) and utters all kinds of curses into it, then he puts the tarbush on again. When somebody curses him then he simply says: *'smi'na* (we have already heard it) and continues on his way.[56]

Nevertheless, due to the presence of various religious communities like that of the Shiites, Ahl-e Haqq, and a smattering of Sunnis, Christians, and Zoroastrians, anti-Semitism in Kermanshah was not as deeply rooted as in some other cities of Persia. Neumark (1884-85) states that "the hatred of Jews, which was prevalent in central Persia, "was not as rife" in Kermanshah.[57] The Jews of Kermanshah even participated in a Shiite ceremony called "'Omar Koshan" along with the Moslem residents of the town, which was held annually on the anniversary of the second Moslem caliph's death when he was burnt in effigy. Jews attended this ceremony because he had set strict rules for Jews during his reign.[58] Therefore, in the 19th through the mid-20th century, the Kermanshah Jewish community was both a sanctuary and a new homeland for refugees from Mashhad, following the forced conversion of its Jewish community and the murder of about thirty-two of them in 1839, and later for the emigrants from Bukhara on their way to Jerusalem.[59] In October 1893, Mullah Yaazghel sent a letter to the *Alliance Israélite Universelle* in Paris from which it may be inferred that the Jewish community of Kermanshah had enjoyed a rather peaceful existence during the first eight decades of nineteenth century, but were subject to some prosecution during its two last decades.[60]

During that period, Jews were repeatedly harassed, attacked and even killed in Kermanshah. Those Jews who had converted to Bahaism ran the double risk of being targeted both as a Jew and a Baha'i. Most if not all cases appear to have been the result of the need to vilify infidels and thus feel better as a Moslem, or to have a scapegoat and easy target to rouse the great

55. Stern 1854, p. 237.
56. Saad 1913, p. 72.
57. Tsadik 2007, p. 108.
58. Kermanshahchi 2007, p. 357. On the *Omar-koshan* festival, see Floor 2005, p. 203-12.
59. Sarshar 2002, pp. 158-60; Kermanshahchi 2007, pp. 354-56.
60. Kermanshahchi 2007, p. 323.

unwashed to settle political local conflicts over the bodies and property of Jews. Some cases of those attacks are mentioned below.

In 1882, Hajj Aqa Mohammad Hasan asked the governor to treat Jews well, but this tolerant attitude changed,[61] because on 29 May 1893, a local Shiite cleric accused a Jew of blaspheming the Prophet. Consequently, fourteen Jewish houses were looted and property was destroyed; the losses amounted 7,000 *tumans*. Fearing for their money and lives, some of the elders (*zqenim*) and notables (*nikhbadim*) of the Jewish community publicly converted to Islam.[62] These converts included seventy members of the family of Hakim Nasir, a prominent Jewish physician, followed by the marriage of his son to the daughter of the chief Moslem clergy member.[63] This family of converted Jews continued to play an important role in local politics. For example, in 1917, the son of Hakim Nasir became governor of Kermanshah.[64]

Persecutions of Jews in Kermanshah also continued thereafter. A letter dated 10 March 1896 written by representatives of the Jewish community, described what happened after the governor of Kermanshah had increased the price of foodstuffs. Conveying their discontent with this development, the population pillaged the Jewish quarter and caused damage amounting 2,000 *tumans*. "Then, they decided to massacre the Jews," and a large number of Jews thus embraced Islam to escape their imminent death. The writers of the letter contended that the olama encouraged the new converts to maltreat their former brethren and incited Moslems against Jews, pushing them to loot the Jews' property and assault (violate) their women and daughters. "The mullahs are much more influential than the Shah and his governors," claimed the Jews.[65] In 1902, two Jewish traveling salesmen were killed near Firuzabad, 36 km outside of Kermanshah. The authorities took no action to find the killers. 'Ala al-Dowleh, the governor, when asked by the Jewish community to take action replied that if they found the killers he would severely punish them. He also prohibited them from complaining about it to Tehran.[66] Sheikh Hadi of Kermanshah was reported in 1904 to have instigated attacks on the Jews of the city.[67] A Turkish Jew was wounded on 24 May 1905 in a caravanserai in town. The Turkish Consul-General protested, but was told that the Jew had interfered with a Persian woman and had to die. Because the Consul-General gave him refuge in his house this caused some concern in the bazaar. The Baghdad Jews, who were British subjects, asked Capt. Gough, the British consul for help. The Director of the *Alliance Israélite Universelle* also wrote to British consul, who took care of French interests as well, asking whether he should close the school or not. Capt. Gough contacted the *kargozar* and everything seemed to have calmed down.[68]

---

61. Kermanshahchi 2007, p. 323.
62. Tsadik 2010, pp. 241.
63. Kermanshahchi 2007, pp. 347-50. Hakim Nasir converted in June1893. *Ruznameh-ye Iran* 1375, vol. 4, p. 3227 (no. 802; 29/06/1893). In 1891, Yusef Jadid al-Islam, a goldsmith, was arrested with his partners in crime for counterfeiting silver coins. *Ruznameh-ye Iran* 1375, vol. 4, p. 2976 (no. 739; 26/01/1891).
64. Mohammad Ali Soltani 1381, p. 379.
65. Tsadik 2010, p. 241.
66. Anonymous 1902, p. 59.
67. Tsadik 2010, p. 248.
68. Political Diaries vol. 1, p. 107.

The Constitutional movement of 1906-07 meant for religious minorities such as Persian Jews that they were equal before the law which opened of a road towards their material and moral restoration. During the first election to the new conservative *Majles* in 1906, members of religious minorities were granted to elect a representative of their own community. Unfortunately, three months after the convening of Parliament, Mozaffar al-Din Shah (r. 1896-1907) died, and under the new Mohammad ʻAli Shah (r. 1907-1909) the constitutional movement very quickly disappointed the high hopes which the liberal elements of the Moslems and Jews in Persia had entertained. Although Persian Jews elected ʻAzizollah Simani, this election soon become a source of conflict between the olama and constitutionalists and, although to avoid such a conflict the Jews had canceled his election, it caused the persecution of Jews in some cities such as Kermanshah. Houses were looted, many Jews were forced to convert, and others were killed.[69]

Anti-Jewish riots again became common, particularly in Kermanshah. In 1908, a Moslem incited the rabble, when Jews protested his intention of wanting to build a house on part of their cemetery. On 25 October 1908 there was a quarrel between a Moslem and a servant of the Alliance; the latter had no blame as confirmed by Persian soldiers. This led to another quarrel and a servant of the Imam Jomʻeh's brother hit a soldier, who took him into the courtyard of the Alliance to punish him. The head of the Alliance, Mr. Sagues ordered the man to be released and asked the Imam Jomʻeh to investigate. Before that could happen a mob gathered attacked the Alliance and took Mr. Sagues to the Friday Mosque threatening him with death. Fortunately, the Imam Jomʻeh arrived and he was released. A few days later Sagues asked for protection for the Jewish quarter as he had heard that it would be raided on the *Ruz-e Qatl*. The British consul contacted the *kargozar*, who was responsible for the Jews, who gave assurances that the quarter would be safe.[70]

One year later, another attack occurred against the Jews of Kermanshah. The Bulletin of the *Alliance Israélite* from Kermanshah dated 31 March 1909 reports that the Jewish ghetto in that city was looted. Twelve hundred Jews became homeless, while the value of property damage amounted to 500,000 *tumans*.[71] This pogrom had been caused by a rumor spread throughout Kermanshah that a Moslem employee, who happened to be a sayyed, had been killed by his Jewish employer, a shopkeeper, to use his blood to make unleavened Passover bread, despite the fact that the man was a Christian convert and thus, did not celebrate Passover.[72] The boy went home, ate and slept, but the next morning he fainted several times and then died. The boy's body was examined by two Persian and one British physician who all told the family that the cause of death was heart failure, which was unrelated to the beating. His older brother then decided not to lodge a complaint. However, some sayyeds, well-known bad characters, saw this sad event as an opportunity to make a name for themselves and forbade the boy's burial, saying that he would be killed if he did. The sayyeds took the body around the city to arouse anger and passion. The following day they threatened the governor that if he did not execute the Jewish

69. Afari 2002, p. 166.
70. Administration Report 1908, p. 59; Political Diaries, vol. 2, p. 405-06,424-25,453.
71. Levy 1335, vol. 3, p. 813.
72. AMFAI, DDSR 1327-K24-P2-97, DDSR 1327-K56-P3-1, DDSR 1327-K56-P3-80, DDSR 1327-K24-P2-84.

Christian their followers would begin rioting. The governor then gave orders to immediately execute the man, after which the rabble started looting anyway, aided and abetted by the governor's soldiers. The British and Russian consuls pressured the governor to protect the *Alliance Israélite Universelle* school, but the Jewish quarter was plundered and even stripped of its doors and windows. No Jews were killed, but many were wounded. There also was a positive aspect to this riot. The leading mullah of Kermanshah condemned the riot and many Jews were saved by armed Moslems who protected them against the raging mob and others who gave them refuge in their homes. After the riot, many Moslems showed sympathy for their Jewish neighbors through gifts of food and clothing. They also established a committee to return as much as possible of the stolen property. It probably was the worst attack against Jews in Kermanshah and even the *New York Times* published an article about it. The governor defended himself saying that he had ordered the execution, without trial, to prevent a riot. The riot had a follow-up. Eleven days later a picture of the Bab was found among the stolen property and in the bazaar tempers and passions ran high. The Jews fearing another attack fled to find sanctuary in the Turkish and British consulates. Fortunately, this was unnecessary, because this time the people listened to the leading mullah (Imam Jom'eh), who took the Jews under his personal protection and had them escorted back to their homes. According to the British consul:

> It is now fully acknowledged that the Jew-Christian who was executed after having been accused of having caused the death of a sayyed apprentice was innocent, as the boy died of natural causes. The boy's mother and brother from the very beginning made it clear that they had no complaints, but the many hooligan Sayyeds in town saw a opportunity for looting and therefore on 27 March the Jewish quarter was looted. Even the governor admits that the executed man was innocent and only executed him to prevent a riot. The attack is much deplored in town and the chief priests are disclaiming any responsibility.

To the consul's astonishment there was much actual sympathy by Moslems who sent food and clothes to the Jews. Capt. Haworth sent 20 *tumans* to the head of the *Alliance* for those without food, but had not expected Moslems to do the same. Many Jews owed their lives to Moslem neighbors and in some cases Moslems actually stood armed in front of their Jewish friends until they could take them to their own homes. Many Jews died of their wounds. "The wounds were all given at very short range usually the looter stood over the Jew, demanding knowledge as to where he kept his money and jewels." The governor charged the *mojtaheds*, who had spoken strongly against the pogrom, with the recovery of the goods and most houses were searched and, as a result, much was recovered. However, the consul feared that most of it would be things of little value as looted carpets wound up in the house of Sardar Jalal, the governor's grandson and houses of other important men, whose houses could not be searched. One Jew claimed he had lost £8,000 in goods, which the consul deemed to be in reality half of that amount. The fact that he knowingly murdered an innocent man did not bother the governor, but he wanted to show the consuls that he did everything to recover the stolen property, because the new year's appointments were not known yet. The recovered property was distributed in the presence of the Mirzas of the British and Russian consuls. Those who had to return goods blamed the consuls for it, but respectable Moslems were very pleased about it. The governor gave the people one month to return the goods looted threatening to take severe action, if they did not. "Notices are stated to have been posted up referring to the various articles which are to be found in the Governor's house, even naming the rooms in which they are to be seen." The British consul could not get copies as they were torn down by the city patrols. Mr. Molitor thought that the notices were the work of Customs employees.[73]

All those events mentioned above show the insecurity of and discrimination against Jews at Kermanshah throughout the Qajar period. At the same time, it also showed that many Moslems were not bigots and showed real humanity by protecting the Jews who were attacked. Also, it seems that after Mohammad 'Ali Shah's deposition and the revival of constitutionalism the situation improved for Jews. Franco, the director of the *Alliance Israélite Universelle* school at Kermanshah, reported that after Nezam al-Saltaneh (1910) had become governor of the city the situation of Jews improved and there was no bloodshed or robbery in the city.[74] In fact, Nezam al-Saltaneh went out of his way to avoid giving ill-intended people an excuse to start anti-Jewish riots. "On 13 August [1910] a certain Moise Abi, professor at the Alliance, was arrested because of relations with a Moslem prostitute. His Persian servant and a woman were also arrested in his house, which is in the Moslem part of town. I immediately contacted the governor and asked him to hand the man over to me in secret in the interest of public order, which he did. After some pressure the man confessed his guilt." Nezam al-Saltaneh asked Knox, the British consul *pro tem* to keep Moise until 15 August, for then he would be able to guarantee his security. Meanwhile, the matter had become known in the bazaar and the governor was forced to ask the consul to detain Moise until he had consulted the *mojtahed*, as this was a religious matter. On 17 August, Nezam al-Saltaneh informed the consul that he had discussed the matter with Aqa Sheikh Mehdi and that Moise would be safe in the *Alliance* school. The consul then sent Moise with a consular *farrash* to the school with the request to the director to ask the Alliance head office to transfer the man to Hamadan, his native city. The consul had done this out of courtesy and appreciation for the governor's handling of the case. He also wrote to Nezam al-Saltaneh that he had taken this step because of Moise's "serious lack of judgment in taking a house in the Musullman [sic] quarter, where his coreligionaries are not willingly tolerated." On 16 August the director asked the British consul to have Moise rehabilitated as both the servant and woman declared that nothing untoward had happened and that the visit concerned a personal matter. The consul declined and the next day Nezam al-Saltaneh informed him that the servant had declared that he had procured women constantly for Moise. He thought it better to release the servant and the woman, strongly pressing upon them not to talk about the matter. Knox suggested that Tehran might sent a sign of appreciation, which Nezam al-Saltaneh might welcome given his waning authority.[75]

The new legal status of non-Moslem minorities means that there were more economic and other opportunities to improve and change their lives. As a result, many young Jews found jobs in tailoring, typesetting, translating, teaching, tutoring, etc. As a result, better civil relations

---

73. Political Diaries, vol. 3, pp. 605-06; FO 248/968, Haworth to Tehran, 28/03/1909; Idem, Haworth to Tehran 11/04/1909.

74. Levy 1335, vol. 3, p. 814.

75. FO 248/999, Knox to Tehran18/08/1910.

between the Jewish minority and the rest of the Persian population came into being.[76] In spite of these improvements, Jews remained stigmatized infidels, because new laws could not erase the centuries of brainwashing of the Moslem majority that Jews were at best to be tolerated and at worst considered to be unclean and thus, to be despised. This also held for the government's attitude. In February 1923, Tehran banned the emigration of Jews, only those leaving on pilgrimage or business were allowed to leave the country, provided they arranged for an appropriate guarantee for their return. On 21 February 1936, without any explanation, Tehran instructed the heads of all local departments throughout the country to dismiss their Jewish employees. Although later many were given functions in the interior of the country, their past service was not taken into account.[77] In January 1944 preparations were made for municipal elections in February in Kermanshah. The governor of Kermanshah asked Tehran whether Jews were also allowed to vote, as the local community had asked, indicating that they still were treated as secondary citizens,[78] although their situation would improve thereafter.

The Balfour declaration in 1917, giving Jews the promise of a homeland, was like a new step in Jewish social life. The declaration played a considerable role in inspiring the Jewish Persian community's involvement in Zionist activities, including the establishment of Zionist organizations.[79] The Jews of Kermanshah played an active role in Zionist activities in Persia. One of the community's early political activists was Shemu'el Yehezkel Haim (1891-1931). A dynamic revolutionary, he was one of the Persian Jewry's most controversial personalities of the era. In 1923, Ḥaim, who was the editor of the first Jewish journal in Persian script, named *Ha-Haim* (started June 1922). In 1923, he was elected as the Jewish representative to the *Majles* (1923-26), because the community was dissatisfied with the inaction of their representative Dr. Loqman, a Tehrani physician.[80] Haim was also acting head of the Zionist organization and immediately after his election he began "a vigorous reorganization of the Jewish Communities, school committees and the Zionist Committee." However, the so-called reorganization, in fact, meant the dissolution of these Jewish bodies, "so that things are even worse than they were before." As a result, despite Haim's efforts to bring the position of Jews in Persia to the notice at the highest level of the government, the Jewish community decided to reinstate their previous *Majles* representative, Dr. Loqman, because "with all his inactivity," he was "preferable to a disruptor." On 2 October 1926, Haim was arrested, accused of being member of a group of military officers, who were accused of plotting the death of Reza Shah, the crown prince, many high military officers and some members of the *Majles* (see Attachment 1 on page 517). On 15 December 1931 Haim was executed after five years of prison.[81] Other early Zionist activists and pious public figures of Kermanshah included Moshe Hay Isaac Kohen Yazdi (1896-1957), author of *Pardes ha-dat* (The orchard of religion, Jerusalem, 1934), who immigrated to Israel

---

76. Levy 1335, vol. 3, pp. 813-14.
77. Political Diaries, vol. 7, p. 265; Idem, vol. 12, pp. 43, 161,
78. FO 371/40177, Kermanshah Diary January 1944.
79. Davidi 2002, p.240.
80. Ayyub Loqman Nehuray (1882-1952), born in Kashan, was a physician in Tehran and *Majles* representative of the Jewish community from 1909 until 1943, except for the period of the fifth *Majles* (1924-26).
81. *The Sentinel*, Friday 29/04/1927, p. 39; Idem, Friday 22/01/1932, p. 27. FO 371/11490, Nicholson to FO, tel. 216, 02/10/1926; Idem, Clive to Chamberlain 20/12/1926 (confidential).

immediately after Israel's independence in 1950. David Davidian (b. 1922), known as Masrur, now residing in Israel, represents a contemporary example of the impact of Persian culture, philosophical issues, literature, and poetic arts on Persian Jews in general and the Jews of Kermanshah in particular, through his poetic compilation, *Kashkul-e Masrur*. Davud Adhami (1916- 2010) is another contemporary intellectual of Kermanshah, whose romantic novel, *Besu-ye kamal* reflects some aspects of the historical and political life of Jews in general and his philosophical views in particular.[82]

EDUCATION

Jewish education in nineteenth century was for boys only and limited to the study Hebrew, the Torah and prayers in the homes of local rabbis. In these Jewish *maktab*s, they learned elements of Hebrew and some Persian literature, which they read and wrote in Hebrew characters. Few learned the Persian script. Girls rarely were taught to read and write, because this was deemed unnecessary.[83] These schools or *maktab*s further imparted to its pupils the values and knowledge required for faithful membership in the religious Jewish community and suitable behavior in the synagogue and at religious ceremonies.[84] Those engaged in trade learned the traditional Persian system of accounting called *siyaq* from family members.[85]

Since the 19th century, changes in Persian society occurred, which also affected Persian Jews and their way of education changed and a new system came into being. The first group that became involved in the education of Jews were Christian missionaries and their aim was to spread Christianity. It seems that the plight of the Persian Jews, their poverty, their lack of schools and hospitals, their moral degeneration, famine and disease, made them fertile soil for the Christian missionary activities. However, they initially did not succeed in establishing a missionary school in 1894 in Kermanshah.[86] There is a letter sent to the Rev. James Hawkes asking to send a teacher to Kermanshah because their children were not allowed to enter Moslem *maktab*s, this letter was signed by some people with Jewish and Christian names (1 March 1894). However, the Rev. Hawkes' request to open a school for Christian and Jewish children in Kermanshah was not granted by the government in Tehran.[87] It was only in 1902 that Christian missionaries opened a school in the city. With the establishment of modern schools, including those by American missionaries, Jewish children also could receive a modern education there. At the missionary school, of course, the missionaries also preached Christianity to the pupils (see chapter two).

In 1904, the *Alliance Israélite Universelle* (AIU) opened a modern school in Kermanshah, twenty years after obtaining Naser al-Din Shah's permission to open AIU schools in Persia by

82. Pirnazar 2014, online edition.
83. Spector and Menachem 2003, p. 382.
84. Cohen 1986, p. 26.
85. Nikbakht 2002, p. 200.
86. Fischel 1950, p. 148.
87. AMFAI, DDSR,1311-K23-P20. For the correspondence between Hawkes and the Persian authorities as well as between the American Legation in Tehran and the Persian authorities and the State Department (January-July 1892), see US Government 1895, vol. 3, pp. 486-92.

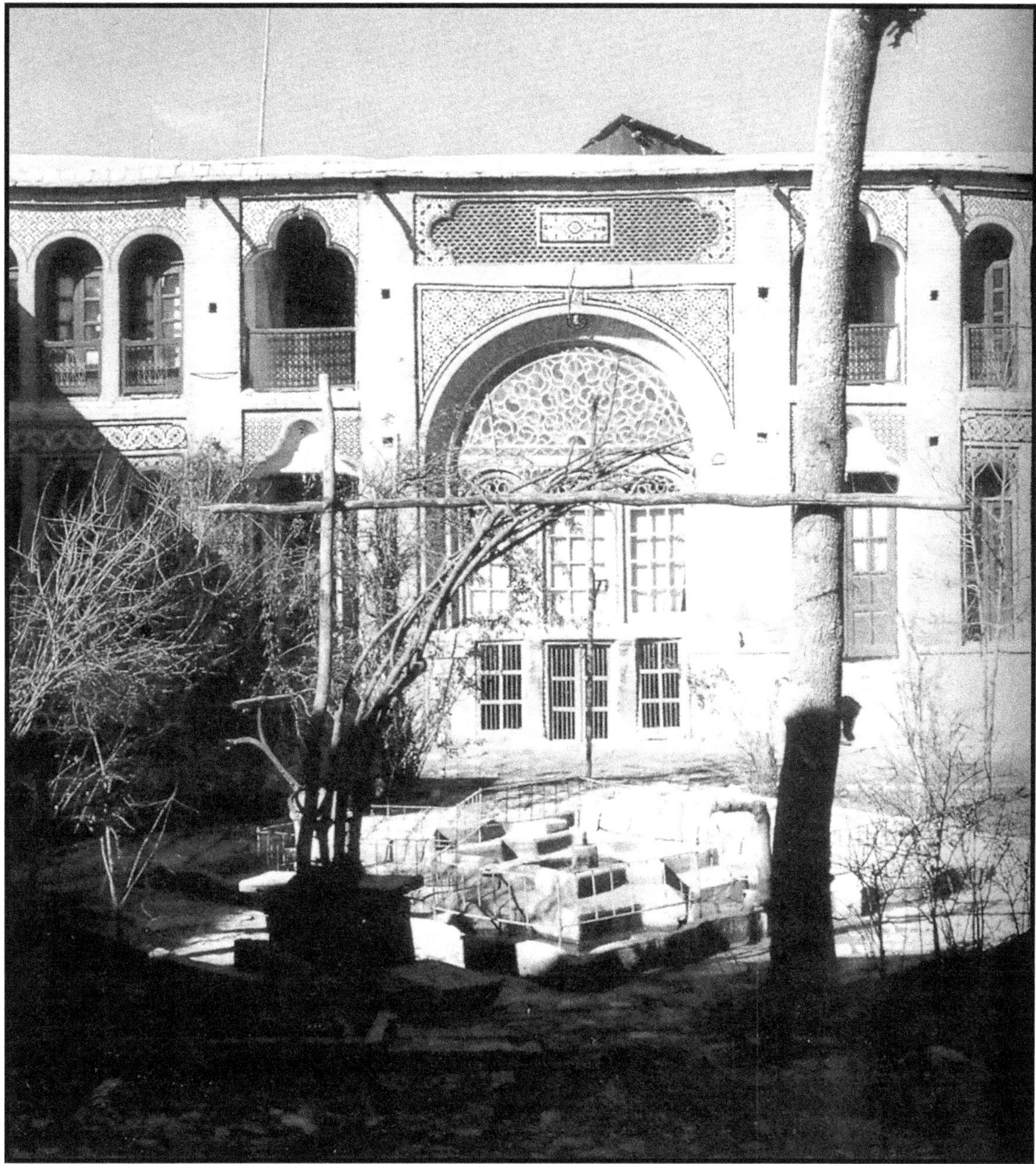

Fig Appendix I.2 Alliance School in Kermanshah (1930s).
Source: Source: Sarshar 2002, 232.

Adolph Cremieux in France, who wanted to provide modern education in a Jewish environment. The *Alliance* school had two branches for boys and girls. In 1904, the Kermanshah school had only 20 girl students.[88] Initially, a teacher called Sidi was the Principal of the school, but in the first years of the Constitution, until 1908, a man named Sagues (Sageh, Sagez) took his place. Thereafter Messrs. Cohen (December 1908-November 1909), Franco (November 1909-October

88. Cohen 1986, p. 26.

Fig Appendix I.3 (top): Alliance School board of directors.
Fig Appendix I.4: Ettehad (Alliance) girls' school (1930s)
Source: Source: Sarshar 2002, 233

1919) and Mirza Hasan Khan Khattat (until December 1934) held this function.[89] In June 1913, Jewish merchants, who held a large part of the trade, discussed the payment of 1 *shahi* per imported bale. It was then decided that one-third of the revenues would be paid to the *Alliance* school.[90]

Non-Jewish students were also accepted at the *Alliance* school. On 8 February 1915, a memorial was held in commemoration of the founder of the *Alliance Israélite*, Narsice Levy, who died in Paris. Soleyman Mirza, one of the local princes and a leader of the Democrats, was one of the speakers and expressed his thanks on behalf the people of Kermanshah for the founder's school, which was such a benefit to the town, where no difference was made between Jew of Moslem and he hoped that the friendly relations between the communities would endure.[91]

Table I.2: Number of pupils at the Alliance Israelite School 1932-1936

Year	Boys	Girls
1932/33	580	285
1933/34	615	296
1934/35	457	296
1935/36	452	291
1938/39	538	436

Source: Netzer 1997, vol. 2, pp. 123-25.

The *Alliance* school like all other institutions had both negative and positive sides: At this school courses such as Arabic, Jewish theology, French language, mathematics, natural sciences, physics, history and geography were taught. But compared with the AIU's early presence in Persia, it may be noted that the *Alliance* schools showed a marked drop given to the status of biblical and liturgical studies. These subjects, which constituted the main component of the *maktab* syllabus, were now allocated only a few class hours weekly. In 1930 it was reported that in Kermanshah students aged 15-18 could barely read the Bible and translated the passages mechanically.[92]

Furthermore, school principles looked down on Judeo-Persian idiom, never teaching to appreciate it as a manifestation of an original and popular Jewish culture. This negative attitude toward Judeo-Persian argot had a doubly negative consequence: first, it tarnished the self-image of students and local teachers, themselves trained at *Alliance* schools in Persia, who began to scorn their own dialects. Second, it increased the risk of mutual alienation between school administrators and the local Jewish population. Most AIU representatives in Persia belittled the local teachers, whom they called "the natives." In

89. Nategh 1370; Yeroushalmi 2010, p. ix; Administration Report 1905-06, p. 50; Soltani 1381, vol. 1, p. 286 (who, erroneously, has October 1901 as the starting date).

90. Soltani 1381, vol. 1, p. 290.

91. FO 248/1112 Kermanshah Diary 12/02/1915.

92. Silberstein's letter from Kermanshah, No. 9, 16 June 1930, in AIUA, File XE 105, as quoted in Cohen 1986, p. 28.

1904, Sidi wrote of two rabbis, former teachers at the *maktab* in Kermanshah: "They are better at bookbinding than teaching. Their service to civilization so far was meager. In the 'new regime' which we establish, their work will be more fruitful.[93]

Appendix fig I. 5: Jews gathered in the Alliance School to recover their belongings after a pillaging of the Mahalleh (1909). Source: Sarshar 2002, 453.

93. Sidi's letter from Kermanshah, No. 6, 16 June 1904, in AIUA, File XIVE 150, as quoted in Cohen 1986, p. 27.

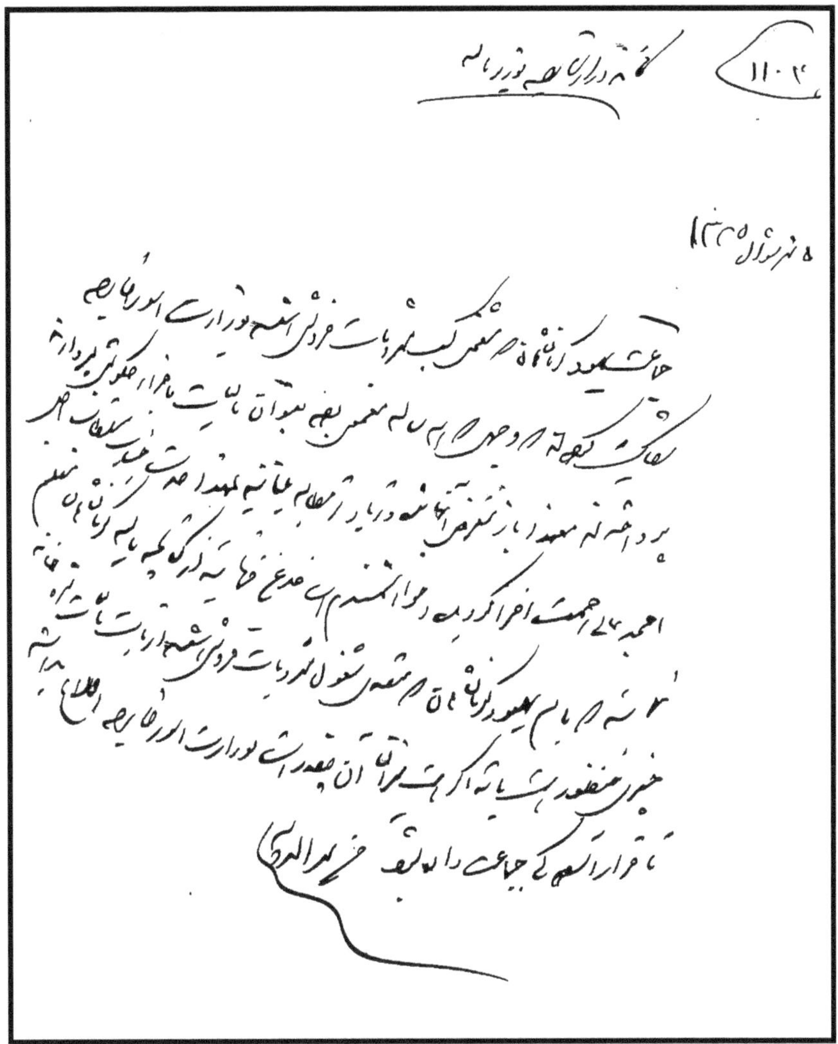

No.1. AMFAI, DDSR, 1325-K12-P2-71

کاغذ وزارت خارجه به
وزیر مالیه
۵ شهر شوال۱۳۲۵
جماعت یهود کرمانشاهان
که مشغول کسب مشروبات
فروشی است به وزارت
امور خارجه شکایت کرده
اند که وجهی که هر ساله
معمول به وجه مالیات به
اجزاء حکومتی پرداخته
اند، پرداخته اند. معهذا باز
متعرض آنها شده و زیادتر
مطالبه می نمایند. لهذا خدمت
جناب مستطاب اجل امجد
عالی زحمت افزا گردیده
و خواهشمند است غدغن
فرمایند از کتابچه مالیه
کرمانشاهان معلوم نمایید
که به اسم یهود کرمانشاهان
که ... مشغول مشروبات
فروشی هستند از مالیات ...
خانه چیزی منظور هست یا
نه؟ اگر هست میزان آن چقدر است به وزارت خارجه اطلاع دهید تا قرار آسودگی جماعت داده شود.
محمد علی علاءالدوله

A letter from the Minister of Foreign Affairs to the Minister of Finance, 5 Shavval 1325/11 November 1907

The Jewish community of Kermanshah, which is engaged in the liquor trade, has complained to the Ministry of Foreign Affairs that it has paid its taxes to the government annually. However, the authorities asked them to pay more. Therefore, based on the Kermanshah tax register, please confirm that the Jews of Kermanshah, who are engaged in the sale of liquor, need to pay a tax for the wine house or not? If yes, how much is the tax? Please let the Ministry of Foreign Affairs know so that the community may be given peace of mind.

Mohammad `Ali `Ala al-Dowleh

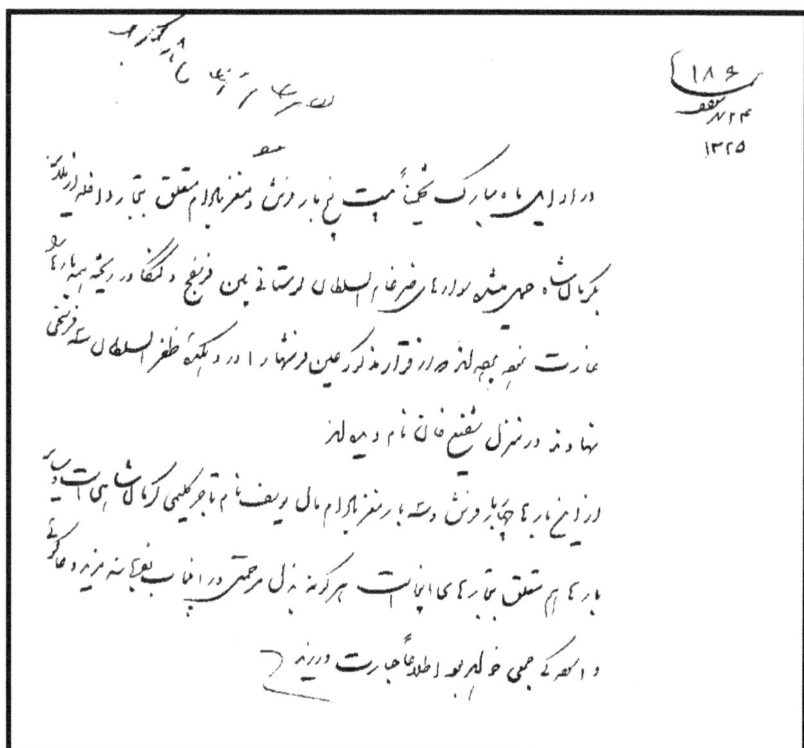

No.2 DDSR, 1325-K11-P9-233

نمره ۱۸۶
در اوایل ماه مبارک تخمینا
بیست پنج بار فرش و مغزبادام
متعلق به تجار داخله از ملایر
به کرمانشاه حمل می شده
سوارهای ضرغام السلطان
لرستانی بین فرسنج و کنگاور
ریخته همه بارها را غارت
نموده برده اند که از قرار
معلوم عین فرش ها را در
دهکده ضفرالسلطان سه
فرسخی نهاوند در منزل شفیع
خان نام دیده اند.
از این بارها چهار بار فرش و
سه بار مغز بادام مال یوسف
نام تاجر کلیمی کرمانشاهی
است و سایر بارها هم متعلق به تجارهای اینجاست. هرگونه مرحمتی در این باب بفرمایند مزید دعاگویی و آسودگی
جمعی خواهد بود.
اطلاعا جسارت ورزید.

No 186

In the beginning of this month 25 loads of carpets and almonds, which belonged to local merchants, was being carried from Malayer to Kermanshah. Between Farsanj and Kangavar, Zargham al-Saltaneh Lorestani's horsemen attacked them and looted the goods. The same carpets were seen in the house of someone called Shafi` Khan in a village beloning to Zargham al-Saltaneh at 3 farsakh from Nehavand.

Four loads of those carpets and three loads of the almond belong to Yusef, a Jewish merchant from Kermanshah and the rest also belong to [other] merchants from here.

Any kind of favor regarding this issue is highly appreciated will much increase their prayers and peace of mind.

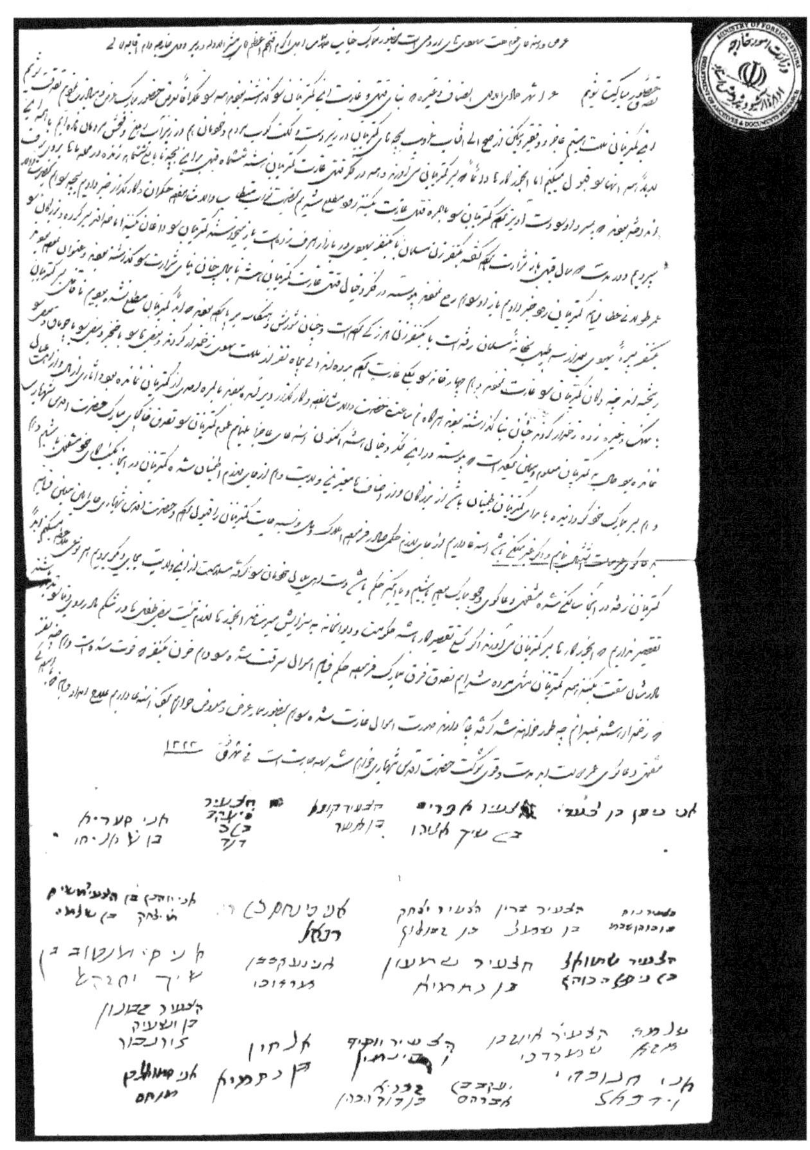

NO.5 DDSR1323-K22-P4.1-300

عرض و استدعای عموم ملت یهودی های ... است به حضور مبارک جناب جلالت مآب اجل اکرم افخم اعظم آقای مشیرالدوله وزیر دول خارجه دام اقباله عالی

تصدق حضور مبارکت شویم ۱۶ شهر جمادی الاول اصناف و غیره که بنای قتل و غارت این کمترینان را گذاشته بودند همه را تلگرافا به عرض حضور مبارک عرض و مبادرت نمودیم. تصدقت شویم این کمترینان ملت هستیم عاجز و فقیر و مسکین از صبح الی آفتاب غروب بچه های کمترینان در زیر دست و لگدکوب مردم و خودمان هم در زیر آب دهن و فحش مردم مانده ایم. با همه این ... هم آنها را قبول می کنیم اما آنجور کارها دائما که بر کمترینان می آورند و همه در فکر قتل غارت کمترینان هستند شش ماه قبل براین بچه نابالغ شش ماهه زنده در محله ما به روی برف انداخته بودند که بمیرد و او یک دست اویز ... کمترینان شود بالمره قتل غارت بکنند. زود مطلع شدیم به حضرت نواب مستطاب والا شاهزاده حکمران و کارگزار خبر دادیم بچه را هم به حضرت والا سپردیم و در مدت دوسال قبل باز شرارت کرده گفتند یک نفر زن مسلمان با یک نفر یهودی در بازار حرف زده است باز می خواستند کمترینان را داغان کنند اما خداوند سپر کرده و بزرگان را عمر طولانی عطا نماید. کمترینان آنها را خبر دادیم باز او را هم رفع نمودند پیوسته در فکر خیال قتل غارت کمترینان، همیشه تا به حال چنان بنای شرارت را گذاشته بودند و عنوان نموده بودند یک نفر پسر یهودی بعد از سه طبیب به خانه زن مسلمان رفته و هرزگی کرده است و چنان شورش و هنگامه برپا کرده بودند که ابدا کمترینان مطلع نشده بودیم ناغافل به سر کمترینان ریخته اند چند دکان کمترینان را غارت نمودند و بام چهار خانه را بکلی غارت کرده برده اند و الی پنجاه نفر از ملت یهودی زخمدار کردند و بعضی را با خنجر و بعضی را با چماق و بعضی را با سنگ و غیره زده زخمدار کردند چنان بنا گذاشته بودند هرگاه نیم ساعت حضرت والا شاهزاده و کارگزار دیر امده بودند بالمره احدی از کمترینان باقی نمانده بود و آثاری از مال و عهد عیال نمانده بود. حال به کمترینان معلوم و معین گردیده است که پیوسته در این فکر و خیال هستند.

اکنون استدعای عاجزانه می نماییم عموم کمترینان را تصدق خاک پای مبارک حضرت اقدس شهریاری و هم به سر خود گردانیده یا برای کمترینان اطمینان؟ باش از بزرگان و اصناف تا معتبرین ولایت و هم ازجای ... اطمینان شده کمترینان در اینجا به کسب کار خود مشغول باشیم و هم دعا گوی ...... و اگر غیر ممکن باشد از جای لازم حکم فرموده املاک و مال و نسیه جات کمترینان را قبول کرده و حضرت اقدس شهریاری جای امن معین فرمایند کمترینان رفته در آنجا ساکن شده مشغول دعاگویی وجود مبارک بوده باشیم یا اینکه حکم باشد دست اهل عیال خودمان را گرفته سلامت از این ولایت بجای دیگر برویم هر نوعی ملاحظه می کنیم ابدا تقصیر نداریم که آنجور کارها به سر کمترینان می آورند و اگر کسی تقصرکار باشد حکومت و دیوانخانه به سزایش می رسانند.

آنجورها لازم نیست برخی طفلی مادر شکم .... و مادرشان سقت بکنند همه کمترینان شهر مرده شده ایم تصدق فرق مبارک فرموده حکم .... اموال سرقت شده شود هم خون یک نفر که فوت شده است و هم چند نفر که زخمدار هستند نمیدانم چطور خواهند شد گرفته .... دارند.

صورت اموال غارت شده را هم به حضور شما عرض و معروض خواهم کرد استدعا داریم علاج امور فرمایند که با آسودگی .... دعاگوی عمر دولت ابد مدت و قوی شوکت حضرت اقدس شهریاری خواهیم شد.

زیاده جسارت است

فی شهر فوق سنه ۱۳۲۳

A letter from the Jewish community to Moshir al-Dowleh, the Minister of Foreign Affairs. On the 16th of Jamadi al-Avval, when the guilds and others engaged in plundering and killing in the Jewish ghetto, we [the Jewish community] informed Your Excellency by telegraph. We are the lowest and poorest class in [society], and from sunrise to sunset our children are treated badly and trampled upon by other people and we also have remained the target of spitting and cursing. Despite all this, we accept all that disrespect, but they continuously behave badly toward us and all of them contemplate killing and plundering these insignificant ones. Six months ago, they took a 6-months old baby and left it alive under the snow to die so as to have an excuse to immediately plunder and kill these insignificant ones.

We quickly became aware of it and informed H.E. the prince-governor and the karguzar and delivered the child to H.E. Two years ago, they said that a Moslem woman had talked with a Jew in the bazaar and again they wanted to attack these insignificant ones, but God protected us, and we immediately informed the authorities and they stopped them. They [people] always think about plundering these insignificant ones and once again a rumor was put about that a Jewish boy after having seen three doctors went to the house of a Moslem woman and had done all kinds of bad things with her. We knew nothing about this and suddenly they attacked these insignificant ones and plundered some shops of these insignificant ones and totally destroyed the roof of four houses. Some 50 persons of the Jewish community were injured; some were struck with a dagger, some with a cudgel, and some with stones and the like. If H.E. the prince-governor and the these insignificant ones would have arrived half an hour later [to the ghetto], none of these insignificant ones would have been alive and no trade of their goods and family would have remained. Now, these insignificant ones are sure that [people of the city] are always thinking about it [i.e., plundering and killing us].

We're beseeching Y.E. to ensure the safety of these insignificant ones and enable us to live here [Kermanshah] and engage in our livelihoods and we beg you, if it is not possible, to please order to select a safe place for the property and wives of these insignificant ones where these insignificant ones may move to and live or that we emigrate to another province. These insignificant ones have done nothing to justify being treated like this and if somebody has behaved badly they will turn him over to the government for punishment.

There is no need to [take] a child from the mother's belly ... to kill the mother, all these insignificant ones would have died. Please issue an order for the return of the plundered goods, the recompense for one person who died and for the wounded ones. The list of plundered goods will be sent to Y.E. Please resolve this issue so that we may pray for the eternal life of the state an the ruler.

[Apology for] the liberty taken
In the above month 1323/1905

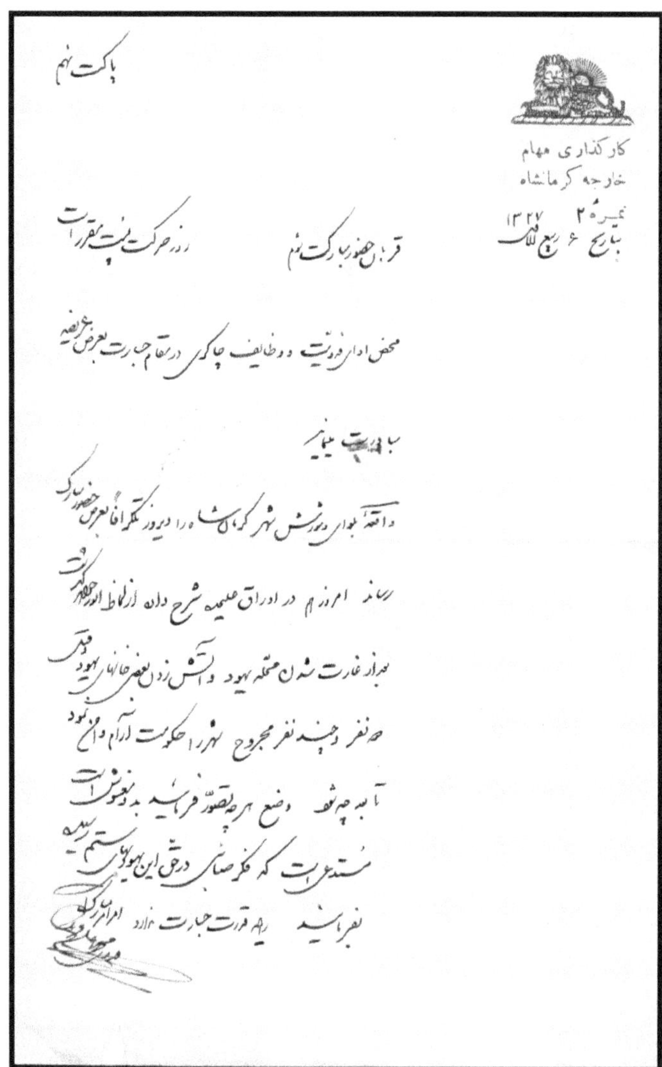

NO.6 DDSR1327-K24-P2-97

کارگزاری مهام خارجه کرمانشاهان
۲ ربیع الاول ۱۳۲۷
قربان حضور مبارکت شوم روز حرکت پست مقرر است
محض ادای فدویت و ادای چاکری در مقام جسارت به عرض عریضه مبادرت می نماید واقعه بلوا و شورش شهر کرمانشاهان را دیروز تلگرافا به عرض حضور مبارک رساند. امروز هم در اوراق علیحده شرح داده از لحاظ امور خواهد گذشت. بعد از غارت محله یهود و آتش زدن بعضی خانه های یهود و قتل دو نفر و چند نفر مجروح شهر را حکومت آرام و امن نمود، تا بعد چه شود.
وضع هرچه تصور فرمایید بد و مغشوش است، مستعی است که فکر صائبی در حق این یهودی های ستم دیده بفرمایید.
زیاده قدرت جسارت ندارد
فدوی محمد علی فرید الملک؟

Office of karguzar of Kermanshahan

2 Rabi` al-Avval 1327/22 March 1909

Yesterday, I sent a report about the disturbances and riots in Kermanshahan by telegraph. Today, I will send you separately a report on the situation. After looting the Jewish quarter, the burning of some Jewish houses and the killing of two people and injuring some others, the government has the situation under control.

The situation is very bad and please think of this poor tyrannized Jewish people.

Yours Sincerely

Mohammad `Ali Farid al-Molk

NO.7 DDSR1327-K56-P3-13

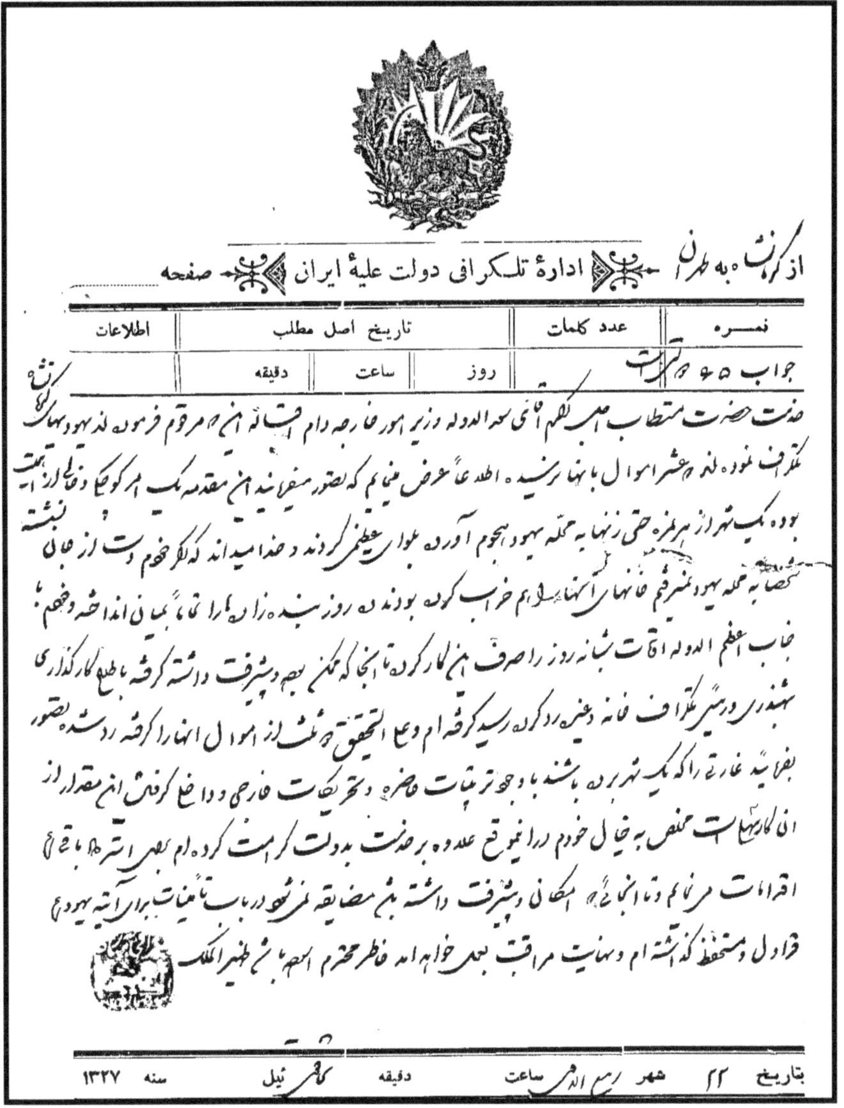

از کرمانشاه به طهران اداره تلگرافی دولت علیه ایران صفحه

نمره	عدد کلمات	تاریخ اصل مطلب			اطلاعات
		روز	ساعت	دقیقه	

بتاریخ ۲۲ شهر ربیع الاول ساعت دقیقه سنه ۱۳۲۷

از کرمانشاه به تهران
۲۲ ربیع الاول ۱۳۲۷

خدمت حضرت مستطاب اجل اکرم آقای سعدالدوله وزیر امور خارجه دام اقباله این که مرقوم فرموده اند یهودی های کرمانشاه تلگراف نموده اند که عشر اموال به آنها نرسیده اطلاعا عرض می نماییم که تصور می فرمایند این مقدمه یک امر کوچک و خالی از اهمیت بوده یک شهر از هر نمره حتی زنها به محله یهود هجوم آورده بلوای عظیمی کردند و خدا می داند که اگر خودم دست از جان نشسته شخصا به محله یهود نمی رفتم خانه های آنها را هم خراب کرده بودند. ده روز بنده زاده ها را تماما به میان انداخته و خودم با جناب اعظم الدوله اوقات شبانه روز را صرف این کار کرده تا آنجا که ممکن بوده و پیشرفت داشته گرفته به اطلاع کارگزاری شهبندری و رییس تلگرافخانه و غیره رد کرده رسید گرفته ام و علی تحقیق دو ثلث از اموال آنها را گرفته رد شده تصور بفرمایید غارتی را که یک شهر برده باشند با وجود ترتیبات حاضره و تحریکات خارجی و داخلی گرفتن این مقدار از آنها کار سهل است مخلص به خیال خودم در این موقع علاوه بر خدمت به دولت کرامت کرده ام برای استرداد باقی هم اقدامات می نمایم و تا انجایی که امکان پیشرفت داشته باشد مضایقه نمی شود در باب تامینات برای آتیه یهود هم قراول و مستحفظ گذاشته ام و نهایت مراقبت به عمل خواهد آمد. خاطر محترم آسوده باشد

ظهیرالملک

22 Rabi` al-Avval 1327/12 April 1909.

It is brought to the attention of H.E. Sa`d al-Dowleh, the Minister of Foreign Affairs that the Jewish community of Kermanshah had telegraphed that they have not received one tenth of their plundered goods. There was a very major crisis in the city, everybody, even women rushed to the Jewish quarter and God knows, if I personally had not gone there, they [people] might also have destroyed their houses.

My sons were helping for ten days; A`zam al-Dowleh and I were doing our best to get the plundered goods back and delivered to the office of the karguzar. Till now, two third's of the plundered goods have been returned. Just think about it, a crisis in which the whole city was involved, plus the foreign and domestic agitation, does not make it easy to get the total amount back.

I will make arrangements to get the remaining amount. I will do my utmost for the safety of the Jews and have set guards for their quarter.

Zahir al-Molk

از کرمانشاه به طهران

اداره تلگرافی دولت علیهٔ ایران

اطلاعات	تاریخ اصل		عدد کلمات	نمره
		۱۸۸		۱۴

NO.8 DDSR1327-K56-P3-1

تلگراف از کرمانشاه به طهران

توسط وزارت جلیله امور خارجه به خاک پای معدلت پیرای اقدس شاهنشاهی ارواحنا فداه. چنانچه به وسایل متعدده به عرض رسیده در پنجم این ماه جمعی از مسلمانان کرمانشاه بقعتا؟ به محله یهود ریخته، سیصد خانوار را به کلی غارت و چند نفر را مجروح و مقتول ساختند. ایالت جلیله به اتفاق بعضی از علما اقدامات غیرتمندانه در استرداد منهوبات به عمل آوردند اعم از اینکه یک عشر از اموال این مظلومان مسترد نگشته شخص قاتل که مرتکب قتل و جرح شده است علنا به قتا خود اقرار و افتخار می نماید بلکه همه روزه این مظلومان را تهدید و تخویف می نماید، عیال و اطفال این بدبختان خواب و آرام ندارند اجمالا ظلمی بر این بی کسان وارد که زمان بخت النصر همچه اتفاقی نیافتاده، ملجا و پناهی جز آستان معدلت بنیان ملوکانه نداریم با کمال تضرع و ...؟ اولا تایید و نصرت تبریز سلطنت را از حق تعالی مسئلت می نماییم، ثانیا استدعای عاجزانه داریم در جواب این عریضه تلگرافی جهان مطاع بر دفع قاتل و استرداد منهوبات و آسایش مظلومان شرف صدور یابد که این ملت ضعیف شاه پرست آسوده خاطر به دعاگویی ذات اقدس همایونی مشغول باشیم.

جماعت یهود کرمانشاهان

۲۴ ربیع الاول ۱۳۲۷

Telegraph from Kermanshah to Tehran

From the Ministry of Foreign Affairs to His Majesty the Shahenshah.

As we had informed you before, on the fifth day of this month, a group of Moslems attacked the Jewish quarter and plundered about 300 families and injured and killed some others.

The governor and some of the olama tried to distribute the plundered goods, but one-tenth of those has not been found and the killer, who murdered and wounded Jews, not only openly confesses the murder and is proud of that, but also threatens these oppressed ones daily. The wives and children of the unfortunate ones don't have a restful sleep and such cruelty has not occurred since Nebuchadnezzar until now and we beg you to reply to this letter and order to have our plundered goods returned and the murderer arrested so that this weak royalist subjects may in peace pray for his holy majesty..

The Jewish community of Kermanshah

24 Rabi` al-Avval 1327/14 April 1909

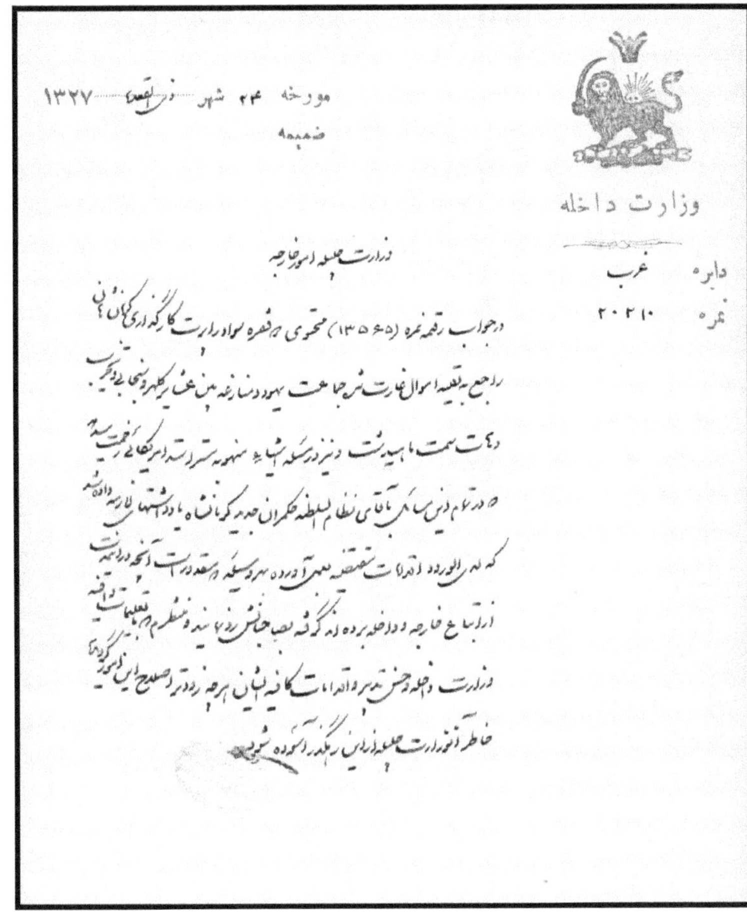

NO.9 DDSR1327-K56-P3-80

وزارت داخله
امور غرب
مورخه ۲۴ شهر ذی القعده ۱۳۲۷
وزارت جلیله امور خارجه
در جواب رقمه نمره (۱۳۵۶۵)
محتوی که فقره سواد راپورت
کارگزاری کرمانشاهان راجع به بقیه
اموال غارت شده جماعت یهود و
منازعه بین عشایر کلهر و سنجابی
و تخریب دهات سمت ماهیدشت و
نیز در مسئله اشیا منهوبه مستر استد
امریکایی زحمت می دهد که در
تمام این مسائل به آقای نظام السلطنه
حکمران جدید کرمانشاه یادداشت های
لازمه داده شده که در؟ ورود اقدامات
مقتضیه به عمل آورده به هر وسیله که
مقدور است آنچه در این مدت از اتباع
داخله و خارجه برده اند، گرفته به
صاحبانشان رد نماید و منتظرم که با
تعلیمات واقعی؟ وزارت داخله و حسن
تدبیر و اقدامات کافیه ایشان هرچه
زودتر اصلاح این امور گردد تا خاطر آن وزارت جلیله از این رهگذر آسوده گردد.

Ministry of Interior

Western Affairs

24 Dhu'-l-Hijjah 1327/5 January 1910

Foreign Ministry Of Affairs

In response to the letter No. 13564 regarding the report of office of karguzar in Kermanshah about the remaining plundered goods of the Jewish community, the conflict between the Kalhor and Sanjabi tribes, the destruction of villages near Mahidasht and the stolen goods of the American Mr. Stead, I should note that we informed Nezam al-Saltaneh, the new governor of Kermanshah, about all these matters, to take effective steps as soon as he arrives in Kermanshah to get back whatever has been taken from national and foreign subjects and we are waiting for the results so that the said Ministry will be satisfied.

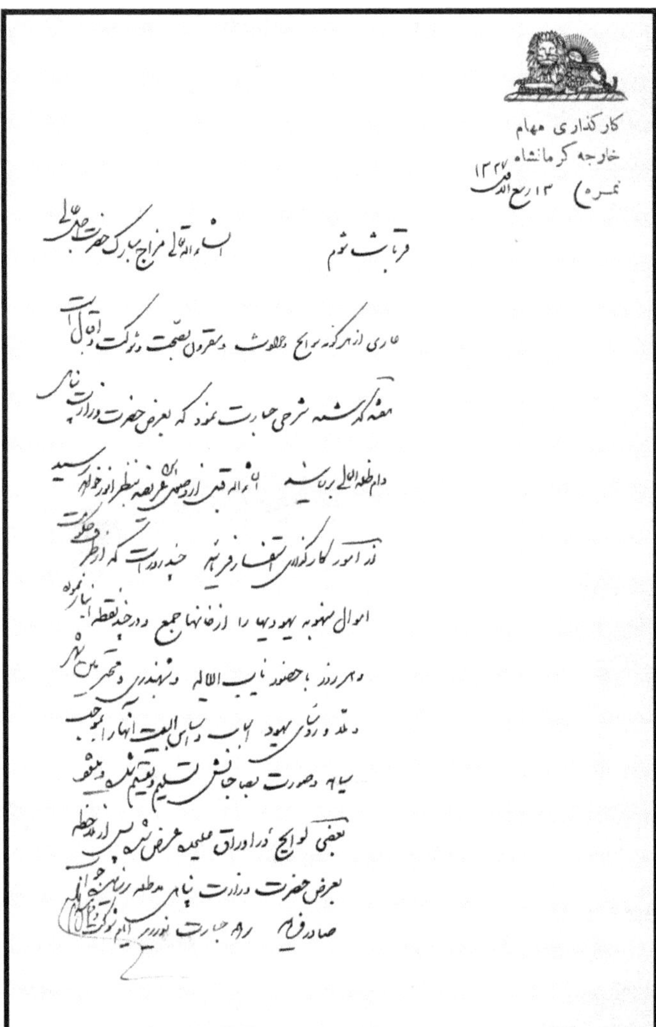
کارگذاری مهام
خارجه کرمانشاه
نمره ( ) ۱۳ ربیع الاول ۱۳۲۷

NO.10 DDSR1327-K24-P2-84

کارگزاری مهام خارجه کرمانشاهان
۱۳ ربیع الاول ۱۳۲۷
قربانت شوم
انشاء اله تعالی مزاج حضرت اجل عالی
عاری از هرگونه سوانح و حوادث و مقرون به صحت و شوکت و اقبال است. هفته گذشته شرحی جسارت نمود که به عرض حضرت وزارت پناهی دام ظله العالی برسانید.
ان شاء الله قبل از وصف؟ این عریضه به نظر انور خواهد رسید.
از امور کارگزاری استفسار فرمایید چند روز است که از طرف حکومت اموال منهوبه یهودی ها را از خانه ها جمع و در چند نقطه انبار نموده و هر روز با حضور نایب الایاله و شهبندری و محترمین شهر و ملا و روئسای یهود اسباب و اساس البیت آنها را به موجب سیاهه و صورت به صاحبانشان تسلیم و تقسیم شد و می شود.
بعضی لوایح که د اوراق علیحده عرض شد، پس از ملاحظه به عرض حضرت وزارت پناه مدظله رسید جواب صادر فرمایید.
زیاده جسارت نمی ورزد
ایام شوکت و اقبال....

The office of kargozar of Kermanshah

13 Rabi` al-Avval 1327/3 April 1909

Hope you are well and everything is fine.

Last week I sent you a report to be delivered to the Minister.

During the last few days we were busy getting back the plundered goods belonging to the Jews, taking them from some houses and storing them in a some safe places and returning them to their owners, in accordance with the list, in the presence of deputy-governor, the [Ottoman] consul, the city's notables and the priest and leaders of the Jews.

NO.11 DDSR1311-K23-P20

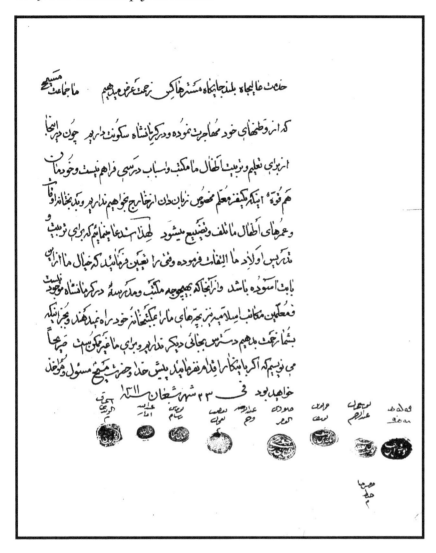

خدمت عالیجاه بلند جایگاه مستر هاکس زحمت عرض میدهیم

ما جماعت مسیح که از دیار های خود مهاجرت نموده و در کرمانشاه سکونت داریم چون در اینجا از برای تعلیم و تربیت اطفال ما مکتب و اسباب درسی فراهم نیست و خودمان هم قوه اینکه یک نفر معلم مخصوص زبان دان از خارج بخواهیم نداریم و بدبختانه اوقات و عمرهای اطفال ما تلف و تضییع می شود. لهذا استدعا می نماییم که برای تربیت و تدریس اولاد ما التفات فرموده وقتی را تعیین فرمایید که خیال ما از این بابت آسوده باشد و از آنجا که به هیچ وجه مکتب و مدرسه در کرمانشاه موجود نیست و معلمین مکاتب اسلامیه نیز بچه های ما را به مکتبخانه خود راه نمیدهند و به جز اینکه به شما زحمت بدهیم دسترس به جای دیگر نداریم و برای ما غیر ممکن است. صریحا می نویسیم که اگر به این کار اقدام نفرمایید پیش خدا و حضرت مسیح مسئول و مواخذ خواهید بود.

فی ۲۳ شهر شعبان سنه ۱۳۱۱

جای مهرها

To Mr. Hoax

We, Christian people, moved from our homes and live in Kermanshah, where there is no school for our children to study and we cannot afford a teacher, who knows foreign languages, from abroad, as we wish. Unfortunately, the life of our children is wasting away. So, we appeal to you to give your attention to the education of our children and give us a time that may set our minds at peace. We have no other choice than you, because there is no school in Kermanshah and teachers of Moslem maktabs don't allow our children into their classes.

Frankly, if you don't accept to do this, you will be responsible before God and Jesus Christ.

23 Shaban 1311/28 February 1894

ATTACHMENT 1

[This Document is the Property of His Britannic Majesty's Government.]

No. 8.—ARCHIVES. 198

[December 20, 1926.]

PERSIA.

CONFIDENTIAL.

SECTION 3. 61

No. 1.

[E 6934/284/34]

Mr. Clive to Sir Austen Chamberlain.—(Received December 20.)

(No. 571.)

Tehran, November 30, 1926.

Sir,

I HAVE the honour to transmit to you herewith a copy of a report addressed to me by the military attaché to this Legation regarding the findings of the court-martial convened to try those officers implicated in the plot said to have been engineered at the end of last summer against the life of His Majesty Reza Shah.

2. The enclosed report gives the sentences imposed by the court-martial on the military officers concerned, but the two civilians implicated still languish in gaol and have yet to be brought to trial. One of them, Mr. Samuel Haim, has been the subject of correspondence between the Foreign Office and the London branch of the Zionist organisation, of which body Mr. Haim was the representative in Persia.

3. There remain many points to be elucidated before the degree of culpability of Mr. Haim in this affair can be established, but it is noteworthy that for a long time past the chief of police and Mr. Haim had been bitter personal enemies. Haim always acted courageously on behalf of his co-religionists and, with parliamentary immunity from arrest to cover him, was never afraid to take up the cudgels in their defence. This attitude evidently exasperated the chief of police, an unscrupulous individual, who resolved to do all that he could to prevent Haim from being elected to the Sixth Legislature.

4. Although Haim soon became aware of the machinations of the chief of police he did not pay much attention to them as, by reason of his popularity with the Jews who were grateful for his fearless protection of their rights, he was certain to be elected by a large majority unless force was used to prevent his election. The chief of police, however, did not scruple to intimidate Haim's chief supporters, threatening them with the displeasure of His Majesty if Haim were returned as their candidate, and it soon became evident that instructions had been issued to the chiefs of the various police commissariats to prevent Haim's election.

5. About this time a Jew, accused of theft, had been brutally flogged by the police in order to wring from him a confession of guilt, and Haim obtained a photograph showing the weals and stripes on the man's back and shoulders. On the occasion of the presentation to His Majesty of a coronation gift from the Jewish community, Haim, who headed the delegation chosen for that purpose, presented the photograph to His Majesty with the prayer that His Majesty might be graciously pleased to prevent in future the meting out of such savage treatment to the Jews. His Majesty promised to take suitable steps and sent for the chief of police. What transpired at this interview is not known, but a few hours later Haim was arrested and put into prison. He was released a few days later, but only to find that during his incarceration the Jewish election had been hurried forward, and no hope remained of his being elected.

6. Rashly he sought to revenge himself. Anonymous leaflets in which threats were made against His Majesty and others were secretly distributed in the town. The police investigated the matter and, rightly or wrongly, the origin of these leaflets was traced to Haim, who was again arrested with others on the charge of conspiring against the life of His Majesty.

7. Rebellions in Azerbaijan and Khorassan broke out at this time, and Salar-ed-Dowleh was still trying to stir up trouble in Kurdistan. The Shah at once suspected that foreign agents were at work. Haim in the course of his duties as Zionist representative had frequently visited this Legation, and unscrupulous persons had evidently tried to make capital out of this fact, with the result that His Majesty even appears at one time to have thought that this Legation was not without knowledge of the plot.

8. Meanwhile, Haim's imprisonment leaves the Zionist organisation in Persia without a responsible head. As it is impossible to say when he will be tried or what the sentence will be, I would suggest that it might be as well if the organisation were

[1488 u—3]

2

to choose another representative to carry out at least provisionally the duties formerly fulfilled by Mr. Haim.

I have, &c.
R. H. CLIVE.

Enclosure in No. 1.

Major Fraser to Mr. Clive.

(No. 412. Confidential.)

Sir,

Tehran, November 23, 1926.

I HAVE the honour to inform you that I was yesterday very confidentially informed of the details of the so-called plot against the Shah to which reference was made in my Summaries of Intelligence Nos. 20 and 23, paragraphs 9 and 8 respectively. My informant was the president of the court-martial that tried the military officers concerned, and I have good reason for believing his version to be true.

2. The conspiracy originated with the Jewish ex-Deputy, Haim, who has for some time been nursing a bitter grudge against the chief of the police, whom he blames for his failure to be re-elected Deputy for the Jews and whom he accuses of wrongful imprisonment. This resentment apparently spread to the whole régime of which the chief of police was a servant. Haim found a willing assistant in Sheikh-ul-Araqeinzadeh, also an ex-Deputy, suffering from a similar grievance aggrevated by the cessation of a monthly allowance previously received from the Shah in return for his support among the smaller mullahs. These two decided to approach Sarhang (Colonel) Mahmud Khan Pouladin, the officer commanding the Pahlavi regiment of infantry, who was, they knew, burning with indignation at a public slight put upon him by his divisional commander, the Shah's favourite general. These three had some conversations regarding the possibility of organising a *coup* to overthrow the present régime. Colonel Mahmud Khan was emphatically of the opinion that nothing could be hoped for from the army in Tehran, the Shah's influence was much too strong. Three other officers and an ex-army doctor, friends of the original conspirators, who were consulted, also condemned the idea as ridiculous, and it was abandoned for the time being. But Haim and Sheikh-ul-Araqeinzadeh decided to relieve their feelings by composing and distributing secretly gelatine leaflets abusing and threatening the Shah. The other members of the party, although aware of it, appear to have had no part in this, except that Colonel Mahmud Khan procured the gelatine. When the mass of evidence had been sifted, no activities other than the above could be proved against any of the accused.

3. The police produced incriminating evidence covering 300 pages. The Shah did not read it, but he did read the police summing-up of the case, which was that the prisoners had been engaged in a plot against his life and throne. He immediately ordered the execution of the principals, and was with difficulty persuaded by the Prime Minister that at least the appearance of a trial was necessary to avoid creating a very bad impression abroad, particularly in America. Having agreed to a court-martial, he personally gave orders to the president of the court (my informant) that the proceedings were to be completed and the executious carried out within twenty-four hours. The general dared to suggest that this would hardly achieve the purpose of preventing unfavourable foreign criticism, as it was public property that the police evidence ran into 300 pages. So hasty a trial might create a bad impression, especially as His Majesty had himself, when Prime Minister a year ago, given Persia a complete penal code. The arguments in favour of the preservation of some appearance of legality having converted the Shah, it was not difficult, as the case progressed, to find more and more legal complications. Details of the case became public, and it was evident that any flagrant infraction of the laws would lead to strong protest. The result was that the civilian accused were handed over to the civil courts for trial and the military court found that it could not legally award more than ten years' imprisonment for the offences substantiated. It has accordingly awarded this punishment to Colonel Mahmud Khan, three years' imprisonment to Major Ahmad Khan, combined in both cases with dismissal from the army, and reduction in rank to the two other military officers brought for trial. Of the civilian accused, Sheikh-ul-Araqeinzadeh has been banished, and judgment has not yet been passed by the civil courts on Haim and the ex-army doctor, Amir Khan.

4. It may be mentioned that during the trial the Shah impressed on the president of the court-martial the necessity for ascertaining whence the conspirators had obtained

3

their support. The general subsequently reported that there was no evidence whatsoever of their having received any encouragement from any source. Haim, it was true, had been a visitor to the British Legation, but during the last year he had been seen more frequently in the Soviet Embassy.

5. I am sending copies of this despatch to the Director of Military Operations and Intelligence, War Office, London, and the Deputy Director of Military Intelligence, India.

I have, &c.
W. A. K. FRASER, *Major, I.A.*,
Military Attaché.

Appendix II

Junkers Air Service, Persia: Flight and Price Schedule

Between	Weekly trips	Travel time by road	Travel time by air	Road distance	Passenger fare	1 kilo merchandise or baggage
		Days	Hours	Miles	US$	US$
Tehran-Baghdad	2	3-4	7.5	600	75	0,75
Tehran-Baku	1	2	8	-	65	0.65
Tehran-Bushire	2	3-5	8	757	80	0.80
Tehran-Hamadan	2	1	2.75	235	30	0.30
Tehran-Isfahan	2	1	2.5	269	30	0.30
Tehran-Kermanshah	2	1.5	4.5	353	40	0.40
Tehran-Meshed	1	2-3	6	581	60	0.60
Tehran-Pahlavi	1	1	2	230	30	0.30
Tehran-Shiraz	2	2.5-3	6	581	60	0.60
Baghdad-Hamadan	2	2-3	4.75	365	55	0.55
Baghdad-Kermanshah	2	1.5-2	2.25	247	40	0.40
Baku-Pahlavi	1	1	3	-	40	0.40
Bushire-Isfahan	2	2-4	5	488	35	0.35
Bushire-Shiraz	2	1-2	1.5	176	28	0.28
Hamadan-Kermanshah	2	0.5-1	1.5	118	15	0.15
Isfahan-Shiraz	2	1-2	3	312	35	0.35

Source: Lingeman 1930, p. 49. Appendix IX.

Appendix III

Notice from the 'Poor Fund Committee' of Kermanshah

McDonall telegraphed to this effect on April 11 and was told that the Minister saw no reason to subscribe.

Notice from the "Poor Fund Committee" of Kermanshah

I can let Mc Donall have 50 T^ns if he considers it necessary that he should subscribe. But the subscription should be made in his own name. M.S.
Tel d/d June 7

Summary

Since all the villages around Kermanshah have been plundered during the last few years, the poor villagers have poured into Kermanshah in search of food. It is to be feared that their general destitution will be the cause of many deaths. Therefore, a committee has been formed under the Presidency of the H.H. Ferma Ferma to collect Relief funds.

Subscriptions to be sent to Haji Abdul Hamid, Tabriz merchant, at Kermanshah & Haji Seyyid Kasim, a Kermanshah merchant, at Kermanshah. Both these merchants are members of the 'Poor Fund Committee'.

(I.B.O. subscribed 100 t. Russian Consul 50 t. L. Dray 25 t. etc. etc. No mention of McDonall having made a subscription)

(ورقه [illegible] هیأت اعانه فقرای کرمانشاهان)

چون بواسطه اتفاقات سوء این دوساله ازقبیل قلت زراعت و حدوث قحطی جماعت کثیری فقیر
و بی خانمان در شهر کرمانشاهان که معبر است جمع شده و متصل هم از عراق عرب میرسیدند و بیم
تلف آنها از گرسنگی و بی منزلی میرفت تشکیل هیئت اعانه و اداره برای تهیه آسایش فقراء و عجزهٔ
غریب و بومی و فرستادن غربا زوار باوطان خود در تحت ریاست عبدالحسین میرزای فرمانفرما شد
و از دهم ربیع الثانی مشغول اجراء این امر خیر شدند و راپورت اقدامات هیئت بطبع رسیده
خدمت عموم بزرگان و محترمین هم نوعان و هم وطنان ایفاد میشود که هر یک میل کنند در این
کار خیر که باعث احیای نفوس جمعی ابناء نوع است همراهی فرمایند [illegible] بابت نان و بابت وجه
اعانه هم که تعیین مبلغ آن بسته بهمت عالی اهل خیر است تقدیم گردد

ادرس محل وصول جواب کرمانشاهان تیمچه فراش باشی حجره حاج عبدالحمید تاجر تبریزی
و حاج سید قاسم تاجر کرمانشاهانی که عضو هیئت اعانه و از هیئت مباشرت هستند

[illegible]
دویست و هشت تومان و پنجهزار

اسامی	مبلغ	اسامی	مبلغ
حاج سید علی رفیس	سی و سه تومان	آقا حسین خلف آقا حسن	سه تومان
حاج تقی چاله چاله	بیست تومان	آقا شیر محمد	سه تومان
حاج ابراهیم	ده تومان	آقا میرزا امین	سه تومان
اولاد حاج علی	ده تومان	آقا محمد حاج نادرویس	سه تومان
آقا محمد حسن زین العابدین	هفت تومان	حاج میرزا محمد	سه تومان
حاج رضا علی	پنجتومان	حاج عباس	سه تومان
حاج تقی شوشتری	پنجتومان	کربلائی آقا برار	سه تومان
حاج محمد علی کاشی	پنجتومان	حاج علی داد	سه تومان
آقا غلامحسین	پنجتومان	کربلائی قاسمخان	دو تومان نیم
آقا عبد الحسین	پنجتومان	حاجی علی اصغر	دو تومان
افتخار اصناف	پنجتومان	حاجی قنبر علی	دو تومان
حاج میر محمود	پنجتومان	مشهدی علی آقا	دو تومان
پسرهای حاج آقا	پنجتومان	حاج غلامعلی	دو تومان
حاج غلامعلی	چهار تومان	حاج علیجان	دو تومان
حاج آقا برار	چهار تومان	حاج کاظم	دو تومان
کربلائی حاج محمد	سه تومان	کربلائی غلامعلی	دو تومان
کربلائی ناصرخان	سه تومان	کربلائی نوروز	دو تومان
حاج علی اکبر و محمد ابراهیم	پنجتومان	آقا سید عباس	دو تومان
آقا علی اکبر حاج نادرویس	سه تومان	آقا محمد رضای شوشتری	دو تومان
حاج محمد باقر	سه تومان	حاج ابوالقاسم	پانزده قران
آقا سید محسن	سه تومان	آقا ابوالقاسم	پانزده قران
آقا سید جعفر	سه تومان	حسینعلی	یکتومان
مشهدی عباس	سه تومان	آقا علی آقا غفور	یکتومان
میرزا احمد	سه تومان		

صورت اسامی اعانه دهندگان برای فقرای کرمانشاهان [illegible] که تا پانزدهم جمادی الاول [illegible] اعانه شده

(اعانه که در ابتداء یکمرتبه مرحمت شده) (جمع وجه نقد هزار و [illegible] پانصد و بیست تومان)

[illegible] مرحمت شده گندم (صد خروار) فرمانفرما مرحمت کرده اند وجه نقد (هزار و پانصد تومان) [illegible]

جناب ژنرال قونسول روس – پنجاه تومان – بانک شاهنشاهی صد تومان [illegible] رئیس بانک شاهنشاهی کرمانشاهان – بیست و پنج تومان

مسیو [illegible] رئیس بانک – ده تومان – مسیو [illegible] آلیانس – بیست تومان – مسیو [illegible] ده تومان – مسیو [illegible] پنجتومان

(اشخاصیکه ماهیانه مرحمت کرده اند در برج حمل) (جمع اعانه اعیان ششصد و هشتاد و پنجتومان و شش قران)

اسامی اعیان	مبلغ	اسامی	مبلغ	اسامی	مبلغ
معتضدالدوله	شصت و هفت تومان	رئیس تلگرافخانه	شش تومان	دکتر همیون خان	چهار تومان
امین الممالک	شصت و چهار تومان	رئیس پستخانه	شش تومان	نصرة السلطان	سه تومان و سه قران
اسعدالدوله	پنجاه تومان	دکتر عبدالله خان	شش تومان	نصیرالاطباء	سه تومان و سه قران
سالار محتشم	پنجاه تومان	اعتضاد الرعایا	شش تومان	سلیمان میرزا	سه تومان
سردار اجلال	پنجاه تومان	محمدباقر میرزا	پنج تومان	دکتر نظامی میرزا احمد خان	سه تومان
صمصام السلطان	پنجاه تومان	محسن میرزا	پنج تومان	میرزا ابوالقاسمخان	سه تومان
حسین قلیخان	سی تومان	معین الکتاب	پنج تومان	میرزا اسدالله خان	سه تومان
حاج چراغعلی خان	بیست تومان	نصیر دیوان	پنج تومان	حاج ابوالفتح خان	سه تومان
اعتماد الرعایا	پانزده تومان	محمد حسن میرزا	پنج تومان	امیر خان	سه تومان
عنایت الله خان	دوازده تومان نیم	رضا خان سرتیپ	پنج تومان	امین اصناف	دو تومان و پنجقران
رئیس قشون	دوازده تومان	اسمعیل آقا	پنج تومان		
امیر مقتدر	ده تومان	ابوالحسن خان	پنج تومان		
سعید دیوان	ده تومان	میرزا عبدالله خان	پنج تومان		
کارگذار	ده تومان	میرزا فضل الله خان	پنج تومان		
رئیس نظمیه	ده تومان	انتصار نظام	پنج تومان		
حاج کلانتر	ده تومان	معین نظام	پنج تومان		
آقا قلیخان	ده تومان	امین همیون	پنج تومان		
میرزا علی اکبرخان	ده تومان	امین الرعایا	پنج تومان		
بنان السلطنه	ده تومان	قوام الایاله	پنج تومان		
آقا سید حسن	ده تومان	انتظام الرعایا	پنج تومان		
حاج آبدار باشی	ده تومان	انتصار الرعایا	پنج تومان		
سالار مظفر	ده تومان	حشمت السلطان	پنج تومان		

[illegible]

اسامی	مبلغ	اسامی	مبلغ	اسامی	مبلغ
[illegible] حسن	بیست و پنجتومان	حاج سید غفور	پنجتومان	آقا فتح الله	سه تومان
[illegible] محمد	بیست تومان	حاج محمد باقر	پنجتومان	آقا عبدالحمید	سه تومان
[illegible] آقا احمد	بیست تومان	حاج محمد جعفر	پنجتومان	برادر میرزا بابا	سه تومان
[illegible] محمدعلی	بیست تومان	ناظم التجار	پنجتومان	آقا تقی	سه تومان
[illegible] التجار	پانزده تومان	آقا خلیل	پنجتومان	آقا میرزا احمد	سه تومان
[illegible] عبدالباقی	پانزده تومان	حاج ابوالحسن	پنجتومان	میرزا حبیب	دو تومان
[illegible] قاسم	پانزده تومان	حاج احمد پشم چی	پنجتومان	مشهدی عباسقلی	یک تومان
[illegible] نصرالله	ده تومان	حاج حسن	پنجتومان		
[illegible] غلامحسین	ده تومان	حاج محمد ابراهیم	پنجتومان		
[illegible] علی بابا	ده تومان	حاج حسین	پنجتومان		
[illegible] محمد حسین	ده تومان	حاج میرزا آقاجان	پنجتومان		
[illegible] عبدالحمید	ده تومان	حاج محمد کاشی	چهارتومان		
حاج غفور	ده تومان	آقا میرزا بابا	چهارتومان		
[illegible] رستم	هفت تومان و نیم	حاج عباس	سه تومان نیم		
[illegible] فرج	هفت تومان و نیم	آقا غلامحسین	سه تومان نیم		
آقا حسین کاشی	هفت تومان و نیم	آقا غلامعلی	سه تومان نیم		
[illegible] غلامعلی	هفت تومان و نیم	حاج احمد یزدی	سه تومان		
[illegible] اسد	هفت تومان و نیم	حاج محمد حسن	سه تومان		
[illegible] صراف باشی	هفت تومان و نیم	آقا علی اکبر کاشی	سه تومان		
[illegible] سید محمد	هفت تومان و نیم	حاج محمد کاشی	سه تومان		
حاج علی اکبر ترک	شش تومان	حاج محمود	سه تومان		
حاج ملا طاهر	شش تومان	کربلائی محمد	سه تومان		
حاج ملا محمد	پنجتومان	آقا سید محمد	سه تومان		
حاج سید مهدی	پنجتومان	شیخ علی اکبر	سه تومان		

(راپورت (نمره) (۲) اقدامات هیئت مباشرت اعانه فقرا از بیستم ربیع الثانی الی یازدهم جمادی الاول)

(۱) روانه نمودن عدهٔ از فقرا باوطان خود موافق صورت ذیل اینها از عتبات عالیات مراجعت کرده و در اینجا حیران و معطل بودند بهمان ترتیب حالی که در نمره اول عرض شده همه را خرجی راه داده روانه [illegible] داشته اسم اینها [illegible] بود در دو نفر علاوه بر آن اشخاصی هستند که در راپورت نمره اول عرض شده که با آنها جمعاً میشوند هشتصد و بیست و چهار نفر ـ

(بیستم ربیع الثانی فرستاده شده پنجاه و سه نفر) (بیست و چهارم ربیع الثانی چهل نفر) (بیست و ششم ایضاً سی و سه نفر) (بیست و هفتم چهل نفر) (چهارم جمادی الاولی چهل و هشت نفر) (پنجم جمادی الاولی پنجاه نفر) (هفتم ایضاً سی و پنج نفر) (نهم ایضاً چهل و سه نفر) (یازدهم ایضاً بیست و چهار نفر) (چهاردهم جمادی الاولی بیست و شش نفر)

(۲) خریداری و تهیه هشتاد عدد بیل و کلنگ و [illegible] خاک کش برای کار کردن و مشغول داشتن فقرای بومی که در گاریخانه با زن و بچه منزل دارند و پس از گرفتن نان مرسومی برای گدائی در کوچه‌های شهر پراکنده شده اسباب زحمت مردم شده‌اند ـ

(۳) کشیدن [illegible] [illegible]

(٤) شروع ساختن خیابان مذکور [illegible] [illegible] ساعت از روز گذشته مشغول کار میشوند تا ظهر پس [illegible] یک نان گرفته سر کار میروند تا یک ساعت بغروب آفتاب دو نان برای شب خود گرفته بمنزل خود که گاریخانه است میروند ـ

(۵) بیرون آمدن ۹ نفر از مریضخانه مخصوص فقرا که هر یک در کمال سختی مریض بودند و بحمدالله با کمال خوبی معالجه شده خارج شدند اسامی آنها از قرار ذیل است ـ

ـ سید احمد رشتی ـ ـ اصغر عراقی ـ ـ حاج عباس [illegible] ـ ـ عزیز اسدآبادی ـ ـ اسمعیل اسدآبادی ـ ـ حسین اصفهانی ـ ـ علی اکبر عراقی ـ ـ بیوه مرحوم عبدالله قم ـ ـ سیده فاطمه ـ

(۶) تولد دو طفل یکی ذکور و یکی اناث در منزل فقرا طفل اناث پدر و مادر داشت اما قادر بر اینکه مولود خود را بپوشانند نبودند و طفل ذکور پدرش حالی بود که در حمله یار محمد خان بشهر از تفنگ اینها ناگهان گلوله خورده و مرده بود مادرش بگاریخانه آمده منزل داشت برای هر دو طفل لباس و برای مادرهاشان مناسب تهیه دیده آسوده شدند برحسب امر حضرت فرمانفرما دختر را شمس الفقرا و پسر را فقیر الله اسم گذاردند

(۷) صورت قندی است که از دهم ربیع الثانی که شروع بجمع آوری فقرا شده است تا کنون که یازدهم جمادی الاولی است از دکان گاریخانه که جمعاً میشود شصت خروار و پنجاه من طبخ و بفقرا داده شده ـ

(دهم ربیع الثانی صدو یازده من) (یازدهم ربیع الثانی صدو شانزده من) (دوازدهم صدو چهل من) (سیزدهم صدو هشتاد و چهار من) (چهاردهم صدو بیست و هشت من) (پانزدهم صدو بیست و هشت من) (شانزدهم صدو چهل و شش من) (هفدهم صدو چهل و شش من) (هجدهم صدو پنجاه من) (نوزدهم صدو پنجاه و شش من) (بیستم صدو شصت و نه من) (بیست و یکم صدو هفتاد و شش من)

(بیست و دوم صد و شصت و چهار من) (بیست و سوم صد و هشتاد من ده سیر) - بیست و چهارم صد و [illegible] و هشت من - - بیست و پنجم صد و نود و نه من سی سیر)

- بیست و ششم دو خروار و چهل و هشت من - - بیست و هفتم صد و هشتاد و هشت من - - بیست و هشتم صد و هشتاد و هشت من و نیم -

- بیست و نهم صد و شصت و یک من - - غره جمادی الاولی صد و هشتاد و یک من - - دوم ایضاً صد و هشتاد و نه من - - سوم صد و هشتاد و نه من -

- چهارم صد و هشتاد و چهار من - - پنجم دو خروار و سه من - - ششم صد و نود من - - هفتم صد و شصت و پنج من - - هشتم صد و هشتاد و چهار من -

- نهم دو خروار - - دهم صد و هشتاد و دو من - - یازدهم صد و پنجاه و هفت من - - دوازدهم صد و شصت و چهار من - - سیزدهم صد و شصت و پنج من -

چهاردهم صد و هشتاد و چهار من - - پانزدهم صد و هشتاد و هفت من تبریز -

(۸) اقداماتی که در جمع آوری وجه اعانه از محترمین اهل بلد شده از بابت قسط ماه اول اعانه که تقبل فرموده بودند تا سه ماه بدهند که صورت

آنچه تاکنون از کیسه فتوت آقایان اهل بلد از شاهزادگان و اعیان و تجار و کسبه وصول داده اند در ورقه ضمیمه این راپورت با اسامی آنها طبع شده

صورت مشروحی که تاکنون شده بنظر محترم قارئین این راپورت میرسد -

(۹) طبع راپورت سابق و ارسال بولایات و ملوکات و محال لازمه برای اطلاع عموم از اقدامات اهل خیر که اگر میل کنند همراهی فرمایند و حضور محترم

که شاید آقایان اهل بلد از محترمین خارجه و داخله و رؤسای خارج شهر با این آقایانی که همراهی با فقرا کرده اند کمک فرمایند -

(۱۰) تعیین یک باب دیگر دکان خبازی برای رسانیدن نان بفقرا و اهل استحقاق آبرومند شهری در دروازه قصابخانه بمباشرت آقا میرزا [illegible]

خبازباشی از تاریخ پنجشنبه دهم شهر جاری که روزی یکخروار نان توسط علماء اعلام بمستحقین اهل بلد داده شود که تا امروز پنجخروار داده شده

(۱۱) جات نمودن دوازده هزار بلیت باسم دکان قصابخانه که هر یک ده سیر نان است که بمستحقین داده شود که برده از آن دکان نان بگیرند

این دکان از وجه اعانه که تازه جمع شده مخصوص فقرای آبرومند شهری دایر گردید که بلیتها را علماء بان اشخاص آبرومند که میشناسند توزیع

نمایند و آنها آمده نان بگیرند -

(۱۲) از اعیان و تجار و اصناف از بزاز و خباز که [illegible] در اداء اعانه همراهی کرده اند [illegible]

داریم که اساس این کار خیر را بانی شدند و در کل و جزو این امر دایم صرف وقت میفرمایند و نیز از جماعت قصابها امتنان داریم که از اول

امر شکنبه گوسفندهای خود را که یکی ده شاهی قیمت دارد برحسب امر ایالت برای قوت فقرا میدهند و امید واریم که سایرین از طبقات

اهل ولایت هم تاسی باین صاحبان فتوت فرموده داخل این کار خیر شوند که در راپورت دیگر اسامی شریف آنها را هم در عداد

اعانه دهندگان درج و عرض نمائیم -

(۱۳) تا این تاریخ آنچه از خیابان که فقرا ساخته اند هشتصد ذرع طول و عرض خیابان همه جا ده ذرع است و از دو طرف هم دو نهر برای

فاضل آب زمستان کشیده شده -

(۱۴) تشریف فرمائی حضرت ایالت در یوم چهاردهم بمنزل فقرا و اظهار غمخواری و مهربانی بفرد فرد آنها و اعطای نفری [illegible] دینار پول

[illegible] بزرگها و متوسطها یکعباسی و اطفال صد دینار که جمعاً [illegible] تومان و سرکشی بدکان خبازی و امتحان نان آن کمال تشکر را داریم

(هیئت مباشرت)

(حاج ساعد همایون) (امین الممالک) (شیخ علی اصغر) (حاج عبدالحمید تاجر تبریزی) (حاج سید قاسم تاجر کرمانشاهانی)

این راپورت در یوم چهارشنبه شانزدهم در محضر کمیسیونی که در تحت ریاست ایالت تشکیل شده بود قرائت گردید و مایه مسرت و امتنان همه شد

آقا محمد مهدی آقا رحیم آقا شیخ هادی اشرف الذاکرین آقا سید رضا حاج ملا حسین سلطان المداحین اسعدالدوله رئیس التجار

مدحت الممالک محمد باقر میرزا حاج هادی بهبهان

Source: FO 248/1073, enclosure in McDouall to Tehran, 24/06/1913.

Appendix IV

Landowners Reaction To New Wheat Assessment Regulations

D.O. No. 12 A/PA

Kermanshah

20th July 1942.

My dear [G.F.] Squire,

As I have just got back from a tour of Senandaj, Hamadan and Malayer you may perhaps be interested in the following information.

2. As far as I could gather all the landlords round Hamadan and Malayer are up in arms about the new scheme for assessing and collecting wheat. The landlords say that they cannot estimate the crop accurately until they see it on the threshing floor and that the new method means "be honest and lose, or bribe us and we agree to your figures." They also say that the arbitration commissions will never function properly. The Finance people say that, as the arbitration commissions will mostly be landowners, they will not be able to cope with landowners who underestimate their crops. Two influential landowners, one in Hamadan and one in Malayer, said that, if the Government were to make one landlord in each area responsible for meeting Government requirements, the Government would get as much wheat as they want. The Ustandar here has also expressed the same opinion. I pass on the above for what it is worth.

3. I was told in Malayer that a landowner named Amin-i-Madani is inciting local landowners not to hand over their wheat to the Government and that he is acting in collusion with his brother Malik-i-Madani who is a deputy in the Majliss. This information was given to me by another landowner named Habib Azoodi (Saham-ul-Mulk) and may be false and due to personal enmity. However, I pass it on for what it is worth.

4. I was rather disturbed by the increase in the discontent expressed by the peasants with whom I talked round Hamadan and Malayer. They are much more vocal than formerly and they all complain that they get no sugar or cloth, and many complain that they get no tea, matches or Kerosine. They say that they have to do all the work to produce grain for the towns and get nothing in return. This increased expression of discontent is all the more disturbing as there have recently been instances of attacks on officials of the Finance Department. One incident took place at Sunghur, north west of Kangavar a crowd of villagers invaded the house of the

local Director of Finance, pulled his hair and beat him mildly. The cause of this outbreak was dissatisfaction at getting no sugar. Another more serious incident took place at Galpaigan on the 17th July. According to the report which reached Malayer 2,000 villagers attacked and burnt the local finance office and 100 troops were sent from Burujird to restore order. This, of course, is probably exaggerated, but an incident did occur and, coupled with the increasing discontent of the country people, makes me somewhat pessimistic as to the future, especially as some landowners have for some time told me that they were apprehensive of trouble among the peasantry.

5. In Burujird recently there was only wheat for 2 days. Hobbins has, I believe, telegraphed to you about this. On my way back from Malayer I stopped at Tuisarkan and called on the bakshdar who was in a state of considerable excitement over the bread situation. It appears that for the needs of the people of this small town 7 Kharvars of wheat daily are necessary, but Ashtiani, who is in charge of wheat collection and distribution in Malayer, Sultanabad, Burujird, Galpaigan and Khurramabad, reduced this amount arbitrarily to 6 Kharvars with the result that there was not enough to go around and the bakers threatened to strike. This story I verified. I have already told you about Ashtiani, who is universally hated by officials, landowners and the people and whom the Security people want removed owing to his virulent anti-British propaganda. It looks to me as if Ashtiani may deliberately be making trouble. He is, of course, protected by Dr Naficy. I am sure, however, that as long as he remains where he is there will be trouble and possibly riots. As his area contains our road to Russia I think he really should be moved before more trouble takes place.

6. The wheat situation here is not good, as Majidzadeh told me today that there was wheat in Kermanshah for only twelve days. Nothing effective has yet been done about hoarding. Popular feeling here is bad owing to the departure of Ghiami, the intrigues of Majidzadeh against the Ustandar and the stagnation of the administration. If the price of bread is put up I am very much afraid there will be riots, which may assume an anti-British complexion, in view of the war news and the increased activity of anti-British propagandists. I do hope that bread will be kept at its current price at any rate for the time being. I have received reliable information that Majidzadeh reported to Tehran that, as the Ustandar was a landowner, he would not support the Finance Department in any way. On this report the Persian Government were thinking of replacing him. This report is in my opinion false. Majidzadeh is openly intriguing against the Ustandar, who is avowedly pro-British, and to a lesser degree against me. As you know I have always backed Majidzadeh but I fear my confidence was misplaced. We need a severe pulling up and I hope he will get it.

7. On the whole things are not good here. Security is getting worse and Pusht-i-Kuh (Ilam), which has so far remained quiet, is showing signs of boiling up. If the Ustandar had a Farmandar in Kermanshah and could leave here and visit Ilam he could probably keep the tribes quiet. Similarly if the Farmandar of Ilam had some tyres for his car he could so something. Can anything be done to get these people some tyres? I have tried Tenth Army but have had no reply.

8. Please forgive this long letter but I wanted to tell you how things are and to ask for any assistance you can give us. The prompt despatch of Tabataba'i, appointed as Farmandar of Shahabad, would help, so would the arrival of a good Farmandar here. Also action to stop these intrigues against the Ustandar by Majidzadeh would greatly assist.

9. In Hamadan and Malayer there is a good deal of bitter criticism pf the Sohaily cabinet among the upper classes, who describe them as "a gang of crooks supported by the British." One landowner said that we were becoming very unpopular in the capital and that the Russians were becoming more popular. But you know more about the capital than I do!!

10. I am sending copies of this letter to General Quinan, Cook, General Mayne and General Wordsworth.

Yours sincerely
F.A.G. Cook

To: G.F. Squqire, Esq.
British Legation
Tehran.

Source: FO 248/1414, Fletcher to Squire, Kermanshah 20/07/1942

Appendix V

Petition of Persian Merchants About The Qarasuran

Translation

To H.B.M. Consul, Kermanshah [23 December 1913]

We beg to make the following petition. Last year the road from Kermanshah to Hamadan was very unsafe, which we brought to your notice and you took action. The Provincial Government took action and the road was put in good order and the money that had been taken in the name of karasurani was stopped and the rate of that road was made satisfactory and now is so. Freight to Hamadan which formerly was twenty tomans a load is now about five tomans and we are all thankful. But as to the road from Mahidasht to Kasr, large sums are taken from the muleteers in the name of karasurani and this amount is added to the freight so that the freight of three tomans a load to Kasr is now twenty tomans, and this is a cause of loss to the firms and it is near that the door of trade will be closed. We beg you that you will bring this matter to the notice of the Province and the Government, in order that as soon as possible they give orders to stop this tyranny, otherwise the goods of British merchants will not be sent to Persia.

(Signed)

For Mir Abdul Baqi & Sons	Seyed Hassan	**On account British firms**	H. Ahmed Hamadani
On account British firm	Toeg & Sofer	**On account British firm**	Ebrahim Yusef
For David Sassoon	Yakub David Kahtan	**On account Meneshi Saleh & Co.**	Seyed Nasrullah
On account Abdela & Mitchel & Co	David Aboodi	**On account Isaacs Brothers**	Yusuf Meyer & Sons
On account Abdela Elias Dungur	Shaul Abdulla Levy (British subject)	**On account Abdullah Elias**	Ezra Salman

Source: FO 248/1073, Enclosure in Consul McDouall's no. 109 of 30/12/1913

[Persian text img 7346

"These agents sell on commission or forward goods on account of the [British] firms, or are their correspondents in Kermanshah. The principal firm here Mir Abdul Baqi and Sons deals with five Manchester firms, and Haji Ahmed Hamadani chiefly forwarding, for several others and the Baghdad firms of Messrs Stephen Lynch and Co. and Messrs Blockie Cree and Co. The Manchester firms are Messrs Isaacs Brothers; David Sassoon & Co; Charles Sassoon & Co; Holdsworth Hougie & Co.; David and Sons; Dungur (2 firms) Shashua Dunoos Somech; Mashal; Abdela & Mitchel; Abdula Elias; and one or two others."

Source: FO 248/1073, McDouall to Townley, no. 109 30/12/1913.

Appendix VI

The Turkish Sanitary Service and the Shiah Pilgrimage

Regulation for 'fresh' bodies. – No fresh body is, in principle, admitted for burial at Kerbela or Nejef, unless death has occurred at a place not more than 12-hours' journey from these towns. Consequently (save in the case of contraband), no such bodies come from other countries, except in cases where, by special request of the relatives, a body dead for less than three years has been admitted to the country. Such requests had been common in recent years, an on each occasion the Board granted permission, provided certain condition were fulfilled in regard to the carriage of the body. These conditions were laid **[34]** down in the 'Regulations respecting Exhumations at Constantinople' dated December 27th, 1862. [...] Each body would be required to be accompanied by a medical certificate to the effect that death had not been due to infectious disease; and that was further required that the body be placed in a lead coffin, of at least 3 millimetres thickness, closed with screws and bound with three iron bands. The medical certificate was required to be visa'ed by the Sanitary Authority and countersigned by the Turkish Consul in the port of departure. **[35]**

Regulations for 'dry' bodies. – Bodies less than three years dead were first prohibited from entering Turkey from Persia in 1871. On January 8th of that year, when the then Shah of Persia was returning from a pilgrimage to the Shiah cities, his representative entered into a convention, to that effect, with Midhat Pasha, then Vali of Baghdad. Later the prohibition was extended in principle to bodies from Turkish territory. Bodies from other countries arrive either by way of Basra or across the Turco-Persian border.

At Basra very few bodies are imported from India. 'Dry' bodies offer no real danger to the public health, according to the Medical Commission, if accompanied by a certificate that death had occurred at least three years before. Such certificate should be delivered by the municipal authority of the place where the corpse had been exhumed, and could be visa'ed by the Sanitary authority and Turkish Consul in the port of departure.

In the case of dry bodies coming from Persia or Russia across the Persian frontier, the only condition actually required is that death shall have occurred at least three years before. The large majority of these bodies come by way of Kermanshah and Khanekin. At Kermanshah, they undergo a first inspection, by a doctor in the service of the Constantinople Board of Health, who delivers to the bearers a certificate, without charge. This certificate has to be stamped by the Turkish Consul in Kermanshah, who makes a charge of P. 50 (8*s*.4d.). On arrival in Khanikin, the bodies are inspected a second time; the Kermanshah certificates are collected and send to Baghdad, the sanitary tax of P. 50 is collected, and a *tezkéré*, or numbered receipt, is delivered, showing the name of the bearer, and the date and place of decease. These *tezkérés* are examined at each town where there is a health office- more particularly at Kazimein and Musseyid- are finally delivered up to the health office at Nejef, or Kerbela in exchange for a 'burial permit.'

Sanitary Contraband' in dead bodies. — Contraband in 'fresh' bodies. It is evidently far more difficult to smuggle a fresh body than a sack or box of bones. Consequently such attempts when they are made at Khanekin, are generally discovered and frustrated. But a certain number of such bodies do evade the authorities and crossing the frontier at some other point, follow devious routes over the desert and ultimately reach the Shiah sites. Still more numerous are the bodies coming from places in Turkish territory beyond the 12-hour cone. It is to be noted that it has [**36**] never been made clear whether a '12-hours' journey' means a journey on horse-back, by camel, in a carriage or on foot. Actually many fresh bodies arrive with certificates from places at least 24 or even 48 hours away from Kerbela or Nejef, by the quickest mode of travelling. In other cases, persons bringing bodies from outside the zone or even from Persia, get the original certificate exchanged for another in some village or town within the 12-hour zone. All these troubles would disappear if the Commission's proposals above set forth were adopted.

It is not rare apparently for corpses to be brought secretly, at night, accompanied by armed bodies of Arabs or Kurds, numbering several score or even hundreds, who bury the corpses in the cemetery outside the town without any formality. Such contraband will probably always exist, for it could only be met by using armed forces superior to others, and in each instance many lives would probably be sacrificed.

Contraband in fresh bodies is largely practised by professional 'contrabandiers' already mentioned. It seems that all the principal towns in Persia and Mesopotamia have representatives or commissioners in the Shiah cities; they are generally grave-diggers, muleteers, khan-keepers, *Khadims*, and even *sayids* and *ulemas*, who thus gain a very considerable income. The bodies are addressed to such commissioners, who go out into the desert to meet them, and give to the bearers false certificates, testifying that death had occurred in the 12-hour zone.

Contraband in 'dry' bodies. This is mainly, if not solely, practised in order to evade the payment of P. 50 sanitary tax at the frontier and P. 50 stamp duty at Kermanshah; but small as these sums may appear, acts of contraband are exceedingly frequent and are often contrived with great ingenuity. The commonest form of contraband is the carriage of bodies by routes avoiding Khanikin and the other towns where there are sanitary offices; and this can only be met by increasing the number and vigilance of the sanitary guards. But there are many other forms of contraband, and gruesome stories are told of the methods practised. Bags of bones are hidden in bales of goods, such as carpets, rice, hay, barley or other grain, in parcels of loaves or in the saddle of a camel. Two of three bodies are placed in a single sack or box, in the hope that they will pass as one body and only be taxed as such. Sometimes a woman will hang round her waist, under the clothes, the bones of a relation, and declaring herself enceinte, will attempt to pass the sanitary officials; but since a female inspector has been added to the staff of Khanikin this form of fraud has ceased. On one occasion a woman was detected carrying in her arms what purported to be an infant, but which proved to be a sack of bones, on which a child's face had been rudely painted; it as only the exaggerated way in which she was caressing the bundle that led to her detection. Shiahs have even been known to reduce the remains of their relations to powder and attempt to pass this through as flour. Briefly every conceivable trick is adopted to smuggle through dry bodies with or as commercial goods. [**37**]

But there is also another form of contraband, which consists in attempting to smuggle through goods with dead bodies. The bodies are placed in a coffin or box, and surrounded by valuable merchandise, such as saffron, camphor and even fruit, in the hope that the coffin or box will not be opened and that the goods will thus escape the heavy customs dues to which they are liable.

Actually the only means of dealing with such forms of contraband lies in the vigilance of the sanitary officials. When detected, a dry body in contraband is seized and kept until claimed and the sanitary dues are paid; no punishment is inflicted; the bearer is however handed over to the local authorities, but as there exists no law or regulations permitting these to inflict a penalty, the offender is immediately released.

Source: Clemow 1916, pp. 35-38.

Number of Arrivals at Khanekin 1909-14

	Paying	Non-paying
1909-10	26,460	1,862
1910-11	48,364	5,232
1911-12	24,682	2,407
1912-13	29,554	6,751
1913-14	19,658	7,242
Average	29,743	4,698
Total	34,442	

Source: Clemow 1916, p. 15.

Nationality of Arrivals at Khanekin

Year	Persians		Russians		Turkish		Hindoos		English		Barbaris		Afghans		Total	
	Paying	Non-paying	Paying	Non-paying	Paying	Non-paying	Paying	Non-paying	Paying	Non-paying	Paying	Non-paying	Paying	Non-paying	Paying	Non-paying
1909-10	21,023	1,591	1,726	188	3520	14	0	...	...	...	...	...	182	67	26,460	1,862
1901-11	42,808	4,941	1,762	198	3,659	27	6	4	...	...	...	...	129	66	48,364	5,231
1911-12	20,450	2,173	896	90	2,887	4	...	3	...	...	381	131	61	6	24,682	2,407
1912-13	26,967	6,613	1,111	125	1,248	10	2	...	...	3	...	...	43	2	20,334	6,754

Source: Clemow 1916, p. 15.

Theses figures only have an approximate value, because the nationality of passengers were registered in a very imperfect manner. "Thus the number of 'Russian' passengers should undoubtedly be much greater and that of 'Persians' much less, as there seems to have been a tendency to register all persons coming from Persian territory as 'Persians'." Clemow 1916, p. 16.

Appendix VII

List of Governors (1797-1947)

Mostafa Qoli Khan Zanganeh	1794-97	the son of Allah Qoli Khan
Mohammad `Ali Khan Shambayati Qajar	1797-98	
Fath `Ali Khan Qajar	1798-1806	
Mohammad `Ali Mirza Dowlatshah	1806-21	
Mohammad Hoseyn Mirza Heshmat al-Dowleh	1821-26	Son of Dowlatshah
Mohammad Taqi Mirza Hosam al-Saltaneh	1826-28	
Mohammad Hoseyn Mirza Heshmat al-Dowleh	1828-34	
Bahram Mirza Mo`ezz al-Dowleh	1834-36	
Manucher Khan Mo`tamed al-Dowleh	1836-38	
Nur Mohammad Khan Qajar	1839-41	
Hajji Khan Shakki, saheb-ekhtiyar	1841-42	
Abdol-Hoseyn Khan Javanshir	1843-44	Nephew of Hajji Khah Shakki
Mohebb `Ali Khan Maku'i	1844-48	
Eskander Khan Sardar	1848-51	
Emamqoli Mirza Qajar `Emad al-Dowleh	1851-71	
Tahmasp Mirza Mo`ayyad al-Dowleh	1871	
Badi` al-Molk Mirza Heshmat al-Saltaneh	1875-76	
Soltan Morad Mirza Hosam al-Saltaneh	1876-79	
Badi` al-Molk Mirza Heshmat al-Saltaneh	1879-80	
GholamReza Khan Shehab al-Molk	1880-81	
`Abdollah Mirza Heshmat al-Dowleh	1881-82	
Mas`ud Mirza Zell al-Soltan	1882-88	
Mahmud Khan Naser al-Molk	1882-83	deputy governor
Hoseyn Khan Qaragozlu Hosam al-Molk	1884-89	deputy governor
Zeyn al-`Abedin Khan Qaragozlu Hosam al-Molk II	1889-92	
Hasan `Ali Khan Garusi Amir Nezam	1892-96	
Zeyn al-`Abedin Khan Qaragozlu Hosam al-Molk II	1896	
Mirza Mohammad Khan Eqbal al-Dowleh Kashani	1897-1902	
Mehdiqoli Khan Majd al-Dowleh	1902-03	
Ahmad Khan Ala' al-Dowleh	1903-04	
Abdol-Hoseyn Mirza Farmanfarma	1903-06	
Zeyn al-`Abedin Khan Hosam al-Molk, Vazir Afkham	January 1906	
prince Seyf al-Dowleh	2/4 till 6/6 1907	

Mobaser al-Saltaneh	pending arrival above 21/3 to 2/4 1907	
Zahir al-Dowleh	27 June till 9 October 1907	
kargozar acting governor	9 Oct to 15 Nov 1907	
Zahir al-Dowleh	15 Nov to 13 Dec 1907	
no governor or deputy governor	15 Dec 1907 to 11 January 1908	
A`zam al-Dowleh	till end 1908	
Azizollah Mirza Zafar al-Saltaneh	May 1908	
Mohammad Reza Khan Zanganeh Zahir al-Molk	as of about August 1908	
Rezaqoli Khan Nezam al-Saltaneh Mafi	05/01-19/11/1910	
Ali Naqi Mirza Rokn al-Dowleh	16/01-30/04/1911	
Jalal al-Din Mohtasham al-Dowleh	Until October 1911	Deputy/acting
A`zam al-Dowleh	11/1911 - 01/1912	acting
Farrokh Khan Ilkhani Kalhor	10/1911-01/1912	Salar al-Dowleh appointee
Mahmud Khan Ilkhani Kalhor	temp. 1912	Salar al-Dowleh appointee
Abdol-Hoseyn Mirza Farmanfarma, Azad al-Saltaneh	January 1912-August 1914	
Sardar-e Ejlal, acting govenor	after August 1914	acting
Lotf `Ali Khan Amir-e Afkham Bakhtiyari	08/01/1915-06/05/1915	
Mo`tasem al-Molk	06-05-1915-?	acting
Mohammad Khan Eqbal al-Dowleh Kashani	?- 01/02/1916	
Schönemann	1915	De-facto
Nezam al-Saltaneh	01-23/1916	
Russian occupation	23/02-30/06/1916	
Naser al-Saltaneh	06/03-28/06/1916	
Turkish occupation	01/07/16-03/1917	
Nezam al-Saltaneh	07/17-03/1917	
Russian occupation	11/03/1917-08/01/1918	
Ali Khan A`zam Sanjabi Amir Koll	07-11/1917	
Taqi Khan Majd al-Molk	11/1917- ?	
Abbas Mirza Salar Lashkar, son of Farmanfarma Firuz Mirza Nosrat al-Dowleh	27/08/1918-03/1919	
Mohammad Rahim Khan Amir Nezam Qaraqozlu	03/1919-13 April 1920	
Sarem al-Dowleh	14 May 1920-12 April 1921	
Mahmud Khan Paludin	12 April 1920-?	Military governor
Thiqeh al-Eslam	April-July 1920	Civil governor

Abu'l-Fazl Mirza`Azud al-Saltaneh	December 1920-March 1921?	
Mokarram al-Molk Qa'emmaqam-e Tabrizi	June 1922 until October-November 1922	
Mohammad Khan Sardar `Azim	November 1922-June? 1923	
Gholam `Ali Mirza Dowlatshahi Mojallal al-Dowleh	August-September 1923-December 1924	
Mohammad Khan Montazam al-Dowleh	January 1925-January 1926	
Nezam al-Dowleh Amir Nuri	1926	1305
Abu'l-Hasan Khan Neysari Amir Heshmat	1927	1306
Asadollah Mirza Molkara Shehab al-Dowleh	1928-33	1307
Mohsen Khan `Aliabadi Eqtedar al-Dowleh	1933	1312
Ahmad Khan Mohsenni `Emad al-Molk	1933	1312
Asadollah Mirza Molkara Shehab al-Dowleh	1934	1313
Mohammad `Ali Rokni Rokn al-Dowleh	1935	1314
Ahmad Begleri	1936	1315
Fathollah Kalantari	1937	1316
Azizollah Nikpay E`zaz al-Dowleh	1938-September 1941	1317
Sarhang Nasehi	September 1941-25 January 1942	Military governor
Ali Khan A`zam Amir Koll Zanganeh	25 January 1942-January 1943	
Dr. Ahmad Salehi	January-August 1943	
Fahim al-Dowleh	October 1943-?	
Jahanshahi	May 1944-19 August 1945	
Fathollah Kalantari	19 August-December 1945	
Abdol-Hoseyn Shabdiz	January 1946	
Shahab al-Dowleh	September 1946-August 1947	
Sardar Akram	August 1947-?	

Source: Footnotes in the text of chapter seven. Soltani 1381, vol. 4, p. 915 gives different names for the governors as of August 1943, which don't agree with those given in the monthly British consular reports and other contemporary British correspondence. For a list of governors in the 19th century with some additional and/or different names, see Rabino 1904, p. 5.

Appendix VIII

Feelings of Persian Officers Contacted in KMS and HDN (24th March till 23rd April 1942)

General Attitude is summed up in this way: "We hate all foreign troops - be it English, Russian or even German. We like them as individuals except the Russians whom we all loathe. We will fight for the British against the Russians any time but against the Germans we cannot say yet. For if the Germans are strong enough to enter Iran it will be useless to fight against them just as it was useless to fight against the British and Russian Forces. We cannot excuse the British from 'bringing in Russians into Iran'. We believe in the British promise of leaving Iran within six months after the war but it will take six years to drive the Russians out. We doubt very much whether the British will stand by us if the Russians occupied Azerbayjan. We appreciate the British way of doing things. They treat us comparatively better because they have (Tamiz) decency. In short, when compared to the 'Khirs' (the Russian bear) we prefer the British but as an army of occupation we dislike them. We have the same feeling on this point as an Englishman would have if the Germans had occupied parts of England. We know good Englishmen appreciate this sentiment, but the Russians do not realise it at all. If any of us shows little independence of thought or speech he is either transferred or demoted and even dismissed in certain cases. (So the British want us to 'hypocrites'). Those who show pro-British feelings are rewarded. Anyway we are grateful to the British for the rise in our pay.

WHY DO WE LIKE THE GERMANS?

To begin with we have, so far, nothing to dislike them for, while we have reasons to dislike the British and hate the Russians. We have been ruled by force for such a long time that we have come to believe in force. The old Shah was feared because of his power. Years of German propaganda, and lack of it on the British side, told us that Germany was going to be the strongest nation in the World. And it is indeed so today. So most of us like Germany for its 'Zor' or power. But very few realise what she has done to France and other small nations. Let the Allies have some smashing victories and maintain it - people will automatically change their opinions in due course of time. Germany, like Iran, was a poor country. She was rising gradually and she wanted raw materials. She was ready to give technical aid in return. Iran needed this and both shook hands with each other. Britain did not need anything from Iran except oil which she already has got - hence she did not bother very much. During all these years of 'Technical Aid'

Germany was also busy 'Politically'. Hence today she has got an advantage over others. But the main thing is her recent successes and so the Victor has all the applause. Those who think and are wise, they know that today the balance of power of the world is against Germany and sooner or later the Axis will collapse.

War. "Next six months will show which side will win. At present, of course there are good omens for the Axis. We believe Japs will do more harm to the British than the Germans have done. Japs will stir up revolt in India. This will produce reactions in the Indian Army overseas. We know many disgruntled Indians in the British Army.

If the British had not helped Russia the latter would have been defeated long ago. The British will be sorry for all the goods she is sending to Russia at present. We believe that English and the Germans will unite one day against the Russians. We have already heard rumours of 'Peace' between the English and the Germans. We fear Iran will be a battleground once again.

Kurdish Troubles."is due to British directly or indirectly. Let the British forces withdraw for a week and we will fix up the Kurds as we did before. Politics is a dirty game and the result is that today we are fighting amongst ourselves. If the Kurds had no 'foreign' support how could it be possible for one of their chiefs to come 'unarmed' into KMS and go about the streets like a Lord. We have heard him say that he has got presents from the British. A few months ago these so called 'Chiefs' bowed before us. Today it is different. "Inglis ma ra be chara kard". (The chief referred to above is one of Mansur son of Jaffar Sultan who has come here to have a 'Talk' with the Persian Government and also see the British authorities).

PROPAGANDA

"British propaganda is a standing joke amongst us. Whenever we want to express something ineffective we say - it is like the British propaganda (Misal-a- Tabliq-e Inglisi Ast). It is difficult to believe what your posters depict. These posters show British successes alone. If your posters showed some damage on your own side - say a couple of dead British soldiers or a tank on fire and lot of Germans on the other side - it would be some sense. But because your propaganda people probably have never been on the front or have no imagination therefore they produce such silly cartoons which have no meaning for us. Judging from results you cannot justify such propaganda.

Another point is the news. Germany and Italy tells us on the same day about the fall or the capture of a city or town. British Radio tells us on the third or fourth day. But we believe both the sides exaggerate.

Your 'Shaipur' is good. But 'Jahan Azad; contains no good pictures. Persian from London Radio is good, but your best propaganda is the inciting of Russians to commit atrocities on Persians and so win a good name for the British!

Good propaganda is giving employment to the people - not to the Syrians and Armenians alone but to the Irani Muslims too."

Source: FO 248/1414, attachment to Col. Fletcher to G.S. Branch. H.Q. Tenth Army, Baghdad, Kermanshah 29/04/1942 (report by 2nd Lt. Kazi). (Col. Fletcher wrote that "his report seems to be a very accurate summary of the attitude of the majority of Persian officers. He did not meet any of the rabidly anti-British ones so that his report does not cover them").

KMS = Kermanshah; HDN = Hamadan

Appendix IX

Fake Telegram from Mullah Abdullah Mazandrani and Mullah Kazem Khorassani

The document was religious and anti-foreign in nature
Extract Translation
Tel: from Mullah Abdullah Mazandrani and Mullah Kazem Khorassani, 26 Jamadi II 1328
4 July 1910

Through H.H. the Naser ul Mulk, to Ministers of Interior and War and the President of the Majliss.

It is obvious that the sacrifices made and the troubles taken by the Ulema, nobles, and the Sardars were for the maintenance of the Constitution, protection of the faith, progress of the country, execution of the laws of Islam, prevention of the extravagance in the finances and its proper spending on the army and other useful purposes and to get rid off some selfish and sensual persons. The object was not to change that despotic regime for another of the same nature under the name of the Constitution and that the officials should try to get each other into different departments of the government, and, instead of forming an army, to create pernicious departments, to be in open revolt against the religion and instead of carrying out the general amnesty already granted and to reduce the taxes new taxes should be put on everything and, that the members of the different departments especially those of the Justice should act in such a way that people should be disgusted with the Constitution, to prevent our orders respecting the papers "Shargh" and "Iran Now" from being carried out, to create trouble after trouble in order to prevent the evacuation of foreign troops which was nearly done.

By Gods will all the nobles and the national Sardars as well as all the inhabitants of Persia are Muslems and the foundation of the Constitution and liberty cannot be based on anything except on Islam which is everlasting.

Those who love the liberty in Paris may proceed to that city and leave Persia into the hands of those who are the wellwishers of the country so that they may do away with the present abuses and draw up the laws, in presence of the Mujteheds who have been introduced to the Majliss, in accordance with the constitutional laws, to prevent all things forbidden in the Mohamedan religion, to have as few members in different departments as possible especially in those of Justice in which most content and most honest people must be employed. Money must be spent on different departments as little as possible and the greatest bulk of the revenue must be spent on the army for the defence of the country and the faith. The Senate should be convoked as soon as possible. Advocates General should be selected from amongst men of knowledge of the Shar and of integrity. A committee must be appointed to censor the press as it is done in Turkey. Educational laws should be sent to us for our observation.

Sd. Abdullah Mazanderani.

Mohamed Kazem Khorassani.

Source: FO 248/999, enclosure to Knox to Legation, 11/07/1910.

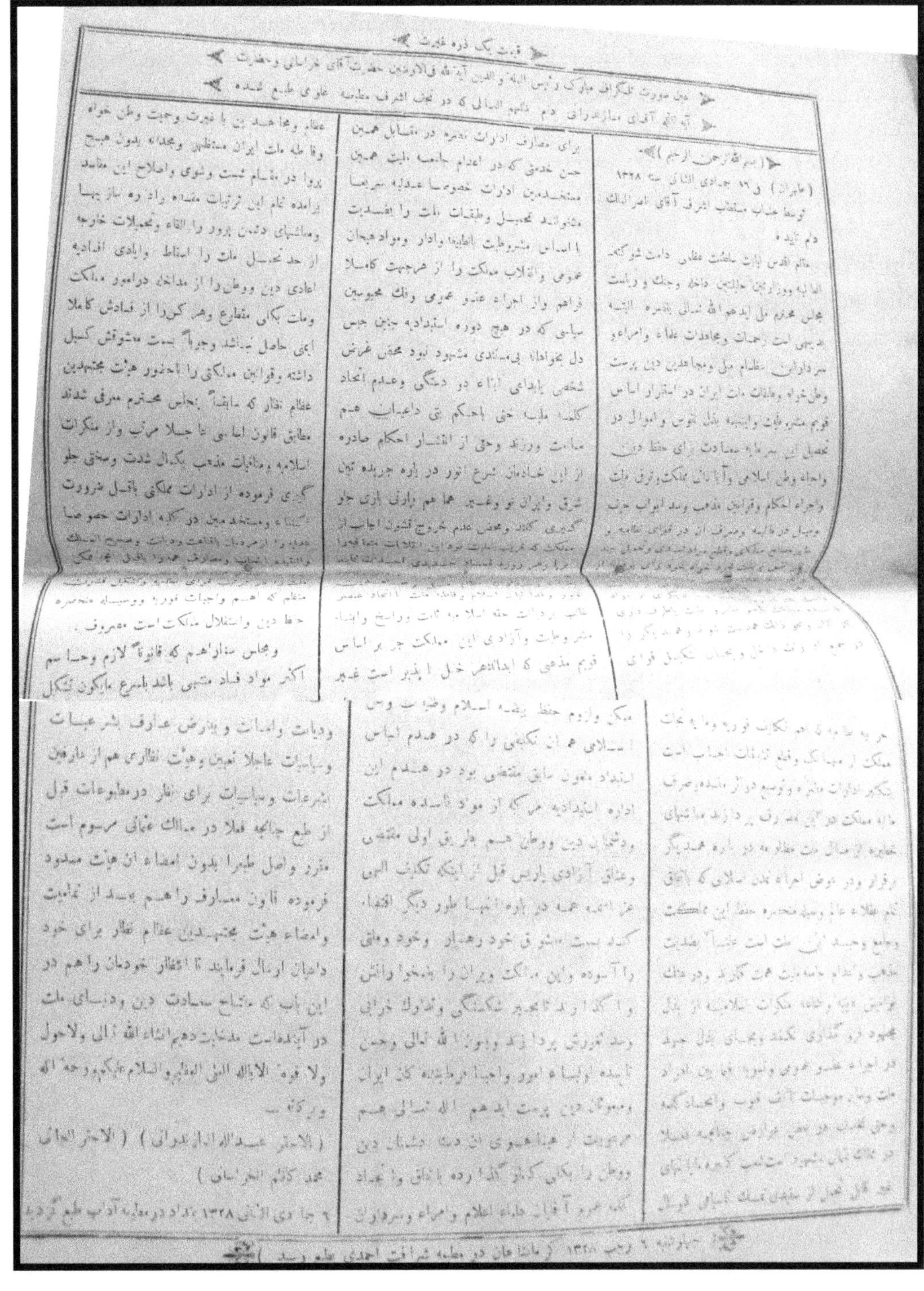

قیمت یک ذره غیرت

متن صورت تلگراف مبارک رئیس الملة والدین آیة الله فی الارضین حضرت آقای خراسانی و حضرت

آیة الله آقای مازندرانی دام ظلهم العالی که در نجف اشرف مطبعه علوی طبع شده

(بسم الله الرحمن الرحیم)

Appendix X

Elections Kermanshah style (1947)

In 1947, in Kermanshah, the Prime Minister made it publicly known that he supported four candidates for the *Majles*: 'Abbas Qubadian, Dr. Mo'aven, 'Aziz Zanganeh and Manuchehr Farmafarmaian. The last two were local leaders of the Democrat party; Aziz Zanganeh was held somewhat in esteem, because of his father Amir Koll, while Farmanfarmaian enjoyed hardly any respect at all. The government departments were urged to only vote for these four candidates. The choice of the two Democrat leaders so incensed the Union of Land Owners and Tribal Leaders that they urged Qubadian to tell his son to see the General Staff and have them changed. He returned saying that the Shah and Gen. Razmara disapproved of both of them and wanted to have Raf'at al-Saltaneh (Hedayat Palizi) and Zahir al-Molk in their place. According to Pullar, the British consul, "the former was extremely right-wing and the latter a man of no experience and little intelligence. If the report is true there appears to be a conflict between the nominees of the Prime Minister and those of the Shah." The landowners were mad at the governor as he chose most of the 'Nazarat' or supervisory members from the Democrat party, which thus would be in control of the elections. [1]

> Apart from the elections nothing of importance happened in this area during the last month. Manoeuvres and tactics were practised by all the candidates and various soundings taken of public opinion. The only notable result of this was the disappearance from the list of candidates of the leader of the local Democrat Party, Manuchehr Farmanfarmayan, whose views and person were not looked on with favour. After a final bid for public opinion he published a document asking the populace to vote for his friends and then departed, according to instructions, to Tehran. Another who fell to the wayside was Dr. Zanganeh, a deputy in the former Majles, who also decided that the atmosphere was unpropitious and left for Tehran. He thus followed the example of another former Deputy, Sasan, who left some time ago having ascertained that his cause was hopeless. Those left in the field were Qubadian, Rafat-us-Saltaneh Pallizzi, Aziz Zanganeh, Dr. Mo'aven, Allameh, and Hayati, while there were one or two minor candidates who were determined to try their luck.
>
> The elections lasted five days and there seems little doubt that they will go to the candidates who had the longest purse behind them. A triumvirate of the first

1. FO 371/45488 Kermanshah Diary December 1946.

three named appears to have been formed, as they were always arm in arm on their way from mosque to mosque. No doubt Pallizzi, who is far from popular, has extended credit to the impecunious Qubadian as a quid pro quo for his tribal votes.

Four polling stations were chosen in different mosques and all were thronged with Kurdish villagers. Many of them were unknown to the authorities and by means of the sejels of their deceased relatives and friends succeeded in voting several times during the first day. Next day two mosques were allotted to villagers and two to townsmen in an effort to obviate the difficulty experienced by the less hardy in attaining the polling room through the throngs of Kurds. Squads of police and gendarmes kept order and the unwanted from voting by strong-armed use of the lash when the more impatient, after waiting for some hours, tried to break through the cordon. The personal servants of Pallizzi and Qubadian were among those successful in arranging for their supporters to break through the cordon. Allameh on the other hand came to appeal to the Consulate to have the elections annulled on account of such methods, his men being unable to vote. The crowds were good humored and treated the whole matter as a joke which cost them nothing whatever it cost their lords and masters. Those who broke through did so by dint of walking over the heads of the crowd and hurling themselves at the police who generally let them fall on the right side for the voting box. In the mosques for the townsmen the same scenes were encated [sic; enacted] repeated and an energetic time was had by all. In at least one mosque the ingenuous villagers were persuaded to hand their voting papers to the trustworthy inspectors who stood around the box and were told that they had done their duty and could depart. There is no evidence available of tampering with the boxes, though would be easier in the small outlying towns where six other polling stations were set up and candidates were not themselves so to the fore.

Source: FO 371/45488, Secret, Kermanshah Diary, January 1947 (Consul H.N. Pullar).

The results of this election were that Qubadian, Palizi, ‘Aziz Zanganeh and Dr. Mo‘aven won. The other candidates complained to Tehran about irregularities, but were referred to the election inspectors. The chief complainant was ‘Allameh, the head of the *‘Edalat* party and anathema to the *Tudeh* party, who lost marginally to Palizi. He claimed to have heard that the governor (*ostandar*) of Kermanshah gave orders on the phone to the two *farmandar*s not to give votes to Allameh and, if given, when counted should be changed. He went to Tehran to complain to Shah and the Prime Minister about the Democrat majority in the election board and the irregularities. Counting the votes took place in one mosque and at each of the outlying stations. The imported villagers returned home.[2]

2. FO 371/45488 Kermanshah Diary February 1947. In 1944, Aziz Zanganeh, the son of Amir Koll, was arrested in Tehran by the British and interned at the concentration camp at Arak. FO 371/40177, Kermanshah Diary January 1944. He was released in June 1944. FO 371/40177, Kermanshah Diary June 1944.

Appendix XI

Quis Custodiet Custodes?

This part of the July 1947 Consular Diary by the British consul H.N. Pullar gives a tongue-in-cheek impression of how government officials and those in league with them enriched themselves. Pullar was convinced that Persian government officials had no sense of civic duty whatsoever and only looked after feathering their own nest. In March 1947, he wrote: "The rich and the directors of government departments live in a kind of fool's paradise as they don't think anything will be done for the town of district and they don't care."[1] Given such a bend of mind and mentality it is no wonder that officials had no care for the integrity of their function and the people, whom they were supposed to serve.

BEGGAR MY NEIGHBOUR.

The following information has been obtained from various sources and is given to show why the people might prefer a strong Shah or Communist doctrine to what they have.

Kermanshah has often been described as the worst town of any size in Iran apart from the south. It has no redeeming features, no aspiring buildings, and until last month, practically no main street. Its inhabitants are said to be among the scruffiest. But there is one good thing which Kermanshah has, even though others may share that grace, and that is the perquisites of office. Given the appeal of the town of Kermanshah, the restricted society, and the doubtful length of his stay the gentleman official can have only one object - to retrieve the amount which he in all probability paid for his post, and make enough for his next down payment and his material comfort. No unusual acumen is required to observe that his opinions are shared by a surprising number of obviously charming and intelligent persons who have realised at once that nothing can be done for such dreadful town or its equally obnoxious inhabitants, and that the best way to see that public money is not wasted is to have it, and as much ill-gotten private gain as possible, put into custody of those who are capable of knowing a good thing when they see it. This high civic mindedness and determination to see that money is not uselessly squandered on or by those who are too poor to benefit therefrom has been instanced in a variety of cases.

His Honour, the Mayor, Jehanshahi, has concluded bargains with the bakers, butchers and fruit sellers by which they may sell at a price above the average. Of course such service is not with a smile only, and its costs each man Rls 50 a day for the Mayor. But the Mayor had to pay Rls 20,000 for his post, supposedly to the Governor-General, and pays a daily impost himself.

1. FO 371/45488, Kermanshah Diary March 1947.

The head of the gendarmerie gets Rls 10,000 a month from his colleague in Qasr-i-Shirin for allowing him to take as many bribes as he can. Six other officers from different towns are acting likewise - generally in co-operation with the police, bakhshdar, and some other official - and paying from Rl. 2,000 to 1,500 a month. Rls. 35,000 a month are paid by Mohammad Beg Lahuni for receiving the salaries of the gendarmes employed in the Avroman area, and the Javanrudis pay Rls. 17,000.

The Police Department cannot of course be outdone and the Chief receives his due 'to keep up with the Browns next door' from the office in charge of traffic so that the latter can levy fines on each bus and taxi leaving Kermanshah.

The poor young rich are in the maws of the Conscription Department which seduces them - no hard task - and indulges in the added pleasures of blackmailing them every six months or so. The tribesmen pay - and then are listed as deserters. The O.C. Troops is believed to turn his blind eye to this practice - and blindness is always expensive. Tea and sugar rations destined for the soldiers and tribesmen are sold by the officers and chiefs, who pay well for the monopoly. In this connexion another young department has unexpectedly winning ways, and that is the Census Department. The difficulty of certifying to the number of persons in the tribes who should receive tea and sugar can only be overcome by a rich uncle. Visiting chieftains are kept in their place until they realise how heinous is the offence of not bringing burnt offerings to the highest.

Tobacco and opium are clearly the Scylla and Charybdis of their growers, but the craft can be steered clear at a cost they are willing to pay. Wheat, unfortunately, shows a great tendency to be adulterated with dirt and becomes earthy - a serious fault involving blood-money of some fifteen to twenty percent.

Malcontents who may have the effrontery and ignorance not to see that these matters work better when done by a team, and who take the case indignantly to court for justice may perhaps find Justice too dazzled to see their point if view. The scales must fall from Justice's eyes. If you want good service you must pay for it.

The system as practised with such success, from the highest official to the lowest, cannot have but an attraction for the rest of the populace who wish to emulate and better their superiors, and, taking it by and large, their attitude is not altogether surprising.

Source: FO 371/45488, Secret, Kermanshah Diary July 1947 (Consul H.N. Pullar)

Appendix XII

Text of Undertaking by Abbas Khan Gubadian Amir Makhsus

TRANSLATION

UNDERTAKING BY ABBAS KHAN GUBADIAN, AMIR MAKHSUS RE/ THE RETURN OF HIS FAMILY TO KALHOR.

At the Ustandari
Kermanshah
15 November 44.

I, the undersigned, take full responsibility if permission be granted for the following persons to return to their own lands and be engaged on working their lands; on no account will they associate themselves in Political or Tribal matters. In the event of any of the under-mentioned persons indulging in Political of Tribal matters, or creating trouble, the O.C. 12 Brigade Kermanshah has full authority to summon the implicated persons, and refuse permission for him to return to his lands: -

Khosrau Khan Gubadian	(Bro. of Amir Makhsus)
Pasha Khan Amiri	(" " ")
Ali Shah Davoudian	(Cousin " ")
Agha Jan, Salar Hishmat	Uncle
Farajullah Hashidi	(Cousin & Head of Munishi)

(Translator's Note: Also, Qassim Khan Davoudian and Ghulam Reza Davoudian, who are cousins of Amir Makhsous and already living on their lands in Gilan - see later Para:)

The transfer of Lands which were given to the Gubadian and Davoudian Family by Persian Govt. has been officially announced. These substituted Lands were divided amongst the heirs of Gubadian and Davuoidian Family, and their shares were specified in the official Title Deed. (Translator's Note: This document is with Amir Makhsous and was read out to the Actg. Ustandar. Copies are with Rais-i-Amlagh Shahabad and with Mr. Hutchinson, Dir. of Finance 5th. Ustan, Kermanshah).

In this document it is stipulated that among all the members of the family they have no right to fight each other, or create disturbance or feud in the family. Each members has the right to protect his own share according to his rights; and if any person tries by force to seize another's property, O.C. 12 Brigade KMS and the Ustandar has full authority to stop the offender and punish him.

Aghai Khosrau Gubadian with 20 head of family will have their residence in Shahabad. He personally is authorised to go out and supervise his lands in Garmasir, provided that he has previously obtained permission from the Farmandar of Shahabad to do so. His family however, must remain in Shahabad.

Aghai Pasha Khan Amiri,[1] with 15 heads of Family are at Shahabad. His residence will be at Shahabad, and he has right to interfere in his lands at Shahabad only. On no account is he to go to Gilan, Aiwan, Karind, etc. It other words, he must stay in Shahabad.

Agha Jan Hishmati, whose small Plot of land is at Gilan, has right to reside at Gilan and be engaged with agricultural affairs; but on no account has he any right to mix himself in Political and Tribal matters.

Farajullah Rashidi, whose lands are at Kifr Avar might reside there. If Kifr Avar is not suitable for his residence he might be permitted to stay on his land at Karind, or at Shahabad.

Davoudian's Family.

Aghai Kerim Khan Davoudian who is at Tehran - his family may reside at Gilan.

Aghai Ali Shah Davoudian is the representative of the Garmasir Lands at Gilan and that area, and has the right to reside in Gilan and carry on with agricultural affairs. But by no means has he any right to interfere with Political or Tribal affairs; and he will be obedient to the bakhshdar of Gilan. His family number about 20 heads.

Aghai Ghulam Reza Davoudian, brother of Kerim Davoudian, who has to support 20 heads of family and for the last 3 years has been residing at Gilan - he may also hereafter reside at Gilan, provided that he concerns himself only with agricultural affairs under the above terms.

I promise to undertake full responsibility for the above-mentioned persons, that they will be obedient and carry on their husbandry matters, and will not mix or indulge in Political or Tribal or Bakhshdar affairs - except to work on their lands which are given to them by the Govt. Their shares will be One-third of irrigated crops and One-quarter of Dry crops. Furthermore, they have no right to encroach or oppress the peasants, except to give them their fair share according to the usual custom.

O.C. 12 Brigade KMS has full authority to take any action in this respect."

---

1. This man was mainly known "as the murderer of his mother and uncle." FO 371/40177, Kermanshah Diary June 1944.

Dated 24/8/23

15 Nov. 44. Signed ... Abbas Gubadian

Endorsement

"On Wednesday 24/8/23 a Meeting was held at the Ustandari in the presence of Col. Pitt Political Adviser Kermanshah, who also represented H.M. Consul KMS, and Col. Shahrukh Shahi O.C. 12 B'de, Aghai Jahanshahi Actg. Ustanbdar 5th Ustan, and Aghai Abbas Qubadian (Amir Makhsous) who signed this Agreement which is approved by the said Meeting with no objection to his family's departure to the above-mentioned places.

Signed Col. Shahrukh Shahi
Jehanshahi

Confirmed no objection from British Authorities

A.R. Pitt, Lt. Col.

Appendix XIII

Who's Who in Kermanshah

[A] FO 248/1204, List of Influential Persons of the Kermanshah Province by Lt. Col. R.L. Kennion, 23/04/1918

[B] AIR 20/663, Maj. Greenhouse, Notes on Kirmanshah Affairs, Chapter VII. Personalities, May 1921, pp. 130-38; see also IOR/R/15/5/95, '1/C Volume II Miscellaneous'. (printed version)

s/o = son of.

Abbas Khan (Amir-e Mo'azzem), chief of the Kalhor, nephew of Soleyman Khan (q.v.). His sister is wife of Salar-e Zafar, Sanjabi. He has always been in close touch with Ali Akbar Khan, Sanjabi, and till recently has been identified with enemy interests. Abbas Khan is intelligent and well informed and has the makings of a better chief of the tribe than his uncle. Age (1918) about 20. [A]

Abdol-Reza Khan. Colonel. Ra'is-e Zhandarmeri-ye Kermanshah. Was educated for 7 years in Vienna and has been attached to the Austrian Army. Was afterwards A.D.C of the Shah. Speaks French, German and a little English. Is cheerful and pleasant to speak to, but it is doubtful what his real politics are, and he is thought to be anti-British at heart. The present ill-discipline of the Gendarmerie in the province does not reflect to his credit. [B]

Abu'l-Fath Mirza. A descendant of the late Emad al-Dowleh. Chief of the Kermanshah police, during Turkish occupation in 1915 and 1916. Sometime governor of Sahneh under the Turks. Belongs to the Democrat party. [A]

Ali Akbar Khan (Sardar Moqtader), age (1918) 38. The most influential chief of the Sanjabis and in Kermanshah generally. Son of the late Shir Khan, Samsam al-Mamalek. This chief has always exercised a prominent influence on tribal policies out of proportion to the strength of his tribe. Before the war the Sanjabis generally were on bad terms with the Turks and when the latter advanced in June 1915 Ali Akbar fought against them. He was afterwards, though the agency of Mohammad Baqer Mirza, won over by German gold and received a monthly payment. On the return of the Russians in the spring of 1917, Ali Akbar Khan retired to the Kuh-e Bamu. Since this time he has always remained in communication with the Germans and has formed the channel of communication between them and their sympathizers in Kermanshah. He was the chief instigator of the attacks on Russian troops by tribesmen in the spring and summer of 1917. In August of this year the Russians made a general peace with the tribes and Ali Akbar Khan and his brother were present at the meeting at Bindar at which this was inaugurated. After this, no further overt acts of hostility were committed against Russian troops but Ali Akbar Khan continued his relations with the enemy. At a meeting with Colonel Kennion in January 1918 the

Sanjabi chiefs and Shahzadeh Soleyman Mirza, who was then their guest, promised to break off their connection with the enemy, but the promise was not kept and Soleyman Mirza was arrested in the camp of Qasem Khan by a force sent from Khaneqin. Since this time relations between our Political officers and the Sanjabi chiefs have remained suspended, and at the present time Ali Akbar is actively working as an enemy agent to raise the Kermanshah tribes against us and cause us trouble on the road to Kermanshah. [A]

Ali Khan (Amir-e Koll, formerly Sardar Ejlal). Grandson of Zaher al-Molk, the well-known head of the Zanganeh tribe. A wealthy landowner, whose family have held the Governorship of Kermanshah from time to time. Has himself on several occasions held post of deputy-governor and has sometimes acted as Governor. During the recent Turkish occupation of Kermanshah received for a short time a stipend from the Germans, but afterwards joined the Russians; was made deputy-governor and when the Russians retired from Kermanshah, he accompanied them. Was made governor of Araq in order to assist Russian operations on the Luristan side, and on Russians returning to Kermanshah in spring of 1917, was made governor of the province. He was removed from the governorship owing to his greed and exactions. His sympathies are with the Conservative party. One daughter is married to Abbas Khan, Kalhor. Two other daughters are married to Mo'azzem al-Dowleh, the son of the locally famous British Agent, Vakil al-Dowleh, Agha Hasan. Amir-e Koll has pleasant manners, is greedy and prodigal. [A]

Ali Morad Khan (Ehtesham al-Mamalek). Chief of Kerind. Age (1918) about 68. Was formerly Sartip of the Kerind regiment and was one of the most influential of the Kermanshah chieftains. Owns land on the road of Sorkheh Dirak, PayTaq, and Qasr-e Shirin. He fought against Gen. Hoseyn Ra'uf when the Turks first invaded Kermanshah. The town of Kerind was looted by them and since then has been pillaged on several occasions by the Russians. At the present time Ali Morad is ruined and broken and has lost all his power. Efforts have been made by the British authorities to restore the prosperity of Kerind by advances for sowing and famine works. In these, however, except in so far as he personally benefitted, Ehtesham has taken little interest. [A]

Amir Arsalan Khan. Sarom Nezam. Zanganeh. Cousin of the late Zaher al-Molk. A wealthy landowner and motavalli of the vaqfs of Mohammad Ali Khan and Sheikh Ali Khan., which have come down from Safavid times. The object of the vaqfs include maintenance of the famous 'Shah Abbasi' caravanserai of the province. [A]

Amir-e Koll (Sardar-e Ejlal). Lives in Kermanshah, where he has much property. Was Governor General of Kermanshah in 1917. He has acted as Governor on several other occasions. Was appointed governor of Thalath (Malayer) in November 1918, but never took up the post. Was elected to the Majles as one of the representatives of Kermanshah in 1920, but never took his seat. He is by birth of the Zanganeh tribe, and has influence over the Othmanavand.

He is a cheery individual , but corrupt to a degree, and lacks character. He is a gambler and intriguer and, though possessing much property, is always in debt.

In April 1921 when the Governor of Kermanshah was arrested, Amir-e Koll's guilty conscience led him to take 'bast' with much rapidity in the British Consulate. However, it appears that he was not wanted so soon returned to his own quarters.

He is father-in-law to Abbas Khan, Kalhor and also to the brothers Mo'azzam al-Dowleh and Raf'at al-Soltaneh. [B]

Agha Rahim. An influential mojtahed of Kermanshah. Moves a good deal in local politics. Is friendly inclined to the British. Venal. [A]

Agha Sayyed Hoseyn Kazzazi. Democrat deputy of Kermanshah. Left Persia with Nezam al-Saltaneh. [A]

Agha Sayyed Rostam. Chief of the Aliolahi sect. Lives at Tushami in Guran country. Has much influence with the tribes. [A]

Ali Pasha Khan, s/o Ya'ub Pasha Khan. One of the most notable of the Hajizadeh family. Provides sowars for the governor and has had governorship of Peyravand, Sahneh, etc. Acts with the Ilkhani. Was an active partisan of the Turks. [A]

Amir-e Nezam. Of the Hajilu tribe (this tribe is a division of the Karagozlus from whom they separated many years ago). He lives at Kabutarahang, about 37 miles N.E. of Hamadan. He is a nephew of Amir-e Afghan, and an elder brother of Sardar-e Akram.

Was educated in England, and speaks English and French. Was Governor-General of Kermanshah in 1919-1920 and his work there is highly spoken of.

After this he wished to go to England for 6 months, but was persuaded to join Sepahdar's cabinet as Minister of War in October 1920.

He remained in office until the coup d'etat of March 1921, when he was imprisoned in Tehran but only for a short time.

He is one of the best Persians, very liberal in his ideas and pro-British. During his time as Governor of Kermanshah he made a genuine effort to administer his office on sound and straightforward lines.

He owns some 40 villages around his home, and can command 250 sowars. [B]

Asad al-Dowleh s/o Jalal al-Din Mirza (Mohtasham al-Dowleh). A wealthy landowner. Worked for Nezam al-Saltaneh during Turkish occupation, but does not identify himself with either political party. Is now (April 1918) deputy-governor. [A]

Asad Khan Beglerbegi. Does not belong to any of the noble families of Kermanshah. Father was governor's farrash-bashi. Has acquired considerable properties. A noxious individual. [A]

Asadollah Beg. Chief of the Qalkhani. Similar character to Qanbar q.v. [A]

Asaf-e A'zam, of Kurdistan. Head of the Vaziri family (Vazirzadeh). Aged 73 years. Nearly blind, but still plays a leading part in Kurdistan affairs, where he is the largest and richest landowner. He is universally loathed for his greed and meanness, and was the cause of many thousands of deaths during the war. At this time, being the owner of most of the land supplying grain to Senneh, he withheld the grain to force it to famine prices. He sent large quantities of grain to Hamadan to sell to the armies of occupation there, while in Senneh, in 1917, he sold it at tumans 200 to 250 per kharvar.

He has encouraged disorder with the object of bringing neighboring estates on the market, and has steadily bought up land until he has acquired a majority of the cultivable area.

He has three sons:

i. Sardar Mo'azzam, weak and indolent. Governor of Galbaghi and Mandumi. Elected representative to the Majles in December 1920.

ii. Sa'd al-Mamalek, governor of Kharvar.

iii. Sa'd al-Soltan, steady, energetic and reliable. Lives in Marring.

He has a brother, Moshir-e Divan, leader of the Aghayan and a social-democrat; a clever and influential man.

Bahador-e Lashkar, s/o Haji Ebrahim Khan (now at Kazimain). Zanganeh. Formerly (and during the Turkish occupation) maintained the governor's sowars for the town. Properties at Daizar taken possession of by the Sanjabis, to whom he is bitterly opposed. This wealthy family, of whom there are numerous members, is known as 'Haji Ebrahim Khanis.' [A]

Bahram Khan (Rashid al-Saltaneh). Principal chief of the Qalkhani section of the Gurans. Has generally opposed the Sanjabi influence with the Gurans. Was at first on good terms with the Russians, but afterwards joined with other Qalkhani chiefs in holding up the Taq-e Gurreh pass. Is well inclined to the British. His instincts are less markedly predatory than the rest of the Qalkhani nobility. [A]

Baqer Khan (Azam al-Saltaneh). Also known as Khan Dara. Chief of the Kakavand, a Lur tribe inhabiting district around Harsin. Fought against the Russians. Is now inclined to be friendly. Together with Sardar-e Amjad (lately made Sardar-e Akram) Hasanavand is head of a Lur confederacy in opposition to Nazar Ali Khan, Amra'i. [A]

'Emad al-Dowleh, head of the family of that name in Kermanshah, where he formerly was Finance Agent. Is now in a similar appointment in Kerman. Was of great assistance to Salar Lashkar, while latter was Governor of Kermanshah, in helping him to enrich himself at the expense of the state. [B]

'Emad al-Ra'aya. Of obscure origin. Employed in Kermanshah police by Turks in 1915, when he was also member of the Democrat Committee. Since the evacuation of Kermanshah by the Turks, has remained active member, until he recently inherited considerable fortune of Amin al-Mamalek, since when he has represented the more moderate Democrat party. [A]

Esma'il Khan (Salar-e Afkham). Son of Ehtesham al-Mamalek (q.v.). Has been acting lately for his father. Is crack brained and greedy. [A]

E'temad-e Homayun, was ra'is-e qoshun in Kermanshah in 1920. When Soleyman Khan and Abbas Khan, the two Kalhor chiefs, were sent away to Tehran on October 192, he was appointed governor of the tribe by Sarem al-Dowleh. In this position he showed himself an able administrator, but at the same time made a large sum of money for his chief out of the tribe. On return of Soleyman Khan in April 1921 he left the tribe hurriedly. [B]

Farajollah Khan. Governor and landowner in Kangavar. Very friendly and useful. [A]

Farrokh Khan. chief of the Ahmadavand, rival of Mehr Ali Khan. Partisan of the Sanjabis. [A]

Fateh Soltan. Chief of the Kuliai, driver of Sardar-e Amjad. Fought against the Russians in 1916 and belongs to the Sanjabi faction. [A]

GholamAli Khan (Salar-e Mansur), s/o Mansur Khan, Mansur al-Molk and titular head of the Guran tribe. Has little power or influence at the present time and has lost much of his property to other chiefs. [A]

Haji Mirza Hoseyn. Kermanshahi s/o Mirza Yayha. Some time Democrat (moderate) vakil of Kermanshah, but did not join the extreme party in Tehran in 1915 or join Nezam al-Saltaneh in Kermanshah. [A]

Haji 'Ezz al-Mamalek, s/o Haji Fakhr al-Molk vali of Kurdistan. Vakil of Kermanshah. Left for Constantinople with Nezam al-Saltameh.

Hoseyn Khan (Sardar Zafar). Age (1918) 29. Chief of the Sanjabis and younger brother of Ali Akbar Khan, q.v. Is believed to be the wealthier of the three brothers, who have always worked in concord. [A]

Hoseyn Qoli Khan (Sardar-e Amjad). Age 38 (1918). Chief of the Kuliais. Was a partisan of the Russians and left with them on the Turks advancing in 1916. Belongs to the anti-Sanjabi faction. [A]

Imam Jom'eh. Abu Ali. Same family as Sheikh Hadi q.v. A mojtahed of some influence. Was much used by the Germans in their propaganda. Venal, full of insincere protestations. [A]

Jahan Bakhsh Khan (Zarghan al-Saltaneh). Soltan. Chief of the Tofangchi section of the Guran. Is a partisan of Soleyman Khan, Kalhor (q.v.) and belongs to the anti-Sanjabi faction. He left Kermanshah with the Russians in 1916 and in the advance on Kermanshah in the spring of 1917 was, together with his brother Sohrab Khan with Colonel Kennion's Kurd sowars. Has since remained a refuge with Soleyman Khan. His property is mostly with Safar Khan and Qambar Soltan. A man of considerable character and a clever intriguer. [A]

Kabuli Sardars. Heydari Qoli Khan and Ja'far Qoli Khan, the sons of Nur Mohammad Khan of Kabul, who was compelled to leave Afghanistan when Lord Roberts retired from there. They suffered much loss at the hands of the Turks. They are entitled to British protection.

They are very pro-British, and in 1920 were awarded the title and insignia pf 'Khan Sahib' at a parade of British troops.

Mahmud Khan, Major in the Gendarmerie. Was sent to Kermanshah by the Prime-Minister Sayyed Ziya al-Din in March 1921 with the object of effecting the arrest of the governor H.H. Sarem al-Dowleh, which he succeeded in doing with the help of Soleyman Khan, Kalhor. He then became Military Governor of Kermanshah. Owing to the ill discipline of the Gendarmes and of the preponderance of Kalhors his position appeared precarious, but up to May 1921 he was still controlling his command without any untoward event. Being quite a stranger to Kermanshah his position was a difficult one, and was not made easier by the obstructive attitude of Colonel Abdol-Reza Khan, who is his senior in the Corps.

He is a strong looking man physically, and gives the impression of quiet efficiency and keenness in his work. [B]

Majid Khan. Chief of Bajlan. A bitter enemy of the Turks who have killed several of his brothers. Was very helpful to the Russians in collecting supplies. A friend of Soleyman Khan, but on bad terms with all the Sanjabi faction. His brother Parviz Khan is with the Turks. [A]

Manuchehr Mirza ('Emad al-Dowleh) s/o of the late 'Emad al-Dowleh. Holds Revenue Office in Kermanshah. Family in Tehran. Speaks French. Has no leanings to either political party. Properties in Chamchemal. Friendly. [A]

Mehr Ali Khan (Salar-e Soltan). Chief of the Ahmadavand. Joined the Russians in 1916. Belongs to the anti-Sanjabi faction. [A]

Mirza Ali Khan. Grandson of the late Mirza Hadi Khan, Kargozar. Sartip. Wealthy landowner of Kermanshah. Rose to prominence during the time of Salar al-Dowleh. Furnished quota of sowars to the Germans in 1915. During second Turkish occupation was in charge of road guards. Is now (1918) in charge of road guards between Kermanshah and Mahidasht. Is friendly. Sympathies conservative but would support authority constituted for the time being. [A]

Mo'aven al-Molk. Of obscure origin. Together with his brother, the late Mo'in-e Ra'aya, rose to some prominence in the service of the governor of Kermanshah before the Persian constitution. Espoused the cause of Salar al-Dowleh. Has not identified himself with any political party. During the present year was appealed to by the governor to restore order in the town which was in a bad state, and has since enjoyed an unofficial position of great authority. Has also been in charge of arranging for supplies for the town during the present famine. Is fairly honest, friendly to British, and against the Sanjabis, who have occupied some of his properties in Mahidasht. [A]

Mo'tazed al-Dowleh, for many years in charge of the Revenue Department in Kermanshah. Is now one of the town's representatives to the Majles. He is getting on in years. Is a partisan of Abbas Khan, Amir-e Mo'azam, Kalhor. [B]

Mofakhkham al-Molk, - Ahmad Khan of Isfahan. Appointed deputy-governor of Kermanshah at the time that Sarem al-Dowleh was appointed Governor. Is a pleasant man, and came with a good reputation from Isfahan. Worked well with us. Was arrested together with his chief, Sarem al-Dowleh on April 12th, 1921, and despatched under guard to Tehran.

Mohammad Baqer Mirza, s/o Mohammad Rahim Mirza (brother of late 'Emad al-Dowleh). A person of great influence in Kermanshah politics. Was chief of Nezam al-Saltaneh's office at Kermanshah during the Turkish occupation. Was particularly active in forcing contributions from people under the name 'ayaneh.' On the return of the Russians in 1917 was deported to Tehran. Is father-in-law to Ali Akbar Khan and Qasem Khan, Sanjabis (q.v.) on whom he has always exercised a baneful influence. [A]

Mohammad Javad Khan (Samsam al-Dowleh), s/o Mehdi Khan. Head of a wealthy Kalhor family that owns property in Mahidasht and elsewhere. Was a Democrat at the time the Persian constitution was formed. Has now no political tendencies. Left Kermanshah with Amir-e Koll when the Russians retired in 1916. Belongs to the anti-Sanjabi faction on account of his lands having been occupied by this tribe. [A]

Mohammad Khan, s/o Farrokh Khan. 'Ilkhani.' The head of the Kalhor family known as 'Hajizadeh,' who came and settled in the city in the time of Mohammad Ali Mirza. Provided sowars for the Germans during the Turkish occupation but being very wealthy would always be on the side of the existing government. [A]

Mohammad Khan. Entesar-e Nezam. Head of the Duruhi Zanganeh family. Owns property in Mahidasht and Dukush Khan. Has the 'Qarasuran' (road guards) on the Khurkhur road to Luristan. [A]

Mohammad Sadeq Mirza. A son of Mohammad Baqer Mirza and understudy of his in tribal politics. [A]

Mojtaheds of Kermanshah: the chief mojtaheds are:

i. Aqa Rahim.
ii. Aqa Sheikh Hadi.
iii. Aqa Imam Jom'eh.
iv. Aqa Mohammad Mehdi (Democrat)

Of them Sheikh Hadi is the least corrupt. Relations of his are Zaher al-Olama and Nezam al-Olama of Harasam. The power of the Mojtaheds is decreasing, but some weight still attaches to their decisions, and we maintained friendly relations with them. [B]

Moqtader al-Dowleh, brother of Salar-e Ashraf (q.v.). Worked for the Turks in various capacities during the occupation by them and is now prepared to work for us. [A]

Nosrat al-Dowleh, H.H. Prince Firuz Mirza, eldest son of Farmanfarma. Was educated in Europe, and speaks French and English fluently. Was in the Cabinet in 1916. Was appointed Governor of Kermanshah in 1918, but never took up the appointment, ceding it to his second brother Salar Lashkar.

Is well-known in England as being one of the authors of the Anglo-Persian Agreement.

Spent 10 days in Kermanshah on his return from Europe in January 1921.

Is an able and highly educated man. The family own most of the land in the Asadabad valley, where they have a large residence.

Has two younger brothers- Salar Lashkar and Mohammad Vali Mirza. Was imprisoned together with his father and younger brother in Tehran by the Prime-Minister in February 1921. [B]

Naser-e Divan, s/o Mohammad Saleh Khan. Of Hajizadeh family. Monshi-bashi of the governor. Married daughter of Ali Morad Khan, Zanganeh, through whom he owns extensive property. Is friendly inclined. [A]

Naser-e Divan, of the Hajizadeh family of Kermanshah. Is a representative to the Majles, and is now in Tehran. Was deputy-governor to Amir-e Nezam, and did not bear a high reputation.

Is at enmity with the Amir-e Koll party and with Sayyed Hasan Owjaq, whom he defeated in the elections. [B]

Nezam al-Saltaneh, a leader of the Persian Nationalist movement. In 1913 was governor of Luristan and Khuzistan. In 1915-1916 set up an independent parliament in Kermanshah. Fled to Constantinople in the spring of 1917.

With regard to his enterprise at Kermanshah, he has since given out that he was actuated by disgust at Russian violation of Persian neutrality, and the manner in which the Russians had overrun his country, and by their conduct in general.

He declares he was not anti-British, and that he took up such position in Kermanshah for the purpose of counteracting German aggression and intrigue, and to prevent the entry of Persia into the war. [B]

Qanbar Soltan. Chief of the Qalkhani. Hereditary and congenial occupation plundering caravans and blackmail on the Taq-e Garreh pass. [A]

Qasem Khan (Sardar-e Naser). Age (1918) 41. Chief of the Sanjabis and the elder brother of Ali Akbar Khan, q.v. [A]

Qavam al-Olama, of the family of Agha Mohammad Ali who came from Najaf in Fath Ali [Shah]'s time. Chief of Democrat Committee in Kermanshah in 1915 and again in 1916. Left Kermanshah with Nezam al-Saltaneh on 1917. Believed now in Constantinople. [A]

Sa'id Abbas. A man of obscure origin. A leader of the Democrat party in Kermanshah. [A]

Seyfollah Mirza, lives in Farmanfarma's house at Janatabad (5 miles S. of Asadabad) where he acts as agent to the Farmanfarma family. He is of princely extraction, and originally came from Tabriz. Now an old man. Is powerful, and can turn out a large number of sowars if necessary.

Simulates friendliness toward the British, but his real feelings are doubtful.

Has made a large amount of money from us on account of road contracts, and his ryots have suffered in consequence. [B]

Sheikh Hadi, s/o Sheikh Abdol-Rahim. Ancestors came from Arabistan in the time of Fath Ali Shah and were given properties near Harasam. A very influential mojtahed of Kermanshah. Refuses to mix himself in politics, but is friendly to the British. [A]

Safar Khan, Soltan. Chief of the Nairizi section of the Guran. An adherent of Ali Akbar Khan, Sanjabi and in close touch with Germans. [A]

Salar-e Ashraf, uncle of Amir-e Koll (q.v) with whom he is not on very good terms. Zanganeh. He acted from time to time as chief of police, chief of the sowars, etc. Is a conservative but poses as a Democrat when it suits him. [A]

Salar-e Mo'ayyed, brother of Naser-e Divan q.v. [A]

Sardar Fateh, s/o Baqer Khan. Is frequently on bad terms with his father. [A]

Sardar-e Lashkar, brother of Naser-e Divan q.v. [A]

Sayyed Hasan Owjaq, lives in Kermanshah where he has much landed property. Is very wealthy. Is a clever man, and has used his religious position and brains to secure great influence among the tribes and townspeople of Kermanshah and district.

Acts as an agent to the Farmanfarma family, for whom he works with great assiduity. [B]

Salar Lashkar, Prince Abbas Mirza, second son of Farmanfarma. Educated at Harrow and Sandhurst. Appointed Governor of Kermanshah in August 1918. Administered the province with firmness, but is very corrupt and made large sums of money by illicit means.

He was recalled to Tehran in July 1919 and given an appointment in the Cabinet.

Was imprisoned together with his father and oldest brother by the Prime-Minister in February 1921. [B]

Samsam al-Dowleh, a representative in Kermanshah of the old Valizadeh family of Kalhor. An affable little man, connected through his mother with the 'Emad al-Dowleh family.

Has Democratic leanings, and is a partisan of Abbas Khan, Kalhor. [B]

Sarem al-Dowleh, Prince Akbar Mirza, son of Zell al-Soltan. Was Minister of Finance in Tehran 1919-1920, and was one of the authors of the Anglo-Persian Agreement. He intrigued against the Prime-Minister, so he was moved to Kermanshah in May 1920 as Governor in relief of Amir-e Nezam. He is a clever man of strong character. Disappointing as Governor owing to his corruption and dilatory methods.

He squeezed the tribes hard, and made large sums of money, particularly from the Kalhor. Was arrested in Kermanshah under order from Tehran on the 12th April 1921by Major Mahmud Khan, assisted by Soleyman Khan, Kalhor. He was despatched forthwith under guard to Tehran. [B]

Sowlat al-Molk, a Tehrani, and relative of Prince Sho'a al-Saltaneh. Was chief of police (ra'is-e nazmiyeh) in Kermanshah 1919-1921. Is one of the Farmanfarma party, but avoids identification with any particular interests, and can be relied upon to work well under any regime. He is tactful, resourceful and popular owing to his comparative honesty. Worked well with us, and kept Kermanshah town in excellent order.

On the occurrence of the coup d'etat introducing Sayyed Ziya al-Din's new regime to Kermanshah in April 1921, he was removed from office, but it is believed he will be re-employed by government. [B]

Sardar Rashid, Abbas Khan of Ruansar, chief of the Bani Ardalan and a leading figure in Kurdistan. He steadily acquired much land there. Has a following of about 1,000 sowars well armed and mounted. His position was so strong as to be looked askance at by the Governors-General of Kurdistan. He never paid revenue. In 1917-1918 he was most anxious to secure his position against the inevitable attacks by Kurdistan Governors-General by obtaining the appointment of Governor himself. This, however, would be impopular, as he is feared without being liked, and is reputed to be untrustworthy and unscrupulous. Consequently his ambition has never been satisfied.

His wife Hamideh Khanom was formerly the wife of his oldest brother Hoseyn Khan, by whom she had a son Gholam Hoseyn Khan, who is now about 12 years old. Hoseyn Khan died of poison, said to have been administered by Sardar Rashid, and it is thought that the son intends to take revenge some day.

Hamideh Khanom has been involved in a liaison with Ali Akbar Khan, Sanjabi, who consequently was always at enmity with Sardar Rashid. The latter's power and influence increased greatly after the removal of Ali Akbar Khan to Tehran in June 1918.

Sardar Rashid would like to see an independent Kurdistan under British protection.

He was suddenly seized by Sharif al-Dowleh the Governor in June 1919, and deported to Tehran. He was released in April 1921 and returned to Ruansar. [B]

Soleyman Khan (Amir-e A'zam) son of the well-known and powerful Kalhor chief Da'ud Khan, who was killed fighting on Salar al-Dowleh's side against the Bakhtiyaris. Refused to join the Turks during the late occupation and took refuge with the Vali of Posht-e Kuh, his rival Abbas Khan taking his place as chief of the Kalhor. On the return of the Russians in 1917 Soleyman Khan joined Colonel Kennion's Kurdish horse and Abbas Khan was driven out. In August 1917 when the Russians made a general pact of peace between the tribes, an agreement to share the chiefship was arrived at, since when the two chiefs have remained outwardly on good terms. Soleyman Khan is weak and greedy and has little real power over the Kalhors. Age (1918) about 38. [A]

Soleyman Mirza, ultra Democrat. Accepted German money in December 1917, and acted as German agent among the tribes, principally with the Sanjabis. He was fanatical on the subject of Persian independence, and freedom from any form of foreign interference.

Was arrested him in 1918 in a Sanjabi camp near Kala Sabzi on account of his intrigues with the German von Dreuffel, and was sent to India. He was released and returned to Persia early in 1921, reaching Kermanshah on the 8th February. He made public speeches in Kermanshah, principally on the subjects of education and unity. He spoke well of his treatment in India, and showed no sign of hostility to us. He is thought to be a scoundrel at heart. [B]

Vakil al-Molk. Nephew of the late Amin al-Mamalek, kadkhoda-bashi. Inherited much of the latter's wealth. Not one of the big families of Kermanshah. Joined Salar al-Dowleh during his last attempt on Persia. Has considerable influence with the Conservative party. [A]

Zaher al-Olama, brother of Sheikh Hadi. [A]

Appendix XIV

Qasr-e Shirin

This border town lies among the foothills of the main mountain chain at an elevation of 1,100 feet on the right bank of the Hulvan River and on the main road from Kermanshah to Baghdad. A large number of people, pilgrims and migratory tribes, are constantly passing through the town and its vicinity. The following is the estimated population of the town and district:

Place	Winter	Summer
Qasr-e Shirin Town	2,500	2,500
Travelers (monthly)	4,000	2,500
Paytaq, Bishewah, Qal`eh Shahin,	3,000	3,000
Sar-e Pol	1,000	1,000
Zohab, with tribes	50,000	1,500
Sanjabi tribe	5,000	-
Kerendis	1,000	-
Total	66,500	10,500

The inhabitants are mostly Arabs, with some Jews and Assyrians.

There is a Customs administration, a telegraph office and a small bazaar. A big stone house on a hill S.W. of the town is the governor's residence. There are several well-built serais. The remainder of the buildings are mean and the streets are narrow.

Grazing taxes are levied 2 qrans per camel, 1 qrans per mule, and 0.5 qran per pony.

Its inhabitants make a living from pilgrims and others who constantly pass through the town and in winter it is the principal market town for the Kermanshah tribes. The banks of the Hulvan are flanked by fruit gardens including figs, dates and melons.

There is good drinking water available from the Hulvan. Fodder is scarce; there is some thin scrub oak at 3 miles in the mountains 3 miles east of the town.

Source: AIR 20/663, pp. 29-31.

BIBLIOGRAPHY

ARCHIVES

AMFAI, ARCHIVE OF THE MINISTRY OF FOREIGN AFFAIRS, IRAN.

DDSR 1311-K23-P20
DDSR 1323-K22-P4.1-300
DDSR, 1325-K12-P2-71
DDSR 1325-K11-P9-233
DDSR 1327-K24-P2-97
DDSR1327-K56-P3-1
DDSR 1327-K56-P3-13
DDSR 1327-K56-P3-80
DDSR 1327-K24-P2-84

BRITISH LIBRARY, INDIA OFFICE, LONDON (UK)

IOR/L/MIL/17/15/11/3, Who's Who in Persia, vol. 2
IOR/L/MIL/17/15/11/8, 'Additions and Corrections to Who's Who in Persia (Volume IV)'
IOR/L/MIL/17/15/11/5, 'Who's Who in Persia (Volume III) Arabistan, Luristan, Isfahan & Bakhtiari'
IOR/L/MIL/17/15/24, 'Military Report on The Anglo-Iranian Oil Company's (South Iranian) Oilfield Area'
IOR/L/MIL/17/15/39, Notes on the Iranian Army. General Staff, India, 1940
IOR/L/MIL/17/15/51, 'Who's who in Mesopotamia, General Staff, India (Serial No.22)'
IOR/L/MIL/17/15/72/1, 'Critical Study of the Campaign in Mesopotamia up to April 1917: Part I - Report'
IOR/L/PS/10/210, Protocol of the Interrogatory ... of Wilhelm Paschen, 31 July 1916, appendix to Meshed Diary no. 33 for week ending the 12th August 1916
IOR/L/PS/10/211, Meshed Diary no. 22 for the week ending 2nd June 1917
IOR/L/PS/10/212, File 211/1912, 'Turkish Arabia Summaries,'
IOR/L/PS/10/231, File 842/1912 'Sanitary Mission to Turco-Persian Frontier'
IOR/L/PS/10/283, File 2612/1912 Pt 1 'Tehran Sanitary Council'
IOR/L/PS/10/284, File 2612/1912 Pt 2 'Persia. Tehran Sanitary Council'
IOR/L/PS/10/463, File 3136/1914 Pt 2 'German War. Situation in Turkish Arabia & Persian Gulf'
IOR/L/PS/10/634/3 (1923-1924);
IOR/L/PS/11/123, P 2560/1917 (22 May 1917-27 Jul 1917)
IOR/L/PS/11/127, P 4038/1917
IOR/L/PS/11/276, P 689/1927
IOR, L/P&S/12/84-87
IOR/L/PS/12/3396, Report of the Administrator General of the Finances of Iran for the months of Ordibehest and Khordad 1323 (April 21-June 21 1944)

IOR/L/PS/18/C144, 'Extracts from Annual Persia Reports, 1906, 1909, 1910, 1911, 1912, 1913 regarding loans, and complete reports for 1908 & 1913'
IOR/L/PS/18/C210, 'Bolshevik Intrigue in Persia since October 1922
IOR/L/PS/20/202, M.G. Gerard, "Notes on a Journey through Kurdistan in the winter of 1881-82" Calcutta, 1883 (Confidential)
IOR/L/PS/20/223, 'Who's who in Persia. Calcutta: General Staff, India, 1916
IOR/L/PS/20/224, 'Biographies of the notables of Fars and certain Persian officials who have served at Shiraz. Delhi: Government of India, 1925
IOR/L/PS/20/260/2, Persia no.1 (1909) Correspondence respecting the affairs of Persia, December 1906 to November 1908
IOR/L/PS/20/261/1, Persia no. 1 (1911), Further Correspondence Respecting the Affairs of Persia
IOR/L/PS/20/261/4, 'Persia. No 3 (1912). Further correspondence respecting the affairs of Persia.'
IOR/L/PS/20/261/5, 'Persia. No 4 (1912) Further correspondence respecting the affairs of Persia'
IOR/L/PS/20/261/6, 'Persia. No 5 (1912). Further correspondence respecting the affairs of Persia'
IOR/L/PS/20/261/7, 'Persia. No 1 (1913). Further correspondence respecting the affairs of Persia'
IOR/R/15/2/1996, 'Who's Who in Mesopotamia, General Staff, India (Serial No. 372)
IOR/R/15/2/1997, 'Who's Who in Mesopotamia, General Staff, India (Serial No. 10)'
IOR/Z/E/4/20/K60 (1849-1850)
IOR/Z/E/4/20/B8 (1849-1850)
IOR/Z/E/4/20/T55 (1849-1850)

NATIONAL ARCHIVES, KEW GARDENS, LONDON (UK)

AIR 20/663, Maj. Greenhouse, Notes on Kirmanshah Affairs, May 1921
FO 60/463, Report on the Trade (1884)
FO 248/789 Kermanshah
FO 248/879 idem
FO 248/906 idem
FO 248/907 idem
FO 248/938 idem
FO 248/968 idem
FO 248/999 idem
FO 248/1031 idem
FO 258/1053 idem
FO 248/1073 idem
FO 248/1112 idem
FO 248/1135 idem
FO 248/1204 idem
FO 248/1293 idem
FO 248/1300 idem
FO 248/1313 idem
FO 248/1314 idem
FO 248/1414 Kermanshah: internal situation
FO 248/1433 Kermanshah: internal situation
FO 248/1451 Kermanshah: internal situation
FO 371/2724 Political Departments: General Correspondence from 1906-1966
FO 371/7829 idem
FO 371/13064 idem
FO 371/21900 Kermanshah Trade Reports

FO 371/31402 Kermanshah situation reports 12/41 to 11/42
FO 371/40177 Kermanshah Diary 12/43-11/44
FO 371/40222 idem
FO 371/45400 idem
FO 371/45488 idem Kermanshah Diaries
FO 416/63 Foreign Office: Confidential Print Persia (Iran)
FO 416/78 idem
FO 416/79 idem
FO 418/80 idem
WORK 10/338 Trade Unions

PRESBYTERIAN HISTORICAL SOCIETY (PHILADELPHIA, USA)

RG 91-19-28 Dr. Hoffman papers
RG 61-3-46idem

BOOKS AND ARTICLES

Abbasi, Mohammad Reza and Badi'i, Parviz eds. 1372/1993. *Gozareshha-ye owza'-ye siyasi, ejtema'i-ye viilayat-e 'ahd-e naseri*. Tehran: Sazman-e Asnad-e Melli.

Abdul-Razak, Rowena 2016. "But what would they think of us?" Propaganda and the Manipulation of the Anglo-Soviet Occupation of Iran, 1941-1946?" *Iranian Studies* 49/5, pp. 817-35.

Abrahamiyan, E. 1983. "A Brief Note Respecting the Trade of the Northern Provinces of Persia, Addressed to T.H. Villiers [1832]," *Iranian Studies* 16, pp. 281-93.

A Correspondent, 1835 a. "A Day in Kermanshah," *The Penny Magazine of the Society for the Diffusion of Useful Knowledge* No. 227, October 17, pp. 404-05.

——— 1835 b, "Dealings in a Bazaar," *The Penny Magazine of the Society for the Diffusion of Useful Knowledge* No. 231, November 7, pp. 438-39.

Adamec, Ludwig 1976. *Historical Gazetteer of Persia*. 4 vols. Graz: Akad. Verlag.

Adamiyat, Fereydun 1348/1969. *Amir Kabir*. Tehran: Khvarezmi.

Adib al-Saltaneh, Hoseyn Sami'i 1332/1953. *Avvalin Qiyam-e Moqaddas-e Melli dar jang-e beyn al-millali-ye avval*. Tehran: Ibn Sina.

Adler, Cyrus ed. 1916. *American Jewish Year Book*, Philadelphia: The Jewish Publication Society of America.

Administration Report = *Administration Report on the Persian Gulf Political Residency for the year (1873 to 1940)* in Government of India. *The Persian Gulf Administration Reports 1873-1947*, 10 vols., Gerrards Cross, Archives Editions, 1986.

Advay, Mazhar 1392/2013. "Jang-e jahani-ye avval, taqabol-e tofangchiha-ye Huramanba qiva-ye Rus (ba takiyeh bar she'ri az Mola Sharif Beysarani," *Payam-e Baharestan* vol. 2, 6/21, pp. 182-206.

Ael 1931. *Po Persii i Mesopotamii*. Leningrad: Oguz.

Afari, Janet 2002. "From Outcasts To Citizen: Jews In Qajar Iran," in Sarshar, Houman 2000, *Esther's children: a portrait of Iranian Jews*. Beverly Hills

Alavi-Kiya, Mohammad Ali and Rostami-Guran, Mohsen 1384/2005. *Tarikh-e Amuzesh va Parvaresh-e Novin-e Kermanshah (1278-1332 h.sh.)*. Kermanshah: Taq-e Bostan.

Al-e Ahmad, 1333

Allemagne, Henri d' 1911. *Du Khorasan au Pays de Bakhtyaris*, 4 vols. Paris.

Alexander, Constance M. 1934. *A Modern Wayfarer in Persia*. London: Stockwell.

Algar, Hamid 1969. Religion and State in Iran 1785-1906. The role of the Ulama in the Qajar Period. Berkeley: UC Press.

Amanat, Abbas 1983. *Cities & Trade: Consul Abbott on the Economy and Society of Persia 1847-1866.* London: Ithaca press.

Anonymous 1840, *The Saturday Magazine*, no. 500, 18 April.

———, 1902. "Israeliten Persiens," *Bericht der Alliance Israelite Universelle vom 1 und 2. Semester.* Paris, pp. 47-68.

———, 1922. *The Continent*, vol. 53, 6 July.

———, 1918. "The Bible in Kermanshah," *The Muslim World* vol. 8, pp. 302-03.

———, 1993. *Ajayeb al-Donya* ed. L. P. Smirnovoi. Mosvow: Nauka.

Ansari, Hormoz 1353/1974. "Dah sal beh onvan-e ma'mur-e Vezarat-e Kharejeh dar Iran va Khavar-e Miyaneh" (an overview of Max Otto Schünemann's unpublished memoirs, "Zehn Jahre als Functionär des Auswärtigen Amtes in Persien und im Vorderen Orient"), *Rahnama-ye ketab* 17/1-3, pp. 126-32.

Anvar, Ya'qub 1331/1952. Memoirs of Ya'qub Anvar during the Muhajirat (under different titles), *Ettala'at-e Haftehgi*, 12th year, No. 597, Bahman 7; No. 598, Bahman 10; No. 599, Bahman 17; No. 600, Bahman 24; No. 601, 1; No. 602, Esfand 8; No. 603, Esfand 15.

AP, see Government of Great Britain, *Accounts and Papers.*

Arasteh, Reza 1967. *Education and Social Awakening in Iran.* Brill: Leiden.

Ardalan, Sheerin 2004. *Les Kurdes Ardalan entre la Perse et l'Empire ottoman.* Paris: Geuthner.

Armstrong, T. B. 1831. *Journal of Travels in the Seat of War during the last Two Campaigns of Russia and Turkey.* London: A. Seguin.

Atkin, Muriel 1980. *Russia and Iran, 1780-1828*, Minneapolis, Minn.

Aubin, Eugene 1907. *La Perse d'aujourd'hui.* Paris: Arman Colin.

Avery, Peter 1967. *Modern Iran*, London.

Axworthy, Michael 2006. *The Sword of Persia. Nader Shah from Tribal warrior to Conquering Tyrant.* London: IB Tauris.

Azari, Shahla 1371/1992. "Qahti va gerani-ye nan (1320-24 shamsi)," *Faslnameh-ye ganjihen-ye asnad* 2/1-2, pp. 4-17.

Azod al-Dowleh, Soltan Ahmad Mirza 2014. *Tarikh-e 'Azodi*, tr. M. M. Eskandari-Qajar. Washington DC: MAGE.

Bader, Ralph H. 1915. "Gum-tragacanth industry in Persia," *Commerce Reports*, vol. 4/4, year 18, Washington DC: US Government, Commerce Department, p. 1054.

Balfour, Patrick 1935. *Grand Tour.* New York: Harcourt, Brace & Co.

Bamberg, James 2000. *British Petroleum and global oil, 1950-1975: the challenge of nationalism.* Cambridge: Cambridge UP.

Bamdad, Mehdi 1347/1968. *Tarikh-e Rejal-e Iran qorun-e 12-13-14.* 6 vols. Tehran: Zavvar.

Bashiri, Ahmad ed. 1367/1988. *Ketab-e Naranji. Gozareshha-ye siyasi-ye vezarat-e kharejeh-ye rusiyeh-ye tzari dar bareh-ye enqelab-e mashruteh-ye Persia* 3 vols. Tehran: Nur.

Basir al-Molk Sistani 1374/1995. *Ruznameh-ye Khaterat-e Basir al-Molk Sistani.* Tehran: Ashna.

Bast, Olivier 1998. *Les Allemands en Perse pendant la première guerre mondiale*, Paris: Peeters.

———, 2002. *La Perse et la Grande Guerre.* Paris: IFPRI.

Bean, C. W. 1942. *The Australian Imperial Force In France During the Main German Offensive. Official History of Australia in the War of 1914–1918, Volume V*, Sydney : Angus and Robertson, Appendix no. 5. Australians in Mesopotamia,

Bélanger, Charles 1838. *Voyage aux Indes-Orientales pedant les années 1825 a 1829* 2 vols. Paris: Arthus Bertrand.

Belge, H.D.T. 1829. "Notice sur M. Devaux, officier français 26/9/1829." *Journal des voyages: découvertes et navigations modernes et archives geographiques du XIX siecle*, vol. 43, p. 349-54.

Bellew, Henry Walter 1999. *From the Indus to the Tigris*. Lahore: Sang-e Meel. [reprint of 1874 edition]

Bembo, Abrosio 2007. *The Travels and Journal of Ambrosio Bembo*. transl. Clara Bargellini. Berkeley: UCLA.

Benjamin, Israel Joseph. 1859. *Eight Years in Asia and Africa from 1846-1855*. Hanover.

Beth Hillel, David 1832. *The Travels of Rabbi David D'Beth Hillel; from Jerusalem, through Arabia, Koordistan, part of Persia and India*. London.

Bidlisi, Saraf Khan 1868. *Cheref-Nameh ou Fastes de la Nation Kourde*. Translated by Francois Bernard Charmoy. 2 vols. St. Petersbourg: Imperial Academy of Sciences.

Bigham, Clive 1897. *A Ride Through Western Asia*. London: MacMillan & Co.

Binder, Henry 1887. *Au Kurdistan*. Paris: Quantin.

Bird, Isabella 1891. *Journeys in Persia and Kurdistan*. 2 vols. London.

Blau, Otto 1858. *Commercielle Zustände Persiens*. Berlin.

Bode, C.A. De 1845. *Travels in Luristan and Arabistan*. 2 vols. London.

Boyle, J. A. 1975. "Dynastic and Political History of the Il-Khans," *Camb. Hist. Iran*, vol. 5, pp. 303-421.

Bleibtreu, J. 1894. Persien. *Das Land der Sonne und des Löwen*. Freiburg im Breisgau: Herder.

Blücher, Wipert von 1949. *Zeitenwende in Iran*, Biberach.

Brugsch, Heinrich. 1863. *Die Reise der K.K. Gesandtschaft nach Persien 1861-1862*, 2 vols. Berlin: J.C. Hinrichs.

Buckingham, J.S. 1971. *Travels in Assyria, Media, and Persia*. Westmead.

Bulletin de l'Alliance Israélite Universelle, 1860-1913. Paris.

Bulmus, Birsen 2012. *Plague, Quarantines and Geopolitics in the Ottoman Empire*, Edinburgh: Edinburgh UP.

Bürgel, J. Christoph 1965. *Die Hofkorrespondenz 'Adud ad-Daulas*. Wiesbaden: Harrassowitz.

Calmard, Jean 2015. "Kermanshah iv. History from the Arab conquest to 1953," *Encyclopedia Iranica*.

Calmeyer, Peter 1996. "Die Landschaft Kambadene," in W. Kleiss and P. Calmeyer, eds., *Bisitun: Ausgrabungen und Forschungen in den Jahren 1963-1967*, Berlin, , pp. 13-14.

Candler, Edmund 1919. *On the Edge of the World*. London-New York: Cassel & Co.

Capenny, S.F.H. 1900. "An Indo-European Highway," *The Scottish Geographical Magazine* vol. 16, pp. 523-34.

Castleman 1942. *Massa'ot Shali'aḥ Ẓefat be-Arzẓot ha-Mizraḥ*. n.p.

Chardin, Jean 1811. *Voyages du chevalier Chardin en Perse et autres lieux de l'Orient*. ed. L. Langles. Paris: Le Normant.

Chelebi, Evliya 2010. *Travels in Iran and The Caucasus, 1647 and 1654*. translated by Hasan Javadi and Willem Floor, Washington DC: Mage.

Clarke J. I. & Clark B.D. 1969. *Kermanshah, an Iranian provincial city*. Durham: University of Durham.

Clemow, F.G. 1916. *Report on Sanitary Matters in Mesopotamia, the Shiah Holy Cities and on the Turco-Persian Frontier*. Calcutta, Superintendent Government Printing India.

Cohen, Avraham 1992. *Ha-Kehillah ha-Yehudit be-Kermanshah*. Jerusalem: No'am.

———, 1986. "Iranian Jewry and the Educational Endeavors of the Alliance Israélite Universelle," *Jewish Social Studies,* vol. 48, pp. 15-44.

Cohanim, Rouhollah 1993. *Golden Treasures*. Los Angeles.

Colvill, W.H. "Sanitary Report on Turkish Arabia," *Transactions of the Bombay Society* N.S. 11 (1872), pp. 32-73.

Cresson, W.P. 1908. *Persia; The Awakening East*. Philadelphia: William Heinemann.

Cronin, Stephanie 2006."Iranian Nationalism and the Government Gendarmerie," in Touraj Atabaki, ed., *Iran and the First World War: Battleground of the Great Powers*, London and New York pp. 43-67.

Curzon, G. N. 1892. *Persia and the Persian Question*, 2 vols., London.

Daryaee, Touraj 2002. *Shahrestaniha i Eranshahr*. Costa Mesa: Mazda.

Davidi, Avi 2002. *"Zionism: Esther's children."* in Sarshar, Houman 2002, *Esther's children: a portrait of Iranian Jews*. Beverly Hills, Calif.: Center for Iranian Jewish Oral History; Philadelphia: Jewish Publication Society.

DCR, see Government of Great Britain, *Diplomatic and Consular Reports*.

Destrée, Annette. 1976. *Les fonctionnaires belges au service de la Perse 1898-1915*. Leiden: Brill.

Dhowqi, Iraj 1386/2007. *Iran va qodratha-ye bozorg dar jang-e jahani-ye dovvom*. Tehran: Pazhang.

Divanbegi, Reza Ali 1351/1972. *Safar-e Mohajerat dar Nakhostin Jang-e Jahani*,
Tehran.

Doty, William F. 1908. "Review of Trade Conditions in Persia", in *Commercial Relations of the United States with Foreign Countries during the Year 1907*. 2 vols. Washington DC: GPO.

Dowlatabadi, Yahya 1362/1983. *Hayat-e Yahya*, 4 vols. Tehran: Attar-Ferdowsi.

Ducrocq, G. 1923. "Les Allemands en Perse", *Revue du Monde Musulman* LIV, pp. 53-199.

Dunsterville, G. L. E. 1920. *The Adventures of Dunsterforce*, London.

Dupré, A. 1819. *Voyage en Perse fait dans les années 1807, 1808, 1809*. 2 vols. Paris: J.G. Dentu.

Dwight, D. H. 1917. "About Rug Books," *The Bookman*, Volume 45/March-August, pp. 614-22.

Ebrahimnejad, Hormuz 2002. "Religion and Medicine in Iran: from relationship to dissocation," *History of Science* 40/1, pp. 91-122.

Ebtehaj, G.H. 1932. *Guide Book on Persia*. Tehran.

Edmonds, C. Cecil John 2010. *East and West of Zagros: Travel, War and Politics in Persia and Iraq 1913-1921*, Yann Richard ed. Leiden: Brill.

Ehtesham al-Dowleh 1366/1987. *Khaterat-e Ehtesham al-Saltaneh*. Tehran: Zavvar.

Elgood, Cyril 1951. *A Medical History of Persia*. Cambeidge: Cambridge UP.

Elwell-Sutton, L. P. 1941. *Modern Iran*, London.

Entner, Marvin L. 1965. *Russo-Persian Commercial Relations, 1828-1914* Gainsville, Fl.

Eqbal, ʻAbbas 1326/1947. "Abeleh-kubi," *Yadgar*, vol. 4/3, pp. 68-72.

Erdmann, Hugo 1918. *Im heiligen Krieg nach Persien*. Berlin: Ullstein & Co.

Esfahani, Mohammad Maʻsum b. Khvajegi 1368/1989. *Kholasat al-Siyar*. Tehran: Elmi.

Eʻtemad al-Saltaneh, Mohammad Hasan Khan 1345/1967. *Ruznameh-ye Khaterat*. ed. Iraj Afshar. Tehran: Amir Kabir.

———, 1363/1984. *Tarikh-e Montazzam-e Naseri*. 3 vols. ed. Mohammad Esmaʻil Rezvani. Tehran: Donya-ye Ketab

———, 1369/1989. *Mer'at al-Boldan*, 4 vols. in 3. Tehran: Daneshgah-e Tehran.

Eʻtezad al-Saltaneh, Ali Qoli Mirza 1370/1991. *Eksir al-Tavarikh*. Tehran: Visman.

Ettehadiyeh, Mansureh; Shams, Esmaʻil and Ruhi, Saʻid eds. 1395/2016. *Naft-e Chiya Sorkh-e Kermanshah*. Tehran: Tarikh-e Iran.

Ettehadiyeh, Mansureh and Sirus Saʻvandiyan ed. 1366/1987. *Gozideh'i az majmuʻeh-ye asnad-e ʻAbdol-Hoseyn Mirza Farmanfarma 1324-45 hijri qamari*. 3 vols. Tehran: Tarik-e Iran.

———, 1369/1990. *Majmuʻeh-ye mokatebat, asnad, khaterat va athar-e Firuz Mirza Farmanfarma (Nosrat al-Dowleh)*. Tehran: Tarikh-e Iran.

Ettehadiyeh, Mansureh ed. 1383/2004, *ʻAbdol-Hoseyn Mirza Farmanfarma*, 2 vols., Tehran, 2004.

——— 2006, "The Iranian Provisional Government," in Touraj Atabaki, ed., *Iran and the First World War: Battleground of the Great Powers*, London, pp. 9-27.

'Eyn al-Saltaneh, Qahraman Mirza Salur 1376/1997. *Ruznameh-ye Khaterat*. 10 vols. eds. Mas'ud Salur and Iraj Afshar. Tehran: Asatir.

Ezz al-Mamalek, Amanollah Ardalan 1332/1953. *Avvalin Qiyam-e Moqaddas-e Melli dar jang-e beyn al-millali-ye avval*. Tehran: Ibn Sina.

Hamadani, Mirza Mohammad Ali Farid al-Molk 1354/1975. Khaterat-e Farid. Tehran: Zavvar.

Farmanfarma'iyan, Mehrmah 1382/2003. *Zendeginameh-ye 'Abdol-Hoseyn Mirza Farmanfarma*. 2 vols. Tehran: Tus.

Fasa'i, Hajj Mirza Hasan Hoseyni 1378/1999. *Farsnameh-ye Naseri*. 2 vols. ed. Mansur Rastgar Fasa'i. Tehran: Amir Kabir.

Ferrier, J.P. 1857. *Caravan Journeys and Wanderings in Persia, Afghanistan etc*. London.

Fischel, Walter J. 1950. "The Jews of Persia," *Jewish Social Studies*, April, pp. 119-160.

Floor, Willem. 1971 a. "The office of kalantar in Qajar Persia," *Journal of the Economic and Social History of the Orient, Journal of the Economic and Social History of the Orient*, vol. 14, pp. 253-68.

———, 1971 b. "The market police in Qajar Persia, the office of darughah-yi bazar and muhtasib," *Die Welt des Islams*, vol. 13, pp. 212-29.

———, 1973. "The police in Qajar Iran," *ZDMG*, vol. 123, pp. 293-315.

———, 1976, The merchants (Tujjar) in Qajar Iran," *Zeitschrift der Morgenlaendische Gesellschaft*", vol. 126, pp. 101-135.

———, 1977, "Bankruptcy in Qajar Iran," *ZDMG*, vol. 127, pp. 61-76.

———, 1983 "Changes and Developments in the judicial system of Qajar Iran," in: *Qajar Iran*, E. Bosworth & C. Hillenbrand eds. (Edinburgh, 1983), pp. 113-147.

———, 1998 *The Persian Textile Industry, Its Products and Their Use 1500-1925* (Paris: Harmattan: 1999

———, 1999 *A Fiscal History of Iran in the Safavid and Qajar Period*. New York: Bibliotheca Persica.

———, 2001. *Safavid Government Institutions*. Costa Mesa: Mazda.

———, 2003 a. *Agriculture in Qajar Iran*. Washington, DC: MAGE.

———, 2003 b. *The Traditional Crafts of Qajar Iran*. Costa Mesa: Mazda.

———, 2004. *Public Health in Qajar Persia*. Washington, DC: MAGE.

———, 2005. *The History of Theater in Iran*. Washington DC: MAGE

———, 2009 a. *Textile Imports into Qajar Iran. Russia versus Great Britain. The Battle for Market Domination*. Costa Mesa: Mazda, 2009

———, 2009 b. *Guilds, Merchants and Ulama in Nineteenth Century Iran*. Washington DC: MAGE.

———, 2009 c. "Kadkhoda," *Encyclopedia Iranica*, vol. XV, Fasc. 3, pp. 328-331 and iranica.com.

———, 2012. "Trade in and position of slaves in southern Iran, 1825-1925" *Studia Iranica* 41/2, pp. 255-94.

———, 2015. *The History of Bread in Iran*. Washington DC: MAGE, 2015

———, 2018 a. *Salar al-Dowleh. A Delusional Prince and Wannabe Shah*. Washington DC: MAGE.

———, 2018 b. *Studies in the Medical History of Iran*. Washington DC: MAGE.

Floyer, Ernest Ayscoghe 1882. *Unexplored Baluchistan*. London.

Fontanier, Victor 1844-46. *Voyage dans l'Inde et dans le golfe Persique. 2 vols. Paris: Ch. Paulin.*

Forbes-Leith, F.A.C. 1925. *By Car to India*. London: Hutchinson & Son.

Fortescue, Capt. L. S. 1920, *Military Report on Tehran and Some Provinces in N.W. Persia*. Tehran, in: FO 248/1300.

Fragner, Bert 1972. *Geschichte der Stadt Hamadan und ihrer Umgebung in den ersten sechs Jahrhunderteb nach der Hijra*. Vienna: University of Vienna.

Fraser, J.B. 1826. *Travels and Adventures in the Persian Provinces and the Southern Banks of the Caspian Sea*. London.

———, 1984. *Narrative of a Journey into Khorasan in the Years 1821 & 1822*. New Delhi.

———, 1840. *Travels in Koordistan*, Mesopotamia &c. London: Richard Bentley.

Ganji, H. M. 1968. "Climate," in W. B. Fisher, ed., *Cambridge History of Iran*, Cambridge: Cambridge UP.

Gehrke, Ulrich 1377/1999. *Pish be suye Sharq*. 2 vols. Tehran: Siyamak translated by Parviz Sadr into Persian from *Persien in der Deutschen Orientpolitik während des Ersten Weltkrieges*, Stuttgart: Kohlhammer, 1961.

Gerard, M.G. 1883. "Notes on a Journey through Kurdistan in the winter of 1881-82" Calcutta, (Confidential) in IOR/L/PS/20/202.

Gleadowe-Newcomen, A.H. 1906. *Report on the British-Indian commercial mission to south-eastern Persia during 1904-1905*. Calcutta.

Gobineau, A. de 1959. *Les Dépêches Diplomatiques.* ed. Adrienne Doris Hytier Geneva-Paris: Droz-Minard.

Golriz, Mas'ud 1357/1978. *Kermanshahan-Kurdistan: shamel-e banaha va asthar-e tarikhi-ye Asadabad - Kangavar - Sahn*. Tehran: Anjoman-e Athar-e Melli.

Government of Great Britain, Parliamentary Papers, *Accounts and Papers* (cited as AP)

AP 30 (1862) LVIII, Report [on the trade of Persia] by Mr. Eastwick, secretary of the Legation.

AP 30-31 (1864) LXI, Remarks by Mr. Consul-General Abbott on the Trade of Tabreez for the Year ending 20th March, 1863.

AP 25-26 (1866) LIV, LV, Report by Mr. Consul-General Abbott on the Trade and Commerce of Tabreez for the Year 1865.

AP 29 (1867-68) LXVIII, Report by Mr. Consul-General Abbott on the Trade and Commerce of Tabreez for the Year 1866.

AP 32 (1867-68) LXVIII, Report by Mr. Consul-General Keith Abbott on the Trade and Commerce of Tabreez for the Year 1866.

AP 68 (1867) Report by Mr. Consul-General Keith Abbott on the Trade and Commerce of Tabreez for the Year 1867.

AP 34 (1866) LXXII, Report [on the trade of Persia] by Mr. W.J. Dickson, secretary of the Legation.

AP 29 (1866) LXVIII, Report by acting consul Henry H. Ongley on the Trade and Commerce of Ghilan for the Year 1866.

AP 29 (1867-68) LXVIII, Report by Mr. Consul-General Abbott on the Trade and Commerce for the Year 1867.

AP 29 (1871) LXV, Report by Mr. Consul-General Jones on the Trade and Commerce of Azerbijan for the Year 1870.

AP 23 (1872) LVIII, Report by Mr. Consul-General Jones on the Trade and Commerce of Tabreez for the Year 1872.

AP 27 (1873) LXXV, Report by Mr. Consul-General Jones on the State of Trade in the Province of Azerbijan for the Year 1872.

AP 30 (1878) LXXV, Report by Mr. Consul-General Jones on the Trade and Commerce of Tabreez for the Year 1877-8.

AP LXXVI (1884-85) LXXVI, Report by Mr. Dickson on the Trade of Persia, Tehran 31/10/1884.

AP 37 (1887) LXXXV or DCR 69, Report for the Year 1885 on the Trade of Tabreez by Mr. Consul-General Abbott.

AP 39 (1895) XCIX or DCR 1569, Report on the Trade of the Province of Azerbaijan for the Year 1894-95 by Cecil G. Wood.

AP 51 (1899), CI. Report on the Trade of the Province of Azerbaijan for the Year 1898-99 by Cecil G. Wood.

Government of Great Britain, *Diplomatic and Consular Reports* (cited as DCR)

DCR 113, Report on the Trade and Industries of Persia by Mr. Herbert, London, 1887.
DCR 590, Misc. Series, Report on the Trade and General Condition of the City and Province of Kermanshah by H.L. Rabino, Agent of the Imperial Bank London, 1903.
DCR 1440, Report on the Trade of the Province of Azerbaijan for the Year 1893-94 by Cecil G. Wood.
DCR 2260, Report on the Trade of the consular district of Ispahan for the Year 1897-98 and 1898-99 by Preece.
DCR 2712, Trade of Bussorah for the Year 1900 by Mr. Wratislaw.
DCR 3043, Trade of Kermanshah and District for the year 1902-03 by Consular Agent H.L. Rabino.
DCR 3189, Trade of Kermanshah and District for the year 1903-04 by Consular Agent H.L. Rabino.
DCR 3420, Trade of Kermanshah and District for the year 1904-05 by Acting Consul H.L. Rabino.
DCR 3507, Report for the Year 1904-05 on the Trade of Azerbaijan by Mr. Wratislaw.
DCR 3683, Report for the Year ended March 20,1906 on the Trade of Kermanshah by Captain H. Cough.
DCR 3865, Trade of Bussorah for the year for the Year 1906.
DCR 3953, Report on the Trade of Kermanshah for the Year 1906-07 by Capt. L. Haworth.
DCR 4100, Report on the Trade of Kermanshah for the Year March 21, 1907 to March 20, 1908 by Capt. L. Haworth.
DCR 4365, Report on the Trade of Kermanshah for the Year 1908-09 by Capt. L. Haworth.
DCR 4487, Report on the Trade of Persia (1910).
DCR 4559, Report on the Trade of Kermanshah for the Year ending March 20, 1910 by Consul McDouall.
DCR 4766, Report on the Trade of Kermanshah for the Year ending March 20, 1911 by Consul McDouall.
DCR 4994, Report on the Trade of Kermanshah for the Year ending March 20, 1912 by Consul McDouall.
DCR 5048, Report on the Trade of the consular district of Ispahan for the Year ending March 20, 1912 by T.G. Grahame.
DCR 5088. Report for the Year ended March 21, 1912 on the Trade of Azerbaijan by N.P. Cowan.
DCR 5204, Report on the Trade of Kermanshah for the Year ending March 20, 1913 by Consul McDouall.
DCR 5254, Report on the Trade of the consular district of Ispahan for the Year ending March 20, 1913 by T.G. Grahame.
DCR 5419, Report on the Trade of Kermanshah for the Year ending March 21, 1914 by Consul McDouall.
DCR 5515, Report for the Year 1913-14 on the Trade of Persia.
DCR 5521, Report on the Trade of the consular district of Ispahan for the Year ending March 20, 1914 by T.G. Grahame.

Government of Great Britain, 1841. *Correspondence relating to Persia*. London: HMSO.
———, 1905. "Persia," in *Mines and Quarries: General Report and Statistics for 1905*.
———, 1910. Persia No. 1 (1910). *Further Correspondence respecting the Affairs of Persia*. London: HMSO.
———, 1911. Persia No.1 (1911) *Further Correspondence respecting the Affairs of Persia*. London: HMSO.

———, 1912. Persia No. 5 (1912). *Further Correspondence respecting the Affairs of Persia.* London: HMSO.
———, 1913. Persia No. 1 (1913). *Further Correspondence respecting the Affairs of Persia.* London: HMSO.
———, 1914. Persia no. 1 (1914). *Further Correspondence respecting the Affairs of Persia.* London: HMSO.
———, 1945. *Persia. Geographical Handbook Series.* Naval Intelligence Division. London.
Gouvernement de France 1914. *Rapports Commerciaux* no. 1079. Perse.
Gray, F.A.G. 1938. *Report on Economic and Commercial Conditions in Iran during 1937.* London: HMSO.
Griscom, Mary Wade 1921. "A Medical Motor Trip Through Persia" *Asia, The American Magazine on the Orient*, vol. 21 (March), pp. 233-240.
Grothe, Hugo 1910. *Wanderungen in Persien.* Berlin: Algemeiner Verein f. Deutsche Literatur.
Gyselen, Rika 1989. *La géographie administrative de l'empire sassanide: les témoignages sigillographiques.* Paris.
Haddad 'Adel, Gholamali; Elmi, Mohammad Jafar; Taromi-Rad, Hassan eds. 2012. *Periodicals of the Muslim World: An Entry from Encyclopaedia of the World of Islam.* London: Ewi Press, p. 79.
Hadow, R. H. 1923. *Report on the Trade and Industry of Persia.* London: HMSO.
———, 1925, *Report on the Trade and Industry of Persia.* London: HMSO.
Hale F. 1920. *From Persian Uplands.* New York: E.P. Dutton & Comp.
Hambly, Gavin R. G. 1991 a. "Iran during the Reigns of Fath Ali Shah and Muhammad Shah,"*Cambridge History of Iran* VII, pp. 144-73.
———,1991 b, "The Traditional Iranian City in the Qajar Period," in *Cambridge History of Iran* VII, pp. 542-89.
Hamed, Mohammad Sadeq and Habibi, Manuchehr 1376/1997 *Tarikh-e San'at-e Barq dar Iran.* Tehran: Tabash-e Barq
Harris W.B. 1896. *From Batum to Baghdad.* Edinburgh-London: Blackwood & Sons.
Hay, Sidney 1937. *By Order of the Shah.* London: Cassell.
Hedayat, Reza Qoli Khan 1339/1960. *Tarikh-e Rowzat al-Safa-ye Naseri.* 10 vols. Tehran: Markazi-Peyruz-Khayyam
Hedges, William 1887-89. *The Diary of William Hedges.* 3 vols. London: Hakluyt.
Heizer, Oscar 1919."Movement of Merchandise to Persia," *Commerce Reports*, vol. 1 Jan-March), year 22, Washington DC: US Government, Commerce Department, pp. 797-98.
———, 1920. "Trade Returns for Baghdad," *Levant Trade Review*, vol. 8/7, pp. 524-26.
Heravi, Mohammad Yusef Riyazi-ye 1372/1993. *'Eyn al-Vaqaye'.* Mohammad Asaf Fekrat ed. Tehran: Enqelab-e Eslami.
Herzfeld, Ernst 1968. *The Persian Empire: Studies in Geography and Ethnography of the Ancient Near East*, ed. Gerold Walser, Wiesbaden.
Hinz, Walther 1938. *Iranische Reise. Eine Forschungsfahrt durch das heutige Persien.* Berlin: Hugo Vermuehler.
Hurner, Rudolph 1896. "Bagdad," US Department of State, *Commercial relations of the United States with foreign countries during the years 1894 and 1895*, 2 vols. Washington DC: GPO, vol. 1, pp. 640-46.
Ibn Muhalhil, Abu-Dulaf Mis'ar, 1955. *Travels in Iran*, tr. V. Minorsky. Cairo.
Issawi, Charles ed. 1967. *The Economic History of the Middle East 1800-1914.* Chicago: Chicago UP.
———, 1971 a. *The Economic History of Iran 1800-1914.* Chicago: Chicago UP.
———, 1971 b. "The Tabriz-Trabzon Trade, 1830-1900: rise and decline of a route," *International Journal of Middle East Studies*, 1/1/, pp. 18-27.
Jackson, A.V. Williams 1909. *Persia Past and Present. A book of travel and research.* London: MacMillan.

———, 1910. *Persia Past and Present. A Book of Research and Travel.* New York: MacMillan.
Jasion, Jan T. 2004. *Tahirih in History: Perspectives on Qurratu'l-'Ayn from East and West.* Los Angeles: Kalimat.
Jaubert, P. A. 1821. *Voyage en Arménie et en Perse, fait dans les années 1805 et 1806*, Paris.
Jones, James Felix 1849. "Narrative of a Journey through Parts of Persia and Kurdistan," *Transactions of the Bombay Geographical Society* viii,
Jones, Geoffrey 1986. *Banking and Empire in Iran.* 2 vols. London: Cambridge UP.
Kashani-Sabet, Firoozeh 2011. *Conceiving Citizens: Women and the Politics of Motherhood in Iran.* Oxford, Oxford UP.
Kasravi, Ahmad, 1350/1971. *Tarikh-e Hejdah Saleh-ye Azerbayjan.* Tehran: Amir Kabir.
Katouzian, Homa 1981. *The Political Economy of Modern Iran 1926-1979.* New York: NY UP.
Keppel, George 1827. *Personal Narrative of a Journey from India to England.* 2 vols. London: Henry Colburn.
Kermanshahchi, Heshmat 2007. *Iranian Jewish community social development in the twentieth century.* Los Angeles.
Keshavarz, Ardashir 1382/2003. *Kermanshah-e ma beh dur nima-ye qadim-e shahr: Uligarshi, khandanha-ye hokumatgar dar Kermanshahan.* Kermanshah: Taq-e Bustan.
Keyhan, Mas'ud. 1310/1931. *Joghrafiya-e Mofassal-e Iran* 3 vols. Tehran: n.p.
Khatunabadi, 'Abdol-Hoseyn al-Hoseyni 1352/1973. *Vaqaye' al-senin va al-a'vām, ya guzareshha-ye saliyeneh az ebteda-ye khelqat ta sal-e 1195 hijri.* Tehran: Eslamiyeh .
Khodadad, Ahmad Ali 1395/2016. *Ruz-e Siyah-e Kargar.* Berkeley: Noghteh.
Kinneir, John MacDonald. 1813. *A geographical memoir of the Persian empire.* London: J. Murray.
Kirsch, Max 1927. *Im Lastkraftwagen von Berlin nach Ispahan.* Berlin: K. F. Koehler.
Küss, Walther 1911. *Handelsratgeber für Persien.* Berlin: n.p.
Lambton, A.K.S. 1953. *Landlord and Peasant in Persia.* Oxford: Oxford UP.
———, 1986. "Kirmanshah," *Encyclopedia of Islam*², vol. V, p. 167b.
La Porte, Joseph de 1771. *Le voyageur français, ou la connaissance de l'ancien et du nouveau Monde*, 3 vols. Paris: L. Cellot.
Laskier, Michael M. 1983. "Aspects of the Activities of the Alliance Israélite Universelle in the Jewish Communities of the Middle East and North Africa: 1860-1918", *Modern Judaism*, 3/2, pp. 147-171.
Laureys, Eric 1996. *Belgen in Perzie 1915-1941. Verwezenlijkingen. verhoudingen en attitudes.* Leuven: Peeters.
Layard A. Henry 1971. *Early Adventures in Persia, Susiana, and Babylonia.* Westmead: Gregg International.
Le Strange, Guy 1966. *The Lands of the Eastern Caliphate.* London.
Levi, Habib 1335/1956. *Tarikh-e Yahud-e Iran.* 3 vols. Tehran: Brukhim.
Lewis, G. Griffin 1913. *The Practical Book of Oriental Rugs*, Philadelphia.
Lingeman, E.R. 1928. *Report on the Finance and Commerce of Persia 1925-1927.* London: HMSO.
——— 1930. *Economic Conditions in Persia.* London: HMSO.
Litten, Wilhelm 1925. *Persische Flitterwochen.* Berlin: Georg Stilke.
Lewis, Bernard 1984. *The Jews of Islam*, Princeton NJ: Princeton UP.
LLoyd, E.H.M. 1956. *Food and Inflation in the Middle East 1940-45.* Standford: Stanford UP.
Lockhart, Laurence 1938. *Nadir Shah. A critical study based mainly upon contemporary sources.* London: Luzac & Co.
———, 1956. *The Fall of the Safavi Dynasty.* Cambridge: Cambridge UP.
Loeb, Laurence D. 1977. *Outcaste the Jewish life in Southern Iran.* New York: Gordon and Breach Science.
Longrigg, Stephen Hemsley 2002. *Four Centuries of Modern Iraq.* Reading: Garnet.

Luft, Paul 2002, "British Policy in Eastern Iran during World War I," in Bast 2002, pp. 45-80.

Lycklama à Nijeholt, T.M. 1873. *Voyage en Russie, au Caucase et en Perse*. 4 vols. Paris-Amsterdam: Arthus Bertrand-C.L. van Langenhuysen.

MacGregor, Major-General Charles Metcalfe 1994. *The Defence of India: A Strategical Study*. Simla.

MacLean, H. W. 1904. *Report on the Conditions and Prospects of British Trade in Persia*. London: HMSO.

MacNamara, Nottidge Charles 1876. *A History of Asiatic Cholera*. London.

Mahdavi, Asghar and Afshar, Iraj 1389/2001, Afshar, Iraj and Mahdavi, Asghar. eds. *Yazd dar Asnad-e Amin al-Zarb* (Tehran: Farhang-e Iran Zamin, Tehran.

Mahrad, Ahmad 1978. *Iran am Vorabend des II. Weltkrieges*. Osnabrück: Eigenverlag.

———, 1979. *Die deutsch-persichen Beziehungen von 1918-1933*. Frankfurt: Peter Lang.

Malekzadeh, Elham; Hamedi, Zahra and Alizadeh-ye Birjandi, Zahra eds. 1392/2013. *Jang-e Jahani-ye Avval va Dovvom dar Iran beh Revayat-e Asnad*. Tehran: Ketabkhaneh-e Markaz-e Asnad-e Majles.

Malekzadeh Hirbod, Hasan 1328/1949. *Sargozasht-e heyrat-angiz*. Tehran.

Mann, Oscar 1909. "Southern Kurdish Folksong in Kermanshah Dialect," *JRAS* 41/4, pp. 1123-24.

Maraghe'i, Zeyn al-'Abedin 1364/1985. *Safarnameh-ye Ebrahim Beg*. Tehran: Afsar.

Mardukh Kurdestani, Sheikh Mohammad 1351/1972. *Tarikh-e Kord va Kordestan va Tavabe' ya Tarikh-e Mardukh*. 2 vols. in one. 2nd ed. n.p.

Martin, Vanessa and Nouraei, Morteza. 2005. "The Role of the *Karguzar* in the Foreign Relations of State and Society of Iran from the mid-nineteenth century to 1921. Part I: Diplomatic Relations," *Journal of the Royal Asiatic Society* XV/3, pp. 261-77.

al-Mas'udi 1965-79. *Moruj al-dhahab va ma'adin al-jowhar*. 7 vols. ed. Charles Pellat. Beirut: al-Jami'ah al-Lubnaniyah.

Matheson, Sylvia A. 1976. *Persia: An Archaeological Guide*. London.

Matthee, Rudi; Floor, Willem; and Clawson, Patrick 2013. *The Monetary History of Iran, 1500-1925*. London: I.B. Tauris.

McCallum, Duncan 1930. *China to Chelsea*. London: Ernest Benn.

McClintic, Eleanor Soukup 1917. "With the Russians in Persia," *American Journal of Nursing* vol. 18/1, pp. 34-40; vol. 18/2, pp. 102-06.

Merritt-Hawkes, O. A. 1935. *Persia – Romance & Reality*. London: Nicholson & Watson.

Milburn, William 1813. *Oriental Commerce*. 2 vols. London: Black, Parry, and Co.

Miles, George C. 1975. "Numismatics," *Cambridge History of Iran* IV, pp. 364-77.

Miller, William M. 1995. *My Persian Pilgrimage: An Autobiography*. Pasadena, Cal.: William Carey Library.

Minorsky, Vladimir tr. 1937. *Hudud al-'Alam, "The Regions of the World": A Persian Geography 372 AH–982 AD*. London: Luzac.

Miroshnikov, L. I. 1963. *Iran in Wor1d War I*, Moscow.

Mitford, Edward Ledwich 1884. *A Land March from England to Ceylon Forty Years Ago*. 2 vols. London: W.H. Allen & Co.

Moberley F.J. 1987. *Operations in Persia, 1914-1919*. London: HMSO.

Mokhber al-Saltaneh 1344/1967. *Khaterat va Khatarat*, Tehran: Zavvar.

Molitor, Auguste 1914. *Contes Persans. Scènes de la Vie réelle et Récit de la Frontière*. Paris: Eugene Figuiere.

Momen, Moojan 2003. "Usuli, Akhbari, Shaykhi, Babi: The Tribulations of a Qazvin Family," *Iranian Studies*, vol. 36/3, pp. 317-37.

al-Moqaddasi 1362/1983. *Ahsan al-Taqasim fi Ma'refat al-aqalim*. 2 vols. Tehran.

Moreen, Vera Basch tr. 1987, *Iranian Jewry's Hour of Peril and Heroism. a study of Babai ibn Lutf's chronicle (1617-1662)*. New York: American Academy for Jewish Research.

———, 1990. *Iranian Jewry during the Afghan Invasion.* Stuttgart: Franz Steiner.
Morgan, Jacques M. de et al. 1894-1905. *Mission scientifique en Perse.* 5 vols., Paris: Ministère de l'Instruction Publique.
Morier, James 1818. *A Second Journey through Persia, Armenia, and Asia Minor ... between the years 1810 and 1816.* London: Longmam, Hurst, Rees, Orme and Browne.
Mostowfi, 'Abdolallah 1324/1945. *Sharh-e Zendagani-ye Man, Tarikh-e Ejtema'i va Edari-ye Dowrah-ye Qajar.* Tehran: Zavvar.
Mostowfi-ye Yazdi, Mohammad Mofid 1989. *Mokhtasar-e Mofid.* 2 vols. ed. Seyf al-Din Najmabadi. Wiesbaden: Reichert.
Motalleb, Motallebi 1384/2005. *Ilat-e Kermanshahan va naqsh-e anha dar qoshun-e Iran-e 'asr-e Qajar.* Tehran: Sazman-e Asnad.
Mounsey, Augustus H. 1872. *A Journey Through the Caucasus and the Interior of Persia.* London: Smith, Elder & Co.
Mumford, John Kimberly 1915. *Oriental Rugs*, New York: Scribner.
Mustawfi, Hamdalllah 1919. *The Geographical Part of the Nuzhat al-Qulub.* tr. Guy Le Strange. Leiden: Brill.
Napier, G.S.F. 1919. "The Road from Baghdad to Baku," *Geographical Journal* 53/1, pp. 1-18.
Naser al-Din Shah 1363/1984. *Safarnameh-ye 'Atabat sal-e 1287 qamari az Naser al-Din-e Qajar.* ed. Iraj Afhsar. Tehran: Ferdowsi-Attar.
Nasiri, Mirza Naqi 2008. *Titles & Emoluments in Safavid Iran.* translated and annotated by Willem Floor. Washington DC: MAGE.
Nategh, Homa 1370/1991. *Karnameh Farhangi Farangi Iran.* Paris: Khavaran.
Nazem, Hossein 1975. *Russia and Great Britain in Iran 1900-1914.* Tehran.
Netzer, Amnon 1997. *Padyavand.* 2 vols. Costa Mesa: Mazda.
———, 2001. "Yahudiyan-e Iran dar avaset-e qarn-e bistom," *Shofar* (a Jewish monthly published in Persian in Long Island) 243 (May).
Neubauer, Adolf ed. 1895. *Mediaeval Jewish Chronicles and Chronological Notes* II, Oxford.
Neumark, Ephraim 1947. *Massa be-erez ha-kedem*, ed. Avrahma Yaari. Jerusalem.
Nikbakht, Faryar 2002. *As with Moses in Egypt: Esther's children.* in Sarshar, Houman 2000, *Esther's children: a portrait of Iranian Jews.* Beverly Hills.
Nikitine, B. 2536/1977. *Khaterat va Safarnameh-ye Mesiyu B. Nikitin.* translated by A1i Mohammad Farahvashi. Tehran:
Olivier, G-A. 1807. *Voyage dans l'empire Ottomane, l'Egypte, et la Perse*, 6 vols. Paris.
Osku'i, Mostafa 1992. *Pazuheshi dar tarikh-e te'yatr-e Iran.* Moscow: Anahita and Progress Publishers.
Otter, Jean 1748. *Voyage en Turquie et en Perse* 2 vols. Paris: les Freres Guerin.
Ouseley, William 1819-23. *Travels in various countries of the East; more particularly Persia.* 3 vols. London: Rodwell and Martin.
Pagès, François de 1797. *Nouveau voyage autour du monde en Asie, Amérique et Afrique, 1788-1790*, 3 vols. Paris: H. J. Jansen.
Petermann, Heinrich 1865. *Reisen im Orient 1852-1855.* Leipzig: Veit & Comp.
Perry, John R. 1979. *Karim Khan Zand, A History of Iran 1747-1779.* Chicago: Chicago UP.
Peterson, Samuel R. 1979. "Painted Tiles at the Takieh Mu'avin al-Mulk (Kirmanshah)," *Akten des VII Internationalen Kongress für Iranische Kunst und Archälogie, München 7-10 September 1976.* Berlin, pp. 618-28.
Pirnazar, Nahid 2010. "Kirmanshah," *The Encyclopedia of Jews.* Leiden: Brill, vol. 3.
———, 2014. "Kermanshah IV. The Jewish Community," *Encyclopedia Iranica* (on-line edition).
Polak, J. E. 1862. "Beitrag zu den agrarischen Verhältnissen in Persien", *Mittheilungen der K.-K. Geogr. Gesellschaft* VI, pp. 107-43.

——— 1865, Persien. *Das Land und seine Bewohner*. 2 vols. Leipzig: Brockhaus.
Political Diaries = *Political Diaries of the Persian Gulf* 1904-1947, 17 vols. n.p. Archive Editions, 1990.
Post, Wilfred 1920. "The Forty-Ninth Star," *The New Armenia* XII/May, pp. 69-72.
Powell, Alexander 1923. *By Camel and Car to the Peacock Throne*. New York: The Century Co
Presbyterian Church 1904. "Eastern Persia. Hamadan," *Hundred and Second Annual Report of the Board of Home Missions of the Presbyterian Church in the U.S.A*. New York.
Presbyterian Church 1908. *Reports of the Missionary and Benevolent Boards and Committees to the General Assembly of the Presbyterian Church in the USA*, Issue 106, 1908.
Presbyterian Church 1915. "Kermanshah Station," Presbyterian Church in the U.S.A., *One Hundred Thirteenth Annual Report of the Board of Home Mission*s, Reports of the Missionary and Benevolent Boards and Committees to the General Assembly.
Presbyterian Church 1919 a. "Kermanshah Station - Medical and Relief work," in *Presbyterian Church in the USA. General Assembly. Reports of the Boards of the Assembly*, New York: 1919.
Presbyterian Church 1919 b. *One Hundred Seventeenth Annual Report of the Home Missions of the Presbyterian Church of the U.S.A*.
Presbyterian Church 1919-20. *Annual Report, By Presbyterian Church in the U.S.A. Board of Foreign Missions*, Volumes 82-83, p. 265-266.
Presbyterian Church 1920. *The Eighty-third Annual Report of the Board of Foreign Missions of the Presbyterian Church in the U.S.A*.
Presbyterian Church 1921. *The Eighty-fourth Annual Report of the Board of Foreign Missions of the Presbyterian Church in the U.S.A*.
Presbyterian Church 1922 a. *The Eighty-fifth Annual Report of the Board of Foreign Missions of the Presbyterian Church in the U.S.A*., 1922.
Presbyterian Church 1922 b. *The Presbyterian Hospital Bulletin*. Chicago, Ill. January 1922, no. 48.
Presbyterian Church 1928. Annual Meeting Actions of the East Persia Mission of the Presbyterian Church in the USA. Daulatabad, August 1-10, 1928.
Pushman, Garabed Thomas 1911. *Art Panels from the Hand Looms of the Far Orient*, Chicago: Pushman Bros.
Qa'emmaqami, Rezaqoli 1334/1955. *Vaqaye'-ye Gharb-e Iran dar Jang-e Avval-e Jahani az Sha'ban 1333 ta Sha'ban*. Arak, n. p.
Qarakhani, Hasan 1353/1974. "Boq'eh-ye Ayyub Ansari dar takab- faramin-e shahan-e Safavi dar bareh mowqufat-e an," *Barrasiha-ye Tarikhi* 9, pp. 71-122.
Qazvini, Mohammad Shafi' 1370/1991. *Qanun-e Qazvini*. ed. Iraj Afshar. Tehran: Talayeh.
Qudsi, Hasan E'zam 1342/1963. *Ketab-e Khaterat-e Man ya Tarikh-e sadsaleh-ye Iran*, 2 vols. Tehran: author.
Rabino, Hyacinthe L. 1905. "Kermanchah." *Revue du Monde Musulman* 38 (March), pp. 1-40.
Rais-Nia, Rahim 2002. "Tabriz et l'intervention des armees etrangeres 1915-1919," in Bast 2002, pp. 293-316.
Rashidirostami, Mahroo 2018. "Performance Traditions of Kurdistan: Towards a More Comprehensive Theatre History," *Iranian Studies*, 51/2, pp. 269-87.
al-Ravandi, Mohammad b. 'Ali b. Soleyman 1921. *Rahat al-Sodur va Ayat al-Sorur*. ed. Mohammad Iqbal. London.
Ravasani, Schapour 1973. *Sowjetrepublik Gilan. Die sozialistische Bewegung im Iran seit Ende des 19. Jhdt. bis 1922*. Berlin: Basis Verlag.
Rawlinson, Henry 1839. "Notes on A March from Zoháb at the Foot of Zagros to Khúzistán and … to Kermánsháh in the Year 1836," *JRGS* 9, pp. 26-116.
Reitlinger, Gerald 1932. *A Tower of Skulls, a journey through Persian and Turkish Armenia* London: Duckworth.

RMM = *Revue du Monde Musulman.*
Rich, Claudius James 1836. *Narrative of a Residence in Koordistan and on the site of ancient Nineveh; with a journal of a voyage doen to the Tigris to Bagdad and an account of a visit to Shirauz and Persepolis*. London: James Duncan.
———, 1839. *Narrative of a Journey to the site of Babylon in 1811 ... with Narrative of a Journey to Persepolis*. London.
Roberts N. S. 1948. *Iran, Economic and Commercial Conditions*. London: HMSO.
Ronaldshay, Lawrence John Lumley Dundas Marquis of Zetland, Earl of 1904. *On the outskirts of empire in Asia*. Edingbugh/London: Blackwood.
Rousseau, M. 1813. "Extrait de l'itinéraire d'un voyage en Perse par la voie de Baghdad," *Fundgrubes des Orients* vol. 3, pp. 85-98.
Rusta'i, Mohsen 1382/2003. *Tarikh-e Tebb va Tebabat dar Iran*, 2 vols. Tehran: Sazman-e Asnad.
Ruznameh-ye Ettefaqiyeh-ye Vaqaye' 1373-74/1994-95. 4 vols. Tehran: Ketabkhaneh- Melli.
Ruznameh-ye Iran 1374/1995. 4 vols. Tehran: Ketabkhaneh- Melli.
Ruznameh-ye Zafar.
Saad, Lamech 1913. *Sechzehn Jahre als Quarantäne-Arzt in der Türkei*. Berlin: Dietrich Reimer-Ernst Vohsen.
Sabar, Yona 1982. *The Folk Literature of the Kurdistani Jews: An Anthology*. New Haven-London: Yale UP.
Safa'i, Ebrahim 1346/1967. *Rahbaran-e Mashruteh*. Tehran: Amir Kabir.
Salar-Behzadi, 'Abdol-Reza 1372/1993. "Mohajerat," *Ayandeh* 19/7-9, pp. 608-37.
Salari, A. 1371/1992. "Takiyeh-e Mo'aven al-Molk," *Mirath-e Farhangi* no. 3.
Saldanha, J.A. 1986. *The Persian Gulf Précis* 8 vols. Gerrards Cross.
Salehi, Nasrollah 2002, "Les fatwas des ulemas persans de Najaf et Kerbela," in Bast 2002, pp. 157-76.
Sanson, M. 1695. *The Present State of Persia*. London.
Santa Cecilia, Leandro di 1757. *Persia. Overo Secondo Viaggio*. Rome.
Sarshar, Houman 2002. *Esther's children: a portrait of Iranian Jews*. Sarshar, Houman 2002. Beverly Hills, Calif.: Center for Iranian Jewish Oral History; Philadelphia: Jewish Publication Society.
Sasani, Khan Malek, 1345/1966. *Yadbudha-ye Sefarat-e Estanbul*, Tehran: Ferdowsi.
Sauer, Emil 1914. "The Mohammerah-Khorremabad Railway," *Daily Consular and Trade Reports*, no. 280 (year 16), 3 December 1913, Washington: GPO, pp. 1105-08.
Sayyah, Hajj 1346/1967. *Khaterat-e Hajj Sayyah ya Dowreh-ye Khowf va Vahshat*. eds. Hamid Sayyah and Seyfollah Golfar. Tehran: Ibn Sina.
Sayyah, Mohammad Ali Mihanpur 1395/2016. *Fedakari dar Rah-e Vatan. Khaterati az safar-e mohajerat va naqsh-e zhandarmeri dar jang-e jahani-ye avval*. ed. Mojtaba Paridar. Tehran: Shirazeh.
Schlimmer, Joh. L. 1970. *Terminologie Medico-Pharmaceutique*. Tehran: Daneshgah.
Scott, Joseph 1905. "The recent cholera epidemic in Persia," *British Medical Journey* 16 September, pp. 620-22.
Schwarz, Paul 1993. *Iran im Mittelalter nach den Arabischen Quellen*. Leipzig: Harrassowitz [reprint, Frankfurt a/M. of 1896-1912 edition].
Sepehr, Ahmad Ali, Mo'arrikh al-Dowleh 1337/1958. *Iran dar Jang-i Bozorg 1914-1918*, Tehran.
Sepehr, Mirza Mohammad Taqi Lesan al-Molk 1337/1958. *Nasekh al-Tavarikh* 3 vols. ed. Jahangir Qa'em-Maqami. Tehran.
Sercey, F.E. de 1928. *Une ambassade extraordinaire: La Perse en 1839-1840*. Paris: L'Artisan du livre.
Shabankareh, Mozaffar b. Mohammad b. Ali 1376/1997. *Majma' al-Ansab*. Tehran: Amir Kabir.
Shamim, Ali 1374/1995. *Iran dar dowreh-ye saltanat-e Qajar*. Tehran: Modabber.
Shahnavaz, Shahbaz 2005. *Britain and the Opening Up of South-West Persia 1880-1914: A Study in Imperialism and Economic Dependence*. New York: Routledge-Curzon.

Sharif Kazemi, Zahra 1396/2017. *Tejarat-e gheyr qanuni. Qachaq-e gandom dar sar-hadat-e gharbi (1304-1324 sh)*. Tehran: Tarikh-e Iran.

Sheil, Lady 1973. *Glimpses of Life and Manners in Persia*. New York:Arno Press.

Shirvani, Zeyn al-Abedin 1315/1897. *Bustan al-Siyaha ya Siyahatnameh*, Tehran.

Simmonds, S. 1935. *Economic Conditions in Iran (Persia)*. London: HMSO.

Sixth Supplement to the London Gazette 26 August 1918.

Singer, Isidore ed. 1916. *The Jewish Encyclopedia*, 12 vols. New York: Funk and Wagnalls.

Skrine, Sir C. 1962. *World War in Iran*, London.

Slaby, Helmut 1982. *Bindenschild und Sonnenlöwe*. Graz.

Soane, E.B. 1926. *To Mesopotamia and Kurdistan in Disguise*. London.

Soltani, Mohammad Ali, 1378/1999. *Ahzab-e siyasi va anjomanha-ye serri dar Kermanshah*. 2 vols. Tehran: Soha.

———,1381/2002. *Joghrafiya-ye Tarikhi va Tarikh-e Mofassal-e Kermanshahan-e Bakhtaran*. 10 vols. Tehran: Soha.

———, ed. 1386/2007. *Nahzat-e Mashrutiyat dar Kermanshah (az arshiv-e ayatollah Hajj Sheykh Mohammad Mehdi Kermanshahi)* . Tehran: Mo'assaseh-ye tahqiqat va towsi'eh-ye 'olum-e ensani.

———, 1384/2005. *Khaterat-e Soltani az Qasr-e Shirin ta Qasr-e Qajar*. Tehran: Mehr.

Southgate, Horatio 1840. *Narrative of a Tour through Armenia, Kurdistan, Persia and Mesopotamia*. 2 vols. New York: D. Appleton & Co.

Spector, Reeva and Menachem, Michael 2003. *The Jews of Middle East and North Africa in Modern Times*. New York: Columbia UP.

Spuler, Berthold 1952. *Iran in Früh-Islamischer Zeit*. Wiesbaden: Steiner.

Stark, Freya 2001. *The Valleys of the Assassins*. New York: The Moden Library.

Stead, Blanche Wilson 1907. "Four months in Kermanshah," *Women's Work*, vol. 22, p. 234.

——— 1911, "An investment worth considering," *The Missionary Review of the World*, vol. 24 (new series) 34 (old series), p. 128.

Stead, F.M. 1908. "From Hamadan, Persia," *The Westminster*, vol. 33, 11 January, p. 18.

Stern, Henry A. 1854. *Dawning Of Light In The East*. London: Charlas H. Purday.

Stocqueler, J.H. 1832. *Fifteen Months' Pilgrimage through untrodden tracts of Khuzistan and Persia*. London: Saunders and Otley.

Sticker, Georg 1908-10. *Abhandlungen aus der Seuchengeschichte*. Giessen.

Stolze F. & Andreas, F.C. 1885. "Die Handelsverhaeltnisse Persiens., in: Dr. A. *Petermanns Mitteilungen. Ergaenzungsheft* nr. 77. Gotha: Justus Perthes.

Sykes, Sir Percy 1969. *The History of Persia*. 2 vols. London: Routledge and Kegan Paul.

al-Tabari 1999. *The History of al-Tabari. The Sasanids, the Byzantines, Lakmids, and Yemen*. tr. E. Bosworth. Albany: New York UP.

Tavernier, Jean-Baptiste 1712. *Les six voyages de Monsieur Jean-Baptiste Tavernier, ecuyer baron d'Aubonne, en Turque, en Perse, et aux Indes*. 6 vols. Rouen: Machuel

Tayarani, Behruz 1372/1993. "Jang-e jahani-ye dovvom, qahti va vakoneshha-ye mardomi dar qebal-e an 1320-24," *Faslnameh-ye ganjihen-ye asnad* 3/9, pp. 20-31.

Temple, B. 1922. *Report on Trade and Transport Conditions in Persia*. London: HMSO.

Teule, Jules Charles 1842. *Pensées et notes critiques extraites du journal de mes voyages dans l'empire du Sultan de Constantinople* 2 vols. Paris ; Arthus Bertrand.

The Hansard, HC Deb

Thévenot, J. de. 1971. *The Travels of [...] into the Levant into three parts*. London, (1686).

Toledano, Ehud R. 1982. *Ottoman Slave Trade and Its Suppression:1840-1890*, Princeton.

Tsadik, Daniel 2003. "The Legal Status of Religious Minorities: Imāmī Shī'ī Law and Iran's Constitutional Revolution", *Islamic Law and Society* vol. 10, pp. 376-407

——— 2005. "Nineteenth century Iranian Jewry," *Journal of British institute of Persian Studies*, vol. 43, pp. 275-282.

——— 2007. *Between foreigners and Shiis*. Stanford.

——— 2009, "Judeo-Persian Communities v. Qajar Period, *Encyclopedia Iranica*, vol. XV, pp. 108-12.

——— 2010. "Jews in the Pre-Constitutional Years: The Shiraz Incident of 1905," *Journal of Iranian Studies*, vol. 43/2, pp. 239-263.

Tucker, Ernest S. 2006. *Nadir Shah's Quest for Legitimacy in Post- Safavid Iran*. Gainsville: Florida UP.

US Government, Surgeon-General's Office 1875, *The Cholera Epidemic of 1873 in the United States*, Washington DC.

———, 1895. *The Executive Documents of the House of Representatives for the third session of the fifty-third Congress 1894-95*. 35 vols. Washington: GPO.

Vahid al-Molk, 'Abdol-Hoseyn Sheybani 1378/1999. *Khaterat-e Mohajerat az dowlat-e movaqqat-e Kermanshah ta komiteh-ye milliyun-e Berlin*. eds. Iraj Afshar and Kaveh Bayat. Tehran Shirazeh.

Vahid Qazvini, Mohammad Taher 1383/2005. *Tarikh-e Jahanara-ye 'Abbasi*. Tehran: Pazhuheshgah-e 'Olum-e Ensani.

Waterfield, Robin E 1973. *Christians in Persia - Assyrians, Armenians, Roman Catholics and Protestants*. London: George Allen & Unwin.

Watt, Donald B. 1967. *Intelligence is not enough*. Putney, VT: The Experiment Press.

Wigham, H.J. 1903. *The Persian Problem*. New York.

Whipple, W.L. 1900. "A Tour to Kermanshah," *The Assembly Herald*, vol. 3/6, October, pp. 813-14.

Wills, C.J. *Persia As It Is* 1886. London: Sampon Low, Marston, Searle & Rivington

———, 1893. *In the Land of the Lion and the Sun*. London: Ward, Lock & Bowden.

Wilson, A. T. 1932. *Persia*. London: Ernest Benn

———, 1941. *S.W. Persia. Letters and Diary of a Young Political Officer 1907-1914*. Oxford: Oxford UP.

Wright, Denis 2001. *The English amongst the Persians*. London: IB Tauris.

Yeroushalmi, David 2009. *The Jews of Iran in the Nineteenth Century: Aspects of History, Community, and Culture*. Boston: Brill.

Yusof, Mohammad and Monshi, Eskandar Beg Torkoman 1317/1938. *Dheyl-e Tarikh-e 'Alamara-ye 'Abbasi*. ed. Soheyli Khvansari. Tehran: Eslamiyeh.

WEBSITES

Molitor 2018 a: Chapter Kermanshah, "1902-1928, 26 ans en Perse," Mémoires intégrales de Lambert Molitor, ed. Elytis, internet, 2018.

Molitor 2018 b: Résumé des événements survenus à Kermanchah lors de l'apparition de Salar ed Dowleh. n.d. (report written by Lambert Molitor, probably 1913) "1902-1928, 26 ans en Perse," Mémoires intégrales de Lambert Molitor, ed. Elytis, internet, 2018.

INDEX

A

B

C

D

E

H

I

J

K

L

M

N

O

P

Q

R

S

T

U

W

Z

READERS' NOTES

CPSIA information can be obtained
at www.ICGtesting.com
Printed in the USA
BVHW081322060619
550310BV00006B/15/P

9 781949 445008